The Complete Tragedies of
William Shakespeare

Start Publishing PD LLC

Cover art: Shutterstock/Taisiya Kozorez

Cover design: Jennifer Do

10 9 8 7 6 5 4 3 2 1

ISBN 979-8-8809-1423-4

Table of Contents

The Tragedy of Titus Andronicus

Dramatis Personae

SATURNINUS, son to the late Emperor of Rome, afterwards Emperor
BASSIANUS, brother to Saturninus
TITUS ANDRONICUS, a noble Roman
MARCUS ANDRONICUS, Tribune of the People, and brother to Titus
Sons to Titus Andronicus:
LUCIUS
QUINTUS
MARTIUS
MUTIUS
YOUNG LUCIUS, a boy, son to Lucius
PUBLIUS, son to Marcus Andronicus
Kinsmen to Titus:
SEMPRONIUS
CAIUS
VALENTINE
AEMILIUS, a noble Roman
Sons to Tamora:
ALARBUS
DEMETRIUS
CHIRON
AARON, a Moor, beloved by Tamora
A CAPTAIN
A MESSENGER
A CLOWN
TAMORA, Queen of the Goths
LAVINIA, daughter to Titus Andronicus
A NURSE, and a black CHILD
Romans and Goths, Senators, Tribunes, Officers, Soldiers, and Attendants

SCENE: Rome and the neighbourhood

ACT I. SCENE I. Rome. Before the Capitol

Flourish. Enter the Tribunes and Senators Aloft; and Then Enter below Saturninus and His Followers at One Door, and Bassianus and His Followers at the Other, with Drums and Trumpets

SATURNINUS: Noble patricians, patrons of my right,
Defend the justice of my cause with arms;
And, countrymen, my loving followers,
Plead my successive title with your swords.
I am his first born son that was the last
That ware the imperial diadem of Rome;
Then let my father's honours live in me,
Nor wrong mine age with this indignity.

BASSIANUS: Romans, friends, followers, favourers of my right,
If ever Bassianus, Caesar's son,
Were gracious in the eyes of royal Rome,
Keep then this passage to the Capitol;
And suffer not dishonour to approach
The imperial seat, to virtue consecrate,
To justice, continence, and nobility;
But let desert in pure election shine;

And, Romans, fight for freedom in your choice.
Enter Marcus Andronicus Aloft, with the Crown
MARCUS: Princes, that strive by factions and by friends
Ambitiously for rule and empery,
Know that the people of Rome, for whom we stand
A special party, have by common voice
In election for the Roman empery
Chosen Andronicus, surnamed Pius
For many good and great deserts to Rome.
A nobler man, a braver warrior,
Lives not this day within the city walls.
He by the Senate is accited home,
From weary wars against the barbarous Goths,
That with his sons, a terror to our foes,
Hath yok'd a nation strong, train'd up in arms.
Ten years are spent since first he undertook
This cause of Rome, and chastised with arms
Our enemies' pride; five times he hath return'd
Bleeding to Rome, bearing his valiant sons
In coffins from the field; and at this day
To the monument of that Andronici
Done sacrifice of expiation,
And slain the noblest prisoner of the Goths.
And now at last, laden with honour's spoils,
Returns the good Andronicus to Rome,
Renowned Titus, flourishing in arms.
Let us entreat, by honour of his name
Whom worthily you would have now succeed,
And in the Capitol and Senate's right,
Whom you pretend to honour and adore,
That you withdraw you and abate your strength,
Dismiss your followers, and, as suitors should,
Plead your deserts in peace and humbleness.
SATURNINUS: How fair the Tribune speaks to calm my thoughts.
BASSIANUS: Marcus Andronicus, so I do affy
In thy uprightness and integrity,
And so I love and honour thee and thine,
Thy noble brother Titus and his sons,
And her to whom my thoughts are humbled all,
Gracious Lavinia, Rome's rich ornament,
That I will here dismiss my loving friends,
And to my fortunes and the people's favour
Commit my cause in balance to be weigh'd.
Exeunt the Soldiers of Bassianus
SATURNINUS: Friends, that have been thus forward in my right,
I thank you all and here dismiss you all,
And to the love and favour of my country
Commit myself, my person, and the cause.
Exeunt the Soldiers of Saturninus
Rome, be as just and gracious unto me
As I am confident and kind to thee.
Open the gates and let me in.
BASSIANUS: Tribunes, and me, a poor competitor.

Flourish. They Go up into the Senate House

Enter a Captain

CAPTAIN: Romans, make way. The good Andronicus,
Patron of virtue, Rome's best champion,
Successful in the battles that he fights,
With honour and with fortune is return'd
From where he circumscribed with his sword
And brought to yoke the enemies of Rome.

Sound Drums and Trumpets, and Then Enter Martius and Mutius, Two of Titus' Sons; and Then Two Men Bearing a Coffin Covered with Black; Then Lucius and Quintus, Two Other Sons; Then Titus Andronicus; and Then Tamora the Queen of Goths, with Her Three Sons, Alarbus, Demetrius, and Chiron, with Aaron the Moor, and Others, as Many as Can Be. Then Set down the Coffin and Titus Speaks

TITUS: Hail, Rome, victorious in thy mourning weeds!
Lo, as the bark that hath discharg'd her fraught
Returns with precious lading to the bay
From whence at first she weigh'd her anchorage,
Cometh Andronicus, bound with laurel boughs,
To re-salute his country with his tears,
Tears of true joy for his return to Rome.
Thou great defender of this Capitol,
Stand gracious to the rites that we intend!
Romans, of five and twenty valiant sons,
Half of the number that King Priam had,
Behold the poor remains, alive and dead!
These that survive let Rome reward with love;
These that I bring unto their latest home,
With burial amongst their ancestors.
Here Goths have given me leave to sheathe my sword.
Titus, unkind, and careless of thine own,
Why suffer'st thou thy sons, unburied yet,
To hover on the dreadful shore of Styx?
Make way to lay them by their brethren.

They Open the Tomb

There greet in silence, as the dead are wont,
And sleep in peace, slain in your country's wars.
O sacred receptacle of my joys,
Sweet cell of virtue and nobility,
How many sons hast thou of mine in store
That thou wilt never render to me more!

LUCIUS: Give us the proudest prisoner of the Goths,
That we may hew his limbs, and on a pile
Ad manes fratrum sacrifice his flesh
Before this earthy prison of their bones,
That so the shadows be not unappeas'd,
Nor we disturb'd with prodigies on earth.

TITUS: I give him you- the noblest that survives,
The eldest son of this distressed queen.

TAMORA: Stay, Roman brethen! Gracious conqueror,
Victorious Titus, rue the tears I shed,
A mother's tears in passion for her son;
And if thy sons were ever dear to thee,
O, think my son to be as dear to me!

Sufficeth not that we are brought to Rome
To beautify thy triumphs, and return
Captive to thee and to thy Roman yoke;
But must my sons be slaughtered in the streets
For valiant doings in their country's cause?
O, if to fight for king and commonweal
Were piety in thine, it is in these.
Andronicus, stain not thy tomb with blood.
Wilt thou draw near the nature of the gods?
Draw near them then in being merciful.
Sweet mercy is nobility's true badge.
Thrice-noble Titus, spare my first-born son.
TITUS: Patient yourself, madam, and pardon me.
These are their brethren, whom your Goths beheld
Alive and dead; and for their brethren slain
Religiously they ask a sacrifice.
To this your son is mark'd, and die he must
T' appease their groaning shadows that are gone.
LUCIUS: Away with him, and make a fire straight;
And with our swords, upon a pile of wood,
Let's hew his limbs till they be clean consum'd.
Exeunt Titus' Sons, with Alarbus
TAMORA: O cruel, irreligious piety!
CHIRON: Was never Scythia half so barbarous!
MESSENGER: Oppose not Scythia to ambitious Rome.
Alarbus goes to rest, and we survive
To tremble under Titus' threat'ning look.
Then, madam, stand resolv'd, but hope withal
The self-same gods that arm'd the Queen of Troy
With opportunity of sharp revenge
Upon the Thracian tyrant in his tent
May favour Tamora, the Queen of Goths-
When Goths were Goths and Tamora was queen-
To quit the bloody wrongs upon her foes.
Re-enter Lucius, Quintus, Martius, and Mutius, the Sons of Andronicus, with Their Swords Bloody
LUCIUS: See, lord and father, how we have perform'd
Our Roman rites: Alarbus' limbs are lopp'd,
And entrails feed the sacrificing fire,
Whose smoke like incense doth perfume the sky.
Remaineth nought but to inter our brethren,
And with loud 'larums welcome them to Rome.
TITUS: Let it be so, and let Andronicus
Make this his latest farewell to their souls.
Sound Trumpets and Lay the Coffin in the Tomb
In peace and honour rest you here, my sons;
Rome's readiest champions, repose you here in rest,
Secure from worldly chances and mishaps!
Here lurks no treason, here no envy swells,
Here grow no damned drugs, here are no storms,
No noise, but silence and eternal sleep.
In peace and honour rest you here, my sons!
Enter Lavinia
LAVINIA: In peace and honour live Lord Titus long;

My noble lord and father, live in fame!
Lo, at this tomb my tributary tears
I render for my brethren's obsequies;
And at thy feet I kneel, with tears of joy
Shed on this earth for thy return to Rome.
O, bless me here with thy victorious hand,
Whose fortunes Rome's best citizens applaud!
TITUS: Kind Rome, that hast thus lovingly reserv'd
The cordial of mine age to glad my heart!
Lavinia, live; outlive thy father's days,
And fame's eternal date, for virtue's praise!
Enter, Above, Marcus Andronicus and Tribunes; Re-enter Saturninus, Bassianus, and Attendants
MARCUS: Long live Lord Titus, my beloved brother,
Gracious triumpher in the eyes of Rome!
TITUS: Thanks, gentle Tribune, noble brother Marcus.
MARCUS: And welcome, nephews, from successful wars,
You that survive and you that sleep in fame.
Fair lords, your fortunes are alike in all
That in your country's service drew your swords;
But safer triumph is this funeral pomp
That hath aspir'd to Solon's happiness
And triumphs over chance in honour's bed.
Titus Andronicus, the people of Rome,
Whose friend in justice thou hast ever been,
Send thee by me, their Tribune and their trust,
This parliament of white and spotless hue;
And name thee in election for the empire
With these our late-deceased Emperor's sons:
Be candidatus then, and put it on,
And help to set a head on headless Rome.
TITUS: A better head her glorious body fits
Than his that shakes for age and feebleness.
What should I don this robe and trouble you?
Be chosen with proclamations to-day,
To-morrow yield up rule, resign my life,
And set abroad new business for you all?
Rome, I have been thy soldier forty years,
And led my country's strength successfully,
And buried one and twenty valiant sons,
Knighted in field, slain manfully in arms,
In right and service of their noble country.
Give me a staff of honour for mine age,
But not a sceptre to control the world.
Upright he held it, lords, that held it last.
MARCUS: Titus, thou shalt obtain and ask the empery.
SATURNINUS: Proud and ambitious Tribune, canst thou tell?
TITUS: Patience, Prince Saturninus.
SATURNINUS: Romans, do me right.
Patricians, draw your swords, and sheathe them not
Till Saturninus be Rome's Emperor.
Andronicus, would thou were shipp'd to hell
Rather than rob me of the people's hearts!
LUCIUS: Proud Saturnine, interrupter of the good

That noble-minded Titus means to thee!
TITUS: Content thee, Prince; I will restore to thee
The people's hearts, and wean them from themselves.
BASSIANUS: Andronicus, I do not flatter thee,
But honour thee, and will do till I die.
My faction if thou strengthen with thy friends,
I will most thankful be; and thanks to men
Of noble minds is honourable meed.
TITUS: People of Rome, and people's Tribunes here,
I ask your voices and your suffrages:
Will ye bestow them friendly on Andronicus?
TRIBUNES: To gratify the good Andronicus,
And gratulate his safe return to Rome,
The people will accept whom he admits.
TITUS: Tribunes, I thank you; and this suit I make,
That you create our Emperor's eldest son,
Lord Saturnine; whose virtues will, I hope,
Reflect on Rome as Titan's rays on earth,
And ripen justice in this commonweal.
Then, if you will elect by my advice,
Crown him, and say 'Long live our Emperor!'
MARCUS: With voices and applause of every sort,
Patricians and plebeians, we create
Lord Saturninus Rome's great Emperor;
And say 'Long live our Emperor Saturnine!'
A Long Flourish till They Come Down
SATURNINUS: Titus Andronicus, for thy favours done
To us in our election this day
I give thee thanks in part of thy deserts,
And will with deeds requite thy gentleness;
And for an onset, Titus, to advance
Thy name and honourable family,
Lavinia will I make my emperess,
Rome's royal mistress, mistress of my heart,
And in the sacred Pantheon her espouse.
Tell me, Andronicus, doth this motion please thee?
TITUS: It doth, my worthy lord, and in this match
I hold me highly honoured of your Grace,
And here in sight of Rome, to Saturnine,
King and commander of our commonweal,
The wide world's Emperor, do I consecrate
My sword, my chariot, and my prisoners,
Presents well worthy Rome's imperious lord;
Receive them then, the tribute that I owe,
Mine honour's ensigns humbled at thy feet.
SATURNINUS: Thanks, noble Titus, father of my life.
How proud I am of thee and of thy gifts
Rome shall record; and when I do forget
The least of these unspeakable deserts,
Romans, forget your fealty to me.
TITUS: To Tamora Now, madam, are you prisoner to an emperor;
To him that for your honour and your state
Will use you nobly and your followers.

SATURNINUS: Aside A goodly lady, trust me; of the hue
That I would choose, were I to choose anew.-
Clear up, fair Queen, that cloudy countenance;
Though chance of war hath wrought this change of cheer,
Thou com'st not to be made a scorn in Rome-
Princely shall be thy usage every way.
Rest on my word, and let not discontent
Daunt all your hopes. Madam, he comforts you
Can make you greater than the Queen of Goths.
Lavinia, you are not displeas'd with this?
LAVINIA: Not I, my lord, sith true nobility
Warrants these words in princely courtesy.
SATURNINUS: Thanks, sweet Lavinia. Romans, let us go.
Ransomless here we set our prisoners free.
Proclaim our honours, lords, with trump and drum.
Flourish
BASSIANUS: Lord Titus, by your leave, this maid is mine.
Seizing Lavinia
TITUS: How, sir! Are you in earnest then, my lord?
BASSIANUS: Ay, noble Titus, and resolv'd withal
To do myself this reason and this right.
MARCUS: Suum cuique is our Roman justice:
This prince in justice seizeth but his own.
LUCIUS: And that he will and shall, if Lucius live.
TITUS: Traitors, avaunt! Where is the Emperor's guard?
Treason, my lord- Lavinia is surpris'd!
SATURNINUS: Surpris'd! By whom?
BASSIANUS: By him that justly may
Bear his betroth'd from all the world away.
Exeunt Bassianus and Marcus with Lavinia
MUTIUS: Brothers, help to convey her hence away,
And with my sword I'll keep this door safe.
Exeunt Lucius, Quintus, and Martius
TITUS: Follow, my lord, and I'll soon bring her back.
MUTIUS: My lord, you pass not here.
TITUS: What, villain boy!
Bar'st me my way in Rome?
MUTIUS: Help, Lucius, help!
Titus Kills Him. During the Fray, Exeunt Saturninus, Tamora, Demetrius, Chiron, and Aaron
Re-enter Lucius
LUCIUS: My lord, you are unjust, and more than so:
In wrongful quarrel you have slain your son.
TITUS: Nor thou nor he are any sons of mine;
My sons would never so dishonour me.
Re-enter Aloft the Emperor with Tamora and Her Two Sons, and Aaron the Moor
Traitor, restore Lavinia to the Emperor.
LUCIUS: Dead, if you will; but not to be his wife,
That is another's lawful promis'd love.
Exit
SATURNINUS: No, Titus, no; the Emperor needs her not,
Nor her, nor thee, nor any of thy stock.
I'll trust by leisure him that mocks me once;
Thee never, nor thy traitorous haughty sons,

Confederates all thus to dishonour me.
Was there none else in Rome to make a stale
But Saturnine? Full well, Andronicus,
Agree these deeds with that proud brag of thine
That saidst I begg'd the empire at thy hands.
TITUS: O monstrous! What reproachful words are these?
SATURNINUS: But go thy ways; go, give that changing piece
To him that flourish'd for her with his sword.
A valiant son-in-law thou shalt enjoy;
One fit to bandy with thy lawless sons,
To ruffle in the commonwealth of Rome.
TITUS: These words are razors to my wounded heart.
SATURNINUS: And therefore, lovely Tamora, Queen of Goths,
That, like the stately Phoebe 'mongst her nymphs,
Dost overshine the gallant'st dames of Rome,
If thou be pleas'd with this my sudden choice,
Behold, I choose thee, Tamora, for my bride
And will create thee Emperess of Rome.
Speak, Queen of Goths, dost thou applaud my choice?
And here I swear by all the Roman gods-
Sith priest and holy water are so near,
And tapers burn so bright, and everything
In readiness for Hymenaeus stand-
I will not re-salute the streets of Rome,
Or climb my palace, till from forth this place
I lead espous'd my bride along with me.
TAMORA: And here in sight of heaven to Rome I swear,
If Saturnine advance the Queen of Goths,
She will a handmaid be to his desires,
A loving nurse, a mother to his youth.
SATURNINUS: Ascend, fair Queen, Pantheon. Lords, accompany
Your noble Emperor and his lovely bride,
Sent by the heavens for Prince Saturnine,
Whose wisdom hath her fortune conquered;
There shall we consummate our spousal rites.
    Exeunt All but Titus
TITUS: I am not bid to wait upon this bride.
Titus, when wert thou wont to walk alone,
Dishonoured thus, and challenged of wrongs?
    Re-enter Marcus, and Titus' Sons, Lucius, Quintus, and Martius
MARCUS: O Titus, see, O, see what thou hast done!
In a bad quarrel slain a virtuous son.
TITUS: No, foolish Tribune, no; no son of mine-
Nor thou, nor these, confederates in the deed
That hath dishonoured all our family;
Unworthy brother and unworthy sons!
LUCIUS: But let us give him burial, as becomes;
Give Mutius burial with our bretheren.
TITUS: Traitors, away! He rests not in this tomb.
This monument five hundred years hath stood,
Which I have sumptuously re-edified;
Here none but soldiers and Rome's servitors
Repose in fame; none basely slain in brawls.

Bury him where you can, he comes not here.
MARCUS: My lord, this is impiety in you.
My nephew Mutius' deeds do plead for him;
He must be buried with his bretheren.
QUINTUS & MARTIUS: And shall, or him we will accompany.
TITUS: 'And shall!' What villain was it spake that word?
QUINTUS: He that would vouch it in any place but here.
TITUS: What, would you bury him in my despite?
MARCUS: No, noble Titus, but entreat of thee
To pardon Mutius and to bury him.
TITUS: Marcus, even thou hast struck upon my crest,
And with these boys mine honour thou hast wounded.
My foes I do repute you every one;
So trouble me no more, but get you gone.
MARTIUS: He is not with himself; let us withdraw.
QUINTUS: Not I, till Mutius' bones be buried.
The Brother and the Sons Kneel
MARCUS: Brother, for in that name doth nature plead-
QUINTUS: Father, and in that name doth nature speak-
TITUS: Speak thou no more, if all the rest will speed.
MARCUS: Renowned Titus, more than half my soul-
LUCIUS: Dear father, soul and substance of us all-
MARCUS: Suffer thy brother Marcus to inter
His noble nephew here in virtue's nest,
That died in honour and Lavinia's cause.
Thou art a Roman- be not barbarous.
The Greeks upon advice did bury Ajax,
That slew himself; and wise Laertes' son
Did graciously plead for his funerals.
Let not young Mutius, then, that was thy joy,
Be barr'd his entrance here.
TITUS: Rise, Marcus, rise;
The dismal'st day is this that e'er I saw,
To be dishonoured by my sons in Rome!
Well, bury him, and bury me the next.
They Put Mutius in the Tomb
LUCIUS: There lie thy bones, sweet Mutius, with thy friends,
Till we with trophies do adorn thy tomb.
ALL: Kneeling No man shed tears for noble Mutius;
He lives in fame that died in virtue's cause.
MARCUS: My lord- to step out of these dreary dumps-
How comes it that the subtle Queen of Goths
Is of a sudden thus advanc'd in Rome?
TITUS: I know not, Marcus, but I know it is-
Whether by device or no, the heavens can tell.
Is she not, then, beholding to the man
That brought her for this high good turn so far?
MARCUS: Yes, and will nobly him remunerate.
Flourish. Re-enter the Emperor, Tamora and Her Two Sons, with the Moor, at One Door; at the Other Door, Bassianus and Lavinia, with Others
SATURNINUS: So, Bassianus, you have play'd your prize:
God give you joy, sir, of your gallant bride!
BASSIANUS: And you of yours, my lord! I say no more,

Nor wish no less; and so I take my leave.
SATURNINUS: Traitor, if Rome have law or we have power,
Thou and thy faction shall repent this rape.
BASSIANUS: Rape, call you it, my lord, to seize my own,
My true betrothed love, and now my wife?
But let the laws of Rome determine all;
Meanwhile am I possess'd of that is mine.
SATURNINUS: 'Tis good, sir. You are very short with us;
But if we live we'll be as sharp with you.
BASSIANUS: My lord, what I have done, as best I may,
Answer I must, and shall do with my life.
Only thus much I give your Grace to know:
By all the duties that I owe to Rome,
This noble gentleman, Lord Titus here,
Is in opinion and in honour wrong'd,
That, in the rescue of Lavinia,
With his own hand did slay his youngest son,
In zeal to you, and highly mov'd to wrath
To be controll'd in that he frankly gave.
Receive him then to favour, Saturnine,
That hath express'd himself in all his deeds
A father and a friend to thee and Rome.
TITUS: Prince Bassianus, leave to plead my deeds.
'Tis thou and those that have dishonoured me.
Rome and the righteous heavens be my judge
How I have lov'd and honoured Saturnine!
TAMORA: My worthy lord, if ever Tamora
Were gracious in those princely eyes of thine,
Then hear me speak indifferently for all;
And at my suit, sweet, pardon what is past.
SATURNINUS: What, madam! be dishonoured openly,
And basely put it up without revenge?
TAMORA: Not so, my lord; the gods of Rome forfend
I should be author to dishonour you!
But on mine honour dare I undertake
For good Lord Titus' innocence in all,
Whose fury not dissembled speaks his griefs.
Then at my suit look graciously on him;
Lose not so noble a friend on vain suppose,
Nor with sour looks afflict his gentle heart.
Aside to Saturninus My lord, be rul'd by me, be won at last;
Dissemble all your griefs and discontents.
You are but newly planted in your throne;
Lest, then, the people, and patricians too,
Upon a just survey take Titus' part,
And so supplant you for ingratitude,
Which Rome reputes to be a heinous sin,
Yield at entreats, and then let me alone:
I'll find a day to massacre them all,
And raze their faction and their family,
The cruel father and his traitorous sons,
To whom I sued for my dear son's life;
And make them know what 'tis to let a queen

Kneel in the streets and beg for grace in vain.-
Come, come, sweet Emperor; come, Andronicus.
Take up this good old man, and cheer the heart
That dies in tempest of thy angry frown.
SATURNINUS: Rise, Titus, rise; my Empress hath prevail'd.
TITUS: I thank your Majesty and her, my lord;
These words, these looks, infuse new life in me.
TAMORA: Titus, I am incorporate in Rome,
A Roman now adopted happily,
And must advise the Emperor for his good.
This day all quarrels die, Andronicus;
And let it be mine honour, good my lord,
That I have reconcil'd your friends and you.
For you, Prince Bassianus, I have pass'd
My word and promise to the Emperor
That you will be more mild and tractable.
And fear not, lords- and you, Lavinia.
By my advice, all humbled on your knees,
You shall ask pardon of his Majesty.
LUCIUS: We do, and vow to heaven and to his Highness
That what we did was mildly as we might,
Tend'ring our sister's honour and our own.
MARCUS: That on mine honour here do I protest.
SATURNINUS: Away, and talk not; trouble us no more.
TAMORA: Nay, nay, sweet Emperor, we must all be friends.
The Tribune and his nephews kneel for grace.
I will not be denied. Sweet heart, look back.
SATURNINUS: Marcus, for thy sake, and thy brother's here,
And at my lovely Tamora's entreats,
I do remit these young men's heinous faults.
Stand up.
Lavinia, though you left me like a churl,
I found a friend; and sure as death I swore
I would not part a bachelor from the priest.
Come, if the Emperor's court can feast two brides,
You are my guest, Lavinia, and your friends.
This day shall be a love-day, Tamora.
TITUS: To-morrow, and it please your Majesty
To hunt the panther and the hart with me,
With horn and hound we'll give your Grace bonjour.
SATURNINUS: Be it so, Titus, and gramercy too.
Exeunt. Sound Trumpets

ACT II. SCENE I. Rome. Before the Palace

Enter Aaron
AARON: Now climbeth Tamora Olympus' top,
Safe out of Fortune's shot, and sits aloft,
Secure of thunder's crack or lightning flash,
Advanc'd above pale envy's threat'ning reach.
As when the golden sun salutes the morn,
And, having gilt the ocean with his beams,
Gallops the zodiac in his glistening coach
And overlooks the highest-peering hills,
So Tamora.

Upon her wit doth earthly honour wait,
And virtue stoops and trembles at her frown.
Then, Aaron, arm thy heart and fit thy thoughts
To mount aloft with thy imperial mistress,
And mount her pitch whom thou in triumph long.
Hast prisoner held, fett'red in amorous chains,
And faster bound to Aaron's charming eyes
Than is Prometheus tied to Caucasus.
Away with slavish weeds and servile thoughts!
I will be bright and shine in pearl and gold,
To wait upon this new-made emperess.
To wait, said I? To wanton with this queen,
This goddess, this Semiramis, this nymph,
This siren that will charm Rome's Saturnine,
And see his shipwreck and his commonweal's.
Hullo! what storm is this?
Enter Chiron and Demetrius, Braving
MESSENGER: Chiron, thy years wants wit, thy wits wants edge
And manners, to intrude where I am grac'd,
And may, for aught thou knowest, affected be.
CHIRON: Demetrius, thou dost over-ween in all;
And so in this, to bear me down with braves.
'Tis not the difference of a year or two
Makes me less gracious or thee more fortunate:
I am as able and as fit as thou
To serve and to deserve my mistress' grace;
And that my sword upon thee shall approve,
And plead my passions for Lavinia's love.
AARON: Aside Clubs, clubs! These lovers will not keep the peace.
MESSENGER: Why, boy, although our mother, unadvis'd,
Gave you a dancing rapier by your side,
Are you so desperate grown to threat your friends?
Go to; have your lath glued within your sheath
Till you know better how to handle it.
CHIRON: Meanwhile, sir, with the little skill I have,
Full well shalt thou perceive how much I dare.
MESSENGER: Ay, boy, grow ye so brave?
They Draw
AARON: Coming Forward Why, how now, lords!
So near the Emperor's palace dare ye draw
And maintain such a quarrel openly?
Full well I wot the ground of all this grudge:
I would not for a million of gold
The cause were known to them it most concerns;
Nor would your noble mother for much more
Be so dishonoured in the court of Rome.
For shame, put up.
MESSENGER: Not I, till I have sheath'd
My rapier in his bosom, and withal
Thrust those reproachful speeches down his throat
That he hath breath'd in my dishonour here.
CHIRON: For that I am prepar'd and full resolv'd,
Foul-spoken coward, that thund'rest with thy tongue,

And with thy weapon nothing dar'st perform.
AARON: Away, I say!
Now, by the gods that warlike Goths adore,
This pretty brabble will undo us all.
Why, lords, and think you not how dangerous
It is to jet upon a prince's right?
What, is Lavinia then become so loose,
Or Bassianus so degenerate,
That for her love such quarrels may be broach'd
Without controlment, justice, or revenge?
Young lords, beware; an should the Empress know
This discord's ground, the music would not please.
CHIRON: I care not, I, knew she and all the world:
I love Lavinia more than all the world.
MESSENGER: Youngling, learn thou to make some meaner choice:
Lavina is thine elder brother's hope.
AARON: Why, are ye mad, or know ye not in Rome
How furious and impatient they be,
And cannot brook competitors in love?
I tell you, lords, you do but plot your deaths
By this device.
CHIRON: Aaron, a thousand deaths
Would I propose to achieve her whom I love.
AARON: To achieve her- how?
MESSENGER: Why mak'st thou it so strange?
She is a woman, therefore may be woo'd;
She is a woman, therefore may be won;
She is Lavinia, therefore must be lov'd.
What, man! more water glideth by the mill
Than wots the miller of; and easy it is
Of a cut loaf to steal a shive, we know.
Though Bassianus be the Emperor's brother,
Better than he have worn Vulcan's badge.
AARON: Aside Ay, and as good as Saturninus may.
MESSENGER: Then why should he despair that knows to court it
With words, fair looks, and liberality?
What, hast not thou full often struck a doe,
And borne her cleanly by the keeper's nose?
AARON: Why, then, it seems some certain snatch or so
Would serve your turns.
CHIRON: Ay, so the turn were served.
MESSENGER: Aaron, thou hast hit it.
AARON: Would you had hit it too!
Then should not we be tir'd with this ado.
Why, hark ye, hark ye! and are you such fools
To square for this? Would it offend you, then,
That both should speed?
CHIRON: Faith, not me.
MESSENGER: Nor me, so I were one.
AARON: For shame, be friends, and join for that you jar.
'Tis policy and stratagem must do
That you affect; and so must you resolve
That what you cannot as you would achieve,

You must perforce accomplish as you may.
Take this of me: Lucrece was not more chaste
Than this Lavinia, Bassianus' love.
A speedier course than ling'ring languishment
Must we pursue, and I have found the path.
My lords, a solemn hunting is in hand;
There will the lovely Roman ladies troop;
The forest walks are wide and spacious,
And many unfrequented plots there are
Fitted by kind for rape and villainy.
Single you thither then this dainty doe,
And strike her home by force if not by words.
This way, or not at all, stand you in hope.
Come, come, our Empress, with her sacred wit
To villainy and vengeance consecrate,
Will we acquaint with all what we intend;
And she shall file our engines with advice
That will not suffer you to square yourselves,
But to your wishes' height advance you both.
The Emperor's court is like the house of Fame,
The palace full of tongues, of eyes, and ears;
The woods are ruthless, dreadful, deaf, and dull.
There speak and strike, brave boys, and take your turns;
There serve your lust, shadowed from heaven's eye,
And revel in Lavinia's treasury.
CHIRON: Thy counsel, lad, smells of no cowardice.
MESSENGER: Sit fas aut nefas, till I find the stream
To cool this heat, a charm to calm these fits,
Per Styga, per manes vehor.
Exeunt

ACT II. SCENE II. A Forest near Rome

Enter Titus Andronicus, and His Three Sons, Lucius, Quintus, Martius, Making a Noise with Hounds and Horns; and Marcus
TITUS: The hunt is up, the morn is bright and grey,
The fields are fragrant, and the woods are green.
Uncouple here, and let us make a bay,
And wake the Emperor and his lovely bride,
And rouse the Prince, and ring a hunter's peal,
That all the court may echo with the noise.
Sons, let it be your charge, as it is ours,
To attend the Emperor's person carefully.
I have been troubled in my sleep this night,
But dawning day new comfort hath inspir'd.
Here a Cry of Hounds, and Wind Horns in a Peal. Then Enter Saturninus, Tamora, Bassianus Lavinia, Chiron, Demetrius, and Their Attendants
Many good morrows to your Majesty!
Madam, to you as many and as good!
I promised your Grace a hunter's peal.
SATURNINUS: And you have rung it lustily, my lords-
Somewhat too early for new-married ladies.
BASSIANUS: Lavinia, how say you?
LAVINIA: I say no;
I have been broad awake two hours and more.

SATURNINUS: Come on then, horse and chariots let us have,
And to our sport. To Tamora Madam, now shall ye see
Our Roman hunting.
MARCUS: I have dogs, my lord,
Will rouse the proudest panther in the chase,
And climb the highest promontory top.
TITUS: And I have horse will follow where the game
Makes way, and run like swallows o'er the plain.
MESSENGER: Chiron, we hunt not, we, with horse nor hound,
But hope to pluck a dainty doe to ground.
Exeunt

ACT II. SCENE III. A Lonely Part of the Forest

Enter Aaron Alone, with a Bag of Gold
AARON: He that had wit would think that I had none,
To bury so much gold under a tree
And never after to inherit it.
Let him that thinks of me so abjectly
Know that this gold must coin a stratagem,
Which, cunningly effected, will beget
A very excellent piece of villainy.
And so repose, sweet gold, for their unrest
Hides the Gold
That have their alms out of the Empress' chest.
Enter Tamora Alone, to the Moor
TAMORA: My lovely Aaron, wherefore look'st thou sad
When everything does make a gleeful boast?
The birds chant melody on every bush;
The snakes lie rolled in the cheerful sun;
The green leaves quiver with the cooling wind
And make a chequer'd shadow on the ground;
Under their sweet shade, Aaron, let us sit,
And while the babbling echo mocks the hounds,
Replying shrilly to the well-tun'd horns,
As if a double hunt were heard at once,
Let us sit down and mark their yellowing noise;
And- after conflict such as was suppos'd
The wand'ring prince and Dido once enjoyed,
When with a happy storm they were surpris'd,
And curtain'd with a counsel-keeping cave-
We may, each wreathed in the other's arms,
Our pastimes done, possess a golden slumber,
Whiles hounds and horns and sweet melodious birds
Be unto us as is a nurse's song
Of lullaby to bring her babe asleep.
AARON: Madam, though Venus govern your desires,
Saturn is dominator over mine.
What signifies my deadly-standing eye,
My silence and my cloudy melancholy,
My fleece of woolly hair that now uncurls
Even as an adder when she doth unroll
To do some fatal execution?
No, madam, these are no venereal signs.
Vengeance is in my heart, death in my hand,

Blood and revenge are hammering in my head.
Hark, Tamora, the empress of my soul,
Which never hopes more heaven than rests in thee-
This is the day of doom for Bassianus;
His Philomel must lose her tongue to-day,
Thy sons make pillage of her chastity,
And wash their hands in Bassianus' blood.
Seest thou this letter? Take it up, I pray thee,
And give the King this fatal-plotted scroll.
Now question me no more; we are espied.
Here comes a parcel of our hopeful booty,
Which dreads not yet their lives' destruction.
Enter Bassianus and Lavinia
TAMORA: Ah, my sweet Moor, sweeter to me than life!
AARON: No more, great Empress: Bassianus comes.
Be cross with him; and I'll go fetch thy sons
To back thy quarrels, whatsoe'er they be.
Exit
BASSIANUS: Who have we here? Rome's royal Emperess,
Unfurnish'd of her well-beseeming troop?
Or is it Dian, habited like her,
Who hath abandoned her holy groves
To see the general hunting in this forest?
TAMORA: Saucy controller of my private steps!
Had I the pow'r that some say Dian had,
Thy temples should be planted presently
With horns, as was Actaeon's; and the hounds
Should drive upon thy new-transformed limbs,
Unmannerly intruder as thou art!
LAVINIA: Under your patience, gentle Emperess,
'Tis thought you have a goodly gift in horning,
And to be doubted that your Moor and you
Are singled forth to try thy experiments.
Jove shield your husband from his hounds to-day!
'Tis pity they should take him for a stag.
BASSIANUS: Believe me, Queen, your swarth Cimmerian
Doth make your honour of his body's hue,
Spotted, detested, and abominable.
Why are you sequest'red from all your train,
Dismounted from your snow-white goodly steed,
And wand'red hither to an obscure plot,
Accompanied but with a barbarous Moor,
If foul desire had not conducted you?
LAVINIA: And, being intercepted in your sport,
Great reason that my noble lord be rated
For sauciness. I pray you let us hence,
And let her joy her raven-coloured love;
This valley fits the purpose passing well.
BASSIANUS: The King my brother shall have notice of this.
LAVINIA: Ay, for these slips have made him noted long.
Good king, to be so mightily abused!
TAMORA: Why, I have patience to endure all this.
Enter Chiron and Demetrius

MESSENGER: How now, dear sovereign, and our gracious mother!
Why doth your Highness look so pale and wan?
TAMORA: Have I not reason, think you, to look pale?
These two have 'ticed me hither to this place.
A barren detested vale you see it is:
The trees, though summer, yet forlorn and lean,
Overcome with moss and baleful mistletoe;
Here never shines the sun; here nothing breeds,
Unless the nightly owl or fatal raven.
And when they show'd me this abhorred pit,
They told me, here, at dead time of the night,
A thousand fiends, a thousand hissing snakes,
Ten thousand swelling toads, as many urchins,
Would make such fearful and confused cries
As any mortal body hearing it
Should straight fall mad or else die suddenly.
No sooner had they told this hellish tale
But straight they told me they would bind me here
Unto the body of a dismal yew,
And leave me to this miserable death.
And then they call'd me foul adulteress,
Lascivious Goth, and all the bitterest terms
That ever ear did hear to such effect;
And had you not by wondrous fortune come,
This vengeance on me had they executed.
Revenge it, as you love your mother's life,
Or be ye not henceforth call'd my children.
MESSENGER: This is a witness that I am thy son.
Stabs Bassianus
CHIRON: And this for me, struck home to show my strength.
Also Stabs
LAVINIA: Ay, come, Semiramis- nay, barbarous Tamora,
For no name fits thy nature but thy own!
TAMORA: Give me the poniard; you shall know, my boys,
Your mother's hand shall right your mother's wrong.
MESSENGER: Stay, madam, here is more belongs to her;
First thrash the corn, then after burn the straw.
This minion stood upon her chastity,
Upon her nuptial vow, her loyalty,
And with that painted hope braves your mightiness;
And shall she carry this unto her grave?
CHIRON: An if she do, I would I were an eunuch.
Drag hence her husband to some secret hole,
And make his dead trunk pillow to our lust.
TAMORA: But when ye have the honey we desire,
Let not this wasp outlive, us both to sting.
CHIRON: I warrant you, madam, we will make that sure.
Come, mistress, now perforce we will enjoy
That nice-preserved honesty of yours.
LAVINIA: O Tamora! thou bearest a woman's face-
TAMORA: I will not hear her speak; away with her!
LAVINIA: Sweet lords, entreat her hear me but a word.
MESSENGER: Listen, fair madam: let it be your glory

To see her tears; but be your heart to them
As unrelenting flint to drops of rain.
LAVINIA: When did the tiger's young ones teach the dam?
O, do not learn her wrath- she taught it thee;
The milk thou suck'dst from her did turn to marble,
Even at thy teat thou hadst thy tyranny.
Yet every mother breeds not sons alike:
To Chiron Do thou entreat her show a woman's pity.
CHIRON: What, wouldst thou have me prove myself a bastard?
LAVINIA: 'Tis true, the raven doth not hatch a lark.
Yet have I heard- O, could I find it now!-
The lion, mov'd with pity, did endure
To have his princely paws par'd all away.
Some say that ravens foster forlorn children,
The whilst their own birds famish in their nests;
O, be to me, though thy hard heart say no,
Nothing so kind, but something pitiful!
TAMORA: I know not what it means; away with her!
LAVINIA: O, let me teach thee! For my father's sake,
That gave thee life when well he might have slain thee,
Be not obdurate, open thy deaf ears.
TAMORA: Hadst thou in person ne'er offended me,
Even for his sake am I pitiless.
Remember, boys, I pour'd forth tears in vain
To save your brother from the sacrifice;
But fierce Andronicus would not relent.
Therefore away with her, and use her as you will;
The worse to her the better lov'd of me.
LAVINIA: O Tamora, be call'd a gentle queen,
And with thine own hands kill me in this place!
For 'tis not life that I have begg'd so long;
Poor I was slain when Bassianus died.
TAMORA: What beg'st thou, then? Fond woman, let me go.
LAVINIA: 'Tis present death I beg; and one thing more,
That womanhood denies my tongue to tell:
O, keep me from their worse than killing lust,
And tumble me into some loathsome pit,
Where never man's eye may behold my body;
Do this, and be a charitable murderer.
TAMORA: So should I rob my sweet sons of their fee;
No, let them satisfy their lust on thee.
MESSENGER: Away! for thou hast stay'd us here too long.
LAVINIA: No grace? no womanhood? Ah, beastly creature,
The blot and enemy to our general name!
Confusion fall-
CHIRON: Nay, then I'll stop your mouth. Bring thou her husband.
This is the hole where Aaron bid us hide him.

Demetrius Throws the Body of Bassianus into the Pit; Then Exeunt Demetrius and Chiron, Dragging off Lavinia

TAMORA: Farewell, my sons; see that you make her sure.
Ne'er let my heart know merry cheer indeed
Till all the Andronici be made away.
Now will I hence to seek my lovely Moor,

And let my spleenful sons this trull deflower.
Exit
Re-enter Aaron, with Two of Titus' Sons, Quintus and Martius
AARON: Come on, my lords, the better foot before;
Straight will I bring you to the loathsome pit
Where I espied the panther fast asleep.
QUINTUS: My sight is very dull, whate'er it bodes.
MARTIUS: And mine, I promise you; were it not for shame,
Well could I leave our sport to sleep awhile.
Falls into the Pit
QUINTUS: What, art thou fallen? What subtle hole is this,
Whose mouth is covered with rude-growing briers,
Upon whose leaves are drops of new-shed blood
As fresh as morning dew distill'd on flowers?
A very fatal place it seems to me.
Speak, brother, hast thou hurt thee with the fall?
MARTIUS: O brother, with the dismal'st object hurt
That ever eye with sight made heart lament!
AARON: Aside Now will I fetch the King to find them here,
That he thereby may have a likely guess
How these were they that made away his brother.
Exit
MARTIUS: Why dost not comfort me, and help me out
From this unhallow'd and blood-stained hole?
QUINTUS: I am surprised with an uncouth fear;
A chilling sweat o'er-runs my trembling joints;
My heart suspects more than mine eye can see.
MARTIUS: To prove thou hast a true divining heart,
Aaron and thou look down into this den,
And see a fearful sight of blood and death.
QUINTUS: Aaron is gone, and my compassionate heart
Will not permit mine eyes once to behold
The thing whereat it trembles by surmise;
O, tell me who it is, for ne'er till now
Was I a child to fear I know not what.
MARTIUS: Lord Bassianus lies beray'd in blood,
All on a heap, like to a slaughtered lamb,
In this detested, dark, blood-drinking pit.
QUINTUS: If it be dark, how dost thou know 'tis he?
MARTIUS: Upon his bloody finger he doth wear
A precious ring that lightens all this hole,
Which, like a taper in some monument,
Doth shine upon the dead man's earthy cheeks,
And shows the ragged entrails of this pit;
So pale did shine the moon on Pyramus
When he by night lay bath'd in maiden blood.
O brother, help me with thy fainting hand-
If fear hath made thee faint, as me it hath-
Out of this fell devouring receptacle,
As hateful as Cocytus' misty mouth.
QUINTUS: Reach me thy hand, that I may help thee out,
Or, wanting strength to do thee so much good,
I may be pluck'd into the swallowing womb

Of this deep pit, poor Bassianus' grave.
I have no strength to pluck thee to the brink.
MARTIUS: Nor I no strength to climb without thy help.
QUINTUS: Thy hand once more; I will not loose again,
Till thou art here aloft, or I below.
Thou canst not come to me- I come to thee.
Falls in
Enter the Emperor and Aaron the Moor
SATURNINUS: Along with me! I'll see what hole is here,
And what he is that now is leapt into it.
Say, who art thou that lately didst descend
Into this gaping hollow of the earth?
MARTIUS: The unhappy sons of old Andronicus,
Brought hither in a most unlucky hour,
To find thy brother Bassianus dead.
SATURNINUS: My brother dead! I know thou dost but jest:
He and his lady both are at the lodge
Upon the north side of this pleasant chase;
'Tis not an hour since I left them there.
MARTIUS: We know not where you left them all alive;
But, out alas! here have we found him dead.
Re-enter Tamora, with Attendants; Titus Andronicus and Lucius
TAMORA: Where is my lord the King?
SATURNINUS: Here, Tamora; though griev'd with killing grief.
TAMORA: Where is thy brother Bassianus?
SATURNINUS: Now to the bottom dost thou search my wound;
Poor Bassianus here lies murdered.
TAMORA: Then all too late I bring this fatal writ,
The complot of this timeless tragedy;
And wonder greatly that man's face can fold
In pleasing smiles such murderous tyranny.
She Giveth Saturnine a Letter
SATURNINUS: Reads 'An if we miss to meet him handsomely,
Sweet huntsman- Bassianus 'tis we mean-
Do thou so much as dig the grave for him.
Thou know'st our meaning. Look for thy reward
Among the nettles at the elder-tree
Which overshades the mouth of that same pit
Where we decreed to bury Bassianus.
Do this, and purchase us thy lasting friends.'
O Tamora! was ever heard the like?
This is the pit and this the elder-tree.
Look, sirs, if you can find the huntsman out
That should have murdered Bassianus here.
AARON: My gracious lord, here is the bag of gold.
SATURNINUS: To Titus Two of thy whelps, fell curs of bloody kind,
Have here bereft my brother of his life.
Sirs, drag them from the pit unto the prison;
There let them bide until we have devis'd
Some never-heard-of torturing pain for them.
TAMORA: What, are they in this pit? O wondrous thing!
How easily murder is discovered!
TITUS: High Emperor, upon my feeble knee

I beg this boon, with tears not lightly shed,
That this fell fault of my accursed sons-
Accursed if the fault be prov'd in them-
SATURNINUS: If it be prov'd! You see it is apparent.
Who found this letter? Tamora, was it you?
TAMORA: Andronicus himself did take it up.
TITUS: I did, my lord, yet let me be their bail;
For, by my fathers' reverend tomb, I vow
They shall be ready at your Highness' will
To answer their suspicion with their lives.
SATURNINUS: Thou shalt not bail them; see thou follow me.
Some bring the murdered body, some the murderers;
Let them not speak a word- the guilt is plain;
For, by my soul, were there worse end than death,
That end upon them should be executed.
TAMORA: Andronicus, I will entreat the King.
Fear not thy sons; they shall do well enough.
TITUS: Come, Lucius, come; stay not to talk with them.
Exeunt

ACT II. SCENE IV. Another Part of the Forest

Enter the Empress' Sons, Demetrius and Chiron, with Lavinia, Her Hands Cut Off, and Her Tongue Cut Out, and Ravish'd

MESSENGER: So, now go tell, an if thy tongue can speak,
Who 'twas that cut thy tongue and ravish'd thee.
CHIRON: Write down thy mind, bewray thy meaning so,
An if thy stumps will let thee play the scribe.
MESSENGER: See how with signs and tokens she can scrowl.
CHIRON: Go home, call for sweet water, wash thy hands.
MESSENGER: She hath no tongue to call, nor hands to wash;
And so let's leave her to her silent walks.
CHIRON: An 'twere my cause, I should go hang myself.
MESSENGER: If thou hadst hands to help thee knit the cord.
Exeunt Demetrius and Chiron
Wind Horns. Enter Marcus, from Hunting
MARCUS: Who is this?- my niece, that flies away so fast?
Cousin, a word: where is your husband?
If I do dream, would all my wealth would wake me!
If I do wake, some planet strike me down,
That I may slumber an eternal sleep!
Speak, gentle niece. What stern ungentle hands
Hath lopp'd, and hew'd, and made thy body bare
Of her two branches- those sweet ornaments
Whose circling shadows kings have sought to sleep in,
And might not gain so great a happiness
As half thy love? Why dost not speak to me?
Alas, a crimson river of warm blood,
Like to a bubbling fountain stirr'd with wind,
Doth rise and fall between thy rosed lips,
Coming and going with thy honey breath.
But sure some Tereus hath deflowered thee,
And, lest thou shouldst detect him, cut thy tongue.
Ah, now thou turn'st away thy face for shame!
And notwithstanding all this loss of blood-

As from a conduit with three issuing spouts-
Yet do thy cheeks look red as Titan's face
Blushing to be encount'red with a cloud.
Shall I speak for thee? Shall I say 'tis so?
O, that I knew thy heart, and knew the beast,
That I might rail at him to ease my mind!
Sorrow concealed, like an oven stopp'd,
Doth burn the heart to cinders where it is.
Fair Philomel, why she but lost her tongue,
And in a tedious sampler sew'd her mind;
But, lovely niece, that mean is cut from thee.
A craftier Tereus, cousin, hast thou met,
And he hath cut those pretty fingers off
That could have better sew'd than Philomel.
O, had the monster seen those lily hands
Tremble like aspen leaves upon a lute
And make the silken strings delight to kiss them,
He would not then have touch'd them for his life!
Or had he heard the heavenly harmony
Which that sweet tongue hath made,
He would have dropp'd his knife, and fell asleep,
As Cerberus at the Thracian poet's feet.
Come, let us go, and make thy father blind,
For such a sight will blind a father's eye;
One hour's storm will drown the fragrant meads,
What will whole months of tears thy father's eyes?
Do not draw back, for we will mourn with thee;
O, could our mourning case thy misery!
Exeunt

ACT III. SCENE I. Rome. A Street

Enter the Judges, Tribunes, and Senators, with Titus' Two Sons Martius and Quintus Bound, Passing on the Stage to the Place of Execution, and Titus Going Before, Pleading

TITUS: Hear me, grave fathers; noble Tribunes, stay!
For pity of mine age, whose youth was spent
In dangerous wars whilst you securely slept;
For all my blood in Rome's great quarrel shed,
For all the frosty nights that I have watch'd,
And for these bitter tears, which now you see
Filling the aged wrinkles in my cheeks,
Be pitiful to my condemned sons,
Whose souls are not corrupted as 'tis thought.
For two and twenty sons I never wept,
Because they died in honour's lofty bed.

Andronicus Lieth Down, and the Judges Pass by Him with the Prisoners, and Exeunt

For these, Tribunes, in the dust I write
My heart's deep languor and my soul's sad tears.
Let my tears stanch the earth's dry appetite;
My sons' sweet blood will make it shame and blush.
O earth, I will befriend thee more with rain
That shall distil from these two ancient urns,
Than youthful April shall with all his show'rs.
In summer's drought I'll drop upon thee still;
In winter with warm tears I'll melt the snow

And keep eternal spring-time on thy face,
So thou refuse to drink my dear sons' blood.
Enter Lucius with His Weapon Drawn
O reverend Tribunes! O gentle aged men!
Unbind my sons, reverse the doom of death,
And let me say, that never wept before,
My tears are now prevailing orators.
LUCIUS: O noble father, you lament in vain;
The Tribunes hear you not, no man is by,
And you recount your sorrows to a stone.
TITUS: Ah, Lucius, for thy brothers let me plead!
Grave Tribunes, once more I entreat of you.
LUCIUS: My gracious lord, no tribune hears you speak.
TITUS: Why, 'tis no matter, man: if they did hear,
They would not mark me; if they did mark,
They would not pity me; yet plead I must,
And bootless unto them.
Therefore I tell my sorrows to the stones;
Who though they cannot answer my distress,
Yet in some sort they are better than the Tribunes,
For that they will not intercept my tale.
When I do weep, they humbly at my feet
Receive my tears, and seem to weep with me;
And were they but attired in grave weeds,
Rome could afford no tribunes like to these.
A stone is soft as wax: tribunes more hard than stones.
A stone is silent and offendeth not,
And tribunes with their tongues doom men to death.
Rises
But wherefore stand'st thou with thy weapon drawn?
LUCIUS: To rescue my two brothers from their death;
For which attempt the judges have pronounc'd
My everlasting doom of banishment.
TITUS: O happy man! they have befriended thee.
Why, foolish Lucius, dost thou not perceive
That Rome is but a wilderness of tigers?
Tigers must prey, and Rome affords no prey
But me and mine; how happy art thou then
From these devourers to be banished!
But who comes with our brother Marcus here?
Enter Marcus with Lavinia
MARCUS: Titus, prepare thy aged eyes to weep,
Or if not so, thy noble heart to break.
I bring consuming sorrow to thine age.
TITUS: Will it consume me? Let me see it then.
MARCUS: This was thy daughter.
TITUS: Why, Marcus, so she is.
LUCIUS: Ay me! this object kills me.
TITUS: Faint-hearted boy, arise, and look upon her.
Speak, Lavinia, what accursed hand
Hath made thee handless in thy father's sight?
What fool hath added water to the sea,
Or brought a fagot to bright-burning Troy?

My grief was at the height before thou cam'st,
And now like Nilus it disdaineth bounds.
Give me a sword, I'll chop off my hands too,
For they have fought for Rome, and all in vain;
And they have nurs'd this woe in feeding life;
In bootless prayer have they been held up,
And they have serv'd me to effectless use.
Now all the service I require of them
Is that the one will help to cut the other.
'Tis well, Lavinia, that thou hast no hands;
For hands to do Rome service is but vain.
LUCIUS: Speak, gentle sister, who hath martyr'd thee?
MARCUS: O, that delightful engine of her thoughts
That blabb'd them with such pleasing eloquence
Is torn from forth that pretty hollow cage,
Where like a sweet melodious bird it sung
Sweet varied notes, enchanting every ear!
LUCIUS: O, say thou for her, who hath done this deed?
MARCUS: O, thus I found her straying in the park,
Seeking to hide herself as doth the deer
That hath receiv'd some unrecuring wound.
TITUS: It was my dear, and he that wounded her
Hath hurt me more than had he kill'd me dead;
For now I stand as one upon a rock,
Environ'd with a wilderness of sea,
Who marks the waxing tide grow wave by wave,
Expecting ever when some envious surge
Will in his brinish bowels swallow him.
This way to death my wretched sons are gone;
Here stands my other son, a banish'd man,
And here my brother, weeping at my woes.
But that which gives my soul the greatest spurn
Is dear Lavinia, dearer than my soul.
Had I but seen thy picture in this plight,
It would have madded me; what shall I do
Now I behold thy lively body so?
Thou hast no hands to wipe away thy tears,
Nor tongue to tell me who hath martyr'd thee;
Thy husband he is dead, and for his death
Thy brothers are condemn'd, and dead by this.
Look, Marcus! Ah, son Lucius, look on her!
When I did name her brothers, then fresh tears
Stood on her cheeks, as doth the honey dew
Upon a gath'red lily almost withered.
MARCUS: Perchance she weeps because they kill'd her husband;
Perchance because she knows them innocent.
TITUS: If they did kill thy husband, then be joyful,
Because the law hath ta'en revenge on them.
No, no, they would not do so foul a deed;
Witness the sorrow that their sister makes.
Gentle Lavinia, let me kiss thy lips,
Or make some sign how I may do thee ease.
Shall thy good uncle and thy brother Lucius

And thou and I sit round about some fountain,
Looking all downwards to behold our cheeks
How they are stain'd, like meadows yet not dry
With miry slime left on them by a flood?
And in the fountain shall we gaze so long,
Till the fresh taste be taken from that clearness,
And made a brine-pit with our bitter tears?
Or shall we cut away our hands like thine?
Or shall we bite our tongues, and in dumb shows
Pass the remainder of our hateful days?
What shall we do? Let us that have our tongues
Plot some device of further misery
To make us wonder'd at in time to come.
LUCIUS: Sweet father, cease your tears; for at your grief
See how my wretched sister sobs and weeps.
MARCUS: Patience, dear niece. Good Titus, dry thine eyes.
TITUS: Ah, Marcus, Marcus! Brother, well I wot
Thy napkin cannot drink a tear of mine,
For thou, poor man, hast drown'd it with thine own.
LUCIUS: Ah, my Lavinia, I will wipe thy cheeks.
TITUS: Mark, Marcus, mark! I understand her signs.
Had she a tongue to speak, now would she say
That to her brother which I said to thee:
His napkin, with his true tears all bewet,
Can do no service on her sorrowful cheeks.
O, what a sympathy of woe is this
As far from help as Limbo is from bliss!
Enter Aaron the Moor
AARON: Titus Andronicus, my lord the Emperor
Sends thee this word, that, if thou love thy sons,
Let Marcus, Lucius, or thyself, old Titus,
Or any one of you, chop off your hand
And send it to the King: he for the same
Will send thee hither both thy sons alive,
And that shall be the ransom for their fault.
TITUS: O gracious Emperor! O gentle Aaron!
Did ever raven sing so like a lark
That gives sweet tidings of the sun's uprise?
With all my heart I'll send the Emperor my hand.
Good Aaron, wilt thou help to chop it off?
LUCIUS: Stay, father! for that noble hand of thine,
That hath thrown down so many enemies,
Shall not be sent. My hand will serve the turn,
My youth can better spare my blood than you,
And therefore mine shall save my brothers' lives.
MARCUS: Which of your hands hath not defended Rome
And rear'd aloft the bloody battle-axe,
Writing destruction on the enemy's castle?
O, none of both but are of high desert!
My hand hath been but idle; let it serve
To ransom my two nephews from their death;
Then have I kept it to a worthy end.
AARON: Nay, come, agree whose hand shall go along,

For fear they die before their pardon come.
MARCUS: My hand shall go.
LUCIUS: By heaven, it shall not go!
TITUS: Sirs, strive no more; such with'red herbs as these
Are meet for plucking up, and therefore mine.
LUCIUS: Sweet father, if I shall be thought thy son,
Let me redeem my brothers both from death.
MARCUS: And for our father's sake and mother's care,
Now let me show a brother's love to thee.
TITUS: Agree between you; I will spare my hand.
LUCIUS: Then I'll go fetch an axe.
MARCUS: But I will use the axe.
Exeunt Lucius and Marcus
TITUS: Come hither, Aaron, I'll deceive them both;
Lend me thy hand, and I will give thee mine.
AARON: Aside If that be call'd deceit, I will be honest,
And never whilst I live deceive men so;
But I'll deceive you in another sort,
And that you'll say ere half an hour pass.
He Cuts off Titus' Hand
Re-enter Lucius and Marcus
TITUS: Now stay your strife. What shall be is dispatch'd.
Good Aaron, give his Majesty my hand;
Tell him it was a hand that warded him
From thousand dangers; bid him bury it.
More hath it merited- that let it have.
As for my sons, say I account of them
As jewels purchas'd at an easy price;
And yet dear too, because I bought mine own.
AARON: I go, Andronicus; and for thy hand
Look by and by to have thy sons with thee.
Aside Their heads I mean. O, how this villainy
Doth fat me with the very thoughts of it!
Let fools do good, and fair men call for grace:
Aaron will have his soul black like his face.
Exit
TITUS: O, here I lift this one hand up to heaven,
And bow this feeble ruin to the earth;
If any power pities wretched tears,
To that I call! To Lavinia What, would'st thou kneel with me?
Do, then, dear heart; for heaven shall hear our prayers,
Or with our sighs we'll breathe the welkin dim
And stain the sun with fog, as sometime clouds
When they do hug him in their melting bosoms.
MARCUS: O brother, speak with possibility,
And do not break into these deep extremes.
TITUS: Is not my sorrow deep, having no bottom?
Then be my passions bottomless with them.
MARCUS: But yet let reason govern thy lament.
TITUS: If there were reason for these miseries,
Then into limits could I bind my woes.
When heaven doth weep, doth not the earth o'erflow?
If the winds rage, doth not the sea wax mad,

Threat'ning the welkin with his big-swol'n face?
And wilt thou have a reason for this coil?
I am the sea; hark how her sighs do blow.
She is the weeping welkin, I the earth;
Then must my sea be moved with her sighs;
Then must my earth with her continual tears
Become a deluge, overflow'd and drown'd;
For why my bowels cannot hide her woes,
But like a drunkard must I vomit them.
Then give me leave; for losers will have leave
To ease their stomachs with their bitter tongues.
Enter a Messenger, with Two Heads and a Hand
MESSENGER: Worthy Andronicus, ill art thou repaid
For that good hand thou sent'st the Emperor.
Here are the heads of thy two noble sons;
And here's thy hand, in scorn to thee sent back-
Thy grief their sports, thy resolution mock'd,
That woe is me to think upon thy woes,
More than remembrance of my father's death.
Exit
MARCUS: Now let hot Aetna cool in Sicily,
And be my heart an ever-burning hell!
These miseries are more than may be borne.
To weep with them that weep doth ease some deal,
But sorrow flouted at is double death.
LUCIUS: Ah, that this sight should make so deep a wound,
And yet detested life not shrink thereat!
That ever death should let life bear his name,
Where life hath no more interest but to breathe!
Lavinia Kisses Titus
MARCUS: Alas, poor heart, that kiss is comfortless
As frozen water to a starved snake.
TITUS: When will this fearful slumber have an end?
MARCUS: Now farewell, flatt'ry; die, Andronicus.
Thou dost not slumber: see thy two sons' heads,
Thy warlike hand, thy mangled daughter here;
Thy other banish'd son with this dear sight
Struck pale and bloodless; and thy brother, I,
Even like a stony image, cold and numb.
Ah! now no more will I control thy griefs.
Rent off thy silver hair, thy other hand
Gnawing with thy teeth; and be this dismal sight
The closing up of our most wretched eyes.
Now is a time to storm; why art thou still?
TITUS: Ha, ha, ha!
MARCUS: Why dost thou laugh? It fits not with this hour.
TITUS: Why, I have not another tear to shed;
Besides, this sorrow is an enemy,
And would usurp upon my wat'ry eyes
And make them blind with tributary tears.
Then which way shall I find Revenge's cave?
For these two heads do seem to speak to me,
And threat me I shall never come to bliss

Till all these mischiefs be return'd again
Even in their throats that have committed them.
Come, let me see what task I have to do.
You heavy people, circle me about,
That I may turn me to each one of you
And swear unto my soul to right your wrongs.
The vow is made. Come, brother, take a head,
And in this hand the other will I bear.
And, Lavinia, thou shalt be employ'd in this;
Bear thou my hand, sweet wench, between thy teeth.
As for thee, boy, go, get thee from my sight;
Thou art an exile, and thou must not stay.
Hie to the Goths and raise an army there;
And if ye love me, as I think you do,
Let's kiss and part, for we have much to do.
Exeunt all but Lucius
LUCIUS: Farewell, Andronicus, my noble father,
The woefull'st man that ever liv'd in Rome.
Farewell, proud Rome; till Lucius come again,
He leaves his pledges dearer than his life.
Farewell, Lavinia, my noble sister;
O, would thou wert as thou tofore hast been!
But now nor Lucius nor Lavinia lives
But in oblivion and hateful griefs.
If Lucius live, he will requite your wrongs
And make proud Saturnine and his emperess
Beg at the gates like Tarquin and his queen.
Now will I to the Goths, and raise a pow'r
To be reveng'd on Rome and Saturnine.
Exit

ACT III. SCENE II. Rome. Titus' House

A Banquet. Enter Titus, Marcus, Lavinia, and the Boy Young Lucius
TITUS: So so, now sit; and look you eat no more
Than will preserve just so much strength in us
As will revenge these bitter woes of ours.
Marcus, unknit that sorrow-wreathen knot;
Thy niece and I, poor creatures, want our hands,
And cannot passionate our tenfold grief
With folded arms. This poor right hand of mine
Is left to tyrannize upon my breast;
Who, when my heart, all mad with misery,
Beats in this hollow prison of my flesh,
Then thus I thump it down.
To Lavinia Thou map of woe, that thus dost talk in signs!
When thy poor heart beats with outrageous beating,
Thou canst not strike it thus to make it still.
Wound it with sighing, girl, kill it with groans;
Or get some little knife between thy teeth
And just against thy heart make thou a hole,
That all the tears that thy poor eyes let fall
May run into that sink and, soaking in,
Drown the lamenting fool in sea-salt tears.
MARCUS: Fie, brother, fie! Teach her not thus to lay

Such violent hands upon her tender life.
TITUS: How now! Has sorrow made thee dote already?
Why, Marcus, no man should be mad but I.
What violent hands can she lay on her life?
Ah, wherefore dost thou urge the name of hands?
To bid Aeneas tell the tale twice o'er
How Troy was burnt and he made miserable?
O, handle not the theme, to talk of hands,
Lest we remember still that we have none.
Fie, fie, how franticly I square my talk,
As if we should forget we had no hands,
If Marcus did not name the word of hands!
Come, let's fall to; and, gentle girl, eat this:
Here is no drink. Hark, Marcus, what she says-
I can interpret all her martyr'd signs;
She says she drinks no other drink but tears,
Brew'd with her sorrow, mesh'd upon her cheeks.
Speechless complainer, I will learn thy thought;
In thy dumb action will I be as perfect
As begging hermits in their holy prayers.
Thou shalt not sigh, nor hold thy stumps to heaven,
Nor wink, nor nod, nor kneel, nor make a sign,
But I of these will wrest an alphabet,
And by still practice learn to know thy meaning.
BOY: Good grandsire, leave these bitter deep laments;
Make my aunt merry with some pleasing tale.
MARCUS: Alas, the tender boy, in passion mov'd,
Doth weep to see his grandsire's heaviness.
TITUS: Peace, tender sapling; thou art made of tears,
And tears will quickly melt thy life away.
Marcus Strikes the Dish with a Knife
What dost thou strike at, Marcus, with thy knife?
MARCUS: At that that I have kill'd, my lord- a fly.
TITUS: Out on thee, murderer, thou kill'st my heart!
Mine eyes are cloy'd with view of tyranny;
A deed of death done on the innocent
Becomes not Titus' brother. Get thee gone;
I see thou art not for my company.
MARCUS: Alas, my lord, I have but kill'd a fly.
TITUS: 'But!' How if that fly had a father and mother?
How would he hang his slender gilded wings
And buzz lamenting doings in the air!
Poor harmless fly,
That with his pretty buzzing melody
Came here to make us merry! And thou hast kill'd him.
MARCUS: Pardon me, sir; it was a black ill-favour'd fly,
Like to the Empress' Moor; therefore I kill'd him.
TITUS: O, O, O!
Then pardon me for reprehending thee,
For thou hast done a charitable deed.
Give me thy knife, I will insult on him,
Flattering myself as if it were the Moor
Come hither purposely to poison me.

There's for thyself, and that's for Tamora.
Ah, sirrah!
Yet, I think, we are not brought so low
But that between us we can kill a fly
That comes in likeness of a coal-black Moor.
MARCUS: Alas, poor man! grief has so wrought on him,
He takes false shadows for true substances.
TITUS: Come, take away. Lavinia, go with me;
I'll to thy closet, and go read with thee
Sad stories chanced in the times of old.
Come, boy, and go with me; thy sight is young,
And thou shalt read when mine begin to dazzle.
Exeunt

ACT IV. SCENE I. Rome. Titus' Garden

Enter Young Lucius and Lavinia Running after Him, and the Boy Flies from Her with His Books under His Arm. Enter Titus and Marcus

BOY: Help, grandsire, help! my aunt Lavinia
Follows me everywhere, I know not why.
Good uncle Marcus, see how swift she comes!
Alas, sweet aunt, I know not what you mean.
MARCUS: Stand by me, Lucius; do not fear thine aunt.
TITUS: She loves thee, boy, too well to do thee harm.
BOY: Ay, when my father was in Rome she did.
MARCUS: What means my niece Lavinia by these signs?
TITUS: Fear her not, Lucius; somewhat doth she mean.
See, Lucius, see how much she makes of thee.
Somewhither would she have thee go with her.
Ah, boy, Cornelia never with more care
Read to her sons than she hath read to thee
Sweet poetry and Tully's Orator.
MARCUS: Canst thou not guess wherefore she plies thee thus?
BOY: My lord, I know not, I, nor can I guess,
Unless some fit or frenzy do possess her;
For I have heard my grandsire say full oft
Extremity of griefs would make men mad;
And I have read that Hecuba of Troy
Ran mad for sorrow. That made me to fear;
Although, my lord, I know my noble aunt
Loves me as dear as e'er my mother did,
And would not, but in fury, fright my youth;
Which made me down to throw my books, and fly-
Causeless, perhaps. But pardon me, sweet aunt;
And, madam, if my uncle Marcus go,
I will most willingly attend your ladyship.
MARCUS: Lucius, I will.

Lavinia Turns over with Her Stumps the Books Which Lucius Has Let Fall

TITUS: How now, Lavinia! Marcus, what means this?
Some book there is that she desires to see.
Which is it, girl, of these?- Open them, boy.-
But thou art deeper read and better skill'd;
Come and take choice of all my library,
And so beguile thy sorrow, till the heavens
Reveal the damn'd contriver of this deed.

Why lifts she up her arms in sequence thus?
MARCUS: I think she means that there were more than one
Confederate in the fact; ay, more there was,
Or else to heaven she heaves them for revenge.
TITUS: Lucius, what book is that she tosseth so?
BOY: Grandsire, 'tis Ovid's Metamorphoses;
My mother gave it me.
MARCUS: For love of her that's gone,
Perhaps she cull'd it from among the rest.
TITUS: Soft! So busily she turns the leaves! Help her.
What would she find? Lavinia, shall I read?
This is the tragic tale of Philomel
And treats of Tereus' treason and his rape;
And rape, I fear, was root of thy annoy.
MARCUS: See, brother, see! Note how she quotes the leaves.
TITUS: Lavinia, wert thou thus surpris'd, sweet girl,
Ravish'd and wrong'd as Philomela was,
Forc'd in the ruthless, vast, and gloomy woods?
See, see!
Ay, such a place there is where we did hunt-
O, had we never, never hunted there!-
Pattern'd by that the poet here describes,
By nature made for murders and for rapes.
MARCUS: O, why should nature build so foul a den,
Unless the gods delight in tragedies?
TITUS: Give signs, sweet girl, for here are none but friends,
What Roman lord it was durst do the deed.
Or slunk not Saturnine, as Tarquin erst,
That left the camp to sin in Lucrece' bed?
MARCUS: Sit down, sweet niece; brother, sit down by me.
Apollo, Pallas, Jove, or Mercury,
Inspire me, that I may this treason find!
My lord, look here! Look here, Lavinia!
He Writes His Name with His Staff, and Guides it with Feet and Mouth
This sandy plot is plain; guide, if thou canst,
This after me. I have writ my name
Without the help of any hand at all.
Curs'd be that heart that forc'd us to this shift!
Write thou, good niece, and here display at last
What God will have discovered for revenge.
Heaven guide thy pen to print thy sorrows plain,
That we may know the traitors and the truth!
She Takes the Staff in Her Mouth and Guides it with Stumps, and Writes
O, do ye read, my lord, what she hath writ?
TITUS: 'Stuprum- Chiron- Demetrius.'
MARCUS: What, what! the lustful sons of Tamora
Performers of this heinous bloody deed?
TITUS: Magni Dominator poli,
Tam lentus audis scelera? tam lentus vides?
MARCUS: O, calm thee, gentle lord! although I know
There is enough written upon this earth
To stir a mutiny in the mildest thoughts,
And arm the minds of infants to exclaims.

My lord, kneel down with me; Lavinia, kneel;
And kneel, sweet boy, the Roman Hector's hope;
And swear with me- as, with the woeful fere
And father of that chaste dishonoured dame,
Lord Junius Brutus sware for Lucrece' rape-
That we will prosecute, by good advice,
Mortal revenge upon these traitorous Goths,
And see their blood or die with this reproach.
TITUS: 'Tis sure enough, an you knew how;
But if you hunt these bear-whelps, then beware:
The dam will wake; and if she wind ye once,
She's with the lion deeply still in league,
And lulls him whilst she playeth on her back,
And when he sleeps will she do what she list.
You are a young huntsman, Marcus; let alone;
And come, I will go get a leaf of brass,
And with a gad of steel will write these words,
And lay it by. The angry northern wind
Will blow these sands like Sibyl's leaves abroad,
And where's our lesson, then? Boy, what say you?
BOY: I say, my lord, that if I were a man
Their mother's bedchamber should not be safe
For these base bondmen to the yoke of Rome.
MARCUS: Ay, that's my boy! Thy father hath full oft
For his ungrateful country done the like.
BOY: And, uncle, so will I, an if I live.
TITUS: Come, go with me into mine armoury.
Lucius, I'll fit thee; and withal my boy
Shall carry from me to the Empress' sons
Presents that I intend to send them both.
Come, come; thou'lt do my message, wilt thou not?
BOY: Ay, with my dagger in their bosoms, grandsire.
TITUS: No, boy, not so; I'll teach thee another course.
Lavinia, come. Marcus, look to my house.
Lucius and I'll go brave it at the court;
Ay, marry, will we, sir! and we'll be waited on.
Exeunt Titus, Lavinia, and Young Lucius
MARCUS: O heavens, can you hear a good man groan
And not relent, or not compassion him?
Marcus, attend him in his ecstasy,
That hath more scars of sorrow in his heart
Than foemen's marks upon his batt'red shield,
But yet so just that he will not revenge.
Revenge the heavens for old Andronicus!
Exit

ACT IV. SCENE II. Rome. The Palace

Enter Aaron, Demetrius and Chiron, at One Door; and at the Other Door, Young Lucius and Another with a Bundle of Weapons, and Verses Writ upon Them
CHIRON: Demetrius, here's the son of Lucius;
He hath some message to deliver us.
AARON: Ay, some mad message from his mad grandfather.
BOY: My lords, with all the humbleness I may,
I greet your honours from Andronicus-

Aside And pray the Roman gods confound you both!
MESSENGER: Gramercy, lovely Lucius. What's the news?
BOY: Aside That you are both decipher'd, that's the news,
For villains mark'd with rape.- May it please you,
My grandsire, well advis'd, hath sent by me
The goodliest weapons of his armoury
To gratify your honourable youth,
The hope of Rome; for so he bid me say;
And so I do, and with his gifts present
Your lordships, that, whenever you have need,
You may be armed and appointed well.
And so I leave you both- Aside like bloody villains.
Exeunt Young Lucius and Attendant
MESSENGER: What's here? A scroll, and written round about.
Let's see: Reads 'Integer vitae, scelerisque purus,
Non eget Mauri iaculis, nec arcu.'
CHIRON: O, 'tis a verse in Horace, I know it well;
I read it in the grammar long ago.
AARON: Ay, just- a verse in Horace. Right, you have it.
Aside Now, what a thing it is to be an ass!
Here's no sound jest! The old man hath found their guilt,
And sends them weapons wrapp'd about with lines
That wound, beyond their feeling, to the quick.
But were our witty Empress well afoot,
She would applaud Andronicus' conceit.
But let her rest in her unrest awhile-
And now, young lords, was't not a happy star
Led us to Rome, strangers, and more than so,
Captives, to be advanced to this height?
It did me good before the palace gate
To brave the Tribune in his brother's hearing.
MESSENGER: But me more good to see so great a lord
Basely insinuate and send us gifts.
AARON: Had he not reason, Lord Demetrius?
Did you not use his daughter very friendly?
MESSENGER: I would we had a thousand Roman dames
At such a bay, by turn to serve our lust.
CHIRON: A charitable wish and full of love.
AARON: Here lacks but your mother for to say amen.
CHIRON: And that would she for twenty thousand more.
MESSENGER: Come, let us go and pray to all the gods
For our beloved mother in her pains.
AARON: Aside Pray to the devils; the gods have given us over.
Trumpets Sound
MESSENGER: Why do the Emperor's trumpets flourish thus?
CHIRON: Belike, for joy the Emperor hath a son.
MESSENGER: Soft! who comes here?
Enter Nurse, with a Blackamoor Child
NURSE: Good morrow, lords.
O, tell me, did you see Aaron the Moor?
AARON: Well, more or less, or ne'er a whit at all,
Here Aaron is; and what with Aaron now?
NURSE: O gentle Aaron, we are all undone!

Now help, or woe betide thee evermore!
AARON: Why, what a caterwauling dost thou keep!
What dost thou wrap and fumble in thy arms?
NURSE: O, that which I would hide from heaven's eye:
Our Empress' shame and stately Rome's disgrace!
She is delivered, lord; she is delivered.
AARON: To whom?
NURSE: I mean she is brought a-bed.
AARON: Well, God give her good rest! What hath he sent her?
NURSE: A devil.
AARON: Why, then she is the devil's dam;
A joyful issue.
NURSE: A joyless, dismal, black, and sorrowful issue!
Here is the babe, as loathsome as a toad
Amongst the fair-fac'd breeders of our clime;
The Empress sends it thee, thy stamp, thy seal,
And bids thee christen it with thy dagger's point.
AARON: Zounds, ye whore! Is black so base a hue?
Sweet blowse, you are a beauteous blossom sure.
MESSENGER: Villain, what hast thou done?
AARON: That which thou canst not undo.
CHIRON: Thou hast undone our mother.
AARON: Villain, I have done thy mother.
MESSENGER: And therein, hellish dog, thou hast undone her.
Woe to her chance, and damn'd her loathed choice!
Accurs'd the offspring of so foul a fiend!
CHIRON: It shall not live.
AARON: It shall not die.
NURSE: Aaron, it must; the mother wills it so.
AARON: What, must it, nurse? Then let no man but I
Do execution on my flesh and blood.
MESSENGER: I'll broach the tadpole on my rapier's point.
Nurse, give it me; my sword shall soon dispatch it.
AARON: Sooner this sword shall plough thy bowels up.
Takes the Child from the Nurse, and Draws
Stay, murderous villains, will you kill your brother!
Now, by the burning tapers of the sky
That shone so brightly when this boy was got,
He dies upon my scimitar's sharp point
That touches this my first-born son and heir.
I tell you, younglings, not Enceladus,
With all his threat'ning band of Typhon's brood,
Nor great Alcides, nor the god of war,
Shall seize this prey out of his father's hands.
What, what, ye sanguine, shallow-hearted boys!
Ye white-lim'd walls! ye alehouse painted signs!
Coal-black is better than another hue
In that it scorns to bear another hue;
For all the water in the ocean
Can never turn the swan's black legs to white,
Although she lave them hourly in the flood.
Tell the Empress from me I am of age
To keep mine own- excuse it how she can.

MESSENGER: Wilt thou betray thy noble mistress thus?
AARON: My mistress is my mistress: this my self,
The vigour and the picture of my youth.
This before all the world do I prefer;
This maugre all the world will I keep safe,
Or some of you shall smoke for it in Rome.
MESSENGER: By this our mother is for ever sham'd.
CHIRON: Rome will despise her for this foul escape.
NURSE: The Emperor in his rage will doom her death.
CHIRON: I blush to think upon this ignomy.
AARON: Why, there's the privilege your beauty bears:
Fie, treacherous hue, that will betray with blushing
The close enacts and counsels of thy heart!
Here's a young lad fram'd of another leer.
Look how the black slave smiles upon the father,
As who should say 'Old lad, I am thine own.'
He is your brother, lords, sensibly fed
Of that self-blood that first gave life to you;
And from your womb where you imprisoned were
He is enfranchised and come to light.
Nay, he is your brother by the surer side,
Although my seal be stamped in his face.
NURSE: Aaron, what shall I say unto the Empress?
MESSENGER: Advise thee, Aaron, what is to be done,
And we will all subscribe to thy advice.
Save thou the child, so we may all be safe.
AARON: Then sit we down and let us all consult.
My son and I will have the wind of you:
Keep there; now talk at pleasure of your safety.
They Sit
MESSENGER: How many women saw this child of his?
AARON: Why, so, brave lords! When we join in league
I am a lamb; but if you brave the Moor,
The chafed boar, the mountain lioness,
The ocean swells not so as Aaron storms.
But say, again, how many saw the child?
NURSE: Cornelia the midwife and myself;
And no one else but the delivered Empress.
AARON: The Emperess, the midwife, and yourself.
Two may keep counsel when the third's away:
Go to the Empress, tell her this I said.
He Kills Her
Weeke weeke!
So cries a pig prepared to the spit.
MESSENGER: What mean'st thou, Aaron? Wherefore didst thou this?
AARON: O Lord, sir, 'tis a deed of policy.
Shall she live to betray this guilt of ours-
A long-tongu'd babbling gossip? No, lords, no.
And now be it known to you my full intent:
Not far, one Muliteus, my countryman-
His wife but yesternight was brought to bed;
His child is like to her, fair as you are.
Go pack with him, and give the mother gold,

And tell them both the circumstance of all,
And how by this their child shall be advanc'd,
And be received for the Emperor's heir
And substituted in the place of mine,
To calm this tempest whirling in the court;
And let the Emperor dandle him for his own.
Hark ye, lords. You see I have given her physic,
Pointing to the Nurse
And you must needs bestow her funeral;
The fields are near, and you are gallant grooms.
This done, see that you take no longer days,
But send the midwife presently to me.
The midwife and the nurse well made away,
Then let the ladies tattle what they please.
CHIRON: Aaron, I see thou wilt not trust the air
With secrets.
MESSENGER: For this care of Tamora,
Herself and hers are highly bound to thee.
Exeunt Demetrius and Chiron, Bearing off the Dead Nurse
AARON: Now to the Goths, as swift as swallow flies,
There to dispose this treasure in mine arms,
And secretly to greet the Empress' friends.
Come on, you thick-lipp'd slave, I'll bear you hence;
For it is you that puts us to our shifts.
I'll make you feed on berries and on roots,
And feed on curds and whey, and suck the goat,
And cabin in a cave, and bring you up
To be a warrior and command a camp.
Exit with the Child

ACT IV. SCENE III. Rome. A Public Place

Enter Titus, Bearing Arrows with Letters on the Ends of Them; with Him Marcus, Young Lucius, and Other Gentlemen, Publius, Sempronius, and Caius, with Bows
TITUS: Come, Marcus, come; kinsmen, this is the way.
Sir boy, let me see your archery;
Look ye draw home enough, and 'tis there straight.
Terras Astrea reliquit,
Be you rememb'red, Marcus; she's gone, she's fled.
Sirs, take you to your tools. You, cousins, shall
Go sound the ocean and cast your nets;
Happily you may catch her in the sea;
Yet there's as little justice as at land.
No; Publius and Sempronius, you must do it;
'Tis you must dig with mattock and with spade,
And pierce the inmost centre of the earth;
Then, when you come to Pluto's region,
I pray you deliver him this petition.
Tell him it is for justice and for aid,
And that it comes from old Andronicus,
Shaken with sorrows in ungrateful Rome.
Ah, Rome! Well, well, I made thee miserable
What time I threw the people's suffrages
On him that thus doth tyrannize o'er me.
Go get you gone; and pray be careful all,

And leave you not a man-of-war unsearch'd.
This wicked Emperor may have shipp'd her hence;
And, kinsmen, then we may go pipe for justice.
MARCUS: O Publius, is not this a heavy case,
To see thy noble uncle thus distract?
PUBLIUS: Therefore, my lords, it highly us concerns
By day and night t' attend him carefully,
And feed his humour kindly as we may
Till time beget some careful remedy.
MARCUS: Kinsmen, his sorrows are past remedy.
Join with the Goths, and with revengeful war
Take wreak on Rome for this ingratitude,
And vengeance on the traitor Saturnine.
TITUS: Publius, how now? How now, my masters?
What, have you met with her?
PUBLIUS: No, my good lord; but Pluto sends you word,
If you will have Revenge from hell, you shall.
Marry, for Justice, she is so employ'd,
He thinks, with Jove in heaven, or somewhere else,
So that perforce you must needs stay a time.
TITUS: He doth me wrong to feed me with delays.
I'll dive into the burning lake below
And pull her out of Acheron by the heels.
Marcus, we are but shrubs, no cedars we,
No big-bon'd men fram'd of the Cyclops' size;
But metal, Marcus, steel to the very back,
Yet wrung with wrongs more than our backs can bear;
And, sith there's no justice in earth nor hell,
We will solicit heaven, and move the gods
To send down justice for to wreak our wrongs.
Come, to this gear. You are a good archer, Marcus.
He Gives Them the Arrows
'Ad Jovem' that's for you; here 'Ad Apollinem.'
'Ad Martem' that's for myself.
Here, boy, 'To Pallas'; here 'To Mercury.'
'To Saturn,' Caius- not to Saturnine:
You were as good to shoot against the wind.
To it, boy. Marcus, loose when I bid.
Of my word, I have written to effect;
There's not a god left unsolicited.
MARCUS: Kinsmen, shoot all your shafts into the court;
We will afflict the Emperor in his pride.
TITUS: Now, masters, draw. They Shoot O, well said, Lucius!
Good boy, in Virgo's lap! Give it Pallas.
MARCUS: My lord, I aim a mile beyond the moon;
Your letter is with Jupiter by this.
TITUS: Ha! ha!
Publius, Publius, hast thou done?
See, see, thou hast shot off one of Taurus' horns.
MARCUS: This was the sport, my lord: when Publius shot,
The Bull, being gall'd, gave Aries such a knock
That down fell both the Ram's horns in the court;
And who should find them but the Empress' villain?

She laugh'd, and told the Moor he should not choose
But give them to his master for a present.
TITUS: Why, there it goes! God give his lordship joy!
Enter the Clown, with a Basket and Two Pigeons in it
News, news from heaven! Marcus, the post is come.
Sirrah, what tidings? Have you any letters?
Shall I have justice? What says Jupiter?
CLOWN: Ho, the gibbet-maker? He says that he hath taken them down again, for the man must not be hang'd till the next week.
TITUS: But what says Jupiter, I ask thee?
CLOWN: Alas, sir, I know not Jupiter; I never drank with him in all my life.
TITUS: Why, villain, art not thou the carrier?
CLOWN: Ay, of my pigeons, sir; nothing else.
TITUS: Why, didst thou not come from heaven?
CLOWN: From heaven! Alas, sir, I never came there. God forbid I should be so bold to press to heaven in my young days. Why, I am going with my pigeons to the Tribunal Plebs, to take up a matter of brawl betwixt my uncle and one of the Emperal's men.
MARCUS: Why, sir, that is as fit as can be to serve for your oration; and let him deliver the pigeons to the Emperor from you.
TITUS: Tell me, can you deliver an oration to the Emperor with a grace?
CLOWN: Nay, truly, sir, I could never say grace in all my life.
TITUS: Sirrah, come hither. Make no more ado,
But give your pigeons to the Emperor;
By me thou shalt have justice at his hands.
Hold, hold! Meanwhile here's money for thy charges.
Give me pen and ink. Sirrah, can you with a grace deliver up a supplication?
CLOWN: Ay, sir.
TITUS: Then here is a supplication for you. And when you come to him, at the first approach you must kneel; then kiss his foot; then deliver up your pigeons; and then look for your reward. I'll be at hand, sir; see you do it bravely.
CLOWN: I warrant you, sir; let me alone.
TITUS: Sirrah, hast thou a knife? Come let me see it.
Here, Marcus, fold it in the oration;
For thou hast made it like a humble suppliant.
And when thou hast given it to the Emperor,
Knock at my door, and tell me what he says.
CLOWN: God be with you, sir; I will.
TITUS: Come, Marcus, let us go. Publius, follow me.
Exeunt

ACT IV. SCENE IV. Rome. Before the Palace

Enter the Emperor, and the Empress and Her Two Sons, Demetrius and Chiron; Lords and Others. The Emperor Brings the Arrows in His Hand That Titus Shot at Him
SATURNINUS: Why, lords, what wrongs are these! Was ever seen
An emperor in Rome thus overborne,
Troubled, confronted thus; and, for the extent
Of egal justice, us'd in such contempt?
My lords, you know, as know the mightful gods,
However these disturbers of our peace

Buzz in the people's ears, there nought hath pass'd
But even with law against the wilful sons
Of old Andronicus. And what an if
His sorrows have so overwhelm'd his wits,
Shall we be thus afflicted in his wreaks,
His fits, his frenzy, and his bitterness?
And now he writes to heaven for his redress.
See, here's 'To Jove' and this 'To Mercury';
This 'To Apollo'; this 'To the God of War'-
Sweet scrolls to fly about the streets of Rome!
What's this but libelling against the Senate,
And blazoning our unjustice every where?
A goodly humour, is it not, my lords?
As who would say in Rome no justice were.
But if I live, his feigned ecstasies
Shall be no shelter to these outrages;
But he and his shall know that justice lives
In Saturninus' health; whom, if she sleep,
He'll so awake as he in fury shall
Cut off the proud'st conspirator that lives.
TAMORA: My gracious lord, my lovely Saturnine,
Lord of my life, commander of my thoughts,
Calm thee, and bear the faults of Titus' age,
Th' effects of sorrow for his valiant sons
Whose loss hath pierc'd him deep and scarr'd his heart;
And rather comfort his distressed plight
Than prosecute the meanest or the best
For these contempts. Aside Why, thus it shall become
High-witted Tamora to gloze with all.
But, Titus, I have touch'd thee to the quick,
Thy life-blood out; if Aaron now be wise,
Then is all safe, the anchor in the port.
Enter Clown
How now, good fellow! Wouldst thou speak with us?
CLOWN: Yes, forsooth, an your mistriship be Emperial.
TAMORA: Empress I am, but yonder sits the Emperor.
CLOWN: 'Tis he.- God and Saint Stephen give you godden. I have brought you a letter and a couple of pigeons here.
Saturninus Reads the Letter
SATURNINUS: Go take him away, and hang him presently.
CLOWN: How much money must I have?
TAMORA: Come, sirrah, you must be hang'd.
CLOWN: Hang'd! by'r lady, then I have brought up a neck to a fair end.
Exit Guarded
SATURNINUS: Despiteful and intolerable wrongs!
Shall I endure this monstrous villainy?
I know from whence this same device proceeds.
May this be borne- as if his traitorous sons
That died by law for murder of our brother
Have by my means been butchered wrongfully?
Go drag the villain hither by the hair;
Nor age nor honour shall shape privilege.

For this proud mock I'll be thy slaughterman,
Sly frantic wretch, that holp'st to make me great,
In hope thyself should govern Rome and me.
Enter Nuntius Aemilius
What news with thee, Aemilius?
AEMILIUS: Arm, my lords! Rome never had more cause.
The Goths have gathered head; and with a power
Of high resolved men, bent to the spoil,
They hither march amain, under conduct
Of Lucius, son to old Andronicus;
Who threats in course of this revenge to do
As much as ever Coriolanus did.
SATURNINUS: Is warlike Lucius general of the Goths?
These tidings nip me, and I hang the head
As flowers with frost, or grass beat down with storms.
Ay, now begins our sorrows to approach.
'Tis he the common people love so much;
Myself hath often heard them say-
When I have walked like a private man-
That Lucius' banishment was wrongfully,
And they have wish'd that Lucius were their emperor.
TAMORA: Why should you fear? Is not your city strong?
SATURNINUS: Ay, but the citizens favour Lucius,
And will revolt from me to succour him.
TAMORA: King, be thy thoughts imperious like thy name!
Is the sun dimm'd, that gnats do fly in it?
The eagle suffers little birds to sing,
And is not careful what they mean thereby,
Knowing that with the shadow of his wings
He can at pleasure stint their melody;
Even so mayest thou the giddy men of Rome.
Then cheer thy spirit; for know thou, Emperor,
I will enchant the old Andronicus
With words more sweet, and yet more dangerous,
Than baits to fish or honey-stalks to sheep,
When as the one is wounded with the bait,
The other rotted with delicious feed.
SATURNINUS: But he will not entreat his son for us.
TAMORA: If Tamora entreat him, then he will;
For I can smooth and fill his aged ears
With golden promises, that, were his heart
Almost impregnable, his old ears deaf,
Yet should both ear and heart obey my tongue.
To Aemilius Go thou before to be our ambassador;
Say that the Emperor requests a parley
Of warlike Lucius, and appoint the meeting
Even at his father's house, the old Andronicus.
SATURNINUS: Aemilius, do this message honourably;
And if he stand on hostage for his safety,
Bid him demand what pledge will please him best.
AEMILIUS: Your bidding shall I do effectually.
Exit
TAMORA: Now will I to that old Andronicus,

And temper him with all the art I have,
To pluck proud Lucius from the warlike Goths.
And now, sweet Emperor, be blithe again,
And bury all thy fear in my devices.
SATURNINUS: Then go successantly, and plead to him.
Exeunt

ACT V. SCENE I. Plains near Rome

Enter Lucius with an Army of Goths with Drums and Colours
LUCIUS: Approved warriors and my faithful friends,
I have received letters from great Rome
Which signifies what hate they bear their Emperor
And how desirous of our sight they are.
Therefore, great lords, be, as your titles witness,
Imperious and impatient of your wrongs;
And wherein Rome hath done you any scath,
Let him make treble satisfaction.
FIRST GOTH: Brave slip, sprung from the great Andronicus,
Whose name was once our terror, now our comfort,
Whose high exploits and honourable deeds
Ingrateful Rome requites with foul contempt,
Be bold in us: we'll follow where thou lead'st,
Like stinging bees in hottest summer's day,
Led by their master to the flow'red fields,
And be aveng'd on cursed Tamora.
ALL THE GOTHS: And as he saith, so say we all with him.
LUCIUS: I humbly thank him, and I thank you all.
But who comes here, led by a lusty Goth?
Enter a Goth, Leading Aaron with His Child in His Arms
SECOND GOTH: Renowned Lucius, from our troops I stray'd
To gaze upon a ruinous monastery;
And as I earnestly did fix mine eye
Upon the wasted building, suddenly
I heard a child cry underneath a wall.
I made unto the noise, when soon I heard
The crying babe controll'd with this discourse:
'Peace, tawny slave, half me and half thy dam!
Did not thy hue bewray whose brat thou art,
Had nature lent thee but thy mother's look,
Villain, thou mightst have been an emperor;
But where the bull and cow are both milk-white,
They never do beget a coal-black calf.
Peace, villain, peace!'- even thus he rates the babe-
'For I must bear thee to a trusty Goth,
Who, when he knows thou art the Empress' babe,
Will hold thee dearly for thy mother's sake.'
With this, my weapon drawn, I rush'd upon him,
Surpris'd him suddenly, and brought him hither
To use as you think needful of the man.
LUCIUS: O worthy Goth, this is the incarnate devil
That robb'd Andronicus of his good hand;
This is the pearl that pleas'd your Empress' eye;
And here's the base fruit of her burning lust.
Say, wall-ey'd slave, whither wouldst thou convey

This growing image of thy fiend-like face?
Why dost not speak? What, deaf? Not a word?
A halter, soldiers! Hang him on this tree,
And by his side his fruit of bastardy.
AARON: Touch not the boy, he is of royal blood.
LUCIUS: Too like the sire for ever being good.
First hang the child, that he may see it sprawl-
A sight to vex the father's soul withal.
Get me a ladder.
A Ladder Brought, Which Aaron Is Made to Climb
AARON: Lucius, save the child,
And bear it from me to the Emperess.
If thou do this, I'll show thee wondrous things
That highly may advantage thee to hear;
If thou wilt not, befall what may befall,
I'll speak no more but 'Vengeance rot you all!'
LUCIUS: Say on; an if it please me which thou speak'st,
Thy child shall live, and I will see it nourish'd.
AARON: An if it please thee! Why, assure thee, Lucius,
'Twill vex thy soul to hear what I shall speak;
For I must talk of murders, rapes, and massacres,
Acts of black night, abominable deeds,
Complots of mischief, treason, villainies,
Ruthful to hear, yet piteously perform'd;
And this shall all be buried in my death,
Unless thou swear to me my child shall live.
LUCIUS: Tell on thy mind; I say thy child shall live.
AARON: Swear that he shall, and then I will begin.
LUCIUS: Who should I swear by? Thou believest no god;
That granted, how canst thou believe an oath?
AARON: What if I do not? as indeed I do not;
Yet, for I know thou art religious
And hast a thing within thee called conscience,
With twenty popish tricks and ceremonies
Which I have seen thee careful to observe,
Therefore I urge thy oath. For that I know
An idiot holds his bauble for a god,
And keeps the oath which by that god he swears,
To that I'll urge him. Therefore thou shalt vow
By that same god- what god soe'er it be
That thou adorest and hast in reverence-
To save my boy, to nourish and bring him up;
Or else I will discover nought to thee.
LUCIUS: Even by my god I swear to thee I will.
AARON: First know thou, I begot him on the Empress.
LUCIUS: O most insatiate and luxurious woman!
AARON: Tut, Lucius, this was but a deed of charity
To that which thou shalt hear of me anon.
'Twas her two sons that murdered Bassianus;
They cut thy sister's tongue, and ravish'd her,
And cut her hands, and trimm'd her as thou sawest.
LUCIUS: O detestable villain! Call'st thou that trimming?
AARON: Why, she was wash'd, and cut, and trimm'd, and 'twas

Trim sport for them which had the doing of it.
LUCIUS: O barbarous beastly villains like thyself!
AARON: Indeed, I was their tutor to instruct them.
That codding spirit had they from their mother,
As sure a card as ever won the set;
That bloody mind, I think, they learn'd of me,
As true a dog as ever fought at head.
Well, let my deeds be witness of my worth.
I train'd thy brethren to that guileful hole
Where the dead corpse of Bassianus lay;
I wrote the letter that thy father found,
And hid the gold within that letter mention'd,
Confederate with the Queen and her two sons;
And what not done, that thou hast cause to rue,
Wherein I had no stroke of mischief in it?
I play'd the cheater for thy father's hand,
And, when I had it, drew myself apart
And almost broke my heart with extreme laughter.
I pried me through the crevice of a wall,
When, for his hand, he had his two sons' heads;
Beheld his tears, and laugh'd so heartily
That both mine eyes were rainy like to his;
And when I told the Empress of this sport,
She swooned almost at my pleasing tale,
And for my tidings gave me twenty kisses.
GOTH: What, canst thou say all this and never blush?
AARON: Ay, like a black dog, as the saying is.
LUCIUS: Art thou not sorry for these heinous deeds?
AARON: Ay, that I had not done a thousand more.
Even now I curse the day- and yet, I think,
Few come within the compass of my curse-
Wherein I did not some notorious ill;
As kill a man, or else devise his death;
Ravish a maid, or plot the way to do it;
Accuse some innocent, and forswear myself;
Set deadly enmity between two friends;
Make poor men's cattle break their necks;
Set fire on barns and hay-stacks in the night,
And bid the owners quench them with their tears.
Oft have I digg'd up dead men from their graves,
And set them upright at their dear friends' door
Even when their sorrows almost was forgot,
And on their skins, as on the bark of trees,
Have with my knife carved in Roman letters
'Let not your sorrow die, though I am dead.'
Tut, I have done a thousand dreadful things
As willingly as one would kill a fly;
And nothing grieves me heartily indeed
But that I cannot do ten thousand more.
LUCIUS: Bring down the devil, for he must not die
So sweet a death as hanging presently.
AARON: If there be devils, would I were a devil,
To live and burn in everlasting fire,

So I might have your company in hell
But to torment you with my bitter tongue!
LUCIUS: Sirs, stop his mouth, and let him speak no more.
Enter Aemilius
GOTH: My lord, there is a messenger from Rome
Desires to be admitted to your presence.
LUCIUS: Let him come near.
Welcome, Aemilius. What's the news from Rome?
AEMILIUS: Lord Lucius, and you Princes of the Goths,
The Roman Emperor greets you all by me;
And, for he understands you are in arms,
He craves a parley at your father's house,
Willing you to demand your hostages,
And they shall be immediately deliver'd.
FIRST GOTH: What says our general?
LUCIUS: Aemilius, let the Emperor give his pledges
Unto my father and my uncle Marcus.
And we will come. March away.
Exeunt

ACT V. SCENE II. Rome. Before Titus' House

Enter Tamora, and Her Two Sons, Demetrius and Chiron, Disguised
TAMORA: Thus, in this strange and sad habiliment,
I will encounter with Andronicus,
And say I am Revenge, sent from below
To join with him and right his heinous wrongs.
Knock at his study, where they say he keeps
To ruminate strange plots of dire revenge;
Tell him Revenge is come to join with him,
And work confusion on his enemies.
They knock and TITUS opens his study door, above
TITUS: Who doth molest my contemplation?
Is it your trick to make me ope the door,
That so my sad decrees may fly away
And all my study be to no effect?
You are deceiv'd; for what I mean to do
See here in bloody lines I have set down;
And what is written shall be executed.
TAMORA: Titus, I am come to talk with thee.
TITUS: No, not a word. How can I grace my talk,
Wanting a hand to give it that accord?
Thou hast the odds of me; therefore no more.
TAMORA: If thou didst know me, thou wouldst talk with me.
TITUS: I am not mad, I know thee well enough:
Witness this wretched stump, witness these crimson lines;
Witness these trenches made by grief and care;
Witness the tiring day and heavy night;
Witness all sorrow that I know thee well
For our proud Empress, mighty Tamora.
Is not thy coming for my other hand?
TAMORA: Know thou, sad man, I am not Tamora:
She is thy enemy and I thy friend.
I am Revenge, sent from th' infernal kingdom
To ease the gnawing vulture of thy mind

By working wreakful vengeance on thy foes.
Come down and welcome me to this world's light;
Confer with me of murder and of death;
There's not a hollow cave or lurking-place,
No vast obscurity or misty vale,
Where bloody murder or detested rape
Can couch for fear but I will find them out;
And in their ears tell them my dreadful name-
Revenge, which makes the foul offender quake.
TITUS: Art thou Revenge? and art thou sent to me
To be a torment to mine enemies?
TAMORA: I am; therefore come down and welcome me.
TITUS: Do me some service ere I come to thee.
Lo, by thy side where Rape and Murder stands;
Now give some surance that thou art Revenge-
Stab them, or tear them on thy chariot wheels;
And then I'll come and be thy waggoner
And whirl along with thee about the globes.
Provide thee two proper palfreys, black as jet,
To hale thy vengeful waggon swift away,
And find out murderers in their guilty caves;
And when thy car is loaden with their heads,
I will dismount, and by thy waggon wheel
Trot, like a servile footman, all day long,
Even from Hyperion's rising in the east
Until his very downfall in the sea.
And day by day I'll do this heavy task,
So thou destroy Rapine and Murder there.
TAMORA: These are my ministers, and come with me.
TITUS: Are they thy ministers? What are they call'd?
TAMORA: Rape and Murder; therefore called so
'Cause they take vengeance of such kind of men.
TITUS: Good Lord, how like the Empress' sons they are!
And you the Empress! But we worldly men
Have miserable, mad, mistaking eyes.
O sweet Revenge, now do I come to thee;
And, if one arm's embracement will content thee,
I will embrace thee in it by and by.
TAMORA: This closing with him fits his lunacy.
Whate'er I forge to feed his brain-sick humours,
Do you uphold and maintain in your speeches,
For now he firmly takes me for Revenge;
And, being credulous in this mad thought,
I'll make him send for Lucius his son,
And whilst I at a banquet hold him sure,
I'll find some cunning practice out of hand
To scatter and disperse the giddy Goths,
Or, at the least, make them his enemies.
See, here he comes, and I must ply my theme.
Enter Titus, below
TITUS: Long have I been forlorn, and all for thee.
Welcome, dread Fury, to my woeful house.
Rapine and Murder, you are welcome too.

How like the Empress and her sons you are!
Well are you fitted, had you but a Moor.
Could not all hell afford you such a devil?
For well I wot the Empress never wags
But in her company there is a Moor;
And, would you represent our queen aright,
It were convenient you had such a devil.
But welcome as you are. What shall we do?
TAMORA: What wouldst thou have us do, Andronicus?
MESSENGER: Show me a murderer, I'll deal with him.
CHIRON: Show me a villain that hath done a rape,
And I am sent to be reveng'd on him.
TAMORA: Show me a thousand that hath done thee wrong,
And I will be revenged on them all.
TITUS: Look round about the wicked streets of Rome,
And when thou find'st a man that's like thyself,
Good Murder, stab him; he's a murderer.
Go thou with him, and when it is thy hap
To find another that is like to thee,
Good Rapine, stab him; he is a ravisher.
Go thou with them; and in the Emperor's court
There is a queen, attended by a Moor;
Well shalt thou know her by thine own proportion,
For up and down she doth resemble thee.
I pray thee, do on them some violent death;
They have been violent to me and mine.
TAMORA: Well hast thou lesson'd us; this shall we do.
But would it please thee, good Andronicus,
To send for Lucius, thy thrice-valiant son,
Who leads towards Rome a band of warlike Goths,
And bid him come and banquet at thy house;
When he is here, even at thy solemn feast,
I will bring in the Empress and her sons,
The Emperor himself, and all thy foes;
And at thy mercy shall they stoop and kneel,
And on them shalt thou ease thy angry heart.
What says Andronicus to this device?
TITUS: Marcus, my brother! 'Tis sad Titus calls.
Enter Marcus
Go, gentle Marcus, to thy nephew Lucius;
Thou shalt inquire him out among the Goths.
Bid him repair to me, and bring with him
Some of the chiefest princes of the Goths;
Bid him encamp his soldiers where they are.
Tell him the Emperor and the Empress too
Feast at my house, and he shall feast with them.
This do thou for my love; and so let him,
As he regards his aged father's life.
MARCUS: This will I do, and soon return again. Exit
TAMORA: Now will I hence about thy business,
And take my ministers along with me.
TITUS: Nay, nay, let Rape and Murder stay with me,
Or else I'll call my brother back again,

And cleave to no revenge but Lucius.
TAMORA: Aside to Her Sons What say you, boys? Will you abide
with him, whiles I go tell my lord the Emperor
How I have govern'd our determin'd jest?
Yield to his humour, smooth and speak him fair,
And tarry with him till I turn again.
TITUS: Aside I knew them all, though they suppos'd me mad,
And will o'er reach them in their own devices,
A pair of cursed hell-hounds and their dam.
MESSENGER: Madam, depart at pleasure; leave us here.
TAMORA: Farewell, Andronicus, Revenge now goes
To lay a complot to betray thy foes.
TITUS: I know thou dost; and, sweet Revenge, farewell.
Exit Tamora
CHIRON: Tell us, old man, how shall we be employ'd?
TITUS: Tut, I have work enough for you to do.
Publius, come hither, Caius, and Valentine.
Enter Publius, Caius, and Valentine
PUBLIUS: What is your will?
TITUS: Know you these two?
PUBLIUS: The Empress' sons, I take them: Chiron, Demetrius.
TITUS: Fie, Publius, fie! thou art too much deceiv'd.
The one is Murder, and Rape is the other's name;
And therefore bind them, gentle Publius-
Caius and Valentine, lay hands on them.
Oft have you heard me wish for such an hour,
And now I find it; therefore bind them sure,
And stop their mouths if they begin to cry.
Exit
They Lay Hold on Chiron and Demetrius
CHIRON: Villains, forbear! we are the Empress' sons.
PUBLIUS: And therefore do we what we are commanded.
Stop close their mouths, let them not speak a word.
Is he sure bound? Look that you bind them fast.
Re-enter Titus Andronicus with a Knife, and Lavinia, with a Basin
TITUS: Come, come, Lavinia; look, thy foes are bound.
Sirs, stop their mouths, let them not speak to me;
But let them hear what fearful words I utter.
O villains, Chiron and Demetrius!
Here stands the spring whom you have stain'd with mud;
This goodly summer with your winter mix'd.
You kill'd her husband; and for that vile fault
Two of her brothers were condemn'd to death,
My hand cut off and made a merry jest;
Both her sweet hands, her tongue, and that more dear
Than hands or tongue, her spotless chastity,
Inhuman traitors, you constrain'd and forc'd.
What would you say, if I should let you speak?
Villains, for shame you could not beg for grace.
Hark, wretches! how I mean to martyr you.
This one hand yet is left to cut your throats,
Whiles that Lavinia 'tween her stumps doth hold
The basin that receives your guilty blood.

You know your mother means to feast with me,
And calls herself Revenge, and thinks me mad.
Hark, villains! I will grind your bones to dust,
And with your blood and it I'll make a paste;
And of the paste a coffin I will rear,
And make two pasties of your shameful heads;
And bid that strumpet, your unhallowed dam,
Like to the earth, swallow her own increase.
This is the feast that I have bid her to,
And this the banquet she shall surfeit on;
For worse than Philomel you us'd my daughter,
And worse than Progne I will be reveng'd.
And now prepare your throats. Lavinia, come,
Receive the blood; and when that they are dead,
Let me go grind their bones to powder small,
And with this hateful liquor temper it;
And in that paste let their vile heads be bak'd.
Come, come, be every one officious
To make this banquet, which I wish may prove
More stern and bloody than the Centaurs' feast.
He Cuts Their Throats So.
Now bring them in, for I will play the cook,
And see them ready against their mother comes.
Exeunt, Bearing the Dead Bodies

ACT V. SCENE III. The Court of Titus' House

Enter Lucius, Marcus, and the Goths, with Aaron Prisoner, and His Child in the Arms of an Attendant

LUCIUS: Uncle Marcus, since 'tis my father's mind
That I repair to Rome, I am content.
FIRST GOTH: And ours with thine, befall what fortune will.
LUCIUS: Good uncle, take you in this barbarous Moor,
This ravenous tiger, this accursed devil;
Let him receive no sust'nance, fetter him,
Till he be brought unto the Empress' face
For testimony of her foul proceedings.
And see the ambush of our friends be strong;
I fear the Emperor means no good to us.
AARON: Some devil whisper curses in my ear,
And prompt me that my tongue may utter forth
The venomous malice of my swelling heart!
LUCIUS: Away, inhuman dog, unhallowed slave!
Sirs, help our uncle to convey him in.
Exeunt Goths with Aaron. Flourish Within the Trumpets Show the Emperor Is at Hand.
Sound Trumpets. Enter Saturninus and Tamora, with Aemilius, Tribunes, Senators, and Others
SATURNINUS: What, hath the firmament more suns than one?
LUCIUS: What boots it thee to can thyself a sun?
MARCUS: Rome's Emperor, and nephew, break the parle;
These quarrels must be quietly debated.
The feast is ready which the careful Titus
Hath ordain'd to an honourable end,
For peace, for love, for league, and good to Rome.
Please you, therefore, draw nigh and take your places.
SATURNINUS: Marcus, we will.

A Table Brought In. The Company Sit down Trumpets Sounding, Enter Titus like a Cook, Placing the Dishes, and Lavinia with a Veil over Her Face; Also Young Lucius, and Others

TITUS: Welcome, my lord; welcome, dread Queen;
Welcome, ye warlike Goths; welcome, Lucius;
And welcome all. Although the cheer be poor,
'Twill fill your stomachs; please you eat of it.
SATURNINUS: Why art thou thus attir'd, Andronicus?
TITUS: Because I would be sure to have all well
To entertain your Highness and your Empress.
TAMORA: We are beholding to you, good Andronicus.
TITUS: An if your Highness knew my heart, you were.
My lord the Emperor, resolve me this:
Was it well done of rash Virginius
To slay his daughter with his own right hand,
Because she was enforc'd, stain'd, and deflower'd?
SATURNINUS: It was, Andronicus.
TITUS: Your reason, mighty lord.
SATURNINUS: Because the girl should not survive her shame,
And by her presence still renew his sorrows.
TITUS: A reason mighty, strong, and effectual;
A pattern, precedent, and lively warrant
For me, most wretched, to perform the like.
Die, die, Lavinia, and thy shame with thee;

He kills her

And with thy shame thy father's sorrow die!
SATURNINUS: What hast thou done, unnatural and unkind?
TITUS: Kill'd her for whom my tears have made me blind.
I am as woeful as Virginius was,
And have a thousand times more cause than he
To do this outrage; and it now is done.
SATURNINUS: What, was she ravish'd? Tell who did the deed.
TITUS: Will't please you eat? Will't please your Highness feed?
TAMORA: Why hast thou slain thine only daughter thus?
TITUS: Not I; 'twas Chiron and Demetrius.
They ravish'd her, and cut away her tongue;
And they, 'twas they, that did her all this wrong.
SATURNINUS: Go, fetch them hither to us presently.
TITUS: Why, there they are, both baked in this pie,
Whereof their mother daintily hath fed,
Eating the flesh that she herself hath bred.
'Tis true, 'tis true: witness my knife's sharp point.

He Stabs the Empress

SATURNINUS: Die, frantic wretch, for this accursed deed!

He Stabs Titus

LUCIUS: Can the son's eye behold his father bleed?
There's meed for meed, death for a deadly deed.

He Stabs Saturninus. A Great Tumult. Lucius, Marcus, and Their Friends Go up into the Balcony

MARCUS: You sad-fac'd men, people and sons of Rome,
By uproars sever'd, as a flight of fowl
Scatter'd by winds and high tempestuous gusts?
O, let me teach you how to knit again
This scattered corn into one mutual sheaf,
These broken limbs again into one body;

Lest Rome herself be bane unto herself,
And she whom mighty kingdoms curtsy to,
Like a forlorn and desperate castaway,
Do shameful execution on herself.
But if my frosty signs and chaps of age,
Grave witnesses of true experience,
Cannot induce you to attend my words,
To Lucius Speak, Rome's dear friend, as erst our ancestor,
When with his solemn tongue he did discourse
To love-sick Dido's sad attending ear
The story of that baleful burning night,
When subtle Greeks surpris'd King Priam's Troy.
Tell us what Sinon hath bewitch'd our ears,
Or who hath brought the fatal engine in
That gives our Troy, our Rome, the civil wound.
My heart is not compact of flint nor steel;
Nor can I utter all our bitter grief,
But floods of tears will drown my oratory
And break my utt'rance, even in the time
When it should move ye to attend me most,
And force you to commiseration.
Here's Rome's young Captain, let him tell the tale;
While I stand by and weep to hear him speak.
LUCIUS: Then, gracious auditory, be it known to you
That Chiron and the damn'd Demetrius
Were they that murd'red our Emperor's brother;
And they it were that ravished our sister.
For their fell faults our brothers were beheaded,
Our father's tears despis'd, and basely cozen'd
Of that true hand that fought Rome's quarrel out
And sent her enemies unto the grave.
Lastly, myself unkindly banished,
The gates shut on me, and turn'd weeping out,
To beg relief among Rome's enemies;
Who drown'd their enmity in my true tears,
And op'd their arms to embrace me as a friend.
I am the turned forth, be it known to you,
That have preserv'd her welfare in my blood
And from her bosom took the enemy's point,
Sheathing the steel in my advent'rous body.
Alas! you know I am no vaunter, I;
My scars can witness, dumb although they are,
That my report is just and full of truth.
But, soft! methinks I do digress too much,
Citing my worthless praise. O, pardon me!
For when no friends are by, men praise themselves.
MARCUS: Now is my turn to speak. Behold the child.
Pointing to the Child in an Attendant's Arms
Of this was Tamora delivered,
The issue of an irreligious Moor,
Chief architect and plotter of these woes.
The villain is alive in Titus' house,
Damn'd as he is, to witness this is true.

Now judge what cause had Titus to revenge
These wrongs unspeakable, past patience,
Or more than any living man could bear.
Now have you heard the truth: what say you, Romans?
Have we done aught amiss, show us wherein,
And, from the place where you behold us pleading,
The poor remainder of Andronici
Will, hand in hand, all headlong hurl ourselves,
And on the ragged stones beat forth our souls,
And make a mutual closure of our house.
Speak, Romans, speak; and if you say we shall,
Lo, hand in hand, Lucius and I will fall.
AEMILIUS: Come, come, thou reverend man of Rome,
And bring our Emperor gently in thy hand,
Lucius our Emperor; for well I know
The common voice do cry it shall be so.
ALL: Lucius, all hail, Rome's royal Emperor!
MARCUS: Go, go into old Titus' sorrowful house,
And hither hale that misbelieving Moor
To be adjudg'd some direful slaught'ring death,
As punishment for his most wicked life.
  Exeunt Some Attendants. Lucius, Marcus, and the Others Descend
ALL: Lucius, all hail, Rome's gracious governor!
LUCIUS: Thanks, gentle Romans! May I govern so
To heal Rome's harms and wipe away her woe!
But, gentle people, give me aim awhile,
For nature puts me to a heavy task.
Stand all aloof; but, uncle, draw you near
To shed obsequious tears upon this trunk.
O, take this warm kiss on thy pale cold lips.
  Kisses Titus
These sorrowful drops upon thy blood-stain'd face,
The last true duties of thy noble son!
MARCUS: Tear for tear and loving kiss for kiss
Thy brother Marcus tenders on thy lips.
O, were the sum of these that I should pay
Countless and infinite, yet would I pay them!
LUCIUS: Come hither, boy; come, come, come, and learn of us
To melt in showers. Thy grandsire lov'd thee well;
Many a time he danc'd thee on his knee,
Sung thee asleep, his loving breast thy pillow;
Many a story hath he told to thee,
And bid thee bear his pretty tales in mind
And talk of them when he was dead and gone.
MARCUS: How many thousand times hath these poor lips,
When they were living, warm'd themselves on thine!
O, now, sweet boy, give them their latest kiss!
Bid him farewell; commit him to the grave;
Do them that kindness, and take leave of them.
BOY: O grandsire, grandsire! ev'n with all my heart
Would I were dead, so you did live again!
O Lord, I cannot speak to him for weeping;
My tears will choke me, if I ope my mouth.

Re-enter Attendants with Aaron
A ROMAN: You sad Andronici, have done with woes;
Give sentence on the execrable wretch
That hath been breeder of these dire events.
LUCIUS: Set him breast-deep in earth, and famish him;
There let him stand and rave and cry for food.
If any one relieves or pities him,
For the offence he dies. This is our doom.
Some stay to see him fast'ned in the earth.
AARON: Ah, why should wrath be mute and fury dumb?
I am no baby, I, that with base prayers
I should repent the evils I have done;
Ten thousand worse than ever yet I did
Would I perform, if I might have my will.
If one good deed in all my life I did,
I do repent it from my very soul.
LUCIUS: Some loving friends convey the Emperor hence,
And give him burial in his father's grave.
My father and Lavinia shall forthwith
Be closed in our household's monument.
As for that ravenous tiger, Tamora,
No funeral rite, nor man in mourning weed,
No mournful bell shall ring her burial;
But throw her forth to beasts and birds to prey.
Her life was beastly and devoid of pity,
And being dead, let birds on her take pity.
Exeunt

END

The Tragedy of Romeo and Juliet

Dramatis Personae

CHORUS.
ESCALUS, Prince of Verona.
PARIS, a young Count, kinsman to the Prince.
MONTAGUE, heads of two houses at variance with each other.
CAPULET, heads of two houses at variance with each other.
AN OLD MAN, of the Capulet family.
ROMEO, son to Montague.
TYBALT, nephew to Lady Capulet.
MERCUTIO, kinsman to the Prince and friend to Romeo.
BENVOLIO, nephew to Montague, and friend to Romeo
TYBALT, nephew to Lady Capulet.
FRIAR LAURENCE, Franciscan.
FRIAR JOHN, Franciscan.
BALTHASAR, servant to Romeo.
ABRAM, servant to Montague.
SAMPSON, servant to Capulet.
GREGORY, servant to Capulet.
PETER, servant to Juliet's nurse.
AN APOTHECARY.
THREE MUSICIANS.
AN OFFICER.
LADY MONTAGUE, wife to Montague.
LADY CAPULET, wife to Capulet.
JULIET, daughter to Capulet.
NURSE TO JULIET.
Citizens of Verona; Gentlemen and Gentlewomen of both houses; Maskers, Torchbearers, Pages, Guards, Watchmen, Servants, and Attendants.

SCENE.: Verona; Mantua.

THE PROLOGUE

Enter Chorus.

CHORUS: Two households, both alike in dignity,
In fair Verona, where we lay our scene,
From ancient grudge break to new mutiny,
Where civil blood makes civil hands unclean.
From forth the fatal loins of these two foes
A pair of star-cross'd lovers take their life;
Whose misadventur'd piteous overthrows
Doth with their death bury their parents' strife.
The fearful passage of their death-mark'd love,
And the continuance of their parents' rage,
Which, but their children's end, naught could remove,
Is now the two hours' traffic of our stage;
The which if you with patient ears attend,
What here shall miss, our toil shall strive to mend.

Exit.

ACT I. SCENE I. Verona. A Public Place.

Enter Sampson and Gregory (With Swords and Bucklers) of the House of Capulet.

SAMPSON: Gregory, on my word, we'll not carry coals.

GREGORY: No, for then we should be colliers.

SAMPSON: I mean, an we be in choler, we'll draw.

GREGORY: Ay, while you live, draw your neck out of collar.

SAMPSON: I strike quickly, being moved.

GREGORY: But thou art not quickly moved to strike.

SAMPSON: A dog of the house of Montague moves me.

GREGORY: To move is to stir, and to be valiant is to stand. Therefore, if thou art moved, thou runn'st away.

SAMPSON: A dog of that house shall move me to stand. I will take the wall of any man or maid of Montague's.

GREGORY: That shows thee a weak slave; for the weakest goes to the wall.

SAMPSON: 'Tis true; and therefore women, being the weaker vessels, are ever thrust to the wall. Therefore I will push Montague's men from the wall and thrust his maids to the wall.

GREGORY: The quarrel is between our masters and us their men.

SAMPSON: 'Tis all one. I will show myself a tyrant. When I have fought with the men, I will be cruel with the maids- I will cut off their heads.

GREGORY: The heads of the maids?

SAMPSON: Ay, the heads of the maids, or their maidenheads. Take it in what sense thou wilt.

GREGORY: They must take it in sense that feel it.

SAMPSON: Me they shall feel while I am able to stand; and 'tis known I am a pretty piece of flesh.

GREGORY: 'Tis well thou art not fish; if thou hadst, thou hadst been poor-John. Draw thy tool! Here comes two of the house of Montagues.

Enter Two Other Servingmen Abram and Balthasar.

SAMPSON: My naked weapon is out. Quarrel! I will back thee.

GREGORY: How? turn thy back and run?

SAMPSON: Fear me not.

GREGORY: No, marry. I fear thee!

SAMPSON: Let us take the law of our sides; let them begin.

GREGORY: I will frown as I pass by, and let them take it as they list.

SAMPSON: Nay, as they dare. I will bite my thumb at them; which is disgrace to them, if they bear it.

ABRAM: Do you bite your thumb at us, sir?

SAMPSON: I do bite my thumb, sir.

ABRAM: Do you bite your thumb at us, sir?

SAMPSON: Aside to Gregory Is the law of our side if I say ay?

GREGORY: Aside to Sampson No.

SAMPSON: No, sir, I do not bite my thumb at you, sir; but I bite my thumb, sir.

GREGORY: Do you quarrel, sir?

ABRAM: Quarrel, sir? No, sir.

SAMPSON: But if you do, sir, am for you. I serve as good a man as you.

ABRAM: No better.

SAMPSON: Well, sir.

Enter Benvolio.
GREGORY: Aside to Sampson Say 'better.' Here comes one of my master's kinsmen.
SAMPSON: Yes, better, sir.
ABRAM: You lie.
SAMPSON: Draw, if you be men. Gregory, remember thy swashing blow.
They fight.
BENVOLIO: Part, fools! Beats down Their Swords.
Put up your swords. You know not what you do.
Enter Tybalt.
TYBALT: What, art thou drawn among these heartless hinds?
Turn thee Benvolio! look upon thy death.
BENVOLIO: I do but keep the peace. Put up thy sword,
Or manage it to part these men with me.
TYBALT: What, drawn, and talk of peace? I hate the word
As I hate hell, all Montagues, and thee.
Have at thee, coward! They fight.
Enter an Officer, and Three or Four Citizens with Clubs or Partisans.
OFFICER: Clubs, bills, and partisans! Strike! beat them down!
CITIZENS: Down with the Capulets! Down with the Montagues!
Enter Old Capulet in His Gown, and His Wife.
CAPULET: What noise is this? Give me my long sword, ho!
WIFE: A crutch, a crutch! Why call you for a sword?
CAPULET: My sword, I say! Old Montague is come
And flourishes his blade in spite of me.
Enter Old Montague and His Wife.
MONTAGUE: Thou villain Capulet!- Hold me not, let me go.
MONTAGUE'S WIFE: Thou shalt not stir one foot to seek a foe.
Enter Prince Escalus, with His Train.
PRINCE: Rebellious subjects, enemies to peace,
Profaners of this neighbour-stained steel-
Will they not hear? What, ho! you men, you beasts,
That quench the fire of your pernicious rage
With purple fountains issuing from your veins!
On pain of torture, from those bloody hands
Throw your mistempered weapons to the ground
And hear the sentence of your moved prince.
Three civil brawls, bred of an airy word
By thee, old Capulet, and Montague,
Have thrice disturb'd the quiet of our streets
And made Verona's ancient citizens
Cast by their grave beseeming ornaments
To wield old partisans, in hands as old,
Cank'red with peace, to part your cank'red hate.
If ever you disturb our streets again,
Your lives shall pay the forfeit of the peace.
For this time all the rest depart away.
You, Capulet, shall go along with me;
And, Montague, come you this afternoon,
To know our farther pleasure in this case,

To old Freetown, our common judgment place.
Once more, on pain of death, all men depart.
Exeunt All but Montague, His Wife, and Benvolio.
MONTAGUE: Who set this ancient quarrel new abroach?
Speak, nephew, were you by when it began?
BENVOLIO: Here were the servants of your adversary
And yours, close fighting ere I did approach.
I drew to part them. In the instant came
The fiery Tybalt, with his sword prepar'd;
Which, as he breath'd defiance to my ears,
He swung about his head and cut the winds,
Who, nothing hurt withal, hiss'd him in scorn.
While we were interchanging thrusts and blows,
Came more and more, and fought on part and part,
Till the Prince came, who parted either part.
MONTAGUE'S WIFE: O, where is Romeo? Saw you him to-day?
Right glad I am he was not at this fray.
BENVOLIO: Madam, an hour before the worshipp'd sun
Peer'd forth the golden window of the East,
A troubled mind drave me to walk abroad;
Where, underneath the grove of sycamore
That westward rooteth from the city's side,
So early walking did I see your son.
Towards him I made; but he was ware of me
And stole into the covert of the wood.
I- measuring his affections by my own,
Which then most sought where most might not be found,
Being one too many by my weary self-
Pursu'd my humour, not Pursuing his,
And gladly shunn'd who gladly fled from me.
MONTAGUE: Many a morning hath he there been seen,
With tears augmenting the fresh morning's dew,
Adding to clouds more clouds with his deep sighs;
But all so soon as the all-cheering sun
Should in the farthest East bean to draw
The shady curtains from Aurora's bed,
Away from light steals home my heavy son
And private in his chamber pens himself,
Shuts up his windows, locks fair daylight
And makes himself an artificial night.
Black and portentous must this humour prove
Unless good counsel may the cause remove.
BENVOLIO: My noble uncle, do you know the cause?
MONTAGUE: I neither know it nor can learn of him
BENVOLIO: Have you importun'd him by any means?
MONTAGUE: Both by myself and many other friend;
But he, his own affections' counsellor,
Is to himself- I will not say how true-
But to himself so secret and so close,

So far from sounding and discovery,
As is the bud bit with an envious worm
Ere he can spread his sweet leaves to the air
Or dedicate his beauty to the sun.
Could we but learn from whence his sorrows grow,
We would as willingly give cure as know.
Enter Romeo.
BENVOLIO: See, where he comes. So please you step aside,
I'll know his grievance, or be much denied.
MONTAGUE: I would thou wert so happy by thy stay
To hear true shrift. Come, madam, let's away,
Exeunt Montague and Wife.
BENVOLIO: Good morrow, cousin.
ROMEO: Is the day so young?
BENVOLIO: But new struck nine.
ROMEO: Ay me! sad hours seem long.
Was that my father that went hence so fast?
BENVOLIO: It was. What sadness lengthens Romeo's hours?
ROMEO: Not having that which having makes them short.
BENVOLIO: In love?
ROMEO: Out-
BENVOLIO: Of love?
ROMEO: Out of her favour where I am in love.
BENVOLIO: Alas that love, so gentle in his view,
Should be so tyrannous and rough in proof!
ROMEO: Alas that love, whose view is muffled still,
Should without eyes see pathways to his will!
Where shall we dine? O me! What fray was here?
Yet tell me not, for I have heard it all.
Here's much to do with hate, but more with love.
Why then, O brawling love! O loving hate!
O anything, of nothing first create!
O heavy lightness! serious vanity!
Misshapen chaos of well-seeming forms!
Feather of lead, bright smoke, cold fire, sick health!
Still-waking sleep, that is not what it is
This love feel I, that feel no love in this.
Dost thou not laugh?
BENVOLIO: No, coz, I rather weep.
ROMEO: Good heart, at what?
BENVOLIO: At thy good heart's oppression.
ROMEO: Why, such is love's transgression.
Griefs of mine own lie heavy in my breast,
Which thou wilt propagate, to have it prest
With more of thine. This love that thou hast shown
Doth add more grief to too much of mine own.
Love is a smoke rais'd with the fume of sighs;
Being purg'd, a fire sparkling in lovers' eyes;
Being vex'd, a sea nourish'd with lovers' tears.

What is it else? A madness most discreet,
A choking gall, and a preserving sweet.
Farewell, my coz.
BENVOLIO: Soft! I will go along.
An if you leave me so, you do me wrong.
ROMEO: Tut! I have lost myself; I am not here:
This is not Romeo, he's some other where.
BENVOLIO: Tell me in sadness, who is that you love?
ROMEO: What, shall I groan and tell thee?
BENVOLIO: Groan? Why, no;
But sadly tell me who.
ROMEO: Bid a sick man in sadness make his will.
Ah, word ill urg'd to one that is so ill!
In sadness, cousin, I do love a woman.
BENVOLIO: I aim'd so near when I suppos'd you lov'd.
ROMEO: A right good markman! And she's fair I love.
BENVOLIO: A right fair mark, fair coz, is soonest hit.
ROMEO: Well, in that hit you miss. She'll not be hit
With Cupid's arrow. She hath Dian's wit,
And, in strong proof of chastity well arm'd,
From Love's weak childish bow she lives unharm'd.
She will not stay the siege of loving terms,
Nor bide th' encounter of assailing eyes,
Nor ope her lap to saint-seducing gold.
O, she's rich in beauty; only poor
That, when she dies, with beauty dies her store.
BENVOLIO: Then she hath sworn that she will still live chaste?
ROMEO: She hath, and in that sparing makes huge waste;
For beauty, starv'd with her severity,
Cuts beauty off from all posterity.
She is too fair, too wise, wisely too fair,
To merit bliss by making me despair.
She hath forsworn to love, and in that vow
Do I live dead that live to tell it now.
BENVOLIO: Be rul'd by me: forget to think of her.
ROMEO: O, teach me how I should forget to think!
BENVOLIO: By giving liberty unto thine eyes.
Examine other beauties.
ROMEO: 'Tis the way
To call hers (exquisite) in question more.
These happy masks that kiss fair ladies' brows,
Being black puts us in mind they hide the fair.
He that is strucken blind cannot forget
The precious treasure of his eyesight lost.
Show me a mistress that is passing fair,
What doth her beauty serve but as a note
Where I may read who pass'd that passing fair?
Farewell. Thou canst not teach me to forget.
BENVOLIO: I'll pay that doctrine, or else die in debt.

Exeunt.

ACT I. SCENE II. A Street.

Enter Capulet, County Paris, and Servant -the Clown.

CAPULET: But Montague is bound as well as I,
In penalty alike; and 'tis not hard, I think,
For men so old as we to keep the peace.
PARIS: Of honourable reckoning are you both,
And pity 'tis you liv'd at odds so long.
But now, my lord, what say you to my suit?
CAPULET: But saying o'er what I have said before:
My child is yet a stranger in the world,
She hath not seen the change of fourteen years;
Let two more summers wither in their pride
Ere we may think her ripe to be a bride.
PARIS: Younger than she are happy mothers made.
CAPULET: And too soon marr'd are those so early made.
The earth hath swallowed all my hopes but she;
She is the hopeful lady of my earth.
But woo her, gentle Paris, get her heart;
My will to her consent is but a part.
An she agree, within her scope of choice
Lies my consent and fair according voice.
This night I hold an old accustom'd feast,
Whereto I have invited many a guest,
Such as I love; and you among the store,
One more, most welcome, makes my number more.
At my poor house look to behold this night
Earth-treading stars that make dark heaven light.
Such comfort as do lusty young men feel
When well apparell'd April on the heel
Of limping Winter treads, even such delight
Among fresh female buds shall you this night
Inherit at my house. Hear all, all see,
And like her most whose merit most shall be;
Which, on more view of many, mine, being one,
May stand in number, though in reck'ning none.
Come, go with me.

To Servant, Giving Him a Paper Go, sirrah,
Trudge about through fair Verona; find those persons out
Whose names are written there, and to them say,
My house and welcome on their pleasure stay-

Exeunt Capulet and Paris.

SERVANT: Find them out whose names are written here? It is written that the shoemaker should meddle with his yard and the tailor with his last, the fisher with his pencil and the painter with his nets; but I am sent to find those persons whose names are here writ, and can never find what names the writing person hath here writ. I must to the learned. In good time!

Enter Benvolio and Romeo.

BENVOLIO: Tut, man, one fire burns out another's burning;
One pain is lessoned by another's anguish;
Turn giddy, and be holp by backward turning;
One desperate grief cures with another's languish.
Take thou some new infection to thy eye,
And the rank poison of the old will die.
ROMEO: Your plantain leaf is excellent for that.
BENVOLIO: For what, I pray thee?
ROMEO: For your broken shin.
BENVOLIO: Why, Romeo, art thou mad?
ROMEO: Not mad, but bound more than a madman is;
Shut up in Prison, kept without my food,
Whipp'd and tormented and- God-den, good fellow.
SERVANT: God gi' go-den. I pray, sir, can you read?
ROMEO: Ay, mine own fortune in my misery.
SERVANT: Perhaps you have learned it without book. But I pray, can you read anything you see?
ROMEO: Ay, If I know the letters and the language.
SERVANT: Ye say honestly. Rest you merry!
ROMEO: Stay, fellow; I can read. He reads.
'Signior Martino and his wife and daughters;
County Anselmo and his beauteous sisters;
The lady widow of Vitruvio;
Signior Placentio and His lovely nieces;
Mercutio and his brother Valentine;
Mine uncle Capulet, his wife, and daughters;
My fair niece Rosaline and Livia;
Signior Valentio and His cousin Tybalt;
Lucio and the lively Helena.'
Gives Back the Paper. A fair assembly. Whither should they come?
SERVANT: Up.
ROMEO: Whither?
SERVANT: To supper, to our house.
ROMEO: Whose house?
SERVANT: My master's.
ROMEO: Indeed I should have ask'd you that before.
SERVANT: Now I'll tell you without asking. My master is the great rich Capulet; and if you be not of the house of Montagues, I pray come and crush a cup of wine. Rest you merry!
Exit.
BENVOLIO: At this same ancient feast of Capulet's
Sups the fair Rosaline whom thou so lov'st;
With all the admired beauties of Verona.
Go thither, and with unattainted eye
Compare her face with some that I shall show,
And I will make thee think thy swan a crow.
ROMEO: When the devout religion of mine eye
Maintains such falsehood, then turn tears to fires;
And these, who, often drown'd, could never die,

Transparent heretics, be burnt for liars!
One fairer than my love? The all-seeing sun
Ne'er saw her match since first the world begun.
BENVOLIO: Tut! you saw her fair, none else being by,
Herself pois'd with herself in either eye;
But in that crystal scales let there be weigh'd
Your lady's love against some other maid
That I will show you shining at this feast,
And she shall scant show well that now seems best.
ROMEO: I'll go along, no such sight to be shown,
But to rejoice in splendour of my own.
Exeunt.

ACT I. SCENE III. Capulet's House.

Enter Capulet's Wife, and Nurse.
WIFE: Nurse, where's my daughter? Call her forth to me.
NURSE: Now, by my maidenhead at twelve year old,
I bade her come. What, lamb! what ladybird!
God forbid! Where's this girl? What, Juliet!
Enter Juliet.
JULIET: How now? Who calls?
NURSE: Your mother.
JULIET: Madam, I am here.
What is your will?
WIFE: This is the matter- Nurse, give leave awhile,
We must talk in secret. Nurse, come back again;
I have rememb'red me, thou's hear our counsel.
Thou knowest my daughter's of a pretty age.
NURSE: Faith, I can tell her age unto an hour.
WIFE: She's not fourteen.
NURSE: I'll lay fourteen of my teeth-
And yet, to my teen be it spoken, I have but four-
She is not fourteen. How long is it now
To Lammastide?
WIFE: A fortnight and odd days.
NURSE: Even or odd, of all days in the year,
Come Lammas Eve at night shall she be fourteen.
Susan and she (God rest all Christian souls!)
Were of an age. Well, Susan is with God;
She was too good for me. But, as I said,
On Lammas Eve at night shall she be fourteen;
That shall she, marry; I remember it well.
'Tis since the earthquake now eleven years;
And she was wean'd (I never shall forget it),
Of all the days of the year, upon that day;
For I had then laid wormwood to my dug,
Sitting in the sun under the dovehouse wall.
My lord and you were then at Mantua.
Nay, I do bear a brain. But, as I said,
When it did taste the wormwood on the nipple

Of my dug and felt it bitter, pretty fool,
To see it tetchy and fall out with the dug!
Shake, quoth the dovehouse! 'Twas no need, I trow,
To bid me trudge.
And since that time it is eleven years,
For then she could stand high-lone; nay, by th' rood,
She could have run and waddled all about;
For even the day before, she broke her brow;
And then my husband (God be with his soul!
'A was a merry man) took up the child.
'Yea,' quoth he, 'dost thou fall upon thy face?
Thou wilt fall backward when thou hast more wit;
Wilt thou not, Jule?' and, by my holidam,
The pretty wretch left crying, and said 'Ay.'
To see now how a jest shall come about!
I warrant, an I should live a thousand yeas,
I never should forget it. 'Wilt thou not, Jule?' quoth he,
And, pretty fool, it stinted, and said 'Ay.'
WIFE: Enough of this. I pray thee hold thy peace.
NURSE: Yes, madam. Yet I cannot choose but laugh
To think it should leave crying and say 'Ay.'
And yet, I warrant, it bad upon it brow
A bump as big as a young cock'rel's stone;
A perilous knock; and it cried bitterly.
'Yea,' quoth my husband, 'fall'st upon thy face?
Thou wilt fall backward when thou comest to age;
Wilt thou not, Jule?' It stinted, and said 'Ay.'
JULIET: And stint thou too, I pray thee, nurse, say I.
NURSE: Peace, I have done. God mark thee to his grace!
Thou wast the prettiest babe that e'er I nurs'd.
An I might live to see thee married once, I have my wish.
WIFE: Marry, that 'marry' is the very theme
I came to talk of. Tell me, daughter Juliet,
How stands your disposition to be married?
JULIET: It is an honour that I dream not of.
NURSE: An honour? Were not I thine only nurse,
I would say thou hadst suck'd wisdom from thy teat.
WIFE: Well, think of marriage now. Younger than you,
Here in Verona, ladies of esteem,
Are made already mothers. By my count,
I was your mother much upon these years
That you are now a maid. Thus then in brief:
The valiant Paris seeks you for his love.
NURSE: A man, young lady! lady, such a man
As all the world- why he's a man of wax.
WIFE: Verona's summer hath not such a flower.
NURSE: Nay, he's a flower, in faith- a very flower.
WIFE: What say you? Can you love the gentleman?
This night you shall behold him at our feast.

Read o'er the volume of young Paris' face,
And find delight writ there with beauty's pen;
Examine every married lineament,
And see how one another lends content;
And what obscur'd in this fair volume lies
Find written in the margent of his eyes,
This precious book of love, this unbound lover,
To beautify him only lacks a cover.
The fish lives in the sea, and 'tis much pride
For fair without the fair within to hide.
That book in many's eyes doth share the glory,
That in gold clasps locks in the golden story;
So shall you share all that he doth possess,
By having him making yourself no less.
NURSE: No less? Nay, bigger! Women grow by men
WIFE: Speak briefly, can you like of Paris' love?
JULIET: I'll look to like, if looking liking move;
But no more deep will I endart mine eye
Than your consent gives strength to make it fly.
Enter Servingman.
SERVANT: Madam, the guests are come, supper serv'd up, you call'd, my young lady ask'd for, the nurse curs'd in the pantry, and everything in extremity. I must hence to wait. I beseech you follow straight.
WIFE: We follow thee.
Exit Servingman. Juliet, the County stays.
NURSE: Go, girl, seek happy nights to happy days.
Exeunt.

ACT I. SCENE IV. A Street.

Enter Romeo, Mercutio, Benvolio, with Five or Six Other Maskers; Torchbearers.
ROMEO: What, shall this speech be spoke for our excuse?
Or shall we on without apology?
BENVOLIO: The date is out of such prolixity.
We'll have no Cupid hoodwink'd with a scarf,
Bearing a Tartar's painted bow of lath,
Scaring the ladies like a crowkeeper;
Nor no without-book prologue, faintly spoke
After the prompter, for our entrance;
But, let them measure us by what they will,
We'll measure them a measure, and be gone.
ROMEO: Give me a torch. I am not for this ambling.
Being but heavy, I will bear the light.
MERCUTIO: Nay, gentle Romeo, we must have you dance.
ROMEO: Not I, believe me. You have dancing shoes
With nimble soles; I have a soul of lead
So stakes me to the ground I cannot move.
MERCUTIO: You are a lover. Borrow Cupid's wings
And soar with them above a common bound.
ROMEO: I am too sore enpierced with his shaft
To soar with his light feathers; and so bound

I cannot bound a pitch above dull woe.
Under love's heavy burthen do I sink.
MERCUTIO: And, to sink in it, should you burthen love-
Too great oppression for a tender thing.
ROMEO: Is love a tender thing? It is too rough,
Too rude, too boist'rous, and it pricks like thorn.
MERCUTIO: If love be rough with you, be rough with love.
Prick love for pricking, and you beat love down.
Give me a case to put my visage in.
A visor for a visor! What care I
What curious eye doth quote deformities?
Here are the beetle brows shall blush for me.
BENVOLIO: Come, knock and enter; and no sooner in
But every man betake him to his legs.
ROMEO: A torch for me! Let wantons light of heart
Tickle the senseless rushes with their heels;
For I am proverb'd with a grandsire phrase,
I'll be a candle-holder and look on;
The game was ne'er so fair, and I am done.
MERCUTIO: Tut! dun's the mouse, the constable's own word!
If thou art Dun, we'll draw thee from the mire
Of this sir-reverence love, wherein thou stick'st
Up to the ears. Come, we burn daylight, ho!
ROMEO: Nay, that's not so.
MERCUTIO: I mean, sir, in delay
We waste our lights in vain, like lamps by day.
Take our good meaning, for our judgment sits
Five times in that ere once in our five wits.
ROMEO: And we mean well, in going to this masque;
But 'tis no wit to go.
MERCUTIO: Why, may one ask?
ROMEO: I dreamt a dream to-night.
MERCUTIO: And so did I.
ROMEO: Well, what was yours?
MERCUTIO: That dreamers often lie.
ROMEO: In bed asleep, while they do dream things true.
MERCUTIO: O, then I see Queen Mab hath been with you.
She is the fairies' midwife, and she comes
In shape no bigger than an agate stone
On the forefinger of an alderman,
Drawn with a team of little atomies
Athwart men's noses as they lie asleep;
Her wagon spokes made of long spinners' legs,
The cover, of the wings of grasshoppers;
Her traces, of the smallest spider's web;
Her collars, of the moonshine's wat'ry beams;
Her whip, of cricket's bone; the lash, of film;
Her wagoner, a small grey-coated gnat,
Not half so big as a round little worm

Prick'd from the lazy finger of a maid;
Her chariot is an empty hazelnut,
Made by the joiner squirrel or old grub,
Time out o' mind the fairies' coachmakers.
And in this state she 'gallops night by night
Through lovers' brains, and then they dream of love;
O'er courtiers' knees, that dream on cursies straight;
O'er lawyers' fingers, who straight dream on fees;
O'er ladies' lips, who straight on kisses dream,
Which oft the angry Mab with blisters plagues,
Because their breaths with sweetmeats tainted are.
Sometime she gallops o'er a courtier's nose,
And then dreams he of smelling out a suit;
And sometime comes she with a tithe-pig's tail
Tickling a parson's nose as 'a lies asleep,
Then dreams he of another benefice.
Sometimes she driveth o'er a soldier's neck,
And then dreams he of cutting foreign throats,
Of breaches, ambuscadoes, Spanish blades,
Of healths five fadom deep; and then anon
Drums in his ear, at which he starts and wakes,
And being thus frighted, swears a prayer or two
And sleeps again. This is that very Mab
That plats the manes of horses in the night
And bakes the elflocks in foul sluttish, hairs,
Which once untangled much misfortune bodes
This is the hag, when maids lie on their backs,
That presses them and learns them first to bear,
Making them women of good carriage.
This is she-
ROMEO: Peace, peace, Mercutio, peace!
Thou talk'st of nothing.
MERCUTIO: True, I talk of dreams;
Which are the children of an idle brain,
Begot of nothing but vain fantasy;
Which is as thin of substance as the air,
And more inconstant than the wind, who wooes
Even now the frozen bosom of the North
And, being anger'd, puffs away from thence,
Turning his face to the dew-dropping South.
BENVOLIO: This wind you talk of blows us from ourselves.
Supper is done, and we shall come too late.
ROMEO: I fear, too early; for my mind misgives
Some consequence, yet hanging in the stars,
Shall bitterly begin his fearful date
With this night's revels and expire the term
Of a despised life, clos'd in my breast,
By some vile forfeit of untimely death.
But he that hath the steerage of my course

Direct my sail! On, lusty gentlemen!
BENVOLIO: Strike, drum.
They March about the Stage. Exeunt.

ACT I. SCENE V. Capulet's House.

Servingmen come forth with napkins.
FIRST SERVANT: Where's Potpan, that he helps not to take away? He shift a trencher! he scrape a trencher!
SECOND SERVANT: When good manners shall lie all in one or two men's hands, and they unwash'd too, 'tis a foul thing.
FIRST SERVANT: Away with the join-stools, remove the court-cubbert, look to the plate. Good thou, save me a piece of marchpane and, as thou loves me, let the porter let in Susan Grindstone and Nell. Anthony, and Potpan!
SECOND SERVANT: Ay, boy, ready.
FIRST SERVANT: You are look'd for and call'd for, ask'd for and sought for, in the great chamber.
THIRD SERVANT: We cannot be here and there too. Cheerly, boys! Be brisk awhile, and the longer liver take all.
Exeunt.
Enter the Maskers; Enter, With Servants, Capulet, His Wife, Juliet, Tybalt, and All the Guests and Gentlewomen to the Maskers.
CAPULET: Welcome, gentlemen! Ladies that have their toes
Unplagu'd with corns will have a bout with you.
Ah ha, my mistresses! which of you all
Will now deny to dance? She that makes dainty,
She I'll swear hath corns. Am I come near ye now?
Welcome, gentlemen! I have seen the day
That I have worn a visor and could tell
A whispering tale in a fair lady's ear,
Such as would please. 'Tis gone, 'tis gone, 'tis gone!
You are welcome, gentlemen! Come, musicians, play.
A hall, a hall! give room! and foot it, girls.
Music Plays, and They Dance.
More light, you knaves! and turn the tables up,
And quench the fire, the room is grown too hot.
Ah, sirrah, this unlook'd-for sport comes well.
Nay, sit, nay, sit, good cousin Capulet,
For you and I are past our dancing days.
How long is't now since last yourself and I
Were in a mask?
SECOND CAPULET: By'r Lady, thirty years.
CAPULET: What, man? 'Tis not so much, 'tis not so much!
'Tis since the nuptial of Lucentio,
Come Pentecost as quickly as it will,
Some five-and-twenty years, and then we mask'd.
SECOND CAPULET: 'Tis more, 'tis more! His son is elder, sir;
His son is thirty.
CAPULET: Will you tell me that?
His son was but a ward two years ago.

ROMEO: To a Servingman What lady's that, which doth enrich the hand
Of yonder knight?
SERVANT: I know not, sir.
ROMEO: O, she doth teach the torches to burn bright!
It seems she hangs upon the cheek of night
Like a rich jewel in an Ethiop's ear-
Beauty too rich for use, for earth too dear!
So shows a snowy dove trooping with crows
As yonder lady o'er her fellows shows.
The measure done, I'll watch her place of stand
And, touching hers, make blessed my rude hand.
Did my heart love till now? Forswear it, sight!
For I ne'er saw true beauty till this night.
TYBALT: This, by his voice, should be a Montague.
Fetch me my rapier, boy. What, dares the slave
Come hither, cover'd with an antic face,
To fleer and scorn at our solemnity?
Now, by the stock and honour of my kin,
To strike him dead I hold it not a sin.
CAPULET: Why, how now, kinsman? Wherefore storm you so?
TYBALT: Uncle, this is a Montague, our foe;
A villain, that is hither come in spite
To scorn at our solemnity this night.
CAPULET: Young Romeo is it?
TYBALT: 'Tis he, that villain Romeo.
CAPULET: Content thee, gentle coz, let him alone.
'A bears him like a portly gentleman,
And, to say truth, Verona brags of him
To be a virtuous and well-govern'd youth.
I would not for the wealth of all this town
Here in my house do him disparagement.
Therefore be patient, take no note of him.
It is my will; the which if thou respect,
Show a fair presence and put off these frowns,
An ill-beseeming semblance for a feast.
TYBALT: It fits when such a villain is a guest.
I'll not endure him.
CAPULET: He shall be endur'd.
What, goodman boy? I say he shall. Go to!
Am I the master here, or you? Go to!
You'll not endure him? God shall mend my soul!
You'll make a mutiny among my guests!
You will set cock-a-hoop! you'll be the man!
TYBALT: Why, uncle, 'tis a shame.
CAPULET: Go to, go to!
You are a saucy boy. Is't so, indeed?
This trick may chance to scathe you. I know what.
You must contrary me! Marry, 'tis time.-
Well said, my hearts!- You are a princox- go!

Be quiet, or- More light, more light!- For shame!
I'll make you quiet; what!- Cheerly, my hearts!
TYBALT: Patience perforce with wilful choler meeting
Makes my flesh tremble in their different greeting.
I will withdraw; but this intrusion shall,
Now seeming sweet, convert to bitt'rest gall.
Exit.
ROMEO: If I profane with my unworthiest hand
This holy shrine, the gentle fine is this:
My lips, two blushing pilgrims, ready stand
To smooth that rough touch with a tender kiss.
JULIET: Good pilgrim, you do wrong your hand too much,
Which mannerly devotion shows in this;
For saints have hands that pilgrims' hands do touch,
And palm to palm is holy palmers' kiss.
ROMEO: Have not saints lips, and holy palmers too?
JULIET: Ay, pilgrim, lips that they must use in pray'r.
ROMEO: O, then, dear saint, let lips do what hands do!
They pray; grant thou, lest faith turn to despair.
JULIET: Saints do not move, though grant for prayers' sake.
ROMEO: Then move not while my prayer's effect I take.
Thus from my lips, by thine my sin is purg'd. Kisses Her.
JULIET: Then have my lips the sin that they have took.
ROMEO: Sin from my lips? O trespass sweetly urg'd!
Give me my sin again. Kisses Her.
JULIET: You kiss by th' book.
NURSE: Madam, your mother craves a word with you.
ROMEO: What is her mother?
NURSE: Marry, bachelor,
Her mother is the lady of the house.
And a good lady, and a wise and virtuous.
I nurs'd her daughter that you talk'd withal.
I tell you, he that can lay hold of her
Shall have the chinks.
ROMEO: Is she a Capulet?
O dear account! my life is my foe's debt.
BENVOLIO: Away, be gone; the sport is at the best.
ROMEO: Ay, so I fear; the more is my unrest.
CAPULET: Nay, gentlemen, prepare not to be gone;
We have a trifling foolish banquet towards.
Is it e'en so? Why then, I thank you all.
I thank you, honest gentlemen. Good night.
More torches here!
Exeunt Maskers.
Come on then, let's to bed.
Ah, sirrah, by my fay, it waxes late;
I'll to my rest.
Exeunt All but Juliet and Nurse.
JULIET: Come hither, nurse. What is yond gentleman?

NURSE: The son and heir of old Tiberio.
JULIET: What's he that now is going out of door?
NURSE: Marry, that, I think, be young Petruchio.
JULIET: What's he that follows there, that would not dance?
NURSE: I know not.
JULIET: Go ask his name.- If he be married,
My grave is like to be my wedding bed.
NURSE: His name is Romeo, and a Montague,
The only son of your great enemy.
JULIET: My only love, sprung from my only hate!
Too early seen unknown, and known too late!
Prodigious birth of love it is to me
That I must love a loathed enemy.
NURSE: What's this? what's this?
JULIET: A rhyme I learnt even now
Of one I danc'd withal.
One Calls Within, 'Juliet.'
NURSE: Anon, anon!
Come, let's away; the strangers all are gone.
Exeunt.

PROLOGUE

Enter Chorus.
CHORUS: Now old desire doth in his deathbed lie,
And young affection gapes to be his heir;
That fair for which love groan'd for and would die,
With tender Juliet match'd, is now not fair.
Now Romeo is belov'd, and loves again,
Alike bewitched by the charm of looks;
But to his foe suppos'd he must complain,
And she steal love's sweet bait from fearful hooks.
Being held a foe, he may not have access
To breathe such vows as lovers use to swear,
And she as much in love, her means much less
To meet her new beloved anywhere;
But passion lends them power, time means, to meet,
Temp'ring extremities with extreme sweet.
Exit.

ACT II. SCENE I. A Lane by the Wall of Capulet's Orchard.

Enter Romeo alone.
ROMEO: Can I go forward when my heart is here?
Turn back, dull earth, and find thy centre out.
Climbs the Wall and Leaps down Within It.
Enter Benvolio with Mercutio.
BENVOLIO: Romeo! my cousin Romeo! Romeo!
MERCUTIO: He is wise,
And, on my life, hath stol'n him home to bed.
BENVOLIO: He ran this way, and leapt this orchard wall.
Call, good Mercutio.
MERCUTIO: Nay, I'll conjure too.

Romeo! humours! madman! passion! lover!
Appear thou in the likeness of a sigh;
Speak but one rhyme, and I am satisfied!
Cry but 'Ay me!' pronounce but 'love' and 'dove';
Speak to my gossip Venus one fair word,
One nickname for her purblind son and heir,
Young Adam Cupid, he that shot so trim
When King Cophetua lov'd the beggar maid!
He heareth not, he stirreth not, be moveth not;
The ape is dead, and I must conjure him.
I conjure thee by Rosaline's bright eyes.
By her high forehead and her scarlet lip,
By her fine foot, straight leg, and quivering thigh,
And the demesnes that there adjacent lie,
That in thy likeness thou appear to us!
BENVOLIO: An if he hear thee, thou wilt anger him.
MERCUTIO: This cannot anger him. 'Twould anger him
To raise a spirit in his mistress' circle
Of some strange nature, letting it there stand
Till she had laid it and conjur'd it down.
That were some spite; my invocation
Is fair and honest: in his mistress' name,
I conjure only but to raise up him.
BENVOLIO: Come, he hath hid himself among these trees
To be consorted with the humorous night.
Blind is his love and best befits the dark.
MERCUTIO: If love be blind, love cannot hit the mark.
Now will he sit under a medlar tree
And wish his mistress were that kind of fruit
As maids call medlars when they laugh alone.
O, Romeo, that she were, O that she were
An open et cetera, thou a pop'rin pear!
Romeo, good night. I'll to my truckle-bed;
This field-bed is too cold for me to sleep.
Come, shall we go?
BENVOLIO: Go then, for 'tis in vain
'To seek him here that means not to be found.
Exeunt.

ACT II. SCENE II. Capulet's Orchard.

Enter Romeo.
ROMEO: He jests at scars that never felt a wound.
Enter Juliet above at a window.
But soft! What light through yonder window breaks?
It is the East, and Juliet is the sun!
Arise, fair sun, and kill the envious moon,
Who is already sick and pale with grief
That thou her maid art far more fair than she.
Be not her maid, since she is envious.
Her vestal livery is but sick and green,

And none but fools do wear it. Cast it off.
It is my lady; O, it is my love!
O that she knew she were!
She speaks, yet she says nothing. What of that?
Her eye discourses; I will answer it.
I am too bold; 'tis not to me she speaks.
Two of the fairest stars in all the heaven,
Having some business, do entreat her eyes
To twinkle in their spheres till they return.
What if her eyes were there, they in her head?
The brightness of her cheek would shame those stars
As daylight doth a lamp; her eyes in heaven
Would through the airy region stream so bright
That birds would sing and think it were not night.
See how she leans her cheek upon her hand!
O that I were a glove upon that hand,
That I might touch that cheek!
JULIET: Ay me!
ROMEO: She speaks.
O, speak again, bright angel! for thou art
As glorious to this night, being o'er my head,
As is a winged messenger of heaven
Unto the white-upturned wond'ring eyes
Of mortals that fall back to gaze on him
When he bestrides the lazy-pacing clouds
And sails upon the bosom of the air.
JULIET: O Romeo, Romeo! wherefore art thou Romeo?
Deny thy father and refuse thy name!
Or, if thou wilt not, be but sworn my love,
And I'll no longer be a Capulet.
ROMEO: Aside Shall I hear more, or shall I speak at this?
JULIET: 'Tis but thy name that is my enemy.
Thou art thyself, though not a Montague.
What's Montague? it is nor hand, nor foot,
Nor arm, nor face, nor any other part
Belonging to a man. O, be some other name!
What's in a name? That which we call a rose
By any other name would smell as sweet.
So Romeo would, were he not Romeo call'd,
Retain that dear perfection which he owes
Without that title. Romeo, doff thy name;
And for that name, which is no part of thee,
Take all myself.
ROMEO: I take thee at thy word.
Call me but love, and I'll be new baptiz'd;
Henceforth I never will be Romeo.
JULIET: What man art thou that, thus bescreen'd in night,
So stumblest on my counsel?
ROMEO: By a name

I know not how to tell thee who I am.
My name, dear saint, is hateful to myself,
Because it is an enemy to thee.
Had I it written, I would tear the word.
JULIET: My ears have yet not drunk a hundred words
Of that tongue's utterance, yet I know the sound.
Art thou not Romeo, and a Montague?
ROMEO: Neither, fair saint, if either thee dislike.
JULIET: How cam'st thou hither, tell me, and wherefore?
The orchard walls are high and hard to climb,
And the place death, considering who thou art,
If any of my kinsmen find thee here.
ROMEO: With love's light wings did I o'erperch these walls;
For stony limits cannot hold love out,
And what love can do, that dares love attempt.
Therefore thy kinsmen are no let to me.
JULIET: If they do see thee, they will murther thee.
ROMEO: Alack, there lies more peril in thine eye
Than twenty of their swords! Look thou but sweet,
And I am proof against their enmity.
JULIET: I would not for the world they saw thee here.
ROMEO: I have night's cloak to hide me from their sight;
And but thou love me, let them find me here.
My life were better ended by their hate
Than death prorogued, wanting of thy love.
JULIET: By whose direction found'st thou out this place?
ROMEO: By love, that first did prompt me to enquire.
He lent me counsel, and I lent him eyes.
I am no pilot; yet, wert thou as far
As that vast shore wash'd with the farthest sea,
I would adventure for such merchandise.
JULIET: Thou knowest the mask of night is on my face;
Else would a maiden blush bepaint my cheek
For that which thou hast heard me speak to-night.
Fain would I dwell on form- fain, fain deny
What I have spoke; but farewell compliment!
Dost thou love me, I know thou wilt say 'Ay';
And I will take thy word. Yet, if thou swear'st,
Thou mayst prove false. At lovers' perjuries,
They say Jove laughs. O gentle Romeo,
If thou dost love, pronounce it faithfully.
Or if thou thinkest I am too quickly won,
I'll frown, and be perverse, and say thee nay,
So thou wilt woo; but else, not for the world.
In truth, fair Montague, I am too fond,
And therefore thou mayst think my haviour light;
But trust me, gentleman, I'll prove more true
Than those that have more cunning to be strange.
I should have been more strange, I must confess,

But that thou overheard'st, ere I was ware,
My true-love passion. Therefore pardon me,
And not impute this yielding to light love,
Which the dark night hath so discovered.
ROMEO: Lady, by yonder blessed moon I swear,
That tips with silver all these fruit-tree tops-
JULIET: O, swear not by the moon, th' inconstant moon,
That monthly changes in her circled orb,
Lest that thy love prove likewise variable.
ROMEO: What shall I swear by?
JULIET: Do not swear at all;
Or if thou wilt, swear by thy gracious self,
Which is the god of my idolatry,
And I'll believe thee.
ROMEO: If my heart's dear love-
JULIET: Well, do not swear. Although I joy in thee,
I have no joy of this contract to-night.
It is too rash, too unadvis'd, too sudden;
Too like the lightning, which doth cease to be
Ere one can say 'It lightens.' Sweet, good night!
This bud of love, by summer's ripening breath,
May prove a beauteous flow'r when next we meet.
Good night, good night! As sweet repose and rest
Come to thy heart as that within my breast!
ROMEO: O, wilt thou leave me so unsatisfied?
JULIET: What satisfaction canst thou have to-night?
ROMEO: Th' exchange of thy love's faithful vow for mine.
JULIET: I gave thee mine before thou didst request it;
And yet I would it were to give again.
ROMEO: Would'st thou withdraw it? For what purpose, love?
JULIET: But to be frank and give it thee again.
And yet I wish but for the thing I have.
My bounty is as boundless as the sea,
My love as deep; the more I give to thee,
The more I have, for both are infinite.
I hear some noise within. Dear love, adieu!
Nurse Calls Within.
Anon, good nurse! Sweet Montague, be true.
Stay but a little, I will come again.
Exit.
ROMEO: O blessed, blessed night! I am afeard,
Being in night, all this is but a dream,
Too flattering-sweet to be substantial.
Enter Juliet Above.
JULIET: Three words, dear Romeo, and good night indeed.
If that thy bent of love be honourable,
Thy purpose marriage, send me word to-morrow,
By one that I'll procure to come to thee,
Where and what time thou wilt perform the rite;

And all my fortunes at thy foot I'll lay
And follow thee my lord throughout the world.
NURSE: (within) Madam!
JULIET: I come, anon.- But if thou meanest not well,
I do beseech thee-
NURSE: (within) Madam!
JULIET: By-and-by I come.-
To cease thy suit and leave me to my grief.
To-morrow will I send.
ROMEO: So thrive my soul-
JULIET: A thousand times good night!
Exit.
ROMEO: A thousand times the worse, to want thy light!
Love goes toward love as schoolboys from their books;
But love from love, towards school with heavy looks.
Enter Juliet Again, Above.
JULIET: Hist! Romeo, hist! O for a falconer's voice
To lure this tassel-gentle back again!
Bondage is hoarse and may not speak aloud;
Else would I tear the cave where Echo lies,
And make her airy tongue more hoarse than mine
With repetition of my Romeo's name.
Romeo!
ROMEO: It is my soul that calls upon my name.
How silver-sweet sound lovers' tongues by night,
Like softest music to attending ears!
JULIET: Romeo!
ROMEO: My dear?
JULIET: At what o'clock to-morrow
Shall I send to thee?
ROMEO: By the hour of nine.
JULIET: I will not fail. 'Tis twenty years till then.
I have forgot why I did call thee back.
ROMEO: Let me stand here till thou remember it.
JULIET: I shall forget, to have thee still stand there,
Rememb'ring how I love thy company.
ROMEO: And I'll still stay, to have thee still forget,
Forgetting any other home but this.
JULIET: 'Tis almost morning. I would have thee gone-
And yet no farther than a wanton's bird,
That lets it hop a little from her hand,
Like a poor prisoner in his twisted gyves,
And with a silk thread plucks it back again,
So loving-jealous of his liberty.
ROMEO: I would I were thy bird.
JULIET: Sweet, so would I.
Yet I should kill thee with much cherishing.
Good night, good night! Parting is such sweet sorrow,
That I shall say good night till it be morrow.

Exit.
ROMEO: Sleep dwell upon thine eyes, peace in thy breast!
Would I were sleep and peace, so sweet to rest!
Hence will I to my ghostly father's cell,
His help to crave and my dear hap to tell.
Exit

ACT II. SCENE III. Friar Laurence's Cell.

Enter Friar Laurence Alone, with a Basket.
FRIAR: The grey-ey'd morn smiles on the frowning night,
Check'ring the Eastern clouds with streaks of light;
And flecked darkness like a drunkard reels
From forth day's path and Titan's fiery wheels.
Non, ere the sun advance his burning eye
The day to cheer and night's dank dew to dry,
I must up-fill this osier cage of ours
With baleful weeds and precious-juiced flowers.
The earth that's nature's mother is her tomb.
What is her burying gave, that is her womb;
And from her womb children of divers kind
We sucking on her natural bosom find;
Many for many virtues excellent,
None but for some, and yet all different.
O, mickle is the powerful grace that lies
In plants, herbs, stones, and their true qualities;
For naught so vile that on the earth doth live
But to the earth some special good doth give;
Nor aught so good but, strain'd from that fair use,
Revolts from true birth, stumbling on abuse.
Virtue itself turns vice, being misapplied,
And vice sometime's by action dignified.
Within the infant rind of this small flower
Poison hath residence, and medicine power;
For this, being smelt, with that part cheers each part;
Being tasted, slays all senses with the heart.
Two such opposed kings encamp them still
In man as well as herbs- grace and rude will;
And where the worser is predominant,
Full soon the canker death eats up that plant.
Enter Romeo.
ROMEO: Good morrow, father.
FRIAR: Benedicite!
What early tongue so sweet saluteth me?
Young son, it argues a distempered head
So soon to bid good morrow to thy bed.
Care keeps his watch in every old man's eye,
And where care lodges sleep will never lie;
But where unbruised youth with unstuff'd brain
Doth couch his limbs, there golden sleep doth reign.
Therefore thy earliness doth me assure

Thou art uprous'd with some distemp'rature;
Or if not so, then here I hit it right-
Our Romeo hath not been in bed to-night.
ROMEO: That last is true-the sweeter rest was mine.
FRIAR: God pardon sin! Wast thou with Rosaline?
ROMEO: With Rosaline, my ghostly father? No.
I have forgot that name, and that name's woe.
FRIAR: That's my good son! But where hast thou been then?
ROMEO: I'll tell thee ere thou ask it me again.
I have been feasting with mine enemy,
Where on a sudden one hath wounded me
That's by me wounded. Both our remedies
Within thy help and holy physic lies.
I bear no hatred, blessed man, for, lo,
My intercession likewise steads my foe.
FRIAR: Be plain, good son, and homely in thy drift
Riddling confession finds but riddling shrift.
ROMEO: Then plainly know my heart's dear love is set
On the fair daughter of rich Capulet;
As mine on hers, so hers is set on mine,
And all combin'd, save what thou must combine
By holy marriage. When, and where, and how
We met, we woo'd, and made exchange of vow,
I'll tell thee as we pass; but this I pray,
That thou consent to marry us to-day.
FRIAR: Holy Saint Francis! What a change is here!
Is Rosaline, that thou didst love so dear,
So soon forsaken? Young men's love then lies
Not truly in their hearts, but in their eyes.
Jesu Maria! What a deal of brine
Hath wash'd thy sallow cheeks for Rosaline!
How much salt water thrown away in waste,
To season love, that of it doth not taste!
The sun not yet thy sighs from heaven clears,
Thy old groans ring yet in mine ancient ears.
Lo, here upon thy cheek the stain doth sit
Of an old tear that is not wash'd off yet.
If e'er thou wast thyself, and these woes thine,
Thou and these woes were all for Rosaline.
And art thou chang'd? Pronounce this sentence then:
Women may fall when there's no strength in men.
ROMEO: Thou chid'st me oft for loving Rosaline.
FRIAR: For doting, not for loving, pupil mine.
ROMEO: And bad'st me bury love.
FRIAR: Not in a grave
To lay one in, another out to have.
ROMEO: I pray thee chide not. She whom I love now
Doth grace for grace and love for love allow.
The other did not so.

FRIAR: O, she knew well
Thy love did read by rote, that could not spell.
But come, young waverer, come go with me.
In one respect I'll thy assistant be;
For this alliance may so happy prove
To turn your households' rancour to pure love.
ROMEO: O, let us hence! I stand on sudden haste.
FRIAR: Wisely, and slow. They stumble that run fast.
Exeunt.

ACT II. SCENE IV. A Street.

Enter Benvolio and Mercutio.
MERCUTIO: Where the devil should this Romeo be?
Came he not home to-night?
BENVOLIO: Not to his father's. I spoke with his man.
MERCUTIO: Why, that same pale hard-hearted wench, that Rosaline,
Torments him so that he will sure run mad.
BENVOLIO: Tybalt, the kinsman to old Capulet,
Hath sent a letter to his father's house.
MERCUTIO: A challenge, on my life.
BENVOLIO: Romeo will answer it.
MERCUTIO: Any man that can write may answer a letter.
BENVOLIO: Nay, he will answer the letter's master, how he dares, being dared.
MERCUTIO: Alas, poor Romeo, he is already dead! stabb'd with a white wench's black eye; shot through the ear with a love song; the very pin of his heart cleft with the blind bow-boy's butt-shaft; and is he a man to encounter Tybalt?
BENVOLIO: Why, what is Tybalt?
MERCUTIO: More than Prince of Cats, I can tell you. O, he's the courageous captain of compliments. He fights as you sing pricksong-keeps time, distance, and proportion; rests me his minim rest, one, two, and the third in your bosom! the very butcher of a silk button, a duellist, a duellist! a gentleman of the very first house, of the first and second cause. Ah, the immortal passado! the punto reverse! the hay.
BENVOLIO: The what?
MERCUTIO: The pox of such antic, lisping, affecting fantasticoes- these new tuners of accent! 'By Jesu, a very good blade! a very tall man! a very good whore!' Why, is not this a lamentable thing, grandsir, that we should be thus afflicted with these strange flies, these fashion-mongers, these pardona-mi's, who stand so much on the new form that they cannot sit at ease on the old bench? O, their bones, their bones!
Enter Romeo.
BENVOLIO: Here comes Romeo! here comes Romeo!
MERCUTIO: Without his roe, like a dried herring. O flesh, flesh, how art thou fishified! Now is he for the numbers that Petrarch flowed in. Laura, to his lady, was but a kitchen wench (marry, she had a better love to berhyme her), Dido a dowdy, Cleopatra a gypsy,

Helen and Hero hildings and harlots, This be a gray eye or so, but not to the purpose. Signior Romeo, bon jour! There's a French salutation to your French slop. You gave us the counterfeit fairly last night.
ROMEO: Good morrow to you both. What counterfeit did I give you?
MERCUTIO: The slip, sir, the slip. Can you not conceive?
ROMEO: Pardon, good Mercutio. My business was great, and in such a case as mine a man may strain courtesy.
MERCUTIO: That's as much as to say, such a case as yours constrains a man to bow in the hams.
ROMEO: Meaning, to cursy.
MERCUTIO: Thou hast most kindly hit it.
ROMEO: A most courteous exposition.
MERCUTIO: Nay, I am the very pink of courtesy.
ROMEO: Pink for flower.
MERCUTIO: Right.
ROMEO: Why, then is my pump well-flower'd.
MERCUTIO: Well said! Follow me this jest now till thou hast worn out thy pump, that, when the single sole of it is worn, the jest may remain, after the wearing, solely singular.
ROMEO: O single-sold jest, solely singular for the singleness!
MERCUTIO: Come between us, good Benvolio! My wits faint.
ROMEO: Swits and spurs, swits and spurs! or I'll cry a match.
MERCUTIO: Nay, if our wits run the wild-goose chase, I am done; for thou hast more of the wild goose in one of thy wits than, I am sure, I have in my whole five. Was I with you there for the goose?
ROMEO: Thou wast never with me for anything when thou wast not there for the goose.
MERCUTIO: I will bite thee by the ear for that jest.
ROMEO: Nay, good goose, bite not!
MERCUTIO: Thy wit is a very bitter sweeting; it is a most sharp sauce.
ROMEO: And is it not, then, well serv'd in to a sweet goose?
MERCUTIO: O, here's a wit of cheveril, that stretches from an inch narrow to an ell broad!
ROMEO: I stretch it out for that word 'broad,' which, added to the goose, proves thee far and wide a broad goose.
MERCUTIO: Why, is not this better now than groaning for love? Now art thou sociable, now art thou Romeo; now art thou what thou art, by art as well as by nature. For this drivelling love is like a great natural that runs lolling up and down to hide his bauble in a hole.
BENVOLIO: Stop there, stop there!
MERCUTIO: Thou desirest me to stop in my tale against the hair.
BENVOLIO: Thou wouldst else have made thy tale large.
MERCUTIO: O, thou art deceiv'd! I would have made it short; for I was come to the whole depth of my tale, and meant indeed to occupy the argument no longer.
ROMEO: Here's goodly gear!
Enter Nurse and Her Man Peter.

MERCUTIO: A sail, a sail!
BENVOLIO: Two, two! a shirt and a smock.
NURSE: Peter!
PETER: Anon.
NURSE: My fan, Peter.
MERCUTIO: Good Peter, to hide her face; for her fan's the fairer face of the two.
NURSE: God ye good morrow, gentlemen.
MERCUTIO: God ye good-den, fair gentlewoman.
NURSE: Is it good-den?
MERCUTIO: 'Tis no less, I tell ye; for the bawdy hand of the dial is now upon the prick of noon.
NURSE: Out upon you! What a man are you!
ROMEO: One, gentlewoman, that God hath made for himself to mar.
NURSE: By my troth, it is well said. 'For himself to mar,' quoth 'a? Gentlemen, can any of you tell me where I may find the young Romeo?
ROMEO: I can tell you; but young Romeo will be older when you have found him than he was when you sought him. I am the youngest of that name, for fault of a worse.
NURSE: You say well.
MERCUTIO: Yea, is the worst well? Very well took, i' faith! wisely, wisely.
NURSE: If you be he, sir, I desire some confidence with you.
BENVOLIO: She will endite him to some supper.
MERCUTIO: A bawd, a bawd, a bawd! So ho!
ROMEO: What hast thou found?
MERCUTIO: No hare, sir; unless a hare, sir, in a lenten pie, that is something stale and hoar ere it be spent

He Walks by Them and Sings.

An old hare hoar,
And an old hare hoar,
Is very good meat in Lent;
But a hare that is hoar
Is too much for a score
When it hoars ere it be spent.

Romeo, will you come to your father's? We'll to dinner thither.
ROMEO: I will follow you.
MERCUTIO: Farewell, ancient lady. Farewell,
Sings lady, lady, lady.

Exeunt Mercutio, Benvolio.

NURSE: Marry, farewell! I Pray you, Sir, what saucy merchant was this that was so full of his ropery?
ROMEO: A gentleman, nurse, that loves to hear himself talk and will speak more in a minute than he will stand to in a month.
NURSE: An 'a speak anything against me, I'll take him down, an 'a were lustier than he is, and twenty such jacks; and if I cannot, I'll find those that shall. Scurvy knave! I am none of his flirt-gills; I am none of his skains-mates. And thou must stand

by too, and suffer every knave to use me at his pleasure!
PETER: I saw no man use you at his pleasure. If I had, my weapon should quickly have been out, I warrant you. I dare draw as soon as another man, if I see occasion in a good quarrel, and the law on my side.
NURSE: Now, afore God, I am so vexed that every part about me quivers. Scurvy knave! Pray you, sir, a word; and, as I told you, my young lady bid me enquire you out. What she bid me say, I will keep to myself; but first let me tell ye, if ye should lead her into a fool's paradise, as they say, it were a very gross kind of behaviour, as they say; for the gentlewoman is young; and therefore, if you should deal double with her, truly it were an ill thing to be off'red to any gentlewoman, and very weak dealing.
ROMEO: Nurse, commend me to thy lady and mistress. I protest unto thee-
NURSE: Good heart, and I faith I will tell her as much. Lord, Lord! she will be a joyful woman.
ROMEO: What wilt thou tell her, nurse? Thou dost not mark me.
NURSE: I will tell her, sir, that you do protest, which, as I take it, is a gentlemanlike offer.
ROMEO: Bid her devise
Some means to come to shrift this afternoon;
And there she shall at Friar Laurence' cell
Be shriv'd and married. Here is for thy pains.
NURSE: No, truly, sir; not a penny.
ROMEO: Go to! I say you shall.
NURSE: This afternoon, sir? Well, she shall be there.
ROMEO: And stay, good nurse, behind the abbey wall.
Within this hour my man shall be with thee
And bring thee cords made like a tackled stair,
Which to the high topgallant of my joy
Must be my convoy in the secret night.
Farewell. Be trusty, and I'll quit thy pains.
Farewell. Commend me to thy mistress.
NURSE: Now God in heaven bless thee! Hark you, sir.
ROMEO: What say'st thou, my dear nurse?
NURSE: Is your man secret? Did you ne'er hear say,
Two may keep counsel, putting one away?
ROMEO: I warrant thee my man's as true as steel.
NURSE: Well, sir, my mistress is the sweetest lady. Lord, Lord! when 'twas a little prating thing- O, there is a nobleman in town, one Paris, that would fain lay knife aboard; but she, good soul, had as lieve see a toad, a very toad, as see him. I anger her sometimes, and tell her that Paris is the properer man; but I'll warrant you, when I say so, she looks as pale as any clout in the versal world. Doth not rosemary and Romeo begin both with a letter?
ROMEO: Ay, nurse; what of that? Both with an R.
NURSE: Ah, mocker! that's the dog's name. R is for the- No; I know it begins with some other letter; and she hath the prettiest

sententtious of it, of you and rosemary, that it would do you good to hear it.

ROMEO: Commend me to thy lady.

NURSE: Ay, a thousand times.

Exit Romeo. Peter!

PETER: Anon.

NURSE: Peter, take my fan, and go before, and apace.

Exeunt.

ACT II. SCENE V. Capulet's Orchard.

Enter Juliet.

JULIET: The clock struck nine when I did send the nurse;
In half an hour she 'promis'd to return.
Perchance she cannot meet him. That's not so.
O, she is lame! Love's heralds should be thoughts,
Which ten times faster glide than the sun's beams
Driving back shadows over low'ring hills.
Therefore do nimble-pinion'd doves draw Love,
And therefore hath the wind-swift Cupid wings.
Now is the sun upon the highmost hill
Of this day's journey, and from nine till twelve
Is three long hours; yet she is not come.
Had she affections and warm youthful blood,
She would be as swift in motion as a ball;
My words would bandy her to my sweet love,
And his to me,
But old folks, many feign as they were dead-
Unwieldy, slow, heavy and pale as lead.

Enter Nurse and Peter.

O God, she comes! O honey nurse, what news?
Hast thou met with him? Send thy man away.

NURSE: Peter, stay at the gate.

Exit Peter.

JULIET: Now, good sweet nurse- O Lord, why look'st thou sad?
Though news be sad, yet tell them merrily;
If good, thou shamest the music of sweet news
By playing it to me with so sour a face.

NURSE: I am aweary, give me leave awhile.
Fie, how my bones ache! What a jaunce have I had!

JULIET: I would thou hadst my bones, and I thy news.
Nay, come, I pray thee speak. Good, good nurse, speak.

NURSE: Jesu, what haste! Can you not stay awhile?
Do you not see that I am out of breath?

JULIET: How art thou out of breath when thou hast breath
To say to me that thou art out of breath?
The excuse that thou dost make in this delay
Is longer than the tale thou dost excuse.
Is thy news good or bad? Answer to that.
Say either, and I'll stay the circumstance.
Let me be satisfied, is't good or bad?

NURSE: Well, you have made a simple choice; you know not how to choose a man. Romeo? No, not he. Though his face be better than any man's, yet his leg excels all men's; and for a hand and a foot, and a body, though they be not to be talk'd on, yet they are past compare. He is not the flower of courtesy, but, I'll warrant him, as gentle as a lamb. Go thy ways, wench; serve God. What, have you din'd at home?
JULIET: No, no. But all this did I know before.
What says he of our marriage? What of that?
NURSE: Lord, how my head aches! What a head have I!
It beats as it would fall in twenty pieces.
My back o' t' other side,- ah, my back, my back!
Beshrew your heart for sending me about
To catch my death with jauncing up and down!
JULIET: I' faith, I am sorry that thou art not well.
Sweet, sweet, Sweet nurse, tell me, what says my love?
NURSE: Your love says, like an honest gentleman, and a courteous, and a kind, and a handsome; and, I warrant, a virtuous- Where is your mother?
JULIET: Where is my mother? Why, she is within.
Where should she be? How oddly thou repliest!
'Your love says, like an honest gentleman,
"Where is your mother?"'
NURSE: O God's Lady dear!
Are you so hot? Marry come up, I trow.
Is this the poultice for my aching bones?
Henceforward do your messages yourself.
JULIET: Here's such a coil! Come, what says Romeo?
NURSE: Have you got leave to go to shrift to-day?
JULIET: I have.
NURSE: Then hie you hence to Friar Laurence' cell;
There stays a husband to make you a wife.
Now comes the wanton blood up in your cheeks:
They'll be in scarlet straight at any news.
Hie you to church; I must another way,
To fetch a ladder, by the which your love
Must climb a bird's nest soon when it is dark.
I am the drudge, and toil in your delight;
But you shall bear the burthen soon at night.
Go; I'll to dinner; hie you to the cell.
JULIET: Hie to high fortune! Honest nurse, farewell.
Exeunt.

ACT II. SCENE VI. Friar Laurence's Cell.

Enter Friar Laurence and Romeo.
FRIAR: So smile the heavens upon this holy act
That after-hours with sorrow chide us not!
ROMEO: Amen, amen! But come what sorrow can,
It cannot countervail the exchange of joy
That one short minute gives me in her sight.

Do thou but close our hands with holy words,
Then love-devouring death do what he dare-
It is enough I may but call her mine.
FRIAR: These violent delights have violent ends
And in their triumph die, like fire and powder,
Which, as they kiss, consume. The sweetest honey
Is loathsome in his own deliciousness
And in the taste confounds the appetite.
Therefore love moderately: long love doth so;
Too swift arrives as tardy as too slow.
Enter Juliet.
Here comes the lady. O, so light a foot
Will ne'er wear out the everlasting flint.
A lover may bestride the gossamer
That idles in the wanton summer air,
And yet not fall; so light is vanity.
JULIET: Good even to my ghostly confessor.
FRIAR: Romeo shall thank thee, daughter, for us both.
JULIET: As much to him, else is his thanks too much.
ROMEO: Ah, Juliet, if the measure of thy joy
Be heap'd like mine, and that thy skill be more
To blazon it, then sweeten with thy breath
This neighbour air, and let rich music's tongue
Unfold the imagin'd happiness that both
Receive in either by this dear encounter.
JULIET: Conceit, more rich in matter than in words,
Brags of his substance, not of ornament.
They are but beggars that can count their worth;
But my true love is grown to such excess
cannot sum up sum of half my wealth.
FRIAR: Come, come with me, and we will make short work;
For, by your leaves, you shall not stay alone
Till Holy Church incorporate two in one.
Exeunt.

ACT III. SCENE I. A Public Place.

Enter Mercutio, Benvolio, and Men.
BENVOLIO: I pray thee, good Mercutio, let's retire.
The day is hot, the Capulets abroad.
And if we meet, we shall not scape a brawl,
For now, these hot days, is the mad blood stirring.
MERCUTIO: Thou art like one of these fellows that, when he enters the confines of a tavern, claps me his sword upon the table and says 'God send me no need of thee!' and by the operation of the second cup draws him on the drawer, when indeed there is no need.
BENVOLIO: Am I like such a fellow?
MERCUTIO: Come, come, thou art as hot a jack in thy mood as any in Italy; and as soon moved to be moody, and as soon moody to be moved.
BENVOLIO: And what to?

MERCUTIO: Nay, an there were two such, we should have none shortly, for one would kill the other. Thou! why, thou wilt quarrel with a man that hath a hair more or a hair less in his beard than thou hast. Thou wilt quarrel with a man for cracking nuts, having no other reason but because thou hast hazel eyes. What eye but such an eye would spy out such a quarrel? Thy head is as full of quarrels as an egg is full of meat; and yet thy head hath been beaten as addle as an egg for quarrelling. Thou hast quarrell'd with a man for coughing in the street, because he hath wakened thy dog that hath lain asleep in the sun. Didst thou not fall out with a tailor for wearing his new doublet before Easter, with another for tying his new shoes with an old riband? And yet thou wilt tutor me from quarrelling!
BENVOLIO: An I were so apt to quarrel as thou art, any man should buy the fee simple of my life for an hour and a quarter.
MERCUTIO: The fee simple? O simple!
Enter Tybalt and Others.
BENVOLIO: By my head, here come the Capulets.
MERCUTIO: By my heel, I care not.
TYBALT: Follow me close, for I will speak to them.
Gentlemen, good den. A word with one of you.
MERCUTIO: And but one word with one of us?
Couple it with something; make it a word and a blow.
TYBALT: You shall find me apt enough to that, sir, an you will give me occasion.
MERCUTIO: Could you not take some occasion without giving
TYBALT: Mercutio, thou consortest with Romeo.
MERCUTIO: Consort? What, dost thou make us minstrels? An thou make minstrels of us, look to hear nothing but discords. Here's my fiddlestick; here's that shall make you dance. Zounds, consort!
BENVOLIO: We talk here in the public haunt of men.
Either withdraw unto some private place
And reason coldly of your grievances,
Or else depart. Here all eyes gaze on us.
MERCUTIO: Men's eyes were made to look, and let them gaze.
I will not budge for no man's pleasure,
Enter Romeo.
TYBALT: Well, peace be with you, sir. Here comes my man.
MERCUTIO: But I'll be hang'd, sir, if he wear your livery.
Marry, go before to field, he'll be your follower!
Your worship in that sense may call him man.
TYBALT: Romeo, the love I bear thee can afford
No better term than this: thou art a villain.
ROMEO: Tybalt, the reason that I have to love thee
Doth much excuse the appertaining rage
To such a greeting. Villain am I none.
Therefore farewell. I see thou knowest me not.
TYBALT: Boy, this shall not excuse the injuries
That thou hast done me; therefore turn and draw.

ROMEO: I do protest I never injur'd thee,
But love thee better than thou canst devise
Till thou shalt know the reason of my love;
And so good Capulet, which name I tender
As dearly as mine own, be satisfied.
MERCUTIO: O calm, dishonourable, vile submission!
Alla stoccata carries it away. Draws.
Tybalt, you ratcatcher, will you walk?
TYBALT: What wouldst thou have with me?
MERCUTIO: Good King of Cats, nothing but one of your nine lives. That I mean to make bold withal, and, as you shall use me hereafter,
dry-beat the rest of the eight. Will you pluck your sword out of
his pitcher by the ears? Make haste, lest mine be about your ears
ere it be out.
TYBALT: I am for you.
Draws.
ROMEO: Gentle Mercutio, put thy rapier up.
MERCUTIO: Come, sir, your passado!
They Fight.
ROMEO: Draw, Benvolio; beat down their weapons.
Gentlemen, for shame! forbear this outrage!
Tybalt, Mercutio, the Prince expressly hath
Forbid this bandying in Verona streets.
Hold, Tybalt! Good Mercutio!
Tybalt under Romeo's arm thrusts Mercutio in, and flies With His Followers.
MERCUTIO: I am hurt.
A plague o' both your houses! I am sped.
Is he gone and hath nothing?
BENVOLIO: What, art thou hurt?
MERCUTIO: Ay, ay, a scratch, a scratch. Marry, 'tis enough.
Where is my page? Go, villain, fetch a surgeon.
Exit Page.
ROMEO: Courage, man. The hurt cannot be much.
MERCUTIO: No, 'tis not so deep as a well, nor so wide as a church door;
but 'tis enough, 'twill serve. Ask for me to-morrow, and you
shall find me a grave man. I am peppered, I warrant, for this
world. A plague o' both your houses! Zounds, a dog, a rat, a
mouse, a cat, to scratch a man to death! a braggart, a rogue, a
villain, that fights by the book of arithmetic! Why the devil
came you between us? I was hurt under your arm.
ROMEO: I thought all for the best.
MERCUTIO: Help me into some house, Benvolio,
Or I shall faint. A plague o' both your houses!
They have made worms' meat of me. I have it,
And soundly too. Your houses!
Exit. Supported by Benvolio.
ROMEO: This gentleman, the Prince's near ally,
My very friend, hath got this mortal hurt
In my behalf- my reputation stain'd

With Tybalt's slander- Tybalt, that an hour
Hath been my kinsman. O sweet Juliet,
Thy beauty hath made me effeminate
And in my temper soft'ned valour's steel
Enter Benvolio.
BENVOLIO: O Romeo, Romeo, brave Mercutio's dead!
That gallant spirit hath aspir'd the clouds,
Which too untimely here did scorn the earth.
ROMEO: This day's black fate on moe days doth depend;
This but begins the woe others must end.
Enter Tybalt.
BENVOLIO: Here comes the furious Tybalt back again.
ROMEO: Alive in triumph, and Mercutio slain?
Away to heaven respective lenity,
And fire-ey'd fury be my conduct now!
Now, Tybalt, take the 'villain' back again
That late thou gavest me; for Mercutio's soul
Is but a little way above our heads,
Staying for thine to keep him company.
Either thou or I, or both, must go with him.
TYBALT: Thou, wretched boy, that didst consort him here,
Shalt with him hence.
ROMEO: This shall determine that.
They Fight. Tybalt Falls.
BENVOLIO: Romeo, away, be gone!
The citizens are up, and Tybalt slain.
Stand not amaz'd. The Prince will doom thee death
If thou art taken. Hence, be gone, away!
ROMEO: O, I am fortune's fool!
BENVOLIO: Why dost thou stay?
Exit Romeo.
Enter Citizens.
CITIZEN: Which way ran he that kill'd Mercutio?
Tybalt, that murtherer, which way ran he?
BENVOLIO: There lies that Tybalt.
CITIZEN: Up, sir, go with me.
I charge thee in the Prince's name obey.
Enter Prince attended, Old Montague, Capulet, their Wives, and others.
PRINCE: Where are the vile beginners of this fray?
BENVOLIO: O noble Prince. I can discover all
The unlucky manage of this fatal brawl.
There lies the man, slain by young Romeo,
That slew thy kinsman, brave Mercutio.
CAPULET: Wife. Tybalt, my cousin! O my brother's child!
O Prince! O husband! O, the blood is spill'd
Of my dear kinsman! Prince, as thou art true,
For blood of ours shed blood of Montague.
O cousin, cousin!
PRINCE: Benvolio, who began this bloody fray?

BENVOLIO: Tybalt, here slain, whom Romeo's hand did stay.
Romeo, that spoke him fair, bid him bethink
How nice the quarrel was, and urg'd withal
Your high displeasure. All this- uttered
With gentle breath, calm look, knees humbly bow'd-
Could not take truce with the unruly spleen
Of Tybalt deaf to peace, but that he tilts
With piercing steel at bold Mercutio's breast;
Who, all as hot, turns deadly point to point,
And, with a martial scorn, with one hand beats
Cold death aside and with the other sends
It back to Tybalt, whose dexterity
Retorts it. Romeo he cries aloud,
'Hold, friends! friends, part!' and swifter than his tongue,
His agile arm beats down their fatal points,
And 'twixt them rushes; underneath whose arm
An envious thrust from Tybalt hit the life
Of stout Mercutio, and then Tybalt fled;
But by-and-by comes back to Romeo,
Who had but newly entertain'd revenge,
And to't they go like lightning; for, ere I
Could draw to part them, was stout Tybalt slain;
And, as he fell, did Romeo turn and fly.
This is the truth, or let Benvolio die.
CAPULET: Wife. He is a kinsman to the Montague;
Affection makes him false, he speaks not true.
Some twenty of them fought in this black strife,
And all those twenty could but kill one life.
I beg for justice, which thou, Prince, must give.
Romeo slew Tybalt; Romeo must not live.
PRINCE: Romeo slew him; he slew Mercutio.
Who now the price of his dear blood doth owe?
MONTAGUE: Not Romeo, Prince; he was Mercutio's friend;
His fault concludes but what the law should end,
The life of Tybalt.
PRINCE: And for that offence
Immediately we do exile him hence.
I have an interest in your hate's proceeding,
My blood for your rude brawls doth lie a-bleeding;
But I'll amerce you with so strong a fine
That you shall all repent the loss of mine.
I will be deaf to pleading and excuses;
Nor tears nor prayers shall purchase out abuses.
Therefore use none. Let Romeo hence in haste,
Else, when he is found, that hour is his last.
Bear hence this body, and attend our will.
Mercy but murders, pardoning those that kill.
Exeunt.

ACT III. SCENE II. Capulet's Orchard.

Enter Juliet alone.
JULIET: Gallop apace, you fiery-footed steeds,
Towards Phoebus' lodging! Such a wagoner
As Phaeton would whip you to the West
And bring in cloudy night immediately.
Spread thy close curtain, love-performing night,
That runaway eyes may wink, and Romeo
Leap to these arms untalk'd of and unseen.
Lovers can see to do their amorous rites
By their own beauties; or, if love be blind,
It best agrees with night. Come, civil night,
Thou sober-suited matron, all in black,
And learn me how to lose a winning match,
Play'd for a pair of stainless maidenhoods.
Hood my unmann'd blood, bating in my cheeks,
With thy black mantle till strange love, grown bold,
Think true love acted simple modesty.
Come, night; come, Romeo; come, thou day in night;
For thou wilt lie upon the wings of night
Whiter than new snow upon a raven's back.
Come, gentle night; come, loving, black-brow'd night;
Give me my Romeo; and, when he shall die,
Take him and cut him out in little stars,
And he will make the face of heaven so fine
That all the world will be in love with night
And pay no worship to the garish sun.
O, I have bought the mansion of a love,
But not possess'd it; and though I am sold,
Not yet enjoy'd. So tedious is this day
As is the night before some festival
To an impatient child that hath new robes
And may not wear them. O, here comes my nurse,
Enter Nurse, with Cords.
And she brings news; and every tongue that speaks
But Romeo's name speaks heavenly eloquence.
Now, nurse, what news? What hast thou there? the cords
That Romeo bid thee fetch?
NURSE: Ay, ay, the cords.
Throws Them Down.
JULIET: Ay me! what news? Why dost thou wring thy hands
NURSE: Ah, weraday! he's dead, he's dead, he's dead!
We are undone, lady, we are undone!
Alack the day! he's gone, he's kill'd, he's dead!
JULIET: Can heaven be so envious?
NURSE: Romeo can,
Though heaven cannot. O Romeo, Romeo!
Who ever would have thought it? Romeo!
JULIET: What devil art thou that dost torment me thus?
This torture should be roar'd in dismal hell.

Hath Romeo slain himself? Say thou but 'I,'
And that bare vowel 'I' shall poison more
Than the death-darting eye of cockatrice.
I am not I, if there be such an 'I';
Or those eyes shut that make thee answer 'I.'
If be be slain, say 'I'; or if not, 'no.'
Brief sounds determine of my weal or woe.
NURSE: I saw the wound, I saw it with mine eyes,
(God save the mark!) here on his manly breast.
A piteous corse, a bloody piteous corse;
Pale, pale as ashes, all bedaub'd in blood,
All in gore-blood. I swounded at the sight.
JULIET: O, break, my heart! poor bankrout, break at once!
To prison, eyes; ne'er look on liberty!
Vile earth, to earth resign; end motion here,
And thou and Romeo press one heavy bier!
NURSE: O Tybalt, Tybalt, the best friend I had!
O courteous Tybalt! honest gentleman
That ever I should live to see thee dead!
JULIET: What storm is this that blows so contrary?
Is Romeo slaught'red, and is Tybalt dead?
My dear-lov'd cousin, and my dearer lord?
Then, dreadful trumpet, sound the general doom!
For who is living, if those two are gone?
NURSE: Tybalt is gone, and Romeo banished;
Romeo that kill'd him, he is banished.
JULIET: O God! Did Romeo's hand shed Tybalt's blood?
NURSE: It did, it did! alas the day, it did!
JULIET: O serpent heart, hid with a flow'ring face!
Did ever dragon keep so fair a cave?
Beautiful tyrant! fiend angelical!
Dove-feather'd raven! wolvish-ravening lamb!
Despised substance of divinest show!
Just opposite to what thou justly seem'st-
A damned saint, an honourable villain!
O nature, what hadst thou to do in hell
When thou didst bower the spirit of a fiend
In mortal paradise of such sweet flesh?
Was ever book containing such vile matter
So fairly bound? O, that deceit should dwell
In such a gorgeous palace!
NURSE: There's no trust,
No faith, no honesty in men; all perjur'd,
All forsworn, all naught, all dissemblers.
Ah, where's my man? Give me some aqua vitae.
These griefs, these woes, these sorrows make me old.
Shame come to Romeo!
JULIET: Blister'd be thy tongue
For such a wish! He was not born to shame.

Upon his brow shame is asham'd to sit;
For 'tis a throne where honour may be crown'd
Sole monarch of the universal earth.
O, what a beast was I to chide at him!
NURSE: Will you speak well of him that kill'd your cousin?
JULIET: Shall I speak ill of him that is my husband?
Ah, poor my lord, what tongue shall smooth thy name
When I, thy three-hours wife, have mangled it?
But wherefore, villain, didst thou kill my cousin?
That villain cousin would have kill'd my husband.
Back, foolish tears, back to your native spring!
Your tributary drops belong to woe,
Which you, mistaking, offer up to joy.
My husband lives, that Tybalt would have slain;
And Tybalt's dead, that would have slain my husband.
All this is comfort; wherefore weep I then?
Some word there was, worser than Tybalt's death,
That murd'red me. I would forget it fain;
But O, it presses to my memory
Like damned guilty deeds to sinners' minds!
'Tybalt is dead, and Romeo- banished.'
That 'banished,' that one word 'banished,'
Hath slain ten thousand Tybalts. Tybalt's death
Was woe enough, if it had ended there;
Or, if sour woe delights in fellowship
And needly will be rank'd with other griefs,
Why followed not, when she said 'Tybalt's dead,'
Thy father, or thy mother, nay, or both,
Which modern lamentation might have mov'd?
But with a rearward following Tybalt's death,
'Romeo is banished'- to speak that word
Is father, mother, Tybalt, Romeo, Juliet,
All slain, all dead. 'Romeo is banished'-
There is no end, no limit, measure, bound,
In that word's death; no words can that woe sound.
Where is my father and my mother, nurse?
NURSE: Weeping and wailing over Tybalt's corse.
Will you go to them? I will bring you thither.
JULIET: Wash they his wounds with tears? Mine shall be spent,
When theirs are dry, for Romeo's banishment.
Take up those cords. Poor ropes, you are beguil'd,
Both you and I, for Romeo is exil'd.
He made you for a highway to my bed;
But I, a maid, die maiden-widowed.
Come, cords; come, nurse. I'll to my wedding bed;
And death, not Romeo, take my maidenhead!
NURSE: Hie to your chamber. I'll find Romeo
To comfort you. I wot well where he is.
Hark ye, your Romeo will be here at night.

I'll to him; he is hid at Laurence' cell.
JULIET: O, find him! give this ring to my true knight
And bid him come to take his last farewell.
Exeunt.

ACT III. SCENE III. Friar Laurence's Cell.

Enter Friar Laurence.
FRIAR: Romeo, come forth; come forth, thou fearful man.
Affliction is enanmour'd of thy parts,
And thou art wedded to calamity.
Enter Romeo.
ROMEO: Father, what news? What is the Prince's doom
What sorrow craves acquaintance at my hand
That I yet know not?
FRIAR: Too familiar
Is my dear son with such sour company.
I bring thee tidings of the Prince's doom.
ROMEO: What less than doomsday is the Prince's doom?
FRIAR: A gentler judgment vanish'd from his lips-
Not body's death, but body's banishment.
ROMEO: Ha, banishment? Be merciful, say 'death';
For exile hath more terror in his look,
Much more than death. Do not say 'banishment.'
FRIAR: Hence from Verona art thou banished.
Be patient, for the world is broad and wide.
ROMEO: There is no world without Verona walls,
But purgatory, torture, hell itself.
Hence banished is banish'd from the world,
And world's exile is death. Then 'banishment'
Is death misterm'd. Calling death 'banishment,'
Thou cut'st my head off with a golden axe
And smilest upon the stroke that murders me.
FRIAR: O deadly sin! O rude unthankfulness!
Thy fault our law calls death; but the kind Prince,
Taking thy part, hath rush'd aside the law,
And turn'd that black word death to banishment.
This is dear mercy, and thou seest it not.
ROMEO: 'Tis torture, and not mercy. Heaven is here,
Where Juliet lives; and every cat and dog
And little mouse, every unworthy thing,
Live here in heaven and may look on her;
But Romeo may not. More validity,
More honourable state, more courtship lives
In carrion flies than Romeo. They may seize
On the white wonder of dear Juliet's hand
And steal immortal blessing from her lips,
Who, even in pure and vestal modesty,
Still blush, as thinking their own kisses sin;
But Romeo may not- he is banished.
This may flies do, when I from this must fly;

They are free men, but I am banished.
And sayest thou yet that exile is not death?
Hadst thou no poison mix'd, no sharp-ground knife,
No sudden mean of death, though ne'er so mean,
But 'banished' to kill me- 'banished'?
O friar, the damned use that word in hell;
Howling attends it! How hast thou the heart,
Being a divine, a ghostly confessor,
A sin-absolver, and my friend profess'd,
To mangle me with that word 'banished'?
FRIAR: Thou fond mad man, hear me a little speak.
ROMEO: O, thou wilt speak again of banishment.
FRIAR: I'll give thee armour to keep off that word;
Adversity's sweet milk, philosophy,
To comfort thee, though thou art banished.
ROMEO: Yet 'banished'? Hang up philosophy!
Unless philosophy can make a Juliet,
Displant a town, reverse a prince's doom,
It helps not, it prevails not. Talk no more.
FRIAR: O, then I see that madmen have no ears.
ROMEO: How should they, when that wise men have no eyes?
FRIAR: Let me dispute with thee of thy estate.
ROMEO: Thou canst not speak of that thou dost not feel.
Wert thou as young as I, Juliet thy love,
An hour but married, Tybalt murdered,
Doting like me, and like me banished,
Then mightst thou speak, then mightst thou tear thy hair,
And fall upon the ground, as I do now,
Taking the measure of an unmade grave.
Knock Within.
FRIAR: Arise; one knocks. Good Romeo, hide thyself.
ROMEO: Not I; unless the breath of heartsick groans,
Mist-like infold me from the search of eyes. Knock.
FRIAR: Hark, how they knock! Who's there? Romeo, arise;
Thou wilt be taken.- Stay awhile!- Stand up; Knock.
Run to my study.- By-and-by!- God's will,
What simpleness is this.- I come, I come! Knock.
Who knocks so hard? Whence come you? What's your will
NURSE: Within Let me come in, and you shall know my errand.
I come from Lady Juliet.
FRIAR: Welcome then.
Enter Nurse.
NURSE: O holy friar, O, tell me, holy friar
Where is my lady's lord, where's Romeo?
FRIAR: There on the ground, with his own tears made drunk.
NURSE: O, he is even in my mistress' case,
Just in her case!
FRIAR: O woeful sympathy!
Piteous predicament!

NURSE: Even so lies she,
Blubb'ring and weeping, weeping and blubbering.
Stand up, stand up! Stand, an you be a man.
For Juliet's sake, for her sake, rise and stand!
Why should you fall into so deep an O?
ROMEO: (rises) Nurse-
NURSE: Ah sir! ah sir! Well, death's the end of all.
ROMEO: Spakest thou of Juliet? How is it with her?
Doth not she think me an old murtherer,
Now I have stain'd the childhood of our joy
With blood remov'd but little from her own?
Where is she? and how doth she! and what says
My conceal'd lady to our cancell'd love?
NURSE: O, she says nothing, sir, but weeps and weeps;
And now falls on her bed, and then starts up,
And Tybalt calls; and then on Romeo cries,
And then down falls again.
ROMEO: As if that name,
Shot from the deadly level of a gun,
Did murther her; as that name's cursed hand
Murder'd her kinsman. O, tell me, friar, tell me,
In what vile part of this anatomy
Doth my name lodge? Tell me, that I may sack
The hateful mansion.
Draws His Dagger.
FRIAR: Hold thy desperate hand.
Art thou a man? Thy form cries out thou art;
Thy tears are womanish, thy wild acts denote
The unreasonable fury of a beast.
Unseemly woman in a seeming man!
Or ill-beseeming beast in seeming both!
Thou hast amaz'd me. By my holy order,
I thought thy disposition better temper'd.
Hast thou slain Tybalt? Wilt thou slay thyself?
And slay thy lady that in thy life lives,
By doing damned hate upon thyself?
Why railest thou on thy birth, the heaven, and earth?
Since birth and heaven and earth, all three do meet
In thee at once; which thou at once wouldst lose.
Fie, fie, thou shamest thy shape, thy love, thy wit,
Which, like a usurer, abound'st in all,
And usest none in that true use indeed
Which should bedeck thy shape, thy love, thy wit.
Thy noble shape is but a form of wax
Digressing from the valour of a man;
Thy dear love sworn but hollow perjury,
Killing that love which thou hast vow'd to cherish;
Thy wit, that ornament to shape and love,
Misshapen in the conduct of them both,

Like powder in a skilless soldier's flask,
is get afire by thine own ignorance,
And thou dismemb'red with thine own defence.
What, rouse thee, man! Thy Juliet is alive,
For whose dear sake thou wast but lately dead.
There art thou happy. Tybalt would kill thee,
But thou slewest Tybalt. There art thou happy too.
The law, that threat'ned death, becomes thy friend
And turns it to exile. There art thou happy.
A pack of blessings light upon thy back;
Happiness courts thee in her best array;
But, like a misbhav'd and sullen wench,
Thou pout'st upon thy fortune and thy love.
Take heed, take heed, for such die miserable.
Go get thee to thy love, as was decreed,
Ascend her chamber, hence and comfort her.
But look thou stay not till the watch be set,
For then thou canst not pass to Mantua,
Where thou shalt live till we can find a time
To blaze your marriage, reconcile your friends,
Beg pardon of the Prince, and call thee back
With twenty hundred thousand times more joy
Than thou went'st forth in lamentation.
Go before, nurse. Commend me to thy lady,
And bid her hasten all the house to bed,
Which heavy sorrow makes them apt unto.
Romeo is coming.
NURSE: O Lord, I could have stay'd here all the night
To hear good counsel. O, what learning is!
My lord, I'll tell my lady you will come.
ROMEO: Do so, and bid my sweet prepare to chide.
NURSE: Here is a ring she bid me give you, sir.
Hie you, make haste, for it grows very late.
  Exit.
ROMEO: How well my comfort is reviv'd by this!
FRIAR: Go hence; good night; and here stands all your state:
Either be gone before the watch be set,
Or by the break of day disguis'd from hence.
Sojourn in Mantua. I'll find out your man,
And he shall signify from time to time
Every good hap to you that chances here.
Give me thy hand. 'Tis late. Farewell; good night.
ROMEO: But that a joy past joy calls out on me,
It were a grief so brief to part with thee.
Farewell.
  Exeunt.

ACT III. SCENE IV. Capulet's House

  Enter Old Capulet, His Wife, and Paris.
CAPULET: Things have fall'n out, sir, so unluckily

That we have had no time to move our daughter.
Look you, she lov'd her kinsman Tybalt dearly,
And so did I. Well, we were born to die.
'Tis very late; she'll not come down to-night.
I promise you, but for your company,
I would have been abed an hour ago.
PARIS: These times of woe afford no tune to woo.
Madam, good night. Commend me to your daughter.
LADY: I will, and know her mind early to-morrow;
To-night she's mew'd up to her heaviness.
CAPULET: Sir Paris, I will make a desperate tender
Of my child's love. I think she will be rul'd
In all respects by me; nay more, I doubt it not.
Wife, go you to her ere you go to bed;
Acquaint her here of my son Paris' love
And bid her (mark you me?) on Wednesday next-
But, soft! what day is this?
PARIS: Monday, my lord.
CAPULET: Monday! ha, ha! Well, Wednesday is too soon.
Thursday let it be- a Thursday, tell her
She shall be married to this noble earl.
Will you be ready? Do you like this haste?
We'll keep no great ado- a friend or two;
For hark you, Tybalt being slain so late,
It may be thought we held him carelessly,
Being our kinsman, if we revel much.
Therefore we'll have some half a dozen friends,
And there an end. But what say you to Thursday?
PARIS: My lord, I would that Thursday were to-morrow.
CAPULET: Well, get you gone. A Thursday be it then.
Go you to Juliet ere you go to bed;
Prepare her, wife, against this wedding day.
Farewell, My lord.- Light to my chamber, ho!
Afore me, It is so very very late
That we may call it early by-and-by.
Good night.
Exeunt

ACT III. SCENE V. Capulet's Orchard.

Enter Romeo and Juliet Aloft, at the Window.
JULIET: Wilt thou be gone? It is not yet near day.
It was the nightingale, and not the lark,
That pierc'd the fearful hollow of thine ear.
Nightly she sings on yond pomegranate tree.
Believe me, love, it was the nightingale.
ROMEO: It was the lark, the herald of the morn;
No nightingale. Look, love, what envious streaks
Do lace the severing clouds in yonder East.
Night's candles are burnt out, and jocund day
Stands tiptoe on the misty mountain tops.

I must be gone and live, or stay and die.
JULIET: Yond light is not daylight; I know it, I.
It is some meteor that the sun exhales
To be to thee this night a torchbearer
And light thee on the way to Mantua.
Therefore stay yet; thou need'st not to be gone.
ROMEO: Let me be ta'en, let me be put to death.
I am content, so thou wilt have it so.
I'll say yon grey is not the morning's eye,
'Tis but the pale reflex of Cynthia's brow;
Nor that is not the lark whose notes do beat
The vaulty heaven so high above our heads.
I have more care to stay than will to go.
Come, death, and welcome! Juliet wills it so.
How is't, my soul? Let's talk; it is not day.
JULIET: It is, it is! Hie hence, be gone, away!
It is the lark that sings so out of tune,
Straining harsh discords and unpleasing sharps.
Some say the lark makes sweet division;
This doth not so, for she divideth us.
Some say the lark and loathed toad chang'd eyes;
O, now I would they had chang'd voices too,
Since arm from arm that voice doth us affray,
Hunting thee hence with hunt's-up to the day!
O, now be gone! More light and light it grows.
ROMEO: More light and light- more dark and dark our woes!
Enter Nurse.
NURSE: Madam!
JULIET: Nurse?
NURSE: Your lady mother is coming to your chamber.
The day is broke; be wary, look about.
JULIET: Then, window, let day in, and let life out.
Exit.
ROMEO: Farewell, farewell! One kiss, and I'll descend.
He Goeth Down.
JULIET: Art thou gone so, my lord, my love, my friend?
I must hear from thee every day in the hour,
For in a minute there are many days.
O, by this count I shall be much in years
Ere I again behold my Romeo!
ROMEO: Farewell!
I will omit no opportunity
That may convey my greetings, love, to thee.
JULIET: O, think'st thou we shall ever meet again?
ROMEO: I doubt it not; and all these woes shall serve
For sweet discourses in our time to come.
JULIET: O God, I have an ill-divining soul!
Methinks I see thee, now thou art below,
As one dead in the bottom of a tomb.

Either my eyesight fails, or thou look'st pale.
ROMEO: And trust me, love, in my eye so do you.
Dry sorrow drinks our blood. Adieu, adieu!
Exit.
JULIET: O Fortune, Fortune! all men call thee fickle.
If thou art fickle, what dost thou with him
That is renown'd for faith? Be fickle, Fortune,
For then I hope thou wilt not keep him long
But send him back.
LADY: Within Ho, daughter! are you up?
JULIET: Who is't that calls? It is my lady mother.
Is she not down so late, or up so early?
What unaccustom'd cause procures her hither?
Enter Mother.
LADY: Why, how now, Juliet?
JULIET: Madam, I am not well.
LADY: Evermore weeping for your cousin's death?
What, wilt thou wash him from his grave with tears?
An if thou couldst, thou couldst not make him live.
Therefore have done. Some grief shows much of love;
But much of grief shows still some want of wit.
JULIET: Yet let me weep for such a feeling loss.
LADY: So shall you feel the loss, but not the friend
Which you weep for.
JULIET: Feeling so the loss,
I cannot choose but ever weep the friend.
LADY: Well, girl, thou weep'st not so much for his death
As that the villain lives which slaughter'd him.
JULIET: What villain, madam?
LADY: That same villain Romeo.
JULIET: Aside Villain and he be many miles asunder.-
God pardon him! I do, with all my heart;
And yet no man like he doth grieve my heart.
LADY: That is because the traitor murderer lives.
JULIET: Ay, madam, from the reach of these my hands.
Would none but I might venge my cousin's death!
LADY: We will have vengeance for it, fear thou not.
Then weep no more. I'll send to one in Mantua,
Where that same banish'd runagate doth live,
Shall give him such an unaccustom'd dram
That he shall soon keep Tybalt company;
And then I hope thou wilt be satisfied.
JULIET: Indeed I never shall be satisfied
With Romeo till I behold him- dead-
Is my poor heart so for a kinsman vex'd.
Madam, if you could find out but a man
To bear a poison, I would temper it;
That Romeo should, upon receipt thereof,
Soon sleep in quiet. O, how my heart abhors

To hear him nam'd and cannot come to him,
To wreak the love I bore my cousin Tybalt
Upon his body that hath slaughter'd him!
LADY: Find thou the means, and I'll find such a man.
But now I'll tell thee joyful tidings, girl.
JULIET: And joy comes well in such a needy time.
What are they, I beseech your ladyship?
LADY: Well, well, thou hast a careful father, child;
One who, to put thee from thy heaviness,
Hath sorted out a sudden day of joy
That thou expects not nor I look'd not for.
JULIET: Madam, in happy time! What day is that?
LADY: Marry, my child, early next Thursday morn
The gallant, young, and noble gentleman,
The County Paris, at Saint Peter's Church,
Shall happily make thee there a joyful bride.
JULIET: Now by Saint Peter's Church, and Peter too,
He shall not make me there a joyful bride!
I wonder at this haste, that I must wed
Ere he that should be husband comes to woo.
I pray you tell my lord and father, madam,
I will not marry yet; and when I do, I swear
It shall be Romeo, whom you know I hate,
Rather than Paris. These are news indeed!
LADY: Here comes your father. Tell him so yourself,
And see how be will take it at your hands.
Enter Capulet and Nurse.
CAPULET: When the sun sets the air doth drizzle dew,
But for the sunset of my brother's son
It rains downright.
How now? a conduit, girl? What, still in tears?
Evermore show'ring? In one little body
Thou counterfeit'st a bark, a sea, a wind:
For still thy eyes, which I may call the sea,
Do ebb and flow with tears; the bark thy body is
Sailing in this salt flood; the winds, thy sighs,
Who, raging with thy tears and they with them,
Without a sudden calm will overset
Thy tempest-tossed body. How now, wife?
Have you delivered to her our decree?
LADY: Ay, sir; but she will none, she gives you thanks.
I would the fool were married to her grave!
CAPULET: Soft! take me with you, take me with you, wife.
How? Will she none? Doth she not give us thanks?
Is she not proud? Doth she not count her blest,
Unworthy as she is, that we have wrought
So worthy a gentleman to be her bridegroom?
JULIET: Not proud you have, but thankful that you have.
Proud can I never be of what I hate,

But thankful even for hate that is meant love.
CAPULET: How, how, how, how, choplogic? What is this?
'Proud'- and 'I thank you'- and 'I thank you not'-
And yet 'not proud'? Mistress minion you,
Thank me no thankings, nor proud me no prouds,
But fettle your fine joints 'gainst Thursday next
To go with Paris to Saint Peter's Church,
Or I will drag thee on a hurdle thither.
Out, you green-sickness carrion I out, you baggage!
You tallow-face!
LADY: Fie, fie! what, are you mad?
JULIET: Good father, I beseech you on my knees,
Hear me with patience but to speak a word.
CAPULET: Hang thee, young baggage! disobedient wretch!
I tell thee what- get thee to church a Thursday
Or never after look me in the face.
Speak not, reply not, do not answer me!
My fingers itch. Wife, we scarce thought us blest
That God had lent us but this only child;
But now I see this one is one too much,
And that we have a curse in having her.
Out on her, hilding!
NURSE: God in heaven bless her!
You are to blame, my lord, to rate her so.
CAPULET: And why, my Lady Wisdom? Hold your tongue,
Good Prudence. Smatter with your gossips, go!
NURSE: I speak no treason.
CAPULET: O, God-i-god-en!
NURSE: May not one speak?
CAPULET: Peace, you mumbling fool!
Utter your gravity o'er a gossip's bowl,
For here we need it not.
LADY: You are too hot.
CAPULET: God's bread I it makes me mad. Day, night, late, early,
At home, abroad, alone, in company,
Waking or sleeping, still my care hath been
To have her match'd; and having now provided
A gentleman of princely parentage,
Of fair demesnes, youthful, and nobly train'd,
Stuff'd, as they say, with honourable parts,
Proportion'd as one's thought would wish a man-
And then to have a wretched puling fool,
A whining mammet, in her fortune's tender,
To answer 'I'll not wed, I cannot love;
I am too young, I pray you pardon me'!
But, an you will not wed, I'll pardon you.
Graze where you will, you shall not house with me.
Look to't, think on't; I do not use to jest.
Thursday is near; lay hand on heart, advise:

An you be mine, I'll give you to my friend;
An you be not, hang, beg, starve, die in the streets,
For, by my soul, I'll ne'er acknowledge thee,
Nor what is mine shall never do thee good.
Trust to't. Bethink you. I'll not be forsworn.
Exit.
JULIET: Is there no pity sitting in the clouds
That sees into the bottom of my grief?
O sweet my mother, cast me not away!
Delay this marriage for a month, a week;
Or if you do not, make the bridal bed
In that dim monument where Tybalt lies.
LADY: Talk not to me, for I'll not speak a word.
Do as thou wilt, for I have done with thee.
Exit.
JULIET: O God!- O nurse, how shall this be prevented?
My husband is on earth, my faith in heaven.
How shall that faith return again to earth
Unless that husband send it me from heaven
By leaving earth? Comfort me, counsel me.
Alack, alack, that heaven should practise stratagems
Upon so soft a subject as myself!
What say'st thou? Hast thou not a word of joy?
Some comfort, nurse.
NURSE: Faith, here it is.
Romeo is banish'd; and all the world to nothing
That he dares ne'er come back to challenge you;
Or if he do, it needs must be by stealth.
Then, since the case so stands as now it doth,
I think it best you married with the County.
O, he's a lovely gentleman!
Romeo's a dishclout to him. An eagle, madam,
Hath not so green, so quick, so fair an eye
As Paris hath. Beshrew my very heart,
I think you are happy in this second match,
For it excels your first; or if it did not,
Your first is dead- or 'twere as good he were
As living here and you no use of him.
JULIET: Speak'st thou this from thy heart?
NURSE: And from my soul too; else beshrew them both.
JULIET: Amen!
NURSE: What?
JULIET: Well, thou hast comforted me marvellous much.
Go in; and tell my lady I am gone,
Having displeas'd my father, to Laurence' cell,
To make confession and to be absolv'd.
NURSE: Marry, I will; and this is wisely done.
Exit.
JULIET: Ancient damnation! O most wicked fiend!

Is it more sin to wish me thus forsworn,
Or to dispraise my lord with that same tongue
Which she hath prais'd him with above compare
So many thousand times? Go, counsellor!
Thou and my bosom henceforth shall be twain.
I'll to the friar to know his remedy.
If all else fail, myself have power to die.
Exit.

ACT IV. SCENE I. Friar Laurence's Cell.

Enter Friar, Laurence and County Paris.
FRIAR: On Thursday, sir? The time is very short.
PARIS: My father Capulet will have it so,
And I am nothing slow to slack his haste.
FRIAR: You say you do not know the lady's mind.
Uneven is the course; I like it not.
PARIS: Immoderately she weeps for Tybalt's death,
And therefore have I little talk'd of love;
For Venus smiles not in a house of tears.
Now, sir, her father counts it dangerous
That she do give her sorrow so much sway,
And in his wisdom hastes our marriage
To stop the inundation of her tears,
Which, too much minded by herself alone,
May be put from her by society.
Now do you know the reason of this haste.
FRIAR: Aside I would I knew not why it should be slow'd.-
Look, sir, here comes the lady toward my cell.
Enter Juliet.
PARIS: Happily met, my lady and my wife!
JULIET: That may be, sir, when I may be a wife.
PARIS: That may be must be, love, on Thursday next.
JULIET: What must be shall be.
FRIAR: That's a certain text.
PARIS: Come you to make confession to this father?
JULIET: To answer that, I should confess to you.
PARIS: Do not deny to him that you love me.
JULIET: I will confess to you that I love him.
PARIS: So will ye, I am sure, that you love me.
JULIET: If I do so, it will be of more price,
Being spoke behind your back, than to your face.
PARIS: Poor soul, thy face is much abus'd with tears.
JULIET: The tears have got small victory by that,
For it was bad enough before their spite.
PARIS: Thou wrong'st it more than tears with that report.
JULIET: That is no slander, sir, which is a truth;
And what I spake, I spake it to my face.
PARIS: Thy face is mine, and thou hast sland'red it.
JULIET: It may be so, for it is not mine own.
Are you at leisure, holy father, now,

Or shall I come to you at evening mass
FRIAR: My leisure serves me, pensive daughter, now.
My lord, we must entreat the time alone.
PARIS: God shield I should disturb devotion!
Juliet, on Thursday early will I rouse ye.
Till then, adieu, and keep this holy kiss.
Exit.
JULIET: O, shut the door! and when thou hast done so,
Come weep with me- past hope, past cure, past help!
FRIAR: Ah, Juliet, I already know thy grief;
It strains me past the compass of my wits.
I hear thou must, and nothing may prorogue it,
On Thursday next be married to this County.
JULIET: Tell me not, friar, that thou hear'st of this,
Unless thou tell me how I may prevent it.
If in thy wisdom thou canst give no help,
Do thou but call my resolution wise
And with this knife I'll help it presently.
God join'd my heart and Romeo's, thou our hands;
And ere this hand, by thee to Romeo's seal'd,
Shall be the label to another deed,
Or my true heart with treacherous revolt
Turn to another, this shall slay them both.
Therefore, out of thy long-experienc'd time,
Give me some present counsel; or, behold,
'Twixt my extremes and me this bloody knife
Shall play the empire, arbitrating that
Which the commission of thy years and art
Could to no issue of true honour bring.
Be not so long to speak. I long to die
If what thou speak'st speak not of remedy.
FRIAR: Hold, daughter. I do spy a kind of hope,
Which craves as desperate an execution
As that is desperate which we would prevent.
If, rather than to marry County Paris
Thou hast the strength of will to slay thyself,
Then is it likely thou wilt undertake
A thing like death to chide away this shame,
That cop'st with death himself to scape from it;
And, if thou dar'st, I'll give thee remedy.
JULIET: O, bid me leap, rather than marry Paris,
From off the battlements of yonder tower,
Or walk in thievish ways, or bid me lurk
Where serpents are; chain me with roaring bears,
Or shut me nightly in a charnel house,
O'ercover'd quite with dead men's rattling bones,
With reeky shanks and yellow chapless skulls;
Or bid me go into a new-made grave
And hide me with a dead man in his shroud-

Things that, to hear them told, have made me tremble-
And I will do it without fear or doubt,
To live an unstain'd wife to my sweet love.
FRIAR: Hold, then. Go home, be merry, give consent
To marry Paris. Wednesday is to-morrow.
To-morrow night look that thou lie alone;
Let not the nurse lie with thee in thy chamber.
Take thou this vial, being then in bed,
And this distilled liquor drink thou off;
When presently through all thy veins shall run
A cold and drowsy humour; for no pulse
Shall keep his native progress, but surcease;
No warmth, no breath, shall testify thou livest;
The roses in thy lips and cheeks shall fade
To paly ashes, thy eyes' windows fall
Like death when he shuts up the day of life;
Each part, depriv'd of supple government,
Shall, stiff and stark and cold, appear like death;
And in this borrowed likeness of shrunk death
Thou shalt continue two-and-forty hours,
And then awake as from a pleasant sleep.
Now, when the bridegroom in the morning comes
To rouse thee from thy bed, there art thou dead.
Then, as the manner of our country is,
In thy best robes uncovered on the bier
Thou shalt be borne to that same ancient vault
Where all the kindred of the Capulets lie.
In the mean time, against thou shalt awake,
Shall Romeo by my letters know our drift;
And hither shall he come; and he and I
Will watch thy waking, and that very night
Shall Romeo bear thee hence to Mantua.
And this shall free thee from this present shame,
If no inconstant toy nor womanish fear
Abate thy valour in the acting it.
JULIET: Give me, give me! O, tell not me of fear!
FRIAR: Hold! Get you gone, be strong and prosperous
In this resolve. I'll send a friar with speed
To Mantua, with my letters to thy lord.
JULIET: Love give me strength! and strength shall help afford.
Farewell, dear father.
Exeunt.

ACT IV. SCENE II. Capulet's House.

Enter Father Capulet, Mother, Nurse, and Servingmen, two or three.
CAPULET: So many guests invite as here are writ.
Exit a Servingman.
Sirrah, go hire me twenty cunning cooks.
SERVANT: You shall have none ill, sir; for I'll try if they can lick
their fingers.

CAPULET: How canst thou try them so?
SERVANT: Marry, sir, 'tis an ill cook that cannot lick his own fingers. Therefore he that cannot lick his fingers goes not with me.
CAPULET: Go, begone.
Exit Servingman.
We shall be much unfurnish'd for this time.
What, is my daughter gone to Friar Laurence?
NURSE: Ay, forsooth.
CAPULET: Well, be may chance to do some good on her.
A peevish self-will'd harlotry it is.
Enter Juliet.
NURSE: See where she comes from shrift with merry look.
CAPULET: How now, my headstrong? Where have you been gadding?
JULIET: Where I have learnt me to repent the sin
Of disobedient opposition
To you and your behests, and am enjoin'd
By holy Laurence to fall prostrate here
To beg your pardon. Pardon, I beseech you!
Henceforward I am ever rul'd by you.
CAPULET: Send for the County. Go tell him of this.
I'll have this knot knit up to-morrow morning.
JULIET: I met the youthful lord at Laurence' cell
And gave him what becomed love I might,
Not stepping o'er the bounds of modesty.
CAPULET: Why, I am glad on't. This is well. Stand up.
This is as't should be. Let me see the County.
Ay, marry, go, I say, and fetch him hither.
Now, afore God, this reverend holy friar,
All our whole city is much bound to him.
JULIET: Nurse, will you go with me into my closet
To help me sort such needful ornaments
As you think fit to furnish me to-morrow?
MOTHER: No, not till Thursday. There is time enough.
CAPULET: Go, nurse, go with her. We'll to church to-morrow.
Exeunt Juliet and Nurse.
MOTHER: We shall be short in our provision.
'Tis now near night.
CAPULET: Tush, I will stir about,
And all things shall be well, I warrant thee, wife.
Go thou to Juliet, help to deck up her.
I'll not to bed to-night; let me alone.
I'll play the housewife for this once. What, ho!
They are all forth; well, I will walk myself
To County Paris, to prepare him up
Against to-morrow. My heart is wondrous light,
Since this same wayward girl is so reclaim'd.
Exeunt.

ACT IV. SCENE III. Juliet's Chamber.

Enter Juliet and Nurse.

JULIET: Ay, those attires are best; but, gentle nurse,
I pray thee leave me to myself to-night;
For I have need of many orisons
To move the heavens to smile upon my state,
Which, well thou knowest, is cross and full of sin.
Enter Mother.
MOTHER: What, are you busy, ho? Need you my help?
JULIET: No, madam; we have cull'd such necessaries
As are behooffull for our state to-morrow.
So please you, let me now be left alone,
And let the nurse this night sit up with you;
For I am sure you have your hands full all
In this so sudden business.
MOTHER: Good night.
Get thee to bed, and rest; for thou hast need.
Exeunt Mother and Nurse.
JULIET: Farewell! God knows when we shall meet again.
I have a faint cold fear thrills through my veins
That almost freezes up the heat of life.
I'll call them back again to comfort me.
Nurse!- What should she do here?
My dismal scene I needs must act alone.
Come, vial.
What if this mixture do not work at all?
Shall I be married then to-morrow morning?
No, No! This shall forbid it. Lie thou there.
Lays down a Dagger.
What if it be a poison which the friar
Subtilly hath minist'red to have me dead,
Lest in this marriage he should be dishonour'd
Because he married me before to Romeo?
I fear it is; and yet methinks it should not,
For he hath still been tried a holy man.
I will not entertain so bad a thought.
How if, when I am laid into the tomb,
I wake before the time that Romeo
Come to redeem me? There's a fearful point!
Shall I not then be stifled in the vault,
To whose foul mouth no healthsome air breathes in,
And there die strangled ere my Romeo comes?
Or, if I live, is it not very like
The horrible conceit of death and night,
Together with the terror of the place-
As in a vault, an ancient receptacle
Where for this many hundred years the bones
Of all my buried ancestors are pack'd;
Where bloody Tybalt, yet but green in earth,
Lies fest'ring in his shroud; where, as they say,
At some hours in the night spirits resort-

Alack, alack, is it not like that I,
So early waking- what with loathsome smells,
And shrieks like mandrakes torn out of the earth,
That living mortals, hearing them, run mad-
O, if I wake, shall I not be distraught,
Environed with all these hideous fears,
And madly play with my forefathers' joints,
And pluck the mangled Tybalt from his shroud.,
And, in this rage, with some great kinsman's bone
As with a club dash out my desp'rate brains?
O, look! methinks I see my cousin's ghost
Seeking out Romeo, that did spit his body
Upon a rapier's point. Stay, Tybalt, stay!
Romeo, I come! this do I drink to thee.
She Drinks And Falls upon Her Bed Within the Curtains.
ACT IV. SCENE IV. Capulet's House.
Enter Lady of the House and Nurse.
LADY: Hold, take these keys and fetch more spices, nurse.
NURSE: They call for dates and quinces in the pastry.
Enter Old Capulet.
CAPULET: Come, stir, stir, stir! The second cock hath crow'd,
The curfew bell hath rung, 'tis three o'clock.
Look to the bak'd meats, good Angelica;
Spare not for cost.
NURSE: Go, you cot-quean, go,
Get you to bed! Faith, you'll be sick to-morrow
For this night's watching.
CAPULET: No, not a whit. What, I have watch'd ere now
All night for lesser cause, and ne'er been sick.
LADY: Ay, you have been a mouse-hunt in your time;
But I will watch you from such watching now.
Exeunt Lady and Nurse.
CAPULET: A jealous hood, a jealous hood!
Enter Three or Four Fellows, with Spits and Logs and Baskets.
What is there? Now, fellow,
Fellow. Things for the cook, sir; but I know not what.
CAPULET: Make haste, make haste.
Exit Fellow.
Sirrah, fetch drier logs.
Call Peter; he will show thee where they are.
Fellow. I have a head, sir, that will find out logs
And never trouble Peter for the matter.
CAPULET: Mass, and well said; a merry whoreson, ha!
Thou shalt be loggerhead.
Exit Fellow.
Good faith, 'tis day.
The County will be here with music straight,
For so he said he would. Play music.
I hear him near.

Nurse! Wife! What, ho! What, nurse, I say!
Enter Nurse.
Go waken Juliet; go and trim her up.
I'll go and chat with Paris. Hie, make haste,
Make haste! The bridegroom he is come already:
Make haste, I say.
Exeunt.

ACT IV. SCENE V. Juliet's Chamber.

Enter Nurse.
NURSE: Mistress! what, mistress! Juliet! Fast, I warrant her, she.
Why, lamb! why, lady! Fie, you slug-abed!
Why, love, I say! madam! sweetheart! Why, bride!
What, not a word? You take your pennyworths now!
Sleep for a week; for the next night, I warrant,
The County Paris hath set up his rest
That you shall rest but little. God forgive me!
Marry, and amen. How sound is she asleep!
I needs must wake her. Madam, madam, madam!
Ay, let the County take you in your bed!
He'll fright you up, i' faith. Will it not be?
Draws Aside the Curtains.
What, dress'd, and in your clothes, and down again?
I must needs wake you. Lady! lady! lady!
Alas, alas! Help, help! My lady's dead!
O weraday that ever I was born!
Some aqua-vitae, ho! My lord! my lady!
Enter Mother.
MOTHER: What noise is here?
NURSE: O lamentable day!
MOTHER: What is the matter?
NURSE: Look, look! O heavy day!
MOTHER: O me, O me! My child, my only life!
Revive, look up, or I will die with thee!
Help, help! Call help.
Enter Father.
FATHER: For shame, bring Juliet forth; her lord is come.
NURSE: She's dead, deceas'd; she's dead! Alack the day!
MOTHER: Alack the day, she's dead, she's dead, she's dead!
CAPULET: Ha! let me see her. Out alas! she's cold,
Her blood is settled, and her joints are stiff;
Life and these lips have long been separated.
Death lies on her like an untimely frost
Upon the sweetest flower of all the field.
NURSE: O lamentable day!
MOTHER: O woful time!
CAPULET: Death, that hath ta'en her hence to make me wail,
Ties up my tongue and will not let me speak.
Enter Friar Laurence and the County Paris, with Musicians.
FRIAR: Come, is the bride ready to go to church?

CAPULET: Ready to go, but never to return.
O son, the night before thy wedding day
Hath Death lain with thy wife. See, there she lies,
Flower as she was, deflowered by him.
Death is my son-in-law, Death is my heir;
My daughter he hath wedded. I will die
And leave him all. Life, living, all is Death's.
PARIS: Have I thought long to see this morning's face,
And doth it give me such a sight as this?
MOTHER: Accurs'd, unhappy, wretched, hateful day!
Most miserable hour that e'er time saw
In lasting labour of his pilgrimage!
But one, poor one, one poor and loving child,
But one thing to rejoice and solace in,
And cruel Death hath catch'd it from my sight!
NURSE: O woe? O woful, woful, woful day!
Most lamentable day, most woful day
That ever ever I did yet behold!
O day! O day! O day! O hateful day!
Never was seen so black a day as this.
O woful day! O woful day!
PARIS: Beguil'd, divorced, wronged, spited, slain!
Most detestable Death, by thee beguil'd,
By cruel cruel thee quite overthrown!
O love! O life! not life, but love in death
CAPULET: Despis'd, distressed, hated, martyr'd, kill'd!
Uncomfortable time, why cam'st thou now
To murther, murther our solemnity?
O child! O child! my soul, and not my child!
Dead art thou, dead! alack, my child is dead,
And with my child my joys are buried!
FRIAR: Peace, ho, for shame! Confusion's cure lives not
In these confusions. Heaven and yourself
Had part in this fair maid! now heaven hath all,
And all the better is it for the maid.
Your part in her you could not keep from death,
But heaven keeps his part in eternal life.
The most you sought was her promotion,
For 'twas your heaven she should be advanc'd;
And weep ye now, seeing she is advanc'd
Above the clouds, as high as heaven itself?
O, in this love, you love your child so ill
That you run mad, seeing that she is well.
She's not well married that lives married long,
But she's best married that dies married young.
Dry up your tears and stick your rosemary
On this fair corse, and, as the custom is,
In all her best array bear her to church;
For though fond nature bids us all lament,

Yet nature's tears are reason's merriment.
CAPULET: All things that we ordained festival
Turn from their office to black funeral-
Our instruments to melancholy bells,
Our wedding cheer to a sad burial feast;
Our solemn hymns to sullen dirges change;
Our bridal flowers serve for a buried corse;
And all things change them to the contrary.
FRIAR: Sir, go you in; and, madam, go with him;
And go, Sir Paris. Every one prepare
To follow this fair corse unto her grave.
The heavens do low'r upon you for some ill;
Move them no more by crossing their high will.
Exeunt. Manent Musicians and Nurse.
FIRST MUSICIAN: Faith, we may put up our pipes and be gone.
NURSE: Honest good fellows, ah, put up, put up!
For well you know this is a pitiful case.
Exit.
FIRST MUSICIAN: Ay, by my troth, the case may be amended.
Enter Peter.
PETER: Musicians, O, musicians, 'Heart's ease,' 'Heart's ease'!
O, an you will have me live, play 'Heart's ease.'
FIRST MUSICIAN: Why 'Heart's ease'',
PETER: O, musicians, because my heart itself plays 'My heart is full of woe.' O, play me some merry dump to comfort me.
FIRST MUSICIAN: Not a dump we! 'Tis no time to play now.
PETER: You will not then?
FIRST MUSICIAN: No.
PETER: I will then give it you soundly.
FIRST MUSICIAN: What will you give us?
PETER: No money, on my faith, but the gleek. I will give you the minstrel.
FIRST MUSICIAN: Then will I give you the serving-creature.
PETER: Then will I lay the serving-creature's dagger on your pate.
I will carry no crotchets. I'll re you, I'll fa you. Do you note me?
FIRST MUSICIAN: An you re us and fa us, you note us.
SECOND MUSICIAN: Pray you put up your dagger, and put out your wit.
PETER: Then have at you with my wit! I will dry-beat you with an iron wit, and put up my iron dagger. Answer me like men.
'When griping grief the heart doth wound,
And doleful dumps the mind oppress,
Then music with her silver sound'-
Why 'silver sound'? Why 'music with her silver sound'?
What say you, Simon Catling?
FIRST MUSICIAN: Marry, sir, because silver hath a sweet sound.
PETER: Pretty! What say You, Hugh Rebeck?
SECOND MUSICIAN: I say 'silver sound' because musicians sound for silver.
PETER: Pretty too! What say you, James Soundpost?
THIRD MUSICIAN: Faith, I know not what to say.

PETER: O, I cry you mercy! you are the singer. I will say for you. It is 'music with her silver sound' because musicians have no gold for sounding.

'Then Music with Her Silver Sound
With Speedy Help Doth Lend Redress.'

Exit.

FIRST MUSICIAN: What a pestilent knave is this same?

SECOND MUSICIAN: Hang him, Jack! Come, we'll in here, tarry for the mourners, and stay dinner.

Exeunt.

ACT V. SCENE I. Mantua. A Street.

Enter Romeo.

ROMEO: If I may trust the flattering truth of sleep
My dreams presage some joyful news at hand.
My bosom's lord sits lightly in his throne,
And all this day an unaccustom'd spirit
Lifts me above the ground with cheerful thoughts.
I dreamt my lady came and found me dead
(Strange dream that gives a dead man leave to think!)
And breath'd such life with kisses in my lips
That I reviv'd and was an emperor.
Ah me! how sweet is love itself possess'd,
When but love's shadows are so rich in joy!

Enter Romeo's Man Balthasar, Booted.

News from Verona! How now, Balthasar?
Dost thou not bring me letters from the friar?
How doth my lady? Is my father well?
How fares my Juliet? That I ask again,
For nothing can be ill if she be well.

BALTHASAR: Then she is well, and nothing can be ill.
Her body sleeps in Capel's monument,
And her immortal part with angels lives.
I saw her laid low in her kindred's vault
And presently took post to tell it you.
O, pardon me for bringing these ill news,
Since you did leave it for my office, sir.

ROMEO: Is it e'en so? Then I defy you, stars!
Thou knowest my lodging. Get me ink and paper
And hire posthorses. I will hence to-night.

BALTHASAR: I do beseech you, sir, have patience.
Your looks are pale and wild and do import
Some misadventure.

ROMEO: Tush, thou art deceiv'd.
Leave me and do the thing I bid thee do.
Hast thou no letters to me from the friar?

BALTHASAR: No, my good lord.

ROMEO: No matter. Get thee gone
And hire those horses. I'll be with thee straight.

Exit Balthasar.

Well, Juliet, I will lie with thee to-night.
Let's see for means. O mischief, thou art swift
To enter in the thoughts of desperate men!
I do remember an apothecary,
And hereabouts 'a dwells, which late I noted
In tatt'red weeds, with overwhelming brows,
Culling of simples. Meagre were his looks,
Sharp misery had worn him to the bones;
And in his needy shop a tortoise hung,
An alligator stuff'd, and other skins
Of ill-shaped fishes; and about his shelves
A beggarly account of empty boxes,
Green earthen pots, bladders, and musty seeds,
Remnants of packthread, and old cakes of roses
Were thinly scattered, to make up a show.
Noting this penury, to myself I said,
'An if a man did need a poison now
Whose sale is present death in Mantua,
Here lives a caitiff wretch would sell it him.'
O, this same thought did but forerun my need,
And this same needy man must sell it me.
As I remember, this should be the house.
Being holiday, the beggar's shop is shut. What, ho! apothecary!
Enter Apothecary.
APOTHECARY: Who calls so loud?
ROMEO: Come hither, man. I see that thou art poor.
Hold, there is forty ducats. Let me have
A dram of poison, such soon-speeding gear
As will disperse itself through all the veins
That the life-weary taker mall fall dead,
And that the trunk may be discharg'd of breath
As violently as hasty powder fir'd
Doth hurry from the fatal cannon's womb.
APOTHECARY: Such mortal drugs I have; but Mantua's law
Is death to any he that utters them.
ROMEO: Art thou so bare and full of wretchedness
And fearest to die? Famine is in thy cheeks,
Need and oppression starveth in thine eyes,
Contempt and beggary hangs upon thy back:
The world is not thy friend, nor the world's law;
The world affords no law to make thee rich;
Then be not poor, but break it and take this.
APOTHECARY: My poverty but not my will consents.
ROMEO: I pay thy poverty and not thy will.
APOTHECARY: Put this in any liquid thing you will
And drink it off, and if you had the strength
Of twenty men, it would dispatch you straight.
ROMEO: There is thy gold- worse poison to men's souls,
Doing more murther in this loathsome world,

Than these poor compounds that thou mayst not sell.
I sell thee poison; thou hast sold me none.
Farewell. Buy food and get thyself in flesh.
Come, cordial and not poison, go with me
To Juliet's grave; for there must I use thee.
Exeunt.

ACT V. SCENE II. Verona. Friar Laurence's Cell.

Enter Friar John to Friar Laurence.
FRIAR JOHN: Holy Franciscan friar, brother, ho!
Enter Friar Laurence.
FRIAR LAURENCE: This same should be the voice of Friar John.
Welcome from Mantua. What says Romeo?
Or, if his mind be writ, give me his letter.
FRIAR JOHN: Going to find a barefoot brother out,
One of our order, to associate me
Here in this city visiting the sick,
And finding him, the searchers of the town,
Suspecting that we both were in a house
Where the infectious pestilence did reign,
Seal'd up the doors, and would not let us forth,
So that my speed to Mantua there was stay'd.
FRIAR LAURENCE Who bare my letter, then, to Romeo?
FRIAR JOHN: I could not send it- here it is again-
Nor get a messenger to bring it thee,
So fearful were they of infection.
FRIAR LAURENCE Unhappy fortune! By my brotherhood,
The letter was not nice, but full of charge,
Of dear import; and the neglecting it
May do much danger. Friar John, go hence,
Get me an iron crow and bring it straight
Unto my cell.
FRIAR JOHN: Brother, I'll go and bring it thee.
Exit.
FRIAR LAURENCE Now, must I to the monument alone.
Within this three hours will fair Juliet wake.
She will beshrew me much that Romeo
Hath had no notice of these accidents;
But I will write again to Mantua,
And keep her at my cell till Romeo come-
Poor living corse, clos'd in a dead man's tomb!
Exit.

ACT V. SCENE III. Verona. A Churchyard; in it the Monument of the Capulets.

Enter Paris and His Page with Flowers and a Torch.
PARIS: Give me thy torch, boy. Hence, and stand aloof.
Yet put it out, for I would not be seen.
Under yond yew tree lay thee all along,
Holding thine ear close to the hollow ground.
So shall no foot upon the churchyard tread
(Being loose, unfirm, with digging up of graves)

But thou shalt hear it. Whistle then to me,
As signal that thou hear'st something approach.
Give me those flowers. Do as I bid thee, go.
PAGE: Aside I am almost afraid to stand alone
Here in the churchyard; yet I will adventure.
Retires.
PARIS: Sweet flower, with flowers thy bridal bed I strew
(O woe! thy canopy is dust and stones)
Which with sweet water nightly I will dew;
Or, wanting that, with tears distill'd by moans.
The obsequies that I for thee will keep
Nightly shall be to strew, thy grave and weep.
Whistle Boy.
The boy gives warning something doth approach.
What cursed foot wanders this way to-night
To cross my obsequies and true love's rite?
What, with a torch? Muffle me, night, awhile.
Retires.
Enter Romeo, and Balthasar with a Torch, a Mattock, and a Crow of Iron.
ROMEO: Give me that mattock and the wrenching iron.
Hold, take this letter. Early in the morning
See thou deliver it to my lord and father.
Give me the light. Upon thy life I charge thee,
Whate'er thou hearest or seest, stand all aloof
And do not interrupt me in my course.
Why I descend into this bed of death
Is partly to behold my lady's face,
But chiefly to take thence from her dead finger
A precious ring- a ring that I must use
In dear employment. Therefore hence, be gone.
But if thou, jealous, dost return to pry
In what I farther shall intend to do,
By heaven, I will tear thee joint by joint
And strew this hungry churchyard with thy limbs.
The time and my intents are savage-wild,
More fierce and more inexorable far
Than empty tigers or the roaring sea.
BALTHASAR: I will be gone, sir, and not trouble you.
ROMEO: So shalt thou show me friendship. Take thou that.
Live, and be prosperous; and farewell, good fellow.
BALTHASAR: Aside For all this same, I'll hide me hereabout.
His looks I fear, and his intents I doubt.
Retires.
ROMEO: Thou detestable maw, thou womb of death,
Gorg'd with the dearest morsel of the earth,
Thus I enforce thy rotten jaws to open,
And in despite I'll cram thee with more food.
Romeo Opens the Tomb.
PARIS: This is that banish'd haughty Montague

That murd'red my love's cousin- with which grief
It is supposed the fair creature died-
And here is come to do some villanous shame
To the dead bodies. I will apprehend him.
Stop thy unhallowed toil, vile Montague!
Can vengeance be pursu'd further than death?
Condemned villain, I do apprehend thee.
Obey, and go with me; for thou must die.
ROMEO: I must indeed; and therefore came I hither.
Good gentle youth, tempt not a desp'rate man.
Fly hence and leave me. Think upon these gone;
Let them affright thee. I beseech thee, youth,
But not another sin upon my head
By urging me to fury. O, be gone!
By heaven, I love thee better than myself,
For I come hither arm'd against myself.
Stay not, be gone. Live, and hereafter say
A madman's mercy bid thee run away.
PARIS: I do defy thy, conjuration
And apprehend thee for a felon here.
ROMEO: Wilt thou provoke me? Then have at thee, boy!
They Fight.
PAGE: O Lord, they fight! I will go call the watch.
Exit. Paris Falls.
PARIS: O, I am slain! If thou be merciful,
Open the tomb, lay me with Juliet.
Dies.
ROMEO: In faith, I will. Let me peruse this face.
Mercutio's kinsman, noble County Paris!
What said my man when my betossed soul
Did not attend him as we rode? I think
He told me Paris should have married Juliet.
Said he not so? or did I dream it so?
Or am I mad, hearing him talk of Juliet
To think it was so? O, give me thy hand,
One writ with me in sour misfortune's book!
I'll bury thee in a triumphant grave.
A grave? O, no, a lanthorn, slaught'red youth,
For here lies Juliet, and her beauty makes
This vault a feasting presence full of light.
Death, lie thou there, by a dead man interr'd.
Lays Him in the Tomb.
How oft when men are at the point of death
Have they been merry! which their keepers call
A lightning before death. O, how may I
Call this a lightning? O my love! my wife!
Death, that hath suck'd the honey of thy breath,
Hath had no power yet upon thy beauty.
Thou art not conquer'd. Beauty's ensign yet

Is crimson in thy lips and in thy cheeks,
And death's pale flag is not advanced there.
Tybalt, liest thou there in thy bloody sheet?
O, what more favour can I do to thee
Than with that hand that cut thy youth in twain
To sunder his that was thine enemy?
Forgive me, cousin.' Ah, dear Juliet,
Why art thou yet so fair? Shall I believe
That unsubstantial Death is amorous,
And that the lean abhorred monster keeps
Thee here in dark to be his paramour?
For fear of that I still will stay with thee
And never from this palace of dim night
Depart again. Here, here will I remain
With worms that are thy chambermaids. O, here
Will I set up my everlasting rest
And shake the yoke of inauspicious stars
From this world-wearied flesh. Eyes, look your last!
Arms, take your last embrace! and, lips, O you
The doors of breath, seal with a righteous kiss
A dateless bargain to engrossing death!
Come, bitter conduct; come, unsavoury guide!
Thou desperate pilot, now at once run on
The dashing rocks thy seasick weary bark!
Here's to my love! Drinks. O true apothecary!
Thy drugs are quick. Thus with a kiss I die. Falls.
Enter Friar Laurence, with Lanthorn, Crow, and Spade.
FRIAR: Saint Francis be my speed! how oft to-night
Have my old feet stumbled at graves! Who's there?
BALTHASAR: Here's one, a friend, and one that knows you well.
FRIAR: Bliss be upon you! Tell me, good my friend,
What torch is yond that vainly lends his light
To grubs and eyeless skulls? As I discern,
It burneth in the Capels' monument.
BALTHASAR: It doth so, holy sir; and there's my master,
One that you love.
FRIAR: Who is it?
BALTHASAR: Romeo.
FRIAR: How long hath he been there?
BALTHASAR: Full half an hour.
FRIAR: Go with me to the vault.
BALTHASAR: I dare not, sir.
My master knows not but I am gone hence,
And fearfully did menace me with death
If I did stay to look on his intents.
FRIAR: Stay then; I'll go alone. Fear comes upon me.
O, much I fear some ill unthrifty thing.
BALTHASAR: As I did sleep under this yew tree here,
I dreamt my master and another fought,

And that my master slew him.
FRIAR: Romeo!
Alack, alack, what blood is this which stains
The stony entrance of this sepulchre?
What mean these masterless and gory swords
To lie discolour'd by this place of peace?
Enters the tomb.
Romeo! O, pale! Who else? What, Paris too?
And steep'd in blood? Ah, what an unkind hour
Is guilty of this lamentable chance! The lady stirs.
Juliet Rises.
JULIET: O comfortable friar! where is my lord?
I do remember well where I should be,
And there I am. Where is my Romeo?
FRIAR: I hear some noise. Lady, come from that nest
Of death, contagion, and unnatural sleep.
A greater power than we can contradict
Hath thwarted our intents. Come, come away.
Thy husband in thy bosom there lies dead;
And Paris too. Come, I'll dispose of thee
Among a sisterhood of holy nuns.
Stay not to question, for the watch is coming.
Come, go, good Juliet. I dare no longer stay.
JULIET: Go, get thee hence, for I will not away.
Exit Friar.
What's here? A cup, clos'd in my true love's hand?
Poison, I see, hath been his timeless end.
O churl! drunk all, and left no friendly drop
To help me after? I will kiss thy lips.
Haply some poison yet doth hang on them
To make me die with a restorative. Kisses Him.
Thy lips are warm!
Chief Watch. Within Lead, boy. Which way?
Yea, noise? Then I'll be brief. O happy dagger!
Snatches Romeo's Dagger.
This is thy sheath; there rest, and let me die.
She Stabs Herself and Falls on Romeo's Body.
Enter Paris's Boy and Watch.
BOY: This is the place. There, where the torch doth burn.
Chief Watch. 'the ground is bloody. Search about the churchyard.
Go, some of you; whoe'er you find attach.
Exeunt Some of the Watch.
Pitiful sight! here lies the County slain;
And Juliet bleeding, warm, and newly dead,
Who here hath lain this two days buried.
Go, tell the Prince; run to the Capulets;
Raise up the Montagues; some others search.
Exeunt Others of the Watch.
We see the ground whereon these woes do lie,

But the true ground of all these piteous woes
We cannot without circumstance descry.
Enter Some of the Watch, with Romeo's Man Balthasar.
SECOND WATCH: Here's Romeo's man.
We found him in the churchyard.
CHIEF WATCH: Hold him in safety till the Prince come hither.
Enter Friar Laurence and another Watchman.
THIRD WATCH: Here is a friar that trembles, sighs, and weeps.
We took this mattock and this spade from him
As he was coming from this churchyard side.
Chief Watch. A great suspicion! Stay the friar too.
Enter the Prince and Attendants.
PRINCE: What misadventure is so early up,
That calls our person from our morning rest?
Enter Capulet and His Wife with Others.
CAPULET: What should it be, that they so shriek abroad?
WIFE: The people in the street cry 'Romeo,'
Some 'Juliet,' and some 'Paris'; and all run,
With open outcry, toward our monument.
PRINCE: What fear is this which startles in our ears?
Chief Watch. Sovereign, here lies the County Paris slain;
And Romeo dead; and Juliet, dead before,
Warm and new kill'd.
PRINCE: Search, seek, and know how this foul murder comes.
CHIEF WATCH: Here is a friar, and slaughter'd Romeo's man,
With instruments upon them fit to open
These dead men's tombs.
CAPULET: O heavens! O wife, look how our daughter bleeds!
This dagger hath mista'en, for, lo, his house
Is empty on the back of Montague,
And it missheathed in my daughter's bosom!
WIFE: O me! this sight of death is as a bell
That warns my old age to a sepulchre.
Enter Montague and Others.
PRINCE: Come, Montague; for thou art early up
To see thy son and heir more early down.
MONTAGUE: Alas, my liege, my wife is dead to-night!
Grief of my son's exile hath stopp'd her breath.
What further woe conspires against mine age?
PRINCE: Look, and thou shalt see.
MONTAGUE: O thou untaught! what manners is in this,
To press before thy father to a grave?
PRINCE: Seal up the mouth of outrage for a while,
Till we can clear these ambiguities
And know their spring, their head, their true descent;
And then will I be general of your woes
And lead you even to death. Meantime forbear,
And let mischance be slave to patience.
Bring forth the parties of suspicion.

FRIAR: I am the greatest, able to do least,
Yet most suspected, as the time and place
Doth make against me, of this direful murther;
And here I stand, both to impeach and purge
Myself condemned and myself excus'd.
PRINCE: Then say it once what thou dost know in this.
FRIAR: I will be brief, for my short date of breath
Is not so long as is a tedious tale.
Romeo, there dead, was husband to that Juliet;
And she, there dead, that Romeo's faithful wife.
I married them; and their stol'n marriage day
Was Tybalt's doomsday, whose untimely death
Banish'd the new-made bridegroom from this city;
For whom, and not for Tybalt, Juliet pin'd.
You, to remove that siege of grief from her,
Betroth'd and would have married her perforce
To County Paris. Then comes she to me
And with wild looks bid me devise some mean
To rid her from this second marriage,
Or in my cell there would she kill herself.
Then gave I her (so tutored by my art)
A sleeping potion; which so took effect
As I intended, for it wrought on her
The form of death. Meantime I writ to Romeo
That he should hither come as this dire night
To help to take her from her borrowed grave,
Being the time the potion's force should cease.
But he which bore my letter, Friar John,
Was stay'd by accident, and yesternight
Return'd my letter back. Then all alone
At the prefixed hour of her waking
Came I to take her from her kindred's vault;
Meaning to keep her closely at my cell
Till I conveniently could send to Romeo.
But when I came, some minute ere the time
Of her awaking, here untimely lay
The noble Paris and true Romeo dead.
She wakes; and I entreated her come forth
And bear this work of heaven with patience;
But then a noise did scare me from the tomb,
And she, too desperate, would not go with me,
But, as it seems, did violence on herself.
All this I know, and to the marriage
Her nurse is privy; and if aught in this
Miscarried by my fault, let my old life
Be sacrific'd, some hour before his time,
Unto the rigour of severest law.
PRINCE: We still have known thee for a holy man.
Where's Romeo's man? What can he say in this?

BALTHASAR: I brought my master news of Juliet's death;
And then in post he came from Mantua
To this same place, to this same monument.
This letter he early bid me give his father,
And threat'ned me with death, going in the vault,
If I departed not and left him there.
PRINCE: Give me the letter. I will look on it.
Where is the County's page that rais'd the watch?
Sirrah, what made your master in this place?
BOY: He came with flowers to strew his lady's grave;
And bid me stand aloof, and so I did.
Anon comes one with light to ope the tomb;
And by-and-by my master drew on him;
And then I ran away to call the watch.
PRINCE: This letter doth make good the friar's words,
Their course of love, the tidings of her death;
And here he writes that he did buy a poison
Of a poor pothecary, and therewithal
Came to this vault to die, and lie with Juliet.
Where be these enemies? Capulet, Montage,
See what a scourge is laid upon your hate,
That heaven finds means to kill your joys with love!
And I, for winking at you, discords too,
Have lost a brace of kinsmen. All are punish'd.
CAPULET: O brother Montague, give me thy hand.
This is my daughter's jointure, for no more
Can I demand.
MONTAGUE: But I can give thee more;
For I will raise her Statue in pure gold,
That whiles Verona by that name is known,
There shall no figure at such rate be set
As that of true and faithful Juliet.
CAPULET: As rich shall Romeo's by his lady's lie-
Poor sacrifices of our enmity!
PRINCE: A glooming peace this morning with it brings.
The sun for sorrow will not show his head.
Go hence, to have more talk of these sad things;
Some shall be pardon'd, and some punished;
For never was a story of more woe
Than this of Juliet and her Romeo.
Exeunt Omnes.

END

The Tragedy of Julius Caesar

Dramatis Personae

JULIUS CAESAR, Roman statesman and general
OCTAVIUS, Triumvir after Caesar's death, later Augustus Caesar, first emperor of Rome
MARK ANTONY, general and friend of Caesar, a Triumvir after his death
LEPIDUS, third member of the Triumvirate
MARCUS BRUTUS, leader of the conspiracy against Caesar
CASSIUS, instigator of the conspiracy
CASCA, conspirator against Caesar
TREBONIUS, conspirator against Caesar
CAIUS LIGARIUS, conspirator against Caesar
DECIUS BRUTUS, conspirator against Caesar
METELLUS CIMBER, conspirator against Caesar
CINNA, conspirator against Caesar
CALPURNIA, wife of Caesar
PORTIA, wife of Brutus
CICERO, senator
POPILIUS, senator
POPILIUS LENA, senator
FLAVIUS, tribune
MARULLUS, tribune
CATO, supportor of Brutus
LUCILIUS, supportor of Brutus
TITINIUS, supportor of Brutus
MESSALA, supportor of Brutus
VOLUMNIUS, supportor of Brutus
ARTEMIDORUS, a teacher of rhetoric
CINNA, a poet
VARRO, servant to Brutus
CLITUS, servant to Brutus
CLAUDIO, servant to Brutus
STRATO, servant to Brutus
LUCIUS, servant to Brutus
DARDANIUS, servant to Brutus
PINDARUS, servant to Cassius
The Ghost of Caesar
A Soothsayer
A Poet, Senators, Citizens, Soldiers, Commoners, Messengers, and Servants

SCENE: Rome, the conspirators' camp near Sardis, and the plains of Philippi.

ACT I. SCENE I. Rome. A Street.

Enter Flavius, Marullus, and Certain Commoners.

FLAVIUS: Hence, home, you idle creatures, get you home.
Is this a holiday? What, know you not,
Being mechanical, you ought not walk
Upon a laboring day without the sign
Of your profession? Speak, what trade art thou?
FIRST COMMONER: Why, sir, a carpenter.

MARULLUS: Where is thy leather apron and thy rule?
What dost thou with thy best apparel on?
You, sir, what trade are you?
SECOND COMMONER: Truly, sir, in respect of a fine workman, I am but, as you would say, a cobbler.
MARULLUS: But what trade art thou? Answer me directly.
SECOND COMMONER: A trade, sir, that, I hope, I may use with a safe conscience, which is indeed, sir, a mender of bad soles.
MARULLUS: What trade, thou knave? Thou naughty knave, what trade?
SECOND COMMONER: Nay, I beseech you, sir, be not out with me; yet, if you be out, sir, I can mend you.
MARULLUS: What mean'st thou by that? Mend me, thou saucy fellow!
SECOND COMMONER: Why, sir, cobble you.
FLAVIUS: Thou art a cobbler, art thou?
SECOND COMMONER: Truly, Sir, all that I live by is with the awl; I meddle with no tradesman's matters, nor women's matters, but with awl. I am indeed, sir, a surgeon to old shoes; when they are in great danger, I recover them. As proper men as ever trod upon neat's leather have gone upon my handiwork.
FLAVIUS: But wherefore art not in thy shop today?
Why dost thou lead these men about the streets?
SECOND COMMONER: Truly, sir, to wear out their shoes to get myself into more work. But indeed, sir, we make holiday to see Caesar and to rejoice in his triumph.
MARULLUS: Wherefore rejoice? What conquest brings he home?
What tributaries follow him to Rome
To grace in captive bonds his chariot wheels?
You blocks, you stones, you worse than senseless things!
O you hard hearts, you cruel men of Rome,
Knew you not Pompey? Many a time and oft
Have you climb'd up to walls and battlements,
To towers and windows, yea, to chimney tops,
Your infants in your arms, and there have sat
The livelong day with patient expectation
To see great Pompey pass the streets of Rome.
And when you saw his chariot but appear,
Have you not made an universal shout
That Tiber trembled underneath her banks
To hear the replication of your sounds
Made in her concave shores?
And do you now put on your best attire?
And do you now cull out a holiday?
And do you now strew flowers in his way
That comes in triumph over Pompey's blood?
Be gone!
Run to your houses, fall upon your knees,
Pray to the gods to intermit the plague
That needs must light on this ingratitude.
FLAVIUS: Go, go, good countrymen, and, for this fault,

Assemble all the poor men of your sort,
Draw them to Tiber banks, and weep your tears
Into the channel, till the lowest stream
Do kiss the most exalted shores of all.
Exeunt all Commoners.
See whether their basest metal be not moved;
They vanish tongue-tied in their guiltiness.
Go you down that way towards the Capitol;
This way will I. Disrobe the images
If you do find them deck'd with ceremonies.
MARULLUS: May we do so?
You know it is the feast of Lupercal.
FLAVIUS: It is no matter; let no images
Be hung with Caesar's trophies. I'll about
And drive away the vulgar from the streets;
So do you too, where you perceive them thick.
These growing feathers pluck'd from Caesar's wing
Will make him fly an ordinary pitch,
Who else would soar above the view of men
And keep us all in servile fearfulness.
Exeunt.

ACT I. SCENE II. A Public Place.

Flourish. Enter Caesar; Antony, for the Course; Calpurnia, Portia, Decius, Cicero, Brutus, Cassius, and Casca; a Great Crowd Follows, among Them a Soothsayer.
CAESAR: Calpurnia!
CASCA: Peace, ho! Caesar speaks.
Music Ceases.
CAESAR: Calpurnia!
CALPURNIA: Here, my lord.
CAESAR: Stand you directly in Antonio's way,
When he doth run his course. Antonio!
ANTONY: Caesar, my lord?
CAESAR: Forget not in your speed, Antonio,
To touch Calpurnia, for our elders say
The barren, touched in this holy chase,
Shake off their sterile curse.
ANTONY: I shall remember.
When Caesar says "Do this," it is perform'd.
CAESAR: Set on, and leave no ceremony out. Flourish.
SOOTHSAYER: Caesar!
CAESAR: Ha! Who calls?
CASCA: Bid every noise be still. Peace yet again!
CAESAR: Who is it in the press that calls on me?
I hear a tongue, shriller than all the music,
Cry "Caesar." Speak, Caesar is turn'd to hear.
SOOTHSAYER: Beware the ides of March.
CAESAR: What man is that?
BRUTUS: A soothsayer you beware the ides of March.
CAESAR: Set him before me let me see his face.

CASSIUS: Fellow, come from the throng; look upon Caesar.
CAESAR: What say'st thou to me now? Speak once again.
SOOTHSAYER: Beware the ides of March.
CAESAR: He is a dreamer; let us leave him. Pass.
Sennet. Exeunt All but Brutus and Cassius.
CALPURNIA: Will you go see the order of the course?
BRUTUS: Not I.
CASSIUS: I pray you, do.
BRUTUS: I am not gamesome; I do lack some part
Of that quick spirit that is in Antony.
Let me not hinder, Cassius, your desires;
I'll leave you.
CASSIUS: Brutus, I do observe you now of late;
I have not from your eyes that gentleness
And show of love as I was wont to have;
You bear too stubborn and too strange a hand
Over your friend that loves you.
BRUTUS: Cassius,
Be not deceived; if I have veil'd my look,
I turn the trouble of my countenance
Merely upon myself. Vexed I am
Of late with passions of some difference,
Conceptions only proper to myself,
Which give some soil perhaps to my behaviors;
But let not therefore my good friends be grieved-
Among which number, Cassius, be you one-
Nor construe any further my neglect
Than that poor Brutus with himself at war
Forgets the shows of love to other men.
CASSIUS: Then, Brutus, I have much mistook your passion,
By means whereof this breast of mine hath buried
Thoughts of great value, worthy cogitations.
Tell me, good Brutus, can you see your face?
BRUTUS: No, Cassius, for the eye sees not itself
But by reflection, by some other things.
CASSIUS: 'Tis just,
And it is very much lamented, Brutus,
That you have no such mirrors as will turn
Your hidden worthiness into your eye
That you might see your shadow. I have heard
Where many of the best respect in Rome,
Except immortal Caesar, speaking of Brutus
And groaning underneath this age's yoke,
Have wish'd that noble Brutus had his eyes.
BRUTUS: Into what dangers would you lead me, Cassius,
That you would have me seek into myself
For that which is not in me?
CASSIUS: Therefore, good Brutus, be prepared to hear,
And since you know you cannot see yourself

So well as by reflection, I your glass
Will modestly discover to yourself
That of yourself which you yet know not of.
And be not jealous on me, gentle Brutus;
Were I a common laugher, or did use
To stale with ordinary oaths my love
To every new protester, if you know
That I do fawn on men and hug them hard
And after scandal them, or if you know
That I profess myself in banqueting
To all the rout, then hold me dangerous.
Flourish and Shout.
BRUTUS: What means this shouting? I do fear the people
Choose Caesar for their king.
CASSIUS: Ay, do you fear it?
Then must I think you would not have it so.
BRUTUS: I would not, Cassius, yet I love him well.
But wherefore do you hold me here so long?
What is it that you would impart to me?
If it be aught toward the general good,
Set honor in one eye and death i' the other
And I will look on both indifferently.
For let the gods so speed me as I love
The name of honor more than I fear death.
CASSIUS: I know that virtue to be in you, Brutus,
As well as I do know your outward favor.
Well, honor is the subject of my story.
I cannot tell what you and other men
Think of this life, but, for my single self,
I had as lief not be as live to be
In awe of such a thing as I myself.
I was born free as Caesar, so were you;
We both have fed as well, and we can both
Endure the winter's cold as well as he.
For once, upon a raw and gusty day,
The troubled Tiber chafing with her shores,
Caesar said to me, "Darest thou, Cassius, now
Leap in with me into this angry flood
And swim to yonder point?" Upon the word,
Accoutred as I was, I plunged in
And bade him follow. So indeed he did.
The torrent roar'd, and we did buffet it
With lusty sinews, throwing it aside
And stemming it with hearts of controversy.
But ere we could arrive the point proposed,
Caesar cried, "Help me, Cassius, or I sink!
I, as Aeneas our great ancestor
Did from the flames of Troy upon his shoulder
The old Anchises bear, so from the waves of Tiber

Did I the tired Caesar. And this man
Is now become a god, and Cassius is
A wretched creature and must bend his body
If Caesar carelessly but nod on him.
He had a fever when he was in Spain,
And when the fit was on him I did mark
How he did shake. 'Tis true, this god did shake;
His coward lips did from their color fly,
And that same eye whose bend doth awe the world
Did lose his luster. I did hear him groan.
Ay, and that tongue of his that bade the Romans
Mark him and write his speeches in their books,
Alas, it cried, "Give me some drink, Titinius,"
As a sick girl. Ye gods! It doth amaze me
A man of such a feeble temper should
So get the start of the majestic world
And bear the palm alone. Shout. Flourish.
BRUTUS: Another general shout!
I do believe that these applauses are
For some new honors that are heap'd on Caesar.
CASSIUS: Why, man, he doth bestride the narrow world
Like a Colossus, and we petty men
Walk under his huge legs and peep about
To find ourselves dishonorable graves.
Men at some time are masters of their fates:
The fault, dear Brutus, is not in our stars,
But in ourselves that we are underlings.
Brutus and Caesar: what should be in that "Caesar"?
Why should that name be sounded more than yours?
Write them together, yours is as fair a name;
Sound them, it doth become the mouth as well;
Weigh them, it is as heavy; conjure with 'em,
"Brutus" will start a spirit as soon as "Caesar."
Now, in the names of all the gods at once,
Upon what meat doth this our Caesar feed
That he is grown so great? Age, thou art shamed!
Rome, thou hast lost the breed of noble bloods!
When went there by an age since the great flood
But it was famed with more than with one man?
When could they say till now that talk'd of Rome
That her wide walls encompass'd but one man?
Now is it Rome indeed, and room enough,
When there is in it but one only man.
O, you and I have heard our fathers say
There was a Brutus once that would have brook'd
The eternal devil to keep his state in Rome
As easily as a king.
BRUTUS: That you do love me, I am nothing jealous;
What you would work me to, I have some aim.

How I have thought of this and of these times,
I shall recount hereafter; for this present,
I would not, so with love I might entreat you,
Be any further moved. What you have said
I will consider; what you have to say
I will with patience hear, and find a time
Both meet to hear and answer such high things.
Till then, my noble friend, chew upon this:
Brutus had rather be a villager
Than to repute himself a son of Rome
Under these hard conditions as this time
Is like to lay upon us.
CASSIUS: I am glad that my weak words
Have struck but thus much show of fire from Brutus.
Re-enter Caesar and His Train.
BRUTUS: The games are done, and Caesar is returning.
CASSIUS: As they pass by, pluck Casca by the sleeve,
And he will, after his sour fashion, tell you
What hath proceeded worthy note today.
BRUTUS: I will do so. But, look you, Cassius,
The angry spot doth glow on Caesar's brow,
And all the rest look like a chidden train:
Calpurnia's cheek is pale, and Cicero
Looks with such ferret and such fiery eyes
As we have seen him in the Capitol,
Being cross'd in conference by some senators.
CASSIUS: Casca will tell us what the matter is.
CAESAR: Antonio!
ANTONY: Caesar?
CAESAR: Let me have men about me that are fat,
Sleek-headed men, and such as sleep o' nights:
Yond Cassius has a lean and hungry look;
He thinks too much; such men are dangerous.
ANTONY: Fear him not, Caesar; he's not dangerous;
He is a noble Roman and well given.
CAESAR: Would he were fatter! But I fear him not,
Yet if my name were liable to fear,
I do not know the man I should avoid
So soon as that spare Cassius. He reads much,
He is a great observer, and he looks
Quite through the deeds of men. He loves no plays,
As thou dost, Antony; he hears no music;
Seldom he smiles, and smiles in such a sort
As if he mock'd himself and scorn'd his spirit
That could be moved to smile at anything.
Such men as he be never at heart's ease
Whiles they behold a greater than themselves,
And therefore are they very dangerous.
I rather tell thee what is to be fear'd

Than what I fear, for always I am Caesar.
Come on my right hand, for this ear is deaf,
And tell me truly what thou think'st of him.

Sennet. Exeunt Caesar and All His Train but Casca.

CASCA: You pull'd me by the cloak; would you speak with me?
BRUTUS: Ay, Casca, tell us what hath chanced today
That Caesar looks so sad.
CASCA: Why, you were with him, were you not?
BRUTUS: I should not then ask Casca what had chanced.
CASCA: Why, there was a crown offered him, and being offered him, he put it by with the back of his hand, thus, and then the people fell ashouting.
BRUTUS: What was the second noise for?
CASCA: Why, for that too.
CASSIUS: They shouted thrice. What was the last cry for?
CASCA: Why, for that too.
BRUTUS: Was the crown offered him thrice?
CASCA: Ay, marry, wast, and he put it by thrice, every time gentler than other, and at every putting by mine honest neighbors shouted.
CASSIUS: Who offered him the crown?
CASCA: Why, Antony.
BRUTUS: Tell us the manner of it, gentle Casca.
CASCA: I can as well be hang'd as tell the manner of it. It was mere foolery; I did not mark it. I saw Mark Antony offer him a crown (yet 'twas not a crown neither, 'twas one of these coronets) and, as I told you, he put it by once. But for all that, to my thinking, he would fain have had it. Then he offered it to him again; then he put it by again. But, to my thinking, he was very loath to lay his fingers off it. And then he offered it the third time; he put it the third time by; and still as he refused it, the rabblement hooted and clapped their chopped hands and threw up their sweaty nightcaps and uttered such a deal of stinking breath because Caesar refused the crown that it had almost choked Caesar, for he swounded and fell down at it. And for mine own part, I durst not laugh for fear of opening my lips and receiving the bad air.
CASSIUS: But, soft, I pray you, what, did Caesars wound?
CASCA: He fell down in the marketplace and foamed at mouth and was speechless.
BRUTUS: 'Tis very like. He hath the falling sickness.
CASSIUS: No, Caesar hath it not, but you, and I,
And honest Casca, we have the falling sickness.
CASCA: I know not what you mean by that, but I am sure Caesar fell down. If the tagrag people did not clap him and hiss him according as he pleased and displeased them, as they use to do the players in the theatre, I am no true man.
BRUTUS: What said he when he came unto himself?
CASCA: Marry, before he fell down, when he perceived the common herd was glad he refused the crown, he plucked me ope his doublet

and offered them his throat to cut. An had been a man of any occupation, if I would not have taken him at a word, I would I might go to hell among the rogues. And so he fell. When he came to himself again, he said, if he had done or said anything amiss, he desired their worships to think it was his infirmity. Three or four wenches where I stood cried, "Alas, good soul!" and forgave him with all their hearts. But there's no heed to be taken of them; if Caesar had stabbed their mothers, they would have done no less.

BRUTUS: And after that he came, thus sad, away?
CASCA: Ay.
CASSIUS: Did Cicero say anything?
CASCA: Ay, he spoke Greek.
CASSIUS: To what effect?
CASCA: Nay, an I tell you that, I'll ne'er look you i' the face again; but those that understood him smiled at one another and shook their heads; but for mine own part, it was Greek to me. I could tell you more news too: Marullus and Flavius, for pulling scarfs off Caesar's images, are put to silence. Fare you well. There was more foolery yet, if could remember it.
CASSIUS: Will you sup with me tonight, Casca?
CASCA: No, I am promised forth.
CASSIUS: Will you dine with me tomorrow?
CASCA: Ay, if I be alive, and your mind hold, and your dinner worth the eating.
CASSIUS: Good, I will expect you.
CASCA: Do so, farewell, both.
Exit.
BRUTUS: What a blunt fellow is this grown to be!
He was quick mettle when he went to school.
CASSIUS: So is he now in execution
Of any bold or noble enterprise,
However he puts on this tardy form.
This rudeness is a sauce to his good wit,
Which gives men stomach to digest his words
With better appetite.
BRUTUS: And so it is. For this time I will leave you.
Tomorrow, if you please to speak with me,
I will come home to you, or, if you will,
Come home to me and I will wait for you.
CASSIUS: I will do so. Till then, think of the world.
Exit Brutus.
Well, Brutus, thou art noble; yet, I see
Thy honorable mettle may be wrought
From that it is disposed; therefore it is meet
That noble minds keep ever with their likes;
For who so firm that cannot be seduced?
Caesar doth bear me hard, but he loves Brutus.
If I were Brutus now and he were Cassius,

He should not humor me. I will this night,
In several hands, in at his windows throw,
As if they came from several citizens,
Writings, all tending to the great opinion
That Rome holds of his name, wherein obscurely
Caesar's ambition shall be glanced at.
And after this let Caesar seat him sure;
For we will shake him, or worse days endure.
Exit.

ACT I. SCENE III. A Street. Thunder and Lightning.

Enter, from Opposite Sides, Casca, with His Sword Drawn, and Cicero.

CICERO: Good even, Casca. Brought you Caesar home?
Why are you breathless, and why stare you so?
CASCA: Are not you moved, when all the sway of earth
Shakes like a thing unfirm? O Cicero,
I have seen tempests when the scolding winds
Have rived the knotty oaks, and I have seen
The ambitious ocean swell and rage and foam
To be exalted with the threatening clouds,
But never till tonight, never till now,
Did I go through a tempest dropping fire.
Either there is a civil strife in heaven,
Or else the world too saucy with the gods
Incenses them to send destruction.
CICERO: Why, saw you anything more wonderful?
CASCA: A common slave- you know him well by sight-
Held up his left hand, which did flame and burn
Like twenty torches join'd, and yet his hand
Not sensible of fire remain'd unscorch'd.
Besides- I ha' not since put up my sword-
Against the Capitol I met a lion,
Who glaz'd upon me and went surly by
Without annoying me. And there were drawn
Upon a heap a hundred ghastly women
Transformed with their fear, who swore they saw
Men all in fire walk up and down the streets.
And yesterday the bird of night did sit
Even at noonday upon the marketplace,
Howling and shrieking. When these prodigies
Do so conjointly meet, let not men say
"These are their reasons; they are natural":
For I believe they are portentous things
Unto the climate that they point upon.
CICERO: Indeed, it is a strange-disposed time.
But men may construe things after their fashion,
Clean from the purpose of the things themselves.
Comes Caesar to the Capitol tomorrow?
CASCA: He doth, for he did bid Antonio
Send word to you he would be there tomorrow.

CICERO: Good then, Casca. This disturbed sky
Is not to walk in.
CASCA: Farewell, Cicero.
Exit Cicero.
Enter Cassius.
CASSIUS: Who's there?
CASCA: A Roman.
CASSIUS: Casca, by your voice.
CASCA: Your ear is good. Cassius, what night is this!
CASSIUS: A very pleasing night to honest men.
CASCA: Who ever knew the heavens menace so?
CASSIUS: Those that have known the earth so full of faults.
For my part, I have walk'd about the streets,
Submitting me unto the perilous night,
And thus unbraced, Casca, as you see,
Have bared my bosom to the thunderstone;
And when the cross blue lightning seem'd to open
The breast of heaven, I did present myself
Even in the aim and very flash of it.
CASCA: But wherefore did you so much tempt the heavens?
It is the part of men to fear and tremble
When the most mighty gods by tokens send
Such dreadful heralds to astonish us.
CASSIUS: You are dull, Casca, and those sparks of life
That should be in a Roman you do want,
Or else you use not. You look pale and gaze
And put on fear and cast yourself in wonder
To see the strange impatience of the heavens.
But if you would consider the true cause
Why all these fires, why all these gliding ghosts,
Why birds and beasts from quality and kind,
Why old men, fools, and children calculate,
Why all these things change from their ordinance,
Their natures, and preformed faculties
To monstrous quality, why, you shall find
That heaven hath infused them with these spirits
To make them instruments of fear and warning
Unto some monstrous state.
Now could I, Casca, name to thee a man
Most like this dreadful night,
That thunders, lightens, opens graves, and roars
As doth the lion in the Capitol,
A man no mightier than thyself or me
In personal action, yet prodigious grown
And fearful, as these strange eruptions are.
CASCA: 'Tis Caesar that you mean, is it not, Cassius?
CASSIUS: Let it be who it is, for Romans now
Have thews and limbs like to their ancestors.
But, woe the while! Our fathers' minds are dead,

And we are govern'd with our mothers' spirits;
Our yoke and sufferance show us womanish.
CASCA: Indeed they say the senators tomorrow
Mean to establish Caesar as a king,
And he shall wear his crown by sea and land
In every place save here in Italy.
CASSIUS: I know where I will wear this dagger then:
Cassius from bondage will deliver Cassius.
Therein, ye gods, you make the weak most strong;
Therein, ye gods, you tyrants do defeat.
Nor stony tower, nor walls of beaten brass,
Nor airless dungeon, nor strong links of iron
Can be retentive to the strength of spirit;
But life, being weary of these worldly bars,
Never lacks power to dismiss itself.
If I know this, know all the world besides,
That part of tyranny that I do bear
I can shake off at pleasure. Thunder still.
CASCA: So can I.
So every bondman in his own hand bears
The power to cancel his captivity.
CASSIUS: And why should Caesar be a tyrant then?
Poor man! I know he would not be a wolf
But that he sees the Romans are but sheep.
He were no lion, were not Romans hinds.
Those that with haste will make a mighty fire
Begin it with weak straws. What trash is Rome,
What rubbish, and what offal, when it serves
For the base matter to illuminate
So vile a thing as Caesar? But, O grief,
Where hast thou led me? I perhaps speak this
Before a willing bondman; then I know
My answer must be made. But I am arm'd,
And dangers are to me indifferent.
CASCA: You speak to Casca, and to such a man
That is no fleering tell-tale. Hold, my hand.
Be factious for redress of all these griefs,
And I will set this foot of mine as far
As who goes farthest.
CASSIUS: There's a bargain made.
Now know you, Casca, I have moved already
Some certain of the noblest-minded Romans
To undergo with me an enterprise
Of honorable-dangerous consequence;
And I do know by this, they stay for me
In Pompey's Porch. For now, this fearful night,
There is no stir or walking in the streets,
And the complexion of the element
In favor's like the work we have in hand,

Most bloody, fiery, and most terrible.
Enter Cinna.
CASCA: Stand close awhile, for here comes one in haste.
CASSIUS: 'Tis Cinna, I do know him by his gait;
He is a friend. Cinna, where haste you so?
CINNA: To find out you. Who's that? Metellus Cimber?
CASSIUS: No, it is Casca, one incorporate
To our attempts. Am I not stay'd for, Cinna?
CINNA: I am glad on't. What a fearful night is this!
There's two or three of us have seen strange sights.
CASSIUS: Am I not stay'd for? Tell me.
CINNA: Yes, you are.
O Cassius, if you could
But win the noble Brutus to our party-
CASSIUS: Be you content. Good Cinna, take this paper,
And look you lay it in the praetor's chair,
Where Brutus may but find it; and throw this
In at his window; set this up with wax
Upon old Brutus' statue. All this done,
Repair to Pompey's Porch, where you shall find us.
Is Decius Brutus and Trebonius there?
CINNA: All but Metellus Cimber, and he's gone
To seek you at your house. Well, I will hie
And so bestow these papers as you bade me.
CASSIUS: That done, repair to Pompey's Theatre.
Exit Cinna.
Come, Casca, you and I will yet ere day
See Brutus at his house. Three parts of him
Is ours already, and the man entire
Upon the next encounter yields him ours.
CASCA: O, he sits high in all the people's hearts,
And that which would appear offense in us,
His countenance, like richest alchemy,
Will change to virtue and to worthiness.
CASSIUS: Him and his worth and our great need of him
You have right well conceited. Let us go,
For it is after midnight, and ere day
We will awake him and be sure of him.
Exeunt.

ACT II. SCENE I. Enter Brutus in His Orchard.

BRUTUS: What, Lucius, ho!
I cannot, by the progress of the stars,
Give guess how near to day. Lucius, I say!
I would it were my fault to sleep so soundly.
When, Lucius, when? Awake, I say! What, Lucius!
Enter Lucius.
LUCIUS: Call'd you, my lord?
BRUTUS: Get me a taper in my study, Lucius.
When it is lighted, come and call me here.

LUCIUS: I will, my lord.
Exit.
BRUTUS: It must be by his death, and, for my part,
I know no personal cause to spurn at him,
But for the general. He would be crown'd:
How that might change his nature, there's the question.
It is the bright day that brings forth the adder
And that craves wary walking. Crown him that,
And then, I grant, we put a sting in him
That at his will he may do danger with.
The abuse of greatness is when it disjoins
Remorse from power, and, to speak truth of Caesar,
I have not known when his affections sway'd
More than his reason. But 'tis a common proof
That lowliness is young ambition's ladder,
Whereto the climber-upward turns his face;
But when he once attains the upmost round,
He then unto the ladder turns his back,
Looks in the clouds, scorning the base degrees
By which he did ascend. So Caesar may;
Then, lest he may, prevent. And, since the quarrel
Will bear no color for the thing he is,
Fashion it thus, that what he is, augmented,
Would run to these and these extremities;
And therefore think him as a serpent's egg
Which hatch'd would as his kind grow mischievous,
And kill him in the shell.
Re-enter Lucius.
LUCIUS: The taper burneth in your closet, sir.
Searching the window for a flint I found
This paper thus seal'd up, and I am sure
It did not lie there when I went to bed.
Gives Him the Letter.
BRUTUS: Get you to bed again, it is not day.
Is not tomorrow, boy, the ides of March?
LUCIUS: I know not, sir.
BRUTUS: Look in the calendar and bring me word.
LUCIUS: I will, sir.
Exit.
BRUTUS: The exhalations whizzing in the air
Give so much light that I may read by them.
Opens the Letter and Reads.
Brutus, thou sleep'st: awake and see thyself!
Shall Rome, etc. Speak, strike, redress!"
"Brutus, thou sleep'st: awake!"
Such instigations have been often dropp'd
Where I have took them up.
"Shall Rome, etc." Thus must I piece it out.
Shall Rome stand under one man's awe? What, Rome?

My ancestors did from the streets of Rome
The Tarquin drive, when he was call'd a king.
"Speak, strike, redress!" Am I entreated
To speak and strike? O Rome, I make thee promise,
If the redress will follow, thou receivest
Thy full petition at the hand of Brutus!
Re-enter Lucius.
LUCIUS: Sir, March is wasted fifteen days.
Knocking within.
BRUTUS: 'Tis good. Go to the gate, somebody knocks.
Exit Lucius.
Since Cassius first did whet me against Caesar
I have not slept.
Between the acting of a dreadful thing
And the first motion, all the interim is
Like a phantasma or a hideous dream;
The genius and the mortal instruments
Are then in council, and the state of man,
Like to a little kingdom, suffers then
The nature of an insurrection.
Re-enter Lucius.
LUCIUS: Sir, 'tis your brother Cassius at the door,
Who doth desire to see you.
BRUTUS: Is he alone?
LUCIUS: No, sir, there are more with him.
BRUTUS: Do you know them?
LUCIUS: No, sir, their hats are pluck'd about their ears,
And half their faces buried in their cloaks,
That by no means I may discover them
By any mark of favor.
BRUTUS: Let 'em enter.
Exit Lucius.
They are the faction. O Conspiracy,
Shamest thou to show thy dangerous brow by night,
When evils are most free? O, then, by day
Where wilt thou find a cavern dark enough
To mask thy monstrous visage? Seek none, Conspiracy;
Hide it in smiles and affability;
For if thou path, thy native semblance on,
Not Erebus itself were dim enough
To hide thee from prevention.
Enter the conspirators, Cassius, Casca, Decius, Cinna, Metellus Cimber, and Trebonius.
CASSIUS: I think we are too bold upon your rest.
Good morrow, Brutus, do we trouble you?
BRUTUS: I have been up this hour, awake all night.
Know I these men that come along with you?
CASSIUS: Yes, every man of them, and no man here
But honors you, and every one doth wish
You had but that opinion of yourself

Which every noble Roman bears of you.
This is Trebonius.
BRUTUS: He is welcome hither.
CASSIUS: This, Decius Brutus.
BRUTUS: He is welcome too.
CASSIUS: This, Casca; this, Cinna; and this, Metellus Cimber.
BRUTUS: They are all welcome.
What watchful cares do interpose themselves
Betwixt your eyes and night?
CASSIUS: Shall I entreat a word? They whisper.
DECIUS: Here lies the east. Doth not the day break here?
CASCA: No.
CINNA: O, pardon, sir, it doth, and yongrey lines
That fret the clouds are messengers of day.
CASCA: You shall confess that you are both deceived.
Here, as I point my sword, the sun arises,
Which is a great way growing on the south,
Weighing the youthful season of the year.
Some two months hence up higher toward the north
He first presents his fire, and the high east
Stands as the Capitol, directly here.
BRUTUS: Give me your hands all over, one by one.
CASSIUS: And let us swear our resolution.
BRUTUS: No, not an oath. If not the face of men,
The sufferance of our souls, the time's abuse-
If these be motives weak, break off betimes,
And every man hence to his idle bed;
So let high-sighted tyranny range on
Till each man drop by lottery. But if these,
As I am sure they do, bear fire enough
To kindle cowards and to steel with valor
The melting spirits of women, then, countrymen,
What need we any spur but our own cause
To prick us to redress? What other bond
Than secret Romans that have spoke the word
And will not palter? And what other oath
Than honesty to honesty engaged
That this shall be or we will fall for it?
Swear priests and cowards and men cautelous,
Old feeble carrions and such suffering souls
That welcome wrongs; unto bad causes swear
Such creatures as men doubt; but do not stain
The even virtue of our enterprise,
Nor the insuppressive mettle of our spirits,
To think that or our cause or our performance
Did need an oath; when every drop of blood
That every Roman bears, and nobly bears,
Is guilty of a several bastardy
If he do break the smallest particle

Of any promise that hath pass'd from him.
CASSIUS: But what of Cicero? Shall we sound him?
I think he will stand very strong with us.
CASCA: Let us not leave him out.
CINNA: No, by no means.
METELLUS: O, let us have him, for his silver hairs
Will purchase us a good opinion,
And buy men's voices to commend our deeds.
It shall be said his judgement ruled our hands;
Our youths and wildness shall no whit appear,
But all be buried in his gravity.
BRUTUS: O, name him not; let us not break with him,
For he will never follow anything
That other men begin.
CASSIUS: Then leave him out.
CASCA: Indeed he is not fit.
DECIUS: Shall no man else be touch'd but only Caesar?
CASSIUS: Decius, well urged. I think it is not meet
Mark Antony, so well beloved of Caesar,
Should outlive Caesar. We shall find of him
A shrewd contriver; and you know his means,
If he improve them, may well stretch so far
As to annoy us all, which to prevent,
Let Antony and Caesar fall together.
BRUTUS: Our course will seem too bloody, Caius Cassius,
To cut the head off and then hack the limbs
Like wrath in death and envy afterwards;
For Antony is but a limb of Caesar.
Let us be sacrificers, but not butchers, Caius.
We all stand up against the spirit of Caesar,
And in the spirit of men there is no blood.
O, that we then could come by Caesar's spirit,
And not dismember Caesar! But, alas,
Caesar must bleed for it! And, gentle friends,
Let's kill him boldly, but not wrathfully;
Let's carve him as a dish fit for the gods,
Not hew him as a carcass fit for hounds;
And let our hearts, as subtle masters do,
Stir up their servants to an act of rage
And after seem to chide 'em. This shall make
Our purpose necessary and not envious,
Which so appearing to the common eyes,
We shall be call'd purgers, not murderers.
And for Mark Antony, think not of him,
For he can do no more than Caesar's arm
When Caesar's head is off.
CASSIUS: Yet I fear him,
For in the ingrated love he bears to Caesar-
BRUTUS: Alas, good Cassius, do not think of him.

If he love Caesar, all that he can do
Is to himself, take thought and die for Caesar.
And that were much he should, for he is given
To sports, to wildness, and much company.
TREBONIUS: There is no fear in him-let him not die,
For he will live and laugh at this hereafter.
Clock Strikes.
BRUTUS: Peace, count the clock.
CASSIUS: The clock hath stricken three.
TREBONIUS: 'Tis time to part.
CASSIUS: But it is doubtful yet
Whether Caesar will come forth today or no,
For he is superstitious grown of late,
Quite from the main opinion he held once
Of fantasy, of dreams, and ceremonies.
It may be these apparent prodigies,
The unaccustom'd terror of this night,
And the persuasion of his augurers
May hold him from the Capitol today.
DECIUS: Never fear that. If he be so resolved,
I can o'ersway him, for he loves to hear
That unicorns may be betray'd with trees,
And bears with glasses, elephants with holes,
Lions with toils, and men with flatterers;
But when I tell him he hates flatterers,
He says he does, being then most flattered.
Let me work;
For I can give his humor the true bent,
And I will bring him to the Capitol.
CASSIUS: Nay, we will all of us be there to fetch him.
BRUTUS: By the eighth hour. Is that the utter most?
CINNA: Be that the uttermost, and fail not then.
METELLUS: Caius Ligarius doth bear Caesar hard,
Who rated him for speaking well of Pompey.
I wonder none of you have thought of him.
BRUTUS: Now, good Metellus, go along by him.
He loves me well, and I have given him reasons;
Send him but hither, and I'll fashion him.
CASSIUS: The morning comes upon 's. We'll leave you, Brutus,
And, friends, disperse yourselves, but all remember
What you have said and show yourselves true Romans.
BRUTUS: Good gentlemen, look fresh and merrily;
Let not our looks put on our purposes,
But bear it as our Roman actors do,
With untired spirits and formal constancy.
And so, good morrow to you every one.
Exeunt all but Brutus.
Boy! Lucius! Fast asleep? It is no matter.
Enjoy the honey-heavy dew of slumber;

Thou hast no figures nor no fantasies,
Which busy care draws in the brains of men;
Therefore thou sleep'st so sound.
Enter Portia.
PORTIA: Brutus, my lord!
BRUTUS: Portia, what mean you? Wherefore rise you now?
It is not for your health thus to commit
Your weak condition to the raw cold morning.
PORTIA: Nor for yours neither. have ungently, Brutus,
Stole from my bed; and yesternight at supper
You suddenly arose and walk'd about,
Musing and sighing, with your arms across;
And when I ask'd you what the matter was,
You stared upon me with ungentle looks.
I urged you further; then you scratch'd your head,
And too impatiently stamp'd with your foot.
Yet I insisted, yet you answer'd not,
But with an angry waiter of your hand
Gave sign for me to leave you. So I did,
Fearing to strengthen that impatience
Which seem'd too much enkindled, and withal
Hoping it was but an effect of humor,
Which sometime hath his hour with every man.
It will not let you eat, nor talk, nor sleep,
And, could it work so much upon your shape
As it hath much prevail'd on your condition,
I should not know you, Brutus. Dear my lord,
Make me acquainted with your cause of grief.
BRUTUS: I am not well in health, and that is all.
PORTIA: Brutus is wise, and, were he not in health,
He would embrace the means to come by it.
BRUTUS: Why, so I do. Good Portia, go to bed.
PORTIA: Is Brutus sick, and is it physical
To walk unbraced and suck up the humors
Of the dank morning? What, is Brutus sick,
And will he steal out of his wholesome bed
To dare the vile contagion of the night
And tempt the rheumy and unpurged air
To add unto his sickness? No, my Brutus,
You have some sick offense within your mind,
Which by the right and virtue of my place
I ought to know of; and, upon my knees,
I charm you, by my once commended beauty,
By all your vows of love and that great vow
Which did incorporate and make us one,
That you unfold to me, yourself, your half,
Why you are heavy and what men tonight
Have had resort to you; for here have been
Some six or seven, who did hide their faces

Even from darkness.
BRUTUS: Kneel not, gentle Portia.
PORTIA: I should not need, if you were gentle Brutus.
Within the bond of marriage, tell me, Brutus,
Is it excepted I should know no secrets
That appertain to you? Am I yourself
But, as it were, in sort or limitation,
To keep with you at meals, comfort your bed,
And talk to you sometimes? Dwell I but in the suburbs
Of your good pleasure? If it be no more,
Portia is Brutus' harlot, not his wife.
BRUTUS: You are my true and honorable wife,
As dear to me as are the ruddy drops
That visit my sad heart.
PORTIA: If this were true, then should I know this secret.
I grant I am a woman, but withal
A woman that Lord Brutus took to wife.
I grant I am a woman, but withal
A woman well reputed, Cato's daughter.
Think you I am no stronger than my sex,
Being so father'd and so husbanded?
Tell me your counsels, I will not disclose 'em.
I have made strong proof of my constancy,
Giving myself a voluntary wound
Here in the thigh. Can I bear that with patience
And not my husband's secrets?
BRUTUS: O ye gods,
Render me worthy of this noble wife! Knocking within.
Hark, hark, one knocks. Portia, go in awhile,
And by and by thy bosom shall partake
The secrets of my heart.
All my engagements I will construe to thee,
All the charactery of my sad brows.
Leave me with haste.
  Exit Portia.
Lucius, who's that knocks?
  Re-enter Lucius with Ligarius.
LUCIUS: Here is a sick man that would speak with you.
BRUTUS: Caius Ligarius, that Metellus spake of.
Boy, stand aside. Caius Ligarius, how?
LIGARIUS: Vouchsafe good morrow from a feeble tongue.
BRUTUS: O, what a time have you chose out, brave Caius,
To wear a kerchief! Would you were not sick!
LIGARIUS: I am not sick, if Brutus have in hand
Any exploit worthy the name of honor.
BRUTUS: Such an exploit have I in hand, Ligarius,
Had you a healthful ear to hear of it.
LIGARIUS: By all the gods that Romans bow before,
I here discard my sickness! Soul of Rome!

Brave son, derived from honorable loins!
Thou, like an exorcist, hast conjured up
My mortified spirit. Now bid me run,
And I will strive with things impossible,
Yea, get the better of them. What's to do?
BRUTUS: A piece of work that will make sick men whole.
LIGARIUS: But are not some whole that we must make sick?
BRUTUS: That must we also. What it is, my Caius,
I shall unfold to thee, as we are going
To whom it must be done.
LIGARIUS: Set on your foot,
And with a heart new-fired I follow you,
To do I know not what; but it sufficeth
That Brutus leads me on.
BRUTUS: Follow me then.
Exeunt.

ACT II. SCENE II. Caesar's House. Thunder and Lightning.

Enter Caesar, in His Nightgown.
CAESAR: Nor heaven nor earth have been at peace tonight.
Thrice hath Calpurnia in her sleep cried out,
"Help, ho! They murther Caesar!" Who's within?
Enter a Servant.
SERVANT: My lord?
CAESAR: Go bid the priests do present sacrifice,
And bring me their opinions of success.
SERVANT: I will, my lord.
Exit.
Enter Calpurnia.
CALPURNIA: What mean you, Caesar? Think you to walk forth?
You shall not stir out of your house today.
CAESAR: Caesar shall forth: the things that threaten'd me
Ne'er look'd but on my back; when they shall see
The face of Caesar, they are vanished.
CALPURNIA: Caesar, I I stood on ceremonies,
Yet now they fright me. There is one within,
Besides the things that we have heard and seen,
Recounts most horrid sights seen by the watch.
A lioness hath whelped in the streets;
And graves have yawn'd, and yielded up their dead;
Fierce fiery warriors fight upon the clouds,
In ranks and squadrons and right form of war,
Which drizzled blood upon the Capitol;
The noise of battle hurtled in the air,
Horses did neigh and dying men did groan,
And ghosts did shriek and squeal about the streets.
O Caesar! These things are beyond all use,
And I do fear them.
CAESAR: What can be avoided
Whose end is purposed by the mighty gods?

Yet Caesar shall go forth, for these predictions
Are to the world in general as to Caesar.
CALPURNIA: When beggars die, there are no comets seen;
The heavens themselves blaze forth the death of princes.
CAESAR: Cowards die many times before their deaths;
The valiant never taste of death but once.
Of all the wonders that I yet have heard,
It seems to me most strange that men should fear
Seeing that death, a necessary end,
Will come when it will come.
Re-enter Servant.
What say the augurers?
SERVANT: They would not have you to stir forth today.
Plucking the entrails of an offering forth,
They could not find a heart within the beast.
CAESAR: The gods do this in shame of cowardice.
Caesar should be a beast without a heart
If he should stay at home today for fear.
No, Caesar shall not. Danger knows full well
That Caesar is more dangerous than he.
We are two lions litter'd in one day,
And I the elder and more terrible.
And Caesar shall go forth.
CALPURNIA: Alas, my lord,
Your wisdom is consumed in confidence.
Do not go forth today. Call it my fear
That keeps you in the house and not your own.
We'll send Mark Antony to the Senate House,
And he shall say you are not well today.
Let me, upon my knee, prevail in this.
CAESAR: Mark Antony shall say I am not well,
And, for thy humor, I will stay at home.
Enter Decius.
Here's Decius Brutus, he shall tell them so.
DECIUS: Caesar, all hail! Good morrow, worthy Caesar!
I come to fetch you to the Senate House.
CAESAR: And you are come in very happy time
To bear my greeting to the senators
And tell them that I will not come today.
Cannot, is false, and that I dare not, falser:
I will not come today. Tell them so, Decius.
CALPURNIA: Say he is sick.
CAESAR: Shall Caesar send a lie?
Have I in conquest stretch'd mine arm so far
To be afeard to tell greybeards the truth?
Decius, go tell them Caesar will not come.
DECIUS: Most mighty Caesar, let me know some cause,
Lest I be laugh'd at when I tell them so.
CAESAR: The cause is in my will: I will not come,

That is enough to satisfy the Senate.
But, for your private satisfaction,
Because I love you, I will let you know.
Calpurnia here, my wife, stays me at home;
She dreamt tonight she saw my statue,
Which, like a fountain with an hundred spouts,
Did run pure blood, and many lusty Romans
Came smiling and did bathe their hands in it.
And these does she apply for warnings and portents
And evils imminent, and on her knee
Hath begg'd that I will stay at home today.
DECIUS: This dream is all amiss interpreted;
It was a vision fair and fortunate.
Your statue spouting blood in many pipes,
In which so many smiling Romans bathed,
Signifies that from you great Rome shall suck
Reviving blood, and that great men shall press
For tinctures, stains, relics, and cognizance.
This by Calpurnia's dream is signified.
CAESAR: And this way have you well expounded it.
DECIUS: I have, when you have heard what I can say.
And know it now, the Senate have concluded
To give this day a crown to mighty Caesar.
If you shall send them word you will not come,
Their minds may change. Besides, it were a mock
Apt to be render'd, for someone to say
"Break up the Senate till another time,
When Caesar's wife shall meet with better dreams."
If Caesar hide himself, shall they not whisper
"Lo, Caesar is afraid"?
Pardon me, Caesar, for my dear dear love
To your proceeding bids me tell you this,
And reason to my love is liable.
CAESAR: How foolish do your fears seem now, Calpurnia!
I am ashamed I did yield to them.
Give me my robe, for I will go.
Enter Publius, Brutus, Ligarius, Metellus, Casca, Trebonius, and Cinna.
And look where Publius is come to fetch me.
PUBLIUS: Good morrow,Caesar.
CAESAR: Welcome, Publius.
What, Brutus, are you stirr'd so early too?
Good morrow, Casca. Caius Ligarius,
Caesar was ne'er so much your enemy
As that same ague which hath made you lean.
What is't o'clock?
BRUTUS: Caesar, 'tis strucken eight.
CAESAR: I thank you for your pains and courtesy.
Enter Antony.
See, Antony, that revels long o' nights,

Is notwithstanding up. Good morrow, Antony.
ANTONY: So to most noble Caesar.
CAESAR: Bid them prepare within.
I am to blame to be thus waited for.
Now, Cinna; now, Metellus; what, Trebonius,
I have an hour's talk in store for you;
Remember that you call on me today;
Be near me, that I may remember you.
TREBONIUS: Caesar, I will. Aside. And so near will I be
That your best friends shall wish I had been further.
CAESAR: Good friends, go in and taste some wine with me,
And we like friends will straightway go together.
BRUTUS: Aside. That every like is not the same, O Caesar,
The heart of Brutus yearns to think upon!
Exeunt.

ACT II. SCENE III. A Street near the Capitol.

Enter Artemidorus, Reading Paper.
ARTEMIDORUS: "Caesar, beware of Brutus; take heed of Cassius; come not near Casca; have an eye to Cinna; trust not Trebonius; mark well Metellus Cimber; Decius Brutus loves thee not; thou hast wronged Caius Ligarius. There is but one mind in all these men, and it is bent against Caesar. If thou beest not immortal, look about you. Security gives way to conspiracy. The mighty gods defend thee!
Thy lover, Artemidorus."
Here will I stand till Caesar pass along,
And as a suitor will I give him this.
My heart laments that virtue cannot live
Out of the teeth of emulation.
If thou read this, O Caesar, thou mayest live;
If not, the Fates with traitors do contrive.
Exit.

ACT II. SCENE IV. Another Part of the Same Street, Before the House of Brutus.

Enter Portia and Lucius.
PORTIA: I prithee, boy, run to the Senate House;
Stay not to answer me, but get thee gone.
Why dost thou stay?
LUCIUS: To know my errand, madam.
PORTIA: I would have had thee there, and here again,
Ere I can tell thee what thou shouldst do there.
O constancy, be strong upon my side!
Set a huge mountain 'tween my heart and tongue!
I have a man's mind, but a woman's might.
How hard it is for women to keep counsel!
Art thou here yet?
LUCIUS: Madam, what should I do?
Run to the Capitol, and nothing else?
And so return to you, and nothing else?
PORTIA: Yes, bring me word, boy, if thy lord look well,

For he went sickly forth; and take good note
What Caesar doth, what suitors press to him.
Hark, boy, what noise is that?
LUCIUS: I hear none, madam.
PORTIA: Prithee, listen well.
I heard a bustling rumor like a fray,
And the wind brings it from the Capitol.
LUCIUS: Sooth, madam, I hear nothing.
Enter the Soothsayer.
PORTIA: Come hither, fellow;
Which way hast thou been?
SOOTHSAYER: At mine own house, good lady.
PORTIA: What is't o'clock?
SOOTHSAYER: About the ninth hour, lady.
PORTIA: Is Caesar yet gone to the Capitol?
SOOTHSAYER: Madam, not yet. I go to take my stand
To see him pass on to the Capitol.
PORTIA: Thou hast some suit to Caesar, hast thou not?
SOOTHSAYER: That I have, lady. If it will please Caesar
To be so good to Caesar as to hear me,
I shall beseech him to befriend himself.
PORTIA: Why, know'st thou any harm's intended towards him?
SOOTHSAYER: None that I know will be, much that I fear may chance.
Good morrow to you. Here the street is narrow,
The throng that follows Caesar at the heels,
Of senators, of praetors, common suitors,
Will crowd a feeble man almost to death.
I'll get me to a place more void and there
Speak to great Caesar as he comes along.
Exit.
PORTIA: I must go in. Ay me, how weak a thing
The heart of woman is! O Brutus,
The heavens speed thee in thine enterprise!
Sure, the boy heard me. Brutus hath a suit
That Caesar will not grant. O, I grow faint.
Run, Lucius, and commend me to my lord;
Say I am merry. Come to me again,
And bring me word what he doth say to thee.
Exeunt Severally.

ACT III. SCENE I. Rome. Before the Capitol; the Senate Sitting Above. A Crowd of People, among Them Artemidorus and the Soothsayer.

Flourish. Enter Caesar, Brutus, Cassius, Casca, Decius, Metellus, Trebonius, Cinna, Antony, Lepidus, Popilius, Publius, and Others.
CAESAR: The ides of March are come.
SOOTHSAYER: Ay, Caesar, but not gone.
A Hail, Caesar! Read this schedule.
DECIUS: Trebonius doth desire you to o'er read,
At your best leisure, this his humble suit.
ARTEMIDORUS: O Caesar, read mine first, for mine's a suit

That touches Caesar nearer. Read it, great Caesar.
CAESAR: What touches us ourself shall be last served.
ARTEMIDORUS: Delay not, Caesar; read it instantly.
CAESAR: What, is the fellow mad?
PUBLIUS: Sirrah, give place.
CASSIUS: What, urge you your petitions in the street?
Come to the Capitol.
Caesar goes up to the Senate House, the rest follow.
POPILIUS: I wish your enterprise today may thrive.
CASSIUS: What enterprise, Popilius?
POPILIUS: Fare you well.
Advances to Caesar.
BRUTUS: What said Popilius Lena?
CASSIUS: He wish'd today our enterprise might thrive.
I fear our purpose is discovered.
BRUTUS: Look, how he makes to Caesar. Mark him.
CASSIUS: Casca,
Be sudden, for we fear prevention.
Brutus, what shall be done? If this be known,
Cassius or Caesar never shall turn back,
For I will slay myself.
BRUTUS: Cassius, be constant.
Popilius Lena speaks not of our purposes;
For, look, he smiles, and Caesar doth not change.
CASSIUS: Trebonius knows his time, for, look you, Brutus,
He draws Mark Antony out of the way.
Exeunt Antony and Trebonius.
DECIUS: Where is Metellus Cimber? Let him
And presently prefer his suit to Caesar.
BRUTUS: He is address'd; press near and second him.
CINNA: Casca, you are the first that rears your hand.
CAESAR: Are we all ready? What is now amiss
That Caesar and his Senate must redress?
METELLUS: Most high, most mighty, and most puissant Caesar,
Metellus Cimber throws before thy seat
An humble heart. Kneels.
CAESAR: I must prevent thee, Cimber.
These couchings and these lowly courtesies
Might fire the blood of ordinary men
And turn preordinance and first decree
Into the law of children. Be not fond
To think that Caesar bears such rebel blood
That will be thaw'd from the true quality
With that which melteth fools- I mean sweet words,
Low-crooked court'sies, and base spaniel-fawning.
Thy brother by decree is banished.
If thou dost bend and pray and fawn for him,
I spurn thee like a cur out of my way.
Know, Caesar doth not wrong, nor without cause

Will he be satisfied.
METELLUS: Is there no voice more worthy than my own,
To sound more sweetly in great Caesar's ear
For the repealing of my banish'd brother?
BRUTUS: I kiss thy hand, but not in flattery, Caesar,
Desiring thee that Publius Cimber may
Have an immediate freedom of repeal.
CAESAR: What, Brutus?
CASSIUS: Pardon, Caesar! Caesar, pardon!
As low as to thy foot doth Cassius fall
To beg enfranchisement for Publius Cimber.
CAESAR: I could be well moved, if I were as you;
If I could pray to move, prayers would move me;
But I am constant as the northern star,
Of whose true-fix'd and resting quality
There is no fellow in the firmament.
The skies are painted with unnumber'd sparks;
They are all fire and every one doth shine;
But there's but one in all doth hold his place.
So in the world, 'tis furnish'd well with men,
And men are flesh and blood, and apprehensive;
Yet in the number I do know but one
That unassailable holds on his rank,
Unshaked of motion; and that I am he,
Let me a little show it, even in this;
That I was constant Cimber should be banish'd,
And constant do remain to keep him so.
CINNA: O Caesar-
CAESAR: Hence! Wilt thou lift up Olympus?
DECIUS: Great Caesar-
CAESAR: Doth not Brutus bootless kneel?
CASCA: Speak, hands, for me!
Casca First, Then the Other Conspirators and Marcus Brutus Stab Caesar.
CAESAR: Et tu, Brute?- Then fall, Caesar! Dies.
CINNA: Liberty! Freedom! Tyranny is dead!
Run hence, proclaim, cry it about the streets.
CASSIUS: Some to the common pulpits and cry out
"Liberty, freedom, and enfranchisement!"
BRUTUS: People and senators, be not affrighted,
Fly not, stand still; ambition's debt is paid.
CASCA: Go to the pulpit, Brutus.
DECIUS: And Cassius too.
BRUTUS: Where's Publius?
CINNA: Here, quite confounded with this mutiny.
METELLUS: Stand fast together, lest some friend of Caesar's
Should chance-
BRUTUS: Talk not of standing. Publius, good cheer,
There is no harm intended to your person,
Nor to no Roman else. So tell them, Publius.

CASSIUS: And leave us, Publius, lest that the people
Rushing on us should do your age some mischief.
BRUTUS: Do so, and let no man abide this deed
But we the doers.
Re-enter Trebonius.
CASSIUS: Where is Antony?
TREBONIUS: Fled to his house amazed.
Men, wives, and children stare, cry out, and run
As it were doomsday.
BRUTUS: Fates, we will know your pleasures.
That we shall die, we know; 'tis but the time
And drawing days out that men stand upon.
CASSIUS: Why, he that cuts off twenty years of life
Cuts off so many years of fearing death.
BRUTUS: Grant that, and then is death a benefit;
So are we Caesar's friends that have abridged
His time of fearing death. Stoop, Romans, stoop,
And let us bathe our hands in Caesar's blood
Up to the elbows, and besmear our swords;
Then walk we forth, even to the marketplace,
And waving our red weapons o'er our heads,
Let's all cry, "Peace, freedom, and liberty!"
CASSIUS: Stoop then, and wash. How many ages hence
Shall this our lofty scene be acted over
In states unborn and accents yet unknown!
BRUTUS: How many times shall Caesar bleed in sport,
That now on Pompey's basis lies along
No worthier than the dust!
CASSIUS: So oft as that shall be,
So often shall the knot of us be call'd
The men that gave their country liberty.
DECIUS: What, shall we forth?
CASSIUS: Ay, every man away.
Brutus shall lead, and we will grace his heels
With the most boldest and best hearts of Rome.
Enter a Servant.
BRUTUS: Soft, who comes here? A friend of Antony's.
SERVANT: Thus, Brutus, did my master bid me kneel,
Thus did Mark Antony bid me fall down,
And, being prostrate, thus he bade me say:
Brutus is noble, wise, valiant, and honest;
Caesar was mighty, bold, royal, and loving.
Say I love Brutus and I honor him;
Say I fear'd Caesar, honor'd him, and loved him.
If Brutus will vouchsafe that Antony
May safely come to him and be resolved
How Caesar hath deserved to lie in death,
Mark Antony shall not love Caesar dead
So well as Brutus living, but will follow

The fortunes and affairs of noble Brutus
Thorough the hazards of this untrod state
With all true faith. So says my master Antony.
BRUTUS: Thy master is a wise and valiant Roman;
I never thought him worse.
Tell him, so please him come unto this place,
He shall be satisfied and, by my honor,
Depart untouch'd.
SERVANT: I'll fetch him presently.
Exit.
BRUTUS: I know that we shall have him well to friend.
CASSIUS: I wish we may, but yet have I a mind
That fears him much, and my misgiving still
Falls shrewdly to the purpose.
Re-enter Antony.
BRUTUS: But here comes Antony. Welcome, Mark Antony.
ANTONY: O mighty Caesar! Dost thou lie so low?
Are all thy conquests, glories, triumphs, spoils,
Shrunk to this little measure? Fare thee well.
I know not, gentlemen, what you intend,
Who else must be let blood, who else is rank.
If I myself, there is no hour so fit
As Caesar's death's hour, nor no instrument
Of half that worth as those your swords, made rich
With the most noble blood of all this world.
I do beseech ye, if you bear me hard,
Now, whilst your purpled hands do reek and smoke,
Fulfill your pleasure. Live a thousand years,
I shall not find myself so apt to die;
No place will please me so, no means of death,
As here by Caesar, and by you cut off,
The choice and master spirits of this age.
BRUTUS: O Antony, beg not your death of us!
Though now we must appear bloody and cruel,
As, by our hands and this our present act
You see we do, yet see you but our hands
And this the bleeding business they have done.
Our hearts you see not; they are pitiful;
And pity to the general wrong of Rome-
As fire drives out fire, so pity pity-
Hath done this deed on Caesar. For your part,
To you our swords have leaden points, Mark Antony;
Our arms in strength of malice, and our hearts
Of brothers' temper, do receive you in
With all kind love, good thoughts, and reverence.
CASSIUS: Your voice shall be as strong as any man's
In the disposing of new dignities.
BRUTUS: Only be patient till we have appeased
The multitude, beside themselves with fear,

And then we will deliver you the cause
Why I, that did love Caesar when I struck him,
Have thus proceeded.
ANTONY: I doubt not of your wisdom.
Let each man render me his bloody hand.
First, Marcus Brutus, will I shake with you;
Next, Caius Cassius, do I take your hand;
Now, Decius Brutus, yours; now yours, Metellus;
Yours, Cinna; and, my valiant Casca, yours;
Though last, not least in love, yours, good Trebonius.
Gentlemen all- alas, what shall I say?
My credit now stands on such slippery ground,
That one of two bad ways you must conceit me,
Either a coward or a flatterer.
That I did love thee, Caesar, O, 'tis true!
If then thy spirit look upon us now,
Shall it not grieve thee dearer than thy death
To see thy Antony making his peace,
Shaking the bloody fingers of thy foes,
Most noble! In the presence of thy corse?
Had I as many eyes as thou hast wounds,
Weeping as fast as they stream forth thy blood,
It would become me better than to close
In terms of friendship with thine enemies.
Pardon me, Julius! Here wast thou bay'd, brave hart,
Here didst thou fall, and here thy hunters stand,
Sign'd in thy spoil, and crimson'd in thy Lethe.
O world, thou wast the forest to this hart,
And this, indeed, O world, the heart of thee.
How like a deer strucken by many princes
Dost thou here lie!
CASSIUS: Mark Antony-
ANTONY: Pardon me, Caius Cassius.
The enemies of Caesar shall say this:
Then, in a friend, it is cold modesty.
CASSIUS: I blame you not for praising Caesar so;
But what compact mean you to have with us?
Will you be prick'd in number of our friends,
Or shall we on, and not depend on you?
ANTONY: Therefore I took your hands, but was indeed
Sway'd from the point by looking down on Caesar.
Friends am I with you all and love you all,
Upon this hope that you shall give me reasons
Why and wherein Caesar was dangerous.
BRUTUS: Or else were this a savage spectacle.
Our reasons are so full of good regard
That were you, Antony, the son of Caesar,
You should be satisfied.
ANTONY: That's all I seek;

And am moreover suitor that I may
Produce his body to the marketplace,
And in the pulpit, as becomes a friend,
Speak in the order of his funeral.
BRUTUS: You shall, Mark Antony.
CASSIUS: Brutus, a word with you.
Aside to Brutus. You know not what you do. Do not consent
That Antony speak in his funeral.
Know you how much the people may be moved
By that which he will utter?
BRUTUS: By your pardon,
I will myself into the pulpit first,
And show the reason of our Caesar's death.
What Antony shall speak, I will protest
He speaks by leave and by permission,
And that we are contented Caesar shall
Have all true rites and lawful ceremonies.
It shall advantage more than do us wrong.
CASSIUS: I know not what may fall; I like it not.
BRUTUS: Mark Antony, here, take you Caesar's body.
You shall not in your funeral speech blame us,
But speak all good you can devise of Caesar,
And say you do't by our permission,
Else shall you not have any hand at all
About his funeral. And you shall speak
In the same pulpit whereto I am going,
After my speech is ended.
ANTONY: Be it so,
I do desire no more.
BRUTUS: Prepare the body then, and follow us.
Exeunt All but Antony.
ANTONY: O, pardon me, thou bleeding piece of earth,
That I am meek and gentle with these butchers!
Thou art the ruins of the noblest man
That ever lived in the tide of times.
Woe to the hand that shed this costly blood!
Over thy wounds now do I prophesy
(Which like dumb mouths do ope their ruby lips
To beg the voice and utterance of my tongue)
A curse shall light upon the limbs of men;
Domestic fury and fierce civil strife
Shall cumber all the parts of Italy;
Blood and destruction shall be so in use,
And dreadful objects so familiar,
That mothers shall but smile when they behold
Their infants quarter'd with the hands of war;
All pity choked with custom of fell deeds,
And Caesar's spirit ranging for revenge,
With Ate by his side come hot from hell,

Shall in these confines with a monarch's voice
Cry "Havoc!" and let slip the dogs of war,
That this foul deed shall smell above the earth
With carrion men, groaning for burial.
Enter a Servant.
You serve Octavius Caesar, do you not?
SERVANT: I do, Mark Antony.
ANTONY: Caesar did write for him to come to Rome.
SERVANT: He did receive his letters, and is coming,
And bid me say to you by word of mouth-
O Caesar! Sees the body.
ANTONY: Thy heart is big; get thee apart and weep.
Passion, I see, is catching, for mine eyes,
Seeing those beads of sorrow stand in thine,
Began to water. Is thy master coming?
SERVANT: He lies tonight within seven leagues of Rome.
ANTONY: Post back with speed and tell him what hath chanced.
Here is a mourning Rome, a dangerous Rome,
No Rome of safety for Octavius yet;
Hie hence, and tell him so. Yet stay awhile,
Thou shalt not back till I have borne this corse
Into the marketplace. There shall I try,
In my oration, how the people take
The cruel issue of these bloody men,
According to the which thou shalt discourse
To young Octavius of the state of things.
Lend me your hand.
Exeunt with Caesar's Body.

ACT III. SCENE II. The Forum.

Enter Brutus and Cassius, and a throng of Citizens.
CITIZENS: We will be satisfied! Let us be satisfied!
BRUTUS: Then follow me and give me audience, friends.
Cassius, go you into the other street
And part the numbers.
Those that will hear me speak, let 'em stay here;
Those that will follow Cassius, go with him;
And public reasons shall be rendered
Of Caesar's death.
FIRST CITIZEN: I will hear Brutus speak.
SECOND CITIZEN: I will hear Cassius and compare their reasons,
When severally we hear them rendered.
Exit Cassius, with Some Citizens. Brutus Goes into the Pulpit.
THIRD CITIZEN: The noble Brutus is ascended. Silence!
BRUTUS: Be patient till the last.
Romans, countrymen, and lovers! Hear me for my cause, and be silent, that you may hear. Believe me for mine honor, and have respect to mine honor, that you may believe. Censure me in your wisdom, and awake your senses, that you may the better judge. If there be any in this assembly, any dear friend of Caesar's, to

him I say that Brutus' love to Caesar was no less than his. If then that friend demand why Brutus rose against Caesar, this is my answer: Not that I loved Caesar less, but that I loved Rome more. Had you rather Caesar were living and die all slaves, than that Caesar were dead to live all freemen? As Caesar loved me, I weep for him; as he was fortunate, I rejoice at it; as he was valiant, I honor him; but as he was ambitious, I slew him. There is tears for his love, joy for his fortune, honor for his valor, and death for his ambition. Who is here so base that would be a bondman? If any, speak, for him have I offended. Who is here so rude that would not be a Roman? If any, speak, for him have I offended. Who is here so vile that will not love his country? If any, speak, for him have I offended. I pause for a reply.
ALL: None, Brutus, none.
BRUTUS: Then none have I offended. I have done no more to Caesar than you shall do to Brutus. The question of his death is enrolled in the Capitol, his glory not extenuated, wherein he was worthy, nor his offenses enforced, for which he suffered death.
Enter Antony and Others, with Caesar's Body.
Here comes his body, mourned by Mark Antony, who, though he had no hand in his death, shall receive the benefit of his dying, a place in the commonwealth, as which of you shall not? With this I depart- that, as I slew my best lover for the good of Rome, I have the same dagger for myself, when it shall please my country to need my death.
ALL: Live, Brutus, live, live!
FIRST CITIZEN: Bring him with triumph home unto his house.
SECOND CITIZEN: Give him a statue with his ancestors.
THIRD CITIZEN: Let him be Caesar.
FOURTH CITIZEN: Caesar's better parts
Shall be crown'd in Brutus.
FIRST CITIZEN: We'll bring him to his house with shouts and clamors.
BRUTUS: My countrymen-
SECOND CITIZEN: Peace! Silence! Brutus speaks.
FIRST CITIZEN: Peace, ho!
BRUTUS: Good countrymen, let me depart alone,
And, for my sake, stay here with Antony.
Do grace to Caesar's corse, and grace his speech
Tending to Caesar's glories, which Mark Antony,
By our permission, is allow'd to make.
I do entreat you, not a man depart,
Save I alone, till Antony have spoke.
Exit.
FIRST CITIZEN: Stay, ho, and let us hear Mark Antony.
THIRD CITIZEN: Let him go up into the public chair;
We'll hear him. Noble Antony, go up.
ANTONY: For Brutus' sake, I am beholding to you.
Goes into the Pulpit.

FOURTH CITIZEN: What does he say of Brutus?
THIRD CITIZEN: He says, for Brutus' sake,
He finds himself beholding to us all.
FOURTH CITIZEN: 'Twere best he speak no harm of Brutus here.
FIRST CITIZEN: This Caesar was a tyrant.
THIRD CITIZEN: Nay, that's certain.
We are blest that Rome is rid of him.
SECOND CITIZEN: Peace! Let us hear what Antony can say.
ANTONY: You gentle Romans-
ALL: Peace, ho! Let us hear him.
ANTONY: Friends, Romans, countrymen, lend me your ears!
I come to bury Caesar, not to praise him.
The evil that men do lives after them,
The good is oft interred with their bones;
So let it be with Caesar. The noble Brutus
Hath told you Caesar was ambitious;
If it were so, it was a grievous fault,
And grievously hath Caesar answer'd it.
Here, under leave of Brutus and the rest-
For Brutus is an honorable man;
So are they all, all honorable men-
Come I to speak in Caesar's funeral.
He was my friend, faithful and just to me;
But Brutus says he was ambitious,
And Brutus is an honorable man.
He hath brought many captives home to Rome,
Whose ransoms did the general coffers fill.
Did this in Caesar seem ambitious?
When that the poor have cried, Caesar hath wept;
Ambition should be made of sterner stuff:
Yet Brutus says he was ambitious,
And Brutus is an honorable man.
You all did see that on the Lupercal
I thrice presented him a kingly crown,
Which he did thrice refuse. Was this ambition?
Yet Brutus says he was ambitious,
And sure he is an honorable man.
I speak not to disprove what Brutus spoke,
But here I am to speak what I do know.
You all did love him once, not without cause;
What cause withholds you then to mourn for him?
O judgement, thou art fled to brutish beasts,
And men have lost their reason. Bear with me;
My heart is in the coffin there with Caesar,
And I must pause till it come back to me.
FIRST CITIZEN: Methinks there is much reason in his sayings.
SECOND CITIZEN: If thou consider rightly of the matter,
Caesar has had great wrong.
THIRD CITIZEN: Has he, masters?

I fear there will a worse come in his place.
FOURTH CITIZEN: Mark'd ye his words? He would not take the crown;
Therefore 'tis certain he was not ambitious.
FIRST CITIZEN: If it be found so, some will dear abide it.
SECOND CITIZEN: Poor soul, his eyes are red as fire with weeping.
THIRD CITIZEN: There's not a nobler man in Rome than Antony.
FOURTH CITIZEN: Now mark him, he begins again to speak.
ANTONY: But yesterday the word of Caesar might
Have stood against the world. Now lies he there,
And none so poor to do him reverence.
O masters! If I were disposed to stir
Your hearts and minds to mutiny and rage,
I should do Brutus wrong and Cassius wrong,
Who, you all know, are honorable men.
I will not do them wrong; I rather choose
To wrong the dead, to wrong myself and you,
Than I will wrong such honorable men.
But here's a parchment with the seal of Caesar;
I found it in his closet, 'tis his will.
Let but the commons hear this testament-
Which, pardon me, I do not mean to read-
And they would go and kiss dead Caesar's wounds
And dip their napkins in his sacred blood,
Yea, beg a hair of him for memory,
And, dying, mention it within their wills,
Bequeathing it as a rich legacy
Unto their issue.
FOURTH CITIZEN: We'll hear the will. Read it, Mark Antony.
ALL: The will, the will! We will hear Caesar's will.
ANTONY: Have patience, gentle friends, I must not read it;
It is not meet you know how Caesar loved you.
You are not wood, you are not stones, but men;
And, being men, hearing the will of Caesar,
It will inflame you, it will make you mad.
'Tis good you know not that you are his heirs,
For if you should, O, what would come of it!
FOURTH CITIZEN: Read the will; we'll hear it, Antony.
You shall read us the will, Caesar's will.
ANTONY: Will you be patient? Will you stay awhile?
I have o'ershot myself to tell you of it.
I fear I wrong the honorable men
Whose daggers have stabb'd Caesar; I do fear it.
FOURTH CITIZEN: They were traitors. Honorable men!
ALL: The will! The testament!
SECOND CITIZEN: They were villains, murtherers. The will!
Read the will!
ANTONY: You will compel me then to read the will?
Then make a ring about the corse of Caesar,
And let me show you him that made the will.

Shall I descend? And will you give me leave?
ALL: Come down.
SECOND CITIZEN: Descend.
He Comes down from the Pulpit.
THIRD CITIZEN: You shall have leave.
FOURTH CITIZEN: A ring, stand round.
FIRST CITIZEN: Stand from the hearse, stand from the body.
SECOND CITIZEN: Room for Antony, most noble Antony.
ANTONY: Nay, press not so upon me, stand far off.
ALL: Stand back; room, bear back!
ANTONY: If you have tears, prepare to shed them now.
You all do know this mantle. I remember
The first time ever Caesar put it on;
'Twas on a summer's evening, in his tent,
That day he overcame the Nervii.
Look, in this place ran Cassius' dagger through;
See what a rent the envious Casca made;
Through this the well-beloved Brutus stabb'd;
And as he pluck'd his cursed steel away,
Mark how the blood of Caesar follow'd it,
As rushing out of doors, to be resolved
If Brutus so unkindly knock'd, or no;
For Brutus, as you know, was Caesar's angel.
Judge, O you gods, how dearly Caesar loved him!
This was the most unkindest cut of all;
For when the noble Caesar saw him stab,
Ingratitude, more strong than traitors' arms,
Quite vanquish'd him. Then burst his mighty heart,
And, in his mantle muffling up his face,
Even at the base of Pompey's statue,
Which all the while ran blood, great Caesar fell.
O, what a fall was there, my countrymen!
Then I, and you, and all of us fell down,
Whilst bloody treason flourish'd over us.
O, now you weep, and I perceive you feel
The dint of pity. These are gracious drops.
Kind souls, what weep you when you but behold
Our Caesar's vesture wounded? Look you here,
Here is himself, marr'd, as you see, with traitors.
FIRST CITIZEN: O piteous spectacle!
SECOND CITIZEN: O noble Caesar!
THIRD CITIZEN: O woeful day!
FOURTH CITIZEN: O traitors villains!
FIRST CITIZEN: O most bloody sight!
SECOND CITIZEN: We will be revenged.
ALL: Revenge! About! Seek! Burn! Fire! Kill!
Slay! Let not a traitor live!
ANTONY: Stay, countrymen.
FIRST CITIZEN: Peace there! Hear the noble Antony.

SECOND CITIZEN: We'll hear him, we'll follow him, we'll die with him.
ANTONY: Good friends, sweet friends, let me not stir you up
To such a sudden flood of mutiny.
They that have done this deed are honorable.
What private griefs they have, alas, I know not,
That made them do it. They are wise and honorable,
And will, no doubt, with reasons answer you.
I come not, friends, to steal away your hearts.
I am no orator, as Brutus is;
But, as you know me all, a plain blunt man,
That love my friend, and that they know full well
That gave me public leave to speak of him.
For I have neither wit, nor words, nor worth,
Action, nor utterance, nor the power of speech,
To stir men's blood. I only speak right on;
I tell you that which you yourselves do know;
Show you sweet Caesar's wounds, poor dumb mouths,
And bid them speak for me. But were I Brutus,
And Brutus Antony, there were an Antony
Would ruffle up your spirits and put a tongue
In every wound of Caesar that should move
The stones of Rome to rise and mutiny.
ALL: We'll mutiny.
FIRST CITIZEN: We'll burn the house of Brutus.
THIRD CITIZEN: Away, then! Come, seek the conspirators.
ANTONY: Yet hear me, countrymen; yet hear me speak.
ALL: Peace, ho! Hear Antony, most noble Antony!
ANTONY: Why, friends, you go to do you know not what.
Wherein hath Caesar thus deserved your loves?
Alas, you know not; I must tell you then.
You have forgot the will I told you of.
ALL: Most true, the will! Let's stay and hear the will.
ANTONY: Here is the will, and under Caesar's seal.
To every Roman citizen he gives,
To every several man, seventy-five drachmas.
SECOND CITIZEN: Most noble Caesar! We'll revenge his death.
THIRD CITIZEN: O royal Caesar!
ANTONY: Hear me with patience.
ALL: Peace, ho!
ANTONY: Moreover, he hath left you all his walks,
His private arbors, and new-planted orchards,
On this side Tiber; he hath left them you,
And to your heirs forever- common pleasures,
To walk abroad and recreate yourselves.
Here was a Caesar! When comes such another?
FIRST CITIZEN: Never, never. Come, away, away!
We'll burn his body in the holy place
And with the brands fire the traitors' houses.

Take up the body.
SECOND CITIZEN: Go fetch fire.
THIRD CITIZEN: Pluck down benches.
FOURTH CITIZEN: Pluck down forms, windows, anything.
Exeunt Citizens with the Body.
ANTONY: Now let it work. Mischief, thou art afoot,
Take thou what course thou wilt.
Enter a Servant.
How now, fellow?
SERVANT: Sir, Octavius is already come to Rome.
ANTONY: Where is he?
SERVANT: He and Lepidus are at Caesar's house.
ANTONY: And thither will I straight to visit him.
He comes upon a wish. Fortune is merry,
And in this mood will give us anything.
SERVANT: I heard him say Brutus and Cassius
Are rid like madmen through the gates of Rome.
ANTONY: Be like they had some notice of the people,
How I had moved them. Bring me to Octavius.
Exeunt.

ACT III. SCENE III. A Street.

Enter Cinna the poet.
CINNA: I dreamt tonight that I did feast with Caesar,
And things unluckily charge my fantasy.
I have no will to wander forth of doors,
Yet something leads me forth.
Enter Citizens.
FIRST CITIZEN: What is your name?
SECOND CITIZEN: Whither are you going?
THIRD CITIZEN: Where do you dwell?
FOURTH CITIZEN: Are you a married man or a bachelor?
SECOND CITIZEN: Answer every man directly.
FIRST CITIZEN: Ay, and briefly.
FOURTH CITIZEN: Ay, and wisely.
THIRD CITIZEN: Ay, and truly, you were best.
CINNA: What is my name? Whither am I going? Where do I dwell? Am I a married man or a bachelor? Then, to answer every man directly and briefly, wisely and truly: wisely I say, I am a bachelor.
SECOND CITIZEN: That's as much as to say they are fools that marry. You'll bear me a bang for that, I fear. Proceed directly.
CINNA: Directly, I am going to Caesar's funeral.
FIRST CITIZEN: As a friend or an enemy?
CINNA: As a friend.
SECOND CITIZEN: That matter is answered directly.
FOURTH CITIZEN: For your dwelling, briefly.
CINNA: Briefly, I dwell by the Capitol.
THIRD CITIZEN: Your name, sir, truly.
CINNA: Truly, my name is Cinna.
FIRST CITIZEN: Tear him to pieces, he's a conspirator.

CINNA: I am Cinna the poet, I am Cinna the poet.
FOURTH CITIZEN: Tear him for his bad verses, tear him for his bad verses.
CINNA: I am not Cinna the conspirator.
FOURTH CITIZEN: It is no matter, his name's Cinna. Pluck but his name out of his heart, and turn him going.
THIRD CITIZEN: Tear him, tear him! Come, brands, ho, firebrands. To Brutus', to Cassius'; burn all. Some to Decius' house, and some to Casca's, some to Ligarius'. Away, go!
Exeunt.
ACT IV. SCENE I. A house in Rome. Antony, Octavius, and Lepidus, seated at a table.
ANTONY: These many then shall die, their names are prick'd.
POPILIUS: Your brother too must die; consent you, Lepidus?
LEPIDUS: I do consent-
POPILIUS: Prick him down, Antony.
LEPIDUS: Upon condition Publius shall not live,
Who is your sister's son, Mark Antony.
ANTONY: He shall not live; look, with a spot I damn him.
But, Lepidus, go you to Caesar's house,
Fetch the will hither, and we shall determine
How to cut off some charge in legacies.
LEPIDUS: What, shall I find you here?
POPILIUS: Or here, or at the Capitol.
Exit Lepidus.
ANTONY: This is a slight unmeritable man,
Meet to be sent on errands. Is it fit,
The three-fold world divided, he should stand
One of the three to share it?
POPILIUS: So you thought him,
And took his voice who should be prick'd to die
In our black sentence and proscription.
ANTONY: Octavius, I have seen more days than you,
And though we lay these honors on this man
To ease ourselves of divers slanderous loads,
He shall but bear them as the ass bears gold,
To groan and sweat under the business,
Either led or driven, as we point the way;
And having brought our treasure where we will,
Then take we down his load and turn him off,
Like to the empty ass, to shake his ears
And graze in commons.
POPILIUS: You may do your will,
But he's a tried and valiant soldier.
ANTONY: So is my horse, Octavius, and for that
I do appoint him store of provender.
It is a creature that I teach to fight,
To wind, to stop, to run directly on,
His corporal motion govern'd by my spirit.
And, in some taste, is Lepidus but so:

He must be taught, and train'd, and bid go forth;
A barren-spirited fellow, one that feeds
On objects, arts, and imitations,
Which, out of use and staled by other men,
Begin his fashion. Do not talk of him
But as a property. And now, Octavius,
Listen great things. Brutus and Cassius
Are levying powers; we must straight make head;
Therefore let our alliance be combined,
Our best friends made, our means stretch'd;
And let us presently go sit in council,
How covert matters may be best disclosed,
And open perils surest answered.
POPILIUS: Let us do so, for we are at the stake,
And bay'd about with many enemies;
And some that smile have in their hearts, I fear,
Millions of mischiefs.
Exeunt.

ACT IV. SCENE II. Camp near Sardis. Before Brutus' Tent. Drum.

Enter Brutus, Lucilius, Lucius, and Soldiers; Titinius and Pindarus Meet Them.
BRUTUS: Stand, ho!
POPILIUS: Give the word, ho, and stand.
BRUTUS: What now, Lucilius, is Cassius near?
POPILIUS: He is at hand, and Pindarus is come
To do you salutation from his master.
BRUTUS: He greets me well. Your master, Pindarus,
In his own change, or by ill officers,
Hath given me some worthy cause to wish
Things done undone; but if he be at hand,
I shall be satisfied.
POPILIUS: I do not doubt
But that my noble master will appear
Such as he is, full of regard and honor.
BRUTUS: He is not doubted. A word, Lucilius,
How he received you. Let me be resolved.
POPILIUS: With courtesy and with respect enough,
But not with such familiar instances,
Nor with such free and friendly conference,
As he hath used of old.
BRUTUS: Thou hast described
A hot friend cooling. Ever note, Lucilius,
When love begins to sicken and decay
It useth an enforced ceremony.
There are no tricks in plain and simple faith;
But hollow men, like horses hot at hand,
Make gallant show and promise of their mettle;
But when they should endure the bloody spur,
They fall their crests and like deceitful jades
Sink in the trial. Comes his army on?

POPILIUS: They meant his night in Sard is to be quarter'd;
The greater part, the horse in general,
Are come with Cassius. Low march within.
BRUTUS: Hark, he is arrived.
March gently on to meet him.
Enter Cassius and His Powers.
CASSIUS: Stand, ho!
BRUTUS: Stand, ho! Speak the word along.
FIRST SOLDIER: Stand!
SECOND SOLDIER:. Stand!
THIRD SOLDIER: Stand!
CASSIUS: Most noble brother, you have done me wrong.
BRUTUS: Judge me, you gods! Wrong I mine enemies?
And, if not so, how should I wrong a brother?
CASSIUS: Brutus, this sober form of yours hides wrongs,
And when you do them-
BRUTUS: Cassius, be content,
Speak your griefs softly, I do know you well.
Before the eyes of both our armies here,
Which should perceive nothing but love from us,
Let us not wrangle. Bid them move away;
Then in my tent, Cassius, enlarge your griefs,
And I will give you audience.
CASSIUS: Pindarus,
Bid our commanders lead their charges off
A little from this ground.
BRUTUS: Lucilius, do you the like, and let no man
Come to our tent till we have done our conference.
Let Lucius and Titinius guard our door.
Exeunt.

ACT IV. SCENE III. Brutus' Tent.

Enter Brutus and Cassius.
CASSIUS: That you have wrong'd me doth appear in this:
You have condemn'd and noted Lucius Pella
For taking bribes here of the Sardians,
Wherein my letters, praying on his side,
Because I knew the man, were slighted off.
BRUTUS: You wrong'd yourself to write in such a case.
CASSIUS: In such a time as this it is not meet
That every nice offense should bear his comment.
BRUTUS: Let me tell you, Cassius, you yourself
Are much condemn'd to have an itching palm,
To sell and mart your offices for gold
To undeservers.
CASSIUS: I an itching palm?
You know that you are Brutus that speaks this,
Or, by the gods, this speech were else your last.
BRUTUS: The name of Cassius honors this corruption,
And chastisement doth therefore hide his head.

CASSIUS: Chastisement?
BRUTUS: Remember March, the ides of March remember.
Did not great Julius bleed for justice' sake?
What villain touch'd his body, that did stab,
And not for justice? What, shall one of us,
That struck the foremost man of all this world
But for supporting robbers, shall we now
Contaminate our fingers with base bribes
And sell the mighty space of our large honors
For so much trash as may be grasped thus?
I had rather be a dog, and bay the moon,
Than such a Roman.
CASSIUS: Brutus, bait not me,
I'll not endure it. You forget yourself
To hedge me in. I am a soldier, I,
Older in practice, abler than yourself
To make conditions.
BRUTUS: Go to, you are not, Cassius.
CASSIUS: I am.
BRUTUS: I say you are not.
CASSIUS: Urge me no more, I shall forget myself;
Have mind upon your health, tempt me no farther.
BRUTUS: Away, slight man!
CASSIUS: Is't possible?
BRUTUS: Hear me, for I will speak.
Must I give way and room to your rash choler?
Shall I be frighted when a madman stares?
CASSIUS: O gods, ye gods! Must I endure all this?
BRUTUS: All this? Ay, more. Fret till your proud heart break.
Go show your slaves how choleric you are,
And make your bondmen tremble. Must I bouge?
Must I observe you? Must I stand and crouch
Under your testy humor? By the gods,
You shall digest the venom of your spleen,
Though it do split you, for, from this day forth,
I'll use you for my mirth, yea, for my laughter,
When you are waspish.
CASSIUS: Is it come to this?
BRUTUS: You say you are a better soldier:
Let it appear so, make your vaunting true,
And it shall please me well. For mine own part,
I shall be glad to learn of noble men.
CASSIUS: You wrong me every way, you wrong me, Brutus.
I said, an elder soldier, not a better.
Did I say "better"?
BRUTUS: If you did, I care not.
CASSIUS: When Caesar lived, he durst not thus have moved me.
BRUTUS: Peace, peace! You durst not so have tempted him.
CASSIUS: I durst not?

BRUTUS: No.
CASSIUS: What, durst not tempt him?
BRUTUS: For your life you durst not.
CASSIUS: Do not presume too much upon my love;
I may do that I shall be sorry for.
BRUTUS: You have done that you should be sorry for.
There is no terror, Cassius, in your threats,
For I am arm'd so strong in honesty,
That they pass by me as the idle wind
Which I respect not. I did send to you
For certain sums of gold, which you denied me,
For I can raise no money by vile means.
By heaven, I had rather coin my heart
And drop my blood for drachmas than to wring
From the hard hands of peasants their vile trash
By any indirection. I did send
To you for gold to pay my legions,
Which you denied me. Was that done like Cassius?
Should I have answer'd Caius Cassius so?
When Marcus Brutus grows so covetous
To lock such rascal counters from his friends,
Be ready, gods, with all your thunderbolts,
Dash him to pieces!
CASSIUS: I denied you not.
BRUTUS: You did.
CASSIUS: I did not. He was but a fool
That brought my answer back. Brutus hath rived my heart.
A friend should bear his friend's infirmities,
But Brutus makes mine greater than they are.
BRUTUS: I do not, till you practise them on me.
CASSIUS: You love me not.
BRUTUS: I do not like your faults.
CASSIUS: A friendly eye could never see such faults.
BRUTUS: A flatterer's would not, though they do appear
As huge as high Olympus.
CASSIUS: Come, Antony, and young Octavius, come,
Revenge yourselves alone on Cassius,
For Cassius is aweary of the world:
Hated by one he loves; braved by his brother;
Check'd like a bondman; all his faults observed,
Set in a notebook, learn'd and conn'd by rote,
To cast into my teeth. O, I could weep
My spirit from mine eyes! There is my dagger,
And here my naked breast; within, a heart
Dearer than Pluto's mine, richer than gold.
If that thou best a Roman, take it forth;
I, that denied thee gold, will give my heart.
Strike, as thou didst at Caesar, for I know,
When thou didst hate him worst, thou lovedst him better

Than ever thou lovedst Cassius.
BRUTUS: Sheathe your dagger.
Be angry when you will, it shall have scope;
Do what you will, dishonor shall be humor.
O Cassius, you are yoked with a lamb,
That carries anger as the flint bears fire,
Who, much enforced, shows a hasty spark
And straight is cold again.
CASSIUS: Hath Cassius lived
To be but mirth and laughter to his Brutus,
When grief and blood ill-temper'd vexeth him?
BRUTUS: When I spoke that, I was ill-temper'd too.
CASSIUS: Do you confess so much? Give me your hand.
BRUTUS: And my heart too.
CASSIUS: O Brutus!
BRUTUS: What's the matter?
CASSIUS: Have not you love enough to bear with me
When that rash humor which my mother gave me
Makes me forgetful?
BRUTUS: Yes, Cassius, and from henceforth,
When you are overearnest with your Brutus,
He'll think your mother chides, and leave you so.
POET: Within. Let me go in to see the generals.
There is some grudge between 'em, 'tis not meet
They be alone.
POPILIUS: Within. You shall not come to them.
POET: Within. Nothing but death shall stay me.
Enter Poet, Followed by Lucilius, Titinius, and Lucius.
CASSIUS: How now, what's the matter?
POET: For shame, you generals! What do you mean?
Love, and be friends, as two such men should be;
For I have seen more years, I'm sure, than ye.
CASSIUS: Ha, ha! How vilely doth this cynic rhyme!
BRUTUS: Get you hence, sirrah; saucy fellow, hence!
CASSIUS: Bear with him, Brutus; 'tis his fashion.
BRUTUS: I'll know his humor when he knows his time.
What should the wars do with these jigging fools?
Companion, hence!
CASSIUS: Away, away, be gone!
Exit Poet.
BRUTUS: Lucilius and Titinius, bid the commanders
Prepare to lodge their companies tonight.
CASSIUS: And come yourselves and bring Messala with you
Immediately to us.
Exeunt Lucilius and Titinius.
BRUTUS: Lucius, a bowl of wine!
Exit Lucius.
CASSIUS: I did not think you could have been so angry.
BRUTUS: O Cassius, I am sick of many griefs.

CASSIUS: Of your philosophy you make no use,
If you give place to accidental evils.
BRUTUS: No man bears sorrow better. Portia is dead.
CASSIUS: Ha? Portia?
BRUTUS: She is dead.
CASSIUS: How 'scaped killing when I cross'd you so?
O insupportable and touching loss!
Upon what sickness?
BRUTUS: Impatient of my absence,
And grief that young Octavius with Mark Antony
Have made themselves so strong- for with her death
That tidings came- with this she fell distract,
And (her attendants absent) swallow'd fire.
CASSIUS: And died so?
BRUTUS: Even so.
CASSIUS: O ye immortal gods!
Re-enter Lucius, with Wine and Taper.
BRUTUS: Speak no more of her. Give me a bowl of wine.
In this I bury all unkindness, Cassius. Drinks.
CASSIUS: My heart is thirsty for that noble pledge.
Fill, Lucius, till the wine o'erswell the cup;
I cannot drink too much of Brutus' love. Drinks.
BRUTUS: Come in, Titinius!
Exit Lucius.
Re-enter Titinius, with Messala.
Welcome, good Messala.
Now sit we close about this taper here,
And call in question our necessities.
CASSIUS: Portia, art thou gone?
BRUTUS: No more, I pray you.
Messala, I have here received letters
That young Octavius and Mark Antony
Come down upon us with a mighty power,
Bending their expedition toward Philippi.
MESSALA: Myself have letters of the selfsame tenure.
BRUTUS: With what addition?
MESSALA: That by proscription and bills of outlawry
Octavius, Antony, and Lepidus
Have put to death an hundred senators.
BRUTUS: There in our letters do not well agree;
Mine speak of seventy senators that died
By their proscriptions, Cicero being one.
CASSIUS: Cicero one!
MESSALA: Cicero is dead,
And by that order of proscription.
Had you your letters from your wife, my lord?
BRUTUS: No, Messala.
MESSALA: Nor nothing in your letters writ of her?
BRUTUS: Nothing, Messala.

MESSALA: That, methinks, is strange.
BRUTUS: Why ask you? Hear you aught of her in yours?
MESSALA: No, my lord.
BRUTUS: Now, as you are a Roman, tell me true.
MESSALA: Then like a Roman bear the truth I tell:
For certain she is dead, and by strange manner.
BRUTUS: Why, farewell, Portia. We must die, Messala.
With meditating that she must die once
I have the patience to endure it now.
MESSALA: Even so great men great losses should endure.
CASSIUS: I have as much of this in art as you,
But yet my nature could not bear it so.
BRUTUS: Well, to our work alive. What do you think
Of marching to Philippi presently?
CASSIUS: I do not think it good.
BRUTUS: Your reason?
CASSIUS: This it is:
'Tis better that the enemy seek us;
So shall he waste his means, weary his soldiers,
Doing himself offense, whilst we lying still
Are full of rest, defense, and nimbleness.
BRUTUS: Good reasons must of force give place to better.
The people 'twixt Philippi and this ground
Do stand but in a forced affection,
For they have grudged us contribution.
The enemy, marching along by them,
By them shall make a fuller number up,
Come on refresh'd, new-added, and encouraged;
From which advantage shall we cut him off
If at Philippi we do face him there,
These people at our back.
CASSIUS: Hear me, good brother.
BRUTUS: Under your pardon. You must note beside
That we have tried the utmost of our friends,
Our legions are brim-full, our cause is ripe:
The enemy increaseth every day;
We, at the height, are ready to decline.
There is a tide in the affairs of men
Which taken at the flood leads on to fortune;
Omitted, all the voyage of their life
Is bound in shallows and in miseries.
On such a full sea are we now afloat,
And we must take the current when it serves,
Or lose our ventures.
CASSIUS: Then, with your will, go on;
We'll along ourselves and meet them at Philippi.
BRUTUS: The deep of night is crept upon our talk,
And nature must obey necessity,
Which we will niggard with a little rest.

There is no more to say?
CASSIUS: No more. Good night.
Early tomorrow will we rise and hence.
BRUTUS: Lucius!
Re-enter Lucius.
My gown.
Exit Lucius.
Farewell, good Messala;
Good night, Titinius; noble, noble Cassius,
Good night and good repose.
CASSIUS: O my dear brother!
This was an ill beginning of the night.
Never come such division 'tween our souls!
Let it not, Brutus.
BRUTUS: Everything is well.
CASSIUS: Good night, my lord.
BRUTUS: Good night, good brother.
TITINIUS: MESSALA. Good night, Lord Brutus.
BRUTUS: Farewell, everyone.
Exeunt all but Brutus.
Re-enter Lucius, with the Gown. Give Me the Gown. Where Is Thy Instrument?
LUCIUS: Here in the tent.
BRUTUS: What, thou speak'st drowsily?
Poor knave, I blame thee not, thou art o'erwatch'd.
Call Claudio and some other of my men,
I'll have them sleep on cushions in my tent.
LUCIUS: Varro and Claudio!
Enter Varro and Claudio.
VARRO: Calls my lord?
BRUTUS: I pray you, sirs, lie in my tent and sleep;
It may be I shall raise you by and by
On business to my brother Cassius.
VARRO: So please you, we will stand and watch your pleasure.
BRUTUS: I would not have it so. Lie down, good sirs.
It may be I shall otherwise bethink me.
Look Lucius, here's the book I sought for so;
I put it in the pocket of my gown.
Varro and Claudio Lie Down.
LUCIUS: I was sure your lordship did not give it me.
BRUTUS: Bear with me, good boy, I am much forgetful.
Canst thou hold up thy heavy eyes awhile,
And touch thy instrument a strain or two?
LUCIUS: Ay, my lord, an't please you.
BRUTUS: It does, my boy.
I trouble thee too much, but thou art willing.
LUCIUS: It is my duty, sir.
BRUTUS: I should not urge thy duty past thy might;
I know young bloods look for a time of rest.
LUCIUS: I have slept, my lord, already.

BRUTUS: It was well done, and thou shalt sleep again;
I will not hold thee long. If I do live,
I will be good to thee. Music, and a song.
This is a sleepy tune. O murtherous slumber,
Layest thou thy leaden mace upon my boy
That plays thee music? Gentle knave, good night.
I will not do thee so much wrong to wake thee.
If thou dost nod, thou break'st thy instrument;
I'll take it from thee; and, good boy, good night.
Let me see, let me see; is not the leaf turn'd down
Where I left reading? Here it is, I think. Sits down.
Enter the Ghost of Caesar.
How ill this taper burns! Ha, who comes here?
I think it is the weakness of mine eyes
That shapes this monstrous apparition.
It comes upon me. Art thou anything?
Art thou some god, some angel, or some devil
That makest my blood cold and my hair to stare?
Speak to me what thou art.
GHOST: Thy evil spirit, Brutus.
BRUTUS: Why comest thou?
GHOST: To tell thee thou shalt see me at Philippi.
BRUTUS: Well, then I shall see thee again?
GHOST: Ay, at Philippi.
BRUTUS: Why, I will see thee at Philippi then.
Exit Ghost.
Now I have taken heart thou vanishest.
Ill spirit, I would hold more talk with thee.
Boy! Lucius! Varro! Claudio! Sirs, awake!
Claudio!
LUCIUS: The strings, my lord, are false.
BRUTUS: He thinks he still is at his instrument.
Lucius, awake!
LUCIUS: My lord?
BRUTUS: Didst thou dream, Lucius, that thou so criedst out?
LUCIUS: My lord, I do not know that I did cry.
BRUTUS: Yes, that thou didst. Didst thou see anything?
LUCIUS: Nothing, my lord.
BRUTUS: Sleep again, Lucius. Sirrah Claudio!
To Varro. Fellow thou, awake!
VARRO: My lord?
CLAUDIO: My lord?
BRUTUS: Why did you so cry out, sirs, in your sleep?
VARRO: CLAUDIO. Did we, my lord?
BRUTUS: Ay, saw you anything?
VARRO: No, my lord, I saw nothing.
CLAUDIO: Nor I, my lord.
BRUTUS: Go and commend me to my brother Cassius;
Bid him set on his powers betimes before,

And we will follow.
VARRO and CLAUDIO: It shall be done, my lord.
Exeunt.

ACT V. SCENE I. The Plains of Philippi.

Enter Octavius, Antony, and their Army.
POPILIUS: Now, Antony, our hopes are answered.
You said the enemy would not come down,
But keep the hills and upper regions.
It proves not so. Their battles are at hand;
They mean to warn us at Philippi here,
Answering before we do demand of them.
ANTONY: Tut, I am in their bosoms, and I know
Wherefore they do it. They could be content
To visit other places, and come down
With fearful bravery, thinking by this face
To fasten in our thoughts that they have courage;
But 'tis not so.
Enter a Messenger.
MESSENGER: Prepare you, generals.
The enemy comes on in gallant show;
Their bloody sign of battle is hung out,
And something to be done immediately.
ANTONY: Octavius, lead your battle softly on,
Upon the left hand of the even field.
POPILIUS: Upon the right hand I, keep thou the left.
ANTONY: Why do you cross me in this exigent?
POPILIUS: I do not cross you, but I will do so.
March. Drum. Enter Brutus, Cassius, and Their Army; Lucilius, Titinius, Messala, and Others.
BRUTUS: They stand, and would have parley.
CASSIUS: Stand fast, Titinius; we must out and talk.
POPILIUS: Mark Antony, shall we give sign of battle?
ANTONY: No, Caesar, we will answer on their charge.
Make forth, the generals would have some words.
POPILIUS: Stir not until the signal not until the signal.
BRUTUS: Words before blows. Is it so, countrymen?
POPILIUS: Not that we love words better, as you do.
BRUTUS: Good words are better than bad strokes, Octavius.
ANTONY: In your bad strokes, Brutus, you give good words.
Witness the hole you made in Caesar's heart,
Crying "Long live! Hail, Caesar!"
CASSIUS: Antony,
The posture of your blows are yet unknown;
But for your words, they rob the Hybla bees,
And leave them honeyless.
ANTONY: Not stingless too.
BRUTUS: O, yes, and soundless too,
For you have stol'n their buzzing, Antony,
And very wisely threat before you sting.

ANTONY: Villains! You did not so when your vile daggers
Hack'd one another in the sides of Caesar.
You show'd your teeth like apes, and fawn'd like hounds,
And bow'd like bondmen, kissing Caesar's feet;
Whilst damned Casca, like a cur, behind
Strooke Caesar on the neck. O you flatterers!
CASSIUS: Flatterers? Now, Brutus, thank yourself.
This tongue had not offended so today,
If Cassius might have ruled.
POPILIUS: Come, come, the cause. If arguing make us sweat,
The proof of it will turn to redder drops.
Look, I draw a sword against conspirators;
When think you that the sword goes up again?
Never, till Caesar's three and thirty wounds
Be well avenged, or till another Caesar
Have added slaughter to the sword of traitors.
BRUTUS: Caesar, thou canst not die by traitors' hands,
Unless thou bring'st them with thee.
POPILIUS: So I hope,
I was not born to die on Brutus' sword.
BRUTUS: O, if thou wert the noblest of thy strain,
Young man, thou couldst not die more honorable.
CASSIUS: A peevish school boy, worthless of such honor,
Join'd with a masker and a reveler!
ANTONY: Old Cassius still!
POPILIUS: Come, Antony, away!
Defiance, traitors, hurl we in your teeth.
If you dare fight today, come to the field;
If not, when you have stomachs.
Exeunt Octavius, Antony, and Their Army.
CASSIUS: Why, now, blow and, swell billow, and swim bark!
The storm is up, and all is on the hazard.
BRUTUS: Ho, Lucilius! Hark, a word with you.
POPILIUS: Stands Forth. My lord?
Brutus and Lucilius Converse Apart.
CASSIUS: Messala!
MESSALA: Stands Forth. What says my general?
CASSIUS: Messala,
This is my birthday, as this very day
Was Cassius born. Give me thy hand, Messala.
Be thou my witness that, against my will,
As Pompey was, am I compell'd to set
Upon one battle all our liberties.
You know that I held Epicurus strong,
And his opinion. Now I change my mind,
And partly credit things that do presage.
Coming from Sardis, on our former ensign
Two mighty eagles fell, and there they perch'd,
Gorging and feeding from our soldiers' hands,

Who to Philippi here consorted us.
This morning are they fled away and gone,
And in their steads do ravens, crows, and kites
Fly o'er our heads and downward look on us,
As we were sickly prey. Their shadows seem
A canopy most fatal, under which
Our army lies, ready to give up the ghost.
MESSALA: Believe not so.
CASSIUS: I but believe it partly,
For I am fresh of spirit and resolved
To meet all perils very constantly.
BRUTUS: Even so, Lucilius.
CASSIUS: Now, most noble Brutus,
The gods today stand friendly that we may,
Lovers in peace, lead on our days to age!
But, since the affairs of men rest still incertain,
Let's reason with the worst that may befall.
If we do lose this battle, then is this
The very last time we shall speak together.
What are you then determined to do?
BRUTUS: Even by the rule of that philosophy
By which I did blame Cato for the death
Which he did give himself- I know not how,
But I do find it cowardly and vile,
For fear of what might fall, so to prevent
The time of life- arming myself with patience
To stay the providence of some high powers
That govern us below.
CASSIUS: Then, if we lose this battle,
You are contented to be led in triumph
Thorough the streets of Rome?
BRUTUS: No, Cassius, no. Think not, thou noble Roman,
That ever Brutus will go bound to Rome;
He bears too great a mind. But this same day
Must end that work the ides of March begun.
And whether we shall meet again I know not.
Therefore our everlasting farewell take.
Forever, and forever, farewell, Cassius!
If we do meet again, why, we shall smile;
If not, why then this parting was well made.
CASSIUS: Forever and forever farewell, Brutus!
If we do meet again, we'll smile indeed;
If not, 'tis true this parting was well made.
BRUTUS: Why then, lead on. O, that a man might know
The end of this day's business ere it come!
But it sufficeth that the day will end,
And then the end is known. Come, ho! Away!
Exeunt.

ACT V. SCENE II. The Field of Battle.

Alarum. Enter Brutus and Messala.

BRUTUS: Ride, ride, Messala, ride, and give these bills
Unto the legions on the other side. Loud alarum.
Let them set on at once, for I perceive
But cold demeanor in Octavia's wing,
And sudden push gives them the overthrow.
Ride, ride, Messala. Let them all come down.

Exeunt.

ACT V. SCENE III. Another Part of the Field.

Alarums. Enter Cassius and Titinius.

CASSIUS: O, look, Titinius, look, the villains fly!
Myself have to mine own turn'd enemy.
This ensign here of mine was turning back;
I slew the coward, and did take it from him.

TITINIUS: O Cassius, Brutus gave the word too early,
Who, having some advantage on Octavius,
Took it too eagerly. His soldiers fell to spoil,
Whilst we by Antony are all enclosed.

Enter Pindarus.

POPILIUS: Fly further off, my lord, fly further off;
Mark Antony is in your tents, my lord;
Fly, therefore, noble Cassius, fly far off.

CASSIUS: This hill is far enough. Look, look, Titinius:
Are those my tents where I perceive the fire?

TITINIUS: They are, my lord.

CASSIUS: Titinius, if thou lovest me,
Mount thou my horse and hide thy spurs in him,
Till he have brought thee up to yonder troops
And here again, that I may rest assured
Whether yond troops are friend or enemy.

TITINIUS: I will be here again, even with a thought.

Exit.

CASSIUS: Go, Pindarus, get higher on that hill;
My sight was ever thick; regard Titinius,
And tell me what thou notest about the field.

Pindarus Ascends the Hill.

This day I breathed first: time is come round,
And where I did begin, there shall I end;
My life is run his compass. Sirrah, what news?

POPILIUS: Above. O my lord!

CASSIUS: What news?

POPILIUS: Above. Titinius is enclosed round about
With horsemen, that make to him on the spur;
Yet he spurs on. Now they are almost on him.
Now, Titinius! Now some light. O, he lights too.
He's ta'en Shout. And, hark! They shout for joy.

CASSIUS: Come down; behold no more.
O, coward that I am, to live so long,

To see my best friend ta'en before my face!
Pindarus descends.
Come hither, sirrah.
In Parthia did I take thee prisoner,
And then I swore thee, saving of thy life,
That whatsoever I did bid thee do,
Thou shouldst attempt it. Come now, keep thine oath;
Now be a freeman, and with this good sword,
That ran through Caesar's bowels, search this bosom.
Stand not to answer: here, take thou the hilts;
And when my face is cover'd, as 'tis now,
Guide thou the sword.
Pindarus Stabs Him.
Caesar, thou art revenged,
Even with the sword that kill'd thee. Dies.
POPILIUS: So, I am free, yet would not so have been,
Durst I have done my will. O Cassius!
Far from this country Pindarus shall run,
Where never Roman shall take note of him.
Exit.
Re-enter Titinius with Messala.
MESSALA: It is but change, Titinius, for Octavius
Is overthrown by noble Brutus' power,
As Cassius' legions are by Antony.
TITINIUS: These tidings would well comfort Cassius.
MESSALA: Where did you leave him?
TITINIUS: All disconsolate,
With Pindarus his bondman, on this hill.
MESSALA: Is not that he that lies upon the ground?
TITINIUS: He lies not like the living. O my heart!
MESSALA: Is not that he?
TITINIUS: No, this was he, Messala,
But Cassius is no more. O setting sun,
As in thy red rays thou dost sink to night,
So in his red blood Cassius' day is set,
The sun of Rome is set! Our day is gone;
Clouds, dews, and dangers come; our deeds are done!
Mistrust of my success hath done this deed.
MESSALA: Mistrust of good success hath done this deed.
O hateful error, melancholy's child,
Why dost thou show to the apt thoughts of men
The things that are not? O error, soon conceived,
Thou never comest unto a happy birth,
But kill'st the mother that engender'd thee!
TITINIUS: What, Pindarus! Where art thou, Pindarus?
MESSALA: Seek him, Titinius, whilst I go to meet
The noble Brutus, thrusting this report
Into his ears. I may say "thrusting" it,
For piercing steel and darts envenomed

Shall be as welcome to the ears of Brutus
As tidings of this sight.
TITINIUS: Hie you, Messala,
And I will seek for Pindarus the while.
Exit Messala.
Why didst thou send me forth, brave Cassius?
Did I not meet thy friends? And did not they
Put on my brows this wreath of victory,
And bid me give it thee? Didst thou not hear their shouts?
Alas, thou hast misconstrued everything!
But, hold thee, take this garland on thy brow;
Thy Brutus bid me give it thee, and I
Will do his bidding. Brutus, come apace,
And see how I regarded Caius Cassius.
By your leave, gods, this is a Roman's part.
Come, Cassius' sword, and find Titinius' heart.
Kills Himself.
Alarum. Re-enter Messala, with Brutus, Young Cato, and Others.
BRUTUS: Where, where, Messala, doth his body lie?
MESSALA: Lo, yonder, and Titinius mourning it.
BRUTUS: Titinius' face is upward.
CATO: He is slain.
BRUTUS: O Julius Caesar, thou art mighty yet!
Thy spirit walks abroad, and turns our swords
In our own proper entrails. Low alarums.
CATO: Brave Titinius!
Look whe'er he have not crown'd dead Cassius!
BRUTUS: Are yet two Romans living such as these?
The last of all the Romans, fare thee well!
It is impossible that ever Rome
Should breed thy fellow. Friends, I owe moe tears
To this dead man than you shall see me pay.
I shall find time, Cassius, I shall find time.
Come therefore, and to Thasos send his body;
His funerals shall not be in our camp,
Lest it discomfort us. Lucilius, come,
And come, young Cato; let us to the field.
Labio and Flavio, set our battles on.
'Tis three o'clock, and Romans, yet ere night
We shall try fortune in a second fight.
Exeunt.

ACT V. SCENE IV. Another Part of the Field.

Alarum. Enter, Fighting, Soldiers of Both Armies; Then Brutus, Young Cato, Lucilius, and Others.

BRUTUS: Yet, countrymen, O, yet hold up your heads!
CATO: What bastard doth not? Who will go with me?
I will proclaim my name about the field.
I am the son of Marcus Cato, ho!
A foe to tyrants, and my country's friend.

I am the son of Marcus Cato, ho!
BRUTUS: And I am Brutus, Marcus Brutus, I;
Brutus, my country's friend; know me for Brutus!
Exit.
POPILIUS: O young and noble Cato, art thou down?
Why, now thou diest as bravely as Titinius,
And mayst be honor'd, being Cato's son.
FIRST SOLDIER: Yield, or thou diest.
POPILIUS: Only I yield to die.
Offers Money.
There is so much that thou wilt kill me straight:
Kill Brutus, and be honor'd in his death.
FIRST SOLDIER: We must not. A noble prisoner!
SECOND SOLDIER:. Room, ho! Tell Antony, Brutus is ta'en.
FIRST SOLDIER: I'll tell the news. Here comes the general.
Enter Antony.
Brutus is ta'en, Brutus is ta'en, my lord.
ANTONY: Where is he?
POPILIUS: Safe, Antony, Brutus is safe enough.
I dare assure thee that no enemy
Shall ever take alive the noble Brutus;
The gods defend him from so great a shame!
When you do find him, or alive or dead,
He will be found like Brutus, like himself.
ANTONY: This is not Brutus, friend, but, I assure you,
A prize no less in worth. Keep this man safe,
Give him all kindness; I had rather have
Such men my friends than enemies. Go on,
And see wheer Brutus be alive or dead,
And bring us word unto Octavius' tent
How everything is chanced.
Exeunt.

ACT V. SCENE V. Another Part of the Field.

Enter Brutus, Dardanius, Clitus, Strato, and Volumnius.
BRUTUS: Come, poor remains of friends, rest on this rock.
CLITUS: Statilius show'd the torchlight, but, my lord,
He came not back. He is or ta'en or slain.
BRUTUS: Sit thee down, Clitus. Slaying is the word:
It is a deed in fashion. Hark thee, Clitus. Whispers.
CLITUS: What, I, my lord? No, not for all the world.
BRUTUS: Peace then, no words.
CLITUS: I'll rather kill myself.
BRUTUS: Hark thee, Dardanius. Whispers.
DARDANIUS: Shall I do such a deed?
CLITUS: O Dardanius!
DARDANIUS: O Clitus!
CLITUS: What ill request did Brutus make to thee?
DARDANIUS: To kill him, Clitus. Look, he meditates.
CLITUS: Now is that noble vessel full of grief,

That it runs over even at his eyes.
BRUTUS: Come hither, good Volumnius, list a word.
VOLUMNIUS: What says my lord?
BRUTUS: Why, this, Volumnius:
The ghost of Caesar hath appear'd to me
Two several times by night; at Sardis once,
And this last night here in Philippi fields.
I know my hour is come.
VOLUMNIUS: Not so, my lord.
BRUTUS: Nay I am sure it is, Volumnius.
Thou seest the world, Volumnius, how it goes;
Our enemies have beat us to the pit; Low alarums.
It is more worthy to leap in ourselves
Than tarry till they push us. Good Volumnius,
Thou know'st that we two went to school together;
Even for that our love of old, I prithee,
Hold thou my sword-hilts, whilst I run on it.
VOLUMNIUS: That's not an office for a friend, my lord.
Alarum Still.
CLITUS: Fly, fly, my lord, there is no tarrying here.
BRUTUS: Farewell to you, and you, and you, Volumnius.
Strato, thou hast been all this while asleep;
Farewell to thee too, Strato. Countrymen,
My heart doth joy that yet in all my life
I found no man but he was true to me.
I shall have glory by this losing day,
More than Octavius and Mark Antony
By this vile conquest shall attain unto.
So, fare you well at once, for Brutus' tongue
Hath almost ended his life's history.
Night hangs upon mine eyes, my bones would rest
That have but labor'd to attain this hour.
Alarum. Cry Within, "Fly, Fly, Fly!"
CLITUS: Fly, my lord, fly.
BRUTUS: Hence! I will follow.
Exeunt Clitus, Dardanius, and Volumnius.
I prithee, Strato, stay thou by thy lord.
Thou art a fellow of a good respect;
Thy life hath had some smatch of honor in it.
Hold then my sword, and turn away thy face,
While I do run upon it. Wilt thou, Strato?
STRATO: Give me your hand first. Fare you well, my lord.
BRUTUS: Farewell, good Strato. Runs on his sword.
Caesar, now be still;
I kill'd not thee with half so good a will. Dies.
Alarum. Retreat. Enter Octavius, Antony, Messala, Lucilius, and the Army.
POPILIUS: What man is that?
MESSALA: My master's man. Strato, where is thy master?
STRATO: Free from the bondage you are in, Messala:

The conquerors can but make a fire of him;
For Brutus only overcame himself,
And no man else hath honor by his death.
POPILIUS: So Brutus should be found. I thank thee, Brutus,
That thou hast proved Lucilius' saying true.
POPILIUS: All that served Brutus, I will entertain them.
Fellow, wilt thou bestow thy time with me?
STRATO: Ay, if Messala will prefer me to you.
POPILIUS: Do so, good Messala.
MESSALA: How died my master, Strato?
STRATO: I held the sword, and he did run on it.
MESSALA: Octavius, then take him to follow thee
That did the latest service to my master.
ANTONY: This was the noblest Roman of them all.
All the conspirators, save only he,
Did that they did in envy of great Caesar;
He only, in a general honest thought
And common good to all, made one of them.
His life was gentle, and the elements
So mix'd in him that Nature might stand up
And say to all the world, "This was a man!"
POPILIUS: According to his virtue let us use him
With all respect and rites of burial.
Within my tent his bones tonight shall lie,
Most like a soldier, ordered honorably.
So call the field to rest, and let's away,
To part the glories of this happy day.
Exeunt.

END

The Tragedy of Julius Caesar

Dramatis Personae

JULIUS CAESAR, Roman statesman and general
OCTAVIUS, Triumvir after Caesar's death, later Augustus Caesar, first emperor of Rome
MARK ANTONY, general and friend of Caesar, a Triumvir after his death
LEPIDUS, third member of the Triumvirate
MARCUS BRUTUS, leader of the conspiracy against Caesar
CASSIUS, instigator of the conspiracy
CASCA, conspirator against Caesar
TREBONIUS, conspirator against Caesar
CAIUS LIGARIUS, conspirator against Caesar
DECIUS BRUTUS, conspirator against Caesar
METELLUS CIMBER, conspirator against Caesar
CINNA, conspirator against Caesar
CALPURNIA, wife of Caesar
PORTIA, wife of Brutus
CICERO, senator
POPILIUS, senator
POPILIUS LENA, senator
FLAVIUS, tribune
MARULLUS, tribune
CATO, supportor of Brutus
LUCILIUS, supportor of Brutus
TITINIUS, supportor of Brutus
MESSALA, supportor of Brutus
VOLUMNIUS, supportor of Brutus
ARTEMIDORUS, a teacher of rhetoric
CINNA, a poet
VARRO, servant to Brutus
CLITUS, servant to Brutus
CLAUDIO, servant to Brutus
STRATO, servant to Brutus
LUCIUS, servant to Brutus
DARDANIUS, servant to Brutus
PINDARUS, servant to Cassius
The Ghost of Caesar
A Soothsayer
A Poet, Senators, Citizens, Soldiers, Commoners, Messengers, and Servants

SCENE: Rome, the conspirators' camp near Sardis, and the plains of Philippi.

ACT I. SCENE I. Rome. A Street.

Enter Flavius, Marullus, and Certain Commoners.

FLAVIUS: Hence, home, you idle creatures, get you home.
Is this a holiday? What, know you not,
Being mechanical, you ought not walk
Upon a laboring day without the sign
Of your profession? Speak, what trade art thou?
FIRST COMMONER: Why, sir, a carpenter.

MARULLUS: Where is thy leather apron and thy rule?
What dost thou with thy best apparel on?
You, sir, what trade are you?
SECOND COMMONER: Truly, sir, in respect of a fine workman, I am but, as you would say, a cobbler.
MARULLUS: But what trade art thou? Answer me directly.
SECOND COMMONER: A trade, sir, that, I hope, I may use with a safe conscience, which is indeed, sir, a mender of bad soles.
MARULLUS: What trade, thou knave? Thou naughty knave, what trade?
SECOND COMMONER: Nay, I beseech you, sir, be not out with me; yet, if you be out, sir, I can mend you.
MARULLUS: What mean'st thou by that? Mend me, thou saucy fellow!
SECOND COMMONER: Why, sir, cobble you.
FLAVIUS: Thou art a cobbler, art thou?
SECOND COMMONER: Truly, Sir, all that I live by is with the awl; I meddle with no tradesman's matters, nor women's matters, but with awl. I am indeed, sir, a surgeon to old shoes; when they are in great danger, I recover them. As proper men as ever trod upon neat's leather have gone upon my handiwork.
FLAVIUS: But wherefore art not in thy shop today?
Why dost thou lead these men about the streets?
SECOND COMMONER: Truly, sir, to wear out their shoes to get myself into more work. But indeed, sir, we make holiday to see Caesar and to rejoice in his triumph.
MARULLUS: Wherefore rejoice? What conquest brings he home?
What tributaries follow him to Rome
To grace in captive bonds his chariot wheels?
You blocks, you stones, you worse than senseless things!
O you hard hearts, you cruel men of Rome,
Knew you not Pompey? Many a time and oft
Have you climb'd up to walls and battlements,
To towers and windows, yea, to chimney tops,
Your infants in your arms, and there have sat
The livelong day with patient expectation
To see great Pompey pass the streets of Rome.
And when you saw his chariot but appear,
Have you not made an universal shout
That Tiber trembled underneath her banks
To hear the replication of your sounds
Made in her concave shores?
And do you now put on your best attire?
And do you now cull out a holiday?
And do you now strew flowers in his way
That comes in triumph over Pompey's blood?
Be gone!
Run to your houses, fall upon your knees,
Pray to the gods to intermit the plague
That needs must light on this ingratitude.
FLAVIUS: Go, go, good countrymen, and, for this fault,

Assemble all the poor men of your sort,
Draw them to Tiber banks, and weep your tears
Into the channel, till the lowest stream
Do kiss the most exalted shores of all.
Exeunt all Commoners.
See whether their basest metal be not moved;
They vanish tongue-tied in their guiltiness.
Go you down that way towards the Capitol;
This way will I. Disrobe the images
If you do find them deck'd with ceremonies.
MARULLUS: May we do so?
You know it is the feast of Lupercal.
FLAVIUS: It is no matter; let no images
Be hung with Caesar's trophies. I'll about
And drive away the vulgar from the streets;
So do you too, where you perceive them thick.
These growing feathers pluck'd from Caesar's wing
Will make him fly an ordinary pitch,
Who else would soar above the view of men
And keep us all in servile fearfulness.
Exeunt.

ACT I. SCENE II. A Public Place.

Flourish. Enter Caesar; Antony, for the Course; Calpurnia, Portia, Decius, Cicero, Brutus, Cassius, and Casca; a Great Crowd Follows, among Them a Soothsayer.
CAESAR: Calpurnia!
CASCA: Peace, ho! Caesar speaks.
Music Ceases.
CAESAR: Calpurnia!
CALPURNIA: Here, my lord.
CAESAR: Stand you directly in Antonio's way,
When he doth run his course. Antonio!
ANTONY: Caesar, my lord?
CAESAR: Forget not in your speed, Antonio,
To touch Calpurnia, for our elders say
The barren, touched in this holy chase,
Shake off their sterile curse.
ANTONY: I shall remember.
When Caesar says "Do this," it is perform'd.
CAESAR: Set on, and leave no ceremony out. Flourish.
SOOTHSAYER: Caesar!
CAESAR: Ha! Who calls?
CASCA: Bid every noise be still. Peace yet again!
CAESAR: Who is it in the press that calls on me?
I hear a tongue, shriller than all the music,
Cry "Caesar." Speak, Caesar is turn'd to hear.
SOOTHSAYER: Beware the ides of March.
CAESAR: What man is that?
BRUTUS: A soothsayer you beware the ides of March.
CAESAR: Set him before me let me see his face.

CASSIUS: Fellow, come from the throng; look upon Caesar.
CAESAR: What say'st thou to me now? Speak once again.
SOOTHSAYER: Beware the ides of March.
CAESAR: He is a dreamer; let us leave him. Pass.
Sennet. Exeunt All but Brutus and Cassius.
CALPURNIA: Will you go see the order of the course?
BRUTUS: Not I.
CASSIUS: I pray you, do.
BRUTUS: I am not gamesome; I do lack some part
Of that quick spirit that is in Antony.
Let me not hinder, Cassius, your desires;
I'll leave you.
CASSIUS: Brutus, I do observe you now of late;
I have not from your eyes that gentleness
And show of love as I was wont to have;
You bear too stubborn and too strange a hand
Over your friend that loves you.
BRUTUS: Cassius,
Be not deceived; if I have veil'd my look,
I turn the trouble of my countenance
Merely upon myself. Vexed I am
Of late with passions of some difference,
Conceptions only proper to myself,
Which give some soil perhaps to my behaviors;
But let not therefore my good friends be grieved-
Among which number, Cassius, be you one-
Nor construe any further my neglect
Than that poor Brutus with himself at war
Forgets the shows of love to other men.
CASSIUS: Then, Brutus, I have much mistook your passion,
By means whereof this breast of mine hath buried
Thoughts of great value, worthy cogitations.
Tell me, good Brutus, can you see your face?
BRUTUS: No, Cassius, for the eye sees not itself
But by reflection, by some other things.
CASSIUS: 'Tis just,
And it is very much lamented, Brutus,
That you have no such mirrors as will turn
Your hidden worthiness into your eye
That you might see your shadow. I have heard
Where many of the best respect in Rome,
Except immortal Caesar, speaking of Brutus
And groaning underneath this age's yoke,
Have wish'd that noble Brutus had his eyes.
BRUTUS: Into what dangers would you lead me, Cassius,
That you would have me seek into myself
For that which is not in me?
CASSIUS: Therefore, good Brutus, be prepared to hear,
And since you know you cannot see yourself

So well as by reflection, I your glass
Will modestly discover to yourself
That of yourself which you yet know not of.
And be not jealous on me, gentle Brutus;
Were I a common laugher, or did use
To stale with ordinary oaths my love
To every new protester, if you know
That I do fawn on men and hug them hard
And after scandal them, or if you know
That I profess myself in banqueting
To all the rout, then hold me dangerous.
Flourish and Shout.
BRUTUS: What means this shouting? I do fear the people
Choose Caesar for their king.
CASSIUS: Ay, do you fear it?
Then must I think you would not have it so.
BRUTUS: I would not, Cassius, yet I love him well.
But wherefore do you hold me here so long?
What is it that you would impart to me?
If it be aught toward the general good,
Set honor in one eye and death i' the other
And I will look on both indifferently.
For let the gods so speed me as I love
The name of honor more than I fear death.
CASSIUS: I know that virtue to be in you, Brutus,
As well as I do know your outward favor.
Well, honor is the subject of my story.
I cannot tell what you and other men
Think of this life, but, for my single self,
I had as lief not be as live to be
In awe of such a thing as I myself.
I was born free as Caesar, so were you;
We both have fed as well, and we can both
Endure the winter's cold as well as he.
For once, upon a raw and gusty day,
The troubled Tiber chafing with her shores,
Caesar said to me, "Darest thou, Cassius, now
Leap in with me into this angry flood
And swim to yonder point?" Upon the word,
Accoutred as I was, I plunged in
And bade him follow. So indeed he did.
The torrent roar'd, and we did buffet it
With lusty sinews, throwing it aside
And stemming it with hearts of controversy.
But ere we could arrive the point proposed,
Caesar cried, "Help me, Cassius, or I sink!
I, as Aeneas our great ancestor
Did from the flames of Troy upon his shoulder
The old Anchises bear, so from the waves of Tiber

Did I the tired Caesar. And this man
Is now become a god, and Cassius is
A wretched creature and must bend his body
If Caesar carelessly but nod on him.
He had a fever when he was in Spain,
And when the fit was on him I did mark
How he did shake. 'Tis true, this god did shake;
His coward lips did from their color fly,
And that same eye whose bend doth awe the world
Did lose his luster. I did hear him groan.
Ay, and that tongue of his that bade the Romans
Mark him and write his speeches in their books,
Alas, it cried, "Give me some drink, Titinius,"
As a sick girl. Ye gods! It doth amaze me
A man of such a feeble temper should
So get the start of the majestic world
And bear the palm alone. Shout. Flourish.
BRUTUS: Another general shout!
I do believe that these applauses are
For some new honors that are heap'd on Caesar.
CASSIUS: Why, man, he doth bestride the narrow world
Like a Colossus, and we petty men
Walk under his huge legs and peep about
To find ourselves dishonorable graves.
Men at some time are masters of their fates:
The fault, dear Brutus, is not in our stars,
But in ourselves that we are underlings.
Brutus and Caesar: what should be in that "Caesar"?
Why should that name be sounded more than yours?
Write them together, yours is as fair a name;
Sound them, it doth become the mouth as well;
Weigh them, it is as heavy; conjure with 'em,
"Brutus" will start a spirit as soon as "Caesar."
Now, in the names of all the gods at once,
Upon what meat doth this our Caesar feed
That he is grown so great? Age, thou art shamed!
Rome, thou hast lost the breed of noble bloods!
When went there by an age since the great flood
But it was famed with more than with one man?
When could they say till now that talk'd of Rome
That her wide walls encompass'd but one man?
Now is it Rome indeed, and room enough,
When there is in it but one only man.
O, you and I have heard our fathers say
There was a Brutus once that would have brook'd
The eternal devil to keep his state in Rome
As easily as a king.
BRUTUS: That you do love me, I am nothing jealous;
What you would work me to, I have some aim.

How I have thought of this and of these times,
I shall recount hereafter; for this present,
I would not, so with love I might entreat you,
Be any further moved. What you have said
I will consider; what you have to say
I will with patience hear, and find a time
Both meet to hear and answer such high things.
Till then, my noble friend, chew upon this:
Brutus had rather be a villager
Than to repute himself a son of Rome
Under these hard conditions as this time
Is like to lay upon us.
CASSIUS: I am glad that my weak words
Have struck but thus much show of fire from Brutus.
Re-enter Caesar and His Train.
BRUTUS: The games are done, and Caesar is returning.
CASSIUS: As they pass by, pluck Casca by the sleeve,
And he will, after his sour fashion, tell you
What hath proceeded worthy note today.
BRUTUS: I will do so. But, look you, Cassius,
The angry spot doth glow on Caesar's brow,
And all the rest look like a chidden train:
Calpurnia's cheek is pale, and Cicero
Looks with such ferret and such fiery eyes
As we have seen him in the Capitol,
Being cross'd in conference by some senators.
CASSIUS: Casca will tell us what the matter is.
CAESAR: Antonio!
ANTONY: Caesar?
CAESAR: Let me have men about me that are fat,
Sleek-headed men, and such as sleep o' nights:
Yond Cassius has a lean and hungry look;
He thinks too much; such men are dangerous.
ANTONY: Fear him not, Caesar; he's not dangerous;
He is a noble Roman and well given.
CAESAR: Would he were fatter! But I fear him not,
Yet if my name were liable to fear,
I do not know the man I should avoid
So soon as that spare Cassius. He reads much,
He is a great observer, and he looks
Quite through the deeds of men. He loves no plays,
As thou dost, Antony; he hears no music;
Seldom he smiles, and smiles in such a sort
As if he mock'd himself and scorn'd his spirit
That could be moved to smile at anything.
Such men as he be never at heart's ease
Whiles they behold a greater than themselves,
And therefore are they very dangerous.
I rather tell thee what is to be fear'd

Than what I fear, for always I am Caesar.
Come on my right hand, for this ear is deaf,
And tell me truly what thou think'st of him.

Sennet. Exeunt Caesar and All His Train but Casca.

CASCA: You pull'd me by the cloak; would you speak with me?

BRUTUS: Ay, Casca, tell us what hath chanced today
That Caesar looks so sad.

CASCA: Why, you were with him, were you not?

BRUTUS: I should not then ask Casca what had chanced.

CASCA: Why, there was a crown offered him, and being offered him, he put it by with the back of his hand, thus, and then the people fell ashouting.

BRUTUS: What was the second noise for?

CASCA: Why, for that too.

CASSIUS: They shouted thrice. What was the last cry for?

CASCA: Why, for that too.

BRUTUS: Was the crown offered him thrice?

CASCA: Ay, marry, wast, and he put it by thrice, every time gentler than other, and at every putting by mine honest neighbors shouted.

CASSIUS: Who offered him the crown?

CASCA: Why, Antony.

BRUTUS: Tell us the manner of it, gentle Casca.

CASCA: I can as well be hang'd as tell the manner of it. It was mere foolery; I did not mark it. I saw Mark Antony offer him a crown (yet 'twas not a crown neither, 'twas one of these coronets) and, as I told you, he put it by once. But for all that, to my thinking, he would fain have had it. Then he offered it to him again; then he put it by again. But, to my thinking, he was very loath to lay his fingers off it. And then he offered it the third time; he put it the third time by; and still as he refused it, the rabblement hooted and clapped their chopped hands and threw up their sweaty nightcaps and uttered such a deal of stinking breath because Caesar refused the crown that it had almost choked Caesar, for he swounded and fell down at it. And for mine own part, I durst not laugh for fear of opening my lips and receiving the bad air.

CASSIUS: But, soft, I pray you, what, did Caesars wound?

CASCA: He fell down in the marketplace and foamed at mouth and was speechless.

BRUTUS: 'Tis very like. He hath the falling sickness.

CASSIUS: No, Caesar hath it not, but you, and I,
And honest Casca, we have the falling sickness.

CASCA: I know not what you mean by that, but I am sure Caesar fell down. If the tagrag people did not clap him and hiss him according as he pleased and displeased them, as they use to do the players in the theatre, I am no true man.

BRUTUS: What said he when he came unto himself?

CASCA: Marry, before he fell down, when he perceived the common herd was glad he refused the crown, he plucked me ope his doublet and offered them his throat to cut. An had been a man of any occupation, if I would not have taken him at a word, I would I might go to hell among the rogues. And so he fell. When he came to himself again, he said, if he had done or said anything amiss, he desired their worships to think it was his infirmity. Three or four wenches where I stood cried, "Alas, good soul!" and forgave him with all their hearts. But there's no heed to be taken of them; if Caesar had stabbed their mothers, they would have done no less.

BRUTUS: And after that he came, thus sad, away?

CASCA: Ay.

CASSIUS: Did Cicero say anything?

CASCA: Ay, he spoke Greek.

CASSIUS: To what effect?

CASCA: Nay, an I tell you that, I'll ne'er look you i' the face again; but those that understood him smiled at one another and shook their heads; but for mine own part, it was Greek to me. I could tell you more news too: Marullus and Flavius, for pulling scarfs off Caesar's images, are put to silence. Fare you well. There was more foolery yet, if could remember it.

CASSIUS: Will you sup with me tonight, Casca?

CASCA: No, I am promised forth.

CASSIUS: Will you dine with me tomorrow?

CASCA: Ay, if I be alive, and your mind hold, and your dinner worth the eating.

CASSIUS: Good, I will expect you.

CASCA: Do so, farewell, both.

Exit.

BRUTUS: What a blunt fellow is this grown to be!
He was quick mettle when he went to school.

CASSIUS: So is he now in execution
Of any bold or noble enterprise,
However he puts on this tardy form.
This rudeness is a sauce to his good wit,
Which gives men stomach to digest his words
With better appetite.

BRUTUS: And so it is. For this time I will leave you.
Tomorrow, if you please to speak with me,
I will come home to you, or, if you will,
Come home to me and I will wait for you.

CASSIUS: I will do so. Till then, think of the world.

Exit Brutus.

Well, Brutus, thou art noble; yet, I see
Thy honorable mettle may be wrought
From that it is disposed; therefore it is meet
That noble minds keep ever with their likes;
For who so firm that cannot be seduced?
Caesar doth bear me hard, but he loves Brutus.
If I were Brutus now and he were Cassius,

He should not humor me. I will this night,
In several hands, in at his windows throw,
As if they came from several citizens,
Writings, all tending to the great opinion
That Rome holds of his name, wherein obscurely
Caesar's ambition shall be glanced at.
And after this let Caesar seat him sure;
For we will shake him, or worse days endure.
Exit.

ACT I. SCENE III. A Street. Thunder and Lightning.

Enter, from Opposite Sides, Casca, with His Sword Drawn, and Cicero.

CICERO: Good even, Casca. Brought you Caesar home?
Why are you breathless, and why stare you so?
CASCA: Are not you moved, when all the sway of earth
Shakes like a thing unfirm? O Cicero,
I have seen tempests when the scolding winds
Have rived the knotty oaks, and I have seen
The ambitious ocean swell and rage and foam
To be exalted with the threatening clouds,
But never till tonight, never till now,
Did I go through a tempest dropping fire.
Either there is a civil strife in heaven,
Or else the world too saucy with the gods
Incenses them to send destruction.
CICERO: Why, saw you anything more wonderful?
CASCA: A common slave- you know him well by sight-
Held up his left hand, which did flame and burn
Like twenty torches join'd, and yet his hand
Not sensible of fire remain'd unscorch'd.
Besides- I ha' not since put up my sword-
Against the Capitol I met a lion,
Who glaz'd upon me and went surly by
Without annoying me. And there were drawn
Upon a heap a hundred ghastly women
Transformed with their fear, who swore they saw
Men all in fire walk up and down the streets.
And yesterday the bird of night did sit
Even at noonday upon the marketplace,
Howling and shrieking. When these prodigies
Do so conjointly meet, let not men say
"These are their reasons; they are natural":
For I believe they are portentous things
Unto the climate that they point upon.
CICERO: Indeed, it is a strange-disposed time.
But men may construe things after their fashion,
Clean from the purpose of the things themselves.
Comes Caesar to the Capitol tomorrow?
CASCA: He doth, for he did bid Antonio
Send word to you he would be there tomorrow.

CICERO: Good then, Casca. This disturbed sky
Is not to walk in.
CASCA: Farewell, Cicero.
Exit Cicero.
Enter Cassius.
CASSIUS: Who's there?
CASCA: A Roman.
CASSIUS: Casca, by your voice.
CASCA: Your ear is good. Cassius, what night is this!
CASSIUS: A very pleasing night to honest men.
CASCA: Who ever knew the heavens menace so?
CASSIUS: Those that have known the earth so full of faults.
For my part, I have walk'd about the streets,
Submitting me unto the perilous night,
And thus unbraced, Casca, as you see,
Have bared my bosom to the thunderstone;
And when the cross blue lightning seem'd to open
The breast of heaven, I did present myself
Even in the aim and very flash of it.
CASCA: But wherefore did you so much tempt the heavens?
It is the part of men to fear and tremble
When the most mighty gods by tokens send
Such dreadful heralds to astonish us.
CASSIUS: You are dull, Casca, and those sparks of life
That should be in a Roman you do want,
Or else you use not. You look pale and gaze
And put on fear and cast yourself in wonder
To see the strange impatience of the heavens.
But if you would consider the true cause
Why all these fires, why all these gliding ghosts,
Why birds and beasts from quality and kind,
Why old men, fools, and children calculate,
Why all these things change from their ordinance,
Their natures, and preformed faculties
To monstrous quality, why, you shall find
That heaven hath infused them with these spirits
To make them instruments of fear and warning
Unto some monstrous state.
Now could I, Casca, name to thee a man
Most like this dreadful night,
That thunders, lightens, opens graves, and roars
As doth the lion in the Capitol,
A man no mightier than thyself or me
In personal action, yet prodigious grown
And fearful, as these strange eruptions are.
CASCA: 'Tis Caesar that you mean, is it not, Cassius?
CASSIUS: Let it be who it is, for Romans now
Have thews and limbs like to their ancestors.
But, woe the while! Our fathers' minds are dead,

And we are govern'd with our mothers' spirits;
Our yoke and sufferance show us womanish.
CASCA: Indeed they say the senators tomorrow
Mean to establish Caesar as a king,
And he shall wear his crown by sea and land
In every place save here in Italy.
CASSIUS: I know where I will wear this dagger then:
Cassius from bondage will deliver Cassius.
Therein, ye gods, you make the weak most strong;
Therein, ye gods, you tyrants do defeat.
Nor stony tower, nor walls of beaten brass,
Nor airless dungeon, nor strong links of iron
Can be retentive to the strength of spirit;
But life, being weary of these worldly bars,
Never lacks power to dismiss itself.
If I know this, know all the world besides,
That part of tyranny that I do bear
I can shake off at pleasure. Thunder still.
CASCA: So can I.
So every bondman in his own hand bears
The power to cancel his captivity.
CASSIUS: And why should Caesar be a tyrant then?
Poor man! I know he would not be a wolf
But that he sees the Romans are but sheep.
He were no lion, were not Romans hinds.
Those that with haste will make a mighty fire
Begin it with weak straws. What trash is Rome,
What rubbish, and what offal, when it serves
For the base matter to illuminate
So vile a thing as Caesar? But, O grief,
Where hast thou led me? I perhaps speak this
Before a willing bondman; then I know
My answer must be made. But I am arm'd,
And dangers are to me indifferent.
CASCA: You speak to Casca, and to such a man
That is no fleering tell-tale. Hold, my hand.
Be factious for redress of all these griefs,
And I will set this foot of mine as far
As who goes farthest.
CASSIUS: There's a bargain made.
Now know you, Casca, I have moved already
Some certain of the noblest-minded Romans
To undergo with me an enterprise
Of honorable-dangerous consequence;
And I do know by this, they stay for me
In Pompey's Porch. For now, this fearful night,
There is no stir or walking in the streets,
And the complexion of the element
In favor's like the work we have in hand,

Most bloody, fiery, and most terrible.
Enter Cinna.
CASCA: Stand close awhile, for here comes one in haste.
CASSIUS: 'Tis Cinna, I do know him by his gait;
He is a friend. Cinna, where haste you so?
CINNA: To find out you. Who's that? Metellus Cimber?
CASSIUS: No, it is Casca, one incorporate
To our attempts. Am I not stay'd for, Cinna?
CINNA: I am glad on't. What a fearful night is this!
There's two or three of us have seen strange sights.
CASSIUS: Am I not stay'd for? Tell me.
CINNA: Yes, you are.
O Cassius, if you could
But win the noble Brutus to our party-
CASSIUS: Be you content. Good Cinna, take this paper,
And look you lay it in the praetor's chair,
Where Brutus may but find it; and throw this
In at his window; set this up with wax
Upon old Brutus' statue. All this done,
Repair to Pompey's Porch, where you shall find us.
Is Decius Brutus and Trebonius there?
CINNA: All but Metellus Cimber, and he's gone
To seek you at your house. Well, I will hie
And so bestow these papers as you bade me.
CASSIUS: That done, repair to Pompey's Theatre.
Exit Cinna.
Come, Casca, you and I will yet ere day
See Brutus at his house. Three parts of him
Is ours already, and the man entire
Upon the next encounter yields him ours.
CASCA: O, he sits high in all the people's hearts,
And that which would appear offense in us,
His countenance, like richest alchemy,
Will change to virtue and to worthiness.
CASSIUS: Him and his worth and our great need of him
You have right well conceited. Let us go,
For it is after midnight, and ere day
We will awake him and be sure of him.
Exeunt.

ACT II. SCENE I. Enter Brutus in His Orchard.

BRUTUS: What, Lucius, ho!
I cannot, by the progress of the stars,
Give guess how near to day. Lucius, I say!
I would it were my fault to sleep so soundly.
When, Lucius, when? Awake, I say! What, Lucius!
Enter Lucius.
LUCIUS: Call'd you, my lord?
BRUTUS: Get me a taper in my study, Lucius.
When it is lighted, come and call me here.

LUCIUS: I will, my lord.
Exit.
BRUTUS: It must be by his death, and, for my part,
I know no personal cause to spurn at him,
But for the general. He would be crown'd:
How that might change his nature, there's the question.
It is the bright day that brings forth the adder
And that craves wary walking. Crown him that,
And then, I grant, we put a sting in him
That at his will he may do danger with.
The abuse of greatness is when it disjoins
Remorse from power, and, to speak truth of Caesar,
I have not known when his affections sway'd
More than his reason. But 'tis a common proof
That lowliness is young ambition's ladder,
Whereto the climber-upward turns his face;
But when he once attains the upmost round,
He then unto the ladder turns his back,
Looks in the clouds, scorning the base degrees
By which he did ascend. So Caesar may;
Then, lest he may, prevent. And, since the quarrel
Will bear no color for the thing he is,
Fashion it thus, that what he is, augmented,
Would run to these and these extremities;
And therefore think him as a serpent's egg
Which hatch'd would as his kind grow mischievous,
And kill him in the shell.
Re-enter Lucius.
LUCIUS: The taper burneth in your closet, sir.
Searching the window for a flint I found
This paper thus seal'd up, and I am sure
It did not lie there when I went to bed.
Gives Him the Letter.
BRUTUS: Get you to bed again, it is not day.
Is not tomorrow, boy, the ides of March?
LUCIUS: I know not, sir.
BRUTUS: Look in the calendar and bring me word.
LUCIUS: I will, sir.
Exit.
BRUTUS: The exhalations whizzing in the air
Give so much light that I may read by them.
Opens the Letter and Reads.
Brutus, thou sleep'st: awake and see thyself!
Shall Rome, etc. Speak, strike, redress!"
"Brutus, thou sleep'st: awake!"
Such instigations have been often dropp'd
Where I have took them up.
"Shall Rome, etc." Thus must I piece it out.
Shall Rome stand under one man's awe? What, Rome?

My ancestors did from the streets of Rome
The Tarquin drive, when he was call'd a king.
"Speak, strike, redress!" Am I entreated
To speak and strike? O Rome, I make thee promise,
If the redress will follow, thou receivest
Thy full petition at the hand of Brutus!
Re-enter Lucius.
LUCIUS: Sir, March is wasted fifteen days.
Knocking within.
BRUTUS: 'Tis good. Go to the gate, somebody knocks.
Exit Lucius.
Since Cassius first did whet me against Caesar
I have not slept.
Between the acting of a dreadful thing
And the first motion, all the interim is
Like a phantasma or a hideous dream;
The genius and the mortal instruments
Are then in council, and the state of man,
Like to a little kingdom, suffers then
The nature of an insurrection.
Re-enter Lucius.
LUCIUS: Sir, 'tis your brother Cassius at the door,
Who doth desire to see you.
BRUTUS: Is he alone?
LUCIUS: No, sir, there are more with him.
BRUTUS: Do you know them?
LUCIUS: No, sir, their hats are pluck'd about their ears,
And half their faces buried in their cloaks,
That by no means I may discover them
By any mark of favor.
BRUTUS: Let 'em enter.
Exit Lucius.
They are the faction. O Conspiracy,
Shamest thou to show thy dangerous brow by night,
When evils are most free? O, then, by day
Where wilt thou find a cavern dark enough
To mask thy monstrous visage? Seek none, Conspiracy;
Hide it in smiles and affability;
For if thou path, thy native semblance on,
Not Erebus itself were dim enough
To hide thee from prevention.
Enter the conspirators, Cassius, Casca, Decius, Cinna, Metellus Cimber, and Trebonius.
CASSIUS: I think we are too bold upon your rest.
Good morrow, Brutus, do we trouble you?
BRUTUS: I have been up this hour, awake all night.
Know I these men that come along with you?
CASSIUS: Yes, every man of them, and no man here
But honors you, and every one doth wish
You had but that opinion of yourself

Which every noble Roman bears of you.
This is Trebonius.
BRUTUS: He is welcome hither.
CASSIUS: This, Decius Brutus.
BRUTUS: He is welcome too.
CASSIUS: This, Casca; this, Cinna; and this, Metellus Cimber.
BRUTUS: They are all welcome.
What watchful cares do interpose themselves
Betwixt your eyes and night?
CASSIUS: Shall I entreat a word? They whisper.
DECIUS: Here lies the east. Doth not the day break here?
CASCA: No.
CINNA: O, pardon, sir, it doth, and yongrey lines
That fret the clouds are messengers of day.
CASCA: You shall confess that you are both deceived.
Here, as I point my sword, the sun arises,
Which is a great way growing on the south,
Weighing the youthful season of the year.
Some two months hence up higher toward the north
He first presents his fire, and the high east
Stands as the Capitol, directly here.
BRUTUS: Give me your hands all over, one by one.
CASSIUS: And let us swear our resolution.
BRUTUS: No, not an oath. If not the face of men,
The sufferance of our souls, the time's abuse-
If these be motives weak, break off betimes,
And every man hence to his idle bed;
So let high-sighted tyranny range on
Till each man drop by lottery. But if these,
As I am sure they do, bear fire enough
To kindle cowards and to steel with valor
The melting spirits of women, then, countrymen,
What need we any spur but our own cause
To prick us to redress? What other bond
Than secret Romans that have spoke the word
And will not palter? And what other oath
Than honesty to honesty engaged
That this shall be or we will fall for it?
Swear priests and cowards and men cautelous,
Old feeble carrions and such suffering souls
That welcome wrongs; unto bad causes swear
Such creatures as men doubt; but do not stain
The even virtue of our enterprise,
Nor the insuppressive mettle of our spirits,
To think that or our cause or our performance
Did need an oath; when every drop of blood
That every Roman bears, and nobly bears,
Is guilty of a several bastardy
If he do break the smallest particle

Of any promise that hath pass'd from him.
CASSIUS: But what of Cicero? Shall we sound him?
I think he will stand very strong with us.
CASCA: Let us not leave him out.
CINNA: No, by no means.
METELLUS: O, let us have him, for his silver hairs
Will purchase us a good opinion,
And buy men's voices to commend our deeds.
It shall be said his judgement ruled our hands;
Our youths and wildness shall no whit appear,
But all be buried in his gravity.
BRUTUS: O, name him not; let us not break with him,
For he will never follow anything
That other men begin.
CASSIUS: Then leave him out.
CASCA: Indeed he is not fit.
DECIUS: Shall no man else be touch'd but only Caesar?
CASSIUS: Decius, well urged. I think it is not meet
Mark Antony, so well beloved of Caesar,
Should outlive Caesar. We shall find of him
A shrewd contriver; and you know his means,
If he improve them, may well stretch so far
As to annoy us all, which to prevent,
Let Antony and Caesar fall together.
BRUTUS: Our course will seem too bloody, Caius Cassius,
To cut the head off and then hack the limbs
Like wrath in death and envy afterwards;
For Antony is but a limb of Caesar.
Let us be sacrificers, but not butchers, Caius.
We all stand up against the spirit of Caesar,
And in the spirit of men there is no blood.
O, that we then could come by Caesar's spirit,
And not dismember Caesar! But, alas,
Caesar must bleed for it! And, gentle friends,
Let's kill him boldly, but not wrathfully;
Let's carve him as a dish fit for the gods,
Not hew him as a carcass fit for hounds;
And let our hearts, as subtle masters do,
Stir up their servants to an act of rage
And after seem to chide 'em. This shall make
Our purpose necessary and not envious,
Which so appearing to the common eyes,
We shall be call'd purgers, not murderers.
And for Mark Antony, think not of him,
For he can do no more than Caesar's arm
When Caesar's head is off.
CASSIUS: Yet I fear him,
For in the ingrated love he bears to Caesar-
BRUTUS: Alas, good Cassius, do not think of him.

If he love Caesar, all that he can do
Is to himself, take thought and die for Caesar.
And that were much he should, for he is given
To sports, to wildness, and much company.
TREBONIUS: There is no fear in him-let him not die,
For he will live and laugh at this hereafter.
Clock Strikes.
BRUTUS: Peace, count the clock.
CASSIUS: The clock hath stricken three.
TREBONIUS: 'Tis time to part.
CASSIUS: But it is doubtful yet
Whether Caesar will come forth today or no,
For he is superstitious grown of late,
Quite from the main opinion he held once
Of fantasy, of dreams, and ceremonies.
It may be these apparent prodigies,
The unaccustom'd terror of this night,
And the persuasion of his augurers
May hold him from the Capitol today.
DECIUS: Never fear that. If he be so resolved,
I can o'ersway him, for he loves to hear
That unicorns may be betray'd with trees,
And bears with glasses, elephants with holes,
Lions with toils, and men with flatterers;
But when I tell him he hates flatterers,
He says he does, being then most flattered.
Let me work;
For I can give his humor the true bent,
And I will bring him to the Capitol.
CASSIUS: Nay, we will all of us be there to fetch him.
BRUTUS: By the eighth hour. Is that the utter most?
CINNA: Be that the uttermost, and fail not then.
METELLUS: Caius Ligarius doth bear Caesar hard,
Who rated him for speaking well of Pompey.
I wonder none of you have thought of him.
BRUTUS: Now, good Metellus, go along by him.
He loves me well, and I have given him reasons;
Send him but hither, and I'll fashion him.
CASSIUS: The morning comes upon 's. We'll leave you, Brutus,
And, friends, disperse yourselves, but all remember
What you have said and show yourselves true Romans.
BRUTUS: Good gentlemen, look fresh and merrily;
Let not our looks put on our purposes,
But bear it as our Roman actors do,
With untired spirits and formal constancy.
And so, good morrow to you every one.
Exeunt all but Brutus.
Boy! Lucius! Fast asleep? It is no matter.
Enjoy the honey-heavy dew of slumber;

Thou hast no figures nor no fantasies,
Which busy care draws in the brains of men;
Therefore thou sleep'st so sound.
Enter Portia.
PORTIA: Brutus, my lord!
BRUTUS: Portia, what mean you? Wherefore rise you now?
It is not for your health thus to commit
Your weak condition to the raw cold morning.
PORTIA: Nor for yours neither. have ungently, Brutus,
Stole from my bed; and yesternight at supper
You suddenly arose and walk'd about,
Musing and sighing, with your arms across;
And when I ask'd you what the matter was,
You stared upon me with ungentle looks.
I urged you further; then you scratch'd your head,
And too impatiently stamp'd with your foot.
Yet I insisted, yet you answer'd not,
But with an angry waiter of your hand
Gave sign for me to leave you. So I did,
Fearing to strengthen that impatience
Which seem'd too much enkindled, and withal
Hoping it was but an effect of humor,
Which sometime hath his hour with every man.
It will not let you eat, nor talk, nor sleep,
And, could it work so much upon your shape
As it hath much prevail'd on your condition,
I should not know you, Brutus. Dear my lord,
Make me acquainted with your cause of grief.
BRUTUS: I am not well in health, and that is all.
PORTIA: Brutus is wise, and, were he not in health,
He would embrace the means to come by it.
BRUTUS: Why, so I do. Good Portia, go to bed.
PORTIA: Is Brutus sick, and is it physical
To walk unbraced and suck up the humors
Of the dank morning? What, is Brutus sick,
And will he steal out of his wholesome bed
To dare the vile contagion of the night
And tempt the rheumy and unpurged air
To add unto his sickness? No, my Brutus,
You have some sick offense within your mind,
Which by the right and virtue of my place
I ought to know of; and, upon my knees,
I charm you, by my once commended beauty,
By all your vows of love and that great vow
Which did incorporate and make us one,
That you unfold to me, yourself, your half,
Why you are heavy and what men tonight
Have had resort to you; for here have been
Some six or seven, who did hide their faces

Even from darkness.
BRUTUS: Kneel not, gentle Portia.
PORTIA: I should not need, if you were gentle Brutus.
Within the bond of marriage, tell me, Brutus,
Is it excepted I should know no secrets
That appertain to you? Am I yourself
But, as it were, in sort or limitation,
To keep with you at meals, comfort your bed,
And talk to you sometimes? Dwell I but in the suburbs
Of your good pleasure? If it be no more,
Portia is Brutus' harlot, not his wife.
BRUTUS: You are my true and honorable wife,
As dear to me as are the ruddy drops
That visit my sad heart.
PORTIA: If this were true, then should I know this secret.
I grant I am a woman, but withal
A woman that Lord Brutus took to wife.
I grant I am a woman, but withal
A woman well reputed, Cato's daughter.
Think you I am no stronger than my sex,
Being so father'd and so husbanded?
Tell me your counsels, I will not disclose 'em.
I have made strong proof of my constancy,
Giving myself a voluntary wound
Here in the thigh. Can I bear that with patience
And not my husband's secrets?
BRUTUS: O ye gods,
Render me worthy of this noble wife! Knocking within.
Hark, hark, one knocks. Portia, go in awhile,
And by and by thy bosom shall partake
The secrets of my heart.
All my engagements I will construe to thee,
All the charactery of my sad brows.
Leave me with haste.
Exit Portia.
Lucius, who's that knocks?
Re-enter Lucius with Ligarius.
LUCIUS: Here is a sick man that would speak with you.
BRUTUS: Caius Ligarius, that Metellus spake of.
Boy, stand aside. Caius Ligarius, how?
LIGARIUS: Vouchsafe good morrow from a feeble tongue.
BRUTUS: O, what a time have you chose out, brave Caius,
To wear a kerchief! Would you were not sick!
LIGARIUS: I am not sick, if Brutus have in hand
Any exploit worthy the name of honor.
BRUTUS: Such an exploit have I in hand, Ligarius,
Had you a healthful ear to hear of it.
LIGARIUS: By all the gods that Romans bow before,
I here discard my sickness! Soul of Rome!

Brave son, derived from honorable loins!
Thou, like an exorcist, hast conjured up
My mortified spirit. Now bid me run,
And I will strive with things impossible,
Yea, get the better of them. What's to do?
BRUTUS: A piece of work that will make sick men whole.
LIGARIUS: But are not some whole that we must make sick?
BRUTUS: That must we also. What it is, my Caius,
I shall unfold to thee, as we are going
To whom it must be done.
LIGARIUS: Set on your foot,
And with a heart new-fired I follow you,
To do I know not what; but it sufficeth
That Brutus leads me on.
BRUTUS: Follow me then.
Exeunt.

ACT II. SCENE II. Caesar's House. Thunder and Lightning.

Enter Caesar, in His Nightgown.
CAESAR: Nor heaven nor earth have been at peace tonight.
Thrice hath Calpurnia in her sleep cried out,
"Help, ho! They murther Caesar!" Who's within?
Enter a Servant.
SERVANT: My lord?
CAESAR: Go bid the priests do present sacrifice,
And bring me their opinions of success.
SERVANT: I will, my lord.
Exit.
Enter Calpurnia.
CALPURNIA: What mean you, Caesar? Think you to walk forth?
You shall not stir out of your house today.
CAESAR: Caesar shall forth: the things that threaten'd me
Ne'er look'd but on my back; when they shall see
The face of Caesar, they are vanished.
CALPURNIA: Caesar, I I stood on ceremonies,
Yet now they fright me. There is one within,
Besides the things that we have heard and seen,
Recounts most horrid sights seen by the watch.
A lioness hath whelped in the streets;
And graves have yawn'd, and yielded up their dead;
Fierce fiery warriors fight upon the clouds,
In ranks and squadrons and right form of war,
Which drizzled blood upon the Capitol;
The noise of battle hurtled in the air,
Horses did neigh and dying men did groan,
And ghosts did shriek and squeal about the streets.
O Caesar! These things are beyond all use,
And I do fear them.
CAESAR: What can be avoided
Whose end is purposed by the mighty gods?

Yet Caesar shall go forth, for these predictions
Are to the world in general as to Caesar.
CALPURNIA: When beggars die, there are no comets seen;
The heavens themselves blaze forth the death of princes.
CAESAR: Cowards die many times before their deaths;
The valiant never taste of death but once.
Of all the wonders that I yet have heard,
It seems to me most strange that men should fear
Seeing that death, a necessary end,
Will come when it will come.
Re-enter Servant.
What say the augurers?
SERVANT: They would not have you to stir forth today.
Plucking the entrails of an offering forth,
They could not find a heart within the beast.
CAESAR: The gods do this in shame of cowardice.
Caesar should be a beast without a heart
If he should stay at home today for fear.
No, Caesar shall not. Danger knows full well
That Caesar is more dangerous than he.
We are two lions litter'd in one day,
And I the elder and more terrible.
And Caesar shall go forth.
CALPURNIA: Alas, my lord,
Your wisdom is consumed in confidence.
Do not go forth today. Call it my fear
That keeps you in the house and not your own.
We'll send Mark Antony to the Senate House,
And he shall say you are not well today.
Let me, upon my knee, prevail in this.
CAESAR: Mark Antony shall say I am not well,
And, for thy humor, I will stay at home.
Enter Decius.
Here's Decius Brutus, he shall tell them so.
DECIUS: Caesar, all hail! Good morrow, worthy Caesar!
I come to fetch you to the Senate House.
CAESAR: And you are come in very happy time
To bear my greeting to the senators
And tell them that I will not come today.
Cannot, is false, and that I dare not, falser:
I will not come today. Tell them so, Decius.
CALPURNIA: Say he is sick.
CAESAR: Shall Caesar send a lie?
Have I in conquest stretch'd mine arm so far
To be afeard to tell greybeards the truth?
Decius, go tell them Caesar will not come.
DECIUS: Most mighty Caesar, let me know some cause,
Lest I be laugh'd at when I tell them so.
CAESAR: The cause is in my will: I will not come,

That is enough to satisfy the Senate.
But, for your private satisfaction,
Because I love you, I will let you know.
Calpurnia here, my wife, stays me at home;
She dreamt tonight she saw my statue,
Which, like a fountain with an hundred spouts,
Did run pure blood, and many lusty Romans
Came smiling and did bathe their hands in it.
And these does she apply for warnings and portents
And evils imminent, and on her knee
Hath begg'd that I will stay at home today.
DECIUS: This dream is all amiss interpreted;
It was a vision fair and fortunate.
Your statue spouting blood in many pipes,
In which so many smiling Romans bathed,
Signifies that from you great Rome shall suck
Reviving blood, and that great men shall press
For tinctures, stains, relics, and cognizance.
This by Calpurnia's dream is signified.
CAESAR: And this way have you well expounded it.
DECIUS: I have, when you have heard what I can say.
And know it now, the Senate have concluded
To give this day a crown to mighty Caesar.
If you shall send them word you will not come,
Their minds may change. Besides, it were a mock
Apt to be render'd, for someone to say
"Break up the Senate till another time,
When Caesar's wife shall meet with better dreams."
If Caesar hide himself, shall they not whisper
"Lo, Caesar is afraid"?
Pardon me, Caesar, for my dear dear love
To your proceeding bids me tell you this,
And reason to my love is liable.
CAESAR: How foolish do your fears seem now, Calpurnia!
I am ashamed I did yield to them.
Give me my robe, for I will go.
Enter Publius, Brutus, Ligarius, Metellus, Casca, Trebonius, and Cinna.
And look where Publius is come to fetch me.
PUBLIUS: Good morrow,Caesar.
CAESAR: Welcome, Publius.
What, Brutus, are you stirr'd so early too?
Good morrow, Casca. Caius Ligarius,
Caesar was ne'er so much your enemy
As that same ague which hath made you lean.
What is't o'clock?
BRUTUS: Caesar, 'tis strucken eight.
CAESAR: I thank you for your pains and courtesy.
Enter Antony.
See, Antony, that revels long o' nights,

Is notwithstanding up. Good morrow, Antony.
ANTONY: So to most noble Caesar.
CAESAR: Bid them prepare within.
I am to blame to be thus waited for.
Now, Cinna; now, Metellus; what, Trebonius,
I have an hour's talk in store for you;
Remember that you call on me today;
Be near me, that I may remember you.
TREBONIUS: Caesar, I will. Aside. And so near will I be
That your best friends shall wish I had been further.
CAESAR: Good friends, go in and taste some wine with me,
And we like friends will straightway go together.
BRUTUS: Aside. That every like is not the same, O Caesar,
The heart of Brutus yearns to think upon!
Exeunt.

ACT II. SCENE III. A Street near the Capitol.

Enter Artemidorus, Reading Paper.
ARTEMIDORUS: "Caesar, beware of Brutus; take heed of Cassius; come not near Casca; have an eye to Cinna; trust not Trebonius; mark well Metellus Cimber; Decius Brutus loves thee not; thou hast wronged Caius Ligarius. There is but one mind in all these men, and it is bent against Caesar. If thou beest not immortal, look about you. Security gives way to conspiracy. The mighty gods defend thee!
Thy lover, Artemidorus."
Here will I stand till Caesar pass along,
And as a suitor will I give him this.
My heart laments that virtue cannot live
Out of the teeth of emulation.
If thou read this, O Caesar, thou mayest live;
If not, the Fates with traitors do contrive.
Exit.

ACT II. SCENE IV. Another Part of the Same Street, Before the House of Brutus.

Enter Portia and Lucius.
PORTIA: I prithee, boy, run to the Senate House;
Stay not to answer me, but get thee gone.
Why dost thou stay?
LUCIUS: To know my errand, madam.
PORTIA: I would have had thee there, and here again,
Ere I can tell thee what thou shouldst do there.
O constancy, be strong upon my side!
Set a huge mountain 'tween my heart and tongue!
I have a man's mind, but a woman's might.
How hard it is for women to keep counsel!
Art thou here yet?
LUCIUS: Madam, what should I do?
Run to the Capitol, and nothing else?
And so return to you, and nothing else?
PORTIA: Yes, bring me word, boy, if thy lord look well,

For he went sickly forth; and take good note
What Caesar doth, what suitors press to him.
Hark, boy, what noise is that?
LUCIUS: I hear none, madam.
PORTIA: Prithee, listen well.
I heard a bustling rumor like a fray,
And the wind brings it from the Capitol.
LUCIUS: Sooth, madam, I hear nothing.
Enter the Soothsayer.
PORTIA: Come hither, fellow;
Which way hast thou been?
SOOTHSAYER: At mine own house, good lady.
PORTIA: What is't o'clock?
SOOTHSAYER: About the ninth hour, lady.
PORTIA: Is Caesar yet gone to the Capitol?
SOOTHSAYER: Madam, not yet. I go to take my stand
To see him pass on to the Capitol.
PORTIA: Thou hast some suit to Caesar, hast thou not?
SOOTHSAYER: That I have, lady. If it will please Caesar
To be so good to Caesar as to hear me,
I shall beseech him to befriend himself.
PORTIA: Why, know'st thou any harm's intended towards him?
SOOTHSAYER: None that I know will be, much that I fear may chance.
Good morrow to you. Here the street is narrow,
The throng that follows Caesar at the heels,
Of senators, of praetors, common suitors,
Will crowd a feeble man almost to death.
I'll get me to a place more void and there
Speak to great Caesar as he comes along.
Exit.
PORTIA: I must go in. Ay me, how weak a thing
The heart of woman is! O Brutus,
The heavens speed thee in thine enterprise!
Sure, the boy heard me. Brutus hath a suit
That Caesar will not grant. O, I grow faint.
Run, Lucius, and commend me to my lord;
Say I am merry. Come to me again,
And bring me word what he doth say to thee.
Exeunt Severally.

ACT III. SCENE I. Rome. Before the Capitol; the Senate Sitting Above. A Crowd of People, among Them Artemidorus and the Soothsayer.

Flourish. Enter Caesar, Brutus, Cassius, Casca, Decius, Metellus, Trebonius, Cinna, Antony, Lepidus, Popilius, Publius, and Others.

CAESAR: The ides of March are come.
SOOTHSAYER: Ay, Caesar, but not gone.
A Hail, Caesar! Read this schedule.
DECIUS: Trebonius doth desire you to o'er read,
At your best leisure, this his humble suit.
ARTEMIDORUS: O Caesar, read mine first, for mine's a suit

That touches Caesar nearer. Read it, great Caesar.
CAESAR: What touches us ourself shall be last served.
ARTEMIDORUS: Delay not, Caesar; read it instantly.
CAESAR: What, is the fellow mad?
PUBLIUS: Sirrah, give place.
CASSIUS: What, urge you your petitions in the street?
Come to the Capitol.
Caesar goes up to the Senate House, the rest follow.
POPILIUS: I wish your enterprise today may thrive.
CASSIUS: What enterprise, Popilius?
POPILIUS: Fare you well.
Advances to Caesar.
BRUTUS: What said Popilius Lena?
CASSIUS: He wish'd today our enterprise might thrive.
I fear our purpose is discovered.
BRUTUS: Look, how he makes to Caesar. Mark him.
CASSIUS: Casca,
Be sudden, for we fear prevention.
Brutus, what shall be done? If this be known,
Cassius or Caesar never shall turn back,
For I will slay myself.
BRUTUS: Cassius, be constant.
Popilius Lena speaks not of our purposes;
For, look, he smiles, and Caesar doth not change.
CASSIUS: Trebonius knows his time, for, look you, Brutus,
He draws Mark Antony out of the way.
Exeunt Antony and Trebonius.
DECIUS: Where is Metellus Cimber? Let him
And presently prefer his suit to Caesar.
BRUTUS: He is address'd; press near and second him.
CINNA: Casca, you are the first that rears your hand.
CAESAR: Are we all ready? What is now amiss
That Caesar and his Senate must redress?
METELLUS: Most high, most mighty, and most puissant Caesar,
Metellus Cimber throws before thy seat
An humble heart. Kneels.
CAESAR: I must prevent thee, Cimber.
These couchings and these lowly courtesies
Might fire the blood of ordinary men
And turn preordinance and first decree
Into the law of children. Be not fond
To think that Caesar bears such rebel blood
That will be thaw'd from the true quality
With that which melteth fools- I mean sweet words,
Low-crooked court'sies, and base spaniel-fawning.
Thy brother by decree is banished.
If thou dost bend and pray and fawn for him,
I spurn thee like a cur out of my way.
Know, Caesar doth not wrong, nor without cause

Will he be satisfied.
METELLUS: Is there no voice more worthy than my own,
To sound more sweetly in great Caesar's ear
For the repealing of my banish'd brother?
BRUTUS: I kiss thy hand, but not in flattery, Caesar,
Desiring thee that Publius Cimber may
Have an immediate freedom of repeal.
CAESAR: What, Brutus?
CASSIUS: Pardon, Caesar! Caesar, pardon!
As low as to thy foot doth Cassius fall
To beg enfranchisement for Publius Cimber.
CAESAR: I could be well moved, if I were as you;
If I could pray to move, prayers would move me;
But I am constant as the northern star,
Of whose true-fix'd and resting quality
There is no fellow in the firmament.
The skies are painted with unnumber'd sparks;
They are all fire and every one doth shine;
But there's but one in all doth hold his place.
So in the world, 'tis furnish'd well with men,
And men are flesh and blood, and apprehensive;
Yet in the number I do know but one
That unassailable holds on his rank,
Unshaked of motion; and that I am he,
Let me a little show it, even in this;
That I was constant Cimber should be banish'd,
And constant do remain to keep him so.
CINNA: O Caesar-
CAESAR: Hence! Wilt thou lift up Olympus?
DECIUS: Great Caesar-
CAESAR: Doth not Brutus bootless kneel?
CASCA: Speak, hands, for me!

Casca First, Then the Other Conspirators and Marcus Brutus Stab Caesar.

CAESAR: Et tu, Brute?- Then fall, Caesar! Dies.
CINNA: Liberty! Freedom! Tyranny is dead!
Run hence, proclaim, cry it about the streets.
CASSIUS: Some to the common pulpits and cry out
"Liberty, freedom, and enfranchisement!"
BRUTUS: People and senators, be not affrighted,
Fly not, stand still; ambition's debt is paid.
CASCA: Go to the pulpit, Brutus.
DECIUS: And Cassius too.
BRUTUS: Where's Publius?
CINNA: Here, quite confounded with this mutiny.
METELLUS: Stand fast together, lest some friend of Caesar's
Should chance-
BRUTUS: Talk not of standing. Publius, good cheer,
There is no harm intended to your person,
Nor to no Roman else. So tell them, Publius.

CASSIUS: And leave us, Publius, lest that the people
Rushing on us should do your age some mischief.
BRUTUS: Do so, and let no man abide this deed
But we the doers.
Re-enter Trebonius.
CASSIUS: Where is Antony?
TREBONIUS: Fled to his house amazed.
Men, wives, and children stare, cry out, and run
As it were doomsday.
BRUTUS: Fates, we will know your pleasures.
That we shall die, we know; 'tis but the time
And drawing days out that men stand upon.
CASSIUS: Why, he that cuts off twenty years of life
Cuts off so many years of fearing death.
BRUTUS: Grant that, and then is death a benefit;
So are we Caesar's friends that have abridged
His time of fearing death. Stoop, Romans, stoop,
And let us bathe our hands in Caesar's blood
Up to the elbows, and besmear our swords;
Then walk we forth, even to the marketplace,
And waving our red weapons o'er our heads,
Let's all cry, "Peace, freedom, and liberty!"
CASSIUS: Stoop then, and wash. How many ages hence
Shall this our lofty scene be acted over
In states unborn and accents yet unknown!
BRUTUS: How many times shall Caesar bleed in sport,
That now on Pompey's basis lies along
No worthier than the dust!
CASSIUS: So oft as that shall be,
So often shall the knot of us be call'd
The men that gave their country liberty.
DECIUS: What, shall we forth?
CASSIUS: Ay, every man away.
Brutus shall lead, and we will grace his heels
With the most boldest and best hearts of Rome.
Enter a Servant.
BRUTUS: Soft, who comes here? A friend of Antony's.
SERVANT: Thus, Brutus, did my master bid me kneel,
Thus did Mark Antony bid me fall down,
And, being prostrate, thus he bade me say:
Brutus is noble, wise, valiant, and honest;
Caesar was mighty, bold, royal, and loving.
Say I love Brutus and I honor him;
Say I fear'd Caesar, honor'd him, and loved him.
If Brutus will vouchsafe that Antony
May safely come to him and be resolved
How Caesar hath deserved to lie in death,
Mark Antony shall not love Caesar dead
So well as Brutus living, but will follow

The fortunes and affairs of noble Brutus
Thorough the hazards of this untrod state
With all true faith. So says my master Antony.
BRUTUS: Thy master is a wise and valiant Roman;
I never thought him worse.
Tell him, so please him come unto this place,
He shall be satisfied and, by my honor,
Depart untouch'd.
SERVANT: I'll fetch him presently.
Exit.
BRUTUS: I know that we shall have him well to friend.
CASSIUS: I wish we may, but yet have I a mind
That fears him much, and my misgiving still
Falls shrewdly to the purpose.
Re-enter Antony.
BRUTUS: But here comes Antony. Welcome, Mark Antony.
ANTONY: O mighty Caesar! Dost thou lie so low?
Are all thy conquests, glories, triumphs, spoils,
Shrunk to this little measure? Fare thee well.
I know not, gentlemen, what you intend,
Who else must be let blood, who else is rank.
If I myself, there is no hour so fit
As Caesar's death's hour, nor no instrument
Of half that worth as those your swords, made rich
With the most noble blood of all this world.
I do beseech ye, if you bear me hard,
Now, whilst your purpled hands do reek and smoke,
Fulfill your pleasure. Live a thousand years,
I shall not find myself so apt to die;
No place will please me so, no means of death,
As here by Caesar, and by you cut off,
The choice and master spirits of this age.
BRUTUS: O Antony, beg not your death of us!
Though now we must appear bloody and cruel,
As, by our hands and this our present act
You see we do, yet see you but our hands
And this the bleeding business they have done.
Our hearts you see not; they are pitiful;
And pity to the general wrong of Rome-
As fire drives out fire, so pity pity-
Hath done this deed on Caesar. For your part,
To you our swords have leaden points, Mark Antony;
Our arms in strength of malice, and our hearts
Of brothers' temper, do receive you in
With all kind love, good thoughts, and reverence.
CASSIUS: Your voice shall be as strong as any man's
In the disposing of new dignities.
BRUTUS: Only be patient till we have appeased
The multitude, beside themselves with fear,

And then we will deliver you the cause
Why I, that did love Caesar when I struck him,
Have thus proceeded.
ANTONY: I doubt not of your wisdom.
Let each man render me his bloody hand.
First, Marcus Brutus, will I shake with you;
Next, Caius Cassius, do I take your hand;
Now, Decius Brutus, yours; now yours, Metellus;
Yours, Cinna; and, my valiant Casca, yours;
Though last, not least in love, yours, good Trebonius.
Gentlemen all- alas, what shall I say?
My credit now stands on such slippery ground,
That one of two bad ways you must conceit me,
Either a coward or a flatterer.
That I did love thee, Caesar, O, 'tis true!
If then thy spirit look upon us now,
Shall it not grieve thee dearer than thy death
To see thy Antony making his peace,
Shaking the bloody fingers of thy foes,
Most noble! In the presence of thy corse?
Had I as many eyes as thou hast wounds,
Weeping as fast as they stream forth thy blood,
It would become me better than to close
In terms of friendship with thine enemies.
Pardon me, Julius! Here wast thou bay'd, brave hart,
Here didst thou fall, and here thy hunters stand,
Sign'd in thy spoil, and crimson'd in thy Lethe.
O world, thou wast the forest to this hart,
And this, indeed, O world, the heart of thee.
How like a deer strucken by many princes
Dost thou here lie!
CASSIUS: Mark Antony-
ANTONY: Pardon me, Caius Cassius.
The enemies of Caesar shall say this:
Then, in a friend, it is cold modesty.
CASSIUS: I blame you not for praising Caesar so;
But what compact mean you to have with us?
Will you be prick'd in number of our friends,
Or shall we on, and not depend on you?
ANTONY: Therefore I took your hands, but was indeed
Sway'd from the point by looking down on Caesar.
Friends am I with you all and love you all,
Upon this hope that you shall give me reasons
Why and wherein Caesar was dangerous.
BRUTUS: Or else were this a savage spectacle.
Our reasons are so full of good regard
That were you, Antony, the son of Caesar,
You should be satisfied.
ANTONY: That's all I seek;

And am moreover suitor that I may
Produce his body to the marketplace,
And in the pulpit, as becomes a friend,
Speak in the order of his funeral.
BRUTUS: You shall, Mark Antony.
CASSIUS: Brutus, a word with you.
Aside to Brutus. You know not what you do. Do not consent
That Antony speak in his funeral.
Know you how much the people may be moved
By that which he will utter?
BRUTUS: By your pardon,
I will myself into the pulpit first,
And show the reason of our Caesar's death.
What Antony shall speak, I will protest
He speaks by leave and by permission,
And that we are contented Caesar shall
Have all true rites and lawful ceremonies.
It shall advantage more than do us wrong.
CASSIUS: I know not what may fall; I like it not.
BRUTUS: Mark Antony, here, take you Caesar's body.
You shall not in your funeral speech blame us,
But speak all good you can devise of Caesar,
And say you do't by our permission,
Else shall you not have any hand at all
About his funeral. And you shall speak
In the same pulpit whereto I am going,
After my speech is ended.
ANTONY: Be it so,
I do desire no more.
BRUTUS: Prepare the body then, and follow us.
Exeunt All but Antony.
ANTONY: O, pardon me, thou bleeding piece of earth,
That I am meek and gentle with these butchers!
Thou art the ruins of the noblest man
That ever lived in the tide of times.
Woe to the hand that shed this costly blood!
Over thy wounds now do I prophesy
(Which like dumb mouths do ope their ruby lips
To beg the voice and utterance of my tongue)
A curse shall light upon the limbs of men;
Domestic fury and fierce civil strife
Shall cumber all the parts of Italy;
Blood and destruction shall be so in use,
And dreadful objects so familiar,
That mothers shall but smile when they behold
Their infants quarter'd with the hands of war;
All pity choked with custom of fell deeds,
And Caesar's spirit ranging for revenge,
With Ate by his side come hot from hell,

Shall in these confines with a monarch's voice
Cry "Havoc!" and let slip the dogs of war,
That this foul deed shall smell above the earth
With carrion men, groaning for burial.
Enter a Servant.
You serve Octavius Caesar, do you not?
SERVANT: I do, Mark Antony.
ANTONY: Caesar did write for him to come to Rome.
SERVANT: He did receive his letters, and is coming,
And bid me say to you by word of mouth-
O Caesar! Sees the body.
ANTONY: Thy heart is big; get thee apart and weep.
Passion, I see, is catching, for mine eyes,
Seeing those beads of sorrow stand in thine,
Began to water. Is thy master coming?
SERVANT: He lies tonight within seven leagues of Rome.
ANTONY: Post back with speed and tell him what hath chanced.
Here is a mourning Rome, a dangerous Rome,
No Rome of safety for Octavius yet;
Hie hence, and tell him so. Yet stay awhile,
Thou shalt not back till I have borne this corse
Into the marketplace. There shall I try,
In my oration, how the people take
The cruel issue of these bloody men,
According to the which thou shalt discourse
To young Octavius of the state of things.
Lend me your hand.
Exeunt with Caesar's Body.

ACT III. SCENE II. The Forum.

Enter Brutus and Cassius, and a throng of Citizens.
CITIZENS: We will be satisfied! Let us be satisfied!
BRUTUS: Then follow me and give me audience, friends.
Cassius, go you into the other street
And part the numbers.
Those that will hear me speak, let 'em stay here;
Those that will follow Cassius, go with him;
And public reasons shall be rendered
Of Caesar's death.
FIRST CITIZEN: I will hear Brutus speak.
SECOND CITIZEN: I will hear Cassius and compare their reasons,
When severally we hear them rendered.
Exit Cassius, with Some Citizens. Brutus Goes into the Pulpit.
THIRD CITIZEN: The noble Brutus is ascended. Silence!
BRUTUS: Be patient till the last.
Romans, countrymen, and lovers! Hear me for my cause, and be silent, that you may hear. Believe me for mine honor, and have respect to mine honor, that you may believe. Censure me in your wisdom, and awake your senses, that you may the better judge. If there be any in this assembly, any dear friend of Caesar's, to

him I say that Brutus' love to Caesar was no less than his. If then that friend demand why Brutus rose against Caesar, this is my answer: Not that I loved Caesar less, but that I loved Rome more. Had you rather Caesar were living and die all slaves, than that Caesar were dead to live all freemen? As Caesar loved me, I weep for him; as he was fortunate, I rejoice at it; as he was valiant, I honor him; but as he was ambitious, I slew him. There is tears for his love, joy for his fortune, honor for his valor, and death for his ambition. Who is here so base that would be a bondman? If any, speak, for him have I offended. Who is here so rude that would not be a Roman? If any, speak, for him have I offended. Who is here so vile that will not love his country? If any, speak, for him have I offended. I pause for a reply.
ALL: None, Brutus, none.
BRUTUS: Then none have I offended. I have done no more to Caesar than you shall do to Brutus. The question of his death is enrolled in the Capitol, his glory not extenuated, wherein he was worthy, nor his offenses enforced, for which he suffered death.
Enter Antony and Others, with Caesar's Body.
Here comes his body, mourned by Mark Antony, who, though he had no hand in his death, shall receive the benefit of his dying, a place in the commonwealth, as which of you shall not? With this I depart- that, as I slew my best lover for the good of Rome, I have the same dagger for myself, when it shall please my country to need my death.
ALL: Live, Brutus, live, live!
FIRST CITIZEN: Bring him with triumph home unto his house.
SECOND CITIZEN: Give him a statue with his ancestors.
THIRD CITIZEN: Let him be Caesar.
FOURTH CITIZEN: Caesar's better parts
Shall be crown'd in Brutus.
FIRST CITIZEN: We'll bring him to his house with shouts and clamors.
BRUTUS: My countrymen-
SECOND CITIZEN: Peace! Silence! Brutus speaks.
FIRST CITIZEN: Peace, ho!
BRUTUS: Good countrymen, let me depart alone,
And, for my sake, stay here with Antony.
Do grace to Caesar's corse, and grace his speech
Tending to Caesar's glories, which Mark Antony,
By our permission, is allow'd to make.
I do entreat you, not a man depart,
Save I alone, till Antony have spoke.
Exit.
FIRST CITIZEN: Stay, ho, and let us hear Mark Antony.
THIRD CITIZEN: Let him go up into the public chair;
We'll hear him. Noble Antony, go up.
ANTONY: For Brutus' sake, I am beholding to you.
Goes into the Pulpit.

FOURTH CITIZEN: What does he say of Brutus?
THIRD CITIZEN: He says, for Brutus' sake,
He finds himself beholding to us all.
FOURTH CITIZEN: 'Twere best he speak no harm of Brutus here.
FIRST CITIZEN: This Caesar was a tyrant.
THIRD CITIZEN: Nay, that's certain.
We are blest that Rome is rid of him.
SECOND CITIZEN: Peace! Let us hear what Antony can say.
ANTONY: You gentle Romans-
ALL: Peace, ho! Let us hear him.
ANTONY: Friends, Romans, countrymen, lend me your ears!
I come to bury Caesar, not to praise him.
The evil that men do lives after them,
The good is oft interred with their bones;
So let it be with Caesar. The noble Brutus
Hath told you Caesar was ambitious;
If it were so, it was a grievous fault,
And grievously hath Caesar answer'd it.
Here, under leave of Brutus and the rest-
For Brutus is an honorable man;
So are they all, all honorable men-
Come I to speak in Caesar's funeral.
He was my friend, faithful and just to me;
But Brutus says he was ambitious,
And Brutus is an honorable man.
He hath brought many captives home to Rome,
Whose ransoms did the general coffers fill.
Did this in Caesar seem ambitious?
When that the poor have cried, Caesar hath wept;
Ambition should be made of sterner stuff:
Yet Brutus says he was ambitious,
And Brutus is an honorable man.
You all did see that on the Lupercal
I thrice presented him a kingly crown,
Which he did thrice refuse. Was this ambition?
Yet Brutus says he was ambitious,
And sure he is an honorable man.
I speak not to disprove what Brutus spoke,
But here I am to speak what I do know.
You all did love him once, not without cause;
What cause withholds you then to mourn for him?
O judgement, thou art fled to brutish beasts,
And men have lost their reason. Bear with me;
My heart is in the coffin there with Caesar,
And I must pause till it come back to me.
FIRST CITIZEN: Methinks there is much reason in his sayings.
SECOND CITIZEN: If thou consider rightly of the matter,
Caesar has had great wrong.
THIRD CITIZEN: Has he, masters?

I fear there will a worse come in his place.
FOURTH CITIZEN: Mark'd ye his words? He would not take the crown;
Therefore 'tis certain he was not ambitious.
FIRST CITIZEN: If it be found so, some will dear abide it.
SECOND CITIZEN: Poor soul, his eyes are red as fire with weeping.
THIRD CITIZEN: There's not a nobler man in Rome than Antony.
FOURTH CITIZEN: Now mark him, he begins again to speak.
ANTONY: But yesterday the word of Caesar might
Have stood against the world. Now lies he there,
And none so poor to do him reverence.
O masters! If I were disposed to stir
Your hearts and minds to mutiny and rage,
I should do Brutus wrong and Cassius wrong,
Who, you all know, are honorable men.
I will not do them wrong; I rather choose
To wrong the dead, to wrong myself and you,
Than I will wrong such honorable men.
But here's a parchment with the seal of Caesar;
I found it in his closet, 'tis his will.
Let but the commons hear this testament-
Which, pardon me, I do not mean to read-
And they would go and kiss dead Caesar's wounds
And dip their napkins in his sacred blood,
Yea, beg a hair of him for memory,
And, dying, mention it within their wills,
Bequeathing it as a rich legacy
Unto their issue.
FOURTH CITIZEN: We'll hear the will. Read it, Mark Antony.
ALL: The will, the will! We will hear Caesar's will.
ANTONY: Have patience, gentle friends, I must not read it;
It is not meet you know how Caesar loved you.
You are not wood, you are not stones, but men;
And, being men, hearing the will of Caesar,
It will inflame you, it will make you mad.
'Tis good you know not that you are his heirs,
For if you should, O, what would come of it!
FOURTH CITIZEN: Read the will; we'll hear it, Antony.
You shall read us the will, Caesar's will.
ANTONY: Will you be patient? Will you stay awhile?
I have o'ershot myself to tell you of it.
I fear I wrong the honorable men
Whose daggers have stabb'd Caesar; I do fear it.
FOURTH CITIZEN: They were traitors. Honorable men!
ALL: The will! The testament!
SECOND CITIZEN: They were villains, murtherers. The will!
Read the will!
ANTONY: You will compel me then to read the will?
Then make a ring about the corse of Caesar,
And let me show you him that made the will.

Shall I descend? And will you give me leave?
ALL: Come down.
SECOND CITIZEN: Descend.
He Comes down from the Pulpit.
THIRD CITIZEN: You shall have leave.
FOURTH CITIZEN: A ring, stand round.
FIRST CITIZEN: Stand from the hearse, stand from the body.
SECOND CITIZEN: Room for Antony, most noble Antony.
ANTONY: Nay, press not so upon me, stand far off.
ALL: Stand back; room, bear back!
ANTONY: If you have tears, prepare to shed them now.
You all do know this mantle. I remember
The first time ever Caesar put it on;
'Twas on a summer's evening, in his tent,
That day he overcame the Nervii.
Look, in this place ran Cassius' dagger through;
See what a rent the envious Casca made;
Through this the well-beloved Brutus stabb'd;
And as he pluck'd his cursed steel away,
Mark how the blood of Caesar follow'd it,
As rushing out of doors, to be resolved
If Brutus so unkindly knock'd, or no;
For Brutus, as you know, was Caesar's angel.
Judge, O you gods, how dearly Caesar loved him!
This was the most unkindest cut of all;
For when the noble Caesar saw him stab,
Ingratitude, more strong than traitors' arms,
Quite vanquish'd him. Then burst his mighty heart,
And, in his mantle muffling up his face,
Even at the base of Pompey's statue,
Which all the while ran blood, great Caesar fell.
O, what a fall was there, my countrymen!
Then I, and you, and all of us fell down,
Whilst bloody treason flourish'd over us.
O, now you weep, and I perceive you feel
The dint of pity. These are gracious drops.
Kind souls, what weep you when you but behold
Our Caesar's vesture wounded? Look you here,
Here is himself, marr'd, as you see, with traitors.
FIRST CITIZEN: O piteous spectacle!
SECOND CITIZEN: O noble Caesar!
THIRD CITIZEN: O woeful day!
FOURTH CITIZEN: O traitors villains!
FIRST CITIZEN: O most bloody sight!
SECOND CITIZEN: We will be revenged.
ALL: Revenge! About! Seek! Burn! Fire! Kill!
Slay! Let not a traitor live!
ANTONY: Stay, countrymen.
FIRST CITIZEN: Peace there! Hear the noble Antony.

SECOND CITIZEN: We'll hear him, we'll follow him, we'll die with him.
ANTONY: Good friends, sweet friends, let me not stir you up
To such a sudden flood of mutiny.
They that have done this deed are honorable.
What private griefs they have, alas, I know not,
That made them do it. They are wise and honorable,
And will, no doubt, with reasons answer you.
I come not, friends, to steal away your hearts.
I am no orator, as Brutus is;
But, as you know me all, a plain blunt man,
That love my friend, and that they know full well
That gave me public leave to speak of him.
For I have neither wit, nor words, nor worth,
Action, nor utterance, nor the power of speech,
To stir men's blood. I only speak right on;
I tell you that which you yourselves do know;
Show you sweet Caesar's wounds, poor dumb mouths,
And bid them speak for me. But were I Brutus,
And Brutus Antony, there were an Antony
Would ruffle up your spirits and put a tongue
In every wound of Caesar that should move
The stones of Rome to rise and mutiny.
ALL: We'll mutiny.
FIRST CITIZEN: We'll burn the house of Brutus.
THIRD CITIZEN: Away, then! Come, seek the conspirators.
ANTONY: Yet hear me, countrymen; yet hear me speak.
ALL: Peace, ho! Hear Antony, most noble Antony!
ANTONY: Why, friends, you go to do you know not what.
Wherein hath Caesar thus deserved your loves?
Alas, you know not; I must tell you then.
You have forgot the will I told you of.
ALL: Most true, the will! Let's stay and hear the will.
ANTONY: Here is the will, and under Caesar's seal.
To every Roman citizen he gives,
To every several man, seventy-five drachmas.
SECOND CITIZEN: Most noble Caesar! We'll revenge his death.
THIRD CITIZEN: O royal Caesar!
ANTONY: Hear me with patience.
ALL: Peace, ho!
ANTONY: Moreover, he hath left you all his walks,
His private arbors, and new-planted orchards,
On this side Tiber; he hath left them you,
And to your heirs forever- common pleasures,
To walk abroad and recreate yourselves.
Here was a Caesar! When comes such another?
FIRST CITIZEN: Never, never. Come, away, away!
We'll burn his body in the holy place
And with the brands fire the traitors' houses.

Take up the body.
SECOND CITIZEN: Go fetch fire.
THIRD CITIZEN: Pluck down benches.
FOURTH CITIZEN: Pluck down forms, windows, anything.
Exeunt Citizens with the Body.
ANTONY: Now let it work. Mischief, thou art afoot,
Take thou what course thou wilt.
Enter a Servant.
How now, fellow?
SERVANT: Sir, Octavius is already come to Rome.
ANTONY: Where is he?
SERVANT: He and Lepidus are at Caesar's house.
ANTONY: And thither will I straight to visit him.
He comes upon a wish. Fortune is merry,
And in this mood will give us anything.
SERVANT: I heard him say Brutus and Cassius
Are rid like madmen through the gates of Rome.
ANTONY: Be like they had some notice of the people,
How I had moved them. Bring me to Octavius.
Exeunt.

ACT III. SCENE III. A Street.

Enter Cinna the poet.
CINNA: I dreamt tonight that I did feast with Caesar,
And things unluckily charge my fantasy.
I have no will to wander forth of doors,
Yet something leads me forth.
Enter Citizens.
FIRST CITIZEN: What is your name?
SECOND CITIZEN: Whither are you going?
THIRD CITIZEN: Where do you dwell?
FOURTH CITIZEN: Are you a married man or a bachelor?
SECOND CITIZEN: Answer every man directly.
FIRST CITIZEN: Ay, and briefly.
FOURTH CITIZEN: Ay, and wisely.
THIRD CITIZEN: Ay, and truly, you were best.
CINNA: What is my name? Whither am I going? Where do I dwell? Am I a married man or a bachelor? Then, to answer every man directly and briefly, wisely and truly: wisely I say, I am a bachelor.
SECOND CITIZEN: That's as much as to say they are fools that marry. You'll bear me a bang for that, I fear. Proceed directly.
CINNA: Directly, I am going to Caesar's funeral.
FIRST CITIZEN: As a friend or an enemy?
CINNA: As a friend.
SECOND CITIZEN: That matter is answered directly.
FOURTH CITIZEN: For your dwelling, briefly.
CINNA: Briefly, I dwell by the Capitol.
THIRD CITIZEN: Your name, sir, truly.
CINNA: Truly, my name is Cinna.
FIRST CITIZEN: Tear him to pieces, he's a conspirator.

CINNA: I am Cinna the poet, I am Cinna the poet.
FOURTH CITIZEN: Tear him for his bad verses, tear him for his bad verses.
CINNA: I am not Cinna the conspirator.
FOURTH CITIZEN: It is no matter, his name's Cinna. Pluck but his name out of his heart, and turn him going.
THIRD CITIZEN: Tear him, tear him! Come, brands, ho, firebrands. To Brutus', to Cassius'; burn all. Some to Decius' house, and some to Casca's, some to Ligarius'. Away, go!
Exeunt.
ACT IV. SCENE I. A house in Rome. Antony, Octavius, and Lepidus, seated at a table.
ANTONY: These many then shall die, their names are prick'd.
POPILIUS: Your brother too must die; consent you, Lepidus?
LEPIDUS: I do consent-
POPILIUS: Prick him down, Antony.
LEPIDUS: Upon condition Publius shall not live,
Who is your sister's son, Mark Antony.
ANTONY: He shall not live; look, with a spot I damn him.
But, Lepidus, go you to Caesar's house,
Fetch the will hither, and we shall determine
How to cut off some charge in legacies.
LEPIDUS: What, shall I find you here?
POPILIUS: Or here, or at the Capitol.
Exit Lepidus.
ANTONY: This is a slight unmeritable man,
Meet to be sent on errands. Is it fit,
The three-fold world divided, he should stand
One of the three to share it?
POPILIUS: So you thought him,
And took his voice who should be prick'd to die
In our black sentence and proscription.
ANTONY: Octavius, I have seen more days than you,
And though we lay these honors on this man
To ease ourselves of divers slanderous loads,
He shall but bear them as the ass bears gold,
To groan and sweat under the business,
Either led or driven, as we point the way;
And having brought our treasure where we will,
Then take we down his load and turn him off,
Like to the empty ass, to shake his ears
And graze in commons.
POPILIUS: You may do your will,
But he's a tried and valiant soldier.
ANTONY: So is my horse, Octavius, and for that
I do appoint him store of provender.
It is a creature that I teach to fight,
To wind, to stop, to run directly on,
His corporal motion govern'd by my spirit.
And, in some taste, is Lepidus but so:

He must be taught, and train'd, and bid go forth;
A barren-spirited fellow, one that feeds
On objects, arts, and imitations,
Which, out of use and staled by other men,
Begin his fashion. Do not talk of him
But as a property. And now, Octavius,
Listen great things. Brutus and Cassius
Are levying powers; we must straight make head;
Therefore let our alliance be combined,
Our best friends made, our means stretch'd;
And let us presently go sit in council,
How covert matters may be best disclosed,
And open perils surest answered.
POPILIUS: Let us do so, for we are at the stake,
And bay'd about with many enemies;
And some that smile have in their hearts, I fear,
Millions of mischiefs.
Exeunt.

ACT IV. SCENE II. Camp near Sardis. Before Brutus' Tent. Drum.

Enter Brutus, Lucilius, Lucius, and Soldiers; Titinius and Pindarus Meet Them.
BRUTUS: Stand, ho!
POPILIUS: Give the word, ho, and stand.
BRUTUS: What now, Lucilius, is Cassius near?
POPILIUS: He is at hand, and Pindarus is come
To do you salutation from his master.
BRUTUS: He greets me well. Your master, Pindarus,
In his own change, or by ill officers,
Hath given me some worthy cause to wish
Things done undone; but if he be at hand,
I shall be satisfied.
POPILIUS: I do not doubt
But that my noble master will appear
Such as he is, full of regard and honor.
BRUTUS: He is not doubted. A word, Lucilius,
How he received you. Let me be resolved.
POPILIUS: With courtesy and with respect enough,
But not with such familiar instances,
Nor with such free and friendly conference,
As he hath used of old.
BRUTUS: Thou hast described
A hot friend cooling. Ever note, Lucilius,
When love begins to sicken and decay
It useth an enforced ceremony.
There are no tricks in plain and simple faith;
But hollow men, like horses hot at hand,
Make gallant show and promise of their mettle;
But when they should endure the bloody spur,
They fall their crests and like deceitful jades
Sink in the trial. Comes his army on?

POPILIUS: They meant his night in Sard is to be quarter'd;
The greater part, the horse in general,
Are come with Cassius. Low march within.
BRUTUS: Hark, he is arrived.
March gently on to meet him.
Enter Cassius and His Powers.
CASSIUS: Stand, ho!
BRUTUS: Stand, ho! Speak the word along.
FIRST SOLDIER: Stand!
SECOND SOLDIER:. Stand!
THIRD SOLDIER: Stand!
CASSIUS: Most noble brother, you have done me wrong.
BRUTUS: Judge me, you gods! Wrong I mine enemies?
And, if not so, how should I wrong a brother?
CASSIUS: Brutus, this sober form of yours hides wrongs,
And when you do them-
BRUTUS: Cassius, be content,
Speak your griefs softly, I do know you well.
Before the eyes of both our armies here,
Which should perceive nothing but love from us,
Let us not wrangle. Bid them move away;
Then in my tent, Cassius, enlarge your griefs,
And I will give you audience.
CASSIUS: Pindarus,
Bid our commanders lead their charges off
A little from this ground.
BRUTUS: Lucilius, do you the like, and let no man
Come to our tent till we have done our conference.
Let Lucius and Titinius guard our door.
Exeunt.

ACT IV. SCENE III. Brutus' Tent.

Enter Brutus and Cassius.
CASSIUS: That you have wrong'd me doth appear in this:
You have condemn'd and noted Lucius Pella
For taking bribes here of the Sardians,
Wherein my letters, praying on his side,
Because I knew the man, were slighted off.
BRUTUS: You wrong'd yourself to write in such a case.
CASSIUS: In such a time as this it is not meet
That every nice offense should bear his comment.
BRUTUS: Let me tell you, Cassius, you yourself
Are much condemn'd to have an itching palm,
To sell and mart your offices for gold
To undeservers.
CASSIUS: I an itching palm?
You know that you are Brutus that speaks this,
Or, by the gods, this speech were else your last.
BRUTUS: The name of Cassius honors this corruption,
And chastisement doth therefore hide his head.

CASSIUS: Chastisement?
BRUTUS: Remember March, the ides of March remember.
Did not great Julius bleed for justice' sake?
What villain touch'd his body, that did stab,
And not for justice? What, shall one of us,
That struck the foremost man of all this world
But for supporting robbers, shall we now
Contaminate our fingers with base bribes
And sell the mighty space of our large honors
For so much trash as may be grasped thus?
I had rather be a dog, and bay the moon,
Than such a Roman.
CASSIUS: Brutus, bait not me,
I'll not endure it. You forget yourself
To hedge me in. I am a soldier, I,
Older in practice, abler than yourself
To make conditions.
BRUTUS: Go to, you are not, Cassius.
CASSIUS: I am.
BRUTUS: I say you are not.
CASSIUS: Urge me no more, I shall forget myself;
Have mind upon your health, tempt me no farther.
BRUTUS: Away, slight man!
CASSIUS: Is't possible?
BRUTUS: Hear me, for I will speak.
Must I give way and room to your rash choler?
Shall I be frighted when a madman stares?
CASSIUS: O gods, ye gods! Must I endure all this?
BRUTUS: All this? Ay, more. Fret till your proud heart break.
Go show your slaves how choleric you are,
And make your bondmen tremble. Must I bouge?
Must I observe you? Must I stand and crouch
Under your testy humor? By the gods,
You shall digest the venom of your spleen,
Though it do split you, for, from this day forth,
I'll use you for my mirth, yea, for my laughter,
When you are waspish.
CASSIUS: Is it come to this?
BRUTUS: You say you are a better soldier:
Let it appear so, make your vaunting true,
And it shall please me well. For mine own part,
I shall be glad to learn of noble men.
CASSIUS: You wrong me every way, you wrong me, Brutus.
I said, an elder soldier, not a better.
Did I say "better"?
BRUTUS: If you did, I care not.
CASSIUS: When Caesar lived, he durst not thus have moved me.
BRUTUS: Peace, peace! You durst not so have tempted him.
CASSIUS: I durst not?

BRUTUS: No.
CASSIUS: What, durst not tempt him?
BRUTUS: For your life you durst not.
CASSIUS: Do not presume too much upon my love;
I may do that I shall be sorry for.
BRUTUS: You have done that you should be sorry for.
There is no terror, Cassius, in your threats,
For I am arm'd so strong in honesty,
That they pass by me as the idle wind
Which I respect not. I did send to you
For certain sums of gold, which you denied me,
For I can raise no money by vile means.
By heaven, I had rather coin my heart
And drop my blood for drachmas than to wring
From the hard hands of peasants their vile trash
By any indirection. I did send
To you for gold to pay my legions,
Which you denied me. Was that done like Cassius?
Should I have answer'd Caius Cassius so?
When Marcus Brutus grows so covetous
To lock such rascal counters from his friends,
Be ready, gods, with all your thunderbolts,
Dash him to pieces!
CASSIUS: I denied you not.
BRUTUS: You did.
CASSIUS: I did not. He was but a fool
That brought my answer back. Brutus hath rived my heart.
A friend should bear his friend's infirmities,
But Brutus makes mine greater than they are.
BRUTUS: I do not, till you practise them on me.
CASSIUS: You love me not.
BRUTUS: I do not like your faults.
CASSIUS: A friendly eye could never see such faults.
BRUTUS: A flatterer's would not, though they do appear
As huge as high Olympus.
CASSIUS: Come, Antony, and young Octavius, come,
Revenge yourselves alone on Cassius,
For Cassius is aweary of the world:
Hated by one he loves; braved by his brother;
Check'd like a bondman; all his faults observed,
Set in a notebook, learn'd and conn'd by rote,
To cast into my teeth. O, I could weep
My spirit from mine eyes! There is my dagger,
And here my naked breast; within, a heart
Dearer than Pluto's mine, richer than gold.
If that thou best a Roman, take it forth;
I, that denied thee gold, will give my heart.
Strike, as thou didst at Caesar, for I know,
When thou didst hate him worst, thou lovedst him better

Than ever thou lovedst Cassius.
BRUTUS: Sheathe your dagger.
Be angry when you will, it shall have scope;
Do what you will, dishonor shall be humor.
O Cassius, you are yoked with a lamb,
That carries anger as the flint bears fire,
Who, much enforced, shows a hasty spark
And straight is cold again.
CASSIUS: Hath Cassius lived
To be but mirth and laughter to his Brutus,
When grief and blood ill-temper'd vexeth him?
BRUTUS: When I spoke that, I was ill-temper'd too.
CASSIUS: Do you confess so much? Give me your hand.
BRUTUS: And my heart too.
CASSIUS: O Brutus!
BRUTUS: What's the matter?
CASSIUS: Have not you love enough to bear with me
When that rash humor which my mother gave me
Makes me forgetful?
BRUTUS: Yes, Cassius, and from henceforth,
When you are overearnest with your Brutus,
He'll think your mother chides, and leave you so.
POET: Within. Let me go in to see the generals.
There is some grudge between 'em, 'tis not meet
They be alone.
POPILIUS: Within. You shall not come to them.
POET: Within. Nothing but death shall stay me.
Enter Poet, Followed by Lucilius, Titinius, and Lucius.
CASSIUS: How now, what's the matter?
POET: For shame, you generals! What do you mean?
Love, and be friends, as two such men should be;
For I have seen more years, I'm sure, than ye.
CASSIUS: Ha, ha! How vilely doth this cynic rhyme!
BRUTUS: Get you hence, sirrah; saucy fellow, hence!
CASSIUS: Bear with him, Brutus; 'tis his fashion.
BRUTUS: I'll know his humor when he knows his time.
What should the wars do with these jigging fools?
Companion, hence!
CASSIUS: Away, away, be gone!
Exit Poet.
BRUTUS: Lucilius and Titinius, bid the commanders
Prepare to lodge their companies tonight.
CASSIUS: And come yourselves and bring Messala with you
Immediately to us.
Exeunt Lucilius and Titinius.
BRUTUS: Lucius, a bowl of wine!
Exit Lucius.
CASSIUS: I did not think you could have been so angry.
BRUTUS: O Cassius, I am sick of many griefs.

CASSIUS: Of your philosophy you make no use,
If you give place to accidental evils.
BRUTUS: No man bears sorrow better. Portia is dead.
CASSIUS: Ha? Portia?
BRUTUS: She is dead.
CASSIUS: How 'scaped killing when I cross'd you so?
O insupportable and touching loss!
Upon what sickness?
BRUTUS: Impatient of my absence,
And grief that young Octavius with Mark Antony
Have made themselves so strong- for with her death
That tidings came- with this she fell distract,
And (her attendants absent) swallow'd fire.
CASSIUS: And died so?
BRUTUS: Even so.
CASSIUS: O ye immortal gods!
  Re-enter Lucius, with Wine and Taper.
BRUTUS: Speak no more of her. Give me a bowl of wine.
In this I bury all unkindness, Cassius. Drinks.
CASSIUS: My heart is thirsty for that noble pledge.
Fill, Lucius, till the wine o'erswell the cup;
I cannot drink too much of Brutus' love. Drinks.
BRUTUS: Come in, Titinius!
  Exit Lucius.
  Re-enter Titinius, with Messala.
Welcome, good Messala.
Now sit we close about this taper here,
And call in question our necessities.
CASSIUS: Portia, art thou gone?
BRUTUS: No more, I pray you.
Messala, I have here received letters
That young Octavius and Mark Antony
Come down upon us with a mighty power,
Bending their expedition toward Philippi.
MESSALA: Myself have letters of the selfsame tenure.
BRUTUS: With what addition?
MESSALA: That by proscription and bills of outlawry
Octavius, Antony, and Lepidus
Have put to death an hundred senators.
BRUTUS: There in our letters do not well agree;
Mine speak of seventy senators that died
By their proscriptions, Cicero being one.
CASSIUS: Cicero one!
MESSALA: Cicero is dead,
And by that order of proscription.
Had you your letters from your wife, my lord?
BRUTUS: No, Messala.
MESSALA: Nor nothing in your letters writ of her?
BRUTUS: Nothing, Messala.

MESSALA: That, methinks, is strange.
BRUTUS: Why ask you? Hear you aught of her in yours?
MESSALA: No, my lord.
BRUTUS: Now, as you are a Roman, tell me true.
MESSALA: Then like a Roman bear the truth I tell:
For certain she is dead, and by strange manner.
BRUTUS: Why, farewell, Portia. We must die, Messala.
With meditating that she must die once
I have the patience to endure it now.
MESSALA: Even so great men great losses should endure.
CASSIUS: I have as much of this in art as you,
But yet my nature could not bear it so.
BRUTUS: Well, to our work alive. What do you think
Of marching to Philippi presently?
CASSIUS: I do not think it good.
BRUTUS: Your reason?
CASSIUS: This it is:
'Tis better that the enemy seek us;
So shall he waste his means, weary his soldiers,
Doing himself offense, whilst we lying still
Are full of rest, defense, and nimbleness.
BRUTUS: Good reasons must of force give place to better.
The people 'twixt Philippi and this ground
Do stand but in a forced affection,
For they have grudged us contribution.
The enemy, marching along by them,
By them shall make a fuller number up,
Come on refresh'd, new-added, and encouraged;
From which advantage shall we cut him off
If at Philippi we do face him there,
These people at our back.
CASSIUS: Hear me, good brother.
BRUTUS: Under your pardon. You must note beside
That we have tried the utmost of our friends,
Our legions are brim-full, our cause is ripe:
The enemy increaseth every day;
We, at the height, are ready to decline.
There is a tide in the affairs of men
Which taken at the flood leads on to fortune;
Omitted, all the voyage of their life
Is bound in shallows and in miseries.
On such a full sea are we now afloat,
And we must take the current when it serves,
Or lose our ventures.
CASSIUS: Then, with your will, go on;
We'll along ourselves and meet them at Philippi.
BRUTUS: The deep of night is crept upon our talk,
And nature must obey necessity,
Which we will niggard with a little rest.

There is no more to say?
CASSIUS: No more. Good night.
Early tomorrow will we rise and hence.
BRUTUS: Lucius!
Re-enter Lucius.
My gown.
Exit Lucius.
Farewell, good Messala;
Good night, Titinius; noble, noble Cassius,
Good night and good repose.
CASSIUS: O my dear brother!
This was an ill beginning of the night.
Never come such division 'tween our souls!
Let it not, Brutus.
BRUTUS: Everything is well.
CASSIUS: Good night, my lord.
BRUTUS: Good night, good brother.
TITINIUS: MESSALA. Good night, Lord Brutus.
BRUTUS: Farewell, everyone.
Exeunt all but Brutus.
Re-enter Lucius, with the Gown. Give Me the Gown. Where Is Thy Instrument?
LUCIUS: Here in the tent.
BRUTUS: What, thou speak'st drowsily?
Poor knave, I blame thee not, thou art o'erwatch'd.
Call Claudio and some other of my men,
I'll have them sleep on cushions in my tent.
LUCIUS: Varro and Claudio!
Enter Varro and Claudio.
VARRO: Calls my lord?
BRUTUS: I pray you, sirs, lie in my tent and sleep;
It may be I shall raise you by and by
On business to my brother Cassius.
VARRO: So please you, we will stand and watch your pleasure.
BRUTUS: I would not have it so. Lie down, good sirs.
It may be I shall otherwise bethink me.
Look Lucius, here's the book I sought for so;
I put it in the pocket of my gown.
Varro and Claudio Lie Down.
LUCIUS: I was sure your lordship did not give it me.
BRUTUS: Bear with me, good boy, I am much forgetful.
Canst thou hold up thy heavy eyes awhile,
And touch thy instrument a strain or two?
LUCIUS: Ay, my lord, an't please you.
BRUTUS: It does, my boy.
I trouble thee too much, but thou art willing.
LUCIUS: It is my duty, sir.
BRUTUS: I should not urge thy duty past thy might;
I know young bloods look for a time of rest.
LUCIUS: I have slept, my lord, already.

BRUTUS: It was well done, and thou shalt sleep again;
I will not hold thee long. If I do live,
I will be good to thee. Music, and a song.
This is a sleepy tune. O murtherous slumber,
Layest thou thy leaden mace upon my boy
That plays thee music? Gentle knave, good night.
I will not do thee so much wrong to wake thee.
If thou dost nod, thou break'st thy instrument;
I'll take it from thee; and, good boy, good night.
Let me see, let me see; is not the leaf turn'd down
Where I left reading? Here it is, I think. Sits down.
Enter the Ghost of Caesar.
How ill this taper burns! Ha, who comes here?
I think it is the weakness of mine eyes
That shapes this monstrous apparition.
It comes upon me. Art thou anything?
Art thou some god, some angel, or some devil
That makest my blood cold and my hair to stare?
Speak to me what thou art.
GHOST: Thy evil spirit, Brutus.
BRUTUS: Why comest thou?
GHOST: To tell thee thou shalt see me at Philippi.
BRUTUS: Well, then I shall see thee again?
GHOST: Ay, at Philippi.
BRUTUS: Why, I will see thee at Philippi then.
Exit Ghost.
Now I have taken heart thou vanishest.
Ill spirit, I would hold more talk with thee.
Boy! Lucius! Varro! Claudio! Sirs, awake!
Claudio!
LUCIUS: The strings, my lord, are false.
BRUTUS: He thinks he still is at his instrument.
Lucius, awake!
LUCIUS: My lord?
BRUTUS: Didst thou dream, Lucius, that thou so criedst out?
LUCIUS: My lord, I do not know that I did cry.
BRUTUS: Yes, that thou didst. Didst thou see anything?
LUCIUS: Nothing, my lord.
BRUTUS: Sleep again, Lucius. Sirrah Claudio!
To Varro. Fellow thou, awake!
VARRO: My lord?
CLAUDIO: My lord?
BRUTUS: Why did you so cry out, sirs, in your sleep?
VARRO: CLAUDIO. Did we, my lord?
BRUTUS: Ay, saw you anything?
VARRO: No, my lord, I saw nothing.
CLAUDIO: Nor I, my lord.
BRUTUS: Go and commend me to my brother Cassius;
Bid him set on his powers betimes before,

And we will follow.
VARRO and CLAUDIO: It shall be done, my lord.
Exeunt.

ACT V. SCENE I. The Plains of Philippi.

Enter Octavius, Antony, and their Army.
POPILIUS: Now, Antony, our hopes are answered.
You said the enemy would not come down,
But keep the hills and upper regions.
It proves not so. Their battles are at hand;
They mean to warn us at Philippi here,
Answering before we do demand of them.
ANTONY: Tut, I am in their bosoms, and I know
Wherefore they do it. They could be content
To visit other places, and come down
With fearful bravery, thinking by this face
To fasten in our thoughts that they have courage;
But 'tis not so.
Enter a Messenger.
MESSENGER: Prepare you, generals.
The enemy comes on in gallant show;
Their bloody sign of battle is hung out,
And something to be done immediately.
ANTONY: Octavius, lead your battle softly on,
Upon the left hand of the even field.
POPILIUS: Upon the right hand I, keep thou the left.
ANTONY: Why do you cross me in this exigent?
POPILIUS: I do not cross you, but I will do so.
March. Drum. Enter Brutus, Cassius, and Their Army; Lucilius, Titinius, Messala, and Others.
BRUTUS: They stand, and would have parley.
CASSIUS: Stand fast, Titinius; we must out and talk.
POPILIUS: Mark Antony, shall we give sign of battle?
ANTONY: No, Caesar, we will answer on their charge.
Make forth, the generals would have some words.
POPILIUS: Stir not until the signal not until the signal.
BRUTUS: Words before blows. Is it so, countrymen?
POPILIUS: Not that we love words better, as you do.
BRUTUS: Good words are better than bad strokes, Octavius.
ANTONY: In your bad strokes, Brutus, you give good words.
Witness the hole you made in Caesar's heart,
Crying "Long live! Hail, Caesar!"
CASSIUS: Antony,
The posture of your blows are yet unknown;
But for your words, they rob the Hybla bees,
And leave them honeyless.
ANTONY: Not stingless too.
BRUTUS: O, yes, and soundless too,
For you have stol'n their buzzing, Antony,
And very wisely threat before you sting.

ANTONY: Villains! You did not so when your vile daggers
Hack'd one another in the sides of Caesar.
You show'd your teeth like apes, and fawn'd like hounds,
And bow'd like bondmen, kissing Caesar's feet;
Whilst damned Casca, like a cur, behind
Strooke Caesar on the neck. O you flatterers!
CASSIUS: Flatterers? Now, Brutus, thank yourself.
This tongue had not offended so today,
If Cassius might have ruled.
POPILIUS: Come, come, the cause. If arguing make us sweat,
The proof of it will turn to redder drops.
Look, I draw a sword against conspirators;
When think you that the sword goes up again?
Never, till Caesar's three and thirty wounds
Be well avenged, or till another Caesar
Have added slaughter to the sword of traitors.
BRUTUS: Caesar, thou canst not die by traitors' hands,
Unless thou bring'st them with thee.
POPILIUS: So I hope,
I was not born to die on Brutus' sword.
BRUTUS: O, if thou wert the noblest of thy strain,
Young man, thou couldst not die more honorable.
CASSIUS: A peevish school boy, worthless of such honor,
Join'd with a masker and a reveler!
ANTONY: Old Cassius still!
POPILIUS: Come, Antony, away!
Defiance, traitors, hurl we in your teeth.
If you dare fight today, come to the field;
If not, when you have stomachs.
Exeunt Octavius, Antony, and Their Army.
CASSIUS: Why, now, blow and, swell billow, and swim bark!
The storm is up, and all is on the hazard.
BRUTUS: Ho, Lucilius! Hark, a word with you.
POPILIUS: Stands Forth. My lord?
Brutus and Lucilius Converse Apart.
CASSIUS: Messala!
MESSALA: Stands Forth. What says my general?
CASSIUS: Messala,
This is my birthday, as this very day
Was Cassius born. Give me thy hand, Messala.
Be thou my witness that, against my will,
As Pompey was, am I compell'd to set
Upon one battle all our liberties.
You know that I held Epicurus strong,
And his opinion. Now I change my mind,
And partly credit things that do presage.
Coming from Sardis, on our former ensign
Two mighty eagles fell, and there they perch'd,
Gorging and feeding from our soldiers' hands,

Who to Philippi here consorted us.
This morning are they fled away and gone,
And in their steads do ravens, crows, and kites
Fly o'er our heads and downward look on us,
As we were sickly prey. Their shadows seem
A canopy most fatal, under which
Our army lies, ready to give up the ghost.
MESSALA: Believe not so.
CASSIUS: I but believe it partly,
For I am fresh of spirit and resolved
To meet all perils very constantly.
BRUTUS: Even so, Lucilius.
CASSIUS: Now, most noble Brutus,
The gods today stand friendly that we may,
Lovers in peace, lead on our days to age!
But, since the affairs of men rest still incertain,
Let's reason with the worst that may befall.
If we do lose this battle, then is this
The very last time we shall speak together.
What are you then determined to do?
BRUTUS: Even by the rule of that philosophy
By which I did blame Cato for the death
Which he did give himself- I know not how,
But I do find it cowardly and vile,
For fear of what might fall, so to prevent
The time of life- arming myself with patience
To stay the providence of some high powers
That govern us below.
CASSIUS: Then, if we lose this battle,
You are contented to be led in triumph
Thorough the streets of Rome?
BRUTUS: No, Cassius, no. Think not, thou noble Roman,
That ever Brutus will go bound to Rome;
He bears too great a mind. But this same day
Must end that work the ides of March begun.
And whether we shall meet again I know not.
Therefore our everlasting farewell take.
Forever, and forever, farewell, Cassius!
If we do meet again, why, we shall smile;
If not, why then this parting was well made.
CASSIUS: Forever and forever farewell, Brutus!
If we do meet again, we'll smile indeed;
If not, 'tis true this parting was well made.
BRUTUS: Why then, lead on. O, that a man might know
The end of this day's business ere it come!
But it sufficeth that the day will end,
And then the end is known. Come, ho! Away!
Exeunt.

ACT V. SCENE II. The Field of Battle.

Alarum. Enter Brutus and Messala.

BRUTUS: Ride, ride, Messala, ride, and give these bills
Unto the legions on the other side. Loud alarum.
Let them set on at once, for I perceive
But cold demeanor in Octavia's wing,
And sudden push gives them the overthrow.
Ride, ride, Messala. Let them all come down.

Exeunt.

ACT V. SCENE III. Another Part of the Field.

Alarums. Enter Cassius and Titinius.

CASSIUS: O, look, Titinius, look, the villains fly!
Myself have to mine own turn'd enemy.
This ensign here of mine was turning back;
I slew the coward, and did take it from him.

TITINIUS: O Cassius, Brutus gave the word too early,
Who, having some advantage on Octavius,
Took it too eagerly. His soldiers fell to spoil,
Whilst we by Antony are all enclosed.

Enter Pindarus.

POPILIUS: Fly further off, my lord, fly further off;
Mark Antony is in your tents, my lord;
Fly, therefore, noble Cassius, fly far off.

CASSIUS: This hill is far enough. Look, look, Titinius:
Are those my tents where I perceive the fire?

TITINIUS: They are, my lord.

CASSIUS: Titinius, if thou lovest me,
Mount thou my horse and hide thy spurs in him,
Till he have brought thee up to yonder troops
And here again, that I may rest assured
Whether yond troops are friend or enemy.

TITINIUS: I will be here again, even with a thought.

Exit.

CASSIUS: Go, Pindarus, get higher on that hill;
My sight was ever thick; regard Titinius,
And tell me what thou notest about the field.

Pindarus Ascends the Hill.

This day I breathed first: time is come round,
And where I did begin, there shall I end;
My life is run his compass. Sirrah, what news?

POPILIUS: Above. O my lord!

CASSIUS: What news?

POPILIUS: Above. Titinius is enclosed round about
With horsemen, that make to him on the spur;
Yet he spurs on. Now they are almost on him.
Now, Titinius! Now some light. O, he lights too.
He's ta'en Shout. And, hark! They shout for joy.

CASSIUS: Come down; behold no more.
O, coward that I am, to live so long,

To see my best friend ta'en before my face!
Pindarus descends.
Come hither, sirrah.
In Parthia did I take thee prisoner,
And then I swore thee, saving of thy life,
That whatsoever I did bid thee do,
Thou shouldst attempt it. Come now, keep thine oath;
Now be a freeman, and with this good sword,
That ran through Caesar's bowels, search this bosom.
Stand not to answer: here, take thou the hilts;
And when my face is cover'd, as 'tis now,
Guide thou the sword.
Pindarus Stabs Him.
Caesar, thou art revenged,
Even with the sword that kill'd thee. Dies.
POPILIUS: So, I am free, yet would not so have been,
Durst I have done my will. O Cassius!
Far from this country Pindarus shall run,
Where never Roman shall take note of him.
Exit.
Re-enter Titinius with Messala.
MESSALA: It is but change, Titinius, for Octavius
Is overthrown by noble Brutus' power,
As Cassius' legions are by Antony.
TITINIUS: These tidings would well comfort Cassius.
MESSALA: Where did you leave him?
TITINIUS: All disconsolate,
With Pindarus his bondman, on this hill.
MESSALA: Is not that he that lies upon the ground?
TITINIUS: He lies not like the living. O my heart!
MESSALA: Is not that he?
TITINIUS: No, this was he, Messala,
But Cassius is no more. O setting sun,
As in thy red rays thou dost sink to night,
So in his red blood Cassius' day is set,
The sun of Rome is set! Our day is gone;
Clouds, dews, and dangers come; our deeds are done!
Mistrust of my success hath done this deed.
MESSALA: Mistrust of good success hath done this deed.
O hateful error, melancholy's child,
Why dost thou show to the apt thoughts of men
The things that are not? O error, soon conceived,
Thou never comest unto a happy birth,
But kill'st the mother that engender'd thee!
TITINIUS: What, Pindarus! Where art thou, Pindarus?
MESSALA: Seek him, Titinius, whilst I go to meet
The noble Brutus, thrusting this report
Into his ears. I may say "thrusting" it,
For piercing steel and darts envenomed

Shall be as welcome to the ears of Brutus
As tidings of this sight.
TITINIUS: Hie you, Messala,
And I will seek for Pindarus the while.
Exit Messala.
Why didst thou send me forth, brave Cassius?
Did I not meet thy friends? And did not they
Put on my brows this wreath of victory,
And bid me give it thee? Didst thou not hear their shouts?
Alas, thou hast misconstrued everything!
But, hold thee, take this garland on thy brow;
Thy Brutus bid me give it thee, and I
Will do his bidding. Brutus, come apace,
And see how I regarded Caius Cassius.
By your leave, gods, this is a Roman's part.
Come, Cassius' sword, and find Titinius' heart.
Kills Himself.
Alarum. Re-enter Messala, with Brutus, Young Cato, and Others.
BRUTUS: Where, where, Messala, doth his body lie?
MESSALA: Lo, yonder, and Titinius mourning it.
BRUTUS: Titinius' face is upward.
CATO: He is slain.
BRUTUS: O Julius Caesar, thou art mighty yet!
Thy spirit walks abroad, and turns our swords
In our own proper entrails. Low alarums.
CATO: Brave Titinius!
Look whe'er he have not crown'd dead Cassius!
BRUTUS: Are yet two Romans living such as these?
The last of all the Romans, fare thee well!
It is impossible that ever Rome
Should breed thy fellow. Friends, I owe moe tears
To this dead man than you shall see me pay.
I shall find time, Cassius, I shall find time.
Come therefore, and to Thasos send his body;
His funerals shall not be in our camp,
Lest it discomfort us. Lucilius, come,
And come, young Cato; let us to the field.
Labio and Flavio, set our battles on.
'Tis three o'clock, and Romans, yet ere night
We shall try fortune in a second fight.
Exeunt.

ACT V. SCENE IV. Another Part of the Field.

Alarum. Enter, Fighting, Soldiers of Both Armies; Then Brutus, Young Cato, Lucilius, and Others.
BRUTUS: Yet, countrymen, O, yet hold up your heads!
CATO: What bastard doth not? Who will go with me?
I will proclaim my name about the field.
I am the son of Marcus Cato, ho!
A foe to tyrants, and my country's friend.

I am the son of Marcus Cato, ho!
BRUTUS: And I am Brutus, Marcus Brutus, I;
Brutus, my country's friend; know me for Brutus!
Exit.
POPILIUS: O young and noble Cato, art thou down?
Why, now thou diest as bravely as Titinius,
And mayst be honor'd, being Cato's son.
FIRST SOLDIER: Yield, or thou diest.
POPILIUS: Only I yield to die.
Offers Money.
There is so much that thou wilt kill me straight:
Kill Brutus, and be honor'd in his death.
FIRST SOLDIER: We must not. A noble prisoner!
SECOND SOLDIER:. Room, ho! Tell Antony, Brutus is ta'en.
FIRST SOLDIER: I'll tell the news. Here comes the general.
Enter Antony.
Brutus is ta'en, Brutus is ta'en, my lord.
ANTONY: Where is he?
POPILIUS: Safe, Antony, Brutus is safe enough.
I dare assure thee that no enemy
Shall ever take alive the noble Brutus;
The gods defend him from so great a shame!
When you do find him, or alive or dead,
He will be found like Brutus, like himself.
ANTONY: This is not Brutus, friend, but, I assure you,
A prize no less in worth. Keep this man safe,
Give him all kindness; I had rather have
Such men my friends than enemies. Go on,
And see wheer Brutus be alive or dead,
And bring us word unto Octavius' tent
How everything is chanced.
Exeunt.

ACT V. SCENE V. Another Part of the Field.

Enter Brutus, Dardanius, Clitus, Strato, and Volumnius.
BRUTUS: Come, poor remains of friends, rest on this rock.
CLITUS: Statilius show'd the torchlight, but, my lord,
He came not back. He is or ta'en or slain.
BRUTUS: Sit thee down, Clitus. Slaying is the word:
It is a deed in fashion. Hark thee, Clitus. Whispers.
CLITUS: What, I, my lord? No, not for all the world.
BRUTUS: Peace then, no words.
CLITUS: I'll rather kill myself.
BRUTUS: Hark thee, Dardanius. Whispers.
DARDANIUS: Shall I do such a deed?
CLITUS: O Dardanius!
DARDANIUS: O Clitus!
CLITUS: What ill request did Brutus make to thee?
DARDANIUS: To kill him, Clitus. Look, he meditates.
CLITUS: Now is that noble vessel full of grief,

That it runs over even at his eyes.
BRUTUS: Come hither, good Volumnius, list a word.
VOLUMNIUS: What says my lord?
BRUTUS: Why, this, Volumnius:
The ghost of Caesar hath appear'd to me
Two several times by night; at Sardis once,
And this last night here in Philippi fields.
I know my hour is come.
VOLUMNIUS: Not so, my lord.
BRUTUS: Nay I am sure it is, Volumnius.
Thou seest the world, Volumnius, how it goes;
Our enemies have beat us to the pit; Low alarums.
It is more worthy to leap in ourselves
Than tarry till they push us. Good Volumnius,
Thou know'st that we two went to school together;
Even for that our love of old, I prithee,
Hold thou my sword-hilts, whilst I run on it.
VOLUMNIUS: That's not an office for a friend, my lord.
Alarum Still.
CLITUS: Fly, fly, my lord, there is no tarrying here.
BRUTUS: Farewell to you, and you, and you, Volumnius.
Strato, thou hast been all this while asleep;
Farewell to thee too, Strato. Countrymen,
My heart doth joy that yet in all my life
I found no man but he was true to me.
I shall have glory by this losing day,
More than Octavius and Mark Antony
By this vile conquest shall attain unto.
So, fare you well at once, for Brutus' tongue
Hath almost ended his life's history.
Night hangs upon mine eyes, my bones would rest
That have but labor'd to attain this hour.
Alarum. Cry Within, "Fly, Fly, Fly!"
CLITUS: Fly, my lord, fly.
BRUTUS: Hence! I will follow.
Exeunt Clitus, Dardanius, and Volumnius.
I prithee, Strato, stay thou by thy lord.
Thou art a fellow of a good respect;
Thy life hath had some smatch of honor in it.
Hold then my sword, and turn away thy face,
While I do run upon it. Wilt thou, Strato?
STRATO: Give me your hand first. Fare you well, my lord.
BRUTUS: Farewell, good Strato. Runs on his sword.
Caesar, now be still;
I kill'd not thee with half so good a will. Dies.
Alarum. Retreat. Enter Octavius, Antony, Messala, Lucilius, and the Army.
POPILIUS: What man is that?
MESSALA: My master's man. Strato, where is thy master?
STRATO: Free from the bondage you are in, Messala:

The conquerors can but make a fire of him;
For Brutus only overcame himself,
And no man else hath honor by his death.
POPILIUS: So Brutus should be found. I thank thee, Brutus,
That thou hast proved Lucilius' saying true.
POPILIUS: All that served Brutus, I will entertain them.
Fellow, wilt thou bestow thy time with me?
STRATO: Ay, if Messala will prefer me to you.
POPILIUS: Do so, good Messala.
MESSALA: How died my master, Strato?
STRATO: I held the sword, and he did run on it.
MESSALA: Octavius, then take him to follow thee
That did the latest service to my master.
ANTONY: This was the noblest Roman of them all.
All the conspirators, save only he,
Did that they did in envy of great Caesar;
He only, in a general honest thought
And common good to all, made one of them.
His life was gentle, and the elements
So mix'd in him that Nature might stand up
And say to all the world, "This was a man!"
POPILIUS: According to his virtue let us use him
With all respect and rites of burial.
Within my tent his bones tonight shall lie,
Most like a soldier, ordered honorably.
So call the field to rest, and let's away,
To part the glories of this happy day.
Exeunt.

END

The Tragedy of Hamlet, Prince of Denmark

Dramatis Personae

CLAUDIUS, King of Denmark.
HAMLET, son to the former, and nephew to the present king.
POLONIUS, Lord Chamberlain.
HORATIO, friend to Hamlet.
LAERTES, son to Polonius.
VOLTEMAND, courtier.
CORNELIUS, courtier.
ROSENCRANTZ, courtier.
GUILDENSTERN, courtier.
OSRIC, courtier.
A GENTLEMAN, courtier.
A PRIEST.
MARCELLUS, officer.
BERNARDO, officer.
FRANCISCO, a soldier
REYNALDO, servant to Polonius.
PLAYERS.
LUCIANUS.
TWO CLOWNS
GRAVEDIGGERS.
FORTINBRAS, Prince of Norway.
A NORWEGIAN CAPTAIN.
ENGLISH AMBASSADORS.
GETRUDE, Queen of Denmark, mother to Hamlet.
OPHELIA, daughter to Polonius.
GHOST of Hamlet's Father.
Lords, ladies, Officers, Soldiers, Sailors, Messengers, Attendants.

SCENE.- Elsinore.

ACT I. SCENE I. Elsinore. A Platform Before the Castle.

Enter Two Sentinels-First, Francisco, Who Paces up and down at His Post; Then Bernardo, Who Approaches Him.

BERNARDO: Who's there.?
FRANCISCO: Nay, answer me. Stand and unfold yourself.
BERNARDO: Long live the King!
FRANCISCO: Bernardo?
BERNARDO: He.
FRANCISCO: You come most carefully upon your hour.
BERNARDO: 'Tis now struck twelve. Get thee to bed, Francisco.
FRANCISCO: For this relief much thanks. 'Tis bitter cold,
And I am sick at heart.
BERNARDO: Have you had quiet guard?
FRANCISCO: Not a mouse stirring.
BERNARDO: Well, good night.
If you do meet Horatio and Marcellus,
The rivals of my watch, bid them make haste.

Enter Horatio and Marcellus.

FRANCISCO: I think I hear them. Stand, ho! Who is there?
HORATIO: Friends to this ground.
MARCELLUS: And liegemen to the Dane.
FRANCISCO: Give you good night.

MARCELLUS: O, farewell, honest soldier.
Who hath reliev'd you?
FRANCISCO: Bernardo hath my place.
Give you good night.
Exit.
MARCELLUS: Holla, Bernardo!
BERNARDO: Say-
What, is Horatio there ?
HORATIO: A piece of him.
BERNARDO: Welcome, Horatio. Welcome, good Marcellus.
MARCELLUS: What, has this thing appear'd again to-night?
BERNARDO: I have seen nothing.
MARCELLUS: Horatio says 'tis but our fantasy,
And will not let belief take hold of him
Touching this dreaded sight, twice seen of us.
Therefore I have entreated him along,
With us to watch the minutes of this night,
That, if again this apparition come,
He may approve our eyes and speak to it.
HORATIO: Tush, tush, 'twill not appear.
BERNARDO: Sit down awhile,
And let us once again assail your ears,
That are so fortified against our story,
What we two nights have seen.
HORATIO: Well, sit we down,
And let us hear Bernardo speak of this.
BERNARDO: Last night of all,
When yond same star that's westward from the pole
Had made his course t' illume that part of heaven
Where now it burns, Marcellus and myself,
The bell then beating one-
Enter Ghost.
MARCELLUS: Peace! break thee off! Look where it comes again!
BERNARDO: In the same figure, like the King that's dead.
MARCELLUS: Thou art a scholar; speak to it, Horatio.
BERNARDO: Looks it not like the King? Mark it, Horatio.
HORATIO: Most like. It harrows me with fear and wonder.
BERNARDO: It would be spoke to.
MARCELLUS: Question it, Horatio.
HORATIO: What art thou that usurp'st this time of night
Together with that fair and warlike form
In which the majesty of buried Denmark
Did sometimes march? By heaven I charge thee speak!
MARCELLUS: It is offended.
BERNARDO: See, it stalks away!
HORATIO: Stay! Speak, speak! I charge thee speak!
Exit Ghost.
MARCELLUS: 'Tis gone and will not answer.
BERNARDO: How now, Horatio? You tremble and look pale.
Is not this something more than fantasy?
What think you on't?
HORATIO: Before my God, I might not this believe
Without the sensible and true avouch

Of mine own eyes.
MARCELLUS: Is it not like the King?
HORATIO: As thou art to thyself.
Such was the very armour he had on
When he th' ambitious Norway combated.
So frown'd he once when, in an angry parle,
He smote the sledded Polacks on the ice.
'Tis strange.
MARCELLUS: Thus twice before, and jump at this dead hour,
With martial stalk hath he gone by our watch.
HORATIO: In what particular thought to work I know not;
But, in the gross and scope of my opinion,
This bodes some strange eruption to our state.
MARCELLUS: Good now, sit down, and tell me he that knows,
Why this same strict and most observant watch
So nightly toils the subject of the land,
And why such daily cast of brazen cannon
And foreign mart for implements of war;
Why such impress of shipwrights, whose sore task
Does not divide the Sunday from the week.
What might be toward, that this sweaty haste
Doth make the night joint-labourer with the day?
Who is't that can inform me?
HORATIO: That can I.
At least, the whisper goes so. Our last king,
Whose image even but now appear'd to us,
Was, as you know, by Fortinbras of Norway,
Thereto prick'd on by a most emulate pride,
Dar'd to the combat; in which our valiant Hamlet
(For so this side of our known world esteem'd him)
Did slay this Fortinbras; who, by a seal'd compact,
Well ratified by law and heraldry,
Did forfeit, with his life, all those his lands
Which he stood seiz'd of, to the conqueror;
Against the which a moiety competent
Was gaged by our king; which had return'd
To the inheritance of Fortinbras,
Had he been vanquisher, as, by the same comart
And carriage of the article design'd,
His fell to Hamlet. Now, sir, young Fortinbras,
Of unimproved mettle hot and full,
Hath in the skirts of Norway, here and there,
Shark'd up a list of lawless resolutes,
For food and diet, to some enterprise
That hath a stomach in't; which is no other,
As it doth well appear unto our state,
But to recover of us, by strong hand
And terms compulsatory, those foresaid lands
So by his father lost; and this, I take it,
Is the main motive of our preparations,
The source of this our watch, and the chief head
Of this post-haste and romage in the land.
BERNARDO: I think it be no other but e'en so.

Well may it sort that this portentous figure
Comes armed through our watch, so like the King
That was and is the question of these wars.
HORATIO: A mote it is to trouble the mind's eye.
In the most high and palmy state of Rome,
A little ere the mightiest Julius fell,
The graves stood tenantless, and the sheeted dead
Did squeak and gibber in the Roman streets;
As stars with trains of fire, and dews of blood,
Disasters in the sun; and the moist star
Upon whose influence Neptune's empire stands
Was sick almost to doomsday with eclipse.
And even the like precurse of fierce events,
As harbingers preceding still the fates
And prologue to the omen coming on,
Have heaven and earth together demonstrated
Unto our climature and countrymen.
Enter Ghost Again.
But soft! behold! Lo, where it comes again!
I'll cross it, though it blast me.- Stay illusion!
Spreads His Arms.
If thou hast any sound, or use of voice,
Speak to me.
If there be any good thing to be done,
That may to thee do ease, and, race to me,
Speak to me.
If thou art privy to thy country's fate,
Which happily foreknowing may avoid,
O, speak!
Or if thou hast uphoarded in thy life
Extorted treasure in the womb of earth
(For which, they say, you spirits oft walk in death),
The Cock Crows.
Speak of it! Stay, and speak!- Stop it, Marcellus!
MARCELLUS: Shall I strike at it with my partisan?
HORATIO: Do, if it will not stand.
BERNARDO: 'Tis here!
HORATIO: 'Tis here!
MARCELLUS: 'Tis gone!
Exit Ghost.
We do it wrong, being so majestical,
To offer it the show of violence;
For it is as the air, invulnerable,
And our vain blows malicious mockery.
BERNARDO: It was about to speak, when the cock crew.
HORATIO: And then it started, like a guilty thing
Upon a fearful summons. I have heard
The cock, that is the trumpet to the morn,
Doth with his lofty and shrill-sounding throat
Awake the god of day; and at his warning,
Whether in sea or fire, in earth or air,
Th' extravagant and erring spirit hies
To his confine; and of the truth herein

This present object made probation.
MARCELLUS: It faded on the crowing of the cock.
Some say that ever, 'gainst that season comes
Wherein our Saviour's birth is celebrated,
The bird of dawning singeth all night long;
And then, they say, no spirit dare stir abroad,
The nights are wholesome, then no planets strike,
No fairy takes, nor witch hath power to charm,
So hallow'd and so gracious is the time.
HORATIO: So have I heard and do in part believe it.
But look, the morn, in russet mantle clad,
Walks o'er the dew of yon high eastward hill.
Break we our watch up; and by my advice
Let us impart what we have seen to-night
Unto young Hamlet; for, upon my life,
This spirit, dumb to us, will speak to him.
Do you consent we shall acquaint him with it,
As needful in our loves, fitting our duty?
Let's do't, I pray; and I this morning know
Where we shall find him most conveniently.
Exeunt.

ACT II. SCENE II. Elsinore. A Room of State in the Castle.

Flourish. Enter Claudius, King of Denmark, Gertrude the Queen, Hamlet, Polonius, Laertes and His Sister Ophelia, Voltemand, Cornelius, Lords Attendant.
KING CLAUDIUS: Though yet of Hamlet our dear brother's death
The memory be green, and that it us befitted
To bear our hearts in grief, and our whole kingdom
To be contracted in one brow of woe,
Yet so far hath discretion fought with nature
That we with wisest sorrow think on him
Together with remembrance of ourselves.
Therefore our sometime sister, now our queen,
Th' imperial jointress to this warlike state,
Have we, as 'twere with a defeated joy,
With an auspicious, and a dropping eye,
With mirth in funeral, and with dirge in marriage,
In equal scale weighing delight and dole,
Taken to wife; nor have we herein barr'd
Your better wisdoms, which have freely gone
With this affair along. For all, our thanks.
Now follows, that you know, young Fortinbras,
Holding a weak supposal of our worth,
Or thinking by our late dear brother's death
Our state to be disjoint and out of frame,
Colleagued with this dream of his advantage,
He hath not fail'd to pester us with message
Importing the surrender of those lands
Lost by his father, with all bands of law,
To our most valiant brother. So much for him.
Now for ourself and for this time of meeting.
Thus much the business is: we have here writ
To Norway, uncle of young Fortinbras,
Who, impotent and bedrid, scarcely hears

Of this his nephew's purpose, to suppress
His further gait herein, in that the levies,
The lists, and full proportions are all made
Out of his subject; and we here dispatch
You, good Cornelius, and you, Voltemand,
For bearers of this greeting to old Norway,
Giving to you no further personal power
To business with the King, more than the scope
Of these dilated articles allow.
Gives a Paper.
Farewell, and let your haste commend your duty.
CORNELIUS: Volt. In that, and all things, will we show our duty.
KING CLAUDIUS: We doubt it nothing. Heartily farewell.
Exeunt Voltemand and Cornelius.
And now, Laertes, what's the news with you?
You told us of some suit. What is't, Laertes?
You cannot speak of reason to the Dane
And lose your voice. What wouldst thou beg, Laertes,
That shall not be my offer, not thy asking?
The head is not more native to the heart,
The hand more instrumental to the mouth,
Than is the throne of Denmark to thy father.
What wouldst thou have, Laertes?
LAERTES: My dread lord,
Your leave and favour to return to France;
From whence though willingly I came to Denmark
To show my duty in your coronation,
Yet now I must confess, that duty done,
My thoughts and wishes bend again toward France
And bow them to your gracious leave and pardon.
KING CLAUDIUS: Have you your father's leave? What says Polonius?
POLONIUS: He hath, my lord, wrung from me my slow leave
By laboursome petition, and at last
Upon his will I seal'd my hard consent.
I do beseech you give him leave to go.
KING CLAUDIUS: Take thy fair hour, Laertes. Time be thine,
And thy best graces spend it at thy will!
But now, my cousin Hamlet, and my son-
HAMLET: Aside A little more than kin, and less than kind!
KING CLAUDIUS: How is it that the clouds still hang on you?
HAMLET: Not so, my lord. I am too much i' th' sun.
QUEEN GETRUDE: Good Hamlet, cast thy nighted colour off,
And let thine eye look like a friend on Denmark.
Do not for ever with thy vailed lids
Seek for thy noble father in the dust.
Thou know'st 'tis common. All that lives must die,
Passing through nature to eternity.
HAMLET: Ay, madam, it is common.
QUEEN GETRUDE: If it be,
Why seems it so particular with thee?
HAMLET: Seems, madam, Nay, it is. I know not 'seems.'
'Tis not alone my inky cloak, good mother,
Nor customary suits of solemn black,

Nor windy suspiration of forc'd breath,
No, nor the fruitful river in the eye,
Nor the dejected havior of the visage,
Together with all forms, moods, shapes of grief,
'That can denote me truly. These indeed seem,
For they are actions that a man might play;
But I have that within which passeth show-
These but the trappings and the suits of woe.
KING CLAUDIUS: 'Tis sweet and commendable in your nature, Hamlet,
To give these mourning duties to your father;
But you must know, your father lost a father;
That father lost, lost his, and the survivor bound
In filial obligation for some term
To do obsequious sorrow. But to persever
In obstinate condolement is a course
Of impious stubbornness. 'Tis unmanly grief;
It shows a will most incorrect to heaven,
A heart unfortified, a mind impatient,
An understanding simple and unschool'd;
For what we know must be, and is as common
As any the most vulgar thing to sense,
Why should we in our peevish opposition
Take it to heart? Fie! 'tis a fault to heaven,
A fault against the dead, a fault to nature,
To reason most absurd, whose common theme
Is death of fathers, and who still hath cried,
From the first corse till he that died to-day,
'This must be so.' We pray you throw to earth
This unprevailing woe, and think of us
As of a father; for let the world take note
You are the most immediate to our throne,
And with no less nobility of love
Than that which dearest father bears his son
Do I impart toward you. For your intent
In going back to school in Wittenberg,
It is most retrograde to our desire;
And we beseech you, bend you to remain
Here in the cheer and comfort of our eye,
Our chiefest courtier, cousin, and our son.
QUEEN GETRUDE: Let not thy mother lose her prayers, Hamlet.
I pray thee stay with us, go not to Wittenberg.
HAMLET: I shall in all my best obey you, madam.
KING CLAUDIUS: Why, 'tis a loving and a fair reply.
Be as ourself in Denmark. Madam, come.
This gentle and unforc'd accord of Hamlet
Sits smiling to my heart; in grace whereof,
No jocund health that Denmark drinks to-day
But the great cannon to the clouds shall tell,
And the King's rouse the heaven shall bruit again,
Respeaking earthly thunder. Come away.
Flourish. Exeunt all but Hamlet.
HAMLET: O that this too too solid flesh would melt,
Thaw, and resolve itself into a dew!

Or that the Everlasting had not fix'd
His canon 'gainst self-slaughter! O God! God!
How weary, stale, flat, and unprofitable
Seem to me all the uses of this world!
Fie on't! ah, fie! 'Tis an unweeded garden
That grows to seed; things rank and gross in nature
Possess it merely. That it should come to this!
But two months dead! Nay, not so much, not two.
So excellent a king, that was to this
Hyperion to a satyr; so loving to my mother
That he might not beteem the winds of heaven
Visit her face too roughly. Heaven and earth!
Must I remember? Why, she would hang on him
As if increase of appetite had grown
By what it fed on; and yet, within a month-
Let me not think on't! Frailty, thy name is woman!-
A little month, or ere those shoes were old
With which she followed my poor father's body
Like Niobe, all tears- why she, even she
(O God! a beast that wants discourse of reason
Would have mourn'd longer) married with my uncle;
My father's brother, but no more like my father
Than I to Hercules. Within a month,
Ere yet the salt of most unrighteous tears
Had left the flushing in her galled eyes,
She married. O, most wicked speed, to post
With such dexterity to incestuous sheets!
It is not, nor it cannot come to good.
But break my heart, for I must hold my tongue!
Enter Horatio, Marcellus, and Bernardo.
HORATIO: Hail to your lordship!
HAMLET: I am glad to see you well.
Horatio!- or I do forget myself.
HORATIO: The same, my lord, and your poor servant ever.
HAMLET: Sir, my good friend- I'll change that name with you.
And what make you from Wittenberg, Horatio? Marcellus?
MARCELLUS: My good lord!
HAMLET: I am very glad to see you.- To Bernardo Good even, sir.-
But what, in faith, make you from Wittenberg?
HORATIO: A truant disposition, good my lord.
HAMLET: I would not hear your enemy say so,
Nor shall you do my ear that violence
To make it truster of your own report
Against yourself. I know you are no truant.
But what is your affair in Elsinore?
We'll teach you to drink deep ere you depart.
HORATIO: My lord, I came to see your father's funeral.
HAMLET: I prithee do not mock me, fellow student.
I think it was to see my mother's wedding.
HORATIO: Indeed, my lord, it followed hard upon.
HAMLET: Thrift, thrift, Horatio! The funeral bak'd meats
Did coldly furnish forth the marriage tables.
Would I had met my dearest foe in heaven

Or ever I had seen that day, Horatio!
My father- methinks I see my father.
HORATIO: O, where, my lord?
HAMLET: In my mind's eye, Horatio.
HORATIO: I saw him once. He was a goodly king.
HAMLET: He was a man, take him for all in all.
I shall not look upon his like again.
HORATIO: My lord, I think I saw him yesternight.
HAMLET: Saw? who?
HORATIO: My lord, the King your father.
HAMLET: The King my father?
HORATIO: Season your admiration for a while
With an attent ear, till I may deliver
Upon the witness of these gentlemen,
This marvel to you.
HAMLET: For God's love let me hear!
HORATIO: Two nights together had these gentlemen
(Marcellus and Bernardo) on their watch
In the dead vast and middle of the night
Been thus encount'red. A figure like your father,
Armed at point exactly, cap-a-pe,
Appears before them and with solemn march
Goes slow and stately by them. Thrice he walk'd
By their oppress'd and fear-surprised eyes,
Within his truncheon's length; whilst they distill'd
Almost to jelly with the act of fear,
Stand dumb and speak not to him. This to me
In dreadful secrecy impart they did,
And I with them the third night kept the watch;
Where, as they had deliver'd, both in time,
Form of the thing, each word made true and good,
The apparition comes. I knew your father.
These hands are not more like.
HAMLET: But where was this?
MARCELLUS: My lord, upon the platform where we watch'd.
HAMLET: Did you not speak to it?
HORATIO: My lord, I did;
But answer made it none. Yet once methought
It lifted up it head and did address
Itself to motion, like as it would speak;
But even then the morning cock crew loud,
And at the sound it shrunk in haste away
And vanish'd from our sight.
HAMLET: 'Tis very strange.
HORATIO: As I do live, my honour'd lord, 'tis true;
And we did think it writ down in our duty
To let you know of it.
HAMLET: Indeed, indeed, sirs. But this troubles me.
Hold you the watch to-night?
BOTH: Marcellus and Bernardo We do, my lord.
HAMLET: Arm'd, say you?
BOTH: Arm'd, my lord.
HAMLET: From top to toe?

BOTH: My lord, from head to foot.
HAMLET: Then saw you not his face?
HORATIO: O, yes, my lord! He wore his beaver up.
HAMLET: What, look'd he frowningly.
HORATIO: A countenance more in sorrow than in anger.
HAMLET: Pale or red?
HORATIO: Nay, very pale.
HAMLET: And fix'd his eyes upon you?
HORATIO: Most constantly.
HAMLET: I would I had been there.
HORATIO: It would have much amaz'd you.
HAMLET: Very like, very like. Stay'd it long?
HORATIO: While one with moderate haste might tell a hundred.
BOTH: Longer, longer.
HORATIO: Not when I saw't.
HAMLET: His beard was grizzled- no?
HORATIO: It was, as I have seen it in his life,
A sable silver'd.
HAMLET: I will watch to-night.
Perchance 'twill walk again.
HORATIO: I warr'nt it will.
HAMLET: If it assume my noble father's person,
I'll speak to it, though hell itself should gape
And bid me hold my peace. I pray you all,
If you have hitherto conceal'd this sight,
Let it be tenable in your silence still;
And whatsoever else shall hap to-night,
Give it an understanding but no tongue.
I will requite your loves. So, fare you well.
Upon the platform, 'twixt eleven and twelve,
I'll visit you.
ALL: Our duty to your honour.
HAMLET: Your loves, as mine to you. Farewell.
Exeunt All but Hamlet.
My father's spirit- in arms? All is not well.
I doubt some foul play. Would the night were come!
Till then sit still, my soul. Foul deeds will rise,
Though all the earth o'erwhelm them, to men's eyes.
Exit.

ACT II. SCENE III. Elsinore. A Room in the House of Polonius.

Enter Laertes and Ophelia.
LAERTES: My necessaries are embark'd. Farewell.
And, sister, as the winds give benefit
And convoy is assistant, do not sleep,
But let me hear from you.
OPHELIA: Do you doubt that?
LAERTES: For Hamlet, and the trifling of his favour,
Hold it a fashion, and a toy in blood;
A violet in the youth of primy nature,
Forward, not permanent- sweet, not lasting;
The perfume and suppliance of a minute;
No more.
OPHELIA: No more but so?

LAERTES: Think it no more.
For nature crescent does not grow alone
In thews and bulk; but as this temple waxes,
The inward service of the mind and soul
Grows wide withal. Perhaps he loves you now,
And now no soil nor cautel doth besmirch
The virtue of his will; but you must fear,
His greatness weigh'd, his will is not his own;
For he himself is subject to his birth.
He may not, as unvalued persons do,
Carve for himself, for on his choice depends
The safety and health of this whole state,
And therefore must his choice be circumscrib'd
Unto the voice and yielding of that body
Whereof he is the head. Then if he says he loves you,
It fits your wisdom so far to believe it
As he in his particular act and place
May give his saying deed; which is no further
Than the main voice of Denmark goes withal.
Then weigh what loss your honour may sustain
If with too credent ear you list his songs,
Or lose your heart, or your chaste treasure open
To his unmast'red importunity.
Fear it, Ophelia, fear it, my dear sister,
And keep you in the rear of your affection,
Out of the shot and danger of desire.
The chariest maid is prodigal enough
If she unmask her beauty to the moon.
Virtue itself scopes not calumnious strokes.
The canker galls the infants of the spring
Too oft before their buttons be disclos'd,
And in the morn and liquid dew of youth
Contagious blastments are most imminent.
Be wary then; best safety lies in fear.
Youth to itself rebels, though none else near.
OPHELIA: I shall th' effect of this good lesson keep
As watchman to my heart. But, good my brother,
Do not as some ungracious pastors do,
Show me the steep and thorny way to heaven,
Whiles, like a puff'd and reckless libertine,
Himself the primrose path of dalliance treads
And recks not his own rede.
LAERTES: O, fear me not!
Enter Polonius.
I stay too long. But here my father comes.
A double blessing is a double grace;
Occasion smiles upon a second leave.
POLONIUS: Yet here, Laertes? Aboard, aboard, for shame!
The wind sits in the shoulder of your sail,
And you are stay'd for. There- my blessing with thee!
And these few precepts in thy memory
Look thou character. Give thy thoughts no tongue,
Nor any unproportion'd thought his act.

Be thou familiar, but by no means vulgar:
Those friends thou hast, and their adoption tried,
Grapple them unto thy soul with hoops of steel;
But do not dull thy palm with entertainment
Of each new-hatch'd, unfledg'd comrade. Beware
Of entrance to a quarrel; but being in,
Bear't that th' opposed may beware of thee.
Give every man thine ear, but few thy voice;
Take each man's censure, but reserve thy judgment.
Costly thy habit as thy purse can buy,
But not express'd in fancy; rich, not gaudy;
For the apparel oft proclaims the man,
And they in France of the best rank and station
Are most select and generous, chief in that.
Neither a borrower nor a lender be;
For loan oft loses both itself and friend,
And borrowing dulls the edge of husbandry.
This above all- to thine own self be true,
And it must follow, as the night the day,
Thou canst not then be false to any man.
Farewell. My blessing season this in thee!
LAERTES: Most humbly do I take my leave, my lord.
POLONIUS: The time invites you. Go, your servants tend.
LAERTES: Farewell, Ophelia, and remember well
What I have said to you.
OPHELIA: 'Tis in my memory lock'd,
And you yourself shall keep the key of it.
LAERTES: Farewell.
Exit.
POLONIUS: What is't, Ophelia, he hath said to you?
OPHELIA: So please you, something touching the Lord Hamlet.
POLONIUS: Marry, well bethought!
'Tis told me he hath very oft of late
Given private time to you, and you yourself
Have of your audience been most free and bounteous.
If it be so- as so 'tis put on me,
And that in way of caution- I must tell you
You do not understand yourself so clearly
As it behooves my daughter and your honour.
What is between you? Give me up the truth.
OPHELIA: He hath, my lord, of late made many tenders
Of his affection to me.
POLONIUS: Affection? Pooh! You speak like a green girl,
Unsifted in such perilous circumstance.
Do you believe his tenders, as you call them?
OPHELIA: I do not know, my lord, what I should think,
POLONIUS: Marry, I will teach you! Think yourself a baby
That you have ta'en these tenders for true pay,
Which are not sterling. Tender yourself more dearly,
Or (not to crack the wind of the poor phrase,
Running it thus) you'll tender me a fool.
OPHELIA: My lord, he hath importun'd me with love
In honourable fashion.

POLONIUS: Ay, fashion you may call it. Go to, go to!
OPHELIA: And hath given countenance to his speech, my lord,
With almost all the holy vows of heaven.
POLONIUS: Ay, springes to catch woodcocks! I do know,
When the blood burns, how prodigal the soul
Lends the tongue vows. These blazes, daughter,
Giving more light than heat, extinct in both
Even in their promise, as it is a-making,
You must not take for fire. From this time
Be something scanter of your maiden presence.
Set your entreatments at a higher rate
Than a command to parley. For Lord Hamlet,
Believe so much in him, that he is young,
And with a larger tether may he walk
Than may be given you. In few, Ophelia,
Do not believe his vows; for they are brokers,
Not of that dye which their investments show,
But mere implorators of unholy suits,
Breathing like sanctified and pious bawds,
The better to beguile. This is for all:
I would not, in plain terms, from this time forth
Have you so slander any moment leisure
As to give words or talk with the Lord Hamlet.
Look to't, I charge you. Come your ways.
OPHELIA: I shall obey, my lord.
Exeunt.

ACT II. SCENE IV. Elsinore. The Platform Before the Castle.

Enter Hamlet, Horatio, and Marcellus.
HAMLET: The air bites shrewdly; it is very cold.
HORATIO: It is a nipping and an eager air.
HAMLET: What hour now?
HORATIO: I think it lacks of twelve.
MARCELLUS: No, it is struck.
HORATIO: Indeed? I heard it not. It then draws near the season
Wherein the spirit held his wont to walk.
A Flourish of Trumpets, and Two Pieces Go Off.
What does this mean, my lord?
HAMLET: The King doth wake to-night and takes his rouse,
Keeps wassail, and the swagg'ring upspring reels,
And, as he drains his draughts of Rhenish down,
The kettledrum and trumpet thus bray out
The triumph of his pledge.
HORATIO: Is it a custom?
HAMLET: Ay, marry, is't;
But to my mind, though I am native here
And to the manner born, it is a custom
More honour'd in the breach than the observance.
This heavy-headed revel east and west
Makes us traduc'd and tax'd of other nations;
They clip us drunkards and with swinish phrase
Soil our addition; and indeed it takes
From our achievements, though perform'd at height,
The pith and marrow of our attribute.

So oft it chances in particular men
That, for some vicious mole of nature in them,
As in their birth,- wherein they are not guilty,
Since nature cannot choose his origin,-
By the o'ergrowth of some complexion,
Oft breaking down the pales and forts of reason,
Or by some habit that too much o'erleavens
The form of plausive manners, that these men
Carrying, I say, the stamp of one defect,
Being nature's livery, or fortune's star,
Their virtues else- be they as pure as grace,
As infinite as man may undergo-
Shall in the general censure take corruption
From that particular fault. The dram of e'il
Doth all the noble substance often dout To his own scandal.
Enter Ghost.
HORATIO: Look, my lord, it comes!
HAMLET: Angels and ministers of grace defend us!
Be thou a spirit of health or goblin damn'd,
Bring with thee airs from heaven or blasts from hell,
Be thy intents wicked or charitable,
Thou com'st in such a questionable shape
That I will speak to thee. I'll call thee Hamlet,
King, father, royal Dane. O, answer me?
Let me not burst in ignorance, but tell
Why thy canoniz'd bones, hearsed in death,
Have burst their cerements; why the sepulchre
Wherein we saw thee quietly inurn'd,
Hath op'd his ponderous and marble jaws
To cast thee up again. What may this mean
That thou, dead corse, again in complete steel,
Revisits thus the glimpses of the moon,
Making night hideous, and we fools of nature
So horridly to shake our disposition
With thoughts beyond the reaches of our souls?
Say, why is this? wherefore? What should we do?
Ghost Beckons Hamlet.
HORATIO: It beckons you to go away with it,
As if it some impartment did desire
To you alone.
MARCELLUS: Look with what courteous action
It waves you to a more removed ground.
But do not go with it!
HORATIO: No, by no means!
HAMLET: It will not speak. Then will I follow it.
HORATIO: Do not, my lord!
HAMLET: Why, what should be the fear?
I do not set my life at a pin's fee;
And for my soul, what can it do to that,
Being a thing immortal as itself?
It waves me forth again. I'll follow it.
HORATIO: What if it tempt you toward the flood, my lord,
Or to the dreadful summit of the cliff

That beetles o'er his base into the sea,
And there assume some other, horrible form
Which might deprive your sovereignty of reason
And draw you into madness? Think of it.
The very place puts toys of desperation,
Without more motive, into every brain
That looks so many fadoms to the sea
And hears it roar beneath.
HAMLET: It waves me still.
Go on. I'll follow thee.
MARCELLUS: You shall not go, my lord.
HAMLET: Hold off your hands!
HORATIO: Be rul'd. You shall not go.
HAMLET: My fate cries out
And makes each petty artire in this body
As hardy as the Nemean lion's nerve.
Ghost Beckons.
Still am I call'd. Unhand me, gentlemen.
By heaven, I'll make a ghost of him that lets me!-
I say, away!- Go on. I'll follow thee.
Exeunt Ghost and Hamlet.
HORATIO: He waxes desperate with imagination.
MARCELLUS: Let's follow. 'Tis not fit thus to obey him.
HORATIO: Have after. To what issue wail this come?
MARCELLUS: Something is rotten in the state of Denmark.
HORATIO: Heaven will direct it.
MARCELLUS: Nay, let's follow him.
Exeunt.

ACT I. SCENE V. Elsinore. The Castle. Another Part of the Fortifications.

Enter Ghost and Hamlet.
HAMLET: Whither wilt thou lead me? Speak! I'll go no further.
GHOST: Mark me.
HAMLET: I will.
GHOST: My hour is almost come,
When I to sulph'rous and tormenting flames
Must render up myself.
HAMLET: Alas, poor ghost!
GHOST: Pity me not, but lend thy serious hearing
To what I shall unfold.
HAMLET: Speak. I am bound to hear.
GHOST: So art thou to revenge, when thou shalt hear.
HAMLET: What?
GHOST: I am thy father's spirit,
Doom'd for a certain term to walk the night,
And for the day confin'd to fast in fires,
Till the foul crimes done in my days of nature
Are burnt and purg'd away. But that I am forbid
To tell the secrets of my prison house,
I could a tale unfold whose lightest word
Would harrow up thy soul, freeze thy young blood,
Make thy two eyes, like stars, start from their spheres,
Thy knotted and combined locks to part,
And each particular hair to stand an end

Like quills upon the fretful porpentine.
But this eternal blazon must not be
To ears of flesh and blood. List, list, O, list!
If thou didst ever thy dear father love-
HAMLET: O God!
GHOST: Revenge his foul and most unnatural murther.
HAMLET: Murther?
GHOST: Murther most foul, as in the best it is;
But this most foul, strange, and unnatural.
HAMLET: Haste me to know't, that I, with wings as swift
As meditation or the thoughts of love,
May sweep to my revenge.
GHOST: I find thee apt;
And duller shouldst thou be than the fat weed
That rots itself in ease on Lethe wharf,
Wouldst thou not stir in this. Now, Hamlet, hear.
'Tis given out that, sleeping in my orchard,
A serpent stung me. So the whole ear of Denmark
Is by a forged process of my death
Rankly abus'd. But know, thou noble youth,
The serpent that did sting thy father's life
Now wears his crown.
HAMLET: O my prophetic soul! My uncle?
GHOST: Ay, that incestuous, that adulterate beast,
With witchcraft of his wit, with traitorous gifts-
O wicked wit and gifts, that have the power
So to seduce!- won to his shameful lust
The will of my most seeming-virtuous queen.
O Hamlet, what a falling-off was there,
From me, whose love was of that dignity
That it went hand in hand even with the vow
I made to her in marriage, and to decline
Upon a wretch whose natural gifts were poor
To those of mine!
But virtue, as it never will be mov'd,
Though lewdness court it in a shape of heaven,
So lust, though to a radiant angel link'd,
Will sate itself in a celestial bed
And prey on garbage.
But soft! methinks I scent the morning air.
Brief let me be. Sleeping within my orchard,
My custom always of the afternoon,
Upon my secure hour thy uncle stole,
With juice of cursed hebona in a vial,
And in the porches of my ears did pour
The leperous distilment; whose effect
Holds such an enmity with blood of man
That swift as quicksilverr it courses through
The natural gates and alleys of the body,
And with a sudden vigour it doth posset
And curd, like eager droppings into milk,
The thin and wholesome blood. So did it mine;
And a most instant tetter bark'd about,

Most lazar-like, with vile and loathsome crust
All my smooth body.
Thus was I, sleeping, by a brother's hand
Of life, of crown, of queen, at once dispatch'd;
Cut off even in the blossoms of my sin,
Unhous'led, disappointed, unanel'd,
No reckoning made, but sent to my account
With all my imperfections on my head.
HAMLET: O, horrible! O, horrible! most horrible!
GHOST: If thou hast nature in thee, bear it not.
Let not the royal bed of Denmark be
A couch for luxury and damned incest.
But, howsoever thou pursuest this act,
Taint not thy mind, nor let thy soul contrive
Against thy mother aught. Leave her to heaven,
And to those thorns that in her bosom lodge
To prick and sting her. Fare thee well at once.
The glowworm shows the matin to be near
And gins to pale his uneffectual fire.
Adieu, adieu, adieu! Remember me.
Exit.
HAMLET: O all you host of heaven! O earth! What else?
And shall I couple hell? Hold, hold, my heart!
And you, my sinews, grow not instant old,
But bear me stiffly up. Remember thee?
Ay, thou poor ghost, while memory holds a seat
In this distracted globe. Remember thee?
Yea, from the table of my memory
I'll wipe away all trivial fond records,
All saws of books, all forms, all pressures past
That youth and observation copied there,
And thy commandment all alone shall live
Within the book and volume of my brain,
Unmix'd with baser matter. Yes, by heaven!
O most pernicious woman!
O villain, villain, smiling, damned villain!
My tables! Meet it is I set it down
That one may smile, and smile, and be a villain;
At least I am sure it may be so in Denmark.
Writes.
So, uncle, there you are. Now to my word:
It is 'Adieu, adieu! Remember me.'
I have sworn't.
HORATIO: (within) My lord, my lord!
Enter Horatio and Marcellus.
MARCELLUS: Lord Hamlet!
HORATIO: Heaven secure him!
HAMLET: So be it!
MARCELLUS: Illo, ho, ho, my lord!
HAMLET: Hillo, ho, ho, boy! Come, bird, come.
MARCELLUS: How is't, my noble lord?
HORATIO: What news, my lord?
MARCELLUS: O, wonderful!

HORATIO: Good my lord, tell it.
HAMLET: No, you will reveal it.
HORATIO: Not I, my lord, by heaven!
MARCELLUS: Nor I, my lord.
HAMLET: How say you then? Would heart of man once think it?
But you'll be secret?
BOTH: Ay, by heaven, my lord.
HAMLET: There's neer a villain dwelling in all Denmark
But he's an arrant knave.
HORATIO: There needs no ghost, my lord, come from the grave
To tell us this.
HAMLET: Why, right! You are in the right!
And so, without more circumstance at all,
I hold it fit that we shake hands and part;
You, as your business and desires shall point you,
For every man hath business and desire,
Such as it is; and for my own poor part,
Look you, I'll go pray.
HORATIO: These are but wild and whirling words, my lord.
HAMLET: I am sorry they offend you, heartily;
Yes, faith, heartily.
HORATIO: There's no offence, my lord.
HAMLET: Yes, by Saint Patrick, but there is, Horatio,
And much offence too. Touching this vision here,
It is an honest ghost, that let me tell you.
For your desire to know what is between us,
O'ermaster't as you may. And now, good friends,
As you are friends, scholars, and soldiers,
Give me one poor request.
HORATIO: What is't, my lord? We will.
HAMLET: Never make known what you have seen to-night.
BOTH: My lord, we will not.
HAMLET: Nay, but swear't.
HORATIO: In faith,
My lord, not I.
MARCELLUS: Nor I, my lord- in faith.
HAMLET: Upon my sword.
MARCELLUS: We have sworn, my lord, already.
HAMLET: Indeed, upon my sword, indeed.
Ghost Cries under the Stage.
GHOST: Swear.
HAMLET: Aha boy, say'st thou so? Art thou there, truepenny?
Come on! You hear this fellow in the cellarage.
Consent to swear.
HORATIO: Propose the oath, my lord.
HAMLET: Never to speak of this that you have seen.
Swear by my sword.

GHOST: Beneath Swear.
HAMLET: Hic et ubique? Then we'll shift our ground.
Come hither, gentlemen,
And lay your hands again upon my sword.
Never to speak of this that you have heard:

Swear by my sword.
GHOST: Beneath Swear by his sword.
HAMLET: Well said, old mole! Canst work i' th' earth so fast?
A worthy pioner! Once more remove, good friends."
HORATIO: O day and night, but this is wondrous strange!
HAMLET: And therefore as a stranger give it welcome.
There are more things in heaven and earth, Horatio,
Than are dreamt of in your philosophy.
But come!
Here, as before, never, so help you mercy,
How strange or odd soe'er I bear myself
(As I perchance hereafter shall think meet
To put an antic disposition on),
That you, at such times seeing me, never shall,
With arms encumb'red thus, or this head-shake,
Or by pronouncing of some doubtful phrase,
As 'Well, well, we know,' or 'We could, an if we would,'
Or 'If we list to speak,' or 'There be, an if they might,'
Or such ambiguous giving out, to note
That you know aught of me- this is not to do,
So grace and mercy at your most need help you, Swear.
GHOST: Beneath Swear.
They Swear.
HAMLET: Rest, rest, perturbed spirit! So, gentlemen,
With all my love I do commend me to you;
And what so poor a man as Hamlet is
May do t' express his love and friending to you,
God willing, shall not lack. Let us go in together;
And still your fingers on your lips, I pray.
The time is out of joint. O cursed spite
That ever I was born to set it right!
Nay, come, let's go together.
Exeunt.

ACT II. SCENE I. Elsinore. A Room in the House of Polonius.

Enter Polonius and Reynaldo.
POLONIUS: Give him this money and these notes, Reynaldo.
REYNALDO: I will, my lord.
POLONIUS: You shall do marvell's wisely, good Reynaldo,
Before You visit him, to make inquire
Of his behaviour.
REYNALDO: My lord, I did intend it.
POLONIUS: Marry, well said, very well said. Look you, sir,
Enquire me first what Danskers are in Paris;
And how, and who, what means, and where they keep,
What company, at what expense; and finding
By this encompassment and drift of question
That they do know my son, come you more nearer
Than your particular demands will touch it.
Take you, as 'twere, some distant knowledge of him;
As thus, 'I know his father and his friends,
And in part him.' Do you mark this, Reynaldo?
REYNALDO: Ay, very well, my lord.
POLONIUS: 'And in part him, but,' you may say, 'not well.

But if't be he I mean, he's very wild
Addicted so and so'; and there put on him
What forgeries you please; marry, none so rank
As may dishonour him- take heed of that;
But, sir, such wanton, wild, and usual slips
As are companions noted and most known
To youth and liberty.
REYNALDO: As gaming, my lord.
POLONIUS: Ay, or drinking, fencing, swearing, quarrelling,
Drabbing. You may go so far.
REYNALDO: My lord, that would dishonour him.
POLONIUS: Faith, no, as you may season it in the charge.
You must not put another scandal on him,
That he is open to incontinency.
That's not my meaning. But breathe his faults so quaintly
That they may seem the taints of liberty,
The flash and outbreak of a fiery mind,
A savageness in unreclaimed blood,
Of general assault.
REYNALDO: But, my good lord-
POLONIUS: Wherefore should you do this?
REYNALDO: Ay, my lord,
I would know that.
POLONIUS: Marry, sir, here's my drift,
And I believe it is a fetch of warrant.
You laying these slight sullies on my son
As 'twere a thing a little soil'd i' th' working,
Mark you,
Your party in converse, him you would sound,
Having ever seen in the prenominate crimes
The youth you breathe of guilty, be assur'd
He closes with you in this consequence:
'Good sir,' or so, or 'friend,' or 'gentleman'-
According to the phrase or the addition
Of man and country-
REYNALDO: Very good, my lord.
POLONIUS: And then, sir, does 'a this- 'a does- What was I about to say?
By the mass, I was about to say something! Where did I leave?
REYNALDO: At 'closes in the consequence,' at 'friend or so,' and
GENTLEMAN:'
POLONIUS: At 'closes in the consequence'- Ay, marry!
He closes thus: 'I know the gentleman.
I saw him yesterday, or t'other day,
Or then, or then, with such or such; and, as you say,
There was 'a gaming; there o'ertook in's rouse;
There falling out at tennis'; or perchance,
'I saw him enter such a house of sale,'
Videlicet, a brothel, or so forth.
See you now-
Your bait of falsehood takes this carp of truth;
And thus do we of wisdom and of reach,
With windlasses and with assays of bias,
By indirections find directions out.

So, by my former lecture and advice,
Shall you my son. You have me, have you not
REYNALDO: My lord, I have.
POLONIUS: God b' wi' ye, fare ye well!
REYNALDO: Good my lord!
Going.
POLONIUS: Observe his inclination in yourself.
REYNALDO: I shall, my lord.
POLONIUS: And let him ply his music.
REYNALDO: Well, my lord.
POLONIUS: Farewell!
Exit Reynaldo.
Enter Ophelia.
How now, Ophelia? What's the matter?
OPHELIA: O my lord, my lord, I have been so affrighted!
POLONIUS: With what, i' th' name of God I
OPHELIA: My lord, as I was sewing in my closet,
Lord Hamlet, with his doublet all unbrac'd,
No hat upon his head, his stockings foul'd,
Ungart'red, and down-gyved to his ankle;
Pale as his shirt, his knees knocking each other,
And with a look so piteous in purport
As if he had been loosed out of hell
To speak of horrors- he comes before me.
POLONIUS: Mad for thy love?
OPHELIA: My lord, I do not know,
But truly I do fear it.
POLONIUS: What said he?
OPHELIA: He took me by the wrist and held me hard;
Then goes he to the length of all his arm,
And, with his other hand thus o'er his brow,
He falls to such perusal of my face
As he would draw it. Long stay'd he so.
At last, a little shaking of mine arm,
And thrice his head thus waving up and down,
He rais'd a sigh so piteous and profound
As it did seem to shatter all his bulk
And end his being. That done, he lets me go,
And with his head over his shoulder turn'd
He seem'd to find his way without his eyes,
For out o' doors he went without their help
And to the last bended their light on me.
POLONIUS: Come, go with me. I will go seek the King.
This is the very ecstasy of love,
Whose violent property fordoes itself
And leads the will to desperate undertakings
As oft as any passion under heaven
That does afflict our natures. I am sorry.
What, have you given him any hard words of late?
OPHELIA: No, my good lord; but, as you did command,
I did repel his letters and denied
His access to me.
POLONIUS: That hath made him mad.

I am sorry that with better heed and judgment
I had not quoted him. I fear'd he did but trifle
And meant to wrack thee; but beshrew my jealousy!
By heaven, it is as proper to our age
To cast beyond ourselves in our opinions
As it is common for the younger sort
To lack discretion. Come, go we to the King.
This must be known; which, being kept close, might move
More grief to hide than hate to utter love.
Come.
Exeunt.

ACT II. SCENE II. Elsinore. A Room in the Castle.

Flourish. Enter King and Queen, Rosencrantz and Guildenstern, cum Aliis.
KING CLAUDIUS: Welcome, dear Rosencrantz and Guildenstern.
Moreover that we much did long to see you,
The need we have to use you did provoke
Our hasty sending. Something have you heard
Of Hamlet's transformation. So I call it,
Sith nor th' exterior nor the inward man
Resembles that it was. What it should be,
More than his father's death, that thus hath put him
So much from th' understanding of himself,
I cannot dream of. I entreat you both
That, being of so young clays brought up with him,
And since so neighbour'd to his youth and haviour,
That you vouchsafe your rest here in our court
Some little time; so by your companies
To draw him on to pleasures, and to gather
So much as from occasion you may glean,
Whether aught to us unknown afflicts him thus
That, open'd, lies within our remedy.
QUEEN GETRUDE: Good gentlemen, he hath much talk'd of you,
And sure I am two men there are not living
To whom he more adheres. If it will please you
To show us so much gentry and good will
As to expend your time with us awhile
For the supply and profit of our hope,
Your visitation shall receive such thanks
As fits a king's remembrance.
ROSENCRANTZ: Both your Majesties
Might, by the sovereign power you have of us,
Put your dread pleasures more into command
Than to entreaty.
GUILDENSTERN: But we both obey,
And here give up ourselves, in the full bent,
To lay our service freely at your feet,
To be commanded.
KING CLAUDIUS: Thanks, Rosencrantz and gentle Guildenstern.
QUEEN GETRUDE: Thanks, Guildenstern and gentle Rosencrantz.
And I beseech you instantly to visit
My too much changed son.- Go, some of you,
And bring these gentlemen where Hamlet is.
GUILDENSTERN: Heavens make our presence and our practices

Pleasant and helpful to him!
QUEEN GETRUDE: Ay, amen!
Exeunt Rosencrantz and Guildenstern, With Some Attendants.
Enter Polonius.
POLONIUS: Th' ambassadors from Norway, my good lord,
Are joyfully return'd.
KING CLAUDIUS: Thou still hast been the father of good news.
POLONIUS: Have I, my lord? Assure you, my good liege,
I hold my duty as I hold my soul,
Both to my God and to my gracious king;
And I do think- or else this brain of mine
Hunts not the trail of policy so sure
As it hath us'd to do- that I have found
The very cause of Hamlet's lunacy.
KING CLAUDIUS: O, speak of that! That do I long to hear.
POLONIUS: Give first admittance to th' ambassadors.
My news shall be the fruit to that great feast.
KING CLAUDIUS: Thyself do grace to them, and bring them in.
Exit Polonius.
He tells me, my dear Gertrude, he hath found
The head and source of all your son's distemper.
QUEEN GETRUDE: I doubt it is no other but the main,
His father's death and our o'erhasty marriage.
KING CLAUDIUS: Well, we shall sift him.
Enter Polonius, Voltemand, and Cornelius.
Welcome, my good friends.
Say, Voltemand, what from our brother Norway?
VOLTEMAND: Most fair return of greetings and desires.
Upon our first, he sent out to suppress
His nephew's levies; which to him appear'd
To be a preparation 'gainst the Polack,
But better look'd into, he truly found
It was against your Highness; whereat griev'd,
That so his sickness, age, and impotence
Was falsely borne in hand, sends out arrests
On Fortinbras; which he, in brief, obeys,
Receives rebuke from Norway, and, in fine,
Makes vow before his uncle never more
To give th' assay of arms against your Majesty.
Whereon old Norway, overcome with joy,
Gives him three thousand crowns in annual fee
And his commission to employ those soldiers,
So levied as before, against the Polack;
With an entreaty, herein further shown,
Gives a Paper.
That it might please you to give quiet pass
Through your dominions for this enterprise,
On such regards of safety and allowance
As therein are set down.
KING CLAUDIUS: It likes us well;
And at our more consider'd time we'll read,
Answer, and think upon this business.
Meantime we thank you for your well-took labour.

Go to your rest; at night we'll feast together.
Most welcome home!
Exeunt Ambassadors.
POLONIUS: This business is well ended.
My liege, and madam, to expostulate
What majesty should be, what duty is,
Why day is day, night is night, and time is time.
Were nothing but to waste night, day, and time.
Therefore, since brevity is the soul of wit,
And tediousness the limbs and outward flourishes,
I will be brief. Your noble son is mad.
Mad call I it; for, to define true madness,
What is't but to be nothing else but mad?
But let that go.
QUEEN GETRUDE: More matter, with less art.
POLONIUS: Madam, I swear I use no art at all.
That he is mad, 'tis true: 'tis true 'tis pity;
And pity 'tis 'tis true. A foolish figure!
But farewell it, for I will use no art.
Mad let us grant him then. And now remains
That we find out the cause of this effect-
Or rather say, the cause of this defect,
For this effect defective comes by cause.
Thus it remains, and the remainder thus. Perpend.
I have a daughter (have while she is mine),
Who in her duty and obedience, mark,
Hath given me this. Now gather, and surmise.
Reads the Letter.
'To the celestial, and my soul's idol, the most beautified Ophelia,'-
That's an ill phrase, a vile phrase; 'beautified' is a vile phrase.
But you shall hear. Thus:
Reads.
'In her excellent white bosom, these, etc.'
QUEEN GETRUDE: Came this from Hamlet to her?
POLONIUS: Good madam, stay awhile. I will be faithful. Reads.
'Doubt thou the stars are fire;
Doubt that the sun doth move;
Doubt truth to be a liar;
But never doubt I love.

'O dear Ophelia, I am ill at these numbers; I have not art to reckon my groans; but that I love thee best, O most best, believe it. Adieu.

'Thine evermore, most dear lady, whilst this machine is to him,
Hamlet.'

This, in obedience, hath my daughter shown me;
And more above, hath his solicitings,
As they fell out by time, by means, and place,
All given to mine ear.
KING CLAUDIUS: But how hath she
Receiv'd his love?
POLONIUS: What do you think of me?

KING CLAUDIUS: As of a man faithful and honourable.
POLONIUS: I would fain prove so. But what might you think,
When I had seen this hot love on the wing
(As I perceiv'd it, I must tell you that,
Before my daughter told me), what might you,
Or my dear Majesty your queen here, think,
If I had play'd the desk or table book,
Or given my heart a winking, mute and dumb,
Or look'd upon this love with idle sight?
What might you think? No, I went round to work
And my young mistress thus I did bespeak:
'Lord Hamlet is a prince, out of thy star.
This must not be.' And then I prescripts gave her,
That she should lock herself from his resort,
Admit no messengers, receive no tokens.
Which done, she took the fruits of my advice,
And he, repulsed, a short tale to make,
Fell into a sadness, then into a fast,
Thence to a watch, thence into a weakness,
Thence to a lightness, and, by this declension,
Into the madness wherein now he raves,
And all we mourn for.
KING CLAUDIUS: Do you think 'tis this?
QUEEN GETRUDE: it may be, very like.
POLONIUS: Hath there been such a time- I would fain know that-
That I have Positively said ''Tis so,'
When it prov'd otherwise.?
KING CLAUDIUS: Not that I know.
POLONIUS: Points to His Head and Shoulder Take this from this,
if this be otherwise.
If circumstances lead me, I will find
Where truth is hid, though it were hid indeed
Within the centre.
KING CLAUDIUS: How may we try it further?
POLONIUS: You know sometimes he walks four hours together
Here in the lobby.
QUEEN GETRUDE: So he does indeed.
POLONIUS: At such a time I'll loose my daughter to him.
Be you and I behind an arras then.
Mark the encounter. If he love her not,
And he not from his reason fall'n thereon
Let me be no assistant for a state,
But keep a farm and carters.
KING CLAUDIUS: We will try it.
Enter Hamlet, Reading on a Book.
QUEEN GETRUDE: But look where sadly the poor wretch comes reading.
POLONIUS: Away, I do beseech you, both away
I'll board him presently. O, give me leave.
Exeunt King and Queen, With Attendants.
How does my good Lord Hamlet?
HAMLET: Well, God-a-mercy.
POLONIUS: Do you know me, my lord?
HAMLET: Excellent well. You are a fishmonger.

POLONIUS: Not I, my lord.
HAMLET: Then I would you were so honest a man.
POLONIUS: Honest, my lord?
HAMLET: Ay, sir. To be honest, as this world goes, is to be one man pick'd out of ten thousand.
POLONIUS: That's very true, my lord.
HAMLET: For if the sun breed maggots in a dead dog, being a god kissing carrion- Have you a daughter?
POLONIUS: I have, my lord.
HAMLET: Let her not walk i' th' sun. Conception is a blessing, but not as your daughter may conceive. Friend, look to't.
POLONIUS: Aside How say you by that? Still harping on my daughter. Yet he knew me not at first. He said I was a fishmonger. He is far gone, far gone! And truly in my youth I suff'red much extremity for love- very near this. I'll speak to him again.- What do you read, my lord?
HAMLET: Words, words, words.
POLONIUS: What is the matter, my lord?
HAMLET: Between who?
POLONIUS: I mean, the matter that you read, my lord.
HAMLET: Slanders, sir; for the satirical rogue says here that old men have grey beards; that their faces are wrinkled; their eyes purging thick amber and plum-tree gum; and that they have a plentiful lack of wit, together with most weak hams. All which, sir, though I most powerfully and potently believe, yet I hold it not honesty to have it thus set down; for you yourself, sir, should be old as I am if, like a crab, you could go backward.
POLONIUS: Aside Though this be madness, yet there is a method in't.- Will You walk out of the air, my lord?
HAMLET: Into my grave?
POLONIUS: Indeed, that is out o' th' air. Aside How pregnant sometimes his replies are! a happiness that often madness hits on, which reason and sanity could not so prosperously be delivered of. I will leave him and suddenly contrive the means of meeting between him and my daughter.- My honourable lord, I will most humbly take my leave of you.
HAMLET: You cannot, sir, take from me anything that I will more willingly part withal- except my life, except my life, except my life.
Enter Rosencrantz and Guildenstern.
POLONIUS: Fare you well, my lord.
HAMLET: These tedious old fools!
POLONIUS: You go to seek the Lord Hamlet. There he is.
ROSENCRANTZ: To Polonius God save you, sir!
Exit Polonius.
GUILDENSTERN: My honour'd lord!
ROSENCRANTZ: My most dear lord!
HAMLET: My excellent good friends! How dost thou, Guildenstern? Ah, Rosencrantz! Good lads, how do ye both?
ROSENCRANTZ: As the indifferent children of the earth.
GUILDENSTERN: Happy in that we are not over-happy.
On Fortune's cap we are not the very button.
HAMLET: Nor the soles of her shoe?
ROSENCRANTZ: Neither, my lord.

HAMLET: Then you live about her waist, or in the middle of her favours?
GUILDENSTERN: Faith, her privates we.
HAMLET: In the secret parts of Fortune? O! most true! she is a strumpet. What news ?
ROSENCRANTZ: None, my lord, but that the world's grown honest.
HAMLET: Then is doomsday near! But your news is not true. Let me question more in particular. What have you, my good friends, deserved at the hands of Fortune that she sends you to prison hither?
GUILDENSTERN: Prison, my lord?
HAMLET: Denmark's a prison.
ROSENCRANTZ: Then is the world one.
HAMLET: A goodly one; in which there are many confines, wards, and dungeons, Denmark being one o' th' worst.
ROSENCRANTZ: We think not so, my lord.
HAMLET: Why, then 'tis none to you; for there is nothing either good or bad but thinking makes it so. To me it is a prison.
ROSENCRANTZ: Why, then your ambition makes it one. 'Tis too narrow for your mind.
HAMLET: O God, I could be bounded in a nutshell and count myself a king of infinite space, were it not that I have bad dreams.
GUILDENSTERN: Which dreams indeed are ambition; for the very substance of the ambitious is merely the shadow of a dream.
HAMLET: A dream itself is but a shadow.
ROSENCRANTZ: Truly, and I hold ambition of so airy and light a quality that it is but a shadow's shadow.
HAMLET: Then are our beggars bodies, and our monarchs and outstretch'd heroes the beggars' shadows. Shall we to th' court? for, by my fay, I cannot reason.
BOTH: We'll wait upon you.
HAMLET: No such matter! I will not sort you with the rest of my servants; for, to speak to you like an honest man, I am most dreadfully attended. But in the beaten way of friendship, what make you at Elsinore?
ROSENCRANTZ: To visit you, my lord; no other occasion.
HAMLET: Beggar that I am, I am even poor in thanks; but I thank you; and sure, dear friends, my thanks are too dear a halfpenny. Were you not sent for? Is it your own inclining? Is it a free visitation? Come, deal justly with me. Come, come! Nay, speak.
GUILDENSTERN: What should we say, my lord?
HAMLET: Why, anything but to th' purpose. You were sent for; and there is a kind of confession in your looks, which your modesties have not craft enough to colour. I know the good King and Queen have sent for you.
ROSENCRANTZ: To what end, my lord?
HAMLET: That you must teach me. But let me conjure you by the rights of our fellowship, by the consonancy of our youth, by the obligation of our ever-preserved love, and by what more dear a better proposer could charge you withal, be even and direct with me, whether you were sent for or no.
ROSENCRANTZ: Aside to Guildenstern What say you?
HAMLET: Aside Nay then, I have an eye of you.- If you love me, hold not off.
GUILDENSTERN: My lord, we were sent for.
HAMLET: I will tell you why. So shall my anticipation prevent your

discovery, and your secrecy to the King and Queen moult no feather. I have of late- but wherefore I know not- lost all my mirth, forgone all custom of exercises; and indeed, it goes so heavily with my disposition that this goodly frame, the earth, seems to me a sterile promontory; this most excellent canopy, the air, look you, this brave o'erhanging firmament, this majestical roof fretted with golden fire- why, it appeareth no other thing to me than a foul and pestilent congregation of vapours. What a piece of work is a man! how noble in reason! how infinite in faculties! in form and moving how express and admirable! in action how like an angel! in apprehension how like a god! the beauty of the world, the paragon of animals! And yet to me what is this quintessence of dust? Man delights not me- no, nor woman neither, though by your smiling you seem to say so.
ROSENCRANTZ: My lord, there was no such stuff in my thoughts.
HAMLET: Why did you laugh then, when I said 'Man delights not me'?
ROSENCRANTZ: To think, my lord, if you delight not in man, what lenten entertainment the players shall receive from you. We coted them on the way, and hither are they coming to offer you service.
HAMLET: He that plays the king shall be welcome- his Majesty shall have tribute of me; the adventurous knight shall use his foil and target; the lover shall not sigh gratis; the humorous man shall end his part in peace; the clown shall make those laugh whose lungs are tickle o' th' sere; and the lady shall say her mind freely, or the blank verse shall halt fort. What players are they?
ROSENCRANTZ: Even those you were wont to take such delight in, the tragedians of the city.
HAMLET: How chances it they travel? Their residence, both in reputation and profit, was better both ways.
ROSENCRANTZ: I think their inhibition comes by the means of the late innovation.
HAMLET: Do they hold the same estimation they did when I was in the city? Are they so follow'd?
ROSENCRANTZ: No indeed are they not.
HAMLET: How comes it? Do they grow rusty?
ROSENCRANTZ: Nay, their endeavour keeps in the wonted pace; but there is, sir, an eyrie of children, little eyases, that cry out on the top of question and are most tyrannically clapp'd fort. These are now the fashion, and so berattle the common stages (so they call them) that many wearing rapiers are afraid of goosequills and dare scarce come thither.
HAMLET: What, are they children? Who maintains 'em? How are they escoted? Will they pursue the quality no longer than they can sing? Will they not say afterwards, if they should grow themselves to common players (as it is most like, if their means are no better), their writers do them wrong to make them exclaim against their own succession.
ROSENCRANTZ: Faith, there has been much to do on both sides; and the nation holds it no sin to tarre them to controversy. There was, for a while, no money bid for argument unless the poet and the player went to cuffs in the question.
HAMLET: Is't possible?
GUILDENSTERN: O, there has been much throwing about of brains.

HAMLET: Do the boys carry it away?
ROSENCRANTZ: Ay, that they do, my lord- Hercules and his load too.
HAMLET: It is not very strange; for my uncle is King of Denmark, and those that would make mows at him while my father lived give twenty, forty, fifty, a hundred ducats apiece for his picture in little. 'Sblood, there is something in this more than natural, if philosophy could find it out.

Flourish for the Players.

GUILDENSTERN: There are the players.
HAMLET: Gentlemen, you are welcome to Elsinore. Your hands, come! Th' appurtenance of welcome is fashion and ceremony. Let me comply with you in this garb, lest my extent to the players (which I tell you must show fairly outwards) should more appear like entertainment than yours. You are welcome. But my uncle-father and aunt-mother are deceiv'd.
GUILDENSTERN: In what, my dear lord?
HAMLET: I am but mad north-north-west. When the wind is southerly I know a hawk from a handsaw.

Enter Polonius.

POLONIUS: Well be with you, gentlemen!
HAMLET: Hark you, Guildenstern- and you too- at each ear a hearer! That great baby you see there is not yet out of his swaddling clouts.
ROSENCRANTZ: Happily he's the second time come to them; for they say an old man is twice a child.
HAMLET: I will prophesy he comes to tell me of the players. Mark it.- You say right, sir; a Monday morning; twas so indeed.
POLONIUS: My lord, I have news to tell you.
HAMLET: My lord, I have news to tell you. When Roscius was an actor in Rome-
POLONIUS: The actors are come hither, my lord.
HAMLET: Buzz, buzz!
POLONIUS: Upon my honour-
HAMLET: Then came each actor on his ass-
POLONIUS: The best actors in the world, either for tragedy, comedy, history, pastoral, pastoral-comical, historical-pastoral, tragical-historical, tragical-comical-historical-pastoral; scene individable, or poem unlimited. Seneca cannot be too heavy, nor Plautus too light. For the law of writ and the liberty, these are the only men.
HAMLET: O Jephthah, judge of Israel, what a treasure hadst thou!
POLONIUS: What treasure had he, my lord?
HAMLET: Why,

'One fair daughter, and no more,
The which he loved passing well.'

POLONIUS: Aside Still on my daughter.
HAMLET: Am I not i' th' right, old Jephthah?
POLONIUS: If you call me Jephthah, my lord, I have a daughter that I love passing well.
HAMLET: Nay, that follows not.
POLONIUS: What follows then, my lord?
HAMLET: Why,
'As by lot, God wot,'
and then, you know,
'It came to pass, as most like it was.'
The first row of the pious chanson will show you more;

for look where my abridgment comes.

Enter Four or Five Players.

You are welcome, masters; welcome, all.- I am glad to see thee well.- Welcome, good friends.- O, my old friend? Why, thy face is valanc'd since I saw thee last. Com'st' thou to' beard me in Denmark?- What, my young lady and mistress? By'r Lady, your ladyship is nearer to heaven than when I saw you last by the altitude of a chopine. Pray God your voice, like a piece of uncurrent gold, be not crack'd within the ring.- Masters, you are all welcome. We'll e'en to't like French falconers, fly at anything we see. We'll have a speech straight. Come, give us a taste of your quality. Come, a passionate speech.

FIRST PLAYER: What speech, my good lord?

HAMLET: I heard thee speak me a speech once, but it was never acted; or if it was, not above once; for the play, I remember, pleas'd not the million, 'twas caviary to the general; but it was (as I receiv'd it, and others, whose judgments in such matters cried in the top of mine) an excellent play, well digested in the scenes, set down with as much modesty as cunning. I remember one said there were no sallets in the lines to make the matter savoury, nor no matter in the phrase that might indict the author of affectation; but call'd it an honest method, as wholesome as sweet, and by very much more handsome than fine. One speech in't I chiefly lov'd. 'Twas AEneas' tale to Dido, and thereabout of it especially where he speaks of Priam's slaughter. If it live in your memory, begin at this line- let me see, let me see:
'The rugged Pyrrhus, like th' Hyrcanian beast-'
'Tis not so; it begins with Pyrrhus:

'The rugged Pyrrhus, he whose sable arms,
Black as his purpose, did the night resemble
When he lay couched in the ominous horse,
Hath now this dread and black complexion smear'd
With heraldry more dismal. Head to foot
Now is be total gules, horridly trick'd
With blood of fathers, mothers, daughters, sons,
Bak'd and impasted with the parching streets,
That lend a tyrannous and a damned light
To their lord's murther. Roasted in wrath and fire,
And thus o'ersized with coagulate gore,
With eyes like carbuncles, the hellish Pyrrhus
Old grandsire Priam seeks.'

So, proceed you.

POLONIUS: Fore God, my lord, well spoken, with good accent and good discretion.

FIRST PLAYER: 'Anon he finds him,
Striking too short at Greeks. His antique sword,
Rebellious to his arm, lies where it falls,
Repugnant to command. Unequal match'd,
Pyrrhus at Priam drives, in rage strikes wide;
But with the whiff and wind of his fell sword
Th' unnerved father falls. Then senseless Ilium,
Seeming to feel this blow, with flaming top
Stoops to his base, and with a hideous crash
Takes prisoner Pyrrhus' ear. For lo! his sword,

Which was declining on the milky head
Of reverend Priam, seem'd i' th' air to stick.
So, as a painted tyrant, Pyrrhus stood,
And, like a neutral to his will and matter, did nothing.
But, as we often see, against some storm,
A silence in the heavens, the rack stand still,
The bold winds speechless, and the orb below
As hush as death- anon the dreadful thunder
Doth rend the region; so, after Pyrrhus' pause,
Aroused vengeance sets him new awork;
And never did the Cyclops' hammers fall
On Mars's armour, forg'd for proof eterne,
With less remorse than Pyrrhus' bleeding sword
Now falls on Priam.
Out, out, thou strumpet Fortune! All you gods,
In general synod take away her power;
Break all the spokes and fellies from her wheel,
And bowl the round nave down the hill of heaven,
As low as to the fiends!

POLONIUS: This is too long.

HAMLET: It shall to the barber's, with your beard.- Prithee say on. He's for a jig or a tale of bawdry, or he sleeps. Say on; come to Hecuba.

FIRST PLAYER: 'But who, O who, had seen the mobled queen-'

HAMLET: 'The mobled queen'?

POLONIUS: That's good! 'Mobled queen' is good.

FIRST PLAYER: 'Run barefoot up and down, threat'ning the flames
With bisson rheum; a clout upon that head
Where late the diadem stood, and for a robe,
About her lank and all o'erteemed loins,
A blanket, in the alarm of fear caught up-
Who this had seen, with tongue in venom steep'd
'Gainst Fortune's state would treason have pronounc'd.
But if the gods themselves did see her then,
When she saw Pyrrhus make malicious sport
In Mincing with his sword her husband's limbs,
The instant burst of clamour that she made
(Unless things mortal move them not at all)
Would have made milch the burning eyes of heaven
And passion in the gods.'

POLONIUS: Look, whe'r he has not turn'd his colour, and has tears in's eyes. Prithee no more!

HAMLET: 'Tis well. I'll have thee speak out the rest of this soon.- Good my lord, will you see the players well bestow'd? Do you hear? Let them be well us'd; for they are the abstract and brief chronicles of the time. After your death you were better have a bad epitaph than their ill report while you live.

POLONIUS: My lord, I will use them according to their desert.

HAMLET: God's bodykins, man, much better! Use every man after his desert, and who should scape whipping? Use them after your own honour and dignity. The less they deserve, the more merit is in your bounty. Take them in.

POLONIUS: Come, sirs.

HAMLET: Follow him, friends. We'll hear a play to-morrow.

Exeunt Polonius and Players Except the First.
Dost thou hear me, old friend? Can you play 'The Murther of Gonzago'?
FIRST PLAYER: Ay, my lord.
HAMLET: We'll ha't to-morrow night. You could, for a need, study a speech of some dozen or sixteen lines which I would set down and insert in't, could you not?
FIRST PLAYER: Ay, my lord.
HAMLET: Very well. Follow that lord- and look you mock him not.
Exit First Player.
My good friends, I'll leave you till night. You are welcome to Elsinore.
ROSENCRANTZ: Good my lord!
HAMLET: Ay, so, God b' wi' ye!
Exeunt Rosencrantz and Guildenstern
Now I am alone.
O what a rogue and peasant slave am I!
Is it not monstrous that this player here,
But in a fiction, in a dream of passion,
Could force his soul so to his own conceit
That, from her working, all his visage wann'd,
Tears in his eyes, distraction in's aspect,
A broken voice, and his whole function suiting
With forms to his conceit? And all for nothing!
For Hecuba!
What's Hecuba to him, or he to Hecuba,
That he should weep for her? What would he do,
Had he the motive and the cue for passion
That I have? He would drown the stage with tears
And cleave the general ear with horrid speech;
Make mad the guilty and appal the free,
Confound the ignorant, and amaze indeed
The very faculties of eyes and ears.
Yet I, a dull and muddy-mettled rascal, peak
Like John-a-dreams, unpregnant of my cause,
And can say nothing! No, not for a king,
Upon whose property and most dear life
A damn'd defeat was made. Am I a coward?
Who calls me villain? breaks my pate across?
Plucks off my beard and blows it in my face?
Tweaks me by th' nose? gives me the lie i' th' throat
As deep as to the lungs? Who does me this, ha?
'Swounds, I should take it! for it cannot be
But I am pigeon-liver'd and lack gall
To make oppression bitter, or ere this
I should have fatted all the region kites
With this slave's offal. Bloody bawdy villain!
Remorseless, treacherous, lecherous, kindless villain!
O, vengeance! Why, what an ass am I! This is most brave,
That I, the son of a dear father murther'd,
Prompted to my revenge by heaven and hell,
Must (like a whore) unpack my heart with words
And fall a-cursing like a very drab, a scullion!
Fie upon't! foh! About, my brain! Hum, I have heard
That guilty creatures, sitting at a play,

Have by the very cunning of the scene
Been struck so to the soul that presently
They have proclaim'd their malefactions;
For murther, though it have no tongue, will speak
With most miraculous organ, I'll have these Players
Play something like the murther of my father
Before mine uncle. I'll observe his looks;
I'll tent him to the quick. If he but blench,
I know my course. The spirit that I have seen
May be a devil; and the devil hath power
T' assume a pleasing shape; yea, and perhaps
Out of my weakness and my melancholy,
As he is very potent with such spirits,
Abuses me to damn me. I'll have grounds
More relative than this. The play's the thing
Wherein I'll catch the conscience of the King.
Exit.

ACT III. SCENE I. Elsinore. A Room in the Castle.

Enter King, Queen, Polonius, Ophelia, Rosencrantz, Guildenstern, and Lords.
KING CLAUDIUS: And can you by no drift of circumstance
Get from him why he puts on this confusion,
Grating so harshly all his days of quiet
With turbulent and dangerous lunacy?
ROSENCRANTZ: He does confess he feels himself distracted,
But from what cause he will by no means speak.
GUILDENSTERN: Nor do we find him forward to be sounded,
But with a crafty madness keeps aloof
When we would bring him on to some confession
Of his true state.
QUEEN GETRUDE: Did he receive you well?
ROSENCRANTZ: Most like a gentleman.
GUILDENSTERN: But with much forcing of his disposition.
ROSENCRANTZ: Niggard of question, but of our demands
Most free in his reply.
QUEEN GETRUDE: Did you assay him
To any pastime?
ROSENCRANTZ: Madam, it so fell out that certain players
We o'erraught on the way. Of these we told him,
And there did seem in him a kind of joy
To hear of it. They are here about the court,
And, as I think, they have already order
This night to play before him.
POLONIUS: 'Tis most true;
And he beseech'd me to entreat your Majesties
To hear and see the matter.
KING CLAUDIUS: With all my heart, and it doth much content me
To hear him so inclin'd.
Good gentlemen, give him a further edge
And drive his purpose on to these delights.
ROSENCRANTZ: We shall, my lord.
Exeunt Rosencrantz and Guildenstern.
KING CLAUDIUS: Sweet Gertrude, leave us too;
For we have closely sent for Hamlet hither,

That he, as 'twere by accident, may here
Affront Ophelia.
Her father and myself (lawful espials)
Will so bestow ourselves that, seeing unseen,
We may of their encounter frankly judge
And gather by him, as he is behav'd,
If't be th' affliction of his love, or no,
That thus he suffers for.
QUEEN GETRUDE: I shall obey you;
And for your part, Ophelia, I do wish
That your good beauties be the happy cause
Of Hamlet's wildness. So shall I hope your virtues
Will bring him to his wonted way again,
To both your honours.
OPHELIA: Madam, I wish it may.
Exit Queen.
POLONIUS: Ophelia, walk you here.- Gracious, so please you,
We will bestow ourselves.- To Ophelia Read on this book,
That show of such an exercise may colour
Your loneliness.- We are oft to blame in this,
'Tis too much prov'd, that with devotion's visage
And pious action we do sugar o'er
The Devil himself.
KING CLAUDIUS: Aside O, 'tis too true!
How smart a lash that speech doth give my conscience!
The harlot's cheek, beautied with plast'ring art,
Is not more ugly to the thing that helps it
Than is my deed to my most painted word.
O heavy burthen!
POLONIUS: I hear him coming. Let's withdraw, my lord.
Exeunt King and Polonius.
Enter Hamlet.
HAMLET: To be, or not to be- that is the question:
Whether 'tis nobler in the mind to suffer
The slings and arrows of outrageous fortune
Or to take arms against a sea of troubles,
And by opposing end them. To die- to sleep-
No more; and by a sleep to say we end
The heartache, and the thousand natural shocks
That flesh is heir to. 'Tis a consummation
Devoutly to be wish'd. To die- to sleep.
To sleep- perchance to dream: ay, there's the rub!
For in that sleep of death what dreams may come
When we have shuffled off this mortal coil,
Must give us pause. There's the respect
That makes calamity of so long life.
For who would bear the whips and scorns of time,
Th' oppressor's wrong, the proud man's contumely,
The pangs of despis'd love, the law's delay,
The insolence of office, and the spurns
That patient merit of th' unworthy takes,
When he himself might his quietus make
With a bare bodkin? Who would these fardels bear,

To grunt and sweat under a weary life,
But that the dread of something after death-
The undiscover'd country, from whose bourn
No traveller returns- puzzles the will,
And makes us rather bear those ills we have
Than fly to others that we know not of?
Thus conscience does make cowards of us all,
And thus the native hue of resolution
Is sicklied o'er with the pale cast of thought,
And enterprises of great pith and moment
With this regard their currents turn awry
And lose the name of action.- Soft you now!
The fair Ophelia!- Nymph, in thy orisons
Be all my sins rememb'red.
OPHELIA: Good my lord,
How does your honour for this many a day?
HAMLET: I humbly thank you; well, well, well.
OPHELIA: My lord, I have remembrances of yours
That I have longed long to re-deliver.
I pray you, now receive them.
HAMLET: No, not I!
I never gave you aught.
OPHELIA: My honour'd lord, you know right well you did,
And with them words of so sweet breath compos'd
As made the things more rich. Their perfume lost,
Take these again; for to the noble mind
Rich gifts wax poor when givers prove unkind.
There, my lord.
HAMLET: Ha, ha! Are you honest?
OPHELIA: My lord?
HAMLET: Are you fair?
OPHELIA: What means your lordship?
HAMLET: That if you be honest and fair, your honesty should admit no discourse to your beauty.
OPHELIA: Could beauty, my lord, have better commerce than with honesty?
HAMLET: Ay, truly; for the power of beauty will sooner transform honesty from what it is to a bawd than the force of honesty can translate beauty into his likeness. This was sometime a paradox, but now the time gives it proof. I did love you once.
OPHELIA: Indeed, my lord, you made me believe so.
HAMLET: You should not have believ'd me; for virtue cannot so inoculate our old stock but we shall relish of it. I loved you not.
OPHELIA: I was the more deceived.
HAMLET: Get thee to a nunnery! Why wouldst thou be a breeder of sinners? I am myself indifferent honest, but yet I could accuse me of such things that it were better my mother had not borne me. I am very proud, revengeful, ambitious; with more offences at my beck than I have thoughts to put them in, imagination to give them shape, or time to act them in. What should such fellows as I do, crawling between earth and heaven? We are arrant knaves all; believe none of us. Go thy ways to a nunnery. Where's your father?
OPHELIA: At home, my lord.

HAMLET: Let the doors be shut upon him, that he may play the fool nowhere but in's own house. Farewell.
OPHELIA: O, help him, you sweet heavens!
HAMLET: If thou dost marry, I'll give thee this plague for thy dowry: be thou as chaste as ice, as pure as snow, thou shalt not escape calumny. Get thee to a nunnery. Go, farewell. Or if thou wilt needs marry, marry a fool; for wise men know well enough what monsters you make of them. To a nunnery, go; and quickly too. Farewell.
OPHELIA: O heavenly powers, restore him!
HAMLET: I have heard of your paintings too, well enough. God hath given you one face, and you make yourselves another. You jig, you amble, and you lisp; you nickname God's creatures and make your wantonness your ignorance. Go to, I'll no more on't! it hath made me mad. I say, we will have no moe marriages. Those that are married already- all but one- shall live; the rest shall keep as they are. To a nunnery, go.
Exit.
OPHELIA: O, what a noble mind is here o'erthrown!
The courtier's, scholar's, soldier's, eye, tongue, sword,
Th' expectancy and rose of the fair state,
The glass of fashion and the mould of form,
Th' observ'd of all observers- quite, quite down!
And I, of ladies most deject and wretched,
That suck'd the honey of his music vows,
Now see that noble and most sovereign reason,
Like sweet bells jangled, out of tune and harsh;
That unmatch'd form and feature of blown youth
Blasted with ecstasy. O, woe is me
T' have seen what I have seen, see what I see!
Enter King and Polonius.
KING CLAUDIUS: Love? his affections do not that way tend;
Nor what he spake, though it lack'd form a little,
Was not like madness. There's something in his soul
O'er which his melancholy sits on brood;
And I do doubt the hatch and the disclose
Will be some danger; which for to prevent,
I have in quick determination
Thus set it down: he shall with speed to England
For the demand of our neglected tribute.
Haply the seas, and countries different,
With variable objects, shall expel
This something-settled matter in his heart,
Whereon his brains still beating puts him thus
From fashion of himself. What think you on't?
POLONIUS: It shall do well. But yet do I believe
The origin and commencement of his grief
Sprung from neglected love.- How now, Ophelia?
You need not tell us what Lord Hamlet said.
We heard it all.- My lord, do as you please;
But if you hold it fit, after the play
Let his queen mother all alone entreat him
To show his grief. Let her be round with him;

And I'll be plac'd so please you, in the ear
Of all their conference. If she find him not,
To England send him; or confine him where
Your wisdom best shall think.
KING CLAUDIUS: It shall be so.
Madness in great ones must not unwatch'd go.
Exeunt.

ACT III. SCENE II. Elsinore. Hall in the Castle.

Enter Hamlet and Three of the Players.

HAMLET: Speak the speech, I pray you, as I pronounc'd it to you, trippingly on the tongue. But if you mouth it, as many of our players do, I had as live the town crier spoke my lines. Nor do not saw the air too much with your hand, thus, but use all gently; for in the very torrent, tempest, and (as I may say) whirlwind of your passion, you must acquire and beget a temperance that may give it smoothness. O, it offends me to the soul to hear a robustious periwig-pated fellow tear a passion to tatters, to very rags, to split the cars of the groundlings, who (for the most part) are capable of nothing but inexplicable dumb shows and noise. I would have such a fellow whipp'd for o'erdoing Termagant. It out-herods Herod. Pray you avoid it.

PLAYER: I warrant your honour.

HAMLET: Be not too tame neither; but let your own discretion be your tutor. Suit the action to the word, the word to the action; with this special observance, that you o'erstep not the modesty of nature: for anything so overdone is from the purpose of playing, whose end, both at the first and now, was and is, to hold, as 'twere, the mirror up to nature; to show Virtue her own feature, scorn her own image, and the very age and body of the time his form and pressure. Now this overdone, or come tardy off, though it make the unskilful laugh, cannot but make the judicious grieve; the censure of the which one must in your allowance o'erweigh a whole theatre of others. O, there be players that I have seen play, and heard others praise, and that highly (not to speak it profanely), that, neither having the accent of Christians, nor the gait of Christian, pagan, nor man, have so strutted and bellowed that I have thought some of Nature's journeymen had made men, and not made them well, they imitated humanity so abominably.

PLAYER: I hope we have reform'd that indifferently with us, sir.

HAMLET: O, reform it altogether! And let those that play your clowns speak no more than is set down for them. For there be of them that will themselves laugh, to set on some quantity of barren spectators to laugh too, though in the mean time some necessary question of the play be then to be considered. That's villanous and shows a most pitiful ambition in the fool that uses it. Go make you ready.

Exeunt Players.

Enter Polonius, Rosencrantz, and Guildenstern.

How now, my lord? Will the King hear this piece of work?

POLONIUS: And the Queen too, and that presently.

HAMLET: Bid the players make haste,

Exit Polonius.

Will you two help to hasten them?
BOTH: We will, my lord.
Exeunt They Two.
HAMLET: What, ho, Horatio!
Enter Horatio.
HORATIO: Here, sweet lord, at your service.
HAMLET: Horatio, thou art e'en as just a man
As e'er my conversation cop'd withal.
HORATIO: O, my dear lord!
HAMLET: Nay, do not think I flatter;
For what advancement may I hope from thee,
That no revenue hast but thy good spirits
To feed and clothe thee? Why should the poor be flatter'd?
No, let the candied tongue lick absurd pomp,
And crook the pregnant hinges of the knee
Where thrift may follow fawning. Dost thou hear?
Since my dear soul was mistress of her choice
And could of men distinguish, her election
Hath scald thee for herself. For thou hast been
As one, in suff'ring all, that suffers nothing;
A man that Fortune's buffets and rewards
Hast ta'en with equal thanks; and blest are those
Whose blood and judgment are so well commingled
That they are not a pipe for Fortune's finger
To sound what stop she please. Give me that man
That is not passion's slave, and I will wear him
In my heart's core, ay, in my heart of heart,
As I do thee. Something too much of this I
There is a play to-night before the King.
One scene of it comes near the circumstance,
Which I have told thee, of my father's death.
I prithee, when thou seest that act afoot,
Even with the very comment of thy soul
Observe my uncle. If his occulted guilt
Do not itself unkennel in one speech,
It is a damned ghost that we have seen,
And my imaginations are as foul
As Vulcan's stithy. Give him heedful note;
For I mine eyes will rivet to his face,
And after we will both our judgments join
In censure of his seeming.
HORATIO: Well, my lord.
If he steal aught the whilst this play is playing,
And scape detecting, I will pay the theft.
Sound a Flourish. Enter Trumpets and Kettledrums. Danish March. Enter King, Queen, Polonius, Ophelia, Rosencrantz, Guildenstern, and Other Lords Attendant, with the Guard Carrying Torches.
HAMLET: They are coming to the play. I must be idle.
Get you a place.
KING CLAUDIUS: How fares our cousin Hamlet?
HAMLET: Excellent, i' faith; of the chameleon's dish. I eat the air,
promise-cramm'd. You cannot feed capons so.
KING CLAUDIUS: I have nothing with this answer, Hamlet. These words are not mine.
HAMLET: No, nor mine now. To Polonius My lord, you play'd once

i' th' university, you say?
POLONIUS: That did I, my lord, and was accounted a good actor.
HAMLET: What did you enact?
POLONIUS: I did enact Julius Caesar; I was kill'd i' th' Capitol; Brutus kill'd me.
HAMLET: It was a brute part of him to kill so capital a calf there. Be the players ready.
ROSENCRANTZ: Ay, my lord. They stay upon your patience.
QUEEN GETRUDE: Come hither, my dear Hamlet, sit by me.
HAMLET: No, good mother. Here's metal more attractive.
POLONIUS: To the King O, ho! do you mark that?
HAMLET: Lady, shall I lie in your lap?
Sits down at Ophelia's Feet.
OPHELIA: No, my lord.
HAMLET: I mean, my head upon your lap?
OPHELIA: Ay, my lord.
HAMLET: Do you think I meant country matters?
OPHELIA: I think nothing, my lord.
HAMLET: That's a fair thought to lie between maids' legs.
OPHELIA: What is, my lord?
HAMLET: Nothing.
OPHELIA: You are merry, my lord.
HAMLET: Who, I?
OPHELIA: Ay, my lord.
HAMLET: O God, your only jig-maker!
What should a man do but be merry?
For look you how cheerfully my mother looks, and my father died within 's two hours.
OPHELIA: Nay 'tis twice two months, my lord.
HAMLET: So long? Nay then, let the devil wear black, for I'll have a suit of sables. O heavens! die two months ago, and not forgotten yet? Then there's hope a great man's memory may outlive his life half a year. But, by'r Lady, he must build churches then; or else shall he suffer not thinking on, with the hobby-horse, whose epitaph is 'For O, for O, the hobby-horse is forgot!'
Hautboys play. The dumb show enters.

Enter a King and a Queen very lovingly; the Queen embracing him and he her. She kneels, and makes show of protestation unto him. He takes her up, and declines his head upon her neck. He lays him down upon a bank of flowers. She, seeing him asleep, leaves him. Anon comes in a fellow, takes off his crown, kisses it, pours poison in the sleeper's ears, and leaves him. The Queen returns, finds the King dead, and makes passionate action. The Poisoner with some three or four Mutes, comes in again, seem to condole with her. The dead body is carried away. The Poisoner wooes the Queen with gifts; she seems harsh and unwilling awhile, but in the end accepts his love.

Exeunt.
OPHELIA: What means this, my lord?
HAMLET: Marry, this is miching malhecho; it means mischief.
OPHELIA: Belike this show imports the argument of the play.
Enter Prologue.
HAMLET: We shall know by this fellow. The players cannot keep counsel; they'll tell all.
OPHELIA: Will he tell us what this show meant?
HAMLET: Ay, or any show that you'll show him. Be not you asham'd to show, he'll not shame to tell you what it means.

OPHELIA: You are naught, you are naught! I'll mark the play.
PROLOGUE
For us, and for our tragedy,
Here stooping to your clemency,
We beg your hearing patiently.
Exit.
HAMLET: Is this a prologue, or the posy of a ring?
OPHELIA: 'Tis brief, my lord.
HAMLET: As woman's love.
Enter Two Players as King and Queen.
PLAYER KING: Full thirty times hath Phoebus' cart gone round
Neptune's salt wash and Tellus' orbed ground,
And thirty dozed moons with borrowed sheen
About the world have times twelve thirties been,
Since love our hearts, and Hymen did our hands,
Unite comutual in most sacred bands.
PLAYER QUEEN: So many journeys may the sun and moon
Make us again count o'er ere love be done!
But woe is me! you are so sick of late,
So far from cheer and from your former state.
That I distrust you. Yet, though I distrust,
Discomfort you, my lord, it nothing must;
For women's fear and love holds quantity,
In neither aught, or in extremity.
Now what my love is, proof hath made you know;
And as my love is siz'd, my fear is so.
Where love is great, the littlest doubts are fear;
Where little fears grow great, great love grows there.
PLAYER KING: Faith, I must leave thee, love, and shortly too;
My operant powers their functions leave to do.
And thou shalt live in this fair world behind,
Honour'd, belov'd, and haply one as kind
For husband shalt thou-
PLAYER QUEEN: O, confound the rest!
Such love must needs be treason in my breast.
When second husband let me be accurst!
None wed the second but who killed the first.
HAMLET: Aside Wormwood, wormwood!
PLAYER QUEEN: The instances that second marriage move
Are base respects of thrift, but none of love.
A second time I kill my husband dead
When second husband kisses me in bed.
PLAYER KING: I do believe you think what now you speak;
But what we do determine oft we break.
Purpose is but the slave to memory,
Of violent birth, but poor validity;
Which now, like fruit unripe, sticks on the tree,
But fill unshaken when they mellow be.
Most necessary 'tis that we forget
To pay ourselves what to ourselves is debt.
What to ourselves in passion we propose,
The passion ending, doth the purpose lose.
The violence of either grief or joy

Their own enactures with themselves destroy.
Where joy most revels, grief doth most lament;
Grief joys, joy grieves, on slender accident.
This world is not for aye, nor 'tis not strange
That even our loves should with our fortunes change;
For 'tis a question left us yet to prove,
Whether love lead fortune, or else fortune love.
The great man down, you mark his favourite flies,
The poor advanc'd makes friends of enemies;
And hitherto doth love on fortune tend,
For who not needs shall never lack a friend,
And who in want a hollow friend doth try,
Directly seasons him his enemy.
But, orderly to end where I begun,
Our wills and fates do so contrary run
That our devices still are overthrown;
Our thoughts are ours, their ends none of our own.
So think thou wilt no second husband wed;
But die thy thoughts when thy first lord is dead.
PLAYER QUEEN: Nor earth to me give food, nor heaven light,
Sport and repose lock from me day and night,
To desperation turn my trust and hope,
An anchor's cheer in prison be my scope,
Each opposite that blanks the face of joy
Meet what I would have well, and it destroy,
Both here and hence pursue me lasting strife,
If, once a widow, ever I be wife!
HAMLET: If she should break it now!
PLAYER KING: 'Tis deeply sworn. Sweet, leave me here awhile.
My spirits grow dull, and fain I would beguile
The tedious day with sleep.
PLAYER QUEEN: Sleep rock thy brain,
He sleeps.
And never come mischance between us twain!
Exit.
HAMLET: Madam, how like you this play?
QUEEN GETRUDE: The lady doth protest too much, methinks.
HAMLET: O, but she'll keep her word.
KING CLAUDIUS: Have you heard the argument? Is there no offence in't?
HAMLET: No, no! They do but jest, poison in jest; no offence i' th' world.
KING CLAUDIUS: What do you call the play?
HAMLET: 'The Mousetrap.' Marry, how? Tropically. This play is the image of a murther done in Vienna. Gonzago is the duke's name; his wife, Baptista. You shall see anon. 'Tis a knavish piece of work; but what o' that? Your Majesty, and we that have free souls, it touches us not. Let the gall'd jade winch; our withers are unwrung.
Enter Lucianus.
This is one Lucianus, nephew to the King.
OPHELIA: You are as good as a chorus, my lord.
HAMLET: I could interpret between you and your love, if I could see the puppets dallying.

OPHELIA: You are keen, my lord, you are keen.
HAMLET: It would cost you a groaning to take off my edge.
OPHELIA: Still better, and worse.
HAMLET: So you must take your husbands.- Begin, murtherer. Pox, leave thy damnable faces, and begin! Come, the croaking raven doth bellow for revenge.
LUCIANUS: Thoughts black, hands apt, drugs fit, and time agreeing;
Confederate season, else no creature seeing;
Thou mixture rank, of midnight weeds collected,
With Hecate's ban thrice blasted, thrice infected,
Thy natural magic and dire property
On wholesome life usurp immediately.
Pours the Poison in His Ears.
HAMLET: He poisons him i' th' garden for's estate. His name's Gonzago. The story is extant, and written in very choice Italian. You shall see anon how the murtherer gets the love of Gonzago's wife.
OPHELIA: The King rises.
HAMLET: What, frighted with false fire?
QUEEN GETRUDE: How fares my lord?
POLONIUS: Give o'er the play.
KING CLAUDIUS: Give me some light! Away!
ALL: Lights, lights, lights!
Exeunt All but Hamlet and Horatio.
HAMLET: Why, let the strucken deer go weep,
The hart ungalled play;
For some must watch, while some must sleep:
Thus runs the world away.
Would not this, sir, and a forest of feathers- if the rest of my fortunes turn Turk with me-with two Provincial roses on my raz'd shoes, get me a fellowship in a cry of players, sir?
HORATIO: Half a share.
HAMLET: A whole one I!
For thou dost know, O Damon dear,
This realm dismantled was
Of Jove himself; and now reigns here
A very, very- pajock.
HORATIO: You might have rhym'd.
HAMLET: O good Horatio, I'll take the ghost's word for a thousand pound! Didst perceive?
HORATIO: Very well, my lord.
HAMLET: Upon the talk of the poisoning?
HORATIO: I did very well note him.
HAMLET: Aha! Come, some music! Come, the recorders!
For if the King like not the comedy,
Why then, belike he likes it not, perdy.
Come, some music!
Enter Rosencrantz and Guildenstern.
GUILDENSTERN: Good my lord, vouchsafe me a word with you.
HAMLET: Sir, a whole history.
GUILDENSTERN: The King, sir-
HAMLET: Ay, sir, what of him?
GUILDENSTERN: Is in his retirement, marvellous distemper'd.
HAMLET: With drink, sir?

GUILDENSTERN: No, my lord; rather with choler.
HAMLET: Your wisdom should show itself more richer to signify this to the doctor; for me to put him to his purgation would perhaps plunge him into far more choler.
GUILDENSTERN: Good my lord, put your discourse into some frame, and start not so wildly from my affair.
HAMLET: I am tame, sir; pronounce.
GUILDENSTERN: The Queen, your mother, in most great affliction of spirit hath sent me to you.
HAMLET: You are welcome.
GUILDENSTERN: Nay, good my lord, this courtesy is not of the right breed. If it shall please you to make me a wholesome answer, I will do your mother's commandment; if not, your pardon and my return shall be the end of my business.
HAMLET: Sir, I cannot.
GUILDENSTERN: What, my lord?
HAMLET: Make you a wholesome answer; my wit's diseas'd. But, sir, such answer is I can make, you shall command; or rather, as you say, my mother. Therefore no more, but to the matter! My mother, you say-
ROSENCRANTZ: Then thus she says: your behaviour hath struck her into amazement and admiration.
HAMLET: O wonderful son, that can so stonish a mother! But is there no sequel at the heels of this mother's admiration? Impart.
ROSENCRANTZ: She desires to speak with you in her closet ere you go to bed.
HAMLET: We shall obey, were she ten times our mother. Have you any further trade with us?
ROSENCRANTZ: My lord, you once did love me.
HAMLET: And do still, by these pickers and stealers!
ROSENCRANTZ: Good my lord, what is your cause of distemper? You do surely bar the door upon your own liberty, if you deny your griefs to your friend.
HAMLET: Sir, I lack advancement.
ROSENCRANTZ: How can that be, when you have the voice of the King himself for your succession in Denmark?
HAMLET: Ay, sir, but 'while the grass grows'- the proverb is something musty.

Enter the Players with Recorders.

O, the recorders! Let me see one. To withdraw with you- why do you go about to recover the wind of me, as if you would drive me into a toil?
GUILDENSTERN: O my lord, if my duty be too bold, my love is too unmannerly.
HAMLET: I do not well understand that. Will you play upon this pipe?
GUILDENSTERN: My lord, I cannot.
HAMLET: I pray you.
GUILDENSTERN: Believe me, I cannot.
HAMLET: I do beseech you.
GUILDENSTERN: I know, no touch of it, my lord.
HAMLET: It is as easy as lying. Govern these ventages with your fingers and thumbs, give it breath with your mouth, and it will discourse most eloquent music. Look you, these are the stops.
GUILDENSTERN: But these cannot I command to any utt'rance of harmony. I have not the skill.
HAMLET: Why, look you now, how unworthy a thing you make of me! You

would play upon me; you would seem to know my stops; you would pluck out the heart of my mystery; you would sound me from my lowest note to the top of my compass; and there is much music, excellent voice, in this little organ, yet cannot you make it speak. 'Sblood, do you think I am easier to be play'd on than a pipe? Call me what instrument you will, though you can fret me, you cannot play upon me.

Enter Polonius.

God bless you, sir!

POLONIUS: My lord, the Queen would speak with you, and presently.

HAMLET: Do you see yonder cloud that's almost in shape of a camel?

POLONIUS: By th' mass, and 'tis like a camel indeed.

HAMLET: Methinks it is like a weasel.

POLONIUS: It is back'd like a weasel.

HAMLET: Or like a whale.

POLONIUS: Very like a whale.

HAMLET: Then will I come to my mother by-and-by. They fool me to the top of my bent. I will come by-and-by.

POLONIUS: I will say so.

Exit.

HAMLET: 'By-and-by' is easily said.- Leave me, friends.

Exeunt All but Hamlet.

'Tis now the very witching time of night,
When churchyards yawn, and hell itself breathes out
Contagion to this world. Now could I drink hot blood
And do such bitter business as the day
Would quake to look on. Soft! now to my mother!
O heart, lose not thy nature; let not ever
The soul of Nero enter this firm bosom.
Let me be cruel, not unnatural;
I will speak daggers to her, but use none.
My tongue and soul in this be hypocrites-
How in my words somever she be shent,
To give them seals never, my soul, consent!

Exit.

ACT III. SCENE III. A Room in the Castle.

Enter King, Rosencrantz, and Guildenstern.

KING CLAUDIUS: I like him not, nor stands it safe with us
To let his madness range. Therefore prepare you;
I your commission will forthwith dispatch,
And he to England shall along with you.
The terms of our estate may not endure
Hazard so near us as doth hourly grow
Out of his lunacies.

GUILDENSTERN: We will ourselves provide.
Most holy and religious fear it is
To keep those many many bodies safe
That live and feed upon your Majesty.

ROSENCRANTZ: The single and peculiar life is bound
With all the strength and armour of the mind
To keep itself from noyance; but much more
That spirit upon whose weal depends and rests
The lives of many. The cesse of majesty

Dies not alone, but like a gulf doth draw
What's near it with it. It is a massy wheel,
Fix'd on the summit of the highest mount,
To whose huge spokes ten thousand lesser things
Are mortis'd and adjoin'd; which when it falls,
Each small annexment, petty consequence,
Attends the boist'rous ruin. Never alone
Did the king sigh, but with a general groan.
KING CLAUDIUS: Arm you, I pray you, to th', speedy voyage;
For we will fetters put upon this fear,
Which now goes too free-footed.
BOTH: We will haste us.
Exeunt Gentlemen.
Enter Polonius.
POLONIUS: My lord, he's going to his mother's closet.
Behind the arras I'll convey myself
To hear the process. I'll warrant she'll tax him home;
And, as you said, and wisely was it said,
'Tis meet that some more audience than a mother,
Since nature makes them partial, should o'erhear
The speech, of vantage. Fare you well, my liege.
I'll call upon you ere you go to bed
And tell you what I know.
KING CLAUDIUS: Thanks, dear my lord.
Exit Polonius.
O, my offence is rank, it smells to heaven;
It hath the primal eldest curse upon't,
A brother's murther! Pray can I not,
Though inclination be as sharp as will.
My stronger guilt defeats my strong intent,
And, like a man to double business bound,
I stand in pause where I shall first begin,
And both neglect. What if this cursed hand
Were thicker than itself with brother's blood,
Is there not rain enough in the sweet heavens
To wash it white as snow? Whereto serves mercy
But to confront the visage of offence?
And what's in prayer but this twofold force,
To be forestalled ere we come to fall,
Or pardon'd being down? Then I'll look up;
My fault is past. But, O, what form of prayer
Can serve my turn? 'Forgive me my foul murther'?
That cannot be; since I am still possess'd
Of those effects for which I did the murther-
My crown, mine own ambition, and my queen.
May one be pardon'd and retain th' offence?
In the corrupted currents of this world
Offence's gilded hand may shove by justice,
And oft 'tis seen the wicked prize itself
Buys out the law; but 'tis not so above.
There is no shuffling; there the action lies
In his true nature, and we ourselves compell'd,
Even to the teeth and forehead of our faults,

To give in evidence. What then? What rests?
Try what repentance can. What can it not?
Yet what can it when one cannot repent?
O wretched state! O bosom black as death!
O limed soul, that, struggling to be free,
Art more engag'd! Help, angels! Make assay.
Bow, stubborn knees; and heart with strings of steel,
Be soft as sinews of the new-born babe!
All may be well. He kneels.
Enter Hamlet.
HAMLET: Now might I do it pat, now he is praying;
And now I'll do't. And so he goes to heaven,
And so am I reveng'd. That would be scann'd.
A villain kills my father; and for that,
I, his sole son, do this same villain send
To heaven.
Why, this is hire and salary, not revenge!
He took my father grossly, full of bread,
With all his crimes broad blown, as flush as May;
And how his audit stands, who knows save heaven?
But in our circumstance and course of thought,
'Tis heavy with him; and am I then reveng'd,
To take him in the purging of his soul,
When he is fit and seasoned for his passage?
No. Up, sword, and know thou a more horrid hent.
When he is drunk asleep; or in his rage;
Or in th' incestuous pleasure of his bed;
At gaming, swearing, or about some act
That has no relish of salvation in't-
Then trip him, that his heels may kick at heaven,
And that his soul may be as damn'd and black
As hell, whereto it goes. My mother stays.
This physic but prolongs thy sickly days.
Exit.
KING CLAUDIUS: Rises My words fly up, my thoughts remain below.
Words without thoughts never to heaven go. Exit.
ACT III. SCENE IV. The Queen's Closet.
Enter Queen and Polonius.
POLONIUS: He will come straight. Look you lay home to him.
Tell him his pranks have been too broad to bear with,
And that your Grace hath screen'd and stood between
Much heat and him. I'll silence me even here.
Pray you be round with him.
HAMLET: (within) Mother, mother, mother!
QUEEN GETRUDE: I'll warrant you; fear me not. Withdraw; I hear him coming.
Polonius Hides Behind the Arras.
Enter Hamlet.
HAMLET: Now, mother, what's the matter?
QUEEN GETRUDE: Hamlet, thou hast thy father much offended.
HAMLET: Mother, you have my father much offended.
QUEEN GETRUDE: Come, come, you answer with an idle tongue.
HAMLET: Go, go, you question with a wicked tongue.
QUEEN GETRUDE: Why, how now, Hamlet?

HAMLET: What's the matter now?
QUEEN GETRUDE: Have you forgot me?
HAMLET: No, by the rood, not so!
You are the Queen, your husband's brother's wife,
And (would it were not so!) you are my mother.
QUEEN GETRUDE: Nay, then I'll set those to you that can speak.
HAMLET: Come, come, and sit you down. You shall not budge I
You go not till I set you up a glass
Where you may see the inmost part of you.
QUEEN GETRUDE: What wilt thou do? Thou wilt not murther me?
Help, help, ho!
POLONIUS: Behind What, ho! help, help, help!
HAMLET: Draws How now? a rat? Dead for a ducat, dead!
Makes a Pass Through the Arras And Kills Polonius.
POLONIUS: Behind O, I am slain!
QUEEN GETRUDE: O me, what hast thou done?
HAMLET: Nay, I know not. Is it the King?
QUEEN GETRUDE: O, what a rash and bloody deed is this!
HAMLET: A bloody deed- almost as bad, good mother,
As kill a king, and marry with his brother.
QUEEN GETRUDE: As kill a king?
HAMLET: Ay, lady, it was my word.
Lifts up the Arras and Sees Polonius.
Thou wretched, rash, intruding fool, farewell!
I took thee for thy better. Take thy fortune.
Thou find'st to be too busy is some danger.
Leave wringing of your hinds. Peace! sit you down
And let me wring your heart; for so I shall
If it be made of penetrable stuff;
If damned custom have not braz'd it so
That it is proof and bulwark against sense.
QUEEN GETRUDE: What have I done that thou dar'st wag thy tongue
In noise so rude against me?
HAMLET: Such an act
That blurs the grace and blush of modesty;
Calls virtue hypocrite; takes off the rose
From the fair forehead of an innocent love,
And sets a blister there; makes marriage vows
As false as dicers' oaths. O, such a deed
As from the body of contraction plucks
The very soul, and sweet religion makes
A rhapsody of words! Heaven's face doth glow;
Yea, this solidity and compound mass,
With tristful visage, as against the doom,
Is thought-sick at the act.
QUEEN GETRUDE: Ay me, what act,
That roars so loud and thunders in the index?
HAMLET: Look here upon th's picture, and on this,
The counterfeit presentment of two brothers.
See what a grace was seated on this brow;
Hyperion's curls; the front of Jove himself;
An eye like Mars, to threaten and command;
A station like the herald Mercury

New lighted on a heaven-kissing hill:
A combination and a form indeed
Where every god did seem to set his seal
To give the world assurance of a man.
This was your husband. Look you now what follows.
Here is your husband, like a mildew'd ear
Blasting his wholesome brother. Have you eyes?
Could you on this fair mountain leave to feed,
And batten on this moor? Ha! have you eyes
You cannot call it love; for at your age
The heyday in the blood is tame, it's humble,
And waits upon the judgment; and what judgment
Would step from this to this? Sense sure you have,
Else could you not have motion; but sure that sense
Is apoplex'd; for madness would not err,
Nor sense to ecstacy was ne'er so thrall'd
But it reserv'd some quantity of choice
To serve in such a difference. What devil was't
That thus hath cozen'd you at hoodman-blind?
Eyes without feeling, feeling without sight,
Ears without hands or eyes, smelling sans all,
Or but a sickly part of one true sense
Could not so mope.
O shame! where is thy blush? Rebellious hell,
If thou canst mutine in a matron's bones,
To flaming youth let virtue be as wax
And melt in her own fire. Proclaim no shame
When the compulsive ardour gives the charge,
Since frost itself as actively doth burn,
And reason panders will.
QUEEN GETRUDE: O Hamlet, speak no more!
Thou turn'st mine eyes into my very soul,
And there I see such black and grained spots
As will not leave their tinct.
HAMLET: Nay, but to live
In the rank sweat of an enseamed bed,
Stew'd in corruption, honeying and making love
Over the nasty sty!
QUEEN GETRUDE: O, speak to me no more!
These words like daggers enter in mine ears.
No more, sweet Hamlet!
HAMLET: A murtherer and a villain!
A slave that is not twentieth part the tithe
Of your precedent lord; a vice of kings;
A cutpurse of the empire and the rule,
That from a shelf the precious diadem stole
And put it in his pocket!
QUEEN GETRUDE: No more!
Enter the Ghost in His Nightgown.
HAMLET: A king of shreds and patches!-
Save me and hover o'er me with your wings,
You heavenly guards! What would your gracious figure?
QUEEN GETRUDE: Alas, he's mad!

HAMLET: Do you not come your tardy son to chide,
That, laps'd in time and passion, lets go by
Th' important acting of your dread command?
O, say!
GHOST: Do not forget. This visitation
Is but to whet thy almost blunted purpose.
But look, amazement on thy mother sits.
O, step between her and her fighting soul
Conceit in weakest bodies strongest works.
Speak to her, Hamlet.
HAMLET: How is it with you, lady?
QUEEN GETRUDE: Alas, how is't with you,
That you do bend your eye on vacancy,
And with th' encorporal air do hold discourse?
Forth at your eyes your spirits wildly peep;
And, as the sleeping soldiers in th' alarm,
Your bedded hairs, like life in excrements,
Start up and stand an end. O gentle son,
Upon the beat and flame of thy distemper
Sprinkle cool patience! Whereon do you look?
HAMLET: On him, on him! Look you how pale he glares!
His form and cause conjoin'd, preaching to stones,
Would make them capable.- Do not look upon me,
Lest with this piteous action you convert
My stern effects. Then what I have to do
Will want true colour- tears perchance for blood.
QUEEN GETRUDE: To whom do you speak this?
HAMLET: Do you see nothing there?
QUEEN GETRUDE: Nothing at all; yet all that is I see.
HAMLET: Nor did you nothing hear?
QUEEN GETRUDE: No, nothing but ourselves.
HAMLET: Why, look you there! Look how it steals away!
My father, in his habit as he liv'd!
Look where he goes even now out at the portal!
Exit Ghost.
QUEEN GETRUDE: This is the very coinage of your brain.
This bodiless creation ecstasy
Is very cunning in.
HAMLET: Ecstasy?
My pulse as yours doth temperately keep time
And makes as healthful music. It is not madness
That I have utt'red. Bring me to the test,
And I the matter will reword; which madness
Would gambol from. Mother, for love of grace,
Lay not that flattering unction to your soul
That not your trespass but my madness speaks.
It will but skin and film the ulcerous place,
Whiles rank corruption, mining all within,
Infects unseen. Confess yourself to heaven;
Repent what's past; avoid what is to come;
And do not spread the compost on the weeds
To make them ranker. Forgive me this my virtue;
For in the fatness of these pursy times

Virtue itself of vice must pardon beg-
Yea, curb and woo for leave to do him good.
QUEEN GETRUDE: O Hamlet, thou hast cleft my heart in twain.
HAMLET: O, throw away the worser part of it,
And live the purer with the other half,
Good night- but go not to my uncle's bed.
Assume a virtue, if you have it not.
That monster, custom, who all sense doth eat
Of habits evil, is angel yet in this,
That to the use of actions fair and good
He likewise gives a frock or livery,
That aptly is put on. Refrain to-night,
And that shall lend a kind of easiness
To the next abstinence; the next more easy;
For use almost can change the stamp of nature,
And either Master the devil, or throw him out
With wondrous potency. Once more, good night;
And when you are desirous to be blest,
I'll blessing beg of you.- For this same lord,
I do repent; but heaven hath pleas'd it so,
To punish me with this, and this with me,
That I must be their scourge and minister.
I will bestow him, and will answer well
The death I gave him. So again, good night.
I must be cruel, only to be kind;
Thus bad begins, and worse remains behind.
One word more, good lady.
QUEEN GETRUDE: What shall I do?
HAMLET: Not this, by no means, that I bid you do:
Let the bloat King tempt you again to bed;
Pinch wanton on your cheek; call you his mouse;
And let him, for a pair of reechy kisses,
Or paddling in your neck with his damn'd fingers,
Make you to ravel all this matter out,
That I essentially am not in madness,
But mad in craft. 'Twere good you let him know;
For who that's but a queen, fair, sober, wise,
Would from a paddock, from a bat, a gib
Such dear concernings hide? Who would do so?
No, in despite of sense and secrecy,
Unpeg the basket on the house's top,
Let the birds fly, and like the famous ape,
To try conclusions, in the basket creep
And break your own neck down.
QUEEN GETRUDE: Be thou assur'd, if words be made of breath,
And breath of life, I have no life to breathe
What thou hast said to me.
HAMLET: I must to England; you know that?
QUEEN GETRUDE: Alack,
I had forgot! 'Tis so concluded on.
HAMLET: There's letters seal'd; and my two schoolfellows,
Whom I will trust as I will adders fang'd,
They bear the mandate; they must sweep my way

And marshal me to knavery. Let it work;
For 'tis the sport to have the enginer
Hoist with his own petar; and 't shall go hard
But I will delve one yard below their mines
And blow them at the moon. O, 'tis most sweet
When in one line two crafts directly meet.
This man shall set me packing.
I'll lug the guts into the neighbour room.-
Mother, good night.- Indeed, this counsellor
Is now most still, most secret, and most grave,
Who was in life a foolish peating knave.
Come, sir, to draw toward an end with you.
Good night, mother.
Exit the Queen. Then Exit Hamlet, Tugging in Polonius.

ACT IV. SCENE I. Elsinore. A Room in the Castle.

Enter King and Queen, with Rosencrantz and Guildenstern.
KING CLAUDIUS: There's matter in these sighs. These profound heaves
You must translate; 'tis fit we understand them.
Where is your son?
QUEEN GETRUDE: Bestow this place on us a little while.
Exeunt Rosencrantz and Guildenstern.
Ah, mine own lord, what have I seen to-night!
KING CLAUDIUS: What, Gertrude? How does Hamlet?
QUEEN GETRUDE: Mad as the sea and wind when both contend
Which is the mightier. In his lawless fit
Behind the arras hearing something stir,
Whips out his rapier, cries 'A rat, a rat!'
And in this brainish apprehension kills
The unseen good old man.
KING CLAUDIUS: O heavy deed!
It had been so with us, had we been there.
His liberty is full of threats to all-
To you yourself, to us, to every one.
Alas, how shall this bloody deed be answer'd?
It will be laid to us, whose providence
Should have kept short, restrain'd, and out of haunt
This mad young man. But so much was our love
We would not understand what was most fit,
But, like the owner of a foul disease,
To keep it from divulging, let it feed
Even on the pith of life. Where is he gone?
QUEEN GETRUDE: To draw apart the body he hath kill'd;
O'er whom his very madness, like some ore
Among a mineral of metals base,
Shows itself pure. He weeps for what is done.
KING CLAUDIUS: O Gertrude, come away!
The sun no sooner shall the mountains touch
But we will ship him hence; and this vile deed
We must with all our majesty and skill
Both countenance and excuse. Ho, Guildenstern!
Enter Rosencrantz and Guildenstern.
Friends both, go join you with some further aid.
Hamlet in madness hath Polonius slain,

And from his mother's closet hath he dragg'd him.
Go seek him out; speak fair, and bring the body
Into the chapel. I pray you haste in this.
Exeunt Rosencrantz and Guildenstern.
Come, Gertrude, we'll call up our wisest friends
And let them know both what we mean to do
And what's untimely done. So Haply Slander-
Whose whisper o'er the world's diameter,
As level as the cannon to his blank,
Transports his poisoned shot- may miss our name
And hit the woundless air.- O, come away!
My soul is full of discord and dismay.
Exeunt.

ACT IV. SCENE II. Elsinore. A Passage in the Castle.

Enter Hamlet.
HAMLET: Safely stow'd.
GENTLEMEN: (within) Hamlet! Lord Hamlet!
HAMLET: But soft! What noise? Who calls on Hamlet? O, here they come.
Enter Rosencrantz and Guildenstern.
ROSENCRANTZ: What have you done, my lord, with the dead body?
HAMLET: Compounded it with dust, whereto 'tis kin.
ROSENCRANTZ: Tell us where 'tis, that we may take it thence
And bear it to the chapel.
HAMLET: Do not believe it.
ROSENCRANTZ: Believe what?
HAMLET: That I can keep your counsel, and not mine own. Besides, to be demanded of a sponge, what replication should be made by the son of a king?
ROSENCRANTZ: Take you me for a sponge, my lord?
HAMLET: Ay, sir; that soaks up the King's countenance, his rewards, his authorities. But such officers do the King best service in the end. He keeps them, like an ape, in the corner of his jaw; first mouth'd, to be last Swallowed. When he needs what you have glean'd, it is but squeezing you and, sponge, you shall be dry again.
ROSENCRANTZ: I understand you not, my lord.
HAMLET: I am glad of it. A knavish speech sleeps in a foolish ear.
ROSENCRANTZ: My lord, you must tell us where the body is and go with us to the King.
HAMLET: The body is with the King, but the King is not with the body.
The King is a thing-
GUILDENSTERN: A thing, my lord?
HAMLET: Of nothing. Bring me to him. Hide fox, and all after.
Exeunt.

ACT IV. SCENE III. Elsinore. A Room in the Castle.

Enter King.
KING CLAUDIUS: I have sent to seek him and to find the body.
How dangerous is it that this man goes loose!
Yet must not we put the strong law on him.
He's lov'd of the distracted multitude,
Who like not in their judgment, but their eyes;
And where 'tis so, th' offender's scourge is weigh'd,
But never the offence. To bear all smooth and even,

This sudden sending him away must seem
Deliberate pause. Diseases desperate grown
By desperate appliance are reliev'd,
Or not at all.
Enter Rosencrantz.
How now O What hath befall'n?
ROSENCRANTZ: Where the dead body is bestow'd, my lord,
We cannot get from him.
KING CLAUDIUS: But where is he?
ROSENCRANTZ: Without, my lord; guarded, to know your pleasure.
KING CLAUDIUS: Bring him before us.
ROSENCRANTZ: Ho, Guildenstern! Bring in my lord.
Enter Hamlet and Guildenstern With Attendants.
KING CLAUDIUS: Now, Hamlet, where's Polonius?
HAMLET: At supper.
KING CLAUDIUS: At supper? Where?
HAMLET: Not where he eats, but where he is eaten. A certain
convocation of politic worms are e'en at him. Your worm is your
only emperor for diet. We fat all creatures else to fat us, and
we fat ourselves for maggots. Your fat king and your lean beggar
is but variable service- two dishes, but to one table. That's the end.
KING CLAUDIUS: Alas, alas!
HAMLET: A man may fish with the worm that hath eat of a king, and eat
of the fish that hath fed of that worm.
KING CLAUDIUS: What dost thou mean by this?
HAMLET: Nothing but to show you how a king may go a progress through
the guts of a beggar.
KING CLAUDIUS: Where is Polonius?
HAMLET: In heaven. Send thither to see. If your messenger find him not
there, seek him i' th' other place yourself. But indeed, if you
find him not within this month, you shall nose him as you go up
the stair, into the lobby.
KING CLAUDIUS: Go seek him there.
To Attendants.
HAMLET: He will stay till you come.
Exeunt Attendants.
KING CLAUDIUS: Hamlet, this deed, for thine especial safety,-
Which we do tender as we dearly grieve
For that which thou hast done,- must send thee hence
With fiery quickness. Therefore prepare thyself.
The bark is ready and the wind at help,
Th' associates tend, and everything is bent
For England.
HAMLET: For England?
KING CLAUDIUS: Ay, Hamlet.
HAMLET: Good.
KING CLAUDIUS: So is it, if thou knew'st our purposes.
HAMLET: I see a cherub that sees them. But come, for England!
Farewell, dear mother.
KING CLAUDIUS: Thy loving father, Hamlet.
HAMLET: My mother! Father and mother is man and wife; man and wife is one flesh; and so, my
mother. Come, for England!
Exit.

KING CLAUDIUS: Follow him at foot; tempt him with speed aboard.
Delay it not; I'll have him hence to-night.
Away! for everything is seal'd and done
That else leans on th' affair. Pray you make haste.
Exeunt Rosencrantz and Guildenstern
And, England, if my love thou hold'st at aught,-
As my great power thereof may give thee sense,
Since yet thy cicatrice looks raw and red
After the Danish sword, and thy free awe
Pays homage to us,- thou mayst not coldly set
Our sovereign process, which imports at full,
By letters congruing to that effect,
The present death of Hamlet. Do it, England;
For like the hectic in my blood he rages,
And thou must cure me. Till I know 'tis done,
Howe'er my haps, my joys were ne'er begun.
Exit.

ACT IV. SCENE IV. Near Elsinore.

Enter Fortinbras with His Army over the Stage.
FORTINBRAS: Go, Captain, from me greet the Danish king.
Tell him that by his license Fortinbras
Craves the conveyance of a promis'd march
Over his kingdom. You know the rendezvous.
if that his Majesty would aught with us,
We shall express our duty in his eye;
And let him know so.
CAPTAIN: I will do't, my lord.
FORTINBRAS: Go softly on.
Exeunt All but the Captain.
Enter Hamlet, Rosencrantz, Guildenstern, and Others.
HAMLET: Good sir, whose powers are these?
CAPTAIN: They are of Norway, sir.
HAMLET: How purpos'd, sir, I pray you?
CAPTAIN: Against some part of Poland.
HAMLET: Who commands them, sir?
CAPTAIN: The nephew to old Norway, Fortinbras.
HAMLET: Goes it against the main of Poland, sir,
Or for some frontier?
CAPTAIN: Truly to speak, and with no addition,
We go to gain a little patch of ground
That hath in it no profit but the name.
To pay five ducats, five, I would not farm it;
Nor will it yield to Norway or the Pole
A ranker rate, should it be sold in fee.
HAMLET: Why, then the Polack never will defend it.
CAPTAIN: Yes, it is already garrison'd.
HAMLET: Two thousand souls and twenty thousand ducats
Will not debate the question of this straw.
This is th' imposthume of much wealth and peace,
That inward breaks, and shows no cause without
Why the man dies.- I humbly thank you, sir.
CAPTAIN: God b' wi' you, sir.
Exit.

ROSENCRANTZ: Will't please you go, my lord?
HAMLET: I'll be with you straight. Go a little before.
Exeunt all but Hamlet.
How all occasions do inform against me
And spur my dull revenge! What is a man,
If his chief good and market of his time
Be but to sleep and feed? A beast, no more.
Sure he that made us with such large discourse,
Looking before and after, gave us not
That capability and godlike reason
To fust in us unus'd. Now, whether it be
Bestial oblivion, or some craven scruple
Of thinking too precisely on th' event,-
A thought which, quarter'd, hath but one part wisdom
And ever three parts coward,- I do not know
Why yet I live to say 'This thing's to do,'
Sith I have cause, and will, and strength, and means
To do't. Examples gross as earth exhort me.
Witness this army of such mass and charge,
Led by a delicate and tender prince,
Whose spirit, with divine ambition puff'd,
Makes mouths at the invisible event,
Exposing what is mortal and unsure
To all that fortune, death, and danger dare,
Even for an eggshell. Rightly to be great
Is not to stir without great argument,
But greatly to find quarrel in a straw
When honour's at the stake. How stand I then,
That have a father klll'd, a mother stain'd,
Excitements of my reason and my blood,
And let all sleep, while to my shame I see
The imminent death of twenty thousand men
That for a fantasy and trick of fame
Go to their graves like beds, fight for a plot
Whereon the numbers cannot try the cause,
Which is not tomb enough and continent
To hide the slain? O, from this time forth,
My thoughts be bloody, or be nothing worth!
Exit.

ACT IV. SCENE V. Elsinore. A Room in the Castle.

Enter Horatio, Queen, and a Gentleman.
QUEEN GETRUDE: I will not speak with her.
GENTLEMEN: She is importunate, indeed distract.
Her mood will needs be pitied.
QUEEN GETRUDE: What would she have?
GENTLEMEN: She speaks much of her father; says she hears
There's tricks i' th' world, and hems, and beats her heart;
Spurns enviously at straws; speaks things in doubt,
That carry but half sense. Her speech is nothing,
Yet the unshaped use of it doth move
The hearers to collection; they aim at it,
And botch the words up fit to their own thoughts;
Which, as her winks and nods and gestures yield them,

Indeed would make one think there might be thought,
Though nothing sure, yet much unhappily.
HORATIO: 'Twere good she were spoken with; for she may strew
Dangerous conjectures in ill-breeding minds.
QUEEN GETRUDE: Let her come in.
Exit Gentleman.
Aside To my sick soul (as sin's true nature is)
Each toy seems Prologue to some great amiss.
So full of artless jealousy is guilt
It spills itself in fearing to be spilt.
Enter Ophelia Distracted.
OPHELIA: Where is the beauteous Majesty of Denmark?
QUEEN GETRUDE: How now, Ophelia?
OPHELIA: (sings)
How should I your true-love know
From another one?
By his cockle bat and' staff
And his sandal shoon.
QUEEN GETRUDE: Alas, sweet lady, what imports this song?
OPHELIA: Say you? Nay, pray You mark.
(Sings) He is dead and gone, lady,
He is dead and gone;
At his head a grass-green turf,
At his heels a stone.
O, ho!
QUEEN GETRUDE: Nay, but Ophelia-
OPHELIA: Pray you mark.
Sings White his shroud as the mountain snow-
Enter King.
QUEEN GETRUDE: Alas, look here, my lord!
OPHELIA: (Sings)
Larded all with sweet flowers;
Which bewept to the grave did not go
With true-love showers.
KING CLAUDIUS: How do you, pretty lady?
OPHELIA: Well, God dild you! They say the owl was a baker's daughter. Lord, we know what we are, but know not what we may be. God be at your table!
KING CLAUDIUS: Conceit upon her father.
OPHELIA: Pray let's have no words of this; but when they ask, you what it means, say you this:
Sings To-morrow is Saint Valentine's day,
All in the morning bedtime,
And I a maid at your window,
To be your Valentine.
Then up he rose and donn'd his clo'es
And dupp'd the chamber door,
Let in the maid, that out a maid
Never departed more.
KING CLAUDIUS: Pretty Ophelia!
OPHELIA: Indeed, la, without an oath, I'll make an end on't!
Sings By Gis and by Saint Charity,
Alack, and fie for shame!

Young men will do't if they come to't
By Cock, they are to blame.
Quoth she, 'Before you tumbled me,
You promis'd me to wed.'
He answers:
'So would I 'a' done, by yonder sun,
An thou hadst not come to my bed.'
KING CLAUDIUS: How long hath she been thus?
OPHELIA: I hope all will be well. We must be patient; but I cannot choose but weep to think they would lay him i' th' cold ground. My brother shall know of it; and so I thank you for your good counsel. Come, my coach! Good night, ladies. Good night, sweet ladies. Good night, good night.
Exit
KING CLAUDIUS: Follow her close; give her good watch, I pray you.
Exit Horatio.
O, this is the poison of deep grief; it springs
All from her father's death. O Gertrude, Gertrude,
When sorrows come, they come not single spies.
But in battalions! First, her father slain;
Next, Your son gone, and he most violent author
Of his own just remove; the people muddied,
Thick and and unwholesome in their thoughts and whispers
For good Polonius' death, and we have done but greenly
In hugger-mugger to inter him; Poor Ophelia
Divided from herself and her fair-judgment,
Without the which we are Pictures or mere beasts;
Last, and as such containing as all these,
Her brother is in secret come from France;
And wants not buzzers to infect his ear
Feeds on his wonder, keep, himself in clouds,
With pestilent speeches of his father's death,
Wherein necessity, of matter beggar'd,
Will nothing stick Our person to arraign
In ear and ear. O my dear Gertrude, this,
Like to a murd'ring piece, in many places
Give, me superfluous death. A noise within.
QUEEN GETRUDE: Alack, what noise is this?
KING CLAUDIUS: Where are my Switzers? Let them guard the door.
Enter a Messenger.
What is the matter?
MESSENGER: Save Yourself, my lord:
The ocean, overpeering of his list,
Eats not the flats with more impetuous haste
Than Young Laertes, in a riotous head,
O'erbears Your offices. The rabble call him lord;
And, as the world were now but to begin,
Antiquity forgot, custom not known,
The ratifiers and props of every word,
They cry 'Choose we! Laertes shall be king!'
Caps, hands, and tongues applaud it to the clouds,
'Laertes shall be king! Laertes king!'
A Noise Within.

QUEEN GETRUDE: How cheerfully on the false trail they cry!
O, this is counter, you false Danish dogs!
KING CLAUDIUS: The doors are broke.
Enter Laertes with Others.
LAERTES: Where is this king?- Sirs, staid you all without.
ALL: No, let's come in!
LAERTES: I pray you give me leave.
ALL: We will, we will!
LAERTES: I thank you. Keep the door.
Exeunt his Followers.
O thou vile king,
Give me my father!
QUEEN GETRUDE: Calmly, good Laertes.
LAERTES: That drop of blood that's calm proclaims me bastard;
Cries cuckold to my father; brands the harlot
Even here between the chaste unsmirched brows
Of my true mother.
KING CLAUDIUS: What is the cause, Laertes,
That thy rebellion looks so giantlike?
Let him go, Gertrude. Do not fear our person.
There's such divinity doth hedge a king
That treason can but peep to what it would,
Acts little of his will. Tell me, Laertes,
Why thou art thus incens'd. Let him go, Gertrude.
Speak, man.
LAERTES: Where is my father?
KING CLAUDIUS: Dead.
QUEEN GETRUDE: But not by him!
KING CLAUDIUS: Let him demand his fill.
LAERTES: How came he dead? I'll not be juggled with:
To hell, allegiance! vows, to the blackest devil
Conscience and grace, to the profoundest pit!
I dare damnation. To this point I stand,
That both the world, I give to negligence,
Let come what comes; only I'll be reveng'd
Most throughly for my father.
KING CLAUDIUS: Who shall stay you?
LAERTES: My will, not all the world!
And for my means, I'll husband them so well
They shall go far with little.
KING CLAUDIUS: Good Laertes,
If you desire to know the certainty
Of your dear father's death, is't writ in Your revenge
That swoopstake you will draw both friend and foe,
Winner and loser?
LAERTES: None but his enemies.
KING CLAUDIUS: Will you know them then?
LAERTES: To his good friends thus wide I'll ope my arms
And, like the kind life-rend'ring pelican,
Repast them with my blood.
KING CLAUDIUS: Why, now You speak
Like a good child and a true gentleman.
That I am guiltless of your father's death,

And am most sensibly in grief for it,
It shall as level to your judgment pierce
As day does to your eye.
A Noise Within:
'Let her come in.'
LAERTES: How now? What noise is that?
Enter Ophelia.
O heat, dry up my brains! Tears seven times salt
Burn out the sense and virtue of mine eye!
By heaven, thy madness shall be paid by weight
Till our scale turn the beam. O rose of May!
Dear maid, kind sister, sweet Ophelia!
O heavens! is't possible a young maid's wits
Should be as mortal as an old man's life?
Nature is fine in love, and where 'tis fine,
It sends some precious instance of itself
After the thing it loves.
OPHELIA: (sings)
They bore him barefac'd on the bier
(Hey non nony, nony, hey nony)
And in his grave rain'd many a tear.
Fare you well, my dove!
LAERTES: Hadst thou thy wits, and didst persuade revenge,
It could not move thus.
OPHELIA: You must sing 'A-down a-down, and you call him a-down-a.' O, how the wheel becomes it! It is the false steward, that stole his master's daughter.
LAERTES: This nothing's more than matter.
OPHELIA: There's rosemary, that's for remembrance. Pray you, love, remember. And there is pansies, that's for thoughts.
LAERTES: A document in madness! Thoughts and remembrance fitted.
OPHELIA: There's fennel for you, and columbines. There's rue for you, and here's some for me. We may call it herb of grace o' Sundays. O, you must wear your rue with a difference! There's a daisy. I would give you some violets, but they wither'd all when my father died. They say he made a good end.
Sings For bonny sweet Robin is all my joy.
LAERTES: Thought and affliction, passion, hell itself,
She turns to favour and to prettiness.
OPHELIA: (sings)
And will he not come again?
And will he not come again?
No, no, he is dead;
Go to thy deathbed;
He never will come again.
His beard was as white as snow,
All flaxen was his poll.
He is gone, he is gone,
And we cast away moan.
God 'a'mercy on his soul!
And of all Christian souls, I pray God. God b' wi', you.
Exit.
LAERTES: Do you see this, O God?
KING CLAUDIUS: Laertes, I must commune with your grief,

Or you deny me right. Go but apart,
Make choice of whom your wisest friends you will,
And they shall hear and judge 'twixt you and me.
If by direct or by collateral hand
They find us touch'd, we will our kingdom give,
Our crown, our life, and all that we call ours,
To you in satisfaction; but if not,
Be you content to lend your patience to us,
And we shall jointly labour with your soul
To give it due content.
LAERTES: Let this be so.
His means of death, his obscure funeral-
No trophy, sword, nor hatchment o'er his bones,
No noble rite nor formal ostentation,-
Cry to be heard, as 'twere from heaven to earth,
That I must call't in question.
KING CLAUDIUS: So you shall;
And where th' offence is let the great axe fall.
I pray you go with me.
Exeunt

ACT IV. SCENE VI. Elsinore. Another Room in the Castle.

Enter Horatio with an Attendant.
HORATIO: What are they that would speak with me?
SERVANT: Seafaring men, sir. They say they have letters for you.
HORATIO: Let them come in.
Exit Attendant.
I do not know from what part of the world
I should be greeted, if not from Lord Hamlet.
Enter Sailors.
SAILOR: God bless you, sir.
HORATIO: Let him bless thee too.
SAILOR: 'A shall, sir, an't please him. There's a letter for you, sir,- it comes from th' ambassador that was bound for England- if your name be Horatio, as I am let to know it is.
HORATIO: (reads the letter) 'Horatio, when thou shalt have overlook'd this, give these fellows some means to the King. They have letters for him. Ere we were two days old at sea, a pirate of very warlike appointment gave us chase. Finding ourselves too slow of sail, we put on a compelled valour, and in the grapple I boarded them. On the instant they got clear of our ship; so I alone became their prisoner. They have dealt with me like thieves of mercy; but they knew what they did: I am to do a good turn for them. Let the King have the letters I have sent, and repair thou to me with as much speed as thou wouldst fly death. I have words to speak in thine ear will make thee dumb; yet are they much too light for the bore of the matter. These good fellows will bring thee where I am. Rosencrantz and Guildenstern hold their course for England. Of them I have much to tell thee. Farewell.
'He that thou knowest thine, Hamlet.'
Come, I will give you way for these your letters,
And do't the speedier that you may direct me
To him from whom you brought them.
Exeunt.

ACT IV. SCENE VII. Elsinore. Another Room in the Castle.

Enter King and Laertes.
KING CLAUDIUS: Now must your conscience my acquittance seal,
And You must put me in your heart for friend,
Sith you have heard, and with a knowing ear,
That he which hath your noble father slain
Pursued my life.
LAERTES: It well appears. But tell me
Why you proceeded not against these feats
So crimeful and so capital in nature,
As by your safety, wisdom, all things else,
You mainly were stirr'd up.
KING CLAUDIUS: O, for two special reasons,
Which may to you, perhaps, seein much unsinew'd,
But yet to me they are strong. The Queen his mother
Lives almost by his looks; and for myself,-
My virtue or my plague, be it either which,-
She's so conjunctive to my life and soul
That, as the star moves not but in his sphere,
I could not but by her. The other motive
Why to a public count I might not go
Is the great love the general gender bear him,
Who, dipping all his faults in their affection,
Would, like the spring that turneth wood to stone,
Convert his gives to graces; so that my arrows,
Too slightly timber'd for so loud a wind,
Would have reverted to my bow again,
And not where I had aim'd them.
LAERTES: And so have I a noble father lost;
A sister driven into desp'rate terms,
Whose worth, if praises may go back again,
Stood challenger on mount of all the age
For her perfections. But my revenge will come.
KING CLAUDIUS: Break not your sleeps for that. You must not think
That we are made of stuff so flat and dull
That we can let our beard be shook with danger,
And think it pastime. You shortly shall hear more.
I lov'd your father, and we love ourself,
And that, I hope, will teach you to imagine-
Enter a Messenger with Letters.
How now? What news?
MESSENGER: Letters, my lord, from Hamlet:
This to your Majesty; this to the Queen.
KING CLAUDIUS: From Hamlet? Who brought them?
MESSENGER: Sailors, my lord, they say; I saw them not.
They were given me by Claudio; he receiv'd them
Of him that brought them.
KING CLAUDIUS: Laertes, you shall hear them.
Leave us.
Exit Messenger.
Reads'High and Mighty,-You shall know I am set naked on your
kingdom. To-morrow shall I beg leave to see your kingly eyes;
when I shall (first asking your pardon thereunto) recount the

occasion of my sudden and more strange return.
'Hamlet.'
What should this mean? Are all the rest come back?
Or is it some abuse, and no such thing?
LAERTES: Know you the hand?
KING CLAUDIUS: 'Tis Hamlet's character. 'Naked!'
And in a postscript here, he says 'alone.'
Can you advise me?
LAERTES: I am lost in it, my lord. But let him come!
It warms the very sickness in my heart
That I shall live and tell him to his teeth,
'Thus didest thou.'
KING CLAUDIUS: If it be so, Laertes
(As how should it be so? how otherwise?),
Will you be rul'd by me?
LAERTES: Ay my lord,
So you will not o'errule me to a peace.
KING CLAUDIUS: To thine own peace. If he be now return'd
As checking at his voyage, and that he means
No more to undertake it, I will work him
To exploit now ripe in my device,
Under the which he shall not choose but fall;
And for his death no wind
But even his mother shall uncharge the practice
And call it accident.
LAERTES: My lord, I will be rul'd;
The rather, if you could devise it so
That I might be the organ.
KING CLAUDIUS: It falls right.
You have been talk'd of since your travel much,
And that in Hamlet's hearing, for a quality
Wherein they say you shine, Your sun of parts
Did not together pluck such envy from him
As did that one; and that, in my regard,
Of the unworthiest siege.
LAERTES: What part is that, my lord?
KING CLAUDIUS: A very riband in the cap of youth-
Yet needfull too; for youth no less becomes
The light and careless livery that it wears
Thin settled age his sables and his weeds,
Importing health and graveness. Two months since
Here was a gentleman of Normandy.
I have seen myself, and serv'd against, the French,
And they can well on horseback; but this gallant
Had witchcraft in't. He grew unto his seat,
And to such wondrous doing brought his horse
As had he been incorps'd and demi-natur'd
With the brave beast. So far he topp'd my thought
That I, in forgery of shapes and tricks,
Come short of what he did.
LAERTES: A Norman was't?
KING CLAUDIUS: A Norman.
LAERTES: Upon my life, Lamound.

KING CLAUDIUS: The very same.
LAERTES: I know him well. He is the broach indeed
And gem of all the nation.
KING CLAUDIUS: He made confession of you;
And gave you such a masterly report
For art and exercise in your defence,
And for your rapier most especially,
That he cried out 'twould be a sight indeed
If one could match you. The scrimers of their nation
He swore had neither motion, guard, nor eye,
If you oppos'd them. Sir, this report of his
Did Hamlet so envenom with his envy
That he could nothing do but wish and beg
Your sudden coming o'er to play with you.
Now, out of this-
LAERTES: What out of this, my lord?
KING CLAUDIUS: Laertes, was your father dear to you?
Or are you like the painting of a sorrow,
A face without a heart,'
LAERTES: Why ask you this?
KING CLAUDIUS: Not that I think you did not love your father;
But that I know love is begun by time,
And that I see, in passages of proof,
Time qualifies the spark and fire of it.
There lives within the very flame of love
A kind of wick or snuff that will abate it;
And nothing is at a like goodness still;
For goodness, growing to a plurisy,
Dies in his own too-much. That we would do,
We should do when we would; for this 'would' changes,
And hath abatements and delays as many
As there are tongues, are hands, are accidents;
And then this 'should' is like a spendthrift sigh,
That hurts by easing. But to the quick o' th' ulcer!
Hamlet comes back. What would you undertake
To show yourself your father's son in deed
More than in words?
LAERTES: To cut his throat i' th' church!
KING CLAUDIUS: No place indeed should murther sanctuarize;
Revenge should have no bounds. But, good Laertes,
Will you do this? Keep close within your chamber.
Will return'd shall know you are come home.
We'll put on those shall praise your excellence
And set a double varnish on the fame
The Frenchman gave you; bring you in fine together
And wager on your heads. He, being remiss,
Most generous, and free from all contriving,
Will not peruse the foils; so that with ease,
Or with a little shuffling, you may choose
A sword unbated, and, in a pass of practice,
Requite him for your father.
LAERTES: I will do't!
And for that purpose I'll anoint my sword.

I bought an unction of a mountebank,
So mortal that, but dip a knife in it,
Where it draws blood no cataplasm so rare,
Collected from all simples that have virtue
Under the moon, can save the thing from death
This is but scratch'd withal. I'll touch my point
With this contagion, that, if I gall him slightly,
It may be death.
KING CLAUDIUS: Let's further think of this,
Weigh what convenience both of time and means
May fit us to our shape. If this should fall,
And that our drift look through our bad performance.
'Twere better not assay'd. Therefore this project
Should have a back or second, that might hold
If this did blast in proof. Soft! let me see.
We'll make a solemn wager on your cunnings-
I ha't! When in your motion you are hot and dry-
As make your bouts more violent to that end-
And that he calls for drink, I'll have prepar'd him
A chalice for the nonce; whereon but sipping,
If he by chance escape your venom'd stuck,
Our purpose may hold there.- But stay, what noise,
Enter Queen.
How now, sweet queen?
QUEEN GETRUDE: One woe doth tread upon another's heel,
So fast they follow. Your sister's drown'd, Laertes.
LAERTES: Drown'd! O, where?
QUEEN GETRUDE: There is a willow grows aslant a brook,
That shows his hoar leaves in the glassy stream.
There with fantastic garlands did she come
Of crowflowers, nettles, daisies, and long purples,
That liberal shepherds give a grosser name,
But our cold maids do dead men's fingers call them.
There on the pendant boughs her coronet weeds
Clamb'ring to hang, an envious sliver broke,
When down her weedy trophies and herself
Fell in the weeping brook. Her clothes spread wide
And, mermaid-like, awhile they bore her up;
Which time she chaunted snatches of old tunes,
As one incapable of her own distress,
Or like a creature native and indued
Unto that element; but long it could not be
Till that her garments, heavy with their drink,
Pull'd the poor wretch from her melodious lay
To muddy death.
LAERTES: Alas, then she is drown'd?
QUEEN GETRUDE: Drown'd, drown'd.
LAERTES: Too much of water hast thou, poor Ophelia,
And therefore I forbid my tears; but yet
It is our trick; nature her custom holds,
Let shame say what it will. When these are gone,
The woman will be out. Adieu, my lord.
I have a speech of fire, that fain would blaze

But that this folly douts it.
Exit.
KING CLAUDIUS: Let's follow, Gertrude.
How much I had to do to calm his rage I
Now fear I this will give it start again;
Therefore let's follow.
Exeunt.

ACT V. SCENE I. Elsinore. A Churchyard.

Enter Two Clowns, With Spades and Pickaxes.
FIRST CLOWN: Is she to be buried in Christian burial when she wilfully seeks her own salvation?
SECOND CLOWN: I tell thee she is; therefore make her grave straight. The crowner hath sate on her, and finds it Christian burial.
FIRST CLOWN: How can that be, unless she drown'd herself in her own defence?
SECOND CLOWN: Why, 'tis found so.
FIRST CLOWN: It must be se offendendo; it cannot be else. For here lies the point: if I drown myself wittingly, it argues an act; and an act hath three branches-it is to act, to do, and to perform; argal, she drown'd herself wittingly.
SECOND CLOWN: Nay, but hear you, Goodman Delver!
FIRST CLOWN: Give me leave. Here lies the water; good. Here stands the man; good. If the man go to this water and drown himself, it is, will he nill he, he goes- mark you that. But if the water come to him and drown him, he drowns not himself. Argal, he that is not guilty of his own death shortens not his own life.
SECOND CLOWN: But is this law?
FIRST CLOWN: Ay, marry, is't- crowner's quest law.
SECOND CLOWN: Will you ha' the truth an't? If this had not been a gentlewoman, she should have been buried out o' Christian burial.
FIRST CLOWN: Why, there thou say'st! And the more pity that great folk should have count'nance in this world to drown or hang themselves more than their even-Christen. Come, my spade! There is no ancient gentlemen but gard'ners, ditchers, and grave-makers. They hold up Adam's profession.
SECOND CLOWN: Was he a gentleman?
FIRST CLOWN:: 'A was the first that ever bore arms.
SECOND CLOWN: Why, he had none.
FIRST CLOWN:: What, art a heathen? How dost thou understand the Scripture?
The Scripture says Adam digg'd. Could he dig without arms? I'll put another question to thee. If thou answerest me not to the purpose, confess thyself-
SECOND CLOWN: Go to!
FIRST CLOWN:: What is he that builds stronger than either the mason, the shipwright, or the carpenter?
SECOND CLOWN: The gallows-maker; for that frame outlives a thousand tenants.
FIRST CLOWN:: I like thy wit well, in good faith. The gallows does well. But how does it well? It does well to those that do ill. Now, thou dost ill to say the gallows is built stronger than the church. Argal, the gallows may do well to thee. To't again, come!
SECOND CLOWN: Who builds stronger than a mason, a shipwright, or a

carpenter?
FIRST CLOWN:: Ay, tell me that, and unyoke.
SECOND CLOWN: Marry, now I can tell!
FIRST CLOWN:: To't.
SECOND CLOWN: Mass, I cannot tell.
Enter Hamlet and Horatio Afar Off.
FIRST CLOWN:: Cudgel thy brains no more about it, for your dull ass will not mend his pace with beating; and when you are ask'd this question next, say 'a grave-maker.' The houses he makes lasts till doomsday. Go, get thee to Yaughan; fetch me a stoup of liquor.
Exit Second Clown.
Clown Digs And Sings.

In youth when I did love, did love,
Methought it was very sweet;
To contract- O- the time for- a- my behove,
O, methought there- a- was nothing- a- meet.

HAMLET: Has this fellow no feeling of his business, that he sings at grave-making?
HORATIO: Custom hath made it in him a Property of easiness.
HAMLET: 'Tis e'en so. The hand of little employment hath the daintier sense.
FIRST CLOWN:: (sings)

But age with his stealing steps
Hath clawed me in his clutch,
And hath shipped me intil the land,
As if I had never been such.

Throws up a Skull.
HAMLET: That skull had a tongue in it, and could sing once. How the knave jowls it to the ground,as if 'twere Cain's jawbone, that did the first murther! This might be the pate of a Politician, which this ass now o'erreaches; one that would circumvent God, might it not?
HORATIO: It might, my lord.
HAMLET: Or of a courtier, which could say 'Good morrow, sweet lord! How dost thou, good lord?' This might be my Lord Such-a-one, that prais'd my Lord Such-a-one's horse when he meant to beg it- might it not?
HORATIO: Ay, my lord.
HAMLET: Why, e'en so! and now my Lady Worm's, chapless, and knock'd about the mazzard with a sexton's spade. Here's fine revolution, and we had the trick to see't. Did these bones cost no more the breeding but to play at loggets with 'em? Mine ache to think on't.
FIRST CLOWN:: (Sings)

A pickaxe and a spade, a spade,
For and a shrouding sheet;
O, a Pit of clay for to be made
For such a guest is meet.

Throws up Another Skull.
HAMLET: There's another. Why may not that be the skull of a lawyer? Where be his quiddits now, his quillets, his cases, his tenures, and his tricks? Why does he suffer this rude knave now to knock

him about the sconce with a dirty shovel, and will not tell him of his action of battery? Hum! This fellow might be in's time a great buyer of land, with his statutes, his recognizances, his fines, his double vouchers, his recoveries. Is this the fine of his fines, and the recovery of his recoveries, to have his fine pate full of fine dirt? Will his vouchers vouch him no more of his purchases, and double ones too, than the length and breadth of a pair of indentures? The very conveyances of his lands will scarcely lie in this box; and must th' inheritor himself have no more, ha?

HORATIO: Not a jot more, my lord.

HAMLET: Is not parchment made of sheepskins?

HORATIO: Ay, my lord, And of calveskins too.

HAMLET: They are sheep and calves which seek out assurance in that. I will speak to this fellow. Whose grave's this, sirrah?

FIRST CLOWN: Mine, sir.

Sings O, a pit of clay for to be made
For such a guest is meet.

HAMLET: I think it be thine indeed, for thou liest in't.

FIRST CLOWN: You lie out on't, sir, and therefore 'tis not yours. For my part, I do not lie in't, yet it is mine.

HAMLET: Thou dost lie in't, to be in't and say it is thine. 'Tis for the dead, not for the quick; therefore thou liest.

FIRST CLOWN: 'Tis a quick lie, sir; 'twill away again from me to you.

HAMLET: What man dost thou dig it for?

FIRST CLOWN: For no man, sir.

HAMLET: What woman then?

FIRST CLOWN: For none neither.

HAMLET: Who is to be buried in't?

FIRST CLOWN: One that was a woman, sir; but, rest her soul, she's dead.

HAMLET: How absolute the knave is! We must speak by the card, or equivocation will undo us. By the Lord, Horatio, this three years I have taken note of it, the age is grown so picked that the toe of the peasant comes so near the heel of the courtier he galls his kibe.- How long hast thou been a grave-maker?

FIRST CLOWN:: Of all the days i' th' year, I came to't that day that our last king Hamlet overcame Fortinbras.

HAMLET: How long is that since?

FIRST CLOWN: Cannot you tell that? Every fool can tell that. It was the very day that young Hamlet was born- he that is mad, and sent into England.

HAMLET: Ay, marry, why was be sent into England?

FIRST CLOWN:: Why, because 'a was mad. 'A shall recover his wits there; or, if 'a do not, 'tis no great matter there.

HAMLET: Why?

FIRST CLOWN: 'Twill not he seen in him there. There the men are as mad as he.

HAMLET: How came he mad?

FIRST CLOWN: Very strangely, they say.

HAMLET: How strangely?

FIRST CLOWN:: Faith, e'en with losing his wits.

HAMLET: Upon what ground?

FIRST CLOWN:: Why, here in Denmark. I have been sexton here, man and boy thirty years.

HAMLET: How long will a man lie i' th' earth ere he rot?
FIRST CLOWN:: Faith, if 'a be not rotten before 'a die (as we have many pocky corses now-a-days that will scarce hold the laying in, I will last you some eight year or nine year. A tanner will last you nine year.
HAMLET: Why he more than another?
FIRST CLOWN:: Why, sir, his hide is so tann'd with his trade that 'a will keep out water a great while; and your water is a sore decayer of your whoreson dead body. Here's a skull now. This skull hath lien you i' th' earth three-and-twenty years.
HAMLET: Whose was it?
FIRST CLOWN:: A whoreson, mad fellow's it was.
Whose do you think it was?
HAMLET: Nay, I know not.
FIRST CLOWN: A pestilence on him for a mad rogue!
'A pour'd a flagon of
Rhenish on my head once. This same skull, sir, was Yorick's skull, the King's jester.
HAMLET: This?
FIRST CLOWN:: E'en that.
HAMLET: Let me see.
Takes the Skull.
Alas, poor Yorick! I knew him,
Horatio. A fellow of infinite jest, of most excellent fancy. He hath borne me on his back a thousand tunes. And now how abhorred in my imagination it is! My gorge rises at it. Here hung those lips that I have kiss'd I know not how oft. Where be your gibes now? your gambols? your songs? your flashes of merriment that were wont to set the table on a roar? Not one now, to mock your own grinning? Quite chap- fall'n? Now get you to my lady's chamber, and tell her, let her paint an inch thick, to this favour she must come. Make her laugh at that. Prithee, Horatio, tell me one thing.
HORATIO: What's that, my lord?
HAMLET: Dost thou think Alexander look'd o' this fashion i' th' earth?
HORATIO: E'en so.
HAMLET: And smelt so? Pah!
Puts down the Skull.
HORATIO: E'en so, my lord.
HAMLET: To what base uses we may return, Horatio!
Why may not imagination trace the noble dust of
Alexander till he find it stopping a bunghole?
HORATIO: 'Twere to consider too curiously, to consider so.
HAMLET: No, faith, not a jot; but to follow him thither with modesty enough, and likelihood to lead it; as thus: Alexander died, Alexander was buried, Alexander returneth into dust; the dust is earth; of earth we make loam; and why of that loam (whereto he was converted) might they not stop a beer barrel?
Imperious Caesar, dead and turn'd to clay,
Might stop a hole to keep the wind away.
O, that that earth which kept the world in awe
Should patch a wall t' expel the winter's flaw!
But soft! but soft! aside! Here comes the King-

Enter priests with a coffin in funeral procession, King, Queen, Laertes, with Lords attendant.

The Queen, the courtiers. Who is this they follow?
And with such maimed rites? This doth betoken
The corse they follow did with desp'rate hand
Fordo it own life. 'Twas of some estate.
Couch we awhile, and mark.

Retires with Horatio.

LAERTES: What ceremony else?
HAMLET: That is Laertes,
A very noble youth. Mark.
LAERTES: What ceremony else?
PRIEST: Her obsequies have been as far enlarg'd
As we have warranty. Her death was doubtful;
And, but that great command o'ersways the order,
She should in ground unsanctified have lodg'd
Till the last trumpet. For charitable prayers,
Shards, flints, and pebbles should be thrown on her.
Yet here she is allow'd her virgin crants,
Her maiden strewments, and the bringing home
Of bell and burial.
LAERTES: Must there no more be done?
PRIEST: No more be done.
We should profane the service of the dead
To sing a requiem and such rest to her
As to peace-parted souls.
LAERTES: Lay her i' th' earth;
And from her fair and unpolluted flesh
May violets spring! I tell thee, churlish priest,
A minist'ring angel shall my sister be
When thou liest howling.
HAMLET: What, the fair Ophelia?
QUEEN GETRUDE: Sweets to the sweet! Farewell.

Scatters Flowers.

I hop'd thou shouldst have been my Hamlet's wife;
I thought thy bride-bed to have deck'd, sweet maid,
And not have strew'd thy grave.
LAERTES: O, treble woe
Fall ten times treble on that cursed head
Whose wicked deed thy most ingenious sense
Depriv'd thee of! Hold off the earth awhile,
Till I have caught her once more in mine arms.

Leaps in the Grave.

Now pile your dust upon the quick and dead
Till of this flat a mountain you have made
T' o'ertop old Pelion or the skyish head
Of blue Olympus.
HAMLET: Comes Forward What is he whose grief
Bears such an emphasis? whose phrase of sorrow
Conjures the wand'ring stars, and makes them stand
Like wonder-wounded hearers? This is I,
Hamlet the Dane.

Leaps in after Laertes.

LAERTES: The devil take thy soul!
Grapples with Him.
HAMLET: Thou pray'st not well.
I prithee take thy fingers from my throat;
For, though I am not splenitive and rash,
Yet have I in me something dangerous,
Which let thy wisdom fear. Hold off thy hand!
KING CLAUDIUS: Pluck thein asunder.
QUEEN GETRUDE: Hamlet, Hamlet!
ALL: Gentlemen!
HORATIO: Good my lord, be quiet.
The Attendants Part Them, and They Come out of the Grave.
HAMLET: Why, I will fight with him upon this theme
Until my eyelids will no longer wag.
QUEEN GETRUDE: O my son, what theme?
HAMLET: I lov'd Ophelia. Forty thousand brothers
Could not (with all their quantity of love)
Make up my sum. What wilt thou do for her?
KING CLAUDIUS: O, he is mad, Laertes.
QUEEN GETRUDE: For love of God, forbear him!
HAMLET: 'Swounds, show me what thou't do.
Woo't weep? woo't fight? woo't fast? woo't tear thyself?
Woo't drink up esill? eat a crocodile?
I'll do't. Dost thou come here to whine?
To outface me with leaping in her grave?
Be buried quick with her, and so will I.
And if thou prate of mountains, let them throw
Millions of acres on us, till our ground,
Singeing his pate against the burning zone,
Make Ossa like a wart! Nay, an thou'lt mouth,
I'll rant as well as thou.
QUEEN GETRUDE: This is mere madness;
And thus a while the fit will work on him.
Anon, as patient as the female dove
When that her golden couplets are disclos'd,
His silence will sit drooping.
HAMLET: Hear you, sir!
What is the reason that you use me thus?
I lov'd you ever. But it is no matter.
Let Hercules himself do what he may,
The cat will mew, and dog will have his day.
Exit.
KING CLAUDIUS: I pray thee, good Horatio, wait upon him.
Exit Horatio.
To Laertes Strengthen your patience in our last night's speech.
We'll put the matter to the present push.-
Good Gertrude, set some watch over your son.-
This grave shall have a living monument.
An hour of quiet shortly shall we see;
Till then in patience our proceeding be.
Exeunt.

ACT V. SCENE II. Elsinore. A Hall in the Castle.

Enter Hamlet and Horatio.

HAMLET: So much for this, sir; now shall you see the other.
You do remember all the circumstance?
HORATIO: Remember it, my lord!
HAMLET: Sir, in my heart there was a kind of fighting
That would not let me sleep. Methought I lay
Worse than the mutinies in the bilboes. Rashly-
And prais'd be rashness for it; let us know,
Our indiscretion sometime serves us well
When our deep plots do pall; and that should learn us
There's a divinity that shapes our ends,
Rough-hew them how we will-
HORATIO: That is most certain.
HAMLET: Up from my cabin,
My sea-gown scarf'd about me, in the dark
Grop'd I to find out them; had my desire,
Finger'd their packet, and in fine withdrew
To mine own room again; making so bold
(My fears forgetting manners) to unseal
Their grand commission; where I found, Horatio
(O royal knavery!), an exact command,
Larded with many several sorts of reasons,
Importing Denmark's health, and England's too,
With, hoo! such bugs and goblins in my life-
That, on the supervise, no leisure bated,
No, not to stay the finding of the axe,
My head should be struck off.
HORATIO: Is't possible?
HAMLET: Here's the commission; read it at more leisure.
But wilt thou bear me how I did proceed?
HORATIO: I beseech you.
HAMLET: Being thus benetted round with villanies,
Or I could make a prologue to my brains,
They had begun the play. I sat me down;
Devis'd a new commission; wrote it fair.
I once did hold it, as our statists do,
A baseness to write fair, and labour'd much
How to forget that learning; but, sir, now
It did me yeoman's service. Wilt thou know
Th' effect of what I wrote?
HORATIO: Ay, good my lord.
HAMLET: An earnest conjuration from the King,
As England was his faithful tributary,
As love between them like the palm might flourish,
As peace should still her wheaten garland wear
And stand a comma 'tween their amities,
And many such-like as's of great charge,
That, on the view and knowing of these contents,
Without debatement further, more or less,
He should the bearers put to sudden death,
Not shriving time allow'd.
HORATIO: How was this seal'd?

HAMLET: Why, even in that was heaven ordinant.
I had my father's signet in my purse,
which was the model of that Danish seal;
Folded the writ up in the form of th' other,
Subscrib'd it, gave't th' impression, plac'd it safely,
The changeling never known. Now, the next day
Was our sea-fight; and what to this was sequent
Thou know'st already.
HORATIO: So Guildenstern and Rosencrantz go to't.
HAMLET: Why, man, they did make love to this employment!
They are not near my conscience; their defeat
Does by their own insinuation grow.
'Tis dangerous when the baser nature comes
Between the pass and fell incensed points
Of mighty opposites.
HORATIO: Why, what a king is this!
HAMLET: Does it not, thinks't thee, stand me now upon-
He that hath kill'd my king, and whor'd my mother;
Popp'd in between th' election and my hopes;
Thrown out his angle for my Proper life,
And with such coz'nage- is't not perfect conscience
To quit him with this arm? And is't not to be damn'd
To let this canker of our nature come
In further evil?
HORATIO: It must be shortly known to him from England
What is the issue of the business there.
HAMLET: It will be short; the interim is mine,
And a man's life is no more than to say 'one.'
But I am very sorry, good Horatio,
That to Laertes I forgot myself,
For by the image of my cause I see
The portraiture of his. I'll court his favours.
But sure the bravery of his grief did put me
Into a tow'ring passion.
HORATIO: Peace! Who comes here?
Enter Young Osric, a Courtier.
OSRIC: Your lordship is right welcome back to Denmark.
HAMLET: I humbly thank you, sir. Aside to Horatio Dost know this waterfly?
HORATIO: Aside to Hamlet No, my good lord.
HAMLET: Aside to Horatio Thy state is the more gracious; for 'tis a vice to know him. He hath much land, and fertile. Let a beast be lord of beasts, and his crib shall stand at the king's messenger 'Tis a chough; but, as I say, spacious in the possession of dirt.
OSRIC: Sweet lord, if your lordship were at leisure, I should impart a thing to you from his Majesty.
HAMLET: I will receive it, sir, with all diligence of spirit. Put your bonnet to his right use. 'Tis for the head.
OSRIC: I thank your lordship, it is very hot.
HAMLET: No, believe me, 'tis very cold; the wind is northerly.
OSRIC: It is indifferent cold, my lord, indeed.
HAMLET: But yet methinks it is very sultry and hot for my complexion.
OSRIC: Exceedingly, my lord; it is very sultry, as 'twere- I cannot

tell how. But, my lord, his Majesty bade me signify to you that he has laid a great wager on your head. Sir, this is the matter-

HAMLET: I beseech you remember.

Hamlet Moves Him to Put on His Hat.

OSRIC: Nay, good my lord; for mine ease, in good faith. Sir, here is newly come to court Laertes; believe me, an absolute gentleman, full of most excellent differences, of very soft society and great showing. Indeed, to speak feelingly of him, he is the card or calendar of gentry; for you shall find in him the continent of what part a gentleman would see.

HAMLET: Sir, his definement suffers no perdition in you; though, I know, to divide him inventorially would dozy th' arithmetic of memory, and yet but yaw neither in respect of his quick sail. But, in the verity of extolment, I take him to be a soul of great article, and his infusion of such dearth and rareness as, to make true diction of him, his semblable is his mirror, and who else would trace him, his umbrage, nothing more.

OSRIC: Your lordship speaks most infallibly of him.

HAMLET: The concernancy, sir? Why do we wrap the gentleman in our more rawer breath

OSRIC: Sir? Aside to Hamlet Is't not possible to understand in another tongue? You will do't, sir, really.

HAMLET: What imports the nomination of this gentleman

OSRIC: Of Laertes?

HORATIO: Aside His purse is empty already. All's golden words are spent.

HAMLET: Of him, sir.

OSRIC: I know you are not ignorant-

HAMLET: I would you did, sir; yet, in faith, if you did, it would not much approve me. Well, sir?

OSRIC: You are not ignorant of what excellence Laertes is-

HAMLET: I dare not confess that, lest I should compare with him in excellence; but to know a man well were to know himself.

OSRIC: I mean, sir, for his weapon; but in the imputation laid on him by them, in his meed he's unfellowed.

HAMLET: What's his weapon?

OSRIC: Rapier and dagger.

HAMLET: That's two of his weapons- but well.

OSRIC: The King, sir, hath wager'd with him six Barbary horses; against the which he has impon'd, as I take it, six French rapiers and poniards, with their assigns, as girdle, hangers, and so. Three of the carriages, in faith, are very dear to fancy, very responsive to the hilts, most delicate carriages, and of very liberal conceit.

HAMLET: What call you the carriages?

HORATIO: Aside to Hamlet I knew you must be edified by the margent ere you had done.

OSRIC: The carriages, sir, are the hangers.

HAMLET: The phrase would be more germane to the matter if we could carry cannon by our sides. I would it might be hangers till then. But on! Six Barbary horses against six French swords, their assigns, and three liberal-conceited carriages: that's the French bet against the Danish. Why is this all impon'd, as you call it?

OSRIC: The King, sir, hath laid that, in a dozen passes between yourself and him, he shall not exceed you three hits; he hath laid on twelve for nine, and it would come to immediate trial if your lordship would vouchsafe the answer.

HAMLET: How if I answer no?

OSRIC: I mean, my lord, the opposition of your person in trial.

HAMLET: Sir, I will walk here in the hall. If it please his Majesty, it is the breathing time of day with me. Let the foils be brought, the gentleman willing, and the King hold his purpose, I will win for him if I can; if not, I will gain nothing but my shame and the odd hits.

OSRIC: Shall I redeliver you e'en so?

HAMLET: To this effect, sir, after what flourish your nature will.

OSRIC: I commend my duty to your lordship.

HAMLET: Yours, yours.

Exit Osric.

He does well to commend it himself; there are no tongues else for's turn.

HORATIO: This lapwing runs away with the shell on his head.

HAMLET: He did comply with his dug before he suck'd it. Thus has he, and many more of the same bevy that I know the drossy age dotes on, only got the tune of the time and outward habit of encounter-a kind of yesty collection, which carries them through and through the most fann'd and winnowed opinions; and do but blow them to their trial-the bubbles are out,

Enter a Lord.

LORD: My lord, his Majesty commended him to you by young Osric, who brings back to him, that you attend him in the hall. He sends to know if your pleasure hold to play with Laertes, or that you will take longer time.

HAMLET: I am constant to my purposes; they follow the King's pleasure. If his fitness speaks, mine is ready; now or whensoever, provided I be so able as now.

LORD: The King and Queen and all are coming down.

HAMLET: In happy time.

LORD: The Queen desires you to use some gentle entertainment to Laertes before you fall to play.

HAMLET: She well instructs me.

Exit Lord.

HORATIO: You will lose this wager, my lord.

HAMLET: I do not think so. Since he went into France I have been in continual practice. I shall win at the odds. But thou wouldst not think how ill all's here about my heart. But it is no matter.

HORATIO: Nay, good my lord -

HAMLET: It is but foolery; but it is such a kind of gaingiving as would perhaps trouble a woman.

HORATIO: If your mind dislike anything, obey it. I will forestall their repair hither and say you are not fit.

HAMLET: Not a whit, we defy augury; there's a special providence in the fall of a sparrow. If it be now, 'tis not to come', if it be not to come, it will be now; if it be not now, yet it will come: the readiness is all. Since no man knows aught of what he leaves, what is't to leave betimes? Let be.

Enter King, Queen, Laertes, Osric, and Lords, with other Attendants with foils and gauntlets. A table and flagons of wine on it.

KING CLAUDIUS: Come, Hamlet, come, and take this hand from me.
The King Puts Laertes' Hand into Hamlet's.
HAMLET: Give me your pardon, sir. I have done you wrong;
But pardon't, as you are a gentleman.
This presence knows,
And you must needs have heard, how I am punish'd
With sore distraction. What I have done
That might your nature, honour, and exception
Roughly awake, I here proclaim was madness.
Was't Hamlet wrong'd Laertes? Never Hamlet.
If Hamlet from himself be taken away,
And when he's not himself does wrong Laertes,
Then Hamlet does it not, Hamlet denies it.
Who does it, then? His madness. If't be so,
Hamlet is of the faction that is wrong'd;
His madness is poor Hamlet's enemy.
Sir, in this audience,
Let my disclaiming from a purpos'd evil
Free me so far in your most generous thoughts
That I have shot my arrow o'er the house
And hurt my brother.
LAERTES: I am satisfied in nature,
Whose motive in this case should stir me most
To my revenge. But in my terms of honour
I stand aloof, and will no reconcilement
Till by some elder masters of known honour
I have a voice and precedent of peace
To keep my name ungor'd. But till that time
I do receive your offer'd love like love,
And will not wrong it.
HAMLET: I embrace it freely,
And will this brother's wager frankly play.
Give us the foils. Come on.
LAERTES: Come, one for me.
HAMLET: I'll be your foil, Laertes. In mine ignorance
Your skill shall, like a star i' th' darkest night,
Stick fiery off indeed.
LAERTES: You mock me, sir.
HAMLET: No, by this bad.
KING CLAUDIUS: Give them the foils, young Osric. Cousin Hamlet,
You know the wager?
HAMLET: Very well, my lord.
Your Grace has laid the odds o' th' weaker side.
KING CLAUDIUS: I do not fear it, I have seen you both;
But since he is better'd, we have therefore odds.
LAERTES: This is too heavy; let me see another.
HAMLET: This likes me well. These foils have all a length?
Prepare to Play.
OSRIC: Ay, my good lord.
KING CLAUDIUS: Set me the stoups of wine upon that table.
If Hamlet give the first or second hit,
Or quit in answer of the third exchange,
Let all the battlements their ordnance fire;

The King shall drink to Hamlet's better breath,
And in the cup an union shall he throw
Richer than that which four successive kings
In Denmark's crown have worn. Give me the cups;
And let the kettle to the trumpet speak,
The trumpet to the cannoneer without,
The cannons to the heavens, the heaven to earth,
'Now the King drinks to Hamlet.' Come, begin.
And you the judges, bear a wary eye.
HAMLET: Come on, sir.
LAERTES: Come, my lord. They play.
HAMLET: One.
LAERTES: No.
HAMLET: Judgment!
OSRIC: A hit, a very palpable hit.
LAERTES: Well, again!
KING CLAUDIUS: Stay, give me drink. Hamlet, this pearl is thine;
Here's to thy health.
Drum; Trumpets Sound; a Piece Goes off Within.
Give him the cup.
HAMLET: I'll play this bout first; set it by awhile.
Come. (They play.) Another hit. What say you?
LAERTES: A touch, a touch; I do confess't.
KING CLAUDIUS: Our son shall win.
QUEEN GETRUDE: He's fat, and scant of breath.
Here, Hamlet, take my napkin, rub thy brows.
The Queen carouses to thy fortune, Hamlet.
HAMLET: Good madam!
KING CLAUDIUS: Gertrude, do not drink.
QUEEN GETRUDE: I will, my lord; I pray you pardon me. Drinks.
KING CLAUDIUS: Aside It is the poison'd cup; it is too late.
HAMLET: I dare not drink yet, madam; by-and-by.
QUEEN GETRUDE: Come, let me wipe thy face.
LAERTES: My lord, I'll hit him now.
KING CLAUDIUS: I do not think't.
LAERTES: Aside And yet it is almost against my conscience.
HAMLET: Come for the third, Laertes! You but dally.
pray You Pass with your best violence;
I am afeard You make a wanton of me.
LAERTES: Say you so? Come on. Play.
OSRIC: Nothing neither way.
LAERTES: Have at you now!
Laertes Wounds Hamlet; Then in Scuffling, They Change Rapiers, And Hamlet Wounds Laertes.
KING CLAUDIUS: Part them! They are incens'd.
HAMLET: Nay come! again! The Queen falls.
OSRIC: Look to the Queen there, ho!
HORATIO: They bleed on both sides. How is it, my lord?
OSRIC: How is't, Laertes?
LAERTES: Why, as a woodcock to mine own springe, Osric.
I am justly kill'd with mine own treachery.
HAMLET: How does the Queen?
KING CLAUDIUS: She sounds to see them bleed.
QUEEN GETRUDE: No, no! the drink, the drink! O my dear Hamlet!

The drink, the drink! I am poison'd.
Dies.
HAMLET: O villany! Ho! let the door be lock'd.
Treachery! Seek it out.
Laertes Falls.
LAERTES: It is here, Hamlet. Hamlet, thou art slain;
No medicine in the world can do thee good.
In thee there is not half an hour of life.
The treacherous instrument is in thy hand,
Unbated and envenom'd. The foul practice
Hath turn'd itself on me. Lo, here I lie,
Never to rise again. Thy mother's poison'd.
I can no more. The King, the King's to blame.
HAMLET: The point envenom'd too?
Then, venom, to thy work. Hurts the King.
ALL: Treason! treason!
KING CLAUDIUS: O, yet defend me, friends! I am but hurt.
HAMLET: Here, thou incestuous, murd'rous, damned Dane,
Drink off this potion! Is thy union here?
Follow my mother. King dies.
LAERTES: He is justly serv'd.
It is a poison temper'd by himself.
Exchange forgiveness with me, noble Hamlet.
Mine and my father's death come not upon thee,
Nor thine on me! Dies.
HAMLET: Heaven make thee free of it! I follow thee.
I am dead, Horatio. Wretched queen, adieu!
You that look pale and tremble at this chance,
That are but mutes or audience to this act,
Had I but time (as this fell sergeant, Death,
Is strict in his arrest) O, I could tell you-
But let it be. Horatio, I am dead;
Thou liv'st; report me and my cause aright
To the unsatisfied.
HORATIO: Never believe it.
I am more an antique Roman than a Dane.
Here's yet some liquor left.
HAMLET: As th'art a man,
Give me the cup. Let go! By heaven, I'll ha't.
O good Horatio, what a wounded name
(Things standing thus unknown) shall live behind me!
If thou didst ever hold me in thy heart,
Absent thee from felicity awhile,
And in this harsh world draw thy breath in pain,
To tell my story.
March Afar Off, and Shot Within.
What warlike noise is this?
OSRIC: Young Fortinbras, with conquest come from Poland,
To the ambassadors of England gives
This warlike volley.
HAMLET: O, I die, Horatio!
The potent poison quite o'ercrows my spirit.
I cannot live to hear the news from England,

But I do prophesy th' election lights
On Fortinbras. He has my dying voice.
So tell him, with th' occurrents, more and less,
Which have solicited- the rest is silence. Dies.
HORATIO: Now cracks a noble heart.
Good night, sweet prince,
And flights of angels sing thee to thy rest!
March Within.
Why does the drum come hither?
Enter Fortinbras and English Ambassadors, with Drum, Colours, and Attendants.
FORTINBRAS: Where is this sight?
HORATIO: What is it you will see?
If aught of woe or wonder, cease your search.
FORTINBRAS: This quarry cries on havoc. O proud Death,
What feast is toward in thine eternal cell
That thou so many princes at a shot
So bloodily hast struck.
AMBASSADOR: The sight is dismal;
And our affairs from England come too late.
The ears are senseless that should give us bearing
To tell him his commandment is fulfill'd
That Rosencrantz and Guildenstern are dead.
Where should We have our thanks?
HORATIO: Not from his mouth,
Had it th' ability of life to thank you.
He never gave commandment for their death.
But since, so jump upon this bloody question,
You from the Polack wars, and you from England,
Are here arriv'd, give order that these bodies
High on a stage be placed to the view;
And let me speak to the yet unknowing world
How these things came about. So shall You hear
Of carnal, bloody and unnatural acts;
Of accidental judgments, casual slaughters;
Of deaths put on by cunning and forc'd cause;
And, in this upshot, purposes mistook
Fall'n on th' inventors' heads. All this can I
Truly deliver.
FORTINBRAS: Let us haste to hear it,
And call the noblest to the audience.
For me, with sorrow I embrace my fortune.
I have some rights of memory in this kingdom
Which now, to claim my vantage doth invite me.
HORATIO: Of that I shall have also cause to speak,
And from his mouth whose voice will draw on more.
But let this same be presently perform'd,
Even while men's minds are wild, lest more mischance
On plots and errors happen.
FORTINBRAS: Let four captains
Bear Hamlet like a soldier to the stage;
For he was likely, had he been put on,
To have prov'd most royally; and for his passage
The soldiers' music and the rites of war

Speak loudly for him.
Take up the bodies. Such a sight as this
Becomes the field but here shows much amiss.
Go, bid the soldiers shoot.

Exeunt Marching; after the Which a Peal of Ordnance Are Shot Off.

END

The History of Troilus and Cressida

Dramatis Personae

PRIAM, King of Troy
His sons:
HECTOR
TROILUS
PARIS
DEIPHOBUS
HELENUS
MARGARELON, a bastard son of Priam
Trojan commanders:
AENEAS
ANTENOR
CALCHAS, a Trojan priest, taking part with the Greeks
PANDARUS, uncle to Cressida
AGAMEMNON, the Greek general
MENELAUS, his brother
Greek commanders:
ACHILLES
AJAX
ULYSSES
NESTOR
DIOMEDES
PATROCLUS
THERSITES, a deformed and scurrilous Greek
ALEXANDER, servant to Cressida
SERVANT to Troilus
SERVANT to Paris
SERVANT to Diomedes
HELEN, wife to Menelaus
ANDROMACHE, wife to Hector
CASSANDRA, daughter to Priam, a prophetess
CRESSIDA, daughter to Calchas
Trojan and Greek Soldiers, and Attendants

SCENE: Troy and the Greek camp before it

PROLOGUE

In Troy, there lies the scene. From isles of Greece
The princes orgillous, their high blood chaf'd,
Have to the port of Athens sent their ships
Fraught with the ministers and instruments
Of cruel war. Sixty and nine that wore
Their crownets regal from th' Athenian bay
Put forth toward Phrygia; and their vow is made
To ransack Troy, within whose strong immures
The ravish'd Helen, Menelaus' queen,
With wanton Paris sleeps-and that's the quarrel.
To Tenedos they come,
And the deep-drawing barks do there disgorge
Their war-like fraughtage. Now on Dardan plains
The fresh and yet unbruised Greeks do pitch
Their brave pavilions: Priam's six-gated city,

Dardan, and Tymbria, Helias, Chetas, Troien,
And Antenorides, with massy staples
And corresponsive and fulfilling bolts,
Sperr up the sons of Troy.
Now expectation, tickling skittish spirits
On one and other side, Troyan and Greek,
Sets all on hazard-and hither am I come
A Prologue arm'd, but not in confidence
Of author's pen or actor's voice, but suited
In like conditions as our argument,
To tell you, fair beholders, that our play
Leaps o'er the vaunt and firstlings of those broils,
Beginning in the middle; starting thence away,
To what may be digested in a play.
Like or find fault; do as your pleasures are;
Now good or bad, 'tis but the chance of war.

ACT I. SCENE I. Troy. Before Priam's Palace

Enter Troilus Armed, and Pandarus

TROILUS: Call here my varlet; I'll unarm again.
Why should I war without the walls of Troy
That find such cruel battle here within?
Each Troyan that is master of his heart,
Let him to field; Troilus, alas, hath none!
PANDARUS: Will this gear ne'er be mended?
TROILUS: The Greeks are strong, and skilful to their strength,
Fierce to their skill, and to their fierceness valiant;
But I am weaker than a woman's tear,
Tamer than sleep, fonder than ignorance,
Less valiant than the virgin in the night,
And skilless as unpractis'd infancy.
PANDARUS: Well, I have told you enough of this; for my part, I'll not meddle nor make no farther. He that will have a cake out of the wheat must needs tarry the grinding.
TROILUS: Have I not tarried?
PANDARUS: Ay, the grinding; but you must tarry the bolting.
TROILUS: Have I not tarried?
PANDARUS: Ay, the bolting; but you must tarry the leavening.
TROILUS: Still have I tarried.
PANDARUS: Ay, to the leavening; but here's yet in the word 'hereafter' the kneading, the making of the cake, the heating of the oven, and the baking; nay, you must stay the cooling too, or you may chance to burn your lips.
TROILUS: Patience herself, what goddess e'er she be,
Doth lesser blench at suff'rance than I do.
At Priam's royal table do I sit;
And when fair Cressid comes into my thoughts-
So, traitor, then she comes when she is thence.
PANDARUS: Well, she look'd yesternight fairer than ever I saw her look, or any woman else.
TROILUS: I was about to tell thee: when my heart,
As wedged with a sigh, would rive in twain,
Lest Hector or my father should perceive me,
I have, as when the sun doth light a storm,

Buried this sigh in wrinkle of a smile.
But sorrow that is couch'd in seeming gladness
Is like that mirth fate turns to sudden sadness.
PANDARUS: An her hair were not somewhat darker than Helen's- well, go to- there were no more comparison between the women. But, for my part, she is my kinswoman; I would not, as they term it, praise her, but I would somebody had heard her talk yesterday, as I did. I will not dispraise your sister Cassandra's wit; but-
TROILUS: O Pandarus! I tell thee, Pandarus-
When I do tell thee there my hopes lie drown'd,
Reply not in how many fathoms deep
They lie indrench'd. I tell thee I am mad
In Cressid's love. Thou answer'st 'She is fair'-
Pourest in the open ulcer of my heart-
Her eyes, her hair, her cheek, her gait, her voice,
Handlest in thy discourse. O, that her hand,
In whose comparison all whites are ink
Writing their own reproach; to whose soft seizure
The cygnet's down is harsh, and spirit of sense
Hard as the palm of ploughman! This thou tell'st me,
As true thou tell'st me, when I say I love her;
But, saying thus, instead of oil and balm,
Thou lay'st in every gash that love hath given me
The knife that made it.
PANDARUS: I speak no more than truth.
TROILUS: Thou dost not speak so much.
PANDARUS: Faith, I'll not meddle in it. Let her be as she is: if she be fair, 'tis the better for her; an she be not, she has the mends in her own hands.
TROILUS: Good Pandarus! How now, Pandarus!
PANDARUS: I have had my labour for my travail, ill thought on of her and ill thought on of you; gone between and between, but small thanks for my labour.
TROILUS: What, art thou angry, Pandarus? What, with me?
PANDARUS: Because she's kin to me, therefore she's not so fair as Helen. An she were not kin to me, she would be as fair a Friday as Helen is on Sunday. But what care I? I care not an she were a blackamoor; 'tis all one to me.
TROILUS: Say I she is not fair?
PANDARUS: I do not care whether you do or no. She's a fool to stay behind her father. Let her to the Greeks; and so I'll tell her the next time I see her. For my part, I'll meddle nor make no more i' th' matter.
TROILUS: Pandarus!
PANDARUS: Not I.
TROILUS: Sweet Pandarus!
PANDARUS: Pray you, speak no more to me: I will leave all as I found it, and there an end.
Exit. Sound alarum
TROILUS: Peace, you ungracious clamours! Peace, rude sounds!
Fools on both sides! Helen must needs be fair,
When with your blood you daily paint her thus.
I cannot fight upon this argument;

It is too starv'd a subject for my sword.
But Pandarus-O gods, how do you plague me!
I cannot come to Cressid but by Pandar;
And he's as tetchy to be woo'd to woo
As she is stubborn-chaste against all suit.
Tell me, Apollo, for thy Daphne's love,
What Cressid is, what Pandar, and what we?
Her bed is India; there she lies, a pearl;
Between our Ilium and where she resides
Let it be call'd the wild and wand'ring flood;
Ourself the merchant, and this sailing Pandar
Our doubtful hope, our convoy, and our bark.
Alarum. Enter Aeneas
AENEAS: How now, Prince Troilus! Wherefore not afield?
TROILUS: Because not there. This woman's answer sorts,
For womanish it is to be from thence.
What news, Aeneas, from the field to-day?
AENEAS: That Paris is returned home, and hurt.
TROILUS: By whom, Aeneas?
AENEAS: Troilus, by Menelaus.
TROILUS: Let Paris bleed: 'tis but a scar to scorn;
Paris is gor'd with Menelaus' horn.
Alarum
AENEAS: Hark what good sport is out of town to-day!
TROILUS: Better at home, if 'would I might' were 'may.'
But to the sport abroad. Are you bound thither?
AENEAS: In all swift haste.
TROILUS: Come, go we then together.
Exeunt

ACT I. SCENE II. Troy. A Street

Enter Cressida and Her Man Alexander
CRESSIDA: Who were those went by?
ALEXANDER: Queen Hecuba and Helen.
CRESSIDA: And whither go they?
ALEXANDER: Up to the eastern tower,
Whose height commands as subject all the vale,
To see the battle. Hector, whose patience
Is as a virtue fix'd, to-day was mov'd.
He chid Andromache, and struck his armourer;
And, like as there were husbandry in war,
Before the sun rose he was harness'd light,
And to the field goes he; where every flower
Did as a prophet weep what it foresaw
In Hector's wrath.
CRESSIDA: What was his cause of anger?
ALEXANDER: The noise goes, this: there is among the Greeks
A lord of Troyan blood, nephew to Hector;
They call him Ajax.
CRESSIDA: Good; and what of him?
ALEXANDER: They say he is a very man per se,
And stands alone.
CRESSIDA: So do all men, unless they are drunk, sick, or have no legs.

ALEXANDER: This man, lady, hath robb'd many beasts of their particular additions: he is as valiant as a lion, churlish as the bear, slow as the elephant-a man into whom nature hath so crowded humours that his valour is crush'd into folly, his folly sauced with discretion. There is no man hath a virtue that he hath not a glimpse of, nor any man an attaint but he carries some stain of it; he is melancholy without cause and merry against the hair; he hath the joints of every thing; but everything so out of joint that he is a gouty Briareus, many hands and no use, or purblind Argus, all eyes and no sight.
CRESSIDA: But how should this man, that makes me smile, make Hector angry?
ALEXANDER: They say he yesterday cop'd Hector in the battle and struck him down, the disdain and shame whereof hath ever since kept Hector fasting and waking.
Enter Pandarus
CRESSIDA: Who comes here?
ALEXANDER: Madam, your uncle Pandarus.
CRESSIDA: Hector's a gallant man.
ALEXANDER: As may be in the world, lady.
PANDARUS: What's that? What's that?
CRESSIDA: Good morrow, uncle Pandarus.
PANDARUS: Good morrow, cousin Cressid. What do you talk of?- Good morrow, Alexander.-How do you, cousin? When were you at Ilium?
CRESSIDA: This morning, uncle.
PANDARUS: What were you talking of when I came? Was Hector arm'd and gone ere you came to Ilium? Helen was not up, was she?
CRESSIDA: Hector was gone; but Helen was not up.
PANDARUS: E'en so. Hector was stirring early.
CRESSIDA: That were we talking of, and of his anger.
PANDARUS: Was he angry?
CRESSIDA: So he says here.
PANDARUS: True, he was so; I know the cause too; he'll lay about him today, I can tell them that. And there's Troilus will not come far behind him; let them take heed of Troilus, I can tell them that too.
CRESSIDA: What, is he angry too?
PANDARUS: Who, Troilus? Troilus is the better man of the two.
CRESSIDA: O Jupiter! there's no comparison.
PANDARUS: What, not between Troilus and Hector? Do you know a man if you see him?
CRESSIDA: Ay, if I ever saw him before and knew him.
PANDARUS: Well, I say Troilus is Troilus.
CRESSIDA: Then you say as I say, for I am sure he is not Hector.
PANDARUS: No, nor Hector is not Troilus in some degrees.
CRESSIDA: 'Tis just to each of them: he is himself.
PANDARUS: Himself! Alas, poor Troilus! I would he were!
CRESSIDA: So he is.
PANDARUS: Condition I had gone barefoot to India.
CRESSIDA: He is not Hector.
PANDARUS: Himself! no, he's not himself. Would 'a were himself! Well, the gods are above; time must friend or end. Well, Troilus, well! I would my heart were in her body! No, Hector is not a

better man than Troilus.
CRESSIDA: Excuse me.
PANDARUS: He is elder.
CRESSIDA: Pardon me, pardon me.
PANDARUS: Th' other's not come to't; you shall tell me another tale when th' other's come to't. Hector shall not have his wit this year.
CRESSIDA: He shall not need it if he have his own.
PANDARUS: Nor his qualities.
CRESSIDA: No matter.
PANDARUS: Nor his beauty.
CRESSIDA: 'Twould not become him: his own's better.
PANDARUS: YOU have no judgment, niece. Helen herself swore th' other day that Troilus, for a brown favour, for so 'tis, I must confess- not brown neither-
CRESSIDA: No, but brown.
PANDARUS: Faith, to say truth, brown and not brown.
CRESSIDA: To say the truth, true and not true.
PANDARUS: She prais'd his complexion above Paris.
CRESSIDA: Why, Paris hath colour enough.
PANDARUS: So he has.
CRESSIDA: Then Troilus should have too much. If she prais'd him above, his complexion is higher than his; he having colour enough, and the other higher, is too flaming praise for a good complexion. I had as lief Helen's golden tongue had commended Troilus for a copper nose.
PANDARUS: I swear to you I think Helen loves him better than Paris.
CRESSIDA: Then she's a merry Greek indeed.
PANDARUS: Nay, I am sure she does. She came to him th' other day into the compass'd window-and you know he has not past three or four hairs on his chin-
CRESSIDA: Indeed a tapster's arithmetic may soon bring his particulars therein to a total.
PANDARUS: Why, he is very young, and yet will he within three pound lift as much as his brother Hector.
CRESSIDA: Is he so young a man and so old a lifter?
PANDARUS: But to prove to you that Helen loves him: she came and puts me her white hand to his cloven chin-
CRESSIDA: Juno have mercy! How came it cloven?
PANDARUS: Why, you know, 'tis dimpled. I think his smiling becomes him better than any man in all Phrygia.
CRESSIDA: O, he smiles valiantly!
PANDARUS: Does he not?
CRESSIDA: O yes, an 'twere a cloud in autumn!
PANDARUS: Why, go to, then! But to prove to you that Helen loves Troilus-
CRESSIDA: Troilus will stand to the proof, if you'll prove it so.
PANDARUS: Troilus! Why, he esteems her no more than I esteem an addle egg.
CRESSIDA: If you love an addle egg as well as you love an idle head, you would eat chickens i' th' shell.
PANDARUS: I cannot choose but laugh to think how she tickled his chin. Indeed, she has a marvell's white hand, I must needs confess.

CRESSIDA: Without the rack.
PANDARUS: And she takes upon her to spy a white hair on his chin.
CRESSIDA: Alas, poor chin! Many a wart is richer.
PANDARUS: But there was such laughing! Queen Hecuba laugh'd that her eyes ran o'er.
CRESSIDA: With millstones.
PANDARUS: And Cassandra laugh'd.
CRESSIDA: But there was a more temperate fire under the pot of her eyes. Did her eyes run o'er too?
PANDARUS: And Hector laugh'd.
CRESSIDA: At what was all this laughing?
PANDARUS: Marry, at the white hair that Helen spied on Troilus' chin.
CRESSIDA: An't had been a green hair I should have laugh'd too.
PANDARUS: They laugh'd not so much at the hair as at his pretty answer.
CRESSIDA: What was his answer?
PANDARUS: Quoth she 'Here's but two and fifty hairs on your chin, and one of them is white.'
CRESSIDA: This is her question.
PANDARUS: That's true; make no question of that. 'Two and fifty hairs,' quoth he 'and one white. That white hair is my father, and all the rest are his sons.' 'Jupiter!' quoth she 'which of these hairs is Paris my husband?' 'The forked one,' quoth he, 'pluck't out and give it him.' But there was such laughing! and Helen so blush'd, and Paris so chaf'd; and all the rest so laugh'd that it pass'd.
CRESSIDA: So let it now; for it has been a great while going by.
PANDARUS: Well, cousin, I told you a thing yesterday; think on't.
CRESSIDA: So I do.
PANDARUS: I'll be sworn 'tis true; he will weep you, and 'twere a man born in April.
CRESSIDA: And I'll spring up in his tears, an 'twere a nettle against May.

Sound a Retreat

PANDARUS: Hark! they are coming from the field. Shall we stand up here and see them as they pass toward Ilium? Good niece, do, sweet niece Cressida.
CRESSIDA: At your pleasure.
PANDARUS: Here, here, here's an excellent place; here we may see most bravely. I'll tell you them all by their names as they pass by; but mark Troilus above the rest.

Aeneas Passes

CRESSIDA: Speak not so loud.
PANDARUS: That's Aeneas. Is not that a brave man? He's one of the flowers of Troy, I can tell you. But mark Troilus; you shall see anon.

Antenor Passes

CRESSIDA: Who's that?
PANDARUS: That's Antenor. He has a shrewd wit, I can tell you; and he's a man good enough; he's one o' th' soundest judgments in Troy, whosoever, and a proper man of person. When comes Troilus? I'll show you Troilus anon. If he see me, you shall see him nod at me.

CRESSIDA: Will he give you the nod?
PANDARUS: You shall see.
CRESSIDA: If he do, the rich shall have more.

Hector Passes

PANDARUS: That's Hector, that, that, look you, that; there's a fellow! Go thy way, Hector! There's a brave man, niece. O brave Hector! Look how he looks. There's a countenance! Is't not a brave man?
CRESSIDA: O, a brave man!
PANDARUS: Is 'a not? It does a man's heart good. Look you what hacks are on his helmet! Look you yonder, do you see? Look you there. There's no jesting; there's laying on; take't off who will, as they say. There be hacks.
CRESSIDA: Be those with swords?
PANDARUS: Swords! anything, he cares not; an the devil come to him, it's all one. By God's lid, it does one's heart good. Yonder comes Paris, yonder comes Paris.

Paris Passes

Look ye yonder, niece; is't not a gallant man too, is't not? Why, this is brave now. Who said he came hurt home to-day? He's not hurt. Why, this will do Helen's heart good now, ha! Would I could see Troilus now! You shall see Troilus anon.

Helenus Passes

CRESSIDA: Who's that?
PANDARUS: That's Helenus. I marvel where Troilus is. That's Helenus. I think he went not forth to-day. That's Helenus.
CRESSIDA: Can Helenus fight, uncle?
PANDARUS: Helenus! no. Yes, he'll fight indifferent well. I marvel where Troilus is. Hark! do you not hear the people cry 'Troilus'? Helenus is a priest.
CRESSIDA: What sneaking fellow comes yonder?

Troilus Passes

PANDARUS: Where? yonder? That's Deiphobus. 'Tis Troilus. There's a man, niece. Hem! Brave Troilus, the prince of chivalry!
CRESSIDA: Peace, for shame, peace!
PANDARUS: Mark him; note him. O brave Troilus! Look well upon him, niece; look you how his sword is bloodied, and his helm more hack'd than Hector's; and how he looks, and how he goes! O admirable youth! he never saw three and twenty. Go thy way, Troilus, go thy way. Had I a sister were a grace or a daughter a goddess, he should take his choice. O admirable man! Paris? Paris is dirt to him; and, I warrant, Helen, to change, would give an eye to boot.
CRESSIDA: Here comes more.

Common Soldiers Pass

PANDARUS: Asses, fools, dolts! chaff and bran, chaff and bran! porridge after meat! I could live and die in the eyes of Troilus. Ne'er look, ne'er look; the eagles are gone. Crows and daws, crows and daws! I had rather be such a man as Troilus than Agamemnon and all Greece.
CRESSIDA: There is amongst the Greeks Achilles, a better man than Troilus.
PANDARUS: Achilles? A drayman, a porter, a very camel!
CRESSIDA: Well, well.
PANDARUS: Well, well! Why, have you any discretion? Have you any

eyes? Do you know what a man is? Is not birth, beauty, good
shape, discourse, manhood, learning, gentleness, virtue, youth,
liberality, and such like, the spice and salt that season a man?
CRESSIDA: Ay, a minc'd man; and then to be bak'd with no date in
the pie, for then the man's date is out.
PANDARUS: You are such a woman! A man knows not at what ward you lie.
CRESSIDA: Upon my back, to defend my belly; upon my wit, to defend
my wiles; upon my secrecy, to defend mine honesty; my mask, to
defend my beauty; and you, to defend all these; and at all these
wards I lie at, at a thousand watches.
PANDARUS: Say one of your watches.
CRESSIDA: Nay, I'll watch you for that; and that's one of the
chiefest of them too. If I cannot ward what I would not have hit,
I can watch you for telling how I took the blow; unless it swell
past hiding, and then it's past watching
PANDARUS: You are such another!
Enter Troilus' Boy
BOY: Sir, my lord would instantly speak with you.
PANDARUS: Where?
BOY: At your own house; there he unarms him.
PANDARUS: Good boy, tell him I come.
Exit Boy
I doubt he be hurt. Fare ye well, good niece.
CRESSIDA: Adieu, uncle.
PANDARUS: I will be with you, niece, by and by.
CRESSIDA: To bring, uncle.
PANDARUS: Ay, a token from Troilus.
CRESSIDA: By the same token, you are a bawd.
Exit Pandarus
Words, vows, gifts, tears, and love's full sacrifice,
He offers in another's enterprise;
But more in Troilus thousand-fold I see
Than in the glass of Pandar's praise may be,
Yet hold I off. Women are angels, wooing:
Things won are done; joy's soul lies in the doing.
That she belov'd knows nought that knows not this:
Men prize the thing ungain'd more than it is.
That she was never yet that ever knew
Love got so sweet as when desire did sue;
Therefore this maxim out of love I teach:
Achievement is command; ungain'd, beseech.
Then though my heart's content firm love doth bear,
Nothing of that shall from mine eyes appear.
Exit

ACT I. SCENE III. The Grecian Camp. Before Agamemnon's Tent

Sennet. Enter Agamemnon, Nestor, Ulysses, Diomedes, Menelaus, and Others
AGAMEMNON: Princes,
What grief hath set these jaundies o'er your cheeks?
The ample proposition that hope makes
In all designs begun on earth below
Fails in the promis'd largeness; checks and disasters
Grow in the veins of actions highest rear'd,
As knots, by the conflux of meeting sap,

Infects the sound pine, and diverts his grain
Tortive and errant from his course of growth.
Nor, princes, is it matter new to us
That we come short of our suppose so far
That after seven years' siege yet Troy walls stand;
Sith every action that hath gone before,
Whereof we have record, trial did draw
Bias and thwart, not answering the aim,
And that unbodied figure of the thought
That gave't surmised shape. Why then, you princes,
Do you with cheeks abash'd behold our works
And call them shames, which are, indeed, nought else
But the protractive trials of great Jove
To find persistive constancy in men;
The fineness of which metal is not found
In fortune's love? For then the bold and coward,
The wise and fool, the artist and unread,
The hard and soft, seem all affin'd and kin.
But in the wind and tempest of her frown
Distinction, with a broad and powerful fan,
Puffing at all, winnows the light away;
And what hath mass or matter by itself
Lies rich in virtue and unmingled.
NESTOR: With due observance of thy godlike seat,
Great Agamemnon, Nestor shall apply
Thy latest words. In the reproof of chance
Lies the true proof of men. The sea being smooth,
How many shallow bauble boats dare sail
Upon her patient breast, making their way
With those of nobler bulk!
But let the ruffian Boreas once enrage
The gentle Thetis, and anon behold
The strong-ribb'd bark through liquid mountains cut,
Bounding between the two moist elements
Like Perseus' horse. Where's then the saucy boat,
Whose weak untimber'd sides but even now
Co-rivall'd greatness? Either to harbour fled
Or made a toast for Neptune. Even so
Doth valour's show and valour's worth divide
In storms of fortune; for in her ray and brightness
The herd hath more annoyance by the breeze
Than by the tiger; but when the splitting wind
Makes flexible the knees of knotted oaks,
And flies fled under shade-why, then the thing of courage
As rous'd with rage, with rage doth sympathise,
And with an accent tun'd in self-same key
Retorts to chiding fortune.
ULYSSES: Agamemnon,
Thou great commander, nerve and bone of Greece,
Heart of our numbers, soul and only spirit
In whom the tempers and the minds of all
Should be shut up-hear what Ulysses speaks.
Besides the applause and approbation

The which, To Agamemnon most mighty, for thy place and sway,
To Nestor And, thou most reverend, for thy stretch'd-out life,
I give to both your speeches- which were such
As Agamemnon and the hand of Greece
Should hold up high in brass; and such again
As venerable Nestor, hatch'd in silver,
Should with a bond of air, strong as the axle-tree
On which heaven rides, knit all the Greekish ears
To his experienc'd tongue-yet let it please both,
Thou great, and wise, to hear Ulysses speak.
AGAMEMNON: Speak, Prince of Ithaca; and be't of less expect
That matter needless, of importless burden,
Divide thy lips than we are confident,
When rank Thersites opes his mastic jaws,
We shall hear music, wit, and oracle.
ULYSSES: Troy, yet upon his basis, had been down,
And the great Hector's sword had lack'd a master,
But for these instances:
The specialty of rule hath been neglected;
And look how many Grecian tents do stand
Hollow upon this plain, so many hollow factions.
When that the general is not like the hive,
To whom the foragers shall all repair,
What honey is expected? Degree being vizarded,
Th' unworthiest shows as fairly in the mask.
The heavens themselves, the planets, and this centre,
Observe degree, priority, and place,
Insisture, course, proportion, season, form,
Office, and custom, in all line of order;
And therefore is the glorious planet Sol
In noble eminence enthron'd and spher'd
Amidst the other, whose med'cinable eye
Corrects the ill aspects of planets evil,
And posts, like the commandment of a king,
Sans check, to good and bad. But when the planets
In evil mixture to disorder wander,
What plagues and what portents, what mutiny,
What raging of the sea, shaking of earth,
Commotion in the winds! Frights, changes, horrors,
Divert and crack, rend and deracinate,
The unity and married calm of states
Quite from their fixture! O, when degree is shak'd,
Which is the ladder of all high designs,
The enterprise is sick! How could communities,
Degrees in schools, and brotherhoods in cities,
Peaceful commerce from dividable shores,
The primogenity and due of birth,
Prerogative of age, crowns, sceptres, laurels,
But by degree, stand in authentic place?
Take but degree away, untune that string,
And hark what discord follows! Each thing melts
In mere oppugnancy: the bounded waters
Should lift their bosoms higher than the shores,

And make a sop of all this solid globe;
Strength should be lord of imbecility,
And the rude son should strike his father dead;
Force should be right; or, rather, right and wrong-
Between whose endless jar justice resides-
Should lose their names, and so should justice too.
Then everything includes itself in power,
Power into will, will into appetite;
And appetite, an universal wolf,
So doubly seconded with will and power,
Must make perforce an universal prey,
And last eat up himself. Great Agamemnon,
This chaos, when degree is suffocate,
Follows the choking.
And this neglection of degree it is
That by a pace goes backward, with a purpose
It hath to climb. The general's disdain'd
By him one step below, he by the next,
That next by him beneath; so ever step,
Exampl'd by the first pace that is sick
Of his superior, grows to an envious fever
Of pale and bloodless emulation.
And 'tis this fever that keeps Troy on foot,
Not her own sinews. To end a tale of length,
Troy in our weakness stands, not in her strength.
NESTOR: Most wisely hath Ulysses here discover'd
The fever whereof all our power is sick.
AGAMEMNON: The nature of the sickness found, Ulysses,
What is the remedy?
ULYSSES: The great Achilles, whom opinion crowns
The sinew and the forehand of our host,
Having his ear full of his airy fame,
Grows dainty of his worth, and in his tent
Lies mocking our designs; with him Patroclus
Upon a lazy bed the livelong day
Breaks scurril jests;
And with ridiculous and awkward action-
Which, slanderer, he imitation calls-
He pageants us. Sometime, great Agamemnon,
Thy topless deputation he puts on;
And like a strutting player whose conceit
Lies in his hamstring, and doth think it rich
To hear the wooden dialogue and sound
'Twixt his stretch'd footing and the scaffoldage-
Such to-be-pitied and o'er-wrested seeming
He acts thy greatness in; and when he speaks
'Tis like a chime a-mending; with terms unsquar'd,
Which, from the tongue of roaring Typhon dropp'd,
Would seem hyperboles. At this fusty stuff
The large Achilles, on his press'd bed lolling,
From his deep chest laughs out a loud applause;
Cries 'Excellent! 'tis Agamemnon just.
Now play me Nestor; hem, and stroke thy beard,

As he being drest to some oration.'
That's done-as near as the extremest ends
Of parallels, as like Vulcan and his wife;
Yet god Achilles still cries 'Excellent!
'Tis Nestor right. Now play him me, Patroclus,
Arming to answer in a night alarm.'
And then, forsooth, the faint defects of age
Must be the scene of mirth: to cough and spit
And, with a palsy-fumbling on his gorget,
Shake in and out the rivet. And at this sport
Sir Valour dies; cries 'O, enough, Patroclus;
Or give me ribs of steel! I shall split all
In pleasure of my spleen.' And in this fashion
All our abilities, gifts, natures, shapes,
Severals and generals of grace exact,
Achievements, plots, orders, preventions,
Excitements to the field or speech for truce,
Success or loss, what is or is not, serves
As stuff for these two to make paradoxes.
NESTOR: And in the imitation of these twain-
Who, as Ulysses says, opinion crowns
With an imperial voice-many are infect.
Ajax is grown self-will'd and bears his head
In such a rein, in full as proud a place
As broad Achilles; keeps his tent like him;
Makes factious feasts; rails on our state of war
Bold as an oracle, and sets Thersites,
A slave whose gall coins slanders like a mint,
To match us in comparisons with dirt,
To weaken and discredit our exposure,
How rank soever rounded in with danger.
ULYSSES: They tax our policy and call it cowardice,
Count wisdom as no member of the war,
Forestall prescience, and esteem no act
But that of hand. The still and mental parts
That do contrive how many hands shall strike
When fitness calls them on, and know, by measure
Of their observant toil, the enemies' weight-
Why, this hath not a finger's dignity:
They call this bed-work, mapp'ry, closet-war;
So that the ram that batters down the wall,
For the great swinge and rudeness of his poise,
They place before his hand that made the engine,
Or those that with the fineness of their souls
By reason guide his execution.
NESTOR: Let this be granted, and Achilles' horse
Makes many Thetis' sons.
Tucket
AGAMEMNON: What trumpet? Look, Menelaus.
MENELAUS: From Troy.
Enter Aeneas
AGAMEMNON: What would you fore our tent?
AENEAS: Is this great Agamemnon's tent, I pray you?

AGAMEMNON: Even this.
AENEAS: May one that is a herald and a prince
Do a fair message to his kingly eyes?
AGAMEMNON: With surety stronger than Achilles' an
Fore all the Greekish heads, which with one voice
Call Agamemnon head and general.
AENEAS: Fair leave and large security. How may
A stranger to those most imperial looks
Know them from eyes of other mortals?
AGAMEMNON: How?
AENEAS: Ay;
I ask, that I might waken reverence,
And bid the cheek be ready with a blush
Modest as Morning when she coldly eyes
The youthful Phoebus.
Which is that god in office, guiding men?
Which is the high and mighty Agamemnon?
AGAMEMNON: This Troyan scorns us, or the men of Troy
Are ceremonious courtiers.
AENEAS: Courtiers as free, as debonair, unarm'd,
As bending angels; that's their fame in peace.
But when they would seem soldiers, they have galls,
Good arms, strong joints, true swords; and, Jove's accord,
Nothing so full of heart. But peace, Aeneas,
Peace, Troyan; lay thy finger on thy lips.
The worthiness of praise distains his worth,
If that the prais'd himself bring the praise forth;
But what the repining enemy commends,
That breath fame blows; that praise, sole pure, transcends.
AGAMEMNON: Sir, you of Troy, call you yourself Aeneas?
AENEAS: Ay, Greek, that is my name.
AGAMEMNON: What's your affair, I pray you?
AENEAS: Sir, pardon; 'tis for Agamemnon's ears.
AGAMEMNON: He hears nought privately that comes from Troy.
AENEAS: Nor I from Troy come not to whisper with him;
I bring a trumpet to awake his ear,
To set his sense on the attentive bent,
And then to speak.
AGAMEMNON: Speak frankly as the wind;
It is not Agamemnon's sleeping hour.
That thou shalt know, Troyan, he is awake,
He tells thee so himself.
AENEAS: Trumpet, blow loud,
Send thy brass voice through all these lazy tents;
And every Greek of mettle, let him know
What Troy means fairly shall be spoke aloud.
Sound Trumpet
We have, great Agamemnon, here in Troy
A prince called Hector-Priam is his father-
Who in this dull and long-continued truce
Is resty grown; he bade me take a trumpet
And to this purpose speak: Kings, princes, lords!
If there be one among the fair'st of Greece

That holds his honour higher than his ease,
That seeks his praise more than he fears his peril,
That knows his valour and knows not his fear,
That loves his mistress more than in confession
With truant vows to her own lips he loves,
And dare avow her beauty and her worth
In other arms than hers-to him this challenge.
Hector, in view of Troyans and of Greeks,
Shall make it good or do his best to do it:
He hath a lady wiser, fairer, truer,
Than ever Greek did couple in his arms;
And will to-morrow with his trumpet call
Mid-way between your tents and walls of Troy
To rouse a Grecian that is true in love.
If any come, Hector shall honour him;
If none, he'll say in Troy, when he retires,
The Grecian dames are sunburnt and not worth
The splinter of a lance. Even so much.
AGAMEMNON: This shall be told our lovers, Lord Aeneas.
If none of them have soul in such a kind,
We left them all at home. But we are soldiers;
And may that soldier a mere recreant prove
That means not, hath not, or is not in love.
If then one is, or hath, or means to be,
That one meets Hector; if none else, I am he.
NESTOR: Tell him of Nestor, one that was a man
When Hector's grandsire suck'd. He is old now;
But if there be not in our Grecian mould
One noble man that hath one spark of fire
To answer for his love, tell him from me
I'll hide my silver beard in a gold beaver,
And in my vantbrace put this wither'd brawn,
And, meeting him, will tell him that my lady
Was fairer than his grandame, and as chaste
As may be in the world. His youth in flood,
I'll prove this truth with my three drops of blood.
AENEAS: Now heavens forfend such scarcity of youth!
ULYSSES: Amen.
AGAMEMNON: Fair Lord Aeneas, let me touch your hand;
To our pavilion shall I lead you, first.
Achilles shall have word of this intent;
So shall each lord of Greece, from tent to tent.
Yourself shall feast with us before you go,
And find the welcome of a noble foe.
Exeunt All but Ulysses and Nestor
ULYSSES: Nestor!
NESTOR: What says Ulysses?
ULYSSES: I have a young conception in my brain;
Be you my time to bring it to some shape.
NESTOR: What is't?
ULYSSES: This 'tis:
Blunt wedges rive hard knots. The seeded pride
That hath to this maturity blown up

In rank Achilles must or now be cropp'd
Or, shedding, breed a nursery of like evil
To overbulk us all.
NESTOR: Well, and how?
ULYSSES: This challenge that the gallant Hector sends,
However it is spread in general name,
Relates in purpose only to Achilles.
NESTOR: True. The purpose is perspicuous even as substance
Whose grossness little characters sum up;
And, in the publication, make no strain
But that Achilles, were his brain as barren
As banks of Libya-though, Apollo knows,
'Tis dry enough-will with great speed of judgment,
Ay, with celerity, find Hector's purpose
Pointing on him.
ULYSSES: And wake him to the answer, think you?
NESTOR: Why, 'tis most meet. Who may you else oppose
That can from Hector bring those honours off,
If not Achilles? Though 't be a sportful combat,
Yet in this trial much opinion dwells;
For here the Troyans taste our dear'st repute
With their fin'st palate; and trust to me, Ulysses,
Our imputation shall be oddly pois'd
In this vile action; for the success,
Although particular, shall give a scantling
Of good or bad unto the general;
And in such indexes, although small pricks
To their subsequent volumes, there is seen
The baby figure of the giant mas
Of things to come at large. It is suppos'd
He that meets Hector issues from our choice;
And choice, being mutual act of all our souls,
Makes merit her election, and doth boil,
As 'twere from forth us all, a man distill'd
Out of our virtues; who miscarrying,
What heart receives from hence a conquering part,
To steel a strong opinion to themselves?
Which entertain'd, limbs are his instruments,
In no less working than are swords and bows
Directive by the limbs.
ULYSSES: Give pardon to my speech.
Therefore 'tis meet Achilles meet not Hector.
Let us, like merchants, show our foulest wares
And think perchance they'll sell; if not, the lustre
Of the better yet to show shall show the better,
By showing the worst first. Do not consent
That ever Hector and Achilles meet;
For both our honour and our shame in this
Are dogg'd with two strange followers.
NESTOR: I see them not with my old eyes. What are they?
ULYSSES: What glory our Achilles shares from Hector,
Were he not proud, we all should wear with him;
But he already is too insolent;

And it were better parch in Afric sun
Than in the pride and salt scorn of his eyes,
Should he scape Hector fair. If he were foil'd,
Why, then we do our main opinion crush
In taint of our best man. No, make a lott'ry;
And, by device, let blockish Ajax draw
The sort to fight with Hector. Among ourselves
Give him allowance for the better man;
For that will physic the great Myrmidon,
Who broils in loud applause, and make him fall
His crest, that prouder than blue Iris bends.
If the dull brainless Ajax come safe off,
We'll dress him up in voices; if he fail,
Yet go we under our opinion still
That we have better men. But, hit or miss,
Our project's life this shape of sense assumes-
Ajax employ'd plucks down Achilles' plumes.
NESTOR: Now, Ulysses, I begin to relish thy advice;
And I will give a taste thereof forthwith
To Agamemnon. Go we to him straight.
Two curs shall tame each other: pride alone
Must tarre the mastiffs on, as 'twere their bone.
Exeunt

ACT II. SCENE I. The Grecian Camp

Enter Ajax and Thersites
AJAX: Thersites!
THERSITES: Agamemnon-how if he had boils full, an over, generally?
AJAX: Thersites!
THERSITES: And those boils did run-say so. Did not the general run then? Were not that a botchy core?
AJAX: Dog!
THERSITES: Then there would come some matter from him; I see none now.
AJAX: Thou bitch-wolf's son, canst thou not hear? Feel, then.
Strikes Him
THERSITES: The plague of Greece upon thee, thou mongrel beef-witted lord!
AJAX: Speak, then, thou whinid'st leaven, speak. I will beat thee into handsomeness.
THERSITES: I shall sooner rail thee into wit and holiness; but I think thy horse will sooner con an oration than thou learn a prayer without book. Thou canst strike, canst thou? A red murrain o' thy jade's tricks!
AJAX: Toadstool, learn me the proclamation.
THERSITES: Dost thou think I have no sense, thou strikest me thus?
AJAX: The proclamation!
THERSITES: Thou art proclaim'd, a fool, I think.
AJAX: Do not, porpentine, do not; my fingers itch.
THERSITES: I would thou didst itch from head to foot and I had the scratching of thee; I would make thee the loathsomest scab in Greece. When thou art forth in the incursions, thou strikest as slow as another.
AJAX: I say, the proclamation.

THERSITES: Thou grumblest and railest every hour on Achilles; and thou art as full of envy at his greatness as Cerberus is at Proserpina's beauty-ay, that thou bark'st at him.
AJAX: Mistress Thersites!
THERSITES: Thou shouldst strike him.
AJAX: Cobloaf!
THERSITES: He would pun thee into shivers with his fist, as a sailor breaks a biscuit.
AJAX: You whoreson cur!
Strikes Him
THERSITES: Do, do.
AJAX: Thou stool for a witch!
THERSITES: Ay, do, do; thou sodden-witted lord! Thou hast no more brain than I have in mine elbows; an assinico may tutor thee. You scurvy valiant ass! Thou art here but to thrash Troyans, and thou art bought and sold among those of any wit like a barbarian slave. If thou use to beat me, I will begin at thy heel and tell what thou art by inches, thou thing of no bowels, thou!
AJAX: You dog!
THERSITES: You scurvy lord!
AJAX: You cur!
Strikes Him
THERSITES: Mars his idiot! Do, rudeness; do, camel; do, do.
Enter Achilles and Patroclus
ACHILLES: Why, how now, Ajax! Wherefore do you thus?
How now, Thersites! What's the matter, man?
THERSITES: You see him there, do you?
ACHILLES: Ay; what's the matter?
THERSITES: Nay, look upon him.
ACHILLES: So I do. What's the matter?
THERSITES: Nay, but regard him well.
ACHILLES: Well! why, so I do.
THERSITES: But yet you look not well upon him; for who some ever you take him to be, he is Ajax.
ACHILLES: I know that, fool.
THERSITES: Ay, but that fool knows not himself.
AJAX: Therefore I beat thee.
THERSITES: Lo, lo, lo, lo, what modicums of wit he utters! His evasions have ears thus long. I have bobb'd his brain more than he has beat my bones. I will buy nine sparrows for a penny, and his pia mater is not worth the ninth part of a sparrow. This lord, Achilles, Ajax-who wears his wit in his belly and his guts in his head-I'll tell you what I say of him.
ACHILLES: What?
THERSITES: I say this Ajax-
Ajax Offers to Strike Him
ACHILLES: Nay, good Ajax.
THERSITES: Has not so much wit-
ACHILLES: Nay, I must hold you.
THERSITES: As will stop the eye of Helen's needle, for whom he comes to fight.
ACHILLES: Peace, fool.
THERSITES: I would have peace and quietness, but the fool will not-

he there; that he; look you there.
AJAX: O thou damned cur! I shall-
ACHILLES: Will you set your wit to a fool's?
THERSITES: No, I warrant you, the fool's will shame it.
PATROCLUS: Good words, Thersites.
ACHILLES: What's the quarrel?
AJAX: I bade the vile owl go learn me the tenour of the proclamation, and he rails upon me.
THERSITES: I serve thee not.
AJAX: Well, go to, go to.
THERSITES: I serve here voluntary.
ACHILLES: Your last service was suff'rance; 'twas not voluntary. No man is beaten voluntary. Ajax was here the voluntary, and you as under an impress.
THERSITES: E'en so; a great deal of your wit too lies in your sinews, or else there be liars. Hector shall have a great catch an he knock out either of your brains: 'a were as good crack a fusty nut with no kernel.
ACHILLES: What, with me too, Thersites?
THERSITES: There's Ulysses and old Nestor-whose wit was mouldy ere your grandsires had nails on their toes-yoke you like draught oxen, and make you plough up the wars.
ACHILLES: What, what?
THERSITES: Yes, good sooth. To Achilles, to Ajax, to-
AJAX: I shall cut out your tongue.
THERSITES: 'Tis no matter; I shall speak as much as thou afterwards.
PATROCLUS: No more words, Thersites; peace!
THERSITES: I will hold my peace when Achilles' brach bids me, shall I?
ACHILLES: There's for you, Patroclus.
THERSITES: I will see you hang'd like clotpoles ere I come any more to your tents. I will keep where there is wit stirring, and leave the faction of fools.
Exit
PATROCLUS: A good riddance.
ACHILLES: Marry, this, sir, is proclaim'd through all our host,
That Hector, by the fifth hour of the sun,
Will with a trumpet 'twixt our tents and Troy,
To-morrow morning, call some knight to arms
That hath a stomach; and such a one that dare
Maintain I know not what; 'tis trash. Farewell.
AJAX: Farewell. Who shall answer him?
ACHILLES: I know not; 'tis put to lott'ry. Otherwise. He knew his man.
AJAX: O, meaning you! I will go learn more of it.
Exeunt

ACT II. SCENE II. Troy. Priam's Palace

Enter Priam, Hector, Troilus, Paris, and Helenus
PRIAM: After so many hours, lives, speeches, spent,
Thus once again says Nestor from the Greeks:
'Deliver Helen, and all damage else-
As honour, loss of time, travail, expense,
Wounds, friends, and what else dear that is consum'd
In hot digestion of this cormorant war-

Shall be struck off.' Hector, what say you to't?
HECTOR: Though no man lesser fears the Greeks than I,
As far as toucheth my particular,
Yet, dread Priam,
There is no lady of more softer bowels,
More spongy to suck in the sense of fear,
More ready to cry out 'Who knows what follows?'
Than Hector is. The wound of peace is surety,
Surety secure; but modest doubt is call'd
The beacon of the wise, the tent that searches
To th' bottom of the worst. Let Helen go.
Since the first sword was drawn about this question,
Every tithe soul 'mongst many thousand dismes
Hath been as dear as Helen-I mean, of ours.
If we have lost so many tenths of ours
To guard a thing not ours, nor worth to us,
Had it our name, the value of one ten,
What merit's in that reason which denies
The yielding of her up?
TROILUS: Fie, fie, my brother!
Weigh you the worth and honour of a king,
So great as our dread father's, in a scale
Of common ounces? Will you with counters sum
The past-proportion of his infinite,
And buckle in a waist most fathomless
With spans and inches so diminutive
As fears and reasons? Fie, for godly shame!
HELENUS: No marvel though you bite so sharp at reasons,
You are so empty of them. Should not our father
Bear the great sway of his affairs with reasons,
Because your speech hath none that tells him so?
TROILUS: You are for dreams and slumbers, brother priest;
You fur your gloves with reason. Here are your reasons:
You know an enemy intends you harm;
You know a sword employ'd is perilous,
And reason flies the object of all harm.
Who marvels, then, when Helenus beholds
A Grecian and his sword, if he do set
The very wings of reason to his heels
And fly like chidden Mercury from Jove,
Or like a star disorb'd? Nay, if we talk of reason,
Let's shut our gates and sleep. Manhood and honour
Should have hare hearts, would they but fat their thoughts
With this cramm'd reason. Reason and respect
Make livers pale and lustihood deject.
HECTOR: Brother, she is not worth what she doth, cost
The keeping.
TROILUS: What's aught but as 'tis valued?
HECTOR: But value dwells not in particular will:
It holds his estimate and dignity
As well wherein 'tis precious of itself
As in the prizer. 'Tis mad idolatry
To make the service greater than the god-I

And the will dotes that is attributive
To what infectiously itself affects,
Without some image of th' affected merit.
TROILUS: I take to-day a wife, and my election
Is led on in the conduct of my will;
My will enkindled by mine eyes and ears,
Two traded pilots 'twixt the dangerous shores
Of will and judgment: how may I avoid,
Although my will distaste what it elected,
The wife I chose? There can be no evasion
To blench from this and to stand firm by honour.
We turn not back the silks upon the merchant
When we have soil'd them; nor the remainder viands
We do not throw in unrespective sieve,
Because we now are full. It was thought meet
Paris should do some vengeance on the Greeks;
Your breath with full consent benied his sails;
The seas and winds, old wranglers, took a truce,
And did him service. He touch'd the ports desir'd;
And for an old aunt whom the Greeks held captive
He brought a Grecian queen, whose youth and freshness
Wrinkles Apollo's, and makes stale the morning.
Why keep we her? The Grecians keep our aunt.
Is she worth keeping? Why, she is a pearl
Whose price hath launch'd above a thousand ships,
And turn'd crown'd kings to merchants.
If you'll avouch 'twas wisdom Paris went-
As you must needs, for you all cried 'Go, go'-
If you'll confess he brought home worthy prize-
As you must needs, for you all clapp'd your hands,
And cried 'Inestimable!' -why do you now
The issue of your proper wisdoms rate,
And do a deed that never fortune did-
Beggar the estimation which you priz'd
Richer than sea and land? O theft most base,
That we have stol'n what we do fear to keep!
But thieves unworthy of a thing so stol'n
That in their country did them that disgrace
We fear to warrant in our native place!
CASSANDRA: Within Cry, Troyans, cry.
PRIAM: What noise, what shriek is this?
TROILUS: 'Tis our mad sister; I do know her voice.
CASSANDRA: Within Cry, Troyans.
HECTOR: It is Cassandra.
Enter Cassandra, Raving
CASSANDRA: Cry, Troyans, cry. Lend me ten thousand eyes,
And I will fill them with prophetic tears.
HECTOR: Peace, sister, peace.
CASSANDRA: Virgins and boys, mid-age and wrinkled eld,
Soft infancy, that nothing canst but cry,
Add to my clamours. Let us pay betimes
A moiety of that mass of moan to come.
Cry, Troyans, cry. Practise your eyes with tears.

Troy must not be, nor goodly Ilion stand;
Our firebrand brother, Paris, burns us all.
Cry, Troyans, cry, A Helen and a woe!
Cry, cry. Troy burns, or else let Helen go.
Exit
HECTOR: Now, youthful Troilus, do not these high strains
Of divination in our sister work
Some touches of remorse, or is your blood
So madly hot that no discourse of reason,
Nor fear of bad success in a bad cause,
Can qualify the same?
TROILUS: Why, brother Hector,
We may not think the justness of each act
Such and no other than event doth form it;
Nor once deject the courage of our minds
Because Cassandra's mad. Her brain-sick raptures
Cannot distaste the goodness of a quarrel
Which hath our several honours all engag'd
To make it gracious. For my private part,
I am no more touch'd than all Priam's sons;
And Jove forbid there should be done amongst us
Such things as might offend the weakest spleen
To fight for and maintain.
PARIS: Else might the world convince of levity
As well my undertakings as your counsels;
But I attest the gods, your full consent
Gave wings to my propension, and cut of
All fears attending on so dire a project.
For what, alas, can these my single arms?
What propugnation is in one man's valour
To stand the push and enmity of those
This quarrel would excite? Yet, I protest,
Were I alone to pass the difficulties,
And had as ample power as I have will,
Paris should ne'er retract what he hath done
Nor faint in the pursuit.
PRIAM: Paris, you speak
Like one besotted on your sweet delights.
You have the honey still, but these the gall;
So to be valiant is no praise at all.
PARIS: Sir, I propose not merely to myself
The pleasures such a beauty brings with it;
But I would have the soil of her fair rape
Wip'd off in honourable keeping her.
What treason were it to the ransack'd queen,
Disgrace to your great worths, and shame to me,
Now to deliver her possession up
On terms of base compulsion! Can it be
That so degenerate a strain as this
Should once set footing in your generous bosoms?
There's not the meanest spirit on our party
Without a heart to dare or sword to draw
When Helen is defended; nor none so noble

Whose life were ill bestow'd or death unfam'd
Where Helen is the subject. Then, I say,
Well may we fight for her whom we know well
The world's large spaces cannot parallel.
HECTOR: Paris and Troilus, you have both said well;
And on the cause and question now in hand
Have gloz'd, but superficially; not much
Unlike young men, whom Aristode thought
Unfit to hear moral philosophy.
The reasons you allege do more conduce
To the hot passion of distemp'red blood
Than to make up a free determination
'Twixt right and wrong; for pleasure and revenge
Have ears more deaf than adders to the voice
Of any true decision. Nature craves
All dues be rend'red to their owners. Now,
What nearer debt in all humanity
Than wife is to the husband? If this law
Of nature be corrupted through affection;
And that great minds, of partial indulgence
To their benumbed wills, resist the same;
There is a law in each well-order'd nation
To curb those raging appetites that are
Most disobedient and refractory.
If Helen, then, be wife to Sparta's king-
As it is known she is-these moral laws
Of nature and of nations speak aloud
To have her back return'd. Thus to persist
In doing wrong extenuates not wrong,
But makes it much more heavy. Hector's opinion
Is this, in way of truth. Yet, ne'er the less,
My spritely brethren, I propend to you
In resolution to keep Helen still;
For 'tis a cause that hath no mean dependence
Upon our joint and several dignities.
TROILUS: Why, there you touch'd the life of our design.
Were it not glory that we more affected
Than the performance of our heaving spleens,
I would not wish a drop of Troyan blood
Spent more in her defence. But, worthy Hector,
She is a theme of honour and renown,
A spur to valiant and magnanimous deeds,
Whose present courage may beat down our foes,
And fame in time to come canonize us;
For I presume brave Hector would not lose
So rich advantage of a promis'd glory
As smiles upon the forehead of this action
For the wide world's revenue.
HECTOR: I am yours,
You valiant offspring of great Priamus.
I have a roisting challenge sent amongst
The dull and factious nobles of the Greeks
Will strike amazement to their drowsy spirits.

I was advertis'd their great general slept,
Whilst emulation in the army crept.
This, I presume, will wake him.
Exeunt

ACT II. SCENE III. The Grecian Camp. Before the Tent of Achilles

Enter Thersites, Solus

THERSITES: How now, Thersites! What, lost in the labyrinth of thy fury? Shall the elephant Ajax carry it thus? He beats me, and I rail at him. O worthy satisfaction! Would it were otherwise: that I could beat him, whilst he rail'd at me! 'Sfoot, I'll learn to conjure and raise devils, but I'll see some issue of my spiteful execrations. Then there's Achilles, a rare engineer! If Troy be not taken till these two undermine it, the walls will stand till they fall of themselves. O thou great thunder-darter of Olympus, forget that thou art Jove, the king of gods, and, Mercury, lose all the serpentine craft of thy caduceus, if ye take not that little little less-than-little wit from them that they have! which short-arm'd ignorance itself knows is so abundant scarce, it will not in circumvention deliver a fly from a spider without drawing their massy irons and cutting the web. After this, the vengeance on the whole camp! or, rather, the Neapolitan bone-ache! for that, methinks, is the curse depending on those that war for a placket. I have said my prayers; and devil Envy say 'Amen.' What ho! my Lord Achilles!

Enter Patroclus

PATROCLUS: Who's there? Thersites! Good Thersites, come in and rail.

THERSITES: If I could 'a remember'd a gilt counterfeit, thou wouldst not have slipp'd out of my contemplation; but it is no matter; thyself upon thyself! The common curse of mankind, folly and ignorance, be thine in great revenue! Heaven bless thee from a tutor, and discipline come not near thee! Let thy blood be thy direction till thy death. Then if she that lays thee out says thou art a fair corse, I'll be sworn and sworn upon't she never shrouded any but lazars. Amen. Where's Achilles?

PATROCLUS: What, art thou devout? Wast thou in prayer?

THERSITES: Ay, the heavens hear me!

PATROCLUS: Amen.

Enter Achilles

ACHILLES: Who's there?

PATROCLUS: Thersites, my lord.

ACHILLES: Where, where? O, where? Art thou come? Why, my cheese, my digestion, why hast thou not served thyself in to my table so many meals? Come, what's Agamemnon?

THERSITES: Thy commander, Achilles. Then tell me, Patroclus, what's Achilles?

PATROCLUS: Thy lord, Thersites. Then tell me, I pray thee, what's Thersites?

THERSITES: Thy knower, Patroclus. Then tell me, Patroclus, what art thou?

PATROCLUS: Thou must tell that knowest.

ACHILLES: O, tell, tell,

THERSITES: I'll decline the whole question. Agamemnon commands Achilles; Achilles is my lord; I am Patroclus' knower; and Patroclus is a fool.

PATROCLUS: You rascal!

THERSITES: Peace, fool! I have not done.

ACHILLES: He is a privileg'd man. Proceed, Thersites.

THERSITES: Agamemnon is a fool; Achilles is a fool; Thersites is a fool; and, as aforesaid, Patroclus is a fool.

ACHILLES: Derive this; come.

THERSITES: Agamemnon is a fool to offer to command Achilles; Achilles is a fool to be commanded of Agamemnon; Thersites is a fool to serve such a fool; and this Patroclus is a fool positive.

PATROCLUS: Why am I a fool?

THERSITES: Make that demand of the Creator. It suffices me thou art. Look you, who comes here?

ACHILLES: Come, Patroclus, I'll speak with nobody. Come in with me,

THERSITES: Here is such patchery, such juggling, and such knavery. All the argument is a whore and a cuckold-a good quarrel to draw emulous factions and bleed to death upon. Now the dry serpigo on the subject, and war and lechery confound all!

Exit

Enter Agamemnon, Ulysses, Nestor, Diomedes, Ajax, and Calchas

AGAMEMNON: Where is Achilles?

PATROCLUS: Within his tent; but ill-dispos'd, my lord.

AGAMEMNON: Let it be known to him that we are here.
He shent our messengers; and we lay by
Our appertainings, visiting of him.
Let him be told so; lest, perchance, he think
We dare not move the question of our place
Or know not what we are.

PATROCLUS: I shall say so to him.

Exit

ULYSSES: We saw him at the opening of his tent.
He is not sick.

AJAX: Yes, lion-sick, sick of proud heart. You may call it melancholy, if you will favour the man; but, by my head, 'tis pride. But why, why? Let him show us a cause. A word, my lord.

Takes Agamemnon Aside

NESTOR: What moves Ajax thus to bay at him?

ULYSSES: Achilles hath inveigled his fool from him.

NESTOR:Who, Thersites?

ULYSSES: He.

NESTOR: Then will Ajax lack matter, if he have lost his argument

ULYSSES: No; you see he is his argument that has his argument-Achilles.

NESTOR: All the better; their fraction is more our wish than their faction. But it was a strong composure a fool could disunite!

ULYSSES: The amity that wisdom knits not, folly may easily untie.

Re-enter Patroclus

Here comes Patroclus.
NESTOR: No Achilles with him.
ULYSSES: The elephant hath joints, but none for courtesy; his legs are legs for necessity, not for flexure.
PATROCLUS: Achilles bids me say he is much sorry
If any thing more than your sport and pleasure
Did move your greatness and this noble state
To call upon him; he hopes it is no other
But for your health and your digestion sake,
An after-dinner's breath.
AGAMEMNON: Hear you, Patroclus.
We are too well acquainted with these answers;
But his evasion, wing'd thus swift with scorn,
Cannot outfly our apprehensions.
Much attribute he hath, and much the reason
Why we ascribe it to him. Yet all his virtues,
Not virtuously on his own part beheld,
Do in our eyes begin to lose their gloss;
Yea, like fair fruit in an unwholesome dish,
Are like to rot untasted. Go and tell him
We come to speak with him; and you shall not sin
If you do say we think him over-proud
And under-honest, in self-assumption greater
Than in the note of judgment; and worthier than himself
Here tend the savage strangeness he puts on,
Disguise the holy strength of their command,
And underwrite in an observing kind
His humorous predominance; yea, watch
His pettish lunes, his ebbs, his flows, as if
The passage and whole carriage of this action
Rode on his tide. Go tell him this, and ad
That if he overhold his price so much
We'll none of him, but let him, like an engine
Not portable, lie under this report:
Bring action hither; this cannot go to war.
A stirring dwarf we do allowance give
Before a sleeping giant. Tell him so.
PATROCLUS: I shall, and bring his answer presently.
Exit
AGAMEMNON: In second voice we'll not be satisfied;
We come to speak with him. Ulysses, enter you.
Exit Ulysses
AJAX: What is he more than another?
AGAMEMNON: No more than what he thinks he is.
AJAX: Is he so much? Do you not think he thinks himself a better man than I am?
AGAMEMNON: No question.
AJAX: Will you subscribe his thought and say he is?
AGAMEMNON: No, noble Ajax; you are as strong, as valiant, as wise, no less noble, much more gentle, and altogether more tractable.
AJAX: Why should a man be proud? How doth pride grow? I know not what pride is.
AGAMEMNON: Your mind is the clearer, Ajax, and your virtues the

fairer. He that is proud eats up himself. Pride is his own glass, his own trumpet, his own chronicle; and whatever praises itself but in the deed devours the deed in the praise.

Re-enter Ulysses

AJAX: I do hate a proud man as I do hate the engend'ring of toads.
NESTOR: Aside And yet he loves himself: is't not strange?
ULYSSES: Achilles will not to the field to-morrow.
AGAMEMNON: What's his excuse?
ULYSSES: He doth rely on none;
But carries on the stream of his dispose,
Without observance or respect of any,
In will peculiar and in self-admission.
AGAMEMNON: Why will he not, upon our fair request,
Untent his person and share the air with us?
ULYSSES: Things small as nothing, for request's sake only,
He makes important; possess'd he is with greatness,
And speaks not to himself but with a pride
That quarrels at self-breath. Imagin'd worth
Holds in his blood such swol'n and hot discourse
That 'twixt his mental and his active parts
Kingdom'd Achilles in commotion rages,
And batters down himself. What should I say?
He is so plaguy proud that the death tokens of it
Cry 'No recovery.'
AGAMEMNON: Let Ajax go to him.
Dear lord, go you and greet him in his tent.
'Tis said he holds you well; and will be led
At your request a little from himself.
ULYSSES: O Agamemnon, let it not be so!
We'll consecrate the steps that Ajax makes
When they go from Achilles. Shall the proud lord
That bastes his arrogance with his own seam
And never suffers matter of the world
Enter his thoughts, save such as doth revolve
And ruminate himself-shall he be worshipp'd
Of that we hold an idol more than he?
No, this thrice-worthy and right valiant lord
Shall not so stale his palm, nobly acquir'd,
Nor, by my will, assubjugate his merit,
As amply titled as Achilles is,
By going to Achilles.
That were to enlard his fat-already pride,
And add more coals to Cancer when he burns
With entertaining great Hyperion.
This lord go to him! Jupiter forbid,
And say in thunder 'Achilles go to him.'
NESTOR: Aside O, this is well! He rubs the vein of him.
DIOMEDES: Aside And how his silence drinks up this applause!
AJAX: If I go to him, with my armed fist I'll pash him o'er the face.
AGAMEMNON: O, no, you shall not go.
AJAX: An 'a be proud with me I'll pheeze his pride.
Let me go to him.

ULYSSES: Not for the worth that hangs upon our quarrel.
AJAX: A paltry, insolent fellow!
NESTOR: Aside How he describes himself!
AJAX: Can he not be sociable?
ULYSSES: Aside The raven chides blackness.
AJAX: I'll let his humours blood.
AGAMEMNON: Aside He will be the physician that should be the patient.
AJAX: An all men were a my mind-
ULYSSES: Aside Wit would be out of fashion.
AJAX: 'A should not bear it so, 'a should eat's words first.
Shall pride carry it?
NESTOR: Aside An 'twould, you'd carry half.
ULYSSES: Aside 'A would have ten shares.
AJAX: I will knead him, I'll make him supple.
NESTOR: Aside He's not yet through warm. Force him with praises;
pour in, pour in; his ambition is dry.
ULYSSES: To Agamemnon My lord, you feed too much on this dislike.
NESTOR: Our noble general, do not do so.
DIOMEDES: You must prepare to fight without Achilles.
ULYSSES: Why 'tis this naming of him does him harm.
Here is a man-but 'tis before his face;
I will be silent.
NESTOR: Wherefore should you so?
He is not emulous, as Achilles is.
ULYSSES: Know the whole world, he is as valiant.
AJAX: A whoreson dog, that shall palter with us thus!
Would he were a Troyan!
NESTOR: What a vice were it in Ajax now-
ULYSSES: If he were proud.
DIOMEDES: Or covetous of praise.
ULYSSES: Ay, or surly borne.
DIOMEDES: Or strange, or self-affected.
ULYSSES: Thank the heavens, lord, thou art of sweet composure
Praise him that gat thee, she that gave thee suck;
Fam'd be thy tutor, and thy parts of nature
Thrice-fam'd beyond, beyond all erudition;
But he that disciplin'd thine arms to fight-
Let Mars divide eternity in twain
And give him half; and, for thy vigour,
Bull-bearing Milo his addition yield
To sinewy Ajax. I will not praise thy wisdom,
Which, like a bourn, a pale, a shore, confines
Thy spacious and dilated parts. Here's Nestor,
Instructed by the antiquary times-
He must, he is, he cannot but be wise;
But pardon, father Nestor, were your days
As green as Ajax' and your brain so temper'd,
You should not have the eminence of him,
But be as Ajax.
AJAX: Shall I call you father?
NESTOR: Ay, my good son.
DIOMEDES: Be rul'd by him, Lord Ajax.

ULYSSES: There is no tarrying here; the hart Achilles
Keeps thicket. Please it our great general
To call together all his state of war;
Fresh kings are come to Troy. To-morrow
We must with all our main of power stand fast;
And here's a lord-come knights from east to west
And cull their flower, Ajax shall cope the best.
AGAMEMNON: Go we to council. Let Achilles sleep.
Light boats sail swift, though greater hulks draw deep.
Exeunt

ACT III. SCENE I. Troy. Priam's Palace

Music Sounds Within. Enter Pandarus and a Servant
PANDARUS: Friend, you-pray you, a word. Do you not follow the young Lord Paris?
SERVANT: Ay, sir, when he goes before me.
PANDARUS: You depend upon him, I mean?
SERVANT: Sir, I do depend upon the lord.
PANDARUS: You depend upon a notable gentleman; I must needs praise him.
SERVANT: The lord be praised!
PANDARUS: You know me, do you not?
SERVANT: Faith, sir, superficially.
PANDARUS: Friend, know me better: I am the Lord Pandarus.
SERVANT: I hope I shall know your honour better.
PANDARUS: I do desire it.
SERVANT: You are in the state of grace.
PANDARUS: Grace! Not so, friend; honour and lordship are my titles. What music is this?
SERVANT: I do but partly know, sir; it is music in parts.
PANDARUS: Know you the musicians?
SERVANT: Wholly, sir.
PANDARUS: Who play they to?
SERVANT: To the hearers, sir.
PANDARUS: At whose pleasure, friend?
SERVANT: At mine, sir, and theirs that love music.
PANDARUS: Command, I mean, friend.
SERVANT: Who shall I command, sir?
PANDARUS: Friend, we understand not one another: I am to courtly, and thou art too cunning. At whose request do these men play?
SERVANT: That's to't, indeed, sir. Marry, sir, at the request of Paris my lord, who is there in person; with him the mortal Venus, the heart-blood of beauty, love's invisible soul-
PANDARUS: Who, my cousin, Cressida?
SERVANT: No, sir, Helen. Could not you find out that by her attributes?
PANDARUS: It should seem, fellow, that thou hast not seen the Lady
CRESSIDA: I come to speak with Paris from the Prince Troilus; I will make a complimental assault upon him, for my business seethes.
SERVANT: Sodden business! There's a stew'd phrase indeed!
Enter Paris and Helen, Attended
PANDARUS: Fair be to you, my lord, and to all this fair company!
Fair desires, in all fair measure, fairly guide them- especially

to you, fair queen! Fair thoughts be your fair pillow.
HELEN: Dear lord, you are full of fair words.
PANDARUS: You speak your fair pleasure, sweet queen. Fair prince, here is good broken music.
PARIS: You have broke it, cousin; and by my life, you shall make it whole again; you shall piece it out with a piece of your performance.
HELEN: He is full of harmony.
PANDARUS: Truly, lady, no.
HELEN: O, sir-
PANDARUS: Rude, in sooth; in good sooth, very rude.
PARIS: Well said, my lord. Well, you say so in fits.
PANDARUS: I have business to my lord, dear queen. My lord, will you vouchsafe me a word?
HELEN: Nay, this shall not hedge us out. We'll hear you sing, certainly-
PANDARUS: Well sweet queen, you are pleasant with me. But, marry, thus, my lord: my dear lord and most esteemed friend, your brother Troilus-
HELEN: My Lord Pandarus, honey-sweet lord-
PANDARUS: Go to, sweet queen, go to-commends himself most affectionately to you-
HELEN: You shall not bob us out of our melody. If you do, our melancholy upon your head!
PANDARUS: Sweet queen, sweet queen; that's a sweet queen, i' faith.
HELEN: And to make a sweet lady sad is a sour offence.
PANDARUS: Nay, that shall not serve your turn; that shall it not, in truth, la. Nay, I care not for such words; no, no. -And, my lord, he desires you that, if the King call for him at supper, you will make his excuse.
HELEN: My Lord Pandarus!
PANDARUS: What says my sweet queen, my very very sweet queen?
PARIS: What exploit's in hand? Where sups he to-night?
HELEN: Nay, but, my lord-
PANDARUS: What says my sweet queen?-My cousin will fall out with you.
HELEN: You must not know where he sups.
PARIS: I'll lay my life, with my disposer Cressida.
PANDARUS: No, no, no such matter; you are wide. Come, your disposer is sick.
PARIS: Well, I'll make's excuse.
PANDARUS: Ay, good my lord. Why should you say Cressida? No, your poor disposer's sick.
PARIS: I spy.
PANDARUS: You spy! What do you spy?-Come, give me an instrument. Now, sweet queen.
HELEN: Why, this is kindly done.
PANDARUS: My niece is horribly in love with a thing you have, sweet Queen.
HELEN: She shall have it, my lord, if it be not my Lord Paris.
PANDARUS: He! No, she'll none of him; they two are twain.
HELEN: Falling in, after falling out, may make them three.
PANDARUS: Come, come. I'll hear no more of this; I'll sing you a

song now.
HELEN: Ay, ay, prithee now. By my troth, sweet lord, thou hast a fine forehead.
PANDARUS: Ay, you may, you may.
HELEN: Let thy song be love. This love will undo us all. O Cupid, Cupid, Cupid!
PANDARUS: Love! Ay, that it shall, i' faith.
PARIS: Ay, good now, love, love, nothing but love.
PANDARUS: In good troth, it begins so.
Sings

Love, love, nothing but love, still love, still more!
For, oh, love's bow
Shoots buck and doe;
The shaft confounds
Not that it wounds,
But tickles still the sore.
These lovers cry, O ho, they die!
Yet that which seems the wound to kill
Doth turn O ho! to ha! ha! he!
So dying love lives still.
O ho! a while, but ha! ha! ha!
O ho! groans out for ha! ha! ha!-hey ho!

HELEN: In love, i' faith, to the very tip of the nose.
PARIS: He eats nothing but doves, love; and that breeds hot blood, and hot blood begets hot thoughts, and hot thoughts beget hot deeds, and hot deeds is love.
PANDARUS: Is this the generation of love: hot blood, hot thoughts, and hot deeds? Why, they are vipers. Is love a generation of vipers? Sweet lord, who's a-field today?
PARIS: Hector, Deiphobus, Helenus, Antenor, and all the gallantry of Troy. I would fain have arm'd to-day, but my Nell would not have it so. How chance my brother Troilus went not?
HELEN: He hangs the lip at something. You know all, Lord Pandarus.
PANDARUS: Not I, honey-sweet queen. I long to hear how they spend to-day. You'll remember your brother's excuse?
PARIS: To a hair.
PANDARUS: Farewell, sweet queen.
HELEN: Commend me to your niece.
PANDARUS: I will, sweet queen.
Exit. Sound a retreat

PARIS: They're come from the field. Let us to Priam's hall
To greet the warriors. Sweet Helen, I must woo you
To help unarm our Hector. His stubborn buckles,
With these your white enchanting fingers touch'd,
Shall more obey than to the edge of steel
Or force of Greekish sinews; you shall do more
Than all the island kings-disarm great Hector.
HELEN: 'Twill make us proud to be his servant, Paris;
Yea, what he shall receive of us in duty
Gives us more palm in beauty than we have,
Yea, overshines ourself.
PARIS: Sweet, above thought I love thee.
Exeunt

ACT III. SCENE II. Troy. Pandarus' Orchard

Enter Pandarus and Troilus' Boy, Meeting

PANDARUS: How now! Where's thy master? At my cousin Cressida's?

BOY: No, sir; he stays for you to conduct him thither.

Enter Troilus

PANDARUS: O, here he comes. How now, how now!

TROILUS: Sirrah, walk off.

Exit Boy

PANDARUS: Have you seen my cousin?

TROILUS: No, Pandarus. I stalk about her door
Like a strange soul upon the Stygian banks
Staying for waftage. O, be thou my Charon,
And give me swift transportance to these fields
Where I may wallow in the lily beds
Propos'd for the deserver! O gentle Pandar,
From Cupid's shoulder pluck his painted wings,
And fly with me to Cressid!

PANDARUS: Walk here i' th' orchard, I'll bring her straight.

Exit

TROILUS: I am giddy; expectation whirls me round.
Th' imaginary relish is so sweet
That it enchants my sense; what will it be
When that the wat'ry palate tastes indeed
Love's thrice-repured nectar? Death, I fear me;
Swooning destruction; or some joy too fine,
Too subtle-potent, tun'd too sharp in sweetness,
For the capacity of my ruder powers.
I fear it much; and I do fear besides
That I shall lose distinction in my joys;
As doth a battle, when they charge on heaps
The enemy flying.

Re-enter Pandarus

PANDARUS: She's making her ready, she'll come straight; you must be witty now. She does so blush, and fetches her wind so short, as if she were fray'd with a sprite. I'll fetch her. It is the prettiest villain; she fetches her breath as short as a new-ta'en sparrow.

Exit

TROILUS: Even such a passion doth embrace my bosom.
My heart beats thicker than a feverous pulse,
And all my powers do their bestowing lose,
Like vassalage at unawares encount'ring
The eye of majesty.

Re-enter Pandarus with Cressida

PANDARUS: Come, come, what need you blush? Shame's a baby.-Here she is now; swear the oaths now to her that you have sworn to me.-What, are you gone again? You must be watch'd ere you be made tame, must you? Come your ways, come your ways; an you draw backward, we'll put you i' th' fills.-Why do you not speak to her?-Come, draw this curtain and let's see your picture. Alas the day, how loath you are to offend daylight! An 'twere dark, you'd close sooner. So, so; rub on, and kiss the mistress How now, a kiss in fee-farm! Build there, carpenter; the air is

sweet. Nay, you shall fight your hearts out ere I part you. The falcon as the tercel, for all the ducks i' th' river. Go to, go to.
TROILUS: You have bereft me of all words, lady.
PANDARUS: Words pay no debts, give her deeds; but she'll bereave you o' th' deeds too, if she call your activity in question. What, billing again? Here's 'In witness whereof the parties interchangeably.' Come in, come in; I'll go get a fire.
Exit
CRESSIDA: Will you walk in, my lord?
TROILUS: O Cressid, how often have I wish'd me thus!
CRESSIDA: Wish'd, my lord! The gods grant-O my lord!
TROILUS: What should they grant? What makes this pretty abruption? What too curious dreg espies my sweet lady in the fountain of our love?
CRESSIDA: More dregs than water, if my fears have eyes.
TROILUS: Fears make devils of cherubims; they never see truly.
CRESSIDA: Blind fear, that seeing reason leads, finds safer footing than blind reason stumbling without fear. To fear the worst oft cures the worse.
TROILUS: O, let my lady apprehend no fear! In all Cupid's pageant there is presented no monster.
CRESSIDA: Nor nothing monstrous neither?
TROILUS: Nothing, but our undertakings when we vow to weep seas, live in fire, cat rocks, tame tigers; thinking it harder for our mistress to devise imposition enough than for us to undergo any difficulty imposed. This is the monstruosity in love, lady, that the will is infinite, and the execution confin'd; that the desire is boundless, and the act a slave to limit.
CRESSIDA: They say all lovers swear more performance than they are able, and yet reserve an ability that they never perform; vowing more than the perfection of ten, and discharging less than the tenth part of one. They that have the voice of lions and the act of hares, are they not monsters?
TROILUS: Are there such? Such are not we. Praise us as we are tasted, allow us as we prove; our head shall go bare till merit crown it. No perfection in reversion shall have a praise in present. We will not name desert before his birth; and, being born, his addition shall be humble. Few words to fair faith: Troilus shall be such to Cressid as what envy can say worst shall be a mock for his truth; and what truth can speak truest not truer than Troilus.
CRESSIDA: Will you walk in, my lord?
Re-enter Pandarus
PANDARUS: What, blushing still? Have you not done talking yet?
CRESSIDA: Well, uncle, what folly I commit, I dedicate to you.
PANDARUS: I thank you for that; if my lord get a boy of you, you'll give him me. Be true to my lord; if he flinch, chide me for it.
TROILUS: You know now your hostages: your uncle's word and my firm faith.
PANDARUS: Nay, I'll give my word for her too: our kindred, though they be long ere they are wooed, they are constant being won; they are burs, I can tell you; they'll stick where they are thrown.
CRESSIDA: Boldness comes to me now and brings me heart.

Prince Troilus, I have lov'd you night and day
For many weary months.
TROILUS: Why was my Cressid then so hard to win?
CRESSIDA: Hard to seem won; but I was won, my lord,
With the first glance that ever-pardon me.
If I confess much, you will play the tyrant.
I love you now; but till now not so much
But I might master it. In faith, I lie;
My thoughts were like unbridled children, grown
Too headstrong for their mother. See, we fools!
Why have I blabb'd? Who shall be true to us,
When we are so unsecret to ourselves?
But, though I lov'd you well, I woo'd you not;
And yet, good faith, I wish'd myself a man,
Or that we women had men's privilege
Of speaking first. Sweet, bid me hold my tongue,
For in this rapture I shall surely speak
The thing I shall repent. See, see, your silence,
Cunning in dumbness, from my weakness draws
My very soul of counsel. Stop my mouth.
TROILUS: And shall, albeit sweet music issues thence.
PANDARUS: Pretty, i' faith.
CRESSIDA: My lord, I do beseech you, pardon me;
'Twas not my purpose thus to beg a kiss.
I am asham'd. O heavens! what have I done?
For this time will I take my leave, my lord.
TROILUS: Your leave, sweet Cressid!
PANDARUS: Leave! An you take leave till to-morrow morning-
CRESSIDA: Pray you, content you.
TROILUS: What offends you, lady?
CRESSIDA: Sir, mine own company.
TROILUS: You cannot shun yourself.
CRESSIDA: Let me go and try.
I have a kind of self resides with you;
But an unkind self, that itself will leave
To be another's fool. I would be gone.
Where is my wit? I know not what I speak.
TROILUS: Well know they what they speak that speak so wisely.
CRESSIDA: Perchance, my lord, I show more craft than love;
And fell so roundly to a large confession
To angle for your thoughts; but you are wise-
Or else you love not; for to be wise and love
Exceeds man's might; that dwells with gods above.
TROILUS: O that I thought it could be in a woman-
As, if it can, I will presume in you-
To feed for aye her lamp and flames of love;
To keep her constancy in plight and youth,
Outliving beauty's outward, with a mind
That doth renew swifter than blood decays!
Or that persuasion could but thus convince me
That my integrity and truth to you
Might be affronted with the match and weight
Of such a winnowed purity in love.

How were I then uplifted! but, alas,
I am as true as truth's simplicity,
And simpler than the infancy of truth.
CRESSIDA: In that I'll war with you.
TROILUS: O virtuous fight,
When right with right wars who shall be most right!
True swains in love shall in the world to come
Approve their truth by Troilus, when their rhymes,
Full of protest, of oath, and big compare,
Want similes, truth tir'd with iteration-
As true as steel, as plantage to the moon,
As sun to day, as turtle to her mate,
As iron to adamant, as earth to th' centre-
Yet, after all comparisons of truth,
As truth's authentic author to be cited,
'As true as Troilus' shall crown up the verse
And sanctify the numbers.
CRESSIDA: Prophet may you be!
If I be false, or swerve a hair from truth,
When time is old and hath forgot itself,
When waterdrops have worn the stones of Troy,
And blind oblivion swallow'd cities up,
And mighty states characterless are grated
To dusty nothing-yet let memory
From false to false, among false maids in love,
Upbraid my falsehood when th' have said 'As false
As air, as water, wind, or sandy earth,
As fox to lamb, or wolf to heifer's calf,
Pard to the hind, or stepdame to her son'-
Yea, let them say, to stick the heart of falsehood,
'As false as Cressid.'
PANDARUS: Go to, a bargain made; seal it, seal it; I'll be the witness. Here I hold your hand; here my cousin's. If ever you prove false one to another, since I have taken such pains to bring you together, let all pitiful goers- between be call'd to the world's end after my name-call them all Pandars; let all constant men be Troiluses, all false women Cressids, and all brokers between Pandars. Say 'Amen.'
TROILUS: Amen.
CRESSIDA: Amen.
PANDARUS: Amen. Whereupon I will show you a chamber and a bed; which bed, because it shall not speak of your pretty encounters, press it to death. Away!
And Cupid grant all tongue-tied maidens here,
Bed, chamber, pander, to provide this gear!
Exeunt

ACT III. SCENE III. The Greek Camp

Flourish. Enter Agamemnon, Ulysses, Diomedes, Nestor, Ajax, Menelaus, and Calchas
CALCHAS: Now, Princes, for the service I have done,
Th' advantage of the time prompts me aloud
To call for recompense. Appear it to your mind
That, through the sight I bear in things to come,
I have abandon'd Troy, left my possession,

Incurr'd a traitor's name, expos'd myself
From certain and possess'd conveniences
To doubtful fortunes, sequest'ring from me all
That time, acquaintance, custom, and condition,
Made tame and most familiar to my nature;
And here, to do you service, am become
As new into the world, strange, unacquainted-
I do beseech you, as in way of taste,
To give me now a little benefit
Out of those many regist'red in promise,
Which you say live to come in my behalf.
AGAMEMNON: What wouldst thou of us, Troyan? Make demand.
CALCHAS: You have a Troyan prisoner call'd Antenor,
Yesterday took; Troy holds him very dear.
Oft have you-often have you thanks therefore-
Desir'd my Cressid in right great exchange,
Whom Troy hath still denied; but this Antenor,
I know, is such a wrest in their affairs
That their negotiations all must slack
Wanting his manage; and they will almost
Give us a prince of blood, a son of Priam,
In change of him. Let him be sent, great Princes,
And he shall buy my daughter; and her presence
Shall quite strike off all service I have done
In most accepted pain.
AGAMEMNON: Let Diomedes bear him,
And bring us Cressid hither. Calchas shall have
What he requests of us. Good Diomed,
Furnish you fairly for this interchange;
Withal, bring word if Hector will to-morrow
Be answer'd in his challenge. Ajax is ready.
DIOMEDES: This shall I undertake; and 'tis a burden
Which I am proud to bear.
Exeunt Diomedes and Calchas
Achilles and Patroclus Stand in Their Tent
ULYSSES: Achilles stands i' th' entrance of his tent.
Please it our general pass strangely by him,
As if he were forgot; and, Princes all,
Lay negligent and loose regard upon him.
I will come last. 'Tis like he'll question me
Why such unplausive eyes are bent, why turn'd on him?
If so, I have derision med'cinable
To use between your strangeness and his pride,
Which his own will shall have desire to drink.
It may do good. Pride hath no other glass
To show itself but pride; for supple knees
Feed arrogance and are the proud man's fees.
AGAMEMNON: We'll execute your purpose, and put on
A form of strangeness as we pass along.
So do each lord; and either greet him not,
Or else disdainfully, which shall shake him more
Than if not look'd on. I will lead the way.
ACHILLES: What comes the general to speak with me?

You know my mind. I'll fight no more 'gainst Troy.
AGAMEMNON: What says Achilles? Would he aught with us?
NESTOR: Would you, my lord, aught with the general?
ACHILLES: No.
NESTOR: Nothing, my lord.
AGAMEMNON: The better.
Exeunt Agamemnon and Nestor
ACHILLES: Good day, good day.
MENELAUS: How do you? How do you?
Exit
ACHILLES: What, does the cuckold scorn me?
AJAX: How now, Patroclus?
ACHILLES: Good morrow, Ajax.
AJAX: Ha?
ACHILLES: Good morrow.
AJAX: Ay, and good next day too.
Exit
ACHILLES: What mean these fellows? Know they not Achilles?
PATROCLUS: They pass by strangely. They were us'd to bend,
To send their smiles before them to Achilles,
To come as humbly as they us'd to creep
To holy altars.
ACHILLES: What, am I poor of late?
'Tis certain, greatness, once fall'n out with fortune,
Must fall out with men too. What the declin'd is,
He shall as soon read in the eyes of others
As feel in his own fall; for men, like butterflies,
Show not their mealy wings but to the summer;
And not a man for being simply man
Hath any honour, but honour for those honours
That are without him, as place, riches, and favour,
Prizes of accident, as oft as merit;
Which when they fall, as being slippery standers,
The love that lean'd on them as slippery too,
Doth one pluck down another, and together
Die in the fall. But 'tis not so with me:
Fortune and I are friends; I do enjoy
At ample point all that I did possess
Save these men's looks; who do, methinks, find out
Something not worth in me such rich beholding
As they have often given. Here is Ulysses.
I'll interrupt his reading.
How now, Ulysses!
ULYSSES: Now, great Thetis' son!
ACHILLES: What are you reading?
ULYSSES: A strange fellow here
Writes me that man-how dearly ever parted,
How much in having, or without or in-
Cannot make boast to have that which he hath,
Nor feels not what he owes, but by reflection;
As when his virtues shining upon others
Heat them, and they retort that heat again
To the first giver.

ACHILLES: This is not strange, Ulysses.
The beauty that is borne here in the face
The bearer knows not, but commends itself
To others' eyes; nor doth the eye itself-
That most pure spirit of sense-behold itself,
Not going from itself; but eye to eye opposed
Salutes each other with each other's form;
For speculation turns not to itself
Till it hath travell'd, and is mirror'd there
Where it may see itself. This is not strange at all.
ULYSSES: I do not strain at the position-
It is familiar-but at the author's drift;
Who, in his circumstance, expressly proves
That no man is the lord of anything,
Though in and of him there be much consisting,
Till he communicate his parts to others;
Nor doth he of himself know them for aught
Till he behold them formed in th' applause
Where th' are extended; who, like an arch, reverb'rate
The voice again; or, like a gate of steel
Fronting the sun, receives and renders back
His figure and his heat. I was much rapt in this;
And apprehended here immediately
Th' unknown Ajax. Heavens, what a man is there!
A very horse that has he knows not what!
Nature, what things there are
Most abject in regard and dear in use!
What things again most dear in the esteem
And poor in worth! Now shall we see to-morrow-
An act that very chance doth throw upon him-
Ajax renown'd. O heavens, what some men do,
While some men leave to do!
How some men creep in skittish Fortune's-hall,
Whiles others play the idiots in her eyes!
How one man eats into another's pride,
While pride is fasting in his wantonness!
To see these Grecian lords!-why, even already
They clap the lubber Ajax on the shoulder,
As if his foot were on brave Hector's breast,
And great Troy shrinking.
ACHILLES: I do believe it; for they pass'd by me
As misers do by beggars-neither gave to me
Good word nor look. What, are my deeds forgot?
ULYSSES: Time hath, my lord, a wallet at his back,
Wherein he puts alms for oblivion,
A great-siz'd monster of ingratitudes.
Those scraps are good deeds past, which are devour'd
As fast as they are made, forgot as soon
As done. Perseverance, dear my lord,
Keeps honour bright. To have done is to hang
Quite out of fashion, like a rusty mail
In monumental mock'ry. Take the instant way;
For honour travels in a strait so narrow -

Where one but goes abreast. Keep then the path,
For emulation hath a thousand sons
That one by one pursue; if you give way,
Or hedge aside from the direct forthright,
Like to an ent'red tide they all rush by
And leave you hindmost;
Or, like a gallant horse fall'n in first rank,
Lie there for pavement to the abject rear,
O'er-run and trampled on. Then what they do in present,
Though less than yours in past, must o'ertop yours;
For Time is like a fashionable host,
That slightly shakes his parting guest by th' hand;
And with his arms out-stretch'd, as he would fly,
Grasps in the corner. The welcome ever smiles,
And farewell goes out sighing. O, let not virtue seek
Remuneration for the thing it was;
For beauty, wit,
High birth, vigour of bone, desert in service,
Love, friendship, charity, are subjects all
To envious and calumniating Time.
One touch of nature makes the whole world kin-
That all with one consent praise new-born gawds,
Though they are made and moulded of things past,
And give to dust that is a little gilt
More laud than gilt o'er-dusted.
The present eye praises the present object.
Then marvel not, thou great and complete man,
That all the Greeks begin to worship Ajax,
Since things in motion sooner catch the eye
Than what stirs not. The cry went once on thee,
And still it might, and yet it may again,
If thou wouldst not entomb thyself alive
And case thy reputation in thy tent,
Whose glorious deeds but in these fields of late
Made emulous missions 'mongst the gods themselves,
And drave great Mars to faction.
ACHILLES: Of this my privacy
I have strong reasons.
ULYSSES: But 'gainst your privacy
The reasons are more potent and heroical.
'Tis known, Achilles, that you are in love
With one of Priam's daughters.
ACHILLES: Ha! known!
ULYSSES: Is that a wonder?
The providence that's in a watchful state
Knows almost every grain of Plutus' gold;
Finds bottom in th' uncomprehensive deeps;
Keeps place with thought, and almost, like the gods,
Do thoughts unveil in their dumb cradles.
There is a mystery-with whom relation
Durst never meddle-in the soul of state,
Which hath an operation more divine
Than breath or pen can give expressure to.

All the commerce that you have had with Troy
As perfectly is ours as yours, my lord;
And better would it fit Achilles much
To throw down Hector than Polyxena.
But it must grieve young Pyrrhus now at home,
When fame shall in our island sound her trump,
And all the Greekish girls shall tripping sing
'Great Hector's sister did Achilles win;
But our great Ajax bravely beat down him.'
Farewell, my lord. I as your lover speak.
The fool slides o'er the ice that you should break.
Exit
PATROCLUS: To this effect, Achilles, have I mov'd you.
A woman impudent and mannish grown
Is not more loath'd than an effeminate man
In time of action. I stand condemn'd for this;
They think my little stomach to the war
And your great love to me restrains you thus.
Sweet, rouse yourself; and the weak wanton Cupid
Shall from your neck unloose his amorous fold,
And, like a dew-drop from the lion's mane,
Be shook to airy air.
ACHILLES: Shall Ajax fight with Hector?
PATROCLUS: Ay, and perhaps receive much honour by him.
ACHILLES: I see my reputation is at stake;
My fame is shrewdly gor'd.
PATROCLUS: O, then, beware:
Those wounds heal ill that men do give themselves;
Omission to do what is necessary
Seals a commission to a blank of danger;
And danger, like an ague, subtly taints
Even then when they sit idly in the sun.
ACHILLES: Go call Thersites hither, sweet Patroclus.
I'll send the fool to Ajax, and desire him
T' invite the Troyan lords, after the combat,
To see us here unarm'd. I have a woman's longing,
An appetite that I am sick withal,
To see great Hector in his weeds of peace;
To talk with him, and to behold his visage,
Even to my full of view.
Enter Thersites
A labour sav'd!
THERSITES: A wonder!
ACHILLES: What?
THERSITES: Ajax goes up and down the field asking for himself.
ACHILLES: How so?
THERSITES: He must fight singly to-morrow with Hector, and is so prophetically proud of an heroical cudgelling that he raves in saying nothing.
ACHILLES: How can that be?
THERSITES: Why, 'a stalks up and down like a peacock-a stride and a stand; ruminaies like an hostess that hath no arithmetic but her brain to set down her reckoning, bites his lip with a politic

regard, as who should say 'There were wit in this head, an 'twould out'; and so there is; but it lies as coldly in him as fire in a flint, which will not show without knocking. The man's undone for ever; for if Hector break not his neck i' th' combat, he'll break't himself in vainglory. He knows not me. I said 'Good morrow, Ajax'; and he replies 'Thanks, Agamemnon.' What think you of this man that takes me for the general? He's grown a very land fish, languageless, a monster. A plague of opinion! A man may wear it on both sides, like leather jerkin.
ACHILLES: Thou must be my ambassador to him, Thersites.
THERSITES: Who, I? Why, he'll answer nobody; he professes not answering. Speaking is for beggars: he wears his tongue in's arms. I will put on his presence. Let Patroclus make his demands to me, you shall see the pageant of Ajax.
ACHILLES: To him, Patroclus. Tell him I humbly desire the valiant Ajax to invite the most valorous Hector to come unarm'd to my tent; and to procure safe conduct for his person of the magnanimous and most illustrious six-or-seven-times-honour'd Captain General of the Grecian army, et cetera, Agamemnon. Do this.
PATROCLUS: Jove bless great Ajax!
THERSITES: Hum!
PATROCLUS: I come from the worthy Achilles-
THERSITES: Ha!
PATROCLUS: Who most humbly desires you to invite Hector to his tent-
THERSITES: Hum!
PATROCLUS: And to procure safe conduct from Agamemnon.
THERSITES: Agamemnon!
PATROCLUS: Ay, my lord.
THERSITES: Ha!
PATROCLUS: What you say to't?
THERSITES: God buy you, with all my heart.
PATROCLUS: Your answer, sir.
THERSITES: If to-morrow be a fair day, by eleven of the clock it will go one way or other. Howsoever, he shall pay for me ere he has me.
PATROCLUS: Your answer, sir.
THERSITES: Fare ye well, with all my heart.
ACHILLES: Why, but he is not in this tune, is he?
THERSITES: No, but he's out a tune thus. What music will be in him when Hector has knock'd out his brains I know not; but, I am sure, none; unless the fiddler Apollo get his sinews to make catlings on.
ACHILLES: Come, thou shalt bear a letter to him straight.
THERSITES: Let me carry another to his horse; for that's the more capable creature.
ACHILLES: My mind is troubled, like a fountain stirr'd;
And I myself see not the bottom of it.
Exeunt Achilles and Patroclus
THERSITES: Would the fountain of your mind were clear again, that I might water an ass at it. I had rather be a tick in a sheep than such a valiant ignorance.
Exit

ACT IV. SCENE I. Troy. A Street

Enter, at One Side, Aeneas, and Servant with a Torch; at Another, Paris, Deiphobus, Antenor, Diomedes the Grecian, and Others, with Torches
PARIS: See, ho! Who is that there?
DEIPHOBUS: It is the Lord Aeneas.
AENEAS: Is the Prince there in person?
Had I so good occasion to lie long
As you, Prince Paris, nothing but heavenly business
Should rob my bed-mate of my company.
DIOMEDES: That's my mind too. Good morrow, Lord Aeneas.
PARIS: A valiant Greek, Aeneas -take his hand:
Witness the process of your speech, wherein
You told how Diomed, a whole week by days,
Did haunt you in the field.
AENEAS: Health to you, valiant sir,
During all question of the gentle truce;
But when I meet you arm'd, as black defiance
As heart can think or courage execute.
DIOMEDES: The one and other Diomed embraces.
Our bloods are now in calm; and so long health!
But when contention and occasion meet,
By Jove, I'll play the hunter for thy life
With all my force, pursuit, and policy.
AENEAS: And thou shalt hunt a lion, that will fly
With his face backward. In humane gentleness,
Welcome to Troy! now, by Anchises' life,
Welcome indeed! By Venus' hand I swear
No man alive can love in such a sort
The thing he means to kill, more excellently.
DIOMEDES: We sympathise. Jove let Aeneas live,
If to my sword his fate be not the glory,
A thousand complete courses of the sun!
But in mine emulous honour let him die
With every joint a wound, and that to-morrow!
AENEAS: We know each other well.
DIOMEDES:We do; and long to know each other worse.
PARIS: This is the most despiteful'st gentle greeting
The noblest hateful love, that e'er I heard of.
What business, lord, so early?
AENEAS: I was sent for to the King; but why, I know not.
PARIS: His purpose meets you: 'twas to bring this Greek
To Calchas' house, and there to render him,
For the enfreed Antenor, the fair Cressid.
Let's have your company; or, if you please,
Haste there before us. I constantly believe-
Or rather call my thought a certain knowledge-
My brother Troilus lodges there to-night.
Rouse him and give him note of our approach,
With the whole quality wherefore; I fear
We shall be much unwelcome.
AENEAS: That I assure you:
Troilus had rather Troy were borne to Greece
Than Cressid borne from Troy.

PARIS: There is no help;
The bitter disposition of the time
Will have it so. On, lord; we'll follow you.
AENEAS: Good morrow, all.
Exit with servant
PARIS: And tell me, noble Diomed-faith, tell me true,
Even in the soul of sound good-fellowship-
Who in your thoughts deserves fair Helen best,
Myself or Menelaus?
DIOMEDES: Both alike:
He merits well to have her that doth seek her,
Not making any scruple of her soilure,
With such a hell of pain and world of charge;
And you as well to keep her that defend her,
Not palating the taste of her dishonour,
With such a costly loss of wealth and friends.
He like a puling cuckold would drink up
The lees and dregs of a flat tamed piece;
You, like a lecher, out of whorish loins
Are pleas'd to breed out your inheritors.
Both merits pois'd, each weighs nor less nor more;
But he as he, the heavier for a whore.
PARIS: You are too bitter to your country-woman.
DIOMEDES: She's bitter to her country. Hear me, Paris:
For every false drop in her bawdy veins
A Grecian's life hath sunk; for every scruple
Of her contaminated carrion weight
A Troyan hath been slain; since she could speak,
She hath not given so many good words breath
As for her Greeks and Troyans suff'red death.
PARIS: Fair Diomed, you do as chapmen do,
Dispraise the thing that you desire to buy;
But we in silence hold this virtue well:
We'll not commend what we intend to sell.
Here lies our way.
Exeunt

ACT IV. SCENE II. Troy. The Court of Pandarus' House

Enter Troilus and Cressida
TROILUS: Dear, trouble not yourself; the morn is cold.
CRESSIDA: Then, sweet my lord, I'll call mine uncle down;
He shall unbolt the gates.
TROILUS: Trouble him not;
To bed, to bed! Sleep kill those pretty eyes,
And give as soft attachment to thy senses
As infants' empty of all thought!
CRESSIDA: Good morrow, then.
TROILUS: I prithee now, to bed.
CRESSIDA: Are you aweary of me?
TROILUS: O Cressida! but that the busy day,
Wak'd by the lark, hath rous'd the ribald crows,
And dreaming night will hide our joys no longer,
I would not from thee.
CRESSIDA: Night hath been too brief.

TROILUS: Beshrew the witch! with venomous wights she stays
As tediously as hell, but flies the grasps of love
With wings more momentary-swift than thought.
You will catch cold, and curse me.
CRESSIDA: Prithee tarry.
You men will never tarry.
O foolish Cressid! I might have still held off,
And then you would have tarried. Hark! there's one up.
PANDARUS: Within What's all the doors open here?
TROILUS: It is your uncle.
Enter Pandarus
CRESSIDA: A pestilence on him! Now will he be mocking.
I shall have such a life!
PANDARUS: How now, how now! How go maidenheads?
Here, you maid! Where's my cousin Cressid?
CRESSIDA: Go hang yourself, you naughty mocking uncle.
You bring me to do, and then you flout me too.
PANDARUS: To do what? to do what? Let her say what.
What have I brought you to do?
CRESSIDA: Come, come, beshrew your heart! You'll ne'er be good,
Nor suffer others.
PANDARUS: Ha, ha! Alas, poor wretch! a poor capocchia! hast not slept to-night? Would he not, a naughty man, let it sleep? A bugbear take him!
CRESSIDA: Did not I tell you? Would he were knock'd i' th' head!
One Knocks
Who's that at door? Good uncle, go and see.
My lord, come you again into my chamber.
You smile and mock me, as if I meant naughtily.
TROILUS: Ha! ha!
CRESSIDA: Come, you are deceiv'd, I think of no such thing.
Knock How earnestly they knock! Pray you come in:
I would not for half Troy have you seen here.
Exeunt Troilus and Cressida
PANDARUS: Who's there? What's the matter? Will you beat down the door? How now? What's the matter?
Enter Aeneas
AENEAS: Good morrow, lord, good morrow.
PANDARUS: Who's there? My lord Aeneas? By my troth,
I knew you not. What news with you so early?
AENEAS: Is not Prince Troilus here?
PANDARUS: Here! What should he do here?
AENEAS: Come, he is here, my lord; do not deny him.
It doth import him much to speak with me.
PANDARUS: Is he here, say you? It's more than I know, I'll be sworn. For my own part, I came in late. What should he do here?
AENEAS: Who!-nay, then. Come, come, you'll do him wrong ere you are ware; you'll be so true to him to be false to him. Do not you know of him, but yet go fetch him hither; go.
Re-enter Troilus
TROILUS: How now! What's the matter?
AENEAS: My lord, I scarce have leisure to salute you,
My matter is so rash. There is at hand

Paris your brother, and Deiphobus,
The Grecian Diomed, and our Antenor
Deliver'd to us; and for him forthwith,
Ere the first sacrifice, within this hour,
We must give up to Diomedes' hand
The Lady Cressida.
TROILUS: Is it so concluded?
AENEAS: By Priam, and the general state of Troy.
They are at hand and ready to effect it.
TROILUS: How my achievements mock me!
I will go meet them; and, my lord Aeneas,
We met by chance; you did not find me here.
AENEAS: Good, good, my lord, the secrets of neighbour Pandar
Have not more gift in taciturnity.
Exeunt Troilus and Aeneas
PANDARUS: Is't possible? No sooner got but lost? The devil take Antenor! The young prince will go mad. A plague upon Antenor! I would they had broke's neck.
Re-enter Cressida
CRESSIDA: How now! What's the matter? Who was here?
PANDARUS: Ah, ah!
CRESSIDA: Why sigh you so profoundly? Where's my lord? Gone? Tell me, sweet uncle, what's the matter?
PANDARUS: Would I were as deep under the earth as I am above!
CRESSIDA: O the gods! What's the matter?
PANDARUS: Pray thee, get thee in. Would thou hadst ne'er been born! I knew thou wouldst be his death! O, poor gentleman! A plague upon Antenor!
CRESSIDA: Good uncle, I beseech you, on my knees I beseech you, what's the matter?
PANDARUS: Thou must be gone, wench, thou must be gone; thou art chang'd for Antenor; thou must to thy father, and be gone from
TROILUS: 'Twill be his death; 'twill be his bane; he cannot bear it.
CRESSIDA: O you immortal gods! I will not go.
PANDARUS: Thou must.
CRESSIDA: I will not, uncle. I have forgot my father;
I know no touch of consanguinity,
No kin, no love, no blood, no soul so near me
As the sweet Troilus. O you gods divine,
Make Cressid's name the very crown of falsehood,
If ever she leave Troilus! Time, force, and death,
Do to this body what extremes you can,
But the strong base and building of my love
Is as the very centre of the earth,
Drawing all things to it. I'll go in and weep-
PANDARUS: Do, do.
CRESSIDA: Tear my bright hair, and scratch my praised cheeks,
Crack my clear voice with sobs and break my heart,
With sounding 'Troilus.' I will not go from Troy.
Exeunt

ACT IV. SCENE III. Troy. A Street Before Pandarus' House

Enter Paris, Troilus, Aeneas, Deiphobus, Antenor, and Diomedes
PARIS: It is great morning; and the hour prefix'd

For her delivery to this valiant Greek
Comes fast upon. Good my brother Troilus,
Tell you the lady what she is to do
And haste her to the purpose.
TROILUS: Walk into her house.
I'll bring her to the Grecian presently;
And to his hand when I deliver her,
Think it an altar, and thy brother Troilus
A priest, there off'ring to it his own heart.
Exit
PARIS: I know what 'tis to love,
And would, as I shall pity, I could help!
Please you walk in, my lords.
Exeunt

ACT IV. SCENE IV. Troy. Pandarus' House

Enter Pandarus and Cressida
PANDARUS: Be moderate, be moderate.
CRESSIDA: Why tell you me of moderation?
The grief is fine, full, perfect, that I taste,
And violenteth in a sense as strong
As that which causeth it. How can I moderate it?
If I could temporize with my affections
Or brew it to a weak and colder palate,
The like allayment could I give my grief.
My love admits no qualifying dross;
No more my grief, in such a precious loss.
Enter Troilus
PANDARUS: Here, here, here he comes. Ah, sweet ducks!
CRESSIDA: O Troilus! Troilus!
Embracing Him
PANDARUS: What a pair of spectacles is here! Let me embrace too. 'O heart,' as the goodly saying is,
O heart, heavy heart,
Why sigh'st thou without breaking?
where he answers again
Because thou canst not ease thy smart
By friendship nor by speaking.
There was never a truer rhyme. Let us cast away nothing, for we may live to have need of such a verse. We see it, we see it. How now, lambs!
TROILUS: Cressid, I love thee in so strain'd a purity
That the bless'd gods, as angry with my fancy,
More bright in zeal than the devotion which
Cold lips blow to their deities, take thee from me.
CRESSIDA: Have the gods envy?
PANDARUS: Ay, ay, ay; 'tis too plain a case.
CRESSIDA: And is it true that I must go from Troy?
TROILUS: A hateful truth.
CRESSIDA: What, and from Troilus too?
TROILUS: From Troy and Troilus.
CRESSIDA: Is't possible?
TROILUS: And suddenly; where injury of chance
Puts back leave-taking, justles roughly by

All time of pause, rudely beguiles our lips
Of all rejoindure, forcibly prevents
Our lock'd embrasures, strangles our dear vows
Even in the birth of our own labouring breath.
We two, that with so many thousand sighs
Did buy each other, must poorly sell ourselves
With the rude brevity and discharge of one.
Injurious time now with a robber's haste
Crams his rich thievery up, he knows not how.
As many farewells as be stars in heaven,
With distinct breath and consign'd kisses to them,
He fumbles up into a loose adieu,
And scants us with a single famish'd kiss,
Distasted with the salt of broken tears.
AENEAS: Within My lord, is the lady ready?
TROILUS: Hark! you are call'd. Some say the Genius so
Cries 'Come' to him that instantly must die.
Bid them have patience; she shall come anon.
PANDARUS: Where are my tears? Rain, to lay this wind, or my heart will be blown up by th' root?
Exit
CRESSIDA: I must then to the Grecians?
TROILUS: No remedy.
CRESSIDA: A woeful Cressid 'mongst the merry Greeks!
When shall we see again?
TROILUS: Hear me, my love. Be thou but true of heart-
CRESSIDA: I true! how now! What wicked deem is this?
TROILUS: Nay, we must use expostulation kindly,
For it is parting from us.
I speak not 'Be thou true' as fearing thee,
For I will throw my glove to Death himself
That there's no maculation in thy heart;
But 'Be thou true' say I to fashion in
My sequent protestation: be thou true,
And I will see thee.
CRESSIDA: O, you shall be expos'd, my lord, to dangers
As infinite as imminent! But I'll be true.
TROILUS: And I'll grow friend with danger. Wear this sleeve.
CRESSIDA: And you this glove. When shall I see you?
TROILUS: I will corrupt the Grecian sentinels
To give thee nightly visitation.
But yet be true.
CRESSIDA: O heavens! 'Be true' again!
TROILUS: Hear why I speak it, love.
The Grecian youths are full of quality;
They're loving, well compos'd with gifts of nature,
And flowing o'er with arts and exercise.
How novelties may move, and parts with person,
Alas, a kind of godly jealousy,
Which I beseech you call a virtuous sin,
Makes me afeard.
CRESSIDA: O heavens! you love me not.
TROILUS: Die I a villain, then!

In this I do not call your faith in question
So mainly as my merit. I cannot sing,
Nor heel the high lavolt, nor sweeten talk,
Nor play at subtle games-fair virtues all,
To which the Grecians are most prompt and pregnant;
But I can tell that in each grace of these
There lurks a still and dumb-discoursive devil
That tempts most cunningly. But be not tempted.
CRESSIDA: Do you think I will?
TROILUS: No.
But something may be done that we will not;
And sometimes we are devils to ourselves,
When we will tempt the frailty of our powers,
Presuming on their changeful potency.
AENEAS: Within Nay, good my lord!
TROILUS: Come, kiss; and let us part.
PARIS: Within Brother Troilus!
TROILUS: Good brother, come you hither;
And bring Aeneas and the Grecian with you.
CRESSIDA: My lord, will you be true?
TROILUS: Who, I? Alas, it is my vice, my fault!
Whiles others fish with craft for great opinion,
I with great truth catch mere simplicity;
Whilst some with cunning gild their copper crowns,
With truth and plainness I do wear mine bare.
Enter Aeneas, Paris, Antenor, Deiphobus, and Diomedes
Fear not my truth: the moral of my wit
Is 'plain and true'; there's all the reach of it.
Welcome, Sir Diomed! Here is the lady
Which for Antenor we deliver you;
At the port, lord, I'll give her to thy hand,
And by the way possess thee what she is.
Entreat her fair; and, by my soul, fair Greek,
If e'er thou stand at mercy of my sword,
Name Cressid, and thy life shall be as safe
As Priam is in Ilion.
DIOMEDES: Fair Lady Cressid,
So please you, save the thanks this prince expects.
The lustre in your eye, heaven in your cheek,
Pleads your fair usage; and to Diomed
You shall be mistress, and command him wholly.
TROILUS: Grecian, thou dost not use me courteously
To shame the zeal of my petition to the
In praising her. I tell thee, lord of Greece,
She is as far high-soaring o'er thy praises
As thou unworthy to be call'd her servant.
I charge thee use her well, even for my charge;
For, by the dreadful Pluto, if thou dost not,
Though the great bulk Achilles be thy guard,
I'll cut thy throat.
DIOMEDES: O, be not mov'd, Prince Troilus.
Let me be privileg'd by my place and message
To be a speaker free: when I am hence

I'll answer to my lust. And know you, lord,
I'll nothing do on charge: to her own worth
She shall be priz'd. But that you say 'Be't so,'
I speak it in my spirit and honour, 'No.'
TROILUS: Come, to the port. I'll tell thee, Diomed,
This brave shall oft make thee to hide thy head.
Lady, give me your hand; and, as we walk,
To our own selves bend we our needful talk.
Exeunt Troilus, Cressida, and Diomedes Sound Trumpet
PARIS: Hark! Hector's trumpet.
AENEAS: How have we spent this morning!
The Prince must think me tardy and remiss,
That swore to ride before him to the field.
PARIS: 'Tis Troilus' fault. Come, come to field with him.
DEIPHOBUS: Let us make ready straight.
AENEAS: Yea, with a bridegroom's fresh alacrity
Let us address to tend on Hector's heels.
The glory of our Troy doth this day lie
On his fair worth and single chivalry.
Exeunt

ACT IV. SCENE V. The Grecian Camp. Lists Set out

Enter Ajax, Armed; Agamemnon, Achilles, Patroclus, Menelaus, Ulysses, Nestor, and Others
AGAMEMNON: Here art thou in appointment fresh and fair,
Anticipating time with starting courage.
Give with thy trumpet a loud note to Troy,
Thou dreadful Ajax, that the appalled air
May pierce the head of the great combatant,
And hale him hither.
AJAX: Thou, trumpet, there's my purse.
Now crack thy lungs and split thy brazen pipe;
Blow, villain, till thy sphered bias cheek
Out-swell the colic of puff Aquilon'd.
Come, stretch thy chest, and let thy eyes spout blood:
Thou blowest for Hector.
Trumpet Sounds
ULYSSES: No trumpet answers.
ACHILLES: 'Tis but early days.
Enter Diomedes, with Cressida
AGAMEMNON: Is not yond Diomed, with Calchas' daughter?
ULYSSES: 'Tis he, I ken the manner of his gait:
He rises on the toe. That spirit of his
In aspiration lifts him from the earth.
AGAMEMNON: Is this the lady Cressid?
DIOMEDES: Even she.
AGAMEMNON: Most dearly welcome to the Greeks, sweet lady.
NESTOR: Our general doth salute you with a kiss.
ULYSSES: Yet is the kindness but particular;
'Twere better she were kiss'd in general.
NESTOR: And very courtly counsel: I'll begin.
So much for Nestor.
ACHILLES: I'll take that winter from your lips, fair lady.
Achilles bids you welcome.
MENELAUS: I had good argument for kissing once.

PATROCLUS: But that's no argument for kissing now;
For thus popp'd Paris in his hardiment,
And parted thus you and your argument.
ULYSSES: O deadly gall, and theme of all our scorns!
For which we lose our heads to gild his horns.
PATROCLUS: The first was Menelaus' kiss; this, mine-
Kisses Her Again
Patroclus kisses you.
MENELAUS: O, this is trim!
PATROCLUS: Paris and I kiss evermore for him.
MENELAUS: I'll have my kiss, sir. Lady, by your leave.
CRESSIDA: In kissing, do you render or receive?
PATROCLUS: Both take and give.
CRESSIDA: I'll make my match to live,
The kiss you take is better than you give;
Therefore no kiss.
MENELAUS: I'll give you boot; I'll give you three for one.
CRESSIDA: You are an odd man; give even or give none.
MENELAUS: An odd man, lady? Every man is odd.
CRESSIDA: No, Paris is not; for you know 'tis true
That you are odd, and he is even with you.
MENELAUS: You fillip me o' th' head.
CRESSIDA: No, I'll be sworn.
ULYSSES: It were no match, your nail against his horn.
May I, sweet lady, beg a kiss of you?
CRESSIDA: You may.
ULYSSES: I do desire it.
CRESSIDA: Why, beg then.
ULYSSES: Why then, for Venus' sake give me a kiss
When Helen is a maid again, and his.
CRESSIDA: I am your debtor; claim it when 'tis due.
ULYSSES: Never's my day, and then a kiss of you.
DIOMEDES: Lady, a word. I'll bring you to your father.
Exit with Cressida
NESTOR: A woman of quick sense.
ULYSSES: Fie, fie upon her!
There's language in her eye, her cheek, her lip,
Nay, her foot speaks; her wanton spirits look out
At every joint and motive of her body.
O these encounters so glib of tongue
That give a coasting welcome ere it comes,
And wide unclasp the tables of their thoughts
To every ticklish reader! Set them down
For sluttish spoils of opportunity,
And daughters of the game.
Trumpet Within
ALL: The Troyans' trumpet.
Enter Hector, Armed; Aeneas, Troilus, Paris, Helenus, and Other Trojans, with Attendants
AGAMEMNON: Yonder comes the troop.
AENEAS: Hail, all the state of Greece! What shall be done
To him that victory commands? Or do you purpose
A victor shall be known? Will you the knights
Shall to the edge of all extremity

Pursue each other, or shall they be divided
By any voice or order of the field?
Hector bade ask.
AGAMEMNON: Which way would Hector have it?
AENEAS: He cares not; he'll obey conditions.
ACHILLES: 'Tis done like Hector; but securely done,
A little proudly, and great deal misprizing
The knight oppos'd.
AENEAS: If not Achilles, sir,
What is your name?
ACHILLES: If not Achilles, nothing.
AENEAS: Therefore Achilles. But whate'er, know this:
In the extremity of great and little
Valour and pride excel themselves in Hector;
The one almost as infinite as all,
The other blank as nothing. Weigh him well,
And that which looks like pride is courtesy.
This Ajax is half made of Hector's blood;
In love whereof half Hector stays at home;
Half heart, half hand, half Hector comes to seek
This blended knight, half Troyan and half Greek.
ACHILLES: A maiden battle then? O, I perceive you!
Re-enter Diomedes
AGAMEMNON: Here is Sir Diomed. Go, gentle knight,
Stand by our Ajax. As you and Lord Eneas
Consent upon the order of their fight,
So be it; either to the uttermost,
Or else a breath. The combatants being kin
Half stints their strife before their strokes begin.
Ajax and Hector Enter the Lists
ULYSSES: They are oppos'd already.
AGAMEMNON: What Troyan is that same that looks so heavy?
ULYSSES: The youngest son of Priam, a true knight;
Not yet mature, yet matchless; firm of word;
Speaking in deeds and deedless in his tongue;
Not soon provok'd, nor being provok'd soon calm'd;
His heart and hand both open and both free;
For what he has he gives, what thinks he shows,
Yet gives he not till judgment guide his bounty,
Nor dignifies an impair thought with breath;
Manly as Hector, but more dangerous;
For Hector in his blaze of wrath subscribes
To tender objects, but he in heat of action
Is more vindicative than jealous love.
They call him Troilus, and on him erect
A second hope as fairly built as Hector.
Thus says Aeneas, one that knows the youth
Even to his inches, and, with private soul,
Did in great Ilion thus translate him to me.
Alarum. Hector and Ajax Fight
AGAMEMNON: They are in action.
NESTOR: Now, Ajax, hold thine own!
TROILUS: Hector, thou sleep'st;

Awake thee.
AGAMEMNON: His blows are well dispos'd. There, Ajax!
Trumpets Cease
DIOMEDES: You must no more.
AENEAS: Princes, enough, so please you.
AJAX: I am not warm yet; let us fight again.
DIOMEDES: As Hector pleases.
HECTOR: Why, then will I no more.
Thou art, great lord, my father's sister's son,
A cousin-german to great Priam's seed;
The obligation of our blood forbids
A gory emulation 'twixt us twain:
Were thy commixtion Greek and Troyan so
That thou could'st say 'This hand is Grecian all,
And this is Troyan; the sinews of this leg
All Greek, and this all Troy; my mother's blood
Runs on the dexter cheek, and this sinister
Bounds in my father's'; by Jove multipotent,
Thou shouldst not bear from me a Greekish member
Wherein my sword had not impressure made
Of our rank feud; but the just gods gainsay
That any drop thou borrow'dst from thy mother,
My sacred aunt, should by my mortal sword
Be drained! Let me embrace thee, Ajax.
By him that thunders, thou hast lusty arms;
Hector would have them fall upon him thus.
Cousin, all honour to thee!
AJAX: I thank thee, Hector.
Thou art too gentle and too free a man.
I came to kill thee, cousin, and bear hence
A great addition earned in thy death.
HECTOR: Not Neoptolemus so mirable,
On whose bright crest Fame with her loud'st Oyes
Cries 'This is he' could promise to himself
A thought of added honour torn from Hector.
AENEAS: There is expectance here from both the sides
What further you will do.
HECTOR: We'll answer it:
The issue is embracement. Ajax, farewell.
AJAX: If I might in entreaties find success,
As seld I have the chance, I would desire
My famous cousin to our Grecian tents.
DIOMEDES: 'Tis Agamemnon's wish; and great Achilles
Doth long to see unarm'd the valiant Hector.
HECTOR: Aeneas, call my brother Troilus to me,
And signify this loving interview
To the expecters of our Troyan part;
Desire them home. Give me thy hand, my cousin;
I will go eat with thee, and see your knights.
Agamemnon and the Rest of the Greeks Come Forward
AJAX: Great Agamemnon comes to meet us here.
HECTOR: The worthiest of them tell me name by name;
But for Achilles, my own searching eyes

Shall find him by his large and portly size.
AGAMEMNON: Worthy all arms! as welcome as to one
That would be rid of such an enemy.
But that's no welcome. Understand more clear,
What's past and what's to come is strew'd with husks
And formless ruin of oblivion;
But in this extant moment, faith and troth,
Strain'd purely from all hollow bias-drawing,
Bids thee with most divine integrity,
From heart of very heart, great Hector, welcome.
HECTOR: I thank thee, most imperious Agamemnon.
AGAMEMNON: To Troilus My well-fam'd lord of Troy, no less to you.
MENELAUS: Let me confirm my princely brother's greeting.
You brace of warlike brothers, welcome hither.
HECTOR: Who must we answer?
AENEAS: The noble Menelaus.
HECTOR: O you, my lord? By Mars his gauntlet, thanks!
Mock not that I affect the untraded oath;
Your quondam wife swears still by Venus' glove.
She's well, but bade me not commend her to you.
MENELAUS: Name her not now, sir; she's a deadly theme.
HECTOR: O, pardon; I offend.
NESTOR: I have, thou gallant Troyan, seen thee oft,
Labouring for destiny, make cruel way
Through ranks of Greekish youth; and I have seen thee,
As hot as Perseus, spur thy Phrygian steed,
Despising many forfeits and subduements,
When thou hast hung thy advanced sword i' th' air,
Not letting it decline on the declined;
That I have said to some my standers-by
'Lo, Jupiter is yonder, dealing life!'
And I have seen thee pause and take thy breath,
When that a ring of Greeks have hemm'd thee in,
Like an Olympian wrestling. This have I seen;
But this thy countenance, still lock'd in steel,
I never saw till now. I knew thy grandsire,
And once fought with him. He was a soldier good,
But, by great Mars, the captain of us all,
Never like thee. O, let an old man embrace thee;
And, worthy warrior, welcome to our tents.
AENEAS: 'Tis the old Nestor.
HECTOR: Let me embrace thee, good old chronicle,
That hast so long walk'd hand in hand with time.
Most reverend Nestor, I am glad to clasp thee.
NESTOR: I would my arms could match thee in contention
As they contend with thee in courtesy.
HECTOR: I would they could.
NESTOR: Ha!
By this white beard, I'd fight with thee to-morrow.
Well, welcome, welcome! I have seen the time.
ULYSSES: I wonder now how yonder city stands,
When we have here her base and pillar by us.
HECTOR: I know your favour, Lord Ulysses, well.

Ah, sir, there's many a Greek and Troyan dead,
Since first I saw yourself and Diomed
In Ilion on your Greekish embassy.
ULYSSES: Sir, I foretold you then what would ensue.
My prophecy is but half his journey yet;
For yonder walls, that pertly front your town,
Yond towers, whose wanton tops do buss the clouds,
Must kiss their own feet.
HECTOR: I must not believe you.
There they stand yet; and modestly I think
The fall of every Phrygian stone will cost
A drop of Grecian blood. The end crowns all;
And that old common arbitrator, Time,
Will one day end it.
ULYSSES: So to him we leave it.
Most gentle and most valiant Hector, welcome.
After the General, I beseech you next
To feast with me and see me at my tent.
ACHILLES: I shall forestall thee, Lord Ulysses, thou!
Now, Hector, I have fed mine eyes on thee;
I have with exact view perus'd thee, Hector,
And quoted joint by joint.
HECTOR: Is this Achilles?
ACHILLES: I am Achilles.
HECTOR: Stand fair, I pray thee; let me look on thee.
ACHILLES: Behold thy fill.
HECTOR: Nay, I have done already.
ACHILLES: Thou art too brief. I will the second time,
As I would buy thee, view thee limb by limb.
HECTOR: O, like a book of sport thou'lt read me o'er;
But there's more in me than thou understand'st.
Why dost thou so oppress me with thine eye?
ACHILLES: Tell me, you heavens, in which part of his body
Shall I destroy him? Whether there, or there, or there?
That I may give the local wound a name,
And make distinct the very breach whereout
Hector's great spirit flew. Answer me, heavens.
HECTOR: It would discredit the blest gods, proud man,
To answer such a question. Stand again.
Think'st thou to catch my life so pleasantly
As to prenominate in nice conjecture
Where thou wilt hit me dead?
ACHILLES: I tell thee yea.
HECTOR: Wert thou an oracle to tell me so,
I'd not believe thee. Henceforth guard thee well;
For I'll not kill thee there, nor there, nor there;
But, by the forge that stithied Mars his helm,
I'll kill thee everywhere, yea, o'er and o'er.
You wisest Grecians, pardon me this brag.
His insolence draws folly from my lips;
But I'll endeavour deeds to match these words,
Or may I never-
AJAX: Do not chafe thee, cousin;

And you, Achilles, let these threats alone
Till accident or purpose bring you to't.
You may have every day enough of Hector,
If you have stomach. The general state, I fear,
Can scarce entreat you to be odd with him.
HECTOR: I pray you let us see you in the field;
We have had pelting wars since you refus'd
The Grecians' cause.
ACHILLES: Dost thou entreat me, Hector?
To-morrow do I meet thee, fell as death;
To-night all friends.
HECTOR: Thy hand upon that match.
AGAMEMNON: First, all you peers of Greece, go to my tent;
There in the full convive we; afterwards,
As Hector's leisure and your bounties shall
Concur together, severally entreat him.
Beat loud the tambourines, let the trumpets blow,
That this great soldier may his welcome know.
Exeunt All but Troilus and Ulysses
TROILUS: My Lord Ulysses, tell me, I beseech you,
In what place of the field doth Calchas keep?
ULYSSES: At Menelaus' tent, most princely Troilus.
There Diomed doth feast with him to-night,
Who neither looks upon the heaven nor earth,
But gives all gaze and bent of amorous view
On the fair Cressid.
TROILUS: Shall I, sweet lord, be bound to you so much,
After we part from Agamemnon's tent,
To bring me thither?
ULYSSES: You shall command me, sir.
As gentle tell me of what honour was
This Cressida in Troy? Had she no lover there
That wails her absence?
TROILUS: O, sir, to such as boasting show their scars
A mock is due. Will you walk on, my lord?
She was belov'd, she lov'd; she is, and doth;
But still sweet love is food for fortune's tooth.
Exeunt

ACT V. SCENE I. The Grecian Camp. Before the Tent of Achilles

Enter Achilles and Patroclus
ACHILLES: I'll heat his blood with Greekish wine to-night,
Which with my scimitar I'll cool to-morrow.
Patroclus, let us feast him to the height.
PATROCLUS: Here comes Thersites.
Enter Thersites
ACHILLES: How now, thou core of envy!
Thou crusty batch of nature, what's the news?
THERSITES: Why, thou picture of what thou seemest, and idol of idiot worshippers, here's a letter for thee.
ACHILLES: From whence, fragment?
THERSITES: Why, thou full dish of fool, from Troy.
PATROCLUS: Who keeps the tent now?
THERSITES: The surgeon's box or the patient's wound.

PATROCLUS: Well said, Adversity! and what needs these tricks?
THERSITES: Prithee, be silent, boy; I profit not by thy talk; thou art said to be Achilles' male varlet.
PATROCLUS: Male varlet, you rogue! What's that?
THERSITES: Why, his masculine whore. Now, the rotten diseases of the south, the guts-griping ruptures, catarrhs, loads o' gravel in the back, lethargies, cold palsies, raw eyes, dirt-rotten livers, wheezing lungs, bladders full of imposthume, sciaticas, limekilns i' th' palm, incurable bone-ache, and the rivelled fee-simple of the tetter, take and take again such preposterous discoveries!
PATROCLUS: Why, thou damnable box of envy, thou, what meanest thou to curse thus?
THERSITES: Do I curse thee?
PATROCLUS: Why, no, you ruinous butt; you whoreson indistinguishable cur, no.
THERSITES: No! Why art thou, then, exasperate, thou idle immaterial skein of sleid silk, thou green sarcenet flap for a sore eye, thou tassel of a prodigal's purse, thou? Ah, how the poor world is pest'red with such water-flies-diminutives of nature!
PATROCLUS: Out, gall!
THERSITES: Finch egg!
ACHILLES: My sweet Patroclus, I am thwarted quite
From my great purpose in to-morrow's battle.
Here is a letter from Queen Hecuba,
A token from her daughter, my fair love,
Both taxing me and gaging me to keep
An oath that I have sworn. I will not break it.
Fall Greeks; fail fame; honour or go or stay;
My major vow lies here, this I'll obey.
Come, come, Thersites, help to trim my tent;
This night in banqueting must all be spent.
Away, Patroclus!
Exit with Patroclus
THERSITES: With too much blood and too little brain these two may run mad; but, if with too much brain and to little blood they do, I'll be a curer of madmen. Here's Agamemnon, an honest fellow enough, and one that loves quails, but he has not so much brain as ear-wax; and the goodly transformation of Jupiter there, his brother, the bull, the primitive statue and oblique memorial of cuckolds, a thrifty shoeing-horn in a chain, hanging at his brother's leg-to what form but that he is, should wit larded with malice, and malice forced with wit, turn him to? To an ass, were nothing: he is both ass and ox. To an ox, were nothing: he is both ox and ass. To be a dog, a mule, a cat, a fitchew, a toad, a lizard, an owl, a put-tock, or a herring without a roe, I would not care; but to be Menelaus, I would conspire against destiny. Ask me not what I would be, if I were not Thersites; for I care not to be the louse of a lazar, so I were not Menelaus. Hey-day! sprites and fires!
Enter Hector, Troilus, Ajax, Agamemnon, Ulysses, Nestor, Menelaus, and Diomedes, with Lights
AGAMEMNON: We go wrong, we go wrong.
AJAX: No, yonder 'tis;

There, where we see the lights.
HECTOR: I trouble you.
AJAX: No, not a whit.
Re-enter Achilles
ULYSSES: Here comes himself to guide you.
ACHILLES: Welcome, brave Hector; welcome, Princes all.
AGAMEMNON: So now, fair Prince of Troy, I bid good night;
Ajax commands the guard to tend on you.
HECTOR: Thanks, and good night to the Greeks' general.
MENELAUS: Good night, my lord.
HECTOR: Good night, sweet Lord Menelaus.
THERSITES: Sweet draught! 'Sweet' quoth 'a?
Sweet sink, sweet sewer!
ACHILLES: Good night and welcome, both at once, to those
That go or tarry.
AGAMEMNON: Good night.
Exeunt Agamemnon and Menelaus
ACHILLES: Old Nestor tarries; and you too, Diomed,
Keep Hector company an hour or two.
DIOMEDES: I cannot, lord; I have important business,
The tide whereof is now. Good night, great Hector.
HECTOR: Give me your hand.
ULYSSES: Aside to Troilus Follow his torch; he goes to
Calchas' tent; I'll keep you company.
TROILUS: Sweet sir, you honour me.
HECTOR: And so, good night.
Exit Diomedes; Ulysses and Troilus Following
ACHILLES: Come, come, enter my tent.
Exeunt All but Thersites
THERSITES: That same Diomed's a false-hearted rogue, a most unjust knave; I will no more trust him when he leers than I will a serpent when he hisses. He will spend his mouth and promise, like Brabbler the hound; but when he performs, astronomers foretell it: it is prodigious, there will come some change; the sun borrows of the moon when Diomed keeps his word. I will rather leave to see Hector than not to dog him. They say he keeps a Troyan drab, and uses the traitor Calchas' tent. I'll after. Nothing but lechery! All incontinent varlets!
Exit

ACT V. SCENE II. The Grecian Camp. Before Calchas' Tent

Enter Diomedes
DIOMEDES: What, are you up here, ho? Speak.
CALCHAS: Within Who calls?
DIOMEDES: Diomed. Calchas, I think. Where's your daughter?
CALCHAS: Within She comes to you.
Enter Troilus and Ulysses, at a Distance; after Them Thersites.
ULYSSES: Stand Where the Torch May Not Discover Us.
Enter Cressida
TROILUS: Cressid comes forth to him.
DIOMEDES: How now, my charge!
CRESSIDA: Now, my sweet guardian! Hark, a word with you.
Whispers
TROILUS: Yea, so familiar!

ULYSSES: She will sing any man at first sight.
THERSITES: And any man may sing her, if he can take her cliff; she's noted.
DIOMEDES: Will you remember?
CRESSIDA: Remember? Yes.
DIOMEDES: Nay, but do, then;
And let your mind be coupled with your words.
TROILUS: What shall she remember?
ULYSSES: List!
CRESSIDA: Sweet honey Greek, tempt me no more to folly.
THERSITES: Roguery!
DIOMEDES: Nay, then-
CRESSIDA: I'll tell you what-
DIOMEDES: Fo, fo! come, tell a pin; you are a forsworn-
CRESSIDA: In faith, I cannot. What would you have me do?
THERSITES: A juggling trick, to be secretly open.
DIOMEDES: What did you swear you would bestow on me?
CRESSIDA: I prithee, do not hold me to mine oath;
Bid me do anything but that, sweet Greek.
DIOMEDES: Good night.
TROILUS: Hold, patience!
ULYSSES: How now, Troyan!
CRESSIDA: Diomed!
DIOMEDES: No, no, good night; I'll be your fool no more.
TROILUS: Thy better must.
CRESSIDA: Hark! a word in your ear.
TROILUS: O plague and madness!
ULYSSES: You are moved, Prince; let us depart, I pray,
Lest your displeasure should enlarge itself
To wrathful terms. This place is dangerous;
The time right deadly; I beseech you, go.
TROILUS: Behold, I pray you.
ULYSSES: Nay, good my lord, go off;
You flow to great distraction; come, my lord.
TROILUS: I prithee stay.
ULYSSES: You have not patience; come.
TROILUS: I pray you, stay; by hell and all hell's torments,
I will not speak a word.
DIOMEDES: And so, good night.
CRESSIDA: Nay, but you part in anger.
TROILUS: Doth that grieve thee? O withered truth!
ULYSSES: How now, my lord?
TROILUS: By Jove, I will be patient.
CRESSIDA: Guardian! Why, Greek!
DIOMEDES: Fo, fo! adieu! you palter.
CRESSIDA: In faith, I do not. Come hither once again.
ULYSSES: You shake, my lord, at something; will you go?
You will break out.
TROILUS: She strokes his cheek.
ULYSSES: Come, come.
TROILUS: Nay, stay; by Jove, I will not speak a word:
There is between my will and all offences
A guard of patience. Stay a little while.

THERSITES: How the devil luxury, with his fat rump and potato finger, tickles these together! Fry, lechery, fry!
DIOMEDES: But will you, then?
CRESSIDA: In faith, I will, lo; never trust me else.
DIOMEDES: Give me some token for the surety of it.
CRESSIDA: I'll fetch you one.
Exit
ULYSSES: You have sworn patience.
TROILUS: Fear me not, my lord;
I will not be myself, nor have cognition
Of what I feel. I am all patience.
Re-enter Cressida
THERSITES: Now the pledge; now, now, now!
CRESSIDA: Here, Diomed, keep this sleeve.
TROILUS: O beauty! where is thy faith?
ULYSSES: My lord!
TROILUS: I will be patient; outwardly I will.
CRESSIDA: You look upon that sleeve; behold it well.
He lov'd me-O false wench!-Give't me again.
DIOMEDES: Whose was't?
CRESSIDA: It is no matter, now I ha't again.
I will not meet with you to-morrow night.
I prithee, Diomed, visit me no more.
THERSITES: Now she sharpens. Well said, whetstone.
DIOMEDES: I shall have it.
CRESSIDA: What, this?
DIOMEDES: Ay, that.
CRESSIDA: O all you gods! O pretty, pretty pledge!
Thy master now lies thinking on his bed
Of thee and me, and sighs, and takes my glove,
And gives memorial dainty kisses to it,
As I kiss thee. Nay, do not snatch it from me;
He that takes that doth take my heart withal.
DIOMEDES: I had your heart before; this follows it.
TROILUS: I did swear patience.
CRESSIDA: You shall not have it, Diomed; faith, you shall not;
I'll give you something else.
DIOMEDES: I will have this. Whose was it?
CRESSIDA: It is no matter.
DIOMEDES: Come, tell me whose it was.
CRESSIDA: 'Twas one's that lov'd me better than you will.
But, now you have it, take it.
DIOMEDES: Whose was it?
CRESSIDA: By all Diana's waiting women yond,
And by herself, I will not tell you whose.
DIOMEDES: To-morrow will I wear it on my helm,
And grieve his spirit that dares not challenge it.
TROILUS: Wert thou the devil and wor'st it on thy horn,
It should be challeng'd.
CRESSIDA: Well, well, 'tis done, 'tis past; and yet it is not;
I will not keep my word.
DIOMEDES: Why, then farewell;
Thou never shalt mock Diomed again.

CRESSIDA: You shall not go. One cannot speak a word
But it straight starts you.
DIOMEDES: I do not like this fooling.
THERSITES: Nor I, by Pluto; but that that likes not you
Pleases me best.
DIOMEDES: What, shall I come? The hour-
CRESSIDA: Ay, come-O Jove! Do come. I shall be plagu'd.
DIOMEDES: Farewell till then.
CRESSIDA: Good night. I prithee come.
Exit Diomedes
Troilus, farewell! One eye yet looks on thee;
But with my heart the other eye doth see.
Ah, poor our sex! this fault in us I find,
The error of our eye directs our mind.
What error leads must err; O, then conclude,
Minds sway'd by eyes are full of turpitude.
Exit
THERSITES: A proof of strength she could not publish more,
Unless she said 'My mind is now turn'd whore.'
ULYSSES: All's done, my lord.
TROILUS: It is.
ULYSSES: Why stay we, then?
TROILUS: To make a recordation to my soul
Of every syllable that here was spoke.
But if I tell how these two did coact,
Shall I not lie in publishing a truth?
Sith yet there is a credence in my heart,
An esperance so obstinately strong,
That doth invert th' attest of eyes and ears;
As if those organs had deceptious functions
Created only to calumniate.
Was Cressid here?
ULYSSES: I cannot conjure, Troyan.
TROILUS: She was not, sure.
ULYSSES: Most sure she was.
TROILUS: Why, my negation hath no taste of madness.
ULYSSES: Nor mine, my lord. Cressid was here but now.
TROILUS: Let it not be believ'd for womanhood.
Think, we had mothers; do not give advantage
To stubborn critics, apt, without a theme,
For depravation, to square the general sex
By Cressid's rule. Rather think this not Cressid.
ULYSSES: What hath she done, Prince, that can soil our mothers?
TROILUS: Nothing at all, unless that this were she.
THERSITES: Will 'a swagger himself out on's own eyes?
TROILUS: This she? No; this is Diomed's Cressida.
If beauty have a soul, this is not she;
If souls guide vows, if vows be sanctimonies,
If sanctimony be the god's delight,
If there be rule in unity itself,
This was not she. O madness of discourse,
That cause sets up with and against itself!
Bifold authority! where reason can revolt

Without perdition, and loss assume all reason
Without revolt: this is, and is not, Cressid.
Within my soul there doth conduce a fight
Of this strange nature, that a thing inseparate
Divides more wider than the sky and earth;
And yet the spacious breadth of this division
Admits no orifex for a point as subtle
As Ariachne's broken woof to enter.
Instance, O instance! strong as Pluto's gates:
Cressid is mine, tied with the bonds of heaven.
Instance, O instance! strong as heaven itself:
The bonds of heaven are slipp'd, dissolv'd, and loos'd;
And with another knot, five-finger-tied,
The fractions of her faith, orts of her love,
The fragments, scraps, the bits, and greasy relics
Of her o'er-eaten faith, are bound to Diomed.
ULYSSES: May worthy Troilus be half-attach'd
With that which here his passion doth express?
TROILUS: Ay, Greek; and that shall be divulged well
In characters as red as Mars his heart
Inflam'd with Venus. Never did young man fancy
With so eternal and so fix'd a soul.
Hark, Greek: as much as I do Cressid love,
So much by weight hate I her Diomed.
That sleeve is mine that he'll bear on his helm;
Were it a casque compos'd by Vulcan's skill
My sword should bite it. Not the dreadful spout
Which shipmen do the hurricano call,
Constring'd in mass by the almighty sun,
Shall dizzy with more clamour Neptune's ear
In his descent than shall my prompted sword
Falling on Diomed.
THERSITES: He'll tickle it for his concupy.
TROILUS: O Cressid! O false Cressid! false, false, false!
Let all untruths stand by thy stained name,
And they'll seem glorious.
ULYSSES: O, contain yourself;
Your passion draws ears hither.
Enter Aeneas
AENEAS: I have been seeking you this hour, my lord.
Hector, by this, is arming him in Troy;
Ajax, your guard, stays to conduct you home.
TROILUS: Have with you, Prince. My courteous lord, adieu.
Fairwell, revolted fair!-and, Diomed,
Stand fast and wear a castle on thy head.
ULYSSES: I'll bring you to the gates.
TROILUS: Accept distracted thanks.
Exeunt Troilus, Aeneas. And Ulysses
THERSITES: Would I could meet that rogue
Diomed! I would croak like a raven; I would
bode, I would bode. Patroclus will give me
anything for the intelligence of this whore;
the parrot will not do more for an almond than

he for a commodious drab. Lechery, lechery!
Still wars and lechery! Nothing else holds fashion.
A burning devil take them!
Exit

ACT V. SCENE III. Troy. Before Priam's Palace

Enter Hector and Andromache
ANDROMACHE: When was my lord so much ungently temper'd
To stop his ears against admonishment?
Unarm, unarm, and do not fight to-day.
HECTOR: You train me to offend you; get you in.
By all the everlasting gods, I'll go.
ANDROMACHE: My dreams will, sure, prove ominous to the day.
HECTOR: No more, I say.
Enter Cassandra
CASSANDRA: Where is my brother Hector?
ANDROMACHE: Here, sister, arm'd, and bloody in intent.
Consort with me in loud and dear petition,
Pursue we him on knees; for I have dreamt
Of bloody turbulence, and this whole night
Hath nothing been but shapes and forms of slaughter.
CASSANDRA: O, 'tis true!
HECTOR: Ho! bid my trumpet sound.
CASSANDRA: No notes of sally, for the heavens, sweet brother!
HECTOR: Be gone, I say. The gods have heard me swear.
CASSANDRA: The gods are deaf to hot and peevish vows;
They are polluted off'rings, more abhorr'd
Than spotted livers in the sacrifice.
ANDROMACHE: O, be persuaded! Do not count it holy
To hurt by being just. It is as lawful,
For we would give much, to use violent thefts
And rob in the behalf of charity.
CASSANDRA: It is the purpose that makes strong the vow;
But vows to every purpose must not hold.
Unarm, sweet Hector.
HECTOR: Hold you still, I say.
Mine honour keeps the weather of my fate.
Life every man holds dear; but the dear man
Holds honour far more precious dear than life.
Enter Troilus
How now, young man! Mean'st thou to fight to-day?
ANDROMACHE: Cassandra, call my father to persuade.
Exit Cassandra
HECTOR: No, faith, young Troilus; doff thy harness, youth;
I am to-day i' th' vein of chivalry.
Let grow thy sinews till their knots be strong,
And tempt not yet the brushes of the war.
Unarm thee, go; and doubt thou not, brave boy,
I'll stand to-day for thee and me and Troy.
TROILUS: Brother, you have a vice of mercy in you
Which better fits a lion than a man.
HECTOR: What vice is that, good Troilus?
Chide me for it.
TROILUS: When many times the captive Grecian falls,

Even in the fan and wind of your fair sword,
You bid them rise and live.
HECTOR: O, 'tis fair play!
TROILUS: Fool's play, by heaven, Hector.
HECTOR: How now! how now!
TROILUS: For th' love of all the gods,
Let's leave the hermit Pity with our mother;
And when we have our armours buckled on,
The venom'd vengeance ride upon our swords,
Spur them to ruthful work, rein them from ruth!
HECTOR: Fie, savage, fie!
TROILUS: Hector, then 'tis wars.
HECTOR: Troilus, I would not have you fight to-day.
TROILUS: Who should withhold me?
Not fate, obedience, nor the hand of Mars
Beck'ning with fiery truncheon my retire;
Not Priamus and Hecuba on knees,
Their eyes o'ergalled with recourse of tears;
Nor you, my brother, with your true sword drawn,
Oppos'd to hinder me, should stop my way,
But by my ruin.
Re-enter Cassandra, with Priam
CASSANDRA: Lay hold upon him, Priam, hold him fast;
He is thy crutch; now if thou lose thy stay,
Thou on him leaning, and all Troy on thee,
Fall all together.
PRIAM: Come, Hector, come, go back.
Thy wife hath dreamt; thy mother hath had visions;
Cassandra doth foresee; and I myself
Am like a prophet suddenly enrapt
To tell thee that this day is ominous.
Therefore, come back.
HECTOR: Aeneas is a-field;
And I do stand engag'd to many Greeks,
Even in the faith of valour, to appear
This morning to them.
PRIAM: Ay, but thou shalt not go.
HECTOR: I must not break my faith.
You know me dutiful; therefore, dear sir,
Let me not shame respect; but give me leave
To take that course by your consent and voice
Which you do here forbid me, royal Priam.
CASSANDRA: O Priam, yield not to him!
ANDROMACHE: Do not, dear father.
HECTOR: Andromache, I am offended with you.
Upon the love you bear me, get you in.
Exit Andromache
TROILUS: This foolish, dreaming, superstitious girl
Makes all these bodements.
CASSANDRA: O, farewell, dear Hector!
Look how thou diest. Look how thy eye turns pale.
Look how thy wounds do bleed at many vents.
Hark how Troy roars; how Hecuba cries out;

How poor Andromache shrills her dolours forth;
Behold distraction, frenzy, and amazement,
Like witless antics, one another meet,
And all cry, Hector! Hector's dead! O Hector!
TROILUS: Away, away!
CASSANDRA: Farewell!-yet, soft! Hector, I take my leave.
Thou dost thyself and all our Troy deceive.
Exit
HECTOR: You are amaz'd, my liege, at her exclaim.
Go in, and cheer the town; we'll forth, and fight,
Do deeds worth praise and tell you them at night.
PRIAM: Farewell. The gods with safety stand about thee!
Exeunt Severally Priam and Hector. Alarums
TROILUS: They are at it, hark! Proud Diomed, believe,
I come to lose my arm or win my sleeve.
Enter Pandarus
PANDARUS: Do you hear, my lord? Do you hear?
TROILUS: What now?
PANDARUS: Here's a letter come from yond poor girl.
TROILUS: Let me read.
PANDARUS: A whoreson tisick, a whoreson rascally tisick so troubles me, and the foolish fortune of this girl, and what one thing, what another, that I shall leave you one o' th's days; and I have a rheum in mine eyes too, and such an ache in my bones that unless a man were curs'd I cannot tell what to think on't. What says she there?
TROILUS: Words, words, mere words, no matter from the heart;
Th' effect doth operate another way.
Tearing the Letter
Go, wind, to wind, there turn and change together.
My love with words and errors still she feeds,
But edifies another with her deeds.
Exeunt Severally

ACT V. SCENE IV. The Plain Between Troy and the Grecian Camp

Enter Thersites. Excursions
THERSITES: Now they are clapper-clawing one another; I'll go look on. That dissembling abominable varlet, Diomed, has got that same scurvy doting foolish young knave's sleeve of Troy there in his helm. I would fain see them meet, that that same young Troyan ass that loves the whore there might send that Greekish whoremasterly villain with the sleeve back to the dissembling luxurious drab of a sleeve-less errand. A th' t'other side, the policy of those crafty swearing rascals-that stale old mouse-eaten dry cheese, Nestor, and that same dog-fox, Ulysses -is not prov'd worth a blackberry. They set me up, in policy, that mongrel cur, Ajax, against that dog of as bad a kind, Achilles; and now is the cur, Ajax prouder than the cur Achilles, and will not arm to-day; whereupon the Grecians begin to proclaim barbarism, and policy grows into an ill opinion.
Enter Diomedes, Troilus Following

Soft! here comes sleeve, and t'other.
TROILUS: Fly not; for shouldst thou take the river Styx
I would swim after.
DIOMEDES: Thou dost miscall retire.
I do not fly; but advantageous care
Withdrew me from the odds of multitude.
Have at thee.
THERSITES: Hold thy whore, Grecian; now for thy whore,
Troyan-now the sleeve, now the sleeve!
Exeunt Troilus and Diomedes Fighting
Enter Hector
HECTOR: What art thou, Greek? Art thou for Hector's match?
Art thou of blood and honour?
THERSITES: No, no-I am a rascal; a scurvy railing knave; a very filthy rogue.
HECTOR: I do believe thee. Live.
Exit
THERSITES: God-a-mercy, that thou wilt believe me; but a plague break thy neck for frighting me! What's become of the wenching rogues? I think they have swallowed one another. I would laugh at that miracle. Yet, in a sort, lechery eats itself. I'll seek them.
Exit

ACT V. SCENE V. Another Part of the Plain

Enter Diomedes and a Servant
DIOMEDES: Go, go, my servant, take thou Troilus' horse;
Present the fair steed to my lady Cressid.
Fellow, commend my service to her beauty;
Tell her I have chastis'd the amorous Troyan,
And am her knight by proof.
SERVANT: I go, my lord.
Exit
Enter Agamemnon
AGAMEMNON: Renew, renew! The fierce Polydamus
Hath beat down enon; bastard Margarelon
Hath Doreus prisoner,
And stands colossus-wise, waving his beam,
Upon the pashed corses of the kings
Epistrophus and Cedius. Polixenes is slain;
Amphimacus and Thoas deadly hurt;
Patroclus ta'en, or slain; and Palamedes
Sore hurt and bruis'd. The dreadful Sagittary
Appals our numbers. Haste we, Diomed,
To reinforcement, or we perish all.
Enter Nestor
NESTOR: Go, bear Patroclus' body to Achilles,
And bid the snail-pac'd Ajax arm for shame.
There is a thousand Hectors in the field;
Now here he fights on Galathe his horse,
And there lacks work; anon he's there afoot,
And there they fly or die, like scaled sculls
Before the belching whale; then is he yonder,
And there the strawy Greeks, ripe for his edge,

Fall down before him like the mower's swath.
Here, there, and everywhere, he leaves and takes;
Dexterity so obeying appetite
That what he will he does, and does so much
That proof is call'd impossibility.
Enter Ulysses
ULYSSES: O, courage, courage, courage, Princes! Great
Achilles Is arming, weeping, cursing, vowing vengeance.
Patroclus' wounds have rous'd his drowsy blood,
Together with his mangled Myrmidons,
That noseless, handless, hack'd and chipp'd, come to
him, Crying on Hector. Ajax hath lost a friend
And foams at mouth, and he is arm'd and at it,
Roaring for Troilus; who hath done to-day
Mad and fantastic execution,
Engaging and redeeming of himself
With such a careless force and forceless care
As if that luck, in very spite of cunning,
Bade him win all.
Enter Ajax
AJAX: Troilus! thou coward Troilus!
Exit
DIOMEDES: Ay, there, there.
NESTOR: So, so, we draw together.
Exit
Enter Achilles
ACHILLES: Where is this Hector?
Come, come, thou boy-queller, show thy face;
Know what it is to meet Achilles angry.
Hector! where's Hector? I will none but Hector.
Exeunt

ACT V. SCENE VI. Another Part of the Plain

Enter Ajax
AJAX: Troilus, thou coward Troilus, show thy head.
Enter Diomedes
DIOMEDES: Troilus, I say! Where's Troilus?
AJAX: What wouldst thou?
DIOMEDES: I would correct him.
AJAX: Were I the general, thou shouldst have my office
Ere that correction. Troilus, I say! What, Troilus!
Enter Troilus
TROILUS: O traitor Diomed! Turn thy false face, thou traitor,
And pay thy life thou owest me for my horse.
DIOMEDES: Ha! art thou there?
AJAX: I'll fight with him alone. Stand, Diomed.
DIOMEDES: He is my prize. I will not look upon.
TROILUS: Come, both, you cogging Greeks; have at you
Exeunt Fighting
Enter Hector
HECTOR: Yea, Troilus? O, well fought, my youngest brother!
Enter Achilles
ACHILLES: Now do I see thee, ha! Have at thee, Hector!
HECTOR: Pause, if thou wilt.

ACHILLES: I do disdain thy courtesy, proud Troyan.
Be happy that my arms are out of use;
My rest and negligence befriends thee now,
But thou anon shalt hear of me again;
Till when, go seek thy fortune.
Exit
HECTOR: Fare thee well.
I would have been much more a fresher man,
Had I expected thee.
Re-enter Troilus
How now, my brother!
TROILUS: Ajax hath ta'en Aeneas. Shall it be?
No, by the flame of yonder glorious heaven,
He shall not carry him; I'll be ta'en too,
Or bring him off. Fate, hear me what I say:
I reck not though thou end my life to-day.
Exit
Enter One in Armour
HECTOR: Stand, stand, thou Greek; thou art a goodly mark.
No? wilt thou not? I like thy armour well;
I'll frush it and unlock the rivets all
But I'll be master of it. Wilt thou not, beast, abide?
Why then, fly on; I'll hunt thee for thy hide.
Exeunt

ACT V. SCENE VII. Another Part of the Plain

Enter Achilles, with Myrmidons
ACHILLES: Come here about me, you my Myrmidons;
Mark what I say. Attend me where I wheel;
Strike not a stroke, but keep yourselves in breath;
And when I have the bloody Hector found,
Empale him with your weapons round about;
In fellest manner execute your arms.
Follow me, sirs, and my proceedings eye.
It is decreed Hector the great must die.
Exeunt
Enter Menelaus and Paris, Fighting; Then Thersites
THERSITES: The cuckold and the cuckold-maker are at it. Now, bull! now, dog! 'Loo, Paris, 'loo! now my double-horn'd Spartan! 'loo, Paris, 'loo! The bull has the game. Ware horns, ho!
Exeunt Paris and Menelaus
Enter Margarelon
MARGARELON: Turn, slave, and fight.
THERSITES: What art thou?
MARGARELON: A bastard son of Priam's.
THERSITES: I am a bastard too; I love bastards. I am a bastard begot, bastard instructed, bastard in mind, bastard in valour, in everything illegitimate. One bear will not bite another, and wherefore should one bastard? Take heed, the quarrel's most ominous to us: if the son of a whore fight for a whore, he tempts judgment. Farewell, bastard.
Exit
MARGARELON: The devil take thee, coward!
Exit

ACT V. SCENE VIII. Another Part of the Plain

Enter Hector

HECTOR: Most putrified core so fair without,
Thy goodly armour thus hath cost thy life.
Now is my day's work done; I'll take good breath:
Rest, sword; thou hast thy fill of blood and death!

Disarms

Enter Achilles and His Myrmidons

ACHILLES: Look, Hector, how the sun begins to set;
How ugly night comes breathing at his heels;
Even with the vail and dark'ning of the sun,
To close the day up, Hector's life is done.
HECTOR: I am unarm'd; forego this vantage, Greek.
ACHILLES: Strike, fellows, strike; this is the man I seek.

Hector Falls

So, Ilion, fall thou next! Come, Troy, sink down;
Here lies thy heart, thy sinews, and thy bone.
On, Myrmidons, and cry you an amain
'Achilles hath the mighty Hector slain.'

A Retreat Sounded

Hark! a retire upon our Grecian part.
MYRMIDON: The Troyan trumpets sound the like, my lord.
ACHILLES: The dragon wing of night o'erspreads the earth
And, stickler-like, the armies separates.
My half-supp'd sword, that frankly would have fed,
Pleas'd with this dainty bait, thus goes to bed.

Sheathes His Sword

Come, tie his body to my horse's tail;
Along the field I will the Troyan trail. Exeunt

ACT V. SCENE IX. Another Part of the Plain

Sound Retreat. Shout. Enter Agamemnon, Ajax, Menelaus, Nestor, Diomedes, and the Rest, Marching

AGAMEMNON: Hark! hark! what shout is this?
NESTOR: Peace, drums!
SOLDIERS: Within Achilles! Achilles! Hector's slain. Achilles!
DIOMEDES: The bruit is Hector's slain, and by Achilles.
AJAX: If it be so, yet bragless let it be;
Great Hector was as good a man as he.
AGAMEMNON: March patiently along. Let one be sent
To pray Achilles see us at our tent.
If in his death the gods have us befriended;
Great Troy is ours, and our sharp wars are ended.

Exeunt

ACT V. SCENE X. Another Part of the Plain

Enter Aeneas, Paris, Antenor, and Deiphobus

AENEAS: Stand, ho! yet are we masters of the field.
Never go home; here starve we out the night.

Enter Troilus

TROILUS: Hector is slain.
ALL: Hector! The gods forbid!
TROILUS: He's dead, and at the murderer's horse's tail,
In beastly sort, dragg'd through the shameful field.
Frown on, you heavens, effect your rage with speed.

Sit, gods, upon your thrones, and smile at Troy.
I say at once let your brief plagues be mercy,
And linger not our sure destructions on.
AENEAS: My lord, you do discomfort all the host.
TROILUS: You understand me not that tell me so.
I do not speak of flight, of fear of death,
But dare all imminence that gods and men
Address their dangers in. Hector is gone.
Who shall tell Priam so, or Hecuba?
Let him that will a screech-owl aye be call'd
Go in to Troy, and say there 'Hector's dead.'
There is a word will Priam turn to stone;
Make wells and Niobes of the maids and wives,
Cold statues of the youth; and, in a word,
Scare Troy out of itself. But, march away;
Hector is dead; there is no more to say.
Stay yet. You vile abominable tents,
Thus proudly pight upon our Phrygian plains,
Let Titan rise as early as he dare,
I'll through and through you. And, thou great-siz'd coward,
No space of earth shall sunder our two hates;
I'll haunt thee like a wicked conscience still,
That mouldeth goblins swift as frenzy's thoughts.
Strike a free march to Troy. With comfort go;
Hope of revenge shall hide our inward woe.
Enter Pandarus
PANDARUS: But hear you, hear you!
TROILUS: Hence, broker-lackey. Ignominy and shame
Pursue thy life and live aye with thy name!
Exeunt All but Pandarus
PANDARUS: A goodly medicine for my aching bones! world! world! thus is the poor agent despis'd! traitors and bawds, how earnestly are you set a work, and how ill requited! Why should our endeavour be so lov'd, and the performance so loathed? What verse for it? What instance for it? Let me see-

Full merrily the humble-bee doth sing
Till he hath lost his honey and his sting;
And being once subdu'd in armed trail,
Sweet honey and sweet notes together fail.

Good traders in the flesh, set this in your painted cloths. As many as be here of pander's hall,
Your eyes, half out, weep out at Pandar's fall;
Or, if you cannot weep, yet give some groans,
Though not for me, yet for your aching bones.
Brethren and sisters of the hold-door trade,
Some two months hence my will shall here be made.
It should be now, but that my fear is this,
Some galled goose of Winchester would hiss.
Till then I'll sweat and seek about for eases,
And at that time bequeath you my diseases.
Exit

END

The Tragedy of Othello, Moor of Venice

Dramatis Personae
OTHELLO, the Moor, general of the Venetian forces
DESDEMONA, his wife
IAGO, ensign to Othello
EMILIA, his wife, lady-in-waiting to Desdemona
CASSIO, lieutenant to Othello
THE DUKE OF VENICE
BRABANTIO, Venetian Senator, father of Desdemona
GRATIANO, nobleman of Venice, brother of Brabantio
LODOVICO, nobleman of Venice, kinsman of Brabantio
RODERIGO, rejected suitor of Desdemona
BIANCA, mistress of Cassio
MONTANO, a Cypriot official
A Clown in service to Othello
Senators, Sailors, Messengers, Officers, Gentlemen, Musicians, and Attendants

SCENE: Venice and Cyprus

ACT I. SCENE I. Venice. A Street.

Enter Roderigo and Iago.
RODERIGO: Tush, never tell me! I take it much unkindly
That thou, Iago, who hast had my purse
As if the strings were thine, shouldst know of this.
IAGO: 'Sblood, but you will not hear me.
If ever I did dream of such a matter,
Abhor me.
RODERIGO: Thou told'st me thou didst hold him in thy hate.
IAGO: Despise me, if I do not. Three great ones of the city,
In personal suit to make me his lieutenant,
Off-capp'd to him; and, by the faith of man,
I know my price, I am worth no worse a place.
But he, as loving his own pride and purposes,
Evades them, with a bumbast circumstance
Horribly stuff'd with epithets of war,
And, in conclusion,
Nonsuits my mediators; for, "Certes," says he,
"I have already chose my officer."
And what was he?
Forsooth, a great arithmetician,
One Michael Cassio, a Florentine
(A fellow almost damn'd in a fair wife)
That never set a squadron in the field,
Nor the division of a battle knows
More than a spinster; unless the bookish theoric,
Wherein the toged consuls can propose
As masterly as he. Mere prattle without practice
Is all his soldiership. But he, sir, had the election;
And I, of whom his eyes had seen the proof
At Rhodes, at Cyprus, and on other grounds
Christian and heathen, must be belee'd and calm'd
By debitor and creditor. This counter-caster,
He, in good time, must his lieutenant be,
And I- God bless the mark!- his Moorship's ancient.

RODERIGO: By heaven, I rather would have been his hangman.
IAGO: Why, there's no remedy. 'Tis the curse of service,
Preferment goes by letter and affection,
And not by old gradation, where each second
Stood heir to the first. Now, sir, be judge yourself
Whether I in any just term am affined
To love the Moor.
RODERIGO: I would not follow him then.
IAGO: O, sir, content you.
I follow him to serve my turn upon him:
We cannot all be masters, nor all masters
Cannot be truly follow'd. You shall mark
Many a duteous and knee-crooking knave,
That doting on his own obsequious bondage
Wears out his time, much like his master's ass,
For nought but provender, and when he's old, cashier'd.
Whip me such honest knaves. Others there are
Who, trimm'd in forms and visages of duty,
Keep yet their hearts attending on themselves,
And throwing but shows of service on their lords
Do well thrive by them; and when they have lined their coats
Do themselves homage. These fellows have some soul,
And such a one do I profess myself.
For, sir, it is as sure as you are Roderigo,
Were I the Moor, I would not be Iago.
In following him, I follow but myself;
Heaven is my judge, not I for love and duty,
But seeming so, for my peculiar end.
For when my outward action doth demonstrate
The native act and figure of my heart
In complement extern, 'tis not long after
But I will wear my heart upon my sleeve
For daws to peck at: I am not what I am.
RODERIGO: What a full fortune does the thick-lips owe,
If he can carry't thus!
IAGO: Call up her father,
Rouse him, make after him, poison his delight,
Proclaim him in the streets, incense her kinsmen,
And, though he in a fertile climate dwell,
Plague him with flies. Though that his joy be joy,
Yet throw such changes of vexation on't
As it may lose some color.
RODERIGO: Here is her father's house; I'll call aloud.
IAGO: Do, with like timorous accent and dire yell
As when, by night and negligence, the fire
Is spied in populous cities.
RODERIGO: What, ho, Brabantio! Signior Brabantio, ho!
IAGO: Awake! What, ho, Brabantio! Thieves! Thieves! Thieves!
Look to your house, your daughter, and your bags!
Thieves! Thieves!
Brabantio appears above, at a window.
BRABANTIO: What is the reason of this terrible summons?
What is the matter there?

RODERIGO: Signior, is all your family within?
IAGO: Are your doors lock'd?
BRABANTIO: Why? Wherefore ask you this?
IAGO: 'Zounds, sir, you're robb'd! For shame, put on your gown;
Your heart is burst, you have lost half your soul;
Even now, now, very now, an old black ram
Is tupping your white ewe. Arise, arise!
Awake the snorting citizens with the bell,
Or else the devil will make a grandsire of you.
Arise, I say!
BRABANTIO: What, have you lost your wits?
RODERIGO: Most reverend signior, do you know my voice?
BRABANTIO: Not I. What are you?
RODERIGO: My name is Roderigo.
BRABANTIO: The worser welcome.
I have charged thee not to haunt about my doors.
In honest plainness thou hast heard me say
My daughter is not for thee; and now, in madness,
Being full of supper and distempering draughts,
Upon malicious bravery, dost thou come
To start my quiet.
RODERIGO: Sir, sir, sir-
BRABANTIO: But thou must needs be sure
My spirit and my place have in them power
To make this bitter to thee.
RODERIGO: Patience, good sir.
BRABANTIO: What tell'st thou me of robbing? This is Venice;
My house is not a grange.
RODERIGO: Most grave Brabantio,
In simple and pure soul I come to you.
IAGO: 'Zounds, sir, you are one of those that will not serve God, if the devil bid you. Because we come to do you service and you think we are ruffians, you'll have your daughter covered with a Barbary horse; you'll have your nephews neigh to you; you'll have coursers for cousins, and gennets for germans.
BRABANTIO: What profane wretch art thou?
IAGO: I am one, sir, that comes to tell you your daughter and the Moor are now making the beast with two backs.
BRABANTIO: Thou are a villain.
IAGO: You are- a senator.
BRABANTIO: This thou shalt answer; I know thee, Roderigo.
RODERIGO: Sir, I will answer anything. But, I beseech you,
If't be your pleasure and most wise consent,
As partly I find it is, that your fair daughter,
At this odd-even and dull watch o' the night,
Transported with no worse nor better guard
But with a knave of common hire, a gondolier,
To the gross clasps of a lascivious Moor-
If this be known to you, and your allowance,
We then have done you bold and saucy wrongs;
But if you know not this, my manners tell me
We have your wrong rebuke. Do not believe
That, from the sense of all civility,

I thus would play and trifle with your reverence.
Your daughter, if you have not given her leave,
I say again, hath made a gross revolt,
Tying her duty, beauty, wit, and fortunes
In an extravagant and wheeling stranger
Of here and everywhere. Straight satisfy yourself:
If she be in her chamber or your house,
Let loose on me the justice of the state
For thus deluding you.
BRABANTIO: Strike on the tinder, ho!
Give me a taper! Call up all my people!
This accident is not unlike my dream;
Belief of it oppresses me already.
Light, I say, light!
Exit above.
IAGO: Farewell, for I must leave you.
It seems not meet, nor wholesome to my place,
To be produced- as, if I stay, I shall-
Against the Moor; for I do know, the state,
However this may gall him with some check,
Cannot with safety cast him, for he's embark'd
With such loud reason to the Cyprus wars,
Which even now stands in act, that, for their souls,
Another of his fathom they have none
To lead their business; in which regard,
Though I do hate him as I do hell pains,
Yet for necessity of present life,
I must show out a flag and sign of love,
Which is indeed but sign. That you shall surely find him,
Lead to the Sagittary the raised search,
And there will I be with him. So farewell.
Exit.
Enter, Below, Brabantio, in His Nightgown, and Servants with Torches.
BRABANTIO: It is too true an evil: gone she is,
And what's to come of my despised time
Is nought but bitterness. Now, Roderigo,
Where didst thou see her? O unhappy girl!
With the Moor, say'st thou? Who would be a father!
How didst thou know 'twas she? O, she deceives me
Past thought! What said she to you? Get more tapers.
Raise all my kindred. Are they married, think you?
RODERIGO: Truly, I think they are.
BRABANTIO: O heaven! How got she out? O treason of the blood!
Fathers, from hence trust not your daughters' minds
By what you see them act. Is there not charms
By which the property of youth and maidhood
May be abused? Have you not read, Roderigo,
Of some such thing?
RODERIGO: Yes, sir, I have indeed.
BRABANTIO: Call up my brother. O, would you had had her!
Some one way, some another. Do you know
Where we may apprehend her and the Moor?
RODERIGO: I think I can discover him, if you please

To get good guard and go along with me.
BRABANTIO: Pray you, lead on. At every house I'll call;
I may command at most. Get weapons, ho!
And raise some special officers of night.
On, good Roderigo, I'll deserve your pains.
Exeunt.

ACT I. SCENE II. Another Street.

Enter Othello, Iago, and Attendants with Torches.
IAGO: Though in the trade of war I have slain men,
Yet do I hold it very stuff o' the conscience
To do no contrived murther. I lack iniquity
Sometimes to do me service. Nine or ten times
I had thought to have yerk'd him here under the ribs.
OTHELLO: 'Tis better as it is.
IAGO: Nay, but he prated
And spoke such scurvy and provoking terms
Against your honor
That, with the little godliness I have,
I did full hard forbear him. But I pray you, sir,
Are you fast married? Be assured of this,
That the magnifico is much beloved,
And hath in his effect a voice potential
As double as the Duke's. He will divorce you,
Or put upon you what restraint and grievance
The law, with all his might to enforce it on,
Will give him cable.
OTHELLO: Let him do his spite.
My services, which I have done the signiory,
Shall out-tongue his complaints. 'Tis yet to know-
Which, when I know that boasting is an honor,
I shall promulgate- I fetch my life and being
From men of royal siege, and my demerits
May speak unbonneted to as proud a fortune
As this that I have reach'd. For know, Iago,
But that I love the gentle Desdemona,
I would not my unhoused free condition
Put into circumscription and confine
For the sea's worth. But, look! What lights come yond?
IAGO: Those are the raised father and his friends.
You were best go in.
OTHELLO: Not I; I must be found.
My parts, my title, and my perfect soul
Shall manifest me rightly. Is it they?
IAGO: By Janus, I think no.
Enter Cassio and Certain Officers with Torches.
OTHELLO: The servants of the Duke? And my lieutenant?
The goodness of the night upon you, friends!
What is the news?
CASSIO: The Duke does greet you, general,
And he requires your haste-post-haste appearance,
Even on the instant.
OTHELLO: What is the matter, think you?
CASSIO: Something from Cyprus, as I may divine;

It is a business of some heat. The galleys
Have sent a dozen sequent messengers
This very night at one another's heels;
And many of the consuls, raised and met,
Are at the Duke's already. You have been hotly call'd for,
When, being not at your lodging to be found,
The Senate hath sent about three several quests
To search you out.
OTHELLO: 'Tis well I am found by you.
I will but spend a word here in the house
And go with you.
Exit.
CASSIO: Ancient, what makes he here?
IAGO: Faith, he tonight hath boarded a land carack;
If it prove lawful prize, he's made forever.
CASSIO: I do not understand.
IAGO: He's married.
CASSIO: To who?
Re-enter Othello.
IAGO: Marry, to- Come, captain, will you go?
OTHELLO: Have with you.
CASSIO: Here comes another troop to seek for you.
IAGO: It is Brabantio. General, be advised,
He comes to bad intent.
Enter Brabantio, Roderigo, and Officers with Torches and Weapons.
OTHELLO: Holla! Stand there!
RODERIGO: Signior, it is the Moor.
BRABANTIO: Down with him, thief!
They Draw on Both Sides.
IAGO: You, Roderigo! Come, sir, I am for you.
OTHELLO: Keep up your bright swords, for the dew will rust them.
Good signior, you shall more command with years
Than with your weapons.
BRABANTIO: O thou foul thief, where hast thou stow'd my daughter?
Damn'd as thou art, thou hast enchanted her,
For I'll refer me to all things of sense,
If she in chains of magic were not bound,
Whether a maid so tender, fair, and happy,
So opposite to marriage that she shunn'd
The wealthy, curled darlings of our nation,
Would ever have, to incur a general mock,
Run from her guardage to the sooty bosom
Of such a thing as thou- to fear, not to delight.
Judge me the world, if 'tis not gross in sense
That thou hast practiced on her with foul charms,
Abused her delicate youth with drugs or minerals
That weaken motion. I'll have't disputed on;
'Tis probable, and palpable to thinking.
I therefore apprehend and do attach thee
For an abuser of the world, a practicer
Of arts inhibited and out of warrant.
Lay hold upon him. If he do resist,
Subdue him at his peril.

OTHELLO: Hold your hands,
Both you of my inclining and the rest.
Were it my cue to fight, I should have known it
Without a prompter. Where will you that I go
To answer this your charge?
BRABANTIO: To prison, till fit time
Of law and course of direct session
Call thee to answer.
OTHELLO: What if I do obey?
How may the Duke be therewith satisfied,
Whose messengers are here about my side,
Upon some present business of the state
To bring me to him?
FIRST OFFICER: 'Tis true, most worthy signior;
The Duke's in council, and your noble self,
I am sure, is sent for.
BRABANTIO: How? The Duke in council?
In this time of the night? Bring him away;
Mine's not an idle cause. The Duke himself,
Or any of my brothers of the state,
Cannot but feel this wrong as 'twere their own;
For if such actions may have passage free,
Bond slaves and pagans shall our statesmen be.
Exeunt.

ACT I. SCENE III. A Council Chamber.

The Duke and Senators Sitting at a Table; Officers Attending.

DUKE: There is no composition in these news
That gives them credit.
FIRST SENATOR: Indeed they are disproportion'd;
My letters say a hundred and seven galleys.
DUKE: And mine, a hundred and forty.
SECOND SENATOR: And mine, two hundred.
But though they jump not on a just account-
As in these cases, where the aim reports,
'Tis oft with difference- yet do they all confirm
A Turkish fleet, and bearing up to Cyprus.
DUKE: Nay, it is possible enough to judgement.
I do not so secure me in the error,
But the main article I do approve
In fearful sense.
SAILOR: Within. What, ho! What, ho! What, ho!
FIRST OFFICER: A messenger from the galleys.
Enter Sailor.
DUKE: Now, what's the business?
SAILOR: The Turkish preparation makes for Rhodes,
So was I bid report here to the state
By Signior Angelo.
DUKE: How say you by this change?
FIRST SENATOR: This cannot be,
By no assay of reason; 'tis a pageant
To keep us in false gaze. When we consider
The importancy of Cyprus to the Turk,

And let ourselves again but understand
That as it more concerns the Turk than Rhodes,
So may he with more facile question bear it,
For that it stands not in such warlike brace,
But altogether lacks the abilities
That Rhodes is dress'd in. If we make thought of this,
We must not think the Turk is so unskillful
To leave that latest which concerns him first,
Neglecting an attempt of ease and gain,
To wake and wage a danger profitless.
DUKE: Nay, in all confidence, he's not for Rhodes.
FIRST OFFICER: Here is more news.
Enter a Messenger.
MESSENGER: The Ottomites, reverend and gracious,
Steering with due course toward the isle of Rhodes,
Have there injointed them with an after fleet.
FIRST SENATOR: Ay, so I thought. How many, as you guess?
MESSENGER: Of thirty sail; and now they do re-stem
Their backward course, bearing with frank appearance
Their purposes toward Cyprus. Signior Montano,
Your trusty and most valiant servitor,
With his free duty recommends you thus,
And prays you to believe him.
DUKE: 'Tis certain then for Cyprus.
Marcus Luccicos, is not he in town?
FIRST SENATOR: He's now in Florence.
DUKE: Write from us to him, post-post-haste dispatch.
FIRST SENATOR: Here comes Brabantio and the valiant Moor.
Enter Brabantio, Othello, Iago, Roderigo, and Officers.
DUKE: Valiant Othello, we must straight employ you
Against the general enemy Ottoman.
To Brabantio. I did not see you; welcome, gentle signior;
We lack'd your counsel and your help tonight.
BRABANTIO: So did I yours. Good your Grace, pardon me:
Neither my place nor aught I heard of business
Hath raised me from my bed, nor doth the general care
Take hold on me; for my particular grief
Is of so flood-gate and o'erbearing nature
That it engluts and swallows other sorrows,
And it is still itself.
DUKE: Why, what's the matter?
BRABANTIO: My daughter! O, my daughter!
ALL: Dead?
BRABANTIO: Ay, to me.
She is abused, stol'n from me and corrupted
By spells and medicines bought of mountebanks;
For nature so preposterously to err,
Being not deficient, blind, or lame of sense,
Sans witchcraft could not.
DUKE: Whoe'er he be that in this foul proceeding
Hath thus beguiled your daughter of herself
And you of her, the bloody book of law
You shall yourself read in the bitter letter

After your own sense, yea, though our proper son
Stood in your action.
BRABANTIO: Humbly I thank your Grace.
Here is the man, this Moor, whom now, it seems,
Your special mandate for the state affairs
Hath hither brought.
ALL: We are very sorry for't.
DUKE: To Othello. What in your own part can you say to this?
BRABANTIO: Nothing, but this is so.
OTHELLO: Most potent, grave, and reverend signiors,
My very noble and approved good masters,
That I have ta'en away this old man's daughter,
It is most true; true, I have married her;
The very head and front of my offending
Hath this extent, no more. Rude am I in my speech,
And little blest with the soft phrase of peace;
For since these arms of mine had seven years' pith,
Till now some nine moons wasted, they have used
Their dearest action in the tented field,
And little of this great world can I speak,
More than pertains to feats of broil and battle;
And therefore little shall I grace my cause
In speaking for myself. Yet, by your gracious patience,
I will a round unvarnish'd tale deliver
Of my whole course of love: what drugs, what charms,
What conjuration, and what mighty magic-
For such proceeding I am charged withal-
I won his daughter.
BRABANTIO: A maiden never bold,
Of spirit so still and quiet that her motion
Blush'd at herself; and she- in spite of nature,
Of years, of country, credit, everything-
To fall in love with what she fear'd to look on!
It is judgement maim'd and most imperfect,
That will confess perfection so could err
Against all rules of nature, and must be driven
To find out practices of cunning hell
Why this should be. I therefore vouch again
That with some mixtures powerful o'er the blood,
Or with some dram conjured to this effect,
He wrought upon her.
DUKE: To vouch this is no proof,
Without more certain and more overt test
Than these thin habits and poor likelihoods
Of modern seeming do prefer against him.
FIRST SENATOR: But, Othello, speak.
Did you by indirect and forced courses
Subdue and poison this young maid's affections?
Or came it by request, and such fair question
As soul to soul affordeth?
OTHELLO: I do beseech you,
Send for the lady to the Sagittary,
And let her speak of me before her father.

If you do find me foul in her report,
The trust, the office I do hold of you,
Not only take away, but let your sentence
Even fall upon my life.
DUKE: Fetch Desdemona hither.
OTHELLO: Ancient, conduct them; you best know the place.
Exeunt Iago and Attendants.
And till she come, as truly as to heaven
I do confess the vices of my blood,
So justly to your grave ears I'll present
How I did thrive in this fair lady's love
And she in mine.
DUKE: Say it, Othello.
OTHELLO: Her father loved me, oft invited me,
Still question'd me the story of my life
From year to year, the battles, sieges, fortunes,
That I have pass'd.
I ran it through, even from my boyish days
To the very moment that he bade me tell it:
Wherein I spake of most disastrous chances,
Of moving accidents by flood and field,
Of hair-breadth 'scapes i' the imminent deadly breach,
Of being taken by the insolent foe
And sold to slavery, of my redemption thence
And portance in my travels' history;
Wherein of antres vast and deserts idle,
Rough quarries, rocks, and hills whose heads touch heaven,
It was my hint to speak- such was the process-
And of the Cannibals that each other eat,
The Anthropophagi, and men whose heads
Do grow beneath their shoulders. This to hear
Would Desdemona seriously incline;
But still the house affairs would draw her thence,
Which ever as she could with haste dispatch,
She'ld come again, and with a greedy ear
Devour up my discourse; which I observing,
Took once a pliant hour, and found good means
To draw from her a prayer of earnest heart
That I would all my pilgrimage dilate,
Whereof by parcels she had something heard,
But not intentively. I did consent,
And often did beguile her of her tears
When I did speak of some distressful stroke
That my youth suffer'd. My story being done,
She gave me for my pains a world of sighs;
She swore, in faith, 'twas strange, 'twas passing strange;
'Twas pitiful, 'twas wondrous pitiful.
She wish'd she had not heard it, yet she wish'd
That heaven had made her such a man; she thank'd me,
And bade me, if I had a friend that loved her,
I should but teach him how to tell my story,
And that would woo her. Upon this hint I spake:
She loved me for the dangers I had pass'd,

And I loved her that she did pity them.
This only is the witchcraft I have used.
Here comes the lady; let her witness it.
Enter Desdemona, Iago, and Attendants.
DUKE: I think this tale would win my daughter too.
Good Brabantio,
Take up this mangled matter at the best:
Men do their broken weapons rather use
Than their bare hands.
BRABANTIO: I pray you, hear her speak.
If she confess that she was half the wooer,
Destruction on my head, if my bad blame
Light on the man! Come hither, gentle mistress.
Do you perceive in all this noble company
Where most you owe obedience?
DESDEMONA: My noble father,
I do perceive here a divided duty.
To you I am bound for life and education;
My life and education both do learn me
How to respect you; you are the lord of duty,
I am hitherto your daughter. But here's my husband,
And so much duty as my mother show'd
To you, preferring you before her father,
So much I challenge that I may profess
Due to the Moor, my lord.
BRABANTIO: God be with you! I have done.
Please it your Grace, on to the state affairs;
I had rather to adopt a child than get it.
Come hither, Moor.
I here do give thee that with all my heart
Which, but thou hast already, with all my heart
I would keep from thee. For your sake, jewel,
I am glad at soul I have no other child;
For thy escape would teach me tyranny,
To hang clogs on them. I have done, my lord.
DUKE: Let me speak like yourself, and lay a sentence
Which, as a grise or step, may help these lovers
Into your favor.
When remedies are past, the griefs are ended
By seeing the worst, which late on hopes depended.
To mourn a mischief that is past and gone
Is the next way to draw new mischief on.
What cannot be preserved when Fortune takes,
Patience her injury a mockery makes.
The robb'd that smiles steals something from the thief;
He robs himself that spends a bootless grief.
BRABANTIO: So let the Turk of Cyprus us beguile;
We lose it not so long as we can smile.
He bears the sentence well, that nothing bears
But the free comfort which from thence he hears;
But he bears both the sentence and the sorrow
That, to pay grief, must of poor patience borrow.
These sentences, to sugar or to gall,

Being strong on both sides, are equivocal.
But words are words; I never yet did hear
That the bruised heart was pierced through the ear.
I humbly beseech you, proceed to the affairs of state.
DUKE: The Turk with a most mighty preparation makes for Cyprus.
Othello, the fortitude of the place is best known to you; and
though we have there a substitute of most allowed sufficiency,
yet opinion, a sovereign mistress of effects, throws a more safer
voice on you. You must therefore be content to slubber the gloss
of your new fortunes with this more stubborn and boisterous
expedition.
OTHELLO: The tyrant custom, most grave senators,
Hath made the flinty and steel couch of war
My thrice-driven bed of down. I do agnize
A natural and prompt alacrity
I find in hardness and do undertake
These present wars against the Ottomites.
Most humbly therefore bending to your state,
I crave fit disposition for my wife,
Due reference of place and exhibition,
With such accommodation and besort
As levels with her breeding.
DUKE: If you please,
Be't at her father's.
BRABANTIO: I'll not have it so.
OTHELLO: Nor I.
DESDEMONA: Nor I. I would not there reside
To put my father in impatient thoughts
By being in his eye. Most gracious Duke,
To my unfolding lend your prosperous ear,
And let me find a charter in your voice
To assist my simpleness.
DUKE: What would you, Desdemona?
DESDEMONA: That I did love the Moor to live with him,
My downright violence and storm of fortunes
May trumpet to the world. My heart's subdued
Even to the very quality of my lord.
I saw Othello's visage in his mind,
And to his honors and his valiant parts
Did I my soul and fortunes consecrate.
So that, dear lords, if I be left behind,
A moth of peace, and he go to the war,
The rites for which I love him are bereft me,
And I a heavy interim shall support
By his dear absence. Let me go with him.
OTHELLO: Let her have your voices.
Vouch with me, heaven, I therefore beg it not
To please the palate of my appetite,
Nor to comply with heat- the young affects
In me defunct- and proper satisfaction;
But to be free and bounteous to her mind.
And heaven defend your good souls, that you think
I will your serious and great business scant

For she is with me. No, when light-wing'd toys
Of feather'd Cupid seel with wanton dullness
My speculative and officed instruments,
That my disports corrupt and taint my business,
Let housewives make a skillet of my helm,
And all indign and base adversities
Make head against my estimation!
DUKE: Be it as you shall privately determine,
Either for her stay or going. The affair cries haste,
And speed must answer't: you must hence tonight.
DESDEMONA: Tonight, my lord?
DUKE: This night.
OTHELLO: With all my heart.
DUKE: At nine i' the morning here we'll meet again.
Othello, leave some officer behind,
And he shall our commission bring to you,
With such things else of quality and respect
As doth import you.
OTHELLO: So please your Grace, my ancient;
A man he is of honesty and trust.
To his conveyance I assign my wife,
With what else needful your good Grace shall think
To be sent after me.
DUKE: Let it be so.
Good night to everyone. To Brabantio. And, noble signior,
If virtue no delighted beauty lack,
Your son-in-law is far more fair than black.
FIRST SENATOR: Adieu, brave Moor, use Desdemona well.
BRABANTIO: Look to her, Moor, if thou hast eyes to see;
She has deceived her father, and may thee.
Exeunt Duke, Senators, and Officers.
OTHELLO: My life upon her faith! Honest Iago,
My Desdemona must I leave to thee.
I prithee, let thy wife attend on her,
And bring them after in the best advantage.
Come, Desdemona, I have but an hour
Of love, of worldly matters and direction,
To spend with thee. We must obey the time.
Exeunt Othello and Desdemona.
RODERIGO: Iago!
IAGO: What say'st thou, noble heart?
RODERIGO: What will I do, thinkest thou?
IAGO: Why, go to bed and sleep.
RODERIGO: I will incontinently drown myself.
IAGO: If thou dost, I shall never love thee after.
Why, thou silly gentleman!
RODERIGO: It is silliness to live when to live is torment, and then have we a prescription to die when death is our physician.
IAGO: O villainous! I have looked upon the world for four times seven years, and since I could distinguish betwixt a benefit and an injury, I never found man that knew how to love himself. Ere I would say I would drown myself for the love of a guinea hen, I would change my humanity with a baboon.

RODERIGO: What should I do? I confess it is my shame to be so fond, but it is not in my virtue to amend it.
IAGO: Virtue? a fig! 'Tis in ourselves that we are thus or thus. Our bodies are gardens, to the which our wills are gardeners; so that if we will plant nettles or sow lettuce, set hyssop and weed up thyme, supply it with one gender of herbs or distract it with many, either to have it sterile with idleness or manured with industry, why, the power and corrigible authority of this lies in our wills. If the balance of our lives had not one scale of reason to poise another of sensuality, the blood and baseness of our natures would conduct us to most preposterous conclusions. But we have reason to cool our raging motions, our carnal stings, our unbitted lusts; whereof I take this, that you call love, to be a sect or scion.
RODERIGO: It cannot be.
IAGO: It is merely a lust of the blood and a permission of the will. Come, be a man! Drown thyself? Drown cats and blind puppies. I have professed me thy friend, and I confess me knit to thy deserving with cables of perdurable toughness; I could never better stead thee than now. Put money in thy purse; follow thou the wars; defeat thy favor with an usurped beard. I say, put money in thy purse. It cannot be that Desdemona should long continue her love to the Moor- put money in thy purse- nor he his to her. It was a violent commencement, and thou shalt see an answerable sequestration- put but money in thy purse. These Moors are changeable in their wills- fill thy purse with money. The food that to him now is as luscious as locusts, shall be to him shortly as acerb as the coloquintida. She must change for youth; when she is sated with his body, she will find the error of her choice. She must have change, she must; therefore put money in thy purse. If thou wilt needs damn thyself, do it a more delicate way than drowning. Make all the money thou canst. If sanctimony and a frail vow betwixt an erring barbarian and a supersubtle Venetian be not too hard for my wits and all the tribe of hell, thou shalt enjoy her- therefore make money. A pox of drowning thyself! It is clean out of the way. Seek thou rather to be hanged in compassing thy joy than to be drowned and go without her.
RODERIGO: Wilt thou be fast to my hopes, if I depend on the issue?
IAGO: Thou art sure of me- go, make money. I have told thee often, and I retell thee again and again, I hate the Moor. My cause is hearted; thine hath no less reason. Let us be conjunctive in our revenge against him. If thou canst cuckold him, thou dost thyself a pleasure, me a sport. There are many events in the womb of time which will be delivered. Traverse, go, provide thy money. We will have more of this tomorrow. Adieu.
RODERIGO: Where shall we meet i' the morning?
IAGO: At my lodging.
RODERIGO: I'll be with thee betimes.
IAGO: Go to, farewell. Do you hear, Roderigo?
RODERIGO: What say you?
IAGO: No more of drowning, do you hear?
RODERIGO: I am changed; I'll go sell all my land.

Exit.
IAGO: Thus do I ever make my fool my purse;
For I mine own gain'd knowledge should profane
If I would time expend with such a snipe
But for my sport and profit. I hate the Moor,
And it is thought abroad that 'twixt my sheets
He has done my office. I know not if't be true,
But I for mere suspicion in that kind
Will do as if for surety. He holds me well,
The better shall my purpose work on him.
Cassio's a proper man. Let me see now-
To get his place, and to plume up my will
In double knavery- How, how?- Let's see-
After some time, to abuse Othello's ear
That he is too familiar with his wife.
He hath a person and a smooth dispose
To be suspected- framed to make women false.
The Moor is of a free and open nature,
That thinks men honest that but seem to be so,
And will as tenderly be led by the nose
As asses are.
I have't. It is engender'd. Hell and night
Must bring this monstrous birth to the world's light.
Exit.

ACT II. SCENE I. A Seaport in Cyprus. An Open Place near the Quay.

Enter Montano and Two Gentlemen.
MONTANO: What from the cape can you discern at sea?
FIRST GENTLEMAN: Nothing at all. It is a high-wrought flood;
I cannot, 'twixt the heaven and the main, descry a sail.
MONTANO: Methinks the wind hath spoke aloud at land;
A fuller blast ne'er shook our battlements.
If it hath ruffian'd so upon the sea,
What ribs of oak, when mountains melt on them,
Can hold the mortise? What shall we hear of this?
SECOND GENTLEMAN: A segregation of the Turkish fleet.
For do but stand upon the foaming shore,
The chidden billow seems to pelt the clouds;
The wind-shaked surge, with high and monstrous mane,
Seems to cast water on the burning bear,
And quench the guards of the ever-fixed pole.
I never did like molestation view
On the enchafed flood.
MONTANO: If that the Turkish fleet
Be not enshelter'd and embay'd, they are drown'd;
It is impossible to bear it out.
Enter a Third Gentleman.
THIRD GENTLEMAN: News, lads! Our wars are done.
The desperate tempest hath so bang'd the Turks,
That their designment halts. A noble ship of Venice
Hath seen a grievous wreck and sufferance
On most part of their fleet.
MONTANO: How? Is this true?
THIRD GENTLEMAN: The ship is here put in,

A Veronesa. Michael Cassio,
Lieutenant to the warlike Moor, Othello,
Is come on shore; the Moor himself at sea,
And is in full commission here for Cyprus.
MONTANO: I am glad on't; 'tis a worthy governor.
THIRD GENTLEMAN: But this same Cassio, though he speak of comfort
Touching the Turkish loss, yet he looks sadly
And prays the Moor be safe; for they were parted
With foul and violent tempest.
MONTANO: Pray heavens he be,
For I have served him, and the man commands
Like a full soldier. Let's to the seaside, ho!
As well to see the vessel that's come in
As to throw out our eyes for brave Othello,
Even till we make the main and the aerial blue
An indistinct regard.
THIRD GENTLEMAN: Come, let's do so,
For every minute is expectancy
Of more arrivance.
Enter Cassio.
CASSIO: Thanks, you the valiant of this warlike isle,
That so approve the Moor! O, let the heavens
Give him defense against the elements,
For I have lost him on a dangerous sea.
MONTANO: Is she well shipp'd?
CASSIO: His bark is stoutly timber'd, and his pilot
Of very expert and approved allowance;
Therefore my hopes, not surfeited to death,
Stand in bold cure.
A Cry Within, "A Sail, a Sail, a Sail!"
Enter a Fourth Gentleman.
What noise?
FOURTH GENTLEMAN: The town is empty; on the brow o' the sea
Stand ranks of people, and they cry, "A sail!"
CASSIO: My hopes do shape him for the governor.
Guns Heard.
SECOND GENTLEMAN: They do discharge their shot of courtesy-
Our friends at least.
CASSIO: I pray you, sir, go forth,
And give us truth who 'tis that is arrived.
SECOND GENTLEMAN: I shall.
Exit.
MONTANO: But, good lieutenant, is your general wived?
CASSIO: Most fortunately: he hath achieved a maid
That paragons description and wild fame,
One that excels the quirks of blazoning pens,
And in the essential vesture of creation
Does tire the ingener.
Re-enter second Gentleman.
How now! who has put in?
SECOND GENTLEMAN: 'Tis one Iago, ancient to the general.
CASSIO: He has had most favorable and happy speed:
Tempests themselves, high seas, and howling winds,

The gutter'd rocks, and congregated sands,
Traitors ensteep'd to clog the guiltless keel,
As having sense of beauty, do omit
Their mortal natures, letting go safely by
The divine Desdemona.
MONTANO: What is she?
CASSIO: She that I spake of, our great captain's captain,
Left in the conduct of the bold Iago,
Whose footing here anticipates our thoughts
A se'nnight's speed. Great Jove, Othello guard,
And swell his sail with thine own powerful breath,
That he may bless this bay with his tall ship,
Make love's quick pants in Desdemona's arms,
Give renew'd fire to our extincted spirits,
And bring all Cyprus comfort.
Enter Desdemona, Emilia Iago, Roderigo, and Attendants.
O, behold, the riches of the ship is come on shore!
Ye men of Cyprus, let her have your knees.
Hall to thee, lady! And the grace of heaven,
Before, behind thee, and on every hand,
Enwheel thee round!
DESDEMONA: I thank you, valiant Cassio.
What tidings can you tell me of my lord?
CASSIO: He is not yet arrived, nor know I aught
But that he's well and will be shortly here.
DESDEMONA: O, but I fear- How lost you company?
CASSIO: The great contention of the sea and skies
Parted our fellowship- But, hark! a sail.
A Cry Within, "A Sail, a Sail!" Guns Heard.
SECOND GENTLEMAN: They give their greeting to the citadel;
This likewise is a friend.
CASSIO: See for the news.
Exit Gentleman.
Good ancient, you are welcome. To Emilia. Welcome, mistress.
Let it not gall your patience, good Iago,
That I extend my manners; 'tis my breeding
That gives me this bold show of courtesy. Kisses her.
IAGO: Sir, would she give you so much of her lips
As of her tongue she oft bestows on me,
You'ld have enough.
DESDEMONA: Alas, she has no speech.
IAGO: In faith, too much;
I find it still when I have list to sleep.
Marry, before your ladyship I grant,
She puts her tongue a little in her heart
And chides with thinking.
EMILIA: You have little cause to say so.
IAGO: Come on, come on. You are pictures out of doors,
Bells in your parlors, wildcats in your kitchens,
Saints in your injuries, devils being offended,
Players in your housewifery, and housewives in your beds.
DESDEMONA: O, fie upon thee, slanderer!
IAGO: Nay, it is true, or else I am a Turk:

You rise to play, and go to bed to work.
EMILIA: You shall not write my praise.
IAGO: No, let me not.
DESDEMONA: What wouldst thou write of me, if thou shouldst praise me?
IAGO: O gentle lady, do not put me to't,
For I am nothing if not critical.
DESDEMONA: Come on, assay- There's one gone to the harbor?
IAGO: Ay, madam.
DESDEMONA: I am not merry, but I do beguile
The thing I am by seeming otherwise.
Come, how wouldst thou praise me?
IAGO: I am about it, but indeed my invention
Comes from my pate as birdlime does from frieze;
It plucks out brains and all. But my Muse labors,
And thus she is deliver'd.
If she be fair and wise, fairness and wit,
The one's for use, the other useth it.
DESDEMONA: Well praised! How if she be black and witty?
IAGO: If she be black, and thereto have a wit,
She'll find a white that shall her blackness fit.
DESDEMONA: Worse and worse.
EMILIA: How if fair and foolish?
IAGO: She never yet was foolish that was fair,
For even her folly help'd her to an heir.
DESDEMONA: These are old fond paradoxes to make fools laugh i' the alehouse. What miserable praise hast thou for her that's foul and foolish?
IAGO: There's none so foul and foolish thereunto,
But does foul pranks which fair and wise ones do.
DESDEMONA: O heavy ignorance! Thou praisest the worst best. But what praise couldst thou bestow on a deserving woman indeed, one that in the authority of her merit did justly put on the vouch of very malice itself?
IAGO: She that was ever fair and never proud,
Had tongue at will and yet was never loud,
Never lack'd gold and yet went never gay,
Fled from her wish and yet said, "Now I may";
She that, being anger'd, her revenge being nigh,
Bade her wrong stay and her displeasure fly;
She that in wisdom never was so frail
To change the cod's head for the salmon's tail;
She that could think and ne'er disclose her mind,
See suitors following and not look behind;
She was a wight, if ever such wight were-
DESDEMONA: To do what?
IAGO: To suckle fools and chronicle small beer.
DESDEMONA: O most lame and impotent conclusion! Do not learn of him, Emilia, though he be thy husband. How say you, Cassio? Is he not a most profane and liberal counselor?
CASSIO: He speaks home, madam. You may relish him more in the soldier than in the scholar.
IAGO: Aside. He takes her by the palm; ay, well said, whisper.

With as little a web as this will I ensnare as great a fly as Cassio. Ay, smile upon her, do; I will gyve thee in thine own courtship. You say true; 'tis so, indeed. If such tricks as these strip you out of your lieutenantry, it had been better you had not kissed your three fingers so oft, which now again you are most apt to play the sir in. Very good. Well kissed! an excellent courtesy! 'tis so, indeed. Yet again your fingers to your lips? Would they were clyster-pipes for your sake! Trumpet Within. The Moor! I know his trumpet.
CASSIO: 'Tis truly so.
DESDEMONA: Let's meet him and receive him.
CASSIO: Lo, where he comes!
Enter Othello and Attendants.
OTHELLO: O my fair warrior!
DESDEMONA: My dear Othello!
OTHELLO: It gives me wonder great as my content
To see you here before me. O my soul's joy!
If after every tempest come such calms,
May the winds blow till they have waken'd death!
And let the laboring bark climb hills of seas
Olympus-high, and duck again as low
As hell's from heaven! If it were now to die,
'Twere now to be most happy; for I fear
My soul hath her content so absolute
That not another comfort like to this
Succeeds in unknown fate.
DESDEMONA: The heavens forbid
But that our loves and comforts should increase,
Even as our days do grow!
OTHELLO: Amen to that, sweet powers!
I cannot speak enough of this content;
It stops me here; it is too much of joy.
And this, and this, the greatest discords be Kisses her.
That e'er our hearts shall make!
IAGO: Aside. O, you are well tuned now!
But I'll set down the pegs that make this music,
As honest as I am.
OTHELLO: Come, let us to the castle.
News, friends: our wars are done, the Turks are drown'd.
How does my old acquaintance of this isle?
Honey, you shall be well desired in Cyprus;
I have found great love amongst them. O my sweet,
I prattle out of fashion, and I dote
In mine own comforts. I prithee, good Iago,
Go to the bay and disembark my coffers.
Bring thou the master to the citadel;
He is a good one, and his worthiness
Does challenge much respect. Come, Desdemona,
Once more well met at Cyprus.
Exeunt All but Iago and Roderigo.
IAGO: Do thou meet me presently at the harbor. Come hither. If thou be'st valiant- as they say base men being in love have then a nobility in their natures more than is native to them- list me.

The lieutenant tonight watches on the court of guard. First, I must tell thee this: Desdemona is directly in love with him.
RODERIGO: With him? Why, 'tis not possible.
IAGO: Lay thy finger thus, and let thy soul be instructed. Mark me with what violence she first loved the Moor, but for bragging and telling her fantastical lies. And will she love him still for prating? Let not thy discreet heart think it. Her eye must be fed; and what delight shall she have to look on the devil? When the blood is made dull with the act of sport, there should be, again to inflame it and to give satiety a fresh appetite, loveliness in favor, sympathy in years, manners, and beauties- all which the Moor is defective in. Now, for want of these required conveniences, her delicate tenderness will find itself abused, begin to heave the gorge, disrelish and abhor the Moor; very nature will instruct her in it and compel her to some second choice. Now sir, this granted- as it is a most pregnant and unforced position- who stands so eminently in the degree of this fortune as Cassio does? A knave very voluble; no further conscionable than in putting on the mere form of civil and humane seeming, for the better compass of his salt and most hidden loose affection? Why, none, why, none- a slipper and subtle knave, a finder out of occasions, that has an eye can stamp and counterfeit advantages, though true advantage never present itself- a devilish knave! Besides, the knave is handsome, young, and hath all those requisites in him that folly and green minds look after- a pestilent complete knave, and the woman hath found him already.
RODERIGO: I cannot believe that in her; she's full of most blest condition.
IAGO: Blest fig's-end! The wine she drinks is made of grapes. If she had been blest, she would never have loved the Moor. Blest pudding! Didst thou not see her paddle with the palm of his hand? Didst not mark that?
RODERIGO: Yes, that I did; but that was but courtesy.
IAGO: Lechery, by this hand; an index and obscure prologue to the history of lust and foul thoughts. They met so near with their lips that their breaths embraced together. Villainous thoughts, Roderigo! When these mutualities so marshal the way, hard at hand comes the master and main exercise, the incorporate conclusion. Pish! But, sir, be you ruled by me. I have brought you from Venice. Watch you tonight; for the command, I'll lay't upon you. Cassio knows you not. I'll not be far from you. Do you find some occasion to anger Cassio, either by speaking too loud, or tainting his discipline, or from what other course you please, which the time shall more favorably minister.
RODERIGO: Well.
IAGO: Sir, he is rash and very sudden in choler, and haply may strike at you. Provoke him, that he may; for even out of that will I cause these of Cyprus to mutiny, whose qualification shall come into no true taste again but by the displanting of Cassio. So shall you have a shorter journey to your desires by the means I shall then have to prefer them, and the impediment most profitably removed, without the which there were no expectation

of our prosperity.
RODERIGO: I will do this, if I can bring it to any opportunity.
IAGO: I warrant thee. Meet me by and by at the citadel. I must fetch his necessaries ashore. Farewell.
RODERIGO: Adieu.
Exit.
IAGO: That Cassio loves her, I do well believe it;
That she loves him, 'tis apt and of great credit.
The Moor, howbeit that I endure him not,
Is of a constant, loving, noble nature,
And I dare think he'll prove to Desdemona
A most dear husband. Now, I do love her too,
Not out of absolute lust, though peradventure
I stand accountant for as great a sin,
But partly led to diet my revenge,
For that I do suspect the lusty Moor
Hath leap'd into my seat; the thought whereof
Doth like a poisonous mineral gnaw my inwards,
And nothing can or shall content my soul
Till I am even'd with him, wife for wife.
Or failing so, yet that I put the Moor
At least into a jealousy so strong
That judgement cannot cure. Which thing to do,
If this poor trash of Venice, whom I trace
For his quick hunting, stand the putting on,
I'll have our Michael Cassio on the hip,
Abuse him to the Moor in the rank garb
(For I fear Cassio with my nightcap too),
Make the Moor thank me, love me, and reward me
For making him egregiously an ass
And practicing upon his peace and quiet
Even to madness. 'Tis here, but yet confused:
Knavery's plain face is never seen till used.
Exit.

ACT II. SCENE II. A Street.

Enter a Herald with a Proclamation; People Following.
HERALD: It is Othello's pleasure, our noble and valiant general, that upon certain tidings now arrived, importing the mere perdition of the Turkish fleet, every man put himself into triumph; some to dance, some to make bonfires, each man to what sport and revels his addiction leads him; for besides these beneficial news, it is the celebration of his nuptial. So much was his pleasure should be proclaimed. All offices are open, and there is full liberty of feasting from this present hour of five till the bell have told eleven. Heaven bless the isle of Cyprus and our noble general Othello!
Exeunt.

ACT II. SCENE III. A Hall in the Castle.

Enter Othello, Desdemona, Cassio, and Attendants.
OTHELLO: Good Michael, look you to the guard tonight.
Let's teach ourselves that honorable stop,

Not to outsport discretion.
CASSIO: Iago hath direction what to do;
But notwithstanding with my personal eye
Will I look to't.
OTHELLO: Iago is most honest.
Michael, good night. Tomorrow with your earliest
Let me have speech with you. Come, my dear love,
The purchase made, the fruits are to ensue;
That profit's yet to come 'tween me and you.
Good night.
Exeunt Othello, Desdemona, and Attendants.
Enter Iago.
CASSIO: Welcome, Iago; we must to the watch.
IAGO: Not this hour, lieutenant; 'tis not yet ten o' the clock. Our general cast us thus early for the love of his Desdemona; who let us not therefore blame. He hath not yet made wanton the night with her, and she is sport for Jove.
CASSIO: She's a most exquisite lady.
IAGO: And, I'll warrant her, full of game.
CASSIO: Indeed she's a most fresh and delicate creature.
IAGO: What an eye she has! Methinks it sounds a parley to provocation.
CASSIO: An inviting eye; and yet methinks right modest.
IAGO: And when she speaks, is it not an alarum to love?
CASSIO: She is indeed perfection.
IAGO: Well, happiness to their sheets! Come, lieutenant, I have a stope of wine, and here without are a brace of Cyprus gallants that would fain have a measure to the health of black Othello.
CASSIO: Not tonight, good Iago. I have very poor and unhappy brains for drinking. I could well wish courtesy would invent some other custom of entertainment.
IAGO: O, they are our friends! But one cup; I'll drink for you.
CASSIO: I have drunk but one cup tonight, and that was craftily qualified too, and behold what innovation it makes here. I am unfortunate in the infirmity, and dare not task my weakness with any more.
IAGO: What, man! 'Tis a night of revels, the gallants desire it.
CASSIO: Where are they?
IAGO: Here at the door; I pray you, call them in.
CASSIO: I'll do't, but it dislikes me.
Exit.
IAGO: If I can fasten but one cup upon him,
With that which he hath drunk tonight already,
He'll be as full of quarrel and offense
As my young mistress' dog. Now my sick fool Roderigo,
Whom love hath turn'd almost the wrong side out,
To Desdemona hath tonight caroused
Potations pottle-deep; and he's to watch.
Three lads of Cyprus, noble swelling spirits,
That hold their honors in a wary distance,
The very elements of this warlike isle,
Have I tonight fluster'd with flowing cups,
And they watch too. Now, 'mongst this flock of drunkards,

Am I to put our Cassio in some action
That may offend the isle. But here they come.
If consequence do but approve my dream,
My boat sails freely, both with wind and stream.
Re-enter Cassio; with Him Montano and Gentlemen; Servants Following with Wine.
CASSIO: 'Fore God, they have given me a rouse already.
MONTANO: Good faith, a little one; not past a pint, as I am a
SOLDIER:
IAGO: Some wine, ho!
Sings. "And let me the canakin clink, clink;
And let me the canakin clink.
A soldier's a man;
O, man's life's but a span;
Why then let a soldier drink."
Some wine, boys!
CASSIO: 'Fore God, an excellent song.
IAGO: I learned it in England, where indeed they are most potent in potting. Your Dane, your German, and your swag-bellied Hollander- Drink, ho!- are nothing to your English.
CASSIO: Is your Englishman so expert in his drinking?
IAGO: Why, he drinks you with facility your Dane dead drunk; he sweats not to overthrow your Almain; he gives your Hollander a vomit ere the next pottle can be filled.
CASSIO: To the health of our general!
MONTANO: I am for it, lieutenant, and I'll do you justice.
IAGO: O sweet England!
Sings. "King Stephen was and-a worthy peer,
His breeches cost him but a crown;
He held them sixpence all too dear,
With that he call'd the tailor lown.
"He was a wight of high renown,
And thou art but of low degree.
'Tis pride that pulls the country down;
Then take thine auld cloak about thee."
Some wine, ho!
CASSIO: Why, this is a more exquisite song than the other.
IAGO: Will you hear't again?
CASSIO: No, for I hold him to be unworthy of his place that does those things. Well, God's above all, and there be souls must be saved, and there be souls must not be saved.
IAGO: It's true, good lieutenant.
CASSIO: For mine own part- no offense to the general, nor any man of quality- I hope to be saved.
IAGO: And so do I too, lieutenant.
CASSIO: Ay, but, by your leave, not before me; the lieutenant is to be saved before the ancient. Let's have no more of this; let's to our affairs. God forgive us our sins! Gentlemen, let's look to our business. Do not think, gentlemen, I am drunk: this is my ancient, this is my right hand, and this is my left. I am not drunk now; I can stand well enough, and I speak well enough.
ALL: Excellent well.
CASSIO: Why, very well then; you must not think then that I am drunk.

Exit.
MONTANO: To the platform, masters; come, let's set the watch.
IAGO: You see this fellow that is gone before;
He is a soldier fit to stand by Caesar
And give direction. And do but see his vice;
'Tis to his virtue a just equinox,
The one as long as the other. 'Tis pity of him.
I fear the trust Othello puts him in
On some odd time of his infirmity
Will shake this island.
MONTANO: But is he often thus?
IAGO: 'Tis evermore the prologue to his sleep.
He'll watch the horologe a double set,
If drink rock not his cradle.
MONTANO: It were well
The general were put in mind of it.
Perhaps he sees it not, or his good nature
Prizes the virtue that appears in Cassio
And looks not on his evils. Is not this true?
Enter Roderigo.
IAGO: Aside to Him. How now, Roderigo!
I pray you, after the lieutenant; go.
Exit Roderigo.
MONTANO: And 'tis great pity that the noble Moor
Should hazard such a place as his own second
With one of an ingraft infirmity.
It were an honest action to say
So to the Moor.
IAGO: Not I, for this fair island.
I do love Cassio well, and would do much
To cure him of this evil- But, hark! What noise?
A Cry Within, "Help, Help!"
Re-enter Cassio, Driving in Roderigo.
CASSIO: 'Zounds! You rogue! You rascal!
MONTANO: What's the matter, lieutenant?
CASSIO: A knave teach me my duty! But I'll beat the knave into a twiggen bottle.
RODERIGO: Beat me!
CASSIO: Dost thou prate, rogue? Strikes Roderigo.
MONTANO: Nay, good lieutenant; I pray you, sir, hold your hand.
CASSIO: Let me go, sir, or I'll knock you o'er the mazzard.
MONTANO: Come, come, you're drunk.
CASSIO: Drunk? They fight.
IAGO: Aside to Roderigo. Away, I say; go out and cry a mutiny.
Exit Roderigo.
Nay, good lieutenant! God's will, gentlemen!
Help, ho!- Lieutenant- sir- Montano- sir-
Help, masters!- Here's a goodly watch indeed!
A bell rings.
Who's that that rings the bell?- Diablo, ho!
The town will rise. God's will, lieutenant, hold!
You will be shamed forever.
Re-enter Othello and Attendants.

OTHELLO: What is the matter here?
MONTANO: 'Zounds, I bleed still; I am hurt to the death.
Faints.
OTHELLO: Hold, for your lives!
IAGO: Hold, ho! Lieutenant- sir- Montano- gentlemen-
Have you forgot all place of sense and duty?
Hold! the general speaks to you! Hold, hold, for shame!
OTHELLO: Why, how now, ho! from whence ariseth this?
Are we turn'd Turks, and to ourselves do that
Which heaven hath forbid the Ottomites?
For Christian shame, put by this barbarous brawl.
He that stirs next to carve for his own rage
Holds his soul light; he dies upon his motion.
Silence that dreadful bell; it frights the isle
From her propriety. What is the matter, masters?
Honest Iago, that look'st dead with grieving,
Speak: who began this? On thy love, I charge thee.
IAGO: I do not know. Friends all but now, even now,
In quarter, and in terms like bride and groom
Devesting them for bed; and then, but now
(As if some planet had unwitted men),
Swords out, and tilting one at other's breast,
In opposition bloody. I cannot speak
Any beginning to this peevish odds;
And would in action glorious I had lost
Those legs that brought me to a part of it!
OTHELLO: How comes it, Michael, you are thus forgot?
CASSIO: I pray you, pardon me; I cannot speak.
OTHELLO: Worthy Montano, you were wont be civil;
The gravity and stillness of your youth
The world hath noted, and your name is great
In mouths of wisest censure. What's the matter,
That you unlace your reputation thus,
And spend your rich opinion for the name
Of a night-brawler? Give me answer to it.
MONTANO: Worthy Othello, I am hurt to danger.
Your officer, Iago, can inform you-
While I spare speech, which something now offends me-
Of all that I do know. Nor know I aught
By me that's said or done amiss this night,
Unless self-charity be sometimes a vice,
And to defend ourselves it be a sin
When violence assails us.
OTHELLO: Now, by heaven,
My blood begins my safer guides to rule,
And passion, having my best judgement collied,
Assays to lead the way. If I once stir,
Or do but lift this arm, the best of you
Shall sink in my rebuke. Give me to know
How this foul rout began, who set it on,
And he that is approved in this offense,
Though he had twinn'd with me, both at a birth,
Shall lose me. What! in a town of war,

Yet wild, the people's hearts brimful of fear,
To manage private and domestic quarrel,
In night, and on the court and guard of safety!
'Tis monstrous. Iago, who began't?
MONTANO: If partially affined, or leagued in office,
Thou dost deliver more or less than truth,
Thou art no soldier.
IAGO: Touch me not so near:
I had rather have this tongue cut from my mouth
Than it should do offense to Michael Cassio;
Yet, I persuade myself, to speak the truth
Shall nothing wrong him. Thus it is, general.
Montano and myself being in speech,
There comes a fellow crying out for help,
And Cassio following him with determined sword,
To execute upon him. Sir, this gentleman
Steps in to Cassio and entreats his pause.
Myself the crying fellow did pursue,
Lest by his clamor- as it so fell out-
The town might fall in fright. He, swift of foot,
Outran my purpose; and I return'd the rather
For that I heard the clink and fall of swords,
And Cassio high in oath, which till tonight
I ne'er might say before. When I came back-
For this was brief- I found them close together,
At blow and thrust, even as again they were
When you yourself did part them.
More of this matter cannot I report.
But men are men; the best sometimes forget.
Though Cassio did some little wrong to him,
As men in rage strike those that wish them best,
Yet surely Cassio, I believe, received
From him that fled some strange indignity,
Which patience could not pass.
OTHELLO: I know, Iago,
Thy honesty and love doth mince this matter,
Making it light to Cassio. Cassio, I love thee,
But never more be officer of mine.
Re-enter Desdemona, Attended.
Look, if my gentle love be not raised up!
I'll make thee an example.
DESDEMONA: What's the matter?
OTHELLO: All's well now, sweeting; come away to bed.
Sir, for your hurts, myself will be your surgeon.
Lead him off.
Exit Montano, attended.
Iago, look with care about the town,
And silence those whom this vile brawl distracted.
Come, Desdemona, 'tis the soldiers' life.
To have their balmy slumbers waked with strife.
Exeunt All but Iago and Cassio.
IAGO: What, are you hurt, lieutenant?
CASSIO: Ay, past all surgery.

IAGO: Marry, heaven forbid!

CASSIO: Reputation, reputation, reputation! O, I have lost my reputation! I have lost the immortal part of myself, and what remains is bestial. My reputation, Iago, my reputation!

IAGO: As I am an honest man, I thought you had received some bodily wound; there is more sense in that than in reputation. Reputation is an idle and most false imposition; oft got without merit and lost without deserving. You have lost no reputation at all, unless you repute yourself such a loser. What, man! there are ways to recover the general again. You are but now cast in his mood, a punishment more in policy than in malice; even so as one would beat his offenseless dog to affright an imperious lion. Sue to him again, and he's yours.

CASSIO: I will rather sue to be despised than to deceive so good a commander with so slight, so drunken, and so indiscreet an Officer. Drunk? and speak parrot? and squabble? swagger? swear? and discourse fustian with one's own shadow? O thou invisible spirit of wine, if thou hast no name to be known by, let us call thee devil!

IAGO: What was he that you followed with your sword? What had he done to you?

CASSIO: I know not.

IAGO: Is't possible?

CASSIO: I remember a mass of things, but nothing distinctly; a quarrel, but nothing wherefore. O God, that men should put an enemy in their mouths to steal away their brains! that we should, with joy, pleasance, revel, and applause, transform ourselves into beasts!

IAGO: Why, but you are now well enough. How came you thus recovered?

CASSIO: It hath pleased the devil drunkenness to give place to the devil wrath: one unperfectness shows me another, to make me frankly despise myself.

IAGO: Come, you are too severe a moraler. As the time, the place, and the condition of this country stands, I could heartily wish this had not befallen; but since it is as it is, mend it for your own good.

CASSIO: I will ask him for my place again; he shall tell me I am a drunkard! Had I as many mouths as Hydra, such an answer would stop them all. To be now a sensible man, by and by a fool, and presently a beast! O strange! Every inordinate cup is unblest, and the ingredient is a devil.

IAGO: Come, come, good wine is a good familiar creature, if it be well used. Exclaim no more against it. And, good lieutenant, I think you think I love you.

CASSIO: I have well approved it, sir. I drunk!

IAGO: You or any man living may be drunk at some time, man. I'll tell you what you shall do. Our general's wife is now the general. I may say so in this respect, for that he hath devoted and given up himself to the contemplation, mark, and denotement of her parts and graces. Confess yourself freely to her; importune her help to put you in your place again. She is of so free, so kind, so apt, so blessed a disposition, she holds it a vice in her goodness not to do more than she is requested. This broken joint between you and her husband entreat her to splinter; and, my fortunes against any lay worth naming, this crack of your love shall grow stronger than it was before.

CASSIO: You advise me well.

IAGO: I protest, in the sincerity of love and honest kindness.

CASSIO: I think it freely; and betimes in the morning I will beseech the virtuous Desdemona to undertake for me. I am desperate of my fortunes if they check me here.

IAGO: You are in the right. Good night, lieutenant, I must to the Third Serving-Watch.

CASSIO: Good night, honest Iago.

Exit.

IAGO: And what's he then that says I play the villain?
When this advice is free I give and honest,
Probal to thinking, and indeed the course
To win the Moor again? For 'tis most easy
The inclining Desdemona to subdue
In any honest suit. She's framed as fruitful
As the free elements. And then for her
To win the Moor, were't to renounce his baptism,
All seals and symbols of redeemed sin,
His soul is so enfetter'd to her love,
That she may make, unmake, do what she list,
Even as her appetite shall play the god
With his weak function. How am I then a villain
To counsel Cassio to this parallel course,
Directly to his good? Divinity of hell!
When devils will the blackest sins put on,
They do suggest at first with heavenly shows,
As I do now. For whiles this honest fool
Plies Desdemona to repair his fortune,
And she for him pleads strongly to the Moor,
I'll pour this pestilence into his ear,
That she repeals him for her body's lust;
And by how much she strives to do him good,
She shall undo her credit with the Moor.
So will I turn her virtue into pitch,
And out of her own goodness make the net
That shall enmesh them all.

Enter Roderigo.

How now, Roderigo!

RODERIGO: I do follow here in the chase, not like a hound that hunts, but one that fills up the cry. My money is almost spent; I have been tonight exceedingly well cudgeled; and I think the issue will be, I shall have so much experience for my pains; and so, with no money at all and a little more wit, return again to Venice.

IAGO: How poor are they that have not patience!
What wound did ever heal but by degrees?
Thou know'st we work by wit and not by witchcraft,
And wit depends on dilatory time.
Does't not go well? Cassio hath beaten thee,
And thou by that small hurt hast cashier'd Cassio.
Though other things grow fair against the sun,

Yet fruits that blossom first will first be ripe.
Content thyself awhile. By the mass, 'tis morning;
Pleasure and action make the hours seem short.
Retire thee; go where thou art billeted.
Away, I say. Thou shalt know more hereafter.
Nay, get thee gone.
Exit Roderigo.
Two things are to be done:
My wife must move for Cassio to her mistress-
I'll set her on; myself the while to draw the Moor apart,
And bring him jump when he may Cassio find
Soliciting his wife. Ay, that's the way;
Dull not device by coldness and delay.
Exit.

ACT III. SCENE I. Before the Castle.

Enter Cassio and Some Musicians.
CASSIO: Masters, play here, I will content
your pains; Something that's brief; and
bid "Good morrow, general." Music.
Enter Clown.
CLOWN: Why, masters, have your instruments been in Naples, that they speak i' the nose thus?
FIRST MUSICIAN: How, sir, how?
CLOWN: Are these, I pray you, wind instruments?
FIRST MUSICIAN: Ay, marry, are they, sir.
CLOWN: O, thereby hangs a tail.
FIRST MUSICIAN: Whereby hangs a tale, sir?
CLOWN: Marry, sir, by many a wind instrument that I know. But, masters, here's money for you; and the general so likes your music, that he desires you, for love's sake, to make no more noise with it.
FIRST MUSICIAN: Well, sir, we will not.
CLOWN: If you have any music that may not be heard, to't again; but, as they say, to hear music the general does not greatly care.
FIRST MUSICIAN: We have none such, sir.
CLOWN: Then put up your pipes in your bag, for I'll away.
Go, vanish into air, away!
Exeunt Musicians.
CASSIO: Dost thou hear, my honest friend?
CLOWN: No, I hear not your honest friend; I hear you.
CASSIO: Prithee, keep up thy quillets. There's a poor piece of gold for thee. If the gentlewoman that attends the general's wife be stirring, tell her there's one Cassio entreats her a little favor of speech. Wilt thou do this?
CLOWN: She is stirring, sir. If she will stir hither, I shall seem to notify unto her.
CASSIO: Do, good my friend.
Exit Clown.
Enter Iago.
In happy time, Iago.
IAGO: You have not been abed, then?
CASSIO: Why, no; the day had broke

Before we parted. I have made bold, Iago,
To send in to your wife. My suit to her
Is that she will to virtuous Desdemona
Procure me some access.
IAGO: I'll send her to you presently;
And I'll devise a mean to draw the Moor
Out of the way, that your converse and business
May be more free.
CASSIO: I humbly thank you for't.
Exit Iago.
I never knew a Florentine more kind and honest.
Enter Emilia.
EMILIA: Good morrow, good lieutenant. I am sorry
For your displeasure, but all will sure be well.
The general and his wife are talking of it,
And she speaks for you stoutly. The Moor replies
That he you hurt is of great fame in Cyprus
And great affinity and that in wholesome wisdom
He might not but refuse you; but he protests he loves you
And needs no other suitor but his likings
To take the safest occasion by the front
To bring you in again.
CASSIO: Yet, I beseech you,
If you think fit, or that it may be done,
Give me advantage of some brief discourse
With Desdemona alone.
EMILIA: Pray you, come in.
I will bestow you where you shall have time
To speak your bosom freely.
CASSIO: I am much bound to you.
Exeunt.

ACT III. SCENE II. A Room in the Castle.

Enter Othello, Iago, and Gentlemen.
OTHELLO: These letters give, Iago, to the pilot,
And by him do my duties to the Senate.
That done, I will be walking on the works;
Repair there to me.
IAGO: Well, my good lord, I'll do't.
OTHELLO: This fortification, gentlemen, shall we see't?
GENTLEMEN: We'll wait upon your lordship.
Exeunt.

ACT III. SCENE III. The Garden of the Castle.

Enter Desdemona, Cassio, and Emilia.
DESDEMONA: Be thou assured, good Cassio, I will do
All my abilities in thy behalf.
EMILIA: Good madam, do. I warrant it grieves my husband
As if the cause were his.
DESDEMONA: O, that's an honest fellow. Do not doubt, Cassio,
But I will have my lord and you again
As friendly as you were.
CASSIO: Bounteous madam,
Whatever shall become of Michael Cassio,
He's never anything but your true servant.

DESDEMONA: I know't: I thank you. You do love my lord:
You have known him long; and be you well assured
He shall in strangeness stand no farther off
Than in a politic distance.
CASSIO: Ay, but, lady,
That policy may either last so long,
Or feed upon such nice and waterish diet,
Or breed itself so out of circumstances,
That I being absent and my place supplied,
My general will forget my love and service.
DESDEMONA: Do not doubt that. Before Emilia here
I give thee warrant of thy place, assure thee,
If I do vow a friendship, I'll perform it
To the last article. My lord shall never rest;
I'll watch him tame and talk him out of patience;
His bed shall seem a school, his board a shrift;
I'll intermingle everything he does
With Cassio's suit. Therefore be merry, Cassio,
For thy solicitor shall rather die
Than give thy cause away.
Enter Othello and Iago, at a Distance.
EMILIA: Madam, here comes my lord.
CASSIO: Madam, I'll take my leave.
DESDEMONA: Nay, stay and hear me speak.
CASSIO: Madam, not now. I am very ill at ease,
Unfit for mine own purposes.
DESDEMONA: Well, do your discretion.
Exit Cassio.
IAGO: Ha! I like not that.
OTHELLO: What dost thou say?
IAGO: Nothing, my lord; or if- I know not what.
OTHELLO: Was not that Cassio parted from my wife?
IAGO: Cassio, my lord! No, sure, I cannot think it,
That he would steal away so guilty-like,
Seeing you coming.
OTHELLO: I do believe 'twas he.
DESDEMONA: How now, my lord!
I have been talking with a suitor here,
A man that languishes in your displeasure.
OTHELLO: Who is't you mean?
DESDEMONA: Why, your lieutenant, Cassio. Good my lord,
If I have any grace or power to move you,
His present reconciliation take;
For if he be not one that truly loves you,
That errs in ignorance and not in cunning,
I have no judgement in an honest face.
I prithee, call him back.
OTHELLO: Went he hence now?
DESDEMONA: Ay, sooth; so humbled
That he hath left part of his grief with me
To suffer with him. Good love, call him back.
OTHELLO: Not now, sweet Desdemona; some other time.
DESDEMONA: But shall't be shortly?

OTHELLO: The sooner, sweet, for you.
DESDEMONA: Shall't be tonight at supper?
OTHELLO: No, not tonight.
DESDEMONA: Tomorrow dinner then?
OTHELLO: I shall not dine at home;
I meet the captains at the citadel.
DESDEMONA: Why then tomorrow night, or Tuesday morn,
On Tuesday noon, or night, on Wednesday morn.
I prithee, name the time, but let it not
Exceed three days. In faith, he's penitent;
And yet his trespass, in our common reason-
Save that, they say, the wars must make example
Out of their best- is not almost a fault
To incur a private check. When shall he come?
Tell me, Othello. I wonder in my soul,
What you would ask me, that I should deny,
Or stand so mammering on. What? Michael Cassio,
That came awooing with you, and so many a time
When I have spoke of you dispraisingly
Hath ta'en your part- to have so much to do
To bring him in! Trust me, I could do much-
OTHELLO: Prithee, no more. Let him come when he will;
I will deny thee nothing.
DESDEMONA: Why, this is not a boon;
'Tis as I should entreat you wear your gloves,
Or feed on nourishing dishes, or keep you warm,
Or sue to you to do a peculiar profit
To your own person. Nay, when I have a suit
Wherein I mean to touch your love indeed,
It shall be full of poise and difficult weight,
And fearful to be granted.
OTHELLO: I will deny thee nothing,
Whereon, I do beseech thee, grant me this,
To leave me but a little to myself.
DESDEMONA: Shall I deny you? No. Farewell, my lord.
OTHELLO: Farewell, my Desdemona; I'll come to thee straight.
DESDEMONA: Emilia, come. Be as your fancies teach you;
Whate'er you be, I am obedient.
Exeunt Desdemona and Emilia.
OTHELLO: Excellent wretch! Perdition catch my soul,
But I do love thee! and when I love thee not,
Chaos is come again.
IAGO: My noble lord-
OTHELLO: What dost thou say, Iago?
IAGO: Did Michael Cassio, when you woo'd my lady,
Know of your love?
OTHELLO: He did, from first to last. Why dost thou ask?
IAGO: But for a satisfaction of my thought;
No further harm.
OTHELLO: Why of thy thought, Iago?
IAGO: I did not think he had been acquainted with her.
OTHELLO: O, yes, and went between us very oft.
IAGO: Indeed!

OTHELLO: Indeed? ay, indeed. Discern'st thou aught in that?
Is he not honest?
IAGO: Honest, my lord?
OTHELLO: Honest? Ay, honest.
IAGO: My lord, for aught I know.
OTHELLO: What dost thou think?
IAGO: Think, my lord?
OTHELLO: Think, my lord? By heaven, he echoes me,
As if there were some monster in his thought
Too hideous to be shown. Thou dost mean something.
I heard thee say even now, thou like'st not that,
When Cassio left my wife. What didst not like?
And when I told thee he was of my counsel
In my whole course of wooing, thou criedst, "Indeed!"
And didst contract and purse thy brow together,
As if thou then hadst shut up in thy brain
Some horrible conceit. If thou dost love me,
Show me thy thought.
IAGO: My lord, you know I love you.
OTHELLO: I think thou dost;
And for I know thou'rt full of love and honesty
And weigh'st thy words before thou givest them breath,
Therefore these stops of thine fright me the more;
For such things in a false disloyal knave
Are tricks of custom; but in a man that's just
They're close dilations, working from the heart,
That passion cannot rule.
IAGO: For Michael Cassio,
I dare be sworn I think that he is honest.
OTHELLO: I think so too.
IAGO: Men should be what they seem;
Or those that be not, would they might seem none!
OTHELLO: Certain, men should be what they seem.
IAGO: Why then I think Cassio's an honest man.
OTHELLO: Nay, yet there's more in this.
I prithee, speak to me as to thy thinkings,
As thou dost ruminate, and give thy worst of thoughts
The worst of words.
IAGO: Good my lord, pardon me;
Though I am bound to every act of duty,
I am not bound to that all slaves are free to.
Utter my thoughts? Why, say they are vile and false;
As where's that palace whereinto foul things
Sometimes intrude not? Who has a breast so pure,
But some uncleanly apprehensions
Keep leets and law-days, and in session sit
With meditations lawful?
OTHELLO: Thou dost conspire against thy friend, Iago,
If thou but think'st him wrong'd and makest his ear
A stranger to thy thoughts.
IAGO: I do beseech you-
Though I perchance am vicious in my guess,
As, I confess, it is my nature's plague

To spy into abuses, and oft my jealousy
Shapes faults that are not- that your wisdom yet,
From one that so imperfectly conceits,
Would take no notice, nor build yourself a trouble
Out of his scattering and unsure observance.
It were not for your quiet nor your good,
Nor for my manhood, honesty, or wisdom,
To let you know my thoughts.
OTHELLO: What dost thou mean?
IAGO: Good name in man and woman, dear my lord,
Is the immediate jewel of their souls.
Who steals my purse steals trash; 'tis something, nothing;
'Twas mine, 'tis his, and has been slave to thousands;
But he that filches from me my good name
Robs me of that which not enriches him
And makes me poor indeed.
OTHELLO: By heaven, I'll know thy thoughts.
IAGO: You cannot, if my heart were in your hand;
Nor shall not, whilst 'tis in my custody.
OTHELLO: Ha!
IAGO: O, beware, my lord, of jealousy!
It is the green-eyed monster, which doth mock
The meat it feeds on. That cuckold lives in bliss
Who, certain of his fate, loves not his wronger;
But O, what damned minutes tells he o'er
Who dotes, yet doubts, suspects, yet strongly loves!
OTHELLO: O misery!
IAGO: Poor and content is rich, and rich enough;
But riches fineless is as poor as winter
To him that ever fears he shall be poor.
Good heaven, the souls of all my tribe defend
From jealousy!
OTHELLO: Why, why is this?
Think'st thou I'ld make a life of jealousy,
To follow still the changes of the moon
With fresh suspicions? No! To be once in doubt
Is once to be resolved. Exchange me for a goat
When I shall turn the business of my soul
To such exsufflicate and blown surmises,
Matching thy inference. 'Tis not to make me jealous
To say my wife is fair, feeds well, loves company,
Is free of speech, sings, plays, and dances well;
Where virtue is, these are more virtuous.
Nor from mine own weak merits will I draw
The smallest fear or doubt of her revolt;
For she had eyes and chose me. No, Iago,
I'll see before I doubt; when I doubt, prove;
And on the proof, there is no more but this-
Away at once with love or jealousy!
IAGO: I am glad of it, for now I shall have reason
To show the love and duty that I bear you
With franker spirit. Therefore, as I am bound,
Receive it from me. I speak not yet of proof.

Look to your wife; observe her well with Cassio;
Wear your eye thus, not jealous nor secure.
I would not have your free and noble nature
Out of self-bounty be abused. Look to't.
I know our country disposition well;
In Venice they do let heaven see the pranks
They dare not show their husbands; their best conscience
Is not to leave't undone, but keep't unknown.
OTHELLO: Dost thou say so?
IAGO: She did deceive her father, marrying you;
And when she seem'd to shake and fear your looks,
She loved them most.
OTHELLO: And so she did.
IAGO: Why, go to then.
She that so young could give out such a seeming,
To seel her father's eyes up close as oak-
He thought 'twas witchcraft- but I am much to blame;
I humbly do beseech you of your pardon
For too much loving you.
OTHELLO: I am bound to thee forever.
IAGO: I see this hath a little dash'd your spirits.
OTHELLO: Not a jot, not a jot.
IAGO: I'faith, I fear it has.
I hope you will consider what is spoke
Comes from my love. But I do see you're moved;
I am to pray you not to strain my speech
To grosser issues nor to larger reach
Than to suspicion.
OTHELLO: I will not.
IAGO: Should you do so, my lord,
My speech should fall into such vile success
Which my thoughts aim not at. Cassio's my worthy friend-
My lord, I see you're moved.
OTHELLO: No, not much moved.
I do not think but Desdemona's honest.
IAGO: Long live she so! and long live you to think so!
OTHELLO: And yet, how nature erring from itself-
IAGO: Ay, there's the point, as- to be bold with you-
Not to affect many proposed matches
Of her own clime, complexion, and degree,
Whereto we see in all things nature tends-
Foh, one may smell in such a will most rank,
Foul disproportion, thoughts unnatural.
But pardon me. I do not in position
Distinctly speak of her; though I may fear,
Her will, recoiling to her better judgement,
May fall to match you with her country forms,
And happily repent.
OTHELLO: Farewell, farewell.
If more thou dost perceive, let me know more;
Set on thy wife to observe. Leave me, Iago.
IAGO: Going. My lord, I take my leave.
OTHELLO: Why did I marry? This honest creature doubtless

Sees and knows more, much more, than he unfolds.
IAGO: Returning. My lord, I would I might entreat your honor
To scan this thing no further; leave it to time.
Though it be fit that Cassio have his place,
For sure he fills it up with great ability,
Yet, if you please to hold him off awhile,
You shall by that perceive him and his means.
Note if your lady strain his entertainment
With any strong or vehement importunity;
Much will be seen in that. In the meantime,
Let me be thought too busy in my fears-
As worthy cause I have to fear I am-
And hold her free, I do beseech your honor.
OTHELLO: Fear not my government.
IAGO: I once more take my leave.
Exit.
OTHELLO: This fellow's of exceeding honesty,
And knows all qualities, with a learned spirit,
Of human dealings. If I do prove her haggard,
Though that her jesses were my dear heartstrings,
I'ld whistle her off and let her down the wind
To prey at fortune. Haply, for I am black
And have not those soft parts of conversation
That chamberers have, or for I am declined
Into the vale of years- yet that's not much-
She's gone. I am abused, and my relief
Must be to loathe her. O curse of marriage,
That we can call these delicate creatures ours,
And not their appetites! I had rather be a toad,
And live upon the vapor of a dungeon,
Than keep a corner in the thing I love
For others' uses. Yet, 'tis the plague of great ones:
Prerogatived are they less than the base;
'Tis destiny unshunnable, like death.
Even then this forked plague is fated to us
When we do quicken. Desdemona comes:
Re-enter Desdemona and Emilia.
If she be false, O, then heaven mocks itself!
I'll not believe't.
DESDEMONA: How now, my dear Othello!
Your dinner, and the generous islanders
By you invited, do attend your presence.
OTHELLO: I am to blame.
DESDEMONA: Why do you speak so faintly?
Are you not well?
OTHELLO: I have a pain upon my forehead here.
DESDEMONA: Faith, that's with watching; 'twill away again.
Let me but bind it hard, within this hour
It will be well.
OTHELLO: Your napkin is too little;
He Puts the Handkerchief from Him, and She Drops It.
Let it alone. Come, I'll go in with you.
DESDEMONA: I am very sorry that you are not well.

Exeunt Othello and Desdemona.
EMILIA: I am glad I have found this napkin;
This was her first remembrance from the Moor.
My wayward husband hath a hundred times
Woo'd me to steal it; but she so loves the token,
For he conjured her she should ever keep it,
That she reserves it evermore about her
To kiss and talk to. I'll have the work ta'en out,
And give't Iago. What he will do with it
Heaven knows, not I;
I nothing but to please his fantasy.
Re-enter Iago.
IAGO: How now, what do you here alone?
EMILIA: Do not you chide; I have a thing for you.
IAGO: A thing for me? It is a common thing-
EMILIA: Ha!
IAGO: To have a foolish wife.
EMILIA: O, is that all? What will you give me now
For that same handkerchief?
IAGO: What handkerchief?
EMILIA: What handkerchief?
Why, that the Moor first gave to Desdemona,
That which so often you did bid me steal.
IAGO: Hast stol'n it from her?
EMILIA: No, faith; she let it drop by negligence,
And, to the advantage, I being here took't up.
Look, here it is.
IAGO: A good wench; give it me.
EMILIA: What will you do with't, that you have been so earnest
To have me filch it?
IAGO: Snatching it. Why, what is that to you?
EMILIA: If't be not for some purpose of import,
Give't me again. Poor lady, she'll run mad
When she shall lack it.
IAGO: Be not acknown on't; I have use for it.
Go, leave me.
Exit Emilia.
I will in Cassio's lodging lose this napkin,
And let him find it. Trifles light as air
Are to the jealous confirmations strong
As proofs of holy writ; this may do something.
The Moor already changes with my poison:
Dangerous conceits are in their natures poisons,
Which at the first are scarce found to distaste,
But with a little act upon the blood
Burn like the mines of sulphur. I did say so.
Look, where he comes!
Re-enter Othello.
Not poppy, nor mandragora,
Nor all the drowsy syrups of the world,
Shall ever medicine thee to that sweet sleep
Which thou owedst yesterday.
OTHELLO: Ha, ha, false to me?

IAGO: Why, how now, general! No more of that.
OTHELLO: Avaunt! be gone! Thou hast set me on the rack.
I swear 'tis better to be much abused
Than but to know't a little.
IAGO: How now, my lord?
OTHELLO: What sense had I of her stol'n hours of lust?
I saw't not, thought it not, it harm'd not me;
I slept the next night well, was free and merry;
I found not Cassio's kisses on her lips.
He that is robb'd, not wanting what is stol'n,
Let him not know't and he's not robb'd at all.
IAGO: I am sorry to hear this.
OTHELLO: I had been happy if the general camp,
Pioners and all, had tasted her sweet body,
So I had nothing known. O, now forever
Farewell the tranquil mind! Farewell content!
Farewell the plumed troop and the big wars
That make ambition virtue! O, farewell,
Farewell the neighing steed and the shrill trump,
The spirit-stirring drum, the ear-piercing fife,
The royal banner, and all quality,
Pride, pomp, and circumstance of glorious war!
And O you mortal engines, whose rude throats
The immortal Jove's dread clamors counterfeit,
Farewell! Othello's occupation's gone!
IAGO: Is't possible, my lord?
OTHELLO: Villain, be sure thou prove my love a whore;
Be sure of it. Give me the ocular proof;
Or, by the worth of man's eternal soul,
Thou hadst been better have been born a dog
Than answer my waked wrath!
IAGO: Is't come to this?
OTHELLO: Make me to see't; or at the least so prove it,
That the probation bear no hinge nor loop
To hang a doubt on; or woe upon thy life!
IAGO: My noble lord-
OTHELLO: If thou dost slander her and torture me,
Never pray more; abandon all remorse;
On horror's head horrors accumulate;
Do deeds to make heaven weep, all earth amazed;
For nothing canst thou to damnation add
Greater than that.
IAGO: O grace! O heaven defend me!
Are you a man? have you a soul or sense?
God be wi' you; take mine office. O wretched fool,
That livest to make thine honesty a vice!
O monstrous world! Take note, take note, O world,
To be direct and honest is not safe.
I thank you for this profit, and from hence
I'll love no friend sith love breeds such offense.
OTHELLO: Nay, stay; thou shouldst be honest.
IAGO: I should be wise; for honesty's a fool,
And loses that it works for.

OTHELLO: By the world,
I think my wife be honest, and think she is not;
I think that thou art just, and think thou art not.
I'll have some proof. Her name, that was as fresh
As Dian's visage, is now begrimed and black
As mine own face. If there be cords or knives,
Poison or fire, or suffocating streams,
I'll not endure it. Would I were satisfied!
IAGO: I see, sir, you are eaten up with passion;
I do repent me that I put it to you.
You would be satisfied?
OTHELLO: Would? Nay, I will.
IAGO: And may. But, how? how satisfied, my lord?
Would you, the supervisor, grossly gape on?
Behold her topp'd?
OTHELLO: Death and damnation! O!
IAGO: It were a tedious difficulty, I think,
To bring them to that prospect. Damn them then,
If ever mortal eyes do see them bolster
More than their own! What then? how then?
What shall I say? Where's satisfaction?
It is impossible you should see this
Were they as prime as goats, as hot as monkeys,
As salt as wolves in pride, and fools as gross
As ignorance made drunk. But yet, I say,
If imputation and strong circumstances,
Which lead directly to the door of truth,
Will give you satisfaction, you may have't.
OTHELLO: Give me a living reason she's disloyal.
IAGO: I do not like the office;
But sith I am enter'd in this cause so far,
Prick'd to't by foolish honesty and love,
I will go on. I lay with Cassio lately
And, being troubled with a raging tooth,
I could not sleep.
There are a kind of men so loose of soul,
That in their sleeps will mutter their affairs;
One of this kind is Cassio.
In sleep I heard him say, "Sweet Desdemona,
Let us be wary, let us hide our loves";
And then, sir, would he gripe and wring my hand,
Cry, "O sweet creature!" and then kiss me hard,
As if he pluck'd up kisses by the roots,
That grew upon my lips; then laid his leg
Over my thigh, and sigh'd and kiss'd; and then
Cried, "Cursed fate that gave thee to the Moor!"
OTHELLO: O monstrous! monstrous!
IAGO: Nay, this was but his dream.
OTHELLO: But this denoted a foregone conclusion.
'Tis a shrewd doubt, though it be but a dream.
IAGO: And this may help to thicken other proofs
That do demonstrate thinly.
OTHELLO: I'll tear her all to pieces.

IAGO: Nay, but be wise; yet we see nothing done;
She may be honest yet. Tell me but this;
Have you not sometimes seen a handkerchief
Spotted with strawberries in your wife's hand?
OTHELLO: I gave her such a one; 'twas my first gift.
IAGO: I know not that; but such a handkerchief-
I am sure it was your wife's- did I today
See Cassio wipe his beard with.
OTHELLO: If it be that-
IAGO: If it be that, or any that was hers,
It speaks against her with the other proofs.
OTHELLO: O, that the slave had forty thousand lives!
One is too poor, too weak for my revenge.
Now do I see 'tis true. Look here, Iago,
All my fond love thus do I blow to heaven.
'Tis gone.
Arise, black vengeance, from thy hollow hell!
Yield up, O love, thy crown and hearted throne
To tyrannous hate! Swell, bosom, with thy fraught,
For 'tis of aspics' tongues!
IAGO: Yet be content.
OTHELLO: O, blood, blood, blood!
IAGO: Patience, I say; your mind perhaps may change.
OTHELLO: Never, Iago. Like to the Pontic Sea,
Whose icy current and compulsive course
Ne'er feels retiring ebb, but keeps due on
To the Propontic and the Hellespont,
Even so my bloody thoughts, with violent pace,
Shall ne'er look back, ne'er ebb to humble love,
Till that a capable and wide revenge
Swallow them up. Now, by yond marble heaven,
In the due reverence of a sacred vow Kneels.
I here engage my words.
IAGO: Do not rise yet. Kneels.
Witness, you ever-burning lights above,
You elements that clip us round about,
Witness that here Iago doth give up
The execution of his wit, hands, heart,
To wrong'd Othello's service! Let him command,
And to obey shall be in me remorse,
What bloody business ever. They rise.
OTHELLO: I greet thy love,
Not with vain thanks, but with acceptance bounteous,
And will upon the instant put thee to't:
Within these three days let me hear thee say
That Cassio's not alive.
IAGO: My friend is dead, 'tis done at your request;
But let her live.
OTHELLO: Damn her, lewd minx! O, damn her!
Come, go with me apart; I will withdraw,
To furnish me with some swift means of death
For the fair devil. Now art thou my lieutenant.
IAGO: I am your own forever.

Exeunt.

ACT III. SCENE IV. Before the Castle.

Enter Desdemona, Emilia, and Clown.

DESDEMONA: Do you know, sirrah, where Lieutenant Cassio lies?
CLOWN: I dare not say he lies anywhere.
DESDEMONA: Why, man?
CLOWN: He's a soldier; and for one to say a soldier lies, is stabbing.
DESDEMONA: Go to! Where lodges he?
CLOWN: To tell you where he lodges, is to tell you where I lie.
DESDEMONA: Can anything be made of this?
CLOWN: I know not where he lodges, and for me to devise a lodging, and say he lies here or he lies there, were to lie in mine own throat.
DESDEMONA: Can you inquire him out and be edified by report?
CLOWN: I will catechize the world for him; that is, make questions and by them answer.
DESDEMONA: Seek him, bid him come hither. Tell him I have moved my lord on his behalf and hope all will be well.
CLOWN: To do this is within the compass of man's wit, and therefore I will attempt the doing it.

Exit.

DESDEMONA: Where should I lose that handkerchief, Emilia?
EMILIA: I know not, madam.
DESDEMONA: Believe me, I had rather have lost my purse
Full of crusadoes; and, but my noble Moor
Is true of mind and made of no such baseness
As jealous creatures are, it were enough
To put him to ill thinking.
EMILIA: Is he not jealous?
DESDEMONA: Who, he? I think the sun where he was born
Drew all such humors from him.
EMILIA: Look, where he comes.
DESDEMONA: I will not leave him now till Cassio
Be call'd to him.

Enter Othello.

How is't with you, my lord?
OTHELLO: Well, my good lady. Aside. O, hardness to dissemble!
How do you, Desdemona?
DESDEMONA: Well, my good lord.
OTHELLO: Give me your hand. This hand is moist, my lady.
DESDEMONA: It yet has felt no age nor known no sorrow.
OTHELLO: This argues fruitfulness and liberal heart;
Hot, hot, and moist. This hand of yours requires
A sequester from liberty, fasting, and prayer,
Much castigation, exercise devout,
For here's a young and sweating devil here
That commonly rebels. 'Tis a good hand,
A frank one.
DESDEMONA: You may, indeed, say so;
For 'twas that hand that gave away my heart.
OTHELLO: A liberal hand. The hearts of old gave hands;
But our new heraldry is hands, not hearts.
DESDEMONA: I cannot speak of this. Come now, your promise.
OTHELLO: What promise, chuck?

DESDEMONA: I have sent to bid Cassio come speak with you.
OTHELLO: I have a salt and sorry rheum offends me;
Lend me thy handkerchief.
DESDEMONA: Here, my lord.
OTHELLO: That which I gave you.
DESDEMONA: I have it not about me.
OTHELLO: Not?
DESDEMONA: No, faith, my lord.
OTHELLO: That's a fault. That handkerchief
Did an Egyptian to my mother give;
She was a charmer, and could almost read
The thoughts of people. She told her, while she kept it,
'Twould make her amiable and subdue my father
Entirely to her love, but if she lost it
Or made a gift of it, my father's eye
Should hold her loathed and his spirits should hunt
After new fancies. She dying gave it me,
And bid me, when my fate would have me wive,
To give it her. I did so, and take heed on't;
Make it a darling like your precious eye;
To lose't or give't away were such perdition
As nothing else could match.
DESDEMONA: Is't possible?
OTHELLO: 'Tis true; there's magic in the web of it.
A sibyl, that had number'd in the world
The sun to course two hundred compasses,
In her prophetic fury sew'd the work;
The worms were hallow'd that did breed the silk,
And it was dyed in mummy which the skillful
Conserved of maiden's hearts.
DESDEMONA: Indeed! is't true?
OTHELLO: Most veritable; therefore look to't well.
DESDEMONA: Then would to God that I had never seen't!
OTHELLO: Ha! wherefore?
DESDEMONA: Why do you speak so startingly and rash?
OTHELLO: Is't lost? is't gone? speak, is it out o' the way?
DESDEMONA: Heaven bless us!
OTHELLO: Say you?
DESDEMONA: It is not lost; but what an if it were?
OTHELLO: How?
DESDEMONA: I say, it is not lost.
OTHELLO: Fetch't, let me see it.
DESDEMONA: Why, so I can, sir, but I will not now.
This is a trick to put me from my suit.
Pray you, let Cassio be received again.
OTHELLO: Fetch me the handkerchief, my mind misgives.
DESDEMONA: Come, come,
You'll never meet a more sufficient man.
OTHELLO: The handkerchief!
DESDEMONA: I pray, talk me of Cassio.
OTHELLO: The handkerchief!
DESDEMONA: A man that all his time
Hath founded his good fortunes on your love,

Shared dangers with you-
OTHELLO: The handkerchief!
DESDEMONA: In sooth, you are to blame.
OTHELLO: Away!
Exit.
EMILIA: Is not this man jealous?
DESDEMONA: I ne'er saw this before.
Sure there's some wonder in this handkerchief;
I am most unhappy in the loss of it.
EMILIA: 'Tis not a year or two shows us a man.
They are all but stomachs and we all but food;
They eat us hungerly, and when they are full
They belch us. Look you! Cassio and my husband.
Enter Cassio and Iago.
IAGO: There is no other way; 'tis she must do't.
And, lo, the happiness! Go and importune her.
DESDEMONA: How now, good Cassio! What's the news with you?
CASSIO: Madam, my former suit: I do beseech you
That by your virtuous means I may again
Exist and be a member of his love
Whom I with all the office of my heart
Entirely honor. I would not be delay'd.
If my offense be of such mortal kind
That nor my service past nor present sorrows
Nor purposed merit in futurity
Can ransom me into his love again,
But to know so must be my benefit;
So shall I clothe me in a forced content
And shut myself up in some other course
To Fortune's alms.
DESDEMONA: Alas, thrice-gentle Cassio!
My advocation is not now in tune;
My lord is not my lord, nor should I know him
Were he in favor as in humor alter'd.
So help me every spirit sanctified,
As I have spoken for you all my best
And stood within the blank of his displeasure
For my free speech! You must awhile be patient.
What I can do I will; and more I will
Than for myself I dare. Let that suffice you.
IAGO: Is my lord angry?
EMILIA: He went hence but now,
And certainly in strange unquietness.
IAGO: Can he be angry? I have seen the cannon,
When it hath blown his ranks into the air
And, like the devil, from his very arm
Puff'd his own brother. And can he be angry?
Something of moment then. I will go meet him.
There's matter in't indeed if he be angry.
DESDEMONA: I prithee, do so.
Exit Iago.
Something sure of state,
Either from Venice or some unhatch'd practice

Made demonstrable here in Cyprus to him,
Hath puddled his clear spirit; and in such cases
Men's natures wrangle with inferior things,
Though great ones are their object. 'Tis even so;
For let our finger ache, and it indues
Our other healthful members even to that sense
Of pain. Nay, we must think men are not gods,
Nor of them look for such observancy
As fits the bridal. Beshrew me much, Emilia,
I was, unhandsome warrior as I am,
Arraigning his unkindness with my soul;
But now I find I had suborn'd the witness,
And he's indicted falsely.
EMILIA: Pray heaven it be state matters, as you think,
And no conception nor no jealous toy
Concerning you.
DESDEMONA: Alas the day, I never gave him cause!
EMILIA: But jealous souls will not be answer'd so;
They are not ever jealous for the cause,
But jealous for they are jealous. 'Tis a monster
Begot upon itself, born on itself.
DESDEMONA: Heaven keep that monster from Othello's mind!
EMILIA: Lady, amen.
DESDEMONA: I will go seek him. Cassio, walk hereabout.
If I do find him fit, I'll move your suit,
And seek to effect it to my uttermost.
CASSIO: I humbly thank your ladyship.
Exeunt Desdemona and Emilia.
Enter Bianca.
BIANCA: Save you, friend Cassio!
CASSIO: What make you from home?
How is it with you, my most fair Bianca?
I'faith, sweet love, I was coming to your house.
BIANCA: And I was going to your lodging, Cassio.
What, keep a week away? seven days and nights?
Eight score eight hours? and lovers' absent hours,
More tedious than the dial eight score times?
O weary reckoning!
CASSIO: Pardon me, Bianca.
I have this while with leaden thoughts been press'd;
But I shall in a more continuate time
Strike off this score of absence. Sweet Bianca,
Gives Her Desdemona's Handkerchief.
Take me this work out.
BIANCA: O Cassio, whence came this?
This is some token from a newer friend.
To the felt absence now I feel a cause.
Is't come to this? Well, well.
CASSIO: Go to, woman!
Throw your vile guesses in the devil's teeth,
From whence you have them. You are jealous now
That this is from some mistress, some remembrance.
No, by my faith, Bianca.

BIANCA: Why, whose is it?
CASSIO: I know not, sweet. I found it in my chamber.
I like the work well. Ere it be demanded-
As like enough it will- I'ld have it copied.
Take it, and do't; and leave me for this time.
BIANCA: Leave you! wherefore?
CASSIO: I do attend here on the general;
And think it no addition, nor my wish,
To have him see me woman'd.
BIANCA: Why, I pray you?
CASSIO: Not that I love you not.
BIANCA: But that you do not love me.
I pray you, bring me on the way a little,
And say if I shall see you soon at night.
CASSIO: 'Tis but a little way that I can bring you,
For I attend here, but I'll see you soon.
BIANCA: 'Tis very good; I must be circumstanced.
Exeunt.

ACT IV. SCENE I. Cyprus. Before the Castle.

Enter Othello and Iago.
IAGO: Will you think so?
OTHELLO: Think so, Iago?
IAGO: What,
To kiss in private?
OTHELLO: An unauthorized kiss.
IAGO: Or to be naked with her friend in bed
An hour or more, not meaning any harm?
OTHELLO: Naked in bed, Iago, and not mean harm!
It is hypocrisy against the devil.
They that mean virtuously and yet do so,
The devil their virtue tempts and they tempt heaven.
IAGO: So they do nothing, 'tis a venial slip.
But if I give my wife a handkerchief-
OTHELLO: What then?
IAGO: Why, then, 'tis hers, my lord, and being hers,
She may, I think, bestow't on any man.
OTHELLO: She is protectress of her honor too.
May she give that?
IAGO: Her honor is an essence that's not seen;
They have it very oft that have it not.
But for the handkerchief-
OTHELLO: By heaven, I would most gladly have forgot it.
Thou said'st- O, it comes o'er my memory,
As doth the raven o'er the infected house,
Boding to all- he had my handkerchief.
IAGO: Ay, what of that?
OTHELLO: That's not so good now.
IAGO: What,
If I had said I had seen him do you wrong?
Or heard him say- as knaves be such abroad,
Who having, by their own importunate suit,
Or voluntary dotage of some mistress,
Convinced or supplied them, cannot choose

But they must blab-
OTHELLO: Hath he said anything?
IAGO: He hath, my lord; but be you well assured,
No more than he'll unswear.
OTHELLO: What hath he said?
IAGO: Faith, that he did- I know not what he did.
OTHELLO: What? what?
IAGO: Lie-
OTHELLO: With her?
IAGO: With her, on her, what you will.
OTHELLO: Lie with her! lie on her! We say lie on her, when they belie her. Lie with her! 'Zounds, that's fulsome! Handkerchief-confessions- handkerchief! To confess and be hanged for his labor-first, to be hanged, and then to confess. I tremble at it. Nature would not invest herself in such shadowing passion without some instruction. It is not words that shakes me thus. Pish! Noses, ears, and lips. Is't possible? Confess? Handkerchief? O devil!
Falls in a Trance.
IAGO: Work on,
My medicine, work! Thus credulous fools are caught,
And many worthy and chaste dames even thus,
All guiltless, meet reproach. What, ho! My lord!
My lord, I say! Othello!
Enter Cassio.
How now, Cassio!
CASSIO: What's the matter?
IAGO: My lord is fall'n into an epilepsy.
This is his second fit; he had one yesterday.
CASSIO: Rub him about the temples.
IAGO: No, forbear;
The lethargy must have his quiet course.
If not, he foams at mouth, and by and by
Breaks out to savage madness. Look, he stirs.
Do you withdraw yourself a little while,
He will recover straight. When he is gone,
I would on great occasion speak with you.
Exit Cassio.
How is it, general? Have you not hurt your head?
OTHELLO: Dost thou mock me?
IAGO: I mock you? No, by heaven.
Would you would bear your fortune like a man!
OTHELLO: A horned man's a monster and a beast.
IAGO: There's many a beast then in a populous city,
And many a civil monster.
OTHELLO: Did he confess it?
IAGO: Good sir, be a man;
Think every bearded fellow that's but yoked
May draw with you. There's millions now alive
That nightly lie in those unproper beds
Which they dare swear peculiar. Your case is better.
O, 'tis the spite of hell, the fiend's arch-mock,
To lip a wanton in a secure couch,
And to suppose her chaste! No, let me know,

And knowing what I am, I know what she shall be.
OTHELLO: O, thou art wise; 'tis certain.
IAGO: Stand you awhile apart,
Confine yourself but in a patient list.
Whilst you were here o'erwhelmed with your grief-
A passion most unsuiting such a man-
Cassio came hither. I shifted him away,
And laid good 'scuse upon your ecstasy;
Bade him anon return and here speak with me
The which he promised. Do but encave yourself
And mark the fleers, the gibes, and notable scorns,
That dwell in every region of his face;
For I will make him tell the tale anew,
Where, how, how oft, how long ago, and when
He hath and is again to cope your wife.
I say, but mark his gesture. Marry, patience,
Or I shall say you are all in all in spleen,
And nothing of a man.
OTHELLO: Dost thou hear, Iago?
I will be found most cunning in my patience;
But (dost thou hear?) most bloody.
IAGO: That's not amiss;
But yet keep time in all. Will you withdraw?
Othello retires.
Now will I question Cassio of Bianca,
A housewife that by selling her desires
Buys herself bread and clothes. It is a creature
That dotes on Cassio, as 'tis the strumpet's plague
To beguile many and be beguiled by one.
He, when he hears of her, cannot refrain
From the excess of laughter. Here he comes.
Re-enter Cassio.
As he shall smile, Othello shall go mad;
And his unbookish jealousy must construe
Poor Cassio's smiles, gestures, and light behavior
Quite in the wrong. How do you now, lieutenant?
CASSIO: The worser that you give me the addition
Whose want even kills me.
IAGO: Ply Desdemona well, and you are sure on't.
Now, if this suit lay in Bianco's power,
How quickly should you speed!
CASSIO: Alas, poor caitiff!
OTHELLO: Look, how he laughs already!
IAGO: I never knew a woman love man so.
CASSIO: Alas, poor rogue! I think, i'faith, she loves me.
OTHELLO: Now he denies it faintly and laughs it out.
IAGO: Do you hear, Cassio?
OTHELLO: Now he importunes him
To tell it o'er. Go to; well said, well said.
IAGO: She gives it out that you shall marry her.
Do you intend it?
CASSIO: Ha, ha, ha!
OTHELLO: Do you triumph, Roman? Do you triumph?

CASSIO: I marry her! What? A customer! I prithee, bear some charity to my wit; do not think it so unwholesome. Ha, ha, ha!
OTHELLO: So, so, so, so. They laugh that win.
IAGO: Faith, the cry goes that you shall marry her.
CASSIO: Prithee, say true.
IAGO: I am a very villain else.
OTHELLO: Have you scored me? Well.
CASSIO: This is the monkey's own giving out. She is persuaded I will marry her, out of her own love and flattery, not out of my promise.
OTHELLO: Iago beckons me; now he begins the story.
CASSIO: She was here even now; she haunts me in every place. I was the other day talking on the sea bank with certain Venetians, and thither comes the bauble, and, by this hand, she falls me thus about my neck-
OTHELLO: Crying, "O dear Cassio!" as it were; his gesture imports it.
CASSIO: So hangs and lolls and weeps upon me; so hales and pulls me. Ha, ha, ha!
OTHELLO: Now he tells how she plucked him to my chamber. O, I see that nose of yours, but not that dog I shall throw it to.
CASSIO: Well, I must leave her company.
IAGO: Before me! look where she comes.
CASSIO: 'Tis such another fitchew! marry, a perfumed one.
Enter Bianca.
What do you mean by this haunting of me?
BIANCA: Let the devil and his dam haunt you! What did you mean by that same handkerchief you gave me even now? I was a fine fool to take it. I must take out the work? A likely piece of work that you should find it in your chamber and not know who left it there! This is some minx's token, and I must take out the work? There, give it your hobbyhorse. Wheresoever you had it, I'll take out no work on't.
CASSIO: How now, my sweet Bianca! how now! how now!
OTHELLO: By heaven, that should be my handkerchief!
BIANCA: An you'll come to supper tonight, you may; an you will not, come when you are next prepared for.
Exit.
IAGO: After her, after her.
CASSIO: Faith, I must; she'll rail i' the street else.
IAGO: Will you sup there?
CASSIO: Faith, I intend so.
IAGO: Well, I may chance to see you, for I would very fain speak with you.
CASSIO: Prithee, come; will you?
IAGO: Go to; say no more.
Exit Cassio.
OTHELLO: Advancing. How shall I murther him, Iago?
IAGO: Did you perceive how he laughed at his vice?
OTHELLO: O Iago!
IAGO: And did you see the handkerchief?
OTHELLO: Was that mine?
IAGO: Yours, by this hand. And to see how he prizes the foolish woman your wife! She gave it him, and he hath given it his whore.
OTHELLO: I would have him nine years akilling. A fine woman! a fair

woman! a sweet woman!
IAGO: Nay, you must forget that.
OTHELLO: Ay, let her rot, and perish, and be damned tonight, for she shall not live. No, my heart is turned to stone; I strike it, and it hurts my hand. O, the world hath not a sweeter creature. She might lie by an emperor's side, and command him tasks.
IAGO: Nay, that's not your way.
OTHELLO: Hang her! I do but say what she is. So delicate with her needle, an admirable musician. O, she will sing the savageness out of a bear. Of so high and plenteous wit and invention-
IAGO: She's the worse for all this.
OTHELLO: O, a thousand, a thousand times. And then, of so gentle a condition!
IAGO: Ay, too gentle.
OTHELLO: Nay, that's certain. But yet the pity of it, Iago!
O Iago, the pity of it, Iago!
IAGO: If you are so fond over her iniquity, give her patent to offend, for, if it touch not you, it comes near nobody.
OTHELLO: I will chop her into messes. Cuckold me!
IAGO: O, 'tis foul in her.
OTHELLO: With mine officer!
IAGO: That's fouler.
OTHELLO: Get me some poison, Iago, this night. I'll not expostulate with her, lest her body and beauty unprovide my mind again. This night, Iago.
IAGO: Do it not with poison, strangle her in her bed, even the bed she hath contaminated.
OTHELLO: Good, good, the justice of it pleases, very good.
IAGO: And for Cassio, let me be his undertaker. You shall hear more by midnight.
OTHELLO: Excellent good. A Trumpet Within. What trumpet is that same?
IAGO: Something from Venice, sure. 'Tis Lodovico
Come from the Duke. And, see your wife is with him.
Enter Lodovico, Desdemona, and Attendants.
LODOVICO: God save the worthy general!
OTHELLO: With all my heart, sir.
LODOVICO: The Duke and Senators of Venice greet you.
Gives Him a Letter.
OTHELLO: I kiss the instrument of their pleasures.
Opens the Letter, and Reads.
DESDEMONA: And what's the news, good cousin Lodovico?
IAGO: I am very glad to see you, signior;
Welcome to Cyprus.
LODOVICO: I thank you. How does Lieutenant Cassio?
IAGO: Lives, sir.
DESDEMONA: Cousin, there's fall'n between him and my lord
An unkind breech; but you shall make all well.
OTHELLO: Are you sure of that?
DESDEMONA: My lord?
OTHELLO: Reads. "This fail you not to do, as you will-"
LODOVICO: He did not call; he's busy in the paper.
Is there division 'twixt my lord and Cassio?

DESDEMONA: A most unhappy one. I would do much
To atone them, for the love I bear to Cassio.
OTHELLO: Fire and brimstone!
DESDEMONA: My lord?
OTHELLO: Are you wise?
DESDEMONA: What, is he angry?
LODOVICO: May be the letter moved him;
For, as I think, they do command him home,
Deputing Cassio in his government.
DESDEMONA: By my troth, I am glad on't.
OTHELLO: Indeed!
DESDEMONA: My lord?
OTHELLO: I am glad to see you mad.
DESDEMONA: Why, sweet Othello?
OTHELLO: Devil! Strikes her.
DESDEMONA: I have not deserved this.
LODOVICO: My lord, this would not be believed in Venice,
Though I should swear I saw't. 'Tis very much.
Make her amends; she weeps.
OTHELLO: O devil, devil!
If that the earth could teem with woman's tears,
Each drop she falls would prove a crocodile.
Out of my sight!
DESDEMONA: Going. I will not stay to offend you.
LODOVICO: Truly, an obedient lady.
I do beseech your lordship, call her back.
OTHELLO: Mistress!
DESDEMONA: My lord?
OTHELLO: What would you with her, sir?
LODOVICO: Who, I, my lord?
OTHELLO: Ay, you did wish that I would make her turn.
Sir, she can turn and turn, and yet go on,
And turn again; and she can weep, sir, weep;
And she's obedient, as you say, obedient,
Very obedient. Proceed you in your tears.
Concerning this, sir- O well-painted passion!-
I am commanded home. Get you away;
I'll send for you anon. Sir, I obey the mandate,
And will return to Venice. Hence, avaunt!
Exit Desdemona.
Cassio shall have my place. And, sir, tonight,
I do entreat that we may sup together.
You are welcome, sir, to Cyprus. Goats and monkeys!
Exit.
LODOVICO: Is this the noble Moor whom our full Senate
Call all in all sufficient? This the nature
Whom passion could not shake? whose solid virtue
The shot of accident nor dart of chance
Could neither graze nor pierce?
IAGO: He is much changed.
LODOVICO: Are his wits safe? Is he not light of brain?
IAGO: He's that he is. I may not breathe my censure
What he might be: if what he might he is not,

I would to heaven he were!
LODOVICO: What, strike his wife!
IAGO: Faith, that was not so well; yet would I knew
That stroke would prove the worst!
LODOVICO: Is it his use?
Or did the letters work upon his blood,
And new create this fault?
IAGO: Alas, alas!
It is not honesty in me to speak
What I have seen and known. You shall observe him,
And his own courses will denote him so
That I may save my speech. Do but go after,
And mark how he continues.
LODOVICO: I am sorry that I am deceived in him.
Exeunt.

ACT IV. SCENE II. A Room in the Castle.

Enter Othello and Emilia.
OTHELLO: You have seen nothing, then?
EMILIA: Nor ever heard, nor ever did suspect.
OTHELLO: Yes, you have seen Cassio and she together.
EMILIA: But then I saw no harm, and then I heard
Each syllable that breath made up between them.
OTHELLO: What, did they never whisper?
EMILIA: Never, my lord.
OTHELLO: Nor send you out o' the way?
EMILIA: Never.
OTHELLO: To fetch her fan, her gloves, her mask, nor nothing?
EMILIA: Never, my lord.
OTHELLO: That's strange.
EMILIA: I durst, my lord, to wager she is honest,
Lay down my soul at stake. If you think other,
Remove your thought; it doth abuse your bosom.
If any wretch have put this in your head,
Let heaven requite it with the serpent's curse!
For if she be not honest, chaste, and true,
There's no man happy; the purest of their wives
Is foul as slander.
OTHELLO: Bid her come hither; go.
Exit Emilia.
She says enough; yet she's a simple bawd
That cannot say as much. This is a subtle whore,
A closet lock and key of villainous secrets.
And yet she'll kneel and pray; I have seen her do't.
Enter Desdemona with Emilia.
DESDEMONA: My lord, what is your will?
OTHELLO: Pray, chuck, come hither.
DESDEMONA: What is your pleasure?
OTHELLO: Let me see your eyes;
Look in my face.
DESDEMONA: What horrible fancy's this?
OTHELLO: To Emilia. Some of your function, mistress,
Leave procreants alone and shut the door;
Cough, or cry "hem," if anybody come.

Your mystery, your mystery; nay, dispatch.
Exit Emilia.
DESDEMONA: Upon my knees, what doth your speech import?
I understand a fury in your words,
But not the words.
OTHELLO: Why, what art thou?
DESDEMONA: Your wife, my lord, your true and loyal wife.
OTHELLO: Come, swear it, damn thyself;
Lest, being like one of heaven, the devils themselves
Should fear to seize thee. Therefore be double-damn'd;
Swear thou art honest.
DESDEMONA: Heaven doth truly know it.
OTHELLO: Heaven truly knows that thou art false as hell.
DESDEMONA: To whom, my lord? with whom? how am I false?
OTHELLO: O Desdemona! Away! away! away!
DESDEMONA: Alas the heavy day! Why do you weep?
Am I the motive of these tears, my lord?
If haply you my father do suspect
An instrument of this your calling back,
Lay not your blame on me. If you have lost him,
Why, I have lost him too.
OTHELLO: Had it pleased heaven
To try me with affliction, had they rain'd
All kinds of sores and shames on my bare head,
Steep'd me in poverty to the very lips,
Given to captivity me and my utmost hopes,
I should have found in some place of my soul
A drop of patience; but, alas, to make me
A fixed figure for the time of scorn
To point his slow unmoving finger at!
Yet could I bear that too, well, very well;
But there, where I have garner'd up my heart,
Where either I must live or bear no life;
The fountain from the which my current runs,
Or else dries up; to be discarded thence!
Or keep it as a cistern for foul toads
To knot and gender in! Turn thy complexion there,
Patience, thou young and rose-lipp'd cherubin,
Ay, there, look grim as hell!
DESDEMONA: I hope my noble lord esteems me honest.
OTHELLO: O, ay, as summer flies are in the shambles,
That quicken even with blowing. O thou weed,
Who art so lovely fair and smell'st so sweet
That the sense aches at thee, would thou hadst ne'er been born!
DESDEMONA: Alas, what ignorant sin have I committed?
OTHELLO: Was this fair paper, this most goodly book,
Made to write "whore" upon? What committed?
Committed? O thou public commoner!
I should make very forges of my cheeks,
That would to cinders burn up modesty,
Did I but speak thy deeds. What committed!
Heaven stops the nose at it, and the moon winks;
The bawdy wind, that kisses all it meets,

Is hush'd within the hollow mine of earth,
And will not hear it. What committed?
Impudent strumpet!
DESDEMONA: By heaven, you do me wrong.
OTHELLO: Are not you a strumpet?
DESDEMONA: No, as I am a Christian.
If to preserve this vessel for my lord
From any other foul unlawful touch
Be not to be a strumpet, I am none.
OTHELLO: What, not a whore?
DESDEMONA: No, as I shall be saved.
OTHELLO: Is't possible?
DESDEMONA: O, heaven forgive us!
OTHELLO: I cry you mercy then;
I took you for that cunning whore of Venice
That married with Othello. Raises His Voice. You, mistress,
That have the office opposite to Saint Peter,
And keep the gate of hell!
Re-enter Emilia.
You, you, ay, you!
We have done our course; there's money for your pains.
I pray you, turn the key, and keep our counsel. Exit.
EMILIA: Alas, what does this gentleman conceive?
How do you, madam? How do you, my good lady?
DESDEMONA: Faith, half asleep.
EMILIA: Good madam, what's the matter with my lord?
DESDEMONA: With who?
EMILIA: Why, with my lord, madam.
DESDEMONA: Who is thy lord?
EMILIA: He that is yours, sweet lady.
DESDEMONA: I have none. Do not talk to me, Emilia;
I cannot weep, nor answer have I none
But what should go by water. Prithee, tonight
Lay on my bed my wedding sheets. Remember,
And call thy husband hither.
EMILIA: Here's a change indeed!
Exit.
DESDEMONA: 'Tis meet I should be used so, very meet.
How have I been behaved, that he might stick
The small'st opinion on my least misuse?
Re-enter Emilia with Iago.
IAGO: What is your pleasure, madam? How is't with you?
DESDEMONA: I cannot tell. Those that do teach young babes
Do it with gentle means and easy tasks.
He might have chid me so, for in good faith,
I am a child to chiding.
IAGO: What's the matter, lady?
EMILIA: Alas, Iago, my lord hath so bewhored her,
Thrown such despite and heavy terms upon her,
As true hearts cannot bear.
DESDEMONA: Am I that name, Iago?
IAGO: What name, fair lady?
DESDEMONA: Such as she says my lord did say I was.

EMILIA: He call'd her whore; a beggar in his drink
Could not have laid such terms upon his callet.
IAGO: Why did he so?
DESDEMONA: I do not know; I am sure I am none such.
IAGO: Do not weep, do not weep. Alas the day!
EMILIA: Hath she forsook so many noble matches,
Her father and her country and her friends,
To be call'd whore? Would it not make one weep?
DESDEMONA: It is my wretched fortune.
IAGO: Beshrew him for't!
How comes this trick upon him?
DESDEMONA: Nay, heaven doth know.
EMILIA: I will be hang'd, if some eternal villain,
Some busy and insinuating rogue,
Some cogging, cozening slave, to get some office,
Have not devised this slander; I'll be hang'd else.
IAGO: Fie, there is no such man; it is impossible.
DESDEMONA: If any such there be, heaven pardon him!
EMILIA: A halter pardon him! And hell gnaw his bones!
Why should he call her whore? Who keeps her company?
What place? What time? What form? What likelihood?
The Moor's abused by some most villainous knave,
Some base notorious knave, some scurvy fellow.
O heaven, that such companions thou'ldst unfold,
And put in every honest hand a whip
To lash the rascals naked through the world
Even from the east to the west!
IAGO: Speak within door.
EMILIA: O, fie upon them! Some such squire he was
That turn'd your wit the seamy side without,
And made you to suspect me with the Moor.
IAGO: You are a fool; go to.
DESDEMONA: O good Iago,
What shall I do to win my lord again?
Good friend, go to him, for by this light of heaven,
I know not how I lost him. Here I kneel:
If e'er my will did trespass 'gainst his love
Either in discourse of thought or actual deed,
Or that mine eyes, mine ears, or any sense,
Delighted them in any other form,
Or that I do not yet, and ever did,
And ever will, though he do shake me off
To beggarly divorcement, love him dearly,
Comfort forswear me! Unkindness may do much,
And his unkindness may defeat my life,
But never taint my love. I cannot say "whore."
It doth abhor me now I speak the word;
To do the act that might the addition earn
Not the world's mass of vanity could make me.
IAGO: I pray you, be content; 'tis but his humor:
The business of the state does him offense,
And he does chide with you.
DESDEMONA: If 'twere no other-

IAGO: 'Tis but so, I warrant. Trumpets within.
Hark, how these instruments summon to supper!
The messengers of Venice stay the meat.
Go in, and weep not; all things shall be well.
Exeunt Desdemona and Emilia.
Enter Roderigo.
How now, Roderigo!

RODERIGO: I do not find that thou dealest justly with me.

IAGO: What in the contrary?

RODERIGO: Every day thou daffest me with some device, Iago; and rather, as it seems to me now, keepest from me all conveniency than suppliest me with the least advantage of hope. I will indeed no longer endure it; nor am I yet persuaded to put up in peace what already I have foolishly suffered.

IAGO: Will you hear me, Roderigo?

RODERIGO: Faith, I have heard too much, for your words and performances are no kin together.

IAGO: You charge me most unjustly.

RODERIGO: With nought but truth. I have wasted myself out of my means. The jewels you have had from me to deliver to Desdemona would half have corrupted a votarist. You have told me she hath received them and returned me expectations and comforts of sudden respect and acquaintance; but I find none.

IAGO: Well, go to, very well.

RODERIGO: Very well! go to! I cannot go to, man; nor 'tis not very well. By this hand, I say 'tis very scurvy, and begin to find myself fopped in it.

IAGO: Very well.

RODERIGO: I tell you 'tis not very well. I will make myself known to Desdemona. If she will return me my jewels, I will give over my suit and repent my unlawful solicitation; if not, assure yourself I will seek satisfaction of you.

IAGO: You have said now.

RODERIGO: Ay, and said nothing but what I protest intendment of doing.

IAGO: Why, now I see there's mettle in thee; and even from this instant do build on thee a better opinion than ever before. Give me thy hand, Roderigo. Thou hast taken against me a most just exception; but yet, I protest, have dealt most directly in thy affair.

RODERIGO: It hath not appeared.

IAGO: I grant indeed it hath not appeared, and your suspicion is not without wit and judgement. But, Roderigo, if thou hast that in thee indeed, which I have greater reason to believe now than ever, I mean purpose, courage, and valor, this night show it; if thou the next night following enjoy not Desdemona, take me from this world with treachery and devise engines for my life.

RODERIGO: Well, what is it? Is it within reason and compass?

IAGO: Sir, there is especial commission come from Venice to depute Cassio in Othello's place.

RODERIGO: Is that true? Why then Othello and Desdemona return again to Venice.

IAGO: O, no; he goes into Mauritania, and takes away with him the fair Desdemona, unless his abode be lingered here by some

accident; wherein none can be so determinate as the removing of Cassio.
RODERIGO: How do you mean, removing of him?
IAGO: Why, by making him uncapable of Othello's place; knocking out his brains.
RODERIGO: And that you would have me to do?
IAGO: Ay, if you dare do yourself a profit and a right. He sups tonight with a harlotry, and thither will I go to him. He knows not yet of his honorable fortune. If you will watch his going thence, which his will fashion to fall out between twelve and one, you may take him at your pleasure; I will be near to second your attempt, and he shall fall between us. Come, stand not amazed at it, but go along with me; I will show you such a necessity in his death that you shall think yourself bound to put it on him. It is now high supper-time, and the night grows to waste. About it.
RODERIGO: I will hear further reason for this.
IAGO: And you shall be satisfied.
Exeunt.

ACT IV. SCENE III. Another Room in the Castle.

Enter Othello, Lodovico, Desdemona, Emilia, and Attendants.
LODOVICO: I do beseech you, sir, trouble yourself no further.
OTHELLO: O, pardon me; 'twill do me good to walk.
LODOVICO: Madam, good night; I humbly thank your ladyship.
DESDEMONA: Your honor is most welcome.
OTHELLO: Will you walk, sir? O- Desdemona-
DESDEMONA: My lord?
OTHELLO: Get you to bed on the instant; I will be returned forthwith. Dismiss your attendant there; look it be done.
DESDEMONA: I will, my lord.
Exeunt Othello, Lodovico, and Attendants.
EMILIA: How goes it now? He looks gentler than he did.
DESDEMONA: He says he will return incontinent.
He hath commanded me to go to bed,
And bade me to dismiss you.
EMILIA: Dismiss me?
DESDEMONA: It was his bidding; therefore, good Emilia,
Give me my nightly wearing, and adieu.
We must not now displease him.
EMILIA: I would you had never seen him!
DESDEMONA: So would not I. My love doth so approve him,
That even his stubbornness, his checks, his frowns-
Prithee, unpin me- have grace and favor in them.
EMILIA: I have laid those sheets you bade me on the bed.
DESDEMONA: All's one. Good faith, how foolish are our minds!
If I do die before thee, prithee shroud me
In one of those same sheets.
EMILIA: Come, come, you talk.
DESDEMONA: My mother had a maid call'd Barbary;
She was in love, and he she loved proved mad
And did forsake her. She had a song of "willow";
An old thing 'twas, but it express'd her fortune,
And she died singing it. That song tonight
Will not go from my mind; I have much to do

But to go hang my head all at one side
And sing it like poor Barbary. Prithee, dispatch.
EMILIA: Shall I go fetch your nightgown?
DESDEMONA: No, unpin me here.
This Lodovico is a proper man.
EMILIA: A very handsome man.
DESDEMONA: He speaks well.
EMILIA: I know a lady in Venice would have walked barefoot to Palestine for a touch of his nether lip.
DESDEMONA: Sings.
"The poor soul sat sighing by a sycamore tree,
Sing all a green willow;
Her hand on her bosom, her head on her knee,
Sing willow, willow, willow.
The fresh streams ran by her, and murmur'd her moans,
Sing willow, willow, willow;
Her salt tears fell from her, and soften'd the stones-"
Lay be these-
Sings. "Sing willow, willow, willow-"
Prithee, hie thee; he'll come anon-
Sings. "Sing all a green willow must be my garland.
Let nobody blame him; his scorn I approve-"
Nay, that's not next. Hark, who is't that knocks?
EMILIA: It's the wind.
DESDEMONA: Sings.
"I call'd my love false love; but what said he then?
Sing willow, willow, willow.
If I court moe women, you'll couch with moe men-"
So get thee gone; good night. Mine eyes do itch;
Doth that bode weeping?
EMILIA: 'Tis neither here nor there.
DESDEMONA: I have heard it said so. O, these men, these men!
Dost thou in conscience think- tell me, Emilia-
That there be women do abuse their husbands
In such gross kind?
EMILIA: There be some such, no question.
DESDEMONA: Wouldst thou do such a deed for all the world?
EMILIA: Why, would not you?
DESDEMONA: No, by this heavenly light!
EMILIA: Nor I neither by this heavenly light; I might do't as well i' the dark.
DESDEMONA: Wouldst thou do such a deed for all the world?
EMILIA: The world's a huge thing; it is a great price
For a small vice.
DESDEMONA: In troth, I think thou wouldst not.
EMILIA: In troth, I think I should, and undo't when I had done. Marry, I would not do such a thing for a joint-ring, nor for measures of lawn, nor for gowns, petticoats, nor caps, nor any petty exhibition; but, for the whole world- why, who would not make her husband a cuckold to make him a monarch? I should venture purgatory for't.
DESDEMONA: Beshrew me, if I would do such a wrong
For the whole world.

EMILIA: Why, the wrong is but a wrong i' the world; and having the world for your labor, 'tis a wrong in your own world, and you might quickly make it right.
DESDEMONA: I do not think there is any such woman.
EMILIA: Yes, a dozen, and as many to the vantage as would store the world they played for.
But I do think it is their husbands' faults
If wives do fall; say that they slack their duties
And pour our treasures into foreign laps,
Or else break out in peevish jealousies,
Throwing restraint upon us, or say they strike us,
Or scant our former having in despite,
Why, we have galls, and though we have some grace,
Yet have we some revenge. Let husbands know
Their wives have sense like them; they see and smell
And have their palates both for sweet and sour,
As husbands have. What is it that they do
When they change us for others? Is it sport?
I think it is. And doth affection breed it?
I think it doth. Is't frailty that thus errs?
It is so too. And have not we affections,
Desires for sport, and frailty, as men have?
Then let them use us well; else let them know,
The ills we do, their ills instruct us so.
DESDEMONA: Good night, good night. Heaven me such uses send,
Not to pick bad from bad, but by bad mend!
Exeunt.

ACT V. SCENE I. Cyprus. A Street.

Enter Iago and Roderigo:
IAGO: Here, stand behind this bulk; straight will he come.
Wear thy good rapier bare, and put it home.
Quick, quick; fear nothing; I'll be at thy elbow.
It makes us, or it mars us; think on that,
And fix most firm thy resolution.
RODERIGO: Be near at hand; I may miscarry in't.
IAGO: Here, at thy hand, be bold, and take thy stand.
Retires.
RODERIGO: I have no great devotion to the deed;
And yet he hath given me satisfying reasons.
'Tis but a man gone. Forth, my sword; he dies.
IAGO: I have rubb'd this young quat almost to the sense,
And he grows angry. Now, whether he kill Cassio,
Or Cassio him, or each do kill the other,
Every way makes my gain. Live Roderigo,
He calls me to a restitution large
Of gold and jewels that I bobb'd from him,
As gifts to Desdemona;
It must not be. If Cassio do remain,
He hath a daily beauty in his life
That makes me ugly; and besides, the Moor
May unfold me to him; there stand I in much peril.
No, he must die. Be't so. I hear him coming.
Enter Cassio.

RODERIGO: I know his gait; 'tis he. Villain, thou diest!
Makes a pass at Cassio.
CASSIO: That thrust had been mine enemy indeed,
But that my coat is better than thou know'st;
I will make proof of thine. Draws, and wounds Roderigo.
RODERIGO: O, I am slain!
Iago from Behind Wounds Cassio in the Leg, and Exit.
CASSIO: I am maim'd forever. Help, ho! Murther! Murther!
Falls.
Enter Othello.
OTHELLO: The voice of Cassio; Iago keeps his word.
RODERIGO: O, villain that I am!
OTHELLO: It is even so.
CASSIO: O, help, ho! Light! A surgeon!
OTHELLO: 'Tis he. O brave Iago, honest and just,
That hast such noble sense of thy friend's wrong!
Thou teachest me. Minion, your dear lies dead,
And your unblest fate hies. Strumpet, I come!
Forth of my heart those charms, thine eyes, are blotted;
Thy bed lust-stain'd shall with lust's blood be spotted.
Exit.
Enter Lodovico and Gratiano.
CASSIO: What, ho! No watch? No passage? Murther! Murther!
GRATIANO: 'Tis some mischance; the cry is very direful.
CASSIO: O, help!
LODOVICO: Hark!
RODERIGO: O wretched villain!
LODOVICO: Two or three groan; it is a heavy night.
These may be counterfeits; let's think't unsafe
To come in to the cry without more help.
RODERIGO: Nobody come? Then shall I bleed to death.
LODOVICO: Hark!
Re-enter Iago, with a Light.
GRATIANO: Here's one comes in his shirt, with light and weapons.
IAGO: Who's there? Whose noise is this that cries on murther?
LODOVICO: We do not know.
IAGO: Did not you hear a cry?
CASSIO: Here, here! for heaven's sake, help me!
IAGO: What's the matter?
GRATIANO: This is Othello's ancient, as I take it.
LODOVICO: The same indeed; a very valiant fellow.
IAGO: What are you here that cry so grievously?
CASSIO: Iago? O, I am spoil'd, undone by villains!
Give me some help.
IAGO: O me, lieutenant! What villains have done this?
CASSIO: I think that one of them is hereabout,
And cannot make away.
IAGO: O treacherous villains!
To Lodovico and Gratiano. What are you there?
Come in and give some help.
RODERIGO: O, help me here!
CASSIO: That's one of them.
IAGO: O murtherous slave! O villain!

Stabs Roderigo.
RODERIGO: O damn'd Iago! O inhuman dog!
IAGO: Kill men i' the dark! Where be these bloody thieves?
How silent is this town! Ho! Murther! Murther!
What may you be? Are you of good or evil?
LODOVICO: As you shall prove us, praise us.
IAGO: Signior Lodovico?
LODOVICO: He, sir.
IAGO: I cry you mercy. Here's Cassio hurt by villains.
GRATIANO: Cassio?
IAGO: How is't, brother?
CASSIO: My leg is cut in two.
IAGO: Marry, heaven forbid!
Light, gentlemen; I'll bind it with my shirt.
Enter Bianca.
BIANCA: What is the matter, ho? Who is't that cried?
IAGO: Who is't that cried?
BIANCA: O my dear Cassio, my sweet Cassio! O Cassio, Cassio, Cassio!
IAGO: O notable strumpet! Cassio, may you suspect
Who they should be that have thus mangled you?
CASSIO: No.
GRATIANO: I am sorry to find you thus; I have been to seek you.
IAGO: Lend me a garter. So. O, for a chair,
To bear him easily hence!
BIANCA: Alas, he faints! O Cassio, Cassio, Cassio!
IAGO: Gentlemen all, I do suspect this trash
To be a party in this injury.
Patience awhile, good Cassio. Come, come;
Lend me a light. Know we this face or no?
Alas, my friend and my dear countryman
Roderigo? No- yes, sure. O heaven! Roderigo.
GRATIANO: What, of Venice?
IAGO: Even he, sir. Did you know him?
GRATIANO: Know him! ay.
IAGO: Signior Gratiano? I cry you gentle pardon;
These bloody accidents must excuse my manners,
That so neglected you.
GRATIANO: I am glad to see you.
IAGO: How do you, Cassio? O, a chair, a chair!
GRATIANO: Roderigo!
IAGO: He, he, 'tis he. A Chair Brought in. O, that's well said: the chair.
Some good man bear him carefully from hence;
I'll fetch the general's surgeon. To Bianca. For you, mistress,
Save you your labor. He that lies slain here, Cassio,
Was my dear friend; what malice was between you?
CASSIO: None in the world; nor do I know the man.
IAGO: To Bianca. What, look you pale? O, bear him out o' the air.
Cassio and Roderigo are borne off.
Stay you, good gentlemen. Look you pale, mistress?
Do you perceive the gastness of her eye?
Nay, if you stare, we shall hear more anon.
Behold her well; I pray you, look upon her.

Do you see, gentlemen? Nay, guiltiness will speak,
Though tongues were out of use.
Enter Emilia.
EMILIA: 'Las, what's the matter? What's the matter, husband?
IAGO: Cassio hath here been set on in the dark
By Roderigo, and fellows that are 'scaped;
He's almost slain, and Roderigo dead.
EMILIA: Alas, good gentleman! alas, good Cassio!
IAGO: This is the fruit of whoring. Prithee, Emilia,
Go know of Cassio where he supp'd tonight.
What, do you shake at that?
BIANCA: He supp'd at my house; but I therefore shake not.
IAGO: O, did he so? I charge you, go with me.
EMILIA: Fie, fie upon thee, strumpet!
BIANCA: I am no strumpet, but of life as honest
As you that thus abuse me.
EMILIA: As I! foh! fie upon thee!
IAGO: Kind gentlemen, let's go see poor Cassio dress'd.
Come, mistress, you must tell's another tale.
Emilia, run you to the citadel,
And tell my lord and lady what hath happ'd!
Will you go on? Aside. This is the night
That either makes me or fordoes me quite.
Exeunt.

ACT V. SCENE II. A Bedchamber in the Castle. Desdemona in Bed Asleep; a Light Burning.

Enter Othello.
OTHELLO: It is the cause, it is the cause, my soul.
Let me not name it to you, you chaste stars!
It is the cause. Yet I'll not shed her blood,
Nor scar that whiter skin of hers than snow
And smooth as monumental alabaster.
Yet she must die, else she'll betray more men.
Put out the light, and then put out the light.
If I quench thee, thou flaming minister,
I can again thy former light restore,
Should I repent me; but once put out thy light,
Thou cunning'st pattern of excelling nature,
I know not where is that Promethean heat
That can thy light relume. When I have pluck'd the rose,
I cannot give it vital growth again,
It must needs wither; I'll smell it on the tree. Kisses her.
O, balmy breath, that dost almost persuade
Justice to break her sword! One more, one more;
Be thus when thou art dead, and I will kill thee,
And love thee after. One more, and this the last;
So sweet was ne'er so fatal. I must weep,
But they are cruel tears; this sorrow's heavenly,
It strikes where it doth love. She wakes.
DESDEMONA: Who's there? Othello?
OTHELLO: Ay, Desdemona.
DESDEMONA: Will you come to bed, my lord?
OTHELLO: Have you pray'd tonight, Desdemona?
DESDEMONA: Ay, my lord.

OTHELLO: If you bethink yourself of any crime
Unreconciled as yet to heaven and grace,
Solicit for it straight.
DESDEMONA: Alas, my lord, what may you mean by that?
OTHELLO: Well, do it, and be brief; I will walk by.
I would not kill thy unprepared spirit.
No, heaven forfend! I would not kill thy soul.
DESDEMONA: Talk you of killing?
OTHELLO: Ay, I do.
DESDEMONA: Then heaven have mercy on me!
OTHELLO: Amen, with all my heart!
DESDEMONA: If you say so, I hope you will not kill me.
OTHELLO: Hum!
DESDEMONA: And yet I fear you, for you are fatal then
When your eyes roll so. Why I should fear I know not,
Since guiltiness I know not; but yet I feel I fear.
OTHELLO: Think on thy sins.
DESDEMONA: They are loves I bear to you.
OTHELLO: Ay, and for that thou diest.
DESDEMONA: That death's unnatural that kills for loving.
Alas, why gnaw you so your nether lip?
Some bloody passion shakes your very frame.
These are portents; but yet I hope, I hope,
They do not point on me.
OTHELLO: Peace, and be still!
DESDEMONA: I will so. What's the matter?
OTHELLO: That handkerchief which I so loved and gave thee
Thou gavest to Cassio.
DESDEMONA: No, by my life and soul!
Send for the man, and ask him.
OTHELLO: Sweet soul, take heed,
Take heed of perjury; thou are on thy deathbed.
DESDEMONA: Ay, but not yet to die.
OTHELLO: Yes, presently:
Therefore confess thee freely of thy sin,
For to deny each article with oath
Cannot remove nor choke the strong conception
That I do groan withal. Thou art to die.
DESDEMONA: Then Lord have mercy on me!
OTHELLO: I say, amen.
DESDEMONA: And have you mercy too! I never did
Offend you in my life; never loved Cassio
But with such general warranty of heaven
As I might love. I never gave him token.
OTHELLO: By heaven, I saw my handkerchief in 's hand.
O perjured woman! Thou dost stone my heart,
And makest me call what I intend to do
A murther, which I thought a sacrifice.
I saw the handkerchief.
DESDEMONA: He found it then;
I never gave it him. Send for him hither;
Let him confess a truth.
OTHELLO: He hath confess'd.

DESDEMONA: What, my lord?
OTHELLO: That he hath used thee.
DESDEMONA: How? unlawfully?
OTHELLO: Ay.
DESDEMONA: He will not say so.
OTHELLO: No, his mouth is stopp'd;
Honest Iago hath ta'en order for't.
DESDEMONA: O, my fear interprets! What, is he dead?
OTHELLO: Had all his hairs been lives, my great revenge
Had stomach for them all.
DESDEMONA: Alas, he is betray'd, and I undone!
OTHELLO: Out, strumpet! Weep'st thou for him to my face?
DESDEMONA: O, banish me, my lord, but kill me not!
OTHELLO: Down, strumpet!
DESDEMONA: Kill me tomorrow; let me live tonight!
OTHELLO: Nay, if you strive-
DESDEMONA: But half an hour!
OTHELLO: Being done, there is no pause.
DESDEMONA: But while I say one prayer!
OTHELLO: It is too late. He stifles her.
EMILIA: Within. My lord, my lord! What, ho! my lord, my lord!
OTHELLO: What noise is this? Not dead? not yet quite dead?
I that am cruel am yet merciful;
I would not have thee linger in thy pain.
So, so.
EMILIA: Within. What, ho! my lord, my lord!
OTHELLO: Who's there?
EMILIA: Within. O, good my lord, I would speak a word with you!
OTHELLO: Yes, 'tis Emilia. By and by. She's dead.
'Tis like she comes to speak of Cassio's death.
The noise was here. Ha! no more moving?
Still as the grave. Shall she come in? were't good?
I think she stirs again. No. What's best to do?
If she come in, she'll sure speak to my wife.
My wife! My wife! What wife? I have no wife.
O, insupportable! O heavy hour!
Methinks it should be now a huge eclipse
Of sun and moon, and that the affrighted globe
Should yawn at alteration.
EMILIA: Within. I do beseech you
That I may speak with you, O, good my lord!
OTHELLO: I had forgot thee. O, come in, Emilia.
Soft, by and by. Let me the curtains draw.
Where art thou? Unlocks the door.
  Enter Emilia.
What's the matter with thee now?
EMILIA: O, my good lord, yonder's foul murthers done!
OTHELLO: What, now?
EMILIA: But now, my lord.
OTHELLO: It is the very error of the moon;
She comes more nearer earth than she was wont
And makes men mad.
EMILIA: Cassio, my lord, hath kill'd a young Venetian

Call'd Roderigo.
OTHELLO: Roderigo kill'd?
And Cassio kill'd?
EMILIA: No, Cassio is not kill'd.
OTHELLO: Not Cassio kill'd! Then murther's out of tune,
And sweet revenge grows harsh.
DESDEMONA: O, falsely, falsely murther'd!
EMILIA: Alas, what cry is that?
OTHELLO: That? what?
EMILIA: Out, and alas! That was my lady's voice.
Help! help, ho! help! O lady, speak again!
Sweet Desdemona! O sweet mistress, speak!
DESDEMONA: A guiltless death I die.
EMILIA: O, who hath done this deed?
DESDEMONA: Nobody; I myself. Farewell;
Commend me to my kind lord. O, farewell! Dies.
OTHELLO: Why, how should she be murther'd?
EMILIA: Alas, who knows?
OTHELLO: You heard her say herself, it was not I.
EMILIA: She said so; I must needs report the truth.
OTHELLO: She's like a liar gone to burning hell;
'Twas I that kill'd her.
EMILIA: O, the more angel she,
And you the blacker devil!
OTHELLO: She turn'd to folly, and she was a whore.
EMILIA: Thou dost belie her, and thou art a devil.
OTHELLO: She was false as water.
EMILIA: Thou art rash as fire, to say
That she was false. O, she was heavenly true!
OTHELLO: Cassio did top her; ask thy husband else.
O, I were damn'd beneath all depth in hell,
But that I did proceed upon just grounds
To this extremity. Thy husband knew it all.
EMILIA: My husband?
OTHELLO: Thy husband.
EMILIA: That she was false to wedlock?
OTHELLO: Ay, with Cassio. Nay, had she been true,
If heaven would make me such another world
Of one entire and perfect chrysolite,
I'ld not have sold her for it.
EMILIA: My husband?
OTHELLO: Ay, 'twas he that told me first.
An honest man he is, and hates the slime
That sticks on filthy deeds.
EMILIA: My husband?
OTHELLO: What needs this iteration, woman? I say thy husband.
EMILIA: O mistress, villainy hath made mocks with love!
My husband say that she was false!
OTHELLO: He, woman;
I say thy husband. Dost understand the word?
My friend, thy husband, honest, honest Iago.
EMILIA: If he say so, may his pernicious soul
Rot half a grain a day! He lies to the heart.

She was too fond of her most filthy bargain.
OTHELLO: Ha!
EMILIA: Do thy worst;
This deed of thine is no more worthy heaven
Than thou wast worthy her.
OTHELLO: Peace, you were best.
EMILIA: Thou hast not half that power to do me harm
As I have to be hurt. O gull! O dolt!
As ignorant as dirt! Thou hast done a deed-
I care not for thy sword; I'll make thee known,
Though I lost twenty lives. Help! help, ho! help!
The Moor hath kill'd my mistress! Murther, murther!
Enter Montano, Gratiano, Iago, and Others.
MONTANO: What is the matter? How now, general?
EMILIA: O, are you come, Iago? You have done well,
That men must lay their murthers on your neck.
GRATIANO: What is the matter?
EMILIA: Disprove this villain, if thou be'st a man.
He says thou told'st him that his wife was false;
I know thou didst not, thou'rt not such a villain.
Speak, for my heart is full.
IAGO: I told him what I thought, and told no more
Than what he found himself was apt and true.
EMILIA: But did you ever tell him she was false?
IAGO: I did.
EMILIA: You told a lie, an odious, damned lie;
Upon my soul, a lie, a wicked lie!
She false with Cassio? Did you say with Cassio?
IAGO: With Cassio, mistress. Go to, charm your tongue.
EMILIA: I will not charm my tongue; I am bound to speak.
My mistress here lies murther'd in her bed-
ALL: O heavens forfend!
EMILIA: And your reports have set the murther on.
OTHELLO: Nay, stare not, masters; it is true indeed.
GRATIANO: 'Tis a strange truth.
MONTANO: O monstrous act!
EMILIA: Villainy, villainy, villainy!
I think upon't, I think, I smell't, O villainy!
I thought so then. I'll kill myself for grief.
O villainy, villainy!
IAGO: What, are you mad? I charge you, get you home.
EMILIA: Good gentlemen, let me have leave to speak;
'Tis proper I obey him, but not now.
Perchance, Iago, I will ne'er go home.
OTHELLO: O! O! O! Falls on the bed.
EMILIA: Nay, lay thee down and roar;
For thou hast kill'd the sweetest innocent
That e'er did lift up eye.
OTHELLO: Rises. O, she was foul!
I scarce did know you, uncle; there lies your niece,
Whose breath indeed these hands have newly stopp'd.
I know this act shows horrible and grim.
GRATIANO: Poor Desdemon! I am glad thy father's dead.

Thy match was mortal to him, and pure grief
Shore his old thread in twain; did he live now,
This sight would make him do a desperate turn,
Yea, curse his better angel from his side,
And fall to reprobation.
OTHELLO: 'Tis pitiful, but yet Iago knows
That she with Cassio hath the act of shame
A thousand times committed. Cassio confess'd it,
And she did gratify his amorous works
With that recognizance and pledge of love
Which I first gave her. I saw it in his hand,
It was a handkerchief, an antique token
My father gave my mother.
EMILIA: O heaven! O heavenly powers!
IAGO: 'Zounds! Hold your peace.
EMILIA: 'Twill out, 'twill. I peace?
No, I will speak as liberal as the north;
Let heaven and men and devils, let them all,
All, all, cry shame against me, yet I'll speak.
IAGO: Be wise, and get you home.
EMILIA: I will not.
Iago Offers to Stab Emilia.
GRATIANO: Fie!
Your sword upon a woman?
EMILIA: O thou dull Moor! That handkerchief thou speak'st of
I found by fortune and did give my husband,
For often with a solemn earnestness,
More than indeed belong'd to such a trifle,
He begg'd of me to steal it.
IAGO: Villainous whore!
EMILIA: She give it Cassio? No, alas, I found it,
And I did give't my husband.
IAGO: Filth, thou liest!
EMILIA: By heaven, I do not, I do not, gentlemen.
O murtherous coxcomb! What should such a fool
Do with so good a wife?
OTHELLO: Are there not stones in heaven
But what serve for thunder? Precious villain!
He Runs at Iago, but Montano Disarms Him. Iago Stabs Emilia.
GRATIANO: The woman falls; sure, he hath kill'd his wife.
EMILIA: Ay, ay! O, lay me by my mistress' side.
Exit Iago.
GRATIANO: He's gone, but his wife's kill'd.
MONTANO: 'Tis a notorious villain. Take you this weapon,
Which I have here recover'd from the Moor.
Come, guard the door without; let him not pass,
But kill him rather. I'll after that same villain,
For 'tis a damned slave.
Exeunt All but Othello and Emilia.
OTHELLO: I am not valiant neither,
But every puny whipster gets my sword.
But why should honor outlive honesty?
Let it go all.

EMILIA: What did thy song bode, lady?
Hark, canst thou hear me? I will play the swan,
And die in music. Sings. "Willow, willow, willow."
Moor, she was chaste; she loved thee, cruel Moor;
So come my soul to bliss, as I speak true;
So speaking as I think, I die, I die. Dies.
OTHELLO: I have another weapon in this chamber;
It is a sword of Spain, the ice-brook's temper-
O, here it is. Uncle, I must come forth.
GRATIANO: Within. If thou attempt it, it will cost thee dear.
Thou hast no weapon, and perforce must suffer.
OTHELLO: Look in upon me then, and speak with me,
Or, naked as I am, I will assault thee.
Re-enter Gratiano.
GRATIANO: What is the matter?
OTHELLO: Behold, I have a weapon;
A better never did itself sustain
Upon a soldier's thigh. I have seen the day
That with this little arm and this good sword
I have made my way through more impediments
Than twenty times your stop. But, O vain boast!
Who can control his fate? 'Tis not so now.
Be not afraid, though you do see me weapon'd;
Here is my journey's end, here is my butt
And very sea-mark of my utmost sail.
Do you go back dismay'd? 'Tis a lost fear.
Man but a rush against Othello's breast,
And he retires. Where should Othello go?
Now, how dost thou look now? O ill-starr'd wench!
Pale as thy smock! When we shall meet at compt,
This look of thine will hurl my soul from heaven,
And fiends will snatch at it. Cold, cold, my girl?
Even like thy chastity. O cursed, cursed slave!
Whip me, ye devils,
From the possession of this heavenly sight!
Blow me about in winds! Roast me in sulphur!
Wash me in steep-down gulfs of liquid fire!
O Desdemon! dead, Desdemon! dead!
O! O! O!
Enter Lodovico, Montano, Cassio Carried in a Chair, and Officers with Iago, Prisoner.
LODOVICO: Where is this rash and most unfortunate man?
OTHELLO: That's he that was Othello. Here I am.
LODOVICO: Where is that viper? Bring the villain forth.
OTHELLO: I look down towards his feet; but that's a fable.
If that thou be'st a devil, I cannot kill thee. Wounds Iago.
LODOVICO: Wrench his sword from him.
IAGO: I bleed, sir, but not kill'd.
OTHELLO: I am not sorry neither. I'ld have thee live,
For, in my sense, 'tis happiness to die.
LODOVICO: O thou Othello, that wert once so good,
Fall'n in the practice of a damned slave,
What shall be said to thee?
OTHELLO: Why, anything;

An honorable murtherer, if you will,
For nought did I in hate, but all in honor.
LODOVICO: This wretch hath part confess'd his villainy.
Did you and he consent in Cassio's death?
OTHELLO: Ay.
CASSIO: Dear general, I never gave you cause.
OTHELLO: I do believe it, and I ask your pardon.
Will you, I pray, demand that demi-devil
Why he hath thus ensnared my soul and body?
IAGO: Demand me nothing; what you know, you know.
From this time forth I never will speak word.
LODOVICO: What, not to pray?
GRATIANO: Torments will ope your lips.
OTHELLO: Well, thou dost best.
LODOVICO: Sir, you shall understand what hath befall'n,
Which, as I think, you know not. Here is a letter
Found in the pocket of the slain Roderigo,
And here another. The one of them imports
The death of Cassio to be undertook
By Roderigo.
OTHELLO: O villain!
CASSIO: Most heathenish and most gross!
LODOVICO: Now here's another discontented paper,
Found in his pocket too; and this, it seems,
Roderigo meant to have sent this damned villain;
But that, belike, Iago in the interim
Came in and satisfied him.
OTHELLO: O the pernicious caitiff!
How came you, Cassio, by that handkerchief
That was my wife's?
CASSIO: I found it in my chamber;
And he himself confess'd but even now
That there he dropp'd it for a special purpose
Which wrought to his desire.
OTHELLO: O fool! fool! fool!
CASSIO: There is besides in Roderigo's letter,
How he upbraids Iago, that he made him
Brave me upon the watch, whereon it came
That I was cast. And even but now he spake
After long seeming dead, Iago hurt him,
Iago set him on.
LODOVICO: You must forsake this room, and go with us.
Your power and your command is taken off,
And Cassio rules in Cyprus. For this slave,
If there be any cunning cruelty
That can torment him much and hold him long,
It shall be his. You shall close prisoner rest,
Till that the nature of your fault be known
To the Venetian state. Come, bring away.
OTHELLO: Soft you; a word or two before you go.
I have done the state some service, and they know't.
No more of that. I pray you, in your letters,
When you shall these unlucky deeds relate,

Speak of me as I am; nothing extenuate,
Nor set down aught in malice. Then must you speak
Of one that loved not wisely but too well;
Of one not easily jealous, but, being wrought,
Perplex'd in the extreme; of one whose hand,
Like the base Indian, threw a pearl away
Richer than all his tribe; of one whose subdued eyes,
Albeit unused to the melting mood,
Drop tears as fast as the Arabian trees
Their medicinal gum. Set you down this;
And say besides, that in Aleppo once,
Where a malignant and a turban'd Turk
Beat a Venetian and traduced the state,
I took by the throat the circumcised dog
And smote him, thus. Stabs himself.
LODOVICO: O bloody period!
GRATIANO: All that's spoke is marr'd.
OTHELLO: I kiss'd thee ere I kill'd thee. No way but this,
Killing myself, to die upon a kiss.
   Falls on the Bed, and Dies.
CASSIO: This did I fear, but thought he had no weapon;
For he was great of heart.
LODOVICO: To Iago. O Spartan dog,
More fell than anguish, hunger, or the sea!
Look on the tragic loading of this bed;
This is thy work. The object poisons sight;
Let it be hid. Gratiano, keep the house,
And seize upon the fortunes of the Moor,
For they succeed on you. To you, Lord Governor,
Remains the censure of this hellish villain,
The time, the place, the torture. O, enforce it!
Myself will straight aboard, and to the state
This heavy act with heavy heart relate. Exeunt.

END

The Tragedy of King Lear

Dramatis Personae

LEAR, King of Britain.
KING OF FRANCE.
DUKE OF BURGUNDY.
DUKE OF CORNWALL.
DUKE OF ALBANY.
EARL OF KENT.
EARL OF GLOUCESTER.
EDGAR, son of Gloucester.
EDMUND, bastard son to Gloucester.
CURAN, a courtier.
OLD MAN, tenant to Gloucester.
DOCTOR.
LEAR'S FOOL.
OSWALD, steward to Goneril.
A CAPTAIN UNDER EDMUND'S COMMAND.
GENTLEMEN
A Herald.
SERVANTS TO CORNWALL.
GONERIL, daughter to Lear.
REGAN, daughter to Lear.
CORDELIA, daughter to Lear.
Knights attending on Lear, Officers, Messengers, Soldiers, Attendants.

SCENE: Britain.

ACT I. SCENE I. King Lear's Palace.

Enter Kent, Gloucester, and Edmund. Kent and Glouceste Converse. Edmund Stands Back.

KENT: I thought the King had more affected the Duke of Albany than Cornwall.

GLOUCESTER: It did always seem so to us; but now, in the division of the kingdom, it appears not which of the Dukes he values most, for equalities are so weigh'd that curiosity in neither can make choice of either's moiety.

KENT: Is not this your son, my lord?

GLOUCESTER: His breeding, sir, hath been at my charge. I have so often blush'd to acknowledge him that now I am braz'd to't.

KENT: I cannot conceive you.

GLOUCESTER: Sir, this young fellow's mother could; whereupon she grew round-womb'd, and had indeed, sir, a son for her cradle ere she had a husband for her bed. Do you smell a fault?

KENT: I cannot wish the fault undone, the issue of it being so proper.

GLOUCESTER: But I have, sir, a son by order of law, some year elder than this, who yet is no dearer in my account. Though this knave came something saucily into the world before he was sent for, yet was his mother fair, there was good sport at his making, and the whoreson must be acknowledged.- Do you know this noble gentleman,

Edmund?
EDMUND: Comes Forward No, my lord.
GLOUCESTER: My Lord of Kent. Remember him hereafter as my honourable friend.
EDMUND: My services to your lordship.
KENT: I must love you, and sue to know you better.
EDMUND: Sir, I shall study deserving.
GLOUCESTER: He hath been out nine years, and away he shall again.
Sound a Sennet.
The King is coming.
Enter One Bearing a Coronet; Then Lear; Then the Dukes of Albany and Cornwall; Next, Goneril, Regan, Cordelia, with Followers.
LEAR: Attend the lords of France and Burgundy, Gloucester.
GLOUCESTER: I shall, my liege.
Exeunt Gloucester and Edmund.
LEAR: Meantime we shall express our darker purpose.
Give me the map there. Know we have divided
In three our kingdom; and 'tis our fast intent
To shake all cares and business from our age,
Conferring them on younger strengths while we
Unburthen'd crawl toward death. Our son of Cornwall,
And you, our no less loving son of Albany,
We have this hour a constant will to publish
Our daughters' several dowers, that future strife
May be prevented now. The princes, France and Burgundy,
Great rivals in our youngest daughter's love,
Long in our court have made their amorous sojourn,
And here are to be answer'd. Tell me, my daughters
(Since now we will divest us both of rule,
Interest of territory, cares of state),
Which of you shall we say doth love us most?
That we our largest bounty may extend
Where nature doth with merit challenge. Goneril,
Our eldest-born, speak first.
GONERIL: Sir, I love you more than words can wield the matter;
Dearer than eyesight, space, and liberty;
Beyond what can be valued, rich or rare;
No less than life, with grace, health, beauty, honour;
As much as child e'er lov'd, or father found;
A love that makes breath poor, and speech unable.
Beyond all manner of so much I love you.
CORDELIA: Aside What shall Cordelia speak? Love, and be silent.
LEAR: Of all these bounds, even from this line to this,
With shadowy forests and with champains rich'd,
With plenteous rivers and wide-skirted meads,
We make thee lady. To thine and Albany's issue
Be this perpetual.- What says our second daughter,
Our dearest Regan, wife to Cornwall? Speak.
REGAN: Sir, I am made
Of the selfsame metal that my sister is,

And prize me at her worth. In my true heart
I find she names my very deed of love;
Only she comes too short, that I profess
Myself an enemy to all other joys
Which the most precious square of sense possesses,
And find I am alone felicitate
In your dear Highness' love.
CORDELIA: Aside Then poor Cordelia!
And yet not so; since I am sure my love's
More richer than my tongue.
LEAR: To thee and thine hereditary ever
Remain this ample third of our fair kingdom,
No less in space, validity, and pleasure
Than that conferr'd on Goneril.- Now, our joy,
Although the last, not least; to whose young love
The vines of France and milk of Burgundy
Strive to be interest; what can you say to draw
A third more opulent than your sisters? Speak.
CORDELIA: Nothing, my lord.
LEAR: Nothing?
CORDELIA: Nothing.
LEAR: Nothing can come of nothing. Speak again.
CORDELIA: Unhappy that I am, I cannot heave
My heart into my mouth. I love your Majesty
According to my bond; no more nor less.
LEAR: How, how, Cordelia? Mend your speech a little,
Lest it may mar your fortunes.
CORDELIA: Good my lord,
You have begot me, bred me, lov'd me; I
Return those duties back as are right fit,
Obey you, love you, and most honour you.
Why have my sisters husbands, if they say
They love you all? Haply, when I shall wed,
That lord whose hand must take my plight shall carry
Half my love with him, half my care and duty.
Sure I shall never marry like my sisters,
To love my father all.
LEAR: But goes thy heart with this?
CORDELIA: Ay, good my lord.
LEAR: So young, and so untender?
CORDELIA: So young, my lord, and true.
LEAR: Let it be so! thy truth then be thy dower!
For, by the sacred radiance of the sun,
The mysteries of Hecate and the night;
By all the operation of the orbs
From whom we do exist and cease to be;
Here I disclaim all my paternal care,
Propinquity and property of blood,
And as a stranger to my heart and me

Hold thee from this for ever. The barbarous Scythian,
Or he that makes his generation messes
To gorge his appetite, shall to my bosom
Be as well neighbour'd, pitied, and reliev'd,
As thou my sometime daughter.
KENT: Good my liege-
LEAR: Peace, Kent!
Come not between the dragon and his wrath.
I lov'd her most, and thought to set my rest
On her kind nursery.- Hence and avoid my sight!-
So be my grave my peace as here I give
Her father's heart from her! Call France! Who stirs?
Call Burgundy! Cornwall and Albany,
With my two daughters' dowers digest this third;
Let pride, which she calls plainness, marry her.
I do invest you jointly in my power,
Preeminence, and all the large effects
That troop with majesty. Ourself, by monthly course,
With reservation of an hundred knights,
By you to be sustain'd, shall our abode
Make with you by due turns. Only we still retain
The name, and all th' additions to a king. The sway,
Revenue, execution of the rest,
Beloved sons, be yours; which to confirm,
This coronet part betwixt you.
KENT: Royal Lear,
Whom I have ever honour'd as my king,
Lov'd as my father, as my master follow'd,
As my great patron thought on in my prayers-
LEAR: The bow is bent and drawn; make from the shaft.
KENT: Let it fall rather, though the fork invade
The region of my heart! Be Kent unmannerly
When Lear is mad. What wouldst thou do, old man?
Think'st thou that duty shall have dread to speak
When power to flattery bows? To plainness honour's bound
When majesty falls to folly. Reverse thy doom;
And in thy best consideration check
This hideous rashness. Answer my life my judgment,
Thy youngest daughter does not love thee least,
Nor are those empty-hearted whose low sound
Reverbs no hollowness.
LEAR: Kent, on thy life, no more!
KENT: My life I never held but as a pawn
To wage against thine enemies; nor fear to lose it,
Thy safety being the motive.
LEAR: Out of my sight!
KENT: See better, Lear, and let me still remain
The true blank of thine eye.
LEAR: Now by Apollo-

KENT: Now by Apollo, King,
Thou swear'st thy gods in vain.
LEAR: O vassal! miscreant!
Lays His Hand on His Sword.
ALBANY: Corn. Dear sir, forbear!
KENT: Do!
Kill thy physician, and the fee bestow
Upon the foul disease. Revoke thy gift,
Or, whilst I can vent clamour from my throat,
I'll tell thee thou dost evil.
LEAR: Hear me, recreant!
On thine allegiance, hear me!
Since thou hast sought to make us break our vow-
Which we durst never yet- and with strain'd pride
To come between our sentence and our power,-
Which nor our nature nor our place can bear,-
Our potency made good, take thy reward.
Five days we do allot thee for provision
To shield thee from diseases of the world,
And on the sixth to turn thy hated back
Upon our kingdom. If, on the tenth day following,
Thy banish'd trunk be found in our dominions,
The moment is thy death. Away! By Jupiter,
This shall not be revok'd.
KENT: Fare thee well, King. Since thus thou wilt appear,
Freedom lives hence, and banishment is here.
To Cordelia The gods to their dear shelter take thee, maid,
That justly think'st and hast most rightly said!
To Regan and Goneril And your large speeches may your deeds approve,
That good effects may spring from words of love.
Thus Kent, O princes, bids you all adieu;
He'll shape his old course in a country new.
Exit.
Flourish. Enter Gloucester, with France and Burgundy; Attendants.
GLOUCESTER: Here's France and Burgundy, my noble lord.
LEAR: My Lord of Burgundy,
We first address toward you, who with this king
Hath rivall'd for our daughter. What in the least
Will you require in present dower with her,
Or cease your quest of love?
BURGUNDY: Most royal Majesty,
I crave no more than hath your Highness offer'd,
Nor will you tender less.
LEAR: Right noble Burgundy,
When she was dear to us, we did hold her so;
But now her price is fall'n. Sir, there she stands.
If aught within that little seeming substance,
Or all of it, with our displeasure piec'd,
And nothing more, may fitly like your Grace,

She's there, and she is yours.
BURGUNDY: I know no answer.
LEAR: Will you, with those infirmities she owes,
Unfriended, new adopted to our hate,
Dow'r'd with our curse, and stranger'd with our oath,
Take her, or leave her?
BURGUNDY: Pardon me, royal sir.
Election makes not up on such conditions.
LEAR: Then leave her, sir; for, by the pow'r that made me,
I tell you all her wealth. To France For you, great King,
I would not from your love make such a stray
To match you where I hate; therefore beseech you
T' avert your liking a more worthier way
Than on a wretch whom nature is asham'd
Almost t' acknowledge hers.
KING OF FRANCE: This is most strange,
That she that even but now was your best object,
The argument of your praise, balm of your age,
Most best, most dearest, should in this trice of time
Commit a thing so monstrous to dismantle
So many folds of favour. Sure her offence
Must be of such unnatural degree
That monsters it, or your fore-vouch'd affection
Fall'n into taint; which to believe of her
Must be a faith that reason without miracle
Should never plant in me.
CORDELIA: I yet beseech your Majesty,
If for I want that glib and oily art
To speak and purpose not, since what I well intend,
I'll do't before I speak- that you make known
It is no vicious blot, murther, or foulness,
No unchaste action or dishonoured step,
That hath depriv'd me of your grace and favour;
But even for want of that for which I am richer-
A still-soliciting eye, and such a tongue
As I am glad I have not, though not to have it
Hath lost me in your liking.
LEAR: Better thou
Hadst not been born than not t' have pleas'd me better.
KING OF FRANCE: Is it but this- a tardiness in nature
Which often leaves the history unspoke
That it intends to do? My Lord of Burgundy,
What say you to the lady? Love's not love
When it is mingled with regards that stands
Aloof from th' entire point. Will you have her?
She is herself a dowry.
BURGUNDY: Royal Lear,
Give but that portion which yourself propos'd,
And here I take Cordelia by the hand,

Duchess of Burgundy.
LEAR: Nothing! I have sworn; I am firm.
BURGUNDY: I am sorry then you have so lost a father
That you must lose a husband.
CORDELIA: Peace be with Burgundy!
Since that respects of fortune are his love,
I shall not be his wife.
KING OF FRANCE: Fairest Cordelia, that art most rich, being poor;
Most choice, forsaken; and most lov'd, despis'd!
Thee and thy virtues here I seize upon.
Be it lawful I take up what's cast away.
Gods, gods! 'tis strange that from their cold'st neglect
My love should kindle to inflam'd respect.
Thy dow'rless daughter, King, thrown to my chance,
Is queen of us, of ours, and our fair France.
Not all the dukes in wat'rish Burgundy
Can buy this unpriz'd precious maid of me.
Bid them farewell, Cordelia, though unkind.
Thou losest here, a better where to find.
LEAR: Thou hast her, France; let her be thine; for we
Have no such daughter, nor shall ever see
That face of hers again. Therefore be gone
Without our grace, our love, our benison.
Come, noble Burgundy.
Flourish. Exeunt Lear, Burgundy, Cornwall, Albany, Gloucester, and Attendants.
KING OF FRANCE: Bid farewell to your sisters.
CORDELIA: The jewels of our father, with wash'd eyes
Cordelia leaves you. I know you what you are;
And, like a sister, am most loath to call
Your faults as they are nam'd. Use well our father.
To your professed bosoms I commit him;
But yet, alas, stood I within his grace,
I would prefer him to a better place!
So farewell to you both.
GONERIL: Prescribe not us our duties.
REGAN: Let your study
Be to content your lord, who hath receiv'd you
At fortune's alms. You have obedience scanted,
And well are worth the want that you have wanted.
CORDELIA: Time shall unfold what plighted cunning hides.
Who cover faults, at last shame them derides.
Well may you prosper!
KING OF FRANCE: Come, my fair Cordelia.
Exeunt France and Cordelia.
GONERIL: Sister, it is not little I have to say of what most nearly appertains to us both. I think our father will hence to-night.
REGAN: That's most certain, and with you; next month with us.
GONERIL: You see how full of changes his age is. The observation we have made of it hath not been little. He always lov'd our

sister most, and with what poor judgment he hath now cast her off appears too grossly.
REGAN: 'Tis the infirmity of his age; yet he hath ever but slenderly known himself.
GONERIL: The best and soundest of his time hath been but rash; then must we look to receive from his age, not alone the imperfections of long-ingraffed condition, but therewithal the unruly waywardness that infirm and choleric years bring with them.
REGAN: Such unconstant starts are we like to have from him as this of Kent's banishment.
GONERIL: There is further compliment of leave-taking between France and him. Pray you let's hit together. If our father carry authority with such dispositions as he bears, this last surrender of his will but offend us.
REGAN: We shall further think on't.
GONERIL: We must do something, and i' th' heat.
Exeunt.

ACT I. SCENE II. The Earl of Gloucester's Castle.

Enter Edmund the Bastard Solus, with a Letter.
EDMUND: Thou, Nature, art my goddess; to thy law
My services are bound. Wherefore should I
Stand in the plague of custom, and permit
The curiosity of nations to deprive me,
For that I am some twelve or fourteen moonshines
Lag of a brother? Why bastard? wherefore base?
When my dimensions are as well compact,
My mind as generous, and my shape as true,
As honest madam's issue? Why brand they us
With base? with baseness? bastardy? base, base?
Who, in the lusty stealth of nature, take
More composition and fierce quality
Than doth, within a dull, stale, tired bed,
Go to th' creating a whole tribe of fops
Got 'tween asleep and wake? Well then,
Legitimate Edgar, I must have your land.
Our father's love is to the bastard Edmund
As to th' legitimate. Fine word- 'legitimate'!
Well, my legitimate, if this letter speed,
And my invention thrive, Edmund the base
Shall top th' legitimate. I grow; I prosper.
Now, gods, stand up for bastards!
Enter Gloucester.
GLOUCESTER: Kent banish'd thus? and France in choler parted?
And the King gone to-night? subscrib'd his pow'r?
Confin'd to exhibition? All this done
Upon the gad? Edmund, how now? What news?
EDMUND: So please your lordship, none.
Puts up the Letter.
GLOUCESTER: Why so earnestly seek you to put up that letter?

EDMUND: I know no news, my lord.
GLOUCESTER: What paper were you reading?
EDMUND: Nothing, my lord.
GLOUCESTER: No? What needed then that terrible dispatch of it into your pocket? The quality of nothing hath not such need to hide itself. Let's see. Come, if it be nothing, I shall not need spectacles.
EDMUND: I beseech you, sir, pardon me. It is a letter from my brother that I have not all o'er-read; and for so much as I have perus'd, I find it not fit for your o'erlooking.
GLOUCESTER: Give me the letter, sir.
EDMUND: I shall offend, either to detain or give it. The contents, as in part I understand them, are to blame.
GLOUCESTER: Let's see, let's see!
EDMUND: I hope, for my brother's justification, he wrote this but as an essay or taste of my virtue.
GLOUCESTER: reads 'This policy and reverence of age makes the world bitter to the best of our times; keeps our fortunes from us till our oldness cannot relish them. I begin to find an idle and fond bondage in the oppression of aged tyranny, who sways, not as it hath power, but as it is suffer'd. Come to me, that of this I may speak more. If our father would sleep till I wak'd him, you should enjoy half his revenue for ever, and live the beloved of your brother, 'Edgar.' Hum! Conspiracy? 'Sleep till I wak'd him, you should enjoy half his revenue.' My son Edgar! Had he a hand to write this? a heart and brain to breed it in? When came this to you? Who brought it?
EDMUND: It was not brought me, my lord: there's the cunning of it. I found it thrown in at the casement of my closet.
GLOUCESTER: You know the character to be your brother's?
EDMUND: If the matter were good, my lord, I durst swear it were his; but in respect of that, I would fain think it were not.
GLOUCESTER: It is his.
EDMUND: It is his hand, my lord; but I hope his heart is not in the contents.
GLOUCESTER: Hath he never before sounded you in this business?
EDMUND: Never, my lord. But I have heard him oft maintain it to be fit that, sons at perfect age, and fathers declining, the father should be as ward to the son, and the son manage his revenue.
GLOUCESTER: O villain, villain! His very opinion in the letter! Abhorred villain! Unnatural, detested, brutish villain! worse than brutish! Go, sirrah, seek him. I'll apprehend him. Abominable villain! Where is he?
EDMUND: I do not well know, my lord. If it shall please you to suspend your indignation against my brother till you can derive from him better testimony of his intent, you should run a certain course; where, if you violently proceed against him, mistaking his purpose, it would make a great gap in your own honour and shake in pieces the heart of his obedience. I dare pawn down my life for him that he hath writ this to feel my affection to your honour, and to no other pretence of danger.
GLOUCESTER: Think you so?
EDMUND: If your honour judge it meet, I will place you where you shall hear us confer of this and by an auricular assurance have your

satisfaction, and that without any further delay than this very evening.
GLOUCESTER: He cannot be such a monster.
EDMUND: Nor is not, sure.
GLOUCESTER: To his father, that so tenderly and entirely loves him. Heaven and earth! Edmund, seek him out; wind me into him, I pray you; frame the business after your own wisdom. I would unstate myself to be in a due resolution.
EDMUND: I will seek him, sir, presently; convey the business as I shall find means, and acquaint you withal.
GLOUCESTER: These late eclipses in the sun and moon portend no good to us. Though the wisdom of nature can reason it thus and thus, yet nature finds itself scourg'd by the sequent effects. Love cools, friendship falls off, brothers divide. In cities, mutinies; in countries, discord; in palaces, treason; and the bond crack'd 'twixt son and father. This villain of mine comes under the prediction; there's son against father: the King falls from bias of nature; there's father against child. We have seen the best of our time. Machinations, hollowness, treachery, and all ruinous disorders follow us disquietly to our graves. Find out this villain, Edmund; it shall lose thee nothing; do it carefully. And the noble and true-hearted Kent banish'd! his offence, honesty! 'Tis strange.
Exit.
EDMUND: This is the excellent foppery of the world, that, when we are sick in fortune, often the surfeit of our own behaviour, we make guilty of our disasters the sun, the moon, and the stars; as if we were villains on necessity; fools by heavenly compulsion; knaves, thieves, and treachers by spherical pre-dominance; drunkards, liars, and adulterers by an enforc'd obedience of planetary influence; and all that we are evil in, by a divine thrusting on. An admirable evasion of whore-master man, to lay his goatish disposition to the charge of a star! My father compounded with my mother under the Dragon's Tail, and my nativity was under Ursa Major, so that it follows I am rough and lecherous. Fut! I should have been that I am, had the maidenliest star in the firmament twinkled on my bastardizing. Edgar-
Enter Edgar.
and pat! he comes, like the catastrophe of the old comedy. My cue is villainous melancholy, with a sigh like Tom o' Bedlam. O, these eclipses do portend these divisions! Fa, sol, la, mi.
EDGAR: How now, brother Edmund? What serious contemplation are you in?
EDMUND: I am thinking, brother, of a prediction I read this other day, what should follow these eclipses.
EDGAR: Do you busy yourself with that?
EDMUND: I promise you, the effects he writes of succeed unhappily: as of unnaturalness between the child and the parent; death, dearth, dissolutions of ancient amities; divisions in state,

menaces and maledictions against king and nobles; needless diffidences, banishment of friends, dissipation of cohorts, nuptial breaches, and I know not what.

EDGAR: How long have you been a sectary astronomical?

EDMUND: Come, come! When saw you my father last?

EDGAR: The night gone by.

EDMUND: Spake you with him?

EDGAR: Ay, two hours together.

EDMUND: Parted you in good terms? Found you no displeasure in him by word or countenance

EDGAR: None at all.

EDMUND: Bethink yourself wherein you may have offended him; and at my entreaty forbear his presence until some little time hath qualified the heat of his displeasure, which at this instant so rageth in him that with the mischief of your person it would scarcely allay.

EDGAR: Some villain hath done me wrong.

EDMUND: That's my fear. I pray you have a continent forbearance till the speed of his rage goes slower; and, as I say, retire with me to my lodging, from whence I will fitly bring you to hear my lord speak. Pray ye, go! There's my key. If you do stir abroad, go arm'd.

EDGAR: Arm'd, brother?

EDMUND: Brother, I advise you to the best. Go arm'd. I am no honest man if there be any good meaning toward you. I have told you what I have seen and heard; but faintly, nothing like the image and horror of it. Pray you, away!

EDGAR: Shall I hear from you anon?

EDMUND: I do serve you in this business.

Exit Edgar.

A credulous father! and a brother noble,
Whose nature is so far from doing harms
That he suspects none; on whose foolish honesty
My practices ride easy! I see the business.
Let me, if not by birth, have lands by wit;
All with me's meet that I can fashion fit.

Exit.

ACT I. SCENE III. The Duke of Albany's Palace.

Enter Goneril and Her Steward Oswald.

GONERIL: Did my father strike my gentleman for chiding of his fool?

OSWALD: Ay, madam.

GONERIL: By day and night, he wrongs me! Every hour
He flashes into one gross crime or other
That sets us all at odds. I'll not endure it.
His knights grow riotous, and himself upbraids us
On every trifle. When he returns from hunting,
I will not speak with him. Say I am sick.
If you come slack of former services,
You shall do well; the fault of it I'll answer.

Horns Within.

OSWALD: He's coming, madam; I hear him.

GONERIL: Put on what weary negligence you please,
You and your fellows. I'd have it come to question.
If he distaste it, let him to our sister,
Whose mind and mine I know in that are one,
Not to be overrul'd. Idle old man,
That still would manage those authorities
That he hath given away! Now, by my life,
Old fools are babes again, and must be us'd
With checks as flatteries, when they are seen abus'd.
Remember what I have said.
OSWALD: Very well, madam.
GONERIL: And let his knights have colder looks among you.
What grows of it, no matter. Advise your fellows so.
I would breed from hence occasions, and I shall,
That I may speak. I'll write straight to my sister
To hold my very course. Prepare for dinner.
Exeunt.

ACT I. SCENE IV. The Duke of Albany's Palace.

Enter Kent, Disguised.
KENT: If but as well I other accents borrow,
That can my speech defuse, my good intent
May carry through itself to that full issue
For which I raz'd my likeness. Now, banish'd Kent,
If thou canst serve where thou dost stand condemn'd,
So may it come, thy master, whom thou lov'st,
Shall find thee full of labours.
Horns within. Enter Lear, Knights, and Attendants.
LEAR: Let me not stay a jot for dinner; go get it ready.
Exit an Attendant.
How now? What art thou?
KENT: A man, sir.
LEAR: What dost thou profess? What wouldst thou with us?
KENT: I do profess to be no less than I seem, to serve him truly that will put me in trust, to love him that is honest, to converse with him that is wise and says little, to fear judgment, to fight when I cannot choose, and to eat no fish.
LEAR: What art thou?
KENT: A very honest-hearted fellow, and as poor as the King.
LEAR: If thou be'st as poor for a subject as he's for a king, thou art poor enough. What wouldst thou?
KENT: Service.
LEAR: Who wouldst thou serve?
KENT: You.
LEAR: Dost thou know me, fellow?
KENT: No, sir; but you have that in your countenance which I would fain call master.
LEAR: What's that?
KENT: Authority.
LEAR: What services canst thou do?

KENT: I can keep honest counsel, ride, run, mar a curious tale in telling it and deliver a plain message bluntly. That which ordinary men are fit for, I am qualified in, and the best of me is diligence.
LEAR: How old art thou?
KENT: Not so young, sir, to love a woman for singing, nor so old to dote on her for anything. I have years on my back forty-eight.
LEAR: Follow me; thou shalt serve me. If I like thee no worse after dinner, I will not part from thee yet. Dinner, ho, dinner! Where's my knave? my fool? Go you and call my fool hither.
Exit an Attendant.
Enter Oswald the Steward.
You, you, sirrah, where's my daughter?
OSWALD: So please you-
Exit.
LEAR: What says the fellow there? Call the clotpoll back.
Exit a Knight. Where's my fool, ho? I think the world's asleep.
Enter Knight
How now? Where's that mongrel?
KNIGHT: He says, my lord, your daughter is not well.
LEAR: Why came not the slave back to me when I call'd him?
KNIGHT: Sir, he answered me in the roundest manner, he would not.
LEAR: He would not?
KNIGHT: My lord, I know not what the matter is; but to my judgment your Highness is not entertain'd with that ceremonious affection as you were wont. There's a great abatement of kindness appears as well in the general dependants as in the Duke himself also and your daughter.
LEAR: Ha! say'st thou so?
KNIGHT: I beseech you pardon me, my lord, if I be mistaken; for my duty cannot be silent when I think your Highness wrong'd.
LEAR: Thou but rememb'rest me of mine own conception. I have perceived a most faint neglect of late, which I have rather blamed as mine own jealous curiosity than as a very pretence and purpose of unkindness. I will look further into't. But where's my fool? I have not seen him this two days.
KNIGHT: Since my young lady's going into France, sir, the fool hath much pined away.
LEAR: No more of that; I have noted it well. Go you and tell my daughter I would speak with her.
Exit Knight.
Go you, call hither my fool.
Exit an Attendant.
Enter Oswald the Steward.
O, you, sir, you! Come you hither, sir. Who am I, sir?
OSWALD: My lady's father.
LEAR: 'My lady's father'? My lord's knave! You whoreson dog! you slave! you cur!
OSWALD: I am none of these, my lord; I beseech your pardon.

LEAR: Do you bandy looks with me, you rascal?
Strikes Him.
OSWALD: I'll not be strucken, my lord.
KENT: Nor tripp'd neither, you base football player?
Trips up His Heels.
LEAR: I thank thee, fellow. Thou serv'st me, and I'll love thee.
KENT: Come, sir, arise, away! I'll teach you differences. Away, away! If you will measure your lubber's length again, tarry; but away! Go to! Have you wisdom? So.
Pushes Him Out.
LEAR: Now, my friendly knave, I thank thee. There's earnest of thy service.
Gives Money.
Enter Fool.
FOOL: Let me hire him too. Here's my coxcomb.
Offers Kent His Cap.
LEAR: How now, my pretty knave? How dost thou?
FOOL: Sirrah, you were best take my coxcomb.
KENT: Why, fool?
FOOL: Why? For taking one's part that's out of favour. Nay, an thou canst not smile as the wind sits, thou'lt catch cold shortly. There, take my coxcomb! Why, this fellow hath banish'd two on's daughters, and did the third a blessing against his will. If thou follow him, thou must needs wear my coxcomb.- How now, nuncle? Would I had two coxcombs and two daughters!
LEAR: Why, my boy?
FOOL: If I gave them all my living, I'ld keep my coxcombs myself. There's mine! beg another of thy daughters.
LEAR: Take heed, sirrah- the whip.
FOOL: Truth's a dog must to kennel; he must be whipp'd out, when Lady the brach may stand by th' fire and stink.
LEAR: A pestilent gall to me!
FOOL: Sirrah, I'll teach thee a speech.
LEAR: Do.
FOOL: Mark it, nuncle.

Have more than thou showest,
Speak less than thou knowest,
Lend less than thou owest,
Ride more than thou goest,
Learn more than thou trowest,
Set less than thou throwest;
Leave thy drink and thy whore,
And keep in-a-door,
And thou shalt have more
Than two tens to a score.

KENT: This is nothing, fool.
FOOL: Then 'tis like the breath of an unfeed lawyer- you gave me nothing for't. Can you make no use of nothing, nuncle?
LEAR: Why, no, boy. Nothing can be made out of nothing.

FOOL: To Kent Prithee tell him, so much the rent of his land comes to. He will not believe a fool.
LEAR: A bitter fool!
FOOL: Dost thou know the difference, my boy, between a bitter fool and a sweet fool?
LEAR: No, lad; teach me.
FOOL: That lord that counsell'd thee
  To give away thy land,
 Come place him here by me-
  Do thou for him stand.
 The sweet and bitter fool
  Will presently appear;
 The one in motley here,
  The other found out there.
LEAR: Dost thou call me fool, boy?
FOOL: All thy other titles thou hast given away; that thou wast born with.
KENT: This is not altogether fool, my lord.
FOOL: No, faith; lords and great men will not let me. If I had a monopoly out, they would have part on't. And ladies too, they will not let me have all the fool to myself; they'll be snatching. Give me an egg, nuncle, and I'll give thee two crowns.
LEAR: What two crowns shall they be?
FOOL: Why, after I have cut the egg i' th' middle and eat up the meat, the two crowns of the egg. When thou clovest thy crown i' th' middle and gav'st away both parts, thou bor'st thine ass on thy back o'er the dirt. Thou hadst little wit in thy bald crown when thou gav'st thy golden one away. If I speak like myself in this, let him be whipp'd that first finds it so.
Sings Fools had ne'er less grace in a year,
  For wise men are grown foppish;
 They know not how their wits to wear,
  Their manners are so apish.
LEAR: When were you wont to be so full of songs, sirrah?
FOOL: I have us'd it, nuncle, ever since thou mad'st thy daughters thy mother; for when thou gav'st them the rod, and put'st down thine own breeches,
Sings Then they for sudden joy did weep,
  And I for sorrow sung,
 That such a king should play bo-peep
  And go the fools among.
Prithee, nuncle, keep a schoolmaster that can teach thy fool to lie. I would fain learn to lie.
LEAR: An you lie, sirrah, we'll have you whipp'd.
FOOL: I marvel what kin thou and thy daughters are. They'll have me whipp'd for speaking true; thou'lt have me whipp'd for lying; and sometimes I am whipp'd for holding my peace. I had rather be any kind o' thing than a fool! And yet I would not be thee, nuncle. Thou hast pared thy wit o' both sides and left nothing

i' th' middle. Here comes one o' the parings.

Enter Goneril.

LEAR: How now, daughter? What makes that frontlet on? Methinks you are too much o' late i' th' frown.

FOOL: Thou wast a pretty fellow when thou hadst no need to care for her frowning. Now thou art an O without a figure. I am better than thou art now: I am a fool, thou art nothing.

To Goneril Yes, forsooth, I will hold my tongue. So your face bids me, though you say nothing. Mum, mum!

He that keeps nor crust nor crum,
Weary of all, shall want some.-

Points at Lear That's a sheal'd peascod.

GONERIL: Not only, sir, this your all-licens'd fool,
But other of your insolent retinue
Do hourly carp and quarrel, breaking forth
In rank and not-to-be-endured riots. Sir,
I had thought, by making this well known unto you,
To have found a safe redress, but now grow fearful,
By what yourself, too, late have spoke and done,
That you protect this course, and put it on
By your allowance; which if you should, the fault
Would not scape censure, nor the redresses sleep,
Which, in the tender of a wholesome weal,
Might in their working do you that offence
Which else were shame, that then necessity
Must call discreet proceeding.

FOOL: For you know, nuncle,
The hedge-sparrow fed the cuckoo so long
That it had it head bit off by it young.
So out went the candle, and we were left darkling.

LEAR: Are you our daughter?

GONERIL: Come, sir,
I would you would make use of that good wisdom
Whereof I know you are fraught, and put away
These dispositions that of late transform you
From what you rightly are.

FOOL: May not an ass know when the cart draws the horse?
Whoop, Jug, I love thee!

LEAR: Doth any here know me? This is not Lear.
Doth Lear walk thus? speak thus? Where are his eyes?
Either his notion weakens, his discernings
Are lethargied- Ha! waking? 'Tis not so!
Who is it that can tell me who I am?

FOOL: Lear's shadow.

LEAR: I would learn that; for, by the marks of sovereignty,
Knowledge, and reason, I should be false persuaded
I had daughters.

FOOL: Which they will make an obedient father.

LEAR: Your name, fair gentlewoman?

GONERIL: This admiration, sir, is much o' th' savour
Of other your new pranks. I do beseech you
To understand my purposes aright.
As you are old and reverend, you should be wise.
Here do you keep a hundred knights and squires;
Men so disorder'd, so debosh'd, and bold
That this our court, infected with their manners,
Shows like a riotous inn. Epicurism and lust
Make it more like a tavern or a brothel
Than a grac'd palace. The shame itself doth speak
For instant remedy. Be then desir'd
By her that else will take the thing she begs
A little to disquantity your train,
And the remainder that shall still depend
To be such men as may besort your age,
Which know themselves, and you.
LEAR: Darkness and devils!
Saddle my horses! Call my train together!
Degenerate bastard, I'll not trouble thee;
Yet have I left a daughter.
GONERIL: You strike my people, and your disorder'd rabble
Make servants of their betters.
Enter Albany.
LEAR: Woe that too late repents!- O, sir, are you come?
Is it your will? Speak, sir!- Prepare my horses.
Ingratitude, thou marble-hearted fiend,
More hideous when thou show'st thee in a child
Than the sea-monster!
ALBANY: Pray, sir, be patient.
LEAR: To Goneril Detested kite, thou liest!
My train are men of choice and rarest parts,
That all particulars of duty know
And in the most exact regard support
The worships of their name.- O most small fault,
How ugly didst thou in Cordelia show!
Which, like an engine, wrench'd my frame of nature
From the fix'd place; drew from my heart all love
And added to the gall. O Lear, Lear, Lear!
Beat at this gate that let thy folly in
Strikes His Head.
And thy dear judgment out! Go, go, my people.
ALBANY: My lord, I am guiltless, as I am ignorant
Of what hath mov'd you.
LEAR: It may be so, my lord.
Hear, Nature, hear! dear goddess, hear!
Suspend thy purpose, if thou didst intend
To make this creature fruitful.
Into her womb convey sterility;
Dry up in her the organs of increase;

And from her derogate body never spring
A babe to honour her! If she must teem,
Create her child of spleen, that it may live
And be a thwart disnatur'd torment to her.
Let it stamp wrinkles in her brow of youth,
With cadent tears fret channels in her cheeks,
Turn all her mother's pains and benefits
To laughter and contempt, that she may feel
How sharper than a serpent's tooth it is
To have a thankless child! Away, away!
Exit.
ALBANY: Now, gods that we adore, whereof comes this?
GONERIL: Never afflict yourself to know the cause;
But let his disposition have that scope
That dotage gives it.
Enter Lear.
LEAR: What, fifty of my followers at a clap?
Within a fortnight?
ALBANY: What's the matter, sir?
LEAR: I'll tell thee. To Goneril Life and death! I am asham'd
That thou hast power to shake my manhood thus;
That these hot tears, which break from me perforce,
Should make thee worth them. Blasts and fogs upon thee!
Th' untented woundings of a father's curse
Pierce every sense about thee!- Old fond eyes,
Beweep this cause again, I'll pluck ye out,
And cast you, with the waters that you lose,
To temper clay. Yea, is it come to this?
Let it be so. Yet have I left a daughter,
Who I am sure is kind and comfortable.
When she shall hear this of thee, with her nails
She'll flay thy wolvish visage. Thou shalt find
That I'll resume the shape which thou dost think
I have cast off for ever; thou shalt, I warrant thee.
Exeunt Lear, Kent, and Attendants.
GONERIL: Do you mark that, my lord?
ALBANY: I cannot be so partial, Goneril,
To the great love I bear you -
GONERIL: Pray you, content.- What, Oswald, ho!
To the Fool You, sir, more knave than fool, after your master!
FOOL: Nuncle Lear, nuncle Lear, tarry! Take the fool with thee.
A fox when one has caught her,
And such a daughter,
Should sure to the slaughter,
If my cap would buy a halter.
So the fool follows after.
Exit.
GONERIL: This man hath had good counsel! A hundred knights?
'Tis politic and safe to let him keep

At point a hundred knights; yes, that on every dream,
Each buzz, each fancy, each complaint, dislike,
He may enguard his dotage with their pow'rs
And hold our lives in mercy.- Oswald, I say!
ALBANY: Well, you may fear too far.
GONERIL: Safer than trust too far.
Let me still take away the harms I fear,
Not fear still to be taken. I know his heart.
What he hath utter'd I have writ my sister.
If she sustain him and his hundred knights,
When I have show'd th' unfitness-
Enter Oswald the Steward.
How now, Oswald?
What, have you writ that letter to my sister?
OSWALD: Yes, madam.
GONERIL: Take you some company, and away to horse!
Inform her full of my particular fear,
And thereto add such reasons of your own
As may compact it more. Get you gone,
And hasten your return.
Exit Oswald.
No, no, my lord!
This milky gentleness and course of yours,
Though I condemn it not, yet, under pardon,
You are much more at task for want of wisdom
Than prais'd for harmful mildness.
ALBANY: How far your eyes may pierce I cannot tell.
Striving to better, oft we mar what's well.
GONERIL: Nay then-
ALBANY: Well, well; th' event.
Exeunt.

ACT I. SCENE V. Court Before the Duke of Albany's Palace.

Enter Lear, Kent, and Fool.
LEAR: Go you before to Gloucester with these letters. Acquaint my daughter no further with anything you know than comes from her demand out of the letter. If your diligence be not speedy, I shall be there afore you.
KENT: I will not sleep, my lord, till I have delivered your letter.
Exit.
FOOL: If a man's brains were in's heels, were't not in danger of kibes?
LEAR: Ay, boy.
FOOL: Then I prithee be merry. Thy wit shall ne'er go slip-shod.
LEAR: Ha, ha, ha!
FOOL: Shalt see thy other daughter will use thee kindly; for though she's as like this as a crab's like an apple, yet I can tell what I can tell.
LEAR: What canst tell, boy?
FOOL: She'll taste as like this as a crab does to a crab. Thou canst tell why one's nose stands i' th' middle on's face?

LEAR: No.
FOOL: Why, to keep one's eyes of either side's nose, that what a man cannot smell out, 'a may spy into.
LEAR: I did her wrong.
FOOL: Canst tell how an oyster makes his shell?
LEAR: No.
FOOL: Nor I neither; but I can tell why a snail has a house.
LEAR: Why?
FOOL: Why, to put's head in; not to give it away to his daughters, and leave his horns without a case.
LEAR: I will forget my nature. So kind a father!- Be my horses ready?
FOOL: Thy asses are gone about 'em. The reason why the seven stars are no moe than seven is a pretty reason.
LEAR: Because they are not eight?
FOOL: Yes indeed. Thou wouldst make a good fool.
LEAR: To tak't again perforce! Monster ingratitude!
FOOL: If thou wert my fool, nuncle, I'ld have thee beaten for being old before thy time.
LEAR: How's that?
FOOL: Thou shouldst not have been old till thou hadst been wise.
LEAR: O, let me not be mad, not mad, sweet heaven!
Keep me in temper; I would not be mad!
Enter a Gentleman.
How now? Are the horses ready?
GENTLEMEN: Ready, my lord.
LEAR: Come, boy.
FOOL: She that's a maid now, and laughs at my departure,
Shall not be a maid long, unless things be cut shorter
Exeunt.

ACT II. SCENE I. A Court Within the Castle of the Earl of Gloucester.

Enter Edmund the Bastard and Curan, Meeting.
EDMUND: Save thee, Curan.
CURAN: And you, sir. I have been with your father, and given him notice that the Duke of Cornwall and Regan his Duchess will be here with him this night.
EDMUND: How comes that?
CURAN: Nay, I know not. You have heard of the news abroad- I mean the whisper'd ones, for they are yet but ear-kissing arguments?
EDMUND: Not I. Pray you, what are they?
CURAN: Have you heard of no likely wars toward 'twixt the two Dukes of Cornwall and Albany?
EDMUND: Not a word.
CURAN: You may do, then, in time. Fare you well, sir.
Exit.
EDMUND: The Duke be here to-night? The better! best!
This weaves itself perforce into my business.
My father hath set guard to take my brother;
And I have one thing, of a queasy question,

Which I must act. Briefness and fortune, work!
Brother, a word! Descend! Brother, I say!
Enter Edgar.
My father watches. O sir, fly this place!
Intelligence is given where you are hid.
You have now the good advantage of the night.
Have you not spoken 'gainst the Duke of Cornwall?
He's coming hither; now, i' th' night, i' th' haste,
And Regan with him. Have you nothing said
Upon his party 'gainst the Duke of Albany?
Advise yourself.
EDGAR: I am sure on't, not a word.
EDMUND: I hear my father coming. Pardon me!
In cunning I must draw my sword upon you.
Draw, seem to defend yourself; now quit you well.-
Yield! Come before my father. Light, ho, here!
Fly, brother.- Torches, torches!- So farewell.
Exit Edgar.
Some blood drawn on me would beget opinion
Of my more fierce endeavour. Stabs His Arm. I have seen drunkards
Do more than this in sport.- Father, father!-
Stop, stop! No help?
Enter Gloucester, and Servants with Torches.
GLOUCESTER: Now, Edmund, where's the villain?
EDMUND: Here stood he in the dark, his sharp sword out,
Mumbling of wicked charms, conjuring the moon
To stand 's auspicious mistress.
GLOUCESTER: But where is he?
EDMUND: Look, sir, I bleed.
GLOUCESTER: Where is the villain, Edmund?
EDMUND: Fled this way, sir. When by no means he could-
GLOUCESTER: Pursue him, ho! Go after.
Exeunt some Servants.
By no means what?
EDMUND: Persuade me to the murther of your lordship;
But that I told him the revenging gods
'Gainst parricides did all their thunders bend;
Spoke with how manifold and strong a bond
The child was bound to th' father- sir, in fine,
Seeing how loathly opposite I stood
To his unnatural purpose, in fell motion
With his prepared sword he charges home
My unprovided body, lanch'd mine arm;
But when he saw my best alarum'd spirits,
Bold in the quarrel's right, rous'd to th' encounter,
Or whether gasted by the noise I made,
Full suddenly he fled.
GLOUCESTER: Let him fly far.
Not in this land shall he remain uncaught;

And found- dispatch. The noble Duke my master,
My worthy arch and patron, comes to-night.
By his authority I will proclaim it
That he which find, him shall deserve our thanks,
Bringing the murderous caitiff to the stake;
He that conceals him, death.
EDMUND: When I dissuaded him from his intent
And found him pight to do it, with curst speech
I threaten'd to discover him. He replied,
'Thou unpossessing bastard, dost thou think,
If I would stand against thee, would the reposal
Of any trust, virtue, or worth in thee
Make thy words faith'd? No. What I should deny
(As this I would; ay, though thou didst produce
My very character), I'ld turn it all
To thy suggestion, plot, and damned practice;
And thou must make a dullard of the world,
If they not thought the profits of my death
Were very pregnant and potential spurs
To make thee seek it.'
GLOUCESTER: Strong and fast'ned villain!
Would he deny his letter? I never got him.
Tucket Within.
Hark, the Duke's trumpets! I know not why he comes.
All ports I'll bar; the villain shall not scape;
The Duke must grant me that. Besides, his picture
I will send far and near, that all the kingdom
May have due note of him, and of my land,
Loyal and natural boy, I'll work the means
To make thee capable.
Enter Cornwall, Regan, and Attendants.
CORNWALL: How now, my noble friend? Since I came hither
Which I can call but now. I have heard strange news.
REGAN: If it be true, all vengeance comes too short
Which can pursue th' offender. How dost, my lord?
GLOUCESTER: O madam, my old heart is crack'd, it's crack'd!
REGAN: What, did my father's godson seek your life?
He whom my father nam'd? Your Edgar?
GLOUCESTER: O lady, lady, shame would have it hid!
REGAN: Was he not companion with the riotous knights
That tend upon my father?
GLOUCESTER: I know not, madam. 'Tis too bad, too bad!
EDMUND: Yes, madam, he was of that consort.
REGAN: No marvel then though he were ill affected.
'Tis they have put him on the old man's death,
To have th' expense and waste of his revenues.
I have this present evening from my sister
Been well inform'd of them, and with such cautions
That, if they come to sojourn at my house,

I'll not be there.
CORNWALL: Nor I, assure thee, Regan.
Edmund, I hear that you have shown your father
A childlike office.
EDMUND: 'Twas my duty, sir.
GLOUCESTER: He did bewray his practice, and receiv'd
This hurt you see, striving to apprehend him.
CORNWALL: Is he pursued?
GLOUCESTER: Ay, my good lord.
CORNWALL: If he be taken, he shall never more
Be fear'd of doing harm. Make your own purpose,
How in my strength you please. For you, Edmund,
Whose virtue and obedience doth this instant
So much commend itself, you shall be ours.
Natures of such deep trust we shall much need;
You we first seize on.
EDMUND: I shall serve you, sir,
Truly, however else.
GLOUCESTER: For him I thank your Grace.
CORNWALL: You know not why we came to visit you-
REGAN: Thus out of season, threading dark-ey'd night.
Occasions, noble Gloucester, of some poise,
Wherein we must have use of your advice.
Our father he hath writ, so hath our sister,
Of differences, which I best thought it fit
To answer from our home. The several messengers
From hence attend dispatch. Our good old friend,
Lay comforts to your bosom, and bestow
Your needful counsel to our business,
Which craves the instant use.
GLOUCESTER: I serve you, madam.
Your Graces are right welcome.
Exeunt. Flourish.

ACT II. SCENE II. Before Gloucester's Castle.

Enter Kent and Oswald the Steward, Severally.
OSWALD: Good dawning to thee, friend. Art of this house?
KENT: Ay.
OSWALD: Where may we set our horses?
KENT: I' th' mire.
OSWALD: Prithee, if thou lov'st me, tell me.
KENT: I love thee not.
OSWALD: Why then, I care not for thee.
KENT: If I had thee in Lipsbury Pinfold, I would make thee care for me.
OSWALD: Why dost thou use me thus? I know thee not.
KENT: Fellow, I know thee.
OSWALD: What dost thou know me for?
KENT: A knave; a rascal; an eater of broken meats; a base, proud,
shallow, beggarly, three-suited, hundred-pound, filthy,
worsted-stocking knave; a lily-liver'd, action-taking, whoreson,

glass-gazing, superserviceable, finical rogue;
one-trunk-inheriting slave; one that wouldst be a bawd in way of
good service, and art nothing but the composition of a knave,
beggar, coward, pander, and the son and heir of a mongrel bitch;
one whom I will beat into clamorous whining, if thou deny the
least syllable of thy addition.
OSWALD: Why, what a monstrous fellow art thou, thus to rail on one
that's neither known of thee nor knows thee!
KENT: What a brazen-fac'd varlet art thou, to deny thou knowest me!
Is it two days ago since I beat thee and tripp'd up thy heels
before the King?
Draws His Sword.
Draw, you rogue! for, though
it be night, yet the moon shines. I'll make a sop o' th'
moonshine o' you. Draw, you whoreson cullionly barbermonger!
draw!
OSWALD: Away! I have nothing to do with thee.
KENT: Draw, you rascal! You come with letters against the King, and
take Vanity the puppet's part against the royalty of her father.
Draw, you rogue, or I'll so carbonado your shanks! Draw, you
rascal! Come your ways!
OSWALD: Help, ho! murther! help!
KENT: Strike, you slave! Stand, rogue! Stand, you neat slave! Strike!
Beats Him.
OSWALD: Help, ho! murther! murther!
Enter Edmund, with His Rapier Drawn, Gloucester, Cornwall, Regan, Servants.
EDMUND: How now? What's the matter?
Parts Them.
KENT: With you, goodman boy, an you please! Come, I'll flesh ye!
Come on, young master!
GLOUCESTER: Weapons? arms? What's the matter here?
CORNWALL: Keep peace, upon your lives!
He dies that strikes again. What is the matter?
REGAN: The messengers from our sister and the King
CORNWALL: What is your difference? Speak.
OSWALD: I am scarce in breath, my lord.
KENT: No marvel, you have so bestirr'd your valour. You cowardly
rascal, nature disclaims in thee; a tailor made thee.
CORNWALL: Thou art a strange fellow. A tailor make a man?
KENT: Ay, a tailor, sir. A stonecutter or a painter could not have
made him so ill, though he had been but two hours at the trade.
CORNWALL: Speak yet, how grew your quarrel?
OSWALD: This ancient ruffian, sir, whose life I have spar'd
At suit of his grey beard-
KENT: Thou whoreson zed! thou unnecessary letter! My lord, if
you'll give me leave, I will tread this unbolted villain into
mortar and daub the walls of a jakes with him. 'Spare my grey
beard,' you wagtail?
CORNWALL: Peace, sirrah!

You beastly knave, know you no reverence?
KENT: Yes, sir, but anger hath a privilege.
CORNWALL: Why art thou angry?
KENT: That such a slave as this should wear a sword,
Who wears no honesty. Such smiling rogues as these,
Like rats, oft bite the holy cords atwain
Which are too intrinse t' unloose; smooth every passion
That in the natures of their lords rebel,
Bring oil to fire, snow to their colder moods;
Renege, affirm, and turn their halcyon beaks
With every gale and vary of their masters,
Knowing naught (like dogs) but following.
A plague upon your epileptic visage!
Smile you my speeches, as I were a fool?
Goose, an I had you upon Sarum Plain,
I'ld drive ye cackling home to Camelot.
CORNWALL: What, art thou mad, old fellow?
GLOUCESTER: How fell you out? Say that.
KENT: No contraries hold more antipathy
Than I and such a knave.
CORNWALL: Why dost thou call him knave? What is his fault?
KENT: His countenance likes me not.
CORNWALL: No more perchance does mine, or his, or hers.
KENT: Sir, 'tis my occupation to be plain.
I have seen better faces in my time
Than stands on any shoulder that I see
Before me at this instant.
CORNWALL: This is some fellow
Who, having been prais'd for bluntness, doth affect
A saucy roughness, and constrains the garb
Quite from his nature. He cannot flatter, he!
An honest mind and plain- he must speak truth!
An they will take it, so; if not, he's plain.
These kind of knaves I know which in this plainness
Harbour more craft and more corrupter ends
Than twenty silly-ducking observants
That stretch their duties nicely.
KENT: Sir, in good faith, in sincere verity,
Under th' allowance of your great aspect,
Whose influence, like the wreath of radiant fire
On flickering Phoebus' front-
CORNWALL: What mean'st by this?
KENT: To go out of my dialect, which you discommend so much. I know, sir, I am no flatterer. He that beguil'd you in a plain accent was a plain knave, which, for my part, I will not be, though I should win your displeasure to entreat me to't.
CORNWALL: What was th' offence you gave him?
OSWALD: I never gave him any.
It pleas'd the King his master very late

To strike at me, upon his misconstruction;
When he, conjunct, and flattering his displeasure,
Tripp'd me behind; being down, insulted, rail'd
And put upon him such a deal of man
That worthied him, got praises of the King
For him attempting who was self-subdu'd;
And, in the fleshment of this dread exploit,
Drew on me here again.
KENT: None of these rogues and cowards
But Ajax is their fool.
CORNWALL: Fetch forth the stocks!
You stubborn ancient knave, you reverent braggart, we'll teach you-
KENT: Sir, I am too old to learn.
Call not your stocks for me. I serve the King;
On whose employment I was sent to you.
You shall do small respect, show too bold malice
Against the grace and person of my master,
Stocking his messenger.
CORNWALL: Fetch forth the stocks! As I have life and honour,
There shall he sit till noon.
REGAN: Till noon? Till night, my lord, and all night too!
KENT: Why, madam, if I were your father's dog,
You should not use me so.
REGAN: Sir, being his knave, I will.
CORNWALL: This is a fellow of the selfsame colour
Our sister speaks of. Come, bring away the stocks!
Stocks Brought Out.
GLOUCESTER: Let me beseech your Grace not to do so.
His fault is much, and the good King his master
Will check him for't. Your purpos'd low correction
Is such as basest and contemn'dest wretches
For pilf'rings and most common trespasses
Are punish'd with. The King must take it ill
That he, so slightly valued in his messenger,
Should have him thus restrain'd.
CORNWALL: I'll answer that.
REGAN: My sister may receive it much more worse,
To have her gentleman abus'd, assaulted,
For following her affairs. Put in his legs.-
Kent Is Put in the Stocks.
Come, my good lord, away.
Exeunt All but Gloucester and Kent.
GLOUCESTER: I am sorry for thee, friend. 'Tis the Duke's pleasure,
Whose disposition, all the world well knows,
Will not be rubb'd nor stopp'd. I'll entreat for thee.
KENT: Pray do not, sir. I have watch'd and travell'd hard.
Some time I shall sleep out, the rest I'll whistle.
A good man's fortune may grow out at heels.
Give you good morrow!

GLOUCESTER: The Duke 's to blame in this; 'twill be ill taken.
Exit.
KENT: Good King, that must approve the common saw,
Thou out of heaven's benediction com'st
To the warm sun!
Approach, thou beacon to this under globe,
That by thy comfortable beams I may
Peruse this letter. Nothing almost sees miracles
But misery. I know 'tis from Cordelia,
Who hath most fortunately been inform'd
Of my obscured course- and Reads 'shall find time
From this enormous state, seeking to give
Losses their remedies'- All weary and o'erwatch'd,
Take vantage, heavy eyes, not to behold
This shameful lodging.
Fortune, good night; smile once more, turn thy wheel.
Sleeps.

ACT II. SCENE III. The Open Country.

Enter Edgar.
EDGAR: I heard myself proclaim'd,
And by the happy hollow of a tree
Escap'd the hunt. No port is free, no place
That guard and most unusual vigilance
Does not attend my taking. Whiles I may scape,
I will preserve myself; and am bethought
To take the basest and most poorest shape
That ever penury, in contempt of man,
Brought near to beast. My face I'll grime with filth,
Blanket my loins, elf all my hair in knots,
And with presented nakedness outface
The winds and persecutions of the sky.
The country gives me proof and precedent
Of Bedlam beggars, who, with roaring voices,
Strike in their numb'd and mortified bare arms
Pins, wooden pricks, nails, sprigs of rosemary;
And with this horrible object, from low farms,
Poor pelting villages, sheepcotes, and mills,
Sometime with lunatic bans, sometime with prayers,
Enforce their charity. 'Poor Turlygod! poor Tom!'
That's something yet! Edgar I nothing am.
Exit.

ACT II. SCENE IV. Before Gloucester's Castle; Kent in the Stocks.

Enter Lear, Fool, and Gentleman.
LEAR: 'Tis strange that they should so depart from home,
And not send back my messenger.
GENTLEMEN: As I learn'd,
The night before there was no purpose in them
Of this remove.
KENT: Hail to thee, noble master!

LEAR: Ha! Mak'st thou this shame thy pastime?
KENT: No, my lord.
FOOL: Ha, ha! look! he wears cruel garters. Horses are tied by the head, dogs and bears by th' neck, monkeys by th' loins, and men by th' legs. When a man's over-lusty at legs, then he wears wooden nether-stocks.
LEAR: What's he that hath so much thy place mistook
To set thee here?
KENT: It is both he and she-
Your son and daughter.
LEAR: No.
KENT: Yes.
LEAR: No, I say.
KENT: I say yea.
LEAR: No, no, they would not!
KENT: Yes, they have.
LEAR: By Jupiter, I swear no!
KENT: By Juno, I swear ay!
LEAR: They durst not do't;
They would not, could not do't. 'Tis worse than murther
To do upon respect such violent outrage.
Resolve me with all modest haste which way
Thou mightst deserve or they impose this usage,
Coming from us.
KENT: My lord, when at their home
I did commend your Highness' letters to them,
Ere I was risen from the place that show'd
My duty kneeling, came there a reeking post,
Stew'd in his haste, half breathless, panting forth
From Goneril his mistress salutations;
Deliver'd letters, spite of intermission,
Which presently they read; on whose contents,
They summon'd up their meiny, straight took horse,
Commanded me to follow and attend
The leisure of their answer, gave me cold looks,
And meeting here the other messenger,
Whose welcome I perceiv'd had poison'd mine-
Being the very fellow which of late
Display'd so saucily against your Highness-
Having more man than wit about me, drew.
He rais'd the house with loud and coward cries.
Your son and daughter found this trespass worth
The shame which here it suffers.
FOOL: Winter's not gone yet, if the wild geese fly that way.
Fathers that wear rags
Do make their children blind;
But fathers that bear bags
Shall see their children kind.
Fortune, that arrant whore,

Ne'er turns the key to th' poor.
But for all this, thou shalt have as many dolours for thy
daughters as thou canst tell in a year.
LEAR: O, how this mother swells up toward my heart!
Hysterica passio! Down, thou climbing sorrow!
Thy element's below! Where is this daughter?
KENT: With the Earl, sir, here within.
LEAR: Follow me not; stay here.
Exit.
GENTLEMEN: Made you no more offence but what you speak of?
KENT: None.
How chance the King comes with so small a number?
FOOL: An thou hadst been set i' th' stocks for that question,
thou'dst well deserv'd it.
KENT: Why, fool?
FOOL: We'll set thee to school to an ant, to teach thee there's no labouring i' th' winter. All that follow their noses are led by their eyes but blind men, and there's not a nose among twenty but can smell him that's stinking. Let go thy hold when a great wheel runs down a hill, lest it break thy neck with following it; but the great one that goes upward, let him draw thee after. When a wise man gives thee better counsel, give me mine again. I would have none but knaves follow it, since a fool gives it.
That sir which serves and seeks for gain,
And follows but for form,
Will pack when it begins to rain
And leave thee in the storm.
But I will tarry; the fool will stay,
And let the wise man fly.
The knave turns fool that runs away;
The fool no knave, perdy.
KENT: Where learn'd you this, fool?
FOOL: Not i' th' stocks, fool.
Enter Lear and Gloucester
LEAR: Deny to speak with me? They are sick? they are weary?
They have travell'd all the night? Mere fetches-
The images of revolt and flying off!
Fetch me a better answer.
GLOUCESTER: My dear lord,
You know the fiery quality of the Duke,
How unremovable and fix'd he is
In his own course.
LEAR: Vengeance! plague! death! confusion!
Fiery? What quality? Why, Gloucester, Gloucester,
I'ld speak with the Duke of Cornwall and his wife.
GLOUCESTER: Well, my good lord, I have inform'd them so.
LEAR: Inform'd them? Dost thou understand me, man?
GLOUCESTER: Ay, my good lord.
LEAR: The King would speak with Cornwall; the dear father

Would with his daughter speak, commands her service.
Are they inform'd of this? My breath and blood!
Fiery? the fiery Duke? Tell the hot Duke that-
No, but not yet! May be he is not well.
Infirmity doth still neglect all office
Whereto our health is bound. We are not ourselves
When nature, being oppress'd, commands the mind
To suffer with the body. I'll forbear;
And am fallen out with my more headier will,
To take the indispos'd and sickly fit
For the sound man.- Death on my state! Wherefore
Should be sit here? This act persuades me
That this remotion of the Duke and her
Is practice only. Give me my servant forth.
Go tell the Duke and 's wife I'ld speak with them-
Now, presently. Bid them come forth and hear me,
Or at their chamber door I'll beat the drum
Till it cry sleep to death.
GLOUCESTER: I would have all well betwixt you.
Exit.
LEAR: O me, my heart, my rising heart! But down!
FOOL: Cry to it, nuncle, as the cockney did to the eels when she put 'em i' th' paste alive. She knapp'd 'em o' th' coxcombs with a stick and cried 'Down, wantons, down!' 'Twas her brother that, in pure kindness to his horse, buttered his hay.
Enter Cornwall, Regan, Gloucester, Servants.
LEAR: Good morrow to you both.
CORNWALL: Hail to your Grace!
Kent Here Set at Liberty.
REGAN: I am glad to see your Highness.
LEAR: Regan, I think you are; I know what reason
I have to think so. If thou shouldst not be glad,
I would divorce me from thy mother's tomb,
Sepulchring an adultress. To Kent O, are you free?
Some other time for that.- Beloved Regan,
Thy sister's naught. O Regan, she hath tied
Sharp-tooth'd unkindness, like a vulture, here!
Lays His Hand on His Heart.
I can scarce speak to thee. Thou'lt not believe
With how deprav'd a quality- O Regan!
REGAN: I pray you, sir, take patience. I have hope
You less know how to value her desert
Than she to scant her duty.
LEAR: Say, how is that?
REGAN: I cannot think my sister in the least
Would fail her obligation. If, sir, perchance
She have restrain'd the riots of your followers,
'Tis on such ground, and to such wholesome end,
As clears her from all blame.

LEAR: My curses on her!
REGAN: O, sir, you are old!
Nature in you stands on the very verge
Of her confine. You should be rul'd, and led
By some discretion that discerns your state
Better than you yourself. Therefore I pray you
That to our sister you do make return;
Say you have wrong'd her, sir.
LEAR: Ask her forgiveness?
Do you but mark how this becomes the house:
'Dear daughter, I confess that I am old. Kneels.
Age is unnecessary. On my knees I beg
That you'll vouchsafe me raiment, bed, and food.'
REGAN: Good sir, no more! These are unsightly tricks.
Return you to my sister.
LEAR: Rises Never, Regan!
She hath abated me of half my train;
Look'd black upon me; struck me with her tongue,
Most serpent-like, upon the very heart.
All the stor'd vengeances of heaven fall
On her ingrateful top! Strike her young bones,
You taking airs, with lameness!
CORNWALL: Fie, sir, fie!
LEAR: You nimble lightnings, dart your blinding flames
Into her scornful eyes! Infect her beauty,
You fen-suck'd fogs, drawn by the pow'rful sun,
To fall and blast her pride!
REGAN: O the blest gods! so will you wish on me
When the rash mood is on.
LEAR: No, Regan, thou shalt never have my curse.
Thy tender-hefted nature shall not give
Thee o'er to harshness. Her eyes are fierce; but thine
Do comfort, and not burn. 'Tis not in thee
To grudge my pleasures, to cut off my train,
To bandy hasty words, to scant my sizes,
And, in conclusion, to oppose the bolt
Against my coming in. Thou better know'st
The offices of nature, bond of childhood,
Effects of courtesy, dues of gratitude.
Thy half o' th' kingdom hast thou not forgot,
Wherein I thee endow'd.
REGAN: Good sir, to th' purpose.
  Tucket Within.
LEAR: Who put my man i' th' stocks?
CORNWALL: What trumpet's that?
REGAN: I know't- my sister's. This approves her letter,
That she would soon be here.
  Enter Oswald the Steward.
Is your lady come?

LEAR: This is a slave, whose easy-borrowed pride
Dwells in the fickle grace of her he follows.
Out, varlet, from my sight!
CORNWALL: What means your Grace?
Enter Goneril.
LEAR: Who stock'd my servant? Regan, I have good hope
Thou didst not know on't.- Who comes here? O heavens!
If you do love old men, if your sweet sway
Allow obedience- if yourselves are old,
Make it your cause! Send down, and take my part!
To Goneril Art not asham'd to look upon this beard?-
O Regan, wilt thou take her by the hand?
GONERIL: Why not by th' hand, sir? How have I offended?
All's not offence that indiscretion finds
And dotage terms so.
LEAR: O sides, you are too tough!
Will you yet hold? How came my man i' th' stocks?
CORNWALL: I set him there, sir; but his own disorders
Deserv'd much less advancement.
LEAR: You? Did you?
REGAN: I pray you, father, being weak, seem so.
If, till the expiration of your month,
You will return and sojourn with my sister,
Dismissing half your train, come then to me.
I am now from home, and out of that provision
Which shall be needful for your entertainment.
LEAR: Return to her, and fifty men dismiss'd?
No, rather I abjure all roofs, and choose
To wage against the enmity o' th' air,
To be a comrade with the wolf and owl-
Necessity's sharp pinch! Return with her?
Why, the hot-blooded France, that dowerless took
Our youngest born, I could as well be brought
To knee his throne, and, squire-like, pension beg
To keep base life afoot. Return with her?
Persuade me rather to be slave and sumpter
To this detested groom.
Points at Oswald.
GONERIL: At your choice, sir.
LEAR: I prithee, daughter, do not make me mad.
I will not trouble thee, my child; farewell.
We'll no more meet, no more see one another.
But yet thou art my flesh, my blood, my daughter;
Or rather a disease that's in my flesh,
Which I must needs call mine. Thou art a boil,
A plague sore, an embossed carbuncle
In my corrupted blood. But I'll not chide thee.
Let shame come when it will, I do not call it.
I do not bid the Thunder-bearer shoot

Nor tell tales of thee to high-judging Jove.
Mend when thou canst; be better at thy leisure;
I can be patient, I can stay with Regan,
I and my hundred knights.
REGAN: Not altogether so.
I look'd not for you yet, nor am provided
For your fit welcome. Give ear, sir, to my sister;
For those that mingle reason with your passion
Must be content to think you old, and so-
But she knows what she does.
LEAR: Is this well spoken?
REGAN: I dare avouch it, sir. What, fifty followers?
Is it not well? What should you need of more?
Yea, or so many, sith that both charge and danger
Speak 'gainst so great a number? How in one house
Should many people, under two commands,
Hold amity? 'Tis hard; almost impossible.
GONERIL: Why might not you, my lord, receive attendance
From those that she calls servants, or from mine?
REGAN: Why not, my lord? If then they chanc'd to slack ye,
We could control them. If you will come to me
(For now I spy a danger), I entreat you
To bring but five-and-twenty. To no more
Will I give place or notice.
LEAR: I gave you all-
REGAN: And in good time you gave it!
LEAR: Made you my guardians, my depositaries;
But kept a reservation to be followed
With such a number. What, must I come to you
With five-and-twenty, Regan? Said you so?
REGAN: And speak't again my lord. No more with me.
LEAR: Those wicked creatures yet do look well-favour'd
When others are more wicked; not being the worst
Stands in some rank of praise. To Goneril I'll go with thee.
Thy fifty yet doth double five-and-twenty,
And thou art twice her love.
GONERIL: Hear, me, my lord.
What need you five-and-twenty, ten, or five,
To follow in a house where twice so many
Have a command to tend you?
REGAN: What need one?
LEAR: O, reason not the need! Our basest beggars
Are in the poorest thing superfluous.
Allow not nature more than nature needs,
Man's life is cheap as beast's. Thou art a lady:
If only to go warm were gorgeous,
Why, nature needs not what thou gorgeous wear'st
Which scarcely keeps thee warm. But, for true need-
You heavens, give me that patience, patience I need!

You see me here, you gods, a poor old man,
As full of grief as age; wretched in both.
If it be you that stirs these daughters' hearts
Against their father, fool me not so much
To bear it tamely; touch me with noble anger,
And let not women's weapons, water drops,
Stain my man's cheeks! No, you unnatural hags!
I will have such revenges on you both
That all the world shall- I will do such things-
What they are yet, I know not; but they shall be
The terrors of the earth! You think I'll weep.
No, I'll not weep.
I have full cause of weeping, but this heart
Shall break into a hundred thousand flaws
Or ere I'll weep. O fool, I shall go mad!
Exeunt Lear, Gloucester, Kent, and Fool. Storm and Tempest.
CORNWALL: Let us withdraw; 'twill be a storm.
REGAN: This house is little; the old man and 's people
Cannot be well bestow'd.
GONERIL: 'Tis his own blame; hath put himself from rest
And must needs taste his folly.
REGAN: For his particular, I'll receive him gladly,
But not one follower.
GONERIL: So am I purpos'd.
Where is my Lord of Gloucester?
CORNWALL: Followed the old man forth.
Enter Gloucester.
He is return'd.
GLOUCESTER: The King is in high rage.
CORNWALL: Whither is he going?
GLOUCESTER: He calls to horse, but will I know not whither.
CORNWALL: 'Tis best to give him way; he leads himself.
GONERIL: My lord, entreat him by no means to stay.
GLOUCESTER: Alack, the night comes on, and the bleak winds
Do sorely ruffle. For many miles about
There's scarce a bush.
REGAN: O, sir, to wilful men
The injuries that they themselves procure
Must be their schoolmasters. Shut up your doors.
He is attended with a desperate train,
And what they may incense him to, being apt
To have his ear abus'd, wisdom bids fear.
CORNWALL: Shut up your doors, my lord: 'tis a wild night.
My Regan counsels well. Come out o' th' storm.
Exeunt.

ACT III. SCENE I. A Heath.

Storm Still. Enter Kent and a Gentleman at Several Doors.
KENT: Who's there, besides foul weather?
GENTLEMEN: One minded like the weather, most unquietly.

KENT: I know you. Where's the King?
GENTLEMEN: Contending with the fretful elements;
Bids the wind blow the earth into the sea,
Or swell the curled waters 'bove the main,
That things might change or cease; tears his white hair,
Which the impetuous blasts, with eyeless rage,
Catch in their fury and make nothing of;
Strives in his little world of man to outscorn
The to-and-fro-conflicting wind and rain.
This night, wherein the cub-drawn bear would couch,
The lion and the belly-pinched wolf
Keep their fur dry, unbonneted he runs,
And bids what will take all.
KENT: But who is with him?
GENTLEMEN: None but the fool, who labours to outjest
His heart-struck injuries.
KENT: Sir, I do know you,
And dare upon the warrant of my note
Commend a dear thing to you. There is division
(Although as yet the face of it be cover'd
With mutual cunning) 'twixt Albany and Cornwall;
Who have (as who have not, that their great stars
Thron'd and set high?) servants, who seem no less,
Which are to France the spies and speculations
Intelligent of our state. What hath been seen,
Either in snuffs and packings of the Dukes,
Or the hard rein which both of them have borne
Against the old kind King, or something deeper,
Whereof, perchance, these are but furnishings-
But, true it is, from France there comes a power
Into this scattered kingdom, who already,
Wise in our negligence, have secret feet
In some of our best ports and are at point
To show their open banner. Now to you:
If on my credit you dare build so far
To make your speed to Dover, you shall find
Some that will thank you, making just report
Of how unnatural and bemadding sorrow
The King hath cause to plain.
I am a gentleman of blood and breeding,
And from some knowledge and assurance offer
This office to you.
GENTLEMEN: I will talk further with you.
KENT: No, do not.
For confirmation that I am much more
Than my out-wall, open this purse and take
What it contains. If you shall see Cordelia
(As fear not but you shall), show her this ring,
And she will tell you who your fellow is

That yet you do not know. Fie on this storm!
I will go seek the King.
GENTLEMEN: Give me your hand. Have you no more to say?
KENT: Few words, but, to effect, more than all yet:
That, when we have found the King (in which your pain
That way, I'll this), he that first lights on him
Holla the other.
Exeunt Severally

ACT III. SCENE II. Another Part of the Heath.

Storm Still. Enter Lear and Fool.
LEAR: Blow, winds, and crack your cheeks! rage! blow!
You cataracts and hurricanoes, spout
Till you have drench'd our steeples, drown'd the cocks!
You sulph'rous and thought-executing fires,
Vaunt-couriers to oak-cleaving thunderbolts,
Singe my white head! And thou, all-shaking thunder,
Strike flat the thick rotundity o' th' world,
Crack Nature's moulds, all germains spill at once,
That makes ingrateful man!
FOOL: O nuncle, court holy water in a dry house is better than this rain water out o' door. Good nuncle, in, and ask thy daughters blessing! Here's a night pities nether wise men nor fools.
LEAR: Rumble thy bellyful! Spit, fire! spout, rain!
Nor rain, wind, thunder, fire are my daughters.
I tax not you, you elements, with unkindness.
I never gave you kingdom, call'd you children,
You owe me no subscription. Then let fall
Your horrible pleasure. Here I stand your slave,
A poor, infirm, weak, and despis'd old man.
But yet I call you servile ministers,
That will with two pernicious daughters join
Your high-engender'd battles 'gainst a head
So old and white as this! O! O! 'tis foul!
FOOL: He that has a house to put 's head in has a good head-piece.
The codpiece that will house
Before the head has any,
The head and he shall louse:
So beggars marry many.
The man that makes his toe
What he his heart should make
Shall of a corn cry woe,
And turn his sleep to wake.
For there was never yet fair woman but she made mouths in a glass.
Enter Kent.
LEAR: No, I will be the pattern of all patience;
I will say nothing.
KENT: Who's there?
FOOL: Marry, here's grace and a codpiece; that's a wise man and a
FOOL:

KENT: Alas, sir, are you here? Things that love night
Love not such nights as these. The wrathful skies
Gallow the very wanderers of the dark
And make them keep their caves. Since I was man,
Such sheets of fire, such bursts of horrid thunder,
Such groans of roaring wind and rain, I never
Remember to have heard. Man's nature cannot carry
Th' affliction nor the fear.
LEAR: Let the great gods,
That keep this dreadful pudder o'er our heads,
Find out their enemies now. Tremble, thou wretch,
That hast within thee undivulged crimes
Unwhipp'd of justice. Hide thee, thou bloody hand;
Thou perjur'd, and thou simular man of virtue
That art incestuous. Caitiff, in pieces shake
That under covert and convenient seeming
Hast practis'd on man's life. Close pent-up guilts,
Rive your concealing continents, and cry
These dreadful summoners grace. I am a man
More sinn'd against than sinning.
KENT: Alack, bareheaded?
Gracious my lord, hard by here is a hovel;
Some friendship will it lend you 'gainst the tempest.
Repose you there, whilst I to this hard house
(More harder than the stones whereof 'tis rais'd,
Which even but now, demanding after you,
Denied me to come in) return, and force
Their scanted courtesy.
LEAR: My wits begin to turn.
Come on, my boy. How dost, my boy? Art cold?
I am cold myself. Where is this straw, my fellow?
The art of our necessities is strange,
That can make vile things precious. Come, your hovel.
Poor fool and knave, I have one part in my heart
That's sorry yet for thee.
FOOL: Sings
He that has and a little tiny wit-
With hey, ho, the wind and the rain-
Must make content with his fortunes fit,
For the rain it raineth every day.
LEAR: True, my good boy. Come, bring us to this hovel.
Exeunt Lear and Kent.
FOOL: This is a brave night to cool a courtesan. I'll speak a prophecy ere I go:
When priests are more in word than matter;
When brewers mar their malt with water;
When nobles are their tailors' tutors,
No heretics burn'd, but wenches' suitors;
When every case in law is right,

No squire in debt nor no poor knight;
When slanders do not live in tongues,
Nor cutpurses come not to throngs;
When usurers tell their gold i' th' field,
And bawds and whores do churches build:
Then shall the realm of Albion
Come to great confusion.
Then comes the time, who lives to see't,
That going shall be us'd with feet.
This prophecy Merlin shall make, for I live before his time.
Exit.

ACT III. SCENE III. Gloucester's Castle.

Enter Gloucester and Edmund.
GLOUCESTER: Alack, alack, Edmund, I like not this unnatural dealing! When I desir'd their leave that I might pity him, they took from me the use of mine own house, charg'd me on pain of perpetual displeasure neither to speak of him, entreat for him, nor any way sustain him.
EDMUND: Most savage and unnatural!
GLOUCESTER: Go to; say you nothing. There is division betwixt the Dukes, and a worse matter than that. I have received a letter this night- 'tis dangerous to be spoken- I have lock'd the letter in my closet. These injuries the King now bears will be revenged home; there's part of a power already footed; we must incline to the King. I will seek him and privily relieve him. Go you and maintain talk with the Duke, that my charity be not of him perceived. If he ask for me, I am ill and gone to bed. Though I die for't, as no less is threat'ned me, the King my old master must be relieved. There is some strange thing toward, Edmund. Pray you be careful.
Exit.
EDMUND: This courtesy, forbid thee, shall the Duke
Instantly know, and of that letter too.
This seems a fair deserving, and must draw me
That which my father loses- no less than all.
The younger rises when the old doth fall.
Exit.

ACT III. SCENE IV. The Heath. Before a Hovel.

Storm still. Enter Lear, Kent, and Fool.
KENT: Here is the place, my lord. Good my lord, enter.
The tyranny of the open night 's too rough
For nature to endure.
LEAR: Let me alone.
KENT: Good my lord, enter here.
LEAR: Wilt break my heart?
KENT: I had rather break mine own. Good my lord, enter.
LEAR: Thou think'st 'tis much that this contentious storm
Invades us to the skin. So 'tis to thee;
But where the greater malady is fix'd,

The lesser is scarce felt. Thou'dst shun a bear;
But if thy flight lay toward the raging sea,
Thou'dst meet the bear i' th' mouth. When the mind's free,
The body's delicate. The tempest in my mind
Doth from my senses take all feeling else
Save what beats there. Filial ingratitude!
Is it not as this mouth should tear this hand
For lifting food to't? But I will punish home!
No, I will weep no more. In such a night
'To shut me out! Pour on; I will endure.
In such a night as this! O Regan, Goneril!
Your old kind father, whose frank heart gave all!
O, that way madness lies; let me shun that!
No more of that.
KENT: Good my lord, enter here.
LEAR: Prithee go in thyself; seek thine own ease.
This tempest will not give me leave to ponder
On things would hurt me more. But I'll go in.
To the Fool In, boy; go first.- You houseless poverty-
Nay, get thee in. I'll pray, and then I'll sleep.
Exit Fool.
Poor naked wretches, wheresoe'er you are,
That bide the pelting of this pitiless storm,
How shall your houseless heads and unfed sides,
Your loop'd and window'd raggedness, defend you
From seasons such as these? O, I have ta'en
Too little care of this! Take physic, pomp;
Expose thyself to feel what wretches feel,
That thou mayst shake the superflux to them
And show the heavens more just.
EDGAR: Within Fathom and half, fathom and half! Poor Tom!
Enter Fool From the Hovel.
FOOL: Come not in here, nuncle, here's a spirit. Help me, help me!
KENT: Give me thy hand. Who's there?
FOOL: A spirit, a spirit! He says his name's poor Tom.
KENT: What art thou that dost grumble there i' th' straw? Come forth.
Enter Edgar Disguised as a Madman.
EDGAR: Away! the foul fiend follows me! Through the sharp hawthorn
blows the cold wind. Humh! go to thy cold bed, and warm thee.
LEAR: Hast thou given all to thy two daughters, and art thou come to this?
EDGAR: Who gives anything to poor Tom? whom the foul fiend hath led
through fire and through flame, through ford and whirlpool, o'er
bog and quagmire; that hath laid knives under his pillow and
halters in his pew, set ratsbane by his porridge, made him proud
of heart, to ride on a bay trotting horse over four-inch'd
bridges, to course his own shadow for a traitor. Bless thy five
wits! Tom 's acold. O, do de, do de, do de. Bless thee from
whirlwinds, star-blasting, and taking! Do poor Tom some charity,
whom the foul fiend vexes. There could I have him now- and there-

and there again- and there!

Storm Still.

LEAR: What, have his daughters brought him to this pass?
Couldst thou save nothing? Didst thou give 'em all?

FOOL: Nay, he reserv'd a blanket, else we had been all sham'd.

LEAR: Now all the plagues that in the pendulous air
Hang fated o'er men's faults light on thy daughters!

KENT: He hath no daughters, sir.

LEAR: Death, traitor! nothing could have subdu'd nature
To such a lowness but his unkind daughters.
Is it the fashion that discarded fathers
Should have thus little mercy on their flesh?
Judicious punishment! 'Twas this flesh begot
Those pelican daughters.

EDGAR: Pillicock sat on Pillicock's Hill. 'Allow, 'allow, loo, loo!

FOOL: This cold night will turn us all to fools and madmen.

EDGAR: Take heed o' th' foul fiend; obey thy parents: keep thy word justly; swear not; commit not with man's sworn spouse; set not thy sweet heart on proud array. Tom 's acold.

LEAR: What hast thou been?

EDGAR: A servingman, proud in heart and mind; that curl'd my hair, wore gloves in my cap; serv'd the lust of my mistress' heart and did the act of darkness with her; swore as many oaths as I spake words, and broke them in the sweet face of heaven; one that slept in the contriving of lust, and wak'd to do it. Wine lov'd I deeply, dice dearly; and in woman out-paramour'd the Turk. False of heart, light of ear, bloody of hand; hog in sloth, fox in stealth, wolf in greediness, dog in madness, lion in prey. Let not the creaking of shoes nor the rustling of silks betray thy poor heart to woman. Keep thy foot out of brothel, thy hand out of placket, thy pen from lender's book, and defy the foul fiend. Still through the hawthorn blows the cold wind; says suum, mun, hey, no, nonny. Dolphin my boy, my boy, sessa! let him trot by.

Storm Still.

LEAR: Why, thou wert better in thy grave than to answer with thy uncover'd body this extremity of the skies. Is man no more than this? Consider him well. Thou ow'st the worm no silk, the beast no hide, the sheep no wool, the cat no perfume. Ha! Here's three on's are sophisticated! Thou art the thing itself; unaccommodated man is no more but such a poor, bare, forked animal as thou art. Off, off, you lendings! Come, unbutton here.

Tears at His Clothes.

FOOL: Prithee, nuncle, be contented! 'Tis a naughty night to swim in. Now a little fire in a wild field were like an old lecher's heart- a small spark, all the rest on's body cold. Look, here comes a walking fire.

Enter Gloucester with a Torch.

EDGAR: This is the foul fiend Flibbertigibbet.

He begins at curfew, and walks till the first cock.
He gives the web and the pin, squints the eye,
and makes the harelip; mildews the white wheat,
and hurts the poor creature of earth.
Saint Withold footed thrice the 'old;
He met the nightmare, and her nine fold;
Bid her alight
And her troth plight,
And aroint thee, witch, aroint thee!
KENT: How fares your Grace?
LEAR: What's he?
KENT: Who's there? What is't you seek?
GLOUCESTER: What are you there? Your names?
EDGAR: Poor Tom, that eats the swimming frog, the toad, the todpole, the wall-newt and the water; that in the fury of his heart, when the foul fiend rages, eats cow-dung for sallets, swallows the old rat and the ditch-dog, drinks the green mantle of the standing pool; who is whipp'd from tithing to tithing, and stock-punish'd and imprison'd; who hath had three suits to his back, six shirts to his body, horse to ride, and weapons to wear;
But mice and rats, and such small deer,
Have been Tom's food for seven long year.
Beware my follower. Peace, Smulkin! peace, thou fiend!
GLOUCESTER: What, hath your Grace no better company?
EDGAR: The prince of darkness is a gentleman!
Modo he's call'd, and Mahu.
GLOUCESTER: Our flesh and blood is grown so vile, my lord,
That it doth hate what gets it.
EDGAR: Poor Tom 's acold.
GLOUCESTER: Go in with me. My duty cannot suffer
T' obey in all your daughters' hard commands.
Though their injunction be to bar my doors
And let this tyrannous night take hold upon you,
Yet have I ventur'd to come seek you out
And bring you where both fire and food is ready.
LEAR: First let me talk with this philosopher.
What is the cause of thunder?
KENT: Good my lord, take his offer; go into th' house.
LEAR: I'll talk a word with this same learned Theban.
What is your study?
EDGAR: How to prevent the fiend and to kill vermin.
LEAR: Let me ask you one word in private.
KENT: Importune him once more to go, my lord.
His wits begin t' unsettle.
GLOUCESTER: Canst thou blame him?
Storm Still.
His daughters seek his death. Ah, that good Kent!
He said it would be thus- poor banish'd man!

Thou say'st the King grows mad: I'll tell thee, friend,
I am almost mad myself. I had a son,
Now outlaw'd from my blood. He sought my life
But lately, very late. I lov'd him, friend-
No father his son dearer. True to tell thee,
The grief hath craz'd my wits. What a night 's this!
I do beseech your Grace-
LEAR: O, cry you mercy, sir.
Noble philosopher, your company.
EDGAR: Tom's acold.
GLOUCESTER: In, fellow, there, into th' hovel; keep thee warm.
LEAR: Come, let's in all.
KENT: This way, my lord.
LEAR: With him!
I will keep still with my philosopher.
KENT: Good my lord, soothe him; let him take the fellow.
GLOUCESTER: Take him you on.
KENT: Sirrah, come on; go along with us.
LEAR: Come, good Athenian.
GLOUCESTER: No words, no words! hush.
EDGAR: Child Rowland to the dark tower came;
His word was still
Fie, foh, and fum!
I smell the blood of a British man.
Exeunt.

ACT III. SCENE V. Gloucester's Castle.

Enter Cornwall and Edmund.
CORNWALL: I will have my revenge ere I depart his house.
EDMUND: How, my lord, I may be censured, that nature thus gives way to loyalty, something fears me to think of.
CORNWALL: I now perceive it was not altogether your brother's evil disposition made him seek his death; but a provoking merit, set awork by a reproveable badness in himself.
EDMUND: How malicious is my fortune that I must repent to be just! This is the letter he spoke of, which approves him an intelligent party to the advantages of France. O heavens! that this treason were not- or not I the detector!
CORNWALL: Go with me to the Duchess.
EDMUND: If the matter of this paper be certain, you have mighty business in hand.
CORNWALL: True or false, it hath made thee Earl of Gloucester. Seek out where thy father is, that he may be ready for our apprehension.
EDMUND: Aside If I find him comforting the King, it will stuff his suspicion more fully.- I will persever in my course of loyalty, though the conflict be sore between that and my blood.
CORNWALL: I will lay trust upon thee, and thou shalt find a dearer father in my love.
Exeunt.

ACT III. SCENE VI. A Farmhouse near Gloucester's Castle.

Enter Gloucester, Lear, Kent, Fool, and Edgar.

GLOUCESTER: Here is better than the open air; take it thankfully. I will piece out the comfort with what addition I can. I will not be long from you.

KENT: All the power of his wits have given way to his impatience. The gods reward your kindness!

Exit Gloucester.

EDGAR: Frateretto calls me, and tells me Nero is an angler in the lake of darkness. Pray, innocent, and beware the foul fiend.

FOOL: Prithee, nuncle, tell me whether a madman be a gentleman or a yeoman.

LEAR: A king, a king!

FOOL: No, he's a yeoman that has a gentleman to his son; for he's a mad yeoman that sees his son a gentleman before him.

LEAR: To have a thousand with red burning spits
Come hizzing in upon 'em-

EDGAR: The foul fiend bites my back.

FOOL: He's mad that trusts in the tameness of a wolf, a horse's health, a boy's love, or a whore's oath.

LEAR: It shall be done; I will arraign them straight.
To Edgar Come, sit thou here, most learned justicer.
To the Fool Thou, sapient sir, sit here. Now, you she-foxes!

EDGAR: Look, where he stands and glares! Want'st thou eyes at trial, madam?
Come o'er the bourn, Bessy, to me.

FOOL: Her boat hath a leak,
And she must not speak
Why she dares not come over to thee.

EDGAR: The foul fiend haunts poor Tom in the voice of a nightingale. Hoppedance cries in Tom's belly for two white herring. Croak not, black angel; I have no food for thee.

KENT: How do you, sir? Stand you not so amaz'd.
Will you lie down and rest upon the cushions?

LEAR: I'll see their trial first. Bring in their evidence.
To Edgar Thou, robed man of justice, take thy place.
To the Fool And thou, his yokefellow of equity,
Bench by his side.
To Kent You are o' th' commission, sit you too.

EDGAR: Let us deal justly.
Sleepest or wakest thou, jolly shepherd?
Thy sheep be in the corn;
And for one blast of thy minikin mouth
Thy sheep shall take no harm.
Purr! the cat is gray.

LEAR: Arraign her first. 'Tis Goneril. I here take my oath before this honourable assembly, she kicked the poor King her father.

FOOL: Come hither, mistress. Is your name Goneril?

LEAR: She cannot deny it.

FOOL: Cry you mercy, I took you for a joint-stool.
LEAR: And here's another, whose warp'd looks proclaim
What store her heart is made on. Stop her there!
Arms, arms! sword! fire! Corruption in the place!
False justicer, why hast thou let her scape?
EDGAR: Bless thy five wits!
KENT: O pity! Sir, where is the patience now
That you so oft have boasted to retain?
EDGAR: Aside My tears begin to take his part so much
They'll mar my counterfeiting.
LEAR: The little dogs and all,
Tray, Blanch, and Sweetheart, see, they bark at me.
EDGAR: Tom will throw his head at them. Avaunt, you curs!
Be thy mouth or black or white,
Tooth that poisons if it bite;
Mastiff, greyhound, mongrel grim,
Hound or spaniel, brach or lym,
Bobtail tyke or trundle-tall-
Tom will make them weep and wail;
For, with throwing thus my head,
Dogs leap the hatch, and all are fled.
Do de, de, de. Sessa! Come, march to wakes and fairs and market towns. Poor Tom, thy horn is dry.
LEAR: Then let them anatomize Regan. See what breeds about her heart. Is there any cause in nature that makes these hard hearts? To Edgar You, sir- I entertain you for one of my hundred; only I do not like the fashion of your garments. You'll say they are Persian attire; but let them be chang'd.
KENT: Now, good my lord, lie here and rest awhile.
LEAR: Make no noise, make no noise; draw the curtains.
So, so, so. We'll go to supper i' th' morning. So, so, so.
FOOL: And I'll go to bed at noon.
Enter Gloucester.
GLOUCESTER: Come hither, friend. Where is the King my master?
KENT: Here, sir; but trouble him not; his wits are gone.
GLOUCESTER: Good friend, I prithee take him in thy arms.
I have o'erheard a plot of death upon him.
There is a litter ready; lay him in't
And drive towards Dover, friend, where thou shalt meet
Both welcome and protection. Take up thy master.
If thou shouldst dally half an hour, his life,
With thine, and all that offer to defend him,
Stand in assured loss. Take up, take up!
And follow me, that will to some provision
Give thee quick conduct.
KENT: Oppressed nature sleeps.
This rest might yet have balm'd thy broken senses,
Which, if convenience will not allow,
Stand in hard cure.

To the Fool Come, help to bear thy master.
Thou must not stay behind.
GLOUCESTER: Come, come, away!
Exeunt all but Edgar.
EDGAR: When we our betters see bearing our woes,
We scarcely think our miseries our foes.
Who alone suffers suffers most i' th' mind,
Leaving free things and happy shows behind;
But then the mind much sufferance doth o'erskip
When grief hath mates, and bearing fellowship.
How light and portable my pain seems now,
When that which makes me bend makes the King bow,
He childed as I fathered! Tom, away!
Mark the high noises, and thyself bewray
When false opinion, whose wrong thought defiles thee,
In thy just proof repeals and reconciles thee.
What will hap more to-night, safe scape the King!
Lurk, lurk.
Exit.

ACT III. SCENE VII. Gloucester's Castle.

Enter Cornwall, Regan, Goneril, Edmund The Bastard, and Servants.
CORNWALL: To Goneril Post speedily to my lord your husband, show him this letter. The army of France is landed.- Seek out the traitor
GLOUCESTER:
Exeunt some of the Servants.
REGAN: Hang him instantly.
GONERIL: Pluck out his eyes.
CORNWALL: Leave him to my displeasure. Edmund, keep you our sister company. The revenges we are bound to take upon your traitorous father are not fit for your beholding. Advise the Duke where you are going, to a most festinate preparation. We are bound to the like. Our posts shall be swift and intelligent betwixt us.
Farewell, dear sister; farewell, my Lord of Gloucester.
Enter Oswald the Steward.
How now? Where's the King?
OSWALD: My Lord of Gloucester hath convey'd him hence.
Some five or six and thirty of his knights,
Hot questrists after him, met him at gate;
Who, with some other of the lord's dependants,
Are gone with him towards Dover, where they boast
To have well-armed friends.
CORNWALL: Get horses for your mistress.
GONERIL: Farewell, sweet lord, and sister.
CORNWALL: Edmund, farewell.
Exeunt Goneril, Edmund, and Oswald.
Go seek the traitor Gloucester,
Pinion him like a thief, bring him before us.
Exeunt other Servants.
Though well we may not pass upon his life

Without the form of justice, yet our power
Shall do a court'sy to our wrath, which men
May blame, but not control.
Enter Gloucester, Brought in by Two or Three.
Who's there? the traitor?
REGAN: Ingrateful fox! 'tis he.
CORNWALL: Bind fast his corky arms.
GLOUCESTER: What mean, your Graces? Good my friends, consider
You are my guests. Do me no foul play, friends.
CORNWALL: Bind him, I say.
Servants Bind Him.
REGAN: Hard, hard. O filthy traitor!
GLOUCESTER: Unmerciful lady as you are, I am none.
CORNWALL: To this chair bind him. Villain, thou shalt find-
Regan Plucks His Beard.
GLOUCESTER: By the kind gods, 'tis most ignobly done
To pluck me by the beard.
REGAN: So white, and such a traitor!
GLOUCESTER: Naughty lady,
These hairs which thou dost ravish from my chin
Will quicken, and accuse thee. I am your host.
With robber's hands my hospitable favours
You should not ruffle thus. What will you do?
CORNWALL: Come, sir, what letters had you late from France?
REGAN: Be simple-answer'd, for we know the truth.
CORNWALL: And what confederacy have you with the traitors
Late footed in the kingdom?
REGAN: To whose hands have you sent the lunatic King?
Speak.
GLOUCESTER: I have a letter guessingly set down,
Which came from one that's of a neutral heart,
And not from one oppos'd.
CORNWALL: Cunning.
REGAN: And false.
CORNWALL: Where hast thou sent the King?
GLOUCESTER: To Dover.
REGAN: Wherefore to Dover? Wast thou not charg'd at peril-
CORNWALL: Wherefore to Dover? Let him first answer that.
GLOUCESTER: I am tied to th' stake, and I must stand the course.
REGAN: Wherefore to Dover, sir?
GLOUCESTER: Because I would not see thy cruel nails
Pluck out his poor old eyes; nor thy fierce sister
In his anointed flesh stick boarish fangs.
The sea, with such a storm as his bare head
In hell-black night endur'd, would have buoy'd up
And quench'd the steeled fires.
Yet, poor old heart, he holp the heavens to rain.
If wolves had at thy gate howl'd that stern time,
Thou shouldst have said, 'Good porter, turn the key.'

All cruels else subscrib'd. But I shall see
The winged vengeance overtake such children.
CORNWALL: See't shalt thou never. Fellows, hold the chair.
Upon these eyes of thine I'll set my foot.
GLOUCESTER: He that will think to live till he be old,
Give me some help!- O cruel! O ye gods!
REGAN: One side will mock another. Th' other too!
CORNWALL: If you see vengeance-
FIRST SERVANT: Hold your hand, my lord!
I have serv'd you ever since I was a child;
But better service have I never done you
Than now to bid you hold.
REGAN: How now, you dog?
FIRST SERVANT: If you did wear a beard upon your chin,
I'ld shake it on this quarrel.
REGAN: What do you mean?
CORNWALL: My villain! Draw and fight.
FIRST SERVANT: Nay, then, come on, and take the chance of anger.
REGAN: Give me thy sword. A peasant stand up thus?
She Takes a Sword and Runs at Him Behind.
FIRST SERVANT: O, I am slain! My lord, you have one eye left
To see some mischief on him. O! He dies.
CORNWALL: Lest it see more, prevent it. Out, vile jelly!
Where is thy lustre now?
GLOUCESTER: All dark and comfortless! Where's my son Edmund?
Edmund, enkindle all the sparks of nature
To quit this horrid act.
REGAN: Out, treacherous villain!
Thou call'st on him that hates thee. It was he
That made the overture of thy treasons to us;
Who is too good to pity thee.
GLOUCESTER: O my follies! Then Edgar was abus'd.
Kind gods, forgive me that, and prosper him!
REGAN: Go thrust him out at gates, and let him smell
His way to Dover.
Exit one with Gloucester.
How is't, my lord? How look you?
CORNWALL: I have receiv'd a hurt. Follow me, lady.
Turn out that eyeless villain. Throw this slave
Upon the dunghill. Regan, I bleed apace.
Untimely comes this hurt. Give me your arm.
Exit Cornwall, led by Regan.
SECOND SERVANT: I'll never care what wickedness I do,
If this man come to good.
THIRD SERVANT: If she live long,
And in the end meet the old course of death,
Women will all turn monsters.
SECOND SERVANT: Let's follow the old Earl, and get the bedlam
To lead him where he would. His roguish madness

Allows itself to anything.
THIRD SERVANT: Go thou. I'll fetch some flax and whites of eggs
To apply to his bleeding face. Now heaven help him!
Exeunt.

ACT IV. SCENE I. The Heath.

Enter Edgar.
EDGAR: Yet better thus, and known to be contemn'd,
Than still contemn'd and flatter'd. To be worst,
The lowest and most dejected thing of fortune,
Stands still in esperance, lives not in fear.
The lamentable change is from the best;
The worst returns to laughter. Welcome then,
Thou unsubstantial air that I embrace!
The wretch that thou hast blown unto the worst
Owes nothing to thy blasts.
Enter Gloucester, Led by an Old Man.
But who comes here?
My father, poorly led? World, world, O world!
But that thy strange mutations make us hate thee,
Life would not yield to age.
OLD MAN: O my good lord,
I have been your tenant, and your father's tenant,
These fourscore years.
GLOUCESTER: Away, get thee away! Good friend, be gone.
Thy comforts can do me no good at all;
Thee they may hurt.
OLD MAN:: You cannot see your way.
GLOUCESTER: I have no way, and therefore want no eyes;
I stumbled when I saw. Full oft 'tis seen
Our means secure us, and our mere defects
Prove our commodities. Ah dear son Edgar,
The food of thy abused father's wrath!
Might I but live to see thee in my touch,
I'ld say I had eyes again!
OLD MAN: How now? Who's there?
EDGAR: Aside O gods! Who is't can say 'I am at the worst'?
I am worse than e'er I was.
OLD MAN: 'Tis poor mad Tom.
EDGAR: Aside And worse I may be yet. The worst is not
So long as we can say 'This is the worst.'
OLD MAN: Fellow, where goest?
GLOUCESTER: Is it a beggarman?
OLD MAN: Madman and beggar too.
GLOUCESTER: He has some reason, else he could not beg.
I' th' last night's storm I such a fellow saw,
Which made me think a man a worm. My son
Came then into my mind, and yet my mind
Was then scarce friends with him. I have heard more since.
As flies to wanton boys are we to th' gods.

They kill us for their sport.
EDGAR: Aside How should this be?
Bad is the trade that must play fool to sorrow,
Ang'ring itself and others.- Bless thee, master!
GLOUCESTER: Is that the naked fellow?
OLD MAN: Ay, my lord.
GLOUCESTER: Then prithee get thee gone. If for my sake
Thou wilt o'ertake us hence a mile or twain
I' th' way toward Dover, do it for ancient love;
And bring some covering for this naked soul,
Who I'll entreat to lead me.
OLD MAN: Alack, sir, he is mad!
GLOUCESTER: 'Tis the time's plague when madmen lead the blind.
Do as I bid thee, or rather do thy pleasure.
Above the rest, be gone.
OLD MAN: I'll bring him the best 'parel that I have,
Come on't what will.
Exit.
GLOUCESTER: Sirrah naked fellow-
EDGAR: Poor Tom's acold. Aside I cannot daub it further.
GLOUCESTER: Come hither, fellow.
EDGAR: Aside And yet I must.- Bless thy sweet eyes, they bleed.
GLOUCESTER: Know'st thou the way to Dover?
EDGAR: Both stile and gate, horseway and footpath. Poor Tom hath been scar'd out of his good wits. Bless thee, good man's son, from the foul fiend! Five fiends have been in poor Tom at once: of lust, as Obidicut; Hobbididence, prince of dumbness; Mahu, of stealing; Modo, of murder; Flibbertigibbet, of mopping and mowing, who since possesses chambermaids and waiting women. So, bless thee, master!
GLOUCESTER: Here, take this Purse, thou whom the heavens' plagues
Have humbled to all strokes. That I am wretched
Makes thee the happier. Heavens, deal so still!
Let the superfluous and lust-dieted man,
That slaves your ordinance, that will not see
Because he does not feel, feel your pow'r quickly;
So distribution should undo excess,
And each man have enough. Dost thou know Dover?
EDGAR: Ay, master.
GLOUCESTER: There is a cliff, whose high and bending head
Looks fearfully in the confined deep.
Bring me but to the very brim of it,
And I'll repair the misery thou dost bear
With something rich about me. From that place
I shall no leading need.
EDGAR: Give me thy arm.
Poor Tom shall lead thee.
Exeunt.

ACT IV. SCENE II. Before the Duke of Albany's Palace.

Enter Goneril and Edmund The Bastard.

GONERIL: Welcome, my lord. I marvel our mild husband
Not met us on the way.

Enter Oswald The Steward.

Now, where's your master?

OSWALD: Madam, within, but never man so chang'd.
I told him of the army that was landed:
He smil'd at it. I told him you were coming:
His answer was, 'The worse.' Of Gloucester's treachery
And of the loyal service of his son
When I inform'd him, then he call'd me sot
And told me I had turn'd the wrong side out.
What most he should dislike seems pleasant to him;
What like, offensive.

GONERIL: To Edmund Then shall you go no further.
It is the cowish terror of his spirit,
That dares not undertake. He'll not feel wrongs
Which tie him to an answer. Our wishes on the way
May prove effects. Back, Edmund, to my brother.
Hasten his musters and conduct his pow'rs.
I must change arms at home and give the distaff
Into my husband's hands. This trusty servant
Shall pass between us. Ere long you are like to hear
(If you dare venture in your own behalf)
A mistress's command. Wear this. Gives a Favour.
Spare speech.
Decline your head. This kiss, if it durst speak,
Would stretch thy spirits up into the air.
Conceive, and fare thee well.

EDMUND: Yours in the ranks of death!

Exit.

GONERIL: My most dear Gloucester!
O, the difference of man and man!
To thee a woman's services are due;
My fool usurps my body.

OSWALD: Madam, here comes my lord.

Exit.

Enter Albany.

GONERIL: I have been worth the whistle.

ALBANY: O Goneril,
You are not worth the dust which the rude wind
Blows in your face! I fear your disposition.
That nature which contemns it origin
Cannot be bordered certain in itself.
She that herself will sliver and disbranch
From her material sap, perforce must wither
And come to deadly use.

GONERIL: No more! The text is foolish.

ALBANY: Wisdom and goodness to the vile seem vile;
Filths savour but themselves. What have you done?
Tigers, not daughters, what have you perform'd?
A father, and a gracious aged man,
Whose reverence even the head-lugg'd bear would lick,
Most barbarous, most degenerate, have you madded.
Could my good brother suffer you to do it?
A man, a prince, by him so benefited!
If that the heavens do not their visible spirits
Send quickly down to tame these vile offences,
It will come,
Humanity must perforce prey on itself,
Like monsters of the deep.
GONERIL: Milk-liver'd man!
That bear'st a cheek for blows, a head for wrongs;
Who hast not in thy brows an eye discerning
Thine honour from thy suffering; that not know'st
Fools do those villains pity who are punish'd
Ere they have done their mischief. Where's thy drum?
France spreads his banners in our noiseless land,
With plumed helm thy state begins to threat,
Whiles thou, a moral fool, sit'st still, and criest
'Alack, why does he so?'
ALBANY: See thyself, devil!
Proper deformity seems not in the fiend
So horrid as in woman.
GONERIL: O vain fool!
ALBANY: Thou changed and self-cover'd thing, for shame!
Bemonster not thy feature! Were't my fitness
To let these hands obey my blood,
They are apt enough to dislocate and tear
Thy flesh and bones. Howe'er thou art a fiend,
A woman's shape doth shield thee.
GONERIL: Marry, your manhood mew!
Enter a Gentleman.
ALBANY: What news?
GENTLEMEN: O, my good lord, the Duke of Cornwall 's dead,
Slain by his servant, going to put out
The other eye of Gloucester.
ALBANY: Gloucester's eyes?
GENTLEMEN: A servant that he bred, thrill'd with remorse,
Oppos'd against the act, bending his sword
To his great master; who, thereat enrag'd,
Flew on him, and amongst them fell'd him dead;
But not without that harmful stroke which since
Hath pluck'd him after.
ALBANY: This shows you are above,
You justicers, that these our nether crimes
So speedily can venge! But O poor Gloucester!

Lose he his other eye?
GENTLEMEN: Both, both, my lord.
This letter, madam, craves a speedy answer.
'Tis from your sister.
GONERIL: Aside One way I like this well;
But being widow, and my Gloucester with her,
May all the building in my fancy pluck
Upon my hateful life. Another way
The news is not so tart.- I'll read, and answer.
Exit.
ALBANY: Where was his son when they did take his eyes?
GENTLEMEN: Come with my lady hither.
ALBANY: He is not here.
GENTLEMEN: No, my good lord; I met him back again.
ALBANY: Knows he the wickedness?
GENTLEMEN: Ay, my good lord. 'Twas he inform'd against him,
And quit the house on purpose, that their punishment
Might have the freer course.
ALBANY: Gloucester, I live
To thank thee for the love thou show'dst the King,
And to revenge thine eyes. Come hither, friend.
Tell me what more thou know'st.
Exeunt.

ACT IV. SCENE III. The French Camp near Dover.

Enter Kent and a Gentleman.
KENT: Why the King of France is so suddenly gone back know you the reason?
GENTLEMEN: Something he left imperfect in the state, which since his coming forth is thought of, which imports to the kingdom so much fear and danger that his personal return was most required and necessary.
KENT: Who hath he left behind him general?
GENTLEMEN: The Marshal of France, Monsieur La Far.
KENT: Did your letters pierce the Queen to any demonstration of grief?
GENTLEMEN: Ay, sir. She took them, read them in my presence,
And now and then an ample tear trill'd down
Her delicate cheek. It seem'd she was a queen
Over her passion, who, most rebel-like,
Sought to be king o'er her.
KENT: O, then it mov'd her?
GENTLEMEN: Not to a rage. Patience and sorrow strove
Who should express her goodliest. You have seen
Sunshine and rain at once: her smiles and tears
Were like, a better way. Those happy smilets
That play'd on her ripe lip seem'd not to know
What guests were in her eyes, which parted thence
As pearls from diamonds dropp'd. In brief,
Sorrow would be a rarity most belov'd,
If all could so become it.

KENT: Made she no verbal question?
GENTLEMEN: Faith, once or twice she heav'd the name of father
Pantingly forth, as if it press'd her heart;
Cried 'Sisters, sisters! Shame of ladies! Sisters!
Kent! father! sisters! What, i' th' storm? i' th' night?
Let pity not be believ'd!' There she shook
The holy water from her heavenly eyes,
And clamour moisten'd. Then away she started
To deal with grief alone.
KENT: It is the stars,
The stars above us, govern our conditions;
Else one self mate and mate could not beget
Such different issues. You spoke not with her since?
GENTLEMEN: No.
KENT: Was this before the King return'd?
GENTLEMEN: No, since.
KENT: Well, sir, the poor distressed Lear's i' th' town;
Who sometime, in his better tune, remembers
What we are come about, and by no means
Will yield to see his daughter.
GENTLEMEN: Why, good sir?
KENT: A sovereign shame so elbows him; his own unkindness,
That stripp'd her from his benediction, turn'd her
To foreign casualties, gave her dear rights
To his dog-hearted daughters- these things sting
His mind so venomously that burning shame
Detains him from Cordelia.
GENTLEMEN: Alack, poor gentleman!
KENT: Of Albany's and Cornwall's powers you heard not?
GENTLEMEN: 'Tis so; they are afoot.
KENT: Well, sir, I'll bring you to our master Lear
And leave you to attend him. Some dear cause
Will in concealment wrap me up awhile.
When I am known aright, you shall not grieve
Lending me this acquaintance. I pray you go
Along with me.
Exeunt.

ACT IV. SCENE IV. The French Camp.

Enter, with Drum and Colours, Cordelia, Doctor, and Soldiers.
CORDELIA: Alack, 'tis he! Why, he was met even now
As mad as the vex'd sea, singing aloud,
Crown'd with rank fumiter and furrow weeds,
With hardocks, hemlock, nettles, cuckoo flow'rs,
Darnel, and all the idle weeds that grow
In our sustaining corn. A century send forth.
Search every acre in the high-grown field
And bring him to our eye.
Exit an Officer.
What can man's wisdom

In the restoring his bereaved sense?
He that helps him take all my outward worth.
DOCTOR: There is means, madam.
Our foster nurse of nature is repose,
The which he lacks. That to provoke in him
Are many simples operative, whose power
Will close the eye of anguish.
CORDELIA: All blest secrets,
All you unpublish'd virtues of the earth,
Spring with my tears! be aidant and remediate
In the good man's distress! Seek, seek for him!
Lest his ungovern'd rage dissolve the life
That wants the means to lead it.
Enter Messenger.
MESSENGER: News, madam.
The British pow'rs are marching hitherward.
CORDELIA: 'Tis known before. Our preparation stands
In expectation of them. O dear father,
It is thy business that I go about.
Therefore great France
My mourning and important tears hath pitied.
No blown ambition doth our arms incite,
But love, dear love, and our ag'd father's right.
Soon may I hear and see him!
Exeunt.

ACT IV. SCENE V. Gloucester's Castle.

Enter Regan and Oswald The Steward.
REGAN: But are my brother's pow'rs set forth?
OSWALD: Ay, madam.
REGAN: Himself in person there?
OSWALD: Madam, with much ado.
Your sister is the better soldier.
REGAN: Lord Edmund spake not with your lord at home?
OSWALD: No, madam.
REGAN: What might import my sister's letter to him?
OSWALD: I know not, lady.
REGAN: Faith, he is posted hence on serious matter.
It was great ignorance, Gloucester's eyes being out,
To let him live. Where he arrives he moves
All hearts against us. Edmund, I think, is gone,
In pity of his misery, to dispatch
His nighted life; moreover, to descry
The strength o' th' enemy.
OSWALD: I must needs after him, madam, with my letter.
REGAN: Our troops set forth to-morrow. Stay with us.
The ways are dangerous.
OSWALD: I may not, madam.
My lady charg'd my duty in this business.
REGAN: Why should she write to Edmund? Might not you

Transport her purposes by word? Belike,
Something- I know not what- I'll love thee much-
Let me unseal the letter.
OSWALD: Madam, I had rather-
REGAN: I know your lady does not love her husband;
I am sure of that; and at her late being here
She gave strange eliads and most speaking looks
To noble Edmund. I know you are of her bosom.
OSWALD: I, madam?
REGAN: I speak in understanding. Y'are! I know't.
Therefore I do advise you take this note.
My lord is dead; Edmund and I have talk'd,
And more convenient is he for my hand
Than for your lady's. You may gather more.
If you do find him, pray you give him this;
And when your mistress hears thus much from you,
I pray desire her call her wisdom to her.
So farewell.
If you do chance to hear of that blind traitor,
Preferment falls on him that cuts him off.
OSWALD: Would I could meet him, madam! I should show
What party I do follow.
REGAN: Fare thee well.
Exeunt.

ACT IV. SCENE VI. The Country near Dover.

Enter Gloucester, and Edgar Like a Peasant.
GLOUCESTER: When shall I come to th' top of that same hill?
EDGAR: You do climb up it now. Look how we labour.
GLOUCESTER: Methinks the ground is even.
EDGAR: Horrible steep.
Hark, do you hear the sea?
GLOUCESTER: No, truly.
EDGAR: Why, then, your other senses grow imperfect
By your eyes' anguish.
GLOUCESTER: So may it be indeed.
Methinks thy voice is alter'd, and thou speak'st
In better phrase and matter than thou didst.
EDGAR: Y'are much deceiv'd. In nothing am I chang'd
But in my garments.
GLOUCESTER: Methinks y'are better spoken.
EDGAR: Come on, sir; here's the place. Stand still. How fearful
And dizzy 'tis to cast one's eyes so low!
The crows and choughs that wing the midway air
Show scarce so gross as beetles. Halfway down
Hangs one that gathers sampire- dreadful trade!
Methinks he seems no bigger than his head.
The fishermen that walk upon the beach
Appear like mice; and yond tall anchoring bark,
Diminish'd to her cock; her cock, a buoy

Almost too small for sight. The murmuring surge
That on th' unnumb'red idle pebble chafes
Cannot be heard so high. I'll look no more,
Lest my brain turn, and the deficient sight
Topple down headlong.
GLOUCESTER: Set me where you stand.
EDGAR: Give me your hand. You are now within a foot
Of th' extreme verge. For all beneath the moon
Would I not leap upright.
GLOUCESTER: Let go my hand.
Here, friend, is another purse; in it a jewel
Well worth a poor man's taking. Fairies and gods
Prosper it with thee! Go thou further off;
Bid me farewell, and let me hear thee going.
EDGAR: Now fare ye well, good sir.
GLOUCESTER: With all my heart.
EDGAR: Aside. Why I do trifle thus with his despair
Is done to cure it.
GLOUCESTER: O you mighty gods! He kneels.
This world I do renounce, and, in your sights,
Shake patiently my great affliction off.
If I could bear it longer and not fall
To quarrel with your great opposeless wills,
My snuff and loathed part of nature should
Burn itself out. If Edgar live, O, bless him!
Now, fellow, fare thee well.
He Falls Forward and Swoons.
EDGAR: Gone, sir, farewell.-
And yet I know not how conceit may rob
The treasury of life when life itself
Yields to the theft. Had he been where he thought,
By this had thought been past.- Alive or dead?
Ho you, sir! friend! Hear you, sir? Speak!-
Thus might he pass indeed. Yet he revives.
What are you, sir?
GLOUCESTER: Away, and let me die.
EDGAR: Hadst thou been aught but gossamer, feathers, air,
So many fadom down precipitating,
Thou'dst shiver'd like an egg; but thou dost breathe;
Hast heavy substance; bleed'st not; speak'st; art sound.
Ten masts at each make not the altitude
Which thou hast perpendicularly fell.
Thy life is a miracle. Speak yet again.
GLOUCESTER: But have I fall'n, or no?
EDGAR: From the dread summit of this chalky bourn.
Look up a-height. The shrill-gorg'd lark so far
Cannot be seen or heard. Do but look up.
GLOUCESTER: Alack, I have no eyes!
Is wretchedness depriv'd that benefit

To end itself by death? 'Twas yet some comfort
When misery could beguile the tyrant's rage
And frustrate his proud will.
EDGAR: Give me your arm.
Up- so. How is't? Feel you your legs? You stand.
GLOUCESTER: Too well, too well.
EDGAR: This is above all strangeness.
Upon the crown o' th' cliff what thing was that
Which parted from you?
GLOUCESTER: A poor unfortunate beggar.
EDGAR: As I stood here below, methought his eyes
Were two full moons; he had a thousand noses,
Horns whelk'd and wav'd like the enridged sea.
It was some fiend. Therefore, thou happy father,
Think that the clearest gods, who make them honours
Of men's impossibility, have preserv'd thee.
GLOUCESTER: I do remember now. Henceforth I'll bear
Affliction till it do cry out itself
'Enough, enough,' and die. That thing you speak of,
I took it for a man. Often 'twould say
'The fiend, the fiend'- he led me to that place.
EDGAR: Bear free and patient thoughts.
Enter Lear, Mad, Fantastically Dressed with Weeds.
But who comes here?
The safer sense will ne'er accommodate
His master thus.
LEAR: No, they cannot touch me for coming;
I am the King himself.
EDGAR: O thou side-piercing sight!
LEAR: Nature 's above art in that respect. There's your press money. That fellow handles his bow like a crow-keeper. Draw me a clothier's yard. Look, look, a mouse! Peace, peace; this piece of toasted cheese will do't. There's my gauntlet; I'll prove it on a giant. Bring up the brown bills. O, well flown, bird! i' th' clout, i' th' clout! Hewgh! Give the word.
EDGAR: Sweet marjoram.
LEAR: Pass.
GLOUCESTER: I know that voice.
LEAR: Ha! Goneril with a white beard? They flatter'd me like a dog, and told me I had white hairs in my beard ere the black ones were there. To say 'ay' and 'no' to everything I said! 'Ay' and 'no' too was no good divinity. When the rain came to wet me once, and the wind to make me chatter; when the thunder would not peace at my bidding; there I found 'em, there I smelt 'em out. Go to, they are not men o' their words! They told me I was everything. 'Tis a lie- I am not ague-proof.
GLOUCESTER: The trick of that voice I do well remember.
Is't not the King?
LEAR: Ay, every inch a king!

When I do stare, see how the subject quakes.
I pardon that man's life. What was thy cause? Adultery?
Thou shalt not die. Die for adultery? No.
The wren goes to't, and the small gilded fly
Does lecher in my sight.
Let copulation thrive; for Gloucester's bastard son
Was kinder to his father than my daughters
Got 'tween the lawful sheets.
To't, luxury, pell-mell! for I lack soldiers.
Behold yond simp'ring dame,
Whose face between her forks presageth snow,
That minces virtue, and does shake the head
To hear of pleasure's name.
The fitchew nor the soiled horse goes to't
With a more riotous appetite.
Down from the waist they are Centaurs,
Though women all above.
But to the girdle do the gods inherit,
Beneath is all the fiend's.
There's hell, there's darkness, there's the sulphurous pit;
burning, scalding, stench, consumption. Fie, fie, fie! pah, pah!
Give me an ounce of civet, good apothecary, to sweeten my
imagination. There's money for thee.
GLOUCESTER: O, let me kiss that hand!
LEAR: Let me wipe it first; it smells of mortality.
GLOUCESTER: O ruin'd piece of nature! This great world
Shall so wear out to naught. Dost thou know me?
LEAR: I remember thine eyes well enough. Dost thou squiny at me?
No, do thy worst, blind Cupid! I'll not love. Read thou this
challenge; mark but the penning of it.
GLOUCESTER: Were all the letters suns, I could not see one.
EDGAR: Aside I would not take this from report. It is,
And my heart breaks at it.
LEAR: Read.
GLOUCESTER: What, with the case of eyes?
LEAR: O, ho, are you there with me? No eyes in your head, nor no
money in your purse? Your eyes are in a heavy case, your purse
in a light. Yet you see how this world goes.
GLOUCESTER: I see it feelingly.
LEAR: What, art mad? A man may see how the world goes with no eyes.
Look with thine ears. See how yond justice rails upon yond
simple thief. Hark in thine ear. Change places and, handy-dandy,
which is the justice, which is the thief? Thou hast seen a
farmer's dog bark at a beggar?
GLOUCESTER: Ay, sir.
LEAR: And the creature run from the cur? There thou mightst behold
the great image of authority: a dog's obeyed in office.
Thou rascal beadle, hold thy bloody hand!
Why dost thou lash that whore? Strip thine own back.

Thou hotly lusts to use her in that kind
For which thou whip'st her. The usurer hangs the cozener.
Through tatter'd clothes small vices do appear;
Robes and furr'd gowns hide all. Plate sin with gold,
And the strong lance of justice hurtless breaks;
Arm it in rags, a pygmy's straw does pierce it.
None does offend, none- I say none! I'll able 'em.
Take that of me, my friend, who have the power
To seal th' accuser's lips. Get thee glass eyes
And, like a scurvy politician, seem
To see the things thou dost not. Now, now, now, now!
Pull off my boots. Harder, harder! So.
EDGAR: O, matter and impertinency mix'd!
Reason, in madness!
LEAR: If thou wilt weep my fortunes, take my eyes.
I know thee well enough; thy name is Gloucester.
Thou must be patient. We came crying hither;
Thou know'st, the first time that we smell the air
We wawl and cry. I will preach to thee. Mark.
GLOUCESTER: Alack, alack the day!
LEAR: When we are born, we cry that we are come
To this great stage of fools. This' a good block.
It were a delicate stratagem to shoe
A troop of horse with felt. I'll put't in proof,
And when I have stol'n upon these sons-in-law,
Then kill, kill, kill, kill, kill, kill!
Enter a Gentleman With Attendants.
GENTLEMEN: O, here he is! Lay hand upon him.- Sir,
Your most dear daughter-
LEAR: No rescue? What, a prisoner? I am even
The natural fool of fortune. Use me well;
You shall have ransom. Let me have a surgeon;
I am cut to th' brains.
GENTLEMEN: You shall have anything.
LEAR: No seconds? All myself?
Why, this would make a man a man of salt,
To use his eyes for garden waterpots,
Ay, and laying autumn's dust.
GENTLEMEN: Good sir-
LEAR: I will die bravely, like a smug bridegroom. What!
I will be jovial. Come, come, I am a king;
My masters, know you that?
GENTLEMEN: You are a royal one, and we obey you.
LEAR: Then there's life in't. Nay, an you get it, you shall get it
by running. Sa, sa, sa, sa!
Exit Running. Attendants Follow.
GENTLEMEN: A sight most pitiful in the meanest wretch,
Past speaking of in a king! Thou hast one daughter
Who redeems nature from the general curse

Which twain have brought her to.
EDGAR: Hail, gentle sir.
GENTLEMEN: Sir, speed you. What's your will?
EDGAR: Do you hear aught, sir, of a battle toward?
GENTLEMEN: Most sure and vulgar. Every one hears that
Which can distinguish sound.
EDGAR: But, by your favour,
How near's the other army?
GENTLEMEN: Near and on speedy foot. The main descry
Stands on the hourly thought.
EDGAR: I thank you sir. That's all.
GENTLEMEN: Though that the Queen on special cause is here,
Her army is mov'd on.
EDGAR: I thank you, sir
Exit Gentleman.
GLOUCESTER: You ever-gentle gods, take my breath from me;
Let not my worser spirit tempt me again
To die before you please!
EDGAR: Well pray you, father.
GLOUCESTER: Now, good sir, what are you?
EDGAR: A most poor man, made tame to fortune's blows,
Who, by the art of known and feeling sorrows,
Am pregnant to good pity. Give me your hand;
I'll lead you to some biding.
GLOUCESTER: Hearty thanks.
The bounty and the benison of heaven
To boot, and boot!
Enter Oswald the Steward.
OSWALD: A proclaim'd prize! Most happy!
That eyeless head of thine was first fram'd flesh
To raise my fortunes. Thou old unhappy traitor,
Briefly thyself remember. The sword is out
That must destroy thee.
GLOUCESTER: Now let thy friendly hand
Put strength enough to't.
Edgar Interposes.
OSWALD: Wherefore, bold peasant,
Dar'st thou support a publish'd traitor? Hence!
Lest that th' infection of his fortune take
Like hold on thee. Let go his arm.
EDGAR: Chill not let go, zir, without vurther 'cagion.
OSWALD: Let go, slave, or thou diest!
EDGAR: Good gentleman, go your gait, and let poor voke pass. An chud ha' bin zwagger'd out of my life, 'twould not ha' bin zo long as 'tis by a vortnight. Nay, come not near th' old man. Keep out, che vore ye, or Ise try whether your costard or my ballow be the harder. Chill be plain with you.
OSWALD: Out, dunghill!
They Fight.

EDGAR: Chill pick your teeth, zir. Come! No matter vor your foins.
Oswald Falls.
OSWALD: Slave, thou hast slain me. Villain, take my purse.
If ever thou wilt thrive, bury my body,
And give the letters which thou find'st about me
To Edmund Earl of Gloucester. Seek him out
Upon the British party. O, untimely death! Death!
He Dies.
EDGAR: I know thee well. A serviceable villain,
As duteous to the vices of thy mistress
As badness would desire.
GLOUCESTER: What, is he dead?
EDGAR: Sit you down, father; rest you.
Let's see his pockets; these letters that he speaks of
May be my friends. He's dead. I am only sorry
He had no other deathsman. Let us see.
Leave, gentle wax; and, manners, blame us not.
To know our enemies' minds, we'ld rip their hearts;
Their papers, is more lawful. Reads the letter.

'Let our reciprocal vows be rememb'red. You have many opportunities to cut him off. If your will want not, time and place will be fruitfully offer'd. There is nothing done, if he return the conqueror. Then am I the prisoner, and his bed my jail; from the loathed warmth whereof deliver me, and supply the place for your labour.

'Your (wife, so I would say) affectionate servant,
'Goneril.'

O indistinguish'd space of woman's will!
A plot upon her virtuous husband's life,
And the exchange my brother! Here in the sands
Thee I'll rake up, the post unsanctified
Of murtherous lechers; and in the mature time
With this ungracious paper strike the sight
Of the death-practis'd Duke, For him 'tis well
That of thy death and business I can tell.
GLOUCESTER: The King is mad. How stiff is my vile sense,
That I stand up, and have ingenious feeling
Of my huge sorrows! Better I were distract.
So should my thoughts be sever'd from my griefs,
And woes by wrong imaginations lose
The knowledge of themselves.
A Drum Afar Off.
EDGAR: Give me your hand.
Far off methinks I hear the beaten drum.
Come, father, I'll bestow you with a friend. Exeunt.

ACT IV. SCENE VII. A Tent in the French Camp.

Enter Cordelia, Kent, Doctor, and Gentleman.
CORDELIA: O thou good Kent, how shall I live and work
To match thy goodness? My life will be too short

And every measure fail me.
KENT: To be acknowledg'd, madam, is o'erpaid.
All my reports go with the modest truth;
Nor more nor clipp'd, but so.
CORDELIA: Be better suited.
These weeds are memories of those worser hours.
I prithee put them off.
KENT: Pardon, dear madam.
Yet to be known shortens my made intent.
My boon I make it that you know me not
Till time and I think meet.
CORDELIA: Then be't so, my good lord.
To the Doctor How, does the King?
DOCTOR: Madam, sleeps still.
CORDELIA: O you kind gods,
Cure this great breach in his abused nature!
Th' untun'd and jarring senses, O, wind up
Of this child-changed father!
DOCTOR: So please your Majesty
That we may wake the King? He hath slept long.
CORDELIA: Be govern'd by your knowledge, and proceed
I' th' sway of your own will. Is he array'd?
Enter Lear in a Chair Carried by Servants.
GENTLEMEN: Ay, madam. In the heaviness of sleep
We put fresh garments on him.
DOCTOR: Be by, good madam, when we do awake him.
I doubt not of his temperance.
CORDELIA: Very well.
Music.
DOCTOR: Please you draw near. Louder the music there!
CORDELIA: O my dear father, restoration hang
Thy medicine on my lips, and let this kiss
Repair those violent harms that my two sisters
Have in thy reverence made!
KENT: Kind and dear princess!
CORDELIA: Had you not been their father, these white flakes
Had challeng'd pity of them. Was this a face
To be oppos'd against the warring winds?
To stand against the deep dread-bolted thunder?
In the most terrible and nimble stroke
Of quick cross lightning? to watch- poor perdu!-
With this thin helm? Mine enemy's dog,
Though he had bit me, should have stood that night
Against my fire; and wast thou fain, poor father,
To hovel thee with swine and rogues forlorn,
In short and musty straw? Alack, alack!
'Tis wonder that thy life and wits at once
Had not concluded all.- He wakes. Speak to him.
DOCTOR: Madam, do you; 'tis fittest.

CORDELIA: How does my royal lord? How fares your Majesty?
LEAR: You do me wrong to take me out o' th' grave.
Thou art a soul in bliss; but I am bound
Upon a wheel of fire, that mine own tears
Do scald like molten lead.
CORDELIA: Sir, do you know me?
LEAR: You are a spirit, I know. When did you die?
CORDELIA: Still, still, far wide!
DOCTOR: He's scarce awake. Let him alone awhile.
LEAR: Where have I been? Where am I? Fair daylight,
I am mightily abus'd. I should e'en die with pity,
To see another thus. I know not what to say.
I will not swear these are my hands. Let's see.
I feel this pin prick. Would I were assur'd
Of my condition!
CORDELIA: O, look upon me, sir,
And hold your hands in benediction o'er me.
No, sir, you must not kneel.
LEAR: Pray, do not mock me.
I am a very foolish fond old man,
Fourscore and upward, not an hour more nor less;
And, to deal plainly,
I fear I am not in my perfect mind.
Methinks I should know you, and know this man;
Yet I am doubtful; for I am mainly ignorant
What place this is; and all the skill I have
Remembers not these garments; nor I know not
Where I did lodge last night. Do not laugh at me;
For (as I am a man) I think this lady
To be my child Cordelia.
CORDELIA: And so I am! I am!
LEAR: Be your tears wet? Yes, faith. I pray weep not.
If you have poison for me, I will drink it.
I know you do not love me; for your sisters
Have, as I do remember, done me wrong.
You have some cause, they have not.
CORDELIA: No cause, no cause.
LEAR: Am I in France?
KENT: In your own kingdom, sir.
LEAR: Do not abuse me.
DOCTOR: Be comforted, good madam. The great rage
You see is kill'd in him; and yet it is danger
To make him even o'er the time he has lost.
Desire him to go in. Trouble him no more
Till further settling.
CORDELIA: Will't please your Highness walk?
LEAR: You must bear with me.
Pray you now, forget and forgive. I am old and foolish.
Exeunt. Manent Kent and Gentleman.

GENTLEMEN: Holds it true, sir, that the Duke of Cornwall was so slain?
KENT: Most certain, sir.
GENTLEMEN: Who is conductor of his people?
KENT: As 'tis said, the bastard son of Gloucester.
GENTLEMEN: They say Edgar, his banish'd son, is with the Earl of Kent in Germany.
KENT: Report is changeable. 'Tis time to look about; the powers of the kingdom approach apace.
GENTLEMEN: The arbitrement is like to be bloody.
Fare you well, sir.
Exit.
KENT: My point and period will be throughly wrought,
Or well or ill, as this day's battle's fought.
Exit.

ACT V. SCENE I. The British Camp near Dover.

Enter, with Drum and Colours, Edmund, Regan, Gentleman, and Soldiers.
EDMUND: Know of the Duke if his last purpose hold,
Or whether since he is advis'd by aught
To change the course. He's full of alteration
And self-reproving. Bring his constant pleasure.
Exit an Officer.
REGAN: Our sister's man is certainly miscarried.
EDMUND: Tis to be doubted, madam.
REGAN: Now, sweet lord,
You know the goodness I intend upon you.
Tell me- but truly- but then speak the truth-
Do you not love my sister?
EDMUND: In honour'd love.
REGAN: But have you never found my brother's way
To the forfended place?
EDMUND: That thought abuses you.
REGAN: I am doubtful that you have been conjunct
And bosom'd with her, as far as we call hers.
EDMUND: No, by mine honour, madam.
REGAN: I never shall endure her. Dear my lord,
Be not familiar with her.
EDMUND: Fear me not.
She and the Duke her husband!
Enter, with Drum and Colours, Albany, Goneril, Soldiers.
GONERIL: Aside I had rather lose the battle than that sister
Should loosen him and me.
ALBANY: Our very loving sister, well bemet.
Sir, this I hear: the King is come to his daughter,
With others whom the rigour of our state
Forc'd to cry out. Where I could not be honest,
I never yet was valiant. For this business,
It toucheth us as France invades our land,
Not bolds the King, with others whom, I fear,
Most just and heavy causes make oppose.

EDMUND: Sir, you speak nobly.
REGAN: Why is this reason'd?
GONERIL: Combine together 'gainst the enemy;
For these domestic and particular broils
Are not the question here.
ALBANY: Let's then determine
With th' ancient of war on our proceeding.
EDMUND: I shall attend you presently at your tent.
REGAN: Sister, you'll go with us?
GONERIL: No.
REGAN: 'Tis most convenient. Pray you go with us.
GONERIL: Aside O, ho, I know the riddle.- I will go.
As They Are Going Out, Enter Edgar Disguised.
EDGAR: If e'er your Grace had speech with man so poor,
Hear me one word.
ALBANY: I'll overtake you.- Speak.
Exeunt all but Albany and Edgar.
EDGAR: Before you fight the battle, ope this letter.
If you have victory, let the trumpet sound
For him that brought it. Wretched though I seem,
I can produce a champion that will prove
What is avouched there. If you miscarry,
Your business of the world hath so an end,
And machination ceases. Fortune love you!
ALBANY: Stay till I have read the letter.
EDGAR: I was forbid it.
When time shall serve, let but the herald cry,
And I'll appear again.
ALBANY: Why, fare thee well. I will o'erlook thy paper.
Exit Edgar.
Enter Edmund.
EDMUND: The enemy 's in view; draw up your powers.
Here is the guess of their true strength and forces
By diligent discovery; but your haste
Is now urg'd on you.
ALBANY: We will greet the time.
Exit.
EDMUND: To both these sisters have I sworn my love;
Each jealous of the other, as the stung
Are of the adder. Which of them shall I take?
Both? one? or neither? Neither can be enjoy'd,
If both remain alive. To take the widow
Exasperates, makes mad her sister Goneril;
And hardly shall I carry out my side,
Her husband being alive. Now then, we'll use
His countenance for the battle, which being done,
Let her who would be rid of him devise
His speedy taking off. As for the mercy
Which he intends to Lear and to Cordelia-

The battle done, and they within our power,
Shall never see his pardon; for my state
Stands on me to defend, not to debate.
Exit.

ACT V. SCENE II. A Field Between the Two Camps.

Alarum Within. Enter, with Drum and Colours, the Powers of France over the Stage, Cordelia with Her Father in Her Hand, and Exeunt.

Enter Edgar and Gloucester.

EDGAR: Here, father, take the shadow of this tree
For your good host. Pray that the right may thrive.
If ever I return to you again,
I'll bring you comfort.
GLOUCESTER: Grace go with you, sir!
Exit Edgar.
Alarum and Retreat Within. Enter Edgar,
EDGAR: Away, old man! give me thy hand! away!
King Lear hath lost, he and his daughter ta'en.
Give me thy hand! come on!
GLOUCESTER: No further, sir. A man may rot even here.
EDGAR: What, in ill thoughts again? Men must endure
Their going hence, even as their coming hither;
Ripeness is all. Come on.
GLOUCESTER: And that's true too.
Exeunt.

ACT V. SCENE III. The British Camp, near Dover.

Enter, in Conquest, with Drum and Colours, Edmund; Lear and Cordelia as Prisoners; Soldiers, Captain.

EDMUND: Some officers take them away. Good guard
Until their greater pleasures first be known
That are to censure them.
CORDELIA: We are not the first
Who with best meaning have incurr'd the worst.
For thee, oppressed king, am I cast down;
Myself could else outfrown false Fortune's frown.
Shall we not see these daughters and these sisters?
LEAR: No, no, no, no! Come, let's away to prison.
We two alone will sing like birds i' th' cage.
When thou dost ask me blessing, I'll kneel down
And ask of thee forgiveness. So we'll live,
And pray, and sing, and tell old tales, and laugh
At gilded butterflies, and hear poor rogues
Talk of court news; and we'll talk with them too-
Who loses and who wins; who's in, who's out-
And take upon 's the mystery of things,
As if we were God's spies; and we'll wear out,
In a wall'd prison, packs and sects of great ones
That ebb and flow by th' moon.
EDMUND: Take them away.
LEAR: Upon such sacrifices, my Cordelia,

The gods themselves throw incense. Have I caught thee?
He that parts us shall bring a brand from heaven
And fire us hence like foxes. Wipe thine eyes.
The goodyears shall devour 'em, flesh and fell,
Ere they shall make us weep! We'll see 'em starv'd first.
Come.
Exeunt Lear and Cordelia, Guarded.
EDMUND: Come hither, Captain; hark.
Take thou this note Gives a Paper. Go follow them to prison.
One step I have advanc'd thee. If thou dost
As this instructs thee, thou dost make thy way
To noble fortunes. Know thou this, that men
Are as the time is. To be tender-minded
Does not become a sword. Thy great employment
Will not bear question. Either say thou'lt do't,
Or thrive by other means.
CAPTAIN: I'll do't, my lord.
EDMUND: About it! and write happy when th' hast done.
Mark- I say, instantly; and carry it so
As I have set it down.
CAPTAIN: I cannot draw a cart, nor eat dried oats;
If it be man's work, I'll do't.
Exit.
Flourish. Enter Albany, Goneril, Regan, Soldiers.
ALBANY: Sir, you have show'd to-day your valiant strain,
And fortune led you well. You have the captives
Who were the opposites of this day's strife.
We do require them of you, so to use them
As we shall find their merits and our safety
May equally determine.
EDMUND: Sir, I thought it fit
To send the old and miserable King
To some retention and appointed guard;
Whose age has charms in it, whose title more,
To pluck the common bosom on his side
And turn our impress'd lances in our eyes
Which do command them. With him I sent the Queen,
My reason all the same; and they are ready
To-morrow, or at further space, t' appear
Where you shall hold your session. At this time
We sweat and bleed: the friend hath lost his friend;
And the best quarrels, in the heat, are curs'd
By those that feel their sharpness.
The question of Cordelia and her father
Requires a fitter place.
ALBANY: Sir, by your patience,
I hold you but a subject of this war,
Not as a brother.
REGAN: That's as we list to grace him.

Methinks our pleasure might have been demanded
Ere you had spoke so far. He led our powers,
Bore the commission of my place and person,
The which immediacy may well stand up
And call itself your brother.
GONERIL: Not so hot!
In his own grace he doth exalt himself
More than in your addition.
REGAN: In my rights
By me invested, he compeers the best.
GONERIL: That were the most if he should husband you.
REGAN: Jesters do oft prove prophets.
GONERIL: Holla, holla!
That eye that told you so look'd but asquint.
REGAN: Lady, I am not well; else I should answer
From a full-flowing stomach. General,
Take thou my soldiers, prisoners, patrimony;
Dispose of them, of me; the walls are thine.
Witness the world that I create thee here
My lord and master.
GONERIL: Mean you to enjoy him?
ALBANY: The let-alone lies not in your good will.
EDMUND: Nor in thine, lord.
ALBANY: Half-blooded fellow, yes.
REGAN: To Edmund Let the drum strike, and prove my title thine.
ALBANY: Stay yet; hear reason. Edmund, I arrest thee
On capital treason; and, in thine attaint,
This gilded serpent Points to Goneril. For your claim, fair sister,
I bar it in the interest of my wife.
'Tis she is subcontracted to this lord,
And I, her husband, contradict your banes.
If you will marry, make your loves to me;
My lady is bespoke.
GONERIL: An interlude!
ALBANY: Thou art arm'd, Gloucester. Let the trumpet sound.
If none appear to prove upon thy person
Thy heinous, manifest, and many treasons,
There is my pledge Throws down a Glove! I'll prove it on thy heart,
Ere I taste bread, thou art in nothing less
Than I have here proclaim'd thee.
REGAN: Sick, O, sick!
GONERIL: Aside If not, I'll ne'er trust medicine.
EDMUND: There's my exchange
Throws down a Glove. What in the world he is
That names me traitor, villain-like he lies.
Call by thy trumpet. He that dares approach,
On him, on you, who not? I will maintain
My truth and honour firmly.
ALBANY: A herald, ho!

EDMUND: A herald, ho, a herald!
ALBANY: Trust to thy single virtue; for thy soldiers,
All levied in my name, have in my name
Took their discharge.
REGAN: My sickness grows upon me.
ALBANY: She is not well. Convey her to my tent.
Exit Regan, Led.
Enter a Herald.
Come hither, herald. Let the trumpet sound,
And read out this.
CAPTAIN: Sound, trumpet! A trumpet sounds.
HERALD: (reads) 'If any man of quality or degree within the lists of the army will maintain upon Edmund, supposed Earl of Gloucester, that he is a manifold traitor, let him appear by the third sound of the trumpet. He is bold in his defence.'
EDMUND: Sound! First trumpet.
DOCTOR: Again! Second trumpet.
HERALD: Again! Third trumpet.
Trumpet Answers Within.
Enter Edgar, Armed, at the Third Sound, a Trumpet Before Him.
ALBANY: Ask him his purposes, why he appears
Upon this call o' th' trumpet.
HERALD: What are you?
Your name, your quality? and why you answer
This present summons?
EDGAR: Know my name is lost;
By treason's tooth bare-gnawn and canker-bit.
Yet am I noble as the adversary
I come to cope.
ALBANY: Which is that adversary?
EDGAR: What's he that speaks for Edmund Earl of Gloucester?
EDMUND: Himself. What say'st thou to him?
EDGAR: Draw thy sword,
That, if my speech offend a noble heart,
Thy arm may do thee justice. Here is mine.
Behold, it is the privilege of mine honours,
My oath, and my profession. I protest-
Maugre thy strength, youth, place, and eminence,
Despite thy victor sword and fire-new fortune,
Thy valour and thy heart- thou art a traitor;
False to thy gods, thy brother, and thy father;
Conspirant 'gainst this high illustrious prince;
And from th' extremest upward of thy head
To the descent and dust beneath thy foot,
A most toad-spotted traitor. Say thou 'no,'
This sword, this arm, and my best spirits are bent
To prove upon thy heart, whereto I speak,
Thou liest.
EDMUND: In wisdom I should ask thy name;

But since thy outside looks so fair and warlike,
And that thy tongue some say of breeding breathes,
What safe and nicely I might well delay
By rule of knighthood, I disdain and spurn.
Back do I toss those treasons to thy head;
With the hell-hated lie o'erwhelm thy heart;
Which- for they yet glance by and scarcely bruise-
This sword of mine shall give them instant way
Where they shall rest for ever. Trumpets, speak!
Alarums. Fight. Edmund Falls.
ALBANY: Save him, save him!
GONERIL: This is mere practice, Gloucester.
By th' law of arms thou wast not bound to answer
An unknown opposite. Thou art not vanquish'd,
But cozen'd and beguil'd.
ALBANY: Shut your mouth, dame,
Or with this paper shall I stop it. Shows Her Her Letter to Edmund.-
To Edmund. Hold, sir.
To Goneril Thou worse than any name, read thine own evil.
No tearing, lady! I perceive you know it.
GONERIL: Say if I do- the laws are mine, not thine.
Who can arraign me for't?
ALBANY: Most monstrous!
Know'st thou this paper?
GONERIL: Ask me not what I know.
Exit.
ALBANY: Go after her. She's desperate; govern her.
Exit an Officer.
EDMUND: What, you have charg'd me with, that have I done,
And more, much more. The time will bring it out.
'Tis past, and so am I.- But what art thou
That hast this fortune on me? If thou'rt noble,
I do forgive thee.
EDGAR: Let's exchange charity.
I am no less in blood than thou art, Edmund;
If more, the more th' hast wrong'd me.
My name is Edgar and thy father's son.
The gods are just, and of our pleasant vices
Make instruments to scourge us.
The dark and vicious place where thee he got
Cost him his eyes.
EDMUND: Th' hast spoken right; 'tis true.
The wheel is come full circle; I am here.
ALBANY: Methought thy very gait did prophesy
A royal nobleness. I must embrace thee.
Let sorrow split my heart if ever I
Did hate thee, or thy father!
EDGAR: Worthy prince, I know't.
ALBANY: Where have you hid yourself?

How have you known the miseries of your father?
EDGAR: By nursing them, my lord. List a brief tale;
And when 'tis told, O that my heart would burst!
The bloody proclamation to escape
That follow'd me so near (O, our lives' sweetness!
That with the pain of death would hourly die
Rather than die at once!) taught me to shift
Into a madman's rags, t' assume a semblance
That very dogs disdain'd; and in this habit
Met I my father with his bleeding rings,
Their precious stones new lost; became his guide,
Led him, begg'd for him, sav'd him from despair;
Never (O fault!) reveal'd myself unto him
Until some half hour past, when I was arm'd,
Not sure, though hoping of this good success,
I ask'd his blessing, and from first to last
Told him my pilgrimage. But his flaw'd heart
(Alack, too weak the conflict to support!)
'Twixt two extremes of passion, joy and grief,
Burst smilingly.
EDMUND: This speech of yours hath mov'd me,
And shall perchance do good; but speak you on;
You look as you had something more to say.
ALBANY: If there be more, more woful, hold it in;
For I am almost ready to dissolve,
Hearing of this.
EDGAR: This would have seem'd a period
To such as love not sorrow; but another,
To amplify too much, would make much more,
And top extremity.
Whilst I was big in clamour, came there a man,
Who, having seen me in my worst estate,
Shunn'd my abhorr'd society; but then, finding
Who 'twas that so endur'd, with his strong arms
He fastened on my neck, and bellowed out
As he'd burst heaven; threw him on my father;
Told the most piteous tale of Lear and him
That ever ear receiv'd; which in recounting
His grief grew puissant, and the strings of life
Began to crack. Twice then the trumpets sounded,
And there I left him tranc'd.
ALBANY: But who was this?
EDGAR: Kent, sir, the banish'd Kent; who in disguise
Followed his enemy king and did him service
Improper for a slave.
Enter a Gentleman with a Bloody Knife.
GENTLEMEN: Help, help! O, help!
EDGAR: What kind of help?
ALBANY: Speak, man.

EDGAR: What means that bloody knife?
GENTLEMEN: 'Tis hot, it smokes.
It came even from the heart of- O! she's dead!
ALBANY: Who dead? Speak, man.
GENTLEMEN: Your lady, sir, your lady! and her sister
By her is poisoned; she hath confess'd it.
EDMUND: I was contracted to them both. All three
Now marry in an instant.
Enter Kent.
EDGAR: Here comes Kent.
ALBANY: Produce their bodies, be they alive or dead.
Exit Gentleman.
This judgement of the heavens, that makes us tremble
Touches us not with pity. O, is this he?
The time will not allow the compliment
That very manners urges.
KENT: I am come
To bid my king and master aye good night.
Is he not here?
ALBANY: Great thing of us forgot!
Speak, Edmund, where's the King? and where's Cordelia?
The bodies of Goneril and Regan are brought in.
Seest thou this object, Kent?
KENT: Alack, why thus?
EDMUND: Yet Edmund was belov'd.
The one the other poisoned for my sake,
And after slew herself.
ALBANY: Even so. Cover their faces.
EDMUND: I pant for life. Some good I mean to do,
Despite of mine own nature. Quickly send
(Be brief in't) to the castle; for my writ
Is on the life of Lear and on Cordelia.
Nay, send in time.
ALBANY: Run, run, O, run!
EDGAR: To who, my lord? Who has the office? Send
Thy token of reprieve.
EDMUND: Well thought on. Take my sword;
Give it the Captain.
ALBANY: Haste thee for thy life.
Exit Edgar.
EDMUND: He hath commission from thy wife and me
To hang Cordelia in the prison and
To lay the blame upon her own despair
That she fordid herself.
ALBANY: The gods defend her! Bear him hence awhile.
Edmund Is Borne Off.
Enter Lear, with Cordelia Dead in His Arms, Edgar, Captain, and Others Following.
LEAR: Howl, howl, howl, howl! O, you are men of stone.
Had I your tongues and eyes, I'ld use them so

That heaven's vault should crack. She's gone for ever!
I know when one is dead, and when one lives.
She's dead as earth. Lend me a looking glass.
If that her breath will mist or stain the stone,
Why, then she lives.
KENT: Is this the promis'd end?
EDGAR: Or image of that horror?
ALBANY: Fall and cease!
LEAR: This feather stirs; she lives! If it be so,
It is a chance which does redeem all sorrows
That ever I have felt.
KENT: O my good master!
LEAR: Prithee away!
EDGAR: 'Tis noble Kent, your friend.
LEAR: A plague upon you, murderers, traitors all!
I might have sav'd her; now she's gone for ever!
Cordelia, Cordelia! stay a little. Ha!
What is't thou say'st, Her voice was ever soft,
Gentle, and low- an excellent thing in woman.
I kill'd the slave that was a-hanging thee.
CAPTAIN: 'Tis true, my lords, he did.
LEAR: Did I not, fellow?
I have seen the day, with my good biting falchion
I would have made them skip. I am old now,
And these same crosses spoil me. Who are you?
Mine eyes are not o' th' best. I'll tell you straight.
KENT: If fortune brag of two she lov'd and hated,
One of them we behold.
LEAR: This' a dull sight. Are you not Kent?
KENT: The same-
Your servant Kent. Where is your servant Caius?
LEAR: He's a good fellow, I can tell you that.
He'll strike, and quickly too. He's dead and rotten.
KENT: No, my good lord; I am the very man-
LEAR: I'll see that straight.
KENT: That from your first of difference and decay
Have followed your sad steps.
LEAR: You're welcome hither.
KENT: Nor no man else! All's cheerless, dark, and deadly.
Your eldest daughters have fordone themselves,
And desperately are dead.
LEAR: Ay, so I think.
ALBANY: He knows not what he says; and vain is it
That we present us to him.
EDGAR: Very bootless.
Enter a Captain.
CAPTAIN: Edmund is dead, my lord.
ALBANY: That's but a trifle here.
You lords and noble friends, know our intent.

What comfort to this great decay may come
Shall be applied. For us, we will resign,
During the life of this old Majesty,
To him our absolute power;
To Edgar and Kent you to your rights;
With boot, and Such addition as your honours
Have more than merited.- All friends shall taste
The wages of their virtue, and all foes
The cup of their deservings.- O, see, see!
LEAR: And my poor fool is hang'd! No, no, no life!
Why should a dog, a horse, a rat, have life,
And thou no breath at all? Thou'lt come no more,
Never, never, never, never, never!
Pray you undo this button. Thank you, sir.
Do you see this? Look on her! look! her lips!
Look there, look there! He dies.
EDGAR: He faints! My lord, my lord!
KENT: Break, heart; I prithee break!
EDGAR: Look up, my lord.
KENT: Vex not his ghost. O, let him pass! He hates him
That would upon the rack of this tough world
Stretch him out longer.
EDGAR: He is gone indeed.
KENT: The wonder is, he hath endur'd so long.
He but usurp'd his life.
ALBANY: Bear them from hence. Our present business is general woe.
To Kent and Edgar Friends of my soul, you twain
Rule in this realm, and the gor'd state sustain.
KENT: I have a journey, sir, shortly to go.
My master calls me; I must not say no.
ALBANY: The weight of this sad time we must obey,
Speak what we feel, not what we ought to say.
The oldest have borne most; we that are young
Shall never see so much, nor live so long.
Exeunt with a Dead March.

END

The Tragedy of Macbeth

Dramatis Personae

DUNCAN, King of Scotland
MACBETH, Thane of Glamis and Cawdor, a general in the King's army
LADY MACBETH, his wife
MACDUFF, Thane of Fife, a nobleman of Scotland
LADY MACDUFF, his wife
MALCOLM, elder son of Duncan
DONALBAIN, younger son of Duncan
BANQUO, Thane of Lochaber, a general in the King's army
FLEANCE, his son
LENNOX, nobleman of Scotland
ROSS, nobleman of Scotland
MENTEITH nobleman of Scotland
ANGUS, nobleman of Scotland
CAITHNESS, nobleman of Scotland
SIWARD, Earl of Northumberland, general of the English forces
YOUNG SIWARD, his son
SEYTON, attendant to Macbeth
HECATE, Queen of the Witches
The Three Witches
Boy, Son of Macduff
Gentlewoman attending on Lady Macbeth
An English Doctor
A Scottish Doctor
A Sergeant
A Porter
An Old Man
The Ghost of Banquo and other Apparitions
Lords, Gentlemen, Officers, Soldiers, Murtherers, Attendants,
and Messengers

SCENE: Scotland and England

ACT I. SCENE I. A Desert Place. Thunder and Lightning.

Enter Three Witches.
FIRST WITCH: When shall we three meet again?
In thunder, lightning, or in rain?
SECOND WITCH: When the hurlyburly's done,
When the battle's lost and won.
THIRD WITCH: That will be ere the set of sun.
FIRST WITCH: Where the place?
SECOND WITCH: Upon the heath.
THIRD WITCH: There to meet with Macbeth.
FIRST WITCH: I come, Graymalkin.
ALL: Paddock calls. Anon!
Fair is foul, and foul is fair.
Hover through the fog and filthy air.
Exeunt.

ACT I. SCENE II. A Camp near Forres. Alarum Within.

Enter Duncan, Malcolm, Donalbain, Lennox, with Attendants, Meeting a Bleeding Sergeant.
DUNCAN: What bloody man is that? He can report,
As seemeth by his plight, of the revolt
The newest state.

MALCOLM: This is the sergeant
Who like a good and hardy soldier fought
'Gainst my captivity. Hail, brave friend!
Say to the King the knowledge of the broil
As thou didst leave it.
SERGEANT: Doubtful it stood,
As two spent swimmers that do cling together
And choke their art. The merciless Macdonwald-
Worthy to be a rebel, for to that
The multiplying villainies of nature
Do swarm upon him -from the Western Isles
Of kerns and gallowglasses is supplied;
And Fortune, on his damned quarrel smiling,
Show'd like a rebel's whore. But all's too weak;
For brave Macbeth -well he deserves that name-
Disdaining Fortune, with his brandish'd steel,
Which smoked with bloody execution,
Like Valor's minion carved out his passage
Till he faced the slave,
Which ne'er shook hands, nor bade farewell to him,
Till he unseam'd him from the nave to the chaps,
And fix'd his head upon our battlements.
DUNCAN: O valiant cousin! Worthy gentleman!
SERGEANT: As whence the sun 'gins his reflection
Shipwrecking storms and direful thunders break,
So from that spring whence comfort seem'd to come
Discomfort swells. Mark, King of Scotland, mark.
No sooner justice had, with valor arm'd,
Compell'd these skipping kerns to trust their heels,
But the Norweyan lord, surveying vantage,
With furbish'd arms and new supplies of men,
Began a fresh assault.
DUNCAN: Dismay'd not this
Our captains, Macbeth and Banquo.?
SERGEANT: Yes,
As sparrows eagles, or the hare the lion.
If I say sooth, I must report they were
As cannons overcharged with double cracks,
So they doubly redoubled strokes upon the foe.
Except they meant to bathe in reeking wounds,
Or memorize another Golgotha,
I cannot tell-
But I am faint; my gashes cry for help.
DUNCAN: So well thy words become thee as thy wounds;
They smack of honor both. Go get him surgeons.
Exit Sergeant, Attended.
Who comes here?
Enter Ross.
MALCOLM: The worthy Thane of Ross.
LENNOX: What a haste looks through his eyes! So should he look
That seems to speak things strange.
ROSS: God save the King!
DUNCAN: Whence camest thou, worthy Thane?

ROSS: From Fife, great King,
Where the Norweyan banners flout the sky
And fan our people cold.
Norway himself, with terrible numbers,
Assisted by that most disloyal traitor
The Thane of Cawdor, began a dismal conflict,
Till that Bellona's bridegroom, lapp'd in proof,
Confronted him with self-comparisons,
Point against point rebellious, arm 'gainst arm,
Curbing his lavish spirit; and, to conclude,
The victory fell on us.
DUNCAN: Great happiness!
ROSS: That now
Sweno, the Norways' king, craves composition;
Nor would we deign him burial of his men
Till he disbursed, at Saint Colme's Inch,
Ten thousand dollars to our general use.
DUNCAN: No more that Thane of Cawdor shall deceive
Our bosom interest. Go pronounce his present death,
And with his former title greet Macbeth.
ROSS: I'll see it done.
DUNCAN: What he hath lost, noble Macbeth hath won.
Exeunt.

ACT I. SCENE III. A Heath. Thunder.

Enter the Three Witches.
FIRST WITCH: Where hast thou been, sister?
SECOND WITCH: Killing swine.
THIRD WITCH: Sister, where thou?
FIRST WITCH: A sailor's wife had chestnuts in her lap,
And mounch'd, and mounch'd, and mounch'd. "Give me," quoth I.
"Aroint thee, witch!" the rump-fed ronyon cries.
Her husband's to Aleppo gone, master the Tiger;
But in a sieve I'll thither sail,
And, like a rat without a tail,
I'll do, I'll do, and I'll do.
SECOND WITCH: I'll give thee a wind.
FIRST WITCH: Thou'rt kind.
THIRD WITCH: And I another.
FIRST WITCH: I myself have all the other,
And the very ports they blow,
All the quarters that they know
I' the shipman's card.
I will drain him dry as hay:
Sleep shall neither night nor day
Hang upon his penthouse lid;
He shall live a man forbid.
Weary se'nnights nine times nine
Shall he dwindle, peak, and pine;
Though his bark cannot be lost,
Yet it shall be tempest-toss'd.
Look what I have.
SECOND WITCH: Show me, show me.
FIRST WITCH: Here I have a pilot's thumb,

Wreck'd as homeward he did come. Drum within.
THIRD WITCH: A drum, a drum!
Macbeth doth come.
ALL: The weird sisters, hand in hand,
Posters of the sea and land,
Thus do go about, about,
Thrice to thine, and thrice to mine,
And thrice again, to make up nine.
Peace! The charm's wound up.
Enter Macbeth and Banquo.
MACBETH: So foul and fair a day I have not seen.
BANQUO: How far is't call'd to Forres? What are these
So wither'd and so wild in their attire,
That look not like the inhabitants o' the earth,
And yet are on't? Live you? or are you aught
That man may question? You seem to understand me,
By each at once her choppy finger laying
Upon her skinny lips. You should be women,
And yet your beards forbid me to interpret
That you are so.
MACBETH: Speak, if you can. What are you?
FIRST WITCH: All hail, Macbeth, hail to thee, Thane of Glamis!
SECOND WITCH: All hail, Macbeth, hail to thee, Thane of Cawdor!
THIRD WITCH: All hail, Macbeth, that shalt be King hereafter!
BANQUO: Good sir, why do you start, and seem to fear
Things that do sound so fair? I' the name of truth,
Are ye fantastical or that indeed
Which outwardly ye show? My noble partner
You greet with present grace and great prediction
Of noble having and of royal hope,
That he seems rapt withal. To me you speak not.
If you can look into the seeds of time,
And say which grain will grow and which will not,
Speak then to me, who neither beg nor fear
Your favors nor your hate.
FIRST WITCH: Hail!
SECOND WITCH: Hail!
THIRD WITCH: Hail!
FIRST WITCH: Lesser than Macbeth, and greater.
SECOND WITCH: Not so happy, yet much happier.
THIRD WITCH: Thou shalt get kings, though thou be none.
So all hail, Macbeth and Banquo!
FIRST WITCH: Banquo and Macbeth, all hail!
MACBETH: Stay, you imperfect speakers, tell me more.
By Sinel's death I know I am Thane of Glamis;
But how of Cawdor? The Thane of Cawdor lives,
A prosperous gentleman; and to be King
Stands not within the prospect of belief,
No more than to be Cawdor. Say from whence
You owe this strange intelligence, or why
Upon this blasted heath you stop our way
With such prophetic greeting? Speak, I charge you.
Witches Vanish.

BANQUO: The earth hath bubbles as the water has,
And these are of them. Whither are they vanish'd?
MACBETH: Into the air, and what seem'd corporal melted
As breath into the wind. Would they had stay'd!
BANQUO: Were such things here as we do speak about?
Or have we eaten on the insane root
That takes the reason prisoner?
MACBETH: Your children shall be kings.
BANQUO: You shall be King.
MACBETH: And Thane of Cawdor too. Went it not so?
BANQUO: To the selfsame tune and words. Who's here?
Enter Ross and Angus.
ROSS: The King hath happily received, Macbeth,
The news of thy success; and when he reads
Thy personal venture in the rebels' fight,
His wonders and his praises do contend
Which should be thine or his. Silenced with that,
In viewing o'er the rest o' the selfsame day,
He finds thee in the stout Norweyan ranks,
Nothing afeard of what thyself didst make,
Strange images of death. As thick as hail
Came post with post, and every one did bear
Thy praises in his kingdom's great defense,
And pour'd them down before him.
ANGUS: We are sent
To give thee, from our royal master, thanks;
Only to herald thee into his sight,
Not pay thee.
ROSS: And for an earnest of a greater honor,
He bade me, from him, call thee Thane of Cawdor.
In which addition, hail, most worthy Thane,
For it is thine.
BANQUO: What, can the devil speak true?
MACBETH: The Thane of Cawdor lives. Why do you dress me
In borrow'd robes?
ANGUS: Who was the Thane lives yet,
But under heavy judgement bears that life
Which he deserves to lose. Whether he was combined
With those of Norway, or did line the rebel
With hidden help and vantage, or that with both
He labor'd in his country's wreck, I know not;
But treasons capital, confess'd and proved,
Have overthrown him.
MACBETH: Aside. Glamis, and Thane of Cawdor!
The greatest is behind. To Ross and Angus Thanks for your pains.
Aside to Banquo Do you not hope your children shall be kings,
When those that gave the Thane of Cawdor to me
Promised no less to them?
BANQUO: Aside to Macbeth. That, trusted home,
Might yet enkindle you unto the crown,
Besides the Thane of Cawdor. But 'tis strange;
And oftentimes, to win us to our harm,
The instruments of darkness tell us truths,

Win us with honest trifles, to betray's
In deepest consequence-
Cousins, a word, I pray you.
MACBETH: Aside. Two truths are told,
As happy prologues to the swelling act
Of the imperial theme-I thank you, gentlemen.
Aside. This supernatural soliciting
Cannot be ill, cannot be good. If ill,
Why hath it given me earnest of success,
Commencing in a truth? I am Thane of Cawdor.
If good, why do I yield to that suggestion
Whose horrid image doth unfix my hair
And make my seated heart knock at my ribs,
Against the use of nature? Present fears
Are less than horrible imaginings:
My thought, whose murther yet is but fantastical,
Shakes so my single state of man that function
Is smother'd in surmise, and nothing is
But what is not.
BANQUO: Look, how our partner's rapt.
MACBETH: Aside. If chance will have me King, why, chance may crown me
Without my stir.
BANQUO: New honors come upon him,
Like our strange garments, cleave not to their mould
But with the aid of use.
MACBETH: Aside. Come what come may,
Time and the hour runs through the roughest day.
BANQUO: Worthy Macbeth, we stay upon your leisure.
MACBETH: Give me your favor; my dull brain was wrought
With things forgotten. Kind gentlemen, your pains
Are register'd where every day I turn
The leaf to read them. Let us toward the King.
Think upon what hath chanced, and at more time,
The interim having weigh'd it, let us speak
Our free hearts each to other.
BANQUO: Very gladly.
MACBETH: Till then, enough. Come, friends.
Exeunt.

SCENE IV. Forres. The Palace.

Flourish. Enter Duncan, Malcolm, Donalbain, Lennox, and Attendants.
DUNCAN: Is execution done on Cawdor? Are not
Those in commission yet return'd?
MALCOLM: My liege,
They are not yet come back. But I have spoke
With one that saw him die, who did report
That very frankly he confess'd his treasons,
Implored your Highness' pardon, and set forth
A deep repentance. Nothing in his life
Became him like the leaving it; he died
As one that had been studied in his death,
To throw away the dearest thing he owed
As 'twere a careless trifle.
DUNCAN: There's no art

To find the mind's construction in the face:
He was a gentleman on whom I built
An absolute trust.
Enter Macbeth, Banquo, Ross, and Angus.
O worthiest cousin!
The sin of my ingratitude even now
Was heavy on me. Thou art so far before,
That swiftest wing of recompense is slow
To overtake thee. Would thou hadst less deserved,
That the proportion both of thanks and payment
Might have been mine! Only I have left to say,
More is thy due than more than all can pay.
MACBETH: The service and the loyalty lowe,
In doing it, pays itself. Your Highness' part
Is to receive our duties, and our duties
Are to your throne and state, children and servants,
Which do but what they should, by doing everything
Safe toward your love and honor.
DUNCAN: Welcome hither.
I have begun to plant thee, and will labor
To make thee full of growing. Noble Banquo,
That hast no less deserved, nor must be known
No less to have done so; let me infold thee
And hold thee to my heart.
BANQUO: There if I grow,
The harvest is your own.
DUNCAN: My plenteous joys,
Wanton in fullness, seek to hide themselves
In drops of sorrow. Sons, kinsmen, thanes,
And you whose places are the nearest, know
We will establish our estate upon
Our eldest, Malcolm, whom we name hereafter
The Prince of Cumberland; which honor must
Not unaccompanied invest him only,
But signs of nobleness, like stars, shall shine
On all deservers. From hence to Inverness,
And bind us further to you.
MACBETH: The rest is labor, which is not used for you.
I'll be myself the harbinger, and make joyful
The hearing of my wife with your approach;
So humbly take my leave.
DUNCAN: My worthy Cawdor!
MACBETH: Aside. The Prince of Cumberland! That is a step
On which I must fall down, or else o'erleap,
For in my way it lies. Stars, hide your fires;
Let not light see my black and deep desires.
The eye wink at the hand; yet let that be
Which the eye fears, when it is done, to see.
Exit.
DUNCAN: True, worthy Banquo! He is full so valiant,
And in his commendations I am fed;
It is a banquet to me. Let's after him,
Whose care is gone before to bid us welcome.

It is a peerless kinsman. Flourish.
Exeunt.

ACT I. SCENE V. Inverness. Macbeth's Castle.

Enter Lady Macbeth, Reading a Letter.
LADY MACBETH: "They met me in the day of success,
and I have learned by the perfectest report they have
more in them than mortal knowledge.
When I burned in desire to question them further,
they made themselves air, into which they vanished.
Whiles I stood rapt in the wonder of it, came missives from
the King, who all-hailed me 'Thane of Cawdor'; by
which title, before, these weird sisters saluted me and
referred me to the coming on of time with 'Hail,
King that shalt be!' This have I thought good
to deliver thee, my dearest partner of greatness,
that thou mightst not lose the dues of rejoicing,
by being ignorant of what greatness is promised
thee. Lay it to thy heart, and farewell."
Glamis thou art, and Cawdor, and shalt be
What thou art promised. Yet do I fear thy nature.
It is too full o' the milk of human kindness
To catch the nearest way. Thou wouldst be great;
Art not without ambition, but without
The illness should attend it. What thou wouldst highly,
That wouldst thou holily; wouldst not play false,
And yet wouldst wrongly win. Thou'ldst have, great Glamis,
That which cries, "Thus thou must do, if thou have it;
And that which rather thou dost fear to do
Than wishest should be undone." Hie thee hither,
That I may pour my spirits in thine ear,
And chastise with the valor of my tongue
All that impedes thee from the golden round,
Which fate and metaphysical aid doth seem
To have thee crown'd withal.
Enter a Messenger.
What is your tidings?
MESSENGER: The King comes here tonight.
LADY MACBETH: Thou'rt mad to say it!
Is not thy master with him? who, were't so,
Would have inform'd for preparation.
MESSENGER: So please you, it is true; our Thane is coming.
One of my fellows had the speed of him,
Who, almost dead for breath, had scarcely more
Than would make up his message.
LADY MACBETH: Give him tending;
He brings great news.
Exit Messenger.
The raven himself is hoarse
That croaks the fatal entrance of Duncan
Under my battlements. Come, you spirits
That tend on mortal thoughts, unsex me here
And fill me from the crown to the toe top-full
Of direst cruelty! Make thick my blood,

Stop up the access and passage to remorse,
That no compunctious visitings of nature
Shake my fell purpose nor keep peace between
The effect and it! Come to my woman's breasts,
And take my milk for gall, your murthering ministers,
Wherever in your sightless substances
You wait on nature's mischief! Come, thick night,
And pall thee in the dunnest smoke of hell
That my keen knife see not the wound it makes
Nor heaven peep through the blanket of the dark
To cry, "Hold, hold!"
Enter Macbeth.
Great Glamis! Worthy Cawdor!
Greater than both, by the all-hail hereafter!
Thy letters have transported me beyond
This ignorant present, and I feel now
The future in the instant.
MACBETH: My dearest love,
Duncan comes here tonight.
LADY MACBETH: And when goes hence?
MACBETH: Tomorrow, as he purposes.
LADY MACBETH: O, never
Shall sun that morrow see!
Your face, my Thane, is as a book where men
May read strange matters. To beguile the time,
Look like the time; bear welcome in your eye,
Your hand, your tongue; look like the innocent flower,
But be the serpent under it. He that's coming
Must be provided for; and you shall put
This night's great business into my dispatch,
Which shall to all our nights and days to come
Give solely sovereign sway and masterdom.
MACBETH: We will speak further.
LADY MACBETH: Only look up clear;
To alter favor ever is to fear.
Leave all the rest to me.
Exeunt.

ACT I. SCENE VI. Before Macbeth's Castle. Hautboys and Torches.

Enter Duncan, Malcolm, Donalbain, Banquo, Lennox, Macduff, Ross, Angus, and Attendants.
DUNCAN: This castle hath a pleasant seat; the air
Nimbly and sweetly recommends itself
Unto our gentle senses.
BANQUO: This guest of summer,
The temple-haunting martlet, does approve
By his loved mansionry that the heaven's breath
Smells wooingly here. No jutty, frieze,
Buttress, nor coign of vantage, but this bird
Hath made his pendant bed and procreant cradle;
Where they most breed and haunt, I have observed
The air is delicate.
Enter Lady Macbeth.
DUNCAN: See, see, our honor'd hostess!
The love that follows us sometime is our trouble,

Which still we thank as love. Herein I teach you
How you shall bid God 'ield us for your pains,
And thank us for your trouble.
LADY MACBETH: All our service
In every point twice done, and then done double,
Were poor and single business to contend
Against those honors deep and broad wherewith
Your Majesty loads our house. For those of old,
And the late dignities heap'd up to them,
We rest your hermits.
DUNCAN: Where's the Thane of Cawdor?
We coursed him at the heels and had a purpose
To be his purveyor; but he rides well,
And his great love, sharp as his spur, hath holp him
To his home before us. Fair and noble hostess,
We are your guest tonight.
LADY MACBETH: Your servants ever
Have theirs, themselves, and what is theirs, in compt,
To make their audit at your Highness' pleasure,
Still to return your own.
DUNCAN: Give me your hand;
Conduct me to mine host. We love him highly,
And shall continue our graces towards him.
By your leave, hostess.
Exeunt.

ACT I. SCENE VII Macbeth's Castle. Hautboys and Torches.

Enter a Sewer and Divers Servants with Dishes and Service, Who Pass over the Stage. Then Enter Macbeth.

MACBETH: If it were done when 'tis done, then 'twere well
It were done quickly. If the assassination
Could trammel up the consequence, and catch,
With his surcease, success; that but this blow
Might be the be-all and the end-all -here,
But here, upon this bank and shoal of time,
We'ld jump the life to come. But in these cases
We still have judgement here, that we but teach
Bloody instructions, which being taught return
To plague the inventor. This even-handed justice
Commends the ingredients of our poison'd chalice
To our own lips. He's here in double trust:
First, as I am his kinsman and his subject,
Strong both against the deed; then, as his host,
Who should against his murtherer shut the door,
Not bear the knife myself. Besides, this Duncan
Hath borne his faculties so meek, hath been
So clear in his great office, that his virtues
Will plead like angels trumpet-tongued against
The deep damnation of his taking-off,
And pity, like a naked new-born babe
Striding the blast, or heaven's cherubin horsed
Upon the sightless couriers of the air,
Shall blow the horrid deed in every eye,
That tears shall drown the wind. I have no spur

To prick the sides of my intent, but only
Vaulting ambition, which o'erleaps itself
And falls on the other.
Enter Lady Macbeth.
How now, what news?
LADY MACBETH: He has almost supp'd. Why have you left the chamber?
MACBETH: Hath he ask'd for me?
LADY MACBETH: Know you not he has?
MACBETH: We will proceed no further in this business:
He hath honor'd me of late, and I have bought
Golden opinions from all sorts of people,
Which would be worn now in their newest gloss,
Not cast aside so soon.
LADY MACBETH: Was the hope drunk
Wherein you dress'd yourself? Hath it slept since?
And wakes it now, to look so green and pale
At what it did so freely? From this time
Such I account thy love. Art thou afeard
To be the same in thine own act and valor
As thou art in desire? Wouldst thou have that
Which thou esteem'st the ornament of life
And live a coward in thine own esteem,
Letting "I dare not" wait upon "I would"
Like the poor cat i' the adage?
MACBETH: Prithee, peace!
I dare do all that may become a man;
Who dares do more is none.
LADY MACBETH: What beast wast then
That made you break this enterprise to me?
When you durst do it, then you were a man,
And, to be more than what you were, you would
Be so much more the man. Nor time nor place
Did then adhere, and yet you would make both.
They have made themselves, and that their fitness now
Does unmake you. I have given suck and know
How tender 'tis to love the babe that milks me-
I would, while it was smiling in my face,
Have pluck'd my nipple from his boneless gums
And dash'd the brains out had I so sworn as you
Have done to this.
MACBETH: If we should fail?
LADY MACBETH: We fail?
But screw your courage to the sticking-place
And we'll not fail. When Duncan is asleep-
Whereto the rather shall his day's hard journey
Soundly invite him- his two chamberlains
Will I with wine and wassail so convince
That memory, the warder of the brain,
Shall be a fume and the receipt of reason
A limbeck only. When in swinish sleep
Their drenched natures lie as in a death,
What cannot you and I perform upon
The unguarded Duncan? What not put upon

His spongy officers, who shall bear the guilt
Of our great quell?
MACBETH: Bring forth men-children only,
For thy undaunted mettle should compose
Nothing but males. Will it not be received,
When we have mark'd with blood those sleepy two
Of his own chamber and used their very daggers,
That they have done't?
LADY MACBETH: Who dares receive it other,
As we shall make our griefs and clamor roar
Upon his death?
MACBETH: I am settled and bend up
Each corporal agent to this terrible feat.
Away, and mock the time with fairest show:
False face must hide what the false heart doth know.
Exeunt.

ACT II. SCENE I. Inverness. Court of Macbeth's Castle.

Enter Banquo and Fleance, Bearing a Torch Before Him.
BANQUO: How goes the night, boy?
FLEANCE: The moon is down; I have not heard the clock.
BANQUO: And she goes down at twelve.
FLEANCE: I take't 'tis later, sir.
BANQUO: Hold, take my sword. There's husbandry in heaven,
Their candles are all out. Take thee that too.
A heavy summons lies like lead upon me,
And yet I would not sleep. Merciful powers,
Restrain in me the cursed thoughts that nature
Gives way to in repose!
Enter Macbeth and a Servant with a Torch.
Give me my sword.
Who's there?
MACBETH: A friend.
BANQUO: What, sir, not yet at rest? The King's abed.
He hath been in unusual pleasure and
Sent forth great largess to your offices.
This diamond he greets your wife withal,
By the name of most kind hostess, and shut up
In measureless content.
MACBETH: Being unprepared,
Our will became the servant to defect,
Which else should free have wrought.
BANQUO: All's well.
I dreamt last night of the three weird sisters:
To you they have show'd some truth.
MACBETH: I think not of them;
Yet, when we can entreat an hour to serve,
We would spend it in some words upon that business,
If you would grant the time.
BANQUO: At your kind'st leisure.
MACBETH: If you shall cleave to my consent, when 'tis,
It shall make honor for you.
BANQUO: So I lose none
In seeking to augment it, but still keep

My bosom franchised and allegiance clear,
I shall be counsel'd.
MACBETH: Good repose the while.
BANQUO: Thanks, sir, the like to you.
Exeunt Banquo. and Fleance.
MACBETH: Go bid thy mistress, when my drink is ready,
She strike upon the bell. Get thee to bed.
Exit Servant.
Is this a dagger which I see before me,
The handle toward my hand? Come, let me clutch thee.
I have thee not, and yet I see thee still.
Art thou not, fatal vision, sensible
To feeling as to sight? Or art thou but
A dagger of the mind, a false creation,
Proceeding from the heat-oppressed brain?
I see thee yet, in form as palpable
As this which now I draw.
Thou marshal'st me the way that I was going,
And such an instrument I was to use.
Mine eyes are made the fools o' the other senses,
Or else worth all the rest. I see thee still,
And on thy blade and dudgeon gouts of blood,
Which was not so before. There's no such thing:
It is the bloody business which informs
Thus to mine eyes. Now o'er the one half-world
Nature seems dead, and wicked dreams abuse
The curtain'd sleep; witchcraft celebrates
Pale Hecate's offerings; and wither'd Murther,
Alarum'd by his sentinel, the wolf,
Whose howl's his watch, thus with his stealthy pace,
With Tarquin's ravishing strides, towards his design
Moves like a ghost. Thou sure and firm-set earth,
Hear not my steps, which way they walk, for fear
Thy very stones prate of my whereabout,
And take the present horror from the time,
Which now suits with it. Whiles I threat, he lives;
Words to the heat of deeds too cold breath gives.
A Bell Rings.
I go, and it is done; the bell invites me.
Hear it not, Duncan, for it is a knell
That summons thee to heaven, or to hell.
Exit.

ACT II. SCENE II. The Same.

Enter Lady Macbeth.
LADY MACBETH: That which hath made them drunk hath made me bold;
What hath quench'd them hath given me fire. Hark! Peace!
It was the owl that shriek'd, the fatal bellman,
Which gives the stern'st good night. He is about it:
The doors are open, and the surfeited grooms
Do mock their charge with snores. I have drugg'd their possets
That death and nature do contend about them,
Whether they live or die.
MACBETH: Within. Who's there' what, ho!

LADY MACBETH: Alack, I am afraid they have awaked
And 'tis not done. The attempt and not the deed
Confounds us. Hark! I laid their daggers ready;
He could not miss 'em. Had he not resembled
My father as he slept, I had done't.
Enter Macbeth,
My husband!
MACBETH: I have done the deed. Didst thou not hear a noise?
LADY MACBETH: I heard the owl scream and the crickets cry.
Did not you speak?
MACBETH: When?
LADY MACBETH: Now.
MACBETH: As I descended?
LADY MACBETH: Ay.
MACBETH: Hark!
Who lies i' the second chamber?
LADY MACBETH: Donalbain.
MACBETH: This is a sorry sight.
Looks on His Hands.
LADY MACBETH: A foolish thought, to say a sorry sight.
MACBETH: There's one did laugh in 's sleep, and one cried, "Murther!"
That they did wake each other. I stood and heard them,
But they did say their prayers and address'd them
Again to sleep.
LADY MACBETH: There are two lodged together.
MACBETH: One cried, "God bless us!" and "Amen" the other,
As they had seen me with these hangman's hands.
Listening their fear, I could not say "Amen,"
When they did say, "God bless us!"
LADY MACBETH: Consider it not so deeply.
MACBETH: But wherefore could not I pronounce "Amen"?
I had most need of blessing, and "Amen"
Stuck in my throat.
LADY MACBETH: These deeds must not be thought
After these ways; so, it will make us mad.
MACBETH: I heard a voice cry, "Sleep no more!
Macbeth does murther sleep" -the innocent sleep,
Sleep that knits up the ravel'd sleave of care,
The death of each day's life, sore labor's bath,
Balm of hurt minds, great nature's second course,
Chief nourisher in life's feast-
LADY MACBETH: What do you mean?
MACBETH: Still it cried, "Sleep no more!" to all the house;
"Glamis hath murther'd sleep, and therefore Cawdor
Shall sleep no more. Macbeth shall sleep no more."
LADY MACBETH: Who was it that thus cried? Why, worthy Thane,
You do unbend your noble strength, to think
So brainsickly of things. Go, get some water
And wash this filthy witness from your hand.
Why did you bring these daggers from the place?
They must lie there. Go carry them, and smear
The sleepy grooms with blood.

MACBETH: I'll go no more.
I am afraid to think what I have done;
Look on't again I dare not.
LADY MACBETH: Infirm of purpose!
Give me the daggers. The sleeping and the dead
Are but as pictures; 'tis the eye of childhood
That fears a painted devil. If he do bleed,
I'll gild the faces of the grooms withal,
For it must seem their guilt.
Exit. Knocking Within.
MACBETH: Whence is that knocking?
How is't with me, when every noise appals me?
What hands are here? Ha, they pluck out mine eyes!
Will all great Neptune's ocean wash this blood
Clean from my hand? No, this my hand will rather
The multitudinous seas incarnadine,
Making the green one red.
Re-enter Lady Macbeth.
LADY MACBETH: My hands are of your color, but I shame
To wear a heart so white. Knocking Within.
I hear knocking
At the south entry. Retire we to our chamber.
A little water clears us of this deed.
How easy is it then! Your constancy
Hath left you unattended. Knocking Within. Hark, more knocking.
Get on your nightgown, lest occasion call us
And show us to be watchers. Be not lost
So poorly in your thoughts.
MACBETH: To know my deed, 'twere best not know myself.
Knocking Within.
Wake Duncan with thy knocking! I would thou couldst!
Exeunt.

ACT II. SCENE III. The Same.

Enter a Porter. Knocking Within.
PORTER: Here's a knocking indeed! If a man were porter of Hell
Gate, he should have old turning the key. Knocking Within.
Knock, knock, knock! Who's there, i' the name of Belzebub? Here's
a farmer that hanged himself on th' expectation of plenty. Come
in time! Have napkins enow about you; here you'll sweat fort.
Knocking Within. Knock, knock! Who's there, in th' other
devil's name? Faith, here's an equivocator that could swear in
both the scales against either scale, who committed treason
enough for God's sake, yet could not equivocate to heaven. O,
come in, equivocator. Knocking Within. Knock, knock, knock!
Who's there? Faith, here's an English tailor come hither, for
stealing out of a French hose. Come in, tailor; here you may
roast your goose. Knocking Within. Knock, knock! Never at
quiet! What are you? But this place is too cold for hell. I'll
devil-porter it no further. I had thought to have let in some of
all professions, that go the primrose way to the everlasting
bonfire. Knocking Within. Anon, anon! I pray you, remember the Porter.
Opens the Gate.
Enter Macduff and Lennox.

MACDUFF: Was it so late, friend, ere you went to bed,
That you do lie so late?
PORTER: Faith, sir, we were carousing till the second cock; and drink, sir, is a great provoker of three things.
MACDUFF: What three things does drink especially provoke?
PORTER: Marry, sir, nose-painting, sleep, and urine. Lechery, sir, it provokes and unprovokes: it provokes the desire, but it takes away the performance. Therefore much drink may be said to be an equivocator with lechery: it makes him, and it mars him; it sets him on, and it takes him off; it persuades him and disheartens him; makes him stand to and not stand to; in conclusion, equivocates him in a sleep, and giving him the lie, leaves him.
MACDUFF: I believe drink gave thee the lie last night.
PORTER: That it did, sir, i' the very throat on me; but requited him for his lie, and, I think, being too strong for him, though he took up my legs sometime, yet I made shift to cast him.
MACDUFF: Is thy master stirring?
Enter Macbeth.
Our knocking has awaked him; here he comes.
LENNOX: Good morrow, noble sir.
MACBETH: morrow, both.
MACDUFF: Is the King stirring, worthy Thane?
MACBETH: Not yet.
MACDUFF: He did command me to call timely on him;
I have almost slipp'd the hour.
MACBETH: I'll bring you to him.
MACDUFF: I know this is a joyful trouble to you,
But yet 'tis one.
MACBETH: The labor we delight in physics pain.
This is the door.
MACDUFF: I'll make so bold to call,
For 'tis my limited service.
Exit.
LENNOX: Goes the King hence today?
MACBETH: He does; he did appoint so.
LENNOX: The night has been unruly. Where we lay,
Our chimneys were blown down, and, as they say,
Lamentings heard i' the air, strange screams of death,
And prophesying with accents terrible
Of dire combustion and confused events
New hatch'd to the woeful time. The obscure bird
Clamor'd the livelong night. Some say the earth
Was feverous and did shake.
MACBETH: 'Twas a rough fight.
LENNOX: My young remembrance cannot parallel
A fellow to it.
Re-enter Macduff.
MACDUFF: O horror, horror, horror! Tongue nor heart
Cannot conceive nor name thee.
MACBETH: LENNOX. What's the matter?
MACDUFF: Confusion now hath made his masterpiece.
Most sacrilegious murther hath broke ope
The Lord's anointed temple and stole thence

The life o' the building.
MACBETH: What is't you say? the life?
LENNOX: Mean you his Majesty?
MACDUFF: Approach the chamber, and destroy your sight
With a new Gorgon. Do not bid me speak;
See, and then speak yourselves.
Exeunt Macbeth and Lennox.
Awake, awake!
Ring the alarum bell. Murther and treason!
Banquo and Donalbain! Malcolm, awake!
Shake off this downy sleep, death's counterfeit,
And look on death itself! Up, up, and see
The great doom's image! Malcolm! Banquo!
As from your graves rise up, and walk like sprites
To countenance this horror! Ring the bell. Bell rings.
Enter Lady Macbeth.
LADY MACBETH: What's the business,
That such a hideous trumpet calls to parley
The sleepers of the house? Speak, speak!
MACDUFF: O gentle lady,
'Tis not for you to hear what I can speak:
The repetition in a woman's ear
Would murther as it fell.
Enter Banquo.
O Banquo, Banquo!
Our royal master's murther'd.
LADY MACBETH: Woe, alas!
What, in our house?
BANQUO: Too cruel anywhere.
Dear Duff, I prithee, contradict thyself,
And say it is not so.
Re-enter Macbeth and Lennox, with Ross.
MACBETH: Had I but died an hour before this chance,
I had lived a blessed time, for from this instant
There's nothing serious in mortality.
All is but toys; renown and grace is dead,
The wine of life is drawn, and the mere lees
Is left this vault to brag of.
Enter Malcolm and Donalbain.
DONALBAIN: What is amiss?
MACBETH: You are, and do not know't.
The spring, the head, the fountain of your blood
Is stopped, the very source of it is stopp'd.
MACDUFF: Your royal father's murther'd.
MALCOLM: O, by whom?
LENNOX: Those of his chamber, as it seem'd, had done't.
Their hands and faces were all badged with blood;
So were their daggers, which unwiped we found
Upon their pillows.
They stared, and were distracted; no man's life
Was to be trusted with them.
MACBETH: O, yet I do repent me of my fury,
That I did kill them.

MACDUFF: Wherefore did you so?
MACBETH: Who can be wise, amazed, temperate and furious,
Loyal and neutral, in a moment? No man.
The expedition of my violent love
Outrun the pauser reason. Here lay Duncan,
His silver skin laced with his golden blood,
And his gash'd stabs look'd like a breach in nature
For ruin's wasteful entrance; there, the murtherers,
Steep'd in the colors of their trade, their daggers
Unmannerly breech'd with gore. Who could refrain,
That had a heart to love, and in that heart
Courage to make 's love known?
LADY MACBETH: Help me hence, ho!
MACDUFF: Look to the lady.
MALCOLM: Aside to Donalbain. Why do we hold our tongues,
That most may claim this argument for ours?
DONALBAIN: Aside to Malcolm. What should be spoken here,
where our fate,
Hid in an auger hole, may rush and seize us?
Let's away,
Our tears are not yet brew'd.
MALCOLM: Aside to Donalbain. Nor our strong sorrow
Upon the foot of motion.
BANQUO: Look to the lady.
Lady Macbeth Is Carried Out.
And when we have our naked frailties hid,
That suffer in exposure, let us meet
And question this most bloody piece of work
To know it further. Fears and scruples shake us.
In the great hand of God I stand, and thence
Against the undivulged pretense I fight
Of treasonous malice.
MACDUFF: And so do I.
ALL: So all.
MACBETH: Let's briefly put on manly readiness
And meet i' the hall together.
ALL: Well contented.
Exeunt All but Malcolm and Donalbain.
MALCOLM: What will you do? Let's not consort with them.
To show an unfelt sorrow is an office
Which the false man does easy. I'll to England.
DONALBAIN: To Ireland, I; our separated fortune
Shall keep us both the safer. Where we are
There's daggers in men's smiles; the near in blood,
The nearer bloody.
MALCOLM: This murtherous shaft that's shot
Hath not yet lighted, and our safest way
Is to avoid the aim. Therefore to horse;
And let us not be dainty of leave-taking,
But shift away. There's warrant in that theft
Which steals itself when there's no mercy left.
Exeunt.

ACT II. SCENE IV. Outside Macbeth's Castle.

Enter Ross with an Old Man.
OLD MAN: Threescore and ten I can remember well,
Within the volume of which time I have seen
Hours dreadful and things strange, but this sore night
Hath trifled former knowings.
ROSS: Ah, good father,
Thou seest the heavens, as troubled with man's act,
Threaten his bloody stage. By the clock 'tis day,
And yet dark night strangles the traveling lamp.
Is't night's predominance, or the day's shame,
That darkness does the face of earth entomb,
When living light should kiss it?
OLD MAN: 'Tis unnatural,
Even like the deed that's done. On Tuesday last
A falcon towering in her pride of place
Was by a mousing owl hawk'd at and kill'd.
ROSS: And Duncan's horses-a thing most strange and certain-
Beauteous and swift, the minions of their race,
Turn'd wild in nature, broke their stalls, flung out,
Contending 'gainst obedience, as they would make
War with mankind.
OLD MAN: 'Tis said they eat each other.
ROSS: They did so, to the amazement of mine eyes
That look'd upon't.
Enter Macduff.
Here comes the good Macduff.
How goes the world, sir, now?
MACDUFF: Why, see you not?
ROSS: Is't known who did this more than bloody deed?
MACDUFF: Those that Macbeth hath slain.
ROSS: Alas, the day!
What good could they pretend?
MACDUFF: They were suborn'd:
Malcolm and Donalbain, the King's two sons,
Are stol'n away and fled, which puts upon them
Suspicion of the deed.
ROSS: 'Gainst nature still!
Thriftless ambition, that wilt ravin up
Thine own life's means! Then 'tis most like
The sovereignty will fall upon Macbeth.
MACDUFF: He is already named, and gone to Scone
To be invested.
ROSS: Where is Duncan's body?
MACDUFF: Carried to Colmekill,
The sacred storehouse of his predecessors
And guardian of their bones.
ROSS: Will you to Scone?
MACDUFF: No, cousin, I'll to Fife.
ROSS: Well, I will thither.
MACDUFF: Well, may you see things well done there.
Adieu,
Lest our old robes sit easier than our new!

ROSS: Farewell, father.
OLD MAN: God's benison go with you and with those
That would make good of bad and friends of foes!
Exeunt.

ACT III. SCENE I. Forres. The Palace.

Enter Banquo.
BANQUO: Thou hast it now: King, Cawdor, Glamis, all,
As the weird women promised, and I fear
Thou play'dst most foully for't; yet it was said
It should not stand in thy posterity,
But that myself should be the root and father
Of many kings. If there come truth from them
(As upon thee, Macbeth, their speeches shine)
Why, by the verities on thee made good,
May they not be my oracles as well
And set me up in hope? But hush, no more.
Sennet Sounds. Enter Macbeth as King, Lady Macbeth as Queen, Lennox, Ross, Lords, Ladies, and Attendants.
MACBETH: Here's our chief guest.
LADY MACBETH: If he had been forgotten,
It had been as a gap in our great feast
And all thing unbecoming.
MACBETH: Tonight we hold a solemn supper, sir,
And I'll request your presence.
BANQUO: Let your Highness
Command upon me, to the which my duties
Are with a most indissoluble tie
Forever knit.
MACBETH: Ride you this afternoon?
BANQUO: Ay, my good lord.
MACBETH: We should have else desired your good advice,
Which still hath been both grave and prosperous
In this day's council; but we'll take tomorrow.
Is't far you ride'!
BANQUO: As far, my lord, as will fill up the time
'Twixt this and supper. Go not my horse the better,
I must become a borrower of the night
For a dark hour or twain.
MACBETH: Fail not our feast.
BANQUO: My lord, I will not.
MACBETH: We hear our bloody cousins are bestow'd
In England and in Ireland, not confessing
Their cruel parricide, filling their hearers
With strange invention. But of that tomorrow,
When therewithal we shall have cause of state
Craving us jointly. Hie you to horse; adieu,
Till you return at night. Goes Fleance with you?
BANQUO: Ay, my good lord. Our time does call upon 's.
MACBETH: I wish your horses swift and sure of foot,
And so I do commend you to their backs.
Farewell.
Exit Banquo.
Let every man be master of his time

Till seven at night; to make society
The sweeter welcome, we will keep ourself
Till supper time alone. While then, God be with you!
Exeunt all but Macbeth and an Attendant.
Sirrah, a word with you. Attend those men
Our pleasure?
ATTENDANT: They are, my lord, without the palace gate.
MACBETH: Bring them before us.
Exit Attendant.
To be thus is nothing,
But to be safely thus. Our fears in Banquo.
Stick deep, and in his royalty of nature
Reigns that which would be fear'd. 'Tis much he dares,
And, to that dauntless temper of his mind,
He hath a wisdom that doth guide his valor
To act in safety. There is none but he
Whose being I do fear; and under him
My genius is rebuked, as it is said
Mark Antony's was by Caesar. He chid the sisters
When first they put the name of King upon me
And bade them speak to him; then prophet-like
They hail'd him father to a line of kings.
Upon my head they placed a fruitless crown
And put a barren sceptre in my gripe,
Thence to be wrench'd with an unlineal hand,
No son of mine succeeding. If't be so,
For Banquo's issue have I filed my mind,
For them the gracious Duncan have I murther'd,
Put rancors in the vessel of my peace
Only for them, and mine eternal jewel
Given to the common enemy of man,
To make them kings -the seed of Banquo kings!
Rather than so, come, Fate, into the list,
And champion me to the utterance! Who's there?
Re-enter Attendant, with Two Murtherers.
Now go to the door, and stay there till we call.
Exit Attendant.
Was it not yesterday we spoke together?
FIRST MURTHERER: It was, so please your Highness.
MACBETH: Well then, now
Have you consider'd of my speeches? Know
That it was he in the times past which held you
So under fortune, which you thought had been
Our innocent self? This I made good to you
In our last conference, pass'd in probation with you:
How you were borne in hand, how cross'd, the instruments,
Who wrought with them, and all things else that might
To half a soul and to a notion crazed
Say, "Thus did Banquo."
FIRST MURTHERER: You made it known to us.
MACBETH: I did so, and went further, which is now
Our point of second meeting. Do you find
Your patience so predominant in your nature,

That you can let this go? Are you so gospel'd,
To pray for this good man and for his issue,
Whose heavy hand hath bow'd you to the grave
And beggar'd yours forever?
FIRST MURTHERER: We are men, my liege.
MACBETH: Ay, in the catalogue ye go for men,
As hounds and greyhounds, mongrels, spaniels, curs,
Shoughs, waterrugs, and demi-wolves are clept
All by the name of dogs. The valued file
Distinguishes the swift, the slow, the subtle,
The housekeeper, the hunter, every one
According to the gift which bounteous nature
Hath in him closed, whereby he does receive
Particular addition, from the bill
That writes them all alike; and so of men.
Now if you have a station in the file,
Not i' the worst rank of manhood, say it,
And I will put that business in your bosoms
Whose execution takes your enemy off,
Grapples you to the heart and love of us,
Who wear our health but sickly in his life,
Which in his death were perfect.
SECOND MURTHERER: I am one, my liege,
Whom the vile blows and buffets of the world
Have so incensed that I am reckless what
I do to spite the world.
FIRST MURTHERER: And I another
So weary with disasters, tugg'd with fortune,
That I would set my life on any chance,
To mend it or be rid on't.
MACBETH: Both of you
Know Banquo was your enemy.
BOTH MURTHERERS: True, my lord.
MACBETH: So is he mine, and in such bloody distance
That every minute of his being thrusts
Against my near'st of life; and though I could
With barefaced power sweep him from my sight
And bid my will avouch it, yet I must not,
For certain friends that are both his and mine,
Whose loves I may not drop, but wail his fall
Who I myself struck down. And thence it is
That I to your assistance do make love,
Masking the business from the common eye
For sundry weighty reasons.
SECOND MURTHERER: We shall, my lord,
Perform what you command us.
FIRST MURTHERER: Though our lives-
MACBETH: Your spirits shine through you. Within this hour at most
I will advise you where to plant yourselves,
Acquaint you with the perfect spy o' the time,
The moment on't; fort must be done tonight
And something from the palace (always thought
That I require a clearness); and with him-

To leave no rubs nor botches in the work-
Fleance his son, that keeps him company,
Whose absence is no less material to me
Than is his father's, must embrace the fate
Of that dark hour. Resolve yourselves apart;
I'll come to you anon.
BOTH MURTHERERS: We are resolved, my lord.
MACBETH: I'll call upon you straight. Abide within.
Exeunt Murtherers.
It is concluded: Banquo, thy soul's flight,
If it find heaven, must find it out tonight.
Exit.

ACT III. SCENE II. The Palace.

Enter Lady Macbeth and a Servant.
LADY MACBETH: Is Banquo gone from court?
SERVANT: Ay, madam, but returns again tonight.
LADY MACBETH: Say to the King I would attend his leisure
For a few words.
SERVANT: Madam, I will.
Exit.
LADY MACBETH: Nought's had, all's spent,
Where our desire is got without content.
'Tis safer to be that which we destroy
Than by destruction dwell in doubtful joy.
Enter Macbeth.
How now, my lord? Why do you keep alone,
Of sorriest fancies your companions making,
Using those thoughts which should indeed have died
With them they think on? Things without all remedy
Should be without regard. What's done is done.
MACBETH: We have scotch'd the snake, not kill'd it.
She'll close and be herself, whilst our poor malice
Remains in danger of her former tooth.
But let the frame of things disjoint, both the worlds suffer,
Ere we will eat our meal in fear and sleep
In the affliction of these terrible dreams
That shake us nightly. Better be with the dead,
Whom we, to gain our peace, have sent to peace,
Than on the torture of the mind to lie
In restless ecstasy. Duncan is in his grave;
After life's fitful fever he sleeps well.
Treason has done his worst; nor steel, nor poison,
Malice domestic, foreign levy, nothing,
Can touch him further.
LADY MACBETH: Come on,
Gentle my lord, sleek o'er your rugged looks;
Be bright and jovial among your guests tonight.
MACBETH: So shall I, love, and so, I pray, be you.
Let your remembrance apply to Banquo;
Present him eminence, both with eye and tongue:
Unsafe the while, that we
Must lave our honors in these flattering streams,
And make our faces vizards to our hearts,

Disguising what they are.
LADY MACBETH: You must leave this.
MACBETH: O, full of scorpions is my mind, dear wife!
Thou know'st that Banquo and his Fleance lives.
LADY MACBETH: But in them nature's copy's not eterne.
MACBETH: There's comfort yet; they are assailable.
Then be thou jocund. Ere the bat hath flown
His cloister'd flight, ere to black Hecate's summons
The shard-borne beetle with his drowsy hums
Hath rung night's yawning peal, there shall be done
A deed of dreadful note.
LADY MACBETH: What's to be done?
MACBETH: Be innocent of the knowledge, dearest chuck,
Till thou applaud the deed. Come, seeling night,
Scarf up the tender eye of pitiful day,
And with thy bloody and invisible hand
Cancel and tear to pieces that great bond
Which keeps me pale! Light thickens, and the crow
Makes wing to the rooky wood;
Good things of day begin to droop and drowse,
Whiles night's black agents to their preys do rouse.
Thou marvel'st at my words, but hold thee still:
Things bad begun make strong themselves by ill.
So, prithee, go with me.
Exeunt.

ACT III. SCENE III. A Park near the Palace.

Enter three Murtherers.
FIRST MURTHERER: But who did bid thee join with us?
THIRD MURTHERER: Macbeth.
SECOND MURTHERER: He needs not our mistrust, since he delivers
Our offices and what we have to do
To the direction just.
FIRST MURTHERER: Then stand with us.
The west yet glimmers with some streaks of day;
Now spurs the lated traveler apace
To gain the timely inn, and near approaches
The subject of our watch.
THIRD MURTHERER: Hark! I hear horses.
BANQUO: Within. Give us a light there, ho!
SECOND MURTHERER: Then 'tis he; the rest
That are within the note of expectation
Already are i' the court.
FIRST MURTHERER: His horses go about.
THIRD MURTHERER: Almost a mile, but he does usually-
So all men do -from hence to the palace gate
Make it their walk.
SECOND MURTHERER: A light, a light!
Enter Banquo, and Fleance with a Torch.
THIRD MURTHERER: 'Tis he.
FIRST MURTHERER: Stand to't.
BANQUO: It will be rain tonight.
FIRST MURTHERER: Let it come down.
They Set upon Banquo.

BANQUO: O, treachery! Fly, good Fleance, fly, fly, fly!
Thou mayst revenge. O slave! Dies. Fleance escapes.
THIRD MURTHERER: Who did strike out the light?
FIRST MURTHERER: Wast not the way?
THIRD MURTHERER: There's but one down; the son is fled.
SECOND MURTHERER: We have lost
Best half of our affair.
FIRST MURTHERER: Well, let's away and say how much is done.
Exeunt.

ACT III. SCENE IV. A Hall in the Palace. A Banquet Prepared.

Enter Macbeth, Lady Macbeth, Ross, Lennox, Lords, and Attendants.
MACBETH: You know your own degrees; sit down. At first
And last the hearty welcome.
LORDS: Thanks to your Majesty.
MACBETH: Ourself will mingle with society
And play the humble host.
Our hostess keeps her state, but in best time
We will require her welcome.
LADY MACBETH: Pronounce it for me, sir, to all our friends,
For my heart speaks they are welcome.
Enter first Murtherer to the door.
MACBETH: See, they encounter thee with their hearts' thanks.
Both sides are even; here I'll sit i' the midst.
Be large in mirth; anon we'll drink a measure
The table round. Approaches the Door. There's blood upon thy face.
MURTHERER: 'Tis Banquo's then.
MACBETH: 'Tis better thee without than he within.
Is he dispatch'd?
MURTHERER: My lord, his throat is cut; that I did for him.
MACBETH: Thou art the best o' the cut-throats! Yet he's good
That did the like for Fleance. If thou didst it,
Thou art the nonpareil.
MURTHERER: Most royal sir,
Fleance is 'scaped.
MACBETH: Aside. Then comes my fit again. I had else been perfect,
Whole as the marble, founded as the rock,
As broad and general as the casing air;
But now I am cabin'd, cribb'd, confin'd, bound in
To saucy doubts and fears -But Banquo's safe?
MURTHERER: Ay, my good lord. Safe in a ditch he bides,
With twenty trenched gashes on his head,
The least a death to nature.
MACBETH: Thanks for that.
There the grown serpent lies; the worm that's fled
Hath nature that in time will venom breed,
No teeth for the present. Get thee gone. Tomorrow
We'll hear ourselves again.
Exit Murtherer.
LADY MACBETH: My royal lord,
You do not give the cheer. The feast is sold
That is not often vouch'd, while 'tis amaking,
'Tis given with welcome. To feed were best at home;
From thence the sauce to meat is ceremony;

Meeting were bare without it.
MACBETH: Sweet remembrancer!
Now good digestion wait on appetite,
And health on both!
LENNOX: May't please your Highness sit.
The Ghost of Banquo Enters and Sits in Macbeth's Place.
MACBETH: Here had we now our country's honor roof'd,
Were the graced person of our Banquo present,
Who may I rather challenge for unkindness
Than pity for mischance!
ROSS: His absence, sir,
Lays blame upon his promise. Please't your Highness
To grace us with your royal company?
MACBETH: The table's full.
LENNOX: Here is a place reserved, sir.
MACBETH: Where?
LENNOX: Here, my good lord. What is't that moves your Highness?
MACBETH: Which of you have done this?
LORDS: What, my good lord?
MACBETH: Thou canst not say I did it; never shake
Thy gory locks at me.
ROSS: Gentlemen, rise; his Highness is well.
LADY MACBETH: Sit, worthy friends; my lord is often thus,
And hath been from his youth. Pray you, keep seat.
The fit is momentary; upon a thought
He will again be well. If much you note him,
You shall offend him and extend his passion.
Feed, and regard him not-Are you a man?
MACBETH: Ay, and a bold one, that dare look on that
Which might appal the devil.
LADY MACBETH: O proper stuff!
This is the very painting of your fear;
This is the air-drawn dagger which you said
Led you to Duncan. O, these flaws and starts,
Impostors to true fear, would well become
A woman's story at a winter's fire,
Authorized by her grandam. Shame itself!
Why do you make such faces? When all's done,
You look but on a stool.
MACBETH: Prithee, see there! Behold! Look! Lo! How say you?
Why, what care I? If thou canst nod, speak too.
If charnel houses and our graves must send
Those that we bury back, our monuments
Shall be the maws of kites.
Exit Ghost.
LADY MACBETH: What, quite unmann'd in folly?
MACBETH: If I stand here, I saw him.
LADY MACBETH: Fie, for shame!
MACBETH: Blood hath been shed ere now, i' the olden time,
Ere humane statute purged the gentle weal;
Ay, and since too, murthers have been perform'd
Too terrible for the ear. The time has been,
That, when the brains were out, the man would die,

And there an end; but now they rise again,
With twenty mortal murthers on their crowns,
And push us from our stools. This is more strange
Than such a murther is.
LADY MACBETH: My worthy lord,
Your noble friends do lack you.
MACBETH: I do forget.
Do not muse at me, my most worthy friends.
I have a strange infirmity, which is nothing
To those that know me. Come, love and health to all;
Then I'll sit down. Give me some wine, fill full.
I drink to the general joy o' the whole table,
And to our dear friend Banquo, whom we miss.
Would he were here! To all and him we thirst,
And all to all.
LORDS: Our duties and the pledge.
Re-enter Ghost.
MACBETH: Avaunt, and quit my sight! Let the earth hide thee!
Thy bones are marrowless, thy blood is cold;
Thou hast no speculation in those eyes
Which thou dost glare with.
LADY MACBETH: Think of this, good peers,
But as a thing of custom. 'Tis no other,
Only it spoils the pleasure of the time.
MACBETH: What man dare, I dare.
Approach thou like the rugged Russian bear,
The arm'd rhinoceros, or the Hyrcan tiger;
Take any shape but that, and my firm nerves
Shall never tremble. Or be alive again,
And dare me to the desert with thy sword.
If trembling I inhabit then, protest me
The baby of a girl. Hence, horrible shadow!
Unreal mockery, hence!
Exit Ghost.
Why, so, being gone,
I am a man again. Pray you sit still.
LADY MACBETH: You have displaced the mirth, broke the good meeting,
With most admired disorder.
MACBETH: Can such things be,
And overcome us like a summer's cloud,
Without our special wonder? You make me strange
Even to the disposition that I owe
When now I think you can behold such sights
And keep the natural ruby of your cheeks
When mine is blanch'd with fear.
ROSS: What sights, my lord?
LADY MACBETH: I pray you, speak not; he grows worse and worse;
Question enrages him. At once, good night.
Stand not upon the order of your going,
But go at once.
LENNOX: Good night, and better health
Attend his Majesty!
LADY MACBETH: A kind good night to all!

Exeunt All but Macbeth and Lady Macbeth.
MACBETH: will have blood; they say blood will have blood.
Stones have been known to move and trees to speak;
Augures and understood relations have
By maggot pies and choughs and rooks brought forth
The secret'st man of blood. What is the night?
LADY MACBETH: Almost at odds with morning, which is which.
MACBETH: How say'st thou, that Macduff denies his person
At our great bidding?
LADY MACBETH: Did you send to him, sir?
MACBETH: I hear it by the way, but I will send.
There's not a one of them but in his house
I keep a servant feed. I will tomorrow,
And betimes I will, to the weird sisters.
More shall they speak; for now I am bent to know,
By the worst means, the worst. For mine own good
All causes shall give way. I am in blood
Stepp'd in so far that, should I wade no more,
Returning were as tedious as go o'er.
Strange things I have in head that will to hand,
Which must be acted ere they may be scann'd.
LADY MACBETH: You lack the season of all natures, sleep.
MACBETH: Come, we'll to sleep. My strange and self-abuse
Is the initiate fear that wants hard use.
We are yet but young in deed.
Exeunt.

ACT III. SCENE V. A Heath. Thunder.

Enter the Three Witches, Meeting Hecate.
FIRST WITCH: Why, how now, Hecate? You look angerly.
HECATE: Have I not reason, beldams as you are,
Saucy and overbold? How did you dare
To trade and traffic with Macbeth
In riddles and affairs of death,
And I, the mistress of your charms,
The close contriver of all harms,
Was never call'd to bear my part,
Or show the glory of our art?
And, which is worse, all you have done
Hath been but for a wayward son,
Spiteful and wrathful, who, as others do,
Loves for his own ends, not for you.
But make amends now. Get you gone,
And at the pit of Acheron
Meet me i' the morning. Thither he
Will come to know his destiny.
Your vessels and your spells provide,
Your charms and everything beside.
I am for the air; this night I'll spend
Unto a dismal and a fatal end.
Great business must be wrought ere noon:
Upon the corner of the moon
There hangs a vaporous drop profound;
I'll catch it ere it come to ground.

And that distill'd by magic sleights
Shall raise such artificial sprites
As by the strength of their illusion
Shall draw him on to his confusion.
He shall spurn fate, scorn death, and bear
His hopes 'bove wisdom, grace, and fear.
And you all know security
Is mortals' chiefest enemy.
Music and a Song Within,
"Come Away, Come Away."
Hark! I am call'd; my little spirit, see,
Sits in a foggy cloud and stays for me. Exit.
FIRST WITCH: Come, let's make haste; she'll soon be back again.
Exeunt.

ACT III. SCENE VI. Forres. The Palace.

Enter Lennox and Another Lord.
LENNOX: My former speeches have but hit your thoughts,
Which can interpret farther; only I say
Thing's have been strangely borne. The gracious Duncan
Was pitied of Macbeth; marry, he was dead.
And the right valiant Banquo walk'd too late,
Whom, you may say, if't please you, Fleance kill'd,
For Fleance fled. Men must not walk too late.
Who cannot want the thought, how monstrous
It was for Malcolm and for Donalbain
To kill their gracious father? Damned fact!
How it did grieve Macbeth! Did he not straight,
In pious rage, the two delinquents tear
That were the slaves of drink and thralls of sleep?
Was not that nobly done? Ay, and wisely too,
For 'twould have anger'd any heart alive
To hear the men deny't. So that, I say,
He has borne all things well; and I do think
That, had he Duncan's sons under his key-
As, an't please heaven, he shall not -they should find
What 'twere to kill a father; so should Fleance.
But, peace! For from broad words, and 'cause he fail'd
His presence at the tyrant's feast, I hear,
Macduff lives in disgrace. Sir, can you tell
Where he bestows himself?
LORD: The son of Duncan,
From whom this tyrant holds the due of birth,
Lives in the English court and is received
Of the most pious Edward with such grace
That the malevolence of fortune nothing
Takes from his high respect. Thither Macduff
Is gone to pray the holy King, upon his aid
To wake Northumberland and warlike Siward;
That by the help of these, with Him above
To ratify the work, we may again
Give to our tables meat, sleep to our nights,
Free from our feasts and banquets bloody knives,
Do faithful homage, and receive free honors-

All which we pine for now. And this report
Hath so exasperate the King that he
Prepares for some attempt of war.
LENNOX: Sent he to Macduff?
LORD: He did, and with an absolute "Sir, not I,"
The cloudy messenger turns me his back,
And hums, as who should say, "You'll rue the time
That clogs me with this answer."
LENNOX: And that well might
Advise him to a caution, to hold what distance
His wisdom can provide. Some holy angel
Fly to the court of England and unfold
His message ere he come, that a swift blessing
May soon return to this our suffering country
Under a hand accursed!
LORD: I'll send my prayers with him.
Exeunt.

ACT IV. SCENE I. A Cavern. In the Middle, a Boiling Cauldron. Thunder.

Enter the Three Witches.
FIRST WITCH: Thrice the brinded cat hath mew'd.
SECOND WITCH: Thrice and once the hedge-pig whined.
THIRD WITCH: Harpier cries, "'Tis time, 'tis time."
FIRST WITCH: Round about the cauldron go;
In the poison'd entrails throw.
Toad, that under cold stone
Days and nights has thirty-one
Swelter'd venom sleeping got,
Boil thou first i' the charmed pot.
ALL: Double, double, toil and trouble;
Fire burn and cauldron bubble.
SECOND WITCH: Fillet of a fenny snake,
In the cauldron boil and bake;
Eye of newt and toe of frog,
Wool of bat and tongue of dog,
Adder's fork and blind-worm's sting,
Lizard's leg and howlet's wing,
For a charm of powerful trouble,
Like a hell-broth boil and bubble.
ALL: Double, double, toil and trouble;
Fire burn and cauldron bubble.
THIRD WITCH: Scale of dragon, tooth of wolf,
Witch's mummy, maw and gulf
Of the ravin'd salt-sea shark,
Root of hemlock digg'd i' the dark,
Liver of blaspheming Jew,
Gall of goat and slips of yew
Sliver'd in the moon's eclipse,
Nose of Turk and Tartar's lips,
Finger of birth-strangled babe
Ditch-deliver'd by a drab,
Make the gruel thick and slab.
Add thereto a tiger's chawdron,
For the ingredients of our cawdron.

ALL: Double, double, toil and trouble;
Fire burn and cauldron bubble.
SECOND WITCH: Cool it with a baboon's blood,
Then the charm is firm and good.
Enter Hecate to the Other Three Witches.
HECATE: O, well done! I commend your pains,
And everyone shall share i' the gains.
And now about the cauldron sing,
Like elves and fairies in a ring,
Enchanting all that you put in.
Music and a Song, "Black Spirits."
Hecate Retires.
SECOND WITCH: By the pricking of my thumbs,
Something wicked this way comes.
Open, locks,
Whoever knocks!
Enter Macbeth.
MACBETH: How now, you secret, black, and midnight hags?
What is't you do?
ALL: A deed without a name.
MACBETH: I conjure you, by that which you profess
(Howeer you come to know it) answer me:
Though you untie the winds and let them fight
Against the churches, though the yesty waves
Confound and swallow navigation up,
Though bladed corn be lodged and trees blown down,
Though castles topple on their warders' heads,
Though palaces and pyramids do slope
Their heads to their foundations, though the treasure
Of nature's germaines tumble all together
Even till destruction sicken, answer me
To what I ask you.
FIRST WITCH: Speak.
SECOND WITCH: Demand.
THIRD WITCH: We'll answer.
FIRST WITCH: Say, if thou'dst rather hear it from our mouths,
Or from our masters'?
MACBETH: Call 'em, let me see 'em.
FIRST WITCH: Pour in sow's blood that hath eaten
Her nine farrow; grease that's sweaten
From the murtherer's gibbet throw
Into the flame.
ALL: Come, high or low;
Thyself and office deftly show!
Thunder. First Apparition: an armed Head.
MACBETH: Tell me, thou unknown power-
FIRST WITCH: He knows thy thought:
Hear his speech, but say thou nought.
FIRST APPARITION: Macbeth! Macbeth! Macbeth! Beware Macduff,
Beware the Thane of Fife. Dismiss me. Enough.
Descends.
MACBETH: Whate'er thou art, for thy good caution, thanks;
Thou hast harp'd my fear aright. But one word more-

FIRST WITCH: He will not be commanded. Here's another,
More potent than the first.
Thunder. Second Apparition: a bloody Child.
SECOND APPARITION: Macbeth! Macbeth! Macbeth!
MACBETH: Had I three ears, I'd hear thee.
SECOND APPARITION: Be bloody, bold, and resolute: laugh to scorn
The power of man, for none of woman born
Shall harm Macbeth. Descends.
MACBETH: Then live, Macduff. What need I fear of thee?
But yet I'll make assurance double sure,
And take a bond of fate: thou shalt not live,
That I may tell pale-hearted fear it lies,
And sleep in spite of thunder.
Thunder. Third Apparition: a Child Crowned, with a Tree in His Hand.
What is this,
That rises like the issue of a king,
And wears upon his baby brow the round
And top of sovereignty?
ALL: Listen, but speak not to't.
THIRD APPARITION: Be lion-mettled, proud, and take no care
Who chafes, who frets, or where conspirers are.
Macbeth shall never vanquish'd be until
Great Birnam Wood to high Dunsinane Hill
Shall come against him. Descends.
MACBETH: That will never be.
Who can impress the forest, bid the tree
Unfix his earth-bound root? Sweet bodements, good!
Rebellion's head, rise never till the Wood
Of Birnam rise, and our high-placed Macbeth
Shall live the lease of nature, pay his breath
To time and mortal custom. Yet my heart
Throbs to know one thing: tell me, if your art
Can tell so much, shall Banquo's issue ever
Reign in this kingdom?
ALL: Seek to know no more.
MACBETH: I will be satisfied! Deny me this,
And an eternal curse fall on you! Let me know.
Why sinks that cauldron, and what noise is this?
Hautboys.
FIRST WITCH: Show!
SECOND WITCH: Show!
THIRD WITCH: Show!
ALL: Show his eyes, and grieve his heart;
Come like shadows, so depart!
A show of eight Kings, the last with a glass in his hand;
Banquo's Ghost Following.
MACBETH: Thou are too like the spirit of Banquo Down!
Thy crown does sear mine eyeballs. And thy hair,
Thou other gold-bound brow, is like the first.
A third is like the former. Filthy hags!
Why do you show me this? A fourth! Start, eyes!
What, will the line stretch out to the crack of doom?
Another yet! A seventh! I'll see no more!

And yet the eighth appears, who bears a glass
Which shows me many more; and some I see
That twofold balls and treble sceptres carry.
Horrible sight! Now I see 'tis true;
For the blood-bolter'd Banquo smiles upon me,
And points at them for his. What, is this so?
FIRST WITCH: Ay, sir, all this is so. But why
Stands Macbeth thus amazedly?
Come,sisters, cheer we up his sprites,
And show the best of our delights.
I'll charm the air to give a sound,
While you perform your antic round,
That this great King may kindly say
Our duties did his welcome pay.
Music. The Witches Dance and Then Vanish with Hecate.
MACBETH: are they? Gone? Let this pernicious hour
Stand ay accursed in the calendar!
Come in, without there!
Enter Lennox.
LENNOX: What's your Grace's will?
MACBETH: Saw you the weird sisters?
LENNOX: No, my lord.
MACBETH: Came they not by you?
LENNOX: No indeed, my lord.
MACBETH: Infected be the 'air whereon they ride,
And damn'd all those that trust them! I did hear
The galloping of horse. Who wast came by?
LENNOX: 'Tis two or three, my lord, that bring you word
Macduff is fled to England.
MACBETH: Fled to England?
LENNOX: Ay, my good lord.
MACBETH: Aside. Time, thou anticipatest my dread exploits.
The flighty purpose never is o'ertook
Unless the deed go with it. From this moment
The very firstlings of my heart shall be
The firstlings of my hand. And even now,
To crown my thoughts with acts, be it thought and done:
The castle of Macduff I will surprise,
Seize upon Fife, give to the edge o' the sword
His wife, his babes, and all unfortunate souls
That trace him in his line. No boasting like a fool;
This deed I'll do before this purpose cool.
But no more sights! -Where are these gentlemen?
Come, bring me where they are.
Exeunt.

ACT IV. SCENE II. Fife. Macduff's Castle.

Enter Lady Macduff, her Son, and Ross.
LADY MACDUFF: What had he done, to make him fly the land?
ROSS: You must have patience, madam.
LADY MACDUFF: He had none;
His flight was madness. When our actions do not,
Our fears do make us traitors.
ROSS: You know not

Whether it was his wisdom or his fear.
LADY MACDUFF: Wisdom? To leave his wife, to leave his babes,
His mansion, and his titles, in a place
From whence himself does fly? He loves us not;
He wants the natural touch; for the poor wren,
The most diminutive of birds, will fight,
Her young ones in her nest, against the owl.
All is the fear and nothing is the love;
As little is the wisdom, where the flight
So runs against all reason.
ROSS: My dearest coz,
I pray you, school yourself. But for your husband,
He is noble, wise, Judicious, and best knows
The fits o' the season. I dare not speak much further;
But cruel are the times when we are traitors
And do not know ourselves; when we hold rumor
From what we fear, yet know not what we fear,
But float upon a wild and violent sea
Each way and move. I take my leave of you;
Shall not be long but I'll be here again.
Things at the worst will cease or else climb upward
To what they were before. My pretty cousin,
Blessing upon you!
LADY MACDUFF: Father'd he is, and yet he's fatherless.
ROSS: I am so much a fool, should I stay longer,
It would be my disgrace and your discomfort.
I take my leave at once.
Exit.
LADY MACDUFF: Sirrah, your father's dead.
And what will you do now? How will you live?
SON: As birds do, Mother.
LADY MACDUFF: What, with worms and flies?
SON: With what I get, I mean; and so do they.
LADY MACDUFF: Poor bird! Thou'ldst never fear the net nor lime,
The pitfall nor the gin.
SON: Why should I, Mother? Poor birds they are not set for.
My father is not dead, for all your saying.
LADY MACDUFF: Yes, he is dead. How wilt thou do for father?
SON: Nay, how will you do for a husband?
LADY MACDUFF: Why, I can buy me twenty at any market.
SON: Then you'll buy 'em to sell again.
LADY MACDUFF: Thou speak'st with all thy wit, and yet, i' faith,
With wit enough for thee.
SON: Was my father a traitor, Mother?
LADY MACDUFF: Ay, that he was.
SON: What is a traitor?
LADY MACDUFF: Why one that swears and lies.
SON: And be all traitors that do so?
LADY MACDUFF: Everyone that does so is a traitor and must be hanged.
SON: And must they all be hanged that swear and lie?
LADY MACDUFF: Everyone.
SON: Who must hang them?

LADY MACDUFF: Why, the honest men.
SON: Then the liars and swearers are fools, for there are liars and swearers enow to beat the honest men and hang up them.
LADY MACDUFF: Now, God help thee, poor monkey! But how wilt thou do for a father?
SON: If he were dead, you'ld weep for him; if you would not, it were a good sign that I should quickly have a new father.
LADY MACDUFF: Poor prattler, how thou talk'st!
Enter a Messenger.
MESSENGER: Bless you, fair dame! I am not to you known,
Though in your state of honor I am perfect.
I doubt some danger does approach you nearly.
If you will take a homely man's advice,
Be not found here; hence, with your little ones.
To fright you thus, methinks I am too savage;
To do worse to you were fell cruelty,
Which is too nigh your person. Heaven preserve you!
I dare abide no longer.
Exit.
LADY MACDUFF: Whither should I fly?
I have done no harm. But I remember now
I am in this earthly world, where to do harm
Is often laudable, to do good sometime
Accounted dangerous folly. Why then, alas,
Do I put up that womanly defense,
To say I have done no harm -What are these faces?
Enter Murtherers.
FIRST MURTHERER: Where is your husband?
LADY MACDUFF: I hope, in no place so unsanctified
Where such as thou mayst find him.
FIRST MURTHERER: He's a traitor.
SON: Thou liest, thou shag-ear'd villain!
FIRST MURTHERER: What, you egg!
Stabs him.
Young fry of treachery!
SON: He has kill'd me, Mother.
Run away, I pray you! Dies.
Exit Lady Macduff, Crying "Murther!"
Exeunt Murtherers, Following Her.

ACT IV. SCENE III. England. Before the King's Palace.

Enter Malcolm and Macduff.
MALCOLM: Let us seek out some desolate shade and there
Weep our sad bosoms empty.
MACDUFF: Let us rather
Hold fast the mortal sword, and like good men
Bestride our downfall'n birthdom. Each new morn
New widows howl, new orphans cry, new sorrows
Strike heaven on the face, that it resounds
As if it felt with Scotland and yell'd out
Like syllable of dolor.
MALCOLM: What I believe, I'll wall;
What know, believe; and what I can redress,
As I shall find the time to friend, I will.
What you have spoke, it may be so perchance.

This tyrant, whose sole name blisters our tongues,
Was once thought honest. You have loved him well;
He hath not touch'd you yet. I am young, but something
You may deserve of him through me, and wisdom
To offer up a weak, poor, innocent lamb
To appease an angry god.
MACDUFF: I am not treacherous.
MALCOLM: But Macbeth is.
A good and virtuous nature may recoil
In an imperial charge. But I shall crave your pardon;
That which you are, my thoughts cannot transpose.
Angels are bright still, though the brightest fell.
Though all things foul would wear the brows of grace,
Yet grace must still look so.
MACDUFF: I have lost my hopes.
MALCOLM: Perchance even there where I did find my doubts.
Why in that rawness left you wife and child,
Those precious motives, those strong knots of love,
Without leave-taking? I pray you,
Let not my jealousies be your dishonors,
But mine own safeties. You may be rightly just,
Whatever I shall think.
MACDUFF: Bleed, bleed, poor country!
Great tyranny, lay thou thy basis sure,
For goodness dare not check thee. Wear thou thy wrongs;
The title is affeer'd. Fare thee well, lord.
I would not be the villain that thou think'st
For the whole space that's in the tyrant's grasp
And the rich East to boot.
MALCOLM: Be not offended;
I speak not as in absolute fear of you.
I think our country sinks beneath the yoke;
It weeps, it bleeds, and each new day a gash
Is added to her wounds. I think withal
There would be hands uplifted in my right;
And here from gracious England have I offer
Of goodly thousands. But for all this,
When I shall tread upon the tyrant's head,
Or wear it on my sword, yet my poor country
Shall have more vices than it had before,
More suffer and more sundry ways than ever,
By him that shall succeed.
MACDUFF: What should he be?
MALCOLM: It is myself I mean, in whom I know
All the particulars of vice so grafted
That, when they shall be open'd, black Macbeth
Will seem as pure as snow, and the poor state
Esteem him as a lamb, being compared
With my confineless harms.
MACDUFF: Not in the legions
Of horrid hell can come a devil more damn'd
In evils to top Macbeth.
MALCOLM: I grant him bloody,

Luxurious, avaricious, false, deceitful,
Sudden, malicious, smacking of every sin
That has a name. But there's no bottom, none,
In my voluptuousness. Your wives, your daughters,
Your matrons, and your maids could not fill up
The cestern of my lust, and my desire
All continent impediments would o'erbear
That did oppose my will. Better Macbeth
Than such an one to reign.
MACDUFF: Boundless intemperance
In nature is a tyranny; it hath been
The untimely emptying of the happy throne,
And fall of many kings. But fear not yet
To take upon you what is yours. You may
Convey your pleasures in a spacious plenty
And yet seem cold, the time you may so hoodwink.
We have willing dames enough; there cannot be
That vulture in you to devour so many
As will to greatness dedicate themselves,
Finding it so inclined.
MALCOLM: With this there grows
In my most ill-composed affection such
A stanchless avarice that, were I King,
I should cut off the nobles for their lands,
Desire his jewels and this other's house,
And my more-having would be as a sauce
To make me hunger more, that I should forge
Quarrels unjust against the good and loyal,
Destroying them for wealth.
MACDUFF: This avarice
Sticks deeper, grows with more pernicious root
Than summer-seeming lust, and it hath been
The sword of our slain kings. Yet do not fear;
Scotland hath foisons to fill up your will
Of your mere own. All these are portable,
With other graces weigh'd.
MALCOLM: But I have none. The king-becoming graces,
As justice, verity, temperance, stableness,
Bounty, perseverance, mercy, lowliness,
Devotion, patience, courage, fortitude,
I have no relish of them, but abound
In the division of each several crime,
Acting it many ways. Nay, had I power, I should
Pour the sweet milk of concord into hell,
Uproar the universal peace, confound
All unity on earth.
MACDUFF: O Scotland, Scotland!
MALCOLM: If such a one be fit to govern, speak.
I am as I have spoken.
MACDUFF: Fit to govern?
No, not to live. O nation miserable!
With an untitled tyrant bloody-scepter'd,
When shalt thou see thy wholesome days again,

Since that the truest issue of thy throne
By his own interdiction stands accursed
And does blaspheme his breed? Thy royal father
Was a most sainted king; the queen that bore thee,
Oftener upon her knees than on her feet,
Died every day she lived. Fare thee well!
These evils thou repeat'st upon thyself
Have banish'd me from Scotland. O my breast,
Thy hope ends here!
MALCOLM: Macduff, this noble passion,
Child of integrity, hath from my soul
Wiped the black scruples, reconciled my thoughts
To thy good truth and honor. Devilish Macbeth
By many of these trains hath sought to win me
Into his power, and modest wisdom plucks me
From over-credulous haste. But God above
Deal between thee and me! For even now
I put myself to thy direction and
Unspeak mine own detraction; here abjure
The taints and blames I laid upon myself,
For strangers to my nature. I am yet
Unknown to woman, never was forsworn,
Scarcely have coveted what was mine own,
At no time broke my faith, would not betray
The devil to his fellow, and delight
No less in truth than life. My first false speaking
Was this upon myself. What I am truly
Is thine and my poor country's to command.
Whither indeed, before thy here-approach,
Old Siward, with ten thousand warlike men
Already at a point, was setting forth.
Now we'll together, and the chance of goodness
Be like our warranted quarrel! Why are you silent?
MACDUFF: Such welcome and unwelcome things at once
'Tis hard to reconcile.
Enter a Doctor.
MALCOLM: Well, more anon. Comes the King forth, I pray you?
DOCTOR: Ay, sir, there are a crew of wretched souls
That stay his cure. Their malady convinces
The great assay of art, but at his touch,
Such sanctity hath heaven given his hand,
They presently amend.
MALCOLM: I thank you, Doctor.
Exit Doctor.
MACDUFF: What's the disease he means?
MALCOLM: 'Tis call'd the evil:
A most miraculous work in this good King,
Which often, since my here-remain in England,
I have seen him do. How he solicits heaven,
Himself best knows; but strangely-visited people,
All swol'n and ulcerous, pitiful to the eye,
The mere despair of surgery, he cures,
Hanging a golden stamp about their necks

Put on with holy prayers; and 'tis spoken,
To the succeeding royalty he leaves
The healing benediction. With this strange virtue
He hath a heavenly gift of prophecy,
And sundry blessings hang about his throne
That speak him full of grace.
Enter Ross.
MACDUFF: See, who comes here?
MALCOLM: My countryman, but yet I know him not.
MACDUFF: My ever gentle cousin, welcome hither.
MALCOLM: I know him now. Good God, betimes remove
The means that makes us strangers!
ROSS: Sir, amen.
MACDUFF: Stands Scotland where it did?
ROSS: Alas, poor country,
Almost afraid to know itself! It cannot
Be call'd our mother, but our grave. Where nothing,
But who knows nothing, is once seen to smile;
Where sighs and groans and shrieks that rend the air,
Are made, not mark'd; where violent sorrow seems
A modern ecstasy. The dead man's knell
Is there scarce ask'd for who, and good men's lives
Expire before the flowers in their caps,
Dying or ere they sicken.
MACDUFF: O, relation too nice, and yet too true!
MALCOLM: What's the newest grief?
ROSS: That of an hour's age doth hiss the speaker;
Each minute teems a new one.
MACDUFF: How does my wife?
ROSS: Why, well.
MACDUFF: And all my children?
ROSS: Well too.
MACDUFF: The tyrant has not batter'd at their peace?
ROSS: No, they were well at peace when I did leave 'em.
MACDUFF: Be not a niggard of your speech. How goest?
ROSS: When I came hither to transport the tidings,
Which I have heavily borne, there ran a rumor
Of many worthy fellows that were out,
Which was to my belief witness'd the rather,
For that I saw the tyrant's power afoot.
Now is the time of help; your eye in Scotland
Would create soldiers, make our women fight,
To doff their dire distresses.
MALCOLM: Be't their comfort
We are coming thither. Gracious England hath
Lent us good Siward and ten thousand men;
An older and a better soldier none
That Christendom gives out.
ROSS: Would I could answer
This comfort with the like! But I have words
That would be howl'd out in the desert air,
Where hearing should not latch them.
MACDUFF: What concern they?

The general cause? Or is it a fee-grief
Due to some single breast?
ROSS: No mind that's honest
But in it shares some woe, though the main part
Pertains to you alone.
MACDUFF: If it be mine,
Keep it not from me, quickly let me have it.
ROSS: Let not your ears despise my tongue forever,
Which shall possess them with the heaviest sound
That ever yet they heard.
MACDUFF: Humh! I guess at it.
ROSS: Your castle is surprised; your wife and babes
Savagely slaughter'd. To relate the manner
Were, on the quarry of these murther'd deer,
To add the death of you.
MALCOLM: Merciful heaven!
What, man! Neer pull your hat upon your brows;
Give sorrow words. The grief that does not speak
Whispers the o'erfraught heart, and bids it break.
MACDUFF: My children too?
ROSS: Wife, children, servants, all
That could be found.
MACDUFF: And I must be from thence!
My wife kill'd too?
ROSS: I have said.
MALCOLM: Be comforted.
Let's make us medicines of our great revenge,
To cure this deadly grief.
MACDUFF: He has no children. All my pretty ones?
Did you say all? O hell-kite! All?
What, all my pretty chickens and their dam
At one fell swoop?
MALCOLM: Dispute it like a man.
MACDUFF: I shall do so,
But I must also feel it as a man.
I cannot but remember such things were
That were most precious to me. Did heaven look on,
And would not take their part? Sinful Macduff,
They were all struck for thee! Naught that I am,
Not for their own demerits, but for mine,
Fell slaughter on their souls. Heaven rest them now!
MALCOLM: Be this the whetstone of your sword. Let grief
Convert to anger; blunt not the heart, enrage it.
MACDUFF: O, I could play the woman with mine eyes
And braggart with my tongue! But, gentle heavens,
Cut short all intermission; front to front
Bring thou this fiend of Scotland and myself;
Within my sword's length set him; if he 'scape,
Heaven forgive him too!
MALCOLM: This tune goes manly.
Come, go we to the King; our power is ready,
Our lack is nothing but our leave. Macbeth
Is ripe for shaking, and the powers above

Put on their instruments. Receive what cheer you may,
The night is long that never finds the day.
Exeunt.

ACT V. SCENE I. Dunsinane. Anteroom in the Castle.

Enter a Doctor of Physic and a Waiting Gentlewoman.

DOCTOR: I have two nights watched with you, but can perceive no truth in your report. When was it she last walked?

GENTLEWOMAN: Since his Majesty went into the field, have seen her rise from her bed, throw her nightgown upon her, unlock her closet, take forth paper, fold it, write upon't, read it, afterwards seal it, and again return to bed; yet all this while in a most fast sleep.

DOCTOR: A great perturbation in nature, to receive at once the benefit of sleep and do the effects of watching! In this slumbery agitation, besides her walking and other actual performances, what, at any time, have you heard her say?

GENTLEWOMAN: That, sir, which I will not report after her.

DOCTOR: You may to me, and 'tis most meet you should.

GENTLEWOMAN: Neither to you nor anyone, having no witness to confirm my speech.

Enter Lady Macbeth with a Taper.

Lo you, here she comes! This is her very guise, and, upon my life, fast asleep. Observe her; stand close.

DOCTOR: How came she by that light?

GENTLEWOMAN: Why, it stood by her. She has light by her continually; 'tis her command.

DOCTOR: You see, her eyes are open.

GENTLEWOMAN: Ay, but their sense is shut.

DOCTOR: What is it she does now? Look how she rubs her hands.

GENTLEWOMAN: It is an accustomed action with her, to seem thus washing her hands. I have known her continue in this a quarter of an hour.

LADY MACBETH: Yet here's a spot.

DOCTOR: Hark, she speaks! I will set down what comes from her, to satisfy my remembrance the more strongly.

LADY MACBETH: Out, damned spot! Out, I say! One- two -why then 'tis time to do't. Hell is murky. Fie, my lord, fie! A soldier, and afeard? What need we fear who knows it, when none can call our power to account? Yet who would have thought the old man to have had so much blood in him?

DOCTOR: Do you mark that?

LADY MACBETH: The Thane of Fife had a wife; where is she now? What, will these hands neer be clean? No more o' that, my lord, no more o' that. You mar all with this starting.

DOCTOR: Go to, go to; you have known what you should not.

GENTLEWOMAN: She has spoke what she should not, I am sure of that. Heaven knows what she has known.

LADY MACBETH: Here's the smell of the blood still. All the perfumes of Arabia will not sweeten this little hand. Oh, oh, oh!

DOCTOR: What a sigh is there! The heart is sorely charged.

GENTLEWOMAN: I would not have such a heart in my bosom for the dignity of the whole body.

DOCTOR: Well, well, well-

GENTLEWOMAN: Pray God it be, sir.

DOCTOR: This disease is beyond my practice. Yet I have known those which have walked in their sleep who have died holily in their beds.
LADY MACBETH: Wash your hands, put on your nightgown, look not so pale. I tell you yet again, Banquo's buried; he cannot come out on's grave.
DOCTOR: Even so?
LADY MACBETH: To bed, to bed; there's knocking at the gate. Come, come, come, come, give me your hand.What's done cannot be undone. To bed, to bed, to bed.
Exit.
DOCTOR: Will she go now to bed?
GENTLEWOMAN: Directly.
DOCTOR: Foul whisperings are abroad. Unnatural deeds
Do breed unnatural troubles; infected minds
To their deaf pillows will discharge their secrets.
More needs she the divine than the physician.
God, God, forgive us all! Look after her;
Remove from her the means of all annoyance,
And still keep eyes upon her. So good night.
My mind she has mated and amazed my sight.
I think, but dare not speak.
GENTLEWOMAN: Good night, good doctor.
Exeunt.

ACT V. SCENE II. The Country near Dunsinane. Drum and Colors.

Enter Menteith, Caithness, Angus, Lennox, and Soldiers.
MENTEITH: The English power is near, led on by Malcolm,
His uncle Siward, and the good Macduff.
Revenges burn in them, for their dear causes
Would to the bleeding and the grim alarm
Excite the mortified man.
ANGUS: Near Birnam Wood
Shall we well meet them; that way are they coming.
CAITHNESS: Who knows if Donalbain be with his brother?
LENNOX: For certain, sir, he is not; I have a file
Of all the gentry. There is Seward's son
And many unrough youths that even now
Protest their first of manhood.
MENTEITH: What does the tyrant?
CAITHNESS: Great Dunsinane he strongly fortifies.
Some say he's mad; others, that lesser hate him,
Do call it valiant fury; but, for certain,
He cannot buckle his distemper'd cause
Within the belt of rule.
ANGUS: Now does he feel
His secret murthers sticking on his hands,
Now minutely revolts upbraid his faith-breach;
Those he commands move only in command,
Nothing in love. Now does he feel his title
Hang loose about him, like a giant's robe
Upon a dwarfish thief.
MENTEITH: Who then shall blame
His pester'd senses to recoil and start,
When all that is within him does condemn
Itself for being there?

CAITHNESS: Well, march we on
To give obedience where 'tis truly owed.
Meet we the medicine of the sickly weal,
And with him pour we, in our country's purge,
Each drop of us.
LENNOX: Or so much as it needs
To dew the sovereign flower and drown the weeds.
Make we our march towards Birnam.
Exeunt Marching.

ACT V. SCENE III. Dunsinane. A Room in the Castle.

Enter Macbeth, Doctor, and Attendants.
MACBETH: Bring me no more reports; let them fly all!
Till Birnam Wood remove to Dunsinane
I cannot taint with fear. What's the boy Malcolm?
Was he not born of woman? The spirits that know
All mortal consequences have pronounced me thus:
"Fear not, Macbeth; no man that's born of woman
Shall e'er have power upon thee." Then fly, false Thanes,
And mingle with the English epicures!
The mind I sway by and the heart I bear
Shall never sag with doubt nor shake with fear.
Enter a Servant.
The devil damn thee black, thou cream-faced loon!
Where got'st thou that goose look?
SERVANT: There is ten thousand-
MACBETH: Geese, villain?
SERVANT: Soldiers, sir.
MACBETH: Go prick thy face and over-red thy fear,
Thou lily-liver'd boy. What soldiers, patch?
Death of thy soul! Those linen cheeks of thine
Are counselors to fear. What soldiers, whey-face?
SERVANT: The English force, so please you.
MACBETH: Take thy face hence.
Exit Servant.
Seyton-I am sick at heart,
When I behold- Seyton, I say!- This push
Will cheer me ever or disseat me now.
I have lived long enough. My way of life
Is fall'n into the sear, the yellow leaf,
And that which should accompany old age,
As honor, love, obedience, troops of friends,
I must not look to have; but in their stead,
Curses, not loud but deep, mouth-honor, breath,
Which the poor heart would fain deny and dare not.
Seyton!
Enter Seyton.
SEYTON: What's your gracious pleasure?
MACBETH: What news more?
SEYTON: All is confirm'd, my lord, which was reported.
MACBETH: I'll fight, 'til from my bones my flesh be hack'd.
Give me my armor.
SEYTON: 'Tis not needed yet.
MACBETH: I'll put it on.

Send out more horses, skirr the country round,
Hang those that talk of fear. Give me mine armor.
How does your patient, doctor?
DOCTOR: Not so sick, my lord,
As she is troubled with thick-coming fancies,
That keep her from her rest.
MACBETH: Cure her of that.
Canst thou not minister to a mind diseased,
Pluck from the memory a rooted sorrow,
Raze out the written troubles of the brain,
And with some sweet oblivious antidote
Cleanse the stuff'd bosom of that perilous stuff
Which weighs upon the heart?
DOCTOR: Therein the patient
Must minister to himself.
MACBETH: Throw physic to the dogs, I'll none of it.
Come, put mine armor on; give me my staff.
Seyton, send out. Doctor, the Thanes fly from me.
Come, sir, dispatch. If thou couldst, doctor, cast
The water of my land, find her disease
And purge it to a sound and pristine health,
I would applaud thee to the very echo,
That should applaud again. Pull't off, I say.
What rhubarb, cyme, or what purgative drug
Would scour these English hence? Hearst thou of them?
DOCTOR: Ay, my good lord, your royal preparation
Makes us hear something.
MACBETH: Bring it after me.
I will not be afraid of death and bane
Till Birnam Forest come to Dunsinane.
DOCTOR: Aside. Were I from Dunsinane away and clear,
Profit again should hardly draw me here. Exeunt.

ACT V. SCENE IV. Country near Birnam Wood. Drum and Colors.

Enter Malcolm, Old Seward and His Son, Macduff, Menteith, Caithness, Angus, Lennox, Ross, and Soldiers, Marching.

MALCOLM: Cousins, I hope the days are near at hand
That chambers will be safe.
MENTEITH: We doubt it nothing.
SIWARD: What wood is this before us?
MENTEITH: The Wood of Birnam.
MALCOLM: Let every soldier hew him down a bough,
And bear't before him; thereby shall we shadow
The numbers of our host, and make discovery
Err in report of us.
SOLDIERS: It shall be done.
SIWARD: We learn no other but the confident tyrant
Keeps still in Dunsinane and will endure
Our setting down before't.
MALCOLM: 'Tis his main hope;
For where there is advantage to be given,
Both more and less have given him the revolt,
And none serve with him but constrained things
Whose hearts are absent too.

MACDUFF: Let our just censures
Attend the true event, and put we on
Industrious soldiership.
SIWARD: The time approaches
That will with due decision make us know
What we shall say we have and what we owe.
Thoughts speculative their unsure hopes relate,
But certain issue strokes must arbitrate.
Towards which advance the war.
Exeunt Marching.

ACT V. SCENE V. Dunsinane. Within the Castle.

Enter Macbeth, Seyton, and Soldiers, with Drum and Colors.
MACBETH: Hang out our banners on the outward walls;
The cry is still, "They come!" Our castle's strength
Will laugh a siege to scorn. Here let them lie
Till famine and the ague eat them up.
Were they not forced with those that should be ours,
We might have met them dareful, beard to beard,
And beat them backward home.
A Cry of Women Within.
What is that noise?
SEYTON: It is the cry of women, my good lord.
Exit.
MACBETH: I have almost forgot the taste of fears:
The time has been, my senses would have cool'd
To hear a night-shriek, and my fell of hair
Would at a dismal treatise rouse and stir
As life were in't. I have supp'd full with horrors;
Direness, familiar to my slaughterous thoughts,
Cannot once start me.
Re-enter Seyton.
Wherefore was that cry?
SEYTON: The Queen, my lord, is dead.
MACBETH: She should have died hereafter;
There would have been a time for such a word.
Tomorrow, and tomorrow, and tomorrow
Creeps in this petty pace from day to day
To the last syllable of recorded time;
And all our yesterdays have lighted fools
The way to dusty death. Out, out, brief candle!
Life's but a walking shadow, a poor player
That struts and frets his hour upon the stage
And then is heard no more. It is a tale
Told by an idiot, full of sound and fury,
Signifying nothing.
Enter a Messenger.
Thou comest to use thy tongue; thy story quickly.
MESSENGER: Gracious my lord,
I should report that which I say I saw,
But know not how to do it.
MACBETH: Well, say, sir.
MESSENGER: As I did stand my watch upon the hill,
I look'd toward Birnam, and anon, methought,

The Wood began to move.
MACBETH: Liar and slave!
MESSENGER: Let me endure your wrath, if't be not so.
Within this three mile may you see it coming;
I say, a moving grove.
MACBETH: If thou speak'st false,
Upon the next tree shalt thou hang alive,
Till famine cling thee; if thy speech be sooth,
I care not if thou dost for me as much.
I pull in resolution and begin
To doubt the equivocation of the fiend
That lies like truth. "Fear not, till Birnam Wood
Do come to Dunsinane," and now a wood
Comes toward Dunsinane. Arm, arm, and out!
If this which he avouches does appear,
There is nor flying hence nor tarrying here.
I 'gin to be aweary of the sun
And wish the estate o' the world were now undone.
Ring the alarum bell! Blow, wind! Come, wrack!
At least we'll die with harness on our back.
Exeunt.

ACT V. SCENE VI. Dunsinane. Before the Castle.

Enter Malcolm, Old Siward, Macduff, and Their Army, with Boughs. Drum and Colors.
MALCOLM: Now near enough; your leavy screens throw down,
And show like those you are. You, worthy uncle,
Shall with my cousin, your right noble son,
Lead our first battle. Worthy Macduff and we
Shall take upon 's what else remains to do, According to our order.
SIWARD: Fare you well.
Do we but find the tyrant's power tonight,
Let us be beaten if we cannot fight.
MACDUFF: Make all our trumpets speak, give them all breath,
Those clamorous harbingers of blood and death.
Exeunt.

ACT V. SCENE VII. Dunsinane. Before the Castle. Alarums.

Enter Macbeth.
MACBETH: They have tied me to a stake; I cannot fly,
But bear-like I must fight the course. What's he
That was not born of woman? Such a one
Am I to fear, or none.
Enter Young Siward.
YOUNG SIWARD: What is thy name?
MACBETH: Thou'lt be afraid to hear it.
YOUNG SIWARD: No, though thou call'st thyself a hotter name
Than any is in hell.
MACBETH: My name's Macbeth.
YOUNG SIWARD: The devil himself could not pronounce a title
More hateful to mine ear.
MACBETH: No, nor more fearful.
YOUNG SIWARD: O Thou liest, abhorred tyrant; with my sword
I'll prove the lie thou speak'st.
They Fight, and Young Seward Is Slain.
MACBETH: Thou wast born of woman.

But swords I smile at, weapons laugh to scorn,
Brandish'd by man that's of a woman born. Exit.
Alarums. Enter Macduff.
MACDUFF: That way the noise is. Tyrant, show thy face!
If thou best slain and with no stroke of mine,
My wife and children's ghosts will haunt me still.
I cannot strike at wretched kerns, whose arms
Are hired to bear their staves. Either thou, Macbeth,
Or else my sword, with an unbatter'd edge,
I sheathe again undeeded. There thou shouldst be;
By this great clatter, one of greatest note
Seems bruited. Let me find him, Fortune!
And more I beg not.
Exit. Alarums.
Enter Malcolm and Old Siward.
SIWARD: This way, my lord; the castle's gently render'd.
The tyrant's people on both sides do fight,
The noble Thanes do bravely in the war,
The day almost itself professes yours,
And little is to do.
MALCOLM: We have met with foes
That strike beside us.
SIWARD: Enter, sir, the castle.
Exeunt. Alarum.

ACT V. SCENE VIII. Another Part of the Field.

Enter Macbeth.
MACBETH: Why should I play the Roman fool and die
On mine own sword? Whiles I see lives, the gashes
Do better upon them.
Enter Macduff.
MACDUFF: Turn, hell hound, turn!
MACBETH: Of all men else I have avoided thee.
But get thee back, my soul is too much charged
With blood of thine already.
MACDUFF: I have no words.
My voice is in my sword, thou bloodier villain
Than terms can give thee out! They fight.
MACBETH: Thou losest labor.
As easy mayst thou the intrenchant air
With thy keen sword impress as make me bleed.
Let fall thy blade on vulnerable crests;
I bear a charmed life, which must not yield
To one of woman born.
MACDUFF: Despair thy charm,
And let the angel whom thou still hast served
Tell thee, Macduff was from his mother's womb untimely ripp'd.
MACBETH: Accursed be that tongue that tells me so,
For it hath cow'd my better part of man!
And be these juggling fiends no more believed
That patter with us in a double sense,
That keep the word of promise to our ear
And break it to our hope. I'll not fight with thee.
MACDUFF: Then yield thee, coward,

And live to be the show and gaze o' the time.
We'll have thee, as our rarer monsters are,
Painted upon a pole, and underwrit,
"Here may you see the tyrant."
MACBETH: I will not yield,
To kiss the ground before young Malcolm's feet,
And to be baited with the rabble's curse.
Though Birnam Wood be come to Dunsinane,
And thou opposed, being of no woman born,
Yet I will try the last. Before my body
I throw my warlike shield! Lay on, Macduff,
And damn'd be him that first cries, "Hold, enough!"
Exeunt Fighting. Alarums.

ACT V. SCENE IX.

Retreat. Flourish. Enter, with Drum and Colors, Malcolm, Old Siward, Ross, the Other Thanes, and Soldiers.

MALCOLM: I would the friends we miss were safe arrived.
SIWARD: Some must go off, and yet, by these I see,
So great a day as this is cheaply bought.
MALCOLM: Macduff is missing, and your noble son.
ROSS: Your son, my lord, has paid a soldier's debt.
He only lived but till he was a man,
The which no sooner had his prowess confirm'd
In the unshrinking station where he fought,
But like a man he died.
SIWARD: Then he is dead?
ROSS: Ay, and brought off the field. Your cause of sorrow
Must not be measured by his worth, for then it hath no end.
SIWARD: Had he his hurts before?
ROSS: Ay, on the front.
SIWARD: Why then, God's soldier be he!
Had I as many sons as I have hairs,
I would not wish them to a fairer death.
And so his knell is knoll'd.
MALCOLM: He's worth more sorrow,
And that I'll spend for him.
SIWARD: He's worth no more:
They say he parted well and paid his score,
And so God be with him! Here comes newer comfort.
Re-enter Macduff, with Macbeth's Head.
MACDUFF: Hail, King, for so thou art. Behold where stands
The usurper's cursed head. The time is free.
I see thee compass'd with thy kingdom's pearl
That speak my salutation in their minds,
Whose voices I desire aloud with mine- Hail, King of Scotland!
ALL: Hail, King of Scotland! Flourish.
MALCOLM: We shall not spend a large expense of time
Before we reckon with your several loves
And make us even with you. My Thanes and kinsmen,
Henceforth be Earls, the first that ever Scotland
In such an honor named. What's more to do,
Which would be planted newly with the time,
As calling home our exiled friends abroad

That fled the snares of watchful tyranny,
Producing forth the cruel ministers
Of this dead butcher and his fiend-like queen,
Who, as 'tis thought, by self and violent hands
Took off her life; this, and what needful else
That calls upon us, by the grace of Grace
We will perform in measure, time, and place.
So thanks to all at once and to each one,
Whom we invite to see us crown'd at Scone.
Flourish. Exeunt.

END

The Tragedy of Antony and Cleopatra

Dramatis Personae

MARK ANTONY, Triumvirs
OCTAVIUS CAESAR,
M. AEMILIUS LEPIDUS,
SEXTUS POMPEIUS,
DOMITIUS ENOBARBUS, friend to Antony
VENTIDIUS, friend to Antony
EROS, friend to Antony
SCARUS, friend to Antony
DERCETAS, friend to Antony
DEMETRIUS, friend to Antony
PHILO, friend to Antony
MAECENAS, friend to Caesar
AGRIPPA, friend to Caesar
DOLABELLA, friend to Caesar
PROCULEIUS, friend to Caesar
THYREUS, friend to Caesar
GALLUS, friend to Caesar
MENAS, friend to Pompey
MENECRATES, friend to Pompey
VARRIUS, friend to Pompey
TAURUS, Lieutenant-General to Caesar
CANIDIUS, Lieutenant-General to Antony
SILIUS, an Officer in Ventidius's army
EUPHRONIUS, an Ambassador from Antony to Caesar
ALEXAS, attendant on Cleopatra
MARDIAN, attendant on Cleopatra
SELEUCUS, attendant on Cleopatra
DIOMEDES, attendant on Cleopatra
A SOOTHSAYER
A CLOWN
CLEOPATRA, Queen of Egypt
OCTAVIA, sister to Caesar and wife to Antony
CHARMIAN, lady attending on Cleopatra
IRAS lady attending on Cleopatra
Officers, Soldiers, Messengers, and Attendants

SCENE: The Roman Empire

ACT I. SCENE I. Alexandria. Cleopatra's Palace

Enter Demetrius and Philo

PHILO: Nay, but this dotage of our general's
O'erflows the measure. Those his goodly eyes,
That o'er the files and musters of the war
Have glow'd like plated Mars, now bend, now turn,
The office and devotion of their view
Upon a tawny front. His captain's heart,
Which in the scuffles of great fights hath burst
The buckles on his breast, reneges all temper,
And is become the bellows and the fan
To cool a gipsy's lust.

Flourish. Enter Antony, Cleopatra, Her Ladies, the Train, with Eunuchs Fanning Her

Look where they come!

Take but good note, and you shall see in him
The triple pillar of the world transform'd
Into a strumpet's fool. Behold and see.
CLEOPATRA: If it be love indeed, tell me how much.
ANTONY: There's beggary in the love that can be reckon'd.
CLEOPATRA: I'll set a bourn how far to be belov'd.
ANTONY:. Then must thou needs find out new heaven, new earth.
Enter a Messenger
MESSENGER: News, my good lord, from Rome.
ANTONY:. Grates me the sum.
CLEOPATRA: Nay, hear them, Antony.
Fulvia perchance is angry; or who knows
If the scarce-bearded Caesar have not sent
His pow'rful mandate to you: 'Do this or this;
Take in that kingdom and enfranchise that;
Perform't, or else we damn thee.'
ANTONY: How, my love?
CLEOPATRA: Perchance? Nay, and most like,
You must not stay here longer; your dismission
Is come from Caesar; therefore hear it, Antony.
Where's Fulvia's process? Caesar's I would say? Both?
Call in the messengers. As I am Egypt's Queen,
Thou blushest, Antony, and that blood of thine
Is Caesar's homager. Else so thy cheek pays shame
When shrill-tongu'd Fulvia scolds. The messengers!
ANTONY: Let Rome in Tiber melt, and the wide arch
Of the rang'd empire fall! Here is my space.
Kingdoms are clay; our dungy earth alike
Feeds beast as man. The nobleness of life
Is to do thus Embracing, when such a mutual pair
And such a twain can do't, in which I bind,
On pain of punishment, the world to weet
We stand up peerless.
CLEOPATRA: Excellent falsehood!
Why did he marry Fulvia, and not love her?
I'll seem the fool I am not. Antony
Will be himself.
ANTONY: But stirr'd by Cleopatra.
Now for the love of Love and her soft hours,
Let's not confound the time with conference harsh;
There's not a minute of our lives should stretch
Without some pleasure now. What sport to-night?
CLEOPATRA: Hear the ambassadors.
ANTONY: Fie, wrangling queen!
Whom everything becomes- to chide, to laugh,
To weep; whose every passion fully strives
To make itself in thee fair and admir'd.
No messenger but thine, and all alone
To-night we'll wander through the streets and note
The qualities of people. Come, my queen;
Last night you did desire it. Speak not to us.
Exeunt Antony and Cleopatra, with the Train
MESSENGER: Is Caesar with Antonius priz'd so slight?

PHILO: Sir, sometimes when he is not Antony,
He comes too short of that great property
Which still should go with Antony.
MESSENGER: I am full sorry
That he approves the common liar, who
Thus speaks of him at Rome; but I will hope
Of better deeds to-morrow. Rest you happy!
Exeunt

ACT I. SCENE II. Alexandria. Cleopatra's Palace

Enter Charmian, Iras, Alexas, and a Soothsayer
CHARMIAN: Lord Alexas, sweet Alexas, most anything Alexas, almost most absolute Alexas, where's the soothsayer that you prais'd so to th' Queen? O that I knew this husband, which you say must charge his horns with garlands!
ALEXAS: Soothsayer!
SOOTHSAYER: Your will?
CHARMIAN: Is this the man? Is't you, sir, that know things?
SOOTHSAYER: In nature's infinite book of secrecy
A little I can read.
ALEXAS: Show him your hand.
Enter Enobarbus
ENOBARBUS: Bring in the banquet quickly; wine enough
Cleopatra's health to drink.
CHARMIAN: Good, sir, give me good fortune.
SOOTHSAYER: I make not, but foresee.
CHARMIAN: Pray, then, foresee me one.
SOOTHSAYER: You shall be yet far fairer than you are.
CHARMIAN: He means in flesh.
IRAS: No, you shall paint when you are old.
CHARMIAN: Wrinkles forbid!
ALEXAS: Vex not his prescience; be attentive.
CHARMIAN: Hush!
SOOTHSAYER: You shall be more beloving than beloved.
CHARMIAN: I had rather heat my liver with drinking.
ALEXAS: Nay, hear him.
CHARMIAN: Good now, some excellent fortune! Let me be married to three kings in a forenoon, and widow them all. Let me have a child at fifty, to whom Herod of Jewry may do homage. Find me to marry me with Octavius Caesar, and companion me with my mistress.
SOOTHSAYER: You shall outlive the lady whom you serve.
CHARMIAN: O, excellent! I love long life better than figs.
SOOTHSAYER: You have seen and prov'd a fairer former fortune
Than that which is to approach.
CHARMIAN: Then belike my children shall have no names.
Prithee, how many boys and wenches must I have?
SOOTHSAYER: If every of your wishes had a womb,
And fertile every wish, a million.
CHARMIAN: Out, fool! I forgive thee for a witch.
ALEXAS: You think none but your sheets are privy to your wishes.
CHARMIAN: Nay, come, tell Iras hers.
ALEXAS: We'll know all our fortunes.
ENOBARBUS: Mine, and most of our fortunes, to-night, shall be-drunk to bed.

IRAS: There's a palm presages chastity, if nothing else.
CHARMIAN: E'en as the o'erflowing Nilus presageth famine.
IRAS: Go, you wild bedfellow, you cannot soothsay.
CHARMIAN: Nay, if an oily palm be not a fruitful prognostication, I cannot scratch mine ear. Prithee, tell her but worky-day fortune.
SOOTHSAYER: Your fortunes are alike.
IRAS: But how, but how? Give me particulars.
SOOTHSAYER: I have said.
IRAS: Am I not an inch of fortune better than she?
CHARMIAN: Well, if you were but an inch of fortune better than I, where would you choose it?
IRAS: Not in my husband's nose.
CHARMIAN: Our worser thoughts heavens mend! Alexas- come, his fortune, his fortune! O, let him marry a woman that cannot go, sweet Isis, I beseech thee! And let her die too, and give him a worse! And let worse follow worse, till the worst of all follow him laughing to his grave, fiftyfold a cuckold! Good Isis, hear me this prayer, though thou deny me a matter of more weight; good Isis, I beseech thee!
IRAS: Amen. Dear goddess, hear that prayer of the people! For, as it is a heartbreaking to see a handsome man loose-wiv'd, so it is a deadly sorrow to behold a foul knave uncuckolded. Therefore, dear Isis, keep decorum, and fortune him accordingly!
CHARMIAN: Amen.
ALEXAS: Lo now, if it lay in their hands to make me a cuckold, they would make themselves whores but they'ld do't!
Enter Cleopatra
ENOBARBUS: Hush! Here comes Antony.
CHARMIAN: Not he; the Queen.
CLEOPATRA: Saw you my lord?
ENOBARBUS: No, lady.
CLEOPATRA: Was he not here?
CHARMIAN: No, madam.
CLEOPATRA: He was dispos'd to mirth; but on the sudden
A Roman thought hath struck him. Enobarbus!
ENOBARBUS: Madam?
CLEOPATRA: Seek him, and bring him hither. Where's Alexas?
ALEXAS: Here, at your service. My lord approaches.
Enter Antony, with a Messenger and Attendants
CLEOPATRA: We will not look upon him. Go with us.
Exeunt Cleopatra, Enobarbus, and the Rest
MESSENGER: Fulvia thy wife first came into the field.
ANTONY: Against my brother Lucius?
MESSENGER: Ay.
But soon that war had end, and the time's state
Made friends of them, jointing their force 'gainst Caesar,
Whose better issue in the war from Italy
Upon the first encounter drave them.
ANTONY: Well, what worst?
MESSENGER: The nature of bad news infects the teller.
ANTONY: When it concerns the fool or coward. On!
Things that are past are done with me. 'Tis thus:
Who tells me true, though in his tale lie death,

I hear him as he flatter'd.
MESSENGER: Labienus-
This is stiff news- hath with his Parthian force
Extended Asia from Euphrates,
His conquering banner shook from Syria
To Lydia and to Ionia, whilst-
ANTONY: Antony, thou wouldst say.
MESSENGER: O, my lord!
ANTONY: Speak to me home; mince not the general tongue;
Name Cleopatra as she is call'd in Rome.
Rail thou in Fulvia's phrase, and taunt my faults
With such full licence as both truth and malice
Have power to utter. O, then we bring forth weeds
When our quick minds lie still, and our ills told us
Is as our earing. Fare thee well awhile.
MESSENGER: At your noble pleasure.
Exit
ANTONY: From Sicyon, ho, the news! Speak there!
FIRST ATTENDANT: The man from Sicyon- is there such an one?
SECOND ATTENDANT: He stays upon your will.
ANTONY: Let him appear.
These strong Egyptian fetters I must break,
Or lose myself in dotage.
Enter Another Messenger with a Letter
What are you?
SECOND MESSENGER: Fulvia thy wife is dead.
ANTONY: Where died she?
SECOND MESSENGER: In Sicyon.
Her length of sickness, with what else more serious
Importeth thee to know, this bears.
Gives the Letter
ANTONY: Forbear me.
Exit Messenger
There's a great spirit gone! Thus did I desire it.
What our contempts doth often hurl from us
We wish it ours again; the present pleasure,
By revolution low'ring, does become
The opposite of itself. She's good, being gone;
The hand could pluck her back that shov'd her on.
I must from this enchanting queen break off.
Ten thousand harms, more than the ills I know,
My idleness doth hatch. How now, Enobarbus!
Re-enter Enobarbus
ENOBARBUS: What's your pleasure, sir?
ANTONY: I must with haste from hence.
ENOBARBUS: Why, then we kill all our women. We see how mortal an unkindness is to them; if they suffer our departure, death's the word.
ANTONY: I must be gone.
ENOBARBUS: Under a compelling occasion, let women die. It were pity to cast them away for nothing, though between them and a great cause they should be esteemed nothing. Cleopatra, catching but the least noise of this, dies instantly; I have seen her die twenty times upon far poorer moment. I do think there is mettle

in death, which commits some loving act upon her, she hath such a celerity in dying.
ANTONY: She is cunning past man's thought.
ENOBARBUS: Alack, sir, no! Her passions are made of nothing but the finest part of pure love. We cannot call her winds and waters sighs and tears; they are greater storms and tempests than almanacs can report. This cannot be cunning in her; if it be, she makes a show'r of rain as well as Jove.
ANTONY: Would I had never seen her!
ENOBARBUS: O Sir, you had then left unseen a wonderful piece of work, which not to have been blest withal would have discredited your travel.
ANTONY: Fulvia is dead.
ENOBARBUS: Sir?
ANTONY: Fulvia is dead.
ENOBARBUS: Fulvia?
ANTONY: Dead.
ENOBARBUS: Why, sir, give the gods a thankful sacrifice. When it pleaseth their deities to take the wife of a man from him, it shows to man the tailors of the earth; comforting therein that when old robes are worn out there are members to make new. If there were no more women but Fulvia, then had you indeed a cut, and the case to be lamented. This grief is crown'd with consolation: your old smock brings forth a new petticoat; and indeed the tears live in an onion that should water this sorrow.
ANTONY: The business she hath broached in the state
Cannot endure my absence.
ENOBARBUS: And the business you have broach'd here cannot be without you; especially that of Cleopatra's, which wholly depends on your abode.
ANTONY: No more light answers. Let our officers
Have notice what we purpose. I shall break
The cause of our expedience to the Queen,
And get her leave to part. For not alone
The death of Fulvia, with more urgent touches,
Do strongly speak to us; but the letters to
Of many our contriving friends in Rome
Petition us at home. Sextus Pompeius
Hath given the dare to Caesar, and commands
The empire of the sea; our slippery people,
Whose love is never link'd to the deserver
Till his deserts are past, begin to throw
Pompey the Great and all his dignities
Upon his son; who, high in name and power,
Higher than both in blood and life, stands up
For the main soldier; whose quality, going on,
The sides o' th' world may danger. Much is breeding
Which, like the courser's hair, hath yet but life
And not a serpent's poison. Say our pleasure,
To such whose place is under us, requires
Our quick remove from hence.
ENOBARBUS: I shall do't.
Exeunt

ACT I. SCENE III. Alexandria. Cleopatra's Palace

Enter Cleopatra, Charmian, Iras, and Alexas

CLEOPATRA: Where is he?
CHARMIAN: I did not see him since.
CLEOPATRA: See where he is, who's with him, what he does.
I did not send you. If you find him sad,
Say I am dancing; if in mirth, report
That I am sudden sick. Quick, and return.

Exit Alexas

CHARMIAN: Madam, methinks, if you did love him dearly,
You do not hold the method to enforce
The like from him.
CLEOPATRA: What should I do I do not?
CHARMIAN: In each thing give him way; cross him in nothing.
CLEOPATRA: Thou teachest like a fool- the way to lose him.
CHARMIAN: Tempt him not so too far; I wish, forbear;
In time we hate that which we often fear.

Enter Antony

But here comes Antony.
CLEOPATRA: I am sick and sullen.
ANTONY: I am sorry to give breathing to my purpose-
CLEOPATRA: Help me away, dear Charmian; I shall fall.
It cannot be thus long; the sides of nature
Will not sustain it.
ANTONY: Now, my dearest queen-
CLEOPATRA: Pray you, stand farther from me.
ANTONY: What's the matter?
CLEOPATRA: I know by that same eye there's some good news.
What says the married woman? You may go.
Would she had never given you leave to come!
Let her not say 'tis I that keep you here-
I have no power upon you; hers you are.
ANTONY: The gods best know-
CLEOPATRA: O, never was there queen
So mightily betray'd! Yet at the first
I saw the treasons planted.
ANTONY: Cleopatra-
CLEOPATRA: Why should I think you can be mine and true,
Though you in swearing shake the throned gods,
Who have been false to Fulvia? Riotous madness,
To be entangled with those mouth-made vows,
Which break themselves in swearing!
ANTONY: Most sweet queen-
CLEOPATRA: Nay, pray you seek no colour for your going,
But bid farewell, and go. When you sued staying,
Then was the time for words. No going then!
Eternity was in our lips and eyes,
Bliss in our brows' bent, none our parts so poor
But was a race of heaven. They are so still,
Or thou, the greatest soldier of the world,
Art turn'd the greatest liar.
ANTONY: How now, lady!
CLEOPATRA: I would I had thy inches. Thou shouldst know

There were a heart in Egypt.
ANTONY: Hear me, queen:
The strong necessity of time commands
Our services awhile; but my full heart
Remains in use with you. Our Italy
Shines o'er with civil swords: Sextus Pompeius
Makes his approaches to the port of Rome;
Equality of two domestic powers
Breed scrupulous faction; the hated, grown to strength,
Are newly grown to love. The condemn'd Pompey,
Rich in his father's honour, creeps apace
Into the hearts of such as have not thrived
Upon the present state, whose numbers threaten;
And quietness, grown sick of rest, would purge
By any desperate change. My more particular,
And that which most with you should safe my going,
Is Fulvia's death.
CLEOPATRA: Though age from folly could not give me freedom,
It does from childishness. Can Fulvia die?
ANTONY: She's dead, my Queen.
Look here, and at thy sovereign leisure read
The garboils she awak'd. At the last, best.
See when and where she died.
CLEOPATRA: O most false love!
Where be the sacred vials thou shouldst fill
With sorrowful water? Now I see, I see,
In Fulvia's death how mine receiv'd shall be.
ANTONY: Quarrel no more, but be prepar'd to know
The purposes I bear; which are, or cease,
As you shall give th' advice. By the fire
That quickens Nilus' slime, I go from hence
Thy soldier, servant, making peace or war
As thou affects.
CLEOPATRA: Cut my lace, Charmian, come!
But let it be; I am quickly ill and well-
So Antony loves.
ANTONY: My precious queen, forbear,
And give true evidence to his love, which stands
An honourable trial.
CLEOPATRA: So Fulvia told me.
I prithee turn aside and weep for her;
Then bid adieu to me, and say the tears
Belong to Egypt. Good now, play one scene
Of excellent dissembling, and let it look
Like perfect honour.
ANTONY: You'll heat my blood; no more.
CLEOPATRA: You can do better yet; but this is meetly.
ANTONY: Now, by my sword-
CLEOPATRA: And target. Still he mends;
But this is not the best. Look, prithee, Charmian,
How this Herculean Roman does become
The carriage of his chafe.
ANTONY: I'll leave you, lady.

CLEOPATRA: Courteous lord, one word.
Sir, you and I must part- but that's not it.
Sir, you and I have lov'd- but there's not it.
That you know well. Something it is I would-
O, my oblivion is a very Antony,
And I am all forgotten!
ANTONY: But that your royalty
Holds idleness your subject, I should take you
For idleness itself.
CLEOPATRA: 'Tis sweating labour
To bear such idleness so near the heart
As Cleopatra this. But, sir, forgive me;
Since my becomings kill me when they do not
Eye well to you. Your honour calls you hence;
Therefore be deaf to my unpitied folly,
And all the gods go with you! Upon your sword
Sit laurel victory, and smooth success
Be strew'd before your feet!
ANTONY: Let us go. Come.
Our separation so abides and flies
That thou, residing here, goes yet with me,
And I, hence fleeting, here remain with thee.
Away!
Exeunt

ACT I. SCENE IV. Rome. Caesar's House

Enter Octavius Caesar, Reading a Letter; Lepidus, and Their Train
CAESAR: You may see, Lepidus, and henceforth know,
It is not Caesar's natural vice to hate
Our great competitor. From Alexandria
This is the news: he fishes, drinks, and wastes
The lamps of night in revel; is not more manlike
Than Cleopatra, nor the queen of Ptolemy
More womanly than he; hardly gave audience, or
Vouchsaf'd to think he had partners. You shall find there
A man who is the abstract of all faults
That all men follow.
LEPIDUS: I must not think there are
Evils enow to darken all his goodness.
His faults, in him, seem as the spots of heaven,
More fiery by night's blackness; hereditary
Rather than purchas'd; what he cannot change
Than what he chooses.
CAESAR: You are too indulgent. Let's grant it is not
Amiss to tumble on the bed of Ptolemy,
To give a kingdom for a mirth, to sit
And keep the turn of tippling with a slave,
To reel the streets at noon, and stand the buffet
With knaves that smell of sweat. Say this becomes him-
As his composure must be rare indeed
Whom these things cannot blemish- yet must Antony
No way excuse his foils when we do bear
So great weight in his lightness. If he fill'd
His vacancy with his voluptuousness,

Full surfeits and the dryness of his bones
Call on him for't! But to confound such time
That drums him from his sport and speaks as loud
As his own state and ours- 'tis to be chid
As we rate boys who, being mature in knowledge,
Pawn their experience to their present pleasure,
And so rebel to judgment.
Enter a Messenger
LEPIDUS: Here's more news.
MESSENGER: Thy biddings have been done; and every hour,
Most noble Caesar, shalt thou have report
How 'tis abroad. Pompey is strong at sea,
And it appears he is belov'd of those
That only have fear'd Caesar. To the ports
The discontents repair, and men's reports
Give him much wrong'd.
CAESAR: I should have known no less.
It hath been taught us from the primal state
That he which is was wish'd until he were;
And the ebb'd man, ne'er lov'd till ne'er worth love,
Comes dear'd by being lack'd. This common body,
Like to a vagabond flag upon the stream,
Goes to and back, lackeying the varying tide,
To rot itself with motion.
MESSENGER: Caesar, I bring thee word
Menecrates and Menas, famous pirates,
Make the sea serve them, which they ear and wound
With keels of every kind. Many hot inroads
They make in Italy; the borders maritime
Lack blood to think on't, and flush youth revolt.
No vessel can peep forth but 'tis as soon
Taken as seen; for Pompey's name strikes more
Than could his war resisted.
CAESAR: Antony,
Leave thy lascivious wassails. When thou once
Was beaten from Modena, where thou slew'st
Hirtius and Pansa, consuls, at thy heel
Did famine follow; whom thou fought'st against,
Though daintily brought up, with patience more
Than savages could suffer. Thou didst drink
The stale of horses and the gilded puddle
Which beasts would cough at. Thy palate then did deign
The roughest berry on the rudest hedge;
Yea, like the stag when snow the pasture sheets,
The barks of trees thou brows'd. On the Alps
It is reported thou didst eat strange flesh,
Which some did die to look on. And all this-
It wounds thine honour that I speak it now-
Was borne so like a soldier that thy cheek
So much as lank'd not.
LEPIDUS: 'Tis pity of him.
CAESAR: Let his shames quickly
Drive him to Rome. 'Tis time we twain

Did show ourselves i' th' field; and to that end
Assemble we immediate council. Pompey
Thrives in our idleness.
LEPIDUS: To-morrow, Caesar,
I shall be furnish'd to inform you rightly
Both what by sea and land I can be able
To front this present time.
CAESAR: Till which encounter
It is my business too. Farewell.
LEPIDUS: Farewell, my lord. What you shall know meantime
Of stirs abroad, I shall beseech you, sir,
To let me be partaker.
CAESAR: Doubt not, sir;
I knew it for my bond.
Exeunt

ACT I. SCENE V. Alexandria. Cleopatra's Palace

Enter Cleopatra, Charmian, Iras, and Mardian
CLEOPATRA: Charmian!
CHARMIAN: Madam?
CLEOPATRA: Ha, ha!
Give me to drink mandragora.
CHARMIAN: Why, madam?
CLEOPATRA: That I might sleep out this great gap of time
My Antony is away.
CHARMIAN: You think of him too much.
CLEOPATRA: O, 'tis treason!
CHARMIAN: Madam, I trust, not so.
CLEOPATRA: Thou, eunuch Mardian!
MARDIAN: What's your Highness' pleasure?
CLEOPATRA: Not now to hear thee sing; I take no pleasure
In aught an eunuch has. 'Tis well for thee
That, being unseminar'd, thy freer thoughts
May not fly forth of Egypt. Hast thou affections?
MARDIAN: Yes, gracious madam.
CLEOPATRA: Indeed?
MARDIAN: Not in deed, madam; for I can do nothing
But what indeed is honest to be done.
Yet have I fierce affections, and think
What Venus did with Mars.
CLEOPATRA: O Charmian,
Where think'st thou he is now? Stands he or sits he?
Or does he walk? or is he on his horse?
O happy horse, to bear the weight of Antony!
Do bravely, horse; for wot'st thou whom thou mov'st?
The demi-Atlas of this earth, the arm
And burgonet of men. He's speaking now,
Or murmuring 'Where's my serpent of old Nile?'
For so he calls me. Now I feed myself
With most delicious poison. Think on me,
That am with Phoebus' amorous pinches black,
And wrinkled deep in time? Broad-fronted Caesar,
When thou wast here above the ground, I was
A morsel for a monarch; and great Pompey

Would stand and make his eyes grow in my brow;
There would he anchor his aspect and die
With looking on his life.
Enter Alexas
ALEXAS: Sovereign of Egypt, hail!
CLEOPATRA: How much unlike art thou Mark Antony!
Yet, coming from him, that great med'cine hath
With his tinct gilded thee.
How goes it with my brave Mark Antony?
ALEXAS: Last thing he did, dear Queen,
He kiss'd- the last of many doubled kisses-
This orient pearl. His speech sticks in my heart.
CLEOPATRA: Mine ear must pluck it thence.
ALEXAS: 'Good friend,' quoth he
'Say the firm Roman to great Egypt sends
This treasure of an oyster; at whose foot,
To mend the petty present, I will piece
Her opulent throne with kingdoms. All the East,
Say thou, shall call her mistress.' So he nodded,
And soberly did mount an arm-gaunt steed,
Who neigh'd so high that what I would have spoke
Was beastly dumb'd by him.
CLEOPATRA: What, was he sad or merry?
ALEXAS: Like to the time o' th' year between the extremes
Of hot and cold; he was nor sad nor merry.
CLEOPATRA: O well-divided disposition! Note him,
Note him, good Charmian; 'tis the man; but note him!
He was not sad, for he would shine on those
That make their looks by his; he was not merry,
Which seem'd to tell them his remembrance lay
In Egypt with his joy; but between both.
O heavenly mingle! Be'st thou sad or merry,
The violence of either thee becomes,
So does it no man else. Met'st thou my posts?
ALEXAS: Ay, madam, twenty several messengers.
Why do you send so thick?
CLEOPATRA: Who's born that day
When I forget to send to Antony
Shall die a beggar. Ink and paper, Charmian.
Welcome, my good Alexas. Did I, Charmian,
Ever love Caesar so?
CHARMIAN: O that brave Caesar!
CLEOPATRA: Be chok'd with such another emphasis!
Say 'the brave Antony.'
CHARMIAN: The valiant Caesar!
CLEOPATRA: By Isis, I will give thee bloody teeth
If thou with Caesar paragon again
My man of men.
CHARMIAN: By your most gracious pardon,
I sing but after you.
CLEOPATRA: My salad days,
When I was green in judgment, cold in blood,
To say as I said then. But come, away!

Get me ink and paper.
He shall have every day a several greeting,
Or I'll unpeople Egypt.
Exeunt

ACT II. SCENE I. Messina. Pompey's House

Enter Pompey, Menecrates, and Menas, in Warlike Manner
POMPEY: If the great gods be just, they shall assist
The deeds of justest men.
MENECRATES: Know, worthy Pompey,
That what they do delay they not deny.
POMPEY: Whiles we are suitors to their throne, decays
The thing we sue for.
MENECRATES: We, ignorant of ourselves,
Beg often our own harms, which the wise pow'rs
Deny us for our good; so find we profit
By losing of our prayers.
POMPEY: I shall do well.
The people love me, and the sea is mine;
My powers are crescent, and my auguring hope
Says it will come to th' full. Mark Antony
In Egypt sits at dinner, and will make
No wars without doors. Caesar gets money where
He loses hearts. Lepidus flatters both,
Of both is flatter'd; but he neither loves,
Nor either cares for him.
MENAS: Caesar and Lepidus
Are in the field. A mighty strength they carry.
POMPEY: Where have you this? 'Tis false.
MENAS: From Silvius, sir.
POMPEY: He dreams. I know they are in Rome together,
Looking for Antony. But all the charms of love,
Salt Cleopatra, soften thy wan'd lip!
Let witchcraft join with beauty, lust with both;
Tie up the libertine in a field of feasts,
Keep his brain fuming. Epicurean cooks
Sharpen with cloyless sauce his appetite,
That sleep and feeding may prorogue his honour
Even till a Lethe'd dullness-
Enter Varrius
How now, Varrius!
VARRIUS: This is most certain that I shall deliver:
Mark Antony is every hour in Rome
Expected. Since he went from Egypt 'tis
A space for farther travel.
POMPEY: I could have given less matter
A better ear. Menas, I did not think
This amorous surfeiter would have donn'd his helm
For such a petty war; his soldiership
Is twice the other twain. But let us rear
The higher our opinion, that our stirring
Can from the lap of Egypt's widow pluck
The ne'er-lust-wearied Antony.
MENAS: I cannot hope

Caesar and Antony shall well greet together.
His wife that's dead did trespasses to Caesar;
His brother warr'd upon him; although, I think,
Not mov'd by Antony.
POMPEY: I know not, Menas,
How lesser enmities may give way to greater.
Were't not that we stand up against them all,
'Twere pregnant they should square between themselves;
For they have entertained cause enough
To draw their swords. But how the fear of us
May cement their divisions, and bind up
The petty difference we yet not know.
Be't as our gods will have't! It only stands
Our lives upon to use our strongest hands.
Come, Menas.
Exeunt

ACT II. SCENE II. Rome. The House of Lepidus

Enter Enobarbus and Lepidus
LEPIDUS: Good Enobarbus, 'tis a worthy deed,
And shall become you well, to entreat your captain
To soft and gentle speech.
ENOBARBUS: I shall entreat him
To answer like himself. If Caesar move him,
Let Antony look over Caesar's head
And speak as loud as Mars. By Jupiter,
Were I the wearer of Antonius' beard,
I would not shave't to-day.
LEPIDUS: 'Tis not a time
For private stomaching.
ENOBARBUS: Every time
Serves for the matter that is then born in't.
LEPIDUS: But small to greater matters must give way.
ENOBARBUS: Not if the small come first.
LEPIDUS: Your speech is passion;
But pray you stir no embers up. Here comes
The noble Antony.
Enter Antony and Ventidius
Enobarbus. And yonder, Caesar.
Enter Caesar, Maecenas, and Agrippa
ANTONY: If we compose well here, to Parthia.
Hark, Ventidius.
CAESAR: I do not know, Maecenas. Ask Agrippa.
LEPIDUS: Noble friends,
That which combin'd us was most great, and let not
A leaner action rend us. What's amiss,
May it be gently heard. When we debate
Our trivial difference loud, we do commit
Murder in healing wounds. Then, noble partners,
The rather for I earnestly beseech,
Touch you the sourest points with sweetest terms,
Nor curstness grow to th' matter.
ANTONY: 'Tis spoken well.
Were we before our arinies, and to fight,

I should do thus.
Flourish
CAESAR: Welcome to Rome.
ANTONY: Thank you.
CAESAR: Sit.
ANTONY: Sit, sir.
CAESAR: Nay, then.
They Sit
ANTONY: I learn you take things ill which are not so,
Or being, concern you not.
CAESAR: I must be laugh'd at
If, or for nothing or a little,
Should say myself offended, and with you
Chiefly i' the world; more laugh'd at that I should
Once name you derogately when to sound your name
It not concern'd me.
ANTONY: My being in Egypt, Caesar,
What was't to you?
CAESAR: No more than my residing here at Rome
Might be to you in Egypt. Yet, if you there
Did practise on my state, your being in Egypt
Might be my question.
ANTONY: How intend you- practis'd?
CAESAR: You may be pleas'd to catch at mine intent
By what did here befall me. Your wife and brother
Made wars upon me, and their contestation
Was theme for you; you were the word of war.
ANTONY: You do mistake your business; my brother never
Did urge me in his act. I did inquire it,
And have my learning from some true reports
That drew their swords with you. Did he not rather
Discredit my authority with yours,
And make the wars alike against my stomach,
Having alike your cause? Of this my letters
Before did satisfy you. If you'll patch a quarrel,
As matter whole you have not to make it with,
It must not be with this.
CAESAR: You praise yourself
By laying defects of judgment to me; but
You patch'd up your excuses.
ANTONY: Not so, not so;
I know you could not lack, I am certain on't,
Very necessity of this thought, that I,
Your partner in the cause 'gainst which he fought,
Could not with graceful eyes attend those wars
Which fronted mine own peace. As for my wife,
I would you had her spirit in such another!
The third o' th' world is yours, which with a snaffle
You may pace easy, but not such a wife.
ENOBARBUS: Would we had all such wives, that the men might go to wars with the women!
ANTONY: So much uncurbable, her garboils, Caesar,
Made out of her impatience- which not wanted

Shrewdness of policy too- I grieving grant
Did you too much disquiet. For that you must
But say I could not help it.
CAESAR: I wrote to you
When rioting in Alexandria; you
Did pocket up my letters, and with taunts
Did gibe my missive out of audience.
ANTONY: Sir,
He fell upon me ere admitted. Then
Three kings I had newly feasted, and did want
Of what I was i' th' morning; but next day
I told him of myself, which was as much
As to have ask'd him pardon. Let this fellow
Be nothing of our strife; if we contend,
Out of our question wipe him.
CAESAR: You have broken
The article of your oath, which you shall never
Have tongue to charge me with.
LEPIDUS: Soft, Caesar!
ANTONY: No;
Lepidus, let him speak.
The honour is sacred which he talks on now,
Supposing that I lack'd it. But on, Caesar:
The article of my oath-
CAESAR: To lend me arms and aid when I requir'd them,
The which you both denied.
ANTONY: Neglected, rather;
And then when poisoned hours had bound me up
From mine own knowledge. As nearly as I may,
I'll play the penitent to you; but mine honesty
Shall not make poor my greatness, nor my power
Work without it. Truth is, that Fulvia,
To have me out of Egypt, made wars here;
For which myself, the ignorant motive, do
So far ask pardon as befits mine honour
To stoop in such a case.
LEPIDUS: 'Tis noble spoken.
MAECENAS: If it might please you to enforce no further
The griefs between ye- to forget them quite
Were to remember that the present need
Speaks to atone you.
LEPIDUS: Worthily spoken, Maecenas.
ENOBARBUS: Or, if you borrow one another's love for the instant,
you may, when you hear no more words of Pompey, return it again.
You shall have time to wrangle in when you have nothing else to do.
ANTONY: Thou art a soldier only. Speak no more.
ENOBARBUS: That truth should be silent I had almost forgot.
ANTONY: You wrong this presence; therefore speak no more.
ENOBARBUS: Go to, then- your considerate stone!
CAESAR: I do not much dislike the matter, but
The manner of his speech; for't cannot be
We shall remain in friendship, our conditions
So diff'ring in their acts. Yet if I knew

What hoop should hold us stanch, from edge to edge
O' th' world, I would pursue it.
AGRIPPA: Give me leave, Caesar.
CAESAR: Speak, Agrippa.
AGRIPPA: Thou hast a sister by the mother's side,
Admir'd Octavia. Great Mark Antony
Is now a widower.
CAESAR: Say not so, Agrippa.
If Cleopatra heard you, your reproof
Were well deserv'd of rashness.
ANTONY: I am not married, Caesar. Let me hear
Agrippa further speak.
AGRIPPA: To hold you in perpetual amity,
To make you brothers, and to knit your hearts
With an unslipping knot, take Antony
Octavia to his wife; whose beauty claims
No worse a husband than the best of men;
Whose virtue and whose general graces speak
That which none else can utter. By this marriage
All little jealousies, which now seem great,
And all great fears, which now import their dangers,
Would then be nothing. Truths would be tales,
Where now half tales be truths. Her love to both
Would each to other, and all loves to both,
Draw after her. Pardon what I have spoke;
For 'tis a studied, not a present thought,
By duty ruminated.
ANTONY: Will Caesar speak?
CAESAR: Not till he hears how Antony is touch'd
With what is spoke already.
ANTONY: What power is in Agrippa,
If I would say 'Agrippa, be it so,'
To make this good?
CAESAR: The power of Caesar, and
His power unto Octavia.
ANTONY: May I never
To this good purpose, that so fairly shows,
Dream of impediment! Let me have thy hand.
Further this act of grace; and from this hour
The heart of brothers govern in our loves
And sway our great designs!
CAESAR: There is my hand.
A sister I bequeath you, whom no brother
Did ever love so dearly. Let her live
To join our kingdoms and our hearts; and never
Fly off our loves again!
LEPIDUS: Happily, amen!
ANTONY: I did not think to draw my sword 'gainst Pompey;
For he hath laid strange courtesies and great
Of late upon me. I must thank him only,
Lest my remembrance suffer ill report;
At heel of that, defy him.
LEPIDUS: Time calls upon's.

Of us must Pompey presently be sought,
Or else he seeks out us.
ANTONY: Where lies he?
CAESAR: About the Mount Misenum.
ANTONY: What is his strength by land?
CAESAR: Great and increasing; but by sea
He is an absolute master.
ANTONY: So is the fame.
Would we had spoke together! Haste we for it.
Yet, ere we put ourselves in arms, dispatch we
The business we have talk'd of.
CAESAR: With most gladness;
And do invite you to my sister's view,
Whither straight I'll lead you.
ANTONY: Let us, Lepidus,
Not lack your company.
LEPIDUS: Noble Antony,
Not sickness should detain me.
Flourish
Exeunt All but Enobarbus, Agrippa, Maecenas
MAECENAS: Welcome from Egypt, sir.
ENOBARBUS: Half the heart of Caesar, worthy Maecenas! My honourable friend, Agrippa!
AGRIPPA: Good Enobarbus!
MAECENAS: We have cause to be glad that matters are so well digested. You stay'd well by't in Egypt.
ENOBARBUS: Ay, sir; we did sleep day out of countenance and made the night light with drinking.
MAECENAS: Eight wild boars roasted whole at a breakfast, and but twelve persons there. Is this true?
ENOBARBUS: This was but as a fly by an eagle. We had much more monstrous matter of feast, which worthily deserved noting.
MAECENAS: She's a most triumphant lady, if report be square to her.
ENOBARBUS: When she first met Mark Antony she purs'd up his heart, upon the river of Cydnus.
AGRIPPA: There she appear'd indeed! Or my reporter devis'd well for her.
ENOBARBUS: I will tell you.
The barge she sat in, like a burnish'd throne,
Burn'd on the water. The poop was beaten gold;
Purple the sails, and so perfumed that
The winds were love-sick with them; the oars were silver,
Which to the tune of flutes kept stroke, and made
The water which they beat to follow faster,
As amorous of their strokes. For her own person,
It beggar'd all description. She did lie
In her pavilion, cloth-of-gold, of tissue,
O'erpicturing that Venus where we see
The fancy out-work nature. On each side her
Stood pretty dimpled boys, like smiling Cupids,
With divers-colour'd fans, whose wind did seem
To glow the delicate cheeks which they did cool,
And what they undid did.

AGRIPPA: O, rare for Antony!
ENOBARBUS: Her gentlewomen, like the Nereides,
So many mermaids, tended her i' th' eyes,
And made their bends adornings. At the helm
A seeming mermaid steers. The silken tackle
Swell with the touches of those flower-soft hands
That yarely frame the office. From the barge
A strange invisible perfume hits the sense
Of the adjacent wharfs. The city cast
Her people out upon her; and Antony,
Enthron'd i' th' market-place, did sit alone,
Whistling to th' air; which, but for vacancy,
Had gone to gaze on Cleopatra too,
And made a gap in nature.
AGRIPPA: Rare Egyptian!
ENOBARBUS: Upon her landing, Antony sent to her,
Invited her to supper. She replied
It should be better he became her guest;
Which she entreated. Our courteous Antony,
Whom ne'er the word of 'No' woman heard speak,
Being barber'd ten times o'er, goes to the feast,
And for his ordinary pays his heart
For what his eyes eat only.
AGRIPPA: Royal wench!
She made great Caesar lay his sword to bed.
He ploughed her, and she cropp'd.
ENOBARBUS: I saw her once
Hop forty paces through the public street;
And, having lost her breath, she spoke, and panted,
That she did make defect perfection,
And, breathless, pow'r breathe forth.
MAECENAS: Now Antony must leave her utterly.
ENOBARBUS: Never! He will not.
Age cannot wither her, nor custom stale
Her infinite variety. Other women cloy
The appetites they feed, but she makes hungry
Where most she satisfies; for vilest things
Become themselves in her, that the holy priests
Bless her when she is riggish.
MAECENAS: If beauty, wisdom, modesty, can settle
The heart of Antony, Octavia is
A blessed lottery to him.
AGRIPPA: Let us go.
Good Enobarbus, make yourself my guest
Whilst you abide here.
ENOBARBUS: Humbly, sir, I thank you.
Exeunt

ACT II. SCENE III. Rome. Caesar's House

Enter Antony, Caesar, Octavia Between Them
ANTONY: The world and my great office will sometimes
Divide me from your bosom.
OCTAVIA: All which time
Before the gods my knee shall bow my prayers

To them for you.
ANTONY: Good night, sir. My Octavia,
Read not my blemishes in the world's report.
I have not kept my square; but that to come
Shall all be done by th' rule. Good night, dear lady.
OCTAVIA: Good night, sir.
CAESAR: Good night.
Exeunt Caesar and Octavia
Enter Soothsayer
ANTONY: Now, sirrah, you do wish yourself in Egypt?
SOOTHSAYER: Would I had never come from thence, nor you thither!
ANTONY: If you can- your reason.
SOOTHSAYER: I see it in my motion, have it not in my tongue; but yet hie you to Egypt again.
ANTONY: Say to me,
Whose fortunes shall rise higher, Caesar's or mine?
SOOTHSAYER: Caesar's.
Therefore, O Antony, stay not by his side.
Thy daemon, that thy spirit which keeps thee, is
Noble, courageous, high, unmatchable,
Where Caesar's is not; but near him thy angel
Becomes a fear, as being o'erpow'r'd. Therefore
Make space enough between you.
ANTONY: Speak this no more.
SOOTHSAYER: To none but thee; no more but when to thee.
If thou dost play with him at any game,
Thou art sure to lose; and of that natural luck
He beats thee 'gainst the odds. Thy lustre thickens
When he shines by. I say again, thy spirit
Is all afraid to govern thee near him;
But, he away, 'tis noble.
ANTONY: Get thee gone.
Say to Ventidius I would speak with him.
Exit Soothsayer
He shall to Parthia.- Be it art or hap,
He hath spoken true. The very dice obey him;
And in our sports my better cunning faints
Under his chance. If we draw lots, he speeds;
His cocks do win the battle still of mine,
When it is all to nought, and his quails ever
Beat mine, inhoop'd, at odds. I will to Egypt;
And though I make this marriage for my peace,
I' th' East my pleasure lies.
Enter Ventidius
O, come, Ventidius,
You must to Parthia. Your commission's ready;
Follow me and receive't. Exeunt

ACT II. SCENE IV. Rome. A Street

Enter Lepidus, Maecenas, and Agrippa
LEPIDUS: Trouble yourselves no further. Pray you hasten
Your generals after.
AGRIPPA: Sir, Mark Antony
Will e'en but kiss Octavia, and we'll follow.

LEPIDUS: Till I shall see you in your soldier's dress,
Which will become you both, farewell.
MAECENAS: We shall,
As I conceive the journey, be at th' Mount
Before you, Lepidus.
LEPIDUS: Your way is shorter;
My purposes do draw me much about.
You'll win two days upon me.
BOTH: Sir, good success!
LEPIDUS: Farewell.
Exeunt

ACT II. SCENE V. Alexandria. Cleopatra's Palace

Enter Cleopatra, Charmian, Iras, and Alexas
CLEOPATRA: Give me some music- music, moody food
Of us that trade in love.
ALL: The music, ho!
Enter Mardian the Eunuch
CLEOPATRA: Let it alone! Let's to billiards. Come, Charmian.
CHARMIAN: My arm is sore; best play with Mardian.
CLEOPATRA: As well a woman with an eunuch play'd
As with a woman. Come, you'll play with me, sir?
MARDIAN: As well as I can, madam.
CLEOPATRA: And when good will is show'd, though't come too short,
The actor may plead pardon. I'll none now.
Give me mine angle- we'll to th' river. There,
My music playing far off, I will betray
Tawny-finn'd fishes; my bended hook shall pierce
Their slimy jaws; and as I draw them up
I'll think them every one an Antony,
And say 'Ah ha! Y'are caught.'
CHARMIAN: 'Twas merry when
You wager'd on your angling; when your diver
Did hang a salt fish on his hook, which he
With fervency drew up.
CLEOPATRA: That time? O times
I laughed him out of patience; and that night
I laugh'd him into patience; and next morn,
Ere the ninth hour, I drunk him to his bed,
Then put my tires and mantles on him, whilst
I wore his sword Philippan.
Enter a Messenger
O! from Italy?
Ram thou thy fruitful tidings in mine ears,
That long time have been barren.
MESSENGER: Madam, madam-
CLEOPATRA: Antony's dead! If thou say so, villain,
Thou kill'st thy mistress; but well and free,
If thou so yield him, there is gold, and here
My bluest veins to kiss- a hand that kings
Have lipp'd, and trembled kissing.
MESSENGER: First, madam, he is well.
CLEOPATRA: Why, there's more gold.
But, sirrah, mark, we use

To say the dead are well. Bring it to that,
The gold I give thee will I melt and pour
Down thy ill-uttering throat.
MESSENGER: Good madam, hear me.
CLEOPATRA: Well, go to, I will.
But there's no goodness in thy face. If Antony
Be free and healthful- why so tart a favour
To trumpet such good tidings? If not well,
Thou shouldst come like a Fury crown'd with snakes,
Not like a formal man.
MESSENGER: Will't please you hear me?
CLEOPATRA: I have a mind to strike thee ere thou speak'st.
Yet, if thou say Antony lives, is well,
Or friends with Caesar, or not captive to him,
I'll set thee in a shower of gold, and hail
Rich pearls upon thee.
MESSENGER: Madam, he's well.
CLEOPATRA: Well said.
MESSENGER: And friends with Caesar.
CLEOPATRA: Th'art an honest man.
MESSENGER: Caesar and he are greater friends than ever.
CLEOPATRA: Make thee a fortune from me.
MESSENGER: But yet, madam-
CLEOPATRA: I do not like 'but yet.' It does allay
The good precedence; fie upon 'but yet'!
'But yet' is as a gaoler to bring forth
Some monstrous malefactor. Prithee, friend,
Pour out the pack of matter to mine ear,
The good and bad together. He's friends with Caesar;
In state of health, thou say'st; and, thou say'st, free.
MESSENGER: Free, madam! No; I made no such report.
He's bound unto Octavia.
CLEOPATRA: For what good turn?
MESSENGER: For the best turn i' th' bed.
CLEOPATRA: I am pale, Charmian.
MESSENGER: Madam, he's married to Octavia.
CLEOPATRA: The most infectious pestilence upon thee!
Strikes Him Down
MESSENGER: Good madam, patience.
CLEOPATRA: What say you? Hence,
Strikes Him
Horrible villain! or I'll spurn thine eyes
Like balls before me; I'll unhair thy head;
She Hales Him up and Down
Thou shalt be whipp'd with wire and stew'd in brine,
Smarting in ling'ring pickle.
MESSENGER: Gracious madam,
I that do bring the news made not the match.
CLEOPATRA: Say 'tis not so, a province I will give thee,
And make thy fortunes proud. The blow thou hadst
Shall make thy peace for moving me to rage;
And I will boot thee with what gift beside
Thy modesty can beg.

MESSENGER: He's married, madam.
CLEOPATRA: Rogue, thou hast liv'd too long.
Draws a Knife
MESSENGER: Nay, then I'll run.
What mean you, madam? I have made no fault.
Exit
CHARMIAN: Good madam, keep yourself within yourself:
The man is innocent.
CLEOPATRA: Some innocents scape not the thunderbolt.
Melt Egypt into Nile! and kindly creatures
Turn all to serpents! Call the slave again.
Though I am mad, I will not bite him. Call!
CHARMIAN: He is afear'd to come.
CLEOPATRA: I will not hurt him.
These hands do lack nobility, that they strike
A meaner than myself; since I myself
Have given myself the cause.
Enter the Messenger Again
Come hither, sir.
Though it be honest, it is never good
To bring bad news. Give to a gracious message
An host of tongues; but let ill tidings tell
Themselves when they be felt.
MESSENGER: I have done my duty.
CLEOPATRA: Is he married?
I cannot hate thee worser than I do
If thou again say 'Yes.'
MESSENGER: He's married, madam.
CLEOPATRA: The gods confound thee! Dost thou hold there still?
MESSENGER: Should I lie, madam?
CLEOPATRA: O, I would thou didst,
So half my Egypt were submerg'd and made
A cistern for scal'd snakes! Go, get thee hence.
Hadst thou Narcissus in thy face, to me
Thou wouldst appear most ugly. He is married?
MESSENGER: I crave your Highness' pardon.
CLEOPATRA: He is married?
MESSENGER: Take no offence that I would not offend you;
To punish me for what you make me do
Seems much unequal. He's married to Octavia.
CLEOPATRA: O, that his fault should make a knave of thee
That art not what th'art sure of! Get thee hence.
The merchandise which thou hast brought from Rome
Are all too dear for me. Lie they upon thy hand,
And be undone by 'em!
Exit Messenger
CHARMIAN: Good your Highness, patience.
CLEOPATRA: In praising Antony I have disprais'd Caesar.
CHARMIAN: Many times, madam.
CLEOPATRA: I am paid for't now. Lead me from hence,
I faint. O Iras, Charmian! 'Tis no matter.
Go to the fellow, good Alexas; bid him
Report the feature of Octavia, her years,

Her inclination; let him not leave out
The colour of her hair. Bring me word quickly.
Exit Alexas
Let him for ever go- let him not, Charmian-
Though he be painted one way like a Gorgon,
The other way's a Mars. To Mardian
Bid you Alexas
Bring me word how tall she is.- Pity me, Charmian,
But do not speak to me. Lead me to my chamber.
Exeunt

ACT II. SCENE VI. Near Misenum

Flourish. Enter Pompey and Menas at One Door, with Drum and Trumpet; at Another, Caesar, Antony, Lepidus, Enobarbus, Maecenas, Agrippa, with Soldiers Marching
POMPEY: Your hostages I have, so have you mine;
And we shall talk before we fight.
CAESAR: Most meet
That first we come to words; and therefore have we
Our written purposes before us sent;
Which if thou hast considered, let us know
If 'twill tie up thy discontented sword
And carry back to Sicily much tall youth
That else must perish here.
POMPEY: To you all three,
The senators alone of this great world,
Chief factors for the gods: I do not know
Wherefore my father should revengers want,
Having a son and friends, since Julius Caesar,
Who at Philippi the good Brutus ghosted,
There saw you labouring for him. What was't
That mov'd pale Cassius to conspire? and what
Made the all-honour'd honest Roman, Brutus,
With the arm'd rest, courtiers of beauteous freedom,
To drench the Capitol, but that they would
Have one man but a man? And that is it
Hath made me rig my navy, at whose burden
The anger'd ocean foams; with which I meant
To scourge th' ingratitude that despiteful Rome
Cast on my noble father.
CAESAR: Take your time.
ANTONY: Thou canst not fear us, Pompey, with thy sails;
We'll speak with thee at sea; at land thou know'st
How much we do o'er-count thee.
POMPEY: At land, indeed,
Thou dost o'er-count me of my father's house.
But since the cuckoo builds not for himself,
Remain in't as thou mayst.
LEPIDUS: Be pleas'd to tell us-
For this is from the present- how you take
The offers we have sent you.
CAESAR: There's the point.
ANTONY: Which do not be entreated to, but weigh
What it is worth embrac'd.
CAESAR: And what may follow,

To try a larger fortune.
POMPEY: You have made me offer
Of Sicily, Sardinia; and I must
Rid all the sea of pirates; then to send
Measures of wheat to Rome; this 'greed upon,
To part with unhack'd edges and bear back
Our targes undinted.
ALL: That's our offer.
POMPEY: Know, then,
I came before you here a man prepar'd
To take this offer; but Mark Antony
Put me to some impatience. Though I lose
The praise of it by telling, you must know,
When Caesar and your brother were at blows,
Your mother came to Sicily and did find
Her welcome friendly.
ANTONY: I have heard it, Pompey,
And am well studied for a liberal thanks
Which I do owe you.
POMPEY: Let me have your hand.
I did not think, sir, to have met you here.
ANTONY: The beds i' th' East are soft; and thanks to you,
That call'd me timelier than my purpose hither;
For I have gained by't.
CAESAR: Since I saw you last
There is a change upon you.
POMPEY: Well, I know not
What counts harsh fortune casts upon my face;
But in my bosom shall she never come
To make my heart her vassal.
LEPIDUS: Well met here.
POMPEY: I hope so, Lepidus. Thus we are agreed.
I crave our composition may be written,
And seal'd between us.
CAESAR: That's the next to do.
POMPEY: We'll feast each other ere we part, and let's
Draw lots who shall begin.
ANTONY: That will I, Pompey.
POMPEY: No, Antony, take the lot;
But, first or last, your fine Egyptian cookery
Shall have the fame. I have heard that Julius Caesar
Grew fat with feasting there.
ANTONY: You have heard much.
POMPEY: I have fair meanings, sir.
ANTONY: And fair words to them.
POMPEY: Then so much have I heard;
And I have heard Apollodorus carried-
ENOBARBUS: No more of that! He did so.
POMPEY: What, I pray you?
ENOBARBUS: A certain queen to Caesar in a mattress.
POMPEY: I know thee now. How far'st thou, soldier?
ENOBARBUS: Well;
And well am like to do, for I perceive

Four feasts are toward.
POMPEY: Let me shake thy hand.
I never hated thee; I have seen thee fight,
When I have envied thy behaviour.
ENOBARBUS: Sir,
I never lov'd you much; but I ha' prais'd ye
When you have well deserv'd ten times as much
As I have said you did.
POMPEY: Enjoy thy plainness;
It nothing ill becomes thee.
Aboard my galley I invite you all.
Will you lead, lords?
ALL: Show's the way, sir.
POMPEY: Come.
Exeunt All but Enobarbus and Menas
MENAS: Aside Thy father, Pompey, would ne'er have made this treaty.- You and I have known, sir.
ENOBARBUS: At sea, I think.
MENAS: We have, sir.
ENOBARBUS: You have done well by water.
MENAS: And you by land.
ENOBARBUS: I Will praise any man that will praise me; though it cannot be denied what I have done by land.
MENAS: Nor what I have done by water.
ENOBARBUS: Yes, something you can deny for your own safety: you have been a great thief by sea.
MENAS: And you by land.
ENOBARBUS: There I deny my land service. But give me your hand, Menas; if our eyes had authority, here they might take two thieves kissing.
MENAS: All men's faces are true, whatsome'er their hands are.
ENOBARBUS: But there is never a fair woman has a true face.
MENAS: No slander: they steal hearts.
ENOBARBUS: We came hither to fight with you.
MENAS: For my part, I am sorry it is turn'd to a drinking.
Pompey doth this day laugh away his fortune.
ENOBARBUS: If he do, sure he cannot weep't back again.
MENAS: Y'have said, sir. We look'd not for Mark Antony here. Pray you, is he married to Cleopatra?
ENOBARBUS: Caesar' sister is call'd Octavia.
MENAS: True, sir; she was the wife of Caius Marcellus.
ENOBARBUS: But she is now the wife of Marcus Antonius.
MENAS: Pray ye, sir?
ENOBARBUS: 'Tis true.
MENAS: Then is Caesar and he for ever knit together.
ENOBARBUS: If I were bound to divine of this unity, I would not prophesy so.
MENAS: I think the policy of that purpose made more in the marriage than the love of the parties.
ENOBARBUS: I think so too. But you shall find the band that seems to tie their friendship together will be the very strangler of their amity: Octavia is of a holy, cold, and still conversation.
MENAS: Who would not have his wife so?

ENOBARBUS: Not he that himself is not so; which is Mark Antony. He will to his Egyptian dish again; then shall the sighs of Octavia blow the fire up in Caesar, and, as I said before, that which is the strength of their amity shall prove the immediate author of their variance. Antony will use his affection where it is; he married but his occasion here.

MENAS: And thus it may be. Come, sir, will you aboard? I have a health for you.

ENOBARBUS: I shall take it, sir. We have us'd our throats in Egypt.

MENAS: Come, let's away.

Exeunt

ACT. II. SCENE VII. On Board Pompey's Galley, off Misenum

Music Plays. Enter Two or Three Servants with a Banquet

FIRST SERVANT: Here they'll be, man. Some o' their plants are ill-rooted already; the least wind i' th' world will blow them down.

SECOND SERVANT: Lepidus is high-colour'd.

FIRST SERVANT: They have made him drink alms-drink.

SECOND SERVANT: As they pinch one another by the disposition, he cries out 'No more!'; reconciles them to his entreaty and himself to th' drink.

FIRST SERVANT: But it raises the greater war between him and his discretion.

SECOND SERVANT: Why, this it is to have a name in great men's fellowship. I had as lief have a reed that will do me no service as a partizan I could not heave.

FIRST SERVANT: To be call'd into a huge sphere, and not to be seen to move in't, are the holes where eyes should be, which pitifully disaster the cheeks.

A Sennet Sounded. Enter Caesar, Antony, Lepidus, Pompey, Agrippa, Maecenas, Enobarbus, Menas, with Other Captains

ANTONY: To Caesar Thus do they, sir: they take the flow o' th' Nile
By certain scales i' th' pyramid; they know
By th' height, the lowness, or the mean, if dearth
Or foison follow. The higher Nilus swells
The more it promises; as it ebbs, the seedsman
Upon the slime and ooze scatters his grain,
And shortly comes to harvest.

LEPIDUS: Y'have strange serpents there.

ANTONY: Ay, Lepidus.

LEPIDUS: Your serpent of Egypt is bred now of your mud by the operation of your sun; so is your crocodile.

ANTONY: They are so.

POMPEY: Sit- and some wine! A health to Lepidus!

LEPIDUS: I am not so well as I should be, but I'll ne'er out.

ENOBARBUS: Not till you have slept. I fear me you'll be in till then.

LEPIDUS: Nay, certainly, I have heard the Ptolemies' pyramises are very goodly things. Without contradiction I have heard that.

MENAS: Aside to Pompey Pompey, a word.

POMPEY: Aside to Menas Say in mine ear; what is't?

MENAS: Aside to Pompey Forsake thy seat, I do beseech thee, Captain,
And hear me speak a word.

POMPEY: Whispers In's Ear Forbear me till anon-
This wine for Lepidus!

LEPIDUS: What manner o' thing is your crocodile?
ANTONY: It is shap'd, sir, like itself, and it is as broad as it hath breadth; it is just so high as it is, and moves with it own organs. It lives by that which nourisheth it, and the elements once out of it, it transmigrates.
LEPIDUS: What colour is it of?
ANTONY: Of it own colour too.
LEPIDUS: 'Tis a strange serpent.
ANTONY: 'Tis so. And the tears of it are wet.
CAESAR: Will this description satisfy him?
ANTONY: With the health that Pompey gives him, else he is a very epicure.
POMPEY: Aside to Menas Go, hang, sir, hang! Tell me of that!
Away!
Do as I bid you.- Where's this cup I call'd for?
MENAS: Aside to Pompey If for the sake of merit thou wilt hear me, rise from thy stool.
POMPEY: Aside to Menas I think th'art mad. Rises and Walks Aside The matter?
MENAS: I have ever held my cap off to thy fortunes.
POMPEY: Thou hast serv'd me with much faith. What's else to say?-
Be jolly, lords.
ANTONY: These quicksands, Lepidus,
Keep off them, for you sink.
MENAS: Wilt thou be lord of all the world?
POMPEY: What say'st thou?
MENAS: Wilt thou be lord of the whole world? That's twice.
POMPEY: How should that be?
MENAS: But entertain it,
And though you think me poor, I am the man
Will give thee all the world.
POMPEY: Hast thou drunk well?
MENAS: No, Pompey, I have kept me from the cup.
Thou art, if thou dar'st be, the earthly Jove;
Whate'er the ocean pales or sky inclips
Is thine, if thou wilt ha't.
POMPEY: Show me which way.
MENAS: These three world-sharers, these competitors,
Are in thy vessel. Let me cut the cable;
And when we are put off, fall to their throats.
All there is thine.
POMPEY: Ah, this thou shouldst have done,
And not have spoke on't. In me 'tis villainy:
In thee't had been good service. Thou must know
'Tis not my profit that does lead mine honour:
Mine honour, it. Repent that e'er thy tongue
Hath so betray'd thine act. Being done unknown,
I should have found it afterwards well done,
But must condemn it now. Desist, and drink.
MENAS: Aside For this,
I'll never follow thy pall'd fortunes more.
Who seeks, and will not take when once 'tis offer'd,
Shall never find it more.

POMPEY: This health to Lepidus!
ANTONY: Bear him ashore. I'll pledge it for him, Pompey.
ENOBARBUS: Here's to thee, Menas!
MENAS: Enobarbus, welcome!
POMPEY: Fill till the cup be hid.
ENOBARBUS: There's a strong fellow, Menas.
Pointing to the Servant Who Carries off Lepidus
MENAS: Why?
ENOBARBUS: 'A bears the third part of the world, man; see'st not?
MENAS: The third part, then, is drunk. Would it were all,
That it might go on wheels!
ENOBARBUS: Drink thou; increase the reels.
MENAS: Come.
POMPEY: This is not yet an Alexandrian feast.
ANTONY: It ripens towards it. Strike the vessels, ho!
Here's to Caesar!
CAESAR: I could well forbear't.
It's monstrous labour when I wash my brain
And it grows fouler.
ANTONY: Be a child o' th' time.
CAESAR: Possess it, I'll make answer.
But I had rather fast from all four days
Than drink so much in one.
ENOBARBUS: To Antony Ha, my brave emperor!
Shall we dance now the Egyptian Bacchanals
And celebrate our drink?
POMPEY: Let's ha't, good soldier.
ANTONY: Come, let's all take hands,
Till that the conquering wine hath steep'd our sense
In soft and delicate Lethe.
ENOBARBUS: All take hands.
Make battery to our ears with the loud music,
The while I'll place you; then the boy shall sing;
The holding every man shall bear as loud
As his strong sides can volley.
Music Plays. Enobarbus Places Them Hand in Hand
THE SONG
Come, thou monarch of the vine,
Plumpy Bacchus with pink eyne!
In thy fats our cares be drown'd,
With thy grapes our hairs be crown'd.
Cup us till the world go round,
Cup us till the world go round!
CAESAR: What would you more? Pompey, good night. Good brother,
Let me request you off; our graver business
Frowns at this levity. Gentle lords, let's part;
You see we have burnt our cheeks. Strong Enobarb
Is weaker than the wine, and mine own tongue
Splits what it speaks. The wild disguise hath almost
Antick'd us all. What needs more words? Good night.
Good Antony, your hand.
POMPEY: I'll try you on the shore.
ANTONY: And shall, sir. Give's your hand.

POMPEY: O Antony,
You have my father's house- but what? We are friends.
Come, down into the boat.
ENOBARBUS: Take heed you fall not.
Exeunt All but Enobarbus and Menas
Menas, I'll not on shore.
MENAS: No, to my cabin.
These drums! these trumpets, flutes! what!
Let Neptune hear we bid a loud farewell
To these great fellows. Sound and be hang'd, sound out!
Sound a Flourish, with Drums
ENOBARBUS: Hoo! says 'a. There's my cap.
MENAS: Hoo! Noble Captain, come.
Exeunt

ACT III. SCENE I. A Plain in Syria

Enter Ventidius, as it Were in Triumph, with Silius and Other Romans, Officers and Soldiers; the Dead Body of Pacorus Borne Before Him
VENTIDIUS: Now, darting Parthia, art thou struck, and now
Pleas'd fortune does of Marcus Crassus' death
Make me revenger. Bear the King's son's body
Before our army. Thy Pacorus, Orodes,
Pays this for Marcus Crassus.
SILIUS: Noble Ventidius,
Whilst yet with Parthian blood thy sword is warm
The fugitive Parthians follow; spur through Media,
Mesopotamia, and the shelters whither
The routed fly. So thy grand captain, Antony,
Shall set thee on triumphant chariots and
Put garlands on thy head.
VENTIDIUS: O Silius, Silius,
I have done enough. A lower place, note well,
May make too great an act; for learn this, Silius:
Better to leave undone than by our deed
Acquire too high a fame when him we serve's away.
Caesar and Antony have ever won
More in their officer, than person. Sossius,
One of my place in Syria, his lieutenant,
For quick accumulation of renown,
Which he achiev'd by th' minute, lost his favour.
Who does i' th' wars more than his captain can
Becomes his captain's captain; and ambition,
The soldier's virtue, rather makes choice of loss
Than gain which darkens him.
I could do more to do Antonius good,
But 'twould offend him; and in his offence
Should my performance perish.
SILIUS: Thou hast, Ventidius, that
Without the which a soldier and his sword
Grants scarce distinction. Thou wilt write to Antony?
VENTIDIUS: I'll humbly signify what in his name,
That magical word of war, we have effected;
How, with his banners, and his well-paid ranks,
The ne'er-yet-beaten horse of Parthia

We have jaded out o' th' field.
SILIUS: Where is he now?
VENTIDIUS: He purposeth to Athens; whither, with what haste
The weight we must convey with's will permit,
We shall appear before him.- On, there; pass along.
Exeunt

ACT III. SCENE II. Rome. Caesar's House

Enter Agrippa at One Door, Enobarbus at Another
AGRIPPA: What, are the brothers parted?
ENOBARBUS: They have dispatch'd with Pompey; he is gone;
The other three are sealing. Octavia weeps
To part from Rome; Caesar is sad; and Lepidus,
Since Pompey's feast, as Menas says, is troubled
With the green sickness.
AGRIPPA: 'Tis a noble Lepidus.
ENOBARBUS: A very fine one. O, how he loves Caesar!
AGRIPPA: Nay, but how dearly he adores Mark Antony!
ENOBARBUS: Caesar? Why he's the Jupiter of men.
AGRIPPA: What's Antony? The god of Jupiter.
ENOBARBUS: Spake you of Caesar? How! the nonpareil!
AGRIPPA: O, Antony! O thou Arabian bird!
ENOBARBUS: Would you praise Caesar, say 'Caesar'- go no further.
AGRIPPA: Indeed, he plied them both with excellent praises.
ENOBARBUS: But he loves Caesar best. Yet he loves Antony.
Hoo! hearts, tongues, figures, scribes, bards, poets, cannot
Think, speak, cast, write, sing, number- hoo!-
His love to Antony. But as for Caesar,
Kneel down, kneel down, and wonder.
AGRIPPA: Both he loves.
ENOBARBUS: They are his shards, and he their beetle.
Trumpets Within
So-this is to horse. Adieu, noble Agrippa.
AGRIPPA: Good fortune, worthy soldier, and farewell.
Enter Caesar, Antony, Lepidus, and Octavia
ANTONY: No further, sir.
CAESAR: You take from me a great part of myself;
Use me well in't. Sister, prove such a wife
As my thoughts make thee, and as my farthest band
Shall pass on thy approof. Most noble Antony,
Let not the piece of virtue which is set
Betwixt us as the cement of our love
To keep it builded be the ram to batter
The fortress of it; for better might we
Have lov'd without this mean, if on both parts
This be not cherish'd.
ANTONY: Make me not offended
In your distrust.
CAESAR: I have said.
ANTONY: You shall not find,
Though you be therein curious, the least cause
For what you seem to fear. So the gods keep you,
And make the hearts of Romans serve your ends!
We will here part.

CAESAR: Farewell, my dearest sister, fare thee well.
The elements be kind to thee and make
Thy spirits all of comfort! Fare thee well.
OCTAVIA: My noble brother!
ANTONY: The April's in her eyes. It is love's spring,
And these the showers to bring it on. Be cheerful.
OCTAVIA: Sir, look well to my husband's house; and-
CAESAR: What, Octavia?
OCTAVIA: I'll tell you in your ear.
ANTONY: Her tongue will not obey her heart, nor can
Her heart inform her tongue- the swan's down feather,
That stands upon the swell at the full of tide,
And neither way inclines.
ENOBARBUS: Aside to Agrippa Will Caesar weep?
AGRIPPA: Aside to Enobarbus He has a cloud in's face.
ENOBARBUS: Aside to Agrippa He were the worse for that, were he a horse; so is he, being a man.
AGRIPPA: Aside to Enobarbus Why, Enobarbus,
When Antony found Julius Caesar dead,
He cried almost to roaring; and he wept
When at Philippi he found Brutus slain.
ENOBARBUS: Aside to Agrippa That year, indeed, he was troubled with a rheum;
What willingly he did confound he wail'd,
Believe't- till I weep too.
CAESAR: No, sweet Octavia,
You shall hear from me still; the time shall not
Out-go my thinking on you.
ANTONY: Come, sir, come;
I'll wrestle with you in my strength of love.
Look, here I have you; thus I let you go,
And give you to the gods.
CAESAR: Adieu; be happy!
LEPIDUS: Let all the number of the stars give light
To thy fair way!
CAESAR: Farewell, farewell!
Kisses Octavia
ANTONY: Farewell! Trumpets sound.
Exeunt

ACT III. SCENE III. Alexandria. Cleopatra's Palace

Enter Cleopatra, Charmian, Iras, and Alexas
CLEOPATRA: Where is the fellow?
ALEXAS: Half afeard to come.
CLEOPATRA: Go to, go to.
Enter the Messenger as Before
Come hither, sir.
ALEXAS: Good Majesty,
Herod of Jewry dare not look upon you
But when you are well pleas'd.
CLEOPATRA: That Herod's head
I'll have. But how, when Antony is gone,
Through whom I might command it? Come thou near.
MESSENGER: Most gracious Majesty!

CLEOPATRA: Didst thou behold Octavia?
MESSENGER: Ay, dread Queen.
CLEOPATRA: Where?
MESSENGER: Madam, in Rome
I look'd her in the face, and saw her led
Between her brother and Mark Antony.
CLEOPATRA: Is she as tall as me?
MESSENGER: She is not, madam.
CLEOPATRA: Didst hear her speak? Is she shrill-tongu'd or low?
MESSENGER: Madam, I heard her speak: she is low-voic'd.
CLEOPATRA: That's not so good. He cannot like her long.
CHARMIAN: Like her? O Isis! 'tis impossible.
CLEOPATRA: I think so, Charmian. Dull of tongue and dwarfish!
What majesty is in her gait? Remember,
If e'er thou look'dst on majesty.
MESSENGER: She creeps.
Her motion and her station are as one;
She shows a body rather than a life,
A statue than a breather.
CLEOPATRA: Is this certain?
MESSENGER: Or I have no observance.
CHARMIAN: Three in Egypt
Cannot make better note.
CLEOPATRA: He's very knowing;
I do perceive't. There's nothing in her yet.
The fellow has good judgment.
CHARMIAN: Excellent.
CLEOPATRA: Guess at her years, I prithee.
MESSENGER: Madam,
She was a widow.
CLEOPATRA: Widow? Charmian, hark!
MESSENGER: And I do think she's thirty.
CLEOPATRA: Bear'st thou her face in mind? Is't long or round?
MESSENGER: Round even to faultiness.
CLEOPATRA: For the most part, too, they are foolish that are so.
Her hair, what colour?
MESSENGER: Brown, madam; and her forehead
As low as she would wish it.
CLEOPATRA: There's gold for thee.
Thou must not take my former sharpness ill.
I will employ thee back again; I find thee
Most fit for business. Go make thee ready;
Our letters are prepar'd.
Exeunt Messenger
CHARMIAN: A proper man.
CLEOPATRA: Indeed, he is so. I repent me much
That so I harried him. Why, methinks, by him,
This creature's no such thing.
CHARMIAN: Nothing, madam.
CLEOPATRA: The man hath seen some majesty, and should know.
CHARMIAN: Hath he seen majesty? Isis else defend,
And serving you so long!
CLEOPATRA: I have one thing more to ask him yet, good Charmian.

But 'tis no matter; thou shalt bring him to me
Where I will write. All may be well enough.
CHARMIAN: I warrant you, madam.
Exeunt

ACT III. SCENE IV. Athens. Antony's House

Enter Antony and Octavia
ANTONY: Nay, nay, Octavia, not only that-
That were excusable, that and thousands more
Of semblable import- but he hath wag'd
New wars 'gainst Pompey; made his will, and read it
To public ear;
Spoke scandy of me; when perforce he could not
But pay me terms of honour, cold and sickly
He vented them, most narrow measure lent me;
When the best hint was given him, he not took't,
Or did it from his teeth.
OCTAVIA: O my good lord,
Believe not all; or if you must believe,
Stomach not all. A more unhappy lady,
If this division chance, ne'er stood between,
Praying for both parts.
The good gods will mock me presently
When I shall pray 'O, bless my lord and husband!'
Undo that prayer by crying out as loud
'O, bless my brother!' Husband win, win brother,
Prays, and destroys the prayer; no mid-way
'Twixt these extremes at all.
ANTONY: Gentle Octavia,
Let your best love draw to that point which seeks
Best to preserve it. If I lose mine honour,
I lose myself; better I were not yours
Than yours so branchless. But, as you requested,
Yourself shall go between's. The meantime, lady,
I'll raise the preparation of a war
Shall stain your brother. Make your soonest haste;
So your desires are yours.
OCTAVIA: Thanks to my lord.
The Jove of power make me, most weak, most weak,
Your reconciler! Wars 'twixt you twain would be
As if the world should cleave, and that slain men
Should solder up the rift.
ANTONY: When it appears to you where this begins,
Turn your displeasure that way, for our faults
Can never be so equal that your love
Can equally move with them. Provide your going;
Choose your own company, and command what cost
Your heart has mind to.
Exeunt

ACTIII. SCENE V. Athens. Antony's House

Enter Enobarbus and Eros, Meeting
ENOBARBUS: How now, friend Eros!
EROS: There's strange news come, sir.
ENOBARBUS: What, man?

EROS: Caesar and Lepidus have made wars upon Pompey.
ENOBARBUS: This is old. What is the success?
EROS: Caesar, having made use of him in the wars 'gainst Pompey, presently denied him rivality, would not let him partake in the glory of the action; and not resting here, accuses him of letters he had formerly wrote to Pompey; upon his own appeal, seizes him. So the poor third is up, till death enlarge his confine.
ENOBARBUS: Then, world, thou hast a pair of chaps- no more;
And throw between them all the food thou hast,
They'll grind the one the other. Where's Antony?
EROS: He's walking in the garden- thus, and spurns
The rush that lies before him; cries 'Fool Lepidus!'
And threats the throat of that his officer
That murd'red Pompey.
ENOBARBUS: Our great navy's rigg'd.
EROS: For Italy and Caesar. More, Domitius:
My lord desires you presently; my news
I might have told hereafter.
ENOBARBUS: 'Twill be naught;
But let it be. Bring me to Antony.
EROS: Come, sir.
Exeunt

ACT III. SCENE VI. Rome. Caesar's House

Enter Caesar, Agrippa, and Maecenas
CAESAR: Contemning Rome, he has done all this and more
In Alexandria. Here's the manner of't:
I' th' market-place, on a tribunal silver'd,
Cleopatra and himself in chairs of gold
Were publicly enthron'd; at the feet sat
Caesarion, whom they call my father's son,
And all the unlawful issue that their lust
Since then hath made between them. Unto her
He gave the stablishment of Egypt; made her
Of lower Syria, Cyprus, Lydia,
Absolute queen.
MAECENAS: This in the public eye?
CAESAR: I' th' common show-place, where they exercise.
His sons he there proclaim'd the kings of kings:
Great Media, Parthia, and Armenia,
He gave to Alexander; to Ptolemy he assign'd
Syria, Cilicia, and Phoenicia. She
In th' habiliments of the goddess Isis
That day appear'd; and oft before gave audience,
As 'tis reported, so.
MAECENAS: Let Rome be thus
Inform'd.
AGRIPPA: Who, queasy with his insolence
Already, will their good thoughts call from him.
CAESAR: The people knows it, and have now receiv'd
His accusations.
AGRIPPA: Who does he accuse?
CAESAR: Caesar; and that, having in Sicily
Sextus Pompeius spoil'd, we had not rated him

His part o' th' isle. Then does he say he lent me
Some shipping, unrestor'd. Lastly, he frets
That Lepidus of the triumvirate
Should be depos'd; and, being, that we detain
All his revenue.
AGRIPPA: Sir, this should be answer'd.
CAESAR: 'Tis done already, and messenger gone.
I have told him Lepidus was grown too cruel,
That he his high authority abus'd,
And did deserve his change. For what I have conquer'd
I grant him part; but then, in his Armenia
And other of his conquer'd kingdoms,
Demand the like.
MAECENAS: He'll never yield to that.
CAESAR: Nor must not then be yielded to in this.
Enter Octavia, with Her Train
OCTAVIA: Hail, Caesar, and my lord! hail, most dear Caesar!
CAESAR: That ever I should call thee cast-away!
OCTAVIA: You have not call'd me so, nor have you cause.
CAESAR: Why have you stol'n upon us thus? You come not
Like Caesar's sister. The wife of Antony
Should have an army for an usher, and
The neighs of horse to tell of her approach
Long ere she did appear. The trees by th' way
Should have borne men, and expectation fainted,
Longing for what it had not. Nay, the dust
Should have ascended to the roof of heaven,
Rais'd by your populous troops. But you are come
A market-maid to Rome, and have prevented
The ostentation of our love, which left unshown
Is often left unlov'd. We should have met you
By sea and land, supplying every stage
With an augmented greeting.
OCTAVIA: Good my lord,
To come thus was I not constrain'd, but did it
On my free will. My lord, Mark Antony,
Hearing that you prepar'd for war, acquainted
My grieved ear withal; whereon I begg'd
His pardon for return.
CAESAR: Which soon he granted,
Being an obstruct 'tween his lust and him.
OCTAVIA: Do not say so, my lord.
CAESAR: I have eyes upon him,
And his affairs come to me on the wind.
Where is he now?
OCTAVIA: My lord, in Athens.
CAESAR: No, my most wronged sister: Cleopatra
Hath nodded him to her. He hath given his empire
Up to a whore, who now are levying
The kings o' th' earth for war. He hath assembled
Bocchus, the king of Libya; Archelaus
Of Cappadocia; Philadelphos, king
Of Paphlagonia; the Thracian king, Adallas;

King Manchus of Arabia; King of Pont;
Herod of Jewry; Mithridates, king
Of Comagene; Polemon and Amyntas,
The kings of Mede and Lycaonia, with
More larger list of sceptres.
OCTAVIA: Ay me most wretched,
That have my heart parted betwixt two friends,
That does afflict each other!
CAESAR: Welcome hither.
Your letters did withhold our breaking forth,
Till we perceiv'd both how you were wrong led
And we in negligent danger. Cheer your heart;
Be you not troubled with the time, which drives
O'er your content these strong necessities,
But let determin'd things to destiny
Hold unbewail'd their way. Welcome to Rome;
Nothing more dear to me. You are abus'd
Beyond the mark of thought, and the high gods,
To do you justice, make their ministers
Of us and those that love you. Best of comfort,
And ever welcome to us.
AGRIPPA: Welcome, lady.
MAECENAS: Welcome, dear madam.
Each heart in Rome does love and pity you;
Only th' adulterous Antony, most large
In his abominations, turns you off,
And gives his potent regiment to a trull
That noises it against us.
OCTAVIA: Is it so, sir?
CAESAR: Most certain. Sister, welcome. Pray you
Be ever known to patience. My dear'st sister!
Exeunt

ACT III. SCENE VII. Antony's Camp near Actium

Enter Cleopatra and Enobarbus
CLEOPATRA: I will be even with thee, doubt it not.
ENOBARBUS: But why, why,
CLEOPATRA: Thou hast forspoke my being in these wars,
And say'st it is not fit.
ENOBARBUS: Well, is it, is it?
CLEOPATRA: Is't not denounc'd against us? Why should not we
Be there in person?
ENOBARBUS: Aside Well, I could reply:
If we should serve with horse and mares together
The horse were merely lost; the mares would bear
A soldier and his horse.
CLEOPATRA: What is't you say?
ENOBARBUS: Your presence needs must puzzle Antony;
Take from his heart, take from his brain, from's time,
What should not then be spar'd. He is already
Traduc'd for levity; and 'tis said in Rome
That Photinus an eunuch and your maids
Manage this war.
CLEOPATRA: Sink Rome, and their tongues rot

That speak against us! A charge we bear i' th' war,
And, as the president of my kingdom, will
Appear there for a man. Speak not against it;
I will not stay behind.
Enter Antony and Canidius
ENOBARBUS: Nay, I have done.
Here comes the Emperor.
ANTONY: Is it not strange, Canidius,
That from Tarentum and Brundusium
He could so quickly cut the Ionian sea,
And take in Toryne?- You have heard on't, sweet?
CLEOPATRA: Celerity is never more admir'd
Than by the negligent.
ANTONY: A good rebuke,
Which might have well becom'd the best of men
To taunt at slackness. Canidius, we
Will fight with him by sea.
CLEOPATRA: By sea! What else?
CANIDIUS: Why will my lord do so?
ANTONY: For that he dares us to't.
ENOBARBUS: So hath my lord dar'd him to single fight.
CANIDIUS: Ay, and to wage this battle at Pharsalia,
Where Caesar fought with Pompey. But these offers,
Which serve not for his vantage, he shakes off;
And so should you.
ENOBARBUS: Your ships are not well mann'd;
Your mariners are muleteers, reapers, people
Ingross'd by swift impress. In Caesar's fleet
Are those that often have 'gainst Pompey fought;
Their ships are yare; yours heavy. No disgrace
Shall fall you for refusing him at sea,
Being prepar'd for land.
ANTONY: By sea, by sea.
ENOBARBUS: Most worthy sir, you therein throw away
The absolute soldiership you have by land;
Distract your army, which doth most consist
Of war-mark'd footmen; leave unexecuted
Your own renowned knowledge; quite forgo
The way which promises assurance; and
Give up yourself merely to chance and hazard
From firm security.
ANTONY: I'll fight at sea.
CLEOPATRA: I have sixty sails, Caesar none better.
ANTONY: Our overplus of shipping will we burn,
And, with the rest full-mann'd, from th' head of Actium
Beat th' approaching Caesar. But if we fail,
We then can do't at land.
Enter a Messenger
Thy business?
MESSENGER: The news is true, my lord: he is descried;
Caesar has taken Toryne.
ANTONY: Can he be there in person? 'Tis impossible-
Strange that his power should be. Canidius,

Our nineteen legions thou shalt hold by land,
And our twelve thousand horse. We'll to our ship.
Away, my Thetis!
Enter a Soldier
How now, worthy soldier?
SOLDIER: O noble Emperor, do not fight by sea;
Trust not to rotten planks. Do you misdoubt
This sword and these my wounds? Let th' Egyptians
And the Phoenicians go a-ducking; we
Have us'd to conquer standing on the earth
And fighting foot to foot.
ANTONY: Well, well- away.
Exeunt Antony, Cleopatra, and Enobarbus
SOLDIER: By Hercules, I think I am i' th' right.
CANIDIUS: Soldier, thou art; but his whole action grows
Not in the power on't. So our leader's led,
And we are women's men.
SOLDIER: You keep by land
The legions and the horse whole, do you not?
CANIDIUS: Marcus Octavius, Marcus Justeius,
Publicola, and Caelius are for sea;
But we keep whole by land. This speed of Caesar's
Carries beyond belief.
SOLDIER: While he was yet in Rome,
His power went out in such distractions as
Beguil'd all spies.
CANIDIUS: Who's his lieutenant, hear you?
SOLDIER: They say one Taurus.
CANIDIUS: Well I know the man.
Enter a Messenger
MESSENGER: The Emperor calls Canidius.
CANIDIUS: With news the time's with labour and throes forth
Each minute some.
Exeunt

ACT III. SCENE VIII. A Plain near Actium

Enter Caesar, with His Army, Marching
CAESAR: Taurus!
TAURUS: My lord?
CAESAR: Strike not by land; keep whole; provoke not battle
Till we have done at sea. Do not exceed
The prescript of this scroll. Our fortune lies
Upon this jump.
Exeunt

ACT III. SCENE IX. Another Part of the Plain

Enter Antony and Enobarbus
ANTONY: Set we our squadrons on yon side o' th' hill,
In eye of Caesar's battle; from which place
We may the number of the ships behold,
And so proceed accordingly.
Exeunt

ACT III. SCENE X. Another Part of the Plain

Canidius Marcheth with His Land Army One Way over the Stage, and Taurus, the Lieutenant of Caesar, the Other Way. After Their Going in Is Heard the Noise of a Sea-Fight

Alarum. Enter Enobarbus
ENOBARBUS: Naught, naught, all naught! I can behold no longer.
Th' Antoniad, the Egyptian admiral,
With all their sixty, fly and turn the rudder.
To see't mine eyes are blasted.
Enter Scarus
SCARUS: Gods and goddesses,
All the whole synod of them!
ENOBARBUS: What's thy passion?
SCARUS: The greater cantle of the world is lost
With very ignorance; we have kiss'd away
Kingdoms and provinces.
ENOBARBUS: How appears the fight?
SCARUS: On our side like the token'd pestilence,
Where death is sure. Yon ribaudred nag of Egypt-
Whom leprosy o'ertake!- i' th' midst o' th' fight,
When vantage like a pair of twins appear'd,
Both as the same, or rather ours the elder-
The breese upon her, like a cow in June-
Hoists sails and flies.
ENOBARBUS: That I beheld;
Mine eyes did sicken at the sight and could not
Endure a further view.
SCARUS: She once being loof'd,
The noble ruin of her magic, Antony,
Claps on his sea-wing, and, like a doting mallard,
Leaving the fight in height, flies after her.
I never saw an action of such shame;
Experience, manhood, honour, ne'er before
Did violate so itself.
ENOBARBUS: Alack, alack!
Enter Canidius
CANIDIUS: Our fortune on the sea is out of breath,
And sinks most lamentably. Had our general
Been what he knew himself, it had gone well.
O, he has given example for our flight
Most grossly by his own!
ENOBARBUS: Ay, are you thereabouts?
Why then, good night indeed.
CANIDIUS: Toward Peloponnesus are they fled.
SCARUS: 'Tis easy to't; and there I will attend
What further comes.
CANIDIUS: To Caesar will I render
My legions and my horse; six kings already
Show me the way of yielding.
ENOBARBUS: I'll yet follow
The wounded chance of Antony, though my reason
Sits in the wind against me.
Exeunt

ACT III. SCENE XI. Alexandria. Cleopatra's Palace

Enter Antony with Attendants
ANTONY: Hark! the land bids me tread no more upon't;
It is asham'd to bear me. Friends, come hither.

I am so lated in the world that I
Have lost my way for ever. I have a ship
Laden with gold; take that; divide it. Fly,
And make your peace with Caesar.
ALL: Fly? Not we!
ANTONY: I have fled myself, and have instructed cowards
To run and show their shoulders. Friends, be gone;
I have myself resolv'd upon a course
Which has no need of you; be gone.
My treasure's in the harbour, take it. O,
I follow'd that I blush to look upon.
My very hairs do mutiny; for the white
Reprove the brown for rashness, and they them
For fear and doting. Friends, be gone; you shall
Have letters from me to some friends that will
Sweep your way for you. Pray you look not sad,
Nor make replies of loathness; take the hint
Which my despair proclaims. Let that be left
Which leaves itself. To the sea-side straight way.
I will possess you of that ship and treasure.
Leave me, I pray, a little; pray you now;
Nay, do so, for indeed I have lost command;
Therefore I pray you. I'll see you by and by.
Sits Down
Enter Cleopatra, Led by Charmian and Iras, Eros Following
EROS: Nay, gentle madam, to him! Comfort him.
IRAS: Do, most dear Queen.
CHARMIAN: Do? Why, what else?
CLEOPATRA: Let me sit down. O Juno!
ANTONY: No, no, no, no, no.
EROS: See you here, sir?
ANTONY: O, fie, fie, fie!
CHARMIAN: Madam!
IRAS: Madam, O good Empress!
EROS: Sir, sir!
ANTONY: Yes, my lord, yes. He at Philippi kept
His sword e'en like a dancer, while I struck
The lean and wrinkled Cassius; and 'twas I
That the mad Brutus ended; he alone
Dealt on lieutenantry, and no practice had
In the brave squares of war. Yet now- no matter.
CLEOPATRA: Ah, stand by!
EROS: The Queen, my lord, the Queen!
IRAS: Go to him, madam, speak to him.
He is unqualitied with very shame.
CLEOPATRA: Well then, sustain me. O!
EROS. Most noble sir, arise; the Queen approaches.
Her head's declin'd, and death will seize her but
Your comfort makes the rescue.
ANTONY: I have offended reputation-
A most unnoble swerving.
EROS: Sir, the Queen.
ANTONY: O, whither hast thou led me, Egypt? See

How I convey my shame out of thine eyes
By looking back what I have left behind
'Stroy'd in dishonour.
CLEOPATRA: O my lord, my lord,
Forgive my fearful sails! I little thought
You would have followed.
ANTONY: Egypt, thou knew'st too well
My heart was to thy rudder tied by th' strings,
And thou shouldst tow me after. O'er my spirit
Thy full supremacy thou knew'st, and that
Thy beck might from the bidding of the gods
Command me.
CLEOPATRA: O, my pardon!
ANTONY: Now I must
To the young man send humble treaties, dodge
And palter in the shifts of lowness, who
With half the bulk o' th' world play'd as I pleas'd,
Making and marring fortunes. You did know
How much you were my conqueror, and that
My sword, made weak by my affection, would
Obey it on all cause.
CLEOPATRA: Pardon, pardon!
ANTONY: Fall not a tear, I say; one of them rates
All that is won and lost. Give me a kiss;
Even this repays me.
We sent our schoolmaster; is 'a come back?
Love, I am full of lead. Some wine,
Within there, and our viands! Fortune knows
We scorn her most when most she offers blows.
Exeunt

ACT III. SCENE XII. Caesar's Camp in Egypt

Enter Caesar, Agrippa, Dolabella, Thyreus, with Others
CAESAR: Let him appear that's come from Antony.
Know you him?
DOLABELLA: Caesar, 'tis his schoolmaster:
An argument that he is pluck'd, when hither
He sends so poor a pinion of his wing,
Which had superfluous kings for messengers
Not many moons gone by.
Enter Euphronius, Ambassador from Antony
CAESAR: Approach, and speak.
EUPHRONIUS: Such as I am, I come from Antony.
I was of late as petty to his ends
As is the morn-dew on the myrtle leaf
To his grand sea.
CAESAR: Be't so. Declare thine office.
EUPHRONIUS: Lord of his fortunes he salutes thee, and
Requires to live in Egypt; which not granted,
He lessens his requests and to thee sues
To let him breathe between the heavens and earth,
A private man in Athens. This for him.
Next, Cleopatra does confess thy greatness,
Submits her to thy might, and of thee craves

The circle of the Ptolemies for her heirs,
Now hazarded to thy grace.
CAESAR: For Antony,
I have no ears to his request. The Queen
Of audience nor desire shall fail, so she
From Egypt drive her all-disgraced friend,
Or take his life there. This if she perform,
She shall not sue unheard. So to them both.
EUPHRONIUS: Fortune pursue thee!
CAESAR: Bring him through the bands.
Exit Euphronius
To Thyreus To try thy eloquence, now 'tis time. Dispatch;
From Antony win Cleopatra. Promise,
And in our name, what she requires; add more,
From thine invention, offers. Women are not
In their best fortunes strong; but want will perjure
The ne'er-touch'd vestal. Try thy cunning, Thyreus;
Make thine own edict for thy pains, which we
Will answer as a law.
THYREUS: Caesar, I go.
CAESAR: Observe how Antony becomes his flaw,
And what thou think'st his very action speaks
In every power that moves.
THYREUS: Caesar, I shall.
Exeunt

ACT III. SCENE XIII. Alexandria. Cleopatra's Palace

Enter Cleopatra, Enobarbus, Charmian, and Iras
CLEOPATRA: What shall we do, Enobarbus?
ENOBARBUS: Think, and die.
CLEOPATRA: Is Antony or we in fault for this?
ENOBARBUS: Antony only, that would make his will
Lord of his reason. What though you fled
From that great face of war, whose several ranges
Frighted each other? Why should he follow?
The itch of his affection should not then
Have nick'd his captainship, at such a point,
When half to half the world oppos'd, he being
The mered question. 'Twas a shame no less
Than was his loss, to course your flying flags
And leave his navy gazing.
CLEOPATRA: Prithee, peace.
Enter Euphronius, the Ambassador; with Antony
ANTONY: Is that his answer?
EUPHRONIUS: Ay, my lord.
ANTONY: The Queen shall then have courtesy, so she
Will yield us up.
EUPHRONIUS: He says so.
ANTONY: Let her know't.
To the boy Caesar send this grizzled head,
And he will fill thy wishes to the brim
With principalities.
CLEOPATRA: That head, my lord?
ANTONY: To him again. Tell him he wears the rose

Of youth upon him; from which the world should note
Something particular. His coin, ships, legions,
May be a coward's whose ministers would prevail
Under the service of a child as soon
As i' th' command of Caesar. I dare him therefore
To lay his gay comparisons apart,
And answer me declin'd, sword against sword,
Ourselves alone. I'll write it. Follow me.
Exeunt Antony and Euphronius
EUPHRONIUS: Aside Yes, like enough high-battled Caesar will
Unstate his happiness, and be stag'd to th' show
Against a sworder! I see men's judgments are
A parcel of their fortunes, and things outward
Do draw the inward quality after them,
To suffer all alike. That he should dream,
Knowing all measures, the full Caesar will
Answer his emptiness! Caesar, thou hast subdu'd
His judgment too.
Enter a Servant
SERVANT: A messenger from Caesar.
CLEOPATRA: What, no more ceremony? See, my women!
Against the blown rose may they stop their nose
That kneel'd unto the buds. Admit him, sir.
Exit Servant
ENOBARBUS: Aside Mine honesty and I begin to square.
The loyalty well held to fools does make
Our faith mere folly. Yet he that can endure
To follow with allegiance a fall'n lord
Does conquer him that did his master conquer,
And earns a place i' th' story.
Enter Thyreus
CLEOPATRA: Caesar's will?
THYREUS: Hear it apart.
CLEOPATRA: None but friends: say boldly.
THYREUS: So, haply, are they friends to Antony.
ENOBARBUS: He needs as many, sir, as Caesar has,
Or needs not us. If Caesar please, our master
Will leap to be his friend. For us, you know
Whose he is we are, and that is Caesar's.
THYREUS: So.
Thus then, thou most renown'd: Caesar entreats
Not to consider in what case thou stand'st
Further than he is Caesar.
CLEOPATRA: Go on. Right royal!
THYREUS: He knows that you embrace not Antony
As you did love, but as you fear'd him.
CLEOPATRA: O!
THYREUS: The scars upon your honour, therefore, he
Does pity, as constrained blemishes,
Not as deserv'd.
CLEOPATRA: He is a god, and knows
What is most right. Mine honour was not yielded,
But conquer'd merely.

ENOBARBUS: Aside To be sure of that,
I will ask Antony. Sir, sir, thou art so leaky
That we must leave thee to thy sinking, for
Thy dearest quit thee.
Exit
THYREUS: Shall I say to Caesar
What you require of him? For he partly begs
To be desir'd to give. It much would please him
That of his fortunes you should make a staff
To lean upon. But it would warm his spirits
To hear from me you had left Antony,
And put yourself under his shroud,
The universal landlord.
CLEOPATRA: What's your name?
THYREUS: My name is Thyreus.
CLEOPATRA: Most kind messenger,
Say to great Caesar this: in deputation
I kiss his conquring hand. Tell him I am prompt
To lay my crown at 's feet, and there to kneel.
Tell him from his all-obeying breath I hear
The doom of Egypt.
THYREUS: 'Tis your noblest course.
Wisdom and fortune combating together,
If that the former dare but what it can,
No chance may shake it. Give me grace to lay
My duty on your hand.
CLEOPATRA: Your Caesar's father oft,
When he hath mus'd of taking kingdoms in,
Bestow'd his lips on that unworthy place,
As it rain'd kisses.
Re-enter Antony and Enobarbus
ANTONY: Favours, by Jove that thunders!
What art thou, fellow?
THYREUS: One that but performs
The bidding of the fullest man, and worthiest
To have command obey'd.
ENOBARBUS: Aside You will be whipt.
ANTONY: Approach there.- Ah, you kite!- Now, gods and devils!
Authority melts from me. Of late, when I cried 'Ho!'
Like boys unto a muss, kings would start forth
And cry 'Your will?' Have you no ears? I am
Antony yet.
Enter Servants
Take hence this Jack and whip him.
ENOBARBUS: 'Tis better playing with a lion's whelp
Than with an old one dying.
ANTONY: Moon and stars!
Whip him. Were't twenty of the greatest tributaries
That do acknowledge Caesar, should I find them
So saucy with the hand of she here- what's her name
Since she was Cleopatra? Whip him, fellows,
Till like a boy you see him cringe his face,
And whine aloud for mercy. Take him hence.

THYMUS. Mark Antony-
ANTONY: Tug him away. Being whipt,
Bring him again: the Jack of Caesar's shall
Bear us an errand to him.
Exeunt Servants with Thyreus
You were half blasted ere I knew you. Ha!
Have I my pillow left unpress'd in Rome,
Forborne the getting of a lawful race,
And by a gem of women, to be abus'd
By one that looks on feeders?
CLEOPATRA: Good my lord-
ANTONY: You have been a boggler ever.
But when we in our viciousness grow hard-
O misery on't!- the wise gods seel our eyes,
In our own filth drop our clear judgments, make us
Adore our errors, laugh at's while we strut
To our confusion.
CLEOPATRA: O, is't come to this?
ANTONY: I found you as a morsel cold upon
Dead Caesar's trencher. Nay, you were a fragment
Of Cneius Pompey's, besides what hotter hours,
Unregist'red in vulgar fame, you have
Luxuriously pick'd out; for I am sure,
Though you can guess what temperance should be,
You know not what it is.
CLEOPATRA: Wherefore is this?
ANTONY: To let a fellow that will take rewards,
And say 'God quit you!' be familiar with
My playfellow, your hand, this kingly seal
And plighter of high hearts! O that I were
Upon the hill of Basan to outroar
The horned herd! For I have savage cause,
And to proclaim it civilly were like
A halter'd neck which does the hangman thank
For being yare about him.
Re-enter a Servant with Thyreus
Is he whipt?
SERVANT: Soundly, my lord.
ANTONY: Cried he? and begg'd 'a pardon?
SERVANT: He did ask favour.
ANTONY: If that thy father live, let him repent
Thou wast not made his daughter; and be thou sorry
To follow Caesar in his triumph, since
Thou hast been whipt for following him. Henceforth
The white hand of a lady fever thee!
Shake thou to look on't. Get thee back to Caesar;
Tell him thy entertainment; look thou say
He makes me angry with him; for he seems
Proud and disdainful, harping on what I am,
Not what he knew I was. He makes me angry;
And at this time most easy 'tis to do't,
When my good stars, that were my former guides,
Have empty left their orbs and shot their fires

Into th' abysm of hell. If he mislike
My speech and what is done, tell him he has
Hipparchus, my enfranched bondman, whom
He may at pleasure whip or hang or torture,
As he shall like, to quit me. Urge it thou.
Hence with thy stripes, be gone.
Exit Thyreus
CLEOPATRA: Have you done yet?
ANTONY: Alack, our terrene moon
Is now eclips'd, and it portends alone
The fall of Antony.
CLEOPATRA: I must stay his time.
ANTONY: To flatter Caesar, would you mingle eyes
With one that ties his points?
CLEOPATRA: Not know me yet?
ANTONY: Cold-hearted toward me?
CLEOPATRA: Ah, dear, if I be so,
From my cold heart let heaven engender hail,
And poison it in the source, and the first stone
Drop in my neck; as it determines, so
Dissolve my life! The next Caesarion smite!
Till by degrees the memory of my womb,
Together with my brave Egyptians all,
By the discandying of this pelleted storm,
Lie graveless, till the flies and gnats of Nile
Have buried them for prey.
ANTONY: I am satisfied.
Caesar sits down in Alexandria, where
I will oppose his fate. Our force by land
Hath nobly held; our sever'd navy to
Have knit again, and fleet, threat'ning most sea-like.
Where hast thou been, my heart? Dost thou hear, lady?
If from the field I shall return once more
To kiss these lips, I will appear in blood.
I and my sword will earn our chronicle.
There's hope in't yet.
CLEOPATRA: That's my brave lord!
ANTONY: I will be treble-sinew'd, hearted, breath'd,
And fight maliciously. For when mine hours
Were nice and lucky, men did ransom lives
Of me for jests; but now I'll set my teeth,
And send to darkness all that stop me. Come,
Let's have one other gaudy night. Call to me
All my sad captains; fill our bowls once more;
Let's mock the midnight bell.
CLEOPATRA: It is my birthday.
I had thought t'have held it poor; but since my lord
Is Antony again, I will be Cleopatra.
ANTONY: We will yet do well.
CLEOPATRA: Call all his noble captains to my lord.
ANTONY: Do so, we'll speak to them; and to-night I'll force
The wine peep through their scars. Come on, my queen,
There's sap in't yet. The next time I do fight

I'll make death love me; for I will contend
Even with his pestilent scythe.
Exeunt All but Enobarbus
ENOBARBUS: Now he'll outstare the lightning. To be furious
Is to be frighted out of fear, and in that mood
The dove will peck the estridge; and I see still
A diminution in our captain's brain
Restores his heart. When valour preys on reason,
It eats the sword it fights with. I will seek
Some way to leave him.
Exit

ACT IV. SCENE I. Caesar's Camp Before Alexandria

Enter Caesar, Agrippa, and Maecenas, with His Army; Caesar Reading a Letter
CAESAR: He calls me boy, and chides as he had power
To beat me out of Egypt. My messenger
He hath whipt with rods; dares me to personal combat,
Caesar to Antony. Let the old ruffian know
I have many other ways to die, meantime
Laugh at his challenge.
MAECENAS: Caesar must think
When one so great begins to rage, he's hunted
Even to falling. Give him no breath, but now
Make boot of his distraction. Never anger
Made good guard for itself.
CAESAR: Let our best heads
Know that to-morrow the last of many battles
We mean to fight. Within our files there are
Of those that serv'd Mark Antony but late
Enough to fetch him in. See it done;
And feast the army; we have store to do't,
And they have earn'd the waste. Poor Antony!
Exeunt

ACT IV. SCENE II. Alexandria. Cleopatra's Palace

Enter Antony, Cleopatra, Enobarbus, Charmian, Iras, Alexas, with Others
ANTONY: He will not fight with me, Domitius?
ENOBARBUS: No.
ANTONY: Why should he not?
ENOBARBUS: He thinks, being twenty times of better fortune,
He is twenty men to one.
ANTONY: To-morrow, soldier,
By sea and land I'll fight. Or I will live,
Or bathe my dying honour in the blood
Shall make it live again. Woo't thou fight well?
ENOBARBUS: I'll strike, and cry 'Take all.'
ANTONY: Well said; come on.
Call forth my household servants; let's to-night
Be bounteous at our meal.
Enter Three or Four Servitors
Give me thy hand,
Thou has been rightly honest. So hast thou;
Thou, and thou, and thou. You have serv'd me well,
And kings have been your fellows.
CLEOPATRA: Aside to Enobarbus What means this?

ENOBARBUS: Aside to Cleopatra 'Tis one of those odd tricks which sorrow shoots out of the mind.
ANTONY: And thou art honest too.
I wish I could be made so many men,
And all of you clapp'd up together in
An Antony, that I might do you service
So good as you have done.
SERVANT: The gods forbid!
ANTONY: Well, my good fellows, wait on me to-night.
Scant not my cups, and make as much of me
As when mine empire was your fellow too,
And suffer'd my command.
CLEOPATRA: Aside to Enobarbus What does he mean?
ENOBARBUS: Aside to Cleopatra To make his followers weep.
ANTONY: Tend me to-night;
May be it is the period of your duty.
Haply you shall not see me more; or if,
A mangled shadow. Perchance to-morrow
You'll serve another master. I look on you
As one that takes his leave. Mine honest friends,
I turn you not away; but, like a master
Married to your good service, stay till death.
Tend me to-night two hours, I ask no more,
And the gods yield you for't!
ENOBARBUS: What mean you, sir,
To give them this discomfort? Look, they weep;
And I, an ass, am onion-ey'd. For shame!
Transform us not to women.
ANTONY: Ho, ho, ho!
Now the witch take me if I meant it thus!
Grace grow where those drops fall! My hearty friends,
You take me in too dolorous a sense;
For I spake to you for your comfort, did desire you
To burn this night with torches. Know, my hearts,
I hope well of to-morrow, and will lead you
Where rather I'll expect victorious life
Than death and honour. Let's to supper, come,
And drown consideration.
Exeunt

ACT IV. SCENE III. Alexandria. Before Cleopatra's Palace

Enter a Company of Soldiers
FIRST SOLDIER: Brother, good night. To-morrow is the day.
SECOND SOLDIER:. It will determine one way. Fare you well.
Heard you of nothing strange about the streets?
FIRST SOLDIER: Nothing. What news?
SECOND SOLDIER:. Belike 'tis but a rumour. Good night to you.
FIRST SOLDIER: Well, sir, good night.
They Meet Other Soldiers
SECOND SOLDIER:. Soldiers, have careful watch.
FIRST SOLDIER: And you. Good night, good night.
The Two Companies Separate and Place Themselves in Every Corner of the Stage
SECOND SOLDIER:. Here we. And if to-morrow
Our navy thrive, I have an absolute hope
Our landmen will stand up.

THIRD SOLDIER: 'Tis a brave army,
And full of purpose.
Music of the Hautboys Is under the Stage
SECOND SOLDIER:. Peace, what noise?
THIRD SOLDIER: List, list!
SECOND SOLDIER:. Hark!
THIRD SOLDIER: Music i' th' air.
FOURTH SOLDIER: Under the earth.
THIRD SOLDIER: It signs well, does it not?
FOURTH SOLDIER: No.
THIRD SOLDIER: Peace, I say!
What should this mean?
SECOND SOLDIER:. 'Tis the god Hercules, whom Antony lov'd,
Now leaves him.
THIRD SOLDIER: Walk; let's see if other watchmen
Do hear what we do.
SECOND SOLDIER:. How now, masters!
SOLDIERS: Speaking Together How now!
How now! Do you hear this?
FIRST SOLDIER: Ay; is't not strange?
THIRD SOLDIER: Do you hear, masters? Do you hear?
FIRST SOLDIER: Follow the noise so far as we have quarter;
Let's see how it will give off.
SOLDIERS: Content. 'Tis strange.
Exeunt

ACT IV. SCENE IV. Alexandria. Cleopatra's Palace

Enter Antony and Cleopatra, Charmian, Iras, with Others
ANTONY: Eros! mine armour, Eros!
CLEOPATRA: Sleep a little.
ANTONY: No, my chuck. Eros! Come, mine armour, Eros!
Enter Eros with Armour
Come, good fellow, put mine iron on.
If fortune be not ours to-day, it is
Because we brave her. Come.
CLEOPATRA: Nay, I'll help too.
What's this for?
ANTONY: Ah, let be, let be! Thou art
The armourer of my heart. False, false; this, this.
CLEOPATRA: Sooth, la, I'll help. Thus it must be.
ANTONY: Well, well;
We shall thrive now. Seest thou, my good fellow?
Go put on thy defences.
EROS: Briefly, sir.
CLEOPATRA: Is not this buckled well?
ANTONY: Rarely, rarely!
He that unbuckles this, till we do please
To daff't for our repose, shall hear a storm.
Thou fumblest, Eros, and my queen's a squire
More tight at this than thou. Dispatch. O love,
That thou couldst see my wars to-day, and knew'st
The royal occupation! Thou shouldst see
A workman in't.
Enter an Armed Soldier

Good-morrow to thee. Welcome.
Thou look'st like him that knows a warlike charge.
To business that we love we rise betime,
And go to't with delight.
SOLDIER: A thousand, sir,
Early though't be, have on their riveted trim,
And at the port expect you.
Shout. Flourish of Trumpets Within
Enter Captains and Soldiers
CAPTAIN: The morn is fair. Good morrow, General.
ALL: Good morrow, General.
ANTONY: 'Tis well blown, lads.
This morning, like the spirit of a youth
That means to be of note, begins betimes.
So, so. Come, give me that. This way. Well said.
Fare thee well, dame, whate'er becomes of me.
This is a soldier's kiss. Rebukeable,
And worthy shameful check it were, to stand
On more mechanic compliment; I'll leave thee
Now like a man of steel. You that will fight,
Follow me close; I'll bring you to't. Adieu.
Exeunt Antony, Eros, Captains and Soldiers
CHARMIAN: Please you retire to your chamber?
CLEOPATRA: Lead me.
He goes forth gallantly. That he and Caesar might
Determine this great war in single fight!
Then, Antony- but now. Well, on.
Exeunt

ACT IV. SCENE V. Alexandria. Antony's Camp

Trumpets Sound. Enter Antony and Eros, a Soldier Meeting Them
SOLDIER: The gods make this a happy day to Antony!
ANTONY: Would thou and those thy scars had once prevail'd
To make me fight at land!
SOLDIER: Hadst thou done so,
The kings that have revolted, and the soldier
That has this morning left thee, would have still
Followed thy heels.
ANTONY: Who's gone this morning?
SOLDIER: Who?
One ever near thee. Call for Enobarbus,
He shall not hear thee; or from Caesar's camp
Say 'I am none of thine.'
ANTONY: What say'st thou?
SOLDIER: Sir,
He is with Caesar.
EROS: Sir, his chests and treasure
He has not with him.
ANTONY: Is he gone?
SOLDIER: Most certain.
ANTONY: Go, Eros, send his treasure after; do it;
Detain no jot, I charge thee. Write to him-
I will subscribe- gentle adieus and greetings;
Say that I wish he never find more cause

To change a master. O, my fortunes have
Corrupted honest men! Dispatch. Enobarbus!
Exeunt

ACT IV. SCENE VI. Alexandria. Caesar's Camp

Flourish. Enter Agrippa, Caesar, with Dolabella and Enobarbus
CAESAR: Go forth, Agrippa, and begin the fight.
Our will is Antony be took alive;
Make it so known.
AGRIPPA: Caesar, I shall.
Exit
CAESAR: The time of universal peace is near.
Prove this a prosp'rous day, the three-nook'd world
Shall bear the olive freely.
Enter a Messenger
MESSENGER: Antony
Is come into the field.
CAESAR: Go charge Agrippa
Plant those that have revolted in the vant,
That Antony may seem to spend his fury
Upon himself.
Exeunt All but Enobarbus
ENOBARBUS: Alexas did revolt and went to Jewry on
Affairs of Antony; there did dissuade
Great Herod to incline himself to Caesar
And leave his master Antony. For this pains
Casaer hath hang'd him. Canidius and the rest
That fell away have entertainment, but
No honourable trust. I have done ill,
Of which I do accuse myself so sorely
That I will joy no more.
Enter a Soldier of Caesar's
SOLDIER: Enobarbus, Antony
Hath after thee sent all thy treasure, with
His bounty overplus. The messenger
Came on my guard, and at thy tent is now
Unloading of his mules.
ENOBARBUS: I give it you.
SOLDIER: Mock not, Enobarbus.
I tell you true. Best you saf'd the bringer
Out of the host. I must attend mine office,
Or would have done't myself. Your emperor
Continues still a Jove.
Exit
ENOBARBUS: I am alone the villain of the earth,
And feel I am so most. O Antony,
Thou mine of bounty, how wouldst thou have paid
My better service, when my turpitude
Thou dost so crown with gold! This blows my heart.
If swift thought break it not, a swifter mean
Shall outstrike thought; but thought will do't, I feel.
I fight against thee? No! I will go seek
Some ditch wherein to die; the foul'st best fits
My latter part of life.

Exit

ACT IV. SCENE VII. Field of Battle Between the Camps

Alarum. Drums and Trumpets. Enter Agrippa and Others

AGRIPPA: Retire. We have engag'd ourselves too far.
Caesar himself has work, and our oppression
Exceeds what we expected.

Exeunt

Alarums. Enter Antony, and Scarus Wounded

SCARUS: O my brave Emperor, this is fought indeed!
Had we done so at first, we had droven them home
With clouts about their heads.

ANTONY: Thou bleed'st apace.

SCARUS: I had a wound here that was like a T,
But now 'tis made an H.

ANTONY: They do retire.

SCARUS: We'll beat'em into bench-holes. I have yet
Room for six scotches more.

Enter Eros

EROS: They are beaten, sir, and our advantage serves
For a fair victory.

SCARUS: Let us score their backs
And snatch 'em up, as we take hares, behind.
'Tis sport to maul a runner.

ANTONY: I will reward thee
Once for thy sprightly comfort, and tenfold
For thy good valour. Come thee on.

SCARUS: I'll halt after.

Exeunt

ACT IV. SCENE VIII. Under the Walls of Alexandria

Alarum. Enter Antony, Again in a March; Scarus with Others

ANTONY: We have beat him to his camp. Run one before
And let the Queen know of our gests. To-morrow,
Before the sun shall see's, we'll spill the blood
That has to-day escap'd. I thank you all;
For doughty-handed are you, and have fought
Not as you serv'd the cause, but as't had been
Each man's like mine; you have shown all Hectors.
Enter the city, clip your wives, your friends,
Tell them your feats; whilst they with joyful tears
Wash the congealment from your wounds and kiss
The honour'd gashes whole.

Enter Cleopatra, Attended

To Scarus Give me thy hand-
To this great fairy I'll commend thy acts,
Make her thanks bless thee. O thou day o' th' world,
Chain mine arm'd neck. Leap thou, attire and all,
Through proof of harness to my heart, and there
Ride on the pants triumphing.

CLEOPATRA: Lord of lords!
O infinite virtue, com'st thou smiling from
The world's great snare uncaught?

ANTONY: Mine nightingale,
We have beat them to their beds. What, girl! though grey

Do something mingle with our younger brown, yet ha' we
A brain that nourishes our nerves, and can
Get goal for goal of youth. Behold this man;
Commend unto his lips thy favouring hand-
Kiss it, my warrior- he hath fought to-day
As if a god in hate of mankind had
Destroyed in such a shape.
CLEOPATRA: I'll give thee, friend,
An armour all of gold; it was a king's.
ANTONY: He has deserv'd it, were it carbuncled
Like holy Phoebus' car. Give me thy hand.
Through Alexandria make a jolly march;
Bear our hack'd targets like the men that owe them.
Had our great palace the capacity
To camp this host, we all would sup together,
And drink carouses to the next day's fate,
Which promises royal peril. Trumpeters,
With brazen din blast you the city's ear;
Make mingle with our rattling tabourines,
That heaven and earth may strike their sounds together
Applauding our approach.
Exeunt

ACT IV. SCENE IX. Caesar's Camp

Enter a Centurion and His Company; Enobarbus Follows
CENTURION: If we be not reliev'd within this hour,
We must return to th' court of guard. The night
Is shiny, and they say we shall embattle
By th' second hour i' th' morn.
FIRST WATCH: This last day was
A shrewd one to's.
ENOBARBUS: O, bear me witness, night-
SECOND WATCH: What man is this?
FIRST WATCH: Stand close and list him.
ENOBARBUS: Be witness to me, O thou blessed moon,
When men revolted shall upon record
Bear hateful memory, poor Enobarbus did
Before thy face repent!
CENTURION: Enobarbus?
SECOND WATCH: Peace!
Hark further.
ENOBARBUS: O sovereign mistress of true melancholy,
The poisonous damp of night disponge upon me,
That life, a very rebel to my will,
May hang no longer on me. Throw my heart
Against the flint and hardness of my fault,
Which, being dried with grief, will break to powder,
And finish all foul thoughts. O Antony,
Nobler than my revolt is infamous,
Forgive me in thine own particular,
But let the world rank me in register
A master-leaver and a fugitive!
O Antony! O Antony!
Dies

FIRST WATCH: Let's speak to him.
CENTURION: Let's hear him, for the things he speaks
May concern Caesar.
SECOND WATCH: Let's do so. But he sleeps.
CENTURION: Swoons rather; for so bad a prayer as his
Was never yet for sleep.
FIRST WATCH: Go we to him.
SECOND WATCH: Awake, sir, awake; speak to us.
FIRST WATCH: Hear you, sir?
CENTURION: The hand of death hath raught him.
Drums Afar off Hark! the drums
Demurely wake the sleepers. Let us bear him
To th' court of guard; he is of note. Our hour
Is fully out.
SECOND WATCH: Come on, then;
He may recover yet.
Exeunt with the Body

ACT IV. SCENE X. Between the Two Camps

Enter Antony and Scarus, with Their Army
ANTONY: Their preparation is to-day by sea;
We please them not by land.
SCARUS: For both, my lord.
ANTONY: I would they'd fight i' th' fire or i' th' air;
We'd fight there too. But this it is, our foot
Upon the hills adjoining to the city
Shall stay with us- Order for sea is given;
They have put forth the haven-
Where their appointment we may best discover
And look on their endeavour.
Exeunt

ACT IV. SCENE XI. Between the Camps

Enter Caesar and His Army
CAESAR: But being charg'd, we will be still by land,
Which, as I take't, we shall; for his best force
Is forth to man his galleys. To the vales,
And hold our best advantage.
Exeunt

ACT IV. SCENE XII. A Hill near Alexandria

Enter Antony and Scarus
ANTONY: Yet they are not join'd. Where yond pine does stand
I shall discover all. I'll bring thee word
Straight how 'tis like to go.
Exit
SCARUS: Swallows have built
In Cleopatra's sails their nests. The augurers
Say they know not, they cannot tell; look grimly,
And dare not speak their knowledge. Antony
Is valiant and dejected; and by starts
His fretted fortunes give him hope and fear
Of what he has and has not.
Alarum Afar Off, as at a Sea-Fight
Re-enter Antony
ANTONY: All is lost!

This foul Egyptian hath betrayed me.
My fleet hath yielded to the foe, and yonder
They cast their caps up and carouse together
Like friends long lost. Triple-turn'd whore! 'tis thou
Hast sold me to this novice; and my heart
Makes only wars on thee. Bid them all fly;
For when I am reveng'd upon my charm,
I have done all. Bid them all fly; begone.
Exit Scarus
O sun, thy uprise shall I see no more!
Fortune and Antony part here; even here
Do we shake hands. All come to this? The hearts
That spaniel'd me at heels, to whom I gave
Their wishes, do discandy, melt their sweets
On blossoming Caesar; and this pine is bark'd
That overtopp'd them all. Betray'd I am.
O this false soul of Egypt! this grave charm-
Whose eye beck'd forth my wars and call'd them home,
Whose bosom was my crownet, my chief end-
Like a right gypsy hath at fast and loose
Beguil'd me to the very heart of loss.
What, Eros, Eros!
Enter Cleopatra
Ah, thou spell! Avaunt!
CLEOPATRA: Why is my lord enrag'd against his love?
ANTONY: Vanish, or I shall give thee thy deserving
And blemish Caesar's triumph. Let him take thee
And hoist thee up to the shouting plebeians;
Follow his chariot, like the greatest spot
Of all thy sex; most monster-like, be shown
For poor'st diminutives, for doits, and let
Patient Octavia plough thy visage up
With her prepared nails.
Exit Cleopatra
'Tis well th'art gone,
If it be well to live; but better 'twere
Thou fell'st into my fury, for one death
Might have prevented many. Eros, ho!
The shirt of Nessus is upon me; teach me,
Alcides, thou mine ancestor, thy rage;
Let me lodge Lichas on the horns o' th' moon,
And with those hands that grasp'd the heaviest club
Subdue my worthiest self. The witch shall die.
To the young Roman boy she hath sold me, and I fall
Under this plot. She dies for't. Eros, ho!
Exit

ACT IV. SCENE XIII. Alexandria. Cleopatra's Palace

Enter Cleopatra, Charmian, Iras, and Mardian
CLEOPATRA: Help me, my women. O, he is more mad
Than Telamon for his shield; the boar of Thessaly
Was never so emboss'd.
CHARMIAN: To th'monument!
There lock yourself, and send him word you are dead.

The soul and body rive not more in parting
Than greatness going off.
CLEOPATRA: To th' monument!
Mardian, go tell him I have slain myself;
Say that the last I spoke was 'Antony'
And word it, prithee, piteously. Hence, Mardian,
And bring me how he takes my death. To th' monument!
Exeunt

ACT IV. SCENE XIV. CLEOPATRA'S palace

Enter Antony and Eros
ANTONY: Eros, thou yet behold'st me?
EROS: Ay, noble lord.
ANTONY: Sometime we see a cloud that's dragonish;
A vapour sometime like a bear or lion,
A tower'd citadel, a pendent rock,
A forked mountain, or blue promontory
With trees upon't that nod unto the world
And mock our eyes with air. Thou hast seen these signs;
They are black vesper's pageants.
EROS: Ay, my lord.
ANTONY: That which is now a horse, even with a thought
The rack dislimns, and makes it indistinct,
As water is in water.
EROS: It does, my lord.
ANTONY: My good knave Eros, now thy captain is
Even such a body. Here I am Antony;
Yet cannot hold this visible shape, my knave.
I made these wars for Egypt; and the Queen-
Whose heart I thought I had, for she had mine,
Which, whilst it was mine, had annex'd unto't
A million moe, now lost- she, Eros, has
Pack'd cards with Caesar, and false-play'd my glory
Unto an enemy's triumph.
Nay, weep not, gentle Eros; there is left us
Ourselves to end ourselves.
Enter Mardian
O, thy vile lady!
She has robb'd me of my sword.
MARDIAN: No, Antony;
My mistress lov'd thee, and her fortunes mingled
With thine entirely.
ANTONY: Hence, saucy eunuch; peace!
She hath betray'd me, and shall die the death.
MARDIAN: Death of one person can be paid but once,
And that she has discharg'd. What thou wouldst do
Is done unto thy hand. The last she spake
Was 'Antony! most noble Antony!'
Then in the midst a tearing groan did break
The name of Antony; it was divided
Between her heart and lips. She rend'red life,
Thy name so buried in her.
ANTONY: Dead then?
MARDIAN: Dead.

ANTONY: Unarm, Eros; the long day's task is done,
And we must sleep. That thou depart'st hence safe
Does pay thy labour richly. Go.
Exit Mardian
Off, pluck off!
The sevenfold shield of Ajax cannot keep
The battery from my heart. O, cleave, my sides!
Heart, once be stronger than thy continent,
Crack thy frail case. Apace, Eros, apace.-
No more a soldier. Bruised pieces, go;
You have been nobly borne.- From me awhile.
Exit Eros
I will o'ertake thee, Cleopatra, and
Weep for my pardon. So it must be, for now
All length is torture. Since the torch is out,
Lie down, and stray no farther. Now all labour
Mars what it does; yea, very force entangles
Itself with strength. Seal then, and all is done.
Eros!- I come, my queen.- Eros!- Stay for me;
Where souls do couch on flowers, we'll hand in hand,
And with our sprightly port make the ghosts gaze.
Dido and her Aeneas shall want troops,
And all the haunt be ours.- Come, Eros, Eros!
Re-enter Eros
EROS: What would my lord?
ANTONY: Since Cleopatra died,
I have liv'd in such dishonour that the gods
Detest my baseness. I, that with my sword
Quarter'd the world, and o'er green Neptune's back
With ships made cities, condemn myself to lack
The courage of a woman; less noble mind
Than she which by her death our Caesar tells
'I am conqueror of myself.' Thou art sworn, Eros,
That, when the exigent should come- which now
Is come indeed- when I should see behind me
Th' inevitable prosecution of
Disgrace and horror, that, on my command,
Thou then wouldst kill me. Do't; the time is come.
Thou strik'st not me; 'tis Caesar thou defeat'st.
Put colour in thy cheek.
EROS: The gods withhold me!
Shall I do that which all the Parthian darts,
Though enemy, lost aim and could not?
ANTONY: Eros,
Wouldst thou be window'd in great Rome and see
Thy master thus with pleach'd arms, bending down
His corrigible neck, his face subdu'd
To penetrative shame, whilst the wheel'd seat
Of fortunate Caesar, drawn before him, branded
His baseness that ensued?
EROS: I would not see't.
ANTONY: Come, then; for with a wound I must be cur'd.
Draw that thy honest sword, which thou hast worn

Most useful for thy country.
EROS: O, sir, pardon me!
ANTONY: When I did make thee free, swor'st thou not then
To do this when I bade thee? Do it at once,
Or thy precedent services are all
But accidents unpurpos'd. Draw, and come.
EROS: Turn from me then that noble countenance,
Wherein the worship of the whole world lies.
ANTONY: Lo thee!
Turning from Him
EROS: My sword is drawn.
ANTONY: Then let it do at once
The thing why thou hast drawn it.
EROS: My dear master,
My captain and my emperor, let me say,
Before I strike this bloody stroke, farewell.
ANTONY: 'Tis said, man; and farewell.
EROS: Farewell, great chief. Shall I strike now?
ANTONY: Now, Eros.
EROS: Why, there then! Thus do I escape the sorrow
Of Antony's death.
Kills Himself
ANTONY: Thrice nobler than myself!
Thou teachest me, O valiant Eros, what
I should, and thou couldst not. My queen and Eros
Have, by their brave instruction, got upon me
A nobleness in record. But I will be
A bridegroom in my death, and run into't
As to a lover's bed. Come, then; and, Eros,
Thy master dies thy scholar. To do thus
Falling on His Sword
I learn'd of thee. How? not dead? not dead?-
The guard, ho! O, dispatch me!
Enter Dercetas and a Guard
FIRST GUARD: What's the noise?
ANTONY: I have done my work ill, friends. O, make an end
Of what I have begun.
SECOND GUARD: The star is fall'n.
FIRST GUARD: And time is at his period.
ALL: Alas, and woe!
ANTONY: Let him that loves me, strike me dead.
FIRST GUARD: Not I.
SECOND GUARD: Nor I.
THIRD GUARD: Nor any one.
Exeunt Guard
DERCETAS: Thy death and fortunes bid thy followers fly.
This sword but shown to Caesar, with this tidings,
Shall enter me with him.
Enter Diomedes
DIOMEDES: Where's Antony?
DERCETAS: There, Diomed, there.
DIOMEDES: Lives he?
Wilt thou not answer, man?

Exit Dercetas
ANTONY: Art thou there, Diomed? Draw thy sword and give me
Sufficing strokes for death.
DIOMEDES: Most absolute lord,
My mistress Cleopatra sent me to thee.
ANTONY: When did she send thee?
DIOMEDES: Now, my lord.
ANTONY: Where is she?
DIOMEDES: Lock'd in her monument. She had a prophesying fear
Of what hath come to pass; for when she saw-
Which never shall be found- you did suspect
She had dispos'd with Caesar, and that your rage
Would not be purg'd, she sent you word she was dead;
But fearing since how it might work, hath sent
Me to proclaim the truth; and I am come,
I dread, too late.
ANTONY: Too late, good Diomed. Call my guard, I prithee.
DIOMEDES: What, ho! the Emperor's guard! The guard, what ho!
Come, your lord calls!
Enter Four or Five of the Guard of Antony
ANTONY: Bear me, good friends, where Cleopatra bides;
'Tis the last service that I shall command you.
FIRST GUARD: Woe, woe are we, sir, you may not live to wear
All your true followers out.
ALL: Most heavy day!
ANTONY: Nay, good my fellows, do not please sharp fate
To grace it with your sorrows. Bid that welcome
Which comes to punish us, and we punish it,
Seeming to bear it lightly. Take me up.
I have led you oft; carry me now, good friends,
And have my thanks for all.
Exeunt, Hearing Antony

ACT IV. SCENE XV. Alexandria. A Monument

Enter Cleopatra and Her Maids Aloft, with Charmian and Iras
CLEOPATRA: O Charmian, I will never go from hence!
CHARMIAN: Be comforted, dear madam.
CLEOPATRA: No, I will not.
All strange and terrible events are welcome,
But comforts we despise; our size of sorrow,
Proportion'd to our cause, must be as great
As that which makes it.
Enter Diomedes, below
How now! Is he dead?
DIOMEDES: His death's upon him, but not dead.
Look out o' th' other side your monument;
His guard have brought him thither.
Enter, Below, Antony, Borne by the Guard
CLEOPATRA: O sun,
Burn the great sphere thou mov'st in! Darkling stand
The varying shore o' th' world. O Antony,
Antony, Antony! Help, Charmian; help, Iras, help;
Help, friends below! Let's draw him hither.
ANTONY: Peace!

Not Caesar's valour hath o'erthrown Antony,
But Antony's hath triumph'd on itself.
CLEOPATRA: So it should be, that none but Antony
Should conquer Antony; but woe 'tis so!
ANTONY: I am dying, Egypt, dying; only
I here importune death awhile, until
Of many thousand kisses the poor last
I lay upon thy lips.
CLEOPATRA: I dare not, dear.
Dear my lord, pardon! I dare not,
Lest I be taken. Not th' imperious show
Of the full-fortun'd Caesar ever shall
Be brooch'd with me. If knife, drugs, serpents, have
Edge, sting, or operation, I am safe.
Your wife Octavia, with her modest eyes
And still conclusion, shall acquire no honour
Demuring upon me. But come, come, Antony-
Help me, my women- we must draw thee up;
Assist, good friends.
ANTONY: O, quick, or I am gone.
CLEOPATRA: Here's sport indeed! How heavy weighs my lord!
Our strength is all gone into heaviness;
That makes the weight. Had I great Juno's power,
The strong-wing'd Mercury should fetch thee up,
And set thee by Jove's side. Yet come a little.
Wishers were ever fools. O come, come,
They Heave Antony Aloft to Cleopatra
And welcome, welcome! Die where thou hast liv'd.
Quicken with kissing. Had my lips that power,
Thus would I wear them out.
ALL: A heavy sight!
ANTONY: I am dying, Egypt, dying.
Give me some wine, and let me speak a little.
CLEOPATRA: No, let me speak; and let me rail so high
That the false huswife Fortune break her wheel,
Provok'd by my offence.
ANTONY: One word, sweet queen:
Of Caesar seek your honour, with your safety. O!
CLEOPATRA: They do not go together.
ANTONY: Gentle, hear me:
None about Caesar trust but Proculeius.
CLEOPATRA: My resolution and my hands I'll trust;
None about Caesar
ANTONY: The miserable change now at my end
Lament nor sorrow at; but please your thoughts
In feeding them with those my former fortunes
Wherein I liv'd the greatest prince o' th' world,
The noblest; and do now not basely die,
Not cowardly put off my helmet to
My countryman- a Roman by a Roman
Valiantly vanquish'd. Now my spirit is going
I can no more.
CLEOPATRA: Noblest of men, woo't die?

Hast thou no care of me? Shall I abide
In this dull world, which in thy absence is
No better than a sty? O, see, my women,
Antony Dies
The crown o' th' earth doth melt. My lord!
O, wither'd is the garland of the war,
The soldier's pole is fall'n! Young boys and girls
Are level now with men. The odds is gone,
And there is nothing left remarkable
Beneath the visiting moon.
Swoons
CHARMIAN: O, quietness, lady!
IRAS: She's dead too, our sovereign.
CHARMIAN: Lady!
IRAS: Madam!
CHARMIAN: O madam, madam, madam!
IRAS: Royal Egypt, Empress!
CHARMIAN: Peace, peace, Iras!
CLEOPATRA: No more but e'en a woman, and commanded
By such poor passion as the maid that milks
And does the meanest chares. It were for me
To throw my sceptre at the injurious gods;
To tell them that this world did equal theirs
Till they had stol'n our jewel. All's but nought;
Patience is sottish, and impatience does
Become a dog that's mad. Then is it sin
To rush into the secret house of death
Ere death dare come to us? How do you, women?
What, what! good cheer! Why, how now, Charmian!
My noble girls! Ah, women, women, look,
Our lamp is spent, it's out! Good sirs, take heart.
We'll bury him; and then, what's brave, what's noble,
Let's do it after the high Roman fashion,
And make death proud to take us. Come, away;
This case of that huge spirit now is cold.
Ah, women, women! Come; we have no friend
But resolution and the briefest end.
Exeunt; Those above Hearing off Antony's Body

ACT V. SCENE I. Alexandria. Caesar's Camp

Enter Caesar, Agrippa, Dolabella, Maecenas, Gallus, Proculeius, and Others, His Council of War
CAESAR: Go to him, Dolabella, bid him yield;
Being so frustrate, tell him he mocks
The pauses that he makes.
DOLABELLA: Caesar, I shall.
Exit
Enter Dercetas with the Sword of Antony
CAESAR: Wherefore is that? And what art thou that dar'st
Appear thus to us?
DERCETAS: I am call'd Dercetas;
Mark Antony I serv'd, who best was worthy
Best to be serv'd. Whilst he stood up and spoke,
He was my master, and I wore my life
To spend upon his haters. If thou please

To take me to thee, as I was to him
I'll be to Caesar; if thou pleasest not,
I yield thee up my life.
CAESAR: What is't thou say'st?
DERCETAS: I say, O Caesar, Antony is dead.
CAESAR: The breaking of so great a thing should make
A greater crack. The round world
Should have shook lions into civil streets,
And citizens to their dens. The death of Antony
Is not a single doom; in the name lay
A moiety of the world.
DERCETAS: He is dead, Caesar,
Not by a public minister of justice,
Nor by a hired knife; but that self hand
Which writ his honour in the acts it did
Hath, with the courage which the heart did lend it,
Splitted the heart. This is his sword;
I robb'd his wound of it; behold it stain'd
With his most noble blood.
CAESAR: Look you sad, friends?
The gods rebuke me, but it is tidings
To wash the eyes of kings.
AGRIPPA: And strange it is
That nature must compel us to lament
Our most persisted deeds.
MAECENAS: His taints and honours
Wag'd equal with him.
AGRIPPA: A rarer spirit never
Did steer humanity. But you gods will give us
Some faults to make us men. Caesar is touch'd.
MAECENAS: When such a spacious mirror's set before him,
He needs must see himself.
CAESAR: O Antony,
I have follow'd thee to this! But we do lance
Diseases in our bodies. I must perforce
Have shown to thee such a declining day
Or look on thine; we could not stall together
In the whole world. But yet let me lament,
With tears as sovereign as the blood of hearts,
That thou, my brother, my competitor
In top of all design, my mate in empire,
Friend and companion in the front of war,
The arm of mine own body, and the heart
Where mine his thoughts did kindle- that our stars,
Unreconciliable, should divide
Our equalness to this. Hear me, good friends-
Enter an Egyptian
But I will tell you at some meeter season.
The business of this man looks out of him;
We'll hear him what he says. Whence are you?
EGYPTIAN: A poor Egyptian, yet the Queen, my mistress,
Confin'd in all she has, her monument,
Of thy intents desires instruction,

That she preparedly may frame herself
To th' way she's forc'd to.
CAESAR: Bid her have good heart.
She soon shall know of us, by some of ours,
How honourable and how kindly we
Determine for her; for Caesar cannot learn
To be ungentle.
EGYPTIAN: So the gods preserve thee! Exit
CAESAR: Come hither, Proculeius. Go and say
We purpose her no shame. Give her what comforts
The quality of her passion shall require,
Lest, in her greatness, by some mortal stroke
She do defeat us; for her life in Rome
Would be eternal in our triumph. Go,
And with your speediest bring us what she says,
And how you find her.
PROCULEIUS: Caesar, I shall.
Exit
CAESAR: Gallus, go you along.
Exit Gallus
Where's Dolabella, to second Proculeius?
ALL: Dolabella!
CAESAR: Let him alone, for I remember now
How he's employ'd; he shall in time be ready.
Go with me to my tent, where you shall see
How hardly I was drawn into this war,
How calm and gentle I proceeded still
In all my writings. Go with me, and see
What I can show in this.
Exeunt

ACT V. SCENE II. Alexandria. The Monument

Enter Cleopatra, Charmian, Iras, and Mardian
CLEOPATRA: My desolation does begin to make
A better life. 'Tis paltry to be Caesar:
Not being Fortune, he's but Fortune's knave,
A minister of her will; and it is great
To do that thing that ends all other deeds,
Which shackles accidents and bolts up change,
Which sleeps, and never palates more the dug,
The beggar's nurse and Caesar's.
Enter, to the Gates of the Monument, Proculeius, Gallus, and Soldiers
PROCULEIUS: Caesar sends greetings to the Queen of Egypt,
And bids thee study on what fair demands
Thou mean'st to have him grant thee.
CLEOPATRA: What's thy name?
PROCULEIUS: My name is Proculeius.
CLEOPATRA: Antony
Did tell me of you, bade me trust you; but
I do not greatly care to be deceiv'd,
That have no use for trusting. If your master
Would have a queen his beggar, you must tell him
That majesty, to keep decorum, must
No less beg than a kingdom. If he please

To give me conquer'd Egypt for my son,
He gives me so much of mine own as I
Will kneel to him with thanks.
PROCULEIUS: Be of good cheer;
Y'are fall'n into a princely hand; fear nothing.
Make your full reference freely to my lord,
Who is so full of grace that it flows over
On all that need. Let me report to him
Your sweet dependency, and you shall find
A conqueror that will pray in aid for kindness
Where he for grace is kneel'd to.
CLEOPATRA: Pray you tell him
I am his fortune's vassal and I send him
The greatness he has got. I hourly learn
A doctrine of obedience, and would gladly
Look him i' th' face.
PROCULEIUS: This I'll report, dear lady.
Have comfort, for I know your plight is pitied
Of him that caus'd it.
GALLUS: You see how easily she may be surpris'd.
Here Proculeius and Two of the Guard Ascend the Monument by a Ladder Placed Against a Window, and Come Behind Cleopatra. Some of the Guard Unbar and Open the Gates
Guard her till Caesar come.
Exit
IRAS: Royal Queen!
CHARMIAN: O Cleopatra! thou art taken, Queen!
CLEOPATRA: Quick, quick, good hands.
Drawing a Dagger
PROCULEIUS: Hold, worthy lady, hold,
Disarms Her
Do not yourself such wrong, who are in this
Reliev'd, but not betray'd.
CLEOPATRA: What, of death too,
That rids our dogs of languish?
PROCULEIUS: Cleopatra,
Do not abuse my master's bounty by
Th' undoing of yourself. Let the world see
His nobleness well acted, which your death
Will never let come forth.
CLEOPATRA: Where art thou, death?
Come hither, come! Come, come, and take a queen
Worth many babes and beggars!
PROCULEIUS: O, temperance, lady!
CLEOPATRA: Sir, I will eat no meat; I'll not drink, sir;
If idle talk will once be necessary,
I'll not sleep neither. This mortal house I'll ruin,
Do Caesar what he can. Know, sir, that I
Will not wait pinion'd at your master's court,
Nor once be chastis'd with the sober eye
Of dull Octavia. Shall they hoist me up,
And show me to the shouting varletry
Of censuring Rome? Rather a ditch in Egypt
Be gentle grave unto me! Rather on Nilus' mud

Lay me stark-nak'd, and let the water-flies
Blow me into abhorring! Rather make
My country's high pyramides my gibbet,
And hang me up in chains!
PROCULEIUS: You do extend
These thoughts of horror further than you shall
Find cause in Caesar.
Enter Dolabella
DOLABELLA: Proculeius,
What thou hast done thy master Caesar knows,
And he hath sent for thee. For the Queen,
I'll take her to my guard.
PROCULEIUS: So, Dolabella,
It shall content me best. Be gentle to her.
To Cleopatra To Caesar I will speak what you shall please,
If you'll employ me to him.
CLEOPATRA: Say I would die.
Exeunt Proculeius and Soldiers
DOLABELLA: Most noble Empress, you have heard of me?
CLEOPATRA: I cannot tell.
DOLABELLA: Assuredly you know me.
CLEOPATRA: No matter, sir, what I have heard or known.
You laugh when boys or women tell their dreams;
Is't not your trick?
DOLABELLA: I understand not, madam.
CLEOPATRA: I dreamt there was an Emperor Antony-
O, such another sleep, that I might see
But such another man!
DOLABELLA: If it might please ye-
CLEOPATRA: His face was as the heav'ns, and therein stuck
A sun and moon, which kept their course and lighted
The little O, the earth.
DOLABELLA: Most sovereign creature-
CLEOPATRA: His legs bestrid the ocean; his rear'd arm
Crested the world. His voice was propertied
As all the tuned spheres, and that to friends;
But when he meant to quail and shake the orb,
He was as rattling thunder. For his bounty,
There was no winter in't; an autumn 'twas
That grew the more by reaping. His delights
Were dolphin-like: they show'd his back above
The element they liv'd in. In his livery
Walk'd crowns and crownets; realms and islands were
As plates dropp'd from his pocket.
DOLABELLA: Cleopatra-
CLEOPATRA: Think you there was or might be such a man
As this I dreamt of?
DOLABELLA: Gentle madam, no.
CLEOPATRA: You lie, up to the hearing of the gods.
But if there be nor ever were one such,
It's past the size of dreaming. Nature wants stuff
To vie strange forms with fancy; yet t' imagine
An Antony were nature's piece 'gainst fancy,

Condemning shadows quite.
DOLABELLA: Hear me, good madam.
Your loss is, as yourself, great; and you bear it
As answering to the weight. Would I might never
O'ertake pursu'd success, but I do feel,
By the rebound of yours, a grief that smites
My very heart at root.
CLEOPATRA: I thank you, sir.
Know you what Caesar means to do with me?
DOLABELLA: I am loath to tell you what I would you knew.
CLEOPATRA: Nay, pray you, sir.
DOLABELLA: Though he be honourable-
CLEOPATRA: He'll lead me, then, in triumph?
DOLABELLA: Madam, he will. I know't.
Flourish
Within: 'Make Way There-Caesar!'
Enter Caesar; Gallus, Proculeius, Maecenas, Seleucus, and Others of His Train
CAESAR: Which is the Queen of Egypt?
DOLABELLA: It is the Emperor, madam.
Cleopatpa Kneels
CAESAR: Arise, you shall not kneel.
I pray you, rise; rise, Egypt.
CLEOPATRA: Sir, the gods
Will have it thus; my master and my lord
I must obey.
CAESAR: Take to you no hard thoughts.
The record of what injuries you did us,
Though written in our flesh, we shall remember
As things but done by chance.
CLEOPATRA: Sole sir o' th' world,
I cannot project mine own cause so well
To make it clear, but do confess I have
Been laden with like frailties which before
Have often sham'd our sex.
CAESAR: Cleopatra, know
We will extenuate rather than enforce.
If you apply yourself to our intents-
Which towards you are most gentle- you shall find
A benefit in this change; but if you seek
To lay on me a cruelty by taking
Antony's course, you shall bereave yourself
Of my good purposes, and put your children
To that destruction which I'll guard them from,
If thereon you rely. I'll take my leave.
CLEOPATRA: And may, through all the world. 'Tis yours, and we,
Your scutcheons and your signs of conquest, shall
Hang in what place you please. Here, my good lord.
CAESAR: You shall advise me in all for Cleopatra.
CLEOPATRA: This is the brief of money, plate, and jewels,
I am possess'd of. 'Tis exactly valued,
Not petty things admitted. Where's Seleucus?
SELEUCUS: Here, madam.
CLEOPATRA: This is my treasurer; let him speak, my lord,

Upon his peril, that I have reserv'd
To myself nothing. Speak the truth, Seleucus.
SELEUCUS: Madam,
I had rather seal my lips than to my peril
Speak that which is not.
CLEOPATRA: What have I kept back?
SELEUCUS: Enough to purchase what you have made known.
CAESAR: Nay, blush not, Cleopatra; I approve
Your wisdom in the deed.
CLEOPATRA: See, Caesar! O, behold,
How pomp is followed! Mine will now be yours;
And, should we shift estates, yours would be mine.
The ingratitude of this Seleucus does
Even make me wild. O slave, of no more trust
Than love that's hir'd! What, goest thou back? Thou shalt
Go back, I warrant thee; but I'll catch thine eyes
Though they had wings. Slave, soulless villain, dog!
O rarely base!
CAESAR: Good Queen, let us entreat you.
CLEOPATRA: O Caesar, what a wounding shame is this,
That thou vouchsafing here to visit me,
Doing the honour of thy lordliness
To one so meek, that mine own servant should
Parcel the sum of my disgraces by
Addition of his envy! Say, good Caesar,
That I some lady trifles have reserv'd,
Immoment toys, things of such dignity
As we greet modern friends withal; and say
Some nobler token I have kept apart
For Livia and Octavia, to induce
Their mediation- must I be unfolded
With one that I have bred? The gods! It smites me
Beneath the fall I have. To Seleucus Prithee go hence;
Or I shall show the cinders of my spirits
Through th' ashes of my chance. Wert thou a man,
Thou wouldst have mercy on me.
CAESAR: Forbear, Seleucus.
Exit Seleucus
CLEOPATRA: Be it known that we, the greatest, are misthought
For things that others do; and when we fall
We answer others' merits in our name,
Are therefore to be pitied.
CAESAR: Cleopatra,
Not what you have reserv'd, nor what acknowledg'd,
Put we i' th' roll of conquest. Still be't yours,
Bestow it at your pleasure; and believe
Caesar's no merchant, to make prize with you
Of things that merchants sold. Therefore be cheer'd;
Make not your thoughts your prisons. No, dear Queen;
For we intend so to dispose you as
Yourself shall give us counsel. Feed and sleep.
Our care and pity is so much upon you
That we remain your friend; and so, adieu.

CLEOPATRA: My master and my lord!
CAESAR: Not so. Adieu.
Flourish. Exeunt Caesar and His Train
CLEOPATRA: He words me, girls, he words me, that I should not
Be noble to myself. But hark thee, Charmian!
Whispers Charmian
IRAS: Finish, good lady; the bright day is done,
And we are for the dark.
CLEOPATRA: Hie thee again.
I have spoke already, and it is provided;
Go put it to the haste.
CHARMIAN: Madam, I will.
Re-enter Dolabella
DOLABELLA: Where's the Queen?
CHARMIAN: Behold, sir.
Exit
CLEOPATRA: Dolabella!
DOLABELLA: Madam, as thereto sworn by your command,
Which my love makes religion to obey,
I tell you this: Caesar through Syria
Intends his journey, and within three days
You with your children will he send before.
Make your best use of this; I have perform'd
Your pleasure and my promise.
CLEOPATRA: Dolabella,
I shall remain your debtor.
DOLABELLA: I your servant.
Adieu, good Queen; I must attend on Caesar.
CLEOPATRA: Farewell, and thanks.
Exit Dolabella
Now, Iras, what think'st thou?
Thou an Egyptian puppet shall be shown
In Rome as well as I. Mechanic slaves,
With greasy aprons, rules, and hammers, shall
Uplift us to the view; in their thick breaths,
Rank of gross diet, shall we be enclouded,
And forc'd to drink their vapour.
IRAS: The gods forbid!
CLEOPATRA: Nay, 'tis most certain, Iras. Saucy lictors
Will catch at us like strumpets, and scald rhymers
Ballad us out o' tune; the quick comedians
Extemporally will stage us, and present
Our Alexandrian revels; Antony
Shall be brought drunken forth, and I shall see
Some squeaking Cleopatra boy my greatness
I' th' posture of a whore.
IRAS: O the good gods!
CLEOPATRA: Nay, that's certain.
IRAS: I'll never see't, for I am sure mine nails
Are stronger than mine eyes.
CLEOPATRA: Why, that's the way
To fool their preparation and to conquer
Their most absurd intents.

Enter Charmian

Now, Charmian!
Show me, my women, like a queen. Go fetch
My best attires. I am again for Cydnus,
To meet Mark Antony. Sirrah, Iras, go.
Now, noble Charmian, we'll dispatch indeed;
And when thou hast done this chare, I'll give thee leave
To play till doomsday. Bring our crown and all.

Exit Iras. A Noise Within

Wherefore's this noise?

Enter a Guardsman

GUARDSMAN: Here is a rural fellow
That will not be denied your Highness' presence.
He brings you figs.

CLEOPATRA: Let him come in.

Exit Guardsman

What poor an instrument
May do a noble deed! He brings me liberty.
My resolution's plac'd, and I have nothing
Of woman in me. Now from head to foot
I am marble-constant; now the fleeting moon
No planet is of mine.

Re-enter Guardsman and Clown, with a Basket

GUARDSMAN: This is the man.

CLEOPATRA: Avoid, and leave him.

Exit Guardsman

Hast thou the pretty worm of Nilus there
That kills and pains not?

CLOWN: Truly, I have him. But I would not be the party that should desire you to touch him, for his biting is immortal; those that do die of it do seldom or never recover.

CLEOPATRA: Remember'st thou any that have died on't?

CLOWN: Very many, men and women too. I heard of one of them no longer than yesterday: a very honest woman, but something given to lie, as a woman should not do but in the way of honesty; how she died of the biting of it, what pain she felt- truly she makes a very good report o' th' worm. But he that will believe all that they say shall never be saved by half that they do. But this is most falliable, the worm's an odd worm.

CLEOPATRA: Get thee hence; farewell.

CLOWN: I wish you all joy of the worm.

Sets down the Basket

CLEOPATRA: Farewell.

CLOWN: You must think this, look you, that the worm will do his kind.

CLEOPATRA: Ay, ay; farewell.

CLOWN: Look you, the worm is not to be trusted but in the keeping of wise people; for indeed there is no goodness in the worm.

CLEOPATRA: Take thou no care; it shall be heeded.

CLOWN: Very good. Give it nothing, I pray you, for it is not worth the feeding.

CLEOPATRA: Will it eat me?

CLOWN: You must not think I am so simple but I know the devil himself will not eat a woman. I know that a woman is a dish for the gods, if the devil dress her not. But truly, these same whoreson devils do the gods great harm in their women, for in every ten that they make the devils mar five.

CLEOPATRA: Well, get thee gone; farewell.

CLOWN: Yes, forsooth. I wish you joy o' th' worm.

Exit

Re-enter Iras, with a Robe, Crown, Etc.

CLEOPATRA: Give me my robe, put on my crown; I have
Immortal longings in me. Now no more
The juice of Egypt's grape shall moist this lip.
Yare, yare, good Iras; quick. Methinks I hear
Antony call. I see him rouse himself
To praise my noble act. I hear him mock
The luck of Caesar, which the gods give men
To excuse their after wrath. Husband, I come.
Now to that name my courage prove my title!
I am fire and air; my other elements
I give to baser life. So, have you done?
Come then, and take the last warmth of my lips.
Farewell, kind Charmian. Iras, long farewell.

Kisses Them. Iras Falls and Dies

Have I the aspic in my lips? Dost fall?
If thus thou and nature can so gently part,
The stroke of death is as a lover's pinch,
Which hurts and is desir'd. Dost thou lie still?
If thou vanishest, thou tell'st the world
It is not worth leave-taking.

CHARMIAN: Dissolve, thick cloud, and rain, that I may say
The gods themselves do weep.

CLEOPATRA: This proves me base.
If she first meet the curled Antony,
He'll make demand of her, and spend that kiss
Which is my heaven to have. Come, thou mortal wretch,

To an Asp, Which She Applies to Her Breast

With thy sharp teeth this knot intrinsicate
Of life at once untie. Poor venomous fool,
Be angry and dispatch. O couldst thou speak,
That I might hear thee call great Caesar ass
Unpolicied!

CHARMIAN: O Eastern star!

CLEOPATRA: Peace, peace!
Dost thou not see my baby at my breast
That sucks the nurse asleep?

CHARMIAN: O, break! O, break!

CLEOPATRA: As sweet as balm, as soft as air, as gentle-
O Antony! Nay, I will take thee too:

Applying Another Asp to Her Arm

What should I stay-

Dies

CHARMIAN: In this vile world? So, fare thee well.
Now boast thee, death, in thy possession lies
A lass unparallel'd. Downy windows, close;

And golden Phoebus never be beheld
Of eyes again so royal! Your crown's awry;
I'll mend it and then play-
Enter the Guard, Rushing in
FIRST GUARD: Where's the Queen?
CHARMIAN: Speak softly, wake her not.
FIRST GUARD: Caesar hath sent-
CHARMIAN: Too slow a messenger. A
pplies an Asp
O, come apace, dispatch. I partly feel thee.
FIRST GUARD: Approach, ho! All's not well: Caesar's beguil'd.
SECOND GUARD: There's Dolabella sent from Caesar; call him.
FIRST GUARD: What work is here! Charmian, is this well done?
CHARMIAN: It is well done, and fitting for a princes
Descended of so many royal kings.
Ah, soldier!
Charmian Dies
Re-enter Dolabella
DOLABELLA: How goes it here?
SECOND GUARD: All dead.
DOLABELLA: Caesar, thy thoughts
Touch their effects in this. Thyself art coming
To see perform'd the dreaded act which thou
So sought'st to hinder.
Within: 'A Way There, a Way for Caesar!'
Re-enter Caesar and All His Train
DOLABELLA: O sir, you are too sure an augurer:
That you did fear is done.
CAESAR: Bravest at the last,
She levell'd at our purposes, and being royal,
Took her own way. The manner of their deaths?
I do not see them bleed.
DOLABELLA: Who was last with them?
FIRST GUARD: A simple countryman that brought her figs.
This was his basket.
CAESAR: Poison'd then.
FIRST GUARD: O Caesar,
This Charmian liv'd but now; she stood and spake.
I found her trimming up the diadem
On her dead mistress. Tremblingly she stood,
And on the sudden dropp'd.
CAESAR: O noble weakness!
If they had swallow'd poison 'twould appear
By external swelling; but she looks like sleep,
As she would catch another Antony
In her strong toil of grace.
DOLABELLA: Here on her breast
There is a vent of blood, and something blown;
The like is on her arm.
FIRST GUARD: This is an aspic's trail; and these fig-leaves
Have slime upon them, such as th' aspic leaves
Upon the caves of Nile.
CAESAR: Most probable

That so she died; for her physician tells me
She hath pursu'd conclusions infinite
Of easy ways to die. Take up her bed,
And bear her women from the monument.
She shall be buried by her Antony;
No grave upon the earth shall clip in it
A pair so famous. High events as these
Strike those that make them; and their story is
No less in pity than his glory which
Brought them to be lamented. Our army shall
In solemn show attend this funeral,
And then to Rome. Come, Dolabella, see
High order in this great solemnity.
Exeunt

END

The Tragedy of Coriolanus

Dramatis Personae

CAIUS MARCIUS, afterwards CAIUS MARCIUS CORIOLANUS
Generals against the Volscians
TITUS LARTIUS
COMINIUS
MENENIUS AGRIPPA, friend to Coriolanus
Tribunes of the People
SICINIUS VELUTUS
JUNIUS BRUTUS
YOUNG MARCIUS, son to Coriolanus
A ROMAN HERALD
NICANOR, a Roman
TULLUS AUFIDIUS, General of the Volscians
LIEUTENANT, to Aufidius
CONSPIRATORS, With Aufidius
ADRIAN, a Volscian
A CITIZEN of Antium
TWO VOLSCIAN GUARDS
VOLUMNIA, mother to Coriolanus
VIRGILIA, wife to Coriolanus
VALERIA, friend to Virgilia
GENTLEWOMAN attending on Virgilia
Roman and Volscian Senators, Patricians, Aediles, Lictors, Soldiers, Citizens, Messengers, Servants to Aufidius, and other Attendants

ACT I. SCENE I. Rome. A Street

Enter a Company of Mutinous Citizens, with Staves, Clubs, and Other Weapons

FIRST CITIZEN: Before we proceed any further, hear me speak.
ALL: Speak, speak.
FIRST CITIZEN: YOU are all resolv'd rather to die than to famish?
ALL: Resolv'd, resolv'd.
FIRST CITIZEN: First, you know Caius Marcius is chief enemy to the people.
ALL: We know't, we know't.
FIRST CITIZEN: Let us kill him, and we'll have corn at our own price. Is't a verdict?
ALL: No more talking on't; let it be done. Away, away!
SECOND CITIZEN: One word, good Citizens.
FIRST CITIZEN: We are accounted poor citizens, the patricians good. What authority surfeits on would relieve us; if they would yield us but the superfluity while it were wholesome, we might guess they relieved us humanely; but they think we are too dear. The leanness that afflicts us, the object of our misery, is as an inventory to particularize their abundance; our sufferance is a gain to them. Let us revenge this with our pikes ere we become rakes; for the gods know I speak this in hunger for bread, not in thirst for revenge.
SECOND CITIZEN: Would you proceed especially against Caius Marcius?
FIRST CITIZEN: Against him first; he's a very dog to the commonalty.
SECOND CITIZEN: Consider you what services he has done for his country?
FIRST CITIZEN: Very well, and could be content to give him good report for't but that he pays himself with being proud.
SECOND CITIZEN: Nay, but speak not maliciously.

FIRST CITIZEN: I say unto you, what he hath done famously he did it to that end; though soft-conscienc'd men can be content to say it was for his country, he did it to please his mother and to be partly proud, which he is, even to the altitude of his virtue.
SECOND CITIZEN: What he cannot help in his nature you account a vice in him. You must in no way say he is covetous.
FIRST CITIZEN: If I must not, I need not be barren of accusations; he hath faults, with surplus, to tire in repetition. Shouts
Within What shouts are these? The other side o' th' city is risen. Why stay we prating here? To th' Capitol!
ALL: Come, come.
FIRST CITIZEN: Soft! who comes here?
Enter Menenius Agrippa
SECOND CITIZEN: Worthy Menenius Agrippa; one that hath always lov'd the people.
FIRST CITIZEN: He's one honest enough; would all the rest were so!
MENENIUS: What work's, my countrymen, in hand? Where go you
With bats and clubs? The matter? Speak, I pray you.
FIRST CITIZEN: Our business is not unknown to th' Senate; they have had inkling this fortnight what we intend to do, which now we'll show 'em in deeds. They say poor suitors have strong breaths; they shall know we have strong arms too.
MENENIUS: Why, masters, my good friends, mine honest neighbours,
Will you undo yourselves?
FIRST CITIZEN: We cannot, sir; we are undone already.
MENENIUS: I tell you, friends, most charitable care
Have the patricians of you. For your wants,
Your suffering in this dearth, you may as well
Strike at the heaven with your staves as lift them
Against the Roman state; whose course will on
The way it takes, cracking ten thousand curbs
Of more strong link asunder than can ever
Appear in your impediment. For the dearth,
The gods, not the patricians, make it, and
Your knees to them, not arms, must help. Alack,
You are transported by calamity
Thither where more attends you; and you slander
The helms o' th' state, who care for you like fathers,
When you curse them as enemies.
FIRST CITIZEN: Care for us! True, indeed! They ne'er car'd for us yet. Suffer us to famish, and their storehouses cramm'd with grain; make edicts for usury, to support usurers; repeal daily any wholesome act established against the rich, and provide more piercing statutes daily to chain up and restrain the poor. If the wars eat us not up, they will; and there's all the love they bear us.
MENENIUS: Either you must
Confess yourselves wondrous malicious,
Or be accus'd of folly. I shall tell you
A pretty tale. It may be you have heard it;
But, since it serves my purpose, I will venture
To stale't a little more.
FIRST CITIZEN: Well, I'll hear it, sir; yet you must not think to fob off our disgrace with a tale. But, an't please you, deliver.
MENENIUS: There was a time when all the body's members

Rebell'd against the belly; thus accus'd it:
That only like a gulf it did remain
I' th' midst o' th' body, idle and unactive,
Still cupboarding the viand, never bearing
Like labour with the rest; where th' other instruments
Did see and hear, devise, instruct, walk, feel,
And, mutually participate, did minister
Unto the appetite and affection common
Of the whole body. The belly answer'd-
FIRST CITIZEN: Well, sir, what answer made the belly?
MENENIUS: Sir, I shall tell you. With a kind of smile,
Which ne'er came from the lungs, but even thus-
For look you, I may make the belly smile
As well as speak- it tauntingly replied
To th' discontented members, the mutinous parts
That envied his receipt; even so most fitly
As you malign our senators for that
They are not such as you.
FIRST CITIZEN: Your belly's answer- What?
The kingly crowned head, the vigilant eye,
The counsellor heart, the arm our soldier,
Our steed the leg, the tongue our trumpeter,
With other muniments and petty helps
Is this our fabric, if that they-
MENENIUS: What then?
Fore me, this fellow speaks! What then? What then?
FIRST CITIZEN: Should by the cormorant belly be restrain'd,
Who is the sink o' th' body-
MENENIUS: Well, what then?
FIRST CITIZEN: The former agents, if they did complain,
What could the belly answer?
MENENIUS: I will tell you;
If you'll bestow a small- of what you have little-
Patience awhile, you'st hear the belly's answer.
FIRST CITIZEN: Y'are long about it.
MENENIUS: Note me this, good friend:
Your most grave belly was deliberate,
Not rash like his accusers, and thus answered.
'True is it, my incorporate friends,' quoth he
'That I receive the general food at first
Which you do live upon; and fit it is,
Because I am the storehouse and the shop
Of the whole body. But, if you do remember,
I send it through the rivers of your blood,
Even to the court, the heart, to th' seat o' th' brain;
And, through the cranks and offices of man,
The strongest nerves and small inferior veins
From me receive that natural competency
Whereby they live. And though that all at once
You, my good friends'- this says the belly; mark me.
FIRST CITIZEN: Ay, sir; well, well.
MENENIUS: 'Though all at once cannot
See what I do deliver out to each,

Yet I can make my audit up, that all
From me do back receive the flour of all,
And leave me but the bran.' What say you to' t?
FIRST CITIZEN: It was an answer. How apply you this?
MENENIUS: The senators of Rome are this good belly,
And you the mutinous members; for, examine
Their counsels and their cares, digest things rightly
Touching the weal o' th' common, you shall find
No public benefit which you receive
But it proceeds or comes from them to you,
And no way from yourselves. What do you think,
You, the great toe of this assembly?
FIRST CITIZEN: I the great toe? Why the great toe?
MENENIUS: For that, being one o' th' lowest, basest, poorest,
Of this most wise rebellion, thou goest foremost.
Thou rascal, that art worst in blood to run,
Lead'st first to win some vantage.
But make you ready your stiff bats and clubs.
Rome and her rats are at the point of battle;
The one side must have bale.
Enter Caius Marcius
Hail, noble Marcius!
MARCIUS: Thanks. What's the matter, you dissentious rogues
That, rubbing the poor itch of your opinion,
Make yourselves scabs?
FIRST CITIZEN: We have ever your good word.
MARCIUS: He that will give good words to thee will flatter
Beneath abhorring. What would you have, you curs,
That like nor peace nor war? The one affrights you,
The other makes you proud. He that trusts to you,
Where he should find you lions, finds you hares;
Where foxes, geese; you are no surer, no,
Than is the coal of fire upon the ice
Or hailstone in the sun. Your virtue is
To make him worthy whose offence subdues him,
And curse that justice did it. Who deserves greatness
Deserves your hate; and your affections are
A sick man's appetite, who desires most that
Which would increase his evil. He that depends
Upon your favours swims with fins of lead,
And hews down oaks with rushes. Hang ye! Trust ye?
With every minute you do change a mind
And call him noble that was now your hate,
Him vile that was your garland. What's the matter
That in these several places of the city
You cry against the noble Senate, who,
Under the gods, keep you in awe, which else
Would feed on one another? What's their seeking?
MENENIUS: For corn at their own rates, whereof they say
The city is well stor'd.
MARCIUS: Hang 'em! They say!
They'll sit by th' fire and presume to know
What's done i' th' Capitol, who's like to rise,

Who thrives and who declines; side factions, and give out
Conjectural marriages, making parties strong,
And feebling such as stand not in their liking
Below their cobbled shoes. They say there's grain enough!
Would the nobility lay aside their ruth
And let me use my sword, I'd make a quarry
With thousands of these quarter'd slaves, as high
As I could pick my lance.
MENENIUS: Nay, these are almost thoroughly persuaded;
For though abundantly they lack discretion,
Yet are they passing cowardly. But, I beseech you,
What says the other troop?
MARCIUS: They are dissolv'd. Hang 'em!
They said they were an-hungry; sigh'd forth proverbs-
That hunger broke stone walls, that dogs must eat,
That meat was made for mouths, that the gods sent not
Corn for the rich men only. With these shreds
They vented their complainings; which being answer'd,
And a petition granted them- a strange one,
To break the heart of generosity
And make bold power look pale- they threw their caps
As they would hang them on the horns o' th' moon,
Shouting their emulation.
MENENIUS: What is granted them?
MARCIUS: Five tribunes, to defend their vulgar wisdoms,
Of their own choice. One's Junius Brutus-
Sicinius Velutus, and I know not. 'Sdeath!
The rabble should have first unroof'd the city
Ere so prevail'd with me; it will in time
Win upon power and throw forth greater themes
For insurrection's arguing.
MENENIUS: This is strange.
MARCIUS: Go get you home, you fragments.
Enter a Messenger, Hastily
MESSENGER: Where's Caius Marcius?
MARCIUS: Here. What's the matter?
MESSENGER: The news is, sir, the Volsces are in arms.
MARCIUS: I am glad on't; then we shall ha' means to vent
Our musty superfluity. See, our best elders.
Enter Cominius, Titus Lartius, with Other Senators; Junius Brutus and Sicinius Velutus
FIRST SENATOR: Marcius, 'tis true that you have lately told us:
The Volsces are in arms.
MARCIUS: They have a leader,
Tullus Aufidius, that will put you to't.
I sin in envying his nobility;
And were I anything but what I am,
I would wish me only he.
COMINIUS: You have fought together?
MARCIUS: Were half to half the world by th' ears, and he
Upon my party, I'd revolt, to make
Only my wars with him. He is a lion
That I am proud to hunt.
FIRST SENATOR: Then, worthy Marcius,

Attend upon Cominius to these wars.
COMINIUS: It is your former promise.
MARCIUS: Sir, it is;
And I am constant. Titus Lartius, thou
Shalt see me once more strike at Tullus' face.
What, art thou stiff? Stand'st out?
LARTIUS: No, Caius Marcius;
I'll lean upon one crutch and fight with t'other
Ere stay behind this business.
MENENIUS: O, true bred!
FIRST SENATOR: Your company to th' Capitol; where, I know,
Our greatest friends attend us.
LARTIUS: To Cominius Lead you on.
To Marcius Follow Cominius; we must follow you;
Right worthy you priority.
COMINIUS: Noble Marcius!
FIRST SENATOR: To the Citizens Hence to your homes; be gone.
MARCIUS: Nay, let them follow.
The Volsces have much corn: take these rats thither
To gnaw their garners. Worshipful mutineers,
Your valour puts well forth; pray follow.
Citizens Steal Away. Exeunt All but Sicinius and Brutus
SICINIUS: Was ever man so proud as is this Marcius?
BRUTUS: He has no equal.
SICINIUS: When we were chosen tribunes for the people-
BRUTUS: Mark'd you his lip and eyes?
SICINIUS: Nay, but his taunts!
BRUTUS: Being mov'd, he will not spare to gird the gods.
SICINIUS: Bemock the modest moon.
BRUTUS: The present wars devour him! He is grown
Too proud to be so valiant.
SICINIUS: Such a nature,
Tickled with good success, disdains the shadow
Which he treads on at noon. But I do wonder
His insolence can brook to be commanded
Under Cominius.
BRUTUS: Fame, at the which he aims-
In whom already he is well grac'd- cannot
Better be held nor more attain'd than by
A place below the first; for what miscarries
Shall be the general's fault, though he perform
To th' utmost of a man, and giddy censure
Will then cry out of Marcius 'O, if he
Had borne the business!'
SICINIUS: Besides, if things go well,
Opinion, that so sticks on Marcius, shall
Of his demerits rob Cominius.
BRUTUS: Come.
Half all Cominius' honours are to Marcius,
Though Marcius earn'd them not; and all his faults
To Marcius shall be honours, though indeed
In aught he merit not.
SICINIUS: Let's hence and hear

How the dispatch is made, and in what fashion,
More than his singularity, he goes
Upon this present action.
BRUTUS: Let's along.
Exeunt

ACT I. SCENE II. Corioli. The Senate House.

Enter Tullus Aufidius with Senators of Corioli
FIRST SENATOR: So, your opinion is, Aufidius,
That they of Rome are ent'red in our counsels
And know how we proceed.
AUFIDIUS: Is it not yours?
What ever have been thought on in this state
That could be brought to bodily act ere Rome
Had circumvention? 'Tis not four days gone
Since I heard thence; these are the words- I think
I have the letter here;.yes, here it is:
Reads
'They have press'd a power, but it is not known
Whether for east or west. The dearth is great;
The people mutinous; and it is rumour'd,
Cominius, Marcius your old enemy,
Who is of Rome worse hated than of you,
And Titus Lartius, a most valiant Roman,
These three lead on this preparation
Whither 'tis bent. Most likely 'tis for you;
Consider of it.'
FIRST SENATOR: Our army's in the field;
We never yet made doubt but Rome was ready
To answer us.
AUFIDIUS: Nor did you think it folly
To keep your great pretences veil'd till when
They needs must show themselves; which in the hatching,
It seem'd, appear'd to Rome. By the discovery
We shall be short'ned in our aim, which was
To take in many towns ere almost Rome
Should know we were afoot.
SECOND SENATOR: Noble Aufidius,
Take your commission; hie you to your bands;
Let us alone to guard Corioli.
If they set down before's, for the remove
Bring up your army; but I think you'll find
Th' have not prepar'd for us.
AUFIDIUS: O, doubt not that!
I speak from certainties. Nay more,
Some parcels of their power are forth already,
And only hitherward. I leave your honours.
If we and Caius Marcius chance to meet,
'Tis sworn between us we shall ever strike
Till one can do no more.
ALL: The gods assist you!
AUFIDIUS: And keep your honours safe!
FIRST SENATOR: Farewell.
SECOND SENATOR: Farewell.

ALL: Farewell.
Exeunt

ACT I. SCENE III. Rome. Marcius' House

Enter Volumnia and Virgilia, Mother and Wife to Marcius; They Set Them down on Two Low Stools and Sew

VOLUMNIA: I pray you, daughter, sing, or express yourself in a more comfortable sort. If my son were my husband, I should freelier rejoice in that absence wherein he won honour than in the embracements of his bed where he would show most love. When yet he was but tender-bodied, and the only son of my womb; when youth with comeliness pluck'd all gaze his way; when, for a day of kings' entreaties, a mother should not sell him an hour from her beholding; I, considering how honour would become such a person- that it was no better than picture-like to hang by th' wall, if renown made it not stir- was pleas'd to let him seek danger where he was to find fame. To a cruel war I sent him, from whence he return'd his brows bound with oak. I tell thee, daughter, I sprang not more in joy at first hearing he was a man-child than now in first seeing he had proved himself a man.
VIRGILIA: But had he died in the business, madam, how then?
VOLUMNIA: Then his good report should have been my son; I therein would have found issue. Hear me profess sincerely: had I a dozen sons, each in my love alike, and none less dear than thine and my good Marcius, I had rather had eleven die nobly for their country than one voluptuously surfeit out of action.
Enter a Gentlewoman
GENTLEWOMAN: Madam, the Lady Valeria is come to visit you.
VIRGILIA: Beseech you give me leave to retire myself.
VOLUMNIA: Indeed you shall not.
Methinks I hear hither your husband's drum;
See him pluck Aufidius down by th' hair;
As children from a bear, the Volsces shunning him.
Methinks I see him stamp thus, and call thus:
'Come on, you cowards! You were got in fear,
Though you were born in Rome.' His bloody brow
With his mail'd hand then wiping, forth he goes,
Like to a harvest-man that's task'd to mow
Or all or lose his hire.
VIRGILIA: His bloody brow? O Jupiter, no blood!
VOLUMNIA: Away, you fool! It more becomes a man
Than gilt his trophy. The breasts of Hecuba,
When she did suckle Hector, look'd not lovelier
Than Hector's forehead when it spit forth blood
At Grecian sword, contemning. Tell Valeria
We are fit to bid her welcome.
Exit Gentlewoman
VIRGILIA: Heavens bless my lord from fell Aufidius!
VOLUMNIA: He'll beat Aufidius' head below his knee
And tread upon his neck.
Re-enter Gentlewoman, with Valeria and an Usher
VALERIA: My ladies both, good day to you.
VOLUMNIA: Sweet madam!
VIRGILIA: I am glad to see your ladyship.

VALERIA: How do you both? You are manifest housekeepers. What are you sewing here? A fine spot, in good faith. How does your little son?
VIRGILIA: I thank your ladyship; well, good madam.
VOLUMNIA: He had rather see the swords and hear a drum than look upon his schoolmaster.
VALERIA: O' my word, the father's son! I'll swear 'tis a very pretty boy. O' my troth, I look'd upon him a Wednesday half an hour together; has such a confirm'd countenance! I saw him run after a gilded butterfly; and when he caught it he let it go again, and after it again, and over and over he comes, and up again, catch'd it again; or whether his fall enrag'd him, or how 'twas, he did so set his teeth and tear it. O, I warrant, how he mammock'd it!
VOLUMNIA: One on's father's moods.
VALERIA: Indeed, la, 'tis a noble child.
VIRGILIA: A crack, madam.
VALERIA: Come, lay aside your stitchery; I must have you play the idle huswife with me this afternoon.
VIRGILIA: No, good madam; I will not out of doors.
VALERIA: Not out of doors!
VOLUMNIA: She shall, she shall.
VIRGILIA: Indeed, no, by your patience; I'll not over the threshold till my lord return from the wars.
VALERIA: Fie, you confine yourself most unreasonably; come, you must go visit the good lady that lies in.
VIRGILIA: I will wish her speedy strength, and visit her with my prayers; but I cannot go thither.
VOLUMNIA: Why, I pray you?
VIRGILIA: 'Tis not to save labour, nor that I want love.
VALERIA: You would be another Penelope; yet they say all the yarn she spun in Ulysses' absence did but fill Ithaca full of moths. Come, I would your cambric were sensible as your finger, that you might leave pricking it for pity. Come, you shall go with us.
VIRGILIA: No, good madam, pardon me; indeed I will not forth.
VALERIA: In truth, la, go with me; and I'll tell you excellent news of your husband.
VIRGILIA: O, good madam, there can be none yet.
VALERIA: Verily, I do not jest with you; there came news from him last night.
VIRGILIA: Indeed, madam?
VALERIA: In earnest, it's true; I heard a senator speak it. Thus it is: the Volsces have an army forth; against whom Cominius the general is gone, with one part of our Roman power. Your lord and Titus Lartius are set down before their city Corioli; they nothing doubt prevailing and to make it brief wars. This is true, on mine honour; and so, I pray, go with us.
VIRGILIA: Give me excuse, good madam; I will obey you in everything hereafter.
VOLUMNIA: Let her alone, lady; as she is now, she will but disease our better mirth.
VALERIA: In troth, I think she would. Fare you well, then. Come, good sweet lady. Prithee, Virgilia, turn thy solemness out o' door and go along with us.

VIRGILIA: No, at a word, madam; indeed I must not. I wish you much mirth.
VALERIA: Well then, farewell.
Exeunt

ACT I. SCENE IV. Before Corioli

Enter Marcius, Titus Lartius, with Drum and Colours, with Captains and Soldiers. To Them a Messenger
MARCIUS: Yonder comes news; a wager- they have met.
LARTIUS: My horse to yours- no.
MARCIUS: 'Tis done.
LARTIUS: Agreed.
MARCIUS: Say, has our general met the enemy?
MESSENGER: They lie in view, but have not spoke as yet.
LARTIUS: So, the good horse is mine.
MARCIUS: I'll buy him of you.
LARTIUS: No, I'll nor sell nor give him; lend you him I will
For half a hundred years. Summon the town.
MARCIUS: How far off lie these armies?
MESSENGER: Within this mile and half.
MARCIUS: Then shall we hear their 'larum, and they ours.
Now, Mars, I prithee, make us quick in work,
That we with smoking swords may march from hence
To help our fielded friends! Come, blow thy blast.
They Sound a Parley. Enter Two Senators with Others, on the Walls of Corioli
Tullus Aufidius, is he within your walls?
FIRST SENATOR: No, nor a man that fears you less than he:
That's lesser than a little. Drum Afar Off Hark, our drums
Are bringing forth our youth. We'll break our walls
Rather than they shall pound us up; our gates,
Which yet seem shut, we have but pinn'd with rushes;
They'll open of themselves. Alarum Far Off Hark you far off!
There is Aufidius. List what work he makes
Amongst your cloven army.
MARCIUS: O, they are at it!
LARTIUS: Their noise be our instruction. Ladders, ho!
Enter the Army of the Volsces
MARCIUS: They fear us not, but issue forth their city.
Now put your shields before your hearts, and fight
With hearts more proof than shields. Advance, brave Titus.
They do disdain us much beyond our thoughts,
Which makes me sweat with wrath. Come on, my fellows.
He that retires, I'll take him for a Volsce,
And he shall feel mine edge.
Alarum. The Romans Are Beat Back to Their Trenches. Re-enter Marcius, Cursing
MARCIUS: All the contagion of the south light on you,
You shames of Rome! you herd of- Boils and plagues
Plaster you o'er, that you may be abhorr'd
Farther than seen, and one infect another
Against the wind a mile! You souls of geese
That bear the shapes of men, how have you run
From slaves that apes would beat! Pluto and hell!
All hurt behind! Backs red, and faces pale
With flight and agued fear! Mend and charge home,

Or, by the fires of heaven, I'll leave the foe
And make my wars on you. Look to't. Come on;
If you'll stand fast we'll beat them to their wives,
As they us to our trenches. Follow me.
Another Alarum. The Volsces Fly, and Marcius Follows Them to the Gates
So, now the gates are ope; now prove good seconds;
'Tis for the followers fortune widens them,
Not for the fliers. Mark me, and do the like.
Marcius Enters the Gates
FIRST SOLDIER: Fool-hardiness; not I.
SECOND SOLDIER:. Not I.
Marcius Is Shut in
FIRST SOLDIER: See, they have shut him in.
ALL: To th' pot, I warrant him.
Alarum Continues
Re-enter Titus Lartius
LARTIUS: What is become of Marcius?
ALL: Slain, sir, doubtless.
FIRST SOLDIER: Following the fliers at the very heels,
With them he enters; who, upon the sudden,
Clapp'd to their gates. He is himself alone,
To answer all the city.
LARTIUS: O noble fellow!
Who sensibly outdares his senseless sword,
And when it bows stand'st up. Thou art left, Marcius;
A carbuncle entire, as big as thou art,
Were not so rich a jewel. Thou wast a soldier
Even to Cato's wish, not fierce and terrible
Only in strokes; but with thy grim looks and
The thunder-like percussion of thy sounds
Thou mad'st thine enemies shake, as if the world
Were feverous and did tremble.
Re-enter Marcius, Bleeding, Assaulted by the Enemy
FIRST SOLDIER: Look, sir.
LARTIUS: O, 'tis Marcius!
Let's fetch him off, or make remain alike.
They Fight, and All Enter the City

ACT I. SCENE V. Within Corioli. A Street

Enter Certain Romans, with Spoils
FIRST ROMAN: This will I carry to Rome.
SECOND ROMAN: And I this.
THIRD ROMAN:. A murrain on 't! I took this for silver.
Alarum Continues Still Afar Off. Enter Marcius and Titus Lartius with a Trumpeter
MARCIUS: See here these movers that do prize their hours
At a crack'd drachma! Cushions, leaden spoons,
Irons of a doit, doublets that hangmen would
Bury with those that wore them, these base slaves,
Ere yet the fight be done, pack up. Down with them!
Exeunt Pillagers
And hark, what noise the general makes! To him!
There is the man of my soul's hate, Aufidius,
Piercing our Romans; then, valiant Titus, take
Convenient numbers to make good the city;

Whilst I, with those that have the spirit, will haste
To help Cominius.
LARTIUS: Worthy sir, thou bleed'st;
Thy exercise hath been too violent
For a second course of fight.
MARCIUS: Sir, praise me not;
My work hath yet not warm'd me. Fare you well;
The blood I drop is rather physical
Than dangerous to me. To Aufidius thus
I will appear, and fight.
LARTIUS: Now the fair goddess, Fortune,
Fall deep in love with thee, and her great charms
Misguide thy opposers' swords! Bold gentleman,
Prosperity be thy page!
MARCIUS: Thy friend no less
Than those she placeth highest! So farewell.
LARTIUS: Thou worthiest Marcius!
Exit Marcius
Go sound thy trumpet in the market-place;
Call thither all the officers o' th' town,
Where they shall know our mind. Away!
Exeunt

ACT I. SCENE VI. Near the Camp of Cominius

Enter Cominius, as it Were in Retire, with Soldiers
COMINIUS: Breathe you, my friends. Well fought; we are come off
Like Romans, neither foolish in our stands
Nor cowardly in retire. Believe me, sirs,
We shall be charg'd again. Whiles we have struck,
By interims and conveying gusts we have heard
The charges of our friends. The Roman gods,
Lead their successes as we wish our own,
That both our powers, with smiling fronts encount'ring,
May give you thankful sacrifice!
Enter a Messenger
Thy news?
MESSENGER: The citizens of Corioli have issued
And given to Lartius and to Marcius battle;
I saw our party to their trenches driven,
And then I came away.
COMINIUS: Though thou speak'st truth,
Methinks thou speak'st not well. How long is't since?
MESSENGER: Above an hour, my lord.
COMINIUS: 'Tis not a mile; briefly we heard their drums.
How couldst thou in a mile confound an hour,
And bring thy news so late?
MESSENGER: Spies of the Volsces
Held me in chase, that I was forc'd to wheel
Three or four miles about; else had I, sir,
Half an hour since brought my report.
Enter Marcius
COMINIUS: Who's yonder
That does appear as he were flay'd? O gods!
He has the stamp of Marcius, and I have

Before-time seen him thus.
MARCIUS: Come I too late?
COMINIUS: The shepherd knows not thunder from a tabor
More than I know the sound of Marcius' tongue
From every meaner man.
MARCIUS: Come I too late?
COMINIUS: Ay, if you come not in the blood of others,
But mantled in your own.
MARCIUS: O! let me clip ye
In arms as sound as when I woo'd, in heart
As merry as when our nuptial day was done,
And tapers burn'd to bedward.
COMINIUS: Flower of warriors,
How is't with Titus Lartius?
MARCIUS: As with a man busied about decrees:
Condemning some to death and some to exile;
Ransoming him or pitying, threat'ning th' other;
Holding Corioli in the name of Rome
Even like a fawning greyhound in the leash,
To let him slip at will.
COMINIUS: Where is that slave
Which told me they had beat you to your trenches?
Where is he? Call him hither.
MARCIUS: Let him alone;
He did inform the truth. But for our gentlemen,
The common file- a plague! tribunes for them!
The mouse ne'er shunn'd the cat as they did budge
From rascals worse than they.
COMINIUS: But how prevail'd you?
MARCIUS: Will the time serve to tell? I do not think.
Where is the enemy? Are you lords o' th' field?
If not, why cease you till you are so?
COMINIUS: Marcius,
We have at disadvantage fought, and did
Retire to win our purpose.
MARCIUS: How lies their battle? Know you on which side
They have plac'd their men of trust?
COMINIUS: As I guess, Marcius,
Their bands i' th' vaward are the Antiates,
Of their best trust; o'er them Aufidius,
Their very heart of hope.
MARCIUS: I do beseech you,
By all the battles wherein we have fought,
By th' blood we have shed together, by th' vows
We have made to endure friends, that you directly
Set me against Aufidius and his Antiates;
And that you not delay the present, but,
Filling the air with swords advanc'd and darts,
We prove this very hour.
COMINIUS: Though I could wish
You were conducted to a gentle bath
And balms applied to you, yet dare I never
Deny your asking: take your choice of those

That best can aid your action.
MARCIUS: Those are they
That most are willing. If any such be here-
As it were sin to doubt- that love this painting
Wherein you see me smear'd; if any fear
Lesser his person than an ill report;
If any think brave death outweighs bad life
And that his country's dearer than himself;
Let him alone, or so many so minded,
Wave thus to express his disposition,
And follow Marcius.
They All Shout and Wave Their Swords, Take Him up in Their Arms and Cast up Their Caps
O, me alone! Make you a sword of me?
If these shows be not outward, which of you
But is four Volsces? None of you but is
Able to bear against the great Aufidius
A shield as hard as his. A certain number,
Though thanks to all, must I select from all; the rest
Shall bear the business in some other fight,
As cause will be obey'd. Please you to march;
And four shall quickly draw out my command,
Which men are best inclin'd.
COMINIUS: March on, my fellows;
Make good this ostentation, and you shall
Divide in all with us.
Exeunt

ACT I. SCENE VII. The Gates of Corioli

Titus Lartius, Having Set a Guard upon Corioli, Going with Drum and Trumpet Toward Cominius and Caius Marcius, Enters with a Lieutenant, Other Soldiers, and a Scout
LARTIUS: So, let the ports be guarded; keep your duties
As I have set them down. If I do send, dispatch
Those centuries to our aid; the rest will serve
For a short holding. If we lose the field
We cannot keep the town.
LIEUTENANT: Fear not our care, sir.
LARTIUS: Hence, and shut your gates upon's.
Our guider, come; to th' Roman camp conduct us.
Exeunt

ACT I. SCENE VIII. A Field of Battle Between the Roman and the Volscian Camps

Alarum, as in Battle. Enter Marcius and Aufidius at Several Doors
MARCIUS: I'll fight with none but thee, for I do hate thee
Worse than a promise-breaker.
AUFIDIUS: We hate alike:
Not Afric owns a serpent I abhor
More than thy fame and envy. Fix thy foot.
MARCIUS: Let the first budger die the other's slave,
And the gods doom him after!
AUFIDIUS: If I fly, Marcius,
Halloa me like a hare.
MARCIUS: Within these three hours, Tullus,
Alone I fought in your Corioli walls,
And made what work I pleas'd. 'Tis not my blood
Wherein thou seest me mask'd. For thy revenge

Wrench up thy power to th' highest.
AUFIDIUS: Wert thou the Hector
That was the whip of your bragg'd progeny,
Thou shouldst not scape me here.

Here They Fight, and Certain Volsces Come in the Aid of Aufidius. Marcius Fights till They Be Driven in Breathless

Officious, and not valiant, you have sham'd me
In your condemned seconds. Exeunt

ACT I. SCENE IX. The Roman Camp

Flourish. Alarum. A Retreat Is Sounded. Enter, at One Door, Cominius with the Romans; at Another Door, Marcius, with His Arm in a Scarf

COMINIUS: If I should tell thee o'er this thy day's work,
Thou't not believe thy deeds; but I'll report it
Where senators shall mingle tears with smiles;
Where great patricians shall attend, and shrug,
I' th' end admire; where ladies shall be frighted
And, gladly quak'd, hear more; where the dull tribunes,
That with the fusty plebeians hate thine honours,
Shall say against their hearts 'We thank the gods
Our Rome hath such a soldier.'
Yet cam'st thou to a morsel of this feast,
Having fully din'd before.

Enter Titus Lartius, with His Power, from the Pursuit

LARTIUS: O General,
Here is the steed, we the caparison.
Hadst thou beheld-
MARCIUS: Pray now, no more; my mother,
Who has a charter to extol her blood,
When she does praise me grieves me. I have done
As you have done- that's what I can; induc'd
As you have been- that's for my country.
He that has but effected his good will
Hath overta'en mine act.
COMINIUS: You shall not be
The grave of your deserving; Rome must know
The value of her own. 'Twere a concealment
Worse than a theft, no less than a traducement,
To hide your doings and to silence that
Which, to the spire and top of praises vouch'd,
Would seem but modest. Therefore, I beseech you,
In sign of what you are, not to reward
What you have done, before our army hear me.
MARCIUS: I have some wounds upon me, and they smart
To hear themselves remembe'red.
COMINIUS: Should they not,
Well might they fester 'gainst ingratitude
And tent themselves with death. Of all the horses-
Whereof we have ta'en good, and good store- of all
The treasure in this field achiev'd and city,
We render you the tenth; to be ta'en forth
Before the common distribution at
Your only choice.
MARCIUS: I thank you, General,

But cannot make my heart consent to take
A bribe to pay my sword. I do refuse it,
And stand upon my common part with those
That have beheld the doing.
A Long Flourish. They All Cry 'Marcius, Marcius!' Cast up Their Caps and Lances. Cominius and Lartius Stand Bare
May these same instruments which you profane
Never sound more! When drums and trumpets shall
I' th' field prove flatterers, let courts and cities be
Made all of false-fac'd soothing. When steel grows
Soft as the parasite's silk, let him be made
An overture for th' wars. No more, I say.
For that I have not wash'd my nose that bled,
Or foil'd some debile wretch, which without note
Here's many else have done, you shout me forth
In acclamations hyperbolical,
As if I lov'd my little should be dieted
In praises sauc'd with lies.
COMINIUS: Too modest are you;
More cruel to your good report than grateful
To us that give you truly. By your patience,
If 'gainst yourself you be incens'd, we'll put you-
Like one that means his proper harm- in manacles,
Then reason safely with you. Therefore be it known,
As to us, to all the world, that Caius Marcius
Wears this war's garland; in token of the which,
My noble steed, known to the camp, I give him,
With all his trim belonging; and from this time,
For what he did before Corioli, can him
With all th' applause-and clamour of the host,
Caius Marcius Coriolanus.
Bear th' addition nobly ever!
Flourish. Trumpets Sound, and Drums
ALL: Caius Marcius Coriolanus!
CORIOLANUS: I will go wash;
And when my face is fair you shall perceive
Whether I blush or no. Howbeit, I thank you;
I mean to stride your steed, and at all times
To undercrest your good addition
To th' fairness of my power.
COMINIUS: So, to our tent;
Where, ere we do repose us, we will write
To Rome of our success. You, Titus Lartius,
Must to Corioli back. Send us to Rome
The best, with whom we may articulate
For their own good and ours.
LARTIUS: I shall, my lord.
CORIOLANUS: The gods begin to mock me. I, that now
Refus'd most princely gifts, am bound to beg
Of my Lord General.
COMINIUS: Take't- 'tis yours; what is't?
CORIOLANUS: I sometime lay here in Corioli
At a poor man's house; he us'd me kindly.

He cried to me; I saw him prisoner;
But then Aufidius was within my view,
And wrath o'erwhelm'd my pity. I request you
To give my poor host freedom.
COMINIUS: O, well begg'd!
Were he the butcher of my son, he should
Be free as is the wind. Deliver him, Titus.
LARTIUS: Marcius, his name?
CORIOLANUS: By Jupiter, forgot!
I am weary; yea, my memory is tir'd.
Have we no wine here?
COMINIUS: Go we to our tent.
The blood upon your visage dries; 'tis time
It should be look'd to. Come.
Exeunt

ACT I. SCENE X. The Camp of the Volsces

A Flourish. Cornets. Enter Tullus Aufidius Bloody, with Two or Three Soldiers
AUFIDIUS: The town is ta'en.
FIRST SOLDIER: 'Twill be deliver'd back on good condition.
AUFIDIUS: Condition!
I would I were a Roman; for I cannot,
Being a Volsce, be that I am. Condition?
What good condition can a treaty find
I' th' part that is at mercy? Five times, Marcius,
I have fought with thee; so often hast thou beat me;
And wouldst do so, I think, should we encounter
As often as we eat. By th' elements,
If e'er again I meet him beard to beard,
He's mine or I am his. Mine emulation
Hath not that honour in't it had; for where
I thought to crush him in an equal force,
True sword to sword, I'll potch at him some way,
Or wrath or craft may get him.
FIRST SOLDIER: He's the devil.
AUFIDIUS: Bolder, though not so subtle. My valour's poison'd
With only suff'ring stain by him; for him
Shall fly out of itself. Nor sleep nor sanctuary,
Being naked, sick, nor fane nor Capitol,
The prayers of priests nor times of sacrifice,
Embarquements all of fury, shall lift up
Their rotten privilege and custom 'gainst
My hate to Marcius. Where I find him, were it
At home, upon my brother's guard, even there,
Against the hospitable canon, would I
Wash my fierce hand in's heart. Go you to th' city;
Learn how 'tis held, and what they are that must
Be hostages for Rome.
FIRST SOLDIER: Will not you go?
AUFIDIUS: I am attended at the cypress grove; I pray you-
'Tis south the city mills- bring me word thither
How the world goes, that to the pace of it
I may spur on my journey.
FIRST SOLDIER: I shall, sir.

Exeunt

ACT II. SCENE I. Rome. A Public Place

Enter Menenius, with the Two Tribunes of the People, Sicinius and Brutus

MENENIUS: The augurer tells me we shall have news tonight.

BRUTUS: Good or bad?

MENENIUS: Not according to the prayer of the people, for they love not Marcius.

SICINIUS: Nature teaches beasts to know their friends.

MENENIUS: Pray you, who does the wolf love?

SICINIUS: The lamb.

MENENIUS: Ay, to devour him, as the hungry plebeians would the noble Marcius.

BRUTUS: He's a lamb indeed, that baes like a bear.

MENENIUS: He's a bear indeed, that lives fike a lamb. You two are old men; tell me one thing that I shall ask you.

BOTH TRIBUNES: Well, sir.

MENENIUS: In what enormity is Marcius poor in that you two have not in abundance?

BRUTUS: He's poor in no one fault, but stor'd with all.

SICINIUS: Especially in pride.

BRUTUS: And topping all others in boasting.

MENENIUS: This is strange now. Do you two know how you are censured here in the city- I mean of us o' th' right-hand file? Do you?

BOTH TRIBUNES: Why, how are we censur'd?

MENENIUS: Because you talk of pride now- will you not be angry?

BOTH TRIBUNES: Well, well, sir, well.

MENENIUS: Why, 'tis no great matter; for a very little thief of occasion will rob you of a great deal of patience. Give your dispositions the reins, and be angry at your pleasures- at the least, if you take it as a pleasure to you in being so. You blame Marcius for being proud?

BRUTUS: We do it not alone, sir.

MENENIUS: I know you can do very little alone; for your helps are many, or else your actions would grow wondrous single: your abilities are too infant-like for doing much alone. You talk of pride. O that you could turn your eyes toward the napes of your necks, and make but an interior survey of your good selves! O that you could!

BOTH TRIBUNES: What then, sir?

MENENIUS: Why, then you should discover a brace of unmeriting, proud, violent, testy magistrates-alias fools- as any in Rome.

SICINIUS: Menenius, you are known well enough too.

MENENIUS: I am known to be a humorous patrician, and one that loves a cup of hot wine with not a drop of allaying Tiber in't; said to be something imperfect in favouring the first complaint, hasty and tinder-like upon too trivial motion; one that converses more with the buttock of the night than with the forehead of the morning. What I think I utter, and spend my malice in my breath. Meeting two such wealsmen as you are- I cannot call you Lycurguses- if the drink you give me touch my palate adversely, I make a crooked face at it. I cannot say your worships have deliver'd the matter well, when I find the ass in compound with the major part of your syllables; and though I must be content to

bear with those that say you are reverend grave men, yet they lie deadly that tell you you have good faces. If you see this in the map of my microcosm, follows it that I am known well enough too? What harm can your bisson conspectuities glean out of this character, if I be known well enough too?
BRUTUS: Come, sir, come, we know you well enough.
MENENIUS: You know neither me, yourselves, nor any thing. You are ambitious for poor knaves' caps and legs; you wear out a good wholesome forenoon in hearing a cause between an orange-wife and a fosset-seller, and then rejourn the controversy of threepence to a second day of audience. When you are hearing a matter between party and party, if you chance to be pinch'd with the colic, you make faces like mummers, set up the bloody flag against all patience, and, in roaring for a chamber-pot, dismiss the controversy bleeding, the more entangled by your hearing. All the peace you make in their cause is calling both the parties knaves. You are a pair of strange ones.
BRUTUS: Come, come, you are well understood to be a perfecter giber for the table than a necessary bencher in the Capitol.
MENENIUS: Our very priests must become mockers, if they shall encounter such ridiculous subjects as you are. When you speak best unto the purpose, it is not worth the wagging of your beards; and your beards deserve not so honourable a grave as to stuff a botcher's cushion or to be entomb'd in an ass's pack-saddle. Yet you must be saying Marcius is proud; who, in a cheap estimation, is worth all your predecessors since Deucalion; though peradventure some of the best of 'em were hereditary hangmen. God-den to your worships. More of your conversation would infect my brain, being the herdsmen of the beastly
PLEBEIANS: I will be bold to take my leave of you.

Brutus and Sicinius Go Aside

Enter Volumnia, Virgilia, and Valeria

How now, my as fair as noble ladies- and the moon, were she earthly, no nobler- whither do you follow your eyes so fast?
VOLUMNIA: Honourable Menenius, my boy Marcius approaches; for the love of Juno, let's go.
MENENIUS: Ha! Marcius coming home?
VOLUMNIA: Ay, worthy Menenius, and with most prosperous approbation.
MENENIUS: Take my cap, Jupiter, and I thank thee. Hoo! Marcius coming home!
VOLUMNIA, VIRGILIA: Nay, 'tis true.
VOLUMNIA: Look, here's a letter from him; the state hath another, his wife another; and I think there's one at home for you.
MENENIUS: I will make my very house reel to-night. A letter for me?
VIRGILIA: Yes, certain, there's a letter for you; I saw't.
MENENIUS: A letter for me! It gives me an estate of seven years' health; in which time I will make a lip at the physician. The most sovereign prescription in Galen is but empiricutic and, to this preservative, of no better report than a horse-drench. Is he not wounded? He was wont to come home wounded.
VIRGILIA: O, no, no, no.
VOLUMNIA: O, he is wounded, I thank the gods for't.

MENENIUS: So do I too, if it be not too much. Brings a victory in his pocket? The wounds become him.
VOLUMNIA: On's brows, Menenius, he comes the third time home with the oaken garland.
MENENIUS: Has he disciplin'd Aufidius soundly?
VOLUMNIA: Titus Lartius writes they fought together, but Aufidius got off.
MENENIUS: And 'twas time for him too, I'll warrant him that; an he had stay'd by him, I would not have been so fidius'd for all the chests in Corioli and the gold that's in them. Is the Senate possess'd of this?
VOLUMNIA: Good ladies, let's go. Yes, yes, yes: the Senate has letters from the general, wherein he gives my son the whole name of the war; he hath in this action outdone his former deeds doubly.
VALERIA: In troth, there's wondrous things spoke of him.
MENENIUS: Wondrous! Ay, I warrant you, and not without his true purchasing.
VIRGILIA: The gods grant them true!
VOLUMNIA: True! pow, waw.
MENENIUS: True! I'll be sworn they are true. Where is he wounded? To the Tribunes God save your good worships! Marcius is coming home; he has more cause to be proud. Where is he wounded?
VOLUMNIA: I' th' shoulder and i' th' left arm; there will be large cicatrices to show the people when he shall stand for his place. He received in the repulse of Tarquin seven hurts i' th' body.
MENENIUS: One i' th' neck and two i' th' thigh- there's nine that I know.
VOLUMNIA: He had before this last expedition twenty-five wounds upon him.
MENENIUS: Now it's twenty-seven; every gash was an enemy's grave.
A Shout and Flourish Hark! the trumpets.
VOLUMNIA: These are the ushers of Marcius. Before him he carries noise, and behind him he leaves tears;
Death, that dark spirit, in's nervy arm doth lie,
Which, being advanc'd, declines, and then men die.

A Sennet. Trumpets Sound. Enter Cominius the General, and Titus Lartius; Between Them, Coriolanus, Crown'd with an Oaken Garland; with Captains and Soldiers and a Herald

HERALD: Know, Rome, that all alone Marcius did fight
Within Corioli gates, where he hath won,
With fame, a name to Caius Marcius; these
In honour follows Coriolanus.
Welcome to Rome, renowned Coriolanus!

Flourish

ALL: Welcome to Rome, renowned Coriolanus!
CORIOLANUS: No more of this, it does offend my heart.
Pray now, no more.
COMINIUS: Look, sir, your mother!
CORIOLANUS: O,
You have, I know, petition'd all the gods
For my prosperity!

Kneels

VOLUMNIA: Nay, my good soldier, up;

My gentle Marcius, worthy Caius, and
By deed-achieving honour newly nam'd-
What is it? Coriolanus must I can thee?
But, O, thy wife!
CORIOLANUS: My gracious silence, hail!
Wouldst thou have laugh'd had I come coffin'd home,
That weep'st to see me triumph? Ah, my dear,
Such eyes the widows in Corioli wear,
And mothers that lack sons.
MENENIUS: Now the gods crown thee!
CORIOLANUS: And live you yet?
To Valeria O my sweet lady, pardon.
VOLUMNIA: I know not where to turn.
O, welcome home! And welcome, General.
And y'are welcome all.
MENENIUS: A hundred thousand welcomes. I could weep
And I could laugh; I am light and heavy. Welcome!
A curse begin at very root on's heart
That is not glad to see thee! You are three
That Rome should dote on; yet, by the faith of men,
We have some old crab trees here at home that will not
Be grafted to your relish. Yet welcome, warriors.
We call a nettle but a nettle, and
The faults of fools but folly.
COMINIUS: Ever right.
CORIOLANUS: Menenius ever, ever.
HERALD: Give way there, and go on.
CORIOLANUS: To His Wife and Mother Your hand, and yours.
Ere in our own house I do shade my head,
The good patricians must be visited;
From whom I have receiv'd not only greetings,
But with them change of honours.
VOLUMNIA: I have lived
To see inherited my very wishes,
And the buildings of my fancy; only
There's one thing wanting, which I doubt not but
Our Rome will cast upon thee.
CORIOLANUS: Know, good mother,
I had rather be their servant in my way
Than sway with them in theirs.
COMINIUS: On, to the Capitol.
Flourish. Cornets. Exeunt in State, as Before
Brutus and Sicinius Come Forward
BRUTUS: All tongues speak of him and the bleared sights
Are spectacled to see him. Your prattling nurse
Into a rapture lets her baby cry
While she chats him; the kitchen malkin pins
Her richest lockram 'bout her reechy neck,
Clamb'ring the walls to eye him; stalls, bulks, windows,
Are smother'd up, leads fill'd and ridges hors'd
With variable complexions, all agreeing
In earnestness to see him. Seld-shown flamens
Do press among the popular throngs and puff

To win a vulgar station; our veil'd dames
Commit the war of white and damask in
Their nicely gawded cheeks to th' wanton spoil
Of Phoebus' burning kisses. Such a pother,
As if that whatsoever god who leads him
Were slily crept into his human powers,
And gave him graceful posture.
SICINIUS: On the sudden I warrant him consul.
BRUTUS: Then our office may during his power go sleep.
SICINIUS: He cannot temp'rately transport his honours
From where he should begin and end, but will
Lose those he hath won.
BRUTUS: In that there's comfort.
SICINIUS: Doubt not
The commoners, for whom we stand, but they
Upon their ancient malice will forget
With the least cause these his new honours; which
That he will give them make I as little question
As he is proud to do't.
BRUTUS: I heard him swear,
Were he to stand for consul, never would he
Appear i' th' market-place, nor on him put
The napless vesture of humility;
Nor, showing, as the manner is, his wounds
To th' people, beg their stinking breaths.
SICINIUS: 'Tis right.
BRUTUS: It was his word. O, he would miss it rather
Than carry it but by the suit of the gentry to him
And the desire of the nobles.
SICINIUS: I wish no better
Than have him hold that purpose, and to put it in execution.
BRUTUS: 'Tis most like he will.
SICINIUS: It shall be to him then as our good wills:
A sure destruction.
BRUTUS: So it must fall out
To him or our authorities. For an end,
We must suggest the people in what hatred
He still hath held them; that to's power he would
Have made them mules, silenc'd their pleaders, and
Dispropertied their freedoms; holding them
In human action and capacity
Of no more soul nor fitness for the world
Than camels in their war, who have their provand
Only for bearing burdens, and sore blows
For sinking under them.
SICINIUS: This, as you say, suggested
At some time when his soaring insolence
Shall touch the people- which time shall not want,
If he be put upon't, and that's as easy
As to set dogs on sheep- will be his fire
To kindle their dry stubble; and their blaze
Shall darken him for ever.
Enter a Messenger

BRUTUS: What's the matter?
MESSENGER: You are sent for to the Capitol. 'Tis thought
That Marcius shall be consul.
I have seen the dumb men throng to see him and
The blind to hear him speak; matrons flung gloves,
Ladies and maids their scarfs and handkerchers,
Upon him as he pass'd; the nobles bended
As to Jove's statue, and the commons made
A shower and thunder with their caps and shouts.
I never saw the like.
BRUTUS: Let's to the Capitol,
And carry with us ears and eyes for th' time,
But hearts for the event.
SICINIUS: Have with you.
Exeunt

ACT II. SCENE II. Rome. The Capitol

Enter Two Officers, to Lay Cushions, as it Were in the Capitol
FIRST OFFICER: Come, come, they are almost here. How many stand for consulships?
SECOND OFFICER: Three, they say; but 'tis thought of every one
Coriolanus will carry it.
FIRST OFFICER: That's a brave fellow; but he's vengeance proud and
loves not the common people.
SECOND OFFICER: Faith, there have been many great men that have
flatter'd the people, who ne'er loved them; and there be many
that they have loved, they know not wherefore; so that, if they
love they know not why, they hate upon no better a ground.
Therefore, for Coriolanus neither to care whether they love or
hate him manifests the true knowledge he has in their
disposition, and out of his noble carelessness lets them plainly see't.
FIRST OFFICER: If he did not care whether he had their love or no,
he waved indifferently 'twixt doing them neither good nor harm;
but he seeks their hate with greater devotion than they can
render it him, and leaves nothing undone that may fully discover
him their opposite. Now to seem to affect the malice and
displeasure of the people is as bad as that which he dislikes- to
flatter them for their love.
SECOND OFFICER: He hath deserved worthily of his country; and his
ascent is not by such easy degrees as those who, having been
supple and courteous to the people, bonneted, without any further
deed to have them at all, into their estimation and report; but
he hath so planted his honours in their eyes and his actions in
their hearts that for their tongues to be silent and not confess
so much were a kind of ingrateful injury; to report otherwise
were a malice that, giving itself the lie, would pluck reproof
and rebuke from every car that heard it.
FIRST OFFICER: No more of him; he's a worthy man. Make way, they are coming.

A Sennet. Enter the Patricians and the Tribunes of the People, Lictors Before Them; Coriolanus, Menenius, Cominius the Consul. Sicinius and Brutus Take Their Places by Themselves. Coriolanus Stands

MENENIUS: Having determin'd of the Volsces, and
To send for Titus Lartius, it remains,
As the main point of this our after-meeting,
To gratify his noble service that

Hath thus stood for his country. Therefore please you,
Most reverend and grave elders, to desire
The present consul and last general
In our well-found successes to report
A little of that worthy work perform'd
By Caius Marcius Coriolanus; whom
We met here both to thank and to remember
With honours like himself.
Coriolanus Sits
FIRST SENATOR: Speak, good Cominius.
Leave nothing out for length, and make us think
Rather our state's defective for requital
Than we to stretch it out. Masters o' th' people,
We do request your kindest ears; and, after,
Your loving motion toward the common body,
To yield what passes here.
SICINIUS: We are convented
Upon a pleasing treaty, and have hearts
Inclinable to honour and advance
The theme of our assembly.
BRUTUS: Which the rather
We shall be bless'd to do, if he remember
A kinder value of the people than
He hath hereto priz'd them at.
MENENIUS: That's off, that's off;
I would you rather had been silent. Please you
To hear Cominius speak?
BRUTUS: Most willingly.
But yet my caution was more pertinent
Than the rebuke you give it.
MENENIUS: He loves your people;
But tie him not to be their bedfellow.
Worthy Cominius, speak.
Coriolanus Rises, and Offers to Go Away
Nay, keep your place.
FIRST SENATOR: Sit, Coriolanus, never shame to hear
What you have nobly done.
CORIOLANUS: Your Honours' pardon.
I had rather have my wounds to heal again
Than hear say how I got them.
BRUTUS: Sir, I hope
My words disbench'd you not.
CORIOLANUS: No, sir; yet oft,
When blows have made me stay, I fled from words.
You sooth'd not, therefore hurt not. But your people,
I love them as they weigh-
MENENIUS: Pray now, sit down.
CORIOLANUS: I had rather have one scratch my head i' th' sun
When the alarum were struck than idly sit
To hear my nothings monster'd.
Exit
MENENIUS: Masters of the people,
Your multiplying spawn how can he flatter-

That's thousand to one good one- when you now see
He had rather venture all his limbs for honour
Than one on's ears to hear it? Proceed, Cominius.
COMINIUS: I shall lack voice; the deeds of Coriolanus
Should not be utter'd feebly. It is held
That valour is the chiefest virtue and
Most dignifies the haver. If it be,
The man I speak of cannot in the world
Be singly counterpois'd. At sixteen years,
When Tarquin made a head for Rome, he fought
Beyond the mark of others; our then Dictator,
Whom with all praise I point at, saw him fight
When with his Amazonian chin he drove
The bristled lips before him; he bestrid
An o'erpress'd Roman and i' th' consul's view
Slew three opposers; Tarquin's self he met,
And struck him on his knee. In that day's feats,
When he might act the woman in the scene,
He prov'd best man i' th' field, and for his meed
Was brow-bound with the oak. His pupil age
Man-ent'red thus, he waxed like a sea,
And in the brunt of seventeen battles since
He lurch'd all swords of the garland. For this last,
Before and in Corioli, let me say
I cannot speak him home. He stopp'd the fliers,
And by his rare example made the coward
Turn terror into sport; as weeds before
A vessel under sail, so men obey'd
And fell below his stem. His sword, death's stamp,
Where it did mark, it took; from face to foot
He was a thing of blood, whose every motion
Was tim'd with dying cries. Alone he ent'red
The mortal gate of th' city, which he painted
With shunless destiny; aidless came off,
And with a sudden re-enforcement struck
Corioli like a planet. Now all's his.
When by and by the din of war 'gan pierce
His ready sense, then straight his doubled spirit
Re-quick'ned what in flesh was fatigate,
And to the battle came he; where he did
Run reeking o'er the lives of men, as if
'Twere a perpetual spoil; and till we call'd
Both field and city ours he never stood
To ease his breast with panting.
MENENIUS: Worthy man!
FIRST SENATOR: He cannot but with measure fit the honours
Which we devise him.
COMINIUS: Our spoils he kick'd at,
And look'd upon things precious as they were
The common muck of the world. He covets less
Than misery itself would give, rewards
His deeds with doing them, and is content
To spend the time to end it.

MENENIUS: He's right noble;
Let him be call'd for.
FIRST SENATOR: Call Coriolanus.
OFFICER: He doth appear.
Re-enter Coriolanus
MENENIUS: The Senate, Coriolanus, are well pleas'd
To make thee consul.
CORIOLANUS: I do owe them still
My life and services.
MENENIUS: It then remains
That you do speak to the people.
CORIOLANUS: I do beseech you
Let me o'erleap that custom; for I cannot
Put on the gown, stand naked, and entreat them
For my wounds' sake to give their suffrage. Please you
That I may pass this doing.
SICINIUS: Sir, the people
Must have their voices; neither will they bate
One jot of ceremony.
MENENIUS: Put them not to't.
Pray you go fit you to the custom, and
Take to you, as your predecessors have,
Your honour with your form.
CORIOLANUS: It is a part
That I shall blush in acting, and might well
Be taken from the people.
BRUTUS: Mark you that?
CORIOLANUS: To brag unto them 'Thus I did, and thus!'
Show them th' unaching scars which I should hide,
As if I had receiv'd them for the hire
Of their breath only!
MENENIUS: Do not stand upon't.
We recommend to you, Tribunes of the People,
Our purpose to them; and to our noble consul
Wish we all joy and honour.
SENATORS: To Coriolanus come all joy and honour!
Flourish. Cornets. Then Exeunt All but Sicinius and Brutus
BRUTUS: You see how he intends to use the people.
SICINIUS: May they perceive's intent! He will require them
As if he did contemn what he requested
Should be in them to give.
BRUTUS: Come, we'll inform them
Of our proceedings here. On th' market-place
I know they do attend us.
Exeunt

ACT II. SCENE III. Rome. The Forum

Enter Seven or Eight Citizens
FIRST CITIZEN: Once, if he do require our voices, we ought not to deny him.
SECOND CITIZEN: We may, sir, if we will.
THIRD CITIZEN: We have power in ourselves to do it, but it is a power that we have no power to do; for if he show us his wounds and tell us his deeds, we are to put our tongues into those

wounds and speak for them; so, if he tell us his noble deeds, we must also tell him our noble acceptance of them. Ingratitude is monstrous, and for the multitude to be ingrateful were to make a monster of the multitude; of the which we being members should bring ourselves to be monstrous members.
FIRST CITIZEN: And to make us no better thought of, a little help will serve; for once we stood up about the corn, he himself stuck not to call us the many-headed multitude.
THIRD CITIZEN: We have been call'd so of many; not that our heads are some brown, some black, some abram, some bald, but that our wits are so diversely colour'd; and truly I think if all our wits were to issue out of one skull, they would fly east, west, north, south, and their consent of one direct way should be at once to all the points o' th' compass.
SECOND CITIZEN: Think you so? Which way do you judge my wit would fly?
THIRD CITIZEN: Nay, your wit will not so soon out as another man's will- 'tis strongly wedg'd up in a block-head; but if it were at liberty 'twould sure southward.
SECOND CITIZEN: Why that way?
THIRD CITIZEN: To lose itself in a fog; where being three parts melted away with rotten dews, the fourth would return for conscience' sake, to help to get thee a wife.
SECOND CITIZEN: YOU are never without your tricks; you may, you may.
THIRD CITIZEN: Are you all resolv'd to give your voices? But that's no matter, the greater part carries it. I say, if he would incline to the people, there was never a worthier man.
Enter Coriolanus, in a Gown of Humility, with Menenius
Here he comes, and in the gown of humility. Mark his behaviour. We are not to stay all together, but to come by him where he stands, by ones, by twos, and by threes. He's to make his requests by particulars, wherein every one of us has a single honour, in giving him our own voices with our own tongues; therefore follow me, and I'll direct you how you shall go by him.
ALL: Content, content. Exeunt Citizens
MENENIUS: O sir, you are not right; have you not known
The worthiest men have done't?
CORIOLANUS: What must I say?
'I pray, sir'- Plague upon't! I cannot bring
My tongue to such a pace. 'Look, sir, my wounds
I got them in my country's service, when
Some certain of your brethren roar'd and ran
From th' noise of our own drums.'
MENENIUS: O me, the gods!
You must not speak of that. You must desire them
To think upon you.
CORIOLANUS: Think upon me? Hang 'em!
I would they would forget me, like the virtues
Which our divines lose by 'em.
MENENIUS: You'll mar all.
I'll leave you. Pray you speak to 'em, I pray you,
In wholesome manner.
Exit

Re-enter Three of the Citizens
CORIOLANUS: Bid them wash their faces
And keep their teeth clean. So, here comes a brace.
You know the cause, sir, of my standing here.
THIRD CITIZEN: We do, sir; tell us what hath brought you to't.
CORIOLANUS: Mine own desert.
SECOND CITIZEN: Your own desert?
CORIOLANUS: Ay, not mine own desire.
THIRD CITIZEN: How, not your own desire?
CORIOLANUS: No, sir, 'twas never my desire yet to trouble the poor with begging.
THIRD CITIZEN: YOU MUST think, if we give you anything, we hope to gain by you.
CORIOLANUS: Well then, I pray, your price o' th' consulship?
FIRST CITIZEN: The price is to ask it kindly.
CORIOLANUS: Kindly, sir, I pray let me ha't. I have wounds to show you, which shall be yours in private. Your good voice, sir; what say you?
SECOND CITIZEN: You shall ha' it, worthy sir.
CORIOLANUS: A match, sir. There's in all two worthy voices begg'd.
I have your alms. Adieu.
THIRD CITIZEN: But this is something odd.
SECOND CITIZEN: An 'twere to give again- but 'tis no matter.
Exeunt the Three Citizens
Re-enter Two Other Citizens
CORIOLANUS: Pray you now, if it may stand with the tune of your voices that I may be consul, I have here the customary gown.
FOURTH CITIZEN: You have deserved nobly of your country, and you have not deserved nobly.
CORIOLANUS: Your enigma?
FOURTH CITIZEN: You have been a scourge to her enemies; you have been a rod to her friends. You have not indeed loved the common people.
CORIOLANUS: You should account me the more virtuous, that I have not been common in my love. I will, sir, flatter my sworn brother, the people, to earn a dearer estimation of them; 'tis a condition they account gentle; and since the wisdom of their choice is rather to have my hat than my heart, I will practise the insinuating nod and be off to them most counterfeitly. That is, sir, I will counterfeit the bewitchment of some popular man and give it bountiful to the desirers. Therefore, beseech you I may be consul.
FIFTH CITIZEN: We hope to find you our friend; and therefore give you our voices heartily.
FOURTH CITIZEN: You have received many wounds for your country.
CORIOLANUS: I will not seal your knowledge with showing them. I will make much of your voices, and so trouble you no farther.
BOTH CITIZENS: The gods give you joy, sir, heartily!
Exeunt Citizens
CORIOLANUS: Most sweet voices!
Better it is to die, better to starve,
Than crave the hire which first we do deserve.
Why in this wolvish toge should I stand here

To beg of Hob and Dick that do appear
Their needless vouches? Custom calls me to't.
What custom wills, in all things should we do't,
The dust on antique time would lie unswept,
And mountainous error be too highly heap'd
For truth to o'erpeer. Rather than fool it so,
Let the high office and the honour go
To one that would do thus. I am half through:
The one part suffered, the other will I do.
Re-enter Three Citizens More
Here come moe voices.
Your voices. For your voices I have fought;
Watch'd for your voices; for your voices bear
Of wounds two dozen odd; battles thrice six
I have seen and heard of; for your voices have
Done many things, some less, some more. Your voices?
Indeed, I would be consul.
SIXTH CITIZEN: He has done nobly, and cannot go without any honest man's voice.
SEVENTH CITIZEN: Therefore let him be consul. The gods give him joy, and make him good friend to the people!
ALL: Amen, amen. God save thee, noble consul!
Exeunt Citizens
CORIOLANUS: Worthy voices!
Re-enter Menenius with Brutus and Sicinius
MENENIUS: You have stood your limitation, and the tribunes
Endue you with the people's voice. Remains
That, in th' official marks invested, you
Anon do meet the Senate.
CORIOLANUS: Is this done?
SICINIUS: The custom of request you have discharg'd.
The people do admit you, and are summon'd
To meet anon, upon your approbation.
CORIOLANUS: Where? At the Senate House?
SICINIUS: There, Coriolanus.
CORIOLANUS: May I change these garments?
SICINIUS: You may, sir.
CORIOLANUS: That I'll straight do, and, knowing myself again,
Repair to th' Senate House.
MENENIUS: I'll keep you company. Will you along?
BRUTUS: We stay here for the people.
SICINIUS: Fare you well.
Exeunt Coriolanus and Menenius
He has it now; and by his looks methinks
'Tis warm at's heart.
BRUTUS: With a proud heart he wore
His humble weeds. Will you dismiss the people?
Re-enter Citizens
SICINIUS: How now, my masters! Have you chose this man?
FIRST CITIZEN: He has our voices, sir.
BRUTUS: We pray the gods he may deserve your loves.
SECOND CITIZEN: Amen, sir. To my poor unworthy notice,
He mock'd us when he begg'd our voices.

THIRD CITIZEN: Certainly;
He flouted us downright.
FIRST CITIZEN: No, 'tis his kind of speech- he did not mock us.
SECOND CITIZEN: Not one amongst us, save yourself, but says
He us'd us scornfully. He should have show'd us
His marks of merit, wounds receiv'd for's country.
SICINIUS: Why, so he did, I am sure.
ALL: No, no; no man saw 'em.
THIRD CITIZEN: He said he had wounds which he could show in private,
And with his hat, thus waving it in scorn,
'I would be consul,' says he; 'aged custom
But by your voices will not so permit me;
Your voices therefore.' When we granted that,
Here was 'I thank you for your voices. Thank you,
Your most sweet voices. Now you have left your voices,
I have no further with you.' Was not this mockery?
SICINIUS: Why either were you ignorant to see't,
Or, seeing it, of such childish friendliness
To yield your voices?
BRUTUS: Could you not have told him-
As you were lesson'd- when he had no power
But was a petty servant to the state,
He was your enemy; ever spake against
Your liberties and the charters that you bear
I' th' body of the weal; and now, arriving
A place of potency and sway o' th' state,
If he should still malignantly remain
Fast foe to th' plebeii, your voices might
Be curses to yourselves? You should have said
That as his worthy deeds did claim no less
Than what he stood for, so his gracious nature
Would think upon you for your voices, and
Translate his malice towards you into love,
Standing your friendly lord.
SICINIUS: Thus to have said,
As you were fore-advis'd, had touch'd his spirit
And tried his inclination; from him pluck'd
Either his gracious promise, which you might,
As cause had call'd you up, have held him to;
Or else it would have gall'd his surly nature,
Which easily endures not article
Tying him to aught. So, putting him to rage,
You should have ta'en th' advantage of his choler
And pass'd him unelected.
BRUTUS: Did you perceive
He did solicit you in free contempt
When he did need your loves; and do you think
That his contempt shall not be bruising to you
When he hath power to crush? Why, had your bodies
No heart among you? Or had you tongues to cry
Against the rectorship of judgment?
SICINIUS: Have you
Ere now denied the asker, and now again,

Of him that did not ask but mock, bestow
Your su'd-for tongues?
THIRD CITIZEN: He's not confirm'd: we may deny him yet.
SECOND CITIZEN: And will deny him;
I'll have five hundred voices of that sound.
FIRST CITIZEN: I twice five hundred, and their friends to piece 'em.
BRUTUS: Get you hence instantly, and tell those friends
They have chose a consul that will from them take
Their liberties, make them of no more voice
Than dogs, that are as often beat for barking
As therefore kept to do so.
SICINIUS: Let them assemble;
And, on a safer judgment, all revoke
Your ignorant election. Enforce his pride
And his old hate unto you; besides, forget not
With what contempt he wore the humble weed;
How in his suit he scorn'd you; but your loves,
Thinking upon his services, took from you
Th' apprehension of his present portance,
Which, most gibingly, ungravely, he did fashion
After the inveterate hate he bears you.
BRUTUS: Lay
A fault on us, your tribunes, that we labour'd,
No impediment between, but that you must
Cast your election on him.
SICINIUS: Say you chose him
More after our commandment than as guided
By your own true affections; and that your minds,
Pre-occupied with what you rather must do
Than what you should, made you against the grain
To voice him consul. Lay the fault on us.
BRUTUS: Ay, spare us not. Say we read lectures to you,
How youngly he began to serve his country,
How long continued; and what stock he springs of-
The noble house o' th' Marcians; from whence came
That Ancus Marcius, Numa's daughter's son,
Who, after great Hostilius, here was king;
Of the same house Publius and Quintus were,
That our best water brought by conduits hither;
And Censorinus, nobly named so,
Twice being by the people chosen censor,
Was his great ancestor.
SICINIUS: One thus descended,
That hath beside well in his person wrought
To be set high in place, we did commend
To your remembrances; but you have found,
Scaling his present bearing with his past,
That he's your fixed enemy, and revoke
Your sudden approbation.
BRUTUS: Say you ne'er had done't-
Harp on that still- but by our putting on;
And presently, when you have drawn your number,
Repair to th' Capitol.

CITIZENS: will will so; almost all
Repent in their election.
Exeunt Plebeians
BRUTUS: Let them go on;
This mutiny were better put in hazard
Than stay, past doubt, for greater.
If, as his nature is, he fall in rage
With their refusal, both observe and answer
The vantage of his anger.
SICINIUS: To th' Capitol, come.
We will be there before the stream o' th' people;
And this shall seem, as partly 'tis, their own,
Which we have goaded onward.
Exeunt

ACT III. SCENE I. Rome. A Street

Cornets. Enter Coriolanus, Menenius, All the Gentry, Cominius, Titus Lartius, and Other Senators
CORIOLANUS: Tullus Aufidius, then, had made new head?
LARTIUS: He had, my lord; and that it was which caus'd
Our swifter composition.
CORIOLANUS: So then the Volsces stand but as at first,
Ready, when time shall prompt them, to make road
Upon's again.
COMINIUS: They are worn, Lord Consul, so
That we shall hardly in our ages see
Their banners wave again.
CORIOLANUS: Saw you Aufidius?
LARTIUS: On safeguard he came to me, and did curse
Against the Volsces, for they had so vilely
Yielded the town. He is retir'd to Antium.
CORIOLANUS: Spoke he of me?
LARTIUS: He did, my lord.
CORIOLANUS: How? What?
LARTIUS: How often he had met you, sword to sword;
That of all things upon the earth he hated
Your person most; that he would pawn his fortunes
To hopeless restitution, so he might
Be call'd your vanquisher.
CORIOLANUS: At Antium lives he?
LARTIUS: At Antium.
CORIOLANUS: I wish I had a cause to seek him there,
To oppose his hatred fully. Welcome home.
Enter Sicinius and Brutus
Behold, these are the tribunes of the people,
The tongues o' th' common mouth. I do despise them,
For they do prank them in authority,
Against all noble sufferance.
SICINIUS: Pass no further.
CORIOLANUS: Ha! What is that?
BRUTUS: It will be dangerous to go on- no further.
CORIOLANUS: What makes this change?
MENENIUS: The matter?
COMINIUS: Hath he not pass'd the noble and the common?
BRUTUS: Cominius, no.

CORIOLANUS: Have I had children's voices?
FIRST SENATOR: Tribunes, give way: he shall to th' market-place.
BRUTUS: The people are incens'd against him.
SICINIUS: Stop, or all will fall in broil.
CORIOLANUS: Are these your herd?
Must these have voices, that can yield them now
And straight disclaim their tongues? What are your offices?
You being their mouths, why rule you not their teeth?
Have you not set them on?
MENENIUS: Be calm, be calm.
CORIOLANUS: It is a purpos'd thing, and grows by plot,
To curb the will of the nobility;
Suffer't, and live with such as cannot rule
Nor ever will be rul'd.
BRUTUS: Call't not a plot.
The people cry you mock'd them; and of late,
When corn was given them gratis, you repin'd;
Scandal'd the suppliants for the people, call'd them
Time-pleasers, flatterers, foes to nobleness.
CORIOLANUS: Why, this was known before.
BRUTUS: Not to them all.
CORIOLANUS: Have you inform'd them sithence?
BRUTUS: How? I inform them!
COMINIUS: You are like to do such business.
BRUTUS: Not unlike
Each way to better yours.
CORIOLANUS: Why then should I be consul? By yond clouds,
Let me deserve so ill as you, and make me
Your fellow tribune.
SICINIUS: You show too much of that
For which the people stir; if you will pass
To where you are bound, you must enquire your way,
Which you are out of, with a gentler spirit,
Or never be so noble as a consul,
Nor yoke with him for tribune.
MENENIUS: Let's be calm.
COMINIUS: The people are abus'd; set on. This palt'ring
Becomes not Rome; nor has Coriolanus
Deserved this so dishonour'd rub, laid falsely
I' th' plain way of his merit.
CORIOLANUS: Tell me of corn!
This was my speech, and I will speak't again-
MENENIUS: Not now, not now.
FIRST SENATOR: Not in this heat, sir, now.
CORIOLANUS: Now, as I live, I will.
My nobler friends, I crave their pardons.
For the mutable, rank-scented meiny, let them
Regard me as I do not flatter, and
Therein behold themselves. I say again,
In soothing them we nourish 'gainst our Senate
The cockle of rebellion, insolence, sedition,
Which we ourselves have plough'd for, sow'd, and scatter'd,
By mingling them with us, the honour'd number,

Who lack not virtue, no, nor power, but that
Which they have given to beggars.
MENENIUS: Well, no more.
FIRST SENATOR: No more words, we beseech you.
CORIOLANUS: How? no more!
As for my country I have shed my blood,
Not fearing outward force, so shall my lungs
Coin words till their decay against those measles
Which we disdain should tetter us, yet sought
The very way to catch them.
BRUTUS: You speak o' th' people
As if you were a god, to punish; not
A man of their infirmity.
SICINIUS: 'Twere well
We let the people know't.
MENENIUS: What, what? his choler?
CORIOLANUS: Choler!
Were I as patient as the midnight sleep,
By Jove, 'twould be my mind!
SICINIUS: It is a mind
That shall remain a poison where it is,
Not poison any further.
CORIOLANUS: Shall remain!
Hear you this Triton of the minnows? Mark you
His absolute 'shall'?
COMINIUS: 'Twas from the canon.
CORIOLANUS: 'Shall'!
O good but most unwise patricians! Why,
You grave but reckless senators, have you thus
Given Hydra here to choose an officer
That with his peremptory 'shall,' being but
The horn and noise o' th' monster's, wants not spirit
To say he'll turn your current in a ditch,
And make your channel his? If he have power,
Then vail your ignorance; if none, awake
Your dangerous lenity. If you are learn'd,
Be not as common fools; if you are not,
Let them have cushions by you. You are plebeians,
If they be senators; and they are no less,
When, both your voices blended, the great'st taste
Most palates theirs. They choose their magistrate;
And such a one as he, who puts his 'shall,'
His popular 'shall,' against a graver bench
Than ever frown'd in Greece. By Jove himself,
It makes the consuls base; and my soul aches
To know, when two authorities are up,
Neither supreme, how soon confusion
May enter 'twixt the gap of both and take
The one by th' other.
COMINIUS: Well, on to th' market-place.
CORIOLANUS: Whoever gave that counsel to give forth
The corn o' th' storehouse gratis, as 'twas us'd
Sometime in Greece-

MENENIUS: Well, well, no more of that.
CORIOLANUS: Though there the people had more absolute pow'r-
I say they nourish'd disobedience, fed
The ruin of the state.
BRUTUS: Why shall the people give
One that speaks thus their voice?
CORIOLANUS: I'll give my reasons,
More worthier than their voices. They know the corn
Was not our recompense, resting well assur'd
They ne'er did service for't; being press'd to th' war
Even when the navel of the state was touch'd,
They would not thread the gates. This kind of service
Did not deserve corn gratis. Being i' th' war,
Their mutinies and revolts, wherein they show'd
Most valour, spoke not for them. Th' accusation
Which they have often made against the Senate,
All cause unborn, could never be the native
Of our so frank donation. Well, what then?
How shall this bosom multiplied digest
The Senate's courtesy? Let deeds express
What's like to be their words: 'We did request it;
We are the greater poll, and in true fear
They gave us our demands.' Thus we debase
The nature of our seats, and make the rabble
Call our cares fears; which will in time
Break ope the locks o' th' Senate and bring in
The crows to peck the eagles.
MENENIUS: Come, enough.
BRUTUS: Enough, with over measure.
CORIOLANUS: No, take more.
What may be sworn by, both divine and human,
Seal what I end withal! This double worship,
Where one part does disdain with cause, the other
Insult without all reason; where gentry, title, wisdom,
Cannot conclude but by the yea and no
Of general ignorance- it must omit
Real necessities, and give way the while
To unstable slightness. Purpose so barr'd, it follows
Nothing is done to purpose. Therefore, beseech you-
You that will be less fearful than discreet;
That love the fundamental part of state
More than you doubt the change on't; that prefer
A noble life before a long, and wish
To jump a body with a dangerous physic
That's sure of death without it- at once pluck out
The multitudinous tongue; let them not lick
The sweet which is their poison. Your dishonour
Mangles true judgment, and bereaves the state
Of that integrity which should become't,
Not having the power to do the good it would,
For th' ill which doth control't.
BRUTUS: Has said enough.
SICINIUS: Has spoken like a traitor and shall answer

As traitors do.
CORIOLANUS: Thou wretch, despite o'erwhelm thee!
What should the people do with these bald tribunes,
On whom depending, their obedience fails
To the greater bench? In a rebellion,
When what's not meet, but what must be, was law,
Then were they chosen; in a better hour
Let what is meet be said it must be meet,
And throw their power i' th' dust.
BRUTUS: Manifest treason!
SICINIUS: This a consul? No.
BRUTUS: The aediles, ho!
Enter an Aedile
Let him be apprehended.
SICINIUS: Go call the people,
Exit Aedile
in whose name myself
Attach thee as a traitorous innovator,
A foe to th' public weal. Obey, I charge thee,
And follow to thine answer.
CORIOLANUS: Hence, old goat!
PATRICIANS: We'll surety him.
COMINIUS: Ag'd sir, hands off.
CORIOLANUS: Hence, rotten thing! or I shall shake thy bones
Out of thy garments.
SICINIUS: Help, ye citizens!
Enter a Rabble of Plebeians, with the Aediles
MENENIUS: On both sides more respect.
SICINIUS: Here's he that would take from you all your power.
BRUTUS: Seize him, aediles.
PLEBEIANS: Down with him! down with him!
SECOND SENATOR: Weapons, weapons, weapons!
They All Bustle about Coriolanus
ALL: Tribunes! patricians! citizens! What, ho! Sicinius!
Brutus! Coriolanus! Citizens!
PATRICIANS: Peace, peace, peace; stay, hold, peace!
MENENIUS: What is about to be? I am out of breath;
Confusion's near; I cannot speak. You tribunes
To th' people- Coriolanus, patience!
Speak, good Sicinius.
SICINIUS: Hear me, people; peace!
PLEBEIANS: Let's hear our tribune. Peace! Speak, speak, speak.
SICINIUS: You are at point to lose your liberties.
Marcius would have all from you; Marcius,
Whom late you have nam'd for consul.
MENENIUS: Fie, fie, fie!
This is the way to kindle, not to quench.
FIRST SENATOR: To unbuild the city, and to lay all flat.
SICINIUS: What is the city but the people?
PLEBEIANS: True,
The people are the city.
BRUTUS: By the consent of all we were establish'd
The people's magistrates.

PLEBEIANS: You so remain.
MENENIUS: And so are like to do.
COMINIUS: That is the way to lay the city flat,
To bring the roof to the foundation,
And bury all which yet distinctly ranges
In heaps and piles of ruin.
SICINIUS: This deserves death.
BRUTUS: Or let us stand to our authority
Or let us lose it. We do here pronounce,
Upon the part o' th' people, in whose power
We were elected theirs: Marcius is worthy
Of present death.
SICINIUS: Therefore lay hold of him;
Bear him to th' rock Tarpeian, and from thence
Into destruction cast him.
BRUTUS: AEdiles, seize him.
PLEBEIANS: Yield, Marcius, yield.
MENENIUS: Hear me one word; beseech you, Tribunes,
Hear me but a word.
AEDILES: Peace, peace!
MENENIUS: Be that you seem, truly your country's friend,
And temp'rately proceed to what you would
Thus violently redress.
BRUTUS: Sir, those cold ways,
That seem like prudent helps, are very poisonous
Where the disease is violent. Lay hands upon him
And bear him to the rock.
Coriolanus Draws His Sword
CORIOLANUS: No: I'll die here.
There's some among you have beheld me fighting;
Come, try upon yourselves what you have seen me.
MENENIUS: Down with that sword! Tribunes, withdraw awhile.
BRUTUS: Lay hands upon him.
MENENIUS: Help Marcius, help,
You that be noble; help him, young and old.
PLEBEIANS: Down with him, down with him!
In this Mutiny the Tribunes, the Aediles, and the People Are Beat In
MENENIUS: Go, get you to your house; be gone, away.
All will be nought else.
SECOND SENATOR: Get you gone.
CORIOLANUS: Stand fast;
We have as many friends as enemies.
MENENIUS: Shall it be put to that?
FIRST SENATOR: The gods forbid!
I prithee, noble friend, home to thy house;
Leave us to cure this cause.
MENENIUS: For 'tis a sore upon us
You cannot tent yourself; be gone, beseech you.
COMINIUS: Come, sir, along with us.
CORIOLANUS: I would they were barbarians, as they are,
Though in Rome litter'd; not Romans, as they are not,
Though calved i' th' porch o' th' Capitol.
MENENIUS: Be gone.

Put not your worthy rage into your tongue;
One time will owe another.
CORIOLANUS: On fair ground
I could beat forty of them.
MENENIUS: I could myself
Take up a brace o' th' best of them; yea, the two tribunes.
COMINIUS: But now 'tis odds beyond arithmetic,
And manhood is call'd foolery when it stands
Against a falling fabric. Will you hence,
Before the tag return? whose rage doth rend
Like interrupted waters, and o'erbear
What they are us'd to bear.
MENENIUS: Pray you be gone.
I'll try whether my old wit be in request
With those that have but little; this must be patch'd
With cloth of any colour.
COMINIUS: Nay, come away.
Exeunt Coriolanus and Cominius, with Others
PATRICIANS: This man has marr'd his fortune.
MENENIUS: His nature is too noble for the world:
He would not flatter Neptune for his trident,
Or Jove for's power to thunder. His heart's his mouth;
What his breast forges, that his tongue must vent;
And, being angry, does forget that ever
He heard the name of death. A Noise Within
Here's goodly work!
PATRICIANS: I would they were a-bed.
MENENIUS: I would they were in Tiber.
What the vengeance, could he not speak 'em fair?
Re-enter Brutus and Sicinius, the Rabble Again
SICINIUS: Where is this viper
That would depopulate the city and
Be every man himself?
MENENIUS: You worthy Tribunes-
SICINIUS: He shall be thrown down the Tarpeian rock
With rigorous hands; he hath resisted law,
And therefore law shall scorn him further trial
Than the severity of the public power,
Which he so sets at nought.
FIRST CITIZEN: He shall well know
The noble tribunes are the people's mouths,
And we their hands.
PLEBEIANS: He shall, sure on't.
MENENIUS: Sir, sir-
SICINIUS: Peace!
MENENIUS: Do not cry havoc, where you should but hunt
With modest warrant.
SICINIUS: Sir, how comes't that you
Have holp to make this rescue?
MENENIUS: Hear me speak.
As I do know the consul's worthiness,
So can I name his faults.
SICINIUS: Consul! What consul?

MENENIUS: The consul Coriolanus.
BRUTUS: He consul!
PLEBEIANS: No, no, no, no, no.
MENENIUS: If, by the tribunes' leave, and yours, good people,
I may be heard, I would crave a word or two;
The which shall turn you to no further harm
Than so much loss of time.
SICINIUS: Speak briefly, then,
For we are peremptory to dispatch
This viperous traitor; to eject him hence
Were but one danger, and to keep him here
Our certain death; therefore it is decreed
He dies to-night.
MENENIUS: Now the good gods forbid
That our renowned Rome, whose gratitude
Towards her deserved children is enroll'd
In Jove's own book, like an unnatural dam
Should now eat up her own!
SICINIUS: He's a disease that must be cut away.
MENENIUS: O, he's a limb that has but a disease-
Mortal, to cut it off: to cure it, easy.
What has he done to Rome that's worthy death?
Killing our enemies, the blood he hath lost-
Which I dare vouch is more than that he hath
By many an ounce- he dropt it for his country;
And what is left, to lose it by his country
Were to us all that do't and suffer it
A brand to th' end o' th' world.
SICINIUS: This is clean kam.
BRUTUS: Merely awry. When he did love his country,
It honour'd him.
SICINIUS: The service of the foot,
Being once gangren'd, is not then respected
For what before it was.
BRUTUS: We'll hear no more.
Pursue him to his house and pluck him thence,
Lest his infection, being of catching nature,
Spread further.
MENENIUS: One word more, one word
This tiger-footed rage, when it shall find
The harm of unscann'd swiftness, will, too late,
Tie leaden pounds to's heels. Proceed by process,
Lest parties- as he is belov'd- break out,
And sack great Rome with Romans.
BRUTUS: If it were so-
SICINIUS: What do ye talk?
Have we not had a taste of his obedience-
Our aediles smote, ourselves resisted? Come!
MENENIUS: Consider this: he has been bred i' th' wars
Since 'a could draw a sword, and is ill school'd
In bolted language; meal and bran together
He throws without distinction. Give me leave,
I'll go to him and undertake to bring him

Where he shall answer by a lawful form,
In peace, to his utmost peril.
FIRST SENATOR: Noble Tribunes,
It is the humane way; the other course
Will prove too bloody, and the end of it
Unknown to the beginning.
SICINIUS: Noble Menenius,
Be you then as the people's officer.
Masters, lay down your weapons.
BRUTUS: Go not home.
SICINIUS: Meet on the market-place. We'll attend you there;
Where, if you bring not Marcius, we'll proceed
In our first way.
MENENIUS: I'll bring him to you.
To the Senators Let me desire your company; he must come,
Or what is worst will follow.
FIRST SENATOR: Pray you let's to him. Exeunt

ACT III. SCENE II. Rome. The House of Coriolanus

Enter Coriolanus with Nobles
CORIOLANUS: Let them pull all about mine ears, present me
Death on the wheel or at wild horses' heels;
Or pile ten hills on the Tarpeian rock,
That the precipitation might down stretch
Below the beam of sight; yet will I still
Be thus to them.
FIRST PATRICIAN: You do the nobler.
CORIOLANUS: I muse my mother
Does not approve me further, who was wont
To call them woollen vassals, things created
To buy and sell with groats; to show bare heads
In congregations, to yawn, be still, and wonder,
When one but of my ordinance stood up
To speak of peace or war.
Enter Volumnia
I talk of you:
Why did you wish me milder? Would you have me
False to my nature? Rather say I play
The man I am.
VOLUMNIA: O, sir, sir, sir,
I would have had you put your power well on
Before you had worn it out.
CORIOLANUS: Let go.
VOLUMNIA: You might have been enough the man you are
With striving less to be so; lesser had been
The thwartings of your dispositions, if
You had not show'd them how ye were dispos'd,
Ere they lack'd power to cross you.
CORIOLANUS: Let them hang.
VOLUMNIA: Ay, and burn too.
Enter Menenius with the Senators
MENENIUS: Come, come, you have been too rough, something too rough;
You must return and mend it.
FIRST SENATOR: There's no remedy,

Unless, by not so doing, our good city
Cleave in the midst and perish.
VOLUMNIA: Pray be counsell'd;
I have a heart as little apt as yours,
But yet a brain that leads my use of anger
To better vantage.
MENENIUS: Well said, noble woman!
Before he should thus stoop to th' herd, but that
The violent fit o' th' time craves it as physic
For the whole state, I would put mine armour on,
Which I can scarcely bear.
CORIOLANUS: What must I do?
MENENIUS: Return to th' tribunes.
CORIOLANUS: Well, what then, what then?
MENENIUS: Repent what you have spoke.
CORIOLANUS: For them! I cannot do it to the gods;
Must I then do't to them?
VOLUMNIA: You are too absolute;
Though therein you can never be too noble
But when extremities speak. I have heard you say
Honour and policy, like unsever'd friends,
I' th' war do grow together; grant that, and tell me
In peace what each of them by th' other lose
That they combine not there.
CORIOLANUS: Tush, tush!
MENENIUS: A good demand.
VOLUMNIA: If it be honour in your wars to seem
The same you are not, which for your best ends
You adopt your policy, how is it less or worse
That it shall hold companionship in peace
With honour as in war; since that to both
It stands in like request?
CORIOLANUS: Why force you this?
VOLUMNIA: Because that now it lies you on to speak
To th' people, not by your own instruction,
Nor by th' matter which your heart prompts you,
But with such words that are but roted in
Your tongue, though but bastards and syllables
Of no allowance to your bosom's truth.
Now, this no more dishonours you at all
Than to take in a town with gentle words,
Which else would put you to your fortune and
The hazard of much blood.
I would dissemble with my nature where
My fortunes and my friends at stake requir'd
I should do so in honour. I am in this
Your wife, your son, these senators, the nobles;
And you will rather show our general louts
How you can frown, than spend a fawn upon 'em
For the inheritance of their loves and safeguard
Of what that want might ruin.
MENENIUS: Noble lady!
Come, go with us, speak fair; you may salve so,

Not what is dangerous present, but the los
Of what is past.
VOLUMNIA: I prithee now, My son,
Go to them with this bonnet in thy hand;
And thus far having stretch'd it- here be with them-
Thy knee bussing the stones- for in such busines
Action is eloquence, and the eyes of th' ignorant
More learned than the ears- waving thy head,
Which often thus correcting thy-stout heart,
Now humble as the ripest mulberry
That will not hold the handling. Or say to them
Thou art their soldier and, being bred in broils,
Hast not the soft way which, thou dost confess,
Were fit for thee to use, as they to claim,
In asking their good loves; but thou wilt frame
Thyself, forsooth, hereafter theirs, so far
As thou hast power and person.
MENENIUS: This but done
Even as she speaks, why, their hearts were yours;
For they have pardons, being ask'd, as free
As words to little purpose.
VOLUMNIA: Prithee now,
Go, and be rul'd; although I know thou hadst rather
Follow thine enemy in a fiery gulf
Than flatter him in a bower.
Enter Cominius
Here is Cominius.
COMINIUS: I have been i' th' market-place; and, sir, 'tis fit
You make strong party, or defend yourself
By calmness or by absence; all's in anger.
MENENIUS: Only fair speech.
COMINIUS: I think 'twill serve, if he
Can thereto frame his spirit.
VOLUMNIA: He must and will.
Prithee now, say you will, and go about it.
CORIOLANUS: Must I go show them my unbarb'd sconce? Must I
With my base tongue give to my noble heart
A lie that it must bear? Well, I will do't;
Yet, were there but this single plot to lose,
This mould of Marcius, they to dust should grind it,
And throw't against the wind. To th' market-place!
You have put me now to such a part which never
I shall discharge to th' life.
COMINIUS: Come, come, we'll prompt you.
VOLUMNIA: I prithee now, sweet son, as thou hast said
My praises made thee first a soldier, so,
To have my praise for this, perform a part
Thou hast not done before.
CORIOLANUS: Well, I must do't.
Away, my disposition, and possess me
Some harlot's spirit! My throat of war be turn'd,
Which quier'd with my drum, into a pipe
Small as an eunuch or the virgin voice

That babies lulls asleep! The smiles of knaves
Tent in my cheeks, and schoolboys' tears take up
The glasses of my sight! A beggar's tongue
Make motion through my lips, and my arm'd knees,
Who bow'd but in my stirrup, bend like his
That hath receiv'd an alms! I will not do't,
Lest I surcease to honour mine own truth,
And by my body's action teach my mind
A most inherent baseness.
VOLUMNIA: At thy choice, then.
To beg of thee, it is my more dishonour
Than thou of them. Come all to ruin. Let
Thy mother rather feel thy pride than fear
Thy dangerous stoutness; for I mock at death
With as big heart as thou. Do as thou list.
Thy valiantness was mine, thou suck'dst it from me;
But owe thy pride thyself.
CORIOLANUS: Pray be content.
Mother, I am going to the market-place;
Chide me no more. I'll mountebank their loves,
Cog their hearts from them, and come home belov'd
Of all the trades in Rome. Look, I am going.
Commend me to my wife. I'll return consul,
Or never trust to what my tongue can do
I' th' way of flattery further.
VOLUMNIA: Do your will.
Exit
COMINIUS: Away! The tribunes do attend you. Arm yourself
To answer mildly; for they are prepar'd
With accusations, as I hear, more strong
Than are upon you yet.
CORIOLANUS: The word is 'mildly.' Pray you let us go.
Let them accuse me by invention; I
Will answer in mine honour.
MENENIUS: Ay, but mildly.
CORIOLANUS: Well, mildly be it then- mildly.
Exeunt

ACT III. SCENE III. Rome. The Forum

Enter Sicinius and Brutus
BRUTUS: In this point charge him home, that he affects
Tyrannical power. If he evade us there,
Enforce him with his envy to the people,
And that the spoil got on the Antiates
Was ne'er distributed.
Enter an Aedile
What, will he come?
AEDILE: He's coming.
BRUTUS: How accompanied?
AEDILE: With old Menenius, and those senators
That always favour'd him.
SICINIUS: Have you a catalogue
Of all the voices that we have procur'd,
Set down by th' poll?

AEDILE: I have; 'tis ready.
SICINIUS: Have you corrected them by tribes?
AEDILE: I have.
SICINIUS: Assemble presently the people hither;
And when they hear me say 'It shall be so
I' th' right and strength o' th' commons' be it either
For death, for fine, or banishment, then let them,
If I say fine, cry 'Fine!'- if death, cry 'Death!'
Insisting on the old prerogative
And power i' th' truth o' th' cause.
AEDILE: I shall inform them.
BRUTUS: And when such time they have begun to cry,
Let them not cease, but with a din confus'd
Enforce the present execution
Of what we chance to sentence.
AEDILE: Very well.
SICINIUS: Make them be strong, and ready for this hint,
When we shall hap to give't them.
BRUTUS: Go about it.
Exit Aedile
Put him to choler straight. He hath been us'd
Ever to conquer, and to have his worth
Of contradiction; being once chaf'd, he cannot
Be rein'd again to temperance; then he speaks
What's in his heart, and that is there which looks
With us to break his neck.
Enter Coriolanus, Menenius and Cominius, with Others
SICINIUS: Well, here he comes.
MENENIUS: Calmly, I do beseech you.
CORIOLANUS: Ay, as an ostler, that for th' poorest piece
Will bear the knave by th' volume. Th' honour'd gods
Keep Rome in safety, and the chairs of justice
Supplied with worthy men! plant love among's!
Throng our large temples with the shows of peace,
And not our streets with war!
FIRST SENATOR: Amen, amen!
MENENIUS: A noble wish.
Re-enter The.aedile,with the Plebeians
SICINIUS: Draw near, ye people.
AEDILE: List to your tribunes. Audience! peace, I say!
CORIOLANUS: First, hear me speak.
BOTH TRIBUNES: Well, say. Peace, ho!
CORIOLANUS: Shall I be charg'd no further than this present?
Must all determine here?
SICINIUS: I do demand,
If you submit you to the people's voices,
Allow their officers, and are content
To suffer lawful censure for such faults
As shall be prov'd upon you.
CORIOLANUS: I am content.
MENENIUS: Lo, citizens, he says he is content.
The warlike service he has done, consider; think
Upon the wounds his body bears, which show

Like graves i' th' holy churchyard.
CORIOLANUS: Scratches with briers,
Scars to move laughter only.
MENENIUS: Consider further,
That when he speaks not like a citizen,
You find him like a soldier; do not take
His rougher accents for malicious sounds,
But, as I say, such as become a soldier
Rather than envy you.
COMINIUS: Well, well! No more.
CORIOLANUS: What is the matter,
That being pass'd for consul with full voice,
I am so dishonour'd that the very hour
You take it off again?
SICINIUS: Answer to us.
CORIOLANUS: Say then; 'tis true, I ought so.
SICINIUS: We charge you that you have contriv'd to take
From Rome all season'd office, and to wind
Yourself into a power tyrannical;
For which you are a traitor to the people.
CORIOLANUS: How- traitor?
MENENIUS: Nay, temperately! Your promise.
CORIOLANUS: The fires i' th' lowest hell fold in the people!
Call me their traitor! Thou injurious tribune!
Within thine eyes sat twenty thousand deaths,
In thy hands clutch'd as many millions, in
Thy lying tongue both numbers, I would say
'Thou liest' unto thee with a voice as free
As I do pray the gods.
SICINIUS: Mark you this, people?
PLEBEIANS: To th' rock, to th' rock, with him!
SICINIUS: Peace!
We need not put new matter to his charge.
What you have seen him do and heard him speak,
Beating your officers, cursing yourselves,
Opposing laws with strokes, and here defying
Those whose great power must try him- even this,
So criminal and in such capital kind,
Deserves th' extremest death.
BRUTUS: But since he hath
Serv'd well for Rome-
CORIOLANUS: What do you prate of service?
BRUTUS: I talk of that that know it.
CORIOLANUS: You!
MENENIUS: Is this the promise that you made your mother?
COMINIUS: Know, I pray you-
CORIOLANUS: I'll know no further.
Let them pronounce the steep Tarpeian death,
Vagabond exile, flaying, pent to linger
But with a grain a day, I would not buy
Their mercy at the price of one fair word,
Nor check my courage for what they can give,
To have't with saying 'Good morrow.'

SICINIUS: For that he has-
As much as in him lies- from time to time
Envied against the people, seeking means
To pluck away their power; as now at last
Given hostile strokes, and that not in the presence
Of dreaded justice, but on the ministers
That do distribute it- in the name o' th' people,
And in the power of us the tribunes, we,
Ev'n from this instant, banish him our city,
In peril of precipitation
From off the rock Tarpeian, never more
To enter our Rome gates. I' th' people's name,
I say it shall be so.
PLEBEIANS: It shall be so, it shall be so! Let him away!
He's banish'd, and it shall be so.
COMINIUS: Hear me, my masters and my common friends-
SICINIUS: He's sentenc'd; no more hearing.
COMINIUS: Let me speak.
I have been consul, and can show for Rome
Her enemies' marks upon me. I do love
My country's good with a respect more tender,
More holy and profound, than mine own life,
My dear wife's estimate, her womb's increase
And treasure of my loins. Then if I would
Speak that-
SICINIUS: We know your drift. Speak what?
BRUTUS: There's no more to be said, but he is banish'd,
As enemy to the people and his country.
It shall be so.
PLEBEIANS: It shall be so, it shall be so.
CORIOLANUS: YOU common cry of curs, whose breath I hate
As reek o' th' rotten fens, whose loves I prize
As the dead carcasses of unburied men
That do corrupt my air- I banish you.
And here remain with your uncertainty!
Let every feeble rumour shake your hearts;
Your enemies, with nodding of their plumes,
Fan you into despair! Have the power still
To banish your defenders, till at length
Your ignorance- which finds not till it feels,
Making but reservation of yourselves
Still your own foes- deliver you
As most abated captives to some nation
That won you without blows! Despising
For you the city, thus I turn my back;
There is a world elsewhere.
Exeunt Coriolanus, Cominius, Menenius, with the Other Patricians
AEDILE: The people's enemy is gone, is gone!
They All Shout and Throw up Their Caps
PLEBEIANS: Our enemy is banish'd, he is gone! Hoo-oo!
SICINIUS: Go see him out at gates, and follow him,
As he hath follow'd you, with all despite;
Give him deserv'd vexation. Let a guard

Attend us through the city.
PLEBEIANS: Come, come, let's see him out at gates; come!
The gods preserve our noble tribunes! Come.
Exeunt

ACT IV. SCENE I. Rome. Before a Gate of the City

Enter Coriolanus, Volumnia, Virgilia, Menenius, Cominius, with the Young Nobility of Rome
CORIOLANUS: Come, leave your tears; a brief farewell. The beast
With many heads butts me away. Nay, mother,
Where is your ancient courage? You were us'd
To say extremities was the trier of spirits;
That common chances common men could bear;
That when the sea was calm all boats alike
Show'd mastership in floating; fortune's blows,
When most struck home, being gentle wounded craves
A noble cunning. You were us'd to load me
With precepts that would make invincible
The heart that conn'd them.
VIRGILIA: O heavens! O heavens!
CORIOLANUS: Nay, I prithee, woman-
VOLUMNIA: Now the red pestilence strike all trades in Rome,
And occupations perish!
CORIOLANUS: What, what, what!
I shall be lov'd when I am lack'd. Nay, mother,
Resume that spirit when you were wont to say,
If you had been the wife of Hercules,
Six of his labours you'd have done, and sav'd
Your husband so much sweat. Cominius,
Droop not; adieu. Farewell, my wife, my mother.
I'll do well yet. Thou old and true Menenius,
Thy tears are salter than a younger man's
And venomous to thine eyes. My sometime General,
I have seen thee stern, and thou hast oft beheld
Heart-hard'ning spectacles; tell these sad women
'Tis fond to wail inevitable strokes,
As 'tis to laugh at 'em. My mother, you wot well
My hazards still have been your solace; and
Believe't not lightly- though I go alone,
Like to a lonely dragon, that his fen
Makes fear'd and talk'd of more than seen- your son
Will or exceed the common or be caught
With cautelous baits and practice.
VOLUMNIA: My first son,
Whither wilt thou go? Take good Cominius
With thee awhile; determine on some course
More than a wild exposture to each chance
That starts i' th' way before thee.
VIRGILIA: O the gods!
COMINIUS: I'll follow thee a month, devise with the
Where thou shalt rest, that thou mayst hear of us,
And we of thee; so, if the time thrust forth
A cause for thy repeal, we shall not send
O'er the vast world to seek a single man,
And lose advantage, which doth ever cool

I' th' absence of the needer.
CORIOLANUS: Fare ye well;
Thou hast years upon thee, and thou art too full
Of the wars' surfeits to go rove with one
That's yet unbruis'd; bring me but out at gate.
Come, my sweet wife, my dearest mother, and
My friends of noble touch; when I am forth,
Bid me farewell, and smile. I pray you come.
While I remain above the ground you shall
Hear from me still, and never of me aught
But what is like me formerly.
MENENIUS: That's worthily
As any ear can hear. Come, let's not weep.
If I could shake off but one seven years
From these old arms and legs, by the good gods,
I'd with thee every foot.
CORIOLANUS: Give me thy hand.
Come.
Exeunt

ACT IV. SCENE II. Rome. A Street near the Gate

Enter the Two Tribunes, Sicinius and Brutus with the Aedile
SICINIUS: Bid them all home; he's gone, and we'll no further.
The nobility are vex'd, whom we see have sided
In his behalf.
BRUTUS: Now we have shown our power,
Let us seem humbler after it is done
Than when it was a-doing.
SICINIUS: Bid them home.
Say their great enemy is gone, and they
Stand in their ancient strength.
BRUTUS: Dismiss them home.
Exit Aedile
Here comes his mother.
Enter Volumnia, Virgilia, and Menenius
SICINIUS: Let's not meet her.
BRUTUS: Why?
SICINIUS: They say she's mad.
BRUTUS: They have ta'en note of us; keep on your way.
VOLUMNIA: O, Y'are well met; th' hoarded plague o' th' gods
Requite your love!
MENENIUS: Peace, peace, be not so loud.
VOLUMNIA: If that I could for weeping, you should hear-
Nay, and you shall hear some. To Brutus Will you be gone?
VIRGILIA: To Sicinius You shall stay too. I would I had the power
To say so to my husband.
SICINIUS: Are you mankind?
VOLUMNIA: Ay, fool; is that a shame? Note but this, fool:
Was not a man my father? Hadst thou foxship
To banish him that struck more blows for Rome
Than thou hast spoken words?
SICINIUS: O blessed heavens!
VOLUMNIA: Moe noble blows than ever thou wise words;
And for Rome's good. I'll tell thee what- yet go!

Nay, but thou shalt stay too. I would my son
Were in Arabia, and thy tribe before him,
His good sword in his hand.
SICINIUS: What then?
VIRGILIA: What then!
He'd make an end of thy posterity.
VOLUMNIA: Bastards and all.
Good man, the wounds that he does bear for Rome!
MENENIUS: Come, come, peace.
SICINIUS: I would he had continued to his country
As he began, and not unknit himself
The noble knot he made.
BRUTUS: I would he had.
VOLUMNIA: 'I would he had!' 'Twas you incens'd the rabble-
Cats that can judge as fitly of his worth
As I can of those mysteries which heaven
Will not have earth to know.
BRUTUS: Pray, let's go.
VOLUMNIA: Now, pray, sir, get you gone;
You have done a brave deed. Ere you go, hear this:
As far as doth the Capitol exceed
The meanest house in Rome, so far my son-
This lady's husband here, this, do you see?-
Whom you have banish'd does exceed you an.
BRUTUS: Well, well, we'll leave you.
SICINIUS: Why stay we to be baited
With one that wants her wits?
Exeunt Tribunes
VOLUMNIA: Take my prayers with you.
I would the gods had nothing else to do
But to confirm my curses. Could I meet 'em
But once a day, it would unclog my heart
Of what lies heavy to't.
MENENIUS: You have told them home,
And, by my troth, you have cause. You'll sup with me?
VOLUMNIA: Anger's my meat; I sup upon myself,
And so shall starve with feeding. Come, let's go.
Leave this faint puling and lament as I do,
In anger, Juno-like. Come, come, come.
Exeunt Volumnia and Virgilia
MENENIUS: Fie, fie, fie!
Exit

ACT IV. SCENE III. A Highway Between Rome and Antium

Enter a Roman and a Volsce, Meeting
ROMAN: I know you well, sir, and you know me; your name, I think, is Adrian.
VOLSCE: It is so, sir. Truly, I have forgot you.
ROMAN: I am a Roman; and my services are, as you are, against 'em. Know you me yet?
VOLSCE: Nicanor? No!
ROMAN: The same, sir.
VOLSCE: You had more beard when I last saw you, but your favour is well appear'd by your tongue. What's the news in Rome? I have a

note from the Volscian state, to find you out there. You have well saved me a day's journey.
ROMAN: There hath been in Rome strange insurrections: the people against the senators, patricians, and nobles.
VOLSCE: Hath been! Is it ended, then? Our state thinks not so; they are in a most warlike preparation, and hope to come upon them in the heat of their division.
ROMAN: The main blaze of it is past, but a small thing would make it flame again; for the nobles receive so to heart the banishment of that worthy Coriolanus that they are in a ripe aptness to take all power from the people, and to pluck from them their tribunes for ever. This lies glowing, I can tell you, and is almost mature for the violent breaking out.
VOLSCE: Coriolanus banish'd!
ROMAN: Banish'd, sir.
VOLSCE: You will be welcome with this intelligence, Nicanor.
ROMAN: The day serves well for them now. I have heard it said the fittest time to corrupt a man's wife is when she's fall'n out with her husband. Your noble Tullus Aufidius will appear well in these wars, his great opposer, Coriolanus, being now in no request of his country.
VOLSCE: He cannot choose. I am most fortunate thus accidentally to encounter you; you have ended my business, and I will merrily accompany you home.
ROMAN: I shall between this and supper tell you most strange things from Rome, all tending to the good of their adversaries. Have you an army ready, say you?
VOLSCE: A most royal one: the centurions and their charges, distinctly billeted, already in th' entertainment, and to be on foot at an hour's warning.
ROMAN: I am joyful to hear of their readiness, and am the man, I think, that shall set them in present action. So, sir, heartily well met, and most glad of your company.
VOLSCE: You take my part from me, sir. I have the most cause to be glad of yours.
ROMAN: Well, let us go together.

ACT IV. SCENE IV. Antium. Before Aufidius' House

Enter Coriolanus, in Mean Apparel, Disguis'd and Muffled
CORIOLANUS: A goodly city is this Antium. City,
'Tis I that made thy widows: many an heir
Of these fair edifices fore my wars
Have I heard groan and drop. Then know me not.
Lest that thy wives with spits and boys with stones,
In puny battle slay me.
Enter a Citizen
Save you, sir.
CITIZEN: And you.
CORIOLANUS: Direct me, if it be your will,
Where great Aufidius lies. Is he in Antium?
CITIZEN: He is, and feasts the nobles of the state
At his house this night.
CORIOLANUS: Which is his house, beseech you?
CITIZEN: This here before you.

CORIOLANUS: Thank you, sir; farewell. Exit Citizen
O world, thy slippery turns! Friends now fast sworn,
Whose double bosoms seems to wear one heart,
Whose hours, whose bed, whose meal and exercise
Are still together, who twin, as 'twere, in love,
Unseparable, shall within this hour,
On a dissension of a doit, break out
To bitterest enmity; so fellest foes,
Whose passions and whose plots have broke their sleep
To take the one the other, by some chance,
Some trick not worth an egg, shall grow dear friends
And interjoin their issues. So with me:
My birthplace hate I, and my love's upon
This enemy town. I'll enter. If he slay me,
He does fair justice: if he give me way,
I'll do his country service.

ACT IV. SCENE V. Antium. Aufidius' House

Music Plays. Enter a Servingman

FIRST SERVANT: Wine, wine, wine! What service is here! I think our fellows are asleep.

Exit

Enter Another Servingman

SECOND SERVANT:Where's Cotus? My master calls for him.
Cotus!

Exit

Enter Coriolanus

CORIOLANUS: A goodly house. The feast smells well, but I
Appear not like a guest.

Re-enter the first Servingman

FIRST SERVANT: What would you have, friend?
Whence are you? Here's no place for you: pray go to the door.

Exit

CORIOLANUS: I have deserv'd no better entertainment
In being Coriolanus.

Re-enter Second Servingman

SECOND SERVANT: Whence are you, sir? Has the porter his eyes in his head that he gives entrance to such companions? Pray get you out.

CORIOLANUS: Away!

SECOND SERVANT: Away? Get you away.

CORIOLANUS: Now th' art troublesome.

SECOND SERVANT: Are you so brave? I'll have you talk'd with anon.

Enter a Third Servingman. The First Meets Him

THIRD SERVANT: What fellow's this?

FIRST SERVANT: A strange one as ever I look'd on. I cannot get him out o' th' house. Prithee call my master to him.

THIRD SERVANT: What have you to do here, fellow? Pray you avoid the house.

CORIOLANUS: Let me but stand- I will not hurt your hearth.

THIRD SERVANT: What are you?

CORIOLANUS: A gentleman.

THIRD SERVANT: A marv'llous poor one.

CORIOLANUS: True, so I am.

THIRD SERVANT: Pray you, poor gentleman, take up some other station; here's no place for you. Pray you avoid. Come.

CORIOLANUS: Follow your function, go and batten on cold bits.

Pushes Him Away from Him
THIRD SERVANT: What, you will not? Prithee tell my master what a strange guest he has here.
SECOND SERVANT: And I shall.
Exit
THIRD SERVANT: Where dwell'st thou?
CORIOLANUS: Under the canopy.
THIRD SERVANT: Under the canopy?
CORIOLANUS: Ay.
THIRD SERVANT: Where's that?
CORIOLANUS: I' th' city of kites and crows.
THIRD SERVANT: I' th' city of kites and crows!
What an ass it is! Then thou dwell'st with daws too?
CORIOLANUS: No, I serve not thy master.
THIRD SERVANT: How, sir! Do you meddle with my master?
CORIOLANUS: Ay; 'tis an honester service than to meddle with thy mistress. Thou prat'st and prat'st; serve with thy trencher; hence!
Beats Him Away
Enter Aufidius with the Second Servingman
AUFIDIUS: Where is this fellow?
SECOND SERVANT: Here, sir; I'd have beaten him like a dog, but for disturbing the lords within.
AUFIDIUS: Whence com'st thou? What wouldst thou? Thy name?
Why speak'st not? Speak, man. What's thy name?
CORIOLANUS: Unmuffling If, Tullus,
Not yet thou know'st me, and, seeing me, dost not
Think me for the man I am, necessity
Commands me name myself.
AUFIDIUS: What is thy name?
CORIOLANUS: A name unmusical to the Volscians' ears,
And harsh in sound to thine.
AUFIDIUS: Say, what's thy name?
Thou has a grim appearance, and thy face
Bears a command in't; though thy tackle's torn,
Thou show'st a noble vessel. What's thy name?
CORIOLANUS: Prepare thy brow to frown- know'st thou me yet?
AUFIDIUS: I know thee not. Thy name?
CORIOLANUS: My name is Caius Marcius, who hath done
To thee particularly, and to all the Volsces,
Great hurt and mischief; thereto witness may
My surname, Coriolanus. The painful service,
The extreme dangers, and the drops of blood
Shed for my thankless country, are requited
But with that surname- a good memory
And witness of the malice and displeasure
Which thou shouldst bear me. Only that name remains;
The cruelty and envy of the people,
Permitted by our dastard nobles, who
Have all forsook me, hath devour'd the rest,
An suffer'd me by th' voice of slaves to be
Whoop'd out of Rome. Now this extremity
Hath brought me to thy hearth; not out of hope,

Mistake me not, to save my life; for if
I had fear'd death, of all the men i' th' world
I would have 'voided thee; but in mere spite,
To be full quit of those my banishers,
Stand I before thee here. Then if thou hast
A heart of wreak in thee, that wilt revenge
Thine own particular wrongs and stop those maims
Of shame seen through thy country, speed thee straight
And make my misery serve thy turn. So use it
That my revengeful services may prove
As benefits to thee; for I will fight
Against my cank'red country with the spleen
Of all the under fiends. But if so be
Thou dar'st not this, and that to prove more fortunes
Th'art tir'd, then, in a word, I also am
Longer to live most weary, and present
My throat to thee and to thy ancient malice;
Which not to cut would show thee but a fool,
Since I have ever followed thee with hate,
Drawn tuns of blood out of thy country's breast,
And cannot live but to thy shame, unless
It be to do thee service.
AUFIDIUS: O Marcius, Marcius!
Each word thou hast spoke hath weeded from my heart
A root of ancient envy. If Jupiter
Should from yond cloud speak divine things,
And say ''Tis true,' I'd not believe them more
Than thee, all noble Marcius. Let me twine
Mine arms about that body, where against
My grained ash an hundred times hath broke
And scarr'd the moon with splinters; here I clip
The anvil of my sword, and do contest
As hotly and as nobly with thy love
As ever in ambitious strength I did
Contend against thy valour. Know thou first,
I lov'd the maid I married; never man
Sigh'd truer breath; but that I see thee here,
Thou noble thing, more dances my rapt heart
Than when I first my wedded mistress saw
Bestride my threshold. Why, thou Mars, I tell the
We have a power on foot, and I had purpose
Once more to hew thy target from thy brawn,
Or lose mine arm for't. Thou hast beat me out
Twelve several times, and I have nightly since
Dreamt of encounters 'twixt thyself and me-
We have been down together in my sleep,
Unbuckling helms, fisting each other's throat-
And wak'd half dead with nothing. Worthy Marcius,
Had we no other quarrel else to Rome but that
Thou art thence banish'd, we would muster all
From twelve to seventy, and, pouring war
Into the bowels of ungrateful Rome,
Like a bold flood o'erbeat. O, come, go in,

And take our friendly senators by th' hands,
Who now are here, taking their leaves of me
Who am prepar'd against your territories,
Though not for Rome itself.
CORIOLANUS: You bless me, gods!
AUFIDIUS: Therefore, most. absolute sir, if thou wilt have
The leading of thine own revenges, take
Th' one half of my commission, and set down-
As best thou art experienc'd, since thou know'st
Thy country's strength and weakness- thine own ways,
Whether to knock against the gates of Rome,
Or rudely visit them in parts remote
To fright them ere destroy. But come in;
Let me commend thee first to those that shall
Say yea to thy desires. A thousand welcomes!
And more a friend than e'er an enemy;
Yet, Marcius, that was much. Your hand; most welcome!
Exeunt Coriolanus and Aufidius
The Two Servingmen Come Forward
FIRST SERVANT: Here's a strange alteration!
SECOND SERVANT: By my hand, I had thought to have strucken him with a cudgel; and yet my mind gave me his clothes made a false report of him.
FIRST SERVANT: What an arm he has! He turn'd me about with his finger and his thumb, as one would set up a top.
SECOND SERVANT: Nay, I knew by his face that there was something in him; he had, sir, a kind of face, methought- I cannot tell how to term it.
FIRST SERVANT: He had so, looking as it were- Would I were hang'd, but I thought there was more in him than I could think.
SECOND SERVANT: So did I, I'll be sworn. He is simply the rarest man i' th' world.
FIRST SERVANT: I think he is; but a greater soldier than he you wot on.
SECOND SERVANT: Who, my master?
FIRST SERVANT: Nay, it's no matter for that.
SECOND SERVANT: Worth six on him.
FIRST SERVANT: Nay, not so neither; but I take him to be the greater soldier.
SECOND SERVANT: Faith, look you, one cannot tell how to say that; for the defence of a town our general is excellent.
FIRST SERVANT: Ay, and for an assault too.
Re-enter the Third Servingman
THIRD SERVANT: O slaves, I can tell you news- news, you rascals!
BOTH: What, what, what? Let's partake.
THIRD SERVANT: I would not be a Roman, of all nations;
I had as lief be a condemn'd man.
BOTH: Wherefore? wherefore?
THIRD SERVANT: Why, here's he that was wont to thwack our general- Caius Marcius.
FIRST SERVANT: Why do you say 'thwack our general'?
THIRD SERVANT: I do not say 'thwack our general,' but he was always good enough for him.

SECOND SERVANT: Come, we are fellows and friends. He was ever too hard for him, I have heard him say so himself.
FIRST SERVANT: He was too hard for him directly, to say the troth on't; before Corioli he scotch'd him and notch'd him like a carbonado.
SECOND SERVANT: An he had been cannibally given, he might have broil'd and eaten him too.
FIRST SERVANT: But more of thy news!
THIRD SERVANT: Why, he is so made on here within as if he were son and heir to Mars; set at upper end o' th' table; no question asked him by any of the senators but they stand bald before him. Our general himself makes a mistress of him, sanctifies himself with's hand, and turns up the white o' th' eye to his discourse. But the bottom of the news is, our general is cut i' th' middle and but one half of what he was yesterday, for the other has half by the entreaty and grant of the whole table. He'll go, he says, and sowl the porter of Rome gates by th' ears; he will mow all down before him, and leave his passage poll'd.
SECOND SERVANT: And he's as like to do't as any man I can imagine.
THIRD SERVANT: Do't! He will do't; for look you, sir, he has as many friends as enemies; which friends, sir, as it were, durst not- look you, sir- show themselves, as we term it, his friends, whilst he's in directitude.
FIRST SERVANT: Directitude? What's that?
THIRD SERVANT: But when they shall see, sir, his crest up again and the man in blood, they will out of their burrows, like conies after rain, and revel an with him.
FIRST SERVANT: But when goes this forward?
THIRD SERVANT: To-morrow, to-day, presently. You shall have the drum struck up this afternoon; 'tis as it were parcel of their feast, and to be executed ere they wipe their lips.
SECOND SERVANT: Why, then we shall have a stirring world again. This peace is nothing but to rust iron, increase tailors, and breed ballad-makers.
FIRST SERVANT: Let me have war, say I; it exceeds peace as far as day does night; it's spritely, waking, audible, and full of vent. Peace is a very apoplexy, lethargy; mull'd, deaf, sleepy, insensible; a getter of more bastard children than war's a destroyer of men.
SECOND SERVANT: 'Tis so; and as war in some sort may be said to be a ravisher, so it cannot be denied but peace is a great maker of cuckolds.
FIRST SERVANT: Ay, and it makes men hate one another.
THIRD SERVANT: Reason: because they then less need one another. The wars for my money. I hope to see Romans as cheap as Volscians. They are rising, they are rising.
BOTH: In, in, in, in!

Exeunt

ACT IV. SCENE VI. Rome. A Public Place

Enter the Two Tribunes, Sicinius and Brutus

SICINIUS: We hear not of him, neither need we fear him.
His remedies are tame. The present peace
And quietness of the people, which before

Were in wild hurry, here do make his friends
Blush that the world goes well; who rather had,
Though they themselves did suffer by't, behold
Dissentious numbers pest'ring streets than see
Our tradesmen singing in their shops, and going
About their functions friendly.
Enter Menenius
BRUTUS: We stood to't in good time. Is this Menenius?
SICINIUS: 'Tis he, 'tis he. O, he is grown most kind
Of late. Hail, sir!
MENENIUS: Hail to you both!
SICINIUS: Your Coriolanus is not much miss'd
But with his friends. The commonwealth doth stand,
And so would do, were he more angry at it.
MENENIUS: All's well, and might have been much better
He could have temporiz'd.
SICINIUS: Where is he, hear you?
MENENIUS: Nay, I hear nothing; his mother and his wife
Hear nothing from him.
Enter Three or Four Citizens
CITIZENS: The gods preserve you both!
SICINIUS: God-den, our neighbours.
BRUTUS: God-den to you all, god-den to you an.
FIRST CITIZEN: Ourselves, our wives, and children, on our knees
Are bound to pray for you both.
SICINIUS: Live and thrive!
BRUTUS: Farewell, kind neighbours; we wish'd Coriolanus
Had lov'd you as we did.
CITIZENS: Now the gods keep you!
BOTH TRIBUNES: Farewell, farewell.
Exeunt Citizens
SICINIUS: This is a happier and more comely time
Than when these fellows ran about the streets crying confusion.
BRUTUS: Caius Marcius was
A worthy officer i' the war, but insolent,
O'ercome with pride, ambitious past all thinking, self-loving-
SICINIUS: And affecting one sole throne,
Without assistance.
MENENIUS: I think not so.
SICINIUS: We should by this, to all our lamentation,
If he had gone forth consul, found it so.
BRUTUS: The gods have well prevented it, and Rome
Sits safe and still without him.
Enter an Aedile
AEDILE: Worthy tribunes,
There is a slave, whom we have put in prison,
Reports the Volsces with several powers
Are ent'red in the Roman territories,
And with the deepest malice of the war
Destroy what lies before 'em.
MENENIUS: 'Tis Aufidius,
Who, hearing of our Marcius' banishment,
Thrusts forth his horns again into the world,

Which were inshell'd when Marcius stood for Rome,
And durst not once peep out.
SICINIUS: Come, what talk you of Marcius?
BRUTUS: Go see this rumourer whipp'd. It cannot be
The Volsces dare break with us.
MENENIUS: Cannot be!
We have record that very well it can;
And three examples of the like hath been
Within my age. But reason with the fellow
Before you punish him, where he heard this,
Lest you shall chance to whip your information
And beat the messenger who bids beware
Of what is to be dreaded.
SICINIUS: Tell not me.
I know this cannot be.
BRUTUS: Not Possible.
Enter a Messenger
MESSENGER: The nobles in great earnestness are going
All to the Senate House; some news is come
That turns their countenances.
SICINIUS: 'Tis this slave-
Go whip him fore the people's eyes- his raising,
Nothing but his report.
MESSENGER: Yes, worthy sir,
The slave's report is seconded, and more,
More fearful, is deliver'd.
SICINIUS: What more fearful?
MESSENGER: It is spoke freely out of many mouths-
How probable I do not know- that Marcius,
Join'd with Aufidius, leads a power 'gainst Rome,
And vows revenge as spacious as between
The young'st and oldest thing.
SICINIUS: This is most likely!
BRUTUS: Rais'd only that the weaker sort may wish
Good Marcius home again.
SICINIUS: The very trick on 't.
MENENIUS: This is unlikely.
He and Aufidius can no more atone
Than violent'st contrariety.
Enter a Second Messenger
SECOND MESSENGER: You are sent for to the Senate.
A fearful army, led by Caius Marcius
Associated with Aufidius, rages
Upon our territories, and have already
O'erborne their way, consum'd with fire and took
What lay before them.
Enter Cominius
COMINIUS: O, you have made good work!
MENENIUS: What news? what news?
COMINIUS: You have holp to ravish your own daughters and
To melt the city leads upon your pates,
To see your wives dishonour'd to your noses-
MENENIUS: What's the news? What's the news?

COMINIUS: Your temples burned in their cement, and
Your franchises, whereon you stood, confin'd
Into an auger's bore.
MENENIUS: Pray now, your news?
You have made fair work, I fear me. Pray, your news.
If Marcius should be join'd wi' th' Volscians-
COMINIUS: If!
He is their god; he leads them like a thing
Made by some other deity than Nature,
That shapes man better; and they follow him
Against us brats with no less confidence
Than boys pursuing summer butterflies,
Or butchers killing flies.
MENENIUS: You have made good work,
You and your apron men; you that stood so much
Upon the voice of occupation and
The breath of garlic-eaters!
COMINIUS: He'll shake
Your Rome about your ears.
MENENIUS: As Hercules
Did shake down mellow fruit. You have made fair work!
BRUTUS: But is this true, sir?
COMINIUS: Ay; and you'll look pale
Before you find it other. All the regions
Do smilingly revolt, and who resists
Are mock'd for valiant ignorance,
And perish constant fools. Who is't can blame him?
Your enemies and his find something in him.
MENENIUS: We are all undone unless
The noble man have mercy.
COMINIUS: Who shall ask it?
The tribunes cannot do't for shame; the people
Deserve such pity of him as the wolf
Does of the shepherds; for his best friends, if they
Should say 'Be good to Rome'- they charg'd him even
As those should do that had deserv'd his hate,
And therein show'd fike enemies.
MENENIUS: 'Tis true;
If he were putting to my house the brand
That should consume it, I have not the face
To say 'Beseech you, cease.' You have made fair hands,
You and your crafts! You have crafted fair!
COMINIUS: You have brought
A trembling upon Rome, such as was never
S' incapable of help.
BOTH TRIBUNES: Say not we brought it.
MENENIUS: How! Was't we? We lov'd him, but, like beasts
And cowardly nobles, gave way unto your clusters,
Who did hoot him out o' th' city.
COMINIUS: But I fear
They'll roar him in again. Tullus Aufidius,
The second name of men, obeys his points
As if he were his officer. Desperation

Is all the policy, strength, and defence,
That Rome can make against them.
Enter a Troop of Citizens
MENENIUS: Here comes the clusters.
And is Aufidius with him? You are they
That made the air unwholesome when you cast
Your stinking greasy caps in hooting at
Coriolanus' exile. Now he's coming,
And not a hair upon a soldier's head
Which will not prove a whip; as many coxcombs
As you threw caps up will he tumble down,
And pay you for your voices. 'Tis no matter;
If he could burn us all into one coal
We have deserv'd it.
PLEBEIANS: Faith, we hear fearful news.
FIRST CITIZEN: For mine own part,
When I said banish him, I said 'twas pity.
SECOND CITIZEN: And so did I.
THIRD CITIZEN: And so did I; and, to say the truth, so did very many of us. That we did, we did for the best; and though we willingly consented to his banishment, yet it was against our will.
COMINIUS: Y'are goodly things, you voices!
MENENIUS: You have made
Good work, you and your cry! Shall's to the Capitol?
COMINIUS: O, ay, what else?
Exeunt Cominius and Menenius
SICINIUS: Go, masters, get you be not dismay'd;
These are a side that would be glad to have
This true which they so seem to fear. Go home,
And show no sign of fear.
FIRST CITIZEN: The gods be good to us! Come, masters, let's home. I ever said we were i' th' wrong when we banish'd him.
SECOND CITIZEN: So did we all. But come, let's home.
Exeunt Citizens
BRUTUS: I do not like this news.
SICINIUS: Nor I.
BRUTUS: Let's to the Capitol. Would half my wealth
Would buy this for a lie!
SICINIUS: Pray let's go.
Exeunt

ACT IV. SCENE VII. A Camp at a Short Distance from Rome

Enter Aufidius with His Lieutenant
AUFIDIUS: Do they still fly to th' Roman?
LIEUTENANT: I do not know what witchcraft's in him, but
Your soldiers use him as the grace fore meat,
Their talk at table, and their thanks at end;
And you are dark'ned in this action, sir,
Even by your own.
AUFIDIUS: I cannot help it now,
Unless by using means I lame the foot
Of our design. He bears himself more proudlier,
Even to my person, than I thought he would
When first I did embrace him; yet his nature

In that's no changeling, and I must excuse
What cannot be amended.
LIEUTENANT: Yet I wish, sir-
I mean, for your particular- you had not
Join'd in commission with him, but either
Had borne the action of yourself, or else
To him had left it solely.
AUFIDIUS: I understand thee well; and be thou sure,
When he shall come to his account, he knows not
What I can urge against him. Although it seems,
And so he thinks, and is no less apparent
To th' vulgar eye, that he bears all things fairly
And shows good husbandry for the Volscian state,
Fights dragon-like, and does achieve as soon
As draw his sword; yet he hath left undone
That which shall break his neck or hazard mine
Whene'er we come to our account.
LIEUTENANT: Sir, I beseech you, think you he'll carry Rome?
AUFIDIUS: All places yield to him ere he sits down,
And the nobility of Rome are his;
The senators and patricians love him too.
The tribunes are no soldiers, and their people
Will be as rash in the repeal as hasty
To expel him thence. I think he'll be to Rome
As is the osprey to the fish, who takes it
By sovereignty of nature. First he was
A noble servant to them, but he could not
Carry his honours even. Whether 'twas pride,
Which out of daily fortune ever taints
The happy man; whether defect of judgment,
To fail in the disposing of those chances
Which he was lord of; or whether nature,
Not to be other than one thing, not moving
From th' casque to th' cushion, but commanding peace
Even with the same austerity and garb
As he controll'd the war; but one of these-
As he hath spices of them all- not all,
For I dare so far free him- made him fear'd,
So hated, and so banish'd. But he has a merit
To choke it in the utt'rance. So our virtues
Lie in th' interpretation of the time;
And power, unto itself most commendable,
Hath not a tomb so evident as a chair
T' extol what it hath done.
One fire drives out one fire; one nail, one nail;
Rights by rights falter, strengths by strengths do fail.
Come, let's away. When, Caius, Rome is thine,
Thou art poor'st of all; then shortly art thou mine.
Exeunt

ACT V. SCENE I. Rome. A Public Place

Enter Menenius, Cominius, Sicinius and Brutus, the Two Tribunes, with Others
MENENIUS: No, I'll not go. You hear what he hath said
Which was sometime his general, who lov'd him

In a most dear particular. He call'd me father;
But what o' that? Go, you that banish'd him:
A mile before his tent fall down, and knee
The way into his mercy. Nay, if he coy'd
To hear Cominius speak, I'll keep at home.
COMINIUS: He would not seem to know me.
MENENIUS: Do you hear?
COMINIUS: Yet one time he did call me by my name.
I urg'd our old acquaintance, and the drops
That we have bled together. 'Coriolanus'
He would not answer to; forbid all names;
He was a kind of nothing, titleless,
Till he had forg'd himself a name i' th' fire
Of burning Rome.
MENENIUS: Why, so! You have made good work.
A pair of tribunes that have wrack'd for Rome
To make coals cheap- a noble memory!
COMINIUS: I minded him how royal 'twas to pardon
When it was less expected; he replied,
It was a bare petition of a state
To one whom they had punish'd.
MENENIUS: Very well.
Could he say less?
COMINIUS: I offer'd to awaken his regard
For's private friends; his answer to me was,
He could not stay to pick them in a pile
Of noisome musty chaff. He said 'twas folly,
For one poor grain or two, to leave unburnt
And still to nose th' offence.
MENENIUS: For one poor grain or two!
I am one of those. His mother, wife, his child,
And this brave fellow too- we are the grains:
You are the musty chaff, and you are smelt
Above the moon. We must be burnt for you.
SICINIUS: Nay, pray be patient; if you refuse your aid
In this so never-needed help, yet do not
Upbraid's with our distress. But sure, if you
Would be your country's pleader, your good tongue,
More than the instant army we can make,
Might stop our countryman.
MENENIUS: No; I'll not meddle.
SICINIUS: Pray you go to him.
MENENIUS: What should I do?
BRUTUS: Only make trial what your love can do
For Rome, towards Marcius.
MENENIUS: Well, and say that Marcius
Return me, as Cominius is return'd,
Unheard- what then?
But as a discontented friend, grief-shot
With his unkindness? Say't be so?
SICINIUS: Yet your good will
Must have that thanks from Rome after the measure
As you intended well.

MENENIUS: I'll undertake't;
I think he'll hear me. Yet to bite his lip
And hum at good Cominius much unhearts me.
He was not taken well: he had not din'd;
The veins unfill'd, our blood is cold, and then
We pout upon the morning, are unapt
To give or to forgive; but when we have stuff'd
These pipes and these conveyances of our blood
With wine and feeding, we have suppler souls
Than in our priest-like fasts. Therefore I'll watch him
Till he be dieted to my request,
And then I'll set upon him.
BRUTUS: You know the very road into his kindness
And cannot lose your way.
MENENIUS: Good faith, I'll prove him,
Speed how it will. I shall ere long have knowledge
Of my success.
Exit
COMINIUS: He'll never hear him.
SICINIUS: Not?
COMINIUS: I tell you he does sit in gold, his eye
Red as 'twould burn Rome, and his injury
The gaoler to his pity. I kneel'd before him;
'Twas very faintly he said 'Rise'; dismiss'd me
Thus with his speechless hand. What he would do,
He sent in writing after me; what he would not,
Bound with an oath to yield to his conditions;
So that all hope is vain,
Unless his noble mother and his wife,
Who, as I hear, mean to solicit him
For mercy to his country. Therefore let's hence,
And with our fair entreaties haste them on.
Exeunt

ACT V. SCENE II. The Volscian Camp Before Rome

Enter Menenius to the Watch on Guard
FIRST WATCH: Stay. Whence are you?
SECOND WATCH: Stand, and go back.
MENENIUS: You guard like men, 'tis well; but, by your leave,
I am an officer of state and come
To speak with Coriolanus.
FIRST WATCH: From whence?
MENENIUS: From Rome.
FIRST WATCH: YOU may not pass; you must return. Our general
Will no more hear from thence.
SECOND WATCH: You'll see your Rome embrac'd with fire before
You'll speak with Coriolanus.
MENENIUS: Good my friends,
If you have heard your general talk of Rome
And of his friends there, it is lots to blanks
My name hath touch'd your ears: it is Menenius.
FIRST WATCH: Be it so; go back. The virtue of your name
Is not here passable.
MENENIUS: I tell thee, fellow,

Thy general is my lover. I have been
The book of his good acts whence men have read
His fame unparallel'd haply amplified;
For I have ever verified my friends-
Of whom he's chief- with all the size that verity
Would without lapsing suffer. Nay, sometimes,
Like to a bowl upon a subtle ground,
I have tumbled past the throw, and in his praise
Have almost stamp'd the leasing; therefore, fellow,
I must have leave to pass.
FIRST WATCH: Faith, sir, if you had told as many lies in his behalf as you have uttered words in your own, you should not pass here; no, though it were as virtuous to lie as to live chastely. Therefore go back.
MENENIUS: Prithee, fellow, remember my name is Menenius, always factionary on the party of your general.
SECOND WATCH: Howsoever you have been his liar, as you say you have, I am one that, telling true under him, must say you cannot pass. Therefore go back.
MENENIUS: Has he din'd, canst thou tell? For I would not speak with him till after dinner.
FIRST WATCH: You are a Roman, are you?
MENENIUS: I am as thy general is.
FIRST WATCH: Then you should hate Rome, as he does. Can you, when you have push'd out your gates the very defender of them, and in a violent popular ignorance given your enemy your shield, think to front his revenges with the easy groans of old women, the virginal palms of your daughters, or with the palsied intercession of such a decay'd dotant as you seem to be? Can you think to blow out the intended fire your city is ready to flame in with such weak breath as this? No, you are deceiv'd; therefore back to Rome and prepare for your execution. You are condemn'd; our general has sworn you out of reprieve and pardon.
MENENIUS: Sirrah, if thy captain knew I were here, he would use me with estimation.
FIRST WATCH: Come, my captain knows you not.
MENENIUS: I mean thy general.
FIRST WATCH: My general cares not for you. Back, I say; go, lest I let forth your half pint of blood. Back- that's the utmost of your having. Back.
MENENIUS: Nay, but fellow, fellow-
Enter Coriolanus with Aufidius
CORIOLANUS: What's the matter?
MENENIUS: Now, you companion, I'll say an errand for you; you shall know now that I am in estimation; you shall perceive that a Jack guardant cannot office me from my son Coriolanus. Guess but by my entertainment with him if thou stand'st not i' th' state of hanging, or of some death more long in spectatorship and crueller in suffering; behold now presently, and swoon for what's to come upon thee. The glorious gods sit in hourly synod about thy particular prosperity, and love thee no worse than thy old father Menenius does! O my son! my son! thou art preparing fire for us; look thee, here's water to quench it. I was hardly moved to come

to thee; but being assured none but myself could move thee, I have been blown out of your gates with sighs, and conjure thee to pardon Rome and thy petitionary countrymen. The good gods assuage thy wrath, and turn the dregs of it upon this varlet here; this, who, like a block, hath denied my access to thee.

CORIOLANUS: Away!

MENENIUS: How! away!

CORIOLANUS: Wife, mother, child, I know not. My affairs
Are servanted to others. Though I owe
My revenge properly, my remission lies
In Volscian breasts. That we have been familiar,
Ingrate forgetfulness shall poison rather
Than pity note how much. Therefore be gone.
Mine ears against your suits are stronger than
Your gates against my force. Yet, for I lov'd thee,
Take this along; I writ it for thy sake

Gives a Letter

And would have sent it. Another word, Menenius,
I will not hear thee speak. This man, Aufidius,
Was my belov'd in Rome; yet thou behold'st.

AUFIDIUS: You keep a constant temper.

Exeunt Coriolanus and Aufidius

FIRST WATCH: Now, sir, is your name Menenius?

SECOND WATCH: 'Tis a spell, you see, of much power! You know the way home again.

FIRST WATCH: Do you hear how we are shent for keeping your greatness back?

SECOND WATCH: What cause, do you think, I have to swoon?

MENENIUS: I neither care for th' world nor your general; for such things as you, I can scarce think there's any, y'are so slight. He that hath a will to die by himself fears it not from another. Let your general do his worst. For you, be that you are, long; and your misery increase with your age! I say to you, as I was said to: Away!

Exit

FIRST WATCH: A noble fellow, I warrant him.

SECOND WATCH: The worthy fellow is our general; he's the rock, the oak not to be wind-shaken.

Exeunt

ACT V. SCENE III. The Tent of Coriolanus

Enter Coriolanus, Aufidius, and Others

CORIOLANUS: We will before the walls of Rome to-morrow
Set down our host. My partner in this action,
You must report to th' Volscian lords how plainly
I have borne this business.

AUFIDIUS: Only their ends
You have respected; stopp'd your ears against
The general suit of Rome; never admitted
A private whisper- no, not with such friends
That thought them sure of you.

CORIOLANUS: This last old man,
Whom with crack'd heart I have sent to Rome,
Lov'd me above the measure of a father;

Nay, godded me indeed. Their latest refuge
Was to send him; for whose old love I have-
Though I show'd sourly to him- once more offer'd
The first conditions, which they did refuse
And cannot now accept. To grace him only,
That thought he could do more, a very little
I have yielded to; fresh embassies and suits,
Nor from the state nor private friends, hereafter
Will I lend ear to. Shout Within Ha! what shout is this?
Shall I be tempted to infringe my vow
In the same time 'tis made? I will not.
Enter, in Mourning Habits, Virgilia, Volumnia, Valeria, Young Marcius, with Attendants
My wife comes foremost, then the honour'd mould
Wherein this trunk was fram'd, and in her hand
The grandchild to her blood. But out, affection!
All bond and privilege of nature, break!
Let it be virtuous to be obstinate.
What is that curtsy worth? or those doves' eyes,
Which can make gods forsworn? I melt, and am not
Of stronger earth than others. My mother bows,
As if Olympus to a molehill should
In supplication nod; and my young boy
Hath an aspect of intercession which
Great nature cries 'Deny not.' Let the Volsces
Plough Rome and harrow Italy; I'll never
Be such a gosling to obey instinct, but stand
As if a man were author of himself
And knew no other kin.
VIRGILIA: My lord and husband!
CORIOLANUS: These eyes are not the same I wore in Rome.
VIRGILIA: The sorrow that delivers us thus chang'd
Makes you think so.
CORIOLANUS: Like a dull actor now
I have forgot my part and I am out,
Even to a full disgrace. Best of my flesh,
Forgive my tyranny; but do not say,
For that, 'Forgive our Romans.' O, a kiss
Long as my exile, sweet as my revenge!
Now, by the jealous queen of heaven, that kiss
I carried from thee, dear, and my true lip
Hath virgin'd it e'er since. You gods! I prate,
And the most noble mother of the world
Leave unsaluted. Sink, my knee, i' th' earth;
Kneels
Of thy deep duty more impression show
Than that of common sons.
VOLUMNIA: O, stand up blest!
Whilst with no softer cushion than the flint
I kneel before thee, and unproperly
Show duty, as mistaken all this while
Between the child and parent.
Kneels
CORIOLANUS: What's this?

Your knees to me, to your corrected son?
Then let the pebbles on the hungry beach
Fillip the stars; then let the mutinous winds
Strike the proud cedars 'gainst the fiery sun,
Murd'ring impossibility, to make
What cannot be slight work.
VOLUMNIA: Thou art my warrior;
I holp to frame thee. Do you know this lady?
CORIOLANUS: The noble sister of Publicola,
The moon of Rome, chaste as the icicle
That's curdied by the frost from purest snow,
And hangs on Dian's temple- dear Valeria!
VOLUMNIA: This is a poor epitome of yours,
Which by th' interpretation of full time
May show like all yourself.
CORIOLANUS: The god of soldiers,
With the consent of supreme Jove, inform
Thy thoughts with nobleness, that thou mayst prove
To shame unvulnerable, and stick i' th' wars
Like a great sea-mark, standing every flaw,
And saving those that eye thee!
VOLUMNIA: Your knee, sirrah.
CORIOLANUS: That's my brave boy.
VOLUMNIA: Even he, your wife, this lady, and myself,
Are suitors to you.
CORIOLANUS: I beseech you, peace!
Or, if you'd ask, remember this before:
The thing I have forsworn to grant may never
Be held by you denials. Do not bid me
Dismiss my soldiers, or capitulate
Again with Rome's mechanics. Tell me not
Wherein I seem unnatural; desire not
T'allay my rages and revenges with
Your colder reasons.
VOLUMNIA: O, no more, no more!
You have said you will not grant us any thing-
For we have nothing else to ask but that
Which you deny already; yet we will ask,
That, if you fail in our request, the blame
May hang upon your hardness; therefore hear us.
CORIOLANUS: Aufidius, and you Volsces, mark; for we'll
Hear nought from Rome in private. Your request?
VOLUMNIA: Should we be silent and not speak, our raiment
And state of bodies would bewray what life
We have led since thy exile. Think with thyself
How more unfortunate than all living women
Are we come hither; since that thy sight, which should
Make our eyes flow with joy, hearts dance with comforts,
Constrains them weep and shake with fear and sorrow,
Making the mother, wife, and child, to see
The son, the husband, and the father, tearing
His country's bowels out. And to poor we
Thine enmity's most capital: thou bar'st us

Our prayers to the gods, which is a comfort
That all but we enjoy. For how can we,
Alas, how can we for our country pray,
Whereto we are bound, together with thy victory,
Whereto we are bound? Alack, or we must lose
The country, our dear nurse, or else thy person,
Our comfort in the country. We must find
An evident calamity, though we had
Our wish, which side should win; for either thou
Must as a foreign recreant be led
With manacles through our streets, or else
Triumphantly tread on thy country's ruin,
And bear the palm for having bravely shed
Thy wife and children's blood. For myself, son,
I purpose not to wait on fortune till
These wars determine; if I can not persuade thee
Rather to show a noble grace to both parts
Than seek the end of one, thou shalt no sooner
March to assault thy country than to tread-
Trust to't, thou shalt not- on thy mother's womb
That brought thee to this world.
VIRGILIA: Ay, and mine,
That brought you forth this boy to keep your name
Living to time.
BOY: 'A shall not tread on me!
I'll run away till I am bigger, but then I'll fight.
CORIOLANUS: Not of a woman's tenderness to be
Requires nor child nor woman's face to see.
I have sat too long.
Rising
VOLUMNIA: Nay, go not from us thus.
If it were so that our request did tend
To save the Romans, thereby to destroy
The Volsces whom you serve, you might condemn us
As poisonous of your honour. No, our suit
Is that you reconcile them: while the Volsces
May say 'This mercy we have show'd,' the Romans
'This we receiv'd,' and each in either side
Give the all-hail to thee, and cry 'Be blest
For making up this peace!' Thou know'st, great son,
The end of war's uncertain; but this certain,
That, if thou conquer Rome, the benefit
Which thou shalt thereby reap is such a name
Whose repetition will be dogg'd with curses;
Whose chronicle thus writ: 'The man was noble,
But with his last attempt he wip'd it out,
Destroy'd his country, and his name remains
To th' ensuing age abhorr'd.' Speak to me, son.
Thou hast affected the fine strains of honour,
To imitate the graces of the gods,
To tear with thunder the wide cheeks o' th' air,
And yet to charge thy sulphur with a bolt
That should but rive an oak. Why dost not speak?

Think'st thou it honourable for a noble man
Still to remember wrongs? Daughter, speak you:
He cares not for your weeping. Speak thou, boy;
Perhaps thy childishness will move him more
Than can our reasons. There's no man in the world
More bound to's mother, yet here he lets me prate
Like one i' th' stocks. Thou hast never in thy life
Show'd thy dear mother any courtesy,
When she, poor hen, fond of no second brood,
Has cluck'd thee to the wars, and safely home
Loaden with honour. Say my request's unjust,
And spurn me back; but if it he not so,
Thou art not honest, and the gods will plague thee,
That thou restrain'st from me the duty which
To a mother's part belongs. He turns away.
Down, ladies; let us shame him with our knees.
To his surname Coriolanus 'longs more pride
Than pity to our prayers. Down. An end;
This is the last. So we will home to Rome,
And die among our neighbours. Nay, behold's!
This boy, that cannot tell what he would have
But kneels and holds up hands for fellowship,
Does reason our petition with more strength
Than thou hast to deny't. Come, let us go.
This fellow had a Volscian to his mother;
His wife is in Corioli, and his child
Like him by chance. Yet give us our dispatch.
I am hush'd until our city be afire,
And then I'll speak a little.
He Holds Her by the Hand, Silent
CORIOLANUS: O mother, mother!
What have you done? Behold, the heavens do ope,
The gods look down, and this unnatural scene
They laugh at. O my mother, mother! O!
You have won a happy victory to Rome;
But for your son- believe it, O, believe it!-
Most dangerously you have with him prevail'd,
If not most mortal to him. But let it come.
Aufidius, though I cannot make true wars,
I'll frame convenient peace. Now, good Aufidius,
Were you in my stead, would you have heard
A mother less, or granted less, Aufidius?
AUFIDIUS: I was mov'd withal.
CORIOLANUS: I dare be sworn you were!
And, sir, it is no little thing to make
Mine eyes to sweat compassion. But, good sir,
What peace you'fl make, advise me. For my part,
I'll not to Rome, I'll back with you; and pray you
Stand to me in this cause. O mother! wife!
AUFIDIUS: Aside I am glad thou hast set thy mercy and thy honour
At difference in thee. Out of that I'll work
Myself a former fortune.
CORIOLANUS: To the Ladies Ay, by and by;

But we will drink together; and you shall bear
A better witness back than words, which we,
On like conditions, will have counter-seal'd.
Come, enter with us. Ladies, you deserve
To have a temple built you. All the swords
In Italy, and her confederate arms,
Could not have made this peace.
Exeunt

ACT V. SCENE IV. Rome. A Public Place

Enter Menenius and Sicinius
MENENIUS: See you yond coign o' th' Capitol, yond cornerstone?
SICINIUS: Why, what of that?
MENENIUS: If it be possible for you to displace it with your little finger, there is some hope the ladies of Rome, especially his mother, may prevail with him. But I say there is no hope in't; our throats are sentenc'd, and stay upon execution.
SICINIUS: Is't possible that so short a time can alter the condition of a man?
MENENIUS: There is differency between a grub and a butterfly; yet your butterfly was a grub. This Marcius is grown from man to dragon; he has wings, he's more than a creeping thing.
SICINIUS: He lov'd his mother dearly.
MENENIUS: So did he me; and he no more remembers his mother now than an eight-year-old horse. The tartness of his face sours ripe grapes; when he walks, he moves like an engine and the ground shrinks before his treading. He is able to pierce a corslet with his eye, talks like a knell, and his hum is a battery. He sits in his state as a thing made for Alexander. What he bids be done is finish'd with his bidding. He wants nothing of a god but eternity, and a heaven to throne in.
SICINIUS: Yes- mercy, if you report him truly.
MENENIUS: I paint him in the character. Mark what mercy his mother shall bring from him. There is no more mercy in him than there is milk in a male tiger; that shall our poor city find. And all this is 'long of you.
SICINIUS: The gods be good unto us!
MENENIUS: No, in such a case the gods will not be good unto us. When we banish'd him we respected not them; and, he returning to break our necks, they respect not us.
Enter a Messenger
MESSENGER: Sir, if you'd save your life, fly to your house.
The plebeians have got your fellow tribune
And hale him up and down; all swearing if
The Roman ladies bring not comfort home
They'll give him death by inches.
Enter Another Messenger
SICINIUS: What's the news?
SECOND MESSENGER: Good news, good news! The ladies have prevail'd,
The Volscians are dislodg'd, and Marcius gone.
A merrier day did never yet greet Rome,
No, not th' expulsion of the Tarquins.
SICINIUS: Friend,
Art thou certain this is true? Is't most certain?

SECOND MESSENGER: As certain as I know the sun is fire.
Where have you lurk'd, that you make doubt of it?
Ne'er through an arch so hurried the blown tide
As the recomforted through th' gates. Why, hark you!
Trumpets, Hautboys, Drums Beat, All Together
The trumpets, sackbuts, psalteries, and fifes,
Tabors and cymbals, and the shouting Romans,
Make the sun dance. Hark you! A Shout Within
MENENIUS: This is good news.
I will go meet the ladies. This Volumnia
Is worth of consuls, senators, patricians,
A city full; of tribunes such as you,
A sea and land full. You have pray'd well to-day:
This morning for ten thousand of your throats
I'd not have given a doit. Hark, how they joy!
Sound Still with the Shouts
SICINIUS: First, the gods bless you for your tidings; next,
Accept my thankfulness.
SECOND MESSENGER: Sir, we have all
Great cause to give great thanks.
SICINIUS: They are near the city?
MESSENGER: Almost at point to enter.
SICINIUS: We'll meet them,
And help the joy.
Exeunt

ACT V. SCENE V. Rome. A street near the Gate

Enter Two Senators with Volumnia, Virgilia, Valeria, Passing over the Stage, 'With Other Lords
FIRST SENATOR: Behold our patroness, the life of Rome!
Call all your tribes together, praise the gods,
And make triumphant fires; strew flowers before them.
Unshout the noise that banish'd Marcius,
Repeal him with the welcome of his mother;
ALL: Welcome, ladies, welcome!
A Flourish with Drums and Trumpets. Exeunt

ACT V. SCENE VI. Corioli. A Public Place

Enter Tullus Aufidius with Attendents
AUFIDIUS: Go tell the lords o' th' city I am here;
Deliver them this paper' having read it,
Bid them repair to th' market-place, where I,
Even in theirs and in the commons' ears,
Will vouch the truth of it. Him I accuse
The city ports by this hath enter'd and
Intends t' appear before the people, hoping
To purge himself with words. Dispatch.
Exeunt Attendants
Enter Three or Four Conspirators of Aufidius' Faction
Most welcome!
FIRST CONSPIRATOR: How is it with our general?
AUFIDIUS: Even so
As with a man by his own alms empoison'd,
And with his charity slain.
SECOND CONSPIRATOR: Most noble sir,
If you do hold the same intent wherein

You wish'd us parties, we'll deliver you
Of your great danger.
AUFIDIUS: Sir, I cannot tell;
We must proceed as we do find the people.
THIRD CONSPIRATOR: The people will remain uncertain whilst
'Twixt you there's difference; but the fall of either
Makes the survivor heir of all.
AUFIDIUS: I know it;
And my pretext to strike at him admits
A good construction. I rais'd him, and I pawn'd
Mine honour for his truth; who being so heighten'd,
He watered his new plants with dews of flattery,
Seducing so my friends; and to this end
He bow'd his nature, never known before
But to be rough, unswayable, and free.
THIRD CONSPIRATOR: Sir, his stoutness
When he did stand for consul, which he lost
By lack of stooping-
AUFIDIUS: That I would have spoken of.
Being banish'd for't, he came unto my hearth,
Presented to my knife his throat. I took him;
Made him joint-servant with me; gave him way
In all his own desires; nay, let him choose
Out of my files, his projects to accomplish,
My best and freshest men; serv'd his designments
In mine own person; holp to reap the fame
Which he did end all his, and took some pride
To do myself this wrong. Till, at the last,
I seem'd his follower, not partner; and
He wag'd me with his countenance as if
I had been mercenary.
FIRST CONSPIRATOR: So he did, my lord.
The army marvell'd at it; and, in the last,
When he had carried Rome and that we look'd
For no less spoil than glory-
AUFIDIUS: There was it;
For which my sinews shall be stretch'd upon him.
At a few drops of women's rheum, which are
As cheap as lies, he sold the blood and labour
Of our great action; therefore shall he die,
And I'll renew me in his fall. But, hark!
Drums and Trumpets Sound, with Great Shouts of the People
FIRST CONSPIRATOR: Your native town you enter'd like a post,
And had no welcomes home; but he returns
Splitting the air with noise.
SECOND CONSPIRATOR: And patient fools,
Whose children he hath slain, their base throats tear
With giving him glory.
THIRD CONSPIRATOR: Therefore, at your vantage,
Ere he express himself or move the people
With what he would say, let him feel your sword,
Which we will second. When he lies along,
After your way his tale pronounc'd shall bury

His reasons with his body.
AUFIDIUS: Say no more:
Here come the lords.
Enter the Lords of the City
LORDS: You are most welcome home.
AUFIDIUS: I have not deserv'd it.
But, worthy lords, have you with heed perused
What I have written to you?
LORDS: We have.
FIRST LORD: And grieve to hear't.
What faults he made before the last, I think
Might have found easy fines; but there to end
Where he was to begin, and give away
The benefit of our levies, answering us
With our own charge, making a treaty where
There was a yielding- this admits no excuse.
AUFIDIUS: He approaches; you shall hear him.
Enter Coriolanus, Marching with Drum and Colours; the Commoners Being with Him
CORIOLANUS: Hail, lords! I am return'd your soldier;
No more infected with my country's love
Than when I parted hence, but still subsisting
Under your great command. You are to know
That prosperously I have attempted, and
With bloody passage led your wars even to
The gates of Rome. Our spoils we have brought home
Doth more than counterpoise a full third part
The charges of the action. We have made peace
With no less honour to the Antiates
Than shame to th' Romans; and we here deliver,
Subscrib'd by th' consuls and patricians,
Together with the seal o' th' Senate, what
We have compounded on.
AUFIDIUS: Read it not, noble lords;
But tell the traitor in the highest degree
He hath abus'd your powers.
CORIOLANUS: Traitor! How now?
AUFIDIUS: Ay, traitor, Marcius.
CORIOLANUS: Marcius!
AUFIDIUS: Ay, Marcius, Caius Marcius! Dost thou think
I'll grace thee with that robbery, thy stol'n name
Coriolanus, in Corioli?
You lords and heads o' th' state, perfidiously
He has betray'd your business and given up,
For certain drops of salt, your city Rome-
I say your city- to his wife and mother;
Breaking his oath and resolution like
A twist of rotten silk; never admitting
Counsel o' th' war; but at his nurse's tears
He whin'd and roar'd away your victory,
That pages blush'd at him, and men of heart
Look'd wond'ring each at others.
CORIOLANUS: Hear'st thou, Mars?
AUFIDIUS: Name not the god, thou boy of tears-

CORIOLANUS: Ha!
AUFIDIUS: -no more.
CORIOLANUS: Measureless liar, thou hast made my heart
Too great for what contains it. 'Boy'! O slave!
Pardon me, lords, 'tis the first time that ever
I was forc'd to scold. Your judgments, my grave lords,
Must give this cur the lie; and his own notion-
Who wears my stripes impress'd upon him, that
Must bear my beating to his grave- shall join
To thrust the lie unto him.
FIRST LORD: Peace, both, and hear me speak.
CORIOLANUS: Cut me to pieces, Volsces; men and lads,
Stain all your edges on me. 'Boy'! False hound!
If you have writ your annals true, 'tis there
That, like an eagle in a dove-cote, I
Flutter'd your Volscians in Corioli.
Alone I did it. 'Boy'!
AUFIDIUS: Why, noble lords,
Will you be put in mind of his blind fortune,
Which was your shame, by this unholy braggart,
Fore your own eyes and ears?
CONSPIRATORS: Let him die for't.
ALL THE PEOPLE: Tear him to pieces. Do it presently. He kill'd my son. My daughter. He kill'd my cousin Marcus. He kill'd my father.
SECOND LORD: Peace, ho! No outrage- peace!
The man is noble, and his fame folds in
This orb o' th' earth. His last offences to us
Shall have judicious hearing. Stand, Aufidius,
And trouble not the peace.
CORIOLANUS: O that I had him,
With six Aufidiuses, or more- his tribe,
To use my lawful sword!
AUFIDIUS: Insolent villain!
CONSPIRATORS Kill, kill, kill, kill, kill him!
The Conspirators Draw and Kill Coriolanus,who Falls. Aufidius Stands on Him
LORDS: Hold, hold, hold, hold!
AUFIDIUS: My noble masters, hear me speak.
FIRST LORD: O Tullus!
SECOND LORD: Thou hast done a deed whereat valour will weep.
THIRD LORD: Tread not upon him. Masters all, be quiet;
Put up your swords.
AUFIDIUS: My lords, when you shall know- as in this rage,
Provok'd by him, you cannot- the great danger
Which this man's life did owe you, you'll rejoice
That he is thus cut off. Please it your honours
To call me to your Senate, I'll deliver
Myself your loyal servant, or endure
Your heaviest censure.
FIRST LORD: Bear from hence his body,
And mourn you for him. Let him be regarded
As the most noble corse that ever herald
Did follow to his um.
SECOND LORD: His own impatience

Takes from Aufidius a great part of blame.
Let's make the best of it.
AUFIDIUS: My rage is gone,
And I am struck with sorrow. Take him up.
Help, three o' th' chiefest soldiers; I'll be one.
Beat thou the drum, that it speak mournfully;
Trail your steel pikes. Though in this city he
Hath widowed and unchilded many a one,
Which to this hour bewail the injury,
Yet he shall have a noble memory.
Assist. Exeunt, Bearing the Body of Coriolanus
A Dead March Sounded

END

The Life of Timon of Athens

Dramatis Personae

TIMON of Athens
LUCIUS
LUCULLUS
SEMPRONIUS
flattering lords
VENTIDIUS, one of Timon's false friends
ALCIBIADES, an Athenian captain
APEMANTUS, a churlish philosopher
FLAVIUS, steward to Timon
FLAMINIUS
LUCILIUS
SERVILIUS
Timon's servants
CAPHIS
PHILOTUS
TITUS
HORTENSIUS
servants to Timon's creditors
POET PAINTER
JEWELLER
MERCHANT
MERCER
AN OLD ATHENIAN
THREE STRANGERS
A PAGE A FOOL
PHRYNIA
TIMANDRA, mistresses to Alcibiades
CUPID
AMAZONS, in the Masque
Lords, Senators, Officers, Soldiers, Servants, Thieves, and Attendants

SCENE: Athens and the neighbouring woods

ACT I SCENE I. Athens. A Hall in Timon's House

Enter Poet, Painter, Jeweller, Merchant, and Others, at Several Doors.

POET: Good day, sir.
PAINTER: I am glad you're well.
POET: I have not seen you long. How goes the world?
PAINTER: It wears, sir, as it grows.
POET: Ay, that's well known;
But what particular rarity? what strange,
Which manifold record not matches? See,
Magic of bounty! all these spirits thy power
Hath conjur'd to attend! I know the merchant.
PAINTER: I know them both; th' other's a jeweller.
MERCHANT: O, 'tis a worthy lord!
JEWELLER: Nay, that's most fix'd.
MERCHANT: A most incomparable man; breath'd, as it were,
To an untirable and continuate goodness.
He passes.
JEWELLER: I have a jewel here-
MERCHANT: O, pray let's see't: for the Lord Timon, sir?

JEWELLER: If he will touch the estimate: but for that-
POET: When we for recompense have prais'd the vile,
It stains the glory in that happy verse
Which aptly sings the good.
MERCHANT: Looking at the Jewel.
'Tis a good form.
JEWELLER: And rich: here is a water, look ye.
PAINTER: You are rapt, sir, in some work, some dedication
To the great lord.
POET: A thing slipp'd idly from me.
Our poesy is as a gum, which oozes
From whence 'tis nourish'd: the fire i' the flint
Shows not till it be struck; our gentle flame
Provokes itself, and like the current flies
Each bound it chafes. What have you there?
PAINTER: A picture, sir. When comes your book forth?
POET: Upon the heels of my presentment, sir.
Let's see your piece.
PAINTER: 'Tis a good piece.
POET: So 'tis: this comes off well and excellent.
PAINTER: Indifferent.
POET: Admirable! How this grace
Speaks his own standing! what a mental power
This eye shoots forth! how big imagination
Moves in this lip! to the dumbness of the gesture
One might interpret.
PAINTER: It is a pretty mocking of the life.
Here is a touch; is't good?
POET: I'll say of it,
It tutors nature: artificial strife
Lives in these touches, livelier than life.
Enter Certain Senators, Who Pass over the Stage.
PAINTER: How this lord is followed!
POET: The senators of Athens: happy man!
PAINTER: Look, more!
POET: You see this confluence, this great flood of visitors.
I have, in this rough work, shap'd out a man
Whom this beneath world doth embrace and hug
With amplest entertainment: my free drift
Halts not particularly, but moves itself
In a wide sea of wax: no levell'd malice
Infects one comma in the course I hold:
But flies an eagle flight, bold and forth on,
Leaving no tract behind.
PAINTER: How shall I understand you?
POET: I will unbolt to you.
You see how all conditions, how all minds-
As well of glib and slipp'ry creatures as
Of grave and austere quality-tender down
Their services to Lord Timon: his large fortune,
Upon his good and gracious nature hanging,
Subdues and properties to his love and tendance
All sorts of hearts; yea, from the glass-fac'd flatterer

To Apemantus, that few things loves better
Than to abhor himself: even he drops down
The knee before him, and returns in peace
Most rich in Timon's nod.
PAINTER: I saw them speak together.
POET: Sir, I have upon a high and pleasant hill
Feign'd Fortune to be thron'd: the base o' the mount
Is rank'd with all deserts, all kind of natures
That labour on the bosom of this sphere
To propagate their states: amongst them all,
Whose eyes are on this sovereign lady fix'd
One do I personate of Lord Timon's frame,
Whom Fortune with her ivory hand wafts to her;
Whose present grace to present slaves and servants
Translates his rivals.
PAINTER: 'Tis conceiv'd to scope.
This throne, this Fortune, and this hill, methinks,
With one man beckon'd from the rest below,
Bowing his head against the steepy mount
To climb his happiness, would be well express'd
In our condition.
POET: Nay, sir, but hear me on.
All those which were his fellows but of late,
Some better than his value, on the moment
Follow his strides, his lobbies fill with tendance,
Rain sacrificial whisperings in his ear,
Make sacred even his stirrup, and through him
Drink the free air.
PAINTER: Ay, marry, what of these?
POET: When Fortune in her shift and change of mood
Spurns down her late beloved, all his dependants,
Which labour'd after him to the mountain's top
Even on their knees and hands, let him slip down,
Not one accompanying his declining foot.
PAINTER: 'Tis common:
A thousand moral paintings I can show
That shall demonstrate these quick blows of Fortune's
More pregnantly than words. Yet you do well
To show Lord Timon that mean eyes have seen
The foot above the head.

Trumpets Sound. Enter Lord Timon, Addressing Himself Courteously to Every Suitor: a Messenger from Ventidius Talking with Him; Lucilius and Other Servants Following.

TIMON: Imprison'd is he, say you?
MESSENGER: Ay, my good lord. Five talents is his debt,
His means most short, his creditors most strait:
Your honourable letter he desires
To those have shut him up; which, failing,
Periods his comfort.
TIMON: Noble Ventidius! Well:
I am not of that feather to shake off
My friend when he must need me. I do know him
A gentleman that well deserves a help,
Which he shall have: I'll pay the debt and free him.

MESSENGER: Your lordship ever binds him.
TIMON: Commend me to him; I will send his ransom;
And being enfranchis'd, bid him come to me.
'Tis not enough to help the feeble up,
But to support him after. Fare you well.
MESSENGER: All happiness to your honour.
Exit.
Enter an Old Athenian.
OLD ATHENIAN: Lord Timon, hear me speak.
TIMON: Freely, good father.
OLD ATHENIAN: Thou hast a servant nam'd Lucilius.
TIMON: I have so: what of him?
OLD ATHENIAN: Most noble Timon, call the man before thee.
TIMON: Attends he here or no? Lucilius!
LUCILIUS: Here, at your lordship's service.
OLD ATHENIAN: This fellow here, Lord Timon, this thy creature,
By night frequents my house. I am a man
That from my first have been inclin'd to thrift,
And my estate deserves an heir more rais'd
Than one which holds a trencher.
TIMON: Well; what further?
OLD ATHENIAN: One only daughter have I, no kin else,
On whom I may confer what I have got:
The maid is fair, o' the youngest for a bride,
And I have bred her at my dearest cost
In qualities of the best. This man of thine
Attempts her love: I prithee, noble lord,
Join with me to forbid him her resort;
Myself have spoke in vain.
TIMON: The man is honest.
OLD ATHENIAN: Therefore he will be, Timon:
His honesty rewards him in itself;
It must not bear my daughter.
TIMON: Does she love him?
OLD ATHENIAN: She is young and apt:
Our own precedent passions do instruct us
What levity's in youth.
TIMON: To Lucilius Love you the maid?
LUCILIUS: Ay, my good lord, and she accepts of it.
OLD ATHENIAN: If in her marriage my consent be missing,
I call the gods to witness, I will choose
Mine heir from forth the beggars of the world,
And dispossess her all.
TIMON: How shall she be endow'd,
If she be mated with an equal husband?
OLD ATHENIAN: Three talents on the present; in future, all.
TIMON: This gentleman of mine hath serv'd me long:
To build his fortune I will strain a little,
For 'tis a bond in men. Give him thy daughter:
What you bestow, in him I'll counterpoise,
And make him weigh with her.
OLD ATHENIAN: Most noble lord,
Pawn me to this your honour, she is his.

TIMON: My hand to thee; mine honour on my promise.
LUCILIUS: Humbly I thank your lordship. Never may
That state or fortune fall into my keeping
Which is not owed to you!
Exeunt Lucilius and Old Athenian.
POET: Presenting His Poem
Vouchsafe my labour, and long live your lordship!
TIMON: I thank you; you shall hear from me anon:
Go not away. What have you there, my friend?
PAINTER: A piece of painting, which I do beseech
Your lordship to accept.
TIMON: Painting is welcome.
The painting is almost the natural man;
For since dishonour traffics with man's nature,
He is but outside: these pencill'd figures are
Even such as they give out. I like your work;
And you shall find I like it: wait attendance
Till you hear further from me.
PAINTER: The gods preserve you!
TIMON: Well fare you, gentleman: give me your hand;
We must needs dine together. Sir, your jewel
Hath suffered under praise.
JEWELLER: What, my lord! dispraise?
TIMON: A mere satiety of commendations;
If I should pay you for 't as 'tis extoll'd,
It would unclew me quite.
JEWELLER: My lord, 'tis rated
As those which sell would give: but you well know,
Things of like value, differing in the owners,
Are prized by their masters. Believe't, dear lord,
You mend the jewel by the wearing it.
TIMON: Well mock'd.
MERCHANT: No, my good lord; he speaks the common tongue,
Which all men speak with him.
TIMON: Look who comes here. Will you be chid?
Enter Apemantus.
JEWELLER: We'll bear, with your lordship.
MERCHANT: He'll spare none.
TIMON: Good morrow to thee, gentle Apemantus!
APEMANTUS: Till I be gentle, stay thou for thy good morrow;
When thou art Timon's dog, and these knaves honest.
TIMON: Why dost thou call them knaves? thou know'st them not.
APEMANTUS: Are they not Athenians?
TIMON: Yes.
APEMANTUS: Then I repent not.
JEWELLER: You know me, Apemantus?
APEMANTUS: Thou know'st I do; I call'd thee by thy name.
TIMON: Thou art proud, Apemantus.
APEMANTUS: Of nothing so much as that I am not like Timon.
TIMON: Whither art going?
APEMANTUS: To knock out an honest Athenian's brains.
TIMON: That's a deed thou'lt die for.
APEMANTUS: Right, if doing nothing be death by the law.

TIMON: How likest thou this picture, Apemantus?
APEMANTUS: The best, for the innocence.
TIMON: Wrought he not well that painted it?
APEMANTUS: He wrought better that made the painter; and yet he's but a filthy piece of work.
PAINTER: You're a dog.
APEMANTUS: Thy mother's of my generation: what's she, if I be a dog?
TIMON: Wilt dine with me, Apemantus?
APEMANTUS: No; I eat not lords.
TIMON: An thou shouldst, thou'dst anger ladies.
APEMANTUS: O! they eat lords; so they come by great bellies.
TIMON: That's a lascivious apprehension.
APEMANTUS: So thou apprehendest it, take it for thy labour.
TIMON: How dost thou like this jewel, Apemantus?
APEMANTUS: Not so well as plain dealing, which will not cost a man a doit.
TIMON: What dost thou think 'tis worth?
APEMANTUS: Not worth my thinking. How now, poet!
POET: How now, philosopher!
APEMANTUS: Thou liest.
POET: Art not one?
APEMANTUS: Yes.
POET: Then I lie not.
APEMANTUS: Art not a poet?
POET: Yes.
APEMANTUS: Then thou liest: look in thy last work, where thou hast feigned him a worthy fellow.
POET: That's not feigned; he is so.
APEMANTUS: Yes, he is worthy of thee, and to pay thee for thy labour: he that loves to be flattered is worthy o' the flatterer. Heavens, that I were a lord!
TIMON: What wouldst do then, Apemantus?
APEMANTUS: Even as Apemantus does now; hate a lord with my heart.
TIMON: What, thyself?
APEMANTUS: Ay.
TIMON: Wherefore?
APEMANTUS: That I had no angry wit to be a lord. Art not thou a merchant?
MERCHANT: Ay, Apemantus.
APEMANTUS: Traffic confound thee, if the gods will not!
MERCHANT: If traffic do it, the gods do it.
APEMANTUS: Traffic's thy god, and thy god confound thee!
Trumpet Sounds. Enter a Messenger.
TIMON: What trumpet's that?
MESSENGER: 'Tis Alcibiades, and some twenty horse,
All of companionship.
TIMON: Pray entertain them; give them guide to us.
Exeunt Some Attendants.
You must needs dine with me. Go not you hence
Till I have thank'd you; when dinner's done,
Show me this piece. I am joyful of your sights.
Enter Alcibiades, with the His Company.
Most welcome, sir!
They salute.
APEMANTUS: So, so, there!

Aches contract and starve your supple joints!
That there should be small love 'mongst these sweet knaves,
And all this courtesy! The strain of man's bred out
Into baboon and monkey.
ALCIBIADES: Sir, you have sav'd my longing, and I feed
Most hungerly on your sight.
TIMON: Right welcome, sir!
Ere we depart we'll share a bounteous time
In different pleasures. Pray you, let us in.
Exeunt All but Apemantus.
Enter Two Lords.
FIRST LORD: What time o' day is't, Apemantus?
APEMANTUS: Time to be honest.
FIRST LORD: That time serves still.
APEMANTUS: The more accursed thou that still omitt'st it.
SECOND LORD: Thou art going to Lord Timon's feast.
APEMANTUS: Ay; to see meat fill knaves and wine heat fools.
SECOND LORD: Fare thee well, fare thee well.
APEMANTUS: Thou art a fool to bid me farewell twice.
SECOND LORD: Why, Apemantus?
APEMANTUS: Shouldst have kept one to thyself, for I mean to give thee none.
FIRST LORD: Hang thyself!
APEMANTUS: No, I will do nothing at thy bidding: make thy requests to thy friend.
SECOND LORD: Away, unpeaceable dog! or I'll spurn thee hence.
APEMANTUS: I will fly, like a dog, the heels of an ass.
Exit.
FIRST LORD: He's opposite to humanity. Come, shall we in,
And taste Lord Timon's bounty? he outgoes
The very heart of kindness.
SECOND LORD: He pours it out; Plutus, the god of gold,
Is but his steward: no meed but he repays
Sevenfold above itself; no gift to him
But breeds the giver a return exceeding
All use of quittance.
FIRST LORD: The noblest mind he carries
That ever govern'd man.
SECOND LORD: Long may he live in fortunes! Shall we in?
FIRST LORD: I'll keep you company.
Exeunt.

ACT I. SCENE II. The Same. A Room of State in Timon's House.

Hautboys Playing Loud Music. A Great Banquet Served In; Flavius and Others Attending: Then Enter Lord Timon, Alcibiades, Lords, and Senators, Ventidius and Attendants. Then Comes, Dropping after All, Apemantus, Discontentedly, like Himself.

VENTIDIUS: Most honour'd Timon,
It hath pleas'd the gods to remember my father's age,
And call him to long peace.
He is gone happy, and has left me rich:
Then, as in grateful virtue I am bound
To your free heart, I do return those talents,
Doubled with thanks and service, from whose help
I deriv'd liberty.
TIMON: O! by no means,
Honest Ventidius: you mistake my love;

I gave it freely ever; and there's none
Can truly say he gives, if he receives:
If our betters play at that game, we must not dare
To imitate them; faults that are rich are fair.
VENTIDIUS: A noble spirit.
They All Stand Ceremoniously Looking on Timon.
TIMON: Nay, my lords, ceremony was but devis'd at first
To set a gloss on faint deeds, hollow welcomes,
Recanting goodness, sorry ere 'tis shown;
But where there is true friendship there needs none.
Pray, sit; more welcome are ye to my fortunes
Than my fortunes to me.
They sit.
FIRST LORD: My lord, we always have confess'd it.
APEMANTUS: Ho, ho! confess'd it; hang'd it, have you not?
TIMON: O! Apemantus, you are welcome.
APEMANTUS: No,
You shall not make me welcome:
I come to have thee thrust me out of doors.
TIMON: Fie! thou'rt a churl; ye've got a humour there
Does not become a man; 'tis much to blame.
They say, my lords, Ira furor brevis est;
But yond man is ever angry.
Go, let him have a table by himself;
For he does neither affect company,
Nor is he fit for it, indeed.
APEMANTUS: Let me stay at thine apperil, Timon:
I come to observe; I give thee warning on't.
TIMON: I take no heed of thee; thou'rt an Athenian, therefore, welcome.
I myself would have no power; prithee; let my meat make thee
silent.
APEMANTUS: I scorn thy meat; 't'would choke me, for I should
Ne'er flatter thee. O you gods! what a number
Of men eats Timon, and he sees 'em not!
It grieves me to see so many dip their meat
In one man's blood; and all the madness is,
He cheers them up too.
I wonder men dare trust themselves with men:
Methinks they should invite them without knives;
Good for their meat, and safer for their lives.
There's much example for 't; the fellow that
Sits next him now, parts bread with him, pledges
The breath of him in a divided draught,
Is the readiest man to kill him: 't has been prov'd.
If I were a huge man, I should fear to drink at meals;
Lest they should spy my wind-pipe's dangerous notes:
Great men should drink with harness on their throats.
TIMON: My lord, in heart; and let the health go round.
SECOND LORD: Let it flow this way, my good lord.
APEMANTUS: Flow this way! A brave fellow! he keeps his tides well. Those healths will make thee and thy state look ill, Timon.
Here's that which is too weak to be a sinner,
Honest water, which ne'er left man i' the mire:

This and my food are equals; there's no odds:
Feasts are too proud to give thanks to the gods.
Immortal gods, I crave no pelf;
I pray for no man but myself.
Grant I may never prove so fond
To trust man on his oath or bond;
Or a harlot for her weeping;
Or a dog that seems a-sleeping;
Or a keeper with my freedom;
Or my friends, if I should need 'em.
Amen. So fall to't.
Rich men sin, and I eat root.
Eats and Drinks.
Much good dich thy good heart, Apemantus!
TIMON: Captain Alcibiades, your heart's in the field now.
ALCIBIADES: My heart is ever at your service, my lord.
TIMON: You had rather be at a breakfast of enemies than a dinner of friends.
ALCIBIADES: So they were bleeding-new, my lord, there's no meat like 'em: I could wish my best friend at such a feast.
APEMANTUS: 'Would all those flatterers were thine enemies then, that then thou mightst kill 'em, and bid me to 'em.
FIRST LORD: Might we but have that happiness, my lord, that you would once use our hearts, whereby we might express some part of our zeals, we should think ourselves for ever perfect.
TIMON: O, no doubt, my good friends, but the gods themselves have provided that I shall have much help from you: how had you been my friends else? why have you that charitable title from thousands, did not you chiefly belong to my heart? I have told more of you to myself than you can with modesty speak in your own behalf; and thus far I confirm you. O you gods! think I, what need we have any friends if we should ne'er have need of 'em? they were the most needless creatures living, should we ne'er have use for 'em; and would most resemble sweet instruments hung up in cases, that keep their sounds to themselves. Why, I have often wished myself poorer that I might come nearer to you. We are born to do benefits; and what better or properer can we call our own than the riches of our friends? O! what a precious comfort 'tis to have so many, like brothers, commanding one another's fortunes! O joy! e'en made away ere it can be born. Mine eyes cannot hold out water, methinks: to forget their faults, I drink to you.
APEMANTUS: Thou weepest to make them drink, Timon.
SECOND LORD: Joy had the like conception in our eyes,
And, at that instant like a babe, sprung up.
APEMANTUS: Ho, ho! I laugh to think that babe a bastard.
THIRD LORD: I promise you, my lord, you mov'd me much.
APEMANTUS: Much!
Tucket Sounded.
TIMON: What means that trump?
Enter a Servant.
How now!
SERVANT: Please you, my lord, there are certain ladies most desirous of

admittance.
TIMON: Ladies? What are their wills?
SERVANT: There comes with them a forerunner, my lord, which bears that office, to signify their pleasures.
TIMON: I pray, let them be admitted.
Enter Cupid.
CUPID: Hail to thee, worthy Timon; and to all
That of his bounties taste! The five best Senses
Acknowledge thee their patron; and come freely
To gratulate thy plenteous bosom. Th' Ear,
Taste, Touch, Smell, pleas'd from thy table rise;
They only now come but to feast thine eyes.
TIMON: They are welcome all; let 'em have kind admittance:
Music, make their welcome!
Exit Cupid.
FIRST LORD: You see, my lord, how ample you're belov'd.
Music. Re-enter Cupid, with a Masque of Ladies as Amazons, with Lutes in Their Hands, Dancing and Playing.
APEMANTUS: Hoy-day! what a sweep of vanity comes this way:
They dance! they are mad women.
Like madness is the glory of this life,
As this pomp shows to a little oil and root.
We make ourselves fools to disport ourselves;
And spend our flatteries to drink those men
Upon whose age we void it up again,
With poisonous spite and envy.
Who lives that's not depraved or depraves?
Who dies that bears not one spurn to their graves
Of their friend's gift?
I should fear those that dance before me now
Would one day stamp upon me: it has been done:
Men shut their doors against a setting sun.
The Lords Rise from Table, with Much Adoring of Timon; and to Show Their Loves, Each Singles out an Amazon, and All Dance, Men with Women, a Lofty Strain or Two to the Hautboys, and Cease.
TIMON: You have done our pleasures much grace, fair ladies,
Set a fair fashion on our entertainment,
Which was not half so beautiful and kind;
You have added worth unto 't and lustre,
And entertain'd me with mine own device;
I am to thank you for 't.
FIRST LADY: My lord, you take us even at the best.
APEMANTUS: Faith, for the worst is filthy; and would not hold taking, I doubt me.
TIMON: Ladies, there is an idle banquet
Attends you; please you to dispose yourselves.
ALL LADIES: Most thankfully, my lord.
Exeunt Cupid and Ladies.
TIMON: Flavius!
FLAVIUS: My lord!
TIMON: The little casket bring me hither.
FLAVIUS: Yes, my lord. Aside. More jewels yet!
There is no crossing him in 's humour;
Else I should tell him well, i' faith, I should,

When all's spent, he'd be cross'd then, an he could.
'Tis pity bounty had not eyes behind,
That man might ne'er be wretched for his mind.
Exit.
FIRST LORD: Where be our men?
SERVANT: Here, my lord, in readiness.
SECOND LORD: Our horses!
Re-enter Flavius, with the Casket.
TIMON: O, my friends! I have one word to say to you;
Look you, my good lord,
I must entreat you, honour me so much
As to advance this jewel; accept it and wear it,
Kind my lord.
FIRST LORD: I am so far already in your gifts-
ALL: So are we all.
Enter a Servant.
SERVANT: My lord, there are certain nobles of the Senate
Newly alighted and come to visit you.
TIMON: They are fairly welcome.

FLAVIUS: I beseech your honour,
Vouchsafe me a word; it does concern you near.
TIMON: Near! why then, another time I'll hear thee.
I prithee let's be provided to show them entertainment.
FLAVIUS: Aside. I scarce know how.
Enter Another Servant.
SECOND SERVANT: May it please vour honour, Lord Lucius,
Out of his free love, hath presented to you
Four milk-white horses, trapp'd in silver.
TIMON: I shall accept them fairly; let the presents
Be worthily entertain'd.
Enter a Third Servant.
How now! What news?
THIRD SERVANT: Please you, my lord, that honourable gentleman, Lord Lucullus, entreats your company to-morrow to hunt with him, and has sent your honour two brace of greyhounds.
TIMON: I'll hunt with him; and let them be receiv'd,
Not without fair reward.
FLAVIUS: Aside. What will this come to?
He commands us to provide, and give great gifts,
And all out of an empty coffer;
Nor will he know his purse, or yield me this,
To show him what a beggar his heart is,
Being of no power to make his wishes good.
His promises fly so beyond his state
That what he speaks is all in debt; he owes
For every word: he is so kind that he now
Pays interest for 't; his land's put to their books.
Well, would I were gently put out of office
Before I were forc'd out!
Happier he that has no friend to feed
Than such that do e'en enemies exceed.
I bleed inwardly for my lord.

Exit.
TIMON: You do yourselves much wrong;
You bate too much of your own merits;
Here, my lord, a trifle of our love.
SECOND LORD: With more than common thanks I will receive it.
THIRD LORD: O! he's the very soul of bounty!
TIMON: And now I remember, my lord, you gave
Good words the other day of a bay courser
I rode on: it is yours because you lik'd it.
THIRD LORD: O! I beseech you, pardon me, my lord, in that.
TIMON: You may take my word, my lord: I know no man
Can justly praise but what he does affect:
I weigh my friend's affection with mine own.
I'll tell you true; I'll call to you.
ALL LORDS: O! none so welcome!
TIMON: I take all and your several visitations
So kind to heart, 'tis not enough to give;
Methinks, I could deal kingdoms to my friends,
And ne'er be weary. Alcibiades,
Thou art a soldier, therefore seldom rich;
It comes in charity to thee; for all thy living
Is 'mongst the dead, and all the lands thou hast
Lie in a pitch'd field.
ALCIBIADES: Ay, defil'd land, my lord.
FIRST LORD: We are so virtuously bound,-
TIMON: And so am I to you.
SECOND LORD: So infinitely endear'd,-
TIMON: All to you. Lights, more lights!
FIRST LORD: The best of happiness,
Honour, and fortunes, keep with you, Lord Timon!
TIMON: Ready for his friends.
Exeunt Alcibiades, Lords, and etc.
APEMANTUS: What a coil's here!
Serving of becks and jutting out of bums!
I doubt whether their legs be worth the sums
That are given for 'em. Friendship's full of dregs:
Methinks, false hearts should never have sound legs.
Thus honest fools lay out their wealth on curtsies.
TIMON: Now, Apemantus, if thou wert not sullen,
I would be good to thee.
APEMANTUS: No, I'll nothing; for if I should be bribed too, there would be none left to rail upon thee, and then thou wouldst sin the faster. Thou givest so long, Timon, I fear me thou wilt give away thyself in paper shortly: What needs these feasts, pomps, and vain-glories?
TIMON: Nay, an you begin to rail on society once, I am sworn not to give regard to you. Farewell; and come with better music.
Exit.
APEMANTUS: So: Thou wilt not hear me now; thou shalt not then;
I'll lock thy heaven from thee.
O! that men's ears should be
To counsel deaf, but not to flattery!
Exit.

ACT II. SCENE I. Athens. A Room in a Senator's House.

Enter a Senator, with Papers in His Hand.

SENATOR: And late, five thousand: to Varro and to Isidore
He owes nine thousand; besides my former sum,
Which makes it five-and-twenty. Still in motion
Of raging waste! It cannot hold; it will not.
If I want gold, steal but a beggar's dog
And give it Timon, why, the dog coins gold;
If I would sell my horse, and buy twenty more
Better than he, why, give my horse to Timon,
Ask nothing, give it him, it foals me straight,
And able horses. No porter at his gate,
But rather one that smiles and still invites
All that pass by. It cannot hold; no reason
Can found his state in safety. Caphis, ho!
Caphis, I say!

Enter Caphis.

CAPHIS: Here, sir; what is your pleasure?
SENATOR: Get on your cloak, and haste you to Lord Timon;
Importune him for my moneys; be not ceas'd
With slight denial, nor then silenc'd when-
'Commend me to your master'-and the cap
Plays in the right hand, thus;-but tell him,
My uses cry to me; I must serve my turn
Out of mine own; his days and times are past,
And my reliances on his fracted dates
Have smit my credit: I love and honour him,
But must not break my back to heal his finger;
Immediate are my needs, and my relief
Must not be toss'd and turn'd to me in words,
But find supply immediate. Get you gone:
Put on a most importunate aspect,
A visage of demand; for I do fear,
When every feather sticks in his own wing,
Lord Timon will be left a naked gull,
Which flashes now a phoenix. Get you gone.
CAPHIS: I go, sir.
SENATOR: Take the bonds along with you,
And have the dates in compt.
CAPHIS: I will, sir.
SENATOR: Go.

Exeunt.

ACT II. SCENE II. The same. A Hall in Timon's House.

Enter Flavius, with Many Bills in His Hand.

FLAVIUS: No care, no stop! So senseless of expense,
That he will neither know how to maintain it,
Nor cease his flow of riot: takes no account
How things go from him, nor resumes no care
Of what is to continue: never mind
Was to be so unwise, to be so kind.
What shall be done? He will not hear, till feel:
I must be round with him. Now he comes from hunting.
Fie, fie, fie, fie!

Enter Caphis, and the Servants of Isidore and Varro.
CAPHIS: Good even, Varro. What! You come for money?
VARRO'S SERVANT: Is't not your business too?
CAPHIS: It is: and yours too, Isidore?
ISIDORE'S SERVANT: It is so.
CAPHIS: Would we were all discharg'd!
VARRO'S SERVANT: I fear it.
CAPHIS: Here comes the lord!
Enter Timon, Alcibiades, and Lords, Etc.
TIMON: So soon as dinner's done, we'll forth again.
My Alcibiades. With me? what is your will?
CAPHIS: My lord, here is a note of certain dues.
TIMON: Dues! Whence are you?
CAPHIS: Of Athens here, my lord.
TIMON: Go to my steward.
CAPHIS: Please it your lordship, he hath put me off
To the succession of new days this month:
My master is awak'd by great occasion
To call upon his own; and humbly prays you
That with your other noble parts you'll suit
In giving him his right.
TIMON: Mine honest friend,
I prithee, but repair to me next morning.
CAPHIS: Nay, good my lord,-
TIMON: Contain thyself, good friend.
VARRO'S SERVANT: One Varro's servant, my good lord,-
ISIDORE'S SERVANT: From Isidore; he humbly prays your speedy payment.
CAPHIS: If you did know, my lord, my master's wants,-
VARRO'S SERVANT: 'Twas due on forfeiture, my lord, six weeks and past.
ISIDORE'S SERVANT: Your steward puts me off, my lord; and
I am sent expressly to your lordship.
TIMON: Give me breath.
I do beseech you, good my lords, keep on;
I'll wait upon you instantly.
Exeunt Alcibiades and Lords.
To Flavius.Come hither: pray you,
How goes the world, that I am thus encounter'd
With clamorous demands of date-broke bonds,
And the detention of long-since-due debts,
Against my honour?
FLAVIUS: Please you, gentlemen,
The time is unagreeable to this business:
Your importunacy cease till after dinner,
That I may make his lordship understand
Wherefore you are not paid.
TIMON: Do so, my friends.
See them well entertain'd.
Exit.
FLAVIUS: Pray, draw near.
Exit.
Enter Apemantus and Fool.
CAPHIS: Stay, stay; here comes the fool with Apemantus:
Let's ha' some sport with 'em.

VARRO'S SERVANT: Hang him, he'll abuse us!
ISIDORE'S SERVANT: A plague upon him, dog!
VARRO'S SERVANT: How dost, fool?
APEMANTUS: Dost dialogue with thy shadow?
VARRO'S SERVANT: I speak not to thee.
APEMANTUS: No; 'tis to thyself. To the Fool.
Come away.
ISIDORE'S SERVANT: To Varro's Servant There's the fool hangs on your back already.
APEMANTUS: No, thou stand'st single; thou'rt not on him yet.
CAPHIS: Where's the fool now?
APEMANTUS: He last asked the question. Poor rogues and usurers'
men! bawds between gold and want!
ALL SERVANTS: What are we, Apemantus?
APEMANTUS: Asses.
ALL SERVANTS: Why?
APEMANTUS: That you ask me what you are, and do not know yourselves. Speak to 'em, fool.
FOOL: How do you, gentlemen?
ALL SERVANTS: Gramercies, good fool. How does your mistress?
FOOL: She's e'en setting on water to scald such chickens as you
are. Would we could see you at Corinth!
APEMANTUS: Good! gramercy.
Enter Page.
FOOL: Look you, here comes my mistress' page.
PAGE: To the Fool. Why, how now, Captain! what do you in this wise company? How dost
thou, Apemantus?
APEMANTUS: Would I had a rod in my mouth, that I might answer thee
profitably.
PAGE: Prithee, Apemantus, read me the superscription of these
letters: I know not which is which.
APEMANTUS: Canst not read?
PAGE: No.
APEMANTUS: There will little learning die, then, that day thou art
hanged. This is to Lord Timon; this to Alcibiades. Go; thou wast
born a bastard, and thou'lt die a bawd.
PAGE: Thou wast whelped a dog, and thou shalt famish a dog's death.
Answer not; I am gone.
Exit Page.
APEMANTUS: E'en so thou outrunn'st grace.-
Fool, I will go with you to Lord Timon's.
FOOL: Will you leave me there?
APEMANTUS: If Timon stay at home. You three serve three usurers?
ALL SERVANTS: Ay; would they served us!
APEMANTUS: So would I, as good a trick as ever hangman served thief.
FOOL: Are you three usurers' men?
ALL SERVANTS: Ay, fool.
FOOL: I think no usurer but has a fool to his servant: my mistress
is one, and I am her fool. When men come to borrow of your
masters, they approach sadly, and go away merry; but they enter
my mistress' house merrily, and go away sadly: the reason of this?
VARRO'S SERVANT: I could render one.
APEMANTUS: Do it, then, that we may account thee a whoremaster
and a knave; which notwithstanding, thou shalt be no less esteemed.
VARRO'S SERVANT: What is a whoremaster, fool?

FOOL: A fool in good clothes, and something like thee. 'Tis a spirit: sometime 't appears like a lord; sometime like a lawyer; sometime like a philosopher, with two stones more than's artificial one. He is very often like a knight; and generally, in all shapes that man goes up and down in from fourscore to thirteen, this spirit walks in.

VARRO'S SERVANT: Thou art not altogether a fool.

FOOL: Nor thou altogether a wise man:
as much foolery as I have, so much wit thou lackest.

APEMANTUS: That answer might have become Apemantus.

VARRO'S SERVANT: Aside, aside; here comes Lord Timon.

Re-enter Timon and Flavius.

APEMANTUS: Come with me, fool, come.

FOOL: I do not always follow lover, elder brother, and woman; sometime the philosopher.

Exeunt Apemantus and Fool.

FLAVIUS: Pray you walk near: I'll speak with you anon.

Exeunt Servants.

TIMON: You make me marvel: wherefore, ere this time,
Had you not fully laid my state before me,
That I might so have rated my expense
As I had leave of means?

FLAVIUS: You would not hear me,
At many leisures I propos'd.

TIMON: Go to:
Perchance some single vantages you took,
When my indisposition put you back;
And that unaptness made your minister
Thus to excuse yourself.

FLAVIUS: O my good lord!
At many times I brought in my accounts,
Laid them before you; you would throw them off,
And say you found them in mine honesty.
When for some trifling present you have bid me
Return so much, I have shook my head, and wept;
Yea, 'gainst the authority of manners, pray'd you
To hold your hand more close: I did endure
Not seldom, nor no slight checks, when I have
Prompted you in the ebb of your estate
And your great flow of debts. My loved lord,
Though you hear now, too late, yet now's a time,
The greatest of your having lacks a half
To pay your present debts.

TIMON: Let all my land be sold.

FLAVIUS: 'Tis all engag'd, some forfeited and gone;
And what remains will hardly stop the mouth
Of present dues; the future comes apace:
What shall defend the interim? and at length
How goes our reckoning?

TIMON: To Lacedaemon did my land extend.

FLAVIUS: O my good lord! the world is but a word;
Were it all yours to give it in a breath,
How quickly were it gone!

TIMON: You tell me true.
FLAVIUS: If you suspect my husbandry or falsehood,
Call me before the exactest auditors
And set me on the proof. So the gods bless me,
When all our offices have been oppress'd
With riotous feeders, when our vaults have wept
With drunken spilth of wine, when every room
Hath blaz'd with lights and bray'd with minstrelsy,
I have retir'd me to a wasteful cock,
And set mine eyes at flow.
TIMON: Prithee, no more.
FLAVIUS: Heavens! have I said, the bounty of this lord!
How many prodigal bits have slaves and peasants
This night englutted! Who is not Timon's?
What heart, head, sword, force, means, but is Lord Timon's?
Great Timon, noble, worthy, royal Timon!'
Ah! when the means are gone that buy this praise,
The breath is gone whereof this praise is made:
Feast-won, fast-lost; one cloud of winter showers,
These flies are couch'd.
TIMON: Come, sermon me no further;
No villainous bounty yet hath pass'd my heart;
Unwisely, not ignobly, have I given.
Why dost thou weep? Canst thou the conscience lack,
To think I shall lack friends? Secure thy heart;
If I would broach the vessels of my love,
And try the argument of hearts by borrowing,
Men and men's fortunes could I frankly use
As I can bid thee speak.
FLAVIUS: Assurance bless your thoughts!
TIMON: And, in some sort, these wants of mine are crown'd
That I account them blessings; for by these
Shall I try friends. You shall perceive how you
Mistake my fortunes; I am wealthy in my friends.
Within there! Flaminius! Servilius!
Enter Flaminius, Servilius, and Other Servants.
SERVANTS: My lord! my lord!
TIMON: I will dispatch you severally: you to Lord Lucius; to Lord Lucullus you: I hunted with his honour to-day; you, to Sempronius. Commend me to their loves; and I am proud, say, that my occasions have found time to use them toward a supply of money: let the request be fifty talents.
FLAMINIUS: As you have said, my lord.
FLAVIUS: Aside. Lord Lucius and Lucullus? hum!
TIMON: To another Servant. Go you, sir, to the senators,-
Of whom, even to the state's best health, I have
Deserv'd this hearing,-Bid 'em send o' the instant
A thousand talents to me.
FLAVIUS: I have been bold,-
For that I knew it the most general way,-
To them to use your signet and your name;
But they do shake their heads, and I am here
No richer in return.

TIMON: Is't true? can't be?
FLAVIUS: They answer, in a joint and corporate voice,
That now they are at fall, want treasure, cannot
Do what they would; are sorry; you are honourable;
But yet they could have wish'd; they know not;
Something hath been amiss; a noble nature
May catch a wrench; would all were well; 'tis pity;
And so, intending other serious matters,
After distasteful looks, and these hard fractions,
With certain half-caps and cold-moving nods,
They froze me into silence.
TIMON: You gods, reward them!
Prithee, man, look cheerly. These old fellows
Have their ingratitude in them hereditary;
Their blood is cak'd, 'tis cold, it seldom flows;
'Tis lack of kindly warmth they are not kind;
And nature, as it grows again toward earth,
Is fashion'd for the journey, dull and heavy.
To a Servant. Go to Ventidius.-To Flavius.
Prithee, be not sad,
Thou art true and honest; ingenuously I speak,
No blame belongs to thee.-To Servant. Ventidius lately
Buried his father; by whose death he's stepp'd
Into a great estate. When he was poor,
Imprison'd and in scarcity of friends,
I clear'd him with five talents; greet him from me,
Bid him suppose some good necessity
Touches his friend, which craves to be remember'd
With those five talents.
Exit Servant.
To Flavius.That had, give't these fellows
To whom 'tis instant due. Ne'er speak, or think
That Timon's fortunes 'mong his friends can sink.
FLAVIUS: I would I could not think it:
That thought is bounty's foe;
Being free itself, it thinks all others so.
Exeunt.

ACT III. SCENE I. Athens. A Room in Lucullus' House.

Flaminius waiting. Enter a Servant to Him.
SERVANT: I have told my lord of you; he is coming down to you.
FLAMINIUS: I thank you, sir.
Enter Lucullus.
SERVANT: Here's my lord.
LUCULLUS: Aside. One of Lord Timon's men! a gift, I warrant. Why, this hits right; I dreamt of a silver basin and ewer to-night. Flaminius, honest Flaminius, you are very respectively welcome, sir. Fill me some wine.
Exit Servant.
And how does that honourable, complete, freehearted gentleman of Athens, thy very bountiful good lord and master?
FLAMINIUS: His health is well, sir.
LUCULLUS: I am right glad that his health is well, sir. And what hast thou there under thy cloak, pretty Flaminius?

FLAMINIUS: Faith, nothing but an empty box, sir; which in my lord's behalf, I come to entreat your honour to supply; who, having great and instant occasion to use fifty talents, hath sent to your lordship to furnish him, nothing doubting your present assistance therein.
LUCULLIUS: La, la, la, la! 'Nothing doubting,' says he? Alas, good lord! a noble gentleman 'tis, if he would not keep so good a house. Many a time and often I ha' dined with him, and told him on't; and come again to supper to him, of purpose to have him spend less; and yet he would embrace no counsel, take no warning by my coming. Every man has his fault, and honesty is his. I ha' told him on't, but I could ne'er get him from it.
Re-enter Servant with Wine.
SERVANT: Please your lordship, here is the wine.
LUCULLUS: Flaminius, I have noted thee always wise. Here's to thee.
FLAMINIUS: Your lordship speaks your pleasure.
LUCULLUS: I have observed thee always for a towardly prompt spirit, give thee thy due, and one that knows what belongs to reason, and canst use the time well, if the time use thee well: good parts in thee. To Servant.-Get you gone, sirrah.-
Exit Servant.
Draw nearer, honest Flaminius.Thy lord's a bountiful gentleman; but thou art wise, and thou know'st well enough, although thou comest to me, that this is no time to lend money, especially upon bare friendship without security. Here's three solidares for thee: good boy, wink at me, and say thou sawest me not. Fare thee well.
FLAMINIUS: Is't possible the world should so much differ,
And we alive that liv'd? Fly, damned baseness,
To him that worships thee.
Throwing the Money Away.
LUCULLUS: Ha! now I see thou art a fool, and fit for thy master.
Exit.
FLAMINIUS: May these add to the number that may scald thee!
Let molten coin be thy damnation,
Thou disease of a friend, and not himself!
Has friendship such a faint and milky heart
It turns in less than two nights? O you gods!
I feel my master's passion! This slave unto his honour
Has my lord's meat in him:
Why should it thrive and turn to nutriment
When he is turn'd to poison?
O! may diseases only work upon't!
And when he's sick to death, let not that part of nature
Which my lord paid for, be of any power
To expel sickness, but prolong his hour.
Exit.

ACT III. SCENE II. A Public Place.

Enter Lucius, with Three Strangers.
LUCIUS: Who, the Lord Timon? he is my very good friend, and an honourable gentleman.
FIRST STRANGER: We know him for no less, though we are but strangers to him. But I can tell you one thing, my lord, and which I hear from common

rumours: now Lord Timon's happy hours are done and past, and his estate shrinks from him.
LUCIUS: Fie, no, do not believe it; he cannot want for money.
SECOND STRANGER: But believe you this, my lord, that, not long ago, one of his men was with the Lord Lucullus to borrow so many talents, nay, urged extremely for't, and showed what necessity belonged to't, and yet was denied.
LUCIUS: How!
SECOND STRANGER: I tell you, denied, my lord.
LUCIUS: What a strange case was that! now, before the gods, I am ashamed on't. Denied that honourable man! there was very little honour showed in't. For my own part, I must needs confess, I have received some small kindnesses from him, as money, plate, jewels, and such like trifles, nothing comparing to his; yet, had he mistook him, and sent to me, I should ne'er have denied his occasion so many talents.
Enter Servilius.
SERVILIUS: See, by good hap, yonder's my lord; I have sweat to see his honour. To Lucius. My honoured lord!
LUCIUS: Servilius! you are kindly met, sir. Fare thee well: commend me to thy honourable virtuous lord, my very exquisite friend.
SERVILIUS: May it please your honour, my lord hath sent-
LUCIUS: Ha! What has he sent? I am so much endeared to that lord; he's ever sending: how shall I thank him, thinkest thou? And what has he sent now?
SERVILIUS: Has only sent his present occasion now, my lord; requesting your lordship to supply his instant use with so many talents.
LUCIUS: I know his lordship is but merry with me;
He cannot want fifty-five hundred talents.
SERVILIUS: But in the mean time he wants less, my lord.
If his occasion were not virtuous,
I should not urge it half so faithfully.
LUCIUS: Dost thou speak seriously, Servilius?
SERVILIUS: Upon my soul, 'tis true, sir.
LUCIUS: What a wicked beast was I to disfurnish myself against such a good time, when I might ha' shown myself honourable! how unluckily it happened, that I should purchase the day before for a little part, and undo a great deal of honour! Servilius, now, before the gods, I am not able to do; the more beast, I say; I was sending to use Lord Timon myself, these gentlemen can witness; but I would not, for the wealth of Athens, I had done it now. Commend me bountifully to his good lordship; and I hope his honour will conceive the fairest of me, because I have no power to be kin: and tell him this from me, I count it one of my greatest afflictions say, that I cannot pleasure such an honourable gentleman. Good Servilius, will you befriend me so far as to use mine own words to him?
SERVILIUS: Yes, sir, I shall.
LUCIUS: I'll look you out a good turn, Servilius.
Exit Servilius.
True, as you said, Timon is shrunk indeed;
And he that's once denied will hardly speed.
Exit.
FIRST STRANGER: Do you observe this, Hostilius?

SECOND STRANGER: Ay, too well.
FIRST STRANGER: Why, this is the world's soul; and just of the same piece is every flatterer's spirit.
Who can call him
His friend that dips in the same dish? for, in
My knowing, Timon has been this lord's father,
And kept his credit with his purse,
Supported his estate; nay, Timon's money
Has paid his men their wages: He ne'er drinks
But Timon's silver treads upon his lip;
And yet, O! see the monstrousness of man,
When he looks out in an ungrateful shape,
He does deny him, in respect of his,
What charitable men afford to beggars.
THIRD STRANGER: Religion groans at it.
FIRST STRANGER: For mine own part,
I never tasted Timon in my life,
Nor came any of his bounties over me
To mark me for his friend; yet I protest,
For his right noble mind, illustrious virtue,
And honourable carriage,
Had his necessity made use of me,
I would have put my wealth into donation,
And the best half should have return'd to him,
So much I love his heart. But, I perceive,
Men must learn now with pity to dispense;
For policy sits above conscience.
Exeunt.

ACT III. SCENE III. The Same. A Room in Sempronius' House.

Enter Sempronius and a Servant of Timon's.
SEMPRONIUS: Must he needs trouble me in't? Hum! 'bove all others?
He might have tried Lord Lucius, or Lucullus;
And now Ventidius is wealthy too,
Whom he redeem'd from prison: all these
Owe their estates unto him.
SERVANT: My lord,
They have all been touch'd and found base metal, for
They have all denied him.
SEMPRONIUS: How! have they denied him?
Has Ventidius and Lucullus denied him?
And does he send to me? Three? Hum!
It shows but little love or judgment in him:
Must I be his last refuge? His friends, like physicians,
Thrice give him over; must I take the cure upon me?
Has much disgrac'd me in't; I'm angry at him,
That might have known my place. I see no sense for't,
But his occasions might have woo'd me first;
For, in my conscience, I was the first man
That e'er received gift from him:
And does he think so backwardly of me now,
That I'll requite it last? No:
So it may prove an argument of laughter
To the rest, and I 'mongst lords be thought a fool.
I had rather than the worth of thrice the sum,

Had sent to me first, but for my mind's sake;
I'd such a courage to do him good. But now return,
And with their faint reply this answer join;
Who bates mine honour shall not know my coin.
Exit.
SERVANT: Excellent! Your lordship's a goodly villain. The devil knew not what he did when he made man politic; he crossed himself by't: and I cannot think but, in the end the villainies of man will set him clear. How fairly this lord strives to appear foul! takes virtuous copies to be wicked, like those that under hot ardent zeal would set whole realms on fire:
Of such a nature is his politic love.
This was my lord's best hope; now all are fled
Save only the gods. Now his friends are dead,
Doors, that were ne'er acquainted with their wards
Many a bounteous year, must be employ'd
Now to guard sure their master:
And this is all a liberal course allows:
Who cannot keep his wealth must keep his house.
Exit.

ACT III. SCENE IV. A Hall in Timon's House.

Enter Two Servants of Varro, and the Servant of Lucius, Meeting Titus, Hortensius, and Other Servants to Timon's Creditors, Waiting His Coming Out.
FIRST VARRO'S SERVANT: Well met; good morrow, Titus and Hortensius.
TITUS: The like to you, kind Varro.
HORTENSIUS: Lucius! What! do we meet together!
LUCIUS' SERVANT: Ay, and I think one business does command us all; for mine is money.
TITUS: So is theirs and ours.
Enter Philotus.
LUCIUS' SERVANT: And Sir Philotus too!
PHILOTUS: Good day at once.
LUCIUS' SERVANT: Wlcome, good brother.
What do you think the hour?
PHILOTUS: Labouring for nine.
LUCIUS' SERVANT: So much?
PHILOTUS: Is not my lord seen yet?
LUCIUS' SERVANT: Not yet.
PHILOTUS: I wonder on't; he was wont to shine at seven.
LUCIUS' SERVANT: Ay, but the days are waxed shorter with him:
You must consider that a prodigal course
Is like the sun's, but not, like his, recoverable.
I fear, 'Tis deepest winter in Lord Timon's purse;
That is, one may reach deep enough, and yet
Find little.
PHILOTUS: I am of your fear for that.
TITUS: I'll show you how to observe a strange event.
Your lord sends now for money.
HORTENSIUS: Most true, he does.
TITUS: And he wears jewels now of Timon's gift,
For which I wait for money.
HORTENSIUS: It is against my heart.
LUCIUS' SERVANT: Mark, how strange it shows,
Timon in this should pay more than he owes:

And e'en as if your lord should wear rich jewels,
And send for money for 'em.
HORTENSIUS: I'm weary of this charge, the gods can witness:
I know my lord hath spent of Timon's wealth,
And now ingratitude makes it worse than stealth.
FIRST VARRO'S SERVANT: Yes, mine's three thousand crowns; what's yours?
LUCIUS' SERVANT: Five thousand mine.
FIRST VARRO'S SERVANT: 'Tis much deep: and it should seem by the sum, your master's confidence was above mine;
Else, surely, his had equall'd.
Enter Flaminius.
TITUS: One of Lord Timon's men.
LUCIUS' SERVANT: Flaminius! Sir, a word. Pray, is my lord ready to come forth?
FLAMINIUS: No, indeed, he is not.
TITUS: We attend his lordship; pray, signify so much.
FLAMINIUS: I need not tell him that; he knows you are too diligent.
Exit Flaminus.
Enter Flavius, in a Cloak, Muffled.
LUCIUS' SERVANT: Ha! is not that his steward muffled so?
He goes away in a cloud: call him, call him.
TITUS: Do you hear, sir?
SECOND VARRO'S SERVANT: By your leave, sir.
FLAVIUS: What do you ask of me, my friend?
TITUS: We wait for certain money here, sir.
FLAVIUS: Ay,
If money were as certain as your waiting,
'Twere sure enough.
Why then preferr'd you not your sums and bills,
When your false masters eat of my lord's meat?
Then they could smile and fawn upon his debts,
And take down the interest into their gluttonous maws.
You do yourselves but wrong to stir me up;
Let me pass quietly:
Believe't, my lord and I have made an end;
I have no more to reckon, he to spend.
LUCIUS' SERVANT: Ay, but this answer will not serve.
FLAVIUS: If 'twill not serve, 'tis not so base as you;
For you serve knaves.
Exit.
FIRST VARRO'S SERVANT: How! what does his cashiered worship mutter?
SECOND VARRO'S SERVANT: No matter what; he's poor, and that's revenge enough. Who can speak broader than he that has no house to put his head in? such may rail against great buildings.
Enter Servilius.
TITUS: O, here's Servilius; now we shall know some answer.
SERVILIUS: If I might beseech you, gentlemen, to repair some other hour, I should derive much from't; for, take't of my soul, my lord leans wondrously to discontent. His comfortable temper has forsook him; he's much out of health, and keeps his chamber.
LUCIUS' SERVANT: Many do keep their chambers are not sick:
And, if it be so far beyond his health,
Methinks he should the sooner pay his debts,

And make a clear way to the gods.
SERVILIUS: Good gods!
TITUS: We cannot take this for answer, sir.
FLAMINIUS: Within. Servilius, help! my lord! my lord!
Enter Timon, in a Rage; Flaminius Following.
TIMON: What! are my doors oppos'd against my passage?
Have I been ever free, and must my house
Be my retentive enemy, my gaol?
The place which I have feasted, does it now,
Like all mankind, show me an iron heart?
LUCIUS' SERVANT: Put in now, Titus.
TITUS: My lord, here is my bill.
LUCIUS' SERVANT: Here's mine.
HORTENSIUS: And mine, my lord.
BOTH VARRO'S SERVANTS: And ours, my lord.
PHILOTUS: All our bills.
TIMON: Knock me down with 'em: cleave me to the girdle.
LUCIUS' SERVANT: Alas, my lord-
TIMON: Cut my heart in sums.
TITUS: Mine, fifty talents.
TIMON: Tell out my blood.
LUCIUS' SERVANT: Five thousand crowns, my lord.
TIMON: Five thousand drops pays that. What yours? and yours?
FIRST VARRO'S SERVANT: My lord-
SECOND VARRO'S SERVANT: My lord-
TIMON: Tear me, take me; and the gods fall upon you!
Exit.
HORTENSIUS: Faith, I perceive our masters may throw their caps at their money: these debts may well be called desperate ones, for a madman owes 'em.
Exeunt.
Re-enter Timon and Flavius.
TIMON: They have e'en put my breath from me, the slaves.
Creditors? devils!
FLAVIUS: My dear lord-
TIMON: What if it should be so?
FLAMINIUS: My lord-
TIMON: I'll have it so. My steward!
FLAVIUS: Here, my lord.
TIMON: So fitly! Go, bid all my friends again:
Lucius, Lucullus, and Sempronius; all:
I'll once more feast the rascals.
FLAVIUS: O my lord!
You only speak from your distracted soul;
There is not so much left to furnish out
A moderate table.
TIMON: Be it not in thy care: go.
I charge thee, invite them all: let in the tide
Of knaves once more; my cook and I'll provide.
Exeunt.

ACT III. SCENE V. The Same. The Senate House. The Senate Sitting.

FIRST SENATOR: My lord, you have my voice to it: the fault's
Bloody. 'tis necessary he should die;

Nothing emboldens sin so much as mercy.
SECOND SENATOR: Most true; the law shall bruise him.
Enter Alcibiades, Attended.
ALCIBIADES: Honour, health, and compassion to the senate!
FIRST SENATOR: Now, captain.
ALCIBIADES: I am a humble suitor to your virtues;
For pity is the virtue of the law,
And none but tyrants use it cruelly.
It pleases time and fortune to lie heavy
Upon a friend of mine, who, in hot blood
Hath stepp'd into the law, which is past depth
To those that without heed do plunge into't.
He is a man, setting his fate aside,
Of comely virtues;
Nor did he soil the fact with cowardice,-
An honour in him which buys out his fault,-
But, with a noble fury and fair spirit,
Seeing his reputation touch'd to death,
He did oppose his foe;
And with such sober and unnoted passion
He did behave his anger, ere 'twas spent,
As if he had but prov'd an argument.
FIRST SENATOR: You undergo too strict a paradox,
Striving to make an ugly deed look fair:
Your words have took such pains as if they labour'd
To bring manslaughter into form, and set
Quarrelling upon the head of valour; which indeed
Is valour misbegot, and came into the world
When sects and factions were newly born.
He's truly valiant that can wisely suffer
The worst that man can breathe, and make his wrongs
his outsides, to wear them like his raiment, carelessly,
And ne'er prefer his injuries to his heart,
To bring it into danger.
If wrongs be evils, and enforce us kill,
What folly 'tis to hazard life for ill!
ALCIBIADES: My lord,-
FIRST SENATOR: You cannot make gross sins look clear;
To revenge is no valour, but to bear.
ALCIBIADES: My lords, then, under favour, pardon me,
If I speak like a captain.
Why do fond men expose themselves to battle,
And not endure all threats? sleep upon't,
And let the foes quietly cut their throats
Without repugnancy? If there be
Such valour in the bearing, what make we
Abroad? why, then, women are more valiant
That stay at home, if bearing carry it,
And the ass more captain than the lion, the felon
Loaden with irons wiser than the judge,
If wisdom be in suffering. O my lords!
As you are great, be pitifully good:
Who cannot condemn rashness in cold blood?

To kill, I grant, is sin's extremest gust;
But, in defence, by mercy, 'tis most just.
To be in anger is impiety;
But who is man that is not angry?
Weigh but the crime with this.
SECOND SENATOR: You breathe in vain.
ALCIBIADES: In vain! his service done
At Lacedaemon and Byzantium
Were a sufficient briber for his life.
FIRST SENATOR: What's that?
ALCIBIADES: I say, my lords, has done fair service,
And slain in fight many of your enemies.
How full of valour did he bear himself
In the last conflict, and made plenteous wounds!
SECOND SENATOR: He has made too much plenty with 'em;
He's a sworn rioter; he has a sin that often
Drowns him and takes his valour prisoner;
If there were no foes, that were enough
To overcome him; in that beastly fury
He has been known to commit outrages
And cherish factions; 'tis inferr'd to us,
His days are foul and his drink dangerous.
FIRST SENATOR: He dies.
ALCIBIADES: Hard fate! he might have died in war.
My lords, if not for any parts in him,-
Though his right arm might purchase his own time,
And be in debt to none,-yet, more to move you,
Take my deserts to his, and join 'em both;
And, for I know your reverend ages love
Security, I'll pawn my victories, all
My honour to you, upon his good returns.
If by this crime he owes the law his life,
Why, let the war receive't in valiant gore;
For law is strict, and war is nothing more.
FIRST SENATOR: We are for law; he dies: urge it no more,
On height of our displeasure. Friend or brother,
He forfeits his own blood that spills another.
ALCIBIADES: Must it be so? it must not be. My lords,
I do beseech you, know me.
SECOND SENATOR: How!
ALCIBIADES: Call me to your remembrances.
THIRD SENATOR: What!
ALCIBIADES: I cannot think but your age has forgot me;
It could not else be I should prove so base,
To sue, and be denied such common grace.
My wounds ache at you.
FIRST SENATOR: Do you dare our anger?
'Tis in few words, but spacious in effect;
We banish thee for ever.
ALCIBIADES: Banish me!
Banish your dotage; banish usury,
That makes the Senate ugly.
FIRST SENATOR: If, after two days' shine, Athens contain thee,

Attend our weightier judgment. And, not to swell our spirit,
He shall be executed presently.
Exeunt Senators.
ALCIBIADES: Now the gods keep you old enough; that you may live
Only in bone, that none may look on you!
I'm worse than mad: I have kept back their foes,
While they have told their money and let out
Their coin upon large interest; I myself
Rich only in large hurts: all those for this?
Is this the balsam that the usuring senate
Pours into captains' wounds? Banishment!
It comes not ill; I hate not to be banish'd;
It is a cause worthy my spleen and fury,
That I may strike at Athens. I'll cheer up
My discontented troops, and lay for hearts.
'Tis honour with most lands to be at odds;
Soldiers should brook as little wrongs as gods.
Exit.

ACT III. SCENE VI. A Room of State in Timon's House.

Music. Tables Set Out: Servants Attending. Enter Divers Lords, Senators, and Others, at Several Doors.

FIRST LORD: The good time of day to you, sir.
SECOND LORD: I also wish it to you. I think this honourable lord
did but try us this other day.
FIRST LORD: Upon that were my thoughts tiring when we encountered:
I hope it is not so low with him as he made it seem in the trial
of his several friends.
SECOND LORD: It should not be, by the persuasion of his new feasting.
FIRST LORD: I should think so: he hath sent me an earnest inviting,
which many my near occasions did urge me to put off; but he hath
conjured me beyond them, and I must needs appear.
SECOND LORD: In like manner was I in debt to my importunate business, but he would not hear
my excuse. I am sorry, when he sent to borrow of me, that my provision was out.
FIRST LORD: I am sick of that grief too, as I understand how all things go.
SECOND LORD: Every man here's so. What would he have borrowed you?
FIRST LORD: A thousand pieces.
SECOND LORD: A thousand pieces!
FIRST LORD: What of you?
SECOND LORD: He sent to me, sir-here he comes.
Enter Timon and Attendants.
TIMON: With all my heart, gentlemen both; And how fare you?
FIRST LORD: Ever at the best, hearing well of your lordship.
SECOND LORD: The swallow follows not summer more willing than we
your lordship.
TIMON: Aside. Nor more willingly leaves winter; such summer-birds
are men. Gentlemen, our dinner will not recompense this long
stay: feast your ears with the music awhile, if they will fare so
harshly o' the trumpet's sound; we shall to't presently.
FIRST LORD: I hope it remains not unkindly with your lordship that
I return'd you an empty messenger.
TIMON: O! sir, let it not trouble you.
SECOND LORD: My noble lord,-
TIMON: Ah! my good friend, what cheer?

SECOND LORD: My most honourable lord, I am e'en sick of shame, that when your lordship this other day sent to me I was so unfortunate a beggar.
TIMON: Think not on't, sir.
SECOND LORD: If you had sent but two hours before,-
TIMON: Let it not cumber your better remembrance.
The Banquet Brought In.
Come, bring in all together.
SECOND LORD: All covered dishes!
FIRST LORD: Royal cheer, I warrant you.
THIRD LORD: Doubt not that, if money and the season can yield it.
FIRST LORD: How do you? What's the news?
THIRD LORD: Alcibiades is banished: hear you of it?
FIRST AND SECOND LORDS: Alcibiades banished!
THIRD LORD: 'Tis so, be sure of it.
FIRST LORD: How? how?
SECOND LORD: I pray you, upon what?
TIMON: My worthy friends, will you draw near?
THIRD LORD: I'll tell you more anon. Here's a noble feast toward.
SECOND LORD: This is the old man still.
THIRD LORD: Will't hold? will't hold?
SECOND LORD: It does; but time will-and so-
THIRD LORD: I do conceive.
TIMON: Each man to his stool with that spur as he would to the lip of his mistress; your diet shall be in all places alike. Make not a city feast of it, to let the meat cool ere we can agree upon the first place: sit, sit. The gods require our thanks.-
You great benefactors sprinkle our society with thankfulness. For your own gifts make yourselves praised: but reserve still to give, lest your deities be despised. Lend to each man enough, that one need not lend to another; for, were your god-heads to borrow of men, men would forsake the gods. Make the meat be beloved more than the man that gives it. Let no assembly of twenty be without a score of villains: if there sit twelve women at the table, let a dozen of them be as they are. The rest of your foes, O gods! the senators of Athens, together with the common lag of people, what is amiss in them, you gods, make suitable for destruction. For these my present friends, as they are to me nothing, so in nothing bless them, and to nothing are they welcome. Uncover, dogs, and lap.
The Dishes Uncovered Are Full of Warm Water.
SOME SPEAK: What does his lordship mean?
SOME OTHER: I know not.
TIMON: May you a better feast never behold,
You knot of mouth-friends! smoke and lukewarm water
Is your perfection. This is Timon's last;
Who, stuck and spangled with your flatteries,
Washes it off, and sprinkles in your faces
Throwing the Water in Their Faces.
Your reeking villainy. Live loath'd, and long,
Most smiling, smooth, detested parasites,
Courteous destroyers, affable wolves, meek bears,
You fools of fortune, trencher-friends, time's flies,
Cap and knee slaves, vapours, and minute-jacks!

Of man and beast the infinite malady
Crust you quite o'er! What, dost thou go?
Soft! take thy physic first,-thou too,-and thou;-
Stay, I will lend thee money, borrow none.
Throws the Dishes at Them.
What, all in motion? Henceforth be no feast,
Whereat a villain's not a welcome guest.
Burn, house! sink Athens! henceforth hated be
Of Timon man and all humanity!
Exit.
Re-enter the Lords, Senators, and &C.
FIRST LORD: How now, my lords!
SECOND LORD: Know you the quality of Lord Timon's fury?
THIRD LORD: Push! did you see my cap?
FOURTH LORD: I have lost my gown.
FIRST LORD: He's but a mad lord, and nought but humour sways him.
He gave me a jewel th' other day, and now he has beat it out of
my hat: did you see my jewel?
THIRD LORD: Did you see my cap?
SECOND LORD: Here 'tis.
FOURTH LORD: Here lies my gown.
FIRST LORD: Let's make no stay.
SECOND LORD: Lord Timon's mad.
THIRD LORD: I feel't upon my bones.
FOURTH LORD:One day he gives us diamonds, next day stones.
Exeunt.

ACT IV. SCENE I. Without the Walls of Athens

Enter Timon.
TIMON: Let me look back upon thee. O thou wall,
That girdles in those wolves, dive in the earth,
And fence not Athens! Matrons, turn incontinent!
Obedience fail in children! slaves and fools,
Pluck the grave wrinkled senate from the bench,
And minister in their steads! To general filths
Convert, o' the instant, green virginity.
Do't in your parents' eyes! Bankrupts, hold fast;
Rather than render back, out with your knives,
And cut your trusters' throats. Bound servants, steal,-
Large-handed robbers your grave masters are,
And pill by law. Maid, to thy master's bed;
Thy mistress is o' the brothel! Son of sixteen,
Pluck the lin'd crutch from thy old limping sire,
With it beat out his brains! Piety, and fear,
Religion to the gods, peace, justice, truth,
Domestic awe, night-rest and neighbourhood,
Instruction, manners, mysteries and trades,
Degrees, observances, customs and laws,
Decline to your confounding contraries,
And let confusion live! Plagues incident to men,
Your potent and infectious fevers heap
On Athens, ripe for stroke! Thou cold sciatica,
Cripple our senators, that their limbs may halt
As lamely as their manners! Lust and liberty

Creep in the minds and marrows of our youth,
That 'gainst the stream of virtue they may strive,
And drown themselves in riot! Itches, blains,
Sow all the Athenian bosoms, and their crop
Be general leprosy! Breath infect breath,
That their society, as their friendship, may
Be merely poison! Nothing I'll bear from thee
But nakedness, thou detestable town!
Take thou that too, with multiplying bans!
Timon will to the woods; where he shall find
Th' unkindest beast more kinder than mankind.
The gods confound-hear me, you good gods all-
The Athenians both within and out that wall!
And grant, as Timon grows, his hate may grow
To the whole race of mankind, high and low!
Amen.
Exit.

ACT IV. SCENE II. Athens. A Room in Timon's House.

Enter Flavius, with Two or Three Servants.
FIRST SERVANT: Hear you, Master Steward! where's our master?
Are we undone? cast off? nothing remaining?
FLAVIUS: Alack! my fellows, what should I say to you?
Let me be recorded by the righteous gods,
I am as poor as you.
FIRST SERVANT: Such a house broke!
So noble a master fall'n! All gone! and not
One friend to take his fortune by the arm
And go along with him!
SECOND SERVANT: As we do turn our backs
From our companion, thrown into his grave,
So his familiars to his buried fortunes
Slink all away, leave their false vows with him,
Like empty purses pick'd; and his poor self,
A dedicated beggar to the air,
With his disease of all-shunn'd poverty,
Walks, like contempt, alone. More of our fellows.
Enter Other Servants.
FLAVIUS: All broken implements of a ruin'd house.
THIRD SERVANT: Yet do our hearts wear Timon's livery,
That see I by our faces; we are fellows still,
Serving alike in sorrow. Leak'd is our bark,
And we, poor mates, stand on the dying deck,
Hearing the surges threat: we must all part
Into this sea of air.
FLAVIUS: Good fellows all,
The latest of my wealth I'll share amongst you.
Wherever we shall meet, for Timon's sake
Let's yet be fellows; let's shake our heads, and say,
As 'twere a knell unto our master's fortune,
'We have seen better days.' Let each take some;
Giving Them Money.
Nay, put out all your hands. Not one word more:
Thus part we rich in sorrow, parting poor.

They Embrace, and Part Several Ways.
O! the fierce wretchedness that glory brings us.
Who would not wish to be from wealth exempt,
Since riches point to misery and contempt?
Who would be so mock'd with glory? or so live,
But in a dream of friendship?
To have his pomp, and all what state compounds
But only painted, like his varnish'd friends?
Poor honest lord! brought low by his own heart,
Undone by goodness. Strange, unusual blood,
When man's worst sin is he does too much good!
Who then dares to be half so kind agen?
For bounty, that makes gods, does still mar men.
My dearest lord, bless'd, to be most accurs'd,
Rich, only to be wretched, thy great fortunes
Are made thy chief afflictions. Alas! kind lord,
He's flung in rage from this ingrateful seat
Of monstrous friends;
Nor has he with him to supply his life,
Or that which can command it.
I'll follow and enquire him out:
I'll ever serve his mind with my best will;
Whilst I have gold, I'll be his steward still.
Exit.

ACT IV. SCENE III. Woods and Caves near the Sea-Shore.

Enter Timon from the Cave.
TIMON: O blessed breeding sun! draw from the earth
Rotten humidity; below thy sister's orb
Infect the air! Twinn'd brothers of one womb,
Whose procreation, residence and birth,
Scarce is dividant, touch them with several fortunes;
The greater scorns the lesser: not nature,
To whom all sores lay siege, can bear great fortune,
But by contempt of nature.
Raise me this beggar, and deny't that lord;
The senator shall bear contempt hereditary,
The beggar native honour.
It is the pasture lards the rother's sides,
The want that makes him lean. Who dares, who dares,
In purity of manhood stand upright,
And say, 'This man's a flatterer'? if one be,
So are they all; for every grize of fortune
Is smooth'd by that below: the learned pate
Ducks to the golden fool: all is oblique;
There's nothing level in our cursed natures
But direct villainy. Therefore, be abhorr'd
All feasts, societies, and throngs of men!
His semblable, yea, himself, Timon disdains:
Destruction fang mankind! Earth, yield me roots!
Digging.
Who seeks for better of thee, sauce his palate
With thy most operant poison! What is here?
Gold! yellow, glittering, precious gold! No, gods,

I am no idle votarist. Roots, you clear heavens!
Thus much of this will make black white, foul fair,
Wrong right, base noble, old young, coward valiant.
Ha! you gods, why this? What this, you gods? Why, this
Will lug your priests and servants from your sides,
Pluck stout men's pillows from below their head:
This yellow slave
Will knit and break religions; bless the accurs'd,
Make the hoar leprosy ador'd; place thieves,
And give them title, knee, and approbation,
With senators on the bench; this is it
That makes the wappen'd widow wed again;
She, whom the spital-house and ulcerous sores
Would cast the gorge at, this embalms and spices
To the April day again. Come, damned earth,
Thou common whore of mankind, that putt'st odds
Among the rout of nations, I will make thee
Do thy right Nature.-March Afar Off.
Ha! a drum? thou'rt quick,
But yet I'll bury thee: thou'lt go, strong thief,
When gouty keepers of thee cannot stand:
Nay, stay thou out for earnest.
Keeping Some Gold.
Enter Alcibiades, with Drum and Fife, in Warlike Manner; Phrynia and Timandra.
ALCIBIADES: What art thou there? speak.
TIMON: A beast, as thou art. The canker gnaw thy heart,
For showing me again the eyes of man!
ALCIBIADES: What is thy name? Is man so hateful to thee,
That art thyself a man?
TIMON: I am Misanthropos, and hate mankind.
For thy part, I do wish thou wert a dog,
That I might love thee something.
ALCIBIADES: I know thee well,
But in thy fortunes am unlearn'd and strange.
TIMON: I know thee too; and more than that I know thee
I not desire to know. Follow thy drum;
With man's blood paint the ground, gules, gules;
Religious canons, civil laws are cruel;
Then what should war be? This fell whore of thine
Hath in her more destruction than thy sword
For all her cherubin look.
PHRYNIA: Thy lips rot off!
TIMON: I will not kiss thee; then the rot returns
To thine own lips again.
ALCIBIADES: How came the noble Timon to this change?
TIMON: As the moon does, by wanting light to give:
But then renew I could not like the moon;
There were no suns to borrow of.
ALCIBIADES: Noble Timon,
What friendship may I do thee?
TIMON: None, but to maintain my opinion.
ALCIBIADES: What is it, Timon?
TIMON: Promise me friendship, but perform none: if thou wilt not

promise, the gods plague thee, for thou art man! If thou dost
perform, confound thee, for thou art a man!
ALCIBIADES: I have heard in some sort of thy miseries.
TIMON: Thou saw'st them when I had prosperity.
ALCIBIADES: I see them now; then was a blessed time.
TIMON: As thine is now, held with a brace of harlots.
TIMANDRA: Is this the Athenian minion whom the world
Voic'd so regardfully?
TIMON: Art thou Timandra?
TIMANDRA: Yes.
TIMON: Be a whore still; they love thee not that use thee;
Give them diseases, leaving with thee their lust.
Make use of thy salt hours; season the slaves
For tubs and baths; bring down rose-cheeked youth
To the tub-fast and the diet.
TIMANDRA: Hang thee, monster!
ALCIBIADES: Pardon him, sweet Timandra, for his wits
Are drown'd and lost in his calamities.
I have but little gold of late, brave Timon,
The want whereof doth daily make revolt
In my penurious band: I have heard, and griev'd
How cursed Athens, mindless of thy worth,
Forgetting thy great deeds, when neighbour states,
But for thy sword and fortune, trod upon them,-
TIMON: I prithee, beat thy drum, and get thee gone.
ALCIBIADES: I am thy friend, and pity thee, dear Timon.
TIMON: How dost thou pity him whom thou dost trouble?
I had rather be alone.
ALCIBIADES: Why, fare thee well:
Here is some gold for thee.
TIMON: Keep it, I cannot eat it.
ALCIBIADES: When I have laid proud Athens on a heap,-
TIMON: Warr'st thou 'gainst Athens?
ALCIBIADES: Ay, Timon, and have cause.
TIMON: The gods confound them all in thy conquest;
And thee after, when thou hast conquer'd!
ALCIBIADES: Why me, Timon?
TIMON: That, by killing of villains,
Thou wast born to conquer my country.
Put up thy gold: go on,-here's gold,-go on;
Be as a planetary plague, when Jove
Will o'er some high-vic'd city hang his poison
In the sick air: let not thy sword skip one.
Pity not honour'd age for his white beard;
He is an usurer. Strike me the counterfeit matron;
It is her habit only that is honest,
Herself's a bawd. Let not the virgin's cheek
Make soft thy trenchant sword; for those milk paps
That through the window-bars bore at men's eyes,
Are not within the leaf of pity writ,
But set them down horrible traitors. Spare not the babe,
Whose dimpled smiles from fools exhaust their mercy;
Think it a bastard, whom the oracle

Hath doubtfully pronounc'd thy throat shall cut,
And mince it sans remorse. Swear against objects;
Put armour on thine ears and on thine eyes,
Whose proof nor yells of mothers, maids, nor babes,
Nor sight of priests in holy vestments bleeding,
Shall pierce a jot. There's gold to pay thy soldiers:
Make large confusion; and, thy fury spent,
Confounded be thyself! Speak not, be gone.
ALCIBIADES: Hast thou gold yet? I'll take the gold thou giv'st me,
Not all thy counsel.
TIMON: Dost thou, or dost thou not, heaven's curse upon thee!
PHRYNIA AND TIMANDRA: Give us some gold, good Timon:
Hast thou more?
TIMON: Enough to make a whore forswear her trade,
And to make whores a bawd. Hold up, you sluts,
Your aprons mountant: you are not oathable,
Although, I know, you'll swear, terribly swear
Into strong shudders and to heavenly agues,
The immortal gods that hear you, spare your oaths,
I'll trust to your conditions: be whores still;
And he whose pious breath seeks to convert you,
Be strong in whore, allure him, burn him up;
Let your close fire predominate his smoke,
And be no turncoats: yet may your pains, six months,
Be quite contrary: and thatch your poor thin roofs
With burdens of the dead; some that were hang'd,
No matter; wear them, betray with them: whore still;
Paint till a horse may mire upon your face:
A pox of wrinkles!
PHRYNIA AND TIMANDRA: Well, more gold. What then?
Believe't that we'll do anything for gold.
TIMON: Consumptions sow
In hollow bones of man; strike their sharp shins,
And mar men's spurring. Crack the lawyer's voice,
That he may never more false title plead,
Nor sound his quillets shrilly; hoar the flamen,
That scolds against the quality of flesh,
And not believes himself: down with the nose,
Down with it flat; take the bridge quite away
Of him that, his particular to foresee,
Smells from the general weal: make curl'd-pate ruffians bald,
And let the unscarr'd braggarts of the war
Derive some pain from you: plague all,
That your activity may defeat and quell
The source of all erection. There's more gold;
Do you damn others, and let this damn you,
And ditches grave you all!
PHRYNIA AND TIMANDRA: More counsel with more money, bounteous Timon.
TIMON: More whore, more mischief first; I have given you earnest.
ALCIBIADES: Strike up the drum towards Athens! Farewell, Timon:
If I thrive well, I'll visit thee again.
TIMON: If I hope well, I'll never see thee more.
ALCIBIADES: I never did thee harm.

TIMON: Yes, thou spok'st well of me.
ALCIBIADES: Call'st thou that harm?
TIMON: Men daily find it. Get thee away, and take
Thy beagles with thee.
ALCIBIADES: We but offend him. Strike!
Drum Beats. Exeunt All but Timon.
TIMON: That nature, being sick of man's unkindness,
Should yet be hungry! Common mother, thou,
Digging.
Whose womb unmeasurable, and infinite breast,
Teems, and feeds all; whose self-same mettle,
Whereof thy proud child, arrogant man, is puff'd,
Engenders the black toad and adder blue,
The gilded newt and eyeless venom'd worm,
With all the abhorred births below crisp heaven
Whereon Hyperion's quickening fire doth shine;
Yield him, who all thy human sons doth hate,
From forth thy plenteous bosom, one poor root!
Ensear thy fertile and conceptious womb,
Let it no more bring out ingrateful man!
Go great with tigers, dragons, wolves, and bears;
Teem with new monsters, whom thy upward face
Hath to the marbled mansion all above
Never presented! O! a root; dear thanks:
Dry up thy marrows, vines and plough-torn leas;
Whereof ingrateful man, with liquorish draughts
And morsels unctuous, greases his pure mind,
That from it all consideration slips!
Enter Apemantus.
More man! Plague! plague!
APEMANTUS: I was directed hither: men report
Thou dost affect my manners, and dost use them.
TIMON: 'Tis, then, because thou dost not keep a dog
Whom I would imitate: consumption catch thee!
APEMANTUS: This is in thee a nature but infected;
A poor unmanly melancholy sprung
From change of fortune. Why this spade, this place?
This slave-like habit? and these looks of care?
Thy flatterers yet wear silk, drink wine, lie soft,
Hug their diseas'd perfumes, and have forgot
That ever Timon was. Shame not these woods
By putting on the cunning of a carper.
Be thou a flatterer now, and seek to thrive
By that which has undone thee: hinge thy knee
And let his very breath, whom thou'lt observe
Blow off thy cap; praise his most vicious strain,
And call it excellent. Thou wast told thus;
Thou gav'st thine ears, like tapsters that bade welcome,
To knaves and all approachers: 'tis most just
That thou turn rascal; hadst thou wealth again,
Rascals should have't. Do not assume my likeness.
TIMON: Were I like thee I'd throw away myself.
APEMANTUS: Thou hast cast away thyself, being like thyself;

A madman so long, now a fool. What! think'st
That the bleak air, thy boisterous chamberlain,
Will put thy shirt on warm? will these moss'd trees,
That have outliv'd the eagle, page thy heels
And skip when thou point'st out? will the cold brook,
Candied with ice, caudle thy morning taste
To cure thy o'ernight's surfeit? Call the creatures
Whose naked natures live in all the spite
Of wreakful heaven, whose bare unhoused trunks,
To the conflicting elements expos'd,
Answer mere nature; bid them flatter thee;
O! thou shalt find-
TIMON: A fool of thee. Depart.
APEMANTUS: I love thee better now than e'er I did.
TIMON: I hate thee worse.
APEMANTUS: Why?
TIMON: Thou flatter'st misery.
APEMANTUS: I flatter not, but say thou art a caitiff.
TIMON: Why dost thou seek me out?
APEMANTUS: To vex thee.
TIMON: Always a villain's office or a fool's.
Dost please thyself in't?
APEMANTUS: Ay.
TIMON: What! a knave too?
APEMANTUS: If thou didst put this sour-cold habit on
To castigate thy pride, 'twere well; but thou
Dost it enforcedly; thou'dst courtier be again
Wert thou not beggar. Willing misery
Outlives incertain pomp, is crown'd before;
The one is filling still, never complete;
The other, at high wish: best state, contentless,
Hath a distracted and most wretched being,
Worse than the worst, content.
Thou shouldst desire to die, being miserable.
TIMON: Not by his breath that is more miserable.
Thou art a slave, whom Fortune's tender arm
With favour never clasp'd, but bred a dog.
Hadst thou, like us from our first swath, proceeded
The sweet degrees that this brief world affords
To such as may the passive drugs of it
Freely command, thou wouldst have plung'd thyself
In general riot; melted down thy youth
In different beds of lust; and never learn'd
The icy precepts of respect, but follow'd
The sugar'd game before thee. But myself,
Who had the world as my confectionary,
The mouths, the tongues, the eyes, and hearts of men
At duty, more than I could frame employment,
That numberless upon me stuck as leaves
Do on the oak, have with one winter's brush
Fell from their boughs, and left me open, bare
For every storm that blows; I, to bear this,
That never knew but better, is some burden:

Thy nature did commence in sufferance, time
Hath made thee hard in't. Why shouldst thou hate men?
They never flatter'd thee: what hast thou given?
If thou wilt curse, thy father, that poor rag,
Must be thy subject; who in spite put stuff
To some she-beggar and compounded thee
Poor rogue hereditary. Hence! be gone!
If thou hadst not been born the worst of men,
Thou hadst been a knave and flatterer.
APEMANTUS: Art thou proud yet?
TIMON: Ay, that I am not thee.
APEMANTUS: I, that I was
No prodigal.
TIMON: I, that I am one now;
Were all the wealth I have shut up in thee,
I'd give thee leave to hang it. Get thee gone.
That the whole life of Athens were in this!
Thus would I eat it.
Eating a Root.
APEMANTUS: Here; I will mend thy feast.
TIMON: First mend my company, take away thyself.
APEMANTUS: So I shall mend mine own, by the lack of thine.
TIMON: 'Tis not well mended so, it is but botch'd.
If not, I would it were.
APEMANTUS: What wouldst thou have to Athens?
TIMON: Thee thither in a whirlwind. If thou wilt,
Tell them there I have gold; look, so I have.
APEMANTUS: Here is no use for gold.
TIMON: The best and truest;
For here it sleeps and does no hired harm.
APEMANTUS: Where liest o' nights, Timon?
TIMON: Under that's above me.
Where feed'st thou o' days, Apemantus?
APEMANTUS: Where my stomach finds meat; or rather, where I eat it.
TIMON: Would poison were obedient and knew my mind!
APEMANTUS: Where wouldst thou send it?
TIMON: To sauce thy dishes.
APEMANTUS: The middle of humanity thou never knewest, but the
extremity of both ends. When thou wast in thy gilt and thy
perfume, they mock'd thee for too much curiosity; in thy rags
thou know'st none, but art despised for the contrary. There's a
medlar for thee; eat it.
TIMON: On what I hate I feed not.
APEMANTUS: Dost hate a medlar?
TIMON: Ay, though it look like thee.
APEMANTUS: An thou hadst hated medlars sooner, thou shouldst have loved
thyself better now. What man didst thou ever know unthrift
that was beloved after his means?
TIMON: Who, without those means thou talkest of, didst thou ever
know beloved?
APEMANTUS: Myself.
TIMON: I understand thee; thou hadst some means to keep a dog.
APEMANTUS: What things in the world canst thou nearest compare to

thy flatterers?
TIMON: Women nearest; but men, men are the things themselves. What wouldst thou do with the world, Apemantus, if it lay in thy power?
APEMANTUS: Give it the beasts, to be rid of the men.
TIMON: Wouldst thou have thyself fall in the confusion of men, and remain a beast with the beasts?
APEMANTUS: Ay, Timon.
TIMON: A beastly ambition, which the gods grant thee to attain to. If thou wert the lion, the fox would beguile thee; if thou wert the lamb, the fox would eat thee; if thou wert the fox, the lion would suspect thee, when peradventure, thou wert accused by the ass; if thou wert the ass, thy dulness would torment thee, and still thou livedst but as a breakfast to the wolf; if thou wert the wolf, thy greediness would afflict thee, and oft thou shouldst hazard thy life for thy dinner; wert thou the unicorn, pride and wrath would confound thee and make thine own self the conquest of thy fury; wert thou a bear, thou wouldst be killed by the horse; wert thou a horse, thou wouldst be seized by the leopard; wert thou a leopard, thou wert german to the lion, and the spots of thy kindred were jurors on thy life; all thy safety were remotion, and thy defence absence. What beast couldst thou be that were not subject to a beast? and what beast art thou already, that seest not thy loss in transformation!
APEMANTUS: If thou couldst please me with speaking to me, thou mightst have hit upon it here; the commonwealth of Athens is become a forest of beasts.
TIMON: How has the ass broke the wall, that thou art out of the city?
APEMANTUS: Yonder comes a poet and a painter: the plague of company light upon thee! I will fear to catch it, and give way. When I know not what else to do, I'll see thee again.
TIMON: When there is nothing living but thee, thou shalt be welcome. I had rather be a beggar's dog than Apemantus.
APEMANTUS: Thou art the cap of all the fools alive.
TIMON: Would thou wert clean enough to spit upon!
APEMANTUS: A plague on thee! thou art too bad to curse!
TIMON: All villains that do stand by thee are pure.
APEMANTUS: There is no leprosy but what thou speak'st.
TIMON: If I name thee,
I'll beat thee, but I should infect my hands.
APEMANTUS: I would my tongue could rot them off!
TIMON: Away, thou issue of a mangy dog!
Choler does kill me that thou art alive;
I swound to see thee.
APEMANTUS: Would thou wouldst burst!
TIMON: Away,
Thou tedious rogue! I am sorry I shall lose
A stone by thee.
Throws a Stone at Him.
APEMANTUS: Beast!
TIMON: Slave!
APEMANTUS: Toad!

TIMON: Rogue, rogue, rogue!
I am sick of this false world, and will love nought
But even the mere necessities upon't.
Then, Timon, presently prepare thy grave;
Lie where the light foam of the sea may beat
Thy gravestone daily: make thine epitaph,
That death in me at others' lives may laugh.
Looking on the Gold.
O thou sweet king-killer, and dear divorce
'Twixt natural son and sire! thou bright defiler
Of Hymen's purest bed! thou valiant Mars!
Thou ever young, fresh, lov'd, and delicate wooer,
Whose blush doth thaw the consecrated snow
That lies on Dian's lap! thou visible god,
That solder'st close impossibilities,
And mak'st them kiss! that speak'st with every tongue
To every purpose! O thou touch of hearts!
Think, thy slave man rebels, and by thy virtue
Set them into confounding odds, that beasts
May have the world in empire!
APEMANTUS: Would 'twere so:
But not till I am dead; I'll say thou'st gold:
Thou wilt be throng'd to shortly.
TIMON: Throng'd to?
APEMANTUS: Ay.
TIMON: Thy back, I prithee.
APEMANTUS: Live, and love thy misery!
TIMON: Long live so, and so die!
Exit Apemantus.
I am quit. More things like men! Eat, Timon, and abhor them.
Enter Banditti.
FIRST BANDIT: Where should he have this gold? It is some poor fragment, some slender ort of his remainder. The mere want of gold, and the falling-from of his friends, drove him into this melancholy.
SECOND BANDIT: It is noised he hath a mass of treasure.
THIRD BANDIT: Let us make the assay upon him: if he care not for't, he will supply us easily; if he covetously reserve it, how shall's get it?
SECOND BANDIT: True; for he bears it not about him, 'tis hid.
FIRST BANDIT: Is not this he?
BANDITTI: Where?
SECOND BANDIT: 'Tis his description.
THIRD BANDIT: He; I know him.
BANDITTI: Save thee, Timon!
TIMON: Now, thieves?
BANDITTI: Soldiers, not thieves.
TIMON: Both too, and women's sons.
BANDITTI: We are not thieves, but men that much do want.
TIMON: Your greatest want is, you want much of meat.
Why should you want? Behold, the earth hath roots;
Within this mile break forth a hundred springs;
The oaks bear mast, the briars scarlet hips;

The bounteous housewife, Nature, on each bush
Lays her full mess before you. Want! Why want?
FIRST BANDIT: We cannot live on grass, on berries, water,
As beasts and birds and fishes.
TIMON: Nor on the beasts themselves, the birds, and fishes;
You must eat men. Yet thanks I must you con
That you are thieves profess'd, that you work not
In holier shapes; for there is boundless theft
In limited professions. Rascal thieves,
Here's gold. Go, suck the subtle blood o' the grape
Till the high fever seethe your blood to froth,
And so scape hanging: trust not the physician;
His antidotes are poison, and he slays
More than you rob: take wealth and lives together;
Do villainy, do, since you protest to do't,
Like workmen. I'll example you with thievery:
The sun's a thief, and with his great attraction
Robs the vast sea; the moon's an arrant thief,
And her pale fire she snatches from the sun;
The sea's a thief, whose liquid surge resolves
The moon into salt tears; the earth's a thief,
That feeds and breeds by a composture stolen
From general excrement, each thing's a thief;
The laws, your curb and whip, in their rough power
Has uncheck'd theft. Love not yourselves; away!
Rob one another. There's more gold; cut throats;
All that you meet are thieves. To Athens go,
Break open shops; nothing can you steal
But thieves do lose it: steal no less for this
I give you; and gold confound you howsoe'er!
Amen.
THIRD BANDIT: Has almost charm'd me from my profession by persuading me to it.
FIRST BANDIT: 'Tis in the malice of mankind that he thus advises us; not to have us thrive in our mystery.
SECOND BANDIT: I'll believe him as an enemy, and give over my trade.
FIRST BANDIT: Let us first see peace in Athens. There is no time so miserable but a man may be true.
Exeunt Banditti.
Enter Flavius.
FLAVIUS: O you gods!
Is yond despised and ruinous man my lord?
Full of decay and failing? O monument
And wonder of good deeds evilly bestow'd!
What an alteration of honour
Has desperate want made!
What viler thing upon the earth than friends
Who can bring noblest minds to basest ends!
How rarely does it meet with this time's guise,
When man was wish'd to love his enemies!
Grant I may ever love, and rather woo
Those that would mischief me than those that do!
He has caught me in his eye: I will present

My honest grief unto him; and, as my lord,
Still serve him with my life. My dearest master!
Timon Comes Forward.
TIMON: Away! What art thou?
FLAVIUS: Have you forgot me, sir?
TIMON: Why dost ask that? I have forgot all men;
Then, if thou grant'st thou'rt a man, I have forgot thee.
FLAVIUS: An honest poor servant of yours.
TIMON: Then I know thee not:
I never had honest man about me; ay all
I kept were knaves, to serve in meat to villains.
FLAVIUS: The gods are witness,
Ne'er did poor steward wear a truer grief
For his undone lord than mine eyes for you.
TIMON: What! dost thou weep? Come nearer. Then I love thee,
Because thou art a woman, and disclaim'st
Flinty mankind, whose eyes do never give
But thorough lust and laughter. Pity's sleeping:
Strange times, that weep with laughing, not with weeping!
FLAVIUS: I beg of you to know me, good my lord,
To accept my grief, and whilst this poor wealth lasts
To entertain me as your steward still.
TIMON: Had I a steward
So true, so just, and now so comfortable?
It almost turns my dangerous nature mild.
Let me behold thy face. Surely, this man
Was born of woman.
Forgive my general and exceptless rashness,
You perpetual sober gods! I do proclaim
One honest man, mistake me not, but one;
No more, I pray, and he's a steward.
How fain would I have hated all mankind!
And thou redeem'st thyself: but all, save thee,
I fell with curses.
Methinks thou art more honest now than wise;
For, by oppressing and betraying me,
Thou mightst have sooner got another service:
For many so arrive at second masters
Upon their first lord's neck. But tell me true,-
For I must ever doubt, though ne'er so sure,-
Is not thy kindness subtle, covetous,
If not a usuring kindness and as rich men deal gifts,
Expecting in return, twenty for one?
FLAVIUS: No, my most worthy master, in whose breast
Doubt and suspect, alas! are plac'd too late!
You should have fear'd false times when you did feast;
Suspect still comes where an estate is least.
That which I show, heaven knows, is merely love,
Duty and zeal to your unmatched mind,
Care of your food and living; and, believe it,
My most honour'd lord,
For any benefit that points to me,
Either in hope or present, I'd exchange

For this one wish, that you had power and wealth
To requite me by making rich yourself.
TIMON: Look thee, 'tis so! Thou singly honest man,
Here, take: the gods, out of my misery,
Have sent thee treasure. Go, live rich and happy,
But thus condition'd: thou shalt build from men;
Hate all, curse all, show charity to none,
But let the famish'd flesh slide from the bone,
Ere thou relieve the beggar; give to dogs
What thou deny'st to men; let prisons swallow 'em,
Debts wither 'em to nothing; be men like blasted woods,
And may diseases lick up their false bloods!
And so, farewell and thrive.
FLAVIUS: O! let me stay
And comfort you, my master.
TIMON: If thou hatest curses,
Stay not; fly, whilst thou'rt bless'd and free:
Ne'er see thou man, and let me ne'er see thee.
Exeunt severally.

ACT V. SCENE I. The Woods. Before Timon's Cave.

Enter Poet and Painter.

PAINTER: As I took note of the place, it cannot be far where he abides.

POET: What's to be thought of him? Does the rumour hold for true that he is so full of gold?

PAINTER: Certain. Alcibiades reports it; Phrynia and Timandra had gold of him: he likewise enriched poor straggling soldiers with great quantity. 'Tis said he gave unto his steward a mighty sum.

POET: Then this breaking of his has been but a try for his friends?

PAINTER: Nothing else. You shall see him a palm in Athens again, and flourish with the highest. Therefore 'tis not amiss we tender our loves to him in this supposed distress of his; it will show honestly in us, and is very likely to load our purposes with what they travail for, if it be just and true report that goes of his having.

POET: What have you now to present unto him?

PAINTER: Nothing at this time but my visitation; only, I will promise him an excellent piece.

POET: I must serve him so too, tell him of an intent that's coming toward him.

PAINTER: Good as the best. Promising is the very air o' the time; it opens the eyes of expectation. Performance is ever the duller for his act, and, but in the plainer and simpler kind of people, the deed of saying is quite out of use. To promise is most courtly and fashionable; performance is a kind of will or testament which argues a great sickness in his judgment that makes it.

Enter Timon from His Cave.

TIMON: Aside. Excellent workman! Thou canst not paint a man so bad as is thyself.

POET: I am thinking what I shall say I have provided for him. It must be a personating of himself; a satire against the softness of prosperity, with a discovery of the infinite flatteries that

follow youth and opulency.
TIMON: Aside. Must thou needs stand for a villain in thine own work? Wilt thou whip thine own faults in other men? Do so, I have gold for thee.
POET: Nay, let's seek him;
Then do we sin against our own estate
When we may profit meet, and come too late.
PAINTER: True;
When the day serves, before black-corner'd night,
Find what thou want'st by free and offer'd light.
Come.
TIMON: Aside. I'll meet you at the turn. What a god's gold,
That he is worshipp'd in a baser temple
Than where swine feed!
'Tis thou that rigg'st the bark and plough'st the foam,
Settlest admired reverence in a slave.
To thee be worship! and thy saints for aye
Be crown'd with plagues, that thee alone obey!
Fit I meet them.
Advancing from His Cave.
POET: Hail, worthy Timon!
PAINTER: Our late noble master!
TIMON: Have I once liv'd to see two honest men?
POET: Sir,
Having often of your open bounty tasted,
Hearing you were retir'd, your friends fall'n off,
Whose thankless natures-O abhorred spirits!
Not all the whips of heaven are large enough-
What! to you,
Whose star-like nobleness gave life and influence
To their whole being! I am rapt, and cannot cover
The monstrous bulk of this ingratitude
With any size of words.
TIMON: Let it go naked: men may see't the better.
You, that are honest, by being what you are,
Make them best seen and known.
PAINTER: He and myself
Have travail'd in the great shower of your gifts,
And sweetly felt it.
TIMON: Ay, you are honest men.
PAINTER: We are hither come to offer you our service.
TIMON: Most honest men! Why, how shall I requite you?
Can you eat roots, and drink cold water? No?
BOTH: What we can do, we'll do, to do you service.
TIMON: Ye're honest men! Ye've heard that I have gold;
I am sure you have. Speak truth; ye're honest men.
PAINTER: So it is said, my noble lord; but therefore
Came not my friend nor I.
TIMON: Good honest men! Thou draw'st a counterfeit
Best in all Athens. Thou'rt, indeed, the best;
Thou counterfeit'st most lively.
PAINTER: So, so, my lord.
TIMON: E'en so, sir, as I say.

To the Poet.
And for thy fiction,
Why, thy verse swells with stuff so fine and smooth
That thou art even natural in thine art.
But for all this, my honest-natur'd friends,
I must needs say you have a little fault.
Marry, 'tis not monstrous in you; neither wish I
You take much pains to mend.
BOTH: Beseech your honour
To make it known to us.
TIMON: You'll take it ill.
BOTH: Most thankfully, my lord.
TIMON: Will you indeed?
BOTH: Doubt it not, worthy lord.
TIMON: There's never a one of you but trusts a knave
That mightily deceives you.
BOTH: Do we, my lord?
TIMON: Ay, and you hear him cog, see him dissemble,
Know his gross patchery, love him, feed him,
Keep in your bosom; yet remain assur'd
That he's a made-up villain.
PAINTER: I know not such, my lord.
POET: Nor I.
TIMON: Look you, I love you well; I'll give you gold,
Rid me these villains from your companies.
Hang them or stab them, drown them in a draught,
Confound them by some course, and come to me,
I'll give you gold enough.
BOTH: Name them, my lord; let's know them.
TIMON: You that way, and you this, but two in company;
Each man apart, all single and alone,
Yet an arch-villain keeps him company.
To the Painter. If, where thou art, two villians shall not be,
Come not near him.
To the Poet. If thou wouldst not reside
But where one villain is, then him abandon.
Hence! pack! there's gold; you came for gold, ye slaves.
To the Painter. You have work for me; there's payment; hence!
To the Poet. You are an alchemist; make gold of that.
Out, rascal dogs!
Beats Them out and Then Returns to His Cave.
Enter Flavius and Two Senators.
FLAVIUS: It is vain that you would speak with Timon;
For he is set so only to himself
That nothing but himself, which looks like man,
Is friendly with him.
FIRST SENATOR: Bring us to his cave.
It is our part and promise to the Athenians
To speak with Timon.
SECOND SENATOR: At all times alike
Men are not still the same; 'twas time and griefs
That fram'd him thus. Time, with his fairer hand,
Offering the fortunes of his former days,

The former man may make him. Bring us to him,
And chance it as it may.
FLAVIUS: Here is his cave.
Peace and content be here! Lord Timon! Timon!
Look out, and speak to friends. The Athenians
By two of their most reverend Senate greet thee.
Speak to them, noble Timon.
Enter Timon from His Cave.
TIMON: Thou sun that comfort'st, burn! Speak and be hang'd!
For each true word, a blister! and each false
Be as a cauterizing to the root o' the tongue,
Consuming it with speaking!
FIRST SENATOR: Worthy Timon,-
TIMON: Of none but such as you, and you of Timon.
FIRST SENATOR: The senators of Athens greet thee, Timon.
TIMON: I thank them; and would send them back the plague,
Could I but catch it for them.
FIRST SENATOR: O! forget
What we are sorry for ourselves in thee.
The senators with one consent of love
Entreat thee back to Athens, who have thought
On special dignities, which vacant lie
For thy best use and wearing.
SECOND SENATOR: They confess
Toward thee forgetfulness too general, gross;
Which now the public body, which doth seldom
Play the recanter, feeling in itself
A lack of Timon's aid, hath sense withal
Of it own fail, restraining aid to Timon,
And send forth us to make their sorrow'd render,
Together with a recompense more fruitful
Than their offence can weigh down by the dram;
Ay, even such heaps and sums of love and wealth
As shall to thee blot out what wrongs were theirs,
And write in thee the figures of their love,
Ever to read them thine.
TIMON: You witch me in it;
Surprise me to the very brink of tears.
Lend me a fool's heart and a woman's eyes,
And I'll beweep these comforts, worthy senators.
FIRST SENATOR: Therefore so please thee to return with us,
And of our Athens-thine and ours-to take
The captainship, thou shalt be met with thanks,
Allow'd with absolute power, and thy good name
Live with authority. So soon we shall drive back
Of Alcibiades the approaches wild,
Who, like a boar too savage, doth root up
His country's peace.
SECOND SENATOR: And shakes his threat'ning sword
Against the walls of Athens.
FIRST SENATOR: Therefore, Timon,-
TIMON: Well, sir, I will. Therefore I will, sir, thus:
If Alcibiades kill my countrymen,

Let Alcibiades know this of Timon,
That Timon cares not. But if he sack fair Athens,
And take our goodly aged men by the beards,
Giving our holy virgins to the stain
Of contumelious, beastly, mad-brain'd war,
Then let him know, and tell him Timon speaks it,
In pity of our aged and our youth
I cannot choose but tell him that I care not,
And let him take't at worst; for their knives care not
While you have throats to answer. For myself,
There's not a whittle in the unruly camp
But I do prize it at my love before
The reverend'st throat in Athens. So I leave you
To the protection of the prosperous gods,
As thieves to keepers.
FLAVIUS: Stay not, all's in vain.
TIMON: Why, I was writing of my epitaph;
It will be seen to-morrow. My long sickness
Of health and living now begins to mend,
And nothing brings me all things. Go, live still;
Be Alcibiades your plague, you his,
And last so long enough!
FIRST SENATOR: We speak in vain.
TIMON: But yet I love my country, and am not
One that rejoices in the common wrack,
As common bruit doth put it.
FIRST SENATOR: That's well spoke.
TIMON: Commend me to my loving countrymen,-
FIRST SENATOR: These words become your lips as they pass through them.
SECOND SENATOR: And enter in our ears like great triumphers
In their applauding gates.
TIMON: Commend me to them,
And tell them that, to ease them of their griefs,
Their fears of hostile strokes, their aches, losses,
Their pangs of love, with other incident throes
That nature's fragile vessel doth sustain
In life's uncertain voyage, I will some kindness do them:
I'll teach them to prevent wild Alcibiades' wrath.
FIRST SENATOR: I like this well; he will return again.
TIMON: I have a tree, which grows here in my close,
That mine own use invites me to cut down,
And shortly must I fell it. Tell my friends,
Tell Athens, in the sequence of degree
From high to low throughout, that whoso please
To stop affliction, let him take his haste,
Come hither, ere my tree hath felt the axe,
And hang himself. I pray you do my greeting.
FLAVIUS: Trouble him no further; thus you still shall find him.
TIMON: Come not to me again; but say to Athens
Timon hath made his everlasting mansion
Upon the beached verge of the salt flood,
Who once a day with his embossed froth

The turbulent surge shall cover. Thither come,
And let my gravestone be your oracle.
Lips, let sour words go by and language end:
What is amiss, plague and infection mend!
Graves only be men's works and death their gain!
Sun, hide thy beams! Timon hath done his reign.
Exit Timon into His Cave.
FIRST SENATOR: His discontents are unremovably
Coupled to nature.
SECOND SENATOR: Our hope in him is dead. Let us return
And strain what other means is left unto us
In our dear peril.
FIRST SENATOR: It requires swift foot.
Exeunt.

ACT V. SCENE II. Before the Walls of Athens.

Enter Two Other Senators with a Messenger.
FIRST SENATOR: Thou hast painfully discover'd; are his files
As full as thy report?
MESSENGER: I have spoke the least.
Besides, his expedition promises
Present approach.
SECOND SENATOR: We stand much hazard if they bring not Timon.
MESSENGER: I met a courier, one mine ancient friend,
Whom, though in general part we were oppos'd,
Yet our old love had a particular force,
And made us speak like friends. This man was riding
From Alcibiades to Timon's cave
With letters of entreaty, which imported
His fellowship i' the cause against your city,
In part for his sake mov'd.
Enter the Other Senators, from Timon.
FIRST SENATOR: Here come our brothers.
THIRD SENATOR: No talk of Timon, nothing of him expect.
The enemies' drum is heard, and fearful scouring
Doth choke the air with dust. In, and prepare.
Ours is the fall, I fear; our foes the snare.
Exeunt.

ACT V. SCENE III. The Woods. Timon's Cave, and a Rude Tomb Seen.

Enter a Soldier in the Woods, Seeking Timon.
SOLDIER: By all description this should be the place.
Who's here? Speak, ho! No answer! What is this?
Timon is dead, who hath outstretch'd his span.
Some beast rear'd this; here does not live a man.
Dead, sure; and this his grave. What's on this tomb
I cannot read; the character I'll take with wax.
Our captain hath in every figure skill,
An ag'd interpreter, though young in days;
Before proud Athens he's set down by this,
Whose fall the mark of his ambition is.
Exit.

ACT V. SCENE IV. Before the Walls of Athens

Trumpets Sound. Enter Alcibiades with His Powers.
ALCIBIADES: Sound to this coward and lascivious town

Our terrible approach.
A Parley Sounded. The Senators Appear upon the Walls.
Till now you have gone on and fill'd the time
With all licentious measure, making your wills
The scope of justice; till now, myself, and such
As slept within the shadow of your power,
Have wander'd with our travers'd arms, and breath'd
Our sufferance vainly. Now the time is flush,
When crouching marrow, in the bearer strong,
Cries of itself, 'No more!' Now breathless wrong
Shall sit and pant in your great chairs of ease,
And pursy insolence shall break his wind
With fear and horrid flight.
FIRST SENATOR: Noble and young,
When thy first griefs were but a mere conceit,
Ere thou hadst power or we had cause of fear,
We sent to thee, to give thy rages balm,
To wipe out our ingratitude with loves
Above their quantity.
SECOND SENATOR: So did we woo
Transformed Timon to our city's love
By humble message and by promis'd means.
We were not all unkind, nor all deserve
The common stroke of war.
FIRST SENATOR: These walls of ours
Were not erected by their hands from whom
You have receiv'd your griefs; nor are they such
That these great towers, trophies, and schools, should fall
For private faults in them.
SECOND SENATOR: Nor are they living
Who were the motives that you first went out;
Shame, that they wanted cunning, in excess
Hath broke their hearts. March, noble lord,
Into our city with thy banners spread.
By decimation and a tithed death,-
If thy revenges hunger for that food
Which nature loathes,-take thou the destin'd tenth,
And by the hazard of the spotted die
Let die the spotted.
FIRST SENATOR: All have not offended;
For those that were, it is not square to take,
On those that are, revenge: crimes, like lands,
Are not inherited. Then, dear countryman,
Bring in thy ranks, but leave without thy rage;
Spare thy Athenian cradle, and those kin
Which, in the bluster of thy wrath, must fall
With those that have offended. Like a shepherd
Approach the fold and cull th' infected forth,
But kill not all together.
SECOND SENATOR: What thou wilt,
Thou rather shalt enforce it with thy smile
Than hew to 't with thy sword.
FIRST SENATOR: Set but thy foot

Against our rampir'd gates and they shall ope,
So thou wilt send thy gentle heart before
To say thou'lt enter friendly.
SECOND SENATOR: Throw thy glove,
Or any token of thine honour else,
That thou wilt use the wars as thy redress
And not as our confusion, all thy powers
Shall make their harbour in our town till we
Have seal'd thy full desire.
ALCIBIADES: Then there's my glove;
Descend, and open your uncharged ports.
Those enemies of Timon's and mine own,
Whom you yourselves shall set out for reproof,
Fall, and no more. And, to atone your fears
With my more noble meaning, not a man
Shall pass his quarter or offend the stream
Of regular justice in your city's bounds,
But shall be render'd to your public laws
At heaviest answer.
BOTH: 'Tis most nobly spoken.
ALCIBIADES: Descend, and keep your words.
The Senators Descend and Open the Gates.
Enter a Soldier.
SOLDIER: My noble General, Timon is dead;
Entomb'd upon the very hem o' the sea;
And on his gravestone this insculpture, which
With wax I brought away, whose soft impression
Interprets for my poor ignorance.
Alcibiades Reads the Epitaph.
'Here lies a wretched corse, of wretched soul bereft;
Seek not my name. A plague consume you wicked caitiffs left!
Here lie I, Timon, who alive all living men did hate.
Pass by, and curse thy fill; but pass, and stay not here thy gait.'
These well express in thee thy latter spirits.
Though thou abhorr'dst in us our human griefs,
Scorn'dst our brain's flow, and those our droplets which
From niggard nature fall, yet rich conceit
Taught thee to make vast Neptune weep for aye
On thy low grave, on faults forgiven. Dead
Is noble Timon, of whose memory
Hereafter more. Bring me into your city,
And I will use the olive with my sword;
Make war breed peace, make peace stint war, make each
Prescribe to other,as each other's leech.
Let our drums strike.
Exeunt.

END

Cymbeline

Dramatis Personae

CYMBELINE, King of Britain
CLOTEN, son to the Queen by a former husband
POSTHUMUS LEONATUS, a gentleman, husband to Imogen
BELARIUS, a banished lord, disguised under the name of Morgan
GUIDERIUS and ARVIRAGUS, sons to Cymbeline, disguised under the names of POLYDORE and CADWAL, supposed sons to Belarius
PHILARIO, Italian, friend to Posthumus
IACHIMO, Italian, friend to Philario
A FRENCH GENTLEMAN, friend to Philario
CAIUS LUCIUS, General of the Roman Forces
A ROMAN CAPTAIN
TWO BRITISH CAPTAINS
PISANIO, servant to Posthumus
CORNELIUS, a physician
TWO LORDS of Cymbeline's court
TWO GENTLEMEN of the same
TWO GAOLERS
QUEEN, wife to Cymbeline
IMOGEN, daughter to Cymbeline by a former queen
HELEN, a lady attending on Imogen
APPARITIONS
Lords, Ladies, Roman Senators, Tribunes, a Soothsayer, a Dutch Gentleman, a Spanish Gentleman, Musicians, Officers, Captains, Soldiers, Messengers, and Attendants

SCENE: Britain; Italy

ACT I. SCENE I. Britain. The Garden of Cymbeline's Palace

FIRST GENTLEMAN: You do not meet a man but frowns; our bloods
No more obey the heavens than our courtiers
Still seem as does the King's.
SECOND GENTLEMAN: But what's the matter?
FIRST GENTLEMAN: His daughter, and the heir of's kingdom, whom
He purpos'd to his wife's sole son- a widow
That late he married- hath referr'd herself
Unto a poor but worthy gentleman. She's wedded;
Her husband banish'd; she imprison'd. All
Is outward sorrow, though I think the King
Be touch'd at very heart.
SECOND GENTLEMAN: None but the King?
FIRST GENTLEMAN: He that hath lost her too. So is the Queen,
That most desir'd the match. But not a courtier,
Although they wear their faces to the bent
Of the King's looks, hath a heart that is not
Glad at the thing they scowl at.
SECOND GENTLEMAN: And why so?
FIRST GENTLEMAN: He that hath miss'd the Princess is a thing
Too bad for bad report; and he that hath her-
I mean that married her, alack, good man!
And therefore banish'd- is a creature such
As, to seek through the regions of the earth
For one his like, there would be something failing

In him that should compare. I do not think
So fair an outward and such stuff within
Endows a man but he.
SECOND GENTLEMAN: You speak him far.
FIRST GENTLEMAN: I do extend him, sir, within himself;
Crush him together rather than unfold
His measure duly.
SECOND GENTLEMAN: What's his name and birth?
FIRST GENTLEMAN: I cannot delve him to the root; his father
Was call'd Sicilius, who did join his honour
Against the Romans with Cassibelan,
But had his titles by Tenantius, whom
He serv'd with glory and admir'd success,
So gain'd the sur-addition Leonatus;
And had, besides this gentleman in question,
Two other sons, who, in the wars o' th' time,
Died with their swords in hand; for which their father,
Then old and fond of issue, took such sorrow
That he quit being; and his gentle lady,
Big of this gentleman, our theme, deceas'd
As he was born. The King he takes the babe
To his protection, calls him Posthumus Leonatus,
Breeds him and makes him of his bed-chamber,
Puts to him all the learnings that his time
Could make him the receiver of; which he took,
As we do air, fast as 'twas minist'red,
And in's spring became a harvest, liv'd in court-
Which rare it is to do- most prais'd, most lov'd,
A sample to the youngest; to th' more mature
A glass that feated them; and to the graver
A child that guided dotards. To his mistress,
For whom he now is banish'd- her own price
Proclaims how she esteem'd him and his virtue;
By her election may be truly read
What kind of man he is.
SECOND GENTLEMAN: I honour him
Even out of your report. But pray you tell me,
Is she sole child to th' King?
FIRST GENTLEMAN: His only child.
He had two sons- if this be worth your hearing,
Mark it- the eldest of them at three years old,
I' th' swathing clothes the other, from their nursery
Were stol'n; and to this hour no guess in knowledge
Which way they went.
SECOND GENTLEMAN: How long is this ago?
FIRST GENTLEMAN: Some twenty years.
SECOND GENTLEMAN: That a king's children should be so convey'd,
So slackly guarded, and the search so slow
That could not trace them!
FIRST GENTLEMAN: Howsoe'er 'tis strange,
Or that the negligence may well be laugh'd at,
Yet is it true, sir.
SECOND GENTLEMAN: I do well believe you.

FIRST GENTLEMAN: We must forbear; here comes the gentleman,
The Queen, and Princess.
Exeunt
Enter the Queen, Posthumus, and Imogen
QUEEN: No, be assur'd you shall not find me, daughter,
After the slander of most stepmothers,
Evil-ey'd unto you. You're my prisoner, but
Your gaoler shall deliver you the keys
That lock up your restraint. For you, Posthumus,
So soon as I can win th' offended King,
I will be known your advocate. Marry, yet
The fire of rage is in him, and 'twere good
You lean'd unto his sentence with what patience
Your wisdom may inform you.
POSTHUMUS: Please your Highness,
I will from hence to-day.
QUEEN: You know the peril.
I'll fetch a turn about the garden, pitying
The pangs of barr'd affections, though the King
Hath charg'd you should not speak together.
Exit
IMOGEN: O dissembling courtesy! How fine this tyrant
Can tickle where she wounds! My dearest husband,
I something fear my father's wrath, but nothing-
Always reserv'd my holy duty- what
His rage can do on me. You must be gone;
And I shall here abide the hourly shot
Of angry eyes, not comforted to live
But that there is this jewel in the world
That I may see again.
POSTHUMUS: My queen! my mistress!
O lady, weep no more, lest I give cause
To be suspected of more tenderness
Than doth become a man. I will remain
The loyal'st husband that did e'er plight troth;
My residence in Rome at one Philario's,
Who to my father was a friend, to me
Known but by letter; thither write, my queen,
And with mine eyes I'll drink the words you send,
Though ink be made of gall.
Re-enter Queen
QUEEN: Be brief, I pray you.
If the King come, I shall incur I know not
How much of his displeasure. Aside Yet I'll move him
To walk this way. I never do him wrong
But he does buy my injuries, to be friends;
Pays dear for my offences.
Exit
POSTHUMUS: Should we be taking leave
As long a term as yet we have to live,
The loathness to depart would grow. Adieu!
IMOGEN: Nay, stay a little.
Were you but riding forth to air yourself,

Such parting were too petty. Look here, love:
This diamond was my mother's; take it, heart;
But keep it till you woo another wife,
When Imogen is dead.
POSTHUMUS: How, how? Another?
You gentle gods, give me but this I have,
And sear up my embracements from a next
With bonds of death! Remain, remain thou here
Puts on the Ring
While sense can keep it on. And, sweetest, fairest,
As I my poor self did exchange for you,
To your so infinite loss, so in our trifles
I still win of you. For my sake wear this;
It is a manacle of love; I'll place it
Upon this fairest prisoner.
Puts a Bracelet on Her Arm
IMOGEN: O the gods!
When shall we see again?
Enter Cymbeline and Lords
POSTHUMUS: Alack, the King!
CYMBELINE: Thou basest thing, avoid; hence from my sight
If after this command thou fraught the court
With thy unworthiness, thou diest. Away!
Thou'rt poison to my blood.
POSTHUMUS: The gods protect you,
And bless the good remainders of the court!
I am gone.
Exit
IMOGEN: There cannot be a pinch in death
More sharp than this is.
CYMBELINE: O disloyal thing,
That shouldst repair my youth, thou heap'st
A year's age on me!
IMOGEN: I beseech you, sir,
Harm not yourself with your vexation.
I am senseless of your wrath; a touch more rare
Subdues all pangs, all fears.
CYMBELINE: Past grace? obedience?
IMOGEN: Past hope, and in despair; that way past grace.
CYMBELINE: That mightst have had the sole son of my queen!
IMOGEN: O blessed that I might not! I chose an eagle,
And did avoid a puttock.
CYMBELINE: Thou took'st a beggar, wouldst have made my throne
A seat for baseness.
IMOGEN: No; I rather added
A lustre to it.
CYMBELINE: O thou vile one!
IMOGEN: Sir,
It is your fault that I have lov'd Posthumus.
You bred him as my playfellow, and he is
A man worth any woman; overbuys me
Almost the sum he pays.
CYMBELINE: What, art thou mad?

IMOGEN: Almost, sir. Heaven restore me! Would I were
A neat-herd's daughter, and my Leonatus
Our neighbour shepherd's son!
Re-enter Queen
CYMBELINE: Thou foolish thing!
To the Queen They were again together. You have done
Not after our command. Away with her,
And pen her up.
QUEEN: Beseech your patience.- Peace,
Dear lady daughter, peace!- Sweet sovereign,
Leave us to ourselves, and make yourself some comfort
Out of your best advice.
CYMBELINE: Nay, let her languish
A drop of blood a day and, being aged,
Die of this folly.
Exit, with Lords
Enter Pisanio
QUEEN: Fie! you must give way.
Here is your servant. How now, sir! What news?
PISANIO: My lord your son drew on my master.
QUEEN: Ha!
No harm, I trust, is done?
PISANIO: There might have been,
But that my master rather play'd than fought,
And had no help of anger; they were parted
By gentlemen at hand.
QUEEN: I am very glad on't.
IMOGEN: Your son's my father's friend; he takes his part
To draw upon an exile! O brave sir!
I would they were in Afric both together;
Myself by with a needle, that I might prick
The goer-back. Why came you from your master?
PISANIO: On his command. He would not suffer me
To bring him to the haven; left these notes
Of what commands I should be subject to,
When't pleas'd you to employ me.
QUEEN: This hath been
Your faithful servant. I dare lay mine honour
He will remain so.
PISANIO: I humbly thank your Highness.
QUEEN: Pray walk awhile.
IMOGEN: About some half-hour hence,
Pray you speak with me. You shall at least
Go see my lord aboard. For this time leave me.
Exeunt

ACT I. SCENE II. Britain. A Public Place

Enter Cloten and Two Lords
FIRST LORD: Sir, I would advise you to shift a shirt; the violence of action hath made you reek as a sacrifice. Where air comes out, air comes in; there's none abroad so wholesome as that you vent.
CLOTEN: If my shirt were bloody, then to shift it. Have I hurt him?
SECOND LORD: Aside No, faith; not so much as his patience.
FIRST LORD: Hurt him! His body's a passable carcass if he be not

hurt. It is a throughfare for steel if it be not hurt.
SECOND LORD: Aside His steel was in debt; it went o' th' back side the town.
CLOTEN: The villain would not stand me.
SECOND LORD: Aside No; but he fled forward still, toward your face.
FIRST LORD: Stand you? You have land enough of your own; but he added to your having, gave you some ground.
SECOND LORD: Aside As many inches as you have oceans. Puppies!
CLOTEN: I would they had not come between us.
SECOND LORD: Aside So would I, till you had measur'd how long a fool you were upon the ground.
CLOTEN: And that she should love this fellow, and refuse me!
SECOND LORD: Aside If it be a sin to make a true election, she is damn'd.
FIRST LORD: Sir, as I told you always, her beauty and her brain go not together; she's a good sign, but I have seen small reflection of her wit.
SECOND LORD: Aside She shines not upon fools, lest the reflection should hurt her.
CLOTEN: Come, I'll to my chamber. Would there had been some hurt done!
SECOND LORD: Aside I wish not so; unless it had been the fall of an ass, which is no great hurt.
CLOTEN: You'll go with us?
FIRST LORD: I'll attend your lordship.
CLOTEN: Nay, come, let's go together.
SECOND LORD: Well, my lord.
Exeunt

ACT I. SCENE III. Britain. Cymbeline's Palace

Enter Imogen and Pisanio
IMOGEN: I would thou grew'st unto the shores o' th' haven,
And questioned'st every sail; if he should write,
And I not have it, 'twere a paper lost,
As offer'd mercy is. What was the last
That he spake to thee?
PISANIO: It was: his queen, his queen!
IMOGEN: Then wav'd his handkerchief?
PISANIO: And kiss'd it, madam.
IMOGEN: Senseless linen, happier therein than I!
And that was all?
PISANIO: No, madam; for so long
As he could make me with his eye, or care
Distinguish him from others, he did keep
The deck, with glove, or hat, or handkerchief,
Still waving, as the fits and stirs of's mind
Could best express how slow his soul sail'd on,
How swift his ship.
IMOGEN: Thou shouldst have made him
As little as a crow, or less, ere left
To after-eye him.
PISANIO: Madam, so I did.
IMOGEN: I would have broke mine eyestrings, crack'd them but

To look upon him, till the diminution
Of space had pointed him sharp as my needle;
Nay, followed him till he had melted from
The smallness of a gnat to air, and then
Have turn'd mine eye and wept. But, good Pisanio,
When shall we hear from him?
PISANIO: Be assur'd, madam,
With his next vantage.
IMOGEN: I did not take my leave of him, but had
Most pretty things to say. Ere I could tell him
How I would think on him at certain hours
Such thoughts and such; or I could make him swear
The shes of Italy should not betray
Mine interest and his honour; or have charg'd him,
At the sixth hour of morn, at noon, at midnight,
T' encounter me with orisons, for then
I am in heaven for him; or ere I could
Give him that parting kiss which I had set
Betwixt two charming words, comes in my father,
And like the tyrannous breathing of the north
Shakes all our buds from growing.
Enter a Lady
LADY: The Queen, madam,
Desires your Highness' company.
IMOGEN: Those things I bid you do, get them dispatch'd.
I will attend the Queen.
PISANIO: Madam, I shall.
Exeunt

ACT I. SCENE IV. Rome. Philario's House

Enter Philario, Iachimo, a Frenchman, a Dutchman, and a Spaniard

IACHIMO: Believe it, sir, I have seen him in Britain. He was then of a crescent note, expected to prove so worthy as since he hath been allowed the name of. But I could then have look'd on him without the help of admiration, though the catalogue of his endowments had been tabled by his side, and I to peruse him by items.

PHILARIO: You speak of him when he was less furnish'd than now he is with that which makes him both without and within.

FRENCHMAN: I have seen him in France; we had very many there could behold the sun with as firm eyes as he.

IACHIMO: This matter of marrying his king's daughter, wherein he must be weighed rather by her value than his own, words him, I doubt not, a great deal from the matter.

FRENCHMAN: And then his banishment.

IACHIMO: Ay, and the approbation of those that weep this lamentable divorce under her colours are wonderfully to extend him, be it but to fortify her judgment, which else an easy battery might lay flat, for taking a beggar, without less quality. But how comes it he is to sojourn with you? How creeps acquaintance?

PHILARIO: His father and I were soldiers together, to whom I have been often bound for no less than my life.

Enter Posthumus

Here comes the Briton. Let him be so entertained amongst

you as suits with gentlemen of your knowing to a stranger of his quality. I beseech you all be better known to this gentleman, whom I commend to you as a noble friend of mine. How worthy he is I will leave to appear hereafter, rather than story him in his own hearing.
FRENCHMAN: Sir, we have known together in Orleans.
POSTHUMUS: Since when I have been debtor to you for courtesies, which I will be ever to pay and yet pay still.
FRENCHMAN: Sir, you o'errate my poor kindness. I was glad I did atone my countryman and you; it had been pity you should have been put together with so mortal a purpose as then each bore, upon importance of so slight and trivial a nature.
POSTHUMUS: By your pardon, sir. I was then a young traveller; rather shunn'd to go even with what I heard than in my every action to be guided by others' experiences; but upon my mended judgment- if I offend not to say it is mended- my quarrel was not altogether slight.
FRENCHMAN: Faith, yes, to be put to the arbitrement of swords, and by such two that would by all likelihood have confounded one the other or have fall'n both.
IACHIMO: Can we, with manners, ask what was the difference?
FRENCHMAN: Safely, I think. 'Twas a contention in public, which may, without contradiction, suffer the report. It was much like an argument that fell out last night, where each of us fell in praise of our country mistresses; this gentleman at that time vouching- and upon warrant of bloody affirmation- his to be more fair, virtuous, wise, chaste, constant, qualified, and less attemptable, than any the rarest of our ladies in France.
IACHIMO: That lady is not now living, or this gentleman's opinion, by this, worn out.
POSTHUMUS: She holds her virtue still, and I my mind.
IACHIMO: You must not so far prefer her fore ours of Italy.
POSTHUMUS: Being so far provok'd as I was in France, I would abate her nothing, though I profess myself her adorer, not her friend.
IACHIMO: As fair and as good- a kind of hand-in-hand comparison- had been something too fair and too good for any lady in Britain. If she went before others I have seen as that diamond of yours outlustres many I have beheld, I could not but believe she excelled many; but I have not seen the most precious diamond that is, nor you the lady.
POSTHUMUS: I prais'd her as I rated her. So do I my stone.
IACHIMO: What do you esteem it at?
POSTHUMUS: More than the world enjoys.
IACHIMO: Either your unparagon'd mistress is dead, or she's outpriz'd by a trifle.
POSTHUMUS: You are mistaken: the one may be sold or given, if there were wealth enough for the purchase or merit for the gift; the other is not a thing for sale, and only the gift of the gods.

IACHIMO: Which the gods have given you?
POSTHUMUS: Which by their graces I will keep.
IACHIMO: You may wear her in title yours; but you know strange fowl light upon neighbouring ponds. Your ring may be stol'n too. So your brace of unprizable estimations, the one is but frail and the other casual; a cunning thief, or a that-way-accomplish'd courtier, would hazard the winning both of first and last.
POSTHUMUS: Your Italy contains none so accomplish'd a courtier to convince the honour of my mistress, if in the holding or loss of that you term her frail. I do nothing doubt you have store of thieves; notwithstanding, I fear not my ring.
PHILARIO: Let us leave here, gentlemen.
POSTHUMUS: Sir, with all my heart. This worthy signior, I thank him, makes no stranger of me; we are familiar at first.
IACHIMO: With five times so much conversation I should get ground of your fair mistress; make her go back even to the yielding, had I admittance and opportunity to friend.
POSTHUMUS: No, no.
IACHIMO: I dare thereupon pawn the moiety of my estate to your ring, which, in my opinion, o'ervalues it something. But I make my wager rather against your confidence than her reputation; and, to bar your offence herein too, I durst attempt it against any lady in the world.
POSTHUMUS: You are a great deal abus'd in too bold a persuasion, and I doubt not you sustain what y'are worthy of by your attempt.
IACHIMO: What's that?
POSTHUMUS: A repulse; though your attempt, as you call it, deserve more- a punishment too.
PHILARIO: Gentlemen, enough of this. It came in too suddenly; let it die as it was born, and I pray you be better acquainted.
IACHIMO: Would I had put my estate and my neighbour's on th' approbation of what I have spoke!
POSTHUMUS: What lady would you choose to assail?
IACHIMO: Yours, whom in constancy you think stands so safe. I will lay you ten thousand ducats to your ring that, commend me to the court where your lady is, with no more advantage than the opportunity of a second conference, and I will bring from thence that honour of hers which you imagine so reserv'd.
POSTHUMUS: I will wage against your gold, gold to it. My ring I hold dear as my finger; 'tis part of it.
IACHIMO: You are a friend, and therein the wiser. If you buy ladies' flesh at a million a dram, you cannot preserve it from tainting. But I see you have some religion in you, that you fear.
POSTHUMUS: This is but a custom in your tongue; you bear a graver purpose, I hope.
IACHIMO: I am the master of my speeches, and would undergo what's spoken, I swear.

POSTHUMUS: Will you? I Shall but lend my diamond till your return. Let there be covenants drawn between's. My mistress exceeds in goodness the hugeness of your unworthy thinking. I dare you to this match: here's my ring.
PHILARIO: I will have it no lay.
IACHIMO: By the gods, it is one. If I bring you no sufficient testimony that I have enjoy'd the dearest bodily part of your mistress, my ten thousand ducats are yours; so is your diamond too. If I come off, and leave her in such honour as you have trust in, she your jewel, this your jewel, and my gold are yours- provided I have your commendation for my more free entertainment.
POSTHUMUS: I embrace these conditions; let us have articles betwixt us. Only, thus far you shall answer: if you make your voyage upon her, and give me directly to understand you have prevail'd, I am no further your enemy- she is not worth our debate; if she remain unseduc'd, you not making it appear otherwise, for your ill opinion and th' assault you have made to her chastity you shall answer me with your sword.
IACHIMO: Your hand- a covenant! We will have these things set down by lawful counsel, and straight away for Britain, lest the bargain should catch cold and starve. I will fetch my gold and have our two wagers recorded.
POSTHUMUS: Agreed.
Exeunt Posthumus and Iachimo
FRENCHMAN. Will this hold, think you?
PHILARIO: Signior Iachimo will not from it. Pray let us follow 'em.
Exeunt

ACT I. SCENE V. Britain. Cymbeline's Palace

Enter Queen, Ladies, and Cornelius
QUEEN: Whiles yet the dew's on ground, gather those flowers;
Make haste; who has the note of them?
LADY: I, madam.
QUEEN: Dispatch.
Exeunt Ladies
Now, Master Doctor, have you brought those drugs?
CORNELIUS: Pleaseth your Highness, ay. Here they are, madam.
Presenting a Box
But I beseech your Grace, without offence-
My conscience bids me ask- wherefore you have
Commanded of me these most poisonous compounds
Which are the movers of a languishing death,
But, though slow, deadly?
QUEEN: I wonder, Doctor,
Thou ask'st me such a question. Have I not been
Thy pupil long? Hast thou not learn'd me how
To make perfumes? distil? preserve? yea, so
That our great king himself doth woo me oft
For my confections? Having thus far proceeded-
Unless thou think'st me devilish- is't not meet
That I did amplify my judgment in
Other conclusions? I will try the forces
Of these thy compounds on such creatures as
We count not worth the hanging- but none human-

To try the vigour of them, and apply
Allayments to their act, and by them gather
Their several virtues and effects.
CORNELIUS: Your Highness
Shall from this practice but make hard your heart;
Besides, the seeing these effects will be
Both noisome and infectious.
QUEEN: O, content thee.
Enter Pisanio
Aside Here comes a flattering rascal; upon him
Will I first work. He's for his master,
An enemy to my son.- How now, Pisanio!
Doctor, your service for this time is ended;
Take your own way.
CORNELIUS: Aside I do suspect you, madam;
But you shall do no harm.
QUEEN: To Pisanio Hark thee, a word.
CORNELIUS: Aside I do not like her. She doth think she has
Strange ling'ring poisons. I do know her spirit,
And will not trust one of her malice with
A drug of such damn'd nature. Those she has
Will stupefy and dull the sense awhile,
Which first perchance she'll prove on cats and dogs,
Then afterward up higher; but there is
No danger in what show of death it makes,
More than the locking up the spirits a time,
To be more fresh, reviving. She is fool'd
With a most false effect; and I the truer
So to be false with her.
QUEEN: No further service, Doctor,
Until I send for thee.
CORNELIUS: I humbly take my leave.
Exit
QUEEN: Weeps she still, say'st thou? Dost thou think in time
She will not quench, and let instructions enter
Where folly now possesses? Do thou work.
When thou shalt bring me word she loves my son,
I'll tell thee on the instant thou art then
As great as is thy master; greater, for
His fortunes all lie speechless, and his name
Is at last gasp. Return he cannot, nor
Continue where he is. To shift his being
Is to exchange one misery with another,
And every day that comes comes comes to
A day's work in him. What shalt thou expect
To be depender on a thing that leans,
Who cannot be new built, nor has no friends
So much as but to prop him?
The Queen Drops the Box. Pisanio Takes it up
Thou tak'st up
Thou know'st not what; but take it for thy labour.
It is a thing I made, which hath the King
Five times redeem'd from death. I do not know

What is more cordial. Nay, I prithee take it;
It is an earnest of a further good
That I mean to thee. Tell thy mistress how
The case stands with her; do't as from thyself.
Think what a chance thou changest on; but think
Thou hast thy mistress still; to boot, my son,
Who shall take notice of thee. I'll move the King
To any shape of thy preferment, such
As thou'lt desire; and then myself, I chiefly,
That set thee on to this desert, am bound
To load thy merit richly. Call my women.
Think on my words.
Exit Pisanio
A sly and constant knave,
Not to be shak'd; the agent for his master,
And the remembrancer of her to hold
The hand-fast to her lord. I have given him that
Which, if he take, shall quite unpeople her
Of leigers for her sweet; and which she after,
Except she bend her humour, shall be assur'd
To taste of too.
Re-enter Pisanio and Ladies
So, so. Well done, well done.
The violets, cowslips, and the primroses,
Bear to my closet. Fare thee well, Pisanio;
Think on my words.
Exeunt Queen and Ladies
PISANIO: And shall do.
But when to my good lord I prove untrue
I'll choke myself- there's all I'll do for you.
Exit

ACT I. SCENE VI. Britain. The Palace

Enter Imogen Alone
IMOGEN: A father cruel and a step-dame false;
A foolish suitor to a wedded lady
That hath her husband banish'd. O, that husband!
My supreme crown of grief! and those repeated
Vexations of it! Had I been thief-stol'n,
As my two brothers, happy! but most miserable
Is the desire that's glorious. Blessed be those,
How mean soe'er, that have their honest wills,
Which seasons comfort. Who may this be? Fie!
Enter Pisanio and Iachimo
PISANIO: Madam, a noble gentleman of Rome
Comes from my lord with letters.
IACHIMO: Change you, madam?
The worthy Leonatus is in safety,
And greets your Highness dearly.
Presents a Letter
IMOGEN: Thanks, good sir.
You're kindly welcome.
IACHIMO: Aside All of her that is out of door most rich!
If she be furnish'd with a mind so rare,

She is alone th' Arabian bird, and I
Have lost the wager. Boldness be my friend!
Arm me, audacity, from head to foot!
Or, like the Parthian, I shall flying fight;
Rather, directly fly.
IMOGEN: Reads 'He is one of the noblest note, to whose kindnesses I am most infinitely tied. Reflect upon him accordingly, as you value your trust. Leonatus.'
So far I read aloud;
But even the very middle of my heart
Is warm'd by th' rest and takes it thankfully.
You are as welcome, worthy sir, as I
Have words to bid you; and shall find it so
In all that I can do.
IACHIMO: Thanks, fairest lady.
What, are men mad? Hath nature given them eyes
To see this vaulted arch and the rich crop
Of sea and land, which can distinguish 'twixt
The fiery orbs above and the twinn'd stones
Upon the number'd beach, and can we not
Partition make with spectacles so precious
'Twixt fair and foul?
IMOGEN: What makes your admiration?
IACHIMO: It cannot be i' th' eye, for apes and monkeys,
'Twixt two such shes, would chatter this way and
Contemn with mows the other; nor i' th' judgment,
For idiots in this case of favour would
Be wisely definite; nor i' th' appetite;
Sluttery, to such neat excellence oppos'd,
Should make desire vomit emptiness,
Not so allur'd to feed.
IMOGEN: What is the matter, trow?
IACHIMO: The cloyed will-
That satiate yet unsatisfied desire, that tub
Both fill'd and running- ravening first the lamb,
Longs after for the garbage.
IMOGEN: What, dear sir,
Thus raps you? Are you well?
IACHIMO: Thanks, madam; well.- Beseech you, sir,
Desire my man's abode where I did leave him.
He's strange and peevish.
PISANIO: I was going, sir,
To give him welcome.
Exit
IMOGEN: Continues well my lord? His health beseech you?
IACHIMO: Well, madam.
IMOGEN: Is he dispos'd to mirth? I hope he is.
IACHIMO: Exceeding pleasant; none a stranger there
So merry and so gamesome. He is call'd
The Britain reveller.
IMOGEN: When he was here
He did incline to sadness, and oft-times
Not knowing why.

IACHIMO: I never saw him sad.
There is a Frenchman his companion, one
An eminent monsieur that, it seems, much loves
A Gallian girl at home. He furnaces
The thick sighs from him; whiles the jolly Briton-
Your lord, I mean- laughs from's free lungs, cries 'O,
Can my sides hold, to think that man- who knows
By history, report, or his own proof,
What woman is, yea, what she cannot choose
But must be- will's free hours languish for
Assured bondage?'
IMOGEN: Will my lord say so?
IACHIMO: Ay, madam, with his eyes in flood with laughter.
It is a recreation to be by
And hear him mock the Frenchman. But heavens know
Some men are much to blame.
IMOGEN: Not he, I hope.
IACHIMO: Not he; but yet heaven's bounty towards him might
Be us'd more thankfully. In himself, 'tis much;
In you, which I account his, beyond all talents.
Whilst I am bound to wonder, I am bound
To pity too.
IMOGEN: What do you pity, sir?
IACHIMO: Two creatures heartily.
IMOGEN: Am I one, sir?
You look on me: what wreck discern you in me
Deserves your pity?
IACHIMO: Lamentable! What,
To hide me from the radiant sun and solace
I' th' dungeon by a snuff?
IMOGEN: I pray you, sir,
Deliver with more openness your answers
To my demands. Why do you pity me?
IACHIMO: That others do,
I was about to say, enjoy your- But
It is an office of the gods to venge it,
Not mine to speak on't.
IMOGEN: You do seem to know
Something of me, or what concerns me; pray you-
Since doubting things go ill often hurts more
Than to be sure they do; for certainties
Either are past remedies, or, timely knowing,
The remedy then born- discover to me
What both you spur and stop.
IACHIMO: Had I this cheek
To bathe my lips upon; this hand, whose touch,
Whose every touch, would force the feeler's soul
To th' oath of loyalty; this object, which
Takes prisoner the wild motion of mine eye,
Fixing it only here; should I, damn'd then,
Slaver with lips as common as the stairs
That mount the Capitol; join gripes with hands
Made hard with hourly falsehood- falsehood as

With labour; then by-peeping in an eye
Base and illustrious as the smoky light
That's fed with stinking tallow- it were fit
That all the plagues of hell should at one time
Encounter such revolt.
IMOGEN: My lord, I fear,
Has forgot Britain.
IACHIMO: And himself. Not I
Inclin'd to this intelligence pronounce
The beggary of his change; but 'tis your graces
That from my mutest conscience to my tongue
Charms this report out.
IMOGEN: Let me hear no more.
IACHIMO: O dearest soul, your cause doth strike my heart
With pity that doth make me sick! A lady
So fair, and fasten'd to an empery,
Would make the great'st king double, to be partner'd
With tomboys hir'd with that self exhibition
Which your own coffers yield! with diseas'd ventures
That play with all infirmities for gold
Which rottenness can lend nature! such boil'd stuff
As well might poison poison! Be reveng'd;
Or she that bore you was no queen, and you
Recoil from your great stock.
IMOGEN: Reveng'd?
How should I be reveng'd? If this be true-
As I have such a heart that both mine ears
Must not in haste abuse- if it be true,
How should I be reveng'd?
IACHIMO: Should he make me
Live like Diana's priest betwixt cold sheets,
Whiles he is vaulting variable ramps,
In your despite, upon your purse? Revenge it.
I dedicate myself to your sweet pleasure,
More noble than that runagate to your bed,
And will continue fast to your affection,
Still close as sure.
IMOGEN: What ho, Pisanio!
IACHIMO: Let me my service tender on your lips.
IMOGEN: Away! I do condemn mine ears that have
So long attended thee. If thou wert honourable,
Thou wouldst have told this tale for virtue, not
For such an end thou seek'st, as base as strange.
Thou wrong'st a gentleman who is as far
From thy report as thou from honour; and
Solicits here a lady that disdains
Thee and the devil alike.- What ho, Pisanio!-
The King my father shall be made acquainted
Of thy assault. If he shall think it fit
A saucy stranger in his court to mart
As in a Romish stew, and to expound
His beastly mind to us, he hath a court
He little cares for, and a daughter who

He not respects at all.- What ho, Pisanio!
IACHIMO: O happy Leonatus! I may say
The credit that thy lady hath of thee
Deserves thy trust, and thy most perfect goodness
Her assur'd credit. Blessed live you long,
A lady to the worthiest sir that ever
Country call'd his! and you his mistress, only
For the most worthiest fit! Give me your pardon.
I have spoke this to know if your affiance
Were deeply rooted, and shall make your lord
That which he is new o'er; and he is one
The truest manner'd, such a holy witch
That he enchants societies into him,
Half all men's hearts are his.
IMOGEN: You make amends.
IACHIMO: He sits 'mongst men like a descended god:
He hath a kind of honour sets him of
More than a mortal seeming. Be not angry,
Most mighty Princess, that I have adventur'd
To try your taking of a false report, which hath
Honour'd with confirmation your great judgment
In the election of a sir so rare,
Which you know cannot err. The love I bear him
Made me to fan you thus; but the gods made you,
Unlike all others, chaffless. Pray your pardon.
IMOGEN: All's well, sir; take my pow'r i' th' court for yours.
IACHIMO: My humble thanks. I had almost forgot
T' entreat your Grace but in a small request,
And yet of moment too, for it concerns
Your lord; myself and other noble friends
Are partners in the business.
IMOGEN: Pray what is't?
IACHIMO: Some dozen Romans of us, and your lord-
The best feather of our wing- have mingled sums
To buy a present for the Emperor;
Which I, the factor for the rest, have done
In France. 'Tis plate of rare device, and jewels
Of rich and exquisite form, their values great;
And I am something curious, being strange,
To have them in safe stowage. May it please you
To take them in protection?
IMOGEN: Willingly;
And pawn mine honour for their safety. Since
My lord hath interest in them, I will keep them
In my bedchamber.
IACHIMO: They are in a trunk,
Attended by my men. I will make bold
To send them to you only for this night;
I must aboard to-morrow.
IMOGEN: O, no, no.
IACHIMO: Yes, I beseech; or I shall short my word
By length'ning my return. From Gallia
I cross'd the seas on purpose and on promise

To see your Grace.
IMOGEN: I thank you for your pains.
But not away to-morrow!
IACHIMO: O, I must, madam.
Therefore I shall beseech you, if you please
To greet your lord with writing, do't to-night.
I have outstood my time, which is material
'To th' tender of our present.
IMOGEN: I will write.
Send your trunk to me; it shall safe be kept
And truly yielded you. You're very welcome.
Exeunt

ACT II. SCENE I. Britain. Before Cymbeline's Palace

Enter Cloten and the Two Lords

CLOTEN: Was there ever man had such luck! When I kiss'd the jack, upon an up-cast to be hit away! I had a hundred pound on't; and then a whoreson jackanapes must take me up for swearing, as if I borrowed mine oaths of him, and might not spend them at my pleasure.

FIRST LORD: What got he by that? You have broke his pate with your bowl.

SECOND LORD: Aside If his wit had been like him that broke it, it would have run all out.

CLOTEN: When a gentleman is dispos'd to swear, it is not for any standers-by to curtail his oaths. Ha?

SECOND LORD: No, my lord; Aside nor crop the ears of them.

CLOTEN: Whoreson dog! I give him satisfaction? Would he had been one of my rank!

SECOND LORD: Aside To have smell'd like a fool.

CLOTEN: I am not vex'd more at anything in th' earth. A pox on't! I had rather not be so noble as I am; they dare not fight with me, because of the Queen my mother. Every jackslave hath his bellyful of fighting, and I must go up and down like a cock that nobody can match.

SECOND LORD: Aside You are cock and capon too; and you crow, cock, with your comb on.

CLOTEN: Sayest thou?

SECOND LORD: It is not fit your lordship should undertake every companion that you give offence to.

CLOTEN: No, I know that; but it is fit I should commit offence to my inferiors.

SECOND LORD: Ay, it is fit for your lordship only.

CLOTEN: Why, so I say.

FIRST LORD: Did you hear of a stranger that's come to court to-night?

CLOTEN: A stranger, and I not known on't?

SECOND LORD: Aside He's a strange fellow himself, and knows it not.

FIRST LORD: There's an Italian come, and, 'tis thought, one of Leonatus' friends.

CLOTEN: Leonatus? A banish'd rascal; and he's another, whatsoever he be. Who told you of this stranger?

FIRST LORD: One of your lordship's pages.

CLOTEN: Is it fit I went to look upon him? Is there no derogation in't?

SECOND LORD: You cannot derogate, my lord.

CLOTEN: Not easily, I think.
SECOND LORD: Aside You are a fool granted; therefore your issues, being foolish, do not derogate.
CLOTEN: Come, I'll go see this Italian. What I have lost to-day at bowls I'll win to-night of him. Come, go.
SECOND LORD: I'll attend your lordship.
Exeunt Cloten and First Lord
That such a crafty devil as is his mother
Should yield the world this ass! A woman that
Bears all down with her brain; and this her son
Cannot take two from twenty, for his heart,
And leave eighteen. Alas, poor princess,
Thou divine Imogen, what thou endur'st,
Betwixt a father by thy step-dame govern'd,
A mother hourly coining plots, a wooer
More hateful than the foul expulsion is
Of thy dear husband, than that horrid act
Of the divorce he'd make! The heavens hold firm
The walls of thy dear honour, keep unshak'd
That temple, thy fair mind, that thou mayst stand
T' enjoy thy banish'd lord and this great land!
Exit

ACT II. SCENE II. Britain. Imogen's Bedchamber in Cymbeline's Palace; a Trunk in One Corner

Enter Imogen in Her Bed, and a Lady Attending
IMOGEN: Who's there? My woman? Helen?
LADY: Please you, madam.
IMOGEN: What hour is it?
LADY: Almost midnight, madam.
IMOGEN: I have read three hours then. Mine eyes are weak;
Fold down the leaf where I have left. To bed.
Take not away the taper, leave it burning;
And if thou canst awake by four o' th' clock,
I prithee call me. Sleep hath seiz'd me wholly.
Exit Lady
To your protection I commend me, gods.
From fairies and the tempters of the night
Guard me, beseech ye!
Sleeps. Iachimo Comes from the Trunk
IACHIMO: The crickets sing, and man's o'er-labour'd sense
Repairs itself by rest. Our Tarquin thus
Did softly press the rushes ere he waken'd
The chastity he wounded. Cytherea,
How bravely thou becom'st thy bed! fresh lily,
And whiter than the sheets! That I might touch!
But kiss; one kiss! Rubies unparagon'd,
How dearly they do't! 'Tis her breathing that
Perfumes the chamber thus. The flame o' th' taper
Bows toward her and would under-peep her lids
To see th' enclosed lights, now canopied
Under these windows white and azure, lac'd
With blue of heaven's own tinct. But my design
To note the chamber. I will write all down:

Such and such pictures; there the window; such
Th' adornment of her bed; the arras, figures-
Why, such and such; and the contents o' th' story.
Ah, but some natural notes about her body
Above ten thousand meaner movables
Would testify, t' enrich mine inventory.
O sleep, thou ape of death, lie dull upon her!
And be her sense but as a monument,
Thus in a chapel lying! Come off, come off;
Taking off Her Bracelet
As slippery as the Gordian knot was hard!
'Tis mine; and this will witness outwardly,
As strongly as the conscience does within,
To th' madding of her lord. On her left breast
A mole cinque-spotted, like the crimson drops
I' th' bottom of a cowslip. Here's a voucher
Stronger than ever law could make; this secret
Will force him think I have pick'd the lock and ta'en
The treasure of her honour. No more. To what end?
Why should I write this down that's riveted,
Screw'd to my memory? She hath been reading late
The tale of Tereus; here the leaf's turn'd down
Where Philomel gave up. I have enough.
To th' trunk again, and shut the spring of it.
Swift, swift, you dragons of the night, that dawning
May bare the raven's eye! I lodge in fear;
Though this a heavenly angel, hell is here.
Clock Strikes
One, two, three. Time, time!
Exit into the Trunk

ACT II. SCENE III. Cymbeline's palace. An Ante-Chamber Adjoining Imogen's Apartments

Enter Cloten and Lords

FIRST LORD: Your lordship is the most patient man in loss, the most coldest that ever turn'd up ace.

CLOTEN: It would make any man cold to lose.

FIRST LORD: But not every man patient after the noble temper of your lordship. You are most hot and furious when you win.

CLOTEN: Winning will put any man into courage. If I could get this foolish Imogen, I should have gold enough. It's almost morning, is't not?

FIRST LORD: Day, my lord.

CLOTEN: I would this music would come. I am advised to give her music a mornings; they say it will penetrate.

Enter Musicians

Come on, tune. If you can penetrate her with your fingering, so. We'll try with tongue too. If none will do, let her remain; but I'll never give o'er. First, a very excellent good-conceited thing; after, a wonderful sweet air, with admirable rich words to it- and then let her consider.

SONG

Hark, hark! the lark at heaven's gate sings,
And Phoebus 'gins arise,
His steeds to water at those springs
On chalic'd flow'rs that lies;

And winking Mary-buds begin
To ope their golden eyes.
With everything that pretty bin,
My lady sweet, arise;
Arise, arise!

So, get you gone. If this penetrate, I will consider your music the better; if it do not, it is a vice in her ears which horsehairs and calves' guts, nor the voice of unpaved eunuch to boot, can never amend. Exeunt musicians

Enter Cymbeline and Queen

SECOND LORD: Here comes the King.

CLOTEN: I am glad I was up so late, for that's the reason I was up so early. He cannot choose but take this service I have done fatherly.- Good morrow to your Majesty and to my gracious mother.

CYMBELINE: Attend you here the door of our stern daughter?
Will she not forth?

CLOTEN: I have assail'd her with musics, but she vouchsafes no notice.

CYMBELINE: The exile of her minion is too new;
She hath not yet forgot him; some more time
Must wear the print of his remembrance out,
And then she's yours.

QUEEN: You are most bound to th' King,
Who lets go by no vantages that may
Prefer you to his daughter. Frame yourself
To orderly soliciting, and be friended
With aptness of the season; make denials
Increase your services; so seem as if
You were inspir'd to do those duties which
You tender to her; that you in all obey her,
Save when command to your dismission tends,
And therein you are senseless.

CLOTEN: Senseless? Not so.

Enter a Messenger

MESSENGER: So like you, sir, ambassadors from Rome;
The one is Caius Lucius.

CYMBELINE: A worthy fellow,
Albeit he comes on angry purpose now;
But that's no fault of his. We must receive him
According to the honour of his sender;
And towards himself, his goodness forespent on us,
We must extend our notice. Our dear son,
When you have given good morning to your mistress,
Attend the Queen and us; we shall have need
T' employ you towards this Roman. Come, our queen.

Exeunt All but Cloten

CLOTEN: If she be up, I'll speak with her; if not,
Let her lie still and dream. By your leave, ho! Knocks
I know her women are about her; what
If I do line one of their hands? 'Tis gold
Which buys admittance; oft it doth-yea, and makes
Diana's rangers false themselves, yield up
Their deer to th' stand o' th' stealer; and 'tis gold

Which makes the true man kill'd and saves the thief;
Nay, sometime hangs both thief and true man. What
Can it not do and undo? I will make
One of her women lawyer to me, for
I yet not understand the case myself.
By your leave.
Knocks
Enter a Lady
LADY: Who's there that knocks?
CLOTEN: A gentleman.
LADY: No more?
CLOTEN: Yes, and a gentlewoman's son.
LADY: That's more
Than some whose tailors are as dear as yours
Can justly boast of. What's your lordship's pleasure?
CLOTEN: Your lady's person; is she ready?
LADY: Ay,
To keep her chamber.
CLOTEN: There is gold for you; sell me your good report.
LADY: How? My good name? or to report of you
What I shall think is good? The Princess!
Enter Imogen
CLOTEN: Good morrow, fairest sister. Your sweet hand.
Exit Lady
IMOGEN: Good morrow, sir. You lay out too much pains
For purchasing but trouble. The thanks I give
Is telling you that I am poor of thanks,
And scarce can spare them.
CLOTEN: Still I swear I love you.
IMOGEN: If you but said so, 'twere as deep with me.
If you swear still, your recompense is still
That I regard it not.
CLOTEN: This is no answer.
IMOGEN: But that you shall not say I yield, being silent,
I would not speak. I pray you spare me. Faith,
I shall unfold equal discourtesy
To your best kindness; one of your great knowing
Should learn, being taught, forbearance.
CLOTEN: To leave you in your madness 'twere my sin;
I will not.
IMOGEN: Fools are not mad folks.
CLOTEN: Do you call me fool?
IMOGEN: As I am mad, I do;
If you'll be patient, I'll no more be mad;
That cures us both. I am much sorry, sir,
You put me to forget a lady's manners
By being so verbal; and learn now, for all,
That I, which know my heart, do here pronounce,
By th' very truth of it, I care not for you,
And am so near the lack of charity
To accuse myself I hate you; which I had rather
You felt than make't my boast.
CLOTEN: You sin against

Obedience, which you owe your father. For
The contract you pretend with that base wretch,
One bred of alms and foster'd with cold dishes,
With scraps o' th' court- it is no contract, none.
And though it be allowed in meaner parties-
Yet who than he more mean?- to knit their souls-
On whom there is no more dependency
But brats and beggary- in self-figur'd knot,
Yet you are curb'd from that enlargement by
The consequence o' th' crown, and must not foil
The precious note of it with a base slave,
A hilding for a livery, a squire's cloth,
A pantler- not so eminent!
IMOGEN: Profane fellow!
Wert thou the son of Jupiter, and no more
But what thou art besides, thou wert too base
To be his groom. Thou wert dignified enough,
Even to the point of envy, if 'twere made
Comparative for your virtues to be styl'd
The under-hangman of his kingdom, and hated
For being preferr'd so well.
CLOTEN: The south fog rot him!
IMOGEN: He never can meet more mischance than come
To be but nam'd of thee. His mean'st garment
That ever hath but clipp'd his body is dearer
In my respect than all the hairs above thee,
Were they all made such men. How now, Pisanio!
Enter Pisanio
CLOTEN: 'His garments'! Now the devil-
IMOGEN: To Dorothy my woman hie thee presently.
CLOTEN: 'His garment'!
IMOGEN: I am sprited with a fool;
Frighted, and ang'red worse. Go bid my woman
Search for a jewel that too casually
Hath left mine arm. It was thy master's; shrew me,
If I would lose it for a revenue
Of any king's in Europe! I do think
I saw't this morning; confident I am
Last night 'twas on mine arm; I kiss'd it.
I hope it be not gone to tell my lord
That I kiss aught but he.
PISANIO: 'Twill not be lost.
IMOGEN: I hope so. Go and search.
Exit Pisanio
CLOTEN: You have abus'd me.
'His meanest garment'!
IMOGEN: Ay, I said so, sir.
If you will make 't an action, call witness to 't.
CLOTEN: I will inform your father.
IMOGEN: Your mother too.
She's my good lady and will conceive, I hope,
But the worst of me. So I leave you, sir,
To th' worst of discontent.

Exit
CLOTEN: I'll be reveng'd.
'His mean'st garment'! Well. Exit

ACT II. SCENE IV. Rome. Philario's House

Enter Posthumus and Philario
POSTHUMUS: Fear it not, sir; I would I were so sure
To win the King as I am bold her honour
Will remain hers.
PHILARIO: What means do you make to him?
POSTHUMUS: Not any; but abide the change of time,
Quake in the present winter's state, and wish
That warmer days would come. In these fear'd hopes
I barely gratify your love; they failing,
I must die much your debtor.
PHILARIO: Your very goodness and your company
O'erpays all I can do. By this your king
Hath heard of great Augustus. Caius Lucius
Will do's commission throughly; and I think
He'll grant the tribute, send th' arrearages,
Or look upon our Romans, whose remembrance
Is yet fresh in their grief.
POSTHUMUS: I do believe
Statist though I am none, nor like to be,
That this will prove a war; and you shall hear
The legions now in Gallia sooner landed
In our not-fearing Britain than have tidings
Of any penny tribute paid. Our countrymen
Are men more order'd than when Julius Caesar
Smil'd at their lack of skill, but found their courage
Worthy his frowning at. Their discipline,
Now mingled with their courages, will make known
To their approvers they are people such
That mend upon the world.
Enter Iachimo
PHILARIO: See! Iachimo!
POSTHUMUS: The swiftest harts have posted you by land,
And winds of all the corners kiss'd your sails,
To make your vessel nimble.
PHILARIO: Welcome, sir.
POSTHUMUS: I hope the briefness of your answer made
The speediness of your return.
IACHIMO: Your lady
Is one of the fairest that I have look'd upon.
POSTHUMUS: And therewithal the best; or let her beauty
Look through a casement to allure false hearts,
And be false with them.
IACHIMO: Here are letters for you.
POSTHUMUS: Their tenour good, I trust.
IACHIMO: 'Tis very like.
PHILARIO: Was Caius Lucius in the Britain court
When you were there?
IACHIMO: He was expected then,
But not approach'd.

POSTHUMUS: All is well yet.
Sparkles this stone as it was wont, or is't not
Too dull for your good wearing?
IACHIMO: If I have lost it,
I should have lost the worth of it in gold.
I'll make a journey twice as far t' enjoy
A second night of such sweet shortness which
Was mine in Britain; for the ring is won.
POSTHUMUS: The stone's too hard to come by.
IACHIMO: Not a whit,
Your lady being so easy.
POSTHUMUS: Make not, sir,
Your loss your sport. I hope you know that we
Must not continue friends.
IACHIMO: Good sir, we must,
If you keep covenant. Had I not brought
The knowledge of your mistress home, I grant
We were to question farther; but I now
Profess myself the winner of her honour,
Together with your ring; and not the wronger
Of her or you, having proceeded but
By both your wills.
POSTHUMUS: If you can make't apparent
That you have tasted her in bed, my hand
And ring is yours. If not, the foul opinion
You had of her pure honour gains or loses
Your sword or mine, or masterless leaves both
To who shall find them.
IACHIMO: Sir, my circumstances,
Being so near the truth as I will make them,
Must first induce you to believe- whose strength
I will confirm with oath; which I doubt not
You'll give me leave to spare when you shall find
You need it not.
POSTHUMUS: Proceed.
IACHIMO: First, her bedchamber,
Where I confess I slept not, but profess
Had that was well worth watching-it was hang'd
With tapestry of silk and silver; the story,
Proud Cleopatra when she met her Roman
And Cydnus swell'd above the banks, or for
The press of boats or pride. A piece of work
So bravely done, so rich, that it did strive
In workmanship and value; which I wonder'd
Could be so rarely and exactly wrought,
Since the true life on't was-
POSTHUMUS: This is true;
And this you might have heard of here, by me
Or by some other.
IACHIMO: More particulars
Must justify my knowledge.
POSTHUMUS: So they must,
Or do your honour injury.

IACHIMO: The chimney
Is south the chamber, and the chimneypiece
Chaste Dian bathing. Never saw I figures
So likely to report themselves. The cutter
Was as another nature, dumb; outwent her,
Motion and breath left out.
POSTHUMUS: This is a thing
Which you might from relation likewise reap,
Being, as it is, much spoke of.
IACHIMO: The roof o' th' chamber
With golden cherubins is fretted; her andirons-
I had forgot them- were two winking Cupids
Of silver, each on one foot standing, nicely
Depending on their brands.
POSTHUMUS: This is her honour!
Let it be granted you have seen all this, and praise
Be given to your remembrance; the description
Of what is in her chamber nothing saves
The wager you have laid.
IACHIMO: Then, if you can,
Shows the Bracelet
Be pale. I beg but leave to air this jewel. See!
And now 'tis up again. It must be married
To that your diamond; I'll keep them.
POSTHUMUS: Jove!
Once more let me behold it. Is it that
Which I left with her?
IACHIMO: Sir- I thank her- that.
She stripp'd it from her arm; I see her yet;
Her pretty action did outsell her gift,
And yet enrich'd it too. She gave it me, and said
She priz'd it once.
POSTHUMUS: May be she pluck'd it of
To send it me.
IACHIMO: She writes so to you, doth she?
POSTHUMUS: O, no, no, no! 'tis true. Here, take this too;
Gives the Ring
It is a basilisk unto mine eye,
Kills me to look on't. Let there be no honour
Where there is beauty; truth where semblance; love
Where there's another man. The vows of women
Of no more bondage be to where they are made
Than they are to their virtues, which is nothing.
O, above measure false!
PHILARIO: Have patience, sir,
And take your ring again; 'tis not yet won.
It may be probable she lost it, or
Who knows if one her women, being corrupted
Hath stol'n it from her?
POSTHUMUS: Very true;
And so I hope he came by't. Back my ring.
Render to me some corporal sign about her,
More evident than this; for this was stol'n.

IACHIMO: By Jupiter, I had it from her arm!
POSTHUMUS: Hark you, he swears; by Jupiter he swears.
'Tis true- nay, keep the ring, 'tis true. I am sure
She would not lose it. Her attendants are
All sworn and honourable- they induc'd to steal it!
And by a stranger! No, he hath enjoy'd her.
The cognizance of her incontinency
Is this: she hath bought the name of whore thus dearly.
There, take thy hire; and all the fiends of hell
Divide themselves between you!
PHILARIO: Sir, be patient;
This is not strong enough to be believ'd
Of one persuaded well of.
POSTHUMUS: Never talk on't;
She hath been colted by him.
IACHIMO: If you seek
For further satisfying, under her breast-
Worthy the pressing- lies a mole, right proud
Of that most delicate lodging. By my life,
I kiss'd it; and it gave me present hunger
To feed again, though full. You do remember
This stain upon her?
POSTHUMUS: Ay, and it doth confirm
Another stain, as big as hell can hold,
Were there no more but it.
IACHIMO: Will you hear more?
POSTHUMUS: Spare your arithmetic; never count the turns.
Once, and a million!
IACHIMO: I'll be sworn-
POSTHUMUS: No swearing.
If you will swear you have not done't, you lie;
And I will kill thee if thou dost deny
Thou'st made me cuckold.
IACHIMO: I'll deny nothing.
POSTHUMUS: O that I had her here to tear her limb-meal!
I will go there and do't, i' th' court, before
Her father. I'll do something-
Exit
PHILARIO: Quite besides
The government of patience! You have won.
Let's follow him and pervert the present wrath
He hath against himself.
IACHIMO: With all my heart.
Exeunt

ACT II. SCENE V. Rome. Another Room in Philario's House

Enter Posthumus
POSTHUMUS: Is there no way for men to be, but women
Must be half-workers? We are all bastards,
And that most venerable man which I
Did call my father was I know not where
When I was stamp'd. Some coiner with his tools
Made me a counterfeit; yet my mother seem'd
The Dian of that time. So doth my wife

The nonpareil of this. O, vengeance, vengeance!
Me of my lawful pleasure she restrain'd,
And pray'd me oft forbearance; did it with
A pudency so rosy, the sweet view on't
Might well have warm'd old Saturn; that I thought her
As chaste as unsunn'd snow. O, all the devils!
This yellow Iachimo in an hour- was't not?
Or less!- at first? Perchance he spoke not, but,
Like a full-acorn'd boar, a German one,
Cried 'O!' and mounted; found no opposition
But what he look'd for should oppose and she
Should from encounter guard. Could I find out
The woman's part in me! For there's no motion
That tends to vice in man but I affirm
It is the woman's part. Be it lying, note it,
The woman's; flattering, hers; deceiving, hers;
Lust and rank thoughts, hers, hers; revenges, hers;
Ambitions, covetings, change of prides, disdain,
Nice longing, slanders, mutability,
All faults that man may name, nay, that hell knows,
Why, hers, in part or all; but rather all;
For even to vice
They are not constant, but are changing still
One vice but of a minute old for one
Not half so old as that. I'll write against them,
Detest them, curse them. Yet 'tis greater skill
In a true hate to pray they have their will:
The very devils cannot plague them better.
Exit

ACT III. SCENE I. Britain. A Hall in Cymbeline's Palace

Enter in State, Cymbeline, Queen, Cloten, and Lords at One Door, and at Another Caius Lucius and Attendants

CYMBELINE: Now say, what would Augustus Caesar with us?
LUCIUS: When Julius Caesar- whose remembrance yet
Lives in men's eyes, and will to ears and tongues
Be theme and hearing ever- was in this Britain,
And conquer'd it, Cassibelan, thine uncle,
Famous in Caesar's praises no whit less
Than in his feats deserving it, for him
And his succession granted Rome a tribute,
Yearly three thousand pounds, which by thee lately
Is left untender'd.
QUEEN: And, to kill the marvel,
Shall be so ever.
CLOTEN: There be many Caesars
Ere such another Julius. Britain is
A world by itself, and we will nothing pay
For wearing our own noses.
QUEEN: That opportunity,
Which then they had to take from 's, to resume
We have again. Remember, sir, my liege,
The kings your ancestors, together with
The natural bravery of your isle, which stands

As Neptune's park, ribb'd and pal'd in
With rocks unscalable and roaring waters,
With sands that will not bear your enemies' boats
But suck them up to th' top-mast. A kind of conquest
Caesar made here; but made not here his brag
Of 'came, and saw, and overcame.' With shame-
The first that ever touch'd him- he was carried
From off our coast, twice beaten; and his shipping-
Poor ignorant baubles!- on our terrible seas,
Like egg-shells mov'd upon their surges, crack'd
As easily 'gainst our rocks; for joy whereof
The fam'd Cassibelan, who was once at point-
O, giglot fortune!- to master Caesar's sword,
Made Lud's Town with rejoicing fires bright
And Britons strut with courage.
CLOTEN: Come, there's no more tribute to be paid. Our kingdom is stronger than it was at that time; and, as I said, there is no moe such Caesars. Other of them may have crook'd noses; but to owe such straight arms, none.
CYMBELINE: Son, let your mother end.
CLOTEN: We have yet many among us can gripe as hard as Cassibelan. I do not say I am one; but I have a hand. Why tribute? Why should we pay tribute? If Caesar can hide the sun from us with a blanket, or put the moon in his pocket, we will pay him tribute for light; else, sir, no more tribute, pray you now.
CYMBELINE: You must know,
Till the injurious Romans did extort
This tribute from us, we were free. Caesar's ambition-
Which swell'd so much that it did almost stretch
The sides o' th' world- against all colour here
Did put the yoke upon's; which to shake of
Becomes a warlike people, whom we reckon
Ourselves to be.
CLOTEN: We do.
CYMBELINE: Say then to Caesar,
Our ancestor was that Mulmutius which
Ordain'd our laws- whose use the sword of Caesar
Hath too much mangled; whose repair and franchise
Shall, by the power we hold, be our good deed,
Though Rome be therefore angry. Mulmutius made our laws,
Who was the first of Britain which did put
His brows within a golden crown, and call'd
Himself a king.
LUCIUS: I am sorry, Cymbeline,
That I am to pronounce Augustus Caesar-
Caesar, that hath moe kings his servants than
Thyself domestic officers- thine enemy.
Receive it from me, then: war and confusion
In Caesar's name pronounce I 'gainst thee; look
For fury not to be resisted. Thus defied,
I thank thee for myself.
CYMBELINE: Thou art welcome, Caius.
Thy Caesar knighted me; my youth I spent

Much under him; of him I gather'd honour,
Which he to seek of me again, perforce,
Behoves me keep at utterance. I am perfect
That the Pannonians and Dalmatians for
Their liberties are now in arms, a precedent
Which not to read would show the Britons cold;
So Caesar shall not find them.
LUCIUS: Let proof speak.
CLOTEN: His majesty bids you welcome. Make pastime with us a day or two, or longer. If you seek us afterwards in other terms, you shall find us in our salt-water girdle. If you beat us out of it, it is yours; if you fall in the adventure, our crows shall fare the better for you; and there's an end.
LUCIUS: So, sir.
CYMBELINE: I know your master's pleasure, and he mine;
All the remain is, welcome.
Exeunt

ACT III. SCENE II. Britain. Another Room in Cymbeline's Palace

Enter Pisanio Reading of a Letter
PISANIO: How? of adultery? Wherefore write you not
What monsters her accuse? Leonatus!
O master, what a strange infection
Is fall'n into thy ear! What false Italian-
As poisonous-tongu'd as handed- hath prevail'd
On thy too ready hearing? Disloyal? No.
She's punish'd for her truth, and undergoes,
More goddess-like than wife-like, such assaults
As would take in some virtue. O my master!
Thy mind to her is now as low as were
Thy fortunes. How? that I should murder her?
Upon the love, and truth, and vows, which I
Have made to thy command? I, her? Her blood?
If it be so to do good service, never
Let me be counted serviceable. How look I
That I should seem to lack humanity
So much as this fact comes to? Reads 'Do't. The letter
That I have sent her, by her own command
Shall give thee opportunity.' O damn'd paper,
Black as the ink that's on thee! Senseless bauble,
Art thou a fedary for this act, and look'st
So virgin-like without? Lo, here she comes.
Enter Imogen
I am ignorant in what I am commanded.
IMOGEN: How now, Pisanio!
PISANIO: Madam, here is a letter from my lord.
IMOGEN: Who? thy lord? That is my lord- Leonatus?
O, learn'd indeed were that astronomer
That knew the stars as I his characters-
He'd lay the future open. You good gods,
Let what is here contain'd relish of love,
Of my lord's health, of his content; yet not
That we two are asunder- let that grieve him!
Some griefs are med'cinable; that is one of them,

For it doth physic love- of his content,
All but in that. Good wax, thy leave. Blest be
You bees that make these locks of counsel! Lovers
And men in dangerous bonds pray not alike;
Though forfeiters you cast in prison, yet
You clasp young Cupid's tables. Good news, gods!
Reads

'Justice and your father's wrath, should he take me in his dominion, could not be so cruel to me as you, O the dearest of creatures, would even renew me with your eyes. Take notice that I am in Cambria, at Milford Haven. What your own love will out of this advise you, follow. So he wishes you all happiness that remains loyal to his vow, and your increasing in love

Leonatus Posthumus.'

O for a horse with wings! Hear'st thou, Pisanio?
He is at Milford Haven. Read, and tell me
How far 'tis thither. If one of mean affairs
May plod it in a week, why may not I
Glide thither in a day? Then, true Pisanio-
Who long'st like me to see thy lord, who long'st-
O, let me 'bate!- but not like me, yet long'st,
But in a fainter kind- O, not like me,
For mine's beyond beyond!-say, and speak thick-
Love's counsellor should fill the bores of hearing
To th' smothering of the sense- how far it is
To this same blessed Milford. And by th' way
Tell me how Wales was made so happy as
T' inherit such a haven. But first of all,
How we may steal from hence; and for the gap
That we shall make in time from our hence-going
And our return, to excuse. But first, how get hence.
Why should excuse be born or ere begot?
We'll talk of that hereafter. Prithee speak,
How many score of miles may we well ride
'Twixt hour and hour?
PISANIO: One score 'twixt sun and sun,
Madam, 's enough for you, and too much too.
IMOGEN: Why, one that rode to's execution, man,
Could never go so slow. I have heard of riding wagers
Where horses have been nimbler than the sands
That run i' th' clock's behalf. But this is fool'ry.
Go bid my woman feign a sickness; say
She'll home to her father; and provide me presently
A riding suit, no costlier than would fit
A franklin's huswife.
PISANIO: Madam, you're best consider.
IMOGEN: I see before me, man. Nor here, nor here,
Nor what ensues, but have a fog in them
That I cannot look through. Away, I prithee;
Do as I bid thee. There's no more to say;
Accessible is none but Milford way.
Exeunt

ACT III. SCENE III. Wales. A Mountainous Country with a Cave

Enter from the Cave Belarius, Guiderius, and Arviragus

BELARIUS: A goodly day not to keep house with such
Whose roof's as low as ours! Stoop, boys; this gate
Instructs you how t' adore the heavens, and bows you
To a morning's holy office. The gates of monarchs
Are arch'd so high that giants may jet through
And keep their impious turbans on without
Good morrow to the sun. Hail, thou fair heaven!
We house i' th' rock, yet use thee not so hardly
As prouder livers do.
GUIDERIUS: Hail, heaven!
ARVIRAGUS: Hail, heaven!
BELARIUS: Now for our mountain sport. Up to yond hill,
Your legs are young; I'll tread these flats. Consider,
When you above perceive me like a crow,
That it is place which lessens and sets off;
And you may then revolve what tales I have told you
Of courts, of princes, of the tricks in war.
This service is not service so being done,
But being so allow'd. To apprehend thus
Draws us a profit from all things we see,
And often to our comfort shall we find
The sharded beetle in a safer hold
Than is the full-wing'd eagle. O, this life
Is nobler than attending for a check,
Richer than doing nothing for a bribe,
Prouder than rustling in unpaid-for silk:
Such gain the cap of him that makes him fine,
Yet keeps his book uncross'd. No life to ours!
GUIDERIUS: Out of your proof you speak. We, poor unfledg'd,
Have never wing'd from view o' th' nest, nor know not
What air's from home. Haply this life is best,
If quiet life be best; sweeter to you
That have a sharper known; well corresponding
With your stiff age. But unto us it is
A cell of ignorance, travelling abed,
A prison for a debtor that not dares
To stride a limit.
ARVIRAGUS: What should we speak of
When we are old as you? When we shall hear
The rain and wind beat dark December, how,
In this our pinching cave, shall we discourse.
The freezing hours away? We have seen nothing;
We are beastly: subtle as the fox for prey,
Like warlike as the wolf for what we eat.
Our valour is to chase what flies; our cage
We make a choir, as doth the prison'd bird,
And sing our bondage freely.
BELARIUS: How you speak!
Did you but know the city's usuries,
And felt them knowingly- the art o' th' court,
As hard to leave as keep, whose top to climb

Is certain falling, or so slipp'ry that
The fear's as bad as falling; the toil o' th' war,
A pain that only seems to seek out danger
I' th'name of fame and honour, which dies i' th'search,
And hath as oft a sland'rous epitaph
As record of fair act; nay, many times,
Doth ill deserve by doing well; what's worse-
Must curtsy at the censure. O, boys, this story
The world may read in me; my body's mark'd
With Roman swords, and my report was once
first with the best of note. Cymbeline lov'd me;
And when a soldier was the theme, my name
Was not far off. Then was I as a tree
Whose boughs did bend with fruit; but in one night
A storm, or robbery, call it what you will,
Shook down my mellow hangings, nay, my leaves,
And left me bare to weather.
GUIDERIUS: Uncertain favour!
BELARIUS: My fault being nothing- as I have told you oft-
But that two villains, whose false oaths prevail'd
Before my perfect honour, swore to Cymbeline
I was confederate with the Romans. So
Follow'd my banishment, and this twenty years
This rock and these demesnes have been my world,
Where I have liv'd at honest freedom, paid
More pious debts to heaven than in all
The fore-end of my time. But up to th' mountains!
This is not hunters' language. He that strikes
The venison first shall be the lord o' th' feast;
To him the other two shall minister;
And we will fear no poison, which attends
In place of greater state. I'll meet you in the valleys.
Exeunt Guiderius and Arviragus
How hard it is to hide the sparks of nature!
These boys know little they are sons to th' King,
Nor Cymbeline dreams that they are alive.
They think they are mine; and though train'd up thus meanly
I' th' cave wherein they bow, their thoughts do hit
The roofs of palaces, and nature prompts them
In simple and low things to prince it much
Beyond the trick of others. This Polydore,
The heir of Cymbeline and Britain, who
The King his father call'd Guiderius- Jove!
When on my three-foot stool I sit and tell
The warlike feats I have done, his spirits fly out
Into my story; say 'Thus mine enemy fell,
And thus I set my foot on's neck'; even then
The princely blood flows in his cheek, he sweats,
Strains his young nerves, and puts himself in posture
That acts my words. The younger brother, Cadwal,
Once Arviragus, in as like a figure
Strikes life into my speech, and shows much more
His own conceiving. Hark, the game is rous'd!

O Cymbeline, heaven and my conscience knows
Thou didst unjustly banish me! Whereon,
At three and two years old, I stole these babes,
Thinking to bar thee of succession as
Thou refts me of my lands. Euriphile,
Thou wast their nurse; they took thee for their mother,
And every day do honour to her grave.
Myself, Belarius, that am Morgan call'd,
They take for natural father. The game is up.
Exit

ACT III. SCENE IV. Wales, near Milford Haven

Enter Pisanio and Imogen
IMOGEN: Thou told'st me, when we came from horse, the place
Was near at hand. Ne'er long'd my mother so
To see me first as I have now. Pisanio! Man!
Where is Posthumus? What is in thy mind
That makes thee stare thus? Wherefore breaks that sigh
From th' inward of thee? One but painted thus
Would be interpreted a thing perplex'd
Beyond self-explication. Put thyself
Into a haviour of less fear, ere wildness
Vanquish my staider senses. What's the matter?
Why tender'st thou that paper to me with
A look untender! If't be summer news,
Smile to't before; if winterly, thou need'st
But keep that count'nance still. My husband's hand?
That drug-damn'd Italy hath out-craftied him,
And he's at some hard point. Speak, man; thy tongue
May take off some extremity, which to read
Would be even mortal to me.
PISANIO: Please you read,
And you shall find me, wretched man, a thing
The most disdain'd of fortune.
IMOGEN: Reads 'Thy mistress, Pisanio, hath play'd the strumpet in my bed, the testimonies whereof lie bleeding in me. I speak not out of weak surmises, but from proof as strong as my grief and as certain as I expect my revenge. That part thou, Pisanio, must act for me, if thy faith be not tainted with the breach of hers. Let thine own hands take away her life; I shall give thee opportunity at Milford Haven; she hath my letter for the purpose; where, if thou fear to strike, and to make me certain it is done, thou art the pander to her dishonour, and equally to me disloyal.'
PISANIO: What shall I need to draw my sword? The paper
Hath cut her throat already. No, 'tis slander,
Whose edge is sharper than the sword, whose tongue
Outvenoms all the worms of Nile, whose breath
Rides on the posting winds and doth belie
All corners of the world. Kings, queens, and states,
Maids, matrons, nay, the secrets of the grave,
This viperous slander enters. What cheer, madam?
IMOGEN: False to his bed? What is it to be false?
To lie in watch there, and to think on him?
To weep twixt clock and clock? If sleep charge nature,

To break it with a fearful dream of him,
And cry myself awake? That's false to's bed, is it?
PISANIO: Alas, good lady!
IMOGEN: I false! Thy conscience witness! Iachimo,
Thou didst accuse him of incontinency;
Thou then look'dst like a villain; now, methinks,
Thy favour's good enough. Some jay of Italy,
Whose mother was her painting, hath betray'd him.
Poor I am stale, a garment out of fashion,
And for I am richer than to hang by th' walls
I must be ripp'd. To pieces with me! O,
Men's vows are women's traitors! All good seeming,
By thy revolt, O husband, shall be thought
Put on for villainy; not born where't grows,
But worn a bait for ladies.
PISANIO: Good madam, hear me.
IMOGEN: True honest men being heard, like false Aeneas,
Were, in his time, thought false; and Sinon's weeping
Did scandal many a holy tear, took pity
From most true wretchedness. So thou, Posthumus,
Wilt lay the leaven on all proper men:
Goodly and gallant shall be false and perjur'd
From thy great fail. Come, fellow, be thou honest;
Do thou thy master's bidding; when thou seest him,
A little witness my obedience. Look!
I draw the sword myself; take it, and hit
The innocent mansion of my love, my heart.
Fear not; 'tis empty of all things but grief;
Thy master is not there, who was indeed
The riches of it. Do his bidding; strike.
Thou mayst be valiant in a better cause,
But now thou seem'st a coward.
PISANIO: Hence, vile instrument!
Thou shalt not damn my hand.
IMOGEN: Why, I must die;
And if I do not by thy hand, thou art
No servant of thy master's. Against self-slaughter
There is a prohibition so divine
That cravens my weak hand. Come, here's my heart-
Something's afore't. Soft, soft! we'll no defence!-
Obedient as the scabbard. What is here?
The scriptures of the loyal Leonatus
All turn'd to heresy? Away, away,
Corrupters of my faith! you shall no more
Be stomachers to my heart. Thus may poor fools
Believe false teachers; though those that are betray'd
Do feel the treason sharply, yet the traitor
Stands in worse case of woe. And thou, Posthumus,
That didst set up my disobedience 'gainst the King
My father, and make me put into contempt the suits
Of princely fellows, shalt hereafter find
It is no act of common passage but
A strain of rareness; and I grieve myself

To think, when thou shalt be disedg'd by her
That now thou tirest on, how thy memory
Will then be pang'd by me. Prithee dispatch.
The lamp entreats the butcher. Where's thy knife?
Thou art too slow to do thy master's bidding,
When I desire it too.
PISANIO: O gracious lady,
Since I receiv'd command to do this busines
I have not slept one wink.
IMOGEN: Do't, and to bed then.
PISANIO: I'll wake mine eyeballs first.
IMOGEN: Wherefore then
Didst undertake it? Why hast thou abus'd
So many miles with a pretence? This place?
Mine action and thine own? our horses' labour?
The time inviting thee? the perturb'd court,
For my being absent?- whereunto I never
Purpose return. Why hast thou gone so far
To be unbent when thou hast ta'en thy stand,
Th' elected deer before thee?
PISANIO: But to win time
To lose so bad employment, in the which
I have consider'd of a course. Good lady,
Hear me with patience.
IMOGEN: Talk thy tongue weary- speak.
I have heard I am a strumpet, and mine ear,
Therein false struck, can take no greater wound,
Nor tent to bottom that. But speak.
PISANIO: Then, madam,
I thought you would not back again.
IMOGEN: Most like-
Bringing me here to kill me.
PISANIO: Not so, neither;
But if I were as wise as honest, then
My purpose would prove well. It cannot be
But that my master is abus'd. Some villain,
Ay, and singular in his art, hath done you both
This cursed injury.
IMOGEN: Some Roman courtezan!
PISANIO: No, on my life!
I'll give but notice you are dead, and send him
Some bloody sign of it, for 'tis commanded
I should do so. You shall be miss'd at court,
And that will well confirm it.
IMOGEN: Why, good fellow,
What shall I do the while? where bide? how live?
Or in my life what comfort, when I am
Dead to my husband?
PISANIO: If you'll back to th' court-
IMOGEN: No court, no father, nor no more ado
With that harsh, noble, simple nothing-
That Cloten, whose love-suit hath been to me
As fearful as a siege.

PISANIO: If not at court,
Then not in Britain must you bide.
IMOGEN: Where then?
Hath Britain all the sun that shines? Day, night,
Are they not but in Britain? I' th' world's volume
Our Britain seems as of it, but not in't;
In a great pool a swan's nest. Prithee think
There's livers out of Britain.
PISANIO: I am most glad
You think of other place. Th' ambassador,
Lucius the Roman, comes to Milford Haven
To-morrow. Now, if you could wear a mind
Dark as your fortune is, and but disguise
That which t' appear itself must not yet be
But by self-danger, you should tread a course
Pretty and full of view; yea, happily, near
The residence of Posthumus; so nigh, at least,
That though his actions were not visible, yet
Report should render him hourly to your ear
As truly as he moves.
IMOGEN: O! for such means,
Though peril to my modesty, not death on't,
I would adventure.
PISANIO: Well then, here's the point:
You must forget to be a woman; change
Command into obedience; fear and niceness-
The handmaids of all women, or, more truly,
Woman it pretty self- into a waggish courage;
Ready in gibes, quick-answer'd, saucy, and
As quarrelous as the weasel. Nay, you must
Forget that rarest treasure of your cheek,
Exposing it- but, O, the harder heart!
Alack, no remedy!- to the greedy touch
Of common-kissing Titan, and forget
Your laboursome and dainty trims wherein
You made great Juno angry.
IMOGEN: Nay, be brief;
I see into thy end, and am almost
A man already.
PISANIO: First, make yourself but like one.
Fore-thinking this, I have already fit-
'Tis in my cloak-bag- doublet, hat, hose, all
That answer to them. Would you, in their serving,
And with what imitation you can borrow
From youth of such a season, fore noble Lucius
Present yourself, desire his service, tell him
Wherein you're happy- which will make him know
If that his head have ear in music; doubtless
With joy he will embrace you; for he's honourable,
And, doubling that, most holy. Your means abroad-
You have me, rich; and I will never fail
Beginning nor supplyment.
IMOGEN: Thou art all the comfort

The gods will diet me with. Prithee away!
There's more to be consider'd; but we'll even
All that good time will give us. This attempt
I am soldier to, and will abide it with
A prince's courage. Away, I prithee.
PISANIO: Well, madam, we must take a short farewell,
Lest, being miss'd, I be suspected of
Your carriage from the court. My noble mistress,
Here is a box; I had it from the Queen.
What's in't is precious. If you are sick at sea
Or stomach-qualm'd at land, a dram of this
Will drive away distemper. To some shade,
And fit you to your manhood. May the gods
Direct you to the best!
IMOGEN: Amen. I thank thee.
Exeunt Severally

ACT III. SCENE V. Britain. Cymbeline's Palace

Enter Cymbeline, Queen, Cloten, Lucius, and Lords
CYMBELINE: Thus far; and so farewell.
LUCIUS: Thanks, royal sir.
My emperor hath wrote; I must from hence,
And am right sorry that I must report ye
My master's enemy.
CYMBELINE: Our subjects, sir,
Will not endure his yoke; and for ourself
To show less sovereignty than they, must needs
Appear unkinglike.
LUCIUS: So, sir. I desire of you
A conduct overland to Milford Haven.
Madam, all joy befall your Grace, and you!
CYMBELINE: My lords, you are appointed for that office;
The due of honour in no point omit.
So farewell, noble Lucius.
LUCIUS: Your hand, my lord.
CLOTEN: Receive it friendly; but from this time forth
I wear it as your enemy.
LUCIUS: Sir, the event
Is yet to name the winner. Fare you well.
CYMBELINE: Leave not the worthy Lucius, good my lords,
Till he have cross'd the Severn. Happiness!
Exeunt Lucius and Lords
QUEEN: He goes hence frowning; but it honours us
That we have given him cause.
CLOTEN: 'Tis all the better;
Your valiant Britons have their wishes in it.
CYMBELINE: Lucius hath wrote already to the Emperor
How it goes here. It fits us therefore ripely
Our chariots and our horsemen be in readiness.
The pow'rs that he already hath in Gallia
Will soon be drawn to head, from whence he moves
His war for Britain.
QUEEN: 'Tis not sleepy business,
But must be look'd to speedily and strongly.

CYMBELINE: Our expectation that it would be thus
Hath made us forward. But, my gentle queen,
Where is our daughter? She hath not appear'd
Before the Roman, nor to us hath tender'd
The duty of the day. She looks us like
A thing more made of malice than of duty;
We have noted it. Call her before us, for
We have been too slight in sufferance.
Exit a Messenger
QUEEN: Royal sir,
Since the exile of Posthumus, most retir'd
Hath her life been; the cure whereof, my lord,
'Tis time must do. Beseech your Majesty,
Forbear sharp speeches to her; she's a lady
So tender of rebukes that words are strokes,
And strokes death to her.
Re-enter Messenger
CYMBELINE: Where is she, sir? How
Can her contempt be answer'd?
MESSENGER: Please you, sir,
Her chambers are all lock'd, and there's no answer
That will be given to th' loud of noise we make.
QUEEN: My lord, when last I went to visit her,
She pray'd me to excuse her keeping close;
Whereto constrain'd by her infirmity
She should that duty leave unpaid to you
Which daily she was bound to proffer. This
She wish'd me to make known; but our great court
Made me to blame in memory.
CYMBELINE: Her doors lock'd?
Not seen of late? Grant, heavens, that which I fear
Prove false!
Exit
QUEEN: Son, I say, follow the King.
CLOTEN: That man of hers, Pisanio, her old servant,
I have not seen these two days.
QUEEN: Go, look after.
Exit Cloten
Pisanio, thou that stand'st so for Posthumus!
He hath a drug of mine. I pray his absence
Proceed by swallowing that; for he believes
It is a thing most precious. But for her,
Where is she gone? Haply despair hath seiz'd her;
Or, wing'd with fervour of her love, she's flown
To her desir'd Posthumus. Gone she is
To death or to dishonour, and my end
Can make good use of either. She being down,
I have the placing of the British crown.
Re-enter Cloten
How now, my son?
CLOTEN: 'Tis certain she is fled.
Go in and cheer the King. He rages; none
Dare come about him.

QUEEN: All the better. May
This night forestall him of the coming day!
Exit
CLOTEN: I love and hate her; for she's fair and royal,
And that she hath all courtly parts more exquisite
Than lady, ladies, woman. From every one
The best she hath, and she, of all compounded,
Outsells them all. I love her therefore; but
Disdaining me and throwing favours on
The low Posthumus slanders so her judgment
That what's else rare is chok'd; and in that point
I will conclude to hate her, nay, indeed,
To be reveng'd upon her. For when fools
Shall-
Enter Pisanio
Who is here? What, are you packing, sirrah?
Come hither. Ah, you precious pander! Villain,
Where is thy lady? In a word, or else
Thou art straightway with the fiends.
PISANIO: O good my lord!
CLOTEN: Where is thy lady? or, by Jupiter-
I will not ask again. Close villain,
I'll have this secret from thy heart, or rip
Thy heart to find it. Is she with Posthumus?
From whose so many weights of baseness cannot
A dram of worth be drawn.
PISANIO: Alas, my lord,
How can she be with him? When was she miss'd?
He is in Rome.
CLOTEN: Where is she, sir? Come nearer.
No farther halting! Satisfy me home
What is become of her.
PISANIO: O my all-worthy lord!
CLOTEN: All-worthy villain!
Discover where thy mistress is at once,
At the next word. No more of 'worthy lord'!
Speak, or thy silence on the instant is
Thy condemnation and thy death.
PISANIO: Then, sir,
This paper is the history of my knowledge
Touching her flight.
Presenting a Letter
CLOTEN: Let's see't. I will pursue her
Even to Augustus' throne.
PISANIO: Aside Or this or perish.
She's far enough; and what he learns by this
May prove his travel, not her danger.
CLOTEN: Humh!
PISANIO: Aside I'll write to my lord she's dead. O Imogen,
Safe mayst thou wander, safe return again!
CLOTEN: Sirrah, is this letter true?
PISANIO: Sir, as I think.
CLOTEN: It is Posthumus' hand; I know't. Sirrah, if thou wouldst

not be a villain, but do me true service, undergo those employments wherein I should have cause to use thee with a serious industry- that is, what villainy soe'er I bid thee do, to perform it directly and truly- I would think thee an honest man; thou shouldst neither want my means for thy relief nor my voice for thy preferment.

PISANIO: Well, my good lord.

CLOTEN: Wilt thou serve me? For since patiently and constantly thou hast stuck to the bare fortune of that beggar Posthumus, thou canst not, in the course of gratitude, but be a diligent follower of mine. Wilt thou serve me?

PISANIO: Sir, I will.

CLOTEN: Give me thy hand; here's my purse. Hast any of thy late master's garments in thy possession?

PISANIO: I have, my lord, at my lodging, the same suit he wore when he took leave of my lady and mistress.

CLOTEN: The first service thou dost me, fetch that suit hither. Let it be thy first service; go.

PISANIO: I shall, my lord.

Exit

CLOTEN: Meet thee at Milford Haven! I forgot to ask him one thing; I'll remember't anon. Even there, thou villain Posthumus, will I kill thee. I would these garments were come. She said upon a time- the bitterness of it I now belch from my heart- that she held the very garment of Posthumus in more respect than my noble and natural person, together with the adornment of my qualities. With that suit upon my back will I ravish her; first kill him, and in her eyes. There shall she see my valour, which will then be a torment to her contempt. He on the ground, my speech of insultment ended on his dead body, and when my lust hath dined- which, as I say, to vex her I will execute in the clothes that she so prais'd- to the court I'll knock her back, foot her home again. She hath despis'd me rejoicingly, and I'll be merry in my revenge.

Re-enter Pisanio, with the Clothes

Be those the garments?

PISANIO: Ay, my noble lord.

CLOTEN: How long is't since she went to Milford Haven?

PISANIO: She can scarce be there yet.

CLOTEN: Bring this apparel to my chamber; that is the second thing that I have commanded thee. The third is that thou wilt be a voluntary mute to my design. Be but duteous and true, preferment shall tender itself to thee. My revenge is now at Milford, would I had wings to follow it! Come, and be true.

Exit

PISANIO: Thou bid'st me to my loss; for true to thee
Were to prove false, which I will never be,
To him that is most true. To Milford go,
And find not her whom thou pursuest. Flow, flow,
You heavenly blessings, on her! This fool's speed
Be cross'd with slowness! Labour be his meed!

Exit

ACT III. SCENE VI. Wales. Before the Cave of Belarius

Enter Imogen Alone, in Boy's Clothes

IMOGEN: I see a man's life is a tedious one.
I have tir'd myself, and for two nights together
Have made the ground my bed. I should be sick
But that my resolution helps me. Milford,
When from the mountain-top Pisanio show'd thee,
Thou wast within a ken. O Jove! I think
Foundations fly the wretched; such, I mean,
Where they should be reliev'd. Two beggars told me
I could not miss my way. Will poor folks lie,
That have afflictions on them, knowing 'tis
A punishment or trial? Yes; no wonder,
When rich ones scarce tell true. To lapse in fulness
Is sorer than to lie for need; and falsehood
Is worse in kings than beggars. My dear lord!
Thou art one o' th' false ones. Now I think on thee
My hunger's gone; but even before, I was
At point to sink for food. But what is this?
Here is a path to't; 'tis some savage hold.
I were best not call; I dare not call. Yet famine,
Ere clean it o'erthrow nature, makes it valiant.
Plenty and peace breeds cowards; hardness ever
Of hardiness is mother. Ho! who's here?
If anything that's civil, speak; if savage,
Take or lend. Ho! No answer? Then I'll enter.
Best draw my sword; and if mine enemy
But fear the sword, like me, he'll scarcely look on't.
Such a foe, good heavens!

Exit into the Cave

Enter Belarius, Guiderius, and Arviragus

BELARIUS: You, Polydore, have prov'd best woodman and
Are master of the feast. Cadwal and I
Will play the cook and servant; 'tis our match.
The sweat of industry would dry and die
But for the end it works to. Come, our stomachs
Will make what's homely savoury; weariness
Can snore upon the flint, when resty sloth
Finds the down pillow hard. Now, peace be here,
Poor house, that keep'st thyself!
GUIDERIUS: I am thoroughly weary.
ARVIRAGUS: I am weak with toil, yet strong in appetite.
GUIDERIUS: There is cold meat i' th' cave; we'll browse on that
Whilst what we have kill'd be cook'd.
BELARIUS: Looking into the Cave Stay, come not in.
But that it eats our victuals, I should think
Here were a fairy.
GUIDERIUS: What's the matter, sir?
BELARIUS:. By Jupiter, an angel! or, if not,
An earthly paragon! Behold divineness
No elder than a boy!

Re-enter Imogen

IMOGEN: Good masters, harm me not.

Before I enter'd here I call'd, and thought
To have begg'd or bought what I have took. Good troth,
I have stol'n nought; nor would not though I had found
Gold strew'd i' th' floor. Here's money for my meat.
I would have left it on the board, so soon
As I had made my meal, and parted
With pray'rs for the provider.
GUIDERIUS: Money, youth?
ARVIRAGUS: All gold and silver rather turn to dirt,
As 'tis no better reckon'd but of those
Who worship dirty gods.
IMOGEN: I see you're angry.
Know, if you kill me for my fault, I should
Have died had I not made it.
BELARIUS: Whither bound?
IMOGEN: To Milford Haven.
BELARIUS: What's your name?
IMOGEN: Fidele, sir. I have a kinsman who
Is bound for Italy; he embark'd at Milford;
To whom being going, almost spent with hunger,
I am fall'n in this offence.
BELARIUS: Prithee, fair youth,
Think us no churls, nor measure our good minds
By this rude place we live in. Well encounter'd!
'Tis almost night; you shall have better cheer
Ere you depart, and thanks to stay and eat it.
Boys, bid him welcome.
GUIDERIUS: Were you a woman, youth,
I should woo hard but be your groom. In honesty
I bid for you as I'd buy.
ARVIRAGUS: I'll make't my comfort
He is a man. I'll love him as my brother;
And such a welcome as I'd give to him
After long absence, such is yours. Most welcome!
Be sprightly, for you fall 'mongst friends.
IMOGEN: 'Mongst friends,
If brothers. Aside Would it had been so that they
Had been my father's sons! Then had my prize
Been less, and so more equal ballasting
To thee, Posthumus.
BELARIUS: He wrings at some distress.
GUIDERIUS: Would I could free't!
ARVIRAGUS: Or I, whate'er it be,
What pain it cost, what danger! Gods!
BELARIUS: Whispering Hark, boys.
IMOGEN: Aside Great men,
That had a court no bigger than this cave,
That did attend themselves, and had the virtue
Which their own conscience seal'd them, laying by
That nothing-gift of differing multitudes,
Could not out-peer these twain. Pardon me, gods!
I'd change my sex to be companion with them,
Since Leonatus' false.

BELARIUS: It shall be so.
Boys, we'll go dress our hunt. Fair youth, come in.
Discourse is heavy, fasting; when we have supp'd,
We'll mannerly demand thee of thy story,
So far as thou wilt speak it.
GUIDERIUS: Pray draw near.
ARVIRAGUS: The night to th' owl and morn to th' lark less welcome.
IMOGEN: Thanks, sir.
ARVIRAGUS: I pray draw near.
Exeunt

ACT III. SCENE VII. Rome. A Public Place

Enter Two Roman Senators and Tribunes
FIRST SENATOR: This is the tenour of the Emperor's writ:
That since the common men are now in action
'Gainst the Pannonians and Dalmatians,
And that the legions now in Gallia are
Full weak to undertake our wars against
The fall'n-off Britons, that we do incite
The gentry to this business. He creates
Lucius proconsul; and to you, the tribunes,
For this immediate levy, he commands
His absolute commission. Long live Caesar!
TRIBUNE: Is Lucius general of the forces?
SECOND SENATOR: Ay.
TRIBUNE: Remaining now in Gallia?
FIRST SENATOR: With those legions
Which I have spoke of, whereunto your levy
Must be supplyant. The words of your commission
Will tie you to the numbers and the time
Of their dispatch.
TRIBUNE: We will discharge our duty.
Exeunt

ACT IV. SCENE I. Wales. Near the Cave of Belarius

Enter Cloten Alone
CLOTEN: I am near to th' place where they should meet, if Pisanio have mapp'd it truly. How fit his garments serve me! Why should his mistress, who was made by him that made the tailor, not be fit too? The rather- saving reverence of the word- for 'tis said a woman's fitness comes by fits. Therein I must play the workman. I dare speak it to myself, for it is not vain-glory for a man and his glass to confer in his own chamber- I mean, the lines of my body are as well drawn as his; no less young, more strong, not beneath him in fortunes, beyond him in the advantage of the time, above him in birth, alike conversant in general services, and more remarkable in single oppositions. Yet this imperceiverant thing loves him in my despite. What mortality is! Posthumus, thy head, which now is growing upon thy shoulders, shall within this hour be off; thy mistress enforced; thy garments cut to pieces before her face; and all this done, spurn her home to her father, who may, haply, be a little angry for my so rough usage; but my mother, having power of his testiness, shall turn all into my commendations. My horse is

tied up safe. Out, sword, and to a sore purpose! Fortune, put them into my hand. This is the very description of their meeting-place; and the fellow dares not deceive me.

Exit

ACT IV. SCENE II. Wales. Before the Cave of Belarius

Enter, from the Cave, Belarius, Guiderius, Arviragus, and Imogen

BELARIUS: To Imogen You are not well. Remain here in the cave;
We'll come to you after hunting.
ARVIRAGUS: To Imogen Brother, stay here.
Are we not brothers?
IMOGEN: So man and man should be;
But clay and clay differs in dignity,
Whose dust is both alike. I am very sick.
GUIDERIUS: Go you to hunting; I'll abide with him.
IMOGEN: So sick I am not, yet I am not well;
But not so citizen a wanton as
To seem to die ere sick. So please you, leave me;
Stick to your journal course. The breach of custom
Is breach of all. I am ill, but your being by me
Cannot amend me; society is no comfort
To one not sociable. I am not very sick,
Since I can reason of it. Pray you trust me here.
I'll rob none but myself; and let me die,
Stealing so poorly.
GUIDERIUS: I love thee; I have spoke it.
How much the quantity, the weight as much
As I do love my father.
BELARIUS: What? how? how?
ARVIRAGUS: If it be sin to say so, sir, I yoke me
In my good brother's fault. I know not why
I love this youth, and I have heard you say
Love's reason's without reason. The bier at door,
And a demand who is't shall die, I'd say
'My father, not this youth.'
BELARIUS: Aside O noble strain!
O worthiness of nature! breed of greatness!
Cowards father cowards and base things sire base.
Nature hath meal and bran, contempt and grace.
I'm not their father; yet who this should be
Doth miracle itself, lov'd before me.-
'Tis the ninth hour o' th' morn.
ARVIRAGUS: Brother, farewell.
IMOGEN: I wish ye sport.
ARVIRAGUS: Your health. To Belarius So please you, sir.
IMOGEN: Aside These are kind creatures.
Gods, what lies I have heard!
Our courtiers say all's savage but at court.
Experience, O, thou disprov'st report!
Th' imperious seas breed monsters; for the dish,
Poor tributary rivers as sweet fish.
I am sick still; heart-sick. Pisanio,
I'll now taste of thy drug.

Swallows Some

GUIDERIUS: I could not stir him.
He said he was gentle, but unfortunate;
Dishonestly afflicted, but yet honest.
ARVIRAGUS: Thus did he answer me; yet said hereafter
I might know more.
BELARIUS: To th' field, to th' field!
We'll leave you for this time. Go in and rest.
ARVIRAGUS: We'll not be long away.
BELARIUS: Pray be not sick,
For you must be our huswife.
IMOGEN: Well, or ill,
I am bound to you.
BELARIUS: And shalt be ever.
Exit Imogen into the Cave
This youth, howe'er distress'd, appears he hath had
Good ancestors.
ARVIRAGUS: How angel-like he sings!
GUIDERIUS: But his neat cookery! He cut our roots in characters,
And sauc'd our broths as Juno had been sick,
And he her dieter.
ARVIRAGUS: Nobly he yokes
A smiling with a sigh, as if the sigh
Was that it was for not being such a smile;
The smile mocking the sigh that it would fly
From so divine a temple to commix
With winds that sailors rail at.
GUIDERIUS: I do note
That grief and patience, rooted in him both,
Mingle their spurs together.
ARVIRAGUS: Grow patience!
And let the stinking elder, grief, untwine
His perishing root with the increasing vine!
BELARIUS: It is great morning. Come, away! Who's there?
Enter Cloten
CLOTEN: I cannot find those runagates; that villain
Hath mock'd me. I am faint.
BELARIUS: Those runagates?
Means he not us? I partly know him; 'tis
Cloten, the son o' th' Queen. I fear some ambush.
I saw him not these many years, and yet
I know 'tis he. We are held as outlaws. Hence!
GUIDERIUS: He is but one; you and my brother search
What companies are near. Pray you away;
Let me alone with him.
Exeunt Belarius and Arviragus
CLOTEN: Soft! What are you
That fly me thus? Some villain mountaineers?
I have heard of such. What slave art thou?
GUIDERIUS: A thing
More slavish did I ne'er than answering
'A slave' without a knock.
CLOTEN: Thou art a robber,
A law-breaker, a villain. Yield thee, thief.

GUIDERIUS: To who? To thee? What art thou? Have not I
An arm as big as thine, a heart as big?
Thy words, I grant, are bigger, for I wear not
My dagger in my mouth. Say what thou art;
Why I should yield to thee.
CLOTEN: Thou villain base,
Know'st me not by my clothes?
GUIDERIUS: No, nor thy tailor, rascal,
Who is thy grandfather; he made those clothes,
Which, as it seems, make thee.
CLOTEN: Thou precious varlet,
My tailor made them not.
GUIDERIUS: Hence, then, and thank
The man that gave them thee. Thou art some fool;
I am loath to beat thee.
CLOTEN: Thou injurious thief,
Hear but my name, and tremble.
GUIDERIUS: What's thy name?
CLOTEN: Cloten, thou villain.
GUIDERIUS: Cloten, thou double villain, be thy name,
I cannot tremble at it. Were it toad, or adder, spider,
'Twould move me sooner.
CLOTEN: To thy further fear,
Nay, to thy mere confusion, thou shalt know
I am son to th' Queen.
GUIDERIUS: I'm sorry for't; not seeming
So worthy as thy birth.
CLOTEN: Art not afeard?
GUIDERIUS: Those that I reverence, those I fear- the wise:
At fools I laugh, not fear them.
CLOTEN: Die the death.
When I have slain thee with my proper hand,
I'll follow those that even now fled hence,
And on the gates of Lud's Town set your heads.
Yield, rustic mountaineer.
Exeunt, Fighting
Re-enter Belarius and Arviragus
BELARIUS: No company's abroad.
ARVIRAGUS: None in the world; you did mistake him, sure.
BELARIUS: I cannot tell; long is it since I saw him,
But time hath nothing blurr'd those lines of favour
Which then he wore; the snatches in his voice,
And burst of speaking, were as his. I am absolute
'Twas very Cloten.
ARVIRAGUS: In this place we left them.
I wish my brother make good time with him,
You say he is so fell.
BELARIUS: Being scarce made up,
I mean to man, he had not apprehension
Or roaring terrors; for defect of judgment
Is oft the cease of fear.
Re-enter Guiderius with Cloten's Head
But, see, thy brother.

GUIDERIUS: This Cloten was a fool, an empty purse;
There was no money in't. Not Hercules
Could have knock'd out his brains, for he had none;
Yet I not doing this, the fool had borne
My head as I do his.
BELARIUS: What hast thou done?
GUIDERIUS: I am perfect what: cut off one Cloten's head,
Son to the Queen, after his own report;
Who call'd me traitor, mountaineer, and swore
With his own single hand he'd take us in,
Displace our heads where- thank the gods!- they grow,
And set them on Lud's Town.
BELARIUS: We are all undone.
GUIDERIUS: Why, worthy father, what have we to lose
But that he swore to take, our lives? The law
Protects not us; then why should we be tender
To let an arrogant piece of flesh threat us,
Play judge and executioner all himself,
For we do fear the law? What company
Discover you abroad?
BELARIUS: No single soul
Can we set eye on, but in an safe reason
He must have some attendants. Though his humour
Was nothing but mutation- ay, and that
From one bad thing to worse- not frenzy, not
Absolute madness could so far have rav'd,
To bring him here alone. Although perhaps
It may be heard at court that such as we
Cave here, hunt here, are outlaws, and in time
May make some stronger head- the which he hearing,
As it is like him, might break out and swear
He'd fetch us in; yet is't not probable
To come alone, either he so undertaking
Or they so suffering. Then on good ground we fear,
If we do fear this body hath a tail
More perilous than the head.
ARVIRAGUS: Let ordinance
Come as the gods foresay it. Howsoe'er,
My brother hath done well.
BELARIUS: I had no mind
To hunt this day; the boy Fidele's sickness
Did make my way long forth.
GUIDERIUS: With his own sword,
Which he did wave against my throat, I have ta'en
His head from him. I'll throw't into the creek
Behind our rock, and let it to the sea
And tell the fishes he's the Queen's son, Cloten.
That's all I reck.
Exit
BELARIUS: I fear'twill be reveng'd.
Would, Polydore, thou hadst not done't! though valour
Becomes thee well enough.
ARVIRAGUS: Would I had done't,

So the revenge alone pursu'd me! Polydore,
I love thee brotherly, but envy much
Thou hast robb'd me of this deed. I would revenges,
That possible strength might meet, would seek us through,
And put us to our answer.
BELARIUS: Well, 'tis done.
We'll hunt no more to-day, nor seek for danger
Where there's no profit. I prithee to our rock.
You and Fidele play the cooks; I'll stay
Till hasty Polydore return, and bring him
To dinner presently.
ARVIRAGUS: Poor sick Fidele!
I'll willingly to him; to gain his colour
I'd let a parish of such Cloten's blood,
And praise myself for charity.
Exit
BELARIUS: O thou goddess,
Thou divine Nature, thou thyself thou blazon'st
In these two princely boys! They are as gentle
As zephyrs blowing below the violet,
Not wagging his sweet head; and yet as rough,
Their royal blood enchaf'd, as the rud'st wind
That by the top doth take the mountain pine
And make him stoop to th' vale. 'Tis wonder
That an invisible instinct should frame them
To royalty unlearn'd, honour untaught,
Civility not seen from other, valour
That wildly grows in them, but yields a crop
As if it had been sow'd. Yet still it's strange
What Cloten's being here to us portends,
Or what his death will bring us.
Re-enter Guiderius
GUIDERIUS: Where's my brother?
I have sent Cloten's clotpoll down the stream,
In embassy to his mother; his body's hostage
For his return.
Solemn Music
BELARIUS: My ingenious instrument!
Hark, Polydore, it sounds. But what occasion
Hath Cadwal now to give it motion? Hark!
GUIDERIUS: Is he at home?
BELARIUS: He went hence even now.
GUIDERIUS: What does he mean? Since death of my dear'st mother
It did not speak before. All solemn things
Should answer solemn accidents. The matter?
Triumphs for nothing and lamenting toys
Is jollity for apes and grief for boys.
Is Cadwal mad?
Re-enter Arviragus, with Imogen as Dead, Bearing Her in His Arms
BELARIUS: Look, here he comes,
And brings the dire occasion in his arms
Of what we blame him for!
ARVIRAGUS: The bird is dead

That we have made so much on. I had rather
Have skipp'd from sixteen years of age to sixty,
To have turn'd my leaping time into a crutch,
Than have seen this.
GUIDERIUS: O sweetest, fairest lily!
My brother wears thee not the one half so well
As when thou grew'st thyself.
BELARIUS: O melancholy!
Who ever yet could sound thy bottom? find
The ooze to show what coast thy sluggish crare
Might'st easiliest harbour in? Thou blessed thing!
Jove knows what man thou mightst have made; but I,
Thou diedst, a most rare boy, of melancholy.
How found you him?
ARVIRAGUS: Stark, as you see;
Thus smiling, as some fly had tickled slumber,
Not as death's dart, being laugh'd at; his right cheek
Reposing on a cushion.
GUIDERIUS: Where?
ARVIRAGUS: O' th' floor;
His arms thus leagu'd. I thought he slept, and put
My clouted brogues from off my feet, whose rudeness
Answer'd my steps too loud.
GUIDERIUS: Why, he but sleeps.
If he be gone he'll make his grave a bed;
With female fairies will his tomb be haunted,
And worms will not come to thee.
ARVIRAGUS: With fairest flowers,
Whilst summer lasts and I live here, Fidele,
I'll sweeten thy sad grave. Thou shalt not lack
The flower that's like thy face, pale primrose; nor
The azur'd hare-bell, like thy veins; no, nor
The leaf of eglantine, whom not to slander,
Out-sweet'ned not thy breath. The ruddock would,
With charitable bill- O bill, sore shaming
Those rich-left heirs that let their fathers lie
Without a monument!- bring thee all this;
Yea, and furr'd moss besides, when flow'rs are none,
To winter-ground thy corse-
GUIDERIUS: Prithee have done,
And do not play in wench-like words with that
Which is so serious. Let us bury him,
And not protract with admiration what
Is now due debt. To th' grave.
ARVIRAGUS: Say, where shall's lay him?
GUIDERIUS: By good Euriphile, our mother.
ARVIRAGUS: Be't so;
And let us, Polydore, though now our voices
Have got the mannish crack, sing him to th' ground,
As once to our mother; use like note and words,
Save that Euriphile must be Fidele.
GUIDERIUS: Cadwal,
I cannot sing. I'll weep, and word it with thee;

For notes of sorrow out of tune are worse
Than priests and fanes that lie.
ARVIRAGUS: We'll speak it, then.
BELARIUS: Great griefs, I see, med'cine the less, for Cloten
Is quite forgot. He was a queen's son, boys;
And though he came our enemy, remember
He was paid for that. Though mean and mighty rotting
Together have one dust, yet reverence-
That angel of the world- doth make distinction
Of place 'tween high and low. Our foe was princely;
And though you took his life, as being our foe,
Yet bury him as a prince.
GUIDERIUS: Pray you fetch him hither.
Thersites' body is as good as Ajax',
When neither are alive.
ARVIRAGUS: If you'll go fetch him,
We'll say our song the whilst. Brother, begin.
Exit Belarius
GUIDERIUS: Nay, Cadwal, we must lay his head to th' East;
My father hath a reason for't.
ARVIRAGUS: 'Tis true.
GUIDERIUS: Come on, then, and remove him.
ARVIRAGUS: So. Begin.
SONG
GUIDERIUS: Fear no more the heat o' th' sun
Nor the furious winter's rages;
Thou thy worldly task hast done,
Home art gone, and ta'en thy wages.
Golden lads and girls all must,
As chimney-sweepers, come to dust.
ARVIRAGUS: Fear no more the frown o' th' great;
Thou art past the tyrant's stroke.
Care no more to clothe and eat;
To thee the reed is as the oak.
The sceptre, learning, physic, must
All follow this and come to dust.
GUIDERIUS: Fear no more the lightning flash,
ARVIRAGUS: Nor th' all-dreaded thunder-stone;
GUIDERIUS: Fear not slander, censure rash;
ARVIRAGUS: Thou hast finish'd joy and moan.
BOTH: All lovers young, all lovers must
Consign to thee and come to dust.
GUIDERIUS: No exorciser harm thee!
ARVIRAGUS: Nor no witchcraft charm thee!
GUIDERIUS: Ghost unlaid forbear thee!
ARVIRAGUS: Nothing ill come near thee!
BOTH: Quiet consummation have,
And renowned be thy grave!
Re-enter Belarius with the Body of Cloten
GUIDERIUS: We have done our obsequies. Come, lay him down.
BELARIUS: Here's a few flowers; but 'bout midnight, more.
The herbs that have on them cold dew o' th' night
Are strewings fit'st for graves. Upon their faces.

You were as flow'rs, now wither'd. Even so
These herblets shall which we upon you strew.
Come on, away. Apart upon our knees.
The ground that gave them first has them again.
Their pleasures here are past, so is their pain.
Exeunt All but Imogen
IMOGEN: Awaking Yes, sir, to Milford Haven. Which is the way?
I thank you. By yond bush? Pray, how far thither?
'Ods pittikins! can it be six mile yet?
I have gone all night. Faith, I'll lie down and sleep.
But, soft! no bedfellow. O gods and goddesses!
Seeing the Body
These flow'rs are like the pleasures of the world;
This bloody man, the care on't. I hope I dream;
For so I thought I was a cave-keeper,
And cook to honest creatures. But 'tis not so;
'Twas but a bolt of nothing, shot at nothing,
Which the brain makes of fumes. Our very eyes
Are sometimes, like our judgments, blind. Good faith,
I tremble still with fear; but if there be
Yet left in heaven as small a drop of pity
As a wren's eye, fear'd gods, a part of it!
The dream's here still. Even when I wake it is
Without me, as within me; not imagin'd, felt.
A headless man? The garments of Posthumus?
I know the shape of's leg; this is his hand,
His foot Mercurial, his Martial thigh,
The brawns of Hercules; but his Jovial face-
Murder in heaven! How! 'Tis gone. Pisanio,
All curses madded Hecuba gave the Greeks,
And mine to boot, be darted on thee! Thou,
Conspir'd with that irregulous devil, Cloten,
Hath here cut off my lord. To write and read
Be henceforth treacherous! Damn'd Pisanio
Hath with his forged letters- damn'd Pisanio-
From this most bravest vessel of the world
Struck the main-top. O Posthumus! alas,
Where is thy head? Where's that? Ay me! where's that?
Pisanio might have kill'd thee at the heart,
And left this head on. How should this be? Pisanio?
'Tis he and Cloten; malice and lucre in them
Have laid this woe here. O, 'tis pregnant, pregnant!
The drug he gave me, which he said was precious
And cordial to me, have I not found it
Murd'rous to th' senses? That confirms it home.
This is Pisanio's deed, and Cloten. O!
Give colour to my pale cheek with thy blood,
That we the horrider may seem to those
Which chance to find us. O, my lord, my lord!
Falls Fainting on the Body
Enter Lucius, Captains, and a Soothsayer
CAPTAIN: To them the legions garrison'd in Gallia,
After your will, have cross'd the sea, attending

You here at Milford Haven; with your ships,
They are in readiness.
LUCIUS: But what from Rome?
CAPTAIN: The Senate hath stirr'd up the confiners
And gentlemen of Italy, most willing spirits,
That promise noble service; and they come
Under the conduct of bold Iachimo,
Sienna's brother.
LUCIUS: When expect you them?
CAPTAIN: With the next benefit o' th' wind.
LUCIUS: This forwardness
Makes our hopes fair. Command our present numbers
Be muster'd; bid the captains look to't. Now, sir,
What have you dream'd of late of this war's purpose?
SOOTHSAYER: Last night the very gods show'd me a vision-
I fast and pray'd for their intelligence- thus:
I saw Jove's bird, the Roman eagle, wing'd
From the spongy south to this part of the west,
There vanish'd in the sunbeams; which portends,
Unless my sins abuse my divination,
Success to th' Roman host.
LUCIUS: Dream often so,
And never false. Soft, ho! what trunk is here
Without his top? The ruin speaks that sometime
It was a worthy building. How? a page?
Or dead or sleeping on him? But dead, rather;
For nature doth abhor to make his bed
With the defunct, or sleep upon the dead.
Let's see the boy's face.
CAPTAIN: He's alive, my lord.
LUCIUS: He'll then instruct us of this body. Young one,
Inform us of thy fortunes; for it seems
They crave to be demanded. Who is this
Thou mak'st thy bloody pillow? Or who was he
That, otherwise than noble nature did,
Hath alter'd that good picture? What's thy interest
In this sad wreck? How came't? Who is't? What art thou?
IMOGEN: I am nothing; or if not,
Nothing to be were better. This was my master,
A very valiant Briton and a good,
That here by mountaineers lies slain. Alas!
There is no more such masters. I may wander
From east to occident; cry out for service;
Try many, all good; serve truly; never
Find such another master.
LUCIUS: 'Lack, good youth!
Thou mov'st no less with thy complaining than
Thy master in bleeding. Say his name, good friend.
IMOGEN: Richard du Champ. Aside If I do lie, and do
No harm by it, though the gods hear, I hope
They'll pardon it.- Say you, sir?
LUCIUS: Thy name?
IMOGEN: Fidele, sir.

LUCIUS: Thou dost approve thyself the very same;
Thy name well fits thy faith, thy faith thy name.
Wilt take thy chance with me? I will not say
Thou shalt be so well master'd; but, be sure,
No less belov'd. The Roman Emperor's letters,
Sent by a consul to me, should not sooner
Than thine own worth prefer thee. Go with me.
IMOGEN: I'll follow, sir. But first, an't please the gods,
I'll hide my master from the flies, as deep
As these poor pickaxes can dig; and when
With wild wood-leaves and weeds I ha' strew'd his grave,
And on it said a century of prayers,
Such as I can, twice o'er, I'll weep and sigh;
And leaving so his service, follow you,
So please you entertain me.
LUCIUS: Ay, good youth;
And rather father thee than master thee.
My friends,
The boy hath taught us manly duties; let us
Find out the prettiest daisied plot we can,
And make him with our pikes and partisans
A grave. Come, arm him. Boy, he is preferr'd
By thee to us; and he shall be interr'd
As soldiers can. Be cheerful; wipe thine eyes.
Some falls are means the happier to arise.
Exeunt

ACT IV. SCENE III. Britain. Cymbeline's Palace

Enter Cymbeline, Lords, Pisanio, and Attendants
CYMBELINE: Again! and bring me word how 'tis with her.
Exit an Attendant
A fever with the absence of her son;
A madness, of which her life's in danger. Heavens,
How deeply you at once do touch me! Imogen,
The great part of my comfort, gone; my queen
Upon a desperate bed, and in a time
When fearful wars point at me; her son gone,
So needful for this present. It strikes me past
The hope of comfort. But for thee, fellow,
Who needs must know of her departure and
Dost seem so ignorant, we'll enforce it from thee
By a sharp torture.
PISANIO: Sir, my life is yours;
I humbly set it at your will; but for my mistress,
I nothing know where she remains, why gone,
Nor when she purposes return. Beseech your Highness,
Hold me your loyal servant.
LORD: Good my liege,
The day that she was missing he was here.
I dare be bound he's true and shall perform
All parts of his subjection loyally. For Cloten,
There wants no diligence in seeking him,
And will no doubt be found.
CYMBELINE: The time is troublesome.

To Pisanio We'll slip you for a season; but our jealousy
Does yet depend.
LORD: So please your Majesty,
The Roman legions, all from Gallia drawn,
Are landed on your coast, with a supply
Of Roman gentlemen by the Senate sent.
CYMBELINE: Now for the counsel of my son and queen!
I am amaz'd with matter.
LORD: Good my liege,
Your preparation can affront no less
Than what you hear of. Come more, for more you're ready.
The want is but to put those pow'rs in motion
That long to move.
CYMBELINE: I thank you. Let's withdraw,
And meet the time as it seeks us. We fear not
What can from Italy annoy us; but
We grieve at chances here. Away!
Exeunt All but Pisanio
PISANIO: I heard no letter from my master since
I wrote him Imogen was slain. 'Tis strange.
Nor hear I from my mistress, who did promise
To yield me often tidings. Neither know
What is betid to Cloten, but remain
Perplex'd in all. The heavens still must work.
Wherein I am false I am honest; not true, to be true.
These present wars shall find I love my country,
Even to the note o' th' King, or I'll fall in them.
All other doubts, by time let them be clear'd:
Fortune brings in some boats that are not steer'd.
Exit

ACT IV. SCENE IV. Wales. Before the Cave of Belarius

Enter Belarius, Guiderius, and Arviragus
GUIDERIUS: The noise is round about us.
BELARIUS: Let us from it.
ARVIRAGUS: What pleasure, sir, find we in life, to lock it
From action and adventure?
GUIDERIUS: Nay, what hope
Have we in hiding us? This way the Romans
Must or for Britons slay us, or receive us
For barbarous and unnatural revolts
During their use, and slay us after.
BELARIUS: Sons,
We'll higher to the mountains; there secure us.
To the King's party there's no going. Newness
Of Cloten's death- we being not known, not muster'd
Among the bands-may drive us to a render
Where we have liv'd, and so extort from's that
Which we have done, whose answer would be death,
Drawn on with torture.
GUIDERIUS: This is, sir, a doubt
In such a time nothing becoming you
Nor satisfying us.
ARVIRAGUS: It is not likely

That when they hear the Roman horses neigh,
Behold their quarter'd fires, have both their eyes
And ears so cloy'd importantly as now,
That they will waste their time upon our note,
To know from whence we are.
BELARIUS: O, I am known
Of many in the army. Many years,
Though Cloten then but young, you see, not wore him
From my remembrance. And, besides, the King
Hath not deserv'd my service nor your loves,
Who find in my exile the want of breeding,
The certainty of this hard life; aye hopeless
To have the courtesy your cradle promis'd,
But to be still hot summer's tanlings and
The shrinking slaves of winter.
GUIDERIUS: Than be so,
Better to cease to be. Pray, sir, to th' army.
I and my brother are not known; yourself
So out of thought, and thereto so o'ergrown,
Cannot be questioned.
ARVIRAGUS: By this sun that shines,
I'll thither. What thing is't that I never
Did see man die! scarce ever look'd on blood
But that of coward hares, hot goats, and venison!
Never bestrid a horse, save one that had
A rider like myself, who ne'er wore rowel
Nor iron on his heel! I am asham'd
To look upon the holy sun, to have
The benefit of his blest beams, remaining
So long a poor unknown.
GUIDERIUS: By heavens, I'll go!
If you will bless me, sir, and give me leave,
I'll take the better care; but if you will not,
The hazard therefore due fall on me by
The hands of Romans!
ARVIRAGUS: So say I. Amen.
BELARIUS: No reason I, since of your lives you set
So slight a valuation, should reserve
My crack'd one to more care. Have with you, boys!
If in your country wars you chance to die,
That is my bed too, lads, and there I'll lie.
Lead, lead. Aside The time seems long; their blood thinks scorn
Till it fly out and show them princes born.
Exeunt

ACT V. SCENE I. Britain. The Roman camp

Enter Posthumus Alone, with a Bloody Handkerchief
POSTHUMUS: Yea, bloody cloth, I'll keep thee; for I wish'd
Thou shouldst be colour'd thus. You married ones,
If each of you should take this course, how many
Must murder wives much better than themselves
For wrying but a little! O Pisanio!
Every good servant does not all commands;
No bond but to do just ones. Gods! if you

Should have ta'en vengeance on my faults, I never
Had liv'd to put on this; so had you saved
The noble Imogen to repent, and struck
Me, wretch more worth your vengeance. But alack,
You snatch some hence for little faults; that's love,
To have them fall no more. You some permit
To second ills with ills, each elder worse,
And make them dread it, to the doer's thrift.
But Imogen is your own. Do your best wills,
And make me blest to obey. I am brought hither
Among th' Italian gentry, and to fight
Against my lady's kingdom. 'Tis enough
That, Britain, I have kill'd thy mistress; peace!
I'll give no wound to thee. Therefore, good heavens,
Hear patiently my purpose. I'll disrobe me
Of these Italian weeds, and suit myself
As does a Britain peasant. So I'll fight
Against the part I come with; so I'll die
For thee, O Imogen, even for whom my life
Is every breath a death. And thus unknown,
Pitied nor hated, to the face of peril
Myself I'll dedicate. Let me make men know
More valour in me than my habits show.
Gods, put the strength o' th' Leonati in me!
To shame the guise o' th' world, I will begin
The fashion- less without and more within.

Exit

ACT V. SCENE II. Britain. A Field of Battle Between the British and Roman Camps

Enter Lucius, Iachimo, and the Roman Army at One Door, and the British Army at Another, Leonatus Posthumus Following like a Poor Soldier. They March over and Go Out. Alarums. Then Enter Again, in Skirmish, Iachimo and Posthumus. He Vanquisheth and Disarmeth Iachimo, and Then Leaves Him

IACHIMO: The heaviness and guilt within my bosom
Takes off my manhood. I have belied a lady,
The Princess of this country, and the air on't
Revengingly enfeebles me; or could this carl,
A very drudge of nature's, have subdu'd me
In my profession? Knighthoods and honours borne
As I wear mine are titles but of scorn.
If that thy gentry, Britain, go before
This lout as he exceeds our lords, the odds
Is that we scarce are men, and you are gods.

Exit

The Battle Continues; the Britons Fly; Cymbeline Is Taken. Then Enter to His Rescue Belarius, Guiderius, and Arviragus

BELARIUS: Stand, stand! We have th' advantage of the ground;
The lane is guarded; nothing routs us but
The villainy of our fears.

Guiderius and Arviragus. Stand, Stand, and Fight!

Re-enter Posthumus, and Seconds the Britons; They Rescue Cymbeline, and Exeunt. Then Re-enter Lucius and Iachimo, with Imogen

LUCIUS: Away, boy, from the troops, and save thyself;
For friends kill friends, and the disorder's such

As war were hoodwink'd.
IACHIMO: 'Tis their fresh supplies.
LUCIUS: It is a day turn'd strangely. Or betimes
Let's reinforce or fly.
Exeunt

ACT V. SCENE III. Another Part of the Field

Enter Posthumus and a Britain Lord
LORD: Cam'st thou from where they made the stand?
POSTHUMUS: I did:
Though you, it seems, come from the fliers.
LORD: I did.
POSTHUMUS: No blame be to you, sir, for all was lost,
But that the heavens fought. The King himself
Of his wings destitute, the army broken,
And but the backs of Britons seen, an flying,
Through a strait lane- the enemy, full-hearted,
Lolling the tongue with slaught'ring, having work
More plentiful than tools to do't, struck down
Some mortally, some slightly touch'd, some falling
Merely through fear, that the strait pass was damm'd
With dead men hurt behind, and cowards living
To die with length'ned shame.
LORD: Where was this lane?
POSTHUMUS: Close by the battle, ditch'd, and wall'd with turf,
Which gave advantage to an ancient soldier-
An honest one, I warrant, who deserv'd
So long a breeding as his white beard came to,
In doing this for's country. Athwart the lane
He, with two striplings- lads more like to run
The country base than to commit such slaughter;
With faces fit for masks, or rather fairer
Than those for preservation cas'd or shame-
Made good the passage, cried to those that fled
'Our Britain's harts die flying, not our men.
To darkness fleet souls that fly backwards! Stand;
Or we are Romans and will give you that,
Like beasts, which you shun beastly, and may save
But to look back in frown. Stand, stand!' These three,
Three thousand confident, in act as many-
For three performers are the file when all
The rest do nothing- with this word 'Stand, stand!'
Accommodated by the place, more charming
With their own nobleness, which could have turn'd
A distaff to a lance, gilded pale looks,
Part shame, part spirit renew'd; that some turn'd coward
But by example- O, a sin in war
Damn'd in the first beginners!- gan to look
The way that they did and to grin like lions
Upon the pikes o' th' hunters. Then began
A stop i' th' chaser, a retire; anon
A rout, confusion thick. Forthwith they fly,
Chickens, the way which they stoop'd eagles; slaves,
The strides they victors made; and now our cowards,

Like fragments in hard voyages, became
The life o' th' need. Having found the back-door open
Of the unguarded hearts, heavens, how they wound!
Some slain before, some dying, some their friends
O'erborne i' th' former wave. Ten chas'd by one
Are now each one the slaughterman of twenty.
Those that would die or ere resist are grown
The mortal bugs o' th' field.
LORD: This was strange chance:
A narrow lane, an old man, and two boys.
POSTHUMUS: Nay, do not wonder at it; you are made
Rather to wonder at the things you hear
Than to work any. Will you rhyme upon't,
And vent it for a mock'ry? Here is one:
'Two boys, an old man (twice a boy), a lane,
Preserv'd the Britons, was the Romans' bane.'
LORD: Nay, be not angry, sir.
POSTHUMUS: 'Lack, to what end?
Who dares not stand his foe I'll be his friend;
For if he'll do as he is made to do,
I know he'll quickly fly my friendship too.
You have put me into rhyme.
LORD: Farewell; you're angry.
Exit
POSTHUMUS: Still going? This is a lord! O noble misery,
To be i' th' field and ask 'What news?' of me!
To-day how many would have given their honours
To have sav'd their carcasses! took heel to do't,
And yet died too! I, in mine own woe charm'd,
Could not find death where I did hear him groan,
Nor feel him where he struck. Being an ugly monster,
'Tis strange he hides him in fresh cups, soft beds,
Sweet words; or hath moe ministers than we
That draw his knives i' th' war. Well, I will find him;
For being now a favourer to the Briton,
No more a Briton, I have resum'd again
The part I came in. Fight I will no more,
But yield me to the veriest hind that shall
Once touch my shoulder. Great the slaughter is
Here made by th' Roman; great the answer be
Britons must take. For me, my ransom's death;
On either side I come to spend my breath,
Which neither here I'll keep nor bear again,
But end it by some means for Imogen.
Enter Two British Captains and Soldiers
FIRST CAPTAIN: Great Jupiter be prais'd! Lucius is taken.
'Tis thought the old man and his sons were angels.
SECOND CAPTAIN: There was a fourth man, in a silly habit,
That gave th' affront with them.
FIRST CAPTAIN: So 'tis reported;
But none of 'em can be found. Stand! who's there?
POSTHUMUS: A Roman,
Who had not now been drooping here if seconds

Had answer'd him.
SECOND CAPTAIN: Lay hands on him; a dog!
A leg of Rome shall not return to tell
What crows have peck'd them here. He brags his service,
As if he were of note. Bring him to th' King.

Enter Cymbeline, Belarius, Guiderius, Arviragus, Pisanio, and Roman Captives. The Captains Present Posthumus to Cymbeline, Who Delivers Him over to a Gaoler. Exeunt Omnes

ACT V. SCENE IV. Britain. A Prison

Enter Posthumus and Two Gaolers

FIRST GAOLER: You shall not now be stol'n, you have locks upon you;
So graze as you find pasture.
SECOND GAOLER: Ay, or a stomach.

Exeunt Gaolers

POSTHUMUS: Most welcome, bondage! for thou art a way,
I think, to liberty. Yet am I better
Than one that's sick o' th' gout, since he had rather
Groan so in perpetuity than be cur'd
By th' sure physician death, who is the key
T' unbar these locks. My conscience, thou art fetter'd
More than my shanks and wrists; you good gods, give me
The penitent instrument to pick that bolt,
Then, free for ever! Is't enough I am sorry?
So children temporal fathers do appease;
Gods are more full of mercy. Must I repent,
I cannot do it better than in gyves,
Desir'd more than constrain'd. To satisfy,
If of my freedom 'tis the main part, take
No stricter render of me than my all.
I know you are more clement than vile men,
Who of their broken debtors take a third,
A sixth, a tenth, letting them thrive again
On their abatement; that's not my desire.
For Imogen's dear life take mine; and though
'Tis not so dear, yet 'tis a life; you coin'd it.
'Tween man and man they weigh not every stamp;
Though light, take pieces for the figure's sake;
You rather mine, being yours. And so, great pow'rs,
If you will take this audit, take this life,
And cancel these cold bonds. O Imogen!
I'll speak to thee in silence.

Sleeps

Solemn Music. Enter, as in an Apparition, Sicilius Leonatus, Father to Posthumus, an Old Man Attired like a Warrior; Leading in His Hand an Ancient Matron, His Wife, and Mother to Posthumus, with Music Before Them. Then, after Other Music, Follows the Two Young Leonati, Brothers to Posthumus, with Wounds, as They Died in the Wars. They Circle Posthumus Round as He Lies Sleeping

SICILIUS: No more, thou thunder-master, show
Thy spite on mortal flies.
With Mars fall out, with Juno chide,
That thy adulteries
Rates and revenges.
Hath my poor boy done aught but well,
Whose face I never saw?

I died whilst in the womb he stay'd
 Attending nature's law;
Whose father then, as men report
 Thou orphans' father art,
Thou shouldst have been, and shielded him
 From this earth-vexing smart.
MOTHER: Lucina lent not me her aid,
 But took me in my throes,
That from me was Posthumus ripp'd,
 Came crying 'mongst his foes,
 A thing of pity.
SICILIUS: Great Nature like his ancestry
 Moulded the stuff so fair
That he deserv'd the praise o' th' world
 As great Sicilius' heir.
FIRST BROTHER: When once he was mature for man,
 In Britain where was he
That could stand up his parallel,
 Or fruitful object be
In eye of Imogen, that best
 Could deem his dignity?
MOTHER: With marriage wherefore was he mock'd,
 To be exil'd and thrown
From Leonati seat and cast
From her his dearest one,
 Sweet Imogen?
SICILIUS: Why did you suffer Iachimo,
 Slight thing of Italy,
To taint his nobler heart and brain
 With needless jealousy,
And to become the geck and scorn
 O' th' other's villainy?
SECOND BROTHER: For this from stiller seats we came,
 Our parents and us twain,
That, striking in our country's cause,
 Fell bravely and were slain,
Our fealty and Tenantius' right
 With honour to maintain.
FIRST BROTHER: Like hardiment Posthumus hath
 To Cymbeline perform'd.
Then, Jupiter, thou king of gods,
 Why hast thou thus adjourn'd
The graces for his merits due,
 Being all to dolours turn'd?
SICILIUS: Thy crystal window ope; look out;
 No longer exercise
Upon a valiant race thy harsh
 And potent injuries.
MOTHER: Since, Jupiter, our son is good,
 Take off his miseries.
SICILIUS: Peep through thy marble mansion. Help!
 Or we poor ghosts will cry
To th' shining synod of the rest

Against thy deity.
BROTHERS: Help, Jupiter! or we appeal,
And from thy justice fly.

Jupiter Descends in Thunder and Lightning, Sitting upon an Eagle. He Throws a Thunderbolt. The Ghosts Fall on Their Knees

JUPITER: No more, you petty spirits of region low,
Offend our hearing; hush! How dare you ghosts
Accuse the Thunderer whose bolt, you know,
Sky-planted, batters all rebelling coasts?
Poor shadows of Elysium, hence and rest
Upon your never-withering banks of flow'rs.
Be not with mortal accidents opprest:
No care of yours it is; you know 'tis ours.
Whom best I love I cross; to make my gift,
The more delay'd, delighted. Be content;
Your low-laid son our godhead will uplift;
His comforts thrive, his trials well are spent.
Our Jovial star reign'd at his birth, and in
Our temple was he married. Rise and fade!
He shall be lord of Lady Imogen,
And happier much by his affliction made.
This tablet lay upon his breast, wherein
Our pleasure his full fortune doth confine;
And so, away; no farther with your din
Express impatience, lest you stir up mine.
Mount, eagle, to my palace crystalline.

Ascends

SICILIUS: He came in thunder; his celestial breath
Was sulpherous to smell; the holy eagle
Stoop'd as to foot us. His ascension is
More sweet than our blest fields. His royal bird
Prunes the immortal wing, and cloys his beak,
As when his god is pleas'd.
ALL: Thanks, Jupiter!
SICILIUS: The marble pavement closes, he is enter'd
His radiant roof. Away! and, to be blest,
Let us with care perform his great behest.

Ghosts Vanishes

POSTHUMUS: Waking Sleep, thou has been a grandsire and begot
A father to me; and thou hast created
A mother and two brothers. But, O scorn,
Gone! They went hence so soon as they were born.
And so I am awake. Poor wretches, that depend
On greatness' favour, dream as I have done;
Wake and find nothing. But, alas, I swerve;
Many dream not to find, neither deserve,
And yet are steep'd in favours; so am I,
That have this golden chance, and know not why.
What fairies haunt this ground? A book? O rare one!
Be not, as is our fangled world, a garment
Nobler than that it covers. Let thy effects
So follow to be most unlike our courtiers,
As good as promise.

Reads 'When as a lion's whelp shall, to himself unknown, without seeking find, and be embrac'd by a piece of tender air; and when from a stately cedar shall be lopp'd branches which, being dead many years, shall after revive, be jointed to the old stock, and freshly grow; then shall Posthumus end his miseries, Britain be fortunate and flourish in peace and plenty.'

'Tis still a dream, or else such stuff as madmen
Tongue, and brain not; either both or nothing,
Or senseless speaking, or a speaking such
As sense cannot untie. Be what it is,
The action of my life is like it, which
I'll keep, if but for sympathy.

Re-enter Gaoler

GAOLER: Come, sir, are you ready for death?

POSTHUMUS: Over-roasted rather; ready long ago.

GAOLER: Hanging is the word, sir; if you be ready for that, you are well cook'd.

POSTHUMUS: So, if I prove a good repast to the spectators, the dish pays the shot.

GAOLER: A heavy reckoning for you, sir. But the comfort is, you shall be called to no more payments, fear no more tavern bills, which are often the sadness of parting, as the procuring of mirth. You come in faint for want of meat, depart reeling with too much drink; sorry that you have paid too much, and sorry that you are paid too much; purse and brain both empty; the brain the heavier for being too light, the purse too light, being drawn of heaviness. O, of this contradiction you shall now be quit. O, the charity of a penny cord! It sums up thousands in a trice. You have no true debitor and creditor but it; of what's past, is, and to come, the discharge. Your neck, sir, is pen, book, and counters; so the acquittance follows.

POSTHUMUS: I am merrier to die than thou art to live.

GAOLER: Indeed, sir, he that sleeps feels not the toothache. But a man that were to sleep your sleep, and a hangman to help him to bed, I think he would change places with his officer; for look you, sir, you know not which way you shall go.

POSTHUMUS: Yes indeed do I, fellow.

GAOLER: Your death has eyes in's head, then; I have not seen him so pictur'd. You must either be directed by some that take upon them to know, or to take upon yourself that which I am sure you do not know, or jump the after-inquiry on your own peril. And how you shall speed in your journey's end, I think you'll never return to tell one.

POSTHUMUS: I tell thee, fellow, there are none want eyes to direct them the way I am going, but such as wink and will not use them.

GAOLER: What an infinite mock is this, that a man should have the best use of eyes to see the way of blindness! I am sure hanging's the way of winking.

Enter a Messenger

MESSENGER: Knock off his manacles; bring your prisoner to the King.

POSTHUMUS: Thou bring'st good news: I am call'd to be made free.

GAOLER: I'll be hang'd then.

POSTHUMUS: Thou shalt be then freer than a gaoler; no bolts for the dead.

Exeunt Posthumus and Messenger

GAOLER: Unless a man would marry a gallows and beget young gibbets, I never saw one so prone. Yet, on my conscience, there are verier knaves desire to live, for all he be a Roman; and there be some of them too that die against their wills; so should I, if I were one. I would we were all of one mind, and one mind good. O, there were desolation of gaolers and gallowses! I speak against my present profit, but my wish hath a preferment in't.

Exit

ACT V. SCENE V. Britain. Cymbeline's Tent

Enter Cymbeline, Belarius, Guiderius, Arviragus, Pisanio, Lords, Officers, and Attendants

CYMBELINE: Stand by my side, you whom the gods have made
Preservers of my throne. Woe is my heart
That the poor soldier that so richly fought,
Whose rags sham'd gilded arms, whose naked breast
Stepp'd before targes of proof, cannot be found.
He shall be happy that can find him, if
Our grace can make him so.
BELARIUS: I never saw
Such noble fury in so poor a thing;
Such precious deeds in one that promis'd nought
But beggary and poor looks.
CYMBELINE: No tidings of him?
PISANIO: He hath been search'd among the dead and living,
But no trace of him.
CYMBELINE: To my grief, I am
The heir of his reward;

To Belarius, Guiderius, and Arviragus

which I will add
To you, the liver, heart, and brain, of Britain,
By whom I grant she lives. 'Tis now the time
To ask of whence you are. Report it.
BELARIUS: Sir,
In Cambria are we born, and gentlemen;
Further to boast were neither true nor modest,
Unless I add we are honest.
CYMBELINE: Bow your knees.
Arise my knights o' th' battle; I create you
Companions to our person, and will fit you
With dignities becoming your estates.

Enter Cornelius and Ladies

There's business in these faces. Why so sadly
Greet you our victory? You look like Romans,
And not o' th' court of Britain.
CORNELIUS: Hail, great King!
To sour your happiness I must report
The Queen is dead.
CYMBELINE: Who worse than a physician
Would this report become? But I consider
By med'cine'life may be prolong'd, yet death
Will seize the doctor too. How ended she?
CORNELIUS: With horror, madly dying, like her life;

Which, being cruel to the world, concluded
Most cruel to herself. What she confess'd
I will report, so please you; these her women
Can trip me if I err, who with wet cheeks
Were present when she finish'd.
CYMBELINE: Prithee say.
CORNELIUS: First, she confess'd she never lov'd you; only
Affected greatness got by you, not you;
Married your royalty, was wife to your place;
Abhorr'd your person.
CYMBELINE: She alone knew this;
And but she spoke it dying, I would not
Believe her lips in opening it. Proceed.
CORNELIUS: Your daughter, whom she bore in hand to love
With such integrity, she did confess
Was as a scorpion to her sight; whose life,
But that her flight prevented it, she had
Ta'en off by poison.
CYMBELINE: O most delicate fiend!
Who is't can read a woman? Is there more?
CORNELIUS: More, sir, and worse. She did confess she had
For you a mortal mineral, which, being took,
Should by the minute feed on life, and ling'ring,
By inches waste you. In which time she purpos'd,
By watching, weeping, tendance, kissing, to
O'ercome you with her show; and in time,
When she had fitted you with her craft, to work
Her son into th' adoption of the crown;
But failing of her end by his strange absence,
Grew shameless-desperate, open'd, in despite
Of heaven and men, her purposes, repented
The evils she hatch'd were not effected; so,
Despairing, died.
CYMBELINE: Heard you all this, her women?
LADY: We did, so please your Highness.
CYMBELINE: Mine eyes
Were not in fault, for she was beautiful;
Mine ears, that heard her flattery; nor my heart
That thought her like her seeming. It had been vicious
To have mistrusted her; yet, O my daughter!
That it was folly in me thou mayst say,
And prove it in thy feeling. Heaven mend all!

Enter Lucius, Iachimo, the Soothsayer, and Other Roman Prisoners, Guarded; Posthumus Behind, and Imogen

Thou com'st not, Caius, now for tribute; that
The Britons have raz'd out, though with the loss
Of many a bold one, whose kinsmen have made suit
That their good souls may be appeas'd with slaughter
Of you their captives, which ourself have granted;
So think of your estate.
LUCIUS: Consider, sir, the chance of war. The day
Was yours by accident; had it gone with us,
We should not, when the blood was cool, have threaten'd

Our prisoners with the sword. But since the gods
Will have it thus, that nothing but our lives
May be call'd ransom, let it come. Sufficeth
A Roman with a Roman's heart can suffer.
Augustus lives to think on't; and so much
For my peculiar care. This one thing only
I will entreat: my boy, a Briton born,
Let him be ransom'd. Never master had
A page so kind, so duteous, diligent,
So tender over his occasions, true,
So feat, so nurse-like; let his virtue join
With my request, which I'll make bold your Highness
Cannot deny; he hath done no Briton harm
Though he have serv'd a Roman. Save him, sir,
And spare no blood beside.
CYMBELINE: I have surely seen him;
His favour is familiar to me. Boy,
Thou hast look'd thyself into my grace,
And art mine own. I know not why, wherefore
To say 'Live, boy.' Ne'er thank thy master. Live;
And ask of Cymbeline what boon thou wilt,
Fitting my bounty and thy state, I'll give it;
Yea, though thou do demand a prisoner,
The noblest ta'en.
IMOGEN: I humbly thank your Highness.
LUCIUS: I do not bid thee beg my life, good lad,
And yet I know thou wilt.
IMOGEN: No, no! Alack,
There's other work in hand. I see a thing
Bitter to me as death; your life, good master,
Must shuffle for itself.
LUCIUS: The boy disdains me,
He leaves me, scorns me. Briefly die their joys
That place them on the truth of girls and boys.
Why stands he so perplex'd?
CYMBELINE: What wouldst thou, boy?
I love thee more and more; think more and more
What's best to ask. Know'st him thou look'st on? Speak,
Wilt have him live? Is he thy kin? thy friend?
IMOGEN: He is a Roman, no more kin to me
Than I to your Highness; who, being born your vassal,
Am something nearer.
CYMBELINE: Wherefore ey'st him so?
IMOGEN: I'll tell you, sir, in private, if you please
To give me hearing.
CYMBELINE: Ay, with all my heart,
And lend my best attention. What's thy name?
IMOGEN: Fidele, sir.
CYMBELINE: Thou'rt my good youth, my page;
I'll be thy master. Walk with me; speak freely.
Cymbeline and Imogen Converse Apart
BELARIUS: Is not this boy reviv'd from death?
ARVIRAGUS: One sand another

Not more resembles- that sweet rosy lad
Who died and was Fidele. What think you?
GUIDERIUS: The same dead thing alive.
BELARIUS: Peace, peace! see further. He eyes us not; forbear.
Creatures may be alike; were't he, I am sure
He would have spoke to us.
GUIDERIUS: But we saw him dead.
BELARIUS: Be silent; let's see further.
PISANIO: Aside It is my mistress.
Since she is living, let the time run on
To good or bad.
Cymbeline and Imogen Advance
CYMBELINE: Come, stand thou by our side;
Make thy demand aloud. To Iachimo Sir, step you forth;
Give answer to this boy, and do it freely,
Or, by our greatness and the grace of it,
Which is our honour, bitter torture shall
Winnow the truth from falsehood. On, speak to him.
IMOGEN: My boon is that this gentleman may render
Of whom he had this ring.
POSTHUMUS: Aside What's that to him?
CYMBELINE: That diamond upon your finger, say
How came it yours?
IACHIMO: Thou'lt torture me to leave unspoken that
Which to be spoke would torture thee.
CYMBELINE: How? me?
IACHIMO: I am glad to be constrain'd to utter that
Which torments me to conceal. By villainy
I got this ring; 'twas Leonatus' jewel,
Whom thou didst banish; and- which more may grieve thee,
As it doth me- a nobler sir ne'er liv'd
'Twixt sky and ground. Wilt thou hear more, my lord?
CYMBELINE: All that belongs to this.
IACHIMO: That paragon, thy daughter,
For whom my heart drops blood and my false spirits
Quail to remember- Give me leave, I faint.
CYMBELINE: My daughter? What of her? Renew thy strength;
I had rather thou shouldst live while nature will
Than die ere I hear more. Strive, man, and speak.
IACHIMO: Upon a time- unhappy was the clock
That struck the hour!- was in Rome- accurs'd
The mansion where!- 'twas at a feast- O, would
Our viands had been poison'd, or at least
Those which I heav'd to head!- the good Posthumus-
What should I say? he was too good to be
Where ill men were, and was the best of all
Amongst the rar'st of good ones- sitting sadly
Hearing us praise our loves of Italy
For beauty that made barren the swell'd boast
Of him that best could speak; for feature, laming
The shrine of Venus or straight-pight Minerva,
Postures beyond brief nature; for condition,
A shop of all the qualities that man

Loves woman for; besides that hook of wiving,
Fairness which strikes the eye-
CYMBELINE: I stand on fire.
Come to the matter.
IACHIMO: All too soon I shall,
Unless thou wouldst grieve quickly. This Posthumus,
Most like a noble lord in love and one
That had a royal lover, took his hint;
And not dispraising whom we prais'd- therein
He was as calm as virtue- he began
His mistress' picture; which by his tongue being made,
And then a mind put in't, either our brags
Were crack'd of kitchen trulls, or his description
Prov'd us unspeaking sots.
CYMBELINE: Nay, nay, to th' purpose.
IACHIMO: Your daughter's chastity- there it begins.
He spake of her as Dian had hot dreams
And she alone were cold; whereat I, wretch,
Made scruple of his praise, and wager'd with him
Pieces of gold 'gainst this which then he wore
Upon his honour'd finger, to attain
In suit the place of's bed, and win this ring
By hers and mine adultery. He, true knight,
No lesser of her honour confident
Than I did truly find her, stakes this ring;
And would so, had it been a carbuncle
Of Phoebus' wheel; and might so safely, had it
Been all the worth of's car. Away to Britain
Post I in this design. Well may you, sir,
Remember me at court, where I was taught
Of your chaste daughter the wide difference
'Twixt amorous and villainous. Being thus quench'd
Of hope, not longing, mine Italian brain
Gan in your duller Britain operate
Most vilely; for my vantage, excellent;
And, to be brief, my practice so prevail'd
That I return'd with simular proof enough
To make the noble Leonatus mad,
By wounding his belief in her renown
With tokens thus and thus; averring notes
Of chamber-hanging, pictures, this her bracelet-
O cunning, how I got it!- nay, some marks
Of secret on her person, that he could not
But think her bond of chastity quite crack'd,
I having ta'en the forfeit. Whereupon-
Methinks I see him now-
POSTHUMUS: Coming Forward Ay, so thou dost,
Italian fiend! Ay me, most credulous fool,
Egregious murderer, thief, anything
That's due to all the villains past, in being,
To come! O, give me cord, or knife, or poison,
Some upright justicer! Thou, King, send out
For torturers ingenious. It is I

That all th' abhorred things o' th' earth amend
By being worse than they. I am Posthumus,
That kill'd thy daughter; villain-like, I lie-
That caus'd a lesser villain than myself,
A sacrilegious thief, to do't. The temple
Of virtue was she; yea, and she herself.
Spit, and throw stones, cast mire upon me, set
The dogs o' th' street to bay me. Every villain
Be call'd Posthumus Leonatus, and
Be villainy less than 'twas! O Imogen!
My queen, my life, my wife! O Imogen,
Imogen, Imogen!
IMOGEN: Peace, my lord. Hear, hear!
POSTHUMUS: Shall's have a play of this? Thou scornful page,
There lies thy part.
Strikes Her. She Falls
PISANIO: O gentlemen, help!
Mine and your mistress! O, my lord Posthumus!
You ne'er kill'd Imogen till now. Help, help!
Mine honour'd lady!
CYMBELINE: Does the world go round?
POSTHUMUS: How comes these staggers on me?
PISANIO: Wake, my mistress!
CYMBELINE: If this be so, the gods do mean to strike me
To death with mortal joy.
PISANIO: How fares my mistress?
IMOGEN: O, get thee from my sight;
Thou gav'st me poison. Dangerous fellow, hence!
Breathe not where princes are.
CYMBELINE: The tune of Imogen!
PISANIO: Lady,
The gods throw stones of sulphur on me, if
That box I gave you was not thought by me
A precious thing! I had it from the Queen.
CYMBELINE: New matter still?
IMOGEN: It poison'd me.
CORNELIUS: O gods!
I left out one thing which the Queen confess'd,
Which must approve thee honest. 'If Pisanio
Have' said she 'given his mistress that confection
Which I gave him for cordial, she is serv'd
As I would serve a rat.'
CYMBELINE: What's this, Cornelius?
CORNELIUS: The Queen, sir, very oft importun'd me
To temper poisons for her; still pretending
The satisfaction of her knowledge only
In killing creatures vile, as cats and dogs,
Of no esteem. I, dreading that her purpose
Was of more danger, did compound for her
A certain stuff, which, being ta'en would cease
The present pow'r of life, but in short time
All offices of nature should again
Do their due functions. Have you ta'en of it?

IMOGEN: Most like I did, for I was dead.
BELARIUS: My boys,
There was our error.
GUIDERIUS: This is sure Fidele.
IMOGEN: Why did you throw your wedded lady from you?
Think that you are upon a rock, and now
Throw me again.
Embracing Him
POSTHUMUS: Hang there like fruit, my soul,
Till the tree die!
CYMBELINE: How now, my flesh? my child?
What, mak'st thou me a dullard in this act?
Wilt thou not speak to me?
IMOGEN: Kneeling Your blessing, sir.
BELARIUS: To Guiderius and Arviragus Though you did love this youth, I blame ye not;
You had a motive for't.
CYMBELINE: My tears that fall
Prove holy water on thee! Imogen,
Thy mother's dead.
IMOGEN: I am sorry for't, my lord.
CYMBELINE: O, she was naught, and long of her it was
That we meet here so strangely; but her son
Is gone, we know not how nor where.
PISANIO: My lord,
Now fear is from me, I'll speak troth. Lord Cloten,
Upon my lady's missing, came to me
With his sword drawn, foam'd at the mouth, and swore,
If I discover'd not which way she was gone,
It was my instant death. By accident
I had a feigned letter of my master's
Then in my pocket, which directed him
To seek her on the mountains near to Milford;
Where, in a frenzy, in my master's garments,
Which he enforc'd from me, away he posts
With unchaste purpose, and with oath to violate
My lady's honour. What became of him
I further know not.
GUIDERIUS: Let me end the story:
I slew him there.
CYMBELINE: Marry, the gods forfend!
I would not thy good deeds should from my lips
Pluck a hard sentence. Prithee, valiant youth,
Deny't again.
GUIDERIUS: I have spoke it, and I did it.
CYMBELINE: He was a prince.
GUIDERIUS: A most incivil one. The wrongs he did me
Were nothing prince-like; for he did provoke me
With language that would make me spurn the sea,
If it could so roar to me. I cut off's head,
And am right glad he is not standing here
To tell this tale of mine.
CYMBELINE: I am sorry for thee.

By thine own tongue thou art condemn'd, and must
Endure our law. Thou'rt dead.
IMOGEN: That headless man
I thought had been my lord.
CYMBELINE: Bind the offender,
And take him from our presence.
BELARIUS: Stay, sir King.
This man is better than the man he slew,
As well descended as thyself, and hath
More of thee merited than a band of Clotens
Had ever scar for. To the Guard Let his arms alone;
They were not born for bondage.
CYMBELINE: Why, old soldier,
Wilt thou undo the worth thou art unpaid for
By tasting of our wrath? How of descent
As good as we?
ARVIRAGUS: In that he spake too far.
CYMBELINE: And thou shalt die for't.
BELARIUS: We will die all three;
But I will prove that two on's are as good
As I have given out him. My sons, I must
For mine own part unfold a dangerous speech,
Though haply well for you.
ARVIRAGUS: Your danger's ours.
GUIDERIUS: And our good his.
BELARIUS: Have at it then by leave!
Thou hadst, great King, a subject who
Was call'd Belarius.
CYMBELINE: What of him? He is
A banish'd traitor.
BELARIUS: He it is that hath
Assum'd this age; indeed a banish'd man;
I know not how a traitor.
CYMBELINE: Take him hence,
The whole world shall not save him.
BELARIUS: Not too hot.
First pay me for the nursing of thy sons,
And let it be confiscate all, so soon
As I have receiv'd it.
CYMBELINE: Nursing of my sons?
BELARIUS: I am too blunt and saucy: here's my knee.
Ere I arise I will prefer my sons;
Then spare not the old father. Mighty sir,
These two young gentlemen that call me father,
And think they are my sons, are none of mine;
They are the issue of your loins, my liege,
And blood of your begetting.
CYMBELINE: How? my issue?
BELARIUS: So sure as you your father's. I, old Morgan,
Am that Belarius whom you sometime banish'd.
Your pleasure was my mere offence, my punishment
Itself, and all my treason; that I suffer'd
Was all the harm I did. These gentle princes-

For such and so they are- these twenty years
Have I train'd up; those arts they have as
Could put into them. My breeding was, sir, as
Your Highness knows. Their nurse, Euriphile,
Whom for the theft I wedded, stole these children
Upon my banishment; I mov'd her to't,
Having receiv'd the punishment before
For that which I did then. Beaten for loyalty
Excited me to treason. Their dear loss,
The more of you 'twas felt, the more it shap'd
Unto my end of stealing them. But, gracious sir,
Here are your sons again, and I must lose
Two of the sweet'st companions in the world.
The benediction of these covering heavens
Fall on their heads like dew! for they are worthy
To inlay heaven with stars.
CYMBELINE: Thou weep'st and speak'st.
The service that you three have done is more
Unlike than this thou tell'st. I lost my children.
If these be they, I know not how to wish
A pair of worthier sons.
BELARIUS: Be pleas'd awhile.
This gentleman, whom I call Polydore,
Most worthy prince, as yours, is true Guiderius;
This gentleman, my Cadwal, Arviragus,
Your younger princely son; he, sir, was lapp'd
In a most curious mantle, wrought by th' hand
Of his queen mother, which for more probation
I can with ease produce.
CYMBELINE: Guiderius had
Upon his neck a mole, a sanguine star;
It was a mark of wonder.
BELARIUS: This is he,
Who hath upon him still that natural stamp.
It was wise nature's end in the donation,
To be his evidence now.
CYMBELINE: O, what am I?
A mother to the birth of three? Ne'er mother
Rejoic'd deliverance more. Blest pray you be,
That, after this strange starting from your orbs,
You may reign in them now! O Imogen,
Thou hast lost by this a kingdom.
IMOGEN: No, my lord;
I have got two worlds by't. O my gentle brothers,
Have we thus met? O, never say hereafter
But I am truest speaker! You call'd me brother,
When I was but your sister: I you brothers,
When we were so indeed.
CYMBELINE: Did you e'er meet?
ARVIRAGUS: Ay, my good lord.
GUIDERIUS: And at first meeting lov'd,
Continu'd so until we thought he died.
CORNELIUS: By the Queen's dram she swallow'd.

CYMBELINE: O rare instinct!
When shall I hear all through? This fierce abridgment
Hath to it circumstantial branches, which
Distinction should be rich in. Where? how liv'd you?
And when came you to serve our Roman captive?
How parted with your brothers? how first met them?
Why fled you from the court? and whither? These,
And your three motives to the battle, with
I know not how much more, should be demanded,
And all the other by-dependences,
From chance to chance; but nor the time nor place
Will serve our long interrogatories. See,
Posthumus anchors upon Imogen;
And she, like harmless lightning, throws her eye
On him, her brothers, me, her master, hitting
Each object with a joy; the counterchange
Is severally in all. Let's quit this ground,
And smoke the temple with our sacrifices.
To Belarius Thou art my brother; so we'll hold thee ever.
IMOGEN: You are my father too, and did relieve me
To see this gracious season.
CYMBELINE: All o'erjoy'd
Save these in bonds. Let them be joyful too,
For they shall taste our comfort.
IMOGEN: My good master,
I will yet do you service.
LUCIUS: Happy be you!
CYMBELINE: The forlorn soldier, that so nobly fought,
He would have well becom'd this place and grac'd
The thankings of a king.
POSTHUMUS: I am, sir,
The soldier that did company these three
In poor beseeming; 'twas a fitment for
The purpose I then follow'd. That I was he,
Speak, Iachimo. I had you down, and might
Have made you finish.
IACHIMO: Kneeling I am down again;
But now my heavy conscience sinks my knee,
As then your force did. Take that life, beseech you,
Which I so often owe; but your ring first,
And here the bracelet of the truest princess
That ever swore her faith.
POSTHUMUS: Kneel not to me.
The pow'r that I have on you is to spare you;
The malice towards you to forgive you. Live,
And deal with others better.
CYMBELINE: Nobly doom'd!
We'll learn our freeness of a son-in-law;
Pardon's the word to all.
ARVIRAGUS: You holp us, sir,
As you did mean indeed to be our brother;
Joy'd are we that you are.
POSTHUMUS: Your servant, Princes. Good my lord of Rome,

Call forth your soothsayer. As I slept, methought
Great Jupiter, upon his eagle back'd,
Appear'd to me, with other spritely shows
Of mine own kindred. When I wak'd, I found
This label on my bosom; whose containing
Is so from sense in hardness that I can
Make no collection of it. Let him show
His skill in the construction.
LUCIUS: Philarmonus!
SOOTHSAYER: Here, my good lord.
LUCIUS: Read, and declare the meaning.
SOOTHSAYER: Reads 'When as a lion's whelp shall, to himself
unknown, without seeking find, and be embrac'd by
a piece of tender air; and when from a stately cedar shall
be lopp'd branches which, being dead many years, shall
after revive, be jointed to the old stock, and freshly grow;
then shall Posthumus end his miseries, Britain be fortunate
and flourish in peace and plenty.'
Thou, Leonatus, art the lion's whelp;
The fit and apt construction of thy name,
Being Leo-natus, doth import so much.
To Cymbeline The piece of tender air, thy virtuous daughter,
Which we call 'mollis aer,' and 'mollis aer'
We term it 'mulier'; which 'mulier' I divine
Is this most constant wife, who even now
Answering the letter of the oracle,
Unknown to you, unsought, were clipp'd about
With this most tender air.
CYMBELINE: This hath some seeming.
SOOTHSAYER: The lofty cedar, royal Cymbeline,
Personates thee; and thy lopp'd branches point
Thy two sons forth, who, by Belarius stol'n,
For many years thought dead, are now reviv'd,
To the majestic cedar join'd, whose issue
Promises Britain peace and plenty.
CYMBELINE: Well,
My peace we will begin. And, Caius Lucius,
Although the victor, we submit to Caesar
And to the Roman empire, promising
To pay our wonted tribute, from the which
We were dissuaded by our wicked queen,
Whom heavens in justice, both on her and hers,
Have laid most heavy hand.
SOOTHSAYER: The fingers of the pow'rs above do tune
The harmony of this peace. The vision
Which I made known to Lucius ere the stroke
Of yet this scarce-cold battle, at this instant
Is full accomplish'd; for the Roman eagle,
From south to west on wing soaring aloft,
Lessen'd herself and in the beams o' th' sun
So vanish'd; which foreshow'd our princely eagle,
Th'imperial Caesar, Caesar, should again unite
His favour with the radiant Cymbeline,

Which shines here in the west.
CYMBELINE: Laud we the gods;
And let our crooked smokes climb to their nostrils
From our bless'd altars. Publish we this peace
To all our subjects. Set we forward; let
A Roman and a British ensign wave
Friendly together. So through Lud's Town march;
And in the temple of great Jupiter
Our peace we'll ratify; seal it with feasts.
Set on there! Never was a war did cease,
Ere bloody hands were wash'd, with such a peace.
Exeunt

END

www.ingramcontent.com/pod-product-compliance
Lightning Source LLC
LaVergne TN
LVHW031150200826
846147LV00014B/89
* 9 7 9 8 8 8 0 9 1 4 2 3 4 *